THE COMPLETE SCHOLARSHIP BOOK

2nd Edition

Student Services, L.L.C.

Sourcebooks, Inc.
Naperville, IL

Copyright © 1998 by Student Services, L.L.C.
Cover design copyright © 1998 by Sourcebooks, Inc.

All rights reserved. No part of this book may be reproduced in any form or by any electronic or mechanical means including information storage and retrieval systems—except in the case of brief quotations embodied in critical articles or reviews—without permission in writing from Sourcebooks, Inc.

Published by: **Sourcebooks, Inc.**
P.O. Box 372
Naperville, IL 60566
(630) 961-3900
FAX: (630) 961-2168

This publication is designed to provide accurate and authoritative information in regard to the subject matter covered. It is sold with the understanding that the publisher is not engaged in rendering legal, accounting or other professional service. If legal advice or other expert assistance is required, the services of a competent professional person should be sought.

From a Declaration of Principles Jointly Adopted by a Committee of the
American Bar Association and a Committee of Publishers and Associations

Every effort has been made to provide you with the best, most up-to-date information on private sector financial aid. However, if you discover an award in this book is listed incorrectly, please contact our research department by mail at: Research Department, Student Services, L.L.C., 2250 Commonwealth Avenue, North Chicago, IL 60064.

Disclaimer

Care has been taken in collecting and presenting the material contained in this book; however, Student Services, L.L.C., and Sourcebooks, Inc., do not guarantee its accuracy. Student Services, L.L.C., and Sourcebooks, Inc., are private corporations and are not affiliated in any way with the U.S. Department of Education or any other government agency.

Library of Congress Cataloging-in-Publication Information

The complete scholarship book: the biggest, easiest-to-use guide for getting the most money for college/ Student Services, L.L.C.—2nd ed.
       p.   cm.
  Includes index.
  ISBN 1-57071-390-1 (alk. paper)
    1. Scholarships—United States—Directories.   2. Associations, institutions, etc.—Charitable contributions—United States—Directories.   3. Student aid—United States—Handbooks, manuals, etc.   I. Student Services, L.L.C.
LB2338.C653 1998
378.3'4'0973—dc21   98-7507
                                                                                            CIP

Printed and bound in the United States of America
10 9 8 7 6 5 4 3 2 1

Read This First

Congratulations! You hold in your hands the most comprehensive and thoroughly researched publication ever produced on the subject of college financial aid furnished by non-government organizations. This book lists more than 5,000 sources of college financial aid sponsored by private sector organizations, representing over 130,000 college scholarships, fellowships, grants, and low-interest loans.

About half of the non-government financial aid opportunities listed in this book are college-specific; that is, you would have to attend a particular school to receive the award. The other half of the awards listed in this book are independent of any specific school—you could receive the financial aid no matter which accredited college you attended.

College financial aid from non-government organizations is provided by philanthropic foundations, corporations, employers, professional societies and associations, clubs, religious organizations, and civic service groups.

Eligibility Requirements

Many students think that college financial aid is for someone else—that they are not "poor enough" or "smart enough" to receive aid. In reality, however, college financial aid is awarded for many different reasons, to many different kinds of people. That means your background and personal circumstances could open the door to a wide array of sources of college money. In fact, eligibility for private aid can be based on a variety of criteria, including:

- career objectives,
- gender,
- disabilities,
- financial need,
- academic performance,
- participation in the military,
- race and heritage,
- religious affiliation,
- the state in which you are a resident,
- membership in clubs and associations,
- upcoming school year (freshman, sophomore, junior, senior, graduate, doctorate, postdoctorate),
- work experience.

Types of Assistance

Financial aid for college is offered in three basic forms:

- grants and scholarships,
- fellowships and internships, and
- loans designed especially for students (and parents of students).

Grants and scholarships, sometimes referred to as gift assistance, do not have to be repaid.

Fellowships and internships are monetary awards paid to the student in return for research or work performed according to the guidelines set forth by the sponsor of the award. Fellowships and internships are usually awarded to a student so he or she may gain experience in a particular field of interest.

Student loans, and loans to parents of students, must be repaid. Generally, these loans feature favorable rates of interest and/or deferred payment options.

How to Receive Applications for College Financial Aid from Private Donors

To save time and effort, we suggest that you use a standard form letter when requesting applications and additional information from private donors. Here is a standard form letter that works well:

> <Date>
>
> <Contact Name at Donor Organization>
> <Name of Donor Organization>
> <Donor's Street Address>
> <Donor's City, State Zip>
>
> Dear Sir or Madam:
>
> Please forward an application and any additional information concerning your financial aid program for postsecondary education.
>
> Sincerely,
>
> <Your Name>
> <Your Address>
> <Your City, State Zip>

Be sure to enclose a self-addressed, stamped envelope with your letter.

How to Use This Book

This book lists over 5,000 different sources of college financial aid from private organizations. Many of the scholarships and awards are available to anyone, requiring you to merely fill out an application form or perhaps submit a short essay.

Other donors, however, target their money toward a specific type of student, often based on your prospective majors, academic interests, skills, and personal background. To help you quickly and easily find the awards that are most appropriate to you, *The Complete Scholarship Book* provides you with two ways to find your most likely donors:

- extensive indexes at the end of the book, identifying awards available by major or career objective, ethnic background, gender, religion, marital status, military background of you or your parents, disability, and intercollegiate athletics; and
- an icon system which allows you to scan the sources quickly.

The Icon System

The icons in this book will allow you to visually identify scholarships which may be appropriate for you based on majors and special criteria.

Majors/Career Objective

College majors have been grouped into nine categories to guide you to general fields of study. The following list includes the most common majors within each category and the icon that will identify them.

Business
Accounting
Advertising/Public Relations
Banking/Finance/Insurance
Business Administration
Economics
Human Resources
Management
Marketing
Sales
Transportation

Education
Childhood Development
Early Childhood Education
Education (General)
Education Administration
Elementary Education
Middle-Level Education
Postsecondary Education

Engineering
Aerospace Engineering
Architecture
Aviation
Civil Engineering/Construction
Computer Science
Engineering (General)
Material Science
Surveying/Cartography
Telecommunications

Fine Arts
Art
Filmmaking
Fine Arts (General)
Graphic Design
Music (General)
Performing Arts
Photography

Humanities
Broadcasting/Communications
Classical Studies
English/Literature
Foreign Languages
Humanities (General)
Journalism
Library/Information Sciences
Philosophy
Religion

Medicine
Dentistry
Health Care Management
Medicine/Medical (General)
Nursing
Pharmacy/Pharmacology/Pharmaceutical

Public Health
Therapy (General)
Veterinary Medicine

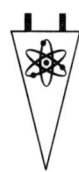

Science
Agriculture
Animal Science
Biology
Chemistry
Ecology/Environmental Science
Energy-Related Studies
Geology
Land Management/Design
Marine Sciences
Mathematics
Meteorology
Physics
Science (General)

Social Sciences
African-American Studies
Anthropology
Archaeology
Foreign Studies
Geography
Government
History
International Relations
Law
Military Science
Political Science
Psychology
Social Sciences (General)
Sociology
Women's Studies

Vocational
Automotive
Court Reporting
Data Processing
Food Services
Funeral Services
Heating/Plumbing/Cooling Industry
Hotel/Motel Management/Administration
Manufacturing
Real Estate
Textiles
Travel and Tourism
Vocational (General)

Special Criteria

The following categories are the most common criteria on which scholarship awards are based. Look for these icons to help find awards for which you may qualify.

Athletics
Almost all scholarships based on athletics are talent-based. Primarily, these scholarships will only be appropriate for you if you plan to compete at the intercollegiate level or major in physical education.

Disability
Many scholarships are available to individuals who are challenged with a mental or physical disability. Awards marked with this icon include those for the blind, hearing impaired, learning disabled, and physically challenged, in addition to several other disabilities.

Ethnic
This category includes scholarships awarded based on race and heritage. The most common are for African-American and Asian-American students, but the range of available awards is truly global and can get very specific. Consider your family background, and be sure to check with the scholarship provider if you are not sure whether you fit its requirements.

Grade Point Average (GPA)
Three cutoffs have been established for the GPA icons—at 2.5+, 3.0+, and 3.5+. Some scholarships' actual requirements may be somewhere between these numbers, so be sure to read the complete listing for the exact GPA criteria.

Military

Scholarships marked with this icon most often require that either you or one of your parents serve or served in the armed forces. Many of these awards are available to veterans or children of veterans of particular military actions or branches of the service. Also, many scholarships are for students whose parents were disabled or killed in military action. Items marked with this icon may also denote a major in military science or a related field.

Religion

Religious groups and organizations offer scholarships to students who are involved in religious or church-related activities, attending or coming from a religious school, or are interested in professional religious study.

Women

This icon identifies scholarships which are available to women only. Please note that many other scholarships are not for women only, but will often give preference to women.

Reading the Listings

Each scholarship listing includes the following information:

- scholarship name,
- amount of the available award or awards,
- deadline for submission of application materials,
- fields/majors of intended study,
- further information you may need in order to apply, and
- the award sponsor's address to write for application forms and additional information.

Identifying the Icons

Major/Career Objective

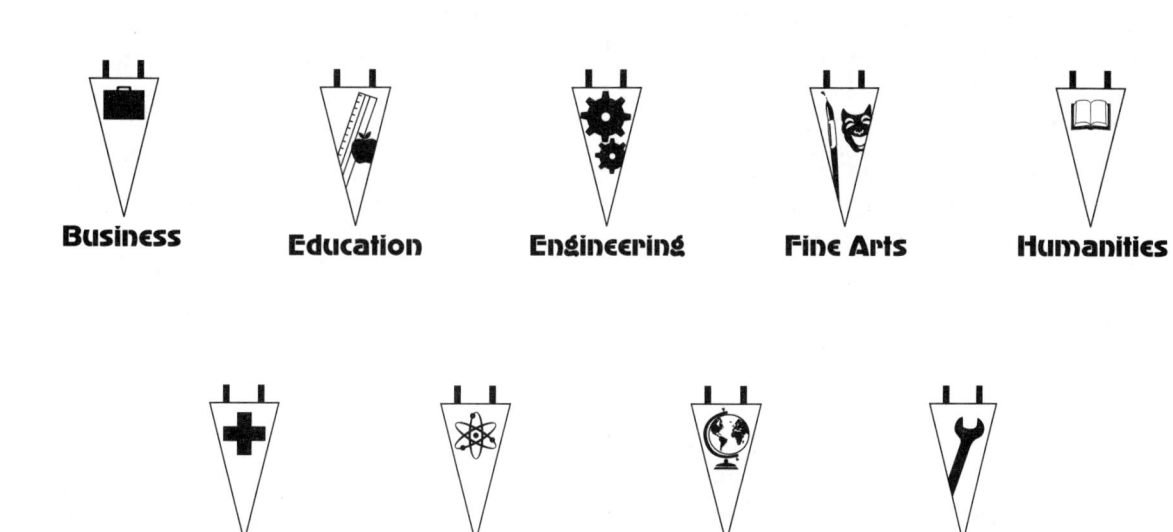

Business Education Engineering Fine Arts Humanities

Medicine Science Social Sciences Vocational

Special Criteria

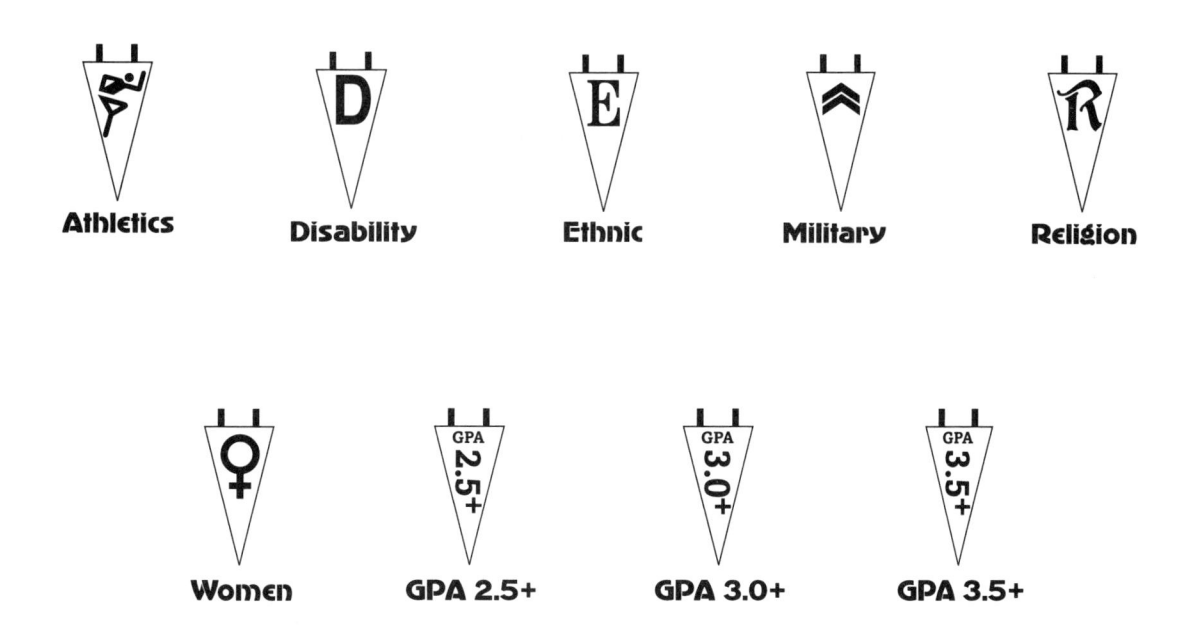

Athletics Disability Ethnic Military Religion

Women GPA 2.5+ GPA 3.0+ GPA 3.5+

Sixty-one Tips for Optimizing Your Money for College

For their help in suggesting and reviewing these tips, Student Services, L.L.C., wishes to thank: Lee Gordon, Executive Associate Director of Financial Aid at Purdue University; Ellen Frishberg, Director of Student Financial Services at Johns Hopkins University; and Derek Bates, President of Student Aid Research Through Technology.

Tip 1 — Prioritize Your Effort According to the Amount of Funding Available from Each Source of College Financial Aid

Each year, approximately $70 billion is made available to college students in the form of financial aid and tax relief. By far, the greatest source of this funding is the federal government. The next biggest source of scholarships and loans, involving several billion dollars, comes from the colleges themselves. Depending on the college, some of these awards will be financial need-based, while other awards will be merit-based (not financial need-based). To determine eligibility for these awards, many colleges require students to fill out a Free Application for Federal Student Aid (FAFSA) form (or a Renewal FAFSA, if applicable) as well as customized, supplemental forms.

As a result, when seeking financial aid for college, three important priorities for most students are to:

- Submit a FAFSA (or Renewal FAFSA).
- Submit a PROFILE form (if required by your college) or any other financial aid form and supporting documents required by the colleges to which you apply.
- Submit any additional forms that may be required by specialized federal loan programs, if applicable.

Depending on where you live and where you will attend college, you may also be eligible to receive financial aid from the $4 billion contributed by state governments. To apply for this aid, additional forms may also be necessary.

To find out more, contact the career center or guidance counseling office at your high school, or the financial aid office at the college(s) to which you will apply.

Beyond these traditional opportunities for college financial aid, another important source is philanthropic foundations, religious organizations, employers, clubs, local governments, corporations, and civic organizations who offer millions of dollars in financial aid through tuition and work-study programs. In fact, over 5,000 such opportunities for scholarships, grants, fellowships, internships, and loans are listed in this book.

However, do not rely solely on the private aid opportunities listed in this book to be your only potential sources of college financial aid. It is always wise to pursue several options, including government and college-sponsored programs.

Tip 2 — Learn All You Can about the College Financial Aid Process

It took twelve years for you to learn enough to be eligible for a college education. With that in mind, please do not be disconcerted if it takes a few weeks to learn how to best finance a college education.

For most parents and students, paying for college is one of the largest investments they will ever make. Yet despite the importance, many parents and students stumble confused through the college financial aid process. That is unfortunate for them but fortunate for you, since you can gain a tremendous advantage by learning thoroughly about college financial aid.

Such knowledge can help you to:

- not miss deadlines,
- position yourself to get a better financial aid package.

Beyond this book, good sources of information include:

- Parent Page; located on the Internet at http://www.fastweb.com/parents.html. Parent Page is an ideal place for parents to meet financial experts, talk with other parents about their financial aid experiences, and learn more on how to help their children obtain scholarships, fellowships, grants, and loans. (Note: even though Parent Page is designed for parents, this site is a tremendous resource for students as well.);
- *The Student Guide to Financial Aid*, written by the U.S. Department of Education;
- the career center or guidance counseling office at your high school;

- the financial aid office at the college(s) to which you will apply;
- *Don't Miss Out: The Ambitious Student's Guide to Financial Aid;*
- financial planners, if they are reputable and specialize in college financing.

Several sites on the Internet offer information about college financial aid. However, be discerning, since the quality of the information available varies. Links to the plethora of financial aid information available via the Internet can be found by accessing: http://www.fastweb.com.

To order a free copy of *The Student Guide to Financial Aid*, call the Federal Student Aid Information Center at 1-800-4-FED-AID, or you can access an electronic version through the Internet at http://www.ed.gov.

Tip 3 Focus on Optimizing, Rather Than Maximizing, Your Financial Aid

To maximize means "to get the most." To optimize means "to get the best." It is critical to focus on optimizing, rather than maximizing, your financial aid.

If you aim to optimize your financial aid, you will stay focused on the right things, including:

- striking the right balance between the quality of your education versus the amount of debt that becomes your burden when you graduate from school;
- improving the composition of your financial aid awards, i.e., increasing the ratio of grants to loans.

On the other hand, it would be easy (though undesirable) to simply maximize your financial aid eligibility. In that case, all you would have to do is apply to the college in the United States in which the Cost of Attendance is highest. According to the federal methodology for determining financial need, that would maximize your financial aid eligibility, since:

| Cost of Attendance at College X | - Expected Family Contribution | = Financial Aid Eligibility for College X |

In this formula, Expected Family Contribution is a constant.[1] In other words, the federal government expects you (and your family) to contribute the same amount of cash out of family resources, regardless of the tuition at the college.

As an example, suppose that the federal government determines your Expected Family Contribution to be $6,000. If you decided to attend College A at which the Cost of Attendance is $10,000, then you would be eligible to receive $4,000 of financial aid:

Cost of Attendance at College A	Expected Family Contribution	Financial Aid Eligibility for College A
$10,000	- $6,000	= $4,000

If you decided to attend College B in which the Cost of Attendance is $25,000, then you would be eligible to receive $19,000 of financial aid:

Cost of Attendance at College B	Expected Family Contribution	Financial Aid Eligibility for College B
$25,000	- $6,000	= $19,000

Therefore, the easiest way to increase your financial aid eligibility is to attend a more expensive college. However, most of this additional eligibility for financial aid may come in the form of loans that will have to be repaid. There is no great honor in graduating from college with the most debt. Yet, that is the folly of people who seek to maximize financial aid eligibility without regard to:

- the ratio of grants to loans,
- the amount of cumulative debt incurred.

Tip 4 Ensure That Cost of Attendance Calculations Include All Reasonable Costs

Since financial aid eligibility is based, in part, on Cost of Attendance, ensure that your Financial Aid Administrator(s) includes all reasonable costs in your Cost of Attendance calculation. For instance:

- If you are dyslexic, you may be able to include costs for special reading devices in the Cost of Attendance calculation.
- If you have children, you may be able to include child care expenses in the Cost of Attendance calculation.

Within reason, be expansive about the items you try to include in Cost of Attendance.

---

[1] You can get a free booklet that describes how Expected Family Contribution is calculated by calling the Federal Student Aid Information Center at 1-800-4-FED-AID.

Tip 5 Submit Your FAFSA Form Early—But Not Too Early

Apply for college financial aid from the federal government as soon as possible after January 1 of the year in which you want to receive the financial aid. For instance, to receive financial aid for the 2000–01 academic year, apply as soon as possible after January 1, 2000.

It is easier to complete the FAFSA form when you (and your parents and/or spouse) have already calculated your federal income tax return, so you may want to consider finishing these tax returns as early as possible. However, you do not have to submit your tax returns prior to submitting your FAFSA form. In fact, you can get an advantage by submitting your FAFSA before most people, even if that means making (reasonably accurate) guesses about the information that is likely to appear on your income tax return. This will increase the chance that all of your financial need will be met.[2]

Tip 6 Submit a FAFSA, Even if You Do Not Think You Will Be Eligible for Federal Financial Aid

To be considered for federal financial aid for college, you must submit a Free Application for Federal Student Aid (FAFSA) form. Even if you think that you will not be eligible for federal financial aid, submit a FAFSA anyway. This is important for four reasons:

- You might be pleasantly surprised by the results; many middle-class people are eligible for federal financial aid (typically, loans with favorable interest rates and payment-deferment options).
- Even if you do not qualify for federal loans with deferred-payment options, you might still qualify for loans with favorable interest rates.
- Submitting a FAFSA is often a prerequisite for many non-federal financial aid programs.
- Being rejected for financial aid from the government is sometimes a pre-condition for private sector awards.

Tip 7 If You are Classified as a "Dependent" Student but Have Unusual Circumstances, Ask Your Financial Aid Administrator to Change Your Status to "Independent"

Students are classified as either dependent or independent because federal student aid programs are based on the idea that students (and their parents, or spouse, if applicable) have the primary responsibility for paying for postsecondary education. According to the federal government, students who have access to parental support (dependent students) should not receive as much need-based federal funds as students who do not have such access to parental support (independent students).

Based on the federal government's methodology for determining Expected Family Contribution, it is generally in your best interest to be considered independent from your parents, rather than dependent on them.

If you are considered dependent, then the income and assets owned by you and your parents will be considered in determining your Expected Family Contribution. If you are considered independent, then only the income and assets owned by you (and your spouse, if married) will be considered.

Declaring yourself to be independent can be advantageous, especially if your parents are wealthy. You are automatically considered to be an independent student if at least one of the following applies to you:

- you will be at least twenty-four years of age on or before December 31st of the year in which you receive the financial aid,
- you are married or have legal dependents other than your spouse,
- you are enrolled in a graduate or professional education program,
- you are an orphan or a ward of the court (or were a ward of the court until age eighteen), or
- you are a veteran of the United States Armed Forces.

Otherwise, you will have to convince the Financial Aid Administrator at your college that unusual circumstances make your situation similar to an independent student. Unusual circumstances include situations that cause your parents to be absolutely unable to help pay for your college education.

---

[2] To avoid having the processor return your FAFSA form to you, do not date or send your FAFSA application before January 1 of the relevant year.

If you think that unusual circumstances make you independent, ask a Financial Aid Administrator at your college to change your status. But remember, the Financial Aid Administrator will not automatically do this. That decision is based on his or her judgment, and it is final—you cannot appeal to the U.S. Department of Education.

Tip 8 Carefully Calculate the Pros and Cons Before Shifting Assets between You and Your Parents

According to the federal methodology for calculating financial need, a dependent student is expected to contribute approximately 35 percent of his or her assets towards current-year college costs. On the other hand, parents are only expected to contribute up to 5.6 percent of their money. For instance, if $10,000 in a mutual fund were in a dependent student's name, he or she would be expected to contribute $10,000 x 35% = $3,500 of that towards current-year college costs. However, if $10,000 in that same mutual fund were in a parent's name, the parent would be expected to contribute only up to $10,000 x 5.6% = $560.

So, should dependent students shift their assets to their parents? Not necessarily, since the parents are probably in a higher income tax bracket and may have to pay in income taxes a higher proportion of their interest and capital gains. As a result, before shifting assets between parents and dependent children, families should carefully calculate the trade-offs between financial aid eligibility and income taxes.

Tip 9 Consider Reducing Reportable Assets by Shifting Assets from Cash to Equity in Your Primary Home

The FAFSA form asks you to report certain assets. Your financial aid eligibility for federal funds will be based, in part, on the amount of assets you report.

You can increase your financial aid eligibility by reducing reportable assets. To do so legally, you need to find acceptable ways to shift funds from reportable assets to non-reportable assets. For the purposes of the FAFSA form, non-reportable assets include equity in your primary home. Therefore, prior to filling out the FAFSA, if you have disposable cash, consider reducing your reportable assets by paying off part of your mortgage.

However, this asset classification-shifting technique only works in some cases, since most high-priced colleges use forms, in addition to the FAFSA, to probe for supplemental financial information, including home equity. This supplemental data can be used in determining eligibility for institutional aid.

Tip 10 Consider Reducing Reportable Assets by Making Large Purchases Prior to Filling Out the FAFSA

Another acceptable way of reducing reportable assets is to get rid of cash by buying a non-reportable asset such as a computer or a car. So, if you were going to make large purchases anyway, do so prior to filling out the FAFSA.

Tip 11 Inform Financial Aid Administrators about Recent Declines in Family Income or Assets

Generally, financial aid forms base the calculation of Expected Family Contribution on income and assets from the prior year. (The greater your income and assets, the more you will be expected to contribute to college costs.)

So, if a calculation based on last year's financial position unfairly overstates your current income or assets, ask a Financial Aid Administrator at your college to make an adjustment. For instance, if you are a dependent student and your father lost his $85,000-a-year job last week, or if your parents divorced nine months ago and you lived just with your mother ever since, this could make you eligible for additional grants or low-interest loans.

Tip 12 Inform Financial Aid Administrators about Atypical Expenses

To increase your financial aid eligibility, ensure that your Financial Aid Administrator is aware of all of your family's relevant costs. For instance, you might be eligible for additional financial aid if:

➤ one or more of your siblings attends an elementary or secondary school in which your parents pay tuition,
➤ you or your parents have documented medical or dental expenses that are not covered by insurance,
➤ you or your parents support elderly relatives.

Tip 13 Try to Establish Residency in the State Where You Will Attend College

Publicly-funded colleges charge in-state students substantially less tuition than they charge out-of-state students for identical educational programs.

If you plan to attend a public college, an easy way to save several thousand dollars is to attend a school that is located in the state where you have already satisfied residency requirements.

Alternatively, if you have strong reasons to attend an out-of-state college, you can try to establish new state residency, wherever the college you attend happens to be located. Guidelines for establishing residency vary, so check with each of the schools that interest you. Generally, some of the factors considered include:

- Do you and/or your parents own property in the state?
- Have you and/or your parents lived primarily in that state during the previous two years?
- Do you possess a drivers license in the state?
- Did you earn a significant portion of your income in the state in the year prior to attending college? Did you file an income tax return for that state?

Tip 14 Consider Attending a Lower-priced College, Particularly if Your Expected Family Contribution Is High

In general, a wealthy student will have to pay most or all of the cost of college tuition without the benefit of government grants. Therefore, the easiest way for a wealthy student to reduce his or her college debt burden is to attend a lower-priced college.

On the other hand, if your family's income and assets are more modest, the difference in the Cost of Attendance between a low-priced and high-priced college may be negated, in whole or in part, by grants and work-study programs, especially if a particular high-priced college is committed to meeting your financial need with an attractive financial aid package.

If you are considering a variety of colleges at which your out-of-pocket costs would be substantially different, your decision can be assisted by comparing graduation rates, job placement rates, graduate school admission rates, and any other factors you value. At many colleges, career counselors can tell you the percentage of students that find jobs within their chosen fields within six months of graduation. Average salary statistics and graduate school admission rates may also be available. Comparing statistics such as these can help you determine whether or not the extra tuition charged by more expensive colleges is worth it.

Keep in mind, highly motivated students can get a great education at almost any accredited college in the United States, no matter how inexpensive; whereas, unmotivated students will get a lousy education even at the most expensive private colleges.

Tip 15 Do Not Absorb More Debt Than You Can Handle

To put college debt in perspective, suppose that after graduation you could afford to pay a maximum of $600 a month towards a total of $70,000 in loans with an average interest rate of 10 percent. Paying off that debt would take over thirty-three years!

Here's another example: It would take over ten years to pay back $20,000 in loans at 10 percent interest if the most you could afford to pay off is $250 a month.

A high debt burden can take a staggering toll on the quality of your life. During the time that every cent is diverted to paying back college loans, you may have to forgo: buying a car, saving for a house, going on vacation, having a big wedding, and perhaps even starting a family.

Be especially wary of building up too much debt on high-interest credit cards.

Tip 16 Consider Attending a Community College for the First Two Years of Postsecondary Education

If you cannot afford the full cost of a four-year college, consider enrolling in a two-year community college for the first two years of your post-secondary education. Community colleges tend to charge an annual tuition that is substantially less than tuition charged by four-year colleges.

If you earn good grades at a community college, you may be able to transfer, as a junior, to a four-year college. Upon graduation from the four-year college, you would enjoy the best of both worlds:

- you would have the prestige of a degree from the four-year college, and
- you would have paid less tuition, in total, than your classmates at the four-year college.

Tip 17 Satisfy Prerequisites at Less Expensive Community Colleges

Some graduate programs and certifications may require prerequisites that were not completed during undergraduate studies. For instance, if a drama student with a bachelor's degree is interested in pursuing a graduate degree in education, he or she may not have taken enough undergraduate math and science courses to receive a state teaching certificate. Often, these prerequisites can be satisfied by taking equivalent courses at an accredited two-year college. This is often a more economical option than taking the course at the more expensive graduate degree school.

Tip 18 Consider Accumulating Credits Faster Than Normal

Suppose you are attending a degree program that takes most students four years to complete. If you finish that degree in three-and-a-half years, you will save 12.5 percent on tuition and will be able to work full-time for half a year longer. If you finish in three years, you will save 25 percent on tuition and will be able to work full-time for a full year longer.

To accumulate credits faster than most people:

- Attend credit courses during intersessions and summer.
- Enroll in as many additional classes per semester or quarter as you can handle.
- Earn credit for college based on recognition that your life experience is equivalent to college-level mastery of a particular subject. This can be demonstrated through the College Board's College-Level Examination Program (CLEP) test or through ACT's Proficiency Examination Program (PEP).
- Earn credit for college during high school by scoring well on advanced placement tests.
- Attend a few college courses while still in high school.

Tip 19 Consider Earning a Three-Year Degree Rather Than a Four-Year Degree

Many fine colleges help students afford postsecondary education by offering degrees that are meant to be earned in three years rather than four. Perhaps this is a good option for you. However, be mindful of the disadvantages:

- Some people believe that four years is required to develop intellectual and occupational skills fully.
- Many people consider their college years to be among the best times of their life. Therefore, why rush if you do not have to?

Tip 20 Consider Combining Degrees

If you are planning to earn multiple degrees anyway, you can save a year's tuition and time by finding a college that will allow you to combine degrees, such as:

- combining a BS with an MBA,
- combining a BA with an MA,
- combining a master's degree with a Ph.D., and
- combining an undergraduate degree with a Master's in Education degree.

Tip 21 Consider Attending a College in an Area Where the Cost of Living is Lower

Tuition is only one component of the Cost of Attendance. Other major costs include food and rent—both of which are affected by the local cost of living. For instance, a hamburger at a fast food chain in Boston, Massachusetts, might cost $1.99, whereas the same hamburger from the same fast food chain might cost only $1.49 in Little Rock, Arkansas. For similar accommodations, rent can also vary considerably from city to city.

In fact, you can save hundreds or thousands of dollars per year by attending a college in an area where the cost of living is lower.

Tip 22 Consider Attending School at Home

A growing number of schools allow you to earn academic credit through distance learning; that is, via computer network, television, and video tapes. In addition, many offer evening classes at satellite facilities that may be located near your home. These approaches can allow you to keep working while earning credit, avoid the expense of moving to another locale, and often, learn at your own pace.

Tip 23 Improve Your Grades and Standardized Test Scores

To enhance their reputations, colleges need to attract outstanding students, especially students who excel academically. As a result, most colleges offer preferential financial aid packages to students with excellent academic records. Generally, the better your grades, the better the financial aid package offered to you by a college.

For instance, suppose that Johnny (who has an 'A' average) and Jimmy (who has a 'B' average) both apply to the same college in which the Cost of Attendance is $10,000. Further, suppose that, according to the federal methodology for determining financial need, Johnny and Jimmy are both expected to contribute the same amount for college out of cash flow: $4,000. Does this mean that Johnny and Jimmy will both be treated the same when the college makes financial aid offers? The answer is "Yes" and "No."

"Yes," Johnny and Jimmy will both be eligible to receive the same amount of financial aid: $6,000.

But "No," since Johnny may get more grants than loans, while Jimmy gets more loans than grants. For instance, Johnny might receive $4,000 in grants and $2,000 in loans, while Jimmy might receive $1,000 in grants and $5,000 in loans. Johnny may get preferential treatment since his 'A' grade average is more desirable to the college.

Tip 24 Improve Your College Grades

To encourage strong academic performance, many colleges offer scholarships for students who continue to earn high grades. Make sure you are aware of the qualification criteria at your college, which might include:

- making the Dean's List,
- attaining a specific grade point average, or
- earning grades that place your academic performance among the top rank of students.

Sometimes, the value of academic scholarships will increase with performance. Substantial scholarships may be available to continuing students who attain grades at the very top of their class.

Tip 25 Apply to Colleges in Which Your Academic Performance Ranks Among the Top 25 Percent of Applicants

Colleges offer their best financial aid packages to their best applicants. Therefore, you can often improve the financial aid package offered to you by applying to colleges in which your academic and extracurricular record is better than most of the other applicants.

For instance, suppose that Janice, who has a 3.7 GPA, applies to a highly competitive college (at which the average GPA among applicants is 3.7) and a moderately competitive college (at which the average GPA among applicants is 3.1). Further, suppose that the Cost of Attendance is the same at the highly competitive college and the moderately competitive college. In that instance, it is likely that Janice will be offered a better financial aid package by the moderately competitive college, since her record compares more favorably to the rest of that college's applicants.

Tip 26 Apply to at Least Three Colleges That Are Likely to Accept You

One of the most direct ways to improve your financial aid choices is to increase the number of colleges to which you apply. By applying to several colleges, you will be offered a variety of different financial aid packages. Based on the schools' particular needs, some of these financial aid offers will be more attractive than others. Even similar schools may make very different offers, for reasons that are difficult to foresee. For instance, you might receive an unexpectedly favorable financial aid offer from a college if they desperately need a harp player for the symphonic orchestra and you are the only harp player that applied.

Applying to a few extra colleges may cost $100 to $150 in extra application fees, but this investment could save thousands of dollars if one of these colleges offers an especially attractive financial aid package.

Some schools use financial aid as a recruiting tool. Others do not.

Tip 27 Choose a Major in an Area Where Demand for Graduating Students Exceeds Supply

Competitive on-campus recruiting motivates employers to offer incentives to students who pursue majors in high demand areas. For instance, if you notice that graduating engineering and computer science students are receiving a large number of job offers, that is a good indication that employer-paid scholarships and high paying summer jobs may also be available. To learn more, check with your campus recruiting office.

Tip 28 Encourage Your Professor(s) to Convert Poor Grades into an Assessment Marked 'Incomplete'

Some grants and scholarships require certain minimum grade point averages. A poor grade will lower your GPA. An incomplete grade, however, will not be factored into the GPA calculation and thus will have the effect of artificially raising your average. Therefore, if your GPA is dangerously close to disqualifying you from an award, then try to encourage your professor to change your worst grade into an assessment marked incomplete.

Incomplete means that you will receive a final grade at some point in the future, after you have had an opportunity to submit additional material to your professor(s) for evaluation.

Tip 29 Money from Grandparents Should Be Paid, in Your Name, Directly to the College

If your grandparents want to help pay for your college tuition, ask them to send money, in your name, directly to the college. In that way, you will get the full benefit of their generosity while avoiding:

- gift tax liability,
- artificially overstating your own assets.

Tip 30 Take Advantage of Tuition Pre-payment Discounts, if Available

Some colleges offer discounts as high as 10 percent if tuition is paid in full by a specific date. Taking advantage of this early payment discount is often better than keeping the money in the bank and paying tuition in installments. If the discount is high enough, and if you have the money available to you anyway, take the discount option.

Tip 31 Take Advantage of Discounts for College Employees and Children of College Employees

Many colleges offer substantial discounts for employees and children of employees. To qualify for the discount, the college employee does not necessarily need to be a professor; the same discount options will often be made available to secretaries and janitors too. As a result, you may be able to save thousands in tuition if you or a parent are able to get a full-time job at a college.

If you are really tight for cash, perhaps you could work at the college full-time and attend courses part-time.

Tip 32 Take Advantage of Discounts for Children of Alumni

To encourage long-term customer loyalty among families, many colleges offer discounts for children of alumni. These discounts can be significant, so find out how much you might save by attending Mom's or Dad's former college.

Tip 33 Start Saving for College as Soon as Possible

College costs can place a severe financial drain on family resources, especially cash flow. Many families make these problems more extreme by waiting too long to start saving for college. Setting aside a few hundred dollars each month for several years, although difficult, is a lot easier than setting aside twenty thousand dollars a year for four years.

To minimize the monthly financial outlay, parents may want to start saving for college as soon as possible, even when their children are just a few years old.

Tip 34 Plan Ahead

To avoid the confusion and frustration that can occur by waiting until the last moment, your family should start to investigate thoroughly the college financial aid process while you are still a high school junior.

In your junior year, it is helpful to:

➤ Gather and review all of the government and college financial aid forms that need to be submitted.

➤ Request additional information from some of the scholarship providers listed in this book.

➤ Create a milestone chart that indicates the deadlines for each financial aid activity and form.

➤ Seek advice from a financial specialist, if appropriate, to reposition family assets in a way that optimizes financial aid eligibility and income tax payments.

➤ Investigate loan options from commercial lenders.

Tip 35 Build Credentials for Scholarships While You Are Still in High School

Many privately-sponsored scholarships are awarded based, in part, on the student's references and extracurricular activities. For instance, a student is more likely to win a scholarship if:

➤ the people who provide references write spectacular comments rather than merely above average comments,

➤ the references come from people who are leaders in their field, rather than from people who have less established reputations,

➤ the student has engaged in activities that demonstrate extraordinary talent and good citizenship.

Therefore, while you are still in high school, it is wise to build your resume and build your reference pool by engaging in extracurricular and volunteer activities that will position you to get excellent references or awards for laudable activities.

Other applicants will have awards from the mayor for helping underprivileged children. What about you?

Tip 36 Leverage Your Athletic Talents

Athletic scholarships are awarded to many students who are capable of competing at an intercollegiate (NCAA Division I or II) level. You do not have to be a high school superstar to receive an athletic scholarship. Colleges need excellent reserve players in addition to superstars. High school superstar athletes who compete in popular sports will likely be approached by college recruiters. However, other high school athletes may need to take a more assertive role in attracting the interest of college coaches. This effort can be worth it, since many colleges set aside considerable money for athletic scholarships and preferential financial aid packages.

To learn more about opportunities for student athletes, contact the National Collegiate Athletic Association (NCAA), a Financial Aid Administrator, your high school coach, or the relevant coaches at the colleges that interest you. The Web site for the National Collegiate Athletic Associate is http://www.ncaa.org.

Tip 37 Build a Portfolio That Can Be Used to Demonstrate Your Accomplishments

To help support your applications for jobs, college admissions, and private scholarships, it is useful to have various sources from which to demonstrate your accomplishments. Therefore, build a portfolio of sources by doing things such as:

➤ videotaping your finest acting performances,

➤ encouraging former employers to write 'To Whom It May Concern' reference letters,

➤ photographing your best artworks,

➤ saving clippings from the newspaper that report on your track and field victories, and

➤ keeping a copy of the certificate you received for winning the science fair.

Tip 38 Find Out Whether Your Parents' Employer(s) Offer College Scholarships

Many big corporations offer college scholarships and tuition reimbursement programs to children of employees. Refer questions about availability and eligibility requirements to the human resources department at your parents' employer(s).

Tip 39 Investigate Company-Sponsored Tuition Plans

If you are already employed, some employers will subsidize the cost of your college tuition if, in return, you promise to work for the employer for a certain number of years upon graduation. In some cases, the employer will grant a leave of absence so you can attend college full-time. More often, however, employers prefer participants to attend college part-time while maintaining a full-time schedule at work.

Generally, participation in company-sponsored tuition plans is based on the quality of work performance rather than previous grades.

As long as you like the employer and the job opportunity, company-sponsored tuition plans can be a great deal. You get substantial tuition subsidies and "guaranteed" employment upon graduation.

Tip 40 Investigate Cooperative Education Opportunities

Cooperative education opportunities combine traditional classroom teaching with off-campus work experience related to your major. In practice, this could mean that you would:

- attend classes in the morning and work in the afternoon (or vice versa);
- work during the day and attend classes during the evenings; or
- attend classes for a semester, then work for a semester, then attend classes for a semester, then work for a semester, etc.

The biggest disadvantage of cooperative education is that it often lengthens the time required to earn a college degree.

The biggest advantages of cooperative education include:

- earning money while you're learning;
- the opportunity to build a strong relationship with a prospective full-time employer, based on work performance rather than grades; and
- graduating from college with more practical experience than students who did not attend a cooperative education program.

Tip 41 Consider Joining the Military

Ignore this idea if you dislike hierarchy, rebel against authority, or conscientiously object to the activities of the military. However, if you would consider it an honor to serve your country as a member of the armed services, the military can be a tremendous source of college financial aid, either before entering the service, while in the service, or as a veteran.

In return for military service, the U.S. armed forces provides several options that help students defray or eliminate their college costs.

For undergraduate students with high SAT or ACT scores, ROTC scholarships are a tremendous source of college financial aid.

- For more information on Army ROTC scholarships and programs, contact 1-800-USA-ROTC.
- For more information on Navy ROTC scholarships and programs, contact 1-800-NAV-ROTC.
- For more information on Marine Corps ROTC scholarships and programs, contact 1-800-NAV-ROTC.
- For more information on Air Force ROTC scholarships and programs, contact 1-800-423-USAF.

Tip 42 If Applicable, Use Your Minority Status to Your Advantage

Have you ever wondered why some financial aid applications ask questions about race and heritage? Do you find this offensive and therefore refuse to answer? If you leave such questions blank, you might be missing out on significant scholarship and grant opportunities.

To promote cultural diversity and understanding, many colleges offer special financial aid opportunities to ethnic minorities. As well, many college scholarships provided by the private sector are also based, in part, on race or ancestry. Even if just one of your parents or grandparents were a member of a minority group, this might improve your financial aid package.

Tip 43 Take a Good Look at Yourself.

Although we often think of ourselves as part of one group—as being a woman, for example, or Italian or Lutheran or African-American—you may actually belong to several groups. A woman, for example, may also be Hispanic, Catholic, and hearing impaired—or have any number of other "minority" attributes. In other words, taking a broader look at your background may reveal aspects that make you eligible for a wider variety of specialized scholarships.

Tip 44 Take Advantage of Your Personal History and Experience

Many scholarships for women, minorities, and people with disabilities focus on certain areas of interest, as well as your heritage, such as scholarships for people of Japanese ancestry who are interested in agriculture, Native Americans who are studying in health-related fields, and disabled people who want to pursue a degree in electronics. So look for financial aid from private donors that reward your activities, work experience, career interests, and goals.

Tip 45 Look for Organizations That Have Your Interests in Mind

Many organizations are interested in advancing the causes of women, minorities, and people with disabilities. Consider:

- corporations that want to be socially responsible,
- associations that wish to support their members,
- minority-based professional associations,
- organizations that want to promote participation from women and minorities in certain activities or sports,
- organizations that support Women's Studies,
- organizations that wish to support single mothers and/or women who have had their college education interrupted,
- organizations that wish to support women and minorities who are pursuing majors in careers in which they have been traditionally underrepresented,
- religious or ethnic organizations that wish to support women and minorities who share their religion or ethnicity.

Tip 46 Find Out What Worked Before

If you are interested in applying for a specific award, find out the qualities of last year's winner. Where there are similarities between you and last year's winner, emphasize those aspects in your application. Where important deficiencies exist, consider upgrading your credentials in those areas. Research grants, in particular, often require you to write a proposal, and fellowships usually require an essay. Try to find samples of previous winning proposals and essays. Often, graduate students are willing to share their accepted proposals with others.

Tip 47 Don't Be Intimidated by Writing Grant Proposals

Writing a research grant proposal can seem like a frightening proposition. But if you find a potential grant that fits your interests, it is worth the effort to apply for two reasons. First, if you don't try, you will certainly not be awarded the grant. Second, if you try and your grant proposal is rejected, you might learn something. That is because research grant rejections often include specific feedback about why the proposal was turned down—and that feedback can help you polish your proposal for your next effort.

Tip 48 Establish a Relationship with Your Financial Aid Administrator

Theoretically, establishing a relationship with your Financial Aid Administrator is not supposed to give you an advantage, since financial aid calculations are based on pre-defined rules and mathematical formulas. However, when borderline situations or unusual circumstances occur, a Financial Aid Administrator is allowed to use discretion. In such situations, the Financial Aid Administrator's decision could mean the difference between receiving $2,000 in loans versus $2,000 in grants. Therefore, the Financial Aid Administrator is an important person to know. Be a face, not just a name.

Tip 49 Understand How a College's Financial Aid Policies Will Affect You

You have the right to receive the following information from the financial aid office at each accredited college:

- the financial assistance that is available, including information on all federal, state, local, private, and institutional financial aid programs;
- the procedures and deadlines for submitting applications for each available financial aid program;
- how the school selects financial aid recipients;
- how the school determines your financial need;

- how the school determines each type and amount of assistance in your financial aid package;
- how and when you'll receive your aid (if granted);
- how the school determines whether you're making satisfactory academic progress, and what happens if you do not;
- the nature, if offered, of a Federal Work-Study job, what the job is, what hours you must work, what your duties will be, what the rate of pay will be, and how and when you will be paid;
- the location, hours, and counseling procedures of the school's financial aid office; and
- the school's refund policy, in the event that you leave the school prior to completing your coursework.

Tip 50 Stay in Touch with Your Financial Aid Office

The college financial aid picture changes from time to time—especially federal and state aid, which is subject to congressional action and shifts in the political climate.

It is also important to let the Financial Aid Office know about changes in your personal situation that may affect your financial status-changes such as increased medical costs or the birth of a child. If the office is aware of such changes, they may be able to make adjustments or find other sources of aid. Also, for short-term problems, many universities maintain an emergency financial aid fund.

Tip 51 Maintain Your Eligibility for Renewable Awards

If you receive an award that can be renewed, ensure that you understand, and do, whatever it takes to maintain eligibility for future years. For instance, many renewable awards will expect you to maintain a predetermined grade average. Sometimes the criteria for renewal will be very creative, such as remaining a non-smoker or doing a certain number of hours of volunteer work.

Tip 52 Pursue Scholarships from Private Donors, Even if the Awards Will Not Reduce Your Out-of-Pocket Payments

You may have heard that winning a scholarship from a private organization is a mixed blessing. That is true for some students, but not others, depending on their financial need. The following example illustrates the possible scenarios.

Scenario 1

Suppose:

- Sally won a $2,000 scholarship for winning a science competition.
- Sally's Cost of Attendance at College 'X' is $10,000, and her Expected Family Contribution is $10,000.
- Sally will be attending College 'X' at which her federal financial aid eligibility is $0.

In this scenario, Sally would benefit fully from the $2,000 scholarship.

Scenario 2

Suppose:

- Sally won a $2,000 scholarship for winning a science competition.
- Sally's Cost of Attendance at College 'Y' is $10,000, and her Expected Family Contribution is $7,000.
- Sally will be attending College 'Y' at which her federal financial aid eligibility is $3,000.

In this scenario, Sally may not benefit financially from the scholarship because the Financial Aid Administrator at College Y will be legally obligated to reduce Sally's federal financial aid eligibility by the amount of the non-government award, from $3,000 to $1,000. So, even though Sally will gain $2,000 from the private donor, she will lose $2,000 in federal financial aid eligibility.

Even if your situation is consistent with Scenario 2 rather than Scenario 1, there are two important reasons to apply for scholarships from private organizations anyway:

- If a private scholarship reduces your federal financial aid eligibility, many Financial Aid Administrators will reduce the loan portion of your federal financial aid package rather than the grant portion.

> Even if you do not benefit financially from the private sector award, you will benefit from the prestige. A scholarship from a private organization will be a great addition to your resume.

Tip 53 Register for Selective Service, if Required by Law

To receive college financial aid from the federal government, you must register, or arrange to register, with the Selective Service, if required by law. The requirement to register applies to males who were born on or after January 1, 1960, are at least eighteen years old, are citizens of the United States or eligible non-citizens, and are not currently on active duty in the armed forces. (Citizens of the Federated States of Micronesia, the Marshall Islands, or Palau are exempt from registering.)

Tip 54 Just Say "No" to Drugs

Being convicted for drug distribution or possession may make you ineligible to receive college financial aid from the federal government.

Tip 55 Double-Check Your Forms for Accuracy...Then Check Them Again

Even small errors or omissions on a financial aid form can cause the form to be rejected and returned to you. By the time you correct the mistake and resubmit the form, the money set aside for the better financial aid programs may have run out. So, read the instructions carefully. Ensure that you answer all questions, use specific numbers rather than ranges (such as $100–$200), write legibly, include correct social security numbers, sign the form, do not write in the margins, etc.

Tip 56 Do Not Rely on Out-of-Date Information or Forms

College financial aid programs, forms, and rules change every year. Relying on information older than one school year, or using old forms, can seriously delay the financial aid process or cause ineligibility. Be sure to use forms that are valid for the upcoming school year.

Tip 57 Get a Job

In an ideal world, students would be able to attend high school and college without having to get a job. Instead, ample time would be available for homework and extracurricular activities, along with a little time left over for relaxing.

Unfortunately, this ideal is not a luxury that most families can afford anymore. To avoid the burden of an unbearable debt after graduating from college, you may need to:

> Get a full-time job during the summer
> Strike a reasonable balance, during the school-year, between your course load and the hours spent at a part-time job

Tip 58 Get a High-Paying Job

If you have to supplement your income by getting a part-time job while attending school, try to limit the number of hours at that job by maximizing earnings per hour. This seems obvious, yet many students sell themselves short by aiming too low. Frying burgers at a fast food chain or washing dishes at a restaurant is an achingly slow way to earn money.

Often, finding a higher paying job is not terribly difficult. The first and most important step is increasing your expectations. For instance, higher expectations will lead you to look for work at restaurants where the tips are big rather than at restaurants where the tips are meager.

As you pursue your job search, be aware that the best jobs are rarely advertised. Discovering excellent jobs often requires knocking on doors and seeking tips from friends. Persistence and a positive attitude are critical.

Remember, in life, you don't always get what you deserve, you get what you settle for.

Everything else being equal, the only time it can pay to accept a lower paying job is when that particular opportunity enriches your education or long-term career prospects.

Tip 59 Check into Residence Hall Counselor Scholarships

Many colleges with on-campus housing need students to serve as counselors for their residence halls, in return for a scholarship that is sometimes worth as much as the value of room and board. Most often, colleges do not announce the availability of these scholarships publicly, so you may have to approach people who are in charge of on-campus residences and dormitories. Generally, Residence Hall Counselors are chosen based more on personal character and leadership than on high grades.

Tip 60 Attend School Half-Time Rather than Part-Time

If you cannot attend school full-time but still want to be eligible for federal financial aid, make sure you register for enough courses to be considered a half-time student rather than just a part-time student. Part-time students do not qualify for most federal financial aid. Minimum attendance requirements to be considered a half-time student are: six semester or quarter hours per academic term for colleges on the semester, trimester, or quarter system; or twelve semester hours or eighteen quarter hours per school year for colleges that use a credit hour system.

Tip 61 Actually Apply

You cannot receive financial aid for awards for which you do not apply. A great number of students "kick the tires" of the financial aid process without following up. These passive students seem to get overwhelmed by the process, or lose interest, or both. Whatever the reason, their loss can be your gain.

However, you must keep motivated. Optimizing your financial aid can be time consuming and exasperating, but it's worth it.

In Summary

Be an informed, educated, and assertive consumer of higher education services and resources. Do not leave your financial aid eligibility to chance. Apply first for college financial aid from the federal government and the colleges you wish to attend, but conduct research on as many additional resources as possible. Read and understand your rights, responsibilities, and opportunities. Be persistent in talking to all of the people who could either help you or direct you to the right resources for help, including high school counselors, members of local civic, women's and minority organizations, and clergy—and, of course, your Financial Aid Administrator.

Admittedly, the process is not always easy or simple—in fact, it can be quite time-consuming, and you will probably have to work to keep yourself motivated. But the effort can be worth it for the short-term benefit of having more money for college and for the long-term opportunities to be found through higher education.

General Awards

1

4-H Development Fund

AMOUNT: $200   DEADLINE: June 1
FIELDS/MAJORS: All Areas of Study

Scholarships for 4-H members from Johnson County, Kansas. Must have been a member for at least five years. Not renewable, but recipients may reapply. Based on completion of one semester or term with a "C" average or above. Write to the address below for details.

Johnson County Extension Office
Lareta Tabor, 4-H Extension Officer
1205 E. Santa Fe St.
Olathe, KS   66061

2

A Call to Action Opportunity Scholarships

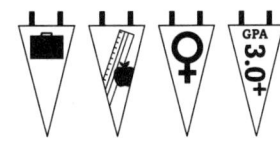

AMOUNT: Maximum: $5000
DEADLINE: August 1
FIELDS/MAJORS: Business, Education, Healthcare, Law Enforcement/Public Service, Mathematics/Science

Open to female California residents wishing to pursue careers in any of the five categories listed above. Applicants must have completed at least two years of postsecondary education, with a minimum GPA of 3.3 and/or four years of work experience. Must be U.S. citizens or legal immigrants and accepted to an accredited California institution. Winners will be notified by telephone, and awards will be presented on October 8. Contact the address listed for further information, or call (916) 445-2841.

Governor's Conference for Women
Office of the Governor, Debbie Olson
State Capitol, First Floor
Sacramento, CA   95814

3

A. Franklin Pilchard Foundation Scholarship

AMOUNT: None Specified   DEADLINE: April 15
FIELDS/MAJORS: All Areas of Study

Open to Illinois high school seniors attending "selected" high schools in Illinois. For use at Illinois colleges or universities. Applicants must check with their high schools to see if the school is participating in the program. Applications and information are available only through the selected schools. NO information is available from the foundation, so please do NOT write for it. Must have a GPA of at least 2.4. Contact your school to see if it is a participating school and to gain information and an application.

McCarthy, Pacilio, Eiesland & Gibbert, P.C.
Certified Public Accountants
1661 Feehanville Dr., St. 120
Mount Prospect, IL   60056

4

AFUD Research Scholar Program, Medical Student Fellowship

AMOUNT: None Specified   DEADLINE: September 1
FIELDS/MAJORS: Urology, Medical Research

Fellowships, awards, and research grants for medical students, researchers, and clinicians in urology and urologic diseases. Renewable. Write to the AFUD at the address below for details.

American Foundation for Urologic Disease, Inc.
Research Scholar Program
300 West Pratt St., Suite 401
Baltimore, MD   21201

5

AFUD Research Scholars, Practicing Urologist's Research Award

AMOUNT: Maximum: $5500   DEADLINE: None Specified
FIELDS/MAJORS: Urology, Nephrology

Research support for postdoctoral, postresidency, and practicing scientists and medical doctors concentrating in the area of urologic diseases and dysfunctions. Peer review is available, if desired, for research proposals. Write to the AFUD at the address below for details.

American Foundation for Urologic Disease, Inc.
Research Program Division
300 West Pratt St., Suite 401
Baltimore, MD   21201

6

A.O. Putnam Memorial Scholarship

AMOUNT: Maximum: $500 DEADLINE: November 15
FIELDS/MAJORS: Industrial Engineering

Scholarships are available for undergraduate industrial engineering majors who are enrolled on a full-time basis, members of the institute, with a GPA of at least 3.4. Preference is given to students with a career interest in management consulting. For freshmen, sophomores, or juniors. Students must be nominated by their IIE department heads. Contact your school's Industrial Engineering Department Head for information.

Institute of Industrial Engineers
Scholarship Program
25 Technology Park/Atlanta
Norcross, GA 30092

7

A.P. Rouch and Louise Rouch Scholarship Grant

AMOUNT: $1000 DEADLINE: May 1
FIELDS/MAJORS: All Areas of Study

Applicants must be residents of the Twin Falls, Idaho, area and demonstrate financial need. Four awards are given annually. Write to address below for details.

Rouch Foundation
C/O First Security Bank, Trust Group
102 Main Ave. South
Twin Falls, ID 83303

8

A.T. Anderson Memorial Scholarship

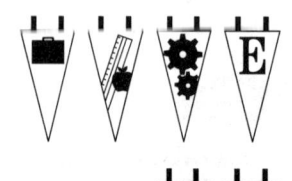

AMOUNT: $1000-$2000
DEADLINE: June 15
FIELDS/MAJORS: Medicine, Natural Resources, Math/Science Secondary Education, Engineering, Sciences, Business

Open to students who are one-quarter American Indian or recognized as a member of a tribe. Must be a member of AISES and enrolled full-time at an accredited institution. $1000 award for undergraduates, and $2000 award for graduates. May reapply each year. Contact the address listed or call (303) 939-0023 for further information.

American Indian Science and Engineering Society
Scholarship Coordinator
5661 Airport Blvd.
Boulder, CO 80301-2339

9

A.T. Cross Scholarship

AMOUNT: $500-$3000 DEADLINE: April 1
FIELDS/MAJORS: All Areas of Study

Scholarships are available for children of full-time employees of A.T. Cross. Write to the address listed for information.

A.T. Cross Company
Employee Communications Administrator
One Albion Road
Lincoln, RI 02865

10

A.W. "Winn" Brindle Memorial Scholarship Loan Fund

AMOUNT: None Specified DEADLINE: None Specified
FIELDS/MAJORS: Fisheries, Food Technology, and Related

Privately funded loans for Alaska residents for studies related to the fishing industry. Renewable for up to eight years. For full-time study. Interest rate is 5%, and recipients are eligible for 50% forgiveness upon graduation and employment in Alaska in the fishing industry. Write to A.W. "Winn" Brindle Memorial Scholarship Loan Program at the address listed or call 1-800-441-2962 for details.

Alaska Commission on Post-Secondary Education
3030 Vintage Blvd.
Juneau, AK 99801

11

A.W. Bodine-Sunkist Memorial Scholarship

AMOUNT: Maximum: $3000 DEADLINE: April 30
FIELDS/MAJORS: All Areas of Study

Scholarships for undergraduate students from agricultural backgrounds in Arizona or California. Renewable. Based on grades, test scores, essay and references. Must have a GPA of at least 3.0. Write to the address listed for details.

Sunkist Growers, Inc.
Claire H. Peters, Administrator
PO Box 7888
Van Nuys, CA 91409

12

AAAA Minority Advertising Intern Program

AMOUNT: $3000   DEADLINE: January 30
FIELDS/MAJORS: Advertising, Communications, Liberal Arts, Marketing

Summer internship program for minority students beyond their junior year of undergraduate work or in graduate school. Must be a U.S. citizen or permanent resident and have a GPA of at least 3.0. Write to the address below for more information.

American Association of Advertising Agencies, Inc.
AAAA Minority Advertising Intern Program
405 Lexington Ave., 18th Floor
New York, NY   10174-1801

13

AACC Undergraduate Scholarship Program

AMOUNT: $1000-$2000   DEADLINE: April 1
FIELDS/MAJORS: Cereal Chemistry and Technology (including Oilseed Chemistry and Technology)

Scholarships for undergraduate students who have completed at least one term and plan to pursue a career in the field of cereal and oilseed science and technology. Must have a college GPA of at least 3.0. Fifteen awards per year. Write to the address below for information and application forms. Please specify that you are interested in the undergraduate awards.

American Association of Cereal Chemists
Scholarship Program
3340 Pilot Knob Road
St. Paul, MN   55121

14

AAS Short-Term Fellowships

AMOUNT: $950-$2850   DEADLINE: January 15
FIELDS/MAJORS: American History, History of Publishing, Eighteenth Century Studies, Etc.

One to three month fellowships in support of research utilizing the collections of the American Antiquarian Society. The AAS has extensive holdings of published materials (books, pamphlets, almanacs, etc.) from antebellum America. Open to Ph.D. students and doctoral candidates engaged in dissertation research. Joint application with the Newberry Library (in Chicago) is encouraged. Write to the Society at the address listed for further information. Please specify the award name when writing.

American Antiquarian Society
Director of Research and Publication
185 Salisbury St., Room 100
Worcester, MA   01609

15

AAS National Endowment for the Humanities Fellowships

AMOUNT: Maximum: $30000   DEADLINE: January 15
FIELDS/MAJORS: American History, History of Publishing, Eighteenth Century Studies

Six- to twelve-month fellowships in support of research utilizing the collections of the American Antiquarian Society. Must hold Ph.D. and be U.S. citizens or legal residents for more than three years. The AAS has extensive holdings of published materials (books, pamphlets, almanacs, etc.) from antebellum America. Joint application with the Newberry Library (in Chicago) is encouraged. Write to the Society at the address listed for further information. Please specify the award name when writing.

American Antiquarian Society
Director of Research and Publication
185 Salisbury St., Room 100
Worcester, MA   01609

16

AAUW Grants

AMOUNT: $1000   DEADLINE: May 15
FIELDS/MAJORS: All Areas of Study

Scholarships for female graduate students from the Norwalk-Westport area or for women (in the same area) who are furthering their education or who are changing careers. Must be a resident of Norwalk, Westport, Wilton, Weston, or Darien. One award is offered annually. Please enclose a legal-sized SASE with your request for an application. Write to Willadean Hart, Chair, at the address below.

American Association of University Women,
   Norwalk-Westport Branch
Chair, Student Grant Committee
36 Colony Road
Westport, CT   06880

17

AAUW-Walnut Creek Scholarships

AMOUNT: None Specified   DEADLINE: March 2
FIELDS/MAJORS: All Areas of Study

Open to women who are U.S. citizens, residents of Contra Costa, and are at least thirty years of age. Must be enrolling as a junior or senior, have a minimum GPA of 2.6 for freshman and sophomore years, and be able to demonstrate financial need. Contact the address listed further information.

American Association of University Women, Walnut Creek
Local Scholarship Fund
PO Box 2322
Walnut Creek, CA   94595

18

Abbie Sargent Memorial Scholarship

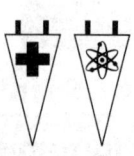

AMOUNT: $200   DEADLINE: March 15
FIELDS/MAJORS: Agriculture, Agribusiness, Horticulture, Veterinary Medicine, Animal Science, Home Economics

Two or three scholarships are available to full- or part-time undergraduates or graduates involved in the studies that are listed above. Must be residents of New Hampshire and demonstrate financial need. Write to the address listed for more information.

Abbie Sargent Memorial Scholarship
295 Sheep Davis Rd.
Concord, NH   03301

19

Abe and Annie Seibel Foundation Educational Loans

AMOUNT: $2500-$3000   DEADLINE: November 1
FIELDS/MAJORS: All Areas of Study

Loans available to Texas residents who are enrolled or planning to attend a Texas college or university to obtain a bachelor's degree. All applicants must have graduated from a Texas high school and have a minimum GPA of 3.0. Write to the address below for details. Information will not be sent to students until the first working day after Christmas.

Abe and Annie Seibel Foundation
C/O United States National Bank, Trust Dept.
PO Box 8210
Galveston, TX   77553

20

Abe and Esther Hagiwara Student Aid Award

AMOUNT: None Specified   DEADLINE: April 1
FIELDS/MAJORS: All Areas of Study

Open to members of the Japanese-American Citizens League who can demonstrate severe financial need. Applications and information may be obtained from local JACL chapters, district offices, and national headquarters at the address listed or (415) 921-5225. Please indicate your level of study and be certain to include a legal-sized SASE.

Japanese-American Citizens League
National Scholarship and Award Program
1765 Sutter St.
San Francisco, CA   94115

21

Abraham A. Spack Fellowship

AMOUNT: None Specified   DEADLINE: April 30
FIELDS/MAJORS: Jewish Education

Awards are available for undergraduate college students who are interested in serving the Jewish people as a Jewish educator. Write to the address below for more information.

Coalition for the Advancement of Jewish Education
261 W. 35th St.
Floor 12A
New York, NY   10001

22

Academic Scholarships

AMOUNT: Maximum: $1000   DEADLINE: April 1
FIELDS/MAJORS: Real Estate

Scholarships for juniors and seniors who are residents of Illinois and are attending two- or four-year schools in Illinois. Based on desire to pursue a career in real estate or a related field, academics, need, and references. Must have completed 30 college credit hours and be U.S. citizens. Write to the address listed for details. Must have a GPA of at least 2.8.

Illinois Real Estate Educational Foundation
3180 Adloff Ln.
PO Box 19451
Springfield, IL   62794

23

ACB of Colorado Scholarships

AMOUNT: Maximum: $1500   DEADLINE: March 1
FIELDS/MAJORS: All Areas of Study

Scholarships are available to legally blind students who are residents of Colorado. Write to the address listed or call (202) 467-5081 or 1-800-424-8666 for details.

American Council of the Blind
Scholarship Coordinator
1155 15th St. NW, Suite 720
Washington, DC   20005

24

ACEC Scholarships

AMOUNT: $2000-$5000   DEADLINE: March 15
FIELDS/MAJORS: Engineering

Applicants must be a junior, senior, or fifth-year student working toward a degree at an accredited ABET university.

Seven to eight awards for $2000 and one award for $5000. Contact your state or regional ACEC organization or write to the address below for details.

American Consulting Engineers Council
Scholarship Program
1015 15th St. NW, #802
Washington, DC 20005-2605

25
ACEC Scholarships

AMOUNT: None Specified DEADLINE: February 15
FIELDS/MAJORS: Engineering, Land Surveying

Applicants must be junior, senior, or fifty-year students working toward a bachelor's degree in an ABET accredited engineering or land survey program at a Florida university. Applicants must also be U.S. citizens or residents of Florida. Based on GPA (must be 3.0 or above), work experience, recommendations, and college activities. Students graduating in December of 1998 are not eligible. Contact your state or regional ACEC organization or write to the address listed for details. Information about National Society of Professional Engineers Scholarships is also available from the Florida Engineering Society.

American Consulting Engineers Council of Florida
Scholarship Coordinator
PO Box 750
Tallahassee, FL 32302

26
ACSM Graduate Women and Minority Scholarship

AMOUNT: Maximum: $1500 DEADLINE: March 27
FIELDS/MAJORS: Sports Medicine

Open to full-time graduate women and minorities who plan to pursue a career in sports medicine or exercise science. Scholarships are renewable for up to four years. Contact the address listed for further information or call (317) 637-9200.

American College of Sports Medicine
Scholarship Coordinator
PO Box 1440
Indianapolis, IN 46206-1440

27
ACSM Human Performance and Injury Research Grant

AMOUNT: Maximum: $2500 DEADLINE: None Specified
FIELDS/MAJORS: Performance, Injury Research

Open to full-time graduate students for research on injury prevention and human performance. Contact the address listed for further information or call (317) 637-9200.

American College of Sports Medicine
Scholarship Coordinator
PO Box 1440
Indianapolis, IN 46206-1440

28
Actuarial Scholarships for Minority Students

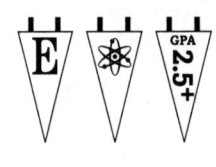

AMOUNT: None Specified DEADLINE: May 1
FIELDS/MAJORS: Actuarial Science

Scholarships for undergraduates who are African-American, Hispanic-American, or Native North American citizens or permanent residents. Must be enrolled/accepted in a program in actuarial science or courses that will serve to prepare the student for an actuarial career. Applicants must demonstrate mathematical ability and evidence of some understanding of the actuarial field. Based on financial need and merit. Write to the address listed for details. Must have a GPA of least 2.5.

Society of Actuaries
Minority Scholarship Coordinator
475 N. Martingale Rd., #800
Schaumburg, IL 60173

29
Addison H. Gibson Student Loan Program

AMOUNT: None Specified DEADLINE: None Specified
FIELDS/MAJORS: All Areas of Study

Low-cost student loans available to residents of western Pennsylvania who have successfully completed one or more years of their undergraduate or graduate education and can demonstrate financial need. Write to the address listed for further information.

Addison H. Gibson Foundation
One PPG Place
Suite 2230
Pittsburgh, PA 15222

30
Adele Kagan Scholarship

AMOUNT: None Specified DEADLINE: March 1
FIELDS/MAJORS: Mathematics, Engineering, and Other Sciences

Scholarships for Jewish men and women living in the Chicago metro area who are identified as having promise for significant contributions in their chosen careers and are in need of financial assistance. For full-time juniors through graduate level. Write to the address below after December 1 for details.

Jewish Vocational Service
Attn: Academic Scholarship Program
One South Franklin St.
Chicago, IL 60606

31
ADMA Scholarships

AMOUNT: Maximum: $1000   DEADLINE: March 15
FIELDS/MAJORS: Aviation Management, General Aviation, Aviation Maintenance, Aircraft, and Powerplant

Open to third- and fourth-year students in an aviation bachelor of science program and to second-year students in an A&P educational program at an accredited aviation technical school. Applicants must have a minimum GPA of 3.0, submit references and an essay, and be able to demonstrate financial need. Recipients will be notified in July. Contact the address listed for further information or call (215) 564-3484.

Aviation Distributors and Manufacturers Assn.
Scholarship Program, Charlotte Keyes
1900 Arch St.
Philadelphia, PA 19103-1498

32
Admiral Mike Boorda Seaman to Admiral Education Assistant Program

AMOUNT: Maximum: $2000   DEADLINE: None Specified
FIELDS/MAJORS: All Areas of Study

Grants for students enrolled in a program leading to a commission in the Navy or Marine Corps. Programs include NROTC, ECP, NESP, MECEP, EEAP, etc. Interest-free loans are also available from the Relief Society. These programs are for undergraduate study only. Write to the address listed for details.

Navy-Marine Corps Relief Society
Education Programs
801 N. Randolph St., Suite 1228
Arlington, VA 22203

33
Adolph Van Pelt, Inc. Scholarship

AMOUNT: $500-$800   DEADLINE: August 1
FIELDS/MAJORS: All Areas of Study

Open to American Indian or Alaskan Native undergraduates and graduate students. Based on financial need and merit. Must have tribal affiliation and proof of enrollment and be at least one-quarter Native American/Alaskan. Recipients are eligible to reapply in subsequent years. Write to the address listed for complete details.

Association on American Indian Affairs, Inc.
Box 268
Sisseton, SD 57262

34
Advanced Graduate Student Member Award

AMOUNT: Maximum: $1000   DEADLINE: March 15
FIELDS/MAJORS: History

Awards available to graduate student members of Phi Alpha Theta for projects leading to the completion of the doctorate degree. Write to address listed or call 1-800-394-8195 for details. Please indicate the name of your chapter. Information may be available from your chapter officers.

Phi Alpha Theta, International Honor Society in History
Headquarters Office
50 College Dr.
Allentown, PA 18104

35
AERA/Spencer Doctoral Research Fellowship Programs

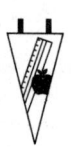

AMOUNT: $4000-$16000   DEADLINE: April 21
FIELDS/MAJORS: Educational Research

Applicants must be full-time doctoral candidates in the U.S. who are at least midway through their program but have not begun their dissertation. The one-year program awards up to $16,000 plus travel funds for professional development activities. The Travel Fellowship awards $4000 to students who wish to take part in professional development activities at their home institutions. Students at institutions that receive research training grants directly from the Spencer Foundation are not eligible but should inquire at their institution about support. Contact the address listed for further information.

American Educational Research Association/Spencer Foundation
AERA/Spencer Fellowship
1230 17th St. NW
Washington, DC 20036-3078

36
Aero Club Memorial Scholarships

AMOUNT: Maximum: $1000   DEADLINE: May 29
FIELDS/MAJORS: Aviation

Open to students between the ages of seventeen and thirty who are interested in pursuing a flying career. Must be residents of the Greater Delaware Valley area and have reached the point of first solo. A personal interview with the scholarship review board in June will be required. Write to the address listed for more information through May 8, 1998.

Aero Club of Pennsylvania
Scholarship Coordinator
PO Box 748
Blue Bell, PA   19422

37
AESF Graduate Scholarships

AMOUNT: $1000   DEADLINE: April 15
FIELDS/MAJORS: Finishing Technologies, Chemical/Environmental Engineering, Materials Science

Awards for graduate students in the above fields. Based on achievement, scholarship potential, and interest in the finishing technologies. For full-time study. Write to the address below for more information.

American Electroplaters and Surface Finishers Society
Central Florida Research Park
12644 Research Parkway
Orlando, FL   32826

38
AESF Undergraduate Scholarships

AMOUNT: $1000   DEADLINE: April 15
FIELDS/MAJORS: Chemistry, Chemical/Environmental Engineering, Metallurgy, Material Science

Awards for juniors or seniors studying in the above fields. Based on achievement, scholarship potential, and interest in the finishing technologies. For full-time study. Write to the address below for more information. Must have a GPA of at least 2.7.

American Electroplaters and Surface Finishers Society
Central Florida Research Park
12644 Research Parkway
Orlando, FL   32826

39
AFCEA Educational Foundation Fellowship

AMOUNT: Maximum: $25000   DEADLINE: February 1
FIELDS/MAJORS: Technology Fields

Two awards are available for scholars or Ph.D. students enrolled full-time in an accredited, degree granting four-year college or university in the U.S. Must be U.S. citizens of good moral character and leadership abilities who demonstrates academic excellence and dedication to completing his/her education. Must also demonstrate financial need. Send a SASE and information on field of study to the address listed or call (703) 631-6149 or 1-800-336-4583 ext. 6149.

Armed Forces Communications and Electronics Association
AFCEA Educational Foundation
4400 Fair Lakes Court
Fairfax, VA   22033

40
AFCEA North Carolina Chapter Scholarships

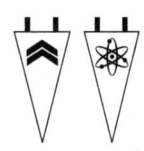

AMOUNT: $500-$2000   DEADLINE: April 15
FIELDS/MAJORS: Physical Sciences

Scholarships for Cumberland County high school students, dependents of North Carolina chapter of the Armed Forces Communications and Electronics Association members, or military service members applying for their first term of full-time college and currently serving in Cumberland County. Write to the address below for details.

Armed Forces Communications and Electronics Assn.,
   NC Chapter
Major Kurt R. Fox, 23D Comm. Squad.
374 Maynard St., Suite H
Pope AFB, NC   28308

41
Affirmative Action Scholarship Program

AMOUNT: Maximum: $6000   DEADLINE: October 31
FIELDS/MAJORS: Library/Information Science

Open to minority students who are graduate students with an interest in librarianship. Extra consideration given to members of the SLA and people who have worked in special libraries, but awards are not limited to these persons. One award per year. Write to the address listed for complete details. Please specify that you are interested in the Affirmative Action Scholarship Program.

Special Libraries Association
SLA Scholarship Committee
1700 Eighteenth St., NW
Washington, DC   20009

42
AFGM International Union Scholarship Program

AMOUNT: $1000   DEADLINE: December 31
FIELDS/MAJORS: All Areas of Study

Scholarships for members of the American Federation of Grain Millers Union or dependent children of AFGM members. For students who will be entering their first year of college or vocational school. Ten awards per year. Write to the address listed for more information.

American Federation of Grain Millers
International Union Scholarship Program
4949 Olson Memorial Highway
Minneapolis, MN   55422

43
AFL-CIO Sponsored Scholarships

AMOUNT: $500 DEADLINE: January 22
FIELDS/MAJORS: All Areas of Study

Scholarships for graduating California high school seniors. Sixty-seven awards per year. Not renewable. No affiliation with the AFL-CIO is required. Must take a scholarship test (administered by the California Labor Federation). Applications are available at your high school. If necessary, write to the office of Albin J. Gruhn, President, at the address below.

California Labor Federation, AFL-CIO
Education Committee
417 Montgomery St., Suite 300
San Francisco, CA   94104

44
African Dissertation Internship Awards

AMOUNT: $20000 DEADLINE: March 2
FIELDS/MAJORS: Agriculture, Education, Health, Humanities, Population

Doctoral dissertation internships are available for African doctoral candidates currently enrolled in U.S. or Canadian institutions to travel to Africa for twelve to eighteen months of supervised doctoral research. U.S. citizens, permanent residents, and Canadian landed immigrants are not eligible. Please write to the address listed for complete information.

Rockefeller Foundation
Fellowship Office
420 Fifth Ave. New York   NY

45
African-American Achievement Scholarship

AMOUNT: Maximum: $3500 DEADLINE: March 15
FIELDS/MAJORS: All Areas of Study

Scholarships are available for African-American undergraduate students pursuing a four-year degree who reside in Hampden, Hampshire, or Franklin Counties in Massachusetts. Write to the address listed for information.

Community Foundation of Western Massachusetts
PO Box 15769
1500 Main St.
Springfield, MA   01115

46
AFSA Scholarship Program

AMOUNT: None Specified DEADLINE: February 6
FIELDS/MAJORS: All Areas of Study

Scholarships for undergraduate dependent children of American Foreign Service personnel (active, retired w/pension, or deceased) who have served abroad with a Foreign Service Agency (defined in the Foreign Service Act of 1980) for at least one year. Write to the address listed or call (202) 944-5504 for details. Must have a GPA of at least 2.0.

American Foreign Service Association
2101 E St. NW
Washington, DC   20037

47
AFSA/AAFSW Art Merit Award Program

AMOUNT: None Specified DEADLINE: February 15
FIELDS/MAJORS: Visual or Musical Arts

Scholarships for high school seniors and college freshmen, sophomores, and juniors who are dependents of American Foreign Service personnel (active, retired w/pension, or deceased) who have served with a Foreign Service Agency (defined in the Foreign Service Act of 1980) for at least one year. Write to the address below for details.

American Foreign Service Association
2101 E St. NW
Washington, DC   20037

48
AFSA/AAFSW Merit Award Program

AMOUNT: $100-$1000 DEADLINE: February 15
FIELDS/MAJORS: All Areas of Study

Scholarships for high school seniors who are dependent children of American Foreign Service personnel (active, retired w/pension, or deceased) who have served abroad with a Foreign Service Agency (defined in the Foreign Service Act of 1980) for at least one year. Thirty-two awards offered annually. Write to the address below for details.

American Foreign Service Association
2101 E St. NW
Washington, DC   20037

49
Agricultural Scholarship Program

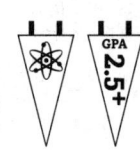

AMOUNT: Maximum: $1500 DEADLINE: April 15
FIELDS/MAJORS: Agriculture

Scholarships are available for high school seniors who are Wisconsin residents or undergraduates, with a commendable academic record and good moral character, who are enrolled in an agriculture program at an accredited college or university. Contact your high school guidance counselor, or write to the address below for information. Must have a GPA of at least 2.5.

Didion Inc.
Scholarship Committee
PO Box 400
Johnson Creek, WI 53038

50
Agricultural Women-in-Network Scholarship

AMOUNT: None Specified DEADLINE: March 1
FIELDS/MAJORS: Agriculture

Award open to agriculture majors, with preference given to women. Must be Oregon residents and U.S. citizens or permanent residents. May be used at four-year schools in any of the following three states: Oregon, Washington, or Idaho. Contact the address listed for further information.

Oregon State Scholarship Commission
Valley River Office Park
1500 Valley River Dr., #100
Eugene, OR 97401

51
AICPA Doctoral Fellowships

AMOUNT: Maximum: $5000 DEADLINE: April 1
FIELDS/MAJORS: Accounting

Doctoral fellowships for students who hold CPA certificates and are applying to or accepted into doctoral programs in accounting. Preference given to students with outstanding academic performance or significant professional experience. Must be a U.S. citizen. Renewable for up to two years. Write to the address below for details. Must have a GPA of at least 3.3.

American Institute of Certified Public Accountants
AICPA Doctoral Fellowships Program
1211 Ave. of the Americas
New York, NY 10036

52
AICPA Minority Scholarships/Fellowships

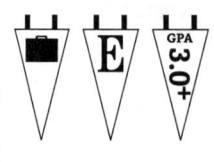

AMOUNT: Maximum: $5000 DEADLINE: July 1
FIELDS/MAJORS: Accounting

Scholarships and fellowships for minority students who are attending school full-time. May be renewed if recipients maintain preset standards. Approximately four hundred awards are offered annually. Write to the address below for details.

American Institute of Certified Public Accountants
Manager, Minority Recruitment
1211 Ave. of the Americas
New York, NY 10036-8775

53
AICPA Scholarships for Minority Accounting Students

AMOUNT: Maximum: $5000 DEADLINE: July 1
FIELDS/MAJORS: Accounting

For U.S. citizens or permanent residents. Must be full-time undergraduate or master level minority students with a GPA of at least 3.0. Must demonstrate financial need and academic achievement. Applicants must have completed 30 semester hours, with at least 6 in accounting. Write to the address below for details.

American Institute of Certified Public Accountants
AICPA Order Dept., Product #870110
PO Box 2209
Jersey City, NJ 07303-2209

54
Aid to Blind Students

AMOUNT: Maximum: $800 DEADLINE: None Specified
FIELDS/MAJORS: All Areas of Study

Scholarship program for undergraduate students in Washington state who are legally blind, to help offset the cost of equipment required because of their visual impairment. Must attend a Washington postsecondary institution. Write to the address below for information.

Washington Higher Education Coordinating Board
917 Lakeridge Way
PO Box 43430
Olympia, WA 98504

55
AIDS Research Loan Repayment Program

AMOUNT: Maximum: $20000 DEADLINE: None Specified
FIELDS/MAJORS: AIDS-Related Research

Special loans are available for research for U.S. citizens or permanent residents with the following (or equivalent) degrees: Ph.D., M.D., D.O., D.D.S., D.M.D., D.V.M., A.D.N./B.S.N. Qualified individuals must sign an initial contract agreeing to perform AIDS research for two years as an NIH employee. Write to the address below for information.

National Institutes of Health
Loan Repayment Programs
7550 Wisconsin Ave., Room 102
Bethesda, MD   20892

56
Aiko Susanna Tashiro Hiratsuka Memorial Scholarship

AMOUNT: None Specified DEADLINE: April 1
FIELDS/MAJORS: Performing Arts

Open to undergraduates who are JACL members majoring in the performing arts. Professional artists are not eligible to apply. Applications and information may be obtained from local JACL chapters, district offices, and the national headquarters at the address listed or call (415) 921-5225. Please indicate your level of study, and be certain to include a legal-sized SASE.

Japanese-American Citizens League
National Scholarship and Award Program
1765 Sutter St.
San Francisco, CA   94115

57
Aileen S. Andrew Science Scholarships

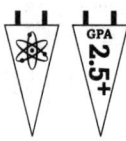

AMOUNT: Maximum: $1000 DEADLINE: November 7
FIELDS/MAJORS: Natural Sciences, Mathematics

Open to outstanding juniors attending any of the ACI member schools. Must have unmet financial need as determined by the financial aid director. Candidates are nominated by a faculty member of the science department and must be recommended by the financial aid office. Contact your financial aid office for further information. Applicants must be recommended by the financial aid office of their school. The school offices will have the information. Must have a GPA of at least 2.9.

Associated Colleges of Illinois
ACI Program Administration
1735 N. Paulina Ave., Loft 401
Chicago. IL   60622

58
Air Force Sergeants' Association

AMOUNT: $500-$3000 DEADLINE: April 15
FIELDS/MAJORS: All Areas of Study

Single, dependent children of AFSA members and/or its auxiliary. For use at accredited institutions. Funds are to be used for tuition, room and board, lunches, books, and transportation costs. Approximately ten awards per year. Must be under twenty-three years old or under. Write for complete details. Be certain to enclose a SASE.

Air Force Sergeants' Association
Scholarship Program
PO Box 50
Temple Hills, MD   20748

59
Air Force Spouse Scholarship

AMOUNT: Maximum: $1000 DEADLINE: None Specified
FIELDS/MAJORS: All Areas of Study

Scholarships awarded to spouses of Air Force active duty, guard, or reserve who are pursuing their undergraduate or graduate degrees. Undergraduates must be enrolled for a minimum of 6 credit hours per semester, and graduates must be attending a minimum of 3 credit hours. Must have a minimum GPA of 3.0. Write to the address listed or call 1-800-727-3337 ext. 4880 for information.

Aerospace Education Foundation
Financial Information Department
1501 Lee Highway
Arlington, VA   22209

60
Air Traffic Control Association Scholarship

AMOUNT: None Specified DEADLINE: May 1
FIELDS/MAJORS: Aeronautics/Aviation

Applicants must be aviation majors, U. S. citizens, and enrolled in or accepted at an accredited college or university. Essays are required. Must have a minimum of 30 semester hours (45 quarter hours) remaining toward bachelor's degree. Write to the address listed for details.

Air Traffic Control Association, Inc.
2300 Clarendon Blvd., Suite 711
Arlington, VA   22201

61
Airline Pilots Association Scholarships

AMOUNT: $3000   DEADLINE: April 1
FIELDS/MAJORS: All Areas of Study

Scholarships available to children of medically retired or deceased members of the Airline Pilots Association. Student must demonstrate financial need and have a minimum GPA of 3.0. Scholarship is renewable by maintaining a 3.0 GPA. Graduating high school seniors or undergraduates may apply. Academics and financial need are considered. Write to the address listed for details.

Airline Pilots Association
Jan Philbrick, President's Department
1625 Massachusetts Ave. NW
Washington, DC   20036

62
AJMAA Scholarship Award

AMOUNT: Maximum: $500   DEADLINE: May 1
FIELDS/MAJORS: All Areas of Study

Awards are available for high school seniors who are members of the American Maine-Anjou Association. Applicants must be under the age of twenty-one. Class rank, academic achievement, and national test scores are also evaluated. Write to the address below for more information.

American Maine-Anjou Association
Scholarship Chairman
760 Livestock Exchange Bldg.
Kansas City, MO   64102

63
AKA Merit Scholarship

AMOUNT: Maximum: $1000   DEADLINE: February 15
FIELDS/MAJORS: All Areas of Study

Available to college students with sophomore status or higher who demonstrate exceptional academic achievement. Applicants must be full-time students planning on completing degree requirements. Write to the address listed for details or call 1-800-653-6528. Must have a GPA of at least 2.8.

Alpha Kappa Alpha Educational Advancement FDN
5656 S. Stony Island Ave.
Chicago, IL   60637

64
Al Qoyawayma Award

AMOUNT: $2000   DEADLINE: June 15
FIELDS/MAJORS: Engineering, Science

Scholarships are available for Native Americans enrolled in a science or engineering program who also show interest or skill in one of the arts (Art, Music, Dance). Must have a GPA of 2.0 or better. Write to the address below for information.

American Indian Science and Engineering Society
Scholarship Coordinator
5661 Airport Blvd.
Boulder, CO   80301-2339

65
ALA/AHA Fellowship in Health Facility Planning and Design

AMOUNT: Maximum: $20000   DEADLINE: January 15
FIELDS/MAJORS: Architecture

Sponsored jointly by the Institute and the American Hospital Association, this fellowship has several options for graduate students to design or study the health facilities field. Write to the address listed for details.

American Institute of Architects/American Hospital
  Association
Fellowship Coordinator
1 North Franklin
Chicago, IL   60611

66
Alabama Power Award

AMOUNT: None Specified   DEADLINE: April 15
FIELDS/MAJORS: Environmental Science

Non-renewable scholarship open to all students from Alabama who are majoring in environmental science. Must be a U.S. citizen or permanent resident. Write to the address below for more information.

University of West Alabama
Office of Admissions
Station 4
Livingston, AL   35470

67
Alabama Student Assistance Program

AMOUNT: $200-$2000 DEADLINE: March 15
FIELDS/MAJORS: All Areas of Study

Need-based assistance program for undergraduate Alabama residents. Priority is given to students who are eligible for a Pell Grant. Students should submit a Student Aid Report. Write to the address listed or call (334) 281-1921 for more information.

Alabama Commission on Higher Education
Financial Aid Office
PO Box 30200
Montgomery, AL 36130

68
Alabama Student Grant Program

AMOUNT: $1200 DEADLINE: None Specified
FIELDS/MAJORS: All Areas of Study

Grants for undergraduate students-both half-time and full-time-who are Alabama residents attending Birmingham-Southern College, Concordia College, Faulkner University, Huntingdon College, Judson College, Miles College, Spring Hill College, Oakwood College, Samford University, Selma University, Southeastern Bible College, Southern Vocational College, Stillman College, and University of Mobile.
Contact your guidance counselor or the financial aid office for more information and an application.

Alabama Commission on Higher Education
PO Box 302000
Montgomery, AL 36130

69
Alabama/Birmingham Legacy Scholarship

AMOUNT: Maximum: $1500 DEADLINE: April 15
FIELDS/MAJORS: Travel and Tourism, Hotel/Motel Management

Awards for Alabama juniors or seniors in one of the areas listed above who are enrolled in any two- or four-year college full-time. Must have a minimum GPA of 3.0. Write to the address listed or call 1-800-682-8886 ext. 4251 for more information.

National Tourism Foundation
546 East Main St.
PO Box 3071
Lexington, KY 40596

70
Alan Camhi '78, Softech Resources, Inc. Scholarship

AMOUNT: Maximum: $250
DEADLINE: March 1
FIELDS/MAJORS: Computer, Information Science

Open to seniors who can demonstrate academic merit. Contact the address listed for further information. Must have a GPA of at least 3.0.

Brooklyn College
Office of the V.P. for Student Life
2113 Boylan Hall
Brooklyn, NY 11210

71
Alaska Airlines Scholarship

AMOUNT: $2000 DEADLINE: July 28
FIELDS/MAJORS: Travel and Tourism

Awards are available for sophomores, juniors, or seniors at the University of Alaska, Fairbanks, the University of Alaska, Anchorage, or the University of Washington who are studying in the field of travel and tourism. Must be U.S. citizens or legal residents and have a GPA of at least 2.5. One award is given annually. Write to the address below for more information.

American Society of Travel Agents
Scholarship Committee
1101 King St., Suite 200
Alexandria, VA 22314

72
Alaska Sea Services Scholarship Program

AMOUNT: Maximum: $1000 DEADLINE: April 30
FIELDS/MAJORS: All Areas of Study

Awards for dependent children of regular/reserve members of the Navy, Marines, or Coast Guard on active duty, retired with pay, deceased, or MIA. Must be a legal resident of Alaska, have high academic standards, and show character, leadership ability, and financial need. Contact address listed for additional information and application.

Navy League Fleet Reserve Association
US Navy League Council 55-151
Box 201510
Anchorage, AK 99520

73
Alaska State Educational Incentive Grant Program

AMOUNT: $100-$1500   DEADLINE: May 31
FIELDS/MAJORS: All Areas of Study

Need-based grants are available to Alaska residents enrolled in their first undergraduate program at eligible Alaska colleges and universities. Must be residents for at least one year, be enrolled full-time, and be able to demonstrate financial need. Write to the address listed or call 1-800-441-2962 for information.

Alaska Commission on Post-secondary Education
3030 Vintage Blvd.
Juneau, AK   99801

74
Alaska Teacher Scholarship Loan Program

AMOUNT: None Specified   DEADLINE: July 1
FIELDS/MAJORS: Education

Special loans are available for Alaska residents who live in rural areas and wish to pursue a secondary or elementary teaching career in a rural area. Applicants must be enrolled in a four-year bachelor's degree in elementary or secondary education or a fifth-year teacher certification program. Write to the address below for information.

Alaska Commission on Post-secondary Education
3030 Vintage Blvd.
Juneau, AK   99801

75
Alaskan Aviation Safety Foundation Scholarships

AMOUNT: None Specified   DEADLINE: March 31
FIELDS/MAJORS: Aviation

Scholarships available to residents of Alaska who are enrolled in an aviation related program in an accredited college, university, trade school, or approved training center. Applicants must have completed at least two semesters, or 30% of the work toward his/her professional goal, or has, at minimum, a private pilot certificate. Write to the address listed or call (907) 243-7237 for details.

Alaskan Aviation Safety Foundation
Scholarship Committee
4340 Postmark Dr.
Anchorage, AK   99502

76
Albert Baker Fund Student Loans

AMOUNT: $2800-$3200   DEADLINE: August 1
FIELDS/MAJORS: All Areas of Study

Applicants must be members of the Mother Church, the First Church of Christ Scientist, Boston, Massachusetts, and be currently active as Christian Scientists. Open to undergraduates, graduates, and Christian Science nurses in training. The $2800 awards are for freshmen and sophomores, and the $3200 awards are for juniors and seniors. Write to the address below for details.

Albert Baker Fund
5 Third St., Suite 717
San Francisco, CA   94103

77
Albert E. and Florence W. Newton Fund

AMOUNT: $100-$1500   DEADLINE: April 1
FIELDS/MAJORS: Nursing

Scholarships are available for Rhode Island resident RNs who are pursuing a B.S.N. degree at a Rhode Island college or university. Approximately fifteen grants offered annually. There are two deadline dates, April 1 and October 1. Write to the address listed for information.

Northwest Community Nursing Association
Ms. Beverly McGuire
PO Box 234
Harmony, RI   02829

78
Albert Einstein Institution Fellows Program

AMOUNT: None Specified   DEADLINE: January 1
FIELDS/MAJORS: Public Policy, Conflict Management, Government

Fellowships for doctoral candidates undertaking dissertation research or writing dissertations, advanced scholars undertaking specific research projects, and practitioners in past or present nonviolent struggles preparing documentation, description, and analysis of conflicts. Must demonstrate in scholarship or practice the capacity to make a significant contribution to the understanding of nonviolent action. Financial awards are normally made for twelve-month periods. Write to the address below for information.

Albert Einstein Institution
Ronald M. McCarthy, Fellows Program
50 Church St.
Cambridge, MA   02138

79
Albert J. Beveridge Grant for Research

AMOUNT: Maximum: $1000 DEADLINE: February 2
FIELDS/MAJORS: Western Hemisphere History

Applicants must be American Historian Association members who are doing doctoral or postdoctoral research in the history of the Western Hemisphere. Twenty-four awards are given annually. Write to the address listed for details.

American Historical Association
Award Administrator
400 A St. SE
Washington, DC   20003

80
Albert O. Halse Memorial Scholarship Award

AMOUNT: Maximum: $1500 DEADLINE: June 5
FIELDS/MAJORS: Architecture

Scholarship awarded to an undergraduate for excellence in architectural delineation and/or architectural models. The student must reside in the Architects League membership area (Bergen, Hudson, Passaic, Sussex, Essex, and Morris counties). Write to the address listed or call (201) 767-9575 for more information.

Architects League of Northern New Jersey
Robert M. Zaccone, AIA
212 White Ave.
Old Tappan, NJ   07675

81
Albert Shanker College Scholarship Fund of Federation of Teachers

AMOUNT: Maximum: $4000 DEADLINE: December 13
FIELDS/MAJORS: All Areas of Study

250 scholarships are available to seniors graduating from a New York City public high school. To be eligible for this program, an applicant must meet the low- income criteria, which is established annually. Proof of family income must be submitted with the application. Official documents (such as tax returns) are the only acceptable proof. Write to the address listed for more details.

United Federation of Teachers
260 Park Ave. South
New York, NY   10010

82
Albert Steiger Memorial Scholarship

AMOUNT: $2500 DEADLINE: March 15
FIELDS/MAJORS: All Areas of Study

Scholarships are available for graduating seniors of Central High School in Springfield, Massachusetts. Two awards are offered annually. Write to the address listed for information.

Community Foundation of Western Massachusetts
PO Box 15769
1500 Main St.
Springfield, MA   01115

83
Albritton Foundation Scholarships

AMOUNT: None Specified DEADLINE: December 31
FIELDS/MAJORS: All Areas of Study

Open to high school seniors, undergraduates, and graduate students who are Texas residents. When requesting information, include a brief introductory letter explaining your educational experience and financial situation. Contact the address listed for further information.

Albritton Foundation
Scholarship Coordinator
5615 Kirby Dr., #310
Houston, TX   77005

84
Alexander and Maude Haedeen Scholarship

AMOUNT: Maximum: $1000 DEADLINE: April 15
FIELDS/MAJORS: All Areas of Study

Available to high school seniors who will be attending college in the U.S. Ninety awards are offered per year. Renewable. For undergraduate study only. Applicants must be U.S. citizens. Write to the address listed for details. Requests for information and applications must be received by the Youth Foundation in January and February.

Youth Foundation, Inc.
36 West 44th St.
New York, NY   10036

85
Alexander Graham Bell College Award

AMOUNT: None Specified DEADLINE: March 1
FIELDS/MAJORS: All Areas of Study

Applicants must be born deaf or became deaf before acquiring language and must use speech/residual hearing or lip-reading as primary communication. Must be a graduating high school senior attending a college or university for hearing students. Write to address below for details.

Alexander Graham Bell Association for the Deaf
Miss America Starts Program
3417 Volta Place NW
Washington, DC 20007

86
Alf M. Diesz Scholarship

AMOUNT: Maximum: $500 DEADLINE: May 1
FIELDS/MAJORS: Law Enforcement/Police Administration

Scholarship for graduating seniors from Dekalb County, Illinois, schools who intend to pursue a career in police science or law enforcement. Must be in top one-half of class. Based on career choice, organizations and activities, and leadership and citizenship. Contact your guidance counselor or your superintendent, or write to the address below for details. Must have a GPA of at least 2.5.

Alf M. Diesz Scholarship Memorial Award
Regional Superintendent of Schools
2301 Sycamore Rd.
Dekalb, IL 60115

87
Alfred and Jane Dewey Scholarship

AMOUNT: $500-$1500 DEADLINE: April 17
FIELDS/MAJORS: All Areas of Study

Open to high school seniors who are Manchester residents. Must be able to demonstrate financial need. Preference given to minorities. Contact the address listed for further information.

Manchester Scholarship Foundation, Inc.
Bruce Comollo, President
20 Hartford Rd.
Manchester, CT 06040

88
Alfred C. Fones Scholarship

AMOUNT: None Specified DEADLINE: April 1
FIELDS/MAJORS: Dental Hygiene Education

Scholarship for bachelor's or graduate degree candidate who has completed their first year of study and intends to be a dental hygiene teacher. Must have a GPA of at least 3.0. Based on need. Write to the address below for more information.

American Dental Hygienists' Association Institute for Oral Health
444 N. Michigan Ave., Suite 3400
Chicago, IL 60611

89
Alice E. Smith Fellowship

AMOUNT: Maximum: $2000 DEADLINE: July 15
FIELDS/MAJORS: American History

An outright grant for any woman doing research in American history. Preference given to graduate research on the history of the Midwest or Wisconsin. Applicants should submit four copies of a two-page, single-spaced letter of application describing her training in historical research and summarizing her current project. Write to the address below for details.

State Historical Society of Wisconsin
State Historian
816 State St.
Madison, WI 53706

90
Alice Koenecke Fellowship

AMOUNT: $2000 DEADLINE: January 15
FIELDS/MAJORS: Home Economics/Related Fields

Applicants must be members of Kappa Omicron Nu and enrolled in a Ph.D. program in home economics. Awards announced April 1. Write to the address below for details.

Kappa Omicron Nu Honor Society
4990 Northwind Dr., Suite 140
East Lansing, MI 48823

91
Alice Yuriko Endo Memorial Scholarship

AMOUNT: None Specified DEADLINE: April 1
FIELDS/MAJORS: Public, Social Service

Open to undergraduates who are members of Japanese ancestry and entering or enrolled at an accredited college or university. Preference given to students residing in the Eastern District Council. Applications and information may be obtained from local JACL chapters, district offices, and the national headquarters at the address listed or call (202) 223-1240. Please indicate your level of study and be certain to include a legal-sized SASE.

Japanese-American Citizens League
National Scholarship and Award Program
1001 Connecticut Ave. NW, #704
Washington, DC 20036

92
All-Teke Academic Team Recognition and John A. Courson Top Scholar Award

AMOUNT: $200-$1000   DEADLINE: March 2
FIELDS/MAJORS: All Areas of Study

Applicants must have junior year, full-time student status and a GPA of 3.5 or above the all men's average. They must also be active members, in good standing, with their chapter. Write to the address listed for more information.

TKE Educational Foundation
8645 Founders Rd.
Indianapolis, IN 46268

93
Allene S. Trushel Trust

AMOUNT: None Specified   DEADLINE: April 15
FIELDS/MAJORS: Medicine, Veterinary, Nursing

Applicants must be graduates of the Oswayo Valley School District. Must complete a minimum of one year (senior year) and reside with a parent or legal guardian within the Oswayo Valley School District. Recipients must be accepted or attending a medical, veterinary, or nursing school. Must have a GPA of at least a 2.0. Write to the address below for more information.

Citizens Trust Co.
10 North Main St.
PO Box 229
Coudersport, PA 16915

94
Allied Health Student Loan-for-Service

AMOUNT: Maximum: $12000   DEADLINE: July 1
FIELDS/MAJORS: See Below

Loans for students who are studying the following areas of health: physical therapy, occupational therapy, speech-language pathology, audiology, pharmacy, nutrition, respiratory care practice, laboratory and radiological technology, mental health services, or emergency medical services. Applicants must be New Mexico residents attending school in New Mexico. Loans may be forgiven if recipients serve in a designated medical shortage area in New Mexico. Write to the address for more information.

New Mexico Commission on Higher Education
Financial Aid and Student Services
PO Box 15910
Santa Fe, NM 87506

95
Allwork Grants

AMOUNT: $2500-$5000   DEADLINE: March 6
FIELDS/MAJORS: Architecture

Awards for New York City residents attending a school in New York to attain a bachelor's degree of architecture. Applicants must demonstrate financial need. Write to the address listed for details.

American Institute of Architects, New York Chapter
Arnold W. Brunner Grant
200 Lexington Ave.
New York, NY 10016

96
Alpha Delta Kappa Scholarship

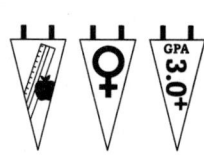

AMOUNT: $400   DEADLINE: April 15
FIELDS/MAJORS: Education

Awards are available for female students who are planning to enter the field of education. Must have financial need and a GPA of at least 3.0. Applicants must be residents of one of the following Ohio counties: Fairfield, Franklin, Hocking, Licking, Perry, or Pickaway. Scholarships will be awarded by June 1. Write to the address below for more information.

Alpha Delta Kappa Educational Sorority, Beta Gamma Chapter
ADK Scholarship Committee
1917 Yorktown Court
Lancaster, OH 43130

97
Alpha Delta Kappa Scholarships

AMOUNT: None Specified   DEADLINE: March 1
FIELDS/MAJORS: Education, Elementary, Secondary

Scholarships for senior or fifth-year elementary or secondary education majors or graduate students enrolled in a fifth-year program leading to a teaching certificate. Must be U.S. citizens or permanent residents and residents of Oregon. Contact your college financial aid office, or write to the address below for details.

Oregon State Scholarship Commission
Attn: Grant Department
1500 Valley River Dr., #100
Eugene, OR 97401

98
Alphonse A. Miele and Theodore Mazza Scholarships

AMOUNT: $1000   DEADLINE: April 15
FIELDS/MAJORS: All Areas of Study

Applicants must be high school seniors and children of Unico members in a city where an active chapter of Unico National is located. Financial need is mandatory. Four awards are given annually. Scholarships are renewable. Write to address below for details. Must have a GPA of at least 2.8.

Unico National
Attn: Scholarship Director
72 Burroughs Pl.
Bloomfield, NJ 07003

99
Alphonso Deal Scholarship Award

AMOUNT: None Specified   DEADLINE: June 1
FIELDS/MAJORS: Law Enforcement, Criminal Justice

Scholarships for graduating high school seniors who plan to attend a two-year college or a university and study law enforcement or a related field. Must be U.S. citizens. Based on character, transcripts, and recommendation. Write to the address listed for details. Must have a GPA of at least 2.9.

National Black Police Association
NBPA Scholarship Award
3251 Mt. Pleasant St. NW
Washington, DC 20010

100
ALTA Endowment Fund Travel Fellowships

AMOUNT: None Specified   DEADLINE: June 30
FIELDS/MAJORS: Translation

Awards are available for outstanding students or beginning translators who would interested in attending the ALTA conference in Richardson, Texas. Write to the address below for more information.

American Literary Translators Association
UTD, MC35
PO Box 830688
Richardson, TX 75083

101
Alumni Chapter-at-Large Grant

AMOUNT: $500   DEADLINE: February 15
FIELDS/MAJORS: Home Economics/Related Fields

Applicants must be Kappa Omicron Nu members. Awarded annually as a project of the alumni chapter-at-large. Awards announced April 15. Write to the address below for details.

Kappa Omicron Nu Honor Society
4990 Northwind Dr., Suite 140
East Lansing, MI 48823

102
Alvan T. and Viola D. Fuller Research Fellowships

AMOUNT: $2500   DEADLINE: February 3
FIELDS/MAJORS: Cancer Research

Summer fellowships for students who are interested in cancer research and are Massachusetts residents. Based on academic standing and demonstrated interest and familiarity with biological or chemical research and laboratory techniques. Write to the address listed for more information.

American Cancer Society, Massachusetts Division
Fuller Committee
30 Speen St.
Framingham, MA 01701

103
Alvin E. Heaps Memorial Scholarship

AMOUNT: None Specified   DEADLINE: July 1
FIELDS/MAJORS: All Areas of Study

Scholarships available to all RWDSU members and their children. Based on academics and extracurricular activities. Write to Stuart Appelbaum, Alvin E. Heaps Memorial Scholarship Committee, at the address below for more information.

Retail, Wholesale, and Department Store Union
Scholarship Committee
30 E. 29th St.
New York, NY 10016

104
Alwin B. Newton Scholarship

AMOUNT: Maximum: $3000   DEADLINE: December 1
FIELDS/MAJORS: Engineering Technology, Heating and Air-Conditioning

This scholarship is designed "to encourage and assist heating, ventilating, air-conditioning, and refrigeration education through scholarships and fellowships." Must have completed at least one semester at an ABET accredited school with a minimum GPA of 3.0. Must have one full year of school remaining and be able to demonstrate financial need. Contact the address listed for further information.

American Society of Heating, Refrigerating, and
  Air-Conditioning Engineers
Scholarship Program
1791 Tullie Circle NE
Atlanta, GA 30329

105
Ambassadors' Business Scholarship

AMOUNT: None Specified DEADLINE: May 1
FIELDS/MAJORS: Business and Related

Scholarship for a Freeborn County high school senior who will be attending a two- or four-year college studying business. Write to the address below for details.

Albert Lea-Freeborn County Chamber of Commerce
Cairns & Ambassador Scholarship Programs
PO Box 686
Albert Lea, MN 56007

106
AMBUCS Scholarships

AMOUNT: $500-$3000 DEADLINE: April 15
FIELDS/MAJORS: Physical, Occupational, Speech/Hearing, Music Therapy, Therapeutic Recreation

Open to students who are U.S. citizens at junior level or above and have a minimum GPA of 3.0. Must be enrolled in one of the fields listed above and be able to demonstrate financial need. Applications are mailed in December. Contact the address listed for further information. Be sure to include a #10 SASE for a reply.

American Business Clubs
AMBUCS Resource Center
PO Box 5127
High Point, NC 27262

107
Amelia Earhart Fellowship Awards

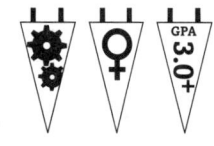

AMOUNT: Maximum: $6000 DEADLINE: November 1
FIELDS/MAJORS: Aerospace Engineering, Aerospace Related Sciences

Open to women graduate students who have a bachelor's degree in a qualifying area of science or engineering. Must have a superior academic record with evidence of potential at a recognized university or college as verified by transcripts, recommendations, and acceptance by an institution of higher learning. Must have completed one year of aerospace related graduate studies by the time the grant is awarded. Recipients will be notified on or before May 15. Write to the address listed for details. Must have a GPA of at least 3.1.

Zonta International Foundation
Amelia Earhart Fellowships
557 W Randolph St.
Chicago, IL 60661

108
Ameren Corporation Scholarships

AMOUNT: Maximum: $2500 DEADLINE: April 15
FIELDS/MAJORS: All Areas of Study

Open to students who are enrolled, full-time undergraduates in colleges in Missouri and Illinois. Applicants must be residents of Missouri and Illinois and be from households that are customers of Union Electric, now known as AmerenUE, or Central Illinois Public Service Co., now as AmerenCIPS. Based on financial need, academics, and character. Contact the address listed for further information, include a SASE for a reply, or call (314) 725-7990. Information also available through e-mail at: schlrshpfd@stlnet.com. Must have a GPA of at least 2.5.

Ameren Corporation
The Scholarship Foundation
8215 Clayton Rd.
St. Louis, MO 63117

109
America's Junior Miss National Scholarship Awards

AMOUNT. $1000-$30000 DEADLINE: None Specified
FIELDS/MAJORS: All Areas of Study

Scholarships are available for the winner, finalists, and other select contestants in the America's Junior Miss Competition. Applicants must be high school seniors who demonstrate scholastic excellence and future potential for outstanding contribution to society. Applicants must never have been married and must be U.S. citizens. Write to the address below for information.

America's Junior Miss Program
PO Box 2786
Mobile, AL 36652

110
American Accounting Association Fellowship Program in Accounting

AMOUNT: $2500 DEADLINE: June 1
FIELDS/MAJORS: Accounting

Fellowships for students entering doctoral programs in accounting with career plans to teach accounting in colleges or universities in the U.S. or Canada. Must be a U.S. or Canadian resident. Foreign students may apply if enrolled in or have a degree from a U.S. or Canadian graduate program. Four or five awards offered annually. Write to Mary Cole, office manager, at the address below for details.

American Accounting Association
5717 Bessie Dr.
Sarasota, FL   34233

111
American Association for Geodetic Surveying Fellowship

AMOUNT: Maximum: $2000   DEADLINE: November 10
FIELDS/MAJORS: Geodetic Surveying, Geodesy

Open to graduate students in a program with a significant focus on geodetic surveying or geodesy at a school of the recipient's choice. Contact the address below for further information.

American Cartographic Association
Lilly Matheson, ACSM Awards Program
5410 Grosvenor Ln., #100
Bethesda, MD   20814-2144

112
American Association for Geodetic Surveying Fellowship

AMOUNT: Maximum: $2000   DEADLINE: November 30
FIELDS/MAJORS: Geodetic Surveying, Geodesy

Open to graduate students in a program with a significant focus upon geodetic surveying or geodesy. Write to the address listed for complete details or call (301) 493-0200.

American Congress on Surveying and Mapping
Ms. Lilly Matheson
5410 Grosvenor Ln., #100
Bethesda, MD   20814

113
American Association of University Women Scholarships

AMOUNT: Maximum: $1000   DEADLINE: March 1
FIELDS/MAJORS: All Areas of Study

Awards offered to female residents of Livermore, Pleasanton, Dublin, or Sunol who have junior or senior standing at an accredited four-year college or university. Based on financial need, GPA, work experience related to the major, letters of recommendation, and personal statements. Write to the address listed for more information. Must have a GPA of at least 2.8.

American Association of University Women, LPD
   Chapter CA
Scholarship Coordinator
PO Box 661
Livermore, CA   94551

114
American Cancer Society Scholarships

AMOUNT: $2250   DEADLINE: April 10
FIELDS/MAJORS: All Areas of Study

Awards for Florida residents who are U.S. citizens and have had a diagnosis of cancer before age twenty-one. Must demonstrate financial need. Applicants must be under twenty-one years of age at time of application. For undergraduate study in any accredited school in Florida. Write to the address below for more information.

American Cancer Society, Florida Division, Inc.
Scholarship Coordinator
3709 W. Jelton Ave.
Tampa, FL   33629

115
American Cancer Society Scholarships

AMOUNT: Maximum: $1000   DEADLINE: April 10
FIELDS/MAJORS: All Areas of Study

Open to undergraduates who have been diagnosed with cancer before the age of twenty-one. Must be residents of Michigan or Indiana and attending any accredited college or university in Michigan or Indiana. Applicants must be under the age of twenty-one at the time of application. Contact the address listed or call (800) 723-0360 for further information.

American Cancer Society Foundation, Great Lakes
   Division
Robert Wood, Chairman
1205 E. Saginaw
Lansing, MI   48906

116
American Cartographic and Geographic Information Society Scholarship

AMOUNT: Maximum: $1000   DEADLINE: November 30
FIELDS/MAJORS: Cartography, Surveying

Open to full-time juniors and seniors enrolled in a cartography or other mapping-science curriculum in a four-year, degree-granting institution. Contact the address listed or (301) 493-0200.

American Congress on Surveying and Mapping
Ms. Lilly Matheson
5410 Grosvenor Ln. #100
Bethesda, MD 20814-2144

117
American Cartographic Association Scholarship Award

AMOUNT: None Specified   DEADLINE: November 10
FIELDS/MAJORS: Cartography

Fellowships are available to recognize outstanding cartography and mapping sciences students and to encourage the pursuit of graduate studies. Write to the address below for information.

American Cartographic Association
Lilly Matheson, ACSM Awards Program
5410 Grosvenor Ln., #100
Bethesda, MD 20814-2144

118
American Chemical Society Minority Scholars Program

AMOUNT: $2500-$5000   DEADLINE: February 28
FIELDS/MAJORS: Chemistry, Biochemistry, Chemical Engineering

Scholarships are open to African-Americans, Hispanic-Americans, and Native Americans who are high school seniors or in college at the freshman through junior levels. Must be planning a career in a chemically related field. Must be U.S. citizens or permanent residents. Approximately fifty to one hundred awards are made annually. Write to the address listed for more information.

American Chemical Society
1155 16th St. NW
Washington, DC 20036

119
American Fellowships, Postdoctoral or Dissertation

AMOUNT: $5000-$27000   DEADLINE: November 15
FIELDS/MAJORS: All Areas of Study

Fellowships for postdoctoral or dissertation research for female scholars. Must be a citizen or permanent resident of the United States. Available for the summer as well as the school year. One-year fellowships and summer programs start June 1. Write to the address listed for more information.

American Association of University Women Educational Foundation
2201 N. Dodge St.
Iowa City, IA 52243

120
American History Scholarships

AMOUNT: $1000-$2000   DEADLINE: February 1
FIELDS/MAJORS: American History

Scholarships available to graduating high school seniors who will be majoring in American history. Foreign students may apply for this award through an overseas chapter of the DAR. Applicants must obtain a letter of sponsorship from a local DAR chapter. Must be U.S. citizens to apply. Contact your local chapter or send a SASE to the address listed for more information. Must have a GPA of at least 2.5.

National Society Daughters of the American Revolution
NSDAR Scholarship Committee
1776 D St. NW
Washington, DC 20006

121
American Indian Endowed Scholarship

AMOUNT: Maximum: $1000   DEADLINE: None Specified
FIELDS/MAJORS: All Areas of Study

Scholarship program for undergraduate Native American students who reside in Washington state and are enrolled in a Washington state schools. Write to the address below for information.

Washington Higher Education Coordinating Board
917 Lakeridge Way
PO Box 43430
Olympia, WA 98504

122
American Indian Scholarship

AMOUNT: Maximum: $500   DEADLINE: July 1
FIELDS/MAJORS: All Areas of Study

Awards available for Native American students at the undergraduate or graduate level. Applicants must have a GPA of at least 2.75 and have proof of Indian blood as indicated in letters or proof papers. Must be able to demonstrate financial need. Preference given to undergraduates. Based on financial need, academics, and ambition. Contact the address listed for further information. Send a SASE for a reply.

National Society Daughters of the American Revolution
American Indians Committee
3738 South Mission Dr.
Lake Havasu City
AZ 86406-4250

123
American Institute of Baking Scholarships

AMOUNT: $500-$3000 DEADLINE: May 1
FIELDS/MAJORS: Baking Industry

Scholarships are awarded on the basis of work experience, formal education, letters of recommendation, and financial need. Over forty private scholarships administered by the Institute are available. There are two deadline dates: November 1 for the spring, and May 1 for the fall. Write to the address listed for details.

American Institute of Baking
Ken Embers, Scholarship Chairman
1213 Bakers Way
Manhattan, KS 66502

124
American Legion "Scout of the Year" Scholarship

AMOUNT: $2000-$8000 DEADLINE: March 1
FIELDS/MAJORS: All Areas of Study

Scholarships are available for high school seniors who are Eagle Scouts in a troop sponsored by an American Legion post or auxiliary unit or are sons of American Legion or auxiliary members. Award must be used within four years of high school graduation. Applicant must be a U.S. citizen. For more information, write to the address below.

American Legion
National Americanism Commission
PO Box 1055
Indianapolis, IN 46206

125
American Legion Auxiliary Memorial Scholarships

AMOUNT: $500 DEADLINE: March 15
FIELDS/MAJORS: All Areas of Study

Scholarships available for Michigan residents who will be or are attending a college or university in Michigan. Applicants must be citizens of the U.S. and daughters of veterans. Write to the address below for additional information.

American Legion Auxiliary, Department of Michigan
212 North Verlinden
Lansing, MI 48915

126
American Legion Auxiliary Memorial Scholarships

AMOUNT: Maximum: $500 DEADLINE: March 15
FIELDS/MAJORS: All Areas of Study

Scholarships are available for Connecticut residents who are children of veterans. Applicant must demonstrate financial need, academic ability, and be less than twenty-four years of age. Five awards are offered, with three going to children of American Legion or Auxiliary members. Must be U.S. citizen. For more information, write to the address below.

American Legion Auxiliary, Department of Connecticut
Second District
PO Box 266
Rocky Hill, CT 06067

127
American Legion Auxiliary National President's Scholarships

AMOUNT: $2000-$2500 DEADLINE: March 10
FIELDS/MAJORS: All Fields of Study

Applicants must be dependents of Veterans of WWI, WWII, Korean, Vietnam, Lebanon, Grenada, Panama, or the Persian Gulf. All applicants must be high school seniors. There are five divisions with five awards offered in each division. Write to your local American Legion Auxiliary for more information. The address shown below does not administer the program; five regional divisions are responsible for the screening process.

American Legion Auxiliary, National Headquarters
PO Box 1055
Indianapolis, IN 46206

128
American Legion Auxiliary Nurses' Scholarships

AMOUNT: Maximum: $400 DEADLINE: May 15
FIELDS/MAJORS: Nursing

Scholarships are available for Arizona residents who are U.S. citizens pursuing a degree as a registered nurse. Applicants must be at least sophomores enrolled at Arizona schools with a GPA of at least C and be children of veterans. Selections based on character, academics, initiative, and financial need. Write to the address below for information. Must have a GPA of at least 2.5.

American Legion Auxiliary, Department of Arizona
Past Presidents' Parley Chairman
4701 N. 19th Ave., #100
Phoenix, AZ 85015-3727

129

American Legion Boy Scout Scholarship

AMOUNT: $200-$1000 DEADLINE: April 30
FIELDS/MAJORS: All Areas of Study

Scholarships for Boy Scouts or Explorer Scouts in an Illinois Troop or Council. Based on a five hundred word essay. Must be a senior in high school. Five awards are given annually. Information and applications can be obtained from the local scout office or from the Department of Illinois American Legion Scout Chairman of the Post, County, District, or Division, or write to the address below for details.

American Legion, Department of Illinois
Legion Scout Chairman
PO Box 2910
Bloomington, IL 61701

130

American Legion Educational Loan

AMOUNT: Maximum: $2000 DEADLINE: None Specified
FIELDS/MAJORS: All Areas of Study

Low cost loans available to residents of South Dakota who are or will be attending a South Dakota college or vocational school. Applicants must be U.S. citizens and children of veterans. Write to the address listed for additional information.

American Legion, Department of South Dakota
Department Adjutant
PO Box 67
Watertown, SD 57201

131

American Legion Scholarships

AMOUNT: $1000 DEADLINE: March 15
FIELDS/MAJORS: All Areas of Study

Scholarships for Illinois residents who will be attending school as an entering freshman. Applicant must be a U.S. citizen and the child of an American Legion or Auxiliary member in Illinois. Based on academic ability and financial need. Twenty awards are offered each year. For more information, write to the address below.

American Legion, Department of Illinois
PO Box 2910
Bloomington, IL 61702

132

American Legion Scholarships

AMOUNT: None Specified DEADLINE: April 1
FIELDS/MAJORS: All Areas of Study

Scholarship for Maryland residents who are less than twenty years old. Applicants must be U.S. citizens and children of a veteran. For full-time study. For more information, write to the address below.

American Legion, Department of Maryland
War Memorial Building
101 N. Gay St., Room E
Baltimore, MD 21202

133

American Medical Technologists Scholarship

AMOUNT: None Specified DEADLINE: April 1
FIELDS/MAJORS: Medical Technology, Dental Assisting, Medical Assisting

Applicant must be a high school graduate or a senior in high school. Also, must be enrolled in, or contemplating enrolling in, a U.S. accredited school to pursue studies in medical laboratory technology, medical assisting, or dental assisting. Write to the address below for details. State your educational interest and career goals, and include a legal-sized SASE with your request.

American Medical Technologists
710 Higgins Rd.
Park Ridge, IL 60068

134

American Medical Women's Association Medical Education Loans

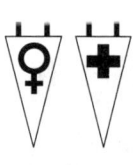

AMOUNT: $2000 DEADLINE: April 30
FIELDS/MAJORS: Medicine, (Medical and Osteopathic)

Loans for women who are members of the American Medical Women's Association. Must be U.S. citizen or permanent resident enrolled in an accredited U.S. medical or osteopathic medicine school. Additional loans may be made to a max. of $4000. Payment and interest deferred until graduation. Write to the address below or call (703) 838-0500) for details.

American Medical Women's Association Foundation
Student Loan Fund
801 N. Fairfax St., Suite 400
Alexandria, VA 22314

135

American Meteorological Society 75th Anniversary Scholarship

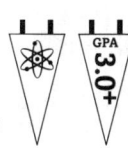

AMOUNT: $2000 DEADLINE: June 16
FIELDS/MAJORS: Metrology, Atmospheric Science

Scholarships for students entering their last year of study toward a degree in one of the fields listed above. Based on academic ability and financial need. Requires a GPA of at least 3.0 and U.S. citizenship or permanent residency. Application forms and further information may be obtained through the AMS headquarters at the address below.

American Meteorological Society
45 Beacon St.
Boston, MA 02108

136

American Meteorological Society Industry Graduate Fellowships

AMOUNT: $15000 DEADLINE: February 20
FIELDS/MAJORS: See Listing of Fields Below

Fellowships for graduate students, must have achieved a bachelor's degree, in their first year of study, who wish to pursue advanced degrees in meteorology, hydrology, atmospheric science, ocean science, or those planning a career in one of the above fields who are currently studying chemistry, computer science, engineering, environmental science, mathematics, or physics. Application forms and further information may be obtained through the AMS headquarters at the address listed.

American Meteorological Society
45 Beacon St.
Boston, MA 02108

137

American Meteorological Society Minority Scholarships

AMOUNT: Maximum: $6000 DEADLINE: January 31
FIELDS/MAJORS: Meteorology, Atmospheric Science, Hydrology, Oceanic Science

Awards for minority students who will be entering their freshman or sophomore year of college planning to study in one of the areas listed above. Write to the address listed for more information.

American Meteorological Society
Attn: Fellowship/Scholarship
45 Beacon St.
Boston, MA 02108

138

American National Can Company Scholarship

AMOUNT: $500-$4000 DEADLINE: March 1
FIELDS/MAJORS: All Areas of Study

Open to children of American National Can Company employees, (current or retired). Must have a minimum GPA of 3.0. Based on high ACT/SAT scores, academic record, and extracurricular activities. Academic progress is required to retain scholarship. Contact the address listed for further information or (312) 399-3000.

American National Can Company
Scholarship Coordinator
8770 W. Bryn Mawr
Chicago, IL 60631-3542

139

American Numismatic Society Fellowship

AMOUNT: Maximum: $3500 DEADLINE: March 1
FIELDS/MAJORS: Numismatics, Classical Studies, Art, and Economic History

Fellowship for graduate students who have completed general examinations for doctorate. Significant utilization of numismatics in dissertation is required. Prior attendance at American Numismatic Society graduate seminar is preferred. Write to the address listed for details.

American Numismatic Society
Broadway at 155th St.
New York, NY 10032

140

American Paralysis Association Research Grants

AMOUNT: Maximum: $50000 DEADLINE: June 1
FIELDS/MAJORS: Paralysis Research

Awards are available for research related to spinal cord injuries and paralysis. Grants are intended for new research projects and are allocated based on scientific merit and adherence to the APA's priorities. Write to the address below for more information.

American Paralysis Association
Ms. Susan P. Howley, Research Director
500 Morris Ave.
Springfield, NJ 07081

141
American Physical Society Minorities Scholarship

AMOUNT: $2000 DEADLINE: February 25
FIELDS/MAJORS: Physics

The American Physical Society has organized this scholarship program for minority freshmen and sophomores majoring in physics. Applicants must be African-American, Native American, or Hispanic, as well as U.S. citizens. Renewable. Ten to twenty awards offered annually. Contact the address listed for more information.

American Physical Society
Scholarship Coordinator
335 E. 45th St.
College Park, MD 20740

142
American Postal Workers Union Scholarships

AMOUNT: Maximum: $1000 DEADLINE: March 1
FIELDS/MAJORS: All Areas of Study

Open to high school seniors who are children of active or deceased members of the American Postal Workers Union. (membership for a year prior to application, or for a year preceding death). Includes the E.C. Hallbeck Memorial Scholarship and The Vocational Scholarship. These sponsors combined offer nineteen awards annually. Contact the local union or write to the address below for details.

American Postal Workers Union, AFL-CIO
Scholarship Programs
1300 L St. NW
Washington, DC 20005

143
American Quarter Horse Youth Association Scholarship

AMOUNT: Maximum: $1000 DEADLINE: May 15
FIELDS/MAJORS: All Areas of Study

Open to members who are eighteen years of age or under and full-time students. Must have a minimum GPA of 3.5. Financial need, references, test scores, and recommendations are required. Usable for undergraduate studies. May be renewed. Contact the address listed for further information.

American Quarter Horse Youth Association
Heath Miller, Director of Youth
PO Box 200
Amarillo, TX 79168-0200

144
American Respiratory Care Foundation Recognition Award

AMOUNT: Maximum: $1000 DEADLINE: June 30
FIELDS/MAJORS: Respiratory Therapy

Open to second-year students in a respiratory therapy program. Based on academics, potential in the career field, and recommendations. Must have a GPA of at least 3.0, provide copy of birth certificate, social security card, immigration visa, or evidence of citizenship. Recipient will be selected by September 1. Write to the address listed for details.

American Respiratory Care Foundation
11030 Ables Ln.
Dallas, TX 75229

145
American Scandinavian Foundation Scholarships

AMOUNT: None Specified DEADLINE: March 15
FIELDS/MAJORS: Business, Art, Science, Music

Scholarships are available for juniors, seniors, and graduate students studying in one of the fields listed above. Applicants must be enrolled in a college or university in the Los Angeles area and demonstrate interest in Scandinavia. Write to the address below for information.

American Scandinavian Foundation of Los Angeles
Ellissa Della Rocca
42 Paloma Ave.
Venice, CA 90291

146
American Society for Eighteenth Century Studies Fellowships

AMOUNT: $800-$2400 DEADLINE: March 1
FIELDS/MAJORS: Eighteenth Century Studies (1660-1815)

Available to postdoctoral scholars for residence at the Newberry to research the era of 1660-1815. Must be a member of the American Society for Eighteenth Century Studies. Stipends are $800 monthly for up to three months. Write to the committee on awards at the address listed or call (312) 255-3666.

Newberry Library
Committee on Awards
60 W. Walton St.
Chicago, IL 60610

147
American Society for Enology and Viticulture Scholarship

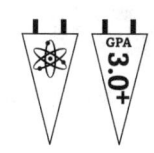

AMOUNT: None Specified   DEADLINE: March 1
FIELDS/MAJORS: Viticulture, Enology

For full-time juniors or above accepted in a four-year accredited college or university program in North America. Must be enrolled in a curriculum stressing a science basic to the wine and grape industry. Undergraduates must have a minimum GPA of 3.0 and graduate students must have at least a 3.2 GPA. Financial need is considered. Formal recognition of the recipients is made at the American Society for Enology and Viticulture's Annual Meeting held each June. Write to the address below for details.

American Society for Enology and Viticulture
Scholarship Committee
PO Box 1855
Davis, CA   95617

148
American Society of Clinical Pathologists Awards

AMOUNT: $1000   DEADLINE: October 31
FIELDS/MAJORS: Cytotechnology, Histology, Medical Lab Technology

Open to outstanding students who are enrolled in cytotechnologists, histologic technician/technologist, medical laboratory technician, or medical technologist programs. Must be enrolled in a NAACLS or CAAHEP accredited program and in your final clinical year of education. Must be a U.S. citizen or permanent resident. Fifty awards offered annually. Write to the address below for more information. Must have a GPA of at least 2.7.

American Society of Clinical Pathologists
2100 West Harrison St.
Chicago, IL   60612

149
American Society of Crime Laboratory Directors Scholarships

AMOUNT: Maximum: $2000   DEADLINE: April 1
FIELDS/MAJORS: Forensic Science

Open to full-time, matriculated undergraduate or graduate students maintaining a GPA of 3.0 or above in an ASCLD recognized forensic science program. Applicants must be nominated by an ASCLD member or an academic advisor. Contact the address listed for further information.

American Society of Crime Laboratory Directors, Inc.
Education and Training Committee
PO Box 496
Lockport, NY   14094

150
American Society of Highway Engineers Scholarships

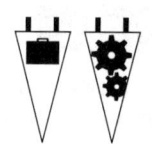

AMOUNT: Maximum: $1000   DEADLINE: March 31
FIELDS/MAJORS: Civil Engineering, Transportation, or Related Field

Awards for students in a four-year college pursuing a bachelor's degree in a transportation related field, preferably civil engineering. Applicants must be U.S. citizens or permanent residents of North Carolina. Contact the address listed for further information.

American Society of Highway Engineers
Carolina Triangle Section
5800 Faringdon Place, #105
Raleigh, NC   27609

151
American Society of Women Accountants Scholarship

AMOUNT: $1000-$1500   DEADLINE: None Specified
FIELDS/MAJORS: Accounting

Open to women who are interested in pursuing a career in accounting. Must be enrolled in college, a university, or an accredited accounting program. Renewable on a yearly basis. Contact your local affiliate for more information or call (312) 644-6610.

American Society of Women Accountants
Program Director
401 N. Michigan Ave., #2400
Chicago, IL   60611

152
American Truckstop Foundation Scholarship

AMOUNT: Maximum: $1000   DEADLINE: June 1
FIELDS/MAJORS: All Areas of Study

Five awards will be given to qualified applicants who are truckstop employees or family members/legal dependents of truckstop employees and NATSO members. Awards given to full-time students at accredited schools. Please write to the address listed for further information and an application.

NATSO Foundation
Chip Deale
PO Box 1285
Alexandria, VA   22313

153
American Water Ski Educational Foundation Scholarships

AMOUNT: None Specified DEADLINE: March 1
FIELDS/MAJORS: All Areas of Study

For active members of the American Water Ski Association/U.S.A Water Ski or donor members of the American Water Ski Association Educational Foundation. Must be a full-time sophomore, junior, or senior at any accredited college or university and be a U.S. citizen. Write to the address listed for additional information.

American Water Ski Educational Foundation
PO Box 2957
Winter Haven, FL   33883

154
American Women in Radio and Television Internships

AMOUNT: Maximum: $1000 DEADLINE: April 10
FIELDS/MAJORS: Radio, TV, Film

One or two internships for Houston area residents or students in the above areas of study who are completing their junior year in local colleges and universities. Internship is served during the summer. Several different companies, TV stations, and radio stations participate in this program. Write for complete details.

American Women in Radio and Television, Houston Chapter
PO Box 980908
Houston, TX   77098

155
Americo Toffoli Scholarship

AMOUNT: None Specified DEADLINE: June 2
FIELDS/MAJORS: All Areas of Study

Open to graduating high school seniors who are sons or daughters of members of a union in good standing with the Colorado AFL-CIO or are members themselves. Six awards are offered per year (three men and three women). Based on academic achievement and a 1000-1500 word essay. Contact your parent's local or write to the address listed for details.

Colorado AFL-CIO
Americo Toffoli Scholarship Committee
2460 W. 26th Ave., Building C, #350
Denver, CO   80211

156
AMHI Scholarships

AMOUNT: $3000 DEADLINE: March 1
FIELDS/MAJORS: All Areas of Study

Scholarships for students who will be high school graduates. Completed or involved in AMHA Horsemastership Program, or involved in 4-H/FFA, or won AHSA and/or AMHA medal for equitation, or placed among top finalists in open competition. Based on ability for serious study, financial need, community service, leadership, and achievement with horses. Five awards offered annually. Send a SASE to the address below for more details.

American Morgan Horse Institute, Inc.
Dane Bettes, AMHI Scholarships
PO Box 837
Shelburne, VT   05482

157
Amity Scholars (of the Oregon Community Foundation)

AMOUNT: None Specified DEADLINE: March 1
FIELDS/MAJORS: All Areas of Study

Amity Scholars (OCF): Amity High School graduating seniors. One-time award. Contact the address listed for further information.

Oregon State Scholarship Commission
Private Awards
1500 Valley River Dr., #100
Eugene, OR   97401-2130

158
AMVETs Memorial Scholarships

AMOUNT: Maximum: $1000 DEADLINE: None Specified
FIELDS/MAJORS: All Areas of Study

Open to AMVET members, their children, or veterans who have exhausted governmental financial aid. Applicants must have completed a two-year course of study at an accredited university or college with a minimum GPA of 2.5. Must be able to demonstrate financial need. Write for details (information may also be available at many high schools). Requests for applications must be postmarked by February 15.

AMVETs National Scholarship Program
Attn: Scholarships
4647 Forbes Blvd.
Lanham, MD   20706

159
An Uncommon Legacy Foundation Scholarship

AMOUNT: Maximum: $1000 DEADLINE: May 1
FIELDS/MAJORS: All Areas of Study

Open to lesbian undergraduates and graduates enrolled in an accredited college or university. Consideration given to academics, honors, financial need, and service to the lesbian/gay community. Primarily to promote the civil rights and well-being of all lesbians in today's society and for future generations. Contact the address listed for further information.

An Uncommon Legacy Foundation, Inc.
Scholarship Committee
150 W. 26th St., #503
New York, NY 10001

160
Andalusia Health Services Repayment Program

AMOUNT: $400-$3000 DEADLINE: April 15
FIELDS/MAJORS: Medicine, Nursing, Laboratory Technology

Open to residents of Covington County, Alabama. Selections based on financial status, academics (at least a "C"), character, and leadership. Recipients must return to Covington County to work or repay the amount received. Renewable. Contact the address listed for further information or (205) 222-5830. Must have a GPA of at least 2.0.

Andalusia Health Services, Inc.
Carolyn Davis, Chamber of Commerce
PO Box 667
Andalusia, AL 36420

161
Andrew K. Ruotolo Memorial Scholarships

AMOUNT: None Specified DEADLINE: June 15
FIELDS/MAJORS: Law

Open to New Jersey residents accepted for admission to a law school or graduate school. Applicants must exhibit an interest in, and commitment to, enhancing the rights and well-being of children through child advocacy programs. Must be able to demonstrate financial need. The Foundation is administered by the Board of Trustees comprised of the Officers of the County Prosecutors Association of New Jersey. Notification of the Trustee's decisions is made in August of each year. Contact the address listed for further information, using the name of the award on the envelope.

County Prosecutors Association of New Jersey Foundation
Scholarship Coordinator
25 Market St., CN 085
Trenton, NJ 08625-0085

162
Andrew Pekema Memorial Scholarship

AMOUNT: $1000-$2000 DEADLINE: April 15
FIELDS/MAJORS: All Areas of Study

Applicant must be a dependent of an Intalco full-time employee, retired full-time, totally disabled, or deceased employee with a minimum of two years Intalco service. Must be a full-time student at an accredited college, university, or technical/trade school. Write to the address below for more information.

Intalco Aluminum Corporation
Holly Karpstein, Chairperson
PO Box 937
Ferndale, WA 98248

163
Andrew W. Mellon Conservation Fellowships

AMOUNT: None Specified DEADLINE: November 7
FIELDS/MAJORS: Art History, Art Conservation

Conservation fellowships are for training in one or more of the following Departments of the Museum: Paintings Conservation, Objects Conservation (includes sculpture, metalwork, glass, ceramics, furniture, and archaeological objects), Musical Instruments, Arms and Armor, Paper Conservation, Textile Conservation, The Costume Institute, and Asian Art Conservation. Fellowships generally are one year. Applicants should have reached an advanced level of experience or training. Write to the address listed for further information.

Metropolitan Museum of Art
Fellowship Programs, Pia Quintano
1000 Fifth Ave.
New York, NY 10028

164
Andrew W. Mellon Research Fellowships

AMOUNT: None Specified DEADLINE: November 7
FIELDS/MAJORS: Art History, Art Conservation, Museum Studies

Open to promising young scholars with commendable research projects related to the Museum's collections. Also open to distinguished visiting scholars from this country and abroad who can serve as teachers and advisors and make their expertise available to catalog and refine the collections. Should have received a doctorate (or completed substantial work toward it). Fellowships generally can last from one to twelve months. Write to the address listed for further information.

Metropolitan Museum of Art
Fellowship Programs, Pia Quintano
1000 Fifth Ave.
New York, NY 10028

165

Angel Flight/Silver Wings Scholarship

AMOUNT: Maximum: $1000 DEADLINE: January 10
FIELDS/MAJORS: All Areas of Study

Applicants must be an active member of Angel Flight/Silver Wings for a minimum of one year. Awards based solely on merit and community service, not on financial need. Applicant should project positive image of ANF/SWS, AFROTC, and USAF. Applicant must also be recommended by ANF/SWS advisor. For junior or senior undergraduates. Write to the address below for details or call the foundation national headquarters at (703) 247-5839.

Aerospace Education Foundation
Financial Information Department
1501 Lee Highway
Arlington, VA 22209

166

Angelina and Pete Costanzo Vocational Scholarship

AMOUNT: None Specified DEADLINE: March 1
FIELDS/MAJORS: All Areas of Study

Open to residents of Clackamas, Columbia, Multnomah, or Washington counties in Oregon. May be high school graduates or GED recipients planning to acquire job skills to enter the work force. These awards are for two-year (or less) programs or schools (vocational, trade, junior college, etc.). Contact the address listed for further information.

Oregon State Scholarship Commission
Private Awards
1500 Valley River Dr., #100
Eugene, OR 97401-2130

167

Ann Arbor Foundation Scholarship

AMOUNT: Maximum: $1000 DEADLINE: None Specified
FIELDS/MAJORS: All Areas of Study

Open to residents of Ann Arbor, Michigan, who are U.S. citizens. Must be high school seniors or undergraduates attending either Washtenaw Community College or Cleary College. Awards usually distributed in May. You must contact the financial aid office at either school for further information. Do NOT write to the address listed.

Ann Arbor Foundation
Scholarship Coordinator
121 W. Washington, #400
Ann Arbor, MI 48104

168

Ann Lane Homemaker Scholarship

AMOUNT: $1000 DEADLINE: March 1
FIELDS/MAJORS: All Areas of Study

Must be graduating high school senior and active member of a local Texas chapter of the Future Homemakers of America. Award based on scholastic achievement, school/community leadership and involvement, and financial need. Write to the address below for further information. Must have a GPA of at least 2.8.

Ann Lane Homemaker Scholarship Committee
C/O Texas Electric Cooperatives Inc.
PO Box 9589
Austin, TX 78766

169

Ann Lane Homemaker Scholarship

AMOUNT: Maximum: $1000 DEADLINE: March 1
FIELDS/MAJORS: Food Science, Nutrition, Food Service, Hospitality, Home Economics

Open to high school seniors who are members of a local Future Homemakers of America, Texas Association chapter. To be used at a Texas college or university during senior year. Must be U.S. citizens and residents of Texas. Based on merit and financial need. Contact the address listed for further information or call (512) 454-0311 ext. 212.

Texas Electric Co-op, Inc.
Dennis Engelke
PO Box 9589
Austin, TX 78766-9589

170

Ann Olson Memorial Doctoral Scholarship

AMOUNT: $3000 DEADLINE: December 1
FIELDS/MAJORS: Oncology Nursing

Scholarships available to doctoral students in the field of oncology nursing. All applicants must be currently licensed registered nurses. Write to the address listed for more information.

Oncology Nursing Foundation
501 Holiday Dr.
Pittsburgh, PA 15220

171
Anna C. Klune Memorial Scholarship

AMOUNT: None Specified DEADLINE: November 1
FIELDS/MAJORS: Marketing

Open to second-year MBA students who are Connecticut residents. Selection based on academics and financial need. Contact the address listed for more information. Must have a GPA of at least 3.0.

American Marketing Association, Connecticut Chapter
Ms. Cathy Dangona, Executive Director
1260 New Britain Ave.
West Hartford, CT 06110

172
Anne A. Agnew Scholarship Program

AMOUNT: Maximum: $1000 DEADLINE: March 1
FIELDS/MAJORS: All Areas of Study

Scholarships for members and children of members of the South Carolina State Employees Association or for deserving others. Must have completed at least one year at a college, university, or trade/vocational school. Based on character, school/community activities, a two hundred word essay, financial need, and leadership potential. Scholarships will be awarded in June. Write to the address listed for details.

South Carolina State Employees Association
Anne A. Agnew Scholarship Foundation
PO Box 5206
Columbia, SC 29250

173
Anne Seaman Memorial Scholarship

AMOUNT: None Specified DEADLINE: July 7
FIELDS/MAJORS: Landscape, Grounds Management, Turf Management, Irrigation Technology

Open to undergraduates planning careers in landscape or grounds management. Extracurricular and community activities will be considered. Winners will be notified by October 1. Contact the address listed for further information.

Professional Grounds Management Society
Scholarship Coordinator
120 Cockeysville Rd., #104
Hunt Valley, MD 21031

174
Annie Gardner Foundation for Student Loans

AMOUNT: None Specified DEADLINE: December 1
FIELDS/MAJORS: All Areas of Study

Loans available for Graves County, Kentucky who are high school seniors or undergraduates. Seniors must have a minimum ACT score of 18, and full-time college students must have a minimum GPA of 2.5. Funds available for vocational training as well. December 1 deadline is for spring semester. March 1 is for fall semester. Contact the address below for further information.

Annie Gardner Foundation
South 6th and College St.
Mayfield, KY 42066

175
Antonio Cirino Memorial Fund

AMOUNT: $2000-$10000 DEADLINE: May 15
FIELDS/MAJORS: Art Education

Scholarships available for residents (of at least five years) of Rhode Island who are at the graduate level in art education programs. Ten awards offered annually. Write to the address listed for information.

Rhode Island Foundation
70 Elm St.
Providence, RI 02903

176
Appalachian Scholarship

AMOUNT: $100-$1000 DEADLINE: July 1
FIELDS/MAJORS: All Areas of Study

Scholarships for undergraduate students who are residents of Appalachia, U.S. citizens or permanent residents, and members of the Presbyterian Church (U.S.A.). Must be able to demonstrate financial need. Write to the address listed for information and an application.

Presbyterian Church (U.S.A.)
Office of Financial Aid for Studies
100 Witherspoon St.
Louisville, KY 40202

177
Appalachian Youth Scholarship

AMOUNT: None Specified DEADLINE: None Specified
FIELDS/MAJORS: All Areas of Study

Program eligibility is limited to youth from the thirty-five Appalachian counties in Alabama. Applicants should be first-time freshmen who graduated high school in the upper third of their class. Write to the address listed for details or call (334) 281-1921. Must have a GPA of at least 2.8.

Alabama Commission on Higher Education
Office of Financial Aid
PO Box 30200
Montgomery, AL 36130

178
Applied Power Manufacturing Engineering Scholarship

AMOUNT: Maximum: $1000   DEADLINE: March 1
FIELDS/MAJORS: Manufacturing Engineering

Open to full-time undergraduates who have completed at least 30 credit hours in an accredited ABET degree program. Applicants must have a minimum GPA of 3.5 and be planning careers in manufacturing engineering. Two awards offered annually. Write to the address listed for more information.

Society of Manufacturing Engineers Education Foundation
One SME Dr.
PO Box 930
Dearborn, MI 48121-0930

179
Appraisal Institute Education Trust Scholarships

AMOUNT: $2000-$3000   DEADLINE: March 15
FIELDS/MAJORS: Real Estate and Related

Scholarships for undergraduate and graduate students of real estate appraisal, land economics, real estate, or allied fields. Must be U.S. citizens. Write to the attention of Charlotte Timms, project coordinator, at the address below for more information.

Appraisal Institute Education Trust
Appraisal Institute
875 N. Michigan Ave., Suite 2400
Chicago, IL 60611

180
APTRA-Clete Roberts Memorial Journalism Scholarship Awards

AMOUNT: $1500   DEADLINE: December 12
FIELDS/MAJORS: Broadcast Journalism

Scholarships are available for broadcast journalism majors enrolled in a college or university in Nevada or California. Applicants must have a career objective in broadcast journalism and be enrolled in a college or university in California or Nevada. Three awards are offered annually. Write to the address listed for information.

Associated Press Television-Radio Association of California/Nevada
Rachel Ambrose, The Associated Press
221 South Figueroa St., #300
Los Angeles, CA 90012

181
APWA/WA Chapter Scholarships

AMOUNT: Maximum: $1000   DEADLINE: January 2
FIELDS/MAJORS: Civil/Structural/Environmental Engineering, Construction Management

Open to full-time juniors and seniors who attend one of the following schools: University of Washington, Seattle University, St. Martin's College, Walla Walla College, Gonzaga University, and Washington State University. Based on academics, activities and interests, and community service. Contact the address below for further information. Must have a GPA of at least 2.8.

American Public Works Association, Washington State Chapter
Chapter Scholarship Committee
411 108th Ave. NE, #400
Bellevue, WA 98004-5515

182
Arby's/Big Brothers/Big Sisters Scholarship

AMOUNT: Maximum: $5000   DEADLINE: March 31
FIELDS/MAJORS: All Areas of Study

Scholarships for persons who are/were a little brother or little sister with an affiliated big brothers/big sisters program in the U.S. For undergraduate study. Two awards per year. Renewable for four years. Contact your local Big Brothers/Big Sisters for more information.

Arby's Foundation and The Big Brothers/Big Sisters Foundation of America
230 North Thirteenth St.
Philadelphia, PA 19107

183
Arc Welding Awards Programs

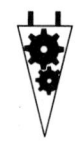

AMOUNT: None Specified   DEADLINE: June 16
FIELDS/MAJORS: Arc Welding, Engineering, Technology

Awards are given to engineering and technology students in solving design engineering or fabricating problems involving the knowledge or application of Arc Welding. Must submit paper in either one of two divisions. Write to the address below for complete details.

James F. Lincoln Arc Welding Foundation
Secretary
PO Box 17035
Cleveland, OH 44117

184

Archbold Scholarship for LPN's, Medical, and Radiology Technicians

AMOUNT: $4000-$6000 DEADLINE: None Specified
FIELDS/MAJORS: Licensed Practical Nursing, Medical Lab, and Radiology Technicians

Awards for students in the above fields of study who are within two years of completing their college course work. Applicants must agree to full-time employment at Archbold Memorial Hospital for one to three years following graduation. Fifty awards are offered only to SW Georgia residents. Write to the address below for more information.

John D. Archbold Memorial Hospital
Gordon Ave. at Mimosa Dr.
Thomasville, GA 31792

185

Architects League Scholastic Achievement Award

AMOUNT: Maximum: $2000 DEADLINE: June 5
FIELDS/MAJORS: Architecture

Scholarship awarded to an undergraduate student for scholastic excellence in architectural design. The student must reside in the Architects League membership area (Bergen, Hudson, Passaic, Sussex, Essex, and Morris counties). Write to the address listed or call (201) 767-9575 for more information.

Architects League of Northern New Jersey
Robert M. Zaccone, AIA
212 White Ave.
Old Tappan, NJ 07675

186

Architectural Study Tour Scholarship

AMOUNT: None Specified DEADLINE: None Specified
FIELDS/MAJORS: Architecture, Architectural History, City Planning, Landscape Architecture

Awards are available for graduate students in any of the fields listed above to participate in the SAH tour of Tidewater, Virginia. All tour expenses are paid for by the society. Applicants must be members of the SAH to apply. Write to the address below for more information.

Society of Architectural Historians
1365 North Astor St.
Chicago, IL 60610

187

Archival Internships

AMOUNT: None Specified DEADLINE: February 15
FIELDS/MAJORS: History, Journalism, Political Science, Library Science, English, Government

Library internships are available to help graduate students gain career-relevant archival experience in a presidential library while contributing constructively to the work of the library. Write to the address listed for information. Must have a GPA of at least 3.1.

John F. Kennedy Library Foundation
Volunteer and Intern Coordinator
John F. Kennedy Library, Columbia Poi
Boston, MA 02125-3313

188

Arizona Chapter Dependent Membership Scholarship

AMOUNT: $1500 DEADLINE: July 28
FIELDS/MAJORS: All Areas of Study

Award available for sophomores attending a two-year college or for juniors or seniors at a four-year institution in Arizona. Applicant must be a dependent of an ASTA Arizona Chapter Active Agency member. Must also be U.S. citizens or legal residents and have a GPA of at least 2.5. One award is given annually. Write to the address below for more information. Must have a GPA of at least 2.5.

American Society of Travel Agents
Scholarship Committee
1101 King St., Suite 200
Alexandria, VA 22314

189

Arizona Chapter Gold Scholarship

AMOUNT: $3000 DEADLINE: July 28
FIELDS/MAJORS: Travel and Tourism

Awards for sophomores, juniors, or seniors studying travel and tourism at an accredited college, university, or proprietary travel school in the state of Arizona. Applicants must be U.S. citizens or permanent residents and have a minimum GPA of 2.5. Based on different criteria such as essays, recommendations, or academics. One award is given annually. Write to the address below for more information. Must have a GPA of at least 2.5.

American Society of Travel Agents
Scholarship Committee
1101 King St., Suite 200
Alexandria, VA 22314

190

Arkansas Academic Challenge Scholarship

AMOUNT: $1500   DEADLINE: July 1
FIELDS/MAJORS: All Areas of Study

Scholarships for graduating Arkansas high school seniors. Must have a GPA of at least 2.5 and an ACT composite of at least 19. For use in public or private Arkansas college or university. Financial need is a major factor. Write to the address below for more details.

Arkansas Department of Higher Education
Financial Aid Division
114 East Capitol
Little Rock, AR   72201

191

Arkansas Funeral Directors Association Scholarships

AMOUNT: Maximum: $500   DEADLINE: January 1
FIELDS/MAJORS: Mortuary Science

Awards for Arkansas residents studying mortuary science. Applicants must have completed an internship at an accredited mortuary school and agree to work in Arkansas for at least two years after graduation. A second deadline date is July 1. Write to the address below for more information.

Arkansas Funeral Directors Association
Penthouse Suite
1123 South University
Little Rock, AR   72204

192

ARMA Records Management Scholarship

AMOUNT: Maximum: $1000   DEADLINE: March 26
FIELDS/MAJORS: Information Systems, Records Management, Library Science, Business Management.

Open to high school seniors who are Connecticut residents planning to attend a four-year school. Selection based on academics, recommendations, work experience, and extracurricular activities. Contact the address listed for further information. Must have a GPA of at least 2.9.

Association of Records Managers and Administrators
Donald Dupont, Dupont Systems, Inc.
465 S. Main St.
Cheshire, CT   06410

193

Armed Forces Health Professions Scholarship Program

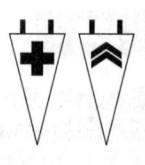

AMOUNT: None Specified   DEADLINE: None Specified
FIELDS/MAJORS: Medicine, Osteopathy, Dentistry, Optometry, Anesthetist Nursing

Awards are available for students in the areas of study above who are members of the U.S. Navy or Naval Reserve. For each year of award, recipient must have one year of active service. No less than three years of active service, regardless of time in the program. Must be a U.S. citizen or permanent resident. Write to the address listed for more information.

Department of the Navy
Chief, Bureau of Medicine and Surgery
Code-512
Washington, DC   20372

194

Armenian Professional Society of the Bay Area Scholarships

AMOUNT: $1000   DEADLINE: November 15
FIELDS/MAJORS: Armenian Studies, Music, Fine Arts, Literature, Journalism, Cinematography

Scholarships for students at the junior level or higher who are enrolled full-time at an accredited four-year college or university and are in need of financial assistance. Applicants must maintain a GPA of 3.2 or higher, be California residents, and be able to demonstrate a substantial involvement in Armenian affairs. Write to the address listed for details. Must have a GPA of at least 3.2.

Armenian Professional Society of the Bay Area
Dr. John Missirian
839 Marina Boulevard
San Francisco, CA   94123

195

Army Aviation Association of America Scholarship

AMOUNT: None Specified   DEADLINE: May 1
FIELDS/MAJORS: All Areas of Study

Open to members or their spouses, siblings, or dependents. Most awards are for high school seniors with a few going to college juniors, seniors, and graduate students. Contact the address listed for further information or call (203) 226-8184.

Army Aviation Association of America Foundation
Scholarship Department
49 Richmondville Ave.
Westport, CT   06880-2000

196
Army Emergency Relief Scholarships

AMOUNT: None Specified   DEADLINE: March 1
FIELDS/MAJORS: All Areas of Study

Scholarships for active Army personnel and for spouses, widows, and children of active, retired, or deceased army personnel. Must be U.S. citizen or permanent resident. Children must be dependents under twenty-two years old. Based on academics, need, and individual accomplishments. For undergraduate study. Renewable. Write to the address below for details. Stafford loans and parent loans for undergraduate studies (PLUS loans) are also available through Army emergency relief. Must have a GPA of at least 2.8.

Army Emergency Relief
Education Department
200 Stovall St.
Alexandria, VA   22332

197
Arnold Ostwald Memorial Science Scholarship

AMOUNT: Maximum: $2000   DEADLINE: March 1
FIELDS/MAJORS: Science

Scholarships are available to legally blind entering freshmen majoring in science. Based on academic ability. Write to the address listed or call (202) 467-5081 or 1-800-424-8666 for details.

American Council of the Blind
Scholarship Coordinator
1155 15th St. NW, Suite 720
Washington, DC   20005

198
Arnold Sadler Memorial Scholarship

AMOUNT: Maximum: $2500   DEADLINE: March 1
FIELDS/MAJORS: Service to the Disabled

Awards for students who are legally blind and are studying in a field of service to the disabled. Write to the address listed or call (202) 467-5081 or 1-800-424-8666 for more information.

American Council of the Blind
Attn: Jessica Beach, Scholarship Admins.
1155 15th St. NW, Suite 720
Washington, DC   20005

199
Arnold W. Brunner Grant

AMOUNT: Maximum: $15000   DEADLINE: November 14
FIELDS/MAJORS: Architecture (research)

Research grants for research at the graduate level or beyond into areas of use and interest to the practice, teaching, or the corpus of knowledge of architecture. Must be a professional architect for at least five years and a U.S. citizen. Write to the address listed for details.

American Institute of Architects, New York Chapter
Arnold W. Brunner Grant
200 Lexington Ave.
New York, NY   10016

200
ARRL Scholarship Honoring Senator Barry Goldwater, K7UGA

AMOUNT: $5000   DEADLINE: February 1
FIELDS/MAJORS: All Areas of Study

Scholarship available to students with a novice class amateur radio license who are enrolled as full-time students in a study program leading to a baccalaureate or higher degree. One award offered annually. Write to the address listed for information.

ARRL Foundation (American Radio Relay League)
Scholarship Program
225 Main St.
Newington, CT   06111

201
Art Institute of Boston Scholarship

AMOUNT: $600   DEADLINE: March 15
FIELDS/MAJORS: Art

Applicants must be seniors in a Massachusetts high school who have been accepted for admission to the Art Institute of Boston. Write to the address below for details, and be sure to include a SASE.

General Federation of Women's Clubs of Massachusetts
700 Beacon St.
Boston, MA   02215

202
Arthur Holstein '34 Scholarship

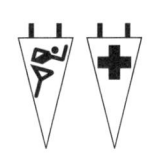

AMOUNT: Maximum: $1000   DEADLINE: March 1
FIELDS/MAJORS: Medicine

Open to a graduating senior athlete who will be attending medical school. Contact the address listed for further information.

Brooklyn College
Office of the V.P. for Student Life
2113 Boylan Hall
Brooklyn, NY 11210

203
Arthur N. Wilson, M.D. Scholarship

AMOUNT: $3000 DEADLINE: January 31
FIELDS/MAJORS: Medicine

Award for medical students of high moral character who attended high school in southeast Alaska and have consistently earned academic honors. A letter of application, high school transcripts from your Alaska high school, and a letter of recommendation from the president of one of the local medical societies in Ketchikan, Juneau, or Sitka, Alaska, will be required. Write to the address listed for more information. Scholarship recipient will be announced by May 1. Must have a GPA of at least 3.0.

American Medical Assn. Education and Research Foundation
Ms. Rita Palulonis
515 N. State St.
Chicago, IL 60610

204
Arthur S. Tuttle Memorial National Scholarship

AMOUNT: $3000-$5000 DEADLINE: February 20
FIELDS/MAJORS: Civil Engineering

Applicant must be a National ASCE member in good standing academically. Financial need and academic performance will be considered in selection. Award is to be used to finance first year of graduate school in a civil engineering program. Write to the address listed or call 1-800-548-ASCE for complete details.

American Society of Civil Engineers
Member Scholarships and Awards
1801 Alexander Bell Dr.
Reston, VA 20191

205
Arthur Weinberg Fellowships for Independent Scholars

AMOUNT: $800 DEADLINE: March 1
FIELDS/MAJORS: History, Humanities, Literature, Social Justice/Reform

Fellowships are available for scholars doing research or working outside the academic setting who need to use the Library's collections. Applicants need not have a Ph.D., but must have demonstrated, through their publications, particular expertise in a field appropriate to the Newberry. Stipends are $800 per month and run from two weeks to three months. Write to the address listed for more details or call (312) 255-3666.

Newberry Library
Committee on Awards
60 W. Walton St.
Chicago, IL 60610

206
ASA Minority Fellowship Program

AMOUNT: $10000 DEADLINE: December 31
FIELDS/MAJORS: Sociology, Mental Health

Applicants must be minority graduate students who have an interest and can express a commitment to the sociological aspects of mental health issues relevant to ethnic and racial minorities. Write to the address below for details.

American Sociological Association
Minority Fellowship Program
1722 N St. NW
Washington, DC 20036

207
ASAE Student Engineer of the Year Scholarship

AMOUNT: Maximum: $1000 DEADLINE: January 30
FIELDS/MAJORS: Agricultural and Biological Engineering

Available for sophomores, juniors, and seniors in agricultural or biological engineering. Must have a minimum GPA of 3.0 and be a student member of ASAE. Based on academic improvement or continued excellence, participation in school and non-school activities, initiative, and responsibility. Committee to make selection by March 15. Write to the address listed for more information. Must have a GPA of at least 3.0.

American Society of Agricultural Engineers
Student Engineer of the Year Scholarship
2950 Niles Rd.
St. Joseph, MI 49085

208
ASCAP Foundation/Rudolf Nissim Award

AMOUNT: $5000 DEADLINE: November 15
FIELDS/MAJORS: Music Composition

ASCAP foundation awards for composers. Candidates must be from an ASCAP school and submission must be an original work that has not been performed professionally. To encourage performance of the work, supplementary funds for rehearsal preparation may be available to the ensemble performing the premiere. Write to Frances Richard at the address below for information.

American Society of Composers, Authors, and Publishers
One Lincoln Plaza
New York, NY 10023

209
ASCAP Foundation Grants to Young Composers

AMOUNT: None Specified   DEADLINE: March 15
FIELDS/MAJORS: Music Composition

ASCAP Foundation grants for young composers. Candidates must be under thirty years of age as of March 15 of the year of application. Applicant must be a U.S. citizen. Awards help young composers continue their studies and develop their skills. Write to Frances Richard at the address below for details.

American Society of Composers, Authors, and Publishers
One Lincoln Plaza
New York, NY 10023

210
ASCAP Lieber and Stoller Music Scholarships

AMOUNT: None Specified   DEADLINE: None Specified
FIELDS/MAJORS: Music

Scholarships available to young songwriters and musicians who are high school seniors in the New York City public school system or the Los Angeles unified school district. Contact your guidance counselor or university music department chair for further information.

American Society of Composers, Authors, and Publishers
One Lincoln Plaza
New York, NY 10023

211
ASCAP Michael Masser Scholarship Honoring Johnny Mercer

AMOUNT: None Specified   DEADLINE: None Specified
FIELDS/MAJORS: All Areas of Study

Scholarships for employees of and immediate family members of the American Society of Composers, Authors, and Publishers Foundation (ASCAP). Contact (or have your parent contact) your ASCAP office.

American Society of Composers, Authors, and Publishers
One Lincoln Plaza
New York, NY 10023

212
ASCSA Summer Sessions

AMOUNT: Maximum: $2950   DEADLINE: February 15
FIELDS/MAJORS: Classical Greek Studies

Awards are available for undergraduates, graduates, and high school and college teachers emphasizing the topography and antiquities of Greece. Write to the address listed for more information.

American School of Classical Studies at Athens
Committee on Admissions and Fellowships
6-8 Charlton St.
Princeton, NJ 08540

213
ASHARE Engineering Technology Scholarship

AMOUNT: Maximum: $3000   DEADLINE: May 1
FIELDS/MAJORS: Engineering Technology

Award for full-time students seeking a two-year degree in engineering technology. Programs designed "to encourage the student to continue his/her preparation for service in the heating, ventilating, air-conditioning, and refrigeration industry." Applicant must have completed at least one semester in an ABET accredited school with a 3.0 GPA in order to apply. Applicants will be notified of the Trustees' decision in the summer, and funds will be available by the fall. Write to the address listed for details. Must have a GPA of at least 3.0.

American Society of Heating, Refrigerating, and
  Air-Conditioning Engineers
Manager of Research
1791 Tullie Circle, NE
Atlanta, GA 30329

214
ASHRAE Scholarships

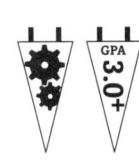

AMOUNT: Maximum: $3000   DEADLINE: December 1
FIELDS/MAJORS: Engineering Technology, Heating/Air-Conditioning Technology

Scholarships designed "to encourage and assist heating, ventilating, air-conditioning, and refrigeration education through scholarships and fellowships." Must have completed at least one semester of study with a minimum GPA of 3.0 in any ABET accredited school. Must have at least one full year of school remaining and be able to demonstrate financial need and character and leadership ability. Contact the address listed for further information. Must have a GPA of at least 3.0.

American Society of Heating, Refrigerating, and
  Air Conditioning Engineers
Scholarship Administrator
1791 Tuillie Circle NE
Atlanta, GA 30329

215

Asian/Pacific Gays and Friends Scholarship

AMOUNT: Maximum: $1000   DEADLINE: September 15
FIELDS/MAJORS: All Areas of Study

Open to gay male Asian and Pacific Islander students pursuing studies primarily in California. Must be enrolled in at least 9 units (if working) or 12 units (if not working). Must have a minimum GPA of 3.0 and be a resident of any of the following five counties: Los Angeles, Orange, Riverside, San Bernardino, or Ventura. Must be involved in gay community leadership and/or activities. Contact the address listed for further information, and be sure to enclose a SASE for a reply. Must have a GPA of at least 3.0.

Fund for Lesbian and Gay Scholarships
Scholarship Coordinator
PO Box 48320
Los Angeles, CA   90048

216

ASID Educational Foundation, S. Harris Memorial Scholarship

AMOUNT: $1500   DEADLINE: March 4
FIELDS/MAJORS: Interior Design

For undergraduates above their sophomore year of study at a degree-granting institution. Based primarily on academic achievements and financial need. Two awards per year. Send a SASE to the address listed for details.

American Society of Interior Designers Educational
   Foundation
Scholarship and Awards Program
608 Massachusetts Ave. NE
Washington, DC   20002

217

ASM Faculty Fellowship Program

AMOUNT: $4000   DEADLINE: February 1
FIELDS/MAJORS: Microbiological Sciences

One- to two-month fellowship for full-time minority undergraduates in the field of microbiological sciences. Applicants must be ASM members and U.S. citizens or permanent residents. This is a joint application with an ASM member faculty mentor. Write to the address below for additional information.

American Society for Microbiology
Office of Education and Training
1325 Massachusetts Ave. NW
Washington, DC   20005

218

ASNE Scholarship Program

AMOUNT: $2000   DEADLINE: February 15
FIELDS/MAJORS: Naval Engineering and Related Fields

Undergraduate and graduate scholarships are available. U.S. citizens and candidates for degree in engineering or physical science only. Based on motivation toward career in naval engineering and scholastic aptitude. Majors that apply: naval architecture, marine, civil, mechanical, aeronautical, and electrical engineering. Students holding advanced degrees are not eligible. For fourth-year undergraduates and first-year master's study. Special consideration may be given to members of the Society and their children. Write to the address below for complete details.

American Society of Naval Engineers
Scholarship Program
1452 Duke St.
Alexandria, VA   22314

219

Associated General Contractors Undergraduate Scholarships

AMOUNT: $1500-$6000   DEADLINE: November 1
FIELDS/MAJORS: Civil Engineering/Construction

The Associated General Contractors of America offers scholarships for undergraduates who are enrolled in a degree program in construction or civil engineering. Renewable up to four years. Must be enrolled at the time of application at the freshman, sophomore, or junior levels. For additional information and applications, write to the address below.

AGC Education and Research Foundation
Director of Programs
1957 E St. NW
Washington, DC   20006

220

Associated Press Minority Summer Internships

AMOUNT: None Specified   DEADLINE: None Specified
FIELDS/MAJORS: Print Editorial, Broadcasting, Photojournalism, Graphic Communications

Minority internship program for full-time upperclassmen or graduate students enrolled in a four-year college or university in the United States. Selection based on a testing process that takes place in an AP bureau or designated testing site. There is no application form. Check the Editor and Publisher International Yearbook at your local library or contact the address below for the location of the nearest AP bureau.

Associated Press
Director of Recruiting
50 Rockefeller Plaza
New York, NY   10020

221
Association for Women in Architecture Scholarships

AMOUNT: $250-$2500 DEADLINE: May 1
FIELDS/MAJORS: Architecture, Interior Design, Landscape Architecture

Open to women who are California residents attending school in California or non-residents attending school in California. Must be sophomore level or above and be able to demonstrate financial need. An essay, references, transcript, and interview in Los Angeles are required. Recipients may reapply. Contact the address listed for further information. Must have a GPA of at least 2.8.

Association for Women in Architecture
Scholarship Coordinator
2550 Beverly Blvd.
Los Angeles, CA   90057

222
Association of Operating Room Scholarships

AMOUNT: None Specified DEADLINE: May 1
FIELDS/MAJORS: Nursing

Open to graduate students and doctoral degree candidates who are members. Applications for fall, 1998, will be available after January 1. Must be an active or associate member of AORN for at least one year prior to deadline date. Number of awards and amounts vary depending on funding. Contact the Foundation via e-mail: tbarlow@aorn.org or at the address listed for further information.

Association of Operating Room Nurses A225
AORN Scholarship, Credentialing Division
10170 E. Mississippi Ave.
Denver, CO   80231

223
Association of State Dam Safety Officials Scholarships

AMOUNT: Maximum: $5000 DEADLINE: February 14
FIELDS/MAJORS: Civil Engineering, Hydrology

Awards open to college juniors and seniors who are U.S. citizens. Must have a minimum GPA of 3.0 for the first two years of college and be pursuing a career in hydraulics, hydrology, or geotechnical disciplines. Based on academics, financial need, and work experience/activities. Announcement of successful candidates will be made in May. Contact the address listed for further information. Must have a GPA of at least 3.0.

Association of State Dam Safety Officials
450 Old East Vine, 2nd Floor
Lexington, KY   40507

224
ASTA Undergraduate Scholarships

AMOUNT: Maximum: $2000 DEADLINE: July 28
FIELDS/MAJORS: Travel and Tourism

Awards are available for undergraduate students who are studying travel and tourism at any four-year school or are enrolled in a proprietary travel school. Must be U.S. citizens or legal residents and have a GPA of at least 2.5. This description includes the American Express, Air Travel Card, Healy, Holland America Line-Westours, Inc., Princess Cruises and Tours, and the George Reinke Scholarships. A total of nine awards are offered annually. Write to the address below for more information. Must have a GPA of at least 2.5.

American Society of Travel Agents
Scholarship Committee
1101 King St., Suite 200
Alexandria, VA   22314

225
Astra Merck Advanced Research Training Awards

AMOUNT: $36000 DEADLINE: September 10
FIELDS/MAJORS: Gastroenterology

Applicants must be M.D.'s currently in a gastroenterology-related field. Awards to help prepare physicians for independent research careers in digestive diseases. Contact the address below for further information or Web sites: http://www.gastro.org; http://www.asge.org; or http://hepar-sfgh.ucsf.edu.

American Digestive Health Foundation
Ms. Irene Kuo
7910 Woodmont Ave. 7th Floor
Bethesda, MD   20814

226
Astrid G. Cates Scholarship Fund

AMOUNT: $500-$750 DEADLINE: March 1
FIELDS/MAJORS: All Areas of Study

Open to undergraduates between the ages of seventeen and twenty-two who are current members of Sons of Norway or children or grandchildren of current Sons of Norway members. Based on financial need, academics, and career goals. Write to the address listed for details.

Sons of Norway Foundation
Sons of Norway
1455 W. Lake St.
Minneapolis, MN   55408

227
ASWA Scholarships

AMOUNT: $2000-$4000 DEADLINE: February 2
FIELDS/MAJORS: Accounting

Four awards are available for accounting students pursuing a bachelor's or a master's degree in a full- or part-time program. Must have completed at least 60 semester hours or 90 quarter hours at an accredited college, university, or professional school. Write to the address listed or call (901) 680-0470 for more information. Must have a GPA of at least 2.8.

American Society of Women Accountants Educational Foundation
Scholarship Coordinator
1255 Lynnfield Rd. #257
Memphis, TN   38119

228
Athlete Scholarship Program

AMOUNT: None Specified   DEADLINE: None Specified
FIELDS/MAJORS: Athletics

Athletic scholarship program for students enrolled at the University of New Mexico, New Mexico State University, Eastern New Mexico University, New Mexico Highlands University, Western New Mexico University, or New Mexico Junior College. For undergraduate study. Contact the Athletics Department or Financial Aid Office at your school.

New Mexico Commission on Higher Education
Financial Aid and Student Services
PO Box 15910
Santa Fe, NM   87506

229
Atkinson Scholarship Program

AMOUNT: Maximum: $5000   DEADLINE: November 1
FIELDS/MAJORS: All Areas of Study

Scholarships and low-cost loans are available to high school seniors who are residents of Sudbury, Massachusetts or are dependents of a full-time town of Sudbury employee and are planning to attend a two- or four-year school or an approved vocational program. Write to the address listed for information.

Sudbury Foundation
Student Aid Program
278 Old Sudbury Road
Sudbury, MA   01776

230
Audio Engineering Society Educational Foundation Grants

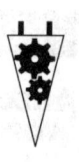

AMOUNT: Maximum: $3000   DEADLINE: May 15
FIELDS/MAJORS: Audio Engineering

Grants for graduate students in audio engineering, based on interest and accomplishments in the field and on faculty recommendations. Renewable for one additional year. Awards usually made in August. Write to the address below for details.

Audio Engineering Society Educational Foundation
60 East 42nd St.
New York, NY   10165

231
Audrey Lumsden-Kouvel Fellowship

AMOUNT: Maximum: $3000   DEADLINE: January 20
FIELDS/MAJORS: Late Medieval or Renaissance Studies

Fellowships are available for postdoctoral scholars wishing to pursue extended research in late medieval or Renaissance studies. Must anticipate being in continuous residence at the Library for at least two months, preferably three. Stipends range up to $3000. Write to the address listed for more details or call (312) 255-3666.

Newberry Library
Committee on Awards, Renaissance Studies
60 W. Walton St.
Chicago, IL   60610

232
Audubon Scholarship

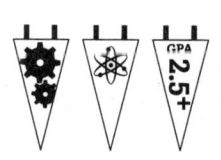

AMOUNT: Maximum: $500   DEADLINE: March 15
FIELDS/MAJORS: Horticulture, Floriculture, Landscape Architecture, Conservation, Forestry, Agronomy, Plant Pathology, Environmental Control, City Planning,

Open to Federated Garden Club Members and teachers and college students for the Audubon Camp of his/her choice. A club member may receive this scholarship once every five years. Winner is responsible for transportation and any increase in fees. The sponsoring Garden Club may pay additional fees, if they desire. Current forms must be used. Contact a local club, the address listed, or (215) 643-0164 for details. Must have a GPA of at least 2.8.

Garden Club Federation of Pennsylvania
Mrs. William A. Lamb, Scholarship Chair
925 Lorien Dr.
Gwynedd Valley, PA   19437-0216

233
Aurora Foundation Scholarships

AMOUNT: $500-$2500   DEADLINE: February 28
FIELDS/MAJORS: All Areas of Study

Scholarships available for graduating high school seniors through graduate students who are residents of the city of Aurora, Kendall County, or southern Kane County. Since these scholarships are so narrowly defined, it is preferred that students contact The Aurora Foundation by telephone to request information, eligibility requirements, and applications. Number of awards varies. Contact the Foundation at (630) 896-7800 Must have a GPA of at least 2.5.

Aurora Foundation
Scholarship Coordinator
111 W. Downer Pl., #312
Aurora, IL   60506

234
Auxiliary Health Career Scholarships

AMOUNT: $500-$1000   DEADLINE: April 1
FIELDS/MAJORS: Healthcare

Open to high school seniors or undergraduates intending to pursue or currently pursuing healthcare careers. Must be residents of Clark or Skamania counties. Contact the address listed or call (360) 256-2035 for further information.

Southwest Washington Medical Center
Scholarship Coordinator
400 N.E. Mother Joseph Pl.
Vancouver, WA   98668

235
Aviation Scholarship Award

AMOUNT: Maximum: $2000   DEADLINE: February 16
FIELDS/MAJORS: Aviation, Aerospace

Open to high school seniors with a minimum GPA of 3.75 who are Virginia residents. Must be planning careers in the aviation field, be under twenty years of age and accepted/enrolled at a technical or four-year institution. For use in freshman year, it is not renewable. Applicants must be U.S. citizens. Contact the address listed for further information or call (804) 973-8341.

Virginia Airport Operators Council
Bryan Willot
201 Bowen Loop
Charlottesville, VA   22911

236
AVIEX Scholarship Essay Contest

AMOUNT: $500-$1500   DEADLINE: June 15
FIELDS/MAJORS: All Areas of Study

Essay contest open to high school juniors and graduating seniors. May be used at a college, university, technical, or vocational school. Essay must be no longer than 750 words on: "What is the greatest challenge facing young people today?" Applicants must have one parent (or both) holding and using a current CDL. Winners will be notified after August 1. Contact the address listed for further information or call (317) 631-0260. You may also pick up an application at the K&W Products booth, #768-770, at the Mid-America Trucking Show.

K&W Products, AVIEX College Scholarship
22 E. Washington, #400, CRE MARCOM
400 Victoria Centre
Indianapolis, IN   46204

237
Avis Rent-a-Car Scholarship

AMOUNT: $2000   DEADLINE: July 28
FIELDS/MAJORS: Travel and Tourism

Awards are available for sophomores, juniors, seniors, or graduate students studying travel and tourism at any institution who have worked part-time in the travel industry. Must be U.S. citizens or legal residents and have a GPA of at least 2.5. One award is given annually. Write to the address below for more information.

American Society of Travel Agents
Scholarship Committee
1101 King St., Suite 200
Alexandria, VA   22314

238
Avon Foundation for Women in Business Studies

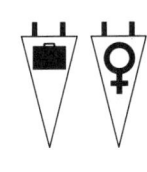

AMOUNT: $1000   DEADLINE: April 15
FIELDS/MAJORS: Business

Women twenty-five or older seeking the necessary education for a career in a business related field. Must be within twenty-four months of graduation. Must demonstrate need and be a U.S. citizen. The preapplication screening form is only available between October 1 and April 1. Up to one hundred scholarships are available. Not for doctoral or correspondence programs or non-degreed programs. Write to the address below for information, and enclose a business-sized SASE.

Business and Professional Women's Foundation
Scholarships
2012 Massachusetts Ave. NW
Washington, DC   20036

239
Award for Academic Excellence

AMOUNT: Maximum: $500   DEADLINE: October 31
FIELDS/MAJORS: Computer Engineering, Computer Science

Open to all undergraduate and graduate IEEE Computer Society members. Initiated with Upsilon Pi Epsilon, award is to encourage academic excellence for members in the computing discipline. Must be full-time students. Based on academic achievement, recommendations, and extracurricular activities related to computing. Write to the address listed for details. Must have a GPA of at least 3.1.

Institute of Electrical and Electronics Engineers, Inc.
IEEE Computer Society
1730 Massachusetts Ave. NW
Washington, DC   20036-1992

240
Awards for Study in Scandinavia

AMOUNT: None Specified   DEADLINE: November 1
FIELDS/MAJORS: Scandinavian Studies

Awards for graduate students who have a well-defined research or study project that makes a stay in Scandinavia essential. Applicants must be U.S. citizens or permanent residents and have completed their undergraduate degree by the start of their project in Scandinavia. Write to the address below for more information.

American-Scandinavian Foundation
725 Park Ave.
New York, NY   10021

241
B'nai Brith Women of Greater Hartford Scholarship

AMOUNT: $200-$500   DEADLINE: June 1
FIELDS/MAJORS: All Areas of Study

Open to Jewish graduating seniors who are residents of the greater Hartford area with average academics. Preference given to relatives of B'nai Brith members. Contact the address listed for further information.

Endowment Foundation of the Jewish Federation of
   Greater Hartford, Inc.
Mrs. Harriet Rosenblit
333 Bloomfield Ave.
West Hartford, CT   06117

242
B. Charles Tiney Memorial ASCE Student Chapter Scholarship

AMOUNT: Maximum: $2000   DEADLINE: February 20
FIELDS/MAJORS: Civil Engineering/Hydraulics

Applicant must be a freshman, sophomore, or junior student ASCE member in good standing. Applicant must demonstrate financial need. Write to the address listed or call 1-800-548-ASCE for complete details.

American Society of Civil Engineers
Member Scholarships and Awards
1801 Alexander Bell Dr.
Reston, VA   20191

243
B.M. Woltman Foundations Scholarship Program

AMOUNT: $200-$3000   DEADLINE: June 1
FIELDS/MAJORS: Theology, Religious Studies

Scholarship grants are available for Texas residents who will be attending Concordia Theological Seminary (Fort Wayne, IN), Concordia Seminary (St. Louis, MO), or Concordia Lutheran College (Austin, TX). Must be members of the Lutheran Church (Missouri Synod). Contact the financial aid office at your school for information.

Lutheran Church-Missouri Synod, Texas District
B.M. Woltman Foundation
7900 E. Highway 290
Austin, TX   78724

244
Baccalaureate Scholarship

AMOUNT: None Specified   DEADLINE: April 1
FIELDS/MAJORS: Dental Hygiene

Scholarships for students who have at least been accepted in a four-year accredited program leading toward a B.A. in dental hygiene. Must have a GPA of at least 3.0. Based on need and career goals. Write to the address below for more information.

American Dental Hygienists' Association Institute for
   Oral Health
444 N. Michigan Ave., Suite 3400
Chicago, IL   60611

245
Bach Organ Scholarship

AMOUNT: Maximum: $500 DEADLINE: June 3
FIELDS/MAJORS: Music-Organ, Piano

Scholarships are available for music majors (piano or organ) who are either Rhode Island residents or who are attending school in Rhode Island. Up to three awards are offered annually. For undergraduate study. Write to the address listed for information.

Rhode Island Foundation
70 Elm St.
Providence, RI   02903

246
Bad Religion Research Award Competition

AMOUNT: $3000-$5000 DEADLINE: April 15
FIELDS/MAJORS: Cultural, Natural Sciences

Open to high school and college/university students in the U.S. This fund, created by the band "Bad Religion," was created to allow students to pursue field-oriented investigations in cultural or natural science. Only applications that entail field-oriented research will be considered. Verification of student status will be required. Contact the address listed for further information about the additional required information and restrictions.

Bad Religion Band Research Fund
Bad Religion Research Award
137 W. 14th St.
New York, NY   10011

247
Barry M. Goldwater Scholarship

AMOUNT: Maximum: $7500 DEADLINE: January 14
FIELDS/MAJORS: Mathematics, Natural Science, Engineering

Scholarships are available for sophomore and junior full-time students who are U.S. citizens, U.S. nationals, or permanent residents. Must have a minimum GPA of 3.0. Applicants must be nominated by their school. Up to three hundred awards offered annually. Contact the faculty representative on campus for complete information.

Barry M. Goldwater Scholarship and Excellence in
   Education Foundation
Goldwater Scholarship Foundation
6225 Brandon Ave., #315
Springfield, VA   22150

248
Bates Scholarships

AMOUNT: Maximum: $2200 DEADLINE: May 1
FIELDS/MAJORS: All Areas of Study

Scholarships are available to minority high school seniors from Arkansas who are pursuing study at an Arkansas college or university. Application forms are available from your high school guidance counselor.

Southwestern Bell Telephone
Bates Scholarships
PO Box 1611, Room 1096
Little Rock, AR   72203

249
Bay Lake Area Lioness Non-Traditional Scholarship

AMOUNT: Maximum: $500 DEADLINE: November 30
FIELDS/MAJORS: All Areas of Study

Applicants must be over twenty-three years of age, residents or Crow Wing or Aitkin counties, and pre-enrolled in a school of their choice. Contact the address listed for further information.

Bay Lake Area Lioness
Dell McAninch
Rt. 2 Box 555
Aitkin, MN   56431

250
Bay State Council of the Blind Scholarships

AMOUNT: Maximum: $1000 DEADLINE: March 1
FIELDS/MAJORS: All Areas of Study

Scholarships are available to legally blind students who are residents of Massachusetts. Write to the address listed or call (202) 467-5081 or 1-800-424-8666 for details.

American Council of the Blind
Scholarship Coordinator
1155 15th St. NW, Suite 720
Washington, DC   20005

251
BCI Graduate Student Scholarship Awards

AMOUNT: $500-$2500 DEADLINE: January 15
FIELDS/MAJORS: Speleology, Bat Research

Awards are available to support student research that will contribute new knowledge essential to conserving bats.

Only projects with direct conservation relevance will be considered for funding. Some relevant research topics include roosting needs, bat feeding behavior, bat nuisance problems, and bat conservation needs. Write to the address listed for more information or call (512) 327-9721.

BAT Conservation International
Scholarship Awards Coordinator
PO Box 162603
Austin, TX 78716

252
Bechtel Undergraduate Fellowship Award

AMOUNT: Maximum: $5000   DEADLINE: None Specified
FIELDS/MAJORS: Construction Engineering

Open to sophomores with a minimum GPA of 3.0. Renewable if recipients maintain a minimum GPA of 3.0. Applicants must be enrolled in any of seventy-nine participating colleges/universities in the U.S and be nominated by the dean. Applicants must be of African-American, Puerto Rican-American, Mexican-American, or Native American descent. Contact the dean's office of your college for further information. Please do NOT contact the Council. They will be unable to respond.

National Action Council for Minorities in Engineering
Scholarship Coordinator
3 W 35th St.
New York, NY 10001-2281

253
Beem Foundation Scholarships

AMOUNT: None Specified   DEADLINE: April 1
FIELDS/MAJORS: Music

Scholarships for music students from Los Angeles County, California. Write to the address below for more information.

Beem Foundation for the Advancement of Music
3864 Grayburn Ave.
Los Angeles, CA 90008

254
Behavioral Sciences Research Training Fellowships

AMOUNT: $30000   DEADLINE: April 1
FIELDS/MAJORS: Epilepsy Research

Open to behavioral scientists to develop expertise in techniques used in working with people with epilepsy. Applicants must have doctoral degrees in a field of the social sciences. Contact the address below for further information.

Epilepsy Foundation of America
Behavioral Sciences Fellowship Program
4351 Garden City Dr.
Landover, MD 20785

255
Behavioral Sciences Student Fellowship, Mary Litty Memorial Fellowship

AMOUNT: Maximum: $2000   DEADLINE: March 1
FIELDS/MAJORS: Behavioral, Social Sciences, Counseling

For students in the behavioral sciences for work on an epilepsy study project. The fellowship is awarded to a student of vocational rehabilitation counseling. An advisor/preceptor must accept responsibility for the study and its supervision. Write to the address below for further information.

Epilepsy Foundation of America
Fellowship Program
4351 Garden City Dr.
Landover, MD 20785

256
Behavioral/Psychosocial Research Grants

AMOUNT: Maximum: $35000   DEADLINE: March 1
FIELDS/MAJORS: Behavioral/Psychosocial Research

Grants for younger faculty or scientists beginning new projects at Massachusetts institutions. Contact the address below for further information.

American Cancer Society
30 Speen St.
Framingham, MA 01701

257
Belden Education Award Program

AMOUNT: Maximum: $3500   DEADLINE: February 1
FIELDS/MAJORS: All Areas of Study

Scholarship program for children of employees of at least one year of Belden Corporation. Applicants must be seniors in high school. Contact the Human Resources Department in your parent(s) facility, or write to the address listed for more information.

Joseph C. Belden Foundation
396 Feather Court
Carol Stream, IL 60188

258
Bement Scholarship Program

AMOUNT: Maximum: $750 DEADLINE: February 15
FIELDS/MAJORS: All Areas of Study

Scholarships for worshipers in churches in the diocese of western Massachusetts. Write to the address below for details.

Episcopal Diocese of Western Massachusetts
37 Chestnut St.
Springfield, MA 01103

259
Benjamin C. Blackburn and Russell W. Myers Scholarships

AMOUNT: $2000 DEADLINE: April 7
FIELDS/MAJORS: Horticulture, Botany, Landscape Architecture, or Related Field

For New Jersey residents who have completed at least 24 hours of college study in one of the fields listed above. Write to the address below for more information.

Friends of the Frelinghuysen Arboretum
53 East Hanover Ave.
PO Box 1295
Morristown, NJ 07962

260
Benjamin Eaton Scholarship Fund

AMOUNT: None Specified DEADLINE: March 1
FIELDS/MAJORS: All Areas of Study

Three scholarships for foster children, one for natural-born children, and one for adopted children of foster parents. Parents must be current members of the National Foster Parent Association. Must apply in senior year of high school for use in college or university study, vocational/job training, correspondence, or other educational pursuits. Write to the address below for more information.

National Foster Parent Association
Benjamin Eaton Scholarship Fund
9 Dartmoor Dr.
Crystal Lake, IL 60014

261
Benton/Bernstein Scholarships

AMOUNT: Maximum: $4000
DEADLINE: March 31
FIELDS/MAJORS: Law, Nursing, Counseling, Social Work

Open to new immigrants and refugees enrolled or accepted into a professional program of study in the areas listed. Applicants must have come to the U.S. with the help of HIAS, Chicago, and have made personal efforts to assist others in the community. Former winners of this scholarship are not eligible to apply. Contact the address listed for further information or call (312) 357-4666. Must have a GPA of at least 3.0.

Hebrew Immigrant Aid Society
Scholarship Coordinator
1 S. Franklin St.
Chicago, IL 60606

262
Benton Soil and Water Conservation Scholarship

AMOUNT: $250 DEADLINE: April 15
FIELDS/MAJORS: Resource Management, Conservation, and Related Fields

Scholarships are available to graduating high school seniors who reside in Benton County, Iowa, and plan to enroll in one of the areas of study that are listed above. One award is given annually. Write to the address below for information.

Benton Soil and Water Conservation District
Scholarship Committee
1705 West D St.
Vinton, IA 52349

263
Berenice Barnard Music Specialist Scholarships

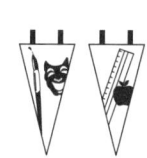

AMOUNT: $500-$1000 DEADLINE: April 8
FIELDS/MAJORS: Music-Education or Performance

Applicants must be from the cities of San Buenaventura or Ojai with good academics and a sincere interest in music. For those with career goals of teaching or performing music. Write to the address listed or call (805) 988-0196 for more information.

Ventura County Community Foundation
1355 Del Norte Road
Camarillo, CA 93010

264
Berkshire District Medical Society Scholarship Loan Program

AMOUNT: $2500   DEADLINE: April 1
FIELDS/MAJORS: Medicine

Must be resident of Berkshire County, Massachusetts, and be accepted into an accredited American or Canadian medical school. Write to the address below for details.

Berkshire District Medical Society
741 North St.
Pittsfield, MA   01201

265
Berna Lou Cartwright Scholarship

AMOUNT: Maximum: $1500   DEADLINE: February 15
FIELDS/MAJORS: Mechanical Engineering

Scholarships for mechanical engineering students entering their final year of undergraduate study. Application must be made in junior year (students enrolled in a five-year program would apply in the fourth year). Must be a student member of ASME and be a U.S. citizen. Information sheets are forwarded to the colleges and universities in the fall of each year. If necessary to write for more details, please be certain to enclose a SASE.

American Society of Mechanical Engineers Auxiliary, Inc.
Ms. Susan Flanders
3556 Stevens Way
Martinez, GA   30907

266
Bernadotte E. Schmitt Grants

AMOUNT: Maximum: $1000   DEADLINE: September 15
FIELDS/MAJORS: History-European, African, or Asian

Ten grants are available to American Historical Association members for research in European, African, and Asian history. Write to the address listed for details.

American Historical Association
Award Administrator
400 A St. SE
Washington, DC   20003

267
Berntsen International Scholarship in Surveying

AMOUNT: Maximum: $1500   DEADLINE: November 30
FIELDS/MAJORS: Surveying

Open to undergraduates studying surveying in a four-year degree program. Please contact address listed for complete information or (301) 493-0200.

American Congress on Surveying and Mapping
Ms. Lilly Matheson
5410 Grosvenor Ln., #100
Bethesda, MD   20814-2144

268
Berntsen International Scholarship in Surveying Technology

AMOUNT: Maximum: $500   DEADLINE: November 30
FIELDS/MAJORS: Surveying

Open to students studying surveying in a two-year program. Please contact address listed for complete information or call (301) 493-0200.

American Congress on Surveying and Mapping
Ms. Lilly Matheson
5410 Grosvenor Ln., #100
Bethesda, MD   20814-2144

269
Bertelsmann's World of Expression Scholarship

AMOUNT: $5000-$15000   DEADLINE: February 1
FIELDS/MAJORS: All Areas of Study

Open to New York City public high school seniors submitting original musical compositions and/or literary composition. Contact the address listed for further information or (212) 930-4520.

Bertelsmann's World of Expression
Scholarship Program Director
1540 Broadway, 43rd Floor
New York, NY   10109-1033

270
Bertha Lamme Westinghouse Scholarships

AMOUNT: $1000   DEADLINE: May 15
FIELDS/MAJORS: Engineering

Applicants must be incoming female freshmen who are pursuing an engineering degree. Three awards per year. Must be U.S. citizens or permanent residents and have a GPA of at least 3.5. Contact the address below for further information. Be certain to enclose a SASE.

Society of Women Engineers
120 Wall St., 11th Floor
New York, NY   10005

271
Bertha P. Singer Scholarship

AMOUNT: None Specified   DEADLINE: March 1
FIELDS/MAJORS: Nursing

Scholarships for Oregon residents enrolled in a nursing program in the state of Oregon. Must have a GPA of at least 3.0. For students entering their sophomore year of study or higher. U.S. Bancorp employees, their children, or near relatives are not eligible to apply for this award. Write to the address listed for details.

Oregon State Scholarship Commission
Attn: Grant Department
1500 Valley River Dr., #100
Eugene, OR   97401

272
Berwind Scholarships

AMOUNT: None Specified   DEADLINE: November 15
FIELDS/MAJORS: All Areas of Study

Awards for students who are children of active, retired, or deceased employees of the Berwind Corporation or its subsidiaries. For high school seniors or graduates entering their first year of study. Approximately five awards are offered annually. Write to the address below for more information.

Charles G. Berwind Foundation
West Tower, Center Square
1500 Market St.
Philadelphia, PA   19102

273
Bessie Coleman Scholarship Award

AMOUNT: Maximum: $5000   DEADLINE: November 14
FIELDS/MAJORS: All Areas of Study

Scholarships are available for African-American graduating high school seniors who reside in Dallas or Tarrant County in Texas and plan to attend a historically black college or university. Family members of *Dallas Weekly* or American Airline employees are not eligible. Write to the address below for information.

Dallas Weekly
PO Box 151789
Dallas, TX   75315-1789

274
Betsy Ross Educational Grants

AMOUNT: None Specified   DEADLINE: March 1
FIELDS/MAJORS: All Areas of Study

Grants for members of the Non-Commissioned Officers Association Auxiliary Division. To be used for preparation for employment or improvement on employable skills. Designed to assist in defraying the cost of taking a course at a local business or technical school. Contact your chapter or the address listed for details.

Non-Commissioned Officers Association Auxiliary
Scholarship Administrator
PO Box 33610
San Antonio, TX   78233-3610

275
Betty Lea Stone Research Fellowship

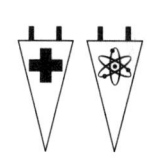

AMOUNT: $3000   DEADLINE: March 1
FIELDS/MAJORS: Cancer Research

Fellowship for a ten-week summer research project. Applicant must be enrolled in a Massachusetts medical school. Contact the address below for further information.

American Cancer Society
30 Speen St.
Framingham, MA   01701

276
Betty Rendel Scholarship

AMOUNT: Maximum: $1000   DEADLINE: None Specified
FIELDS/MAJORS: Government, Political Science, or Economics

Open to undergraduate women who are currently majoring in political science, government, or economics. Contact your local Republican Women's Club, state federation president, or the address listed or call (703) 548-9688 for further information.

National Federation of Republican Women
Scholarship Coordinator
124 North Alfred St.
Alexandria, VA 22314

277
Beulah Frey Scholarship

AMOUNT: None Specified   DEADLINE: March 15
FIELDS/MAJORS: Environmental Studies

Open to graduating high school seniors who are residents of any of the following areas: Allegheny, Armstrong, Beaver, Westmoreland, southern Butler, northern Fayette, and northeastern Washington counties. Applicants must be applying to two- or four-year schools. Contact your high school guidance counselor or the address listed for further information.

Audubon Society of Western Pennsylvania
Sarah Ibershof
614 Dorseyville Rd.
Pittsburgh, PA 15238

278
Bev Sellers Memorial Scholarship

AMOUNT: Maximum: $1000   DEADLINE: February 15
FIELDS/MAJORS: Vocal Music

Awards are available for full-time students studying vocal music in an accredited institution. Must have a GPA of at least 3.0. Based on transcripts, activities, and recommendations. Write to the address listed for more information.

Young Singers Foundation
Attn: Corporate Secretary
667 N. Desert Peach Ct.
Orange, CA 92869

279
Beverly M. McCurdy Scholarship

AMOUNT: None Specified   DEADLINE: None Specified
FIELDS/MAJORS: All Areas of Study

Awards for graduating seniors from Machias High School in Machias, Maine, who plan to pursue a postsecondary education. Contact the Machias High School Guidance Office for more information.

Maine Community Foundation
245 East Maine St.
PO Box 148
Ellsworth, ME 04605

280
Beverly Myers Award

AMOUNT: $200-$500   DEADLINE: April 1
FIELDS/MAJORS: Optometry

Candidates must be senior students currently enrolled in an optician program accredited by the Commission on Opticianry Accreditation. Write to the address below for more information.

National Academy of Opticianry
10111 M.l. King Jr., Hwy., #112
Bowie, MD 20720

281
Bewerber Aus Aller Welt

AMOUNT: $570-$740   DEADLINE: January 31
FIELDS/MAJORS: All Areas of Study, especially Austrian Studies

Open to students for research or study projects at Austrian Universities. Applicants for the program must be between twenty and thirty-five years old with working knowledge of German. Awards are between $570 and $740 monthly for up to nine months. Applicants will be required to submit two letters of recommendation, a supervisor's declaration (a professor at the university in Austria), a health certificate, and transcripts. Contact the address listed for more information or call (212) 759-5165.

Austrian Cultural Institute
Scholarship Coordinator.
950 Third Ave., 20th Floor
New York, NY 10022

282
Bick Bickson Scholarship

AMOUNT: Maximum: $1000   DEADLINE: March 1
FIELDS/MAJORS: Marketing, Law, Travel Industry Management

Open to Hawaii residents. May be going to school in another state but must have family in Hawaii. Employees, volunteers, or board members of the Foundation are not eligible to apply. Contact the address below for further information.

Hawaii Community Scholarship Foundation
College Scholarships
900 Fort St. Mall, #1300
Honolulu, HI 96813

283
Bilingual Teachers of Tomorrow Scholarship

AMOUNT: None Specified   DEADLINE: January 15
FIELDS/MAJORS: Education

Scholarships available for incoming freshmen and transfer students from the Garden City area. Must be committed to teach in the Garden City School District after graduation. Write to the address below for information.

Bilingual Teachers of Tomorrow
Ms. Linda Trujillo
201 Buffalo Jones Ave.
Garden City, KS   67846

284
Bill and Mary Russell Healthcare Scholarship Fund

AMOUNT: None Specified   DEADLINE: July 1
FIELDS/MAJORS: Healthcare, Nursing

Scholarships for students in healthcare or nursing fields. For residents of Missouri and Kansas who are served by the Heartland Health Foundation (generally, northwest Missouri and northeast Kansas). Write to the address below for further information.

Heartland Health Foundation and Voiture 130 of the 40 and 8
801 Faraon St.
St. Joseph, MO   64501

285
Bioquip Products Scholarship and Iselin & Associates Scholarships

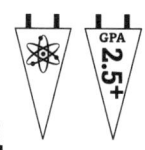

AMOUNT: Maximum: $1500   DEADLINE: May 31
FIELDS/MAJORS: Entomology, Biology, Zoology

Open to students who have accumulated at least 30 semester hours at the time the award is presented. Must have completed at least one course or project in entomology. Interest and academic achievement in biology are considered. Must be enrolled at a recognized university or college in the United States, Canada, or Mexico. Several awards offered annually. Write to the address listed for complete details. Must have a GPA of at least 2.9.

Entomological Society of America
Education Committee
9301 Annapolis Road
Lanham, MD   20706

286
Bishop Greco Graduate Fellowship Program

AMOUNT: Maximum: $2000   DEADLINE: May 1
FIELDS/MAJORS: Special Education

Fellowship for graduate students in a full-time program for the preparation of classroom teachers of mentally retarded children. Applicants also must be a member of the Knights in good standing or the wife, son, or daughter of a member and have a good academic record. Special consideration will be given to students who attend a Catholic graduate school. Write to the secretary of the Committee on Fellowships at the address below for details.

Knights of Columbus
Secretary of the Committee on Fellowship
PO Box 1670
New Haven, CT   06507

287
Bishop W. Bertrand Stevens Foundation Grants and Loans

AMOUNT: None Specified   DEADLINE: May 15
FIELDS/MAJORS: All Areas of Study

Grants of part gift and part loan for residents of the (Episcopal) diocese of Los Angeles (Los Angeles, Orange, Ventura, Santa Barbara, and parts of San Bernardino and Riverside counties). Interview required, 0% interest, repay after graduation. Membership in the Episcopal church is not a requirement. Some preference is given to students planning to attend a seminary. Students in all fields of study are encouraged to apply. Write for details.

Bishop W. Bertrand Stevens Foundation
PO Box 80251
San Marino, CA   91118

288
Blackfeet Higher Education Program

AMOUNT: None Specified   DEADLINE: March 3
FIELDS/MAJORS: All Areas of Study

Scholarships are available for members of the Blackfeet Tribe who are actively pursuing an undergraduate degree in any area of study. Special awards are also available for adult students. Write to the address below for more information.

Blackfeet Tribe
PO Box 850
Browning, MT   59417

289
Blanche Fischer Foundation

AMOUNT: $500   DEADLINE: None Specified
FIELDS/MAJORS: All Areas of Study

Open to disabled or physically handicapped persons (excluding mental problems) residing within the state of Oregon. Must demonstrate financial need, and medical confirmation is required. Write to the address listed for more information.

Blanche Fischer Foundation
7912 SW 35th Ave., Suite 7
Portland, OR   97219

290
Blind Service Association Scholarship Grant Program

AMOUNT: $200-$2500   DEADLINE: March 31
FIELDS/MAJORS: All Areas of Study

Scholarships for legally blind students. For study at college, university, professional, or vocational educational program. Applicants must reside in the six-county Chicago metropolitan area. Applications are available after January 1 by writing to the address below. You must be legally blind to qualify for these awards.

Blind Service Association, Inc.
22 W. Monroe St.
Chicago, IL   60603

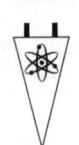

291
Bluebird Society Research Grants-Bluebird Research Grants

AMOUNT: $1000   DEADLINE: December 1
FIELDS/MAJORS: Ornithology: Avian Research and Study-Bluebirds

Research grants available to student, professional, and individual researchers for a research project focused on any of the three species of bluebird from the genus "Sialia." Proposal required. Supported on a one-year basis. Interested persons should write to the address below for further information.

North American Bluebird Society, Inc.
Kevin Berner, Research Comm. Chairman
State University of New York
Cobleskill, NY   12043

292
Bluebird Society Research Grants-General Research Grant

AMOUNT: $1000   DEADLINE: December 1
FIELDS/MAJORS: Ornithology: Avian Research and Study-Bluebirds

Research grants available to student, professional, and individual researchers for a research project focused on any North American cavity-nesting bird species. Proposal required. Supported on a one-year basis. Interested persons should write to the address below for further information.

North American Bluebird Society, Inc.
Kevin Berner, Research Comm. Chairman
State University of New York
Cobleskill, NY   12043

293
Bluebird Society Research Grants-Student Research Grant

AMOUNT: $1000   DEADLINE: December 1
FIELDS/MAJORS: Ornithology: Avian Research and Study-Bluebirds

Student research grant (1) available to a full-time college or university student, for a research project focused on any North American avian cavity-nesting species (genus "Sialia" and cavity-nesting species native to North America). Proposal required. Supported on a one-year basis. Interested students should write to the address below for further information.

North American Bluebird Society, Inc.
Kevin Berner, Research Comm. Chairman
State University of New York
Cobleskill, NY   12043

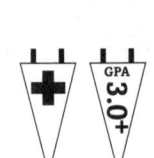

294
Board of Nursing and General Assembly Nursing Scholarships

AMOUNT: $100-$5000   DEADLINE: July 30
FIELDS/MAJORS: Nursing

Open to undergraduate and graduate Virginia residents, for a minimum of one year, who are enrolled full-time in a practical school of nursing in the State of Virginia. Based on academics and financial need. Recipients must practice nursing in Virginia after graduation for one month for every hundred dollars received. Applications will not be accepted prior to April 30. Awards are granted in September. Write to the address listed for details. The financial aid office at your school or Department of Nursing may also have information on this scholarship program. Must have a GPA of at least 3.0.

Virginia Department of Health
Office of Public Health Nursing
PO Box 2448
Richmond, VA   23218

295
Bob East Scholarship

AMOUNT: $1000 DEADLINE: March 1
FIELDS/MAJORS: Photojournalism

Applicants must be undergraduates, planning to pursue a career in newspaper photojournalism. All applicants must submit a portfolio that includes at least five individual prints and a photo essay. Write to Chuck Fadely at the address listed for more information. Be sure to include a business-sized SASE for a reply.

National Press Photographers Foundation
The Miami Herald-Photography Dept.
One Herald Plaza
Miami, FL 33132

296
Bob Eddy/Richard Peck Scholarship

AMOUNT: $1000-$2500 DEADLINE: April 14
FIELDS/MAJORS: Journalism, Communications

Open to college students entering junior or senior year. Must be attending four-year schools. Selections based on academics, dedication to journalism, and financial need. One award is for $1000, one award is for $1500, and the last award is $2500. Contact the address listed for further information. Must have a GPA of at least 3.0.

Connecticut Chapter Society of Professional Journalists
Debra A. Estock
71 Kenwood Ave.
Fairfield, CT 06430

297
Bob Hasson Memorial Scholarship

AMOUNT: None Specified DEADLINE: March 1
FIELDS/MAJORS: All Areas of Study

Open to high school seniors who are Oregon residents and U.S. citizens or permanent residents. May also apply if enrolling in college within twelve months of high school graduation. This is a one time award. Children and grandchildren of owners and officers of collection agencies registered in the State of Oregon are not eligible to apply for this scholarship. Contact the address below for further information.

Oregon State Scholarship Commission
Private Awards
1500 Valley River Dr., #100
Eugene, OR 97401-2130

298
Bob Shannon Memorial Scholarship Fund

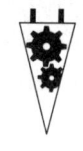

AMOUNT: Maximum: $1000 DEADLINE: May 15
FIELDS/MAJORS: Aviation

Open to students between the ages of sixteen and nineteen who are interested in learning to fly. Must be residents of the Greater Delaware Valley area and be able to utilize the scholarship within one year of the date of the grant. Applicants are expected to contribute the cost of 25% of the training. Write to the address listed for more information.

Aero Club of Pennsylvania, Bob Shannon Scholarship
  Trustees
Mrs. Adelle M. Bedrossian
810 Crum Creek Rd.
Springfield, PA 19064

299
Bobby Briffith Memorial Scholarship

AMOUNT: None Specified DEADLINE: None Specified
FIELDS/MAJORS: All Areas of Study

Open to graduating high school seniors who are residents of Contra Costa County. Award for people who contribute to improving the environment for lesbian, gay, bisexual, and transgendered youth. Contact the address listed for further information. Include a SASE for a reply.

Gay, Lesbian, and Straight Education Network
San Francisco Bay Area Chapter
PO Box 70554
Point Richmond, CA 94807-0554

300
Boettcher Foundation Scholarships

AMOUNT: Maximum: $2800 DEADLINE: February 1
FIELDS/MAJORS: All Areas of Study

Applicants must be Colorado residents who are graduating high school seniors. Other requirements include: upper 7% class rank, 1100 SAT or 27 ACT test score, and U.S. citizenship. Award is for use at Colorado schools only. Renewable. Approximately forty awards are offered annually. The actual awards are for tuition plus $2800 toward room, board, books, etc. Write to the address below for details. Must have a GPA of at least 3.7.

Boettcher Foundation
600 17th St., Suite 2210 South
Denver, CO 80202

301

Bonerty Scholarships

AMOUNT: Maximum: $800 DEADLINE: December 31
FIELDS/MAJORS: All Areas of Study

Must be natural or legally adopted child of an active, retired, or deceased letter carrier who has been a member of the National Association of Letter Carriers for at least one year. Applicant must be a high school senior, planning on attending any state-supported college or university. Requests for applications are available only through *The Postal Record*. Write to the address below for information.

National Association of Letter Carriers
Scholarship Committee
100 Indiana Ave. NW
Washington, DC 20001

302

Bootstrap Scholarship

AMOUNT: None Specified DEADLINE: None Specified
FIELDS/MAJORS: All Areas of Study

Scholarship open to single residents of Sarasota and Manatee counties who are the head of household and will be attending MCC. Must be able to demonstrate financial need. Write to the address below for details.

Selby Foundation
Manatee Community College-Finance Office
PO Box 1849
Bradenton, FL 34206

303

Bound-to-Stay-Bound Books Scholarship

AMOUNT: Maximum: $6000 DEADLINE: March 1
FIELDS/MAJORS: Library Science, Children's Library Service

Applicants must be entering or enrolled in an ALA-accredited program for the master's or beyond the master's with a concentration in children's library services. Must be U.S. or Canadian citizens. Recipients are required to work in a children's library for a minimum of one year after graduation. Write to the address listed or call (312) 280-2163/2165 for details.

American Library Association
Assn. for Library Service to Children
50 E. Huron St.
Chicago, IL 60611

304

Bour Memorial Scholarships

AMOUNT: Maximum: $1000 DEADLINE: April 1
FIELDS/MAJORS: All Areas of Study

Open to graduates of Lafayette County, Missouri, high schools. Recipients may attend colleges of their choice and be able to demonstrate financial need. Contact the address listed for further information or call (816) 259-4661. Must have a GPA of at least 2.7.

Boatman's Bank of Lexington
Delores A. Fischer
1016 Main St.
Lexington, MO 64067

305

Boy Scout of the Year Scholarship

AMOUNT: $400-$2000 DEADLINE: None Specified
FIELDS/MAJORS: All Areas of Study

Scholarships for Iowa residents who are Eagle Scouts. Based upon dedication to church and country, and school/community service. Applicant must be a U.S. citizen. Write to the address listed or call 1-800-365-8387 for additional information or application.

American Legion, Department of Iowa
Department Headquarters
720 Lyon St.
Des Moines, IA 50309

306

BPW Foundation Scholarship

AMOUNT: Maximum: $1000 DEADLINE: March 25
FIELDS/MAJORS: All Areas of Study, Career-oriented Curriculum

Available to women twenty-five years of age or older for undergraduate study. Purpose is for recipients to upgrade their skills for career advancement, to train for a new career field, or to re-enter the job market. Recipients must demonstrate financial need and carry a minimum of 6 credit hours. Send a SASE to the address listed for an application.

Business and Professional Women's Foundation of Maryland, Inc.
Scholarships Coordinator
282 New Mark Esplanade
Rockville, MD 20850

307
BPW Loan Fund for Women in Engineering Studies

AMOUNT: Maximum: $5000   DEADLINE: April 15
FIELDS/MAJORS: Engineering

Loans for women in the final two years of an accredited engineering program. Based on need. Renewable. Must be a U.S. citizen. Write to the address below for details.

Business and Professional Women's Foundation
Loan Programs
2012 Massachusetts Ave. NW
Washington, DC   20036

308
BPW/Sears-Roebuck Loan Fund for Women in Graduate Business Studies

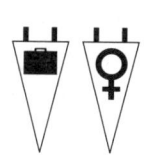

AMOUNT: Maximum: $2500   DEADLINE: April 15
FIELDS/MAJORS: Business Administration

Loans to encourage women to enter programs in business administration. Must demonstrate financial need. May apply annually for additional loans totaling $2500. Must be a U.S. citizen and enrolled in an accredited MBA program. BPW Foundation and Sears-Roebuck Foundation employees are not eligible. Write to address below for details.

Business and Professional Women's Foundation
Loan Programs
2012 Massachusetts Ave., NW
Washington, DC   20036

309
Brian M. Day Scholarships

AMOUNT: Maximum: $3500   DEADLINE: February 20
FIELDS/MAJORS: All Areas of Study

Awards open to Seattle area African-American gay men. Must be able to demonstrate significant financial need and activism in the gay/lesbian community. Contact the address listed for further information.

Greater Seattle Business Association and Pride Foundation
2033 6th Ave., #804
Seattle, WA   98121

310
Brian W. Sullivan Memorial Scholarship

AMOUNT: $1000   DEADLINE: March 15
FIELDS/MAJORS: All Areas of Study

Five scholarships are available for graduating seniors of Cathedral High School in Springfield, Massachusetts. Based on financial need, extracurricular activities, and sports. Write to the address listed for information.

Community Foundation of Western Massachusetts
PO Box 15769
1500 Main St.
Springfield, MA   01115

311
Bridgestone/Firestone Trust Fund Scholarships

AMOUNT: $2000   DEADLINE: February 1
FIELDS/MAJORS: All Areas of Study

Scholarships for Bridgestone/Firestone employees or their children. Retired employees are also invited to apply. Children of employees should apply during the junior year of high school. Forty-six awards are given annually. One time award only. Write to the address below for details.

Bridgestone/Firestone, Inc.
Trust Fund Administrator
50 Century Boulevard
Nashville, TN   37214

312
Bristol Bar Association Scholarships

AMOUNT: None Specified   DEADLINE: April 12
FIELDS/MAJORS: Law

Scholarships for students entering law school who are residents of the city of Bristol, Connecticut, or the surrounding towns of Burlington, Plainville, Terryville, and Plymouth. Based also on need, achievement, and extracurricular activities. Number and amount of awards varies. Contact Attorney Margaret M. Hayes, Chairperson of the Bristol Bar Association Scholarship Committee, for details.

Bristol Bar Association
Anderson, Alden, Hayes & Ziogas, LLC
PO Box 1197
Bristol, CT   06011

313
Bristol Children's Home Fund

AMOUNT: Maximum: $700   DEADLINE: May 1
FIELDS/MAJORS: All Areas of Study

Scholarships are available for residents of Bristol who have lived there for at least four years and wish to or are currently attending a four-year institution. Write to the address listed for information.

Rhode Island Foundation
Mrs. Jessie Huey
26 Acacia Rd.
Bristol, RI   02809

314
British Marshall Scholarships

AMOUNT: Maximum: $24000   DEADLINE: October 15
FIELDS/MAJORS: All Areas of Study

Scholarships for American graduate students to study in a university in the United Kingdom. The primary program's purpose is to allow young Americans, who will one day become leaders, opinion formers, and decision makers in their own country, to study in Great Britain and understand and appreciate British culture. Must be U.S. citizens, under age twenty-six, and have a minimum 3.7 GPA. Write to the address below for complete details.

British Information Services
845 Third Ave.
New York, NY   10022

315
Broome County Medical Society Auxiliary Loan Program

AMOUNT: None Specified   DEADLINE: May 1
FIELDS/MAJORS: Medical

Financial assistance is given to students attending medical school in Broome County or to Broome County residents attending an accredited medical school in the United States or Canada. Assistance is given in the form of a no-interest loan, which students are required to repay within five years of completion of residency training. Write to the address below for further details.

Broome County Medical Society Auxiliary
4513 Old Vestal Road
Vestal, NY   13850

316
Bruce and Marjorie Sundlun Scholarship

AMOUNT: $250-$1000   DEADLINE: May 1
FIELDS/MAJORS: All Areas of Study

One to three scholarships are available for residents of Rhode Island who are single parents returning to school to upgrade their skills. Write to the address listed for information.

Rhode Island Foundation
70 Elm St.
Providence, RI   02903

317
Bruce B. Melchert Scholarship

AMOUNT: Maximum: $300   DEADLINE: June 2
FIELDS/MAJORS: Political Science, Government

Scholarship is available to Tau Kappa Epsilon members who are full-time sophomores, juniors, or seniors pursuing a degree in political science or government, with a GPA of 3.0 or higher. Must be able to demonstrate leadership within his chapter as rush chairman, Prytanis, or other major office and a leader in IFC or other campus organizations. Write to the address listed for more information.

TKE Educational Foundation
8645 Founders Rd.
Indianapolis, IN   46268

318
Bryan Patterson Prize

AMOUNT: $600   DEADLINE: April 1
FIELDS/MAJORS: Vertebrate Paleontology

Grants to support field work by SVP members. Proposals for the award should be for fieldwork and for fieldwork that is imaginative rather than pedestrian; venturesome rather than safe. Write to the address below for details.

Society of Vertebrate Paleontology
W436 Nebraska Hall
University of Nebraska
Lincoln, NE   68588

319
Buffalo Sigma Delta Chi Journalism Scholarships

AMOUNT: Maximum: $1500   DEADLINE: April 30
FIELDS/MAJORS: Journalism, Communications, Writing

Scholarships for juniors, seniors, and graduate students living in western New York, northwestern Pennsylvania, and southern Ontario. Must be majoring in courses leading to a career in one of the above fields. Renewable once. Students in western New York, northwestern Pennsylvania, and southern Ontario should write to the address listed for details.

Society of Professional Journalists, Greater Buffalo Chapter
John C. Connolly, Scholarship Secretary
160 Schimwood Ct.
Getzville, NY   14068

320
Bundeskanzler Scholarships for Germany

AMOUNT: None Specified   DEADLINE: October 31
FIELDS/MAJORS: Humanities, Social Sciences, Law, and Economics of Germany

Scholarships are awarded annually to exceptionally able young Americans for study in such fields as the humanities, social sciences, law, and economics at academic or other appropriate institutions in Germany. Applicants must be U.S. citizens under thirty-two years of age and should have at least a bachelor's degree by the time the award begins. Write to the address listed for more information.

Alexander Von Humboldt Foundation
1055 Thomas Jefferson St. NW, Suite 2020
Washington, DC   20007

321
Bureau of Alcohol, Tobacco, and Firearms Special Agents' Scholarships

AMOUNT: Maximum: $1000   DEADLINE: April 1
FIELDS/MAJORS: Law Enforcement

Scholarships are presented every year to law enforcement explorers whose achievements reflect the high degree of motivation, commitment, and community concern that epitomize the law enforcement profession. Write to the address listed for more information.

Bureau of Alcohol, Tobacco, and Firearms
Office of Liaison and Public Information
650 Massachusetts Ave., Room 8290
Washington, DC   20226

322
Burlington Northern, Santa Fe Pacific Foundation Scholarships

AMOUNT: Maximum: $2500
DEADLINE: March 31
FIELDS/MAJORS: Science, Business, Education, Health Administration

This scholarship is made available to Native American high school seniors who reside in states serviced by the Burlington Northern and Santa Fe Pacific Corporation and its affiliated companies: AZ, CO, KS, MN, MT, NM, ND, OK, SD, WA, and CA. Applicants must be one-quarter Native American or recognized as a member of a tribe. Contact the address listed or call (303) 939-0023 and specify you are interested in the Santa Fe Pacific awards. Must have a GPA of at least 2.8.

American Indian Science and Engineering Society
Scholarship Coordinator
5661 Airport Blvd.
Boulder, CO   80301

323
Burns and Haynes Scholarship

AMOUNT: Maximum: $500   DEADLINE: None Specified
FIELDS/MAJORS: Textile Technology

Scholarships are available for residents of Rhode Island who are studying textile technology. Preference is given to children of members of the National Association of Textile Supervisors. One award is offered annually. Write to the address listed for information.

Rhode Island Foundation
John Reardon
PO Box 325, Village Station
Medway, MA   02053

324
Business Reporting Internship Program for Minorities

AMOUNT: $1000   DEADLINE: November 15
FIELDS/MAJORS: Journalism

Internships consist of summer paid jobs as reporters for business sections of daily newspapers. Includes one week free pre-intern training seminar. $1000 scholarships to successful interns who return to college in the fall. Open to college sophomores and juniors who are U.S. citizens. Contact the address listed for further information or call (609) 452-2820. Applications available August 15 through November 1.

Dow Jones Newspaper Fund
PO Box 300
Princeton, NJ   08543

325
Butler Manufacturing Company Foundation Scholarships

AMOUNT: Maximum: $2000 DEADLINE: February 18
FIELDS/MAJORS: All Areas of Study

Applicants must be children of Butler Manufacturing employees. Scholarships are available for undergraduate study only. U.S. citizenship required. Awarded to graduating high school seniors. Eight renewable awards per year. Have your parent contact his/her human resources department or write to the address below for details.

Butler Manufacturing Company Foundation
BMA Tower, Penn Valley Park
PO Box 419917
Kansas City, MO 64141

326
Byron Community Scholarship

AMOUNT: Maximum: $500 DEADLINE: February 1
FIELDS/MAJORS: All Areas of Study

Open to Byron High School graduates who have been accepted to and are enrolled at an accredited vocational or trade school or college. Winners will be notified in March. Contact the address listed or call (810) 266-5814 or Byron High School office for further information.

Shiawassee Foundation
Inta Davis
PO Box 261
Byron, MI 48418

327
Byron Hanke Fellowships

AMOUNT: Maximum: $2500 DEADLINE: None Specified
FIELDS/MAJORS: Related to Community Associations

Fellowships are available for students enrolled in an accredited master's, doctoral, or law program. Topics must be related to the community associations (cooperative, condominium, and homeowners) research project. Write to the address listed for information.

Community Associations Institute Research Foundation
1630 Duke St.
Alexandria, VA 22314

328
C.J. Davidson Scholarship

AMOUNT: Maximum: $900 DEADLINE: None Specified
FIELDS/MAJORS: Home Economics or Family and Consumer Sciences

Open to graduating high school seniors who have completed one or more years of home economics in school, have an overall high school grade average of 85, and have been active members of an affiliated chapter of FHA for at least two years. Available for use at twelve Texas institutions. Contact the financial aid office at the participating schools, your FHA chapter, or the address listed for further information. Must have a GPA of at least 2.7.

Texas Assn., Future Homemakers of America Assn.
Scholarship Coordinator
PO Box 9616
Austin, TX 78766-9616

329
Cabaniss, Johnston Scholarship

AMOUNT: Maximum: $5000 DEADLINE: June 5
FIELDS/MAJORS: Law

Scholarship is awarded annually to a law student who is a resident of Alabama, is attending an accredited law school in the United States, and will be a second year student. Write to the address listed or call (334) 269-1515 for more information.

Alabama Law Foundation, Inc.
PO Box 671
Montgomery, AL 36101

330
Cabot Corporation Scholarship Program

AMOUNT: $500-$2000 DEADLINE: April 1
FIELDS/MAJORS: All Areas of Study

Scholarships are available for high school seniors who are children of Cabot Corporation employees. Based on scholastic record and participation in extracurricular activities. For full-time undergraduate studies in a four-year program. May spend first two years in a junior or community college. Your parent(s) may receive an application card from their plant manager or the human resources manager. If those two sources do not have the material, you may write to the address listed for information.

Cabot Corporation
Scholarship Program
75 State St.
Boston, MA 02109

331
Cabrillo Civic Clubs Scholarship

AMOUNT: Maximum: $400　DEADLINE: April 1
FIELDS/MAJORS: All Areas of Study

Open to students of Portuguese descent enrolled in an accredited U.S. college or university. Must have a minimum GPA of 3.5. Contact your high school guidance counselor for further information about the other five requirements needed by applicants, or contact the address listed.

Cabrillo Civic Club, #27 of California
Robert Minter, Chairman
3429 Heather Ln.
Ceres, CA　95307

332
Caddie Scholarship Foundation (N.J. Golf Assn.) Scholarships

AMOUNT: $800-$2500　DEADLINE: May 1
FIELDS/MAJORS: All Areas of Study

Scholarships for high school seniors or undergraduates who have caddied for at least one year at a NJSGA club. For full-time study. Based on academics, need, character, and length of service as a caddie. Renewable for four years. Students whose parents are members of a private golf club are not eligible. Write to the address listed for details.

New Jersey State Golf Association
Golf Cottage
1000 Broad St.
Bloomfield, NJ　07003

333
CAEOP and Marjorie Stewart Scholarships

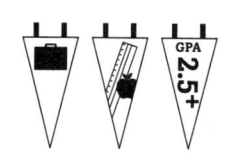

AMOUNT: Maximum: $750　DEADLINE: February 6
FIELDS/MAJORS: Business Education

Open to high school seniors who are Connecticut residents. For study at two- or four-year schools. Based on academic success, financial need, and community service. Contact the address listed for further information. Must have a GPA of at least 2.9.

Connecticut Association of Educational Office Professionals
Ms. M. Baldwin, V.P.
C/O Litchfield Schools
PO Box 110
Litchfield, CT　06759

334
California Farm Bureau Scholarships

AMOUNT: $1500-$2700　DEADLINE: March 1
FIELDS/MAJORS: Agriculture

Open to residents of California. Must be enrolled/accepted by a four-year college or university in California. Must be a U.S. citizen. Selections based on academics, career goals, extracurricular activities, and leadership skills. Write for complete details. Must have a GPA of at least 2.9.

California Farm Bureau Scholarship Foundation
2300 River Plaza Dr.
Sacramento, CA　95833

335
California Scholarship Challenge Program

AMOUNT: Maximum: $500　DEADLINE: April 15
FIELDS/MAJORS: Travel and Tourism, Hotel/Motel Management

Awards for California residents in one of the areas listed above who are enrolled in any two- or four-year college full-time. Must have a GPA of 3.0 or better and be entering junior or senior year. Write to the address listed or call 1-800-682-8886 ext. 4251 for more information.

National Tourism Foundation
546 East Main St.
PO Box 3071
Lexington, KY　40596

336
California Sea Grant State Fellow Program

AMOUNT: None Specified　DEADLINE: March 3
FIELDS/MAJORS: Marine Sciences

Open to graduate students in a marine-related field at a California university. Applicant should demonstrate an interest in marine science and public policy. College seniors are also eligible to apply if they intend to continue school. These internships match students with hosts in the California State Legislature or in state agencies for a nine-month period in Sacramento. Write to the address below for more information.

California Sea Grant System, State Fellow Program
University of California
9500 Gilman Dr.
La Jolla, CA　92093

337
Camden County Hero Scholarship 200 Club

AMOUNT: Maximum: $5000 DEADLINE: March 31
FIELDS/MAJORS: Public Safety

Students who have completed their freshman year in college and who have a parent actively serving or they themselves are serving Camden County in a public safety capacity. Three awards are given annually. Write to the address listed or call Dawn M. Shirley at (609) 768-9656 for more information.

Camden County Hero Scholarship 200 Club
191 White Horse Pike
Berlin, NJ 08009

338
Campus Safety Association Scholarship

AMOUNT: Maximum: $1000 DEADLINE: March 31
FIELDS/MAJORS: Occupational Safety, Environmental Health

Awards for students in academic programs leading to a degree in occupational safety, environmental health, or a related field. Candidates must be in good academic standing and recommended by their college or university. Two awards offered annually. Contact the Financial Aid Office at your school or call (630) 775-2026 for more information. The Financial Aid Administrator must collect the application forms and return them to the National Safety Council. Must have a GPA of at least 2.0.

Campus Safety, Health, and Environmental Management Association
C/O Eve Brouwer, National Safety Council
1121 Spring Lake Dr.
Itasca, IL 60143

339
Canton Student Loan Fund

AMOUNT: Maximum: $3000 DEADLINE: June 1
FIELDS/MAJORS: All Areas of Study

Loans are available for students who graduated from a Stark County high school or any Stark County resident who received a high school diploma through participation in the ABC program. For full-time undergraduate study. Must have a GPA of 2.0 or better. Payments begin three months following graduation. Current interest rate is 6%. The maximum loan repayment term is seven years. Write to the address listed for more information.

Canton Student Loan Foundation
4974 Higbee Ave. NW, #204
Canton, OH 44718

340
Cape Canaveral Chapter Retired Officers Association Scholarship

AMOUNT: Maximum: $2000 DEADLINE: March 31
FIELDS/MAJORS: All Areas of Study

Candidates must be Brevard County, Florida, residents, juniors or seniors, attending any four-year college in the U.S. Must be descendant or ward of an active or retired or deceased (while on active or in retired status) member. Write to the address listed for details. Please be certain to enclose a business-sized SASE with your request.

Retired Officers Association, Cape Canaveral Chapter
TROACC Scholarship Committee
PO Box 254186
Patrick AFB, FL 32925

341
Capitol Hill News Internships

AMOUNT: Maximum: $3000 DEADLINE: None Specified
FIELDS/MAJORS: Electronic Journalism

Internship positions available for recent college graduates with a demonstrated objective of a career in electronic journalism. Preference given to minority applicants. Excellent writing skills are essential. Interns will work side by side with the Washington Press and Congressional Staff to cover the political process. There are two spring internships with a deadline of January 15 and two summer internships with a deadline date of March 2. Each internship is a full-time position for three months with a salary of $1000 per month. Write to the address listed for more information. Must have a GPA of at least 3.2.

Radio and Television News Directors Foundation
RTNDF DC Internships
1000 Connecticut Ave. NW, #615
Washington, DC 20036

342
Captain Dan and Barney Flynn Scholarship

AMOUNT: Maximum: $500 DEADLINE: None Specified
FIELDS/MAJORS: All Areas of Study

Open to graduating seniors at a Corpus Christi high school who are in the NROTC program and plan to attend Texas A&M at Corpus Christi or Del Mar College as full-time students. Must have a minimum GPA of 2.0. Selections based on merit and financial need. Contact the address below for further information.

Coastal Bend Community Foundation
Mercantile Tower MT276
615 N. Upper Broadway, #860
Corpus Christi, TX 78477

343
CAP-College Assistance Program Grants

AMOUNT: $500-$3000 DEADLINE: July 1
FIELDS/MAJORS: All Areas of Study

Scholarships for Dade County, Florida, students enrolled in a full-time undergraduate program. Based on financial need. Must have graduated from a Dade County public high school. Twenty-five hundred awards are offered annually. Contact your high school CAP Advisor, contact your high school guidance office, or write to the address below for details.

College Assistance Program, Inc. (Dade County)
School Board Administration Bldg.
1500 Biscayne Blvd., Room 341
Miami, FL 33132

344
Career Advancement Scholarship Program

AMOUNT: $500-$1000
DEADLINE: April 15
FIELDS/MAJORS: Computer Science, Education, Paralegal, Engineering, or Science

Up to one hundred scholarships for women twenty-five or older. Criteria: within twenty-four months of completing an accredited course of study in the U.S.A. Should lead to entry or advancement in the work force. Must be U.S. citizens. The pre-application screening form is only available between October 1 and April 1. Not for doctoral study, correspondence schools, or non-degreed programs. Write to address below for details.

Business and Professional Women's Foundation Scholarships
2012 Massachusetts Ave. NW
Washington, DC 20036

345
Career Development Awards

AMOUNT: $2000-$3000 DEADLINE: December 1
FIELDS/MAJORS: Nursing, Administration

Awards for continuing education programs that will further professional goals in nursing or administration. Criteria will vary among these awards. All four awards require current employment as staff/registered/administrator-manager nurses. Other criteria will vary slightly. The four awards: Ethics Career Development Award, Josh Gottheil Memorial Bone Marrow Transplant Career Development Awards, Nurse Administrator/Manager Career Development Award, and Pearl Moore Career Development Awards offer a combined total of nine awards ranging from $2000 to $3000 each. Contact the address listed for further information about all the awards.

Oncology Nursing Foundation
501 Holiday Dr.
Pittsburgh, PA 15220

346
Career Development Grants

AMOUNT: $1000-$5000 DEADLINE: January 5
FIELDS/MAJORS: All Areas of Study

Grants to prepare for re-entry into work force or training for a career change. Special consideration is given to qualified AAUW members, minorities, women pursuing their first terminal degrees, and women pursuing degrees in non-traditional fields. Must be U.S. citizens or permanent residents and have earned your last degree at least five years previously. Write to the address listed for more information.

American Association of University Women Educational Foundation
2201 N. Dodge St.
Iowa City, IA 52243

347
Carey Rose Winski Dance Competition

AMOUNT: $500-$1000 DEADLINE: July 24
FIELDS/MAJORS: Dance

Scholarship competition for students who show a talent in dance. Based on performance (in person) in both classical ballet (en pointe for women) and in any eclectic style (jazz, modern, character, etc.). Must be between thirteen and eighteen years old. Competition takes place at the Marjorie Ward Marshall Dance Center located on the Northwestern University Campus in Evanston, Illinois. Write to the address below for details.

Carey Rose Winski Memorial Foundation, Inc.
69 Woodley Rd.
Winnetka, IL 60093

348
Cargill Scholarship Program for Rural America

AMOUNT: Maximum: $1000 DEADLINE: February 16
FIELDS/MAJORS: Agriculture

Over 250 awards available to graduating seniors from farm families who plan to attend the postsecondary institution of their choice. For questions, contact the address listed. For completed applications, send to National FFA Organization, Scholarship Office, PO Box 15160, 5632 Mount Vernon Memorial Highway, Alexandria, VA 22309-0160.

National FFA Foundation
Cargill Scholarship Coordinator
Box 45205
Madison, WI 53744

349

Carl F. Dietz Memorial, Jerry Wilmot, Harold Bettinger Scholarships

AMOUNT: $1000-$2000 DEADLINE: April 1
FIELDS/MAJORS: Horticulture

Scholarships for students in four-year colleges or universities with a major in horticulture. Must have a minimum GPA of 3.0. Award requirements vary slightly. Write to the address below for details. The BPFI also sponsors two awards through Future Farmers of America (check with your FFA advisor).

Bedding Plants Foundation, Inc.
Scholarship Program
PO Box 27241
Lansing, MI 48909

350

Carol Macias Nursing Scholarship

AMOUNT: Maximum: $300 DEADLINE: May 30
FIELDS/MAJORS: Nursing, Healthcare

Scholarships for Santa Paula high school graduates who are enrolled in a school of nursing. Allied fields will also be considered (physician's assistant, physical therapy, etc.). Write to the address below for details.

Carol Macias Nursing Scholarship
Westside Family Practice
247 March St.
Santa Paula, CA 93060

351

Caroline Holt Nursing Scholarships

AMOUNT: Maximum: $500 DEADLINE: February 15
FIELDS/MAJORS: Nursing

Must be undergraduates currently enrolled in an accredited school of nursing and sponsored by a local DAR chapter. Must be U.S. citizens. Second deadline date is August 15. Contact your local chapter or send a SASE to the address listed for details.

National Society Daughters of the American Revolution
NSDAR Scholarship Committee
1776 D St. NW
Washington, DC 20006

352

Carolyn Elizabeth Spivey Memorial Scholarship

AMOUNT: None Specified DEADLINE: April 1
FIELDS/MAJORS: Nursing

Awards for graduating high school seniors or college students with a GPA greater than 2.5 on a 4.0 scale as verified by official transcripts. Applicants must demonstrate economic need, as verified by parent's tax return or other suitable document. Also based on three letters of reference, an essay on the challenge to American families today, and school and community involvement. For more information and an application, contact Nylcare customer service at 1-800-635-3121.

Nylcare/Mid-Atlantic Scholarship Foundation, Inc.
7617 Ora Glen Dr.
Greenbelt, MD 20770

353

Carrol C. Hall Memorial Scholarship

AMOUNT: Maximum: $600 DEADLINE: June 2
FIELDS/MAJORS: Education, Science

Scholarship is available to any undergraduate member of Tau Kappa Epsilon who is earning a degree in education or science and has plans to become a teacher or pursue a profession in science. Must have a GPA of 3.0 or higher and be a full-time student in good standing. Must be able to demonstrate leadership within his chapter, on campus, and in the community. Write to the address listed for more information.

TKE Educational Foundation
8645 Founders Rd.
Indianapolis, IN 46268

354

Carroll L. Birch Award

AMOUNT: $500 DEADLINE: June 30
FIELDS/MAJORS: Medicine

This award is presented to an AMWA student member for the best original research paper. Write to the address below for details.

American Medical Women's Association
Carroll L. Birch Award
801 N. Fairfax St., Suite 400
Alexandria, VA 22314

355
Cartography and Geographic Information Society Scholarship

AMOUNT: Maximum: $1000   DEADLINE: November 10
FIELDS/MAJORS: Cartography

Open to full-time juniors and seniors enrolled in a cartography curriculum in a four-year, degree-granting institution. Contact the address below for further information.

American Cartographic Association
Lilly Matheson, ACSM Awards Program
5410 Grosvenor Ln., #100
Bethesda, MD   20814-2144

356
Cartography Fellowships

AMOUNT: $800   DEADLINE: March 1
FIELDS/MAJORS: Cartography, History of Map-Making

Fellowships available to doctoral candidates or postdoctoral scholars for residence at Newberry. All doctoral requirements must be fulfilled except the dissertation, if candidate does not have Ph.D. projects must be related to the history of cartography and focused on cartographic materials in the library's collections. Stipends are $800 per month for up to two months. Write to the address listed for details or call (312) 255-3666.

Newberry Library
Committee on Awards
60 W. Walton St.
Chicago, IL   60610

357
Casaday-Elmore Ministerial Scholarship

AMOUNT: None Specified   DEADLINE: January 31
FIELDS/MAJORS: Religion/Theology

Applicants must be CAP cadet members with plans to enter the ministry. Write to the address listed for details.

Civil Air Patrol
National Headquarters Cap (TT)
Maxwell AFB, AL   36112

358
CASW-Nate Haseltine Fellowships in Science Writing

AMOUNT: Maximum: $2000   DEADLINE: June 15
FIELDS/MAJORS: Science Writing

Fellowships for students who hold an undergraduate degree in science or journalism. Preference is given to journalists with at least two years of experience. Based on resume, transcript, recommendations, writing samples, and application. Write to the address below for full details. Not for pursuit of careers in public relations or public information work.

Council for the Advancement of Science Writing, Inc.
Ben Patrusky, Executive Director
PO Box 404
Greenlawn, NY   11740

359
Cataract Fire Company #2 Scholarship

AMOUNT: Maximum: $1000   DEADLINE: April 22
FIELDS/MAJORS: All Areas of Study

Scholarships are available for residents of Warwick, Rhode Island, who are graduating high school seniors and are entering a four-year school. Three awards offered annually. Write to the address listed for information.

Warwick Public Schools
Donald R. Staley, Asst. Superintendent
34 Warwick Lake Ave.
Warwick, RI   02889

360
Caterpillar Scholars Awards

AMOUNT: Maximum: $2000   DEADLINE: March 1
FIELDS/MAJORS: Manufacturing Engineering, Manufacturing Engineering Technology

Open to full-time undergraduates who have completed at least 30 credit hours in an ABET accredited program with a minimum GPA of 3.0. Must be planning careers in manufacturing engineering or manufacturing engineering technology. Minority applicants may apply as incoming freshmen. Write to the address listed for details.

Society of Manufacturing Engineering Education Foundation
One SME Dr.
PO Box 930
Dearborn, MI   48121

361
Catherine Beattie Fellowship

AMOUNT: Maximum: $4000 DEADLINE: December 31
FIELDS/MAJORS: Botany or Related Fields

Fellowships are available for graduate students at a botanical garden jointly serving the Center for Plant Conservation and the student's academic research. Open to students with academic qualifications and an interest in rare plant conservation. Preference given to those with an interest in and whose projects focus on the endangered flora of the Carolinas and southeastern U.S. Write to the address listed for information.

Garden Club of America-Center for Plant Conservation
Anukriti Sud, Missouri Botanical Garden
PO Box 299
St. Louis, MO 63166

362
Catherine F. DeCaterina Scholarship

AMOUNT: Maximum: $1000 DEADLINE: April 1
FIELDS/MAJORS: Performing Arts, Writing, Theater Arts

Open to high school seniors who are residents of Virginia, Tennessee, Kentucky, North Carolina, or West Virginia. Applicants must demonstrate a high level of participation in theater arts (on or behind the stage), letters of recommendation, a one page essay, and supporting documents of dedication to the craft of theater will be required. Contact the address listed for further information or call (423) 968-4977.

Appalachian Regional Theater
Theater Bristol, Scholarship Director
512 State St.
Bristol, TN 37620

363
Catherine H. Kenworthy Endowed Scholarship

AMOUNT: Maximum: $1000 DEADLINE: February 15
FIELDS/MAJORS: Horticulture, Floriculture, Landscape Architecture, Conservation, Forestry, Plant Pathology, Environmental Control, City Planning, Land Management

Open to students from high school seniors to graduate level who are Pennsylvania residents. Must have a minimum GPA of 2.8. Must be sponsored by a Federated Garden Club in Pennsylvania and be able to demonstrate financial need. References, a personal letter, (regarding goals, background, and commitment), an official transcript for the current period, and the application signed by the sponsoring club's president will be required. A student may reapply if academics remain high and need is apparent. Contact a local club, the address listed, or (215) 643-0164 for details.

Garden Club Federation of Pennsylvania
Mrs. William A. Lamb, Scholarship Chair
925 Lorien Dr.
Gwynedd Valley, PA 19437-0216

364
Catholic Graduates Club Scholarship

AMOUNT: Maximum: $1000 DEADLINE: March 15
FIELDS/MAJORS: All Areas of Study

Open to Catholic graduating seniors who are residents of Hartford County, Connecticut. For use at a four-year institution. Selections based on strong academics, financial need, and extracurricular and community activities. Contact the address listed for further information.

Catholic Graduates Club of Greater Hartford
Bob Mittica, Scholarship Chairman
PO Box 1501
Hartford, CT 06144

365
CBAI Foundation for Community Banking Scholarship Contest

AMOUNT: Maximum: $1000 DEADLINE: February 10
FIELDS/MAJORS: All Areas of Study

Essay contest open to Illinois seniors sponsored by a Community Bankers Association of Illinois member bank. Essay theme should be: "How Will Community Banks Make a Difference in the 21st Century?" Judges will look for an understanding of what a community bank is and its role in the local economy. Winners selected by April 15. Contact your local community bank member for detailed contest rules and its deadline date. The Foundation headquarters must have the entries (sent from the member banks, not the applicants) by February 20. For information about member locations, call 1-800-736-2224.

Community Bankers Association of Illinois

366
CELSOC Scholarship Award

AMOUNT: Maximum: $6000 DEADLINE: February 16
FIELDS/MAJORS: Engineering, Surveying

Scholarships for juniors, seniors, or graduate students in engineering programs. Must be U.S. citizen, have a GPA of at least 3.2, and plan a career in either consulting engineering or in land surveying. Seven awards are offered annually. Write to the address below for details (information may also be available from your department).

Consulting Engineers and Land Surveyors of California
Scholarship Program
1303 J St., Suite 370
Sacramento, CA 95814

367

Cenex Agriculture Scholarships

AMOUNT: $600   DEADLINE: February 15
FIELDS/MAJORS: Agriculture

Scholarships for students in their first or second year of a two-year program in vocational agriculture at institutions in the Cenex trade area (Great Plains and Mountain States). Application is made through individual schools. Eighty-one scholarships are awarded annually. Contact the financial aid office at your college for information.

Cenex Foundation Scholarship Program
5500 Cenex Dr.
Inver Grove Heights, MN   55077

368

Cenex Cooperative Studies Scholarships

AMOUNT: $750   DEADLINE: March 1
FIELDS/MAJORS: Agriculture

Scholarships for juniors or seniors attending the agriculture college of a participating university in the Cenex trade area. Renewable if awarded as a junior. Seventeen schools participate in this scholarship. Universities select their own recipients. Seventy-nine scholarships are awarded annually. Contact the financial aid office at your school for details.

Cenex Foundation Scholarship Program
5500 Cenex Dr.
Inver Grove Heights, MN   55077

369

Center for Advanced Study in the Visual Arts Fellowships

AMOUNT: None Specified   DEADLINE: November 15
FIELDS/MAJORS: Visual Arts and Related Areas

Fellowships for Ph.D. candidates who have completed all course work except the dissertation. Requires knowledge of two foreign languages related to the topic of the dissertation. Applicants must be U.S. citizens or legal residents. Application must be made through graduate departments of art history (or other appropriate departments). Direct inquiries to the address below.

National Gallery of Art
Center for Advanced Study in Visual Arts
Fellowship Programs
Washington, DC   20565

370

Central Florida Jazz Society Scholarships

AMOUNT: $500-$1500   DEADLINE: May 1
FIELDS/MAJORS: Jazz Music, Vocal Music

Scholarship competition for students who are graduating high school seniors, college freshmen, sophomores, and juniors. Auditions will be held at the University of Central Florida on May 17th. A pre-screening tape must be mailed with the application. Five awards will be offered. For Florida residents or students attending a Florida college or university. Write to the address below for details.

Central Florida Jazz Society
PO Box 540133
Orlando, FL   32854

371

Central Minnesota Arts Board Scholarship Program

AMOUNT: $2000-$8000   DEADLINE: April 1
FIELDS/MAJORS: Art, Music, Dance, Literature, and Theater

Scholarships for graduating high school seniors planning careers in art. Must be residents of Benton, Stearns, Sherburne, or Wright Counties in Minnesota. Based on artistic quality and merit. Write to the address listed or call (320) 253-9517 for details.

Central Minnesota Arts Board
Sandra Beuning
PO Box 1442
St. Cloud, MN   56302

372

Central Pennsylvania Communications Scholarship

AMOUNT: $500   DEADLINE: None Specified
FIELDS/MAJORS: Communications

Scholarships available to male or female communication majors completing their junior year who either attend a college in the central Pennsylvania area or who are residents of the area. Must have a minimum GPA of 3.0. A portfolio of the student's work will be required. Contact the address listed for further information.

Association for Women in Communications, Inc., Central
   PA Chapter
Jennifer Engle
1845 Brubaker Run Rd.
Lancaster, PA   17603

373
Central Virginia Scholarships

AMOUNT: $1000-$5000 DEADLINE: March 4
FIELDS/MAJORS: Liberal Arts

Awards for high school seniors in the Richmond metropolitan area. Program is intended to help bridge the gap for worthy students whose preference is to attend the more expensive private institutions. Applicants must have been admitted to an accredited four-year college or university in the continental U.S. and should intend to pursue a major in liberal arts. One award is offered annually. Students who would like to be considered for this award must contact their high school guidance counselor or principal to be nominated.

Community Foundation Serving Richmond and Central Virginia
1025 Boulders Parkway
Suite 405
Richmond, VA 23225

374
Certificate/Associate Scholarship Program

AMOUNT: None Specified DEADLINE: April 1
FIELDS/MAJORS: Dental Hygiene

Scholarships for students in their second year of a full-time certificate or associates program of an accredited dental school. Minimum GPA of 3.0. Based on need. Write to the address below for more information.

American Dental Hygienists' Association Institute for Oral Health
444 N. Michigan Ave., Suite 3400
Chicago, IL 60611

375
Cesar E. Chavez Scholarship Endowment Fund

AMOUNT: Maximum: $1000 DEADLINE: None Specified
FIELDS/MAJORS: All Areas of Study

Open to children of agricultural and migrant workers who are full-time daytime students at a college or university. Students may be attending a junior college with the intention of transferring to a four-year institution. Must have completed a minimum of fifteen college credits before applying. Must also be a U.S. citizen or permanent resident. Contact the address below for further information. Be sure to include a SASE. Must have a GPA of at least 2.8.

United Farm Workers of America-National Hispanic Scholarship Fund
Ernest Z. Robles, Executive Director
PO Box 728
Novato, CA 94948

376
Charitabulls Scholarship Program

AMOUNT: None Specified DEADLINE: February 6
FIELDS/MAJORS: All Areas of Study

Open to high school seniors in the city of Chicago as well as the surrounding suburbs. Must complete an essay (five hundred words or less). Scholarships are available to students living in the following counties only: McHenry, Lake, Cook, Kane, DuPage, and Will. Three awards per year. Write to the address listed or call (312) 455-4000 for more information.

Chicago Bulls
1901 West Madison St.
Chicago, IL 60612

377
Charles A. Edwards YABA Scholarship Fund

AMOUNT: $500 DEADLINE: March 15
FIELDS/MAJORS: All Areas of Study

Awards for graduating high school seniors who are currently sanctioned Morris County YABA members and have bowled in the YABA program for at least the past three years. Based on academics. Contact the address below for further information.

Morris County Bowling Association
Albert Gonsiska, Jr.
21 Tinc Rd.
Flanders, NJ 07836

378
Charles and Louise Rosenbaum Student Loan Fund

AMOUNT: None Specified DEADLINE: March 29
FIELDS/MAJORS: All Areas of Study

Interest free loans for Jewish graduating high school seniors from Colorado who will be entering their freshmen year of college. Write to the address below for details.

Endowment Fund of the Allied Jewish Federation
300 Dahlia St.
Denver, CO 80222

379

Charles and Lucille King Family Foundation Scholarships

AMOUNT: $2500 DEADLINE: April 30
FIELDS/MAJORS: Television and Film

Awards open to sophomores and juniors. Based on financial need, academics, and letters of recommendation. Must be attending one of a select number of schools in any of the following states: New York, New Jersey, Maine, Maryland, New Hampshire, Vermont, Connecticut, Pennsylvania, or Massachusetts. Contact your department chairperson, bursar, or financial aid office to see if your school has been invited to participate in the scholarship program. If you write to this organization for information and application, you must include a SASE for a reply. Must have a GPA of at least 3.0.

Charles and Lucille King Family Foundation, Inc.
366 Madison Ave., 10th Fl.
New York, NY   10017

380

Charles Clarke Cordle Memorial Scholarship

AMOUNT: $1000 DEADLINE: February 1
FIELDS/MAJORS: All Areas of Study

Scholarship available to students with a general class amateur radio license who are residents of Georgia or Alabama. Must be enrolled full-time at any Georgia or Alabama institution and have a minimum GPA of 2.5. Write to the address listed for information.

ARRL Foundation (American Radio Relay League)
Scholarship Program
225 Main St.
Newington, CT   06111

381

Charles Dubose Scholarship

AMOUNT: $500-$2000 DEADLINE: May 1
FIELDS/MAJORS: Architecture

Open to students who have completed at least two years in a college offering a five-year accredited degree in architecture. Based on academics and financial need. Must be residents of Connecticut. Contact the address listed for further information. Must have a GPA of at least 3.0.

Connecticut Architecture Foundation, Inc.
Judy Edwards, Exec. V.P.
87 Willow St.
New Haven, CT   06511

382

Charles H. Feoppel Educational Loan Trust

AMOUNT: None Specified DEADLINE: May 31
FIELDS/MAJORS: All Areas of Study

Recipients of these low interest loans must be residents of Harrison County, unmarried, and must have completed high school or possess an equivalent certification. Write to the address below for more information.

Huntington National Bank WV
Attn: Trust Department
230 W. Pike St., PO Box 2490
Clarksburg, WV   26302

383

Charles LeGeyt Fortescue Fellowship

AMOUNT: Maximum: $24000 DEADLINE: January 15
FIELDS/MAJORS: Electrical Engineering

The fellowship is for one year of full-time graduate work in electrical engineering at an engineering school of recognized standing located in the U.S. or Canada. Must have bachelor's degree from an engineering school of recognized standing. For beginning graduate students only. Write to the address listed for details.

Institute of Electrical and Electronics Engineers, Awards Board
Secretary of the Fellowship Committee
445 Hoes Ln., PO Box 1331
Piscataway, NJ   08855

384

Charles M. Goethe Memorial Scholarship

AMOUNT: None Specified DEADLINE: June 10
FIELDS/MAJORS: All Areas of Study

Applicants must be members or senior members of the Order of DeMolay or be sons or daughters of a member (or a deceased member) of a constituent Masonic Lodge of the Grand Lodge of Free and Accepted Masons of California. All areas of study are acceptable, but preference will be given to students majoring in eugenics, genetics, biology, or life sciences. Write to the address below for details.

Sacramento Bodies Ancient and Accepted Scottish Rite of Freemasonry
PO Box 19497
Sacramento, CA   95819

385
Charles N. Fisher Memorial Scholarship

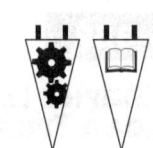

AMOUNT: $1000 DEADLINE: February 1
FIELDS/MAJORS: Electronics, Communications, Related Fields

Scholarship available to students with any class amateur radio license who are enrolled as full-time students in one of the above fields. Applicants must be residents of: Arizona or Los Angeles, Orange, San Diego, or Santa Barbara counties in California. Schools must be regionally accredited. Write to the address listed for information.

ARRL Foundation (American Radio Relay League)
Scholarship Program
225 Main St.
Newington, CT 06111

386
Charles N. Flint Scholarships and the Ebell Scholarship Fund

AMOUNT: Maximum: $2000 DEADLINE: May 1
FIELDS/MAJORS: All Areas of Study

Available to U.S. citizens only. For sophomores, juniors, or seniors who are unmarried and residents of Los Angeles County and attending a college or university in Los Angeles County. Applications are accepted after the deadline date for consideration if vacancies occur. Must have a minimum GPA of 3.25. Further information is available in many college financial aid offices in Los Angeles County, or write to the address below for details.

Ebell of Los Angeles
Attn: Scholarship Chairman
743 S. Lucerne Blvd.
Los Angeles, CA 90005

387
Charles P. Bell Conservation Scholarship

AMOUNT: Maximum: $250 DEADLINE: January 9
FIELDS/MAJORS: Conservation and Related Fields

Scholarships available for sophomores, juniors, or seniors who are Missouri residents (preference will be given to students enrolled in Missouri schools) who are pursuing a degree in a field related to conservation. Write to the address listed or call (573) 840-9673 for details.

Conservation Foundation of Missouri Charitable Trust
728 West Main St.
Jefferson City, MO 65101

388
Charles River District Medical Society Scholarships

AMOUNT: None Specified DEADLINE: April 1
FIELDS/MAJORS: Medicine

Open to first-year medical students enrolled at an approved medical school and a resident of the following towns in the Charles River District: Needham, Newton, Waltham, Wellesley, or Weston. Applications must be received before April 1 of the freshman year, as the scholarship is awarded for the sophomore year. May be renewable for junior year at the discretion of the Committee on Medical Education. Write to the Society at the address below for details.

Charles River District Medical Society
Attn: Scholarship Program
1440 Main St.
Waltham, MA 02154

389
Charlie Carpenter Vocational Scholarship

AMOUNT: $1000 DEADLINE: March 7
FIELDS/MAJORS: All Areas of Study

Awards for Minnesota high school seniors planning to attend a vocational school. Based on academics, financial need, leadership, character, and recommendations. Contact your high school counselor for more information and applications.

Minnesota Federation of Teachers
168 Aurora Ave.
St. Paul, MN 55103

400
Chase Wilson Memorial 4-H Scholarship

AMOUNT: None Specified DEADLINE: May 31
FIELDS/MAJORS: All Areas of Study

Scholarships for members of 4-H based on achievements in 4-H. For residents of Nueces County, Texas. Several awards may be offered. Write to the address below for complete information.

Coastal Bend Community Foundation
Mercantile Tower MT276
615 N. Upper Broadway, #860
Corpus Christi, TX 78477

401
Chateaubriand Fellowship Program

AMOUNT: $10800-$48400 DEADLINE: December 7
FIELDS/MAJORS: Science, Engineering

Open to applicants who are currently working towards their Ph.D. or have completed it in the last three years. Candidates already participating in an exchange program with a French research team or within a university affiliated with the desired host institution in France will receive special consideration. Research would be performed in a French university, school of engineering, or in a public or private laboratory. You may use existing contacts between your laboratory and a French research institution. Must be a U.S. citizen and registered in a U.S. university or in a U.S. National Laboratory. Fellowships are available for a six to twelve month period with a monthly stipend of $1800 for a doctoral fellow and $2200 for a postdoctoral fellow. Contact the address listed for more information.

Embassy of France
Department of Science and Technology
4101 Reservoir Rd. NW
Washington, DC 20007

402
Chemung County Community Foundation Scholarships

AMOUNT: None Specified DEADLINE: March 15
FIELDS/MAJORS: All Areas of Study

Scholarships for residents of Chemung County or employees or children of employees of Artistic Greetings, Inc. Must be attending college with in a fifty-five mile radius of Elmira. Write to the address below for details.

Community Foundation Chemung County Foundation
168 N. Main St.
PO Box 714
Elmira, NY 14902

403
Chester A. Bowser Memorial Scholarship

AMOUNT: Maximum: $2000 DEADLINE: February 15
FIELDS/MAJORS: Library Science, Museum Studies, History

Open to graduate students who have a connection to any of the following counties in Illinois: Cook, Kane, Lake, DuPage, McHenry, and Will. A brief resume of interests and goals will be required. Organizations, such as museums, that offer intern programs are also eligible to apply. Contact the address listed for further information or call (847) 888-1661.

Elgin Genealogical Society
Scholarship Chairman
PO Box 1418
Elgin, IL 60121-1418

404
Chester Dale Fellowship

AMOUNT: Maximum: $16000 DEADLINE: November 15
FIELDS/MAJORS: Western Art, Visual Art, and Other Related Areas

One year fellowship for doctoral student doing dissertation research in the fields of study above. The Dale Fellows may use the grant to study in the U.S. or abroad. Applicants must know two foreign languages related to topic of their dissertation and be U.S. citizens or legal residents. Contact the chairperson of the graduate department of art history at your school (or other appropriate department) or write to the address below for more information.

National Gallery of Art
Center for Study in the Visual Arts
Predoctoral Fellowship Program
Washington, DC 20565

405
Chester Dale Fellowships

AMOUNT: None Specified DEADLINE: November 7
FIELDS/MAJORS: Fine Arts, Art History, Art Conservation

Research grants for three months to one year are available for those whose fields of study are related to the fine arts of the western world and preferably are American citizens under the age of forty. Write to the address listed for further information.

Metropolitan Museum of Art
Fellowship Programs, Pia Quintano
1000 Fifth Ave.
New York, NY 10028

406
Chicago FM Club Scholarship

AMOUNT: $500 DEADLINE: February 1
FIELDS/MAJORS: All Areas of Study

Scholarships are available to students with at least a technician class amateur radio license who have been accepted at a two- or four-year college. Must be a residents of Indiana, Illinois, or Wisconsin. Must be U.S. citizens (or within three months of citizenship). Multiple awards are offered annually. Write to the address listed for information.

ARRL Foundation (American Radio Relay League)
Scholarship Program
225 Main St.
Newington, CT 06111

407
Chicanos for Creative Medicine Scholarships

AMOUNT: $200-$1500 DEADLINE: April 1
FIELDS/MAJORS: Medicine

Awards for students of Chicano/Latino/Hispanic ancestry who are high school students at a school in East Los Angeles or for students at East Los Angeles College who have completed at least 24 units. Based on academics, financial need, recommendations, and personal statements. Fifteen awards are offered annually. Write to the address below for more information.

Chicanos for Creative Medicine
1301 Avenida Cesar Chavez
Monterey Park, CA   91754

408
Child Care Grants

AMOUNT: None Specified DEADLINE: None Specified
FIELDS/MAJORS: All Areas of Study

Funds are available to assist undergraduate and graduate student-parents. Applicants must be enrolled at least part-time in a New Mexico institution of higher learning. Priority is given to residents of New Mexico, but it is not required. Contact the financial aid office at any New Mexico public postsecondary institution.

New Mexico Commission on Higher Education
Financial Aid and Student Services
PO Box 15910
Santa Fe, NM   87506

409
Children of Deceased Servicemembers Program

AMOUNT: Maximum: $2000 DEADLINE: None Specified
FIELDS/MAJORS: All Areas of Study

Open to undergraduate children of servicemembers who died while on active duty or in retired status. Must be enrolled full-time with a minimum GPA of 2.0. Amounts of grants are determined on a case-by-case basis. Includes the USS Stark Memorial Scholarship Fund, which is limited to children and widows of deceased crew members of the USS Stark who perished as a result of the Persian Gulf missile attack on 17 May 1987. Applications available only from NMCS Headquarters. Write for complete details to the address listed.

Navy-Marine Corps Relief Society
Education Programs
801 N. Randolph St., Suite 1228
Arlington, VA   22203

410
China Area Studies Fellowships

AMOUNT: Maximum: $25000 DEADLINE: October 15
FIELDS/MAJORS: Social Sciences, Humanities

Fellowship for Ph.D. candidates for eleven months of advanced study or dissertation research at a Chinese university or research institute. Requires Chinese language proficiency acquired through at least three years of college-level study or its equivalent. Applicants must be U.S. citizens or permanent residents. Write to the address for further information.

American Council of Learned Societies
Office of Fellowships and Grants
228 E. 45th St.
New York, NY   10017

411
Chinese-American Medical Society Scholarships

AMOUNT: $1500 DEADLINE: March 31
FIELDS/MAJORS: Medicine, Dentistry

Awards for medical and dental students of Chinese heritage for completion of their studies in the U.S. Must be able to demonstrate financial need. One award offered annually. Contact the address below for further information.

Chinese American Medical Society
Dr. H.H. Wang, Executive Director
281 Edgewood Ave.
Teaneck, NJ   07666

412
Chinese Professional Club Scholarship

AMOUNT: $500-$1500 DEADLINE: November 29
FIELDS/MAJORS: All Areas of Study

Scholarships are available to graduating high school seniors who are residents of Houston and of Chinese descent. Applicant must be planning to enroll on a full-time basis in any accredited college or university in the U.S. A minimum of ten awards offered annually. Write to the address listed for information. Applications will not be available until June.

Chinese Professional Club
CPC Scholarship Committee
Susannah Wong, Chair
2915 Carnegie
Houston, TX   77005

413
Chiron Therapeutics/H.M. Roussel, Inc./Ortho Biotech Research Fellows

AMOUNT: Maximum: $10000 DEADLINE: June 1
FIELDS/MAJORS: Oncology Research

Awards for postdoctoral, short-term research training that is relevant to oncology nursing. Applicants must be registered nurses who have completed advanced research preparation and have a doctorate in nursing or a related discipline. Contact the address listed for information about all three awards.

Oncology Nursing Foundation
501 Holiday Dr.
Pittsburgh, PA   15220

414
Chiropractic Education Assistance Awards

AMOUNT: Maximum: $3000 DEADLINE: July 1
FIELDS/MAJORS: Chiropractic Medicine

Open to professional students who are/have been Oklahoma residents for a minimum of five years. Must be enrolled at an accredited college of chiropractic medicine and making satisfactory academic progress. Must be recommended by the Oklahoma Board of Chiropractic Examiners and approved by the Oklahoma State Regents for Higher Education. Write to the address listed for more information.

Oklahoma State Regents for Higher Education
Chiropractic Education Assistance Program
500 Education Bldg. State Capitol Complex
Oklahoma City, OK   73105

415
Christa McAuliffe Award for Excellence

AMOUNT: None Specified DEADLINE: January 1
FIELDS/MAJORS: Education

Scholarship program for current teachers, principals, or administrators who wish to continue their education in a Washington state college or university. It is in recognition of their leadership, contributions, and commitment to education. Selections are made in March. Write to the address below for information.

Washington Higher Education Coordinating Board
917 Lakeridge Way
PO Box 43430
Olympia, WA   98504

416
Christa McAuliffe Teacher Scholarship Loan

AMOUNT: $1000 DEADLINE: March 31
FIELDS/MAJORS: Education

Scholarship for students who meet academic requirements and enroll in a program at a Delaware college leading to a teacher qualification. Renewable. Write to the address listed for more information.

Delaware Higher Education Commission
Carvel State Office Building
820 North French St., #4F
Wilmington, DE   19801

417
Christian Record Services Scholarships

AMOUNT: Maximum: $500 DEADLINE: April 1
FIELDS/MAJORS: All Areas of Study

Ten scholarships for legally blind or deaf undergraduate students. Awards are to assist students in becoming more independent and self-supportive. Write to the address listed for more details.

Christian Record Services
4444 S. 52nd St.
Box 6097
Lincoln, NE   68506

418
Christine Sullivan Memorial Scholarship

AMOUNT: Maximum: $500 DEADLINE: May 31
FIELDS/MAJORS: All Areas of Study

Scholarships for Tuloso-Midway graduating seniors. Write to the address below for complete information.

Coastal Bend Community Foundation
Mercantile Tower MT 276
615 N. Upper Broadway, #860
Corpus Christi, TX   78477

419
Chrysalis Scholarship

AMOUNT: $750 DEADLINE: March 1
FIELDS/MAJORS: Geoscience Fields

Scholarships available to women who are candidates for an advanced degree in a geoscience field. Applicants must have had their education interrupted for at least one year.

Applicant must be completing her thesis during the current academic year. Awards will be made by March 31. Write to the address below for further details.

Association for Women Geoscientists Foundation
G & H Production Company
518 17th St., #930
Denver, CO 80202

420
Chrysler Junior Golf Scholarship Program

AMOUNT: $1000 DEADLINE: October 1
FIELDS/MAJORS: All Areas of Study

Awards for junior high or high school students with academic ability and extracurricular activities (including golf). Based on academics, recommendations, and a personal statement. Forty awards per year. Write to the address below for more information.

Chrysler Junior Golf Program Headquarters
Golf Scholarship
75 Rockefeller Plaza, 6th Floor
New York, NY 10019

421
Cicuso Club Scholarship

AMOUNT: Maximum: $500 DEADLINE: April 1
FIELDS/MAJORS: All Areas of Study

Open to high school seniors who are residents of Hartford, Bloomfield, or Windsor, Connecticut. Applicants must be planning to attend four-year schools. Selections based on financial need, academics, and community service. Contact the address listed for further information. Must have a GPA of at least 2.8.

Cicuso Club
Mrs. Estelle M. Cole
19 Durham St.
Hartford, CT 06112

422
Citizens Flag Alliance Scholarship Essay Contest

AMOUNT: $1000-$15000 DEADLINE: March 1
FIELDS/MAJORS: Government, Political Science

Essay contest open to high school students who are U.S. citizens or permanent residents. Contest is to promote student interest in the study of government, the U.S. Constitution, and their rights within it. Essays must be in support of a Constitutional amendment to protect the American Flag from physical desecration. Based on clarity and strength of argumentation, quality, and originality of essay/research. Contact your high school guidance office for further information and an application. Additional contest information, including the mailing address of each states' essay coordinator, is available at the CFA Web site at: http://www.cfa-inc.org.

Citizens Flag Alliance Scholarship Essay Contest

423
Claddagh Club of Enfield Scholarship

AMOUNT: Maximum: $500 DEADLINE: April 30
FIELDS/MAJORS: All Areas of Study

Open to high school seniors and undergraduates who are of Irish heritage and residents of any of the following towns in Connecticut: Enfield, East Windsor, Ellington, Suffield, and Windsor Locks. May be used for two- and four-year institutions. Must be able to demonstrate financial need. Contact the address listed for further information.

Claddagh Club of Enfield, Inc.
John Reardon
45 Skyridge Dr.
Somers, CT 06071

424
Clara Carter Higgins Conservation Scholarship

AMOUNT: Maximum: $1500 DEADLINE: February 15
FIELDS/MAJORS: Environmental Studies/Ecology

Award is open to students who wish to attend a summer course in environmental studies. Two awards are offered annually. Send a SASE to the address below for details.

Garden Club of America
Clara Carter Higgins Scholarship
598 Madison Ave.
New York, NY 10022

425
Clara Stewart Watson Foundation Scholarship

AMOUNT: Maximum: $1000 DEADLINE: March 31
FIELDS/MAJORS: All Areas of Study

Open to graduating high school seniors in Tarrant and Dallas counties. Applicants must be of good moral character, be ranked in the top 5% of class, and be able to demonstrate financial need. Contact the address listed for further information and applications in January. Must have a GPA of at least 3.5.

Nations Bank of Texas, N.A.
Trust Department
100 N. Main
Corsicana, TX 75110

426

Clarence Tabor Memorial Scholarship Award

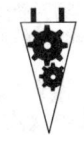

AMOUNT: Maximum: $1500 DEADLINE: June 5
FIELDS/MAJORS: Architecture

Scholarship awarded to a student entering the last year of undergraduate studies in architecture. The student must reside in the Architects League membership area (Bergen, Hudson, Passaic, Sussex, Essex, and Morris counties). Write to the address listed or call (201) 767-9575 for more information.

Architects League of Northern New Jersey
Robert M. Zaccone, AIA
212 White Ave.
Old Tappan, NJ 07675

427

Clark County Association for Home and Community Scholarship

AMOUNT: $250 DEADLINE: May 23
FIELDS/MAJORS: All Areas of Study

Two scholarships for residents of Clark County, Wisconsin, who are in the process of completing one year of higher education beyond high school and will have 24 credits by June. Previous recipients may not reapply. Contact the office at the address below for details.

Clark County Association for Home and Community
PO Box 68
517 Court St., Room 104
Neillsville, WI 54456

428

Clark County Cattlemen's Association Scholarship

AMOUNT: $1000 DEADLINE: July 15
FIELDS/MAJORS: All Areas of Study

Scholarships are available for children of members of the Clark County Cattlemen's Association enrolled in any course of study in any accredited postsecondary institution. Contact address below for complete information.

Purdue University Cooperative Extension Service
9608 Highway 62, Suite 1
Charleston, IN 47111

429

Clark Foundation Scholarships

AMOUNT: None Specified DEADLINE: None Specified
FIELDS/MAJORS: All Areas of Study

Scholarships for graduates of the following school districts in Otsego and Herkimer counties in New York: Cooperstown, Milford, Cherry Valley, Springfield, Boces, Van Hornesville, West Winfield, Schenevus, Richfield Springs, Worcester, Edmeston, or Laurens. Write to the address below for details.

Clark Foundation
Scholarship Office
PO Box 427
Cooperstown, NY 13326

430

Classical Fellowship

AMOUNT: None Specified DEADLINE: November 7
FIELDS/MAJORS: Greek and Roman Art

Applicants must be admitted to a doctoral program in the United States have submitted an outline of a thesis on Greek or Roman art. Thesis outline must have already been accepted by the applicant's advisor at the time of application for this fellowship. Preference will be given to the applicant who, in the opinion of the Grants Committee, will profit most from utilizing the resources of the Department of Greek and Roman Art: its collections, library, photographic, and other archives and the guidance of its curatorial staff. Announcements of awards will be made by February 27. Write to the address listed for details.

Metropolitan Museum of Art
Fellowship Programs, Pia Quintano
1000 Fifth Ave.
New York, NY 10028

431

Clem Jaunich Education Trust

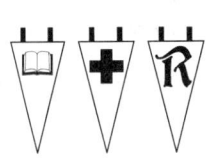

AMOUNT: $1000-$5000 DEADLINE: June 1
FIELDS/MAJORS: Theology, Medicine

Applicants must have attended public or parochial school in the Delano, Minnesota, school district or within seven miles of the city of Delano, Minnesota, and be an undergraduate or graduate student pursuing the study of medicine or theology. Six to eight awards are given annually. Write to address below for details.

Clem Jaunich Education Trust
Parkdale 4, Suite 110
5353 Gamble Dr.
Minneapolis, MN 55416

432
Cletus Ludden and Denver Area Labor Federation Scholarships

AMOUNT: $500-$1500   DEADLINE: May 1
FIELDS/MAJORS: All Areas of Study

Scholarships for students who are members or children of members of a local union in the jurisdiction of the Denver area labor federation (AFL-CIO). Students whose guardians are members are also eligible. Jurisdiction: Adams, Arapahoe, Denver, Douglas, and Jefferson counties. Write to the address below or have your parent contact his/her union.

Denver Area Labor Federation AFL-CIO
Denver Labor Center
360 Acoma St., Room 202
Denver, CO   80223

433
Cleveland Legacy I Scholarship

AMOUNT: Maximum: $500   DEADLINE: April 15
FIELDS/MAJORS: Travel and Tourism, Hotel/Motel Management

Awards for Ohio juniors or seniors in one of the areas listed above who are enrolled in any four-year college full-time. Must have a minimum GPA of 3.0. Write to the address listed or call 1-800-682-8886 ext. 4251 for more information.

National Tourism Foundation
546 East Main St.
PO Box 3071
Lexington, KY   40596

434
Cleveland Legacy II Scholarship

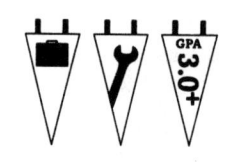

AMOUNT: Maximum: $500   DEADLINE: April 15
FIELDS/MAJORS: Travel and Tourism, Hotel/Motel Management

Awards for Ohio juniors or seniors in one of the areas listed above who are enrolled in any two-year college full-time. Must have a minimum GPA of 3.0. Write to the address listed or call 1-800-682-8886 ext. 4251 for more information.

National Tourism Foundation
546 East Main St.
PO Box 3071
Lexington, KY   40596

435
Cliff Cairns Scholarship

AMOUNT: Maximum: $1000
DEADLINE: April 1
FIELDS/MAJORS: Agriculture, Home Economics

Applicants must be residents of Freeborn County, Minnesota, who are high school seniors. To be used for freshman year. Write to the Cliff Cairns Scholarship Fund at the address listed for details. Must have a GPA of at least 2.8.

Wilson Foods
Scholarship Coordinator
417 Meredith Rd.
Albert Lea, MN   56007

436
Clinical Fellowships

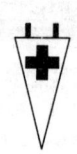

AMOUNT: Maximum: $36000   DEADLINE: October 1
FIELDS/MAJORS: Medical Research-Cystic Fibrosis

Fellowships for early career M.D.'s and Ph.D.'s interested in preparing for a career in academic medicine. Applicants must be eligible for board certification in pediatrics or internal medicine by the time the fellowship begins. Awards are $36000 (first year) and $37500 (second year). Training must encompass diagnostic and therapeutic procedures, comprehensive care, and CF-related research. Applicants must be U.S. citizens or permanent residents. Write to the address below for more information.

Cystic Fibrosis Foundation
Office of Grants Management
6931 Arlington Rd.
Bethesda, MD   20814

437
Clinical Fellowships and Internships

AMOUNT: Maximum: $6000   DEADLINE: March 30
FIELDS/MAJORS: Psychology

Fellowships and internships in cognitive behavior therapy for graduates only. Applicants must have a Ph.D. in psychology or an M.D., R.N., or M.S.W. and be eligible for state certification. Nine awards are given annually. The fellowship program is an eleven-month, two-year program, and the internship is an eleven-month, one-year program. Write to address below for details.

Institute for Rational-Emotive Therapy
Director of Training
45 E. 65th St.
New York, NY   10021

438
Clinical Pharmacology and Postdoctoral Research Fellowships

AMOUNT: $25000 DEADLINE: October 1
FIELDS/MAJORS: Pharmacology, Clinical Pharmacology

Fellowships for Ph.D. candidates and recent recipients of doctorates in pharmacology or a related area to gain and expand research skills through formal training. Tenure is for two years. One career award and three postdoctoral awards. Must be U.S. citizen or permanent resident. Write to the address below for details.

Pharmaceutical Manufacturers Association Foundation, Inc.
1100 15th St. NW
Washington, DC 20005

439
Clinical Training Fellowship

AMOUNT: Maximum: $8340 DEADLINE: January 15
FIELDS/MAJORS: Psychology, Clinical Psychology

Fellowships for minority doctoral students of psychology who are specializing in clinical training. Must be a U.S. citizen or permanent resident enrolled in a full-time academic program. Fellowships are usually awarded for ten months with a monthly stipend of $834. Write to the address below for more information.

American Psychological Association
750 First St. NE
Washington, DC 20002

440
Clinton Helton Scholarship

AMOUNT: Maximum: $1200 DEADLINE: March 1
FIELDS/MAJORS: Manufacturing Engineering, Manufacturing Engineering Technology

Open to full-time undergraduates enrolled in a degree program at one of the following two institutions: Colorado State University or University of Colorado-Boulder. Must have completed at least 30 credit hours and have a minimum GPA of 3.3. Recipients announced in June. Three awards are offered annually. Write to the address listed for more information.

Society of Manufacturing Engineers Education Foundation
One SME Dr.
PO Box 930
Dearborn, MI 48121-0930

441
Cloisters Summer Internship

AMOUNT: Maximum: $2250 DEADLINE: February 6
FIELDS/MAJORS: Art History, Art Conservation, Related Fields

Nine-week internships for freshmen or sophomores who are interested in art and museum careers and enjoy working with children. Program begins in mid-June and runs through mid-August. Participants must join the Education Department of the Cloisters, a branch museum dedicated to the art of medieval Europe. Intensive training provided. Ethnically diverse students are encouraged to apply. Write to the address listed for additional information.

Metropolitan Museum of Art
The Cloisters College Internship Program
Fort Tyron Park
New York, NY 10040

442
Club Foundation Scholarships

AMOUNT: Maximum: $2500 DEADLINE: June 15
FIELDS/MAJORS: Club Management, Hotel/Restaurant Management

For undergraduate students who have completed their freshman year in a four-year college or university. Criteria: at least a 2.5 GPA, financial need, and interest in the club management profession. Write for complete details.

Club Foundation
Scholarship Coordinator
1733 King St.
Alexandria, VA 22314

443
Clyde Russell Scholarship Fund

AMOUNT: Maximum: $10000 DEADLINE: February 1
FIELDS/MAJORS: All Areas of Study

Three different gifts are awarded to high school seniors, full or part-time college students, and citizens of Maine pursuing further educational/cultural opportunities. All awardees must be citizens of Maine. Applicants need to specify which scholarship they are applying for. Write to the address listed for more information.

Maine Education Association
PO Box 2457
Augusta, ME 04338

444
CMP Scholarship Fund

AMOUNT: None Specified   DEADLINE: May 1
FIELDS/MAJORS: All Areas of Study

Awards for graduating seniors from the Central Maine Power Company service area who plan to enroll in any accredited two- or four-year college or university. Applicants must be dependents of CMP employees. Based on personal aspirations, academic achievement, financial need, and the student's contribution to school or community activities. Contact the address listed or the CMP Regional Office at 83 Edison Dr., Augusta, ME., 04336 for more information.

Maine Community Foundation
245 East Maine St.
PO Box 148
Ellsworth, ME   04605

445
Coast Guard Mutual Assistance Education Grants

AMOUNT: Maximum: $1000   DEADLINE: March 7
FIELDS/MAJORS: All Areas of Study

Grants for dependents of Coast Guard members in one of the following categories: active duty, retired, or deceased while on active duty or retired. For undergraduate study in a school accredited by the Department of Education. Must have GPAs of at least 2.0. 150 grants are awarded annually. Write to the address listed or call (202) 267-1682 or 1-800-881-2462 for more details.

U.S. Coast Guard
Commandant (G-ZMA)
2100 2nd St. SW
Washington, DC   20593

446
Coates, Wolff, Russell Memorial Mining Industry Scholarships

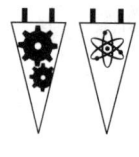

AMOUNT: Maximum: $1000   DEADLINE: December 1
FIELDS/MAJORS: Engineering, Environmental Sciences, Mineral Extractive Disciplines

Awards are available for Wyoming residents of sophomore, junior, or senior standing. Recipients are eligible for award consideration through their senior year. Must have a minimum GPA of 2.25. Write to the address listed for more information.

Society for Mining, Metallurgy, and Exploration,
   Wyoming Section
Scholarship Committee, Mr. Rob Thurman
800 Werner Ct., #352
Casper, WY   82601

447
Coca-Cola Scholars Program

AMOUNT: None Specified   DEADLINE: October 31
FIELDS/MAJORS: All Areas of Study

Scholarships for outstanding high school seniors who have a minimum GPA of 3.0 by end of junior year and live within one of the territories of a participating Coca-Cola bottler (90% participate). Applicants must anticipate graduation from secondary school during the academic year in which the application is made and must be planning to pursue a degree at an accredited U.S. postsecondary institution. Must be U.S. citizens or permanent residents. Applications are only available from your high school guidance counselors.

Coca-Cola Scholars Foundation, Inc.
PO Box 442
Atlanta, GA   30301

448
Cogan Trust Fund Scholarships

AMOUNT: None Specified   DEADLINE: May 5
FIELDS/MAJORS: All Areas of Study

Scholarships for graduating high school seniors from Portsmouth High School or St. Thomas Aquinas High School in Portsmouth, New Hampshire Must have been a resident for at least four years. Based on financial need, leadership, ability, and character. Approximately fifteen to seventeen awards offered annually. Contact the address below for further information.

George T. Cogan Scholarship Trust Fund
C/O Wyman P. Boynton
82 Court St., Box 418
Portsmouth, NH   03801

449
Cole/Stewart Scholarship

AMOUNT: Maximum: $3500   DEADLINE: February 20
FIELDS/MAJORS: All Areas of Study

Awards open to gay/lesbian students who are Washington residents, under the age of twenty-five, and were raised by one or more gay/lesbian parents. May be used at any accredited college or vocational school. Contact the address listed for further information.

Greater Seattle Business Association and Pride Foundation
2033 6th Ave., #804
Seattle, WA   98121

450
Coles-Moultrie Electric Cooperative Scholarships

AMOUNT: $500 DEADLINE: May 28
FIELDS/MAJORS: All Areas of Study

Scholarships for members or dependent children of members of the co-op. Four scholarships are awarded. Applicants who are children of members must be under twenty-one years of age. For use at any accredited school in Illinois. Write to the attention of Sandra Fisher at the address below for details. Applications are also sent to area colleges.

Coles-Moultrie Electric Cooperative
PO Box 709
Mattoon, IL 61938

451
Colgate/Juliette A. Southard Scholarship Trust Fund

AMOUNT: $1000 DEADLINE: January 31
FIELDS/MAJORS: Dental Assisting

Scholarships available to students who have been accepted into an accredited dental assisting program at any level of study and are ADAA members or student members. Must be a U.S. citizen and have a high school diploma or GED to apply. Write to the address below for more information.

American Dental Assistants Association
203 N. LaSalle St., #1320
Chicago, IL 60601

452
College Bound Scholarships

AMOUNT: $500-$50000 DEADLINE: March 1
FIELDS/MAJORS: All Areas of Study

Open to high school seniors who are Chicagoland residents and are attending Chicagoland high schools. These awards are for economically disadvantaged students who have strong academic ambition, character, and motivation and wish to attend college. To qualify, please see the following schedule: If your household population is one, income may not exceed $15,780, if two persons-$21,220, if three persons-$26,660, if four persons-$32,100, if five persons-$37,540, if six persons-$42,980, if seven persons-$48,420, if eight persons-$53,860. For each additional person, add $5,440. There were ten awards offered last year. Contact the address listed for further information.

College Bound, Inc.
Selection Committee
450 Skokie Blvd., #1000
Northbrook, IL 60062

453
College Club of Hartford Scholarship

AMOUNT: $500-$1000 DEADLINE: March 1
FIELDS/MAJORS: All Areas of Study

Open to public high school seniors who are planning to attend a four-year school and are residents of any of the following towns in Connecticut: Avon, Bloomfield, Canton, E. Hartford, Farmington, Glastonbury, Hartford, Newington, Rocky Hill, Simsbury, W. Hartford, Wethersfield, or Windsor. Must be in the upper 10% of class. Selections based on academics, financial need, and community service. Applications available in high school guidance offices. Send completed forms to the address listed. Must have a GPA of at least 3.3.

College Club of Hartford
Ruth E. Falkin, Chairman
354 Fern St.
West Hartford, CT 06119

454
College Club West Scholarship

AMOUNT: Maximum: $1000 DEADLINE: February 15
FIELDS/MAJORS: All Areas of Study

Open to qualified women who are residents of the west side of Greater Cleveland, from West 25th St. out to Avon and Avon Lake. Must be twenty-five or older and currently enrolled in school either obtaining or have completed a baccalaureate or graduate degree. Contact the address listed for further information.

College Club West
Virginia Kazimer
14 Nantucket Row
Rocky River, OH 44116

455
College Internships

AMOUNT: None Specified DEADLINE: None Specified
FIELDS/MAJORS: Military History

Open to undergraduate students at college or university that will grant academic credit for work experience as interns in Military History. Internships are served at address listed. If interested, please write to "Internships" at the address listed or call (202) 433-3839/40/41 for complete information.

U.S. Marine Corps Historical Center
Building 58
Washington Navy Yard
Washington, DC 20374

456
College Scholarship Assistance Program

AMOUNT: None Specified DEADLINE: None Specified
FIELDS/MAJORS: All Areas of Study

Available for Virginia residents who are undergraduates in any college or university in Virginia. Must demonstrate financial need, be enrolled at least half-time, demonstrate academic excellence, and be a U.S. citizen. Graduate students must meet the requirements established by the granting institution. Awards may not exceed normal charges for tuition and fees. Applications available at the financial aid offices of Virginia public institutions where students are planning to attend. Must have a GPA of at least 3.5.

Virginia Council of Higher Education
James Monroe Building
101 N. 14th St.
Richmond, VA 23219

457
Colonel Hayden W. Wagner Memorial Scholarship

AMOUNT: Maximum: $1000 DEADLINE: March 31
FIELDS/MAJORS: All Areas of Study

Scholarships for daughters or granddaughters of Commissioned Officers or Warrant Officers in the U.S. Army who are on active duty, died while on active duty, or retired after at least twenty years of service. For undergraduate study. Renewable. Write to the address listed for details. Specify the officers name, rank, social security number, and dates of active duty when requesting an application. Be sure to include a SASE.

Society of Daughters of the U.S. Army
Janet B. Otto, Scholarship Chairman
7717 Rockledge Court
West Springfield, VA 22152

458
Colorado Society of Certified Public Accountants Scholarships

AMOUNT: Maximum: $750 DEADLINE: November 30
FIELDS/MAJORS: Accounting

Open to declared accounting majors who are Colorado residents attending a Colorado school. Must have completed at least 8 semester hours of accounting courses with a minimum GPA of 3.0. Deadlines are November 30 for winter quarter or spring semester and June 30 for fall. May reapply each time the award is offered. Write to the address listed for details.

Colorado Society of Certified Public Accountants
Scholarship Coordinator
7979 E. Tufts Ave., #500
Denver, CO 80237

459
Colorado Society of Certified Public Accountants Senior Scholarships

AMOUNT: Maximum: $750 DEADLINE: March 1
FIELDS/MAJORS: Accounting

Open to high school seniors with a minimum GPA of 3.75 who are Colorado residents. Must be planning to major in accounting in any accredited Colorado community college, college, or university. These scholarships are awarded for freshman year. Contact your high school counselor or write to the address listed for details.

Colorado Society of Certified Public Accountants
Scholarship Coordinator
7979 E. Tufts Ave., #500
Denver, CO 80237

460
Combined Health Appeal of Greater St. Louis Scholarships

AMOUNT: Maximum: $500 DEADLINE: April 10
FIELDS/MAJORS: Medicine, Healthcare

Scholarships for upperclassmen and graduate students in the St. Louis area studying toward a career in healthcare. Geographic area: St. Louis, Jefferson, Warren, Lincoln, Franklin, and St. Charles counties in Missouri and St.Clair, Monroe, Madison, Clinton, and Randolph counties in Illinois. The foundation does not mail out applications. Information is available at your school or call (314) 729-0606.

Combined Health Appeal of Greater St. Louis
Mr. Philip D. Carlock, Executive Dir.
50 Crestwood Executive Center, #201
St. Louis, MO 63126-1945

461
Commercial Financial Services Scholarship

AMOUNT: Maximum: $5000 DEADLINE: April 1
FIELDS/MAJORS: All Areas of Study

Open to Oklahoma residents who are full-time students pursuing a baccalaureate degree at one of the following schools: University of Oklahoma, Oklahoma State, University of Tulsa, Oral Roberts University, Oklahoma City University, University of Central Oklahoma,

Northeastern State University, or Langston University. Must demonstrate financial need. The scholarships have two components: 1) monetary awards and 2) employment opportunities in summer and after graduation. Write to the address listed for information.

Oklahoma State Regents for Higher Education
Commercial Financial Svcs. Scholarships
500 Education Bldg. State Capitol Complex
Oklahoma City, OK 73105

462
Commitment to Healthcare Award

AMOUNT: Maximum: $1000 DEADLINE: April 1
FIELDS/MAJORS: Health

Award will offer financial assistance to non-traditional students who are working toward advanced degrees, entering an entirely new health field, or pursuing a new career after being out of school or in the work force for some time. Applicants must reside in one of the following counties: Berlin, Green Lake, Markesan, Princeton, Ripon, Wautoma, or Wild Rose in Wisconsin. One to three awards are offered annually. Write to the address listed for further details.

Community Health Network
Community Resources Department
225 Memorial Dr.
Berlin, WI 54923

463
Commonwealth Council of the Blind Scholarships

AMOUNT: Maximum: $2000 DEADLINE: March 1
FIELDS/MAJORS: All Areas of Study

Scholarships are available to legally blind undergraduates who are residents of Virginia, attending a college or university in Virginia. Two awards per year. Write to the address listed or call (202) 467-5081 or 1-800-424-8666 for details.

American Council of the Blind
Scholarship Coordinator
1155 15th St. NW, Suite 720
Washington, DC 20005

464
Communication Disorder Scholarship

AMOUNT: $500 DEADLINE: March 1
FIELDS/MAJORS: Communication Disorders

Applicants must be maintaining legal residence in Massachusetts and present a letter of endorsement from a sponsoring Women's Club in your community. For graduate study in communication disorders. Write to the address below for details, and be sure to include a SASE.

General Federation of Women's Clubs of Massachusetts
Scholarship Chairperson, 245 Dutton Road
PO Box 679
Sudbury, MA 01776

465
Communicative Disorders Scholarship

AMOUNT: Maximum: $1000 DEADLINE: April 1
FIELDS/MAJORS: Speech Language Pathology and/or Audiology

Awards for master's students in the fields above who are from the tri-district area (Lancaster, York, Dauphin, Lebanon, or Chester Counties). Applicants must be U.S. citizens or permanent residents and have a GPA of at least 3.2 coming out of college. Must be enrolled in an ASHA accredited program. One award is offered annually. Write to the address below for more information.

Hear/Say Fund, Inc.
321 Bareview Dr.
Leola, PA 17540

466
Community Arts Administration Internship

AMOUNT: $3000 DEADLINE: May 1
FIELDS/MAJORS: Art Administration

Internship program for North Carolina residents who possess at least a four-year college degree in the field of art administration. Interns work under the supervision of the executive director or another designated staff member who designs training programs. Internship is for three months. At the end of the program, the Council will provide assistance to interns seeking full-time employment. Four internships per year. Write to the address listed for further information.

North Carolina Arts Council
Grants Office
Department of Cultural Resources
Raleigh, NC 27601

467
Community Education Basehor-Linwood District Scholarship

AMOUNT: Maximum: $1000 DEADLINE: June 30
FIELDS/MAJORS: Any Area of Study

Send personal letter stating why you need the scholarship, transcripts, letter from college instructor or advisor, and a letter from a community member or former high school teacher. Must be a full-time student, minimum 12 hours, and have a minimum GPA of 2.0. Must be a resident of Basehor-Linwood and/or graduated high school in the Basehor-Linwood District 458. For more information, contact the address below.

Community Education Dist. #458
Beverly Dumler, Director, Comm. Educ.
PO Box 282
Basehor, KS 66007

468
Community Foundation for Erie County Scholarships

AMOUNT: None Specified   DEADLINE: May 22
FIELDS/MAJORS: All Areas of Study

Scholarships are open to undergraduate and graduate residents of Erie County, New York, who demonstrate financial need. Graduate study is only considered in the areas of Fine Arts, Social Work, Medicine, Architecture, Nursing, and Piano. Undergraduate study in all majors is supported. Renewable. Application must be requested by May 9. Send a SASE to the address shown for details or call (716) 852-2857.

Buffalo Foundation
Gail Johnstone
712 Main St.
Buffalo, NY 14202-1720

469
Community Foundation for Palm Beach/Martin Counties Scholarships

AMOUNT: $750-$2500   DEADLINE: March 1
FIELDS/MAJORS: All Areas of Study

Open to graduating seniors in Palm Beach or Martin County who are residents of those counties. Applicants must plan to be full-time students at an accredited two- or four-year college or university or vocational school and be able to demonstrate financial need. The Foundation administers a number of awards with varying other criteria. See your high school guidance counselor for complete information about individual awards. Contact your high school guidance counselor for information. If additional assistance is required, contact the address listed or call (516) 659-6800 (in Palm Beach) or (561) 288-2069 (in Martin County). Must have a GPA of at least 2.5.

Community Foundation for Palm Beach and Martin
  Counties
Scholarship Coordinator
324 Datura St., #340
West Palm Beach, FL 33401

470
Community Fund Scholarships

AMOUNT: Maximum: $750
DEADLINE: March 1
FIELDS/MAJORS: Arts, Education, Humanities, Social Science

Open to Hawaii residents or students who are attending school in another state but have family in Hawaii. Must have a minimum GPA of 3.0, demonstrate accomplishment and potential for filling a community need, motivation, vision, and financial need. Employees, volunteers, or board members of Hawaii Community Foundation are not eligible to apply. Contact the address below for further information.

Hawaii Community Scholarship Fund
College Scholarships
900 Fort St. Mall, #1300
Honolulu, HI 96813

471
Community Service Scholarships

AMOUNT: $100-$1000   DEADLINE: March 1
FIELDS/MAJORS: All Areas of Study

Open to high school seniors with an average of "C" or better during senior year. Must have completed one hundred or more hours of community service work and be members of Desert Schools Federal Credit Union, (for at least six months), or have a relative who has been a member for at least six months. The first 212 entrants who meet the requirements stated above will receive a $100 U.S. Savings Bond, of those, at least ten will receive a $1000 scholarship. Contact the address listed for further information. Must have a GPA of at least 2.0.

Desert Schools Federal Credit Union
Attn: Marketing
PO Box 11350
Phoenix, AZ 85061-1350

472
Community Services Block Grant

AMOUNT: $750   DEADLINE: April 5
FIELDS/MAJORS: All Areas of Study, Preference Is Given to "High-Tech" Fields

Fifteen scholarships of $750 each are available to low income students who plan to pursue a full-time education, preferably (but not limited to) in high-tech or "growth" fields. Applicant must be planning to attend an accredited Illinois school and reside in Bureau, Carroll, LaSalle, Lee, Marshall, Ogle, Putnam, Stark, or Whiteside counties. Write to the address listed for further information and an application.

Tri-County Opportunities Council
Scholarship Committee
PO Box 610
Rock Falls, IL 61071

473
Competitive Scholarship

AMOUNT: Maximum: $100 DEADLINE: None Specified
FIELDS/MAJORS: All Areas of Study

Grants to encourage out-of-state students who have demonstrated high academic achievement in high school to enroll in public institutions of higher learning in New Mexico. Students must meet certain high school GPA and ACT score requirements. Awarded to high school seniors. Contact the financial aid office at any New Mexico public postsecondary institution. Must have a GPA of at least 2.9.

New Mexico Commission on Higher Education
Financial Aid and Student Services
PO Box 15910
Santa Fe, NM 87506

474
Conagra National Merit Scholarship Program

AMOUNT: None Specified DEADLINE: None Specified
FIELDS/MAJORS: All Areas of Study

Applicants must be children of Conagra employees (including employees who used to work for Beatrice). Must be U.S. citizen. For study at any college or university in the U.S. Renewable. Contact your parent's workplace or write to the address below for details.

Conagra, Inc.
Manager, Community Affairs
One Conagra Dr.
Omaha, NE 68102

475
Concordia Mutual Life Scholarship

AMOUNT: $500-$1000 DEADLINE: March 31
FIELDS/MAJORS: All Areas of Study

Applicants must be high school seniors, college undergraduates, and CMI members having a life insurance or annuity policy for a minimum of one year before the scholarship application deadline. Write to the address below or call 1-800-342-5265 ext. 208 for more information.

Concordia Mutual Life
PO Box 9230
Downers Grove, IL 60515

476
Concrete Research and Education Foundation Scholarships

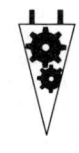

AMOUNT: Maximum: $3000 DEADLINE: January 15
FIELDS/MAJORS: Engineering, Architecture, Material Science

Open to graduate students in the first or second year at an accredited college or university in the U.S. or Canada that offers a graduate program in concrete design, materials, or construction. Must be attending school full-time during the entire fellowship year. The awards include: The Katharine and Bryant Mather, The ACI-W.R.Grace, The V. Mohan Malhotra, The Stewart C. Watson, and The ACI Fellowships. Contact the address listed for further information.

Concrete Research and Education Foundation of ACI International
ACI ConREF
PO Box 9094
Farmington Hills, MI 48333

477
Congressional Science and Engineering Fellowships

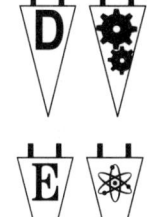

AMOUNT: Maximum: $43000
DEADLINE: January 15
FIELDS/MAJORS: Engineering, Sciences

Applicants must have Ph.D. or equivalent degrees. Persons with master's degrees in engineering and three years professional experience also qualify. Recipients will spend one year working as special legislative assistants on the staffs of members of Congress or Congressional committees. Program begins in September. Must demonstrate exceptional competence in the areas of science or engineering and have some experience in applying personal knowledge toward the solution of societal problems. Minorities and disabled encouraged to apply. Must be U.S. citizens. Federal employees are not eligible. Call (202) 326-6700 or write to the address listed below for more information.

American Association for the Advancement of Science
Fellowship Programs
1200 New York Ave. NW
Washington, DC 20005

478
Connecticut Assn. of Latin Americans in Higher Education Scholarship

AMOUNT: Maximum: $500 DEADLINE: March 10
FIELDS/MAJORS: All Areas of Study

Open to high school seniors and undergraduates who are Connecticut residents, have a Latino background, and have a minimum GPA of 3.0. Based on academic success, community service, and financial need. Contact the address listed for further information.

Connecticut Association of Latin Americans in Higher Education, Inc.
Wilson Luna, Ed D.
Box 2415
Hartford, CT 06146

479
Connecticut Building Congress Scholarships

AMOUNT: $500-$2000 DEADLINE: March 1
FIELDS/MAJORS: Architecture, Engineering, Construction

Awards for high school seniors who can demonstrate financial need, scholastic achievement, and extracurricular/community activities. Must be Connecticut residents. Two to four awards are offered annually. Contact your high school guidance counselor or the address listed for further information and an application. Must have a GPA of at least 3.0.

Connecticut Building Congress
Scholarship Program
2600 Dixwell Ave.
Hamden, CT 06514

480
Connecticut Education Association Minority Scholarship

AMOUNT: Maximum: $500 DEADLINE: May 1
FIELDS/MAJORS: Teaching

Open to high school seniors and college students who are Connecticut residents and entering a teacher preparation program. For use at two- or four-year schools. Applicants must be members of minority groups, have a minimum GPA of 2.75, and be able to demonstrate financial need. Contact the address listed for further information.

Connecticut Education Foundation, Inc.
President
21 Oak St., #500
Hartford, CT 06106-8001

481
Connecticut Law Enforcement Memorial Scholarship

AMOUNT: Maximum: $2000 DEADLINE: May 15
FIELDS/MAJORS: Criminal Justice

Open to high school seniors who are Connecticut residents. For use at two- or four-year schools. Based on academics, community service, and extracurricular activities. Contact the address listed for further information. Must have a GPA of at least 3.0.

Connecticut Law Enforcement Memorial Scholarship Fund
Steven Giordano, Scholarship P.R. Chair
233 Reynolds Bridge Rd.
Thomaston, CT 06787

482
Connecticut League for Nursing Scholarships

AMOUNT: Maximum: $500 DEADLINE: October 1
FIELDS/MAJORS: Nursing

Applicants must be Connecticut residents who are college-level senior nursing students or graduate students attending a Connecticut nursing school only. Must have 20 credits completed in a nursing program. Based on academic achievement and financial need. Write to the address listed for details. Must have a GPA of at least 3.0.

Connecticut League for Nursing
Ms. Diantha R. Morrow, Exec. Dir.
393 Center St., PO Box 365
Wallingford, CT 06492

483
Connecticut Nurserymen's Association, Inc. Scholarships

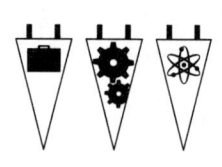

AMOUNT: Maximum: $1000 DEADLINE: April 1
FIELDS/MAJORS: Agriculture, Landscaping, Horticulture, Agricultural Engineering, Agricultural Economics, Floriculture

Awards for high school seniors who can demonstrate financial need, extracurricular activities, scholastic achievement, and community service. Must be a Connecticut resident. One award is for a student going to a four-year school, the second award is for a student going to a two-year school. Contact your high school guidance counselor or Connecticut Nurserymen's Association, Inc., at the address below for further information.

Connecticut Nurserymen's Association, Inc.
PO Box 117
Vernon, CT 06066

484
Connecticut Scholarship Challenge Program

AMOUNT: Maximum: $1000 DEADLINE: April 15
FIELDS/MAJORS: Travel and Tourism, Hotel/Motel Management

Awards for Connecticut residents in one of the areas listed above who are enrolled in any four-year college full-time. Must have a GPA of 3.0 or better and be entering junior or senior year. Write to the address listed or call 1-800-682-8886 ext. 4251 for more information.

National Tourism Foundation
546 East Main St.
PO Box 3071
Lexington, KY 40596

485
Connecticut Sports Writers Alliance Scholarship

AMOUNT: Maximum: $500 DEADLINE: March 15
FIELDS/MAJORS: Sports Journalism

Open to high school seniors who are Connecticut residents. For use at four-year schools. Based on academics, proven ability, and interest in sports journalism as a career. Contact the address listed for further information. Must have a GPA of at least 3.0.

Connecticut Sports Writers Alliance
C/O Waterbury Republican-American
389 Meadow St.
Waterbury, CT 06722

486
Connecticut State DAR Scholarship

AMOUNT: Maximum: $500 DEADLINE: February 15
FIELDS/MAJORS: All Areas of Study

Open to high school seniors who are Connecticut residents and U.S. citizens. Based on academics, citizenship, leadership, and financial need. Contact your high school guidance counselor or send a SASE to the address listed for further information. Must have a GPA of at least 3.0.

CT Daughters of the American Revolution
Chapter Regent
10 Hunter Ln.
Norwalk, CT 06850

487
Connecticut Young Mortgage Bankers Scholarship

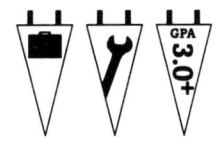

AMOUNT: $500-$1500 DEADLINE: February 24
FIELDS/MAJORS: Banking, Finance, Real Estate, Business

Open to high school seniors who are Connecticut residents. For use at two- or four-year schools. Based on academics, extracurricular activities, and financial need. Contact Ellis Simpson, Consultant, at the address listed for further information. Must have a GPA of at least 3.0.

Connecticut Young Mortgage Bankers Association
Greater Hartford Interracial School Fund, Inc.
PO Box 320644
Hartford, CT 06132

488
Connie and Robert T. Gunter Scholarship

AMOUNT: Maximum: $750 DEADLINE: March 1
FIELDS/MAJORS: Manufacturing Engineering, Manufacturing Technology

Open to full-time undergraduates enrolled in a degree program who have completed at least 30 credit hours. Must have a minimum GPA of 3.5 and be attending any of the three following schools: Georgia Institute of Technology, Georgia Southern College, or Southern College of Technology. One award is offered annually. Write to the address listed for more information.

Society of Manufacturing Engineers Education Foundation
One SME Dr.
PO Box 930
Dearborn, MI 48121-0930

489
Conservation Education Scholarships

AMOUNT: Maximum: $1000 DEADLINE: June 1
FIELDS/MAJORS: Conservation and Related

Scholarships for residents of Crawford County, Pennsylvania, who are studying at the junior or senior level in a conservation-related area. Preference for the $1000 award is given to a student who has successfully attended any of the week-long youth conservation schools. Write to the address below for details.

Crawford County Sportsmen's Council, Inc.
Mr. Neal Williams
19575 Park St.
Meadville, PA 16335

490
Conservation Scholarship

AMOUNT: Maximum: $500 DEADLINE: April 20
FIELDS/MAJORS: Conservation, Agriculture, and Related

Scholarships for graduating high school seniors within the Palomar-Ramona-Julian (San Diego County, California) who will pursue studies in conservation or agriculture. Must have GPAs of at least 2.5. Write to the address listed or call (760) 745-2061 for details.

Resource Conservation District of Greater San Diego County
Rebecca J. Woo, Education Coordinator
332 S. Juniper St., Suite 110
Escondido, CA 92025

491
Consortium for Graduate Study in Management

AMOUNT: None Specified DEADLINE: January 15
FIELDS/MAJORS: Business, Economics

Graduate fellowships for minorities. U.S. citizenship required. Must have received bachelor's degree from accredited institution and must submit GMAT scores. Each fellow undertakes the regular MBA curriculum at one of the eleven consortium graduate schools of business. Must be members of the following minority groups: Native American, African-American, or Hispanic. Write to the address listed or call (314) 935-6364 or fax (314) 935-5014 for details.

Consortium for Graduate Study in Management
200 S. Hanley Rd., Suite 1102
St. Louis, MO 63105

492
Constance L. Lloyd, FACMPE Scholarship

AMOUNT: Maximum: $1500 DEADLINE: June 1
FIELDS/MAJORS: Health Administration, Clinical Healthcare

One award for a female student attending school in the state of Georgia who is pursuing either an administrative or clinically related degree in the healthcare field. Write to the address listed for more information.

American College of Medical Practice Executives
Attn: Ms. Laurie J. Draizen
104 Inverness Terrace East
Englewood, CO 80112

493
Constantinople Armenian Relief Society (CARS) Scholarship

AMOUNT: $400-$600 DEADLINE: July 15
FIELDS/MAJORS: All Areas of Study

Awards for Armenian students enrolled in an accredited college or university at the sophomore level or above. Based mainly on merit and financial need. Write to the address below for more information.

Constantinople Armenian Relief Society
Mr. Berc Araz
66 Stephenville Parkway
Edison, NJ 08820

494
Consulting Engineers Council of Alabama Scholarships

AMOUNT: $1000 DEADLINE: February 28
FIELDS/MAJORS: Engineering

Competition open to engineering students entering their junior, senior, or fifth year (in a five year program) in fall. Applicants must be U.S. citizens. Preference is given to those who demonstrate high scholastic achievement and an understanding of and interest in the consulting engineering profession. Applicant must be enrolled in a program accredited by the accreditation board for engineering and technology. Write to the address below for details.

Consulting Engineers Council of Washington
660 Adams Ave., #333
Montgomery, AL 36104

495
Consulting Engineers Council of Minnesota Scholarships

AMOUNT: Maximum: $1250 DEADLINE: January 23
FIELDS/MAJORS: Consulting Engineering

Open to engineering students in their sophomore and junior years at an accredited engineering school within the state of Minnesota. Based on academics, character, and interest in the field of consulting. Winners will be announced at the Association's annual meeting in June. Contact the address listed for further information or call (612) 593-5533. Must have a GPA of at least 2.8.

Consulting Engineers Council of Minnesota
Mary Detloff, Asst. Executive Director
10201 Wayzata Blvd., #240
Minnetonka, MN 55306

496
Cooperstown Art Association Scholarship

AMOUNT: Maximum: $300 DEADLINE: May 15
FIELDS/MAJORS: Art-Visual, Art-History, Art-Administration

Scholarship for a graduating high school senior who intends to study one of the above areas. Must be a resident of Otsego County, New York. Based on five slides or pieces of art (or three written scholarly works). One award is offered annually. Write to the address below for details.

Cooperstown Art Association
Scholarship Committee
22 Main St.
Cooperstown, NY 13326

497
Copernicus Award

AMOUNT: $500-$1000　DEADLINE: March 2
FIELDS/MAJORS: Science

Scholarships are available for Polish-American students in a science major. Applicants must reside in Wisconsin, be U.S. citizens, and have GPAs of at least 3.0. Write to the address listed or call (414) 744-9029 for information.

Polanki, Polish Women's Cultural Club of Milwaukee
Ms. Valerie Lukaszewicz, Chairperson
4160 S. First St.
Milwaukee, WI　53207

498
Corning Glass Works Scholarship and Jennie M. Kiernan Scholarship

AMOUNT: $500-$1000　DEADLINE: April 15
FIELDS/MAJORS: All Areas of Study

Scholarships are available for residents of Central Falls, Cumberland, Lincoln, or Pawtucket who are graduating high school seniors. Two to three awards offered annually. Contact your principal's office for information.

Rhode Island Foundation
70 Elm St.
Providence, RI　02903

499
Country Doctor Scholarship Program

AMOUNT: None Specified　DEADLINE: May 15
FIELDS/MAJORS: Medicine

Scholarships are available for Georgia resident medical students who plan to practice medicine in a rural area of Georgia upon graduation. Applicants must demonstrate financial need and a strong commitment to practice medicine in a Board-approved Georgia community having a population of fifteen thousand persons or less. All recipients required to sign a contract affirming commitment to practice in an approved community. One year of service credits one year of scholarship. Applications available beginning in January. Write to the address listed for information.

State Medical Education Board of Georgia
County Doctor Scholarship Program
244 Washington St., SW #574J
Atlanta, GA　30334

500
Courage Center Scholarship for People with Disabilities

AMOUNT: Maximum: $1000　DEADLINE: May 31
FIELDS/MAJORS: All Areas of Study

Award open to students with sensory impairments or physical disabilities who want to pursue educational goals or gain technical expertise beyond high school. Based on intentions and achievements. Must be U.S. citizens, residents of Minnesota, already enrolled full-time in accredited institutions, and be able to demonstrate financial need. Scholarships are awarded in July. Contact the address listed for further information.

Courage Center/United Way
Courage Center Scholarship Committee
3915 Golden Valley Rd.
Golden Valley, MN　55422

501
CPCU-Harry Loman Foundation Graduate Grants

AMOUNT: Maximum: $1000　DEADLINE: None Specified
FIELDS/MAJORS: Insurance

Grants are available for graduate students studying full-time or doing research in the property/casualty insurance field. Academics will be considered. This is a matching scholarship that will match, up to $1000, the award granted by local chapters. There are 152 chapters in the U.S. working with local colleges and universities. Write to the address below for information.

CPCU-Harry Loman Foundation
Joyce Natalie, Administrator
720 Providence Road, PO Box 3009
Malvern, PA　19355

502
Cranston Foundation Scholarship Program

AMOUNT: None Specified　DEADLINE: May 1
FIELDS/MAJORS: All Areas of Study

Scholarship is limited to dependent children of Cranston Print Works Company employees only. Write to the address listed for more information.

Cranston Print Works Company
The Trustees
1381 Cranston St.
Cranston, RI　02920

503
Critical Teacher Shortage Student Loan Forgiveness Program

AMOUNT: None Specified DEADLINE: July 15
FIELDS/MAJORS: Education

Open to certified Florida public school teachers. Program provides repayment of educational loans in return for teaching in a critical teacher shortage area. Up to $2500 per year for four years for teachers with undergraduate loans. $5000 per year for up to two years for teachers with graduate loans. Write to the address below for details.

Florida Department of Education
Office of Student Financial Assistance
1344 Florida Education Center
Tallahassee, FL 32399

504
Critical Teacher Shortage Tuition Reimbursement Program

AMOUNT: None Specified DEADLINE: None Specified
FIELDS/MAJORS: Education

Incentive program to encourage Florida public school district employees certified to teach to become certified in or gain a graduate degree in a Critical Teacher Shortage area. Must complete courses with a minimum GPA of 3.0. Get further information from District School Board offices or the office of student financial assistance.

Florida Department of Education
Office of Student Financial Assistance
1344 Florida Education Center
Tallahassee, FL 32399

505
Crop Protection Scholarships-Seniors To Be Returning To Farm

AMOUNT: $1000 DEADLINE: March 15
FIELDS/MAJORS: Agriculture

Ten scholarships for seniors in college who are from farming families (parents or guardians derive majority of income from farming) and plan to return to farming after graduation. Must have a GPA of at least 3.0, be enrolled in an approved agricultural curriculum in a four-year college, and demonstrate leadership potential through extracurricular activities and work. Write to the address below for details.

Successful Farming-Bayer Corporation
1716 Locust St.
Des Moines, IA 50309

506
CSBG Scholarships

AMOUNT: $500 DEADLINE: April 30
FIELDS/MAJORS: All Areas of Study

Scholarships for students of Christian, Clay, Effingham, Fayette, Montgomery, Moultrie, and Shelby counties (Illinois) attending an Illinois institution. Must meet income requirements. Contact your county Outreach Office or write to the address below for details.

CEFS Economic Opportunity Corporation
101 N. Fourth St.
PO Box 928
Effingham, IL 62401

507
CTA Scholarships

AMOUNT: $2000 DEADLINE: February 15
FIELDS/MAJORS: All Areas of Study

Open to active members of CTA or dependent children of members who are active, retired, or deceased. For use at any accredited institution of higher learning for a degree, credential, or vocational program. Thirty-three awards offered annually. Write to the address listed for complete details.

California Teachers Association
C/O CTA Human Rights Department
1705 Murchison Dr., PO Box 921
Burlingame, CA 94011

508
Cushman Scholarship

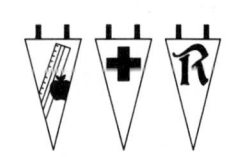

AMOUNT: None Specified DEADLINE: May 1
FIELDS/MAJORS: Medical or Christian Education Fields

Scholarship fund provides scholarship assistance to Hancock County residents pursuing education in the medical or Christian education fields. Write to Patti D'Angelo at the address listed for details.

Maine Community Foundation
245 East Maine St.
PO Box 148
Ellsworth, ME 04605

509
Cutting Edge Scholarship Contest

AMOUNT: $5000 DEADLINE: March 31
FIELDS/MAJORS: All Areas of Study

Open to graduating high school seniors who are legal residents of Michigan, Tennessee, or Washington. Must have a minimum GPA of 2.0 and a proven attendance record. Contest winners selected on completed project's originality and creativity, ability to reach project goals, replication potential in other schools or communities, and impact in the real world. Winners will be notified by May 15. For further information and an official application, contact the address listed or visit the Web site: http://www.mci.com/cuttingedge/TN/rules.shtml.

MCI Cutting Edge Scholars
Scholarship Coordinator
1875 Connecticut Ave. NW, #800
Washington, DC 20009

510
Cuyahoga County Medical Foundation

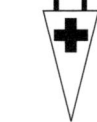

AMOUNT: $500-$1500 DEADLINE: June 1
FIELDS/MAJORS: Medicine, Dentistry, Pharmacy, Nursing, Osteopathy

Student must be a bona fide resident of Cuyahoga County. Students must be attending school for doctor of medicine, osteopathic medicine, dentistry, pharmacy, and nursing. Ten to fifteen awards are offered annually. Write to the address below for more information.

Cuyahoga County Medical Foundation
6000 Rockside Woods Blvd., Suite 150
Cleveland, OH 44131

511
D. Anita Small Science and Business Scholarship

AMOUNT: Maximum: $1500
DEADLINE: March 25
FIELDS/MAJORS: Math, Engineering, Computer Sciences, Physical Sciences, Medical Sciences, Business

Available to women age twenty-one or older who have maintained at least a 3.0 GPA and are pursuing a bachelor's or advanced degree in one of the areas listed above. Recipient must demonstrate financial need and carry a minimum of six credit hours. Send a SASE to the address listed for an application.

Business and Professional Women's Foundation of
    Maryland, Inc.
Scholarship Coordinator
282 New Mark Esplanade
Rockville, MD 20850

512
Daad Fulbright Grants

AMOUNT: None Specified DEADLINE: October 31
FIELDS/MAJORS: Arts, Humanities, Social Sciences

Open to full-time graduates for study or research in Germany for one academic year. Applicants must be U.S. citizens, no older than thirty-two years of age, and have a good command of German. Contact your campus Fulbright program advisor or write to the address listed for further information.

Daad German Academic Exchange Service
Institute of International Education
809 United Nations Plaza
New York, NY 10017

513
Dacor Bacon House Heyward G. Hill Scholarship Program

AMOUNT: Maximum: $2500 DEADLINE: February 15
FIELDS/MAJORS: Foreign Affairs

Scholarships for undergraduate junior and seniors who are dependents of American Foreign Service personnel (active, retired w/ pension, or deceased) who have served with a Foreign Service Agency (defined in the Foreign Service Act of 1980) for at least one year. Approximately twenty awards offered annually. For study toward a career in the Foreign Service or international affairs. Write to the address below for details.

American Foreign Service Association
2101 E St. NW
Washington, DC 20037

514
Dade County Council PTA/PTSA Scholarship

AMOUNT: Maximum: $1000 DEADLINE: April 1
FIELDS/MAJORS: Education

Scholarship for Dade County residents. Must be U.S. citizen and have a GPA of at least 3.0. Financial need is considered, and an education major is preferred. Contact your counselor or CAP advisor for details.

Dade County Council PTA/PTSA
Ms. Ann Thompson
1450 NE 2nd Ave., #103
Miami, FL 33132

515
Dallam Scholarship for History Majors

AMOUNT: Maximum: $750   DEADLINE: March 25
FIELDS/MAJORS: History

Available to women with junior or senior standing who are majoring in history and have maintained at least a 3.0 GPA. Recipient must demonstrate financial need and must carry at least 6 credit hours per semester. Send a SASE to the address listed for an application.

Business and Professional Women's Foundation of Maryland, Inc.
Scholarship Coordinator
282 New Mark Esplanade
Rockville, MD 20850

516
Dan Klepper Outdoor Photography Scholarships

AMOUNT: Maximum: $1000   DEADLINE: November 1
FIELDS/MAJORS: Photography, Video Related

Scholarships open to juniors, seniors, graduate students, and active professionals who are seeking further training. Must be planning to enroll/enrolled in photography or video related courses. For use at an accredited Texas college or university. Winners announced at the TOWA annual meeting, February 21, in Waco, Texas. Contact the address or e-mail listed to request information.
steve.lightfoot@tpwd.state.tx.us

Texas Outdoor Writers Association
TOWA Scholarship
1715 Chamois Knoll
Round Rock, TX 78664

517
Daniel B. Goldberg Scholarship

AMOUNT: Maximum: $3500   DEADLINE: February 1
FIELDS/MAJORS: Finance

Open to full-time students in a master's of finance program preparing for a career in state and local government finance. Applicants must be citizens or permanent residents of the U.S. or Canada. Recommendation from academic advisor or dean of the graduate program will be required. Information may be available from the head of your finance department. If not, write to the address listed or call (312) 977-9700. Applications are available in November for awards in the following spring.

Government Finance Officers Association
Scholarship Committee
180 N. Michigan Ave., Suite 800
Chicago, IL 60601

518
Daniel E. Lambert Memorial Scholarship

AMOUNT: None Specified   DEADLINE: May 1
FIELDS/MAJORS: All Areas of Study

Open to residents of Maine entering their first year or higher of Post High School education or training. Must be U.S. citizens and dependents of veterans. Write to the address listed for more information.

American Legion-Department of Maine
PO Box 900
Waterville, ME 04903

519
Daniella Altfeld-Moreno Scholarships

AMOUNT: Maximum: $3500   DEADLINE: February 20
FIELDS/MAJORS: All Areas of Study

Awards open to Latino/Latina youth (under twenty-one), self-identified gay/lesbian or children of gay/lesbian families. Preference given to students involved in athletics. Contact the address listed for further information.

Greater Seattle Business Association and Pride Foundation
2033 6th Ave., #804
Seattle, WA 98121

520
Danish Sisterhood America National Scholarship

AMOUNT: None Specified   DEADLINE: None Specified
FIELDS/MAJORS: Danish Heritage and Culture

Scholarships for students who are members or dependents of members of the Danish Sisterhood of America. Based on academics and good standing in your local lodge. Write to the address below for more information.

Danish Sisterhood of America
Elizabeth K. Hunter, Scholarship Chairperson
8004 Jasmine Blvd.
Port Richey, FL 34668

521
Dante Aston Memorial Scholarship

AMOUNT: None Specified DEADLINE: April 4
FIELDS/MAJORS: All Areas of Study

Available to Lake County, Ohio, graduating high school seniors. Students must have a GPA of 2.5, proof of financial need, and must submit a five hundred word essay about "what education means to me." Contact the address listed for further information.

Union Congregation Church
Rev. Roderick Coffee
182 West Jackson St.
Painesville, OH 44077

522
Datatel Scholars Foundation

AMOUNT: $700-$2000 DEADLINE: February 28
FIELDS/MAJORS: All Areas of Study

Open to full-time and part-time undergraduate or graduate students attending a secondary, undergraduate, or graduate program at a Datatel client site. Must include name of institute you plan on/are attending to determine if they are part of this program. Write to the address below for more information. Must have a GPA of at least 2.0.

Datatel Scholars Foundation
4375 Fair Lakes Ct.
Fairfax, VA 22033

523
Daughters of Cincinnati Scholarships

AMOUNT: None Specified DEADLINE: March 15
FIELDS/MAJORS: All Areas of Study

Open to female high school seniors who are daughters of commissioned regular active or retired officers in U.S. Army, Navy, Air Force, Marine Corps, or Coast Guard. Based on financial need and merit. Renewable. The sponsor has requested we stress that the award is only for daughters of commissioned officers. Also, please be certain to put your name, address, parent's rank and parent's branch of service on your letter (not just on the outside of the envelope).

Daughters of Cincinnati
Attn: Scholarship Administrator
122 East 58th St.
New York, NY 10022

524
Daughters of the Pioneer of Washington Scholarships

AMOUNT: Maximum: $600 DEADLINE: April 15
FIELDS/MAJORS: History, Education, English

Open to juniors, seniors, and graduate students who are Washington residents. Must be descendants of a pioneer who established residence either in: Washington during or prior to 1870, Oregon during or prior to 1853, Idaho during or prior to 1863, or western Montana during or prior to 1863. One award for attendance at Eastern Washington University and one award for attendance at Western Washington University. Contact the address below for further information.

Memorial Scholarship Fund
Ms. Shirlie Verley, Administrator
150 Kennicott Dr.
Chehalis, WA 98532

525
Dauphin County Conservation District Scholarships

AMOUNT: $500 DEADLINE: September 1
FIELDS/MAJORS: Agriculture, Environmentally Related Fields

Scholarships offered to Dauphin County residents with at least a sophomore standing. Write to address below for details.

Dauphin County Conservation District
Agriculture and Natural Resources Center
1451 Peters Mountain Road
Dauphin, PA 17081

526
Dave Cameron Scholarships

AMOUNT: $500-$2000 DEADLINE: None Specified
FIELDS/MAJORS: All Areas of Study

Open to undergraduates who are residents of York, South Carolina, and have a minimum GPA of 2.0. Based on both financial need and academic achievement. Number of awards varies depending on funding. Contact the address listed for further information. Must enclose a SASE for a reply.

Dave Cameron Educational Foundation
Scholarship Coordinator
PO Box 181
York, SC 29745

527
Davenport Foundation Scholarships in the Arts

AMOUNT: None Specified DEADLINE: July 15
FIELDS/MAJORS: Art, Music, Theater

Open to Barnstable County, Massachusetts, residents in the last two years of undergraduate study or beyond who are studying in the performing or visual arts. Based on need, ability, academics, and proven desire in the field of endeavor. Interviews are an integral part of the granting process. Write to the address listed for details. Must have a GPA of at least 2.8.

John K. and Thirza F. Davenport Foundation
20 North Main St.
South Yarmouth, MA 02664

528
David Baumgardt Memorial Fellowships

AMOUNT: $3000 DEADLINE: November 1
FIELDS/MAJORS: Jewish Studies

Fellowships are available for research at the Leo Baeck Institute for current predoctoral scholars who are studying the social, communal, and intellectual history of German-speaking Jewry. Applicants must be U.S. citizens. Write to the address below for information.

Leo Baeck Institute
Fellowship Programs
129 East 73rd St.
New York, NY 10021

529
David Carlyle Richards III Scholarship

AMOUNT: Maximum: $2000 DEADLINE: None Specified
FIELDS/MAJORS: All Areas of Study

Candidates must be a high school senior from Carroll County, Illinois, and have financial need. Recommendation by school officials is required. Renewable. Information is made available to the superintendents offices of school districts in Carroll County. Contact that office or write to the below address for details.

Anita H. Richards Trust
Attn: Manager
112 Adams St. PO Box 312
Savanna, IL 61074

530
David E. Finley Fellowship, Paul Mellon Fellowship

AMOUNT: $16000 DEADLINE: November 15
FIELDS/MAJORS: Western Art, Visual Arts, and Related Areas

Three-year fellowships are available for doctoral scholars researching for the dissertation. Two years will be spent in Europe in research, and one year will be spent at the National Gallery of Art. Applicants must be U.S. citizens or legal residents. One fellowship is given annually. Write to the address below for information.

National Gallery of Art
Center for Advanced Study in Visual Arts
Predoctoral Fellowship Program
Washington, DC 20565

531
David Family Scholarships

AMOUNT: None Specified DEADLINE: March 1
FIELDS/MAJORS: All Areas of Study

Open to residents of Clackamas, Lane, Linn, Marin, Multnomah, Washington, and Yamhill counties who graduated from Oregon high schools. Must be enrolled at least quarter time in either an undergraduate or graduate program. Must have a minimum GPA of 2.5 and be U.S. citizens or permanent residents. May reapply from year to year for this award. Contact the address listed for further information.

Oregon State Scholarship Commission
Private Awards
1500 Valley River Dr., #100
Eugene, OR 97401-2130

532
David H. Clift Scholarship

AMOUNT: Maximum: $3000 DEADLINE: April 1
FIELDS/MAJORS: Library Science

Applicants must be graduate students who are entering or enrolled in an ALA-accredited master's program and be U.S. or Canadian citizens. Based on academic accomplishment, leadership potential, and desire to pursue a career in librarianship. For students who have completed fewer than 12 semester hours toward master's (by June of preceding year). Write to the address listed or call (312) 280-4281 for details.

American Library Association
Staff Liaison, ALA Scholarship Juries
50 E. Huron St.
Chicago, IL 60611

533
David L. Owens Scholarship

AMOUNT: $10000   DEADLINE: April 1
FIELDS/MAJORS: Water Utility Industry

Scholarship for graduating seniors or master's level students pursuing a degree in the water utility industry. Must be a U.S. citizen. Write to the address below for more information.

National Association of Water Companies
Scholarship Committee
1725 K St. NW, Suite 1212
Washington, DC 20006

534
David M. Lowrey Memorial Scholarship

AMOUNT: Maximum: $1000   DEADLINE: March 1
FIELDS/MAJORS: All Areas of Study

Open to high school seniors who are residents of Hartford and attending one of the three Hartford high schools. Based on academic success and community involvement. Contact the address listed for further information. Must have a GPA of at least 2.8.

Hartford Whalers Foundation
Ms. Mary Lynn Gorman
242 Trumbull St.
Hartford, CT 06103

535
David Rozkuszka Scholarship

AMOUNT: None Specified   DEADLINE: December 1
FIELDS/MAJORS: Library Science

Awards for ALA-accredited master's degree candidate currently working in a library with government documents, with a commitment to government documents librarianship. Write to the address below for additional information.

American Library Association
Susan Tulis, Law Library
University of Virginia, 580 Massie Rd.
Charlottesville, VA 22901

536
David T. Woolsey Scholarship-Hawaii Chapter

AMOUNT: Maximum: $1000   DEADLINE: March 31
FIELDS/MAJORS: Landscape Architecture/Design

Open to third-, fourth-, fifth-year, or graduate students from Hawaii. A personal statement, autobiography, and samples of design work will be required. Write to the address listed for details or call (202) 686-8337.

Landscape Architecture Foundation
Scholarship Program
4401 Connecticut Ave. NW, #500
Washington, DC 20008

537
David Tamotsu Kagiwada Memorial Scholarship

AMOUNT: None Specified   DEADLINE: March 15
FIELDS/MAJORS: Theology

Applicants must be Asian-American members of the Christian Church (Disciples of Christ) who are preparing for the ordained ministry. For full-time study. Financial need is considered. Must have at least a "C+" grade average. Write to the address below for details.

Christian Church (Disciples of Christ)
Attn: Scholarships
PO Box 1986
Indianapolis, IN 46206

538
David Wasserman Scholarships

AMOUNT: $300   DEADLINE: April 15
FIELDS/MAJORS: All Areas of Study

Scholarship for residents of Montgomery County, New York. For undergraduate study only. Write to the address below for details.

David Wasserman Scholarship Fund, Inc.
Adirondack Center
Rte 30 N., Rd #4
Amsterdam, NY 12010

539
D.C. Commission on the Arts and Humanities Grants

AMOUNT: $2500-$20000   DEADLINE: March 17
FIELDS/MAJORS: Arts

Applicants must be artists and reside in Washington D.C. Awards are intended to generate arts endeavors within the Washington D.C. community. Write for further details.

District of Columbia Commission on the Arts and
   Humanities
Stables Art Center
410 Eighth St. NW, Fifth Floor
Washington, DC 20004

540
Debra Levy Neimark Memorial Scholarship

AMOUNT: Maximum: $1500 DEADLINE: April 1
FIELDS/MAJORS: All Areas of Study

One award open to women for vocational education assistance and one award for traditional higher education. Must attend an accredited Florida school. Awards are to help promote higher education and economic self-sufficiency. Contact the address below for further information.

Debra Levy Neimark Scholarship Foundation
Selection Committee
800 Corporate Dr., #602
Ft. Lauderdale, FL 33334

541
DEED (Demonstration of Energy-Efficient Developments) Scholarships

AMOUNT: Maximum: $3000 DEADLINE: December 16
FIELDS/MAJORS: Energy-Related Studies

Graduate or undergraduate students in energy-related disciplines from accredited four-year colleges or universities are eligible. Must have completed a research project to qualify. Project must be specifically geared to electric utilities. Write to the address listed for additional information.

American Public Power Association
DEED Administrator
2301 M St. NW
Washington, DC 20037

542
Deerfield Plastics/Barker Family Scholarship

AMOUNT: Maximum: $1500 DEADLINE: March 15
FIELDS/MAJORS: All Areas of Study

Open to the children of Deerfield Plastics employees. Applicants must apply directly to Deerfield Plastics in Deerfield, Massachusetts. You must contact Deerfield Plastics directly for information and an application.

Community Foundation of Western Massachusetts
PO Box 15769
1500 Main St.
Springfield, MA 01115

543
Defense Policy Science and Engineering Fellowships

AMOUNT: $45000
DEADLINE: January 15
FIELDS/MAJORS: Engineering, Sciences, Defense Technology

Applicants must have Ph.D. or equivalent degrees. Persons with master's degrees in engineering and three years professional experience also qualify. Recipients spend one year working as special assistant for the offices under Secretary of Defense or Army Deputy Assistant Secretary. Program begins in September. Must demonstrate exceptional competence in the areas of science, engineering, or technology and have some interest in applying personal knowledge toward the solution of national security problems. Minority and disabled students are encouraged to apply. Must be U.S. citizens. Federal employees are not eligible. Contact address listed or (202) 326-6760 for more details.

American Association for the Advancement of Science
Fellowship Program
1200 New York Ave. NW
Washington, DC 20005

544
Delaware Nursing Incentive Scholarship Loan

AMOUNT: Maximum: $3000 DEADLINE: March 31
FIELDS/MAJORS: Nursing

Scholarship for students who meet academic requirements and enroll in a nursing program. Commission makes final awards July 1. Write to the address listed for more information.

Delaware Higher Education Commission
Carvel State Office Building
820 North French St., #4F
Wilmington, DE 19801

545
Delaware Scholarship Incentive Program

AMOUNT: Maximum: $1000 DEADLINE: April 15
FIELDS/MAJORS: All Areas of Study

Program for Delaware residents enrolled full-time in a degree program at a Delaware college. In certain instances, Delaware residents attending out-of-state colleges may apply. All recipients must have a GPA of 2.5 or better. Selections are made based on financial need. Awards made on July 1. Write to the address listed for more information.

Delaware Higher Education Commission
Carvel State Office Building
820 North French St., #4F
Wilmington, DE 19801

546
Delbert K. Aman Memorial Scholarships

AMOUNT: Maximum: $500 DEADLINE: March 1
FIELDS/MAJORS: All Areas of Study

Scholarships are available to legally blind students who are residents of South Dakota or attending a South Dakota college or university. For undergraduate study. Write to the address listed or call (202) 467-5081 or 1-800-424-8666 for details.

American Council of the Blind
Scholarship Coordinator
1155 15th St. NW, Suite 720
Washington, DC 20005

547
Delta Gamma Foundation Florence Margaret Harvey Memorial Scholarship

AMOUNT: Maximum: $1000 DEADLINE: April 30
FIELDS/MAJORS: Rehabilitation, Education of Visually Impaired or Blind Persons

Open to legally blind undergraduates and graduates in the field of rehabilitation or education of the visually impaired or blind. Must be U.S. citizens and have exhibited academic excellence. Write to the address listed for complete details or call (212) 502-7771. Must have a GPA of at least 2.9.

American Foundation for the Blind
Scholarship Committee
11 Penn Plaza, Suite 300
New York, NY 10001

548
Delta Kappa Gamma International Scholarships

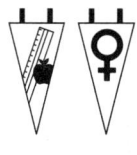

AMOUNT: $1000 DEADLINE: May 15
FIELDS/MAJORS: Education, Child Development

Scholarships are available for female juniors and seniors who are residents of Sarasota County, Florida, and attending school full-time in Florida. Must be majoring in education or child development. Write to the address below for information.

Delta Kappa Gamma International-Gamma Upsilon
C/O Dr. Laura Wiggins
130 Ogden St.
Sarasota, FL 34242

549
Delta Kappa Gamma Scholarship

AMOUNT: $500 DEADLINE: March 1
FIELDS/MAJORS: Education

Scholarships for women who graduated from a Geauga County, Ohio, high school. Must be at least juniors in college. Write to the address below for details.

Delta Kappa Gamma-Omega Chapter
Shirley Haueter, Scholarship Chair
PO Box 865
Chardon, OH 44024

550
Delta Sigma Theta Hartford Alumnae Scholarship

AMOUNT: $500-$1000 DEADLINE: April 1
FIELDS/MAJORS: All Areas of Study

Open to African-American female high school seniors from Hartford, Bloomfield, and Windsor who plan on attending a four-year school. Must be in the top quarter of class and be able to demonstrate leadership, citizenship, and financial need. Contact the address listed for further information. Must have a GPA of at least 2.5.

Delta Sigma Theta Sorority, Inc.
Chairperson, Hartford Alumnae Chapter
PO Box 320079
Hartford, CT 06132

551
Denmark Lions Club Community Fund

AMOUNT: None Specified DEADLINE: April 30
FIELDS/MAJORS: All Areas of Study

Awards to support residents of Denmark, Maine, who are pursuing postsecondary education at the college or technical school level. Contact the Denmark Town Office for more information.

Maine Community Foundation
245 East Maine St.
PO Box 148
Ellsworth, ME 04605

552
Dental Assisting Scholarship Program

AMOUNT: $1000 DEADLINE: September 15
FIELDS/MAJORS: Dental Assisting

Applicant must be a U.S. citizen and must be enrolled full-time as an entering student in a dental assisting program accredited by the Commission on Dental Accreditation of the American Dental Association. Students must have a GPA of 2.8 or above and demonstrate financial need. Students receiving a full scholarship from any other source are ineligible for this scholarship. Recipients may apply to renew the scholarship for a second year provided the student has completed the previous year's academic requirements in good standing. Write to the address below for details.

ADA Endowment and Assistance Fund, Inc.
211 East Chicago Ave.
Chicago, IL 60611

553
Dental Assisting Scholarship Program

AMOUNT: Maximum: $300 DEADLINE: None Specified
FIELDS/MAJORS: Dental Assisting

Scholarships for Florida residents (for at least two years) who have completed at least one semester or quarter in a Florida Board of Dentistry approved program with a GPA of at least 2.0. Program is designed to alleviate shortage of dental assistants in certain parts of Florida. Renewable. Requests for scholarships should be made at least forty-five days before the date the funds are needed. Write to the Florida Dental Health Foundation at the address below for details.

Florida Dental Association
Florida Dental Health Foundation
1111 E. Tennessee St., #102
Tallahassee, FL 32308

554
Dental Hygiene Scholarship Program

AMOUNT: $1000 DEADLINE: August 15
FIELDS/MAJORS: Dental Hygiene

Applicant must be a U.S. citizen and enrolled full-time entering their second year at a dental hygiene school accredited by the Commission on Dental Accreditation of the American Dental Association. Students must have a GPA of 3.0 or above and show financial need. Students receiving a full scholarship from any other source are ineligible for this scholarship. Recipients may apply to renew the scholarship for a second year provided the student has completed the previous year's academic requirements in good standing. Contact the financial aid office at your school for details.

ADA Endowment and Assistance Fund, Inc.
211 East Chicago Ave.
Chicago, IL 60611

555
Dental Student Scholarship

AMOUNT: $2500 DEADLINE: June 15
FIELDS/MAJORS: Dentistry

Applicant must be a U.S. citizen enrolled full-time entering their second year in a dentistry program accredited by the Commission on Accreditation of the American Dental Association. Students must have a GPA of 3.0 or above and demonstrate financial need. Students receiving a full scholarship from any other source are ineligible for this scholarship. Contact the address below for further information.

ADA Endowment and Assistance Fund, Inc.
211 East Chicago Ave.
Chicago, IL 60611

556
Department of Minnesota Scholarships

AMOUNT: $500 DEADLINE: March 15
FIELDS/MAJORS: All Areas of Study

For Minnesota residents who are children/grandchildren of veterans of: WWI, WWII, Korea, Vietnam, Grenada, Lebanon (82-84), or Panama. For study in Minnesota. Must be high school senior with a good scholastic record and a minimum GPA of a "C". Based on character and financial need. Seven awards per year. Information for this award and the National Presidents Scholarship are available from the address listed. Must have a GPA of at least 2.0.

American Legion Auxiliary-Department of Minnesota
State Veterans Service Bldg.
St. Paul, MN 55155

557
Department President's Scholarships

AMOUNT: $1000-$1500 DEADLINE: March 15
FIELDS/MAJORS: All Areas of Study

Open to children (adopted, step, grand or great-grand) of a living, deceased, or disabled discharged veteran who served during these active war dates: 4/6/17-11/11/18, 12/7/41-12/31/46, 6/25/50-1/31/55, 12/22/61-5/7/75, 8/24/82-7/31/84, 12/20/89-1/31/90, or 8/2/90 to cessation. Must be residents of Ohio, sponsored by an Ohio Legion Auxiliary Unit, and preparing to enter freshman year of college. Winners based on Americanism, character, leadership, scholarship, and financial need. Contact the address below for further information. Must have a GPA of at least 2.7.

American Legion Auxiliary-Department of Ohio, Inc.
C. Baughman-Underwood
804 Summit Gardens
Kent, OH 44240

558
Desk and Derrick Educational Trust Scholarships

AMOUNT: $1000 DEADLINE: April 1
FIELDS/MAJORS: Petroleum, Geology

Ten to thirteen awards for college juniors, seniors, or graduate students with a minimum GPA of 3.0. Must be U.S. or Canadian citizens who plan a career in the petroleum or allied industry. Must demonstrate financial need. Contact the address listed for further information.

Desk and Derrick Educational Trust
4823 S. Sheridan Rd.
Suite 308A
Tulsa, OK 74145

559
Diamond State Scholarship

AMOUNT: None Specified DEADLINE: March 31
FIELDS/MAJORS: All Areas of Study

Scholarship for high school seniors who rank in the upper quarter of the class, scored 1200 or better on the SAT or 27 or better on the ACT, and enrolls full-time at an accredited college. Commission makes final awards July 1. Write to the address listed for more information. Must have a GPA of at least 3.0.

Delaware Higher Education Commission
Carvel State Office Building
820 North French St., #4F
Wilmington, DE 19801

560
Dick Horne Foundation Scholarships

AMOUNT: $75-$1200 DEADLINE: None Specified
FIELDS/MAJORS: All Areas of Study

Open to high school seniors planning to attend college or a university. Applicants must be residents of Orangeburg County, South Carolina. Awards based on academics and financial need. Approximately 130 awards offered annually, but the number may vary. Contact the address listed for further information or (803) 534-2096. Must have a GPA of at least 2.8.

Dick Horne Foundation
Scholarship Coordinator
PO Box 306
Orangeburg, SC 29116

561
Dickinson County Education Scholarship

AMOUNT: $300 DEADLINE: January 15
FIELDS/MAJORS: Education

Scholarship available for juniors and seniors in Kansas four-year colleges and universities. Must have graduated from one of five Dickinson County High Schools. Write to the address below for information.

AARTA
Dale Relihan
Box 86
Chapman, KS 67431

562
Disciple Chaplains' Scholarship

AMOUNT: None Specified DEADLINE: March 15
FIELDS/MAJORS: Theology

Applicants must be members of the Christian Church (Disciples of Christ) who are entering first year in seminary. For full-time study. Financial need is considered. Must have better than a "C+" grade average. Write to the address below for details.

Christian Church (Disciples of Christ)
Attn: Scholarships
PO Box 1986
Indianapolis, IN 46206

563
Discover Card Tribute Award Scholarship Program

AMOUNT: $1250-$20000 DEADLINE: January 13
FIELDS/MAJORS: All Areas of Study

Scholarships available for current high school juniors who have a minimum GPA of 2.75 and are U.S. citizens. Must demonstrate accomplishments in four of the following: special talents, leadership, obstacles overcome, unique endeavors, and community service. For use at any two- or four-year school. Contact the address listed for further information.

American Association of School Administrators, Discover Card Services
Discover Card Tribute Award Program
PO Box 9338
Arlington, VA 22219

564
Discovery Research Proposal

AMOUNT: Maximum: $25000 DEADLINE: December 4
FIELDS/MAJORS: Meat Science, Swine Studies

Awards are available for scientists in the areas of pork production. Graduate students as well as postdoctoral scholars are eligible for this award. Requires applicant to submit a research proposal to the council. Write to the address listed or call (515) 223-2600 for more details.

National Pork Producers Council
PO Box 10383
Des Moines, IA 50306

565
Displaced Homemaker Scholarships

AMOUNT: None Specified DEADLINE: September 1
FIELDS/MAJORS: All Areas of Study

Open to Native American mid-life homemakers, both men and women who are unable to fill their educational goals. This program will augment financial sources or help with child care, transportation, and basic living expenses. Must be at least one-quarter Native Indian/Alaskan. Recipients are eligible to reapply in subsequent years. Write to the address below for complete details.

Association on American Indian Affairs, Inc.
Box 268
Sisseton, SD 57262

566
Dissertation and Postdoctoral Research Fellowships

AMOUNT: $1000-$2000 DEADLINE: April 1
FIELDS/MAJORS: Jewish Studies

Eight fellowships are available for postdoctoral candidates or persons at the doctoral dissertation stage for up to three months of active research or writing at the American Jewish Archives. Contact address listed for complete information.

American Jewish Archives
Administrative Director
3101 Clifton Ave.
Cincinnati, OH 45220

567
Dissertation Fellowship

AMOUNT: Maximum: $7500 DEADLINE: May 1
FIELDS/MAJORS: U.S. Military and Naval History

A fellowship is available for doctoral candidates performing dissertation research in an area of history relevant to the Marine Corps. Applicants must be U.S. citizens and have all requirements for the doctoral degree completed by the time of application, except the dissertation. Some portion of the work is expected to be done at the Marine Corps Historical Center in Washington, D.C. Write to the address listed for information.

Marine Corps Historical Center
Building 58
Washington Navy Yard
Washington, DC 20374

568
Dissertation Fellowships

AMOUNT: $8000 DEADLINE: February 1
FIELDS/MAJORS: American Military History

Doctoral dissertation fellowships for civilian Ph.D. candidates at recognized graduate schools. All requirements for Ph.D. (except dissertation) should be completed by September of award year. Must be U.S. citizens or legal residents. Write to the address listed for complete details.

U.S. Army Center of Military History
Dissertation Fellowship Committee
1099 14th St. NW
Washington, DC 20005

569
Dissertation Fellowships

AMOUNT: Maximum: $14500 DEADLINE: November 15
FIELDS/MAJORS: All Areas of Study

Fellowships for women in their final year of writing their dissertations. Applicants must have completed all course work, passed all preliminary exams, and have their dissertation research proposal (or plan) approved by November 15. Must be a U.S. citizen or permanent resident. Awards are for one year beginning July 1. The fellow is expected to devote full-time to the project for the fellowship year. Scholars may apply up to two times for a dissertation fellowship on the same topic. Write to the address listed for more information.

American Association of University Women
2401 Virginia Ave. NW
Washington, DC 20037

570

Dissertation Fellowships

AMOUNT: Maximum: $6000 DEADLINE: September 15
FIELDS/MAJORS: History: Business, Technology, Industry, Economic, Science

Residential fellowships for Ph.D. candidates who have completed all course work and are starting the dissertation process. The dissertation must be within the center's research fields and collecting interests. Programs for post-doctoral scholarly work are also available. Write to address listed for more details.

Hagley Museum and Library
PO Box 3630
Wilmington, DE 19807

571

Dissertation Fellowships

AMOUNT: None Specified DEADLINE: November 1
FIELDS/MAJORS: Music, Drama, Playwriting

Fellowships are available to Ph.D. candidates for dissertation research that is directly related to the musical works of Kurt Weill and to the perpetuation of his artistic legacy. Write to the address listed for information.

Kurt Weill Foundation for Music, Inc.
Joanna C. Lee, Associate Director
7 East 20th St.
New York, NY 10003

572

Dissertation Grants Program

AMOUNT: Maximum: $1500 DEADLINE: February 2
FIELDS/MAJORS: Women's Studies

Doctoral dissertation grants to support use of Schlesinger library materials. Two or more grants each year. Must be matriculated in doctoral program and have completed all course work before application. Must be U.S. citizens or permanent residents. Write to "Dissertation Grants Program" at the address below for details.

Radcliffe College
Arthur and Elizabeth Schlesinger Library
10 Garden St.
Cambridge, MA 02138

573

District 56 Graduate Scholarships

AMOUNT: Maximum: $6000 DEADLINE: April 1
FIELDS/MAJORS: All Areas of Study

Open to students who are graduating from Neah-Kah-Nie high school in Rockaway, Oregon, or any student who has graduated since 1954. Write to the address listed for more information.

Neah-Kah-Nie District 56 Graduate Scholarships, Inc.
Scholarship Coordinator
PO Box 373
Rockaway Beach, OR 97136

574

Doane Educational Trust Fund Scholarship

AMOUNT: None Specified DEADLINE: March 1
FIELDS/MAJORS: All Areas of Study

Open to residents of Wasco County, Oregon. Must be U.S. citizens or permanent residents. Applicants may apply and compete annually. Contact the address listed for further information.

Oregon State Scholarship Commission
Private Awards
1500 Valley River Dr., #100
Eugene, OR 97401-2130

575

Doc Hurley

AMOUNT: Maximum: $1000 DEADLINE: March 1
FIELDS/MAJORS: All Areas of Study

Open to high school seniors whose schools participate in the Doc Hurley Classic. For use at two- or four-year schools. Based on academics, community service, and financial need. Contact the high school director of guidance for further information. Must have a GPA of at least 3.0.

Doc Hurley Scholarship Foundation, Inc.
Greater Hartford Chamber of Commerce
250 Constitution Plaza
Hartford, CT 06103

576

Doctoral and Postdoctoral Fellowship

AMOUNT: $3700-$4300 DEADLINE: November 1
FIELDS/MAJORS: Japanese Studies

Fifteen fellowships available to doctoral or postdoctoral students in the field of Japanese studies who have completed all the academic requirements except the dissertation. Applicants must be able to speak Japanese in order to successfully continue their research in Japan. Write to the address listed for additional information.

Japan Foundation
New York Office
152 West 57th St.
New York, NY 10019

577

Doctoral Dissertation Fellowships in Jewish Studies

AMOUNT: $7000-$9000   DEADLINE: January 5
FIELDS/MAJORS: Jewish Studies

Awards are available for students who have completed all academic requirements for the doctoral degree except the dissertation in the field of Jewish studies. Must be a U.S. citizen or permanent resident and give evidence of a proficiency in a Jewish language. Write to the address listed for more information.

National Foundation for Jewish Culture
330 Seventh Ave.
21st Floor
New York, NY 10001

578

Doctoral Dissertation Fellowships in Law and Social Science

AMOUNT: $15000   DEADLINE: February 2
FIELDS/MAJORS: Law, Social Science

Fellowships are available for Ph.D. candidates who have completed all doctoral requirements except the dissertation. Proposed research must be in the areas of sociolegal studies, social scientific approaches to law, the legal profession, or legal institutions. Fellowships are held in residence at the ABF. All Fellows are provided with personal computers and access to the libraries of Northwestern University and the University of Chicago. Minority students are encouraged to apply. Write to the address listed for information.

American Bar Foundation
Ann Tatalovich, Assistant Director
750 N. Lake Shore Dr.
Chicago, IL 60611

579

Doctoral Dissertation Grant Program

AMOUNT: $10000   DEADLINE: January 31
FIELDS/MAJORS: Purchasing, Business, Management, Logistics, Economics, Industrial Engineering

Doctoral dissertation research grants are available for research that can be applied to the management of the purchasing and materials management functions and to help develop high-potential academicians who will teach and conduct research in the field. For doctoral candidates in an accredited U.S. college or university. Must be U.S. citizens or permanent residents. Write to the address below for information.

National Association of Purchasing Management
Doctoral Research Grant Committee
PO Box 22160
Tempe, AZ 85285

580

Doctoral Dissertation Research in Chinese Studies Scholarships

AMOUNT: Maximum: $10000   DEADLINE: June 30
FIELDS/MAJORS: Humanities, Social Science

Applicants must be doctoral candidates in humanities or social sciences with an approved dissertation prospectus. Enrollment in a university in the U.S. or Canada required. Write to the address listed or call (718) 460-4900 for more information.

China Times Cultural Foundation
136-39 41 Ave., #1A
Flushing, NY 11355

581

Doctoral Fellowship Program in Biomedical Engineering

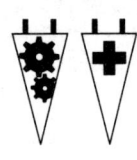

AMOUNT: None Specified   DEADLINE: December 11
FIELDS/MAJORS: Biomedical Engineering

Doctoral fellowships are available to support graduate students of outstanding scholarship, ability, and aptitude for future achievements in Biomedical Engineering Research. Write to the address below for information.

Whitaker Foundation
Fellowship Programs
1700 North Moore St., Suite 2200
Rosslyn, VA 22209

582

Doctoral Fellowships in Art Education

AMOUNT: Maximum: $12500   DEADLINE: November 1
FIELDS/MAJORS: Art Education

Open to doctoral students for the final research and writing stages of their doctoral studies. Must have completed an approved dissertation proposal that is significantly related to discipline-based art education at an accredited university in the U.S. or Canada. Awards will be announced by April 15. Contact the address listed for further information.

Getty Education Institute for the Arts
Dr. Jeffrey H. Patchen
1200 Getty Center Dr., #600
Los Angeles, CA 90049-1683

583
Doctoral Scholarships

AMOUNT: $3000   DEADLINE: February 1
FIELDS/MAJORS: Oncology Nursing

Scholarships available to doctoral students in the field of oncology nursing. All applicants must be currently licensed registered nurses. Three awards offered annually. Write to the address listed for more information.

Oncology Nursing Foundation
501 Holiday Dr.
Pittsburgh, PA 15220

584
Dodd and Dorothy L. Bryan Foundation Student Loans

AMOUNT: Maximum: $4000   DEADLINE: None Specified
FIELDS/MAJORS: All Areas of Study

Loans for Wyoming residents who live in Sheridan, Campbell or Johnson counties. Montana residents may also apply if you live in Powder River, Rosebud, or Big Horn counties. Applicant must live in the above areas at least one year prior to applying. For academic loans, the student must be under the age of twenty-five and have (or had) a minimum GPA of 2.25 and carry 12 credit hours. Contact the address below for further information.

Dodd and Dorothy L Bryan Foundation
PO Box 6287
First Plaza-2 N. Main, #401
Sheridan, WY 82801

585
Don Hall Scholarship

AMOUNT: None Specified   DEADLINE: May 1
FIELDS/MAJORS: All Areas of Study

Awards for graduating seniors from Sangerville pursuing postsecondary education. Preference is given to students showing civic or community involvement, leadership qualities, or environmental efforts. Contact the Executive Committee of the East Sangerville Grange, Box 60, Sangerville, ME, 04443 for more information.

Maine Community Foundation
245 East Maine St.
PO Box 148
Ellsworth, ME 04605

586
Donald A. Fisher Memorial Scholarship

AMOUNT: Maximum: $1000   DEADLINE: June 2
FIELDS/MAJORS: All Areas of Study

Scholarships are available to undergraduates who are members of Tau Kappa Epsilon. Must have demonstrated leadership capability within his chapter, on campus, or in the community. Must have a GPA of 2.5 or higher and be a full-time student in good standing. Write to the address listed for more information.

TKE Educational Foundation
8645 Founders Road
Indianapolis, IN 46268

587
Donald Groves Fund Awards in Numismatics

AMOUNT: None Specified   DEADLINE: None Specified
FIELDS/MAJORS: Numismatics

Grants to support the study and publishing of works involving early American coinage and currency (pre-1800). Funds support travel, research, and publication. Write to the address listed for details.

American Numismatic Society
Broadway at 155th St.
New York, NY 10032

588
Donald Macolm MacArthur

AMOUNT: Maximum: $2500   DEADLINE: March 15
FIELDS/MAJORS: All Fields of Study

Available to students from Scotland coming to the U.S. or U.S. students from one of the following states: Maryland, North Carolina, New Jersey, Pennsylvania, Virginia, West Virginia, Delaware, or Washington D.C. who wish to study in Scotland. Based on need, academics, and goals. Consideration is made for students who continue to enhance their knowledge of Scottish history or culture. Write to James S. McLeod, Chairman of the Charity and Education Committee, at the address listed for details or call (301) 229-6140.

St. Andrew's Society of Washington, D.C.
James McLeod, Chairman
7012 Arandale Rd.
Bethesda, MD 20817-4702

589
Donna Amyx Memorial Scholarship

AMOUNT: None Specified   DEADLINE: April 1
FIELDS/MAJORS: All Areas of Study

Award for child of a Nylcare/Healthplus subscriber who demonstrates need, as verified by parent's tax return for prior year or other suitable documents. Must be a graduating high school senior or college student with a GPA of 2.5 or better. Also based upon three letters of reference, an essay on the challenge to American families today, and involvement in school and community activities. Contact Nylcare customer service at 1-800-635-3121 for more information.

Nylcare/Mid-Atlantic Scholarship Foundation, Inc.
7617 Ora Glen Dr.
Greenbelt, MD 20770

590
Dorchester Board of Trade Scholarships

AMOUNT: $250-$500 DEADLINE: June 4
FIELDS/MAJORS: All Areas of Study

Scholarships awarded to Dorchester residents. Applicants must submit a three to five hundred word essay on the following topic: "My Hero" or "My Heroine." One to four awards are offered annually. Write to the address listed for more details.

Dorchester Board of Trade
PO Box 452
Dorchester, MA 02122

591
Dorchester Woman's Club Scholarship

AMOUNT: $500 DEADLINE: February 15
FIELDS/MAJORS: Music-Voice

Applicant must be a senior in a Massachusetts high school who will enroll in a four-year accredited college or university and present a letter of endorsement from a sponsoring Women's Club in your community. Write to the address below for details, be sure to include a SASE.

General Federation of Women's Clubs of Massachusetts
Chairman, Music Division
245 Dutton Rd., PO Box 679
Sudbury, MA 01776

592
Dorothy Andrews Kabis Memorial Internship

AMOUNT: None Specified DEADLINE: February 21
FIELDS/MAJORS: Government

Open to women who are twenty-one years of age or older. Applicants should have a general knowledge of government, a keen interest in Republican politics, campaign experience, as well as some clerical office skills. This is a one-month unpaid experience, but round-trip airfare is provided. Interns will be housed at Georgetown University. Contact your local Republican Women's Club, state federation president or the address listed or call (703) 548-9688 for further information.

National Federation of Republican Women
Scholarship Coordinator
124 North Alfred St.
Alexandria, VA 22314

593
Dorothy Campbell Memorial Scholarships

AMOUNT: None Specified DEADLINE: March 1
FIELDS/MAJORS: All Areas of Study

Open to female Oregon high school graduates with a minimum GPA of 2.75. A strong and continuing interest in golf will be a factor in the selection process. May be used at any four-year Oregon college. For undergraduate study. Must be an Oregon resident and a U.S. citizen or permanent resident. Contact the address listed for further information.

Oregon State Scholarship Commission
Private Awards
1500 Valley River Dr., #100
Eugene, OR 97401-2130

594
Dorothy E. Schoelzel Memorial Scholarship

AMOUNT: None Specified
DEADLINE: February 1
FIELDS/MAJORS: Education

Open to Connecticut female graduate students in education who have completed at least three years of undergraduate work in education with a minimum GPA of 3.0. Based on future promise, academics, and financial need. Contact the address listed for further information.

West Hartford Women's Club
Ms. Catherine Davidson
109 S. Main St., #A3
West Hartford, CT 06107

595
Dorothy I. Mitstifer Fellowship

AMOUNT: Maximum: $2000 DEADLINE: January 15
FIELDS/MAJORS: Home Economics/Related Fields

Applicants must be chapter advisers of Kappa Omicron Nu and wish to pursue graduate or postgraduate study. Awards will be announced April 1. Write to the address listed for details.

Kappa Omicron Nu Honor Society
4990 Northwind Dr., Suite 140
East Lansing, MI 48823

596
Dorothy Lemke Howarth Scholarship

AMOUNT: Maximum: $2000   DEADLINE: February 1
FIELDS/MAJORS: Engineering

Scholarships for female students who will be sophomores majoring in engineering. Must be a U.S. citizen and have a GPA of at least 3.5. Three awards offered annually. Information and applications for the SWE awards are available from the deans of engineering schools, or write to the address listed for complete details. Please be certain to enclose a SASE.

Society of Women Engineers
Scholarship Selection Committee
120 Wall St., 11th Floor
New York, NY 10005

597
Dorothy Strayer Premier Scholarship

AMOUNT: Maximum: $1000   DEADLINE: January 25
FIELDS/MAJORS: Music

Scholarships for juniors, seniors, and graduate students planning to continue professional musical training who are from one of the following New York counties: Allegany, Cattaraugus, Chautauqua, Erie, Niagara, Orleans, or Wyoming. Write to the address listed for more information.

New York State Federation of Women's Clubs
8th District Music Chairman, D. Blakely
155 Seneca St.
Gowanda, NY 14070

598
Douglas County Community Scholarship

AMOUNT: None Specified   DEADLINE: March 1
FIELDS/MAJORS: All Areas of Study

Open to graduates of Douglas County high schools. Awards may be used at colleges in Oregon, Washington, California, or Idaho. Applicants may apply and compete annually. Must be U.S. citizens or permanent residents to apply. Contact the address listed for further information.

Oregon State Scholarship Commission
Private Awards
1500 Valley River Dr., #100
Eugene, OR 97401-2130

599
DPMA Scholarship

AMOUNT: Maximum: $1000   DEADLINE: March 1
FIELDS/MAJORS: Data Processing, Information Systems, Computer Systems

Open to high school seniors who are Connecticut residents. For use at four-year schools. Based on financial need, reasonable academic success, and school activities. Contact the address listed for further information. Must have a GPA of at least 2.7.

Hartford Chapter, Data Processing Management
   Association
PO Box 562
Hartford, CT 06141

600
Dr. A. F. Zimmerman Award

AMOUNT: $750-$1250   DEADLINE: March 15
FIELDS/MAJORS: History

Applicants must be a student member of Phi Alpha Theta entering a graduate program leading to a master's degree in History. Three awards offered annually. Write to address listed or call 1-800-394-8195 for details. Please indicate the name of your chapter. Information may be available from your chapter officers.

Phi Alpha Theta-International Honor Society in History
Headquarters Office
50 College Dr.
Allentown, PA 18104

601
Dr. Allen Devilbiss Literary Award

AMOUNT: $2000   DEADLINE: None Specified
FIELDS/MAJORS: Respiratory Care

Awards for practitioners and physicians who submit the best papers involving scientific investigations or evaluations on case reports. Must address new technologies or new applications of current technologies in respiratory care. Papers to be published in Respiratory Care. Contact the address listed for further information.

American Respiratory Care Foundation
11030 Ables Ln.
Dallas, TX 75229

602

Dr. G. Layton Grier Scholarship Fund

AMOUNT: $1000 DEADLINE: February 1
FIELDS/MAJORS: Dentistry

Open to full-time dental students entering their second year of study at an accredited dental school, who are residents of Delaware. Based on grades, test scores, recommendations, and an interview. Write to the address below for details.

Delaware State Dental Society
1925 Lovering Ave.
Wilmington, DE 19806

603

Dr. George I. and Eunice A. Tice Scholarships

AMOUNT: Maximum: $500 DEADLINE: January 19
FIELDS/MAJORS: Medicine, Nursing, Psychology, X-ray Technology, or Related Healthcare Fields

Open to students pursuing careers in the medical field at any college, medical, or technical school. Must demonstrate financial need and ability to do well in their chosen medical field. Only high school graduates of north central Iowa are eligible, such as: Black Hawk, Bremer, Butler, Cerra Gorde, Chickasaw, Floyd, Franklin, Grundy, Hamilton, Hancock, Hardin, Howard, Humboldt, Kossuth, Mitchell, Polk, Story, Webster, Winnebago, Worth, and Wright counties. Contact the address listed, be sure to include a business-sized SASE for a reply, or call (515) 422-7740 for further information. Information available after November 17.

North Iowa Mercy Foundation
Mariann Alcorn
1000 4th St. SW
Mason City, IA 50401

604

Dr. Hannah K. Vuolo Memorial Scholarship

AMOUNT: $250 DEADLINE: May 1
FIELDS/MAJORS: Secondary Education

One scholarship is available for residents of New York who will be enrolled in college as an entering freshman. Applicant must be under age twenty-one, a descendant of an American Legion or auxiliary member, and pursuing a degree in secondary education. Based on academic ability and financial need. Write to the address below for additional information.

American Legion-Department of New York
Department Adjutant
112 State St., Suite 400
Albany, NY 12207

605

Dr. Hans and Clara Zimmerman Health Scholar

AMOUNT: Maximum: $1600 DEADLINE: March 1
FIELDS/MAJORS: Health, Pharmacology

Open to sophomores through graduate students who are residents of Hawaii. May be going to school in another state, but must have family in Hawaii. Employees, volunteers, and board members of the Foundation are not eligible to apply. Contact the address below for further information. Must have a GPA of at least 2.5.

Hawaii Community Scholarship Foundation
College Scholarships
900 Fort St. Mall, #1300
Honolulu, HI 96813

606

Dr. Harold Hillenbrand Scholarship

AMOUNT: None Specified DEADLINE: April 1
FIELDS/MAJORS: Dental Hygiene

Scholarships for students who have completed at least one year in a full-time accredited program in dental hygiene. Must have a GPA of at least 3.5. Based on academics, need, and clinical performance. Write to the address below for more information.

American Dental Hygienists' Association Institute for Oral Health
444 N. Michigan Ave., Suite 3400
Chicago, IL 60611

607

Dr. Harry Britenstool Scholarship

AMOUNT: Maximum: $4000 DEADLINE: June 1
FIELDS/MAJORS: All Areas of Study

Open to high school seniors who are/have been registered with the Greater New York Councils, Boy Scouts of America for a minimum of two years. Must have been registered from the five boroughs only. Must be able to demonstrate good academics, financial need, and strong scouting involvement. Write to the address listed for complete details or call (212) 242-1100.

Boy Scouts of America, Greater New York Councils
Britenstool Scholarship Committee
345 Hudson St.
New York, NY 10014

608
Dr. James L. Lawson Memorial Scholarships

AMOUNT: $500 DEADLINE: February 1
FIELDS/MAJORS: Electronics, Communications, Related Fields

Scholarship available to students with a general class amateur radio license, who are residents of: Maine, Massachusetts, Vermont, Rhode Island, New Hampshire, Connecticut, or New York and attend school in their home state. For full-time study. Write to the address listed for information.

ARRL Foundation (American Radio Relay League)
Scholarship Program
225 Main St.
Newington, CT 06111

609
Dr. Jeffrey A. Ferst Valedictorian Memorial Scholarship

AMOUNT: $2000 DEADLINE: March 15
FIELDS/MAJORS: All Areas of Study

Award for the Westfield High School valedictorian, for all areas of study. Contact the address listed for further information.

Community Foundation of Western Massachusetts
PO Box 15769
1500 Main St.
Springfield, MA 01115

610
Dr. John Pine Memorial Award

AMOUNT: Maximum: $1000 DEADLINE: March 15
FIELDS/MAJORS: History

Applicants must be members of Phi Alpha Theta who are advanced graduate students in history. Three awards offered annually. Write to address listed or call 1-800-394-8195 for details. Please indicate the name of your chapter. Information may be available from your chapter officers.

Phi Alpha Theta-International Honor Society in History
Headquarters Office
50 College Dr.
Allentown, PA 18104

611
Dr. Kiyoshi Sonoda Memorial Scholarship

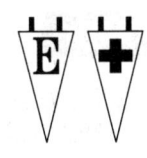

AMOUNT: None Specified DEADLINE: April 1
FIELDS/MAJORS: Dentistry

Applicants must be of Japanese ancestry, majoring in dentistry, and be members of the Japanese American Citizens League. Applications and information may be obtained from local JACL chapters, district offices, and the national headquarters at the address listed or call (415) 921-5225. Please indicate your level of study and be certain to include a legal-sized SASE.

Japanese American Citizens League
National Scholarship and Award Program
1765 Sutter St.
San Francisco, CA 94115

612
Dr. Mae Davidow Memorial Scholarship

AMOUNT: Maximum: $1000 DEADLINE: March 1
FIELDS/MAJORS: All Areas of Study

Applicants must be legally blind entering freshmen who demonstrate outstanding academic achievement. Write to the address listed or call (202) 467-5081 or 1-800-424-8666 for details.

American Council of the Blind
Scholarship Coordinator
1155 15th St. NW, Suite 720
Washington, DC 20005

613
Dr. Pedro Grau Undergraduate Scholarship

AMOUNT: $2500 DEADLINE: June 16
FIELDS/MAJORS: Metrology, Atmospheric Science, Ocean Science, Hydrology

Scholarships for students entering their last year of study toward a degree in one of the fields listed above. Based on academic ability and financial need. Requires a GPA of at least 3.0 and U.S. citizenship or permanent residency. Application forms and further information may be obtained through the AMS headquarters at the address listed.

American Meteorological Society
45 Beacon St.
Boston, MA 02108

614
Dr. Robert L. Rosenthal Memorial Scholarship

AMOUNT: $250-$1600 DEADLINE: March 31
FIELDS/MAJORS: All Areas of Study

Awards are available for Highland High School seniors who have a personal interest in music or are involved musically at Highland High School. Applicants must be ranked in the upper half of their class. Contact the Highland guidance department for more information. Must have a GPA of at least 2.0.

Highland Community Unit School District #5
1800 Lindenthal
Highland, IL 62249

615
Dr. Theodore Von Karman Graduate Scholarship Program

AMOUNT: Maximum: $5000 DEADLINE: None Specified
FIELDS/MAJORS: Engineering, Mathematics, Sciences

Scholarships for graduating ROTC cadets who plan to pursue a graduate degree in engineering, mathematics, or science. Write to the address listed or call 1-800-727-3337 or (703) 247-5839 for details.

Aerospace Education Foundation
Financial Information Department
1501 Lee Highway
Arlington, VA 22209

616
Dr. Tom Anderson Memorial Scholarship

AMOUNT: Maximum: $2000 DEADLINE: April 15
FIELDS/MAJORS: Travel and Tourism, Hotel/Motel Management

Awards for juniors or seniors in one of the areas listed above who are enrolled in a two- or four-year college full-time. Must have a GPA of 3.0 or better. For study anywhere in North America. Write to the address listed or call 1-800-682-8886 ext. 4251 for more information.

National Tourism Foundation
546 East Main St.
PO Box 3071
Lexington, KY 40596

617
Drake Scholarship

AMOUNT: None Specified DEADLINE: April 15
FIELDS/MAJORS: All Areas of Study

Awards for graduating seniors of Brewer High School who plan to pursue a postsecondary degree in any discipline. Contact the Brewer High School Guidance Office for more information.

Maine Community Foundation
245 East Maine St.
PO Box 148
Ellsworth, ME 04605

618
Duane Hanson Scholarship

AMOUNT: Maximum: $3000 DEADLINE: December 1
FIELDS/MAJORS: Engineering Technology, Heating/Air-Conditioning

This scholarship is designed "to encourage and assist heating, ventilating, air-conditioning, and refrigeration education through scholarships and fellowships." Must have completed at least one semester at an ABET accredited school with a minimum GPA of 3.0. Must have one full year of school remaining and be able to demonstrate financial need. Contact the address listed for further information.

American Society of Heating, Refrigerating, and
  Air-Conditioning Engineers
Scholarship Program
1791 Tullie Circle NE
Atlanta, GA 30329

619
DuPont Challenge, Science Essay Awards Program

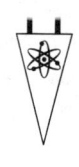

AMOUNT: $50-$1500 DEADLINE: January 30
FIELDS/MAJORS: Science

Scholarships in the form of cash awards are available to graduating high school seniors who enter a winning science-related essay in the DuPont Challenge. Entries must be seven hundred to one thousand words in length and can be on any subject within the realm of science. Must be students in U.S., its territories, or Canada. See your science teacher or guidance counselor for information and an entry form. If unavailable from those sources, write to the address listed.

General Learning Corporation
60 Revere Dr.
Northbrook, IL 60062

620
Duracell/National Urban League Scholarship

AMOUNT: $10000
DEADLINE: April 15
FIELDS/MAJORS: Engineering, Marketing, Finance, Sales, Manufacturing Operations

Scholarships for minority students in their junior year of college. Must be in top quarter of class and have a strong interest in summer employment with Duracell. Contact your local Urban League or write to the address below for details. Must have a GPA of at least 3.0.

National Urban League
500 E. 62nd St.
New York, NY 10021

621
Duracell/National Science Teachers Association Scholarship Contest

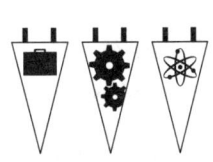

AMOUNT: $200-$20000   DEADLINE: January 14
FIELDS/MAJORS: Engineering, Finance, Marketing, Manufacturing Operations, Sales

Contest for high school students who are U.S. citizens and reside in the United States or U.S. territories. Students design and build working devices powered by Duracell batteries. Will need to submit a two page description and a schematic of the device. Awards are in the form of U.S. Savings Bonds. Applications available in September every year. Contact the address listed for details.

National Science Teachers Association
Duracell/NSTA Scholarship Competition
1840 Wilson Blvd.
Arlington, VA 22201-3000

622
Dwight D. Gardener Scholarship

AMOUNT: Maximum: $2000   DEADLINE: November 15
FIELDS/MAJORS: Industrial Engineering

Scholarships are available for undergraduate industrial engineering majors who are enrolled on a full-time basis and members of the institute with a GPA of at least 3.4 and of junior standing or below. Students must be nominated by their IIE department heads. Four awards offered annually. Contact your school's industrial engineering department head for information.

Institute of Industrial Engineers
Scholarship Program
25 Technology Park/Atlanta
Norcross, GA 30092

623
Dwight David Eisenhower Transportation Fellowship Program

AMOUNT: $1450-$2000   DEADLINE: February 14
FIELDS/MAJORS: Any Fields Related to Transportation

Research-based graduate awards are available to assist in upgrading the total transportation community in the U.S. Must be U.S. citizens who plan to enter the transportation profession. Amounts indicated below are stipends; awards also include tuition and fees. This program administers six separate grants and fellowships. Write to the address below for information.

Federal Highway Administration
901 North Stuart St., Suite 300
National Highway Institute, HHI-20
Arlington, VA 22203

624
E.J. Sierleja Memorial Fellowship

AMOUNT: Maximum: $400   DEADLINE: November 15
FIELDS/MAJORS: Transportation

Scholarships are available for graduate industrial engineering majors who are enrolled on a full-time basis, members of the institute, with a GPA of at least 3.4. Preference is given to students with a career interest in the rail transportation industry. Students must be nominated by their department heads. Contact your school's Industrial Engineering Department Head for information.

Institute of Industrial Engineers
Scholarship Program
25 Technology Park/Atlanta
Norcross, GA 30092

625
E.U. Parker Scholarship

AMOUNT: Maximum: $3000   DEADLINE: March 31
FIELDS/MAJORS: All Areas of Study

Open to full-time students who are legally blind. Contact the address below for further information.

National Federation of the Blind
Mrs. Peggy Elliott, Chairman
814 Fifth Ave.
Grinnell, IA 50112

626
E.W. "Beich" Beichley Scholarship

AMOUNT: Maximum: $1500 DEADLINE: None Specified
FIELDS/MAJORS: Mechanical Engineering

Open to junior and senior ASME members. Must be enrolled in an ABET accredited (or equivalent) program. Selections based on character, academics, leadership, financial need, and potential contribution to the mechanical engineering profession. Contact the address below for further information. Include a SASE for a reply. Must have a GPA of at least 2.9.

American Society of Mechanical Engineers
Nellie Malave
345 E. 47th St.
New York, NY 10017

627
Eagle Scout Scholarship

AMOUNT: $1000-$5000 DEADLINE: December 1
FIELDS/MAJORS: All Areas of Study

Scholarship is available to the current class of Eagle Scouts who have passed their board of review within the last year. Please contact your local Boy Scout chairman for complete information, or write to the address below. Application is made through each state society.

National Society of the Sons of the American Revolution
Scholarship Office
1000 South Fourth St.
Louisville, KY 40203

628
Earl J. Small Growers, Inc. Scholarships

AMOUNT: Maximum: $2000 DEADLINE: April 1
FIELDS/MAJORS: Horticulture

Two scholarships for students in four-year college or university programs in horticulture, with emphasis on greenhouse production. Applicants must be undergraduates and citizens of the U.S. or Canada. Write to the address below for details. The BPFI also sponsors two awards through Future Farmers of America (check with your FFA advisor).

Bedding Plants Foundation, Inc.
Scholarship Program
PO Box 27241
Lansing, MI 48909

629
Earl P. Andrews, Jr. Memorial Scholarship

AMOUNT: $500-$1000 DEADLINE: April 1
FIELDS/MAJORS: All Areas of Study

Open to a minority student based on academic achievement and need. Applicant must have a minimum ACT score of 23 (or SAT equivalent) and a 3.5 GPA. High school transcript and essay outlining career goals are required. Finalists will have a personal interview with the selection committee. Contact the address listed or call (334) 264-6223 for further information.

Central Alabama Community Foundation
412 N. Hull St.
PO Box 11587
Montgomery, AL 36111

630
Earl Warren Legal Training Program General Scholarships

AMOUNT: $3000-$4500 DEADLINE: March 15
FIELDS/MAJORS: Law

Scholarships for entering African-American law students. Preference is given to applicants who express an interest in civil rights or in public interest litigation. Must be a U.S. citizen. Applications are available after November 15. Twenty to twenty-five awards are offered annually. Write to the address below for further information.

Earl Warren Legal Training Program, Inc.
99 Hudson St., Suite 1600
New York, NY 10013

631
East European Research Fellowships

AMOUNT: $15000-$25000 DEADLINE: October 31
FIELDS/MAJORS: Social Sciences and Humanities

Open to doctoral candidates for dissertation research or writing and Ph.D. scholars who provide evidence of degree, field of specialization, research proposal, and project duration. U.S. citizenship or legal residency required. ACLS supports research in the humanities and the humanistic aspects of the social sciences. Fellowships will last for at least six months outside of East Europe. Write to the address listed for complete details.

American Council of Learned Societies
Office of Fellowships and Grants
228 E. 45th St.
New York, NY 10017

632
Easter Seal Society of Iowa Scholarship

AMOUNT: None Specified   DEADLINE: April 15
FIELDS/MAJORS: Rehabilitation

Open to full-time sophomores, juniors, seniors, and graduate students planning a career in the field of rehabilitation. Must be able to demonstrate financial need. Contact the address listed for more information.

Easter Seal Society of Iowa, Inc.
Scholarship Program
PO Box 4002
Des Moines, IA 50333

633
Easter Seal Society of Iowa Scholarships

AMOUNT: $400-$600   DEADLINE: April 15
FIELDS/MAJORS: Rehabilitation/Related Fields

Scholarships for Iowa residents majoring in physical or psychological rehabilitation. For full-time study. Must have a GPA of at least 2.8 and show financial need. Open to college sophomores through graduate students. Six awards per year. Renewable. Write to the address below for details. Application forms are available after January 1 of each year.

Easter Seal Society of Iowa, Inc.
PO Box 4002
Des Moines, IA 50333

634
Eastern Shore Assistance Program

AMOUNT: None Specified   DEADLINE: July 5
FIELDS/MAJORS: All Areas of Study

Awards are available for juniors and seniors who are Virginia residents living in Northampton or Accomack counties and are commuting to the University of Maryland, Eastern Shore, or Salisbury State College. Information is available at the Maryland institutions, or applicants can write to the address listed.

Virginia Council of Higher Education
James Monroe Building
101 North 14th St.
Richmond, VA 23219

635
EBSCO/NMRT Scholarship

AMOUNT: $1000   DEADLINE: December 1
FIELDS/MAJORS: Library and Information Science

Applicants must be ALA/NMRT members who are entering an ALA-accredited master's program or beyond. Must be U.S. or Canadian citizens. Write to NMRT scholarship committee chair, at the address below for details.

California Institute of Technology Library
Pamela Padley, Ca. Tech. Library System
Mail Code 1-32.
Pasadena, CA 91125

636
Ecole Des Chartes Exchange Fellowship

AMOUNT: None Specified   DEADLINE: None Specified
FIELDS/MAJORS: Archival Paleography, Bibliography, History of the Book

Awards provide a monthly stipend and tuition for a graduate student to study at the Ecole Nationale Des Chartes in Paris for up to three months. Applicants must be U.S. citizens and doctoral candidates at any of the consortium schools. Contact the address listed for further information or call (312) 255-3666.

Newberry Library
Committee on Awards-Renaissance Studies
60 W. Walton St.
Chicago, IL 60610

637
Economic Assistance Loans

AMOUNT: None Specified   DEADLINE: None Specified
FIELDS/MAJORS: All Areas of Study

Educational loans for residents of Wisconsin who are veterans or surviving spouses and minor dependent children of deceased eligible veterans, who have not remarried. Loans are also available for purchase of property, debt consolidation, medical expenses, and more. Unspecified number of loans per year. Contact your county veterans service office, listed in your telephone directory under "county government."

Wisconsin Department of Veterans Affairs
PO Box 7843
30 West Mifflin St.
Madison, WI 53707

638
Ed Bradley and Carole Simpson Scholarships

AMOUNT: $2000-$5000   DEADLINE: March 2
FIELDS/MAJORS: Broadcast, Electronic Journalism

Open to minority undergraduates seeking a career in electronic journalism. Must have at least one full year of college remaining. Based on examples of reporting or producing skills on audio or VHS cassettes accompanied by scripts. Previous RTNDF winners are not eligible. Winners will be notified by May 15. Write to the address listed for details.

Radio and Television News Directors Foundation, Inc.
RTNDF Scholarships
1000 Connecticut Ave. NW, Suite 615
Washington, DC 20036

639
Ed E. and Gladys Hurley Foundation Grants

AMOUNT: Maximum: $1000   DEADLINE: May 31
FIELDS/MAJORS: Religion/Theology

Grants available to students who wish to study toward the ministry or other aspects of Protestantism. To support students who, along with their families, are unable to afford such an education. For use at any accredited college or university. Loans are also available for students who are residents of Louisiana, Arkansas, or Texas. Contact Margarie Rays at the address listed for further information or call (318) 226-2110. Must include a SASE for a reply.

Ed E. and Gladys Hurley Foundation
C/O First National Bank of Shreveport
PO Box 21116
Shreveport, LA 71154

640
Ed Taylor Memorial Scholarship Award

AMOUNT: $1000   DEADLINE: June 1
FIELDS/MAJORS: Agriculture

Scholarships are available to agricultural studies students who are studying at Cal Poly or San Luis Obispo College. Write to the address listed or call (714) 863-9028 for more information.

Western Growers Association
Scholarship Fund
PO Box 2130
Newport Beach, CA 92658

641
Eddie Vega Fund

AMOUNT: None Specified   DEADLINE: April 1
FIELDS/MAJORS: Technical Fields, Martial Arts

Scholarships are available for residents of Bridgeport, Easton, Fairfield, Milford, Monroe, Shelton, Stratford, Trumbull, and Westport who will be enrolled as entering college freshmen in the above areas of study. One award is offered annually. Write to the address below for additional information.

Greater Bridgeport Area Foundation
280 State St.
Bridgeport, CT 06604

642
Eddy/Peck Scholarships

AMOUNT: $1000-$2500   DEADLINE: April 13
FIELDS/MAJORS: Journalism

Scholarships are available for Connecticut residents or students attending a Connecticut college or university and majoring in journalism. For students who will be entering their junior or senior year. Three awards offered annually. The journalism department at your college may have details on this award. If not, write to the address listed or call (203) 255-4561 for details.

Connecticut Society of Professional Journalists Foundation
Debra A. Estock, Scholarship Committee
71 Kenwood Ave.
Fairfield, CT 06430

643
Edilia De Montequin Fellowship

AMOUNT: Maximum: $1000   DEADLINE: December 15
FIELDS/MAJORS: Spanish, Portuguese, or Ibero-American Architectural History

Awards available are intended to support junior scholars, including graduate students, but senior scholars may apply. Research proposal must focus on any of the areas listed above. Applicants must have been a member of the Society of Architectural Historians for at least one year before applying. Write to the address listed for more information.

Society of Architectural Historians
1365 North Astor St.
Chicago, IL 60610

644
Edison Int'l. Community College Achievement Awards

AMOUNT: Maximum: $6000
DEADLINE: March 3
FIELDS/MAJORS: Science-Applied, Earth, Physical, Education, Mathematics

Open to transferring community college students who are California residents pursuing a degree in secondary teaching of math or science. Must be a minority or economically or physically disadvantaged and a customer of Southern California Edison. These one-time awards are for use in junior year at a California school. Based on test scores, financial need, and an interview. Contact the address listed for further information or call (818) 302-3503. Must have a GPA of at least 2.8.

Edison International
Scholarship Coordinator
PO Box 800
Rosemead, CA 91770-0800

645
Edith Grace Reynolds Estate Residuary Trust Grants

AMOUNT: Maximum: $1764   DEADLINE: February 15
FIELDS/MAJORS: All Areas of Study

Open to graduates of School District 1, Rensselaer County, New York. Eight to nine awards offered annually, averaging $1764 per award. Contact Michelle Cardillo, Trust Officer, at the address listed for further information or call (518) 486-8500.

Edith Grace Reynolds Estate Residuary Trust
C/O Key Trust Company
PO Box 1965
Albany, NY 12201

646
Edith H. Henderson Scholarship

AMOUNT: Maximum: $1000   DEADLINE: March 31
FIELDS/MAJORS: Landscape Architecture/Design

Open to students enrolled in a landscape architect or design program. Must be enrolled/have participated in a public speaking or creative writing class. A two hundred to four hundred word essay will be required. Write to the address listed for additional information or call (202) 686-8337. Must have a GPA of at least 2.7.

Landscape Architecture Foundation
Scholarship Program
4401 Connecticut Ave. NW, #500
Washington, DC 20008

647
Edmond A. Metzger Scholarship

AMOUNT: $500   DEADLINE: February 1
FIELDS/MAJORS: Electrical Engineering

Scholarship available to students with a novice class amateur radio license who are residents of: Illinois, Indiana, or Wisconsin and attend school in their home state. Must be a member of AARL. For full-time study. Write to the address listed for information.

ARRL Foundation (American Radio Relay League)
Scholarship Program
225 Main St.
Newington, CT 06111

648
Edmund F. Maxwell Scholarships

AMOUNT: Maximum: $3500   DEADLINE: April 30
FIELDS/MAJORS: All Areas of Study

Scholarships for entering freshmen from Washington, particularly the Seattle area, who have a combined SAT score of over 1200. Based on financial need and academics. Write to the address listed for more information. Must have a GPA of at least 3.0.

Edmund F. Maxwell Foundation
Scholarship Coordinator
PO Box 22537
Seattle, WA 98122

649
Edna Aimes Scholarship

AMOUNT: $2000   DEADLINE: March 16
FIELDS/MAJORS: Mental Health

Open to juniors, seniors, and matriculated graduate students in New York State, preparing for a career in mental health to assist in the prevention and treatment of mental illnesses, the promotion of mental health, and the empowerment of adults, children and families whose lives have been affected by mental illnesses. Applicants must be New York residents and be able to demonstrate financial need. Previous recipients of an Edna Aimes Scholarship are not eligible to apply. Contact the address listed for further information or call (518) 434-0439.

Mental Health Association in New York State, Inc.
Edna Aimes Scholarship Committee
169 Central Ave.
Albany, NY 12206

650
Edna Meudt Memorial Scholarship

AMOUNT: $500 DEADLINE: February 1
FIELDS/MAJORS: Poetry

Awards open to juniors or seniors at any accredited college or university. Must submit ten original poems that are judged on or before March 1. Recipients will be announced after April 1. State organizations will be advertising and making available applications and information.

National Federation of State Poetry Societies (NFSPS)
Pj Doyle, NFSPS Scholarship Committee
4242 Stevens
Minneapolis, MN 55409

651
Edna Yelland Memorial Scholarship

AMOUNT: $2000 DEADLINE: May 31
FIELDS/MAJORS: Library Science

Applicants must be a member of an ethnic minority group who is pursuing a graduate library degree in library or information sciences. Must be U.S. citizen or permanent resident and California resident. For study in a master's program at a California library school. Must be able to demonstrate financial need. Request an application form and further information from the address below.

California Library Association
Scholarship Committee
717 K St., Suite 300
Sacramento, CA 95814

652
Education and Health and Human Services Employee Gift-Matching Program

AMOUNT: Maximum: $5000 DEADLINE: None Specified
FIELDS/MAJORS: All Areas of Study

Company matches, (on a two to one basis), up to an annual maximum of $5,000 for each employee gift to a qualified educational institution. Write to the address below for more information.

American Standard Companies Inc.
Corporate Headquarters
One Centennial Ave.
Piscataway, NJ 08855

653
Education and Research Trust Faculty Development Award

AMOUNT: None Specified DEADLINE: January 12
FIELDS/MAJORS: Allergy/Immunology Medical Research

Grants for M.D. members of the American Academy of Allergy and Immunology (or persons who are awaiting acceptance into the academy) who are junior faculty members (either instructors, assistant professors, or equivalent). Applicants must be U.S. or Canadian citizens or permanent residents. Write to the address listed or call (414) 272-6071 for details.

American Academy of Allergy and Immunology
Jerome Schultz
611 E. Wells St.
Milwaukee, WI 53202

654
Education Incentive Loan Forgiveness Program

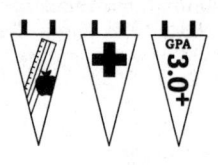

AMOUNT: None Specified DEADLINE: None Specified
FIELDS/MAJORS: Nursing, Education

Forgivable loan program for current or recent (within two years) Idaho high school graduates who wish to pursue a career in either nursing or teaching. Must be an Idaho resident, enrolled in an Idaho school, and agree to work in Idaho for at least two years after graduation. Must have (have had) a minimum GPA of 3.0. Write to the address listed for information.

Idaho State Board of Education
PO Box 83720
Boise, ID 83720

655
Educational Advancement Scholarships and Grants

AMOUNT: $1500 DEADLINE: May 15
FIELDS/MAJORS: Nursing

Applicant must be a registered nurse and a current AACN member who has junior status in an NIN-accredited program. GPA of 3.0 and current employment or employment in last three years as a critical care nurse is required. Write to address below for more information. American Association of Critical Care Nurses has several other scholarships and grants available.

American Association of Critical Care Nurses
Educational Advancement Scholarships
101 Columbia
Aliso Viejo, CA 92656

656

Educational Award

AMOUNT: $500-$1500   DEADLINE: April 21
FIELDS/MAJORS: All Areas of Study

Scholarships for students who are graduating high school seniors or other persons enrolling full-time in postsecondary schools for the first time. Must be a U.S. citizen who resides in one of twenty-two boroughs or townships in Bucks County. Write to the address below for more information.

A. Marlyn Moyer, Jr. Scholarship Foundation
409 Hood Blvd.
Fairless Hills, PA 19030

657

Educational Benefits for Children of Deceased Veterans and Others

AMOUNT: None Specified   DEADLINE: April 15
FIELDS/MAJORS: All Areas of Study

Program for Delaware residents who are children of deceased military veterans or police officers whose cause of death was service related. Renewable. Selections based on financial need. Commission makes final awards July 1. Write to the address listed for more information.

Delaware Higher Education Commission
Carvel State Office Building
820 North French St., #4F
Wilmington, DE 19801

658

Educational Foundation Scholarships

AMOUNT: $1250-$2000   DEADLINE: April 25
FIELDS/MAJORS: Real Estate and Related Fields

Scholarships available to New Jersey residents who are high school seniors planning to attend a four-year school, current undergraduates, and graduates studying real estate. Must be a member of NJAR or a relative of a member. Sixteen awards are offered annually. Interviews held in June, recipients announced shortly thereafter. Write to the address listed for details.

New Jersey Association of Realtors
Educational Foundation Scholarships
PO Box 2098
Edison, NJ 08818

659

Educational Foundation Trust Fund Loans

AMOUNT: $500-$5000   DEADLINE: None Specified
FIELDS/MAJORS: Pharmacy

Loans are available to students in their last two years of pharmacy school in the state of California who plan to pursue their career in the state. Applicants must be U.S. citizens and members of the Academy of Students of Pharmacy chapter at their school. Write to the address listed for more details.

California Pharmacists Association
CPHA Educational Foundation
1112 I St., Suite 300
Sacramento, CA 95814

660

Educational Opportunity Grant

AMOUNT: Maximum: $2500   DEADLINE: None Specified
FIELDS/MAJORS: All Areas of Study

Scholarship program for undergraduate students who have completed their associate degree and wish to pursue their education in a Washington state college or university. Must demonstrate financial need. Write to the address below for information.

Washington Higher Education Coordinating Board
917 Lakeridge Way
PO Box 43430
Olympia, WA 98504

661

Edward Bangs Kelley and Elza Kelley Foundation Scholarships

AMOUNT: None Specified   DEADLINE: None Specified
FIELDS/MAJORS: Healthcare, Medicine

Applicants must be residents of Barnstable County, Massachusetts, whose education will benefit the health and welfare of the communities of the Cape and Islands. Write to the address below for details.

Edward Bangs Kelley and Elza Kelley Foundation
Lock Drawer M
243 South St.
Hyannis, MA 02601

662
Edward C. and Mary Marth Scholarship

AMOUNT: None Specified DEADLINE: March 15
FIELDS/MAJORS: Nursing or Allied Field

Open to seniors graduating from St. Mary's High School in Westfield. Must be planning to attend college or technical school for nursing or an allied field. Contact the address listed for further information.

Community Foundation of Western Massachusetts
PO Box 15769
1500 Main St.
Springfield, MA 01115

663
Edward D. Stone Jr. and Associates Minority Scholarship

AMOUNT: Maximum: $1000 DEADLINE: March 31
FIELDS/MAJORS: Landscape Architecture/Design

Open to minority students in the last two years of undergraduate study. An essay and slides/pictures of applicant's best work will be required. Write to the address listed for details or call (202) 686-8337.

Landscape Architecture Foundation
Scholarship Program
4401 Connecticut Ave. NW, #500
Washington, DC 20008

664
Edward Henderson Student Award

AMOUNT: $500 DEADLINE: December 8
FIELDS/MAJORS: Geriatrics

Award available for a student who has demonstrated a commitment to the field of geriatrics through: leadership in areas pertinent to geriatrics, initiation of new information or programs in geriatrics, or scholarship in geriatrics through original research or reviews. Applicants must be nominated by one faculty member with at least two supporting letters from other faculty. Write to the address listed for more information.

American Geriatrics Society
770 Lexington Ave., Suite 300
New York, NY 10021

665
Edward Leon Duhamel Scholarship

AMOUNT: $500-$1500 DEADLINE: March 1
FIELDS/MAJORS: All Areas of Study

Scholarships are available for the direct descendants of the Franklin Lodge #20 of the Freemasons in Westerly. Write to the address listed for information.

Franklin Lodge
Secretary
PO Box 116
Westerly, RI 02891

666
Edwin G. and Lauretta M. Michael Scholarship

AMOUNT: None Specified DEADLINE: March 15
FIELDS/MAJORS: All Areas of Study

Open to minister's wives who are members of the Christian Church (Disciples of Christ). Must have at least a 2.3 GPA. For full-time study. Write to the address below for details.

Christian Church (Disciples of Christ)
Attn: Scholarships
PO Box 1986
Indianapolis, IN 46206

667
Edwin T. Pratt Memorial Scholarship

AMOUNT: None Specified DEADLINE: None Specified
FIELDS/MAJORS: All Areas of Study

Open to African-Americans who reside in King County and have a high school diploma (or equivalent). Must be planning to enroll or currently enrolled in a vocational, two-, or four-year college in Washington state. Applications available after February 1. Contact the address below for further information. Must included a SASE for a reply.

Urban League of Metropolitan Seattle
Ms. Terry Marsh
105 Fourteenth Ave.
Seattle, WA 98122

668
EEA-Ship Undergraduate Scholarship in Technology Education

AMOUNT: Maximum: $1000   DEADLINE: December 1
FIELDS/MAJORS: Technology Education

Scholarship for members (at least one year) of the International Technology Education Association who are preparing for a career in teaching. Applicant must not be a senior by application deadline. Must have a GPA of 2.5 or greater. Write to "Undergraduate Scholarship" at the address listed for details.

International Technology Education Association
Tom Hughes
1914 Association Dr.
Reston, VA 22091

669
Eileen C. Maddex Fellowship

AMOUNT: Maximum: $2000   DEADLINE: April 1
FIELDS/MAJORS: Home Economics/Related Fields

Applicants must be members of Kappa Omicron Nu and a master's candidate. Awards will be announced May 15. Write to the address listed for details.

Kappa Omicron Nu Honor Society
4990 Northwind Dr., Suite 140
East Lansing, MI 48823

670
Eileen J. Garrett Research Scholarship Award

AMOUNT: Maximum: $3000   DEADLINE: July 15
FIELDS/MAJORS: Parapsychology

Scholarship for undergraduate or graduate students in parapsychology attending an accredited college or university. For persons studying parapsychology directly (not those with merely a general interest in the field). Write to the address below for details.

Parapsychology Foundation, Inc.
Eileen J. Garrett Library
228 E. 71st St.
New York, NY 10021

671
Einar and Eva Lund Haugen Dissertation Scholarship

AMOUNT: $3000   DEADLINE: March 1
FIELDS/MAJORS: Arts, Humanities, Social Sciences

Open to outstanding doctoral candidates who have completed pre-dissertation requirements within the preceding year. The dissertation shall treat a Scandinavian or Scandinavian-American topic. Based on evaluation of the applicant's academic record, three references, thesis proposal work plan, and future professional goals. Awards are usually made in the month of April. Contact the address listed for further information. There are no application forms; direct applications, together with the above described documents, must be received by March 1. Must have a GPA of at least 3.2.

Norwegian-American Historical Society
Chairman, Haugen Scholarship Committee
1510 St. Olaf Ave.
Northfield, MN 55057-1097

672
Eleanor Roosevelt Teacher Fellowships

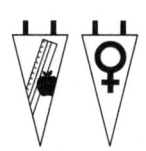

AMOUNT: $1000-$10000   DEADLINE: January 12
FIELDS/MAJORS: Elementary and Secondary School Teaching

The teacher fellowships are designed for elementary and secondary school teachers who are seeking to advance gender equity in the classroom, increase their effectiveness at teaching math and science to girls, and/or tailor their teaching to the needs of minority students and girls at the risk of dropping out. Fellowships available only to female teachers. Applicants must be U.S. citizens or permanent residents, teach full-time at U.S. public schools in grades K-12, have at least five consecutive years full-time teaching experience, and plan to continue teaching for the next five years. Write to the address listed for more information.

American Association of University Women Educational Foundation
2201 N. Dodge St.
Iowa City, IA 52243

673
Elenore M. Francisco Educational Trust Fund Loan

AMOUNT: Maximum: $2500   DEADLINE: None Specified
FIELDS/MAJORS: All Areas of Study

Loan program for graduating seniors of Union County High School in Kentucky. Current rate for loan is 4.755%.

Applicants must maintain a GPA of 2.0. Renewable. Write to the address below for more information.

Morganfield National Bank
Trust Department
PO Box 390
Morganfield, KY 42437

674
Elie Wiesel Prize in Ethics

AMOUNT: $500-$5000   **DEADLINE:** January 22
FIELDS/MAJORS: All Areas of Study

Awards are available to five winners of this annual essay contest. Open to juniors and seniors, the essay theme must be creating an ethical society: personal responsibility and the common good. Should be between three thousand and four thousand words. The prizes are two at $500, one at $1500, one at $2500, and one at $5000. Must be enrolled in a four-year accredited college or university. Contact the address listed for information or call (212) 221-1100. If writing, you must include a SASE for a reply. Must have a GPA of at least 2.8.

Elie Wiesel Foundation for Humanity
Elie Wiesel Prize in Ethics
450 Lexington Ave., #1920
New York, NY 10017

675
Elisabeth M. and Winchell M. Parsons Scholarship

AMOUNT: Maximum: $1500   **DEADLINE:** February 15
FIELDS/MAJORS: Mechanical Engineering

Applicants must be studying toward a doctorate in mechanical engineering. Must be ASME members and U.S. citizens. Write to the address listed for details. Please be certain to enclose a SASE with your request.

American Society of Mechanical Engineers Auxiliary, Inc.
Mrs. Michael G. Snyder
102 Meadow Ridge Dr.
Lynchburg, VA 24503-3829

676
Elizabeth Benson Scholarships

AMOUNT: None Specified   **DEADLINE:** May 1
FIELDS/MAJORS: Interpreting, Transliterating (deaf)

Scholarship for members of the Registry of Interpreters for the Deaf (both the national and affiliate). For full-time study in an interpreting-transliterating preparation program (IPP). Must have a GPA of at least 3.0. and have completed at least two semesters by June 30 of the award year. Award is made at the biannual convention of RID. Write to the address below for details.

Registry of Interpreters for the Deaf, Inc., National Office
Elizabeth Benson Scholarships
8630 Fenton St., #324
Silver Spring, MD 20910

677
Ellen Setterfield Memorial Scholarship

AMOUNT: $3000-$10000   **DEADLINE:** March 31
FIELDS/MAJORS: Social Sciences

Open to legally blind students studying any of the social sciences on the graduate level. Write to the address below for complete details.

National Federation of the Blind
Mrs. Peggy Elliott, Chairman
814 Fifth Ave., Suite 200
Grinnell, IA 50112

678
Ellice T. Johnston Scholarship

AMOUNT: $1000   **DEADLINE:** July 1
FIELDS/MAJORS: Ceramic Art

Renewable scholarship, awarded twice annually, for Oregon or Northern California residents or students. Need is considered but not necessary. Clayfolk members are not eligible. Based on portfolio review. Applicants must have two years of art classes or the equivalent. Write to the address below for details.

Clayfolk
PO Box 274
Talent, OR 97540

679
Elmer H. Schmitz Memorial Scholarship

AMOUNT: Maximum: $350   **DEADLINE:** June 2
FIELDS/MAJORS: All Areas of Study

Awards for undergraduates who are initiated members of Tau Kappa Epsilon and from the state of Wisconsin. Applicants must have demonstrated leadership within his campus, chapter, or the community. Must have a GPA of at least 2.5 and be enrolled in full-time study. Write to the address listed for more information.

TKE Educational Foundation
8645 Founders Road
Indianapolis, IN 46268

680
Eloise Campbell Scholarship

AMOUNT: None Specified   DEADLINE: None Specified
FIELDS/MAJORS: All Areas of Study

Awards for female students from Bowie County, Texas, or Miller County, Arkansas. Must be a member or dependent of a member of the United Daughters of the Confederacy or the Children of the Confederacy. Contact your local chapter of the UDC or write to the address below for more information.

United Daughters of the Confederacy
Education Committee
328 North Ave.
Richmond, VA 23220

681
Elsa Everette Memorial Scholarship

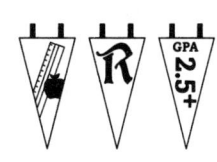

AMOUNT: None Specified   DEADLINE: June 1
FIELDS/MAJORS: Christian Ministry, Education

Open to students from the First Presbyterian Church who are studying for the ministry or Christian education work. Must be from Tulsa, Oklahoma. Write to the address listed for more information. Must have a GPA of at least 2.5.

First Presbyterian Church
Scholarship Fund Program
709 S. Boston Ave.
Tulsa, OK 74119

682
Elsevier Research Initiative Awards

AMOUNT: $25000   DEADLINE: January 9
FIELDS/MAJORS: Gastroenterology Research, Related Fields

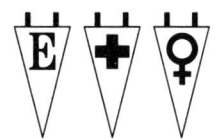

Awards for investigators who possess an M.D. or Ph.D. (or equivalent) and hold faculty positions at universities or institutions. Applicants must also be members of any of the ADHF organizations. Women and minorities are encouraged to apply. Awards to assist reaching career goal of research. Contact the address below for further information or Web sites: http://www.gastro.org; http://asge.org; or http://hepar-sfgh.ucsf.edu.

American Digestive Health Foundation
Ms. Irene Kuo
7910 Woodmont Ave., 7th Floor
Bethesda, MD 20814

683
Elvin S. Douglas, Jr. Scholarship

AMOUNT: None Specified   DEADLINE: April 20
FIELDS/MAJORS: Healthcare, Medicine

Scholarships for Cass County, Missouri residents who are studying in a health-related field. Based on ability, motivation, continuing good progress, and financial need. Write to the committee at the address listed for details.

Elvin S. Douglas, Jr. Scholarship Committee
Linda Wheeler, Chair
PO Box 566
Harrisonville, MO 64701

684
Emanuel Sternberger Educational Fund Loans

AMOUNT: None Specified   DEADLINE: April 30
FIELDS/MAJORS: All Areas of Study

For residents of North Carolina who are entering junior or senior year of college or in graduate school. Loans are renewable. Write to the address below for complete details.

Emanuel Sternberger Educational Fund
Office of the Trustee
PO Box 1735
Greensboro, NC 27402

685
Emblem Club Scholarship Grants

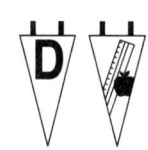

AMOUNT: None Specified   DEADLINE: None Specified
FIELDS/MAJORS: Special Education, Particularly of Deaf and Hearing Impaired

For students enrolled in/accepted to a participating master's degree program that provides training for teachers of deaf and hearing impaired persons. Applicants must be full-time students under the age of fifty with the intention of teaching in the U.S. Students studying special education in other areas will also be considered. Write to the address listed for complete details.

Emblem Club Scholarship Foundation
PO Box 712
San Luis Rey, CA 92068

686

Emergency Aid and Health Professions Scholarships

AMOUNT: $50-$300   DEADLINE: None Specified
FIELDS/MAJORS: All Areas of Study

Scholarships are available for undergraduate Native American or Alaskan Indian full-time undergraduates. Based on financial need, and limited by the availability of scholarship funds. Applicants must be minimally one-quarter degree Indian blood from a federally recognized tribe. Scholarships are available from September 1 through June 1 of the academic year. Write to the address listed for details.

Association on American Indian Affairs, Inc.
Box 268
Sisseton, SD 57262

687

Emergency Educational Fund Grant

AMOUNT: None Specified   DEADLINE: None Specified
FIELDS/MAJORS: All Areas of Study

Assistance is available to undergraduate students who are children of deceased or totally incapacitated Elks. Applicants must be U.S. citizens, unmarried, and under the age of twenty-three. For full-time study at any U.S. college or university. Contact BPO Elks Lodge where your parent was/is a member for more information. Applications must be filed between June 1 and December 31. See their Web site for additional information: http://www.elks.org/enf/enf_scholar.cfm

Elks National Foundation
Scholarship Coordinator
2750 N. Lakeview Ave.
Chicago, IL 60614

688

Emergency Secondary Education Loan

AMOUNT: Maximum: $2500   DEADLINE: April 1
FIELDS/MAJORS: Education

Scholarships open to full-time undergraduates or graduate students pursuing a secondary education teaching certification at an approved Arkansas school. Applicant must be an Arkansas resident. Repayment of loan is forgiven at 20% for each year taught in approved subject shortage areas in Arkansas secondary schools after graduation. Write to the address below for details.

Arkansas Department of Higher Education
Financial Aid Division
114 East Capitol
Little Rock, AR 72201

689

Emilia Polak Scholarship

AMOUNT: Maximum: $500   DEADLINE: February 15
FIELDS/MAJORS: Agriculture, Roman Catholic Divinity

One award is given to a Rhode Island resident of Polish-American descent studying agriculture or planning to enroll in Roman Catholic Divinity School. Write to the address listed or call (401) 831-7177 for more information.

Rhode Island Polonia Scholarship Foundation
Foundation Office
866 Atwells Ave.
Providence, RI 02909

690

Emily Chaison Gold Award Scholarship

AMOUNT: Maximum: $500   DEADLINE: April 30
FIELDS/MAJORS: All Areas of Study

Open to high school seniors who are Connecticut residents, registered Girl Scouts, and Gold Award recipients. Selection based on community service and commitment to Girl Scouting. Contact the address listed for further information.

Six Girl Scout Councils in Connecticut
Ms. Eileen Lawlor
529 Danbury Rd.
Wilton, CT 06897

691

ENA Foundation Doctoral Scholarship

AMOUNT: Maximum: $4500   DEADLINE: April 1
FIELDS/MAJORS: Nursing

Scholarship is for a nurse pursuing a doctoral degree. Write to the address below for more information.

Emergency Nurses Association (ENA) Foundation
Funding Program
216 Higgins Rd.
Park Ridge, IL 60068

692

ENA Foundation Research Grant

AMOUNT: Maximum: $10000   DEADLINE: June 1
FIELDS/MAJORS: Nursing

Scholarship is for nurses to advance their specialized practice of emergency nursing. Write to the address below for more information.

Emergency Nurses Association (ENA) Foundation
Funding Program
216 Higgins Rd.
Park Ridge, IL 60068

693
ENA Foundation Special Project/Program Development Grants

AMOUNT: Maximum: $2000 DEADLINE: June 1
FIELDS/MAJORS: Nursing

Scholarship is for nurses to enhance the care of emergency patients. Write to the address below for more information.

Emergency Nurses Association (ENA) Foundation
Funding Program
216 Higgins Rd.
Park Ridge, IL 60068

694
ENA Foundation Undergraduate Scholarship

AMOUNT: Maximum: $2000 DEADLINE: April 1
FIELDS/MAJORS: Nursing

Open to nurses pursuing undergraduate degrees in nursing. Three awards offered annually. Write to the address below for more information.

Emergency Nurses Association (ENA) Foundation
Funding Program
216 Higgins Rd.
Park Ridge, IL 60068

695
ENA Foundation/Emergency Medicine Foundation Team Research Grant

AMOUNT: Maximum: $10000 DEADLINE: February 20
FIELDS/MAJORS: Medicine, Nursing

Scholarship is for physicians and nurses to improve clinical research in emergency care. Contact Emergency Medicine Foundation, PO Box 619911, Dallas, TX 75261-9911 for more information.

Emergency Nurses Association (ENA) Foundation
Funding Program
216 Higgins Rd.
Park Ridge, IL 60068

696
ENA Foundation/ Sigma Theta Tau Joint Research Grant

AMOUNT: Maximum: $6000 DEADLINE: March 1
FIELDS/MAJORS: Nursing

Scholarship is for emergency nurses advancing their specialized practice. Write to the address below for more information.

Emergency Nurses Association (ENA) Foundation
Funding Program
216 Higgins Rd.
Park Ridge, IL 60068

697
Endoscopic Research Awards

AMOUNT: $25000 DEADLINE: September 3
FIELDS/MAJORS: Endoscopic Research

Candidates must be M.D.'s currently in a gastroenterology-related and endoscopic practice in institutions or private practice. Awards will be made to individual members or to trainees sponsored by an individual member of the ADHF partner societies. Contact the address below for further information or Web sites: http://www.gastro.org; http://asge.org; or http://hepar-sfgh.uscf.edu.

American Digestive Health Foundation
Ms. Irene Kuo
7910 Woodmont Ave., 7th Floor
Bethesda, MD 20814

698
Energy Research Summer Fellowships

AMOUNT: Maximum: $3000 DEADLINE: January 1
FIELDS/MAJORS: Electrochemistry and Related Fields

Open to graduate students enrolled in a college or university in the U.S. or Canada. Applicants must be studying a field related to the objectives of the Electrochemical Society. May be renewed. This program is supported by the U.S. Department of Energy. Five awards offered annually. Contact the address listed for more information or call (609) 737-1902.

Electrochemical Society, Inc.
Scholarship Coordinator
10 S. Main St.
Pennington, NJ 08534

699
Engineering Dissertation Fellowships

AMOUNT: Maximum: $14500 DEADLINE: November 17
FIELDS/MAJORS: Engineering

Fellowships are available to those women who have successfully completed all required course work and exams by November 17. Awards are to be used for the final year of doctoral work. Fellowships cannot cover tuition for additional course work. Degree should be received at the end of the award year. Fellow is expected to devote full-time to the project during the award year. Write to the address listed for more information.

American Association of University Women Educational
  Foundation
2201 N. Dodge St.
Iowa City, IA 52243

700
Engineering Scholarships for Minority High School Seniors

AMOUNT: $500-$1000 DEADLINE: March 1
FIELDS/MAJORS: Engineering

Scholarships are for Hispanic-American and African-American high school seniors who are in the top quarter of their class and have at least a 3.0 GPA. Must be U.S. citizens and plan to study engineering. Contact the address below for further information.

National Society of Professional Engineers Education
  Foundation
1420 King St.
Alexandria, VA 22314

701
Enid Hall Griswold Memorial Scholarship

AMOUNT: Maximum: $1000 DEADLINE: February 15
FIELDS/MAJORS: Political Science, Government, History, Economics

Open to juniors or seniors in a four-year school. Applicants must be U.S. citizens and obtain a letter of sponsorship from a local DAR chapter. These awards are not renewable. The number of awards is unspecified. Contact your local chapter or send a SASE to the address listed for more information.

National Society Daughters of the American Revolution
NSDAR Scholarship Committee
1776 D St. NW
Washington, DC 20006

702
Environmental Protection Scholarships

AMOUNT: None Specified DEADLINE: February 15
FIELDS/MAJORS: Chemistry, Civil/Chemical Engineering, Geology, Agronomy, Soil Science

Contractual scholarships for full-time students from junior through graduate level. Students must agree to work full-time for the Kentucky National Resources and Environmental Protection Cabinet after graduation. Must have good academic standing and a letter of recommendation from a faculty advisor. An essay will also be required. Write to the address listed for details. Must have a GPA of at least 2.8.

Kentucky Water Resources Research Institute
Scholarship Program Coordinator
233 Mining and Mineral Resources
Lexington, KY 40506

703
Environmental Toxicology and Chemistry (SETAC) Fellowship

AMOUNT: $15000 DEADLINE: September 1
FIELDS/MAJORS: Environmental Chemistry and Toxicology

Awards are available for predoctoral students pursuing dissertation research in the areas of environmental chemistry or toxicology. Write to the address below for more information.

Society of Environmental Toxicology and Chemistry
Mr. Rodney Parrish, Executive Director
1010 North 12th Ave.
Pensacola, FL 32501

704
EPA Environmental Science and Engineering Fellowships

AMOUNT: Maximum: $43000
DEADLINE: January 15
FIELDS/MAJORS: Engineering, Environmental, and Conservational Sciences

Applicants must have Ph.D. or equivalent degrees. Persons with master's degrees in engineering and three years professional experience also qualify. Recipients spend one year working as special assistant for the EPA. Program begins in September. Must demonstrate exceptional competence in the areas of environmental sciences or engineering and have some interest in applying personal knowledge toward the solution of global conservation efforts. Minority and disabled students encouraged to apply. Must be U.S. citizens. Federal employees are not eligible. Contact the address listed or call (202) 326-6760 for more details.

American Association for the Advancement of Science
Fellowships Program
1200 New York Ave. NW
Washington, DC 20005

705
Equine Scholarship

AMOUNT: None Specified   DEADLINE: July 1
FIELDS/MAJORS: All Areas of Study

Open to West Virginia high school seniors and undergraduates who must have been properly recognized entrants in previous State Fair of West Virginia Open Horse Shows. Recommendations from principals, counselors, or advisors will be considered along with academic ability. Contact the address below for further information.

State Fair of West Virginia
Manager, State Fair of West Virginia
PO Drawer 986
Lewisburg, WV 24901

706
Eric and Bette Friedheim, H. Neil Mecaskey, and Treadway Scholarships

AMOUNT: Maximum: $500   DEADLINE: April 15
FIELDS/MAJORS: Travel and Tourism, Hotel/Motel Management

Awards for juniors or seniors in one of the areas listed above who are enrolled in a four-year college full-time. Must have a GPA of 3.0 or better. For study anywhere in North America. Write to the address listed or call 1-800-682-8886 ext. 4251 for more information about all three awards.

National Tourism Foundation
546 East Main St.
PO Box 3071
Lexington, KY 40596

707
Erik Barnouw Award

AMOUNT: $500   DEADLINE: December 1
FIELDS/MAJORS: American History

Award given in recognition of an outstanding documentary film concerned with American history, the study of American history, and/or the promotion of history as a lifetime habit. Only films completed after January 1 of the year you are entering are eligible. One or two awards are given annually. Write to the address listed for more information.

Organization of American Historians
Award and Prize Committee Coordinator
112 N. Bryan St.
Bloomington, IN 47408

708
Ernest Manchester Memorial Scholarship

AMOUNT: Maximum: $200   DEADLINE: July 30
FIELDS/MAJORS: Agriculture, Environmental Resource Management, Conservation

Scholarship offered to a junior or senior studying one of the above programs at a Pennsylvania college or university. Must be a resident of Bradford County. Write to the address below for details.

Bradford County Conservation District
Stoll Natural Resource Center
RR 5 Box 5030C
Towanda, PA 18848

709
Esther Dachslager Scholarship

AMOUNT: None Specified   DEADLINE: None Specified
FIELDS/MAJORS: Education

Awards for graduating seniors from Cony High School who are pursuing degrees in education at the college level. Contact the Cony High School Guidance Office for more information.

Maine Community Foundation
245 East Maine St.
PO Box 148
Ellsworth, ME 04605

710
Ethel J. Viles Scholarship Fund

AMOUNT: None Specified   DEADLINE: None Specified
FIELDS/MAJORS: All Areas of Study

Awards for female graduating seniors from Cony High School who plan to attend a college or university in Maine. Based on character and academic achievement. Contact the Cony High School Guidance Office for more information.

Maine Community Foundation
245 East Maine St.
PO Box 148
Ellsworth, ME 04605

711
Ethnic Diversity College Scholarships

AMOUNT: Maximum: $750 DEADLINE: November 30
FIELDS/MAJORS: Accounting

Open to minority undergraduates and graduates who are Colorado residents. Must have completed at least one intermediate accounting class with a minimum GPA of 3.0 and be a declared accounting major. Must have completed at least 8 semester hours of accounting courses. Write to the address listed for details, or call Gena Mantz (303) 773-2877 for more information.

Colorado Society of Certified Public Accountants
Scholarship Coordinator
7979 E. Tufts Ave., #500
Denver, CO 80237

712
Ethnic Diversity Scholarships

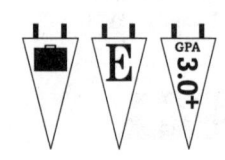

AMOUNT: Maximum: $750 DEADLINE: March 1
FIELDS/MAJORS: Accounting

Open to minority high school seniors who are Colorado residents. Must have a minimum GPA of 3.0 and be enrolled in a Colorado community college, college, or university. Selections are based primarily on academics. Write to the address listed for details.

Colorado Society of Certified Public Accountants
Scholarship Coordinator
7979 E. Tufts Ave., #500
Denver, CO 80237

713
Ethnic Minority and Women's Enhancement Programs

AMOUNT: $1400 DEADLINE: February 15
FIELDS/MAJORS: Intercollegiate Athletics Administration

Post-graduate scholarships, internships, and curricula vitae bank for women and minorities who intend to pursue careers in coaching, officiating, or athletic administration. Ten awards for women and ten for minorities. Contact the athletic director of the financial aid office at an NCAA member institution for details, or write to the director of personal development at the address below for details.

National Collegiate Athletic Association
6201 College Blvd.
Overland Park, KS 66211

714
Ethnic Minority Fellowship Program

AMOUNT: $11946 DEADLINE: January 15
FIELDS/MAJORS: Nursing, Behavioral Sciences, Clinical Research, Biomedical Research, Mental Health

Fellowships for minorities with a commitment to a career in nursing related to minority mental health and/or the research training program for careers in behavioral science or the clinical training program for careers in psychiatric nursing. For pre or postdoctoral study. Must be a U.S. citizen or permanent resident and a R.N. Write to the address below for more information.

American Nurse's Association, Inc.
Minority Fellowships Office
600 Maryland Ave. SW, Suite 100 West
Washington, DC 20024

715
Eugene "Gene" Sallee, W4YFR Memorial Scholarship

AMOUNT: $500 DEADLINE: February 1
FIELDS/MAJORS: All Areas of Study

Scholarship available to students with at least a technician plus class amateur radio license who are residents of Georgia. Must have a minimum GPA of 3.0. Write to the address listed for information.

ARRL Foundation (American Radio Relay League)
Scholarship Program
225 Main St.
Newington, CT 06111

716
Eugene C. Beach Memorial Scholarship

AMOUNT: Maximum: $350 DEADLINE: June 2
FIELDS/MAJORS: All Areas of Study

Scholarships are available to undergraduates who are members of Tau Kappa Epsilon. Must have demonstrated leadership capability within his chapter, on campus, or in the community. Must have a GPA of 2.5 or higher and be a full-time student in good standing. Write to the address listed for more information.

TKE Educational Foundation
8645 Founders Road
Indianapolis, IN 46268

717
Eugene Rotary Scholarship

AMOUNT: None Specified DEADLINE: March 1
FIELDS/MAJORS: All Areas of Study

Open to graduating seniors of the Eugene or Bethel School Districts. Awards may be used at the University of Oregon, Lane Community College, or Northwestern Christian College. These are one-time awards. Rotarians or their relatives are not eligible for this award. Must be U.S. citizens or permanent residents and residents of Oregon to apply. Contact the address below for further information.

Oregon State Scholarship Commission
Private Awards
1500 Valley River Dr., #100
Eugene, OR 97401-2130

718
Eugenia Bradford Roberts Memorial Scholarship

AMOUNT: Maximum: $1000 DEADLINE: March 31
FIELDS/MAJORS: All Areas of Study

Scholarships for daughters or granddaughters of Career Commissioned Officers (including Warrant) currently active in the U.S. Army or who retired after twenty years or died while on duty. Preference given to the student best qualified academically and most deserving of financial assistance. Eight renewable scholarships per year. Write to the address listed for details. Please include name, rank, and social security number of qualifying parent when requesting application. Be certain to include a SASE.

Society of Daughters of the U.S. Army
Janet B. Otto, Scholarship Chairman
7717 Rockledge Court
West Springfield, VA 22152

719
Evans Scholars Foundation

AMOUNT: None Specified DEADLINE: November 1
FIELDS/MAJORS: All Areas of Study

Candidates must have completed their junior year in high school, rank in the upper quarter of their class, and demonstrate financial need. Must have a superior caddie record for a minimum of two years and be recommended by club officials. Approximately 225 scholarships awarded annually. Application forms are available from your local club or sponsoring association. Write to the address listed for further information and more specific limitations on where you may attend school. Must have a GPA of at least 3.0.

Evans Scholars Foundation
Western Golf Association
Golf, IL 60029

720
Excel Temps Endowment for Excellence in Continuing Education

AMOUNT: Maximum: $500 DEADLINE: June 1
FIELDS/MAJORS: All Areas of Study

Two awards for Albuquerque residents who are currently enrolled part-time at an accredited school to advance career. Applicants must be age twenty-one or over and have a GPA of at least 3.0. Applicants must be working full-time. Write to the address listed for more information.

Albuquerque Community Foundation
PO Box 36960
Albuquerque, NM 87176

721
Exceptional Financial Need Scholarship Program

AMOUNT: None Specified DEADLINE: None Specified
FIELDS/MAJORS: Medicine, Dentistry, Osteopathic Medicine

Awards for full-time students in a health professions program who display exceptional financial need. Must be U.S. citizens or permanent residents. Contact the financial aid office at the school you attend.

Bureau of Health Professions
Student Assistance Division
5600 Fishers Ln.
Rockville, MD 20857

722
Exceptional Student Fellowships

AMOUNT: Maximum: $3000 DEADLINE: February 15
FIELDS/MAJORS: Business, Accounting, Actuarial/Computer Science, Insurance, Finance, Management, Marketing, Statistics

Open to full-time college juniors and seniors at time of application who have a 3.6 or higher GPA and are enrolled in a business-related major. Must be U.S. citizens and be able to demonstrate significant leadership in extracurricular activities. Fifty awards offered annually. Applicants must be nominated by the dean or department head. Contact the head of your department, write to the address listed for more information, or call (309) 766-2039. Applications are available from November 1 to February 1.

State Farm Companies Foundation
Scholarship Coordinator
1 State Farm Plaza SC-3
Bloomington, IL 61710

723
F. Charles Ruling N6FR Memorial Scholarship

AMOUNT: $1000 DEADLINE: February 1
FIELDS/MAJORS: Electronics, Communications

Scholarship available to students with a general class amateur radio license. For full-time study. Write to the address listed for information.

ARRL Foundation (American Radio Relay League)
Scholarship Program
225 Main St.
Newington, CT 06111

724
F. Gordon Davis Scholarship

AMOUNT: Maximum: $1000 DEADLINE: April 1
FIELDS/MAJORS: Journalism, Public Relations, Communications

Open to Michigan residents who are seniors or graduate students in accredited schools in Michigan. Must be preparing for a career in not-for-profit or healthcare communications. Must have a minimum GPA of 3.0. Award notification will take place via mail in May. Contact your school's financial aid office, academic department, the address listed, or (619) 592-4409 for further information.

Michigan Healthcare Communicators Assn.
Thomas Hogenson, RN, Public Relations Mg
Mecosta County General Hospital
Big Rapids, MI 49307

725
Faculty/Administrators Development

AMOUNT: None Specified DEADLINE: June 1
FIELDS/MAJORS: Education

Minority American teachers or administrators at, or alumni of, sponsoring Arkansas public colleges or universities, who have been admitted as full-time, in-residence doctoral program students. Write to the address below for more information.

Arkansas Department of Higher Education
Financial Aid Division
114 East Capitol
Little Rock, AR 72201

726
Falcon Foundation Scholarships

AMOUNT: Maximum: $3000 DEADLINE: April 30
FIELDS/MAJORS: Air Force Military Career

Scholarships for students entering the USAF Academy. Applicant must be between the ages of seventeen and twenty-one on July 1 of the year they are admitted to prep school. Must be a U.S. citizen and plan to follow a lifetime career as an officer in the U.S. Air Force after graduation. One hundred awards are offered annually. Contact address below for further information.

Falcon Foundation
3116 Academy Dr., #200
USAF Academy, CO 80840

727
Family Scholarships

AMOUNT: $3000-$12000 DEADLINE: December 1
FIELDS/MAJORS: All Areas of Study

Scholarships are for sons and daughters of current Westinghouse employees or employees of wholly-owned subsidiaries of Westinghouse. Only sons and daughters of employees from business units are eligible. Applicant's parents must be employed by Westinghouse for a period of at least one year. Fifty awards are offered annually. Contact the human resources department where your parent is (or was, if deceased, retired, or disabled) employed. Request information and a Family Scholarship application.

Westinghouse Foundation
Six Gateway Center
11 Stanwix St.
Pittsburgh, PA 15222

728
Fannie and John Hertz Foundation Graduate Fellowship Program

AMOUNT: $20000 DEADLINE: February 25
FIELDS/MAJORS: Applied Physical Sciences

Applicants must have at least a bachelor's degree to be eligible for these fellowships for doctoral studies in the physical sciences. Tenable at thirty-four different graduate schools. Must have a GPA of at least 3.8 (during the last two years of undergraduate work) and be a U.S. citizen (or in process of naturalization). Students pursuing both Ph.D. and professional degrees such as joint or parallel Ph.D./M.D., Ph.D./LL.D. or Ph.D./MBA are not eligible. Renewable. Write to the address listed for complete details.

Fannie and John Hertz Foundation
PO Box 5032
Livermore, CA 94551

729
Farm Foundation Extension Fellowships

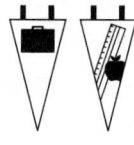

AMOUNT: None Specified
DEADLINE: March 1
FIELDS/MAJORS: Social and Political Sciences, Education, Business Administration, Agriculture

Scholarships for agricultural extension workers. Emphasis is placed on improving managerial and supervisory abilities. Candidates must be recommended by extension director, accepted by the university selected, and approved by the committee of the Farm Foundation. For graduate study. Write for complete details.

Farm Foundation
1211 W. 22nd St.
Oak Brook, IL 60521

730
Farmington UNICO Scholarship

AMOUNT: Maximum: $1000   DEADLINE: May 1
FIELDS/MAJORS: All Areas of Study

Open to graduating high school seniors who are residents of Farmington or West Hartford. For use at four-year schools. Must be able to demonstrate scholastic achievement and financial need. Contact the address listed for further information. Must have a GPA of at least 2.7.

UNICO Farmington Chapter
Joseph A. Mercaldi
10 Maiden Ln.
Farmington, CT 06032

731
Fashion Design Student Scholarship

AMOUNT: $2000   DEADLINE: June 30
FIELDS/MAJORS: Fashion Design

Awards for students in a fashion design or merchandising program who are from the San Antonio, Texas, area. Must have a GPA of at least 3.0. Applicant may not be a member of the Fashion Group, Inc., a professional or business designer. Write to the address below for more information.

Fashion Group International, Inc.
Adrian Highsmith
14006 Bluff Park
San Antonio, TX 78216

732
Father Anthony J. O'Driscoll Memorial Scholarship Award

AMOUNT: $500   DEADLINE: July 1
FIELDS/MAJORS: All Areas of Study

Scholarship available to New Jersey students entering their freshmen year in an accredited four-year college. Applicants must be members of the American Legion or Auxiliary or descendants of a member. Boy's/girl's state students are also eligible. Write to the address listed for additional information.

American Legion Press Club of New Jersey
Jack W. Kuepfer, ALPC Education Chairman
68 Merrill Road
Clifton, NJ 07012

733
Father James B. MacElwane Annual Awards

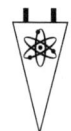

AMOUNT: $100-$300   DEADLINE: June 14
FIELDS/MAJORS: Meteorology, Atmospheric Sciences

Awards are available from the American Meteorological Society for the top three papers submitted by undergraduate students on the subject of atmospheric science or meteorology. One award is given annually. Write to address shown for details. A bulletin listing more information about this award may be posted in your department. Must have a GPA of at least 3.0.

American Meteorological Society
45 Beacon St.
Boston, MA 02108

734
Father Joseph P. Fitzgerald and Puerto Rican Bar Association Scholarship

AMOUNT: Maximum: $1000   DEADLINE: March 1
FIELDS/MAJORS: Law

Open to Latino students attending law school in the United States. Based on need, academic promise, and Latino community involvement. Generally, must be already enrolled into a J.D. program. Contact the address listed for complete information.

Puerto Rican Legal Defense and Education Fund, Inc.
99 Hudson St.
New York, NY 10013

735
Fay T. Barnes Scholarship Trust

AMOUNT: $3000-$12000 DEADLINE: January 30
FIELDS/MAJORS: All Areas of Study

Scholarships available to graduating high school seniors residing in Travis or Williamson County, Texas. Applicants must plan to attend a Texas college or university and possess a minimum GPA of 3.0. Contact your high school counselor for more information.

Texas Commerce Bank-National Association
700 Lavaca
PO Box 550
Austin, TX 78789

736
FCER Fellowships and Student Research Awards

AMOUNT: None Specified DEADLINE: March 1
FIELDS/MAJORS: Chiropractic Medicine

Fellowships are awarded primarily to graduate Chiropractors pursuing advanced degrees, usually leading to a doctorate. Student research awards are designed to stimulate interest in chiropractic research. Contact the address listed for details.

Foundation for Chiropractic Education and Research
1701 Clarendon Blvd.
Arlington, VA 22209

737
FEEA Scholarships

AMOUNT: $300-$1750 DEADLINE: May 8
FIELDS/MAJORS: All Areas of Study

Open to employees (at least three years) or dependents of employees of either the federal government or the U.S. Postal Service. Applicants must have a minimum overall GPA of 3.0 for the last full year of school. Must be enrolled in a two- or four-year school, graduate, or post-graduate program. An essay will be required. Based on academic merit. Write to the address listed for details. Please include two business-sized SASE for a reply. Requests for information without the return envelopes included will not be processed.

Federal Employee Education and Assistance Fund
Educational Programs
8441 W. Bowles Ave., Suite 200
Littleton, CO 80123

738
FEEA Student Loans

AMOUNT: None Specified DEADLINE: None Specified
FIELDS/MAJORS: All Areas of Study

Educational loans for employees or children of employees of either the federal government or the U.S. Postal Service. Employee must have been employed for at least three years. For undergraduate study. Write to the address listed for details. Please enclose a SASE for reply.

Federal Employee Education and Assistance Fund
Educational Programs
8441 W. Bowles Ave., Suite 200
Littleton, CO 80123

739
Field Cooperative Association Loans

AMOUNT: Maximum: $2000 DEADLINE: None Specified
FIELDS/MAJORS: All Areas of Study

Loans for Mississippi residents in at least their junior undergraduate year. Academic record, financial need, and financial responsibility are used to evaluate loan requests. Interest is 6% per year, and repayment starts three months after graduation. Renewable four times. Write to the address below for details. Must have a GPA of at least 2.1.

Field Cooperative Association, Inc.
2506 Lakeland Dr., Suite 607
PO Box 5054
Jackson, MS 39296

740
FEL-PRO Automotive Technicians Scholarships

AMOUNT: Maximum: $500 DEADLINE: May 1
FIELDS/MAJORS: Automotive, Diesel, Heavy Equipment Mechanics

Scholarships open to graduating high school seniors, high school graduates, or equivalent who plan to enroll or are currently enrolled in a full-time course of study. Must be currently studying or planning on studying auto, diesel, heavy equipment, or agricultural equipment mechanics. Contact Celene Peurye at the address listed for further information. Must enclose a SASE for a reply. Applications will be mailed in February.

FEL-PRO, Inc., Scholarship Program
Celene Peurye
7450 N. McCormick Blvd. Box C1103
Skokie, IL 60076-8103

741
Fellowship and Career Opportunity Grants

AMOUNT: $100-$8000 DEADLINE: October 1
FIELDS/MAJORS: Visual, Performing, Theater, and Literary Arts

Awards for professional artists who are legal residents of the state of Minnesota. Must be over eighteen years of age to apply. Based primarily on the quality of work and merit of the artist's career plans. Please be aware of the following: the deadline date for the visual award is August 15; the deadline date for the performing award is September 15. Both awards have a maximum value of $8000. The deadline date for the theater and literary arts awards is October 1. Value ranges from $100 to $1500. Write to the address below for more information.

Minnesota State Arts Board
Park Square Court
400 Sibley St., Suite 200
Saint Paul, MN 55101

742
Fellowship Awards in Pharmacology-Morphology

AMOUNT: $28585 DEADLINE: January 15
FIELDS/MAJORS: Pharmacology-Morphology

Postdoctoral fellowships to support research in drug actions, specifically cellular and tissue changes. Fellowships are for two years. Five awards annually. Must be U.S. citizen or permanent resident. Write to the address below for details.

Pharmaceutical Manufacturers Association Foundation, Inc.
1100 15th St. NW
Washington, DC 20005

743
Fellowship in Aerospace History

AMOUNT: $21000-$30000 DEADLINE: February 1
FIELDS/MAJORS: American Aerospace History

Fellowships are available to Ph.D.'s and Ph.D. candidates at the dissertation stage. Must have superior academic ability to engage in significant and sustained advanced research in NASA aerospace science, technology, management, or policy. Applicants must be U.S. citizens. Write to the address listed for details.

American Historical Association-NASA
AHA Administrative Assistant
400 A St. SE
Washington, DC 20003

744
Fellowship in Roman Studies

AMOUNT: Maximum: $5000 DEADLINE: March 1
FIELDS/MAJORS: Numismatics, Byzantine Studies, Classical Studies

Fellowship for research in residence at the society to study the ancient Roman world using the facilities and collections of the society. Applicants must be U.S. citizens associated with a North American institute of higher learning. Write to the address listed for details.

American Numismatic Society
Broadway at 155th St.
New York, NY 10032

745
Fellowship of United Methodists in Music and Worship Arts

AMOUNT: None Specified DEADLINE: March 1
FIELDS/MAJORS: Church Music, Worship Arts

Open to a full-time music degree candidate either entering as a freshman or already in an accredited university, college, School of Theology, or doing special education in worship or the arts related to worship. Write to the address listed for more information.

Fellowship of United Methodists in Music and Worship Arts
PO Box 24787
Nashville, TN 37202

746
Fellowship on Women and Public Policy

AMOUNT: None Specified DEADLINE: May 30
FIELDS/MAJORS: All Areas of Study

Fellowships are available to encourage greater participation of women in the public policy process, develop public policy leaders, and encourage the formulation of state policy that recognizes and responds to the need of women and families. Applicants must be female graduate students with at least 12 credit hours completed in an accredited New York university and planning to continue education in New York. Write to the address below for information.

University at Albany, Center for Women in Government
Joeanna Hurston Brown, Director
135 Western Ave, Draper Hall, Room 302
Albany, NY 12222

747
Fellowship Program in Academic Medicine

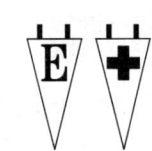

AMOUNT: Maximum: $6000 DEADLINE: August 31
FIELDS/MAJORS: Biomedical Research and Academic Medicine

Scholarships, fellowships, and awards for minority medical students. Minorities are defined here as African-American, American Indian (including Eskimos, Alaskan Aleuts, Hawaiian natives), Mexican-American, and mainland Puerto Rican. Must be U.S. citizens. Thirty-five awards are presented annually. There are two deadlines: May 31 deadline is for renewal applicants, and August 31 deadline is for new applicants. Send a SASE to the address listed for additional information.

National Medical Fellowships, Inc.
110 West 32nd St., 8th Floor
New York, NY 10001

748
Fellowship Research Grants

AMOUNT: Maximum: $20200
DEADLINE: None Specified
FIELDS/MAJORS: Government, International Affairs, Philosophy, Economics

Research grants are available to individuals for postdoctoral research. The applicant must be associated with educational or research institutions, and the effort supported should lead to the advancement of knowledge through teaching, lecturing, or publication. Write to the address below for information.

Earhart Foundation
2200 Green Road, Suite H
Ann Arbor, MI 48105

749
Fellowships at the Smithsonian Astrophysical Observatory

AMOUNT: None Specified DEADLINE: None Specified
FIELDS/MAJORS: Astronomy, Astrophysics, and Related Fields

Fellowships are available to graduate and postgraduate students at the Smithsonian Astrophysical Observatory. Write to address below for details. Request the publication "Smithsonian Opportunities for Research and Study."

Smithsonian Astrophysical Observatory
Office of the Director
60 Garden St., Mailstop 47
Cambridge, MA 02138

750
Fellowships for Advanced Predoctoral Training in Pharmaceutics

AMOUNT: $12000 DEADLINE: October 1
FIELDS/MAJORS: Pharmacology, Pharmacy, Academic Pharmaceutics

Advanced predoctoral fellowships to support promising students during thesis research. Fellowships are for one to two years. Must be U.S. citizen or permanent resident. Write to the address below for details. Additional funding for research expenses is available.

Pharmaceutical Manufacturers Association Foundation, Inc.
1100 15th St. NW
Washington, DC 20005

751
Fellowships for Careers in Clinical Pharmacology

AMOUNT: $25000 DEADLINE: October 1
FIELDS/MAJORS: Pharmacology, Toxicology, Morphology, Pharmaceutics

Research starter grants open to postdoctoral instructors, assistant professors, and investigators. This program is intended to assist them in establishing careers as independent investigators in pharmacology, toxicology, morphology, and pharmaceutics. Applicants must be U.S. citizens. Write to the address below for details.

Pharmaceutical Manufacturers Association Foundation, Inc.
1100 15th St. NW
Washington, DC 20005

752
Fellowships in Arts and the Humanities

AMOUNT: None Specified DEADLINE: None Specified
FIELDS/MAJORS: Arts and Humanities

Postdoctoral fellowships offered as a year or six-month visiting fellowship at selected academic and non-academic institutions. Will support scholars and writers whose research aids understanding of contemporary social and cultural issues. For a list of host institutions offering fellowships please write to "Arts and Humanities Fellowships" at the address below.

Rockefeller Foundation
Arts and Humanities Division
420 Fifth Ave.
New York, NY 10018-2702

753
Fellowships in Geriatric Clinical Pharmacology

AMOUNT: Maximum: $50000   DEADLINE: November 3
FIELDS/MAJORS: Clinical Pharmacology, Geriatrics

Candidates must be board certified or eligible by July 1, 1998, with special training or interest in geriatrics or clinical pharmacology. Awards are for two years of training in these areas of study. Based on candidates' abilities, promise, and evidence of commitment to a career in geriatric clinical pharmacology, and qualifications of the faculty member who will be a mentor. Write to the address listed for more information.

Merck Co. Foundation/American Federation for Aging Research
Scholarships Coordinator
1414 Ave. of the Americas, 18th Floor
New York, NY 10019

754
Ferdinand Torres Scholarship

AMOUNT: Maximum: $1000   DEADLINE: April 30
FIELDS/MAJORS: All Areas of Study

Open to students who are legally blind and present evidence of economic need. Must legally reside in the U.S. but need not be citizens. Preference given to applicants residing in the New York City metropolitan area and new immigrants. Write to the address listed for more information or call (212) 502-7661.

American Foundation for the Blind
Scholarship Committee
11 Penn Plaza, #300
New York, NY 10001

755
Fernando R. Ayuso Award

AMOUNT: Maximum: $5000   DEADLINE: October 15
FIELDS/MAJORS: Travel, Tourism

Open to U.S. citizens who have a high school diploma and at least two years worth of credit at an accredited college or university. Must have been involved in a professional capacity in the travel industry for a minimum of two years or have been studying the travel and tourism industry for at least two years. A letter of recommendation from an employer or professor will be required along with a five hundred word essay. This award pays transatlantic transportation, registration, local transportation, accommodations, and food at the International Travel Fair of Madrid. Winner will be notified in December. Contact the address listed for further information.

ASTA Scholarship Foundation, Inc.
Ayuso Scholarship
1101 King St.
Alexandria, VA 22314

756
Fine Arts and Music Grants

AMOUNT: $570-$5130   DEADLINE: January 31
FIELDS/MAJORS: Music, Arts

Open to advanced students for study of the Fine Arts at Austrian Universities. Applicants for the program must be between twenty and thirty-five years old with working knowledge of German. Awards are $570 monthly for up to nine months. Applicants will be required to submit two letters of recommendation, a supervisor's declaration (a professor at the university in Austria), a health certificate, and transcripts. Contact the address listed for more information or call (212) 759-5165. Must have a GPA of at least 2.8.

Austrian Cultural Institute
Scholarship Coordinator.
950 Third Ave., 20th Floor
New York, NY 10022

757
Fire Fighter and Peace Officer Survivors Scholarship

AMOUNT: None Specified   DEADLINE: None Specified
FIELDS/MAJORS: All Areas of Study

Grants for New Mexico residents attending New Mexico schools who are children or spouses of fire fighters or peace officers who were killed in the line of duty. Children must be under twenty-one years of age Contact the financial aid office at any New Mexico public postsecondary institution for more information.

New Mexico Commission on Higher Education
Financial Aid and Student Services
PO Box 15910
Santa Fe, NM 87506

758
First Catholic Slovak Ladies Association Member Scholarships

AMOUNT: $800   DEADLINE: March 1
FIELDS/MAJORS: All Areas of Study

Scholarships for members in good standing of the First Catholic Slovak Ladies Association (for at least three years prior to application) and on a $1000 legal reserve certificate, a $5000 term certificate, or an annuity certificate. Membership standing shall be verified from the records of the member's local branch and at the home office. Must be enrolled in or accepted by any accredited four-year college in the U.S. or Canada in order to pursue a bachelor's degree. Awards are made for one academic year. Eighty awards offered annually. Write to the address listed for details.

First Catholic Slovak Ladies Association
Director of Fraternal Scholarship Aid
24950 Chagrin Blvd.
Beachwood, OH 44122

759
First Marine Division Association Scholarships

AMOUNT: None Specified DEADLINE: None Specified
FIELDS/MAJORS: All Areas of Study

For dependents of deceased or 100% permanently disabled veterans of service with the First Marine Division, or in a unit assigned to, attached to, or in support of the First Marine Division. Must be full-time undergraduates attending an accredited college, university, or higher technical trade school. Write to the address listed for complete details.

First Marine Division Association, Inc.
14325 Willard Rd., #107
Chantilly, VA 22021

760
First Presbyterian Church Scholarship Fund

AMOUNT: None Specified DEADLINE: June 1
FIELDS/MAJORS: All Areas of Study

Scholarships for undergraduate or graduate students from Tulsa, Oklahoma, who are members of the First Presbyterian Church and are attending an accredited college or university. Based primarily on need, academic performance, and individual potential. Includes the Clarence Warren, Harry Allen, Ethel Francis Crate, Christian Vocation-Wallingford, and General Scholarships. Crate scholarships are for junior or senior undergraduates only. The Christian Vocation-Wallingford Scholarships are for students pursuing a Christian vocation. Write to the address listed for more specific details. Must have a GPA of at least 2.7.

First Presbyterian Church
Scholarship Fund Program
709 S. Boston Ave.
Tulsa, OK 74119

761
First Year Ph.D. Fellowships for African-American Students

AMOUNT: Maximum: $6000 DEADLINE: November 1
FIELDS/MAJORS: Political Science

Open to African-American graduates of a baccalaureate institution in the U.S. enrolling in a doctoral program in the following academic year. Applicants must have a record of outstanding academic achievement and be U.S. citizens. Write to the address for further information. Must have a GPA of at least 3.2.

American Political Science Association
Director of Minority Affairs
1527 New Hampshire Ave. NW
Washington, DC 20036

762
First Year Ph.D. Fellowships for Latino(a) Students

AMOUNT: Maximum: $6000 DEADLINE: November 1
FIELDS/MAJORS: Political Science

Open to Latino/Latina graduates of a baccalaureate institution in the U.S. enrolling in a doctoral program in the following year. Applicants must have a record of outstanding academic achievement and be U.S. citizens. Write to the address listed for further information. Must have a GPA of at least 3.2.

American Political Science Association
Director of Minority Affairs
1527 New Hampshire Ave. NW
Washington, DC 20036

763
First Year Ph.D. Fellowships for Native Americans

AMOUNT: Maximum: $6000 DEADLINE: November 1
FIELDS/MAJORS: Political Science

Fellowships open to Native Americans who graduated from a baccalaureate institution in the U.S. and will be enrolling in a political science doctoral program the following academic year. Applicants must have a record of outstanding academic achievement and be U.S. citizens. Contact the address listed for further information. Must have a GPA of at least 3.2.

American Political Science Association
Director of Minority Affairs
1527 New Hampshire Ave. NW
Washington, DC 20036

764
Five College Fellowship Program for Minority Scholars

AMOUNT: $25000 DEADLINE: None Specified
FIELDS/MAJORS: All Areas of Study

Program for minority graduate students in the final phase of the doctoral degree. While the emphasis is on completing the dissertation, fellows may be expected to teach a single one-semester course within the hosting department. Applicants must attend Amherst, Hampshire, Mount Holyoke, or Smith Colleges or the University of Massachusetts. Write to the address below for more information. Award also includes office space, housing assistance, and library privileges at the Five Colleges.

Five Colleges, Inc.
Fellowship Program Committee
97 Spring St.
Amherst, MA 01002

765
Fleet Reserve Association Scholarships

AMOUNT: None Specified DEADLINE: April 15
FIELDS/MAJORS: All Areas of Study

Children of the Fleet Reserve Association members (in good standing as of April 1 of year award is made). Based on financial need, academics, character, and leadership. Open to high school seniors and college and graduate students. Also available is the Fleet Reserve Association award for children of active, retired with pay, or deceased USN, USMC, or USCG personnel. Write to the address listed for complete details.

Fleet Reserve Association
FRA Scholarship Administrator
125 N. West St.
Alexandria, VA 22314

766
Fleet Scholars Work/ Study Scholarship

AMOUNT: $1000 DEADLINE: April 30
FIELDS/MAJORS: All Areas of Study, Preference Given to Business

Open to minority graduating high school seniors who are residents of Hartford and surrounding towns. For use at a four-year school. Must be able to demonstrate academic success and financial need. Each of the scholarships include $1000 and summer/vacation employment. Contact the address listed for further information. Must have a GPA of at least 2.7.

Fleet Bank NA
Ms. Maxine R. Deanat
1 Constitution Plaza
Hartford, CT 06115-1600

767
Fleischman Awards

AMOUNT: None Specified DEADLINE: November 14
FIELDS/MAJORS: All Areas of Study

Open to graduating high school seniors who have attended grades seven through twelve in Santa Barbara County. Must have an unweighted GPA of at least 3.8 and have a strong record of participation in activities benefiting the community. Contact your high school guidance counselor for more information. You can also contact the Foundation for information.

Santa Barbara Foundation
Student Aid Programs
15 East Carrillo St.
Santa Barbara, CA 93101

768
Flemish Community Fellowship

AMOUNT: None Specified
DEADLINE: January 15
FIELDS/MAJORS: Art, Music, Humanities, Social/Political Science, Law, Economics

Fellowships are available to American postgraduate students who wish to study at a Flemish university in Flanders, Belgium. Awards are given to candidates doing research in one of the fields listed above or in the science/medical fields, and their affiliation with the Flemish community. Applicant must hold at least a bachelor's degree, be under age thirty-five, and be a U.S. citizen. Write to the address below for information.

Embassy of Belgium
Flemish Community Fellowship
3330 Garfield St. NW
Washington, DC 20008

769
Flemish Community Scholarships

AMOUNT: None Specified
DEADLINE: January 15
FIELDS/MAJORS: Art, Music, Humanities, Social/Political Sciences, Law. Economics, Sciences

Open to sophomores who want to spend their junior or senior year at a Flemish university, conservatory of music, or art academy affiliated with the Flemish community. Must be U.S. citizens and have a minimum GPA of 3.2. Contact the address below for further information.

Embassy of Belgium
Attache of the Flemish Community
3330 Garfield St. NW
Washington, DC 20008

770

Flora M. Von Der Ahe Scholarship

AMOUNT: None Specified   DEADLINE: March 1
FIELDS/MAJORS: All Areas of Study

Scholarship for graduates from Umatilla County high schools who had a GPA of at least 2.5. For study at Oregon colleges. Applicants must be U.S. residents and may apply and compete annually. U.S. Bancorp employees, their children, or near relatives are not eligible to apply for this award. Contact your financial aid office or write to the address listed for details.

Oregon State Scholarship Commission
Attn: Grant Department
1500 Valley River Dr., #100
Eugene, OR 97401

771

Flora Rogge College Scholarship

AMOUNT: $1000   DEADLINE: March 7
FIELDS/MAJORS: Education

Awards for Minnesota high school seniors planning to pursue a career in teaching. Based on academics, financial need, leadership, character, and recommendations. Contact your high school counselor for more information and applications.

Minnesota Federation of Teachers
168 Aurora Ave.
St. Paul, MN 55103

772

Florence A. Carter Fellowships in Leukemia Research

AMOUNT: $25000   DEADLINE: January 31
FIELDS/MAJORS: Leukemia Research

Fellowships for investigative efforts in the area of leukemia research. Appropriate clinical research considered as well. Supporting letters from your institution describing their interest and focus on leukemia, proposed research with specifically stated goals, budget, and qualifications of the Chief and young (under forty) investigators will be required. Institution must agree to provide a report of the findings at the conclusion of the fellowship period. Contact the address listed for further information. Recipients will be announced by May 1.

American Medical Assn. Education and Research Foundation
Rita M. Palulonis
515 N. State St.
Chicago, IL 60610

773

Florida College Student of the Year Award

AMOUNT: Maximum: $30000   DEADLINE: February 1
FIELDS/MAJORS: All Areas of Study

Scholarships are available for Florida students enrolled on at least a half-time basis at any accredited Florida school. Applicant must have completed at least 30 credit hours, have a GPA of at least 3.2, and demonstrate financial self-reliance by working and/or receiving scholarships. Based on involvement in college and community activities. There are twenty awards offered annually. One award is for "Student of the Year" named, with six finalists, and thirteen honorable mention winners who share the total of $30,000. Write to the address below for information. Must include a SASE with $1 worth of postage to receive an answer.

Florida Leader Magazine
PO Box 14081
Gainesville, FL 32604

774

Florida Engineering Foundation Scholarship

AMOUNT: Maximum: $1000   DEADLINE: February 15
FIELDS/MAJORS: Engineering

Scholarships for juniors and seniors in a Florida university engineering program. Applicant must have a minimum GPA of 3.0 and be a U.S. citizen or a Florida resident. Must be recommended by an engineering faculty member. Contact the address listed for further information.

Florida Engineering Foundation
Florida Engineering Society
PO Box 750, Scholarship Coordinator
Tallahassee, FL 32302

775

Florida Engineering Society Engineering Scholarships

AMOUNT: Maximum: $1000   DEADLINE: February 15
FIELDS/MAJORS: Engineering

Open to high school seniors who are U.S. citizens and have a minimum GPA of 3.5. Must be enrolled in an engineering program accredited by the Engineering Accreditation Commission of the Accreditation Board for Engineering and Technology (ABET). Write to the address listed for details.

Florida Engineering Society
Scholarship Coordinator
PO Box 750
Tallahassee, FL 32302

776
Florida Library Association Graduate Grants

AMOUNT: $2000 DEADLINE: March 1
FIELDS/MAJORS: Library Science

Grants for master's level library science students attending Florida State University or the University of South Florida. Must be a Florida resident. Write to the address below for additional information.

Florida Library Association
Chair, FLA Scholarship Committee
1133 W. Morse Blvd., Suite 201
Winter Park, FL 32789

777
Florida Peanut Producers Association Scholarships

AMOUNT: $750 DEADLINE: July 1
FIELDS/MAJORS: All Areas of Study

Scholarships for sons and daughters of active peanut farmers in Florida. Award is intended for use at a Florida college. Two awards per year, one for a male and one for a female. Membership in the FFPA is not necessary. Write to the address below for details.

Florida Peanut Producers Association
Scholarship Award Committee
PO Box 447
Graceville, FL 32440

778
Florida Scholarship Challenge Program

AMOUNT: Maximum: $500 DEADLINE: April 15
FIELDS/MAJORS: Travel and Tourism, Hotel/Motel Management

Awards for Florida residents in one of the areas listed above who are enrolled in any four-year college full-time. Must have a GPA of 3.0 or better and be entering junior or senior year. Write to the address listed or call 1-800-682-8886 ext. 4251 for more information.

National Tourism Foundation
546 East Main St.
PO Box 3071
Lexington, KY 40596

779
Florida Student Assistance Grants

AMOUNT: $200-$1500 DEADLINE: April 15
FIELDS/MAJORS: All Areas of Study

Florida resident for at least one year. Proven need of required financial help. Must be full-time undergraduate student at an eligible Florida institution. Open to U.S. citizens or eligible non-citizens. For more details, contact the address below or your high school guidance counselor.

Florida Department of Education
Office of Student Financial Assistance
1344 Florida Education Center
Tallahassee, FL 32399

780
Florida Teacher Scholarship and Forgivable Loan Program

AMOUNT: $1500-$8000 DEADLINE: March 1
FIELDS/MAJORS: Education

Loans for full-time juniors, seniors, or graduate students enrolled in a state-approved teacher education program that leads to certification. Recipients then work in a critical teacher shortage area. Scholarships for freshmen and sophomores who plan to make teaching a career. Write to the address below for details. Must have a GPA of at least 2.5.

Florida Department of Education
Office of Student Financial Assistance
1344 Florida Education Center
Tallahassee, FL 32399

781
Florida Undergraduate Scholars Fund

AMOUNT: $2500 DEADLINE: April 1
FIELDS/MAJORS: Liberal Arts, Education

Open to high school seniors who are/have been Florida residents for at least one year and are outstanding students. For two- and four-year Florida colleges. Applications are available from your guidance counselor or high school principal. Write to the address below for complete details. Must have a GPA of at least 3.5.

Florida Department of Education
Office of Student Financial Assistance
1344 Florida Education Center
Tallahassee, FL 32399

782
Florida Work Experience Program

AMOUNT: None Specified   DEADLINE: None Specified
FIELDS/MAJORS: All Areas of Study

Open to undergraduates who are/have been a Florida resident for at least one year. May be enrolled half-time at a Florida institution. Provides need-based employment that will complement educational goals. Contact the financial aid office at the school you plan to attend or write to the address below for details.

Florida Department of Education
Office of Student Financial Assistance
1344 Florida Education Center
Tallahassee, FL 32399

783
Floyd Cargill Scholarship

AMOUNT: Maximum: $750   DEADLINE: June 15
FIELDS/MAJORS: All Areas of Study

Award for an outstanding blind student enrolled in an academic, vocational, technical, or professional training program in Illinois beyond the high school level. Applicants must be legally blind, U.S. citizens from the state of Illinois. Write to the address listed or call 217-523-4967 for more information.

Illinois Council of the Blind
PO Box 1336
Springfield, IL 62705

784
Floyd Qualls Memorial Scholarships

AMOUNT: Maximum: $2500   DEADLINE: March 1
FIELDS/MAJORS: All Areas of Study

Scholarships are for legally blind applicants who have been admitted for vocational/technical, professional, or academic studies at postsecondary levels. Write to the address listed or call (202) 467-5081 or 1-800-424-8666 for details.

American Council of the Blind
Scholarship Coordinator
1155 15th St. NW, Suite 720
Washington, DC 20005

785
Foods and Nutrition/Plant and Crop Science Scholarship

AMOUNT: $1900   DEADLINE: November 1
FIELDS/MAJORS: All Areas of Study

Scholarships for members of Minnesota 4-H or FFA clubs who have been active in production or nutrition areas of plant and soil science projects or food science and nutrition projects. To be used for educational expenses at a postsecondary school. Money will be held in trust if the winner does not attend school immediately. Four awards are given annually. Write to the address below for details.

Minnesota Soybean Research and Promotion Council
360 Pierce Ave., Suite 110
North Mankato, MN 56003

786
Ford Foundation Doctoral Fellowships for Minorities

AMOUNT: $7500-$18000
DEADLINE: November 15
FIELDS/MAJORS: Social and Life Sciences, Humanities, Engineering, Math, Physics

Approximately fifty predoctoral and twenty-nine dissertation fellowships for doctoral students. Must be U.S. citizens or U.S. nationals of African-American, Native American, Hispanic, Alaskan Native, or Native Pacific Islander descent. Contact your fellowship office or write to the address listed for details.

National Research Council
The Fellowship Office/FFPD
2101 Constitution Ave. NW
Washington, DC 20418

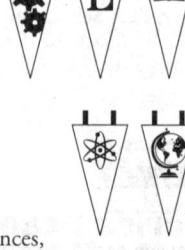

787
Ford Foundation Postdoctoral Fellowships for Minorities

AMOUNT: Maximum: $25000
DEADLINE: January 5
FIELDS/MAJORS: Social and Life Sciences, Humanities, Engineering, Math, Physics

Postdoctoral fellowships are available for scholars in the fields above. Renewable. Must be U.S. citizen or U.S. national and of African-American, Native American, Hispanic, Native Alaskan, or Native Pacific Islander descent. Twenty-five awards offered annually. Contact your fellowship office or write to the address listed for details.

National Research Council
The Fellowship Office/FFPD
2101 Constitution Ave., NW
Washington, DC 20418

788
Ford Opportunity Program Scholarship

AMOUNT: None Specified DEADLINE: March 1
FIELDS/MAJORS: All Areas of Study

Open to Oregon residents who are single heads of household with custody of a dependent child or children. May be used at Oregon colleges only. Must be U.S. citizens or permanent residents to apply. Contact the address below for further information.

Oregon State Scholarship Commission
Private Awards
1500 Valley River Dr., #100
Eugene, OR 97401-2130

789
Ford Scholars Scholarship

AMOUNT: None Specified DEADLINE: March 1
FIELDS/MAJORS: All Areas of Study

Open to Oregon graduating high school seniors or students who will be entering their junior year at an Oregon four-year college. Must have a minimum GPA of 3.0 and be U.S. citizens or permanent residents. These awards are for undergraduate study at any Oregon college. Contact the address below for further information.

Oregon State Scholarship Commission
Private Awards
1500 Valley River Rd., #100
Eugene, OR 97401-2130

790
Fort Peck Tribal Higher Education Program

AMOUNT: None Specified DEADLINE: July 15
FIELDS/MAJORS: All Areas of Study

Applicants must be members of the Fort Peck Assiniboine and Sioux Tribes of the Fort Peck Reservation. Must be a high school graduate or possess a GED certificate and enrolled, or accepted for enrollment, in an accredited college or university. Must have a GPA of 2.0 or higher. Selections based on financial need. Sixty to one hundred awards offered annually. Deadlines for applications are July 15 for fall quarter, December 1 for winter quarter, March 1 for spring quarter, and May 1 for summer quarter (college seniors). Write to the address below for more information.

Fort Peck Tribal Education Department
PO Box 1027
Poplar, MT 59255

791
Foundation for Seacoast Health Scholarship Program

AMOUNT: $1000-$10000 DEADLINE: February 1
FIELDS/MAJORS: Medical Lab/Secretary/Technology, Optometry, Pharmacology, Social Work, Nutrition, Medicine, Biomedical Engineering, Counseling/Mental Health, Gerontology, Healthcare Management, Home Healthcare, Dentistry, Physical or Health Education, Public Health, Speech Pathology, and Veterinary Medicine.

Applicants must be residents of: Portsmouth, North Hampton, Greenland, Rye, Newington, or New Castle in New Hampshire; or Kittery, Eliot, or York in Maine. Based on academics, work experience, and school/community participation. Contact the address listed for further information.

Foundation for Seacoast Health
PO Box 4606
Portsmouth, NH 03802

792
Founders Fund Scholarship

AMOUNT: $500-$5000 DEADLINE: None Specified
FIELDS/MAJORS: All Areas of Study

Applicants must be members or dependents of members of Beta Theta Pi in good standing. Previous winners are not eligible. Sixty awards are offered annually. Write to the address below for details.

Beta Theta Pi Foundation
Scholarship Coordinator
5134 Bonham Rd, PO Box 6277
Oxford, OH 45056

793
Founders Fund Vocational Aid Grants

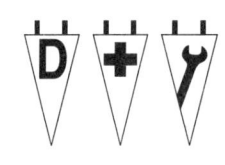

AMOUNT: Maximum: $150 DEADLINE: None Specified
FIELDS/MAJORS: Radiology, Dental Hygiene, Vocational/Technical Training

Open to undergraduates or students in vocational training. Preference given to students with disabilities. Also open to mature students who have not worked outside the home or are the sole supporters of families. Must have graduated high school. Last year, forty students were awarded $150 each. Contact the address listed for further information or call (312) 427-4410.

Altrusa International Foundation, Inc.
Josie Lucente
332 S. Michigan Ave., #1123
Chicago, IL 60604

794
Fourth Degree Pro Deo and Pro Patria Scholarships

AMOUNT: Maximum: $1500 DEADLINE: March 1
FIELDS/MAJORS: All Areas of Study

Scholarships for high school seniors planning to attend a Catholic college in the U.S. Must be members of the Knights of Columbus or children of active or deceased members. Renewable for up to four years. Write to the address listed for details.

Knights of Columbus
Rev. Donald Barry, SJ, Director of Aid
PO Box 1670
New Haven, CT 06507

795
Fran Johnson Scholarship for Non-Traditional Students

AMOUNT: $500-$1000 DEADLINE: April 1
FIELDS/MAJORS: Floriculture

Scholarship for undergraduate or graduate student who is re-entering school after an absence of at least five years. Must be enrolled in an accredited four-year school in the U.S. or Canada. Open to U.S. and Canadian citizens. Write to the address below for details.

Bedding Plants Foundation, Inc.
Scholarship Program
PO Box 27241
Lansing, MI 48909

796
Frances M. Peacock Scholarship for Native Bird Habitat

AMOUNT: Maximum: $4000 DEADLINE: January 15
FIELDS/MAJORS: Ornithology

Scholarships are available for seniors and graduate students in ornithology, to study areas in the United States that provide winter or summer habitat for threatened and endangered native birds. Write to the address listed for information.

Garden Club of America-Cornell Lab of Ornithology
Scott Sutcliffe
159 Sapsucker Woods Road
Ithaca, NY 14850

797
Frances M. Schwartz Fellowship

AMOUNT: Maximum: $2000 DEADLINE: March 1
FIELDS/MAJORS: Numismatics, Museum Studies, Art and Economic History, Classical Studies

Applicants must have a bachelor's degree or equivalent. The fellowship supports the work and study of numismatic and museum methodology at the society. Write to the address listed for details.

American Numismatic Society
Broadway at 155th St.
New York, NY 10032

798
Francis C. Allen Fellowship

AMOUNT: None Specified DEADLINE: None Specified
FIELDS/MAJORS: Humanities, Social Sciences

Open to female Native American graduate students. Candidates may be working in any graduate or pre-professional field, but Allen Fellows are encouraged in the areas of humanities and social sciences. Recipient will be expected to spend most of her tenure in residency at Newberry's Center for American Indian History. Financial support varies according to need. Write to the address listed or call (312) 255-3666 for additional information.

Newberry Library
Center of History of the American Indian
60 West Walton
Chicago, IL 60610

799
Francis J. Flynn Memorial Scholarship

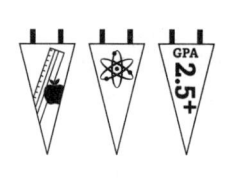

AMOUNT: Maximum: $600 DEADLINE: June 2
FIELDS/MAJORS: Mathematics, Education

Scholarship is available to undergraduate Tau Kappa Epsilon members who are full-time students pursuing a degree in mathematics or education. Must have a minimum GPA of 2.75. Applicants should have a record of leadership within their chapters and campus organizations. Preference will first be given to members of Theta-Sigma Chapter, but if no qualified candidate applies, the award will be open to any member of TKE. Write to the address listed for more information.

TKE Educational Foundation
8645 Founders Road
Indianapolis, IN 46268

800
Francis Ouimet Scholarship

AMOUNT: $500-$2500 DEADLINE: December 1
FIELDS/MAJORS: All Areas of Study

Awards granted to high school and college students who were caddies or worked in a golf environment for three or more years at any Massachusetts Golf Club. This is available for undergraduate study at a community college or four-year college or university. Over 250 awards per year. Write to the address below for complete details.

Francis Ouimet Caddie Scholarship Fund
Golf House
190 Park Rd.
Weston, MA 02193

801
Francis P. Matthews and John E. Swift Educational Trust Scholarships

AMOUNT: None Specified DEADLINE: None Specified
FIELDS/MAJORS: All Areas of Study

Applicants must be children of members of the Order who were either in the military and killed or disabled in a war or conflict, or were policemen or firemen killed or disabled in the line of duty. Must attend a Catholic school. For undergraduate study. Write to the address below for details.

Knights of Columbus
Director of Scholarship Aid
PO Box 1670
New Haven, CT 06507

802
Frank L. Greathouse Governmental Accounting Scholarship

AMOUNT: Maximum: $2000 DEADLINE: February 1
FIELDS/MAJORS: Accounting

Open to full-time seniors preparing for a career in state or local government. Applicants must be citizens of the U.S. or Canada. Recommendation from academic advisor or accounting program chair will be required. Contact the department head for further information, write to the address listed, or call (312) 977-9700.

Government Finance Officers Association
Scholarship Committee
180 N. Michigan Ave., #800
Chicago, IL 60601

803
Frank W. Jendrysik, Jr. Memorial Scholarship

AMOUNT: None Specified DEADLINE: March 15
FIELDS/MAJORS: All Areas of Study

Open to residents of Chicopee, Holyoke, or Springfield in Massachusetts. Contact the address listed for further information.

Community Foundation of Western Massachusetts
PO Box 15769
1500 Main St.
Springfield, MA 01115

804
Frank Walton Horn Memorial Scholarship

AMOUNT: $3000 DEADLINE: March 31
FIELDS/MAJORS: Architecture, Engineering

Open to full-time students who are legally blind. Students may be in any area of study, but architecture or engineering majors are preferred. Write to the address below for complete details.

National Federation of the Blind
Mrs. Peggy Elliott, Chairman
805 Fifth Ave.
Grinnell, IA 50112

805
Frank William and Dorothy Given Miller ASME Auxiliary Scholarship

AMOUNT: Maximum: $1500 DEADLINE: None Specified
FIELDS/MAJORS: Mechanical Engineering

Open to junior and senior ASME members. Must be enrolled in an accredited ABET (or equivalent) program. Selections based on character, integrity, leadership, and potential contribution to the mechanical engineering profession. Must be U.S. citizens and residents of North America. Contact the address below for further information. Include a SASE for a reply.

American Society of Mechanical Engineers
Nellie Malave
345 E. 47th St.
New York, NY 10017

806

Frank's Foundation Fund Scholarship

AMOUNT: None Specified
DEADLINE: March 1
FIELDS/MAJORS: Nursing, Theology

Open to high school seniors, undergraduates, and graduate students who are residents of any of the following Oregon counties: Deschutes, Crook, Jefferson, Harney, Lake, Grant, and Klamath. Must be U.S. citizens or permanent residents to apply. High school seniors must have a minimum GPA of 2.5, and continuing college students must have at least a 2.0. U.S. Bancorp employees, their children, or near relatives are not eligible to apply for this award. Contact the address below for further information.

Oregon State Scholarship Commission
Private Awards
1500 Valley River Dr., #100
Eugene, OR 97401-2130

807

Franklin Lindsey Student Aid Loan Fund

AMOUNT: Maximum: $3000   DEADLINE: None Specified
FIELDS/MAJORS: All Areas of Study

Loans for full-time students attending college or a university in Texas. Must have a GPA of at least 2.0 and have completed at least one year or 24 hours of study. Both student and co-signer must be U.S. citizens. Write to the address listed for details. Recipients must have co-signers for their loans.

Texas Commerce Bank-Austin, Franklin Lindsey Student
   Aid Loan Fund
Trust Department, Attn: Polly Randell
PO Box 550
Austin, TX 78789

808

Franz Werfel Scholarship

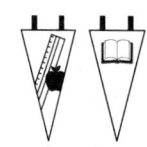

AMOUNT: $3605-$7305   DEADLINE: January 31
FIELDS/MAJORS: Austrian Literature

Open to professors teaching Austrian literature at American universities. Award consists of $740 monthly for up to nine months, $190, a book gift amount of $380, and a book budget of $75 per month. Other benefits continue after consumption of original grant. Designed to enable research at Austrian archives, libraries, and other institutions. Contact the address listed for further information or (212) 759-5165.

Austrian Cultural Institute
Scholarship Coordinator
950 Third St., 20th Floor
New York, NY 10022

809

Fraternal College Scholarship Program

AMOUNT: $500-$2000   DEADLINE: January 1
FIELDS/MAJORS: All Areas of Study

Scholarships for members of Modern Woodmen of America who are high school seniors enrolling in a four-year college. Must be in the top one-half of high school class. Thirty-six awards offered annually. Write to the address listed for details. Must have a GPA of at least 2.0.

Modern Woodmen of America
Fraternal Scholarship Administrator
1701 1st Ave.
Rock Island, IL 61201

810

Fraternal Non-Traditional Scholarship Program

AMOUNT: Maximum: $1000   DEADLINE: December 1
FIELDS/MAJORS: All Areas of Study

Applicants must be at least age twenty-five or older by the date of the application deadline. Must be a beneficial member of Royal Neighbors of America for at least two years. Must be attending school full-time. Write to the address below for more information.

Royal Neighbors of America
Fraternal Scholarship Program
230 16th St.
Rock Island, IL 61201

811

Fraternal Order of Police Lodge 89 Scholarship

AMOUNT: Maximum: $1000   DEADLINE: January 15
FIELDS/MAJORS: All Areas of Study

Open to seniors in Prince George's County high schools. Must have a minimum GPA of 2.5 and be able to demonstrate leadership skills. Contact the address listed for further information or call (301) 449-6488.

Prince George's County Scholarship Fund
Ms. Helen V. Page, Scholarship Secretary
6901 Temple Hills Rd.
Temple Hills, MD 20748

812

Fred A. Bryan Collegiate Students Fund Grants

AMOUNT: None Specified   DEADLINE: March 1
FIELDS/MAJORS: All Areas of Study

Open to graduating seniors from South Bend, Indiana, who are/or were Boy Scouts. Grant renewable up to four years. Amount of award varies from year to year. Write to the address below for complete details.

Fred A. Bryan Collegiate Students Fund
C/O Norwest Bank Indiana, NA, Trust Dept.
112 W. Jefferson Blvd.
South Bend, IN 46601

813
Fred and Shirley Brown Memorial Scholarship

AMOUNT: Maximum: $500   DEADLINE: March 15
FIELDS/MAJORS: All Areas of Study

Open to graduating high school seniors in Durham or Orange counties. Must be able to demonstrate academic achievement, leadership potential, and financial need. Preference given to students attending a public college or university in North Carolina. Letters of notification will be mailed to all applicants by May 15. Contact the address listed for further information. Must have a GPA of at least 2.9.

Triangle Community Foundation
Ellen F. Grisset, Dir. Philanthropic Svcs
PO Box 12834
Research Triangle Pk., NC 27709

814
Fred G. Zahn Scholarship

AMOUNT: $1500   DEADLINE: April 15
FIELDS/MAJORS: All Areas of Study

Awards for graduates of Washington high schools who attend schools in Washington state. Must have a GPA of 3.75. Preference is given to junior and senior college students. Contact any college within the state of Washington for information or applications.

Seattle-First National Bank
Trust Department
PO Box 2296
Tacoma, WA 98401

815
Fred R. McDaniel Memorial Scholarship

AMOUNT: $500   DEADLINE: February 1
FIELDS/MAJORS: Electronics, Communications, Related Fields

Scholarship available to students with a general class amateur radio license who are residents of and attend school in: Texas, Oklahoma, Alaska, New Mexico, Louisiana, or Michigan. For full-time study only. Applicants must have a minimum GPA of 3.0. Write to the address listed for information.

ARRL Foundation (American Radio Relay League)
Scholarship Program
225 Main St.
Newington, CT 06111

816
Frederic G. Melcher Scholarships

AMOUNT: Maximum: $6000   DEADLINE: April 1
FIELDS/MAJORS: Library Science, Children's

Applicants must be graduate students entering an ALA-accredited master's program and specializing in children's libraries. Must be U.S. or Canadian citizens. Recipients are expected to work in the children's library field for a minimum of one year. Write to the address listed or call (312) 280-2163/65 for details.

American Library Association
Assn. for Library Service to Children
50 E. Huron St.
Chicago, IL 60611

817
Frederick A Downes Scholarship

AMOUNT: Maximum: $2500   DEADLINE: April 30
FIELDS/MAJORS: Vocational/Technical

Scholarships are available to legally blind undergraduate students who are twenty-two years of age or younger and are enrolled in a course of study leading to a degree or vocational credentials. Applicants must be U.S. citizens. Based on academics and financial need. Contact the address listed for further information or call (212) 502-7600.

American Foundation for the Blind
Julie Tucker, Scholarship Coordinator
11 Penn Plaza #300
New York, NY 10001

818
Frederick J. Benson Scholarship

AMOUNT: $1000-$4000   DEADLINE: None Specified
FIELDS/MAJORS: All Areas of Study

Scholarships are available for residents of Block Island who are of sophomore standing or above. Applicant must have lived on Block Island for eight years or more or attended high school there for at least three years. Two awards offered annually. Write to the address listed for information.

Rhode Island Foundation
Ms. Michelle Phelan
PO Box B-2
Block Island, RI 02807

819
Freedom of Choice Grant

AMOUNT: Maximum: $2614 DEADLINE: March 1
FIELDS/MAJORS: All Areas of Study

The freedom of choice grant is designed to further assist students who are residents of Indiana with the tuition costs at a private undergraduate institution in the state of Indiana. Applicants must be U.S. citizens or permanent residents. Based primarily on financial need. May be renewed if acceptable progress toward degree is made. Write to the address below for complete information.

Indiana Student Assistance Commission
150 W. Market St., Fifth Floor
Indianapolis, IN 46204

820
Freeman Fellowship

AMOUNT: $3000-$5000 DEADLINE: February 20
FIELDS/MAJORS: Civil Engineering

Applicant must be a National ASCE member in the first year of graduate study. Award to be used for experiments, observations, and compilations to discover new and accurate data that will be useful in engineering, particularly hydraulics. Write to the address listed or call 1-800-548-ASCE for complete details.

American Society of Civil Engineers
Member Scholarships and Award
1801 Alexander Bell Dr.
Reston, VA 20191

821
Fresno-Madera Medical Society Scholarships

AMOUNT: $1000 DEADLINE: May 15
FIELDS/MAJORS: Medicine

Applicants must be legal residents of Fresno or Madera counties, California, for at least one year and be attending or accepted in a medical school. Based on need, academics, and prospects for completion of curriculum. Write to the address below for complete details.

Fresno-Madera Medical Society
Scholarship Foundation
PO Box 31
Fresno, CA 93707

822
Friedrich Ebert Doctoral Research Fellowships

AMOUNT: None Specified DEADLINE: February 28
FIELDS/MAJORS: German Studies (Political Science, Sociology, History, Economics)

Fellowships for students in the above area of study who have an approved dissertation proposal. Applicants must be U.S. citizens and provide evidence that they have knowledge of German that is adequate for research purposes. Approximately five awards offered annually. These fellowships are for stays in Germany for between five and twelve months. Write to the address below for more information.

Friedrich Ebert Foundation
New York Office
950 Third Ave., 28th Floor
New York, NY 10022

823
Friedrich Ebert Postdoctoral/Young Scholar Fellowships

AMOUNT: None Specified DEADLINE: February 28
FIELDS/MAJORS: German Studies (Political Science, Sociology, History, Economics)

Fellowships for scholars in the above area of study who have a Ph.D. and at least two years of research or teaching experience at a university or institution. Applicants must be U.S. citizens and be able to prove that they have a knowledge of German that is adequate for their research purposes. Approximately five awards offered annually. Write to the address below for more information.

Friedrich Ebert Foundation
New York Office
950 Third Ave., 28th Floor
New York, NY 10022

824
Friedrich Ebert Pre-Dissertation/ Advanced Graduate Fellowships

AMOUNT: None Specified DEADLINE: February 28
FIELDS/MAJORS: German Studies (Political Science, Sociology, History, Economics)

Fellowships for students in the above area of studies who intend to pursue a doctoral degree. Applicants must be U.S. citizens, have completed two years of graduate study, and provide proof that they have knowledge of German. Approximately five awards offered annually. These fellowships will be granted for stays of between five and twelve months in Germany. Write to the address below for more information.

Friedrich Ebert Foundation
New York Office
950 Third Ave., 28th Floor
New York, NY 10022

825
Friends of Rochester Hills Public Library Scholarship

AMOUNT: $2000 DEADLINE: August 1
FIELDS/MAJORS: Library Science

Awards for graduate students from the greater Rochester area who are studying in the area of library science. Must be currently enrolled or accepted in an accredited program. Must be a U.S. citizen. One award per year. Write to the address below for more information.

Friends of Rochester Hills Public Library
Scholarship Committee
500 Olde Town Road
Rochester, MI 48307

826
Fritchof and Marion Saliness Memorial Student Loan Fund

AMOUNT: None Specified DEADLINE: June 1
FIELDS/MAJORS: All Areas of Study

Low cost loans are available to students residing in Saginaw County who are attending or who plan to attend a public college or university in Michigan. Applicants must have a GPA of at least 2.0, demonstrate financial need, and be at least sixteen years old but not more than thirty years old. Repayment of loan will begin nine months after graduation and must be completed in six years. Write to the address listed for more information.

Second National Bank of Saginaw
Trust Department
101 N. Washington Ave.
Saginaw, MI 48607

827
FTE Undergraduate Scholarship in Technology Education

AMOUNT: Maximum: $1000 DEADLINE: December 1
FIELDS/MAJORS: Technology Education

Scholarship for members (at least one year) of the International Technology Education Association who are preparing for a career in teaching. Applicant must not be a senior by application deadline. Must have a GPA of 2.5 or greater. Write to "Undergraduate Scholarship" at the address listed for details.

International Technology Education Association
Tom Hughes
1914 Association Dr.
Reston, VA 22091

828
Fukunaga Scholarships in Business Administration

AMOUNT: $1500-$2000 DEADLINE: April 15
FIELDS/MAJORS: Business Administration

Scholarships for Hawaii residents pursuing a four-year degree in business. Program is designed to encourage graduating high school seniors, but students who are already attending college will also be considered. Must have a GPA of at least 3.0. Twelve to sixteen awards are offered annually. Write to the address below for more details.

Fukunaga Scholarship Foundation
Scholarship Selection Committee
PO Box 2788
Honolulu, HI 96803

829
Fulbright Awards

AMOUNT: None Specified DEADLINE: None Specified
FIELDS/MAJORS: International Studies

Available to master's degree candidates to foster mutual understanding among nations through educational and cultural exchanges. The program enables U.S. students to benefit from unique resources and gain international competence in an increasingly interdependent world. Must be U.S. citizen at the time of application. Write to the address listed for information.

Institute of International Education
Fulbright Awards
809 United Nations Plaza
New York, NY 10017

830
Full Tuition Fellowships

AMOUNT: None Specified DEADLINE: February 15
FIELDS/MAJORS: All Areas of Study

Fellowships based on merit are available to VSC students for the May through January sessions. Write to the address listed or call (802) 635-2727 for more information.

Vermont Studio Center
Office of Financial Aid
Box 613
Johnson, VT 05656

831
Fund for Lesbian and Gay Scholarships

AMOUNT: None Specified DEADLINE: September 15
FIELDS/MAJORS: All Areas of Study

Open to gay, lesbian, bisexual, and transgendered students who are enrolled in a college, university, or trade school. Must be able to demonstrate financial need. Must be involved in community affairs. Contact the address listed for further information, and be sure to enclose a SASE for a reply. Must have a GPA of at least 3.0.

Whitman-Brooks
Scholarship Fund
PO Box 48320
Los Angeles, CA 90048-0320

832
Fund for Podiatric Medical Education

AMOUNT: None Specified DEADLINE: May 1
FIELDS/MAJORS: Podiatric Medicine

Open to third and fourth year students studying podiatric medicine at any of the following seven schools: Barry University School of Podiatric Medicine, California College of Podiatric Medicine, College of Podiatric Medicine and Surgery, Scholl College of Podiatric Medicine, New York College of Podiatric Medicine, Ohio College of Podiatric Medicine, and the Pennsylvania College of Podiatric Medicine. Information available at the financial aid offices of the listed participating schools.

Fund for Podiatric Medical Education
9312 Old Georgetown Rd.
Bethesda, MD 20814

833
Future Teachers Scholarship Program

AMOUNT: Maximum: $1500 DEADLINE: None Specified
FIELDS/MAJORS: Education

Open to students seeking certification in teaching fields designated by the State Department of Education as in critical need of teachers. (Critical areas for 1995-96 were special education, science, early childhood, foreign language). Applicants must be Oklahoma residents who graduated in the top 15% of their high school graduating class. Must be enrolled in or accepted to a professional education program at an accredited Oklahoma college or university. Nomination by your school president is required. Write to the address listed for information. Must have a GPA of at least 3.0.

Oklahoma State Regents for Higher Education
Future Teachers Scholarship Program
500 Education Bldg. State Capitol Complex
Oklahoma City, OK 73105

834
G.I. Dependents Scholarship Program

AMOUNT: None Specified DEADLINE: None Specified
FIELDS/MAJORS: All Areas of Study

Students who are children or spouses of eligible Alabama veterans and who attend public postsecondary educational institutions in Alabama as undergraduates. The parent must have served ninety or more days of continuous active federal military service and have been a legal resident of Alabama for a year prior to military duty. Write to the address below for details.

Alabama Department of Veterans Affairs
PO Box 1509
Montgomery, AL 36102

835
Gabriel J. Brown Trust Loan

AMOUNT: None Specified DEADLINE: None Specified
FIELDS/MAJORS: All Areas of Study

Loans available to students who are residents of North Dakota with an interest rate of 6%. Must have completed 48 semester hours and have a GPA of 2.5 or better. Applications are available at Bismarck State College or the finance office of any four-year college or university in North Dakota or from the address listed.

Gabriel J. Brown Trust Loan Fund
112 Ave. E West
Bismarck, ND 58501

836
GAE Scholarships

AMOUNT: Maximum: $1000 DEADLINE: March 20
FIELDS/MAJORS: Teaching

Open to graduating seniors currently attending a fully accredited public Georgia high school who will attend a fully accredited Georgia college or university. Winning candidates will show the greatest potential as a teacher, have a minimum GPA of 3.0, and be bona fide residents of Georgia. Contact the address listed for further information.

Georgia Association of Educators
GFIE Scholarship Awards
3951 Snapfinger Parkway, Suite 400
Decatur, GA 30035-3203

837
Garden Club of America Awards for Summer Environmental Studies

AMOUNT: Maximum: $1500 DEADLINE: February 15
FIELDS/MAJORS: Environmental Studies

Financial aid toward a summer course in environmental studies to encourage studies and careers in the field. For sophomores through graduate students. Two or more awards offered annually. Write to the address listed for more details.

Garden Club of America
Ms. Shelley Burch
598 Madison Ave.
New York, NY 10022

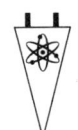

838
Garden Club of America Awards in Tropical Botany

AMOUNT: Maximum: $5500 DEADLINE: December 31
FIELDS/MAJORS: Tropical Botany

Financial aid for study in tropical botany. Awards for field study to Ph.D. candidates. Two awards offered annually. Write to the address listed for more details.

Garden Club of America
Ms. Marlar Oo, World Wildlife Fund
1250 24th St. NW
Washington, DC 20037

839
Garden Club of Ohio Scholarships

AMOUNT: $1500-$3000 DEADLINE: February 1
FIELDS/MAJORS: See Below

Scholarships for Ohio residents who are juniors, seniors, or graduate students in one of the following areas of study at any college. Fields include horticulture, floriculture, landscape design, botany, forestry, conservation, agronomy, plant pathology, city planning, and environmental sciences. Must have a GPA of 3.0. Contact your local Garden Club District or write to the address below for further information.

Garden Club of Ohio, Inc.
Mrs. Charles Blum
338 Emmett St.
Crestline, OH 44827

840
Garden Clubs Advanced Scholarships

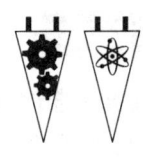

AMOUNT: Maximum: $3500 DEADLINE: March 1
FIELDS/MAJORS: Horticulture, Floriculture, Landscape Design, City Planning, Land Management

Scholarships for juniors, seniors, and graduate students in the above areas of study. Application is made through your state of legal residence. Must be a U.S. citizen or permanent resident. Thirty-two awards offered annually. Contact your State Garden Club. If the address is unknown, write to the address listed to request the scholarship chairperson for your state.

National Council of State Garden Clubs, Inc.
Mrs. Kathleen Romine
4401 Magnolia Ave.
St. Louis, MO 63110

841
Garland Duncan Scholarships

AMOUNT: Maximum: $2500 DEADLINE: None Specified
FIELDS/MAJORS: Mechanical Engineering

Open to members of ASME who are juniors and seniors. Selections based on character, integrity, leadership, scholastics, and financial need. Must be enrolled in an ABET accredited (or equivalent) program. One or two awards are offered annually. Contact the address below for further information. Include a SASE for a reply. Must have a GPA of at least 3.0.

American Society of Mechanical Engineers
Nellie Malave
345 E. 47th St.
New York, NY 10017

842
Gary Gross, OD, Memorial Scholarship

AMOUNT: Maximum: $2500 DEADLINE: None Specified
FIELDS/MAJORS: Optometry

Two awards are available for fourth-year optometry students who reside in and plan to practice in one of the member states of the North Central States Optometric Council (Illinois, Iowa, Michigan, Minnesota, Nebraska, North/South Dakota, Wisconsin). Requires an essay (1000 to 1500 words) on "Professionalism and Ethical Practice in Optometry." Write to the address listed or call (301) 984-4734 for information.

American Optometric Foundation
6110 Executive Blvd., Suite 506
Rockville, MD 20852

843
Gary Merrill Memorial Fund

AMOUNT: None Specified DEADLINE: April 1
FIELDS/MAJORS: Political Science or Government Studies

Scholarship support for a Maine resident who will be a second-, third-, or fourth-year student enrolled in a Maine college or university and majoring in political science or government studies. Write to Patti D'Angelo at the address listed for details.

Maine Community Foundation
245 East Maine St.
PO Box 148
Ellsworth, ME 04605

844
Gas Capital Scholarship Program

AMOUNT: None Specified DEADLINE: February 15
FIELDS/MAJORS: Petroleum Related

Scholarships for students from Southwestern counties (South and West of Finney County plus Greeley County) in Kansas. Must have completed at least three semesters at a college (including two-year programs) or university (or be in graduate school). Minimum GPA 2.5. Additional information and application forms are available at the Chamber of Commerce at the address below.

Gas Capital Scholarship Program
C/O Hugoton Chamber of Commerce
630 South Main
Hugoton, KS 67951

845
Gay and Lesbian Business Association of Santa Barbara Scholarship

AMOUNT: None Specified DEADLINE: July 1
FIELDS/MAJORS: All Areas of Study

Open to lesbian, gay, or bisexual students enrolled in an accredited postsecondary educational institution in Santa Barbara County. Selection based on financial need, academics, LGB awareness, and community/extracurricular activities. Contact the address listed for further information. Must have a GPA of at least 3.0.

Gay and Lesbian Business Association of Santa Barbara
Scholarship Coordinator
PO Box 90907
Santa Barbara, CA 93190-0907

846
Gay Wallentine Memorial Nurse's Scholarship

AMOUNT: $500-$1600 DEADLINE: July 15
FIELDS/MAJORS: Nursing.

Scholarship offered to nursing students attending a North Dakota college or university affiliated with St. Alexius Medical Center. To apply, send a letter stating educational background and any academic or practical preparation. Award is based on need of assistance, goals and career plans, and three non-related references. Write to the address listed for more details.

St. Alexius Medical Center Foundation
Box 5510
Bismarck, ND 58502

847
GCSAA Turfgrass Students Essay Contest

AMOUNT: $400-$1600 DEADLINE: March 31
FIELDS/MAJORS: Turfgrass Management

The contest is open to students of any age enrolled in formal turfgrass science or golf course management programs. Essays must examine environmentally-related topics such as integrated pest management, protecting water quality, etc. Three awards are given annually. Write for complete details.

Golf Course Superintendents Association of America
Scholarship and Research Committee
1421 Research Park Dr.
Lawrence, KS 66049

848
GEM Fellowships

AMOUNT: Maximum: $12000
DEADLINE: December 1
FIELDS/MAJORS: Engineering, Sciences, Mathematics

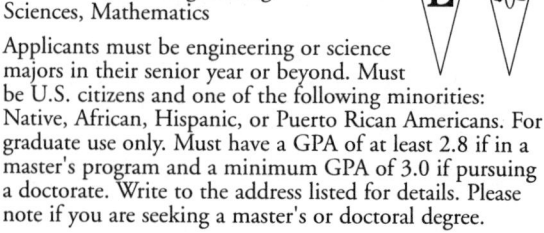

Applicants must be engineering or science majors in their senior year or beyond. Must be U.S. citizens and one of the following minorities: Native, African, Hispanic, or Puerto Rican Americans. For graduate use only. Must have a GPA of at least 2.8 if in a master's program and a minimum GPA of 3.0 if pursuing a doctorate. Write to the address listed for details. Please note if you are seeking a master's or doctoral degree.

Consortium for Graduate Degrees for Minorities
GEM Central Office
PO Box 537
Notre Dame, IN 46556

849
General Electric Scholarship Program

AMOUNT: None Specified   DEADLINE: January 15
FIELDS/MAJORS: All Areas of Study

Scholarships for dependent children of General Electric Company employees. Must be a graduating high school senior. Write to the address below or call 1-800-537-4180 for more information.

General Electric Scholarship Program
C/O Citizens Scholarship Foundation
PO Box 297
St. Peter, MN 56082

850
General Emmett Paige Scholarships

AMOUNT: Maximum: $2000
DEADLINE: March 1
FIELDS/MAJORS: Technology Fields

Awards are available for undergraduates who were on active duty or veterans of the military services or to their dependents. Must be enrolled in an accredited institution in the U.S. Must be a U.S. citizen of good moral character who demonstrates academic excellence, dedication to completing postsecondary education, and a GPA of 3.4. Must also demonstrate financial need. Send a SASE, along with information on the name of the school you are attending, field of study, GPA, and school year to the address listed or call (703) 631-4147 or 1-800-336-4583 ext. 6147.

Armed Forces Communications and Electronics
   Association
AFCEA Educational Foundation
4400 Fair Lakes Court
Fairfax, VA 22033

851
General Fund Scholarships

AMOUNT: $1000   DEADLINE: February 1
FIELDS/MAJORS: All Areas of Study

Scholarships are available to students with any class amateur radio license who are enrolled as full-time students in any area of study. Multiple awards offered annually. Write to the address listed for information.

ARRL Foundation (American Radio Relay League)
Scholarship Program
225 Main St.
Newington, CT 06111

852
General Henry H. Arnold Education Grant Program

AMOUNT: Maximum: $1500   DEADLINE: March 20
FIELDS/MAJORS: All Areas of Study

Scholarships are available for children of active duty, retired, or deceased Air Force personnel. Must have a minimum GPA of 2.0, be a U.S. citizen, and be under age twenty-four. For undergraduate study. Write to the address listed for more details.

Air Force Aid Society
Education Assistance Department
1745 Jeff Davis Highway, Suite 202
Arlington, VA 22202

853
General John A. Wickham Scholarships

AMOUNT: Maximum: $2000   DEADLINE: May 1
FIELDS/MAJORS: Electrical/Computer Engineering, Computer Science, Physics, Mathematics

Awards are available for sophomores and juniors enrolled full-time in an accredited degree-granting, four-year college or university in the U.S. Must be a U.S. citizen of good moral character and leadership abilities who demonstrates academic excellence and dedication to completing his/her education. Must also demonstrate financial need and have a minimum GPA of 3.4 on a 4.0 scale. Write to the address listed or call (703) 631-6149 or 1-800-336-4583 ext. 6149 for more information. Include a SASE for a reply.

Armed Forces Communications and Electronics
   Association
AFCEA Educational Foundation
4400 Fair Lakes Court
Fairfax, VA 22033

854
General Motors Engineering Scholarship

AMOUNT: None Specified   DEADLINE: None Specified
FIELDS/MAJORS: Electrical/Industrial/Mechanical Engineering

Open to first semester sophomores who have a minimum GPA of 3.2 and are enrolled at any of the following historically black colleges or universities: Atlanta University Center, Florida A&M, Howard University, North Carolina A&T University, Prairie View A&M University, Southern University A&M College, Tennessee State University, and Tuskegee University. Contact the financial aid office at your school for information and an application.

United Negro College Fund
Scholarship Program
PO Box 10444
Fairfax, VA 22031-4511

855
Genesee Valley Foundations for the Future Scholarship

AMOUNT: $500 DEADLINE: May 1
FIELDS/MAJORS: Special Education, Human Services, Occupational and Physical Therapy

Scholarships available to high school seniors residing in either Livingston or Wyoming County. Applicants must be entering a field that will benefit persons with developmental disabilities. Recipient must have already been accepted to a four or two year university, college, or community college. Write to the address below for details.

Livingston-Wyoming Association for Retarded Citizens
Attn: GVFF Scholarship Committee
18 Main St.
Mt. Morris, NY 14510

856
Genevieve Starcher Foundation Scholarships

AMOUNT: Maximum: $1000 DEADLINE: May 31
FIELDS/MAJORS: All Fields of Study.

Scholarships offered to graduates of Ripley High School or to those living in the Ripley area while attending college. Applications are available from Jean Crow at United National Bank in Ripley and Ripley High School. Write to address below for details.

Genevieve Starcher Educational Foundation
Kathryn S. Goodwin, Ph.D., Chairman
PO Box 266
Ripley, WV 25271

857
George Choy Memorial Scholarship

AMOUNT: None Specified DEADLINE: June 15
FIELDS/MAJORS: All Areas of Study

Open to gay, lesbian, bisexual, and transgendered Asian and Pacific Islander graduating high school seniors. Must be graduating from a high school in one of the following counties: Alameda, Contra Costa, Marin, San Francisco, San Mateo, Santa Clara, Napa, Sonoma, or Solano and have a minimum GPA of 3.0. Must be accepted to or in the process of applying to an institution of higher learning. Contact the address listed for further information, and be sure to enclose a SASE for a reply.

Horizons Foundation
Scholarship Coordinator
870 Market St. #1155
San Francisco, CA 94102

858
George E. Stifel Scholarship Foundation

AMOUNT: $1000-$25000 DEADLINE: June 1
FIELDS/MAJORS: All Areas of Study

Scholarships for residents of Ohio County, West Virginia, and for students who graduated from Ohio County public schools. Contact address below for complete information.

George E. Stifel Scholarship Foundation
C/O Security National Bank
PO Box 511
Wheeling, WV 26003

859
George H. and Margaret B. McDonnell Family Scholarship

AMOUNT: None Specified DEADLINE: March 15
FIELDS/MAJORS: Social Work

Open to a Holyoke Catholic High School graduate pursuing a career in social work or an allied field. Contact the address listed for further information.

Community Foundation of Western Massachusetts
PO Box 15769
1500 Main St.
Springfield, MA 01115

860
George H. Brooker Collegiate Scholarship

AMOUNT: $1000-$2500 DEADLINE: March 15
FIELDS/MAJORS: Real Estate

Open to full-time juniors, seniors, and graduate students who are enrolled in accredited institutions in the U.S. Applicants must have completed at least two courses in real estate, (or intend to do so), and have a minimum GPA of 3.0. Applicants must be U.S. citizens of Alaskan Native, Native American, Asian, African-American, Mexican, Chicano, Hispanic, Puerto Rican, or Pacific Islander descent. Must demonstrate financial need, academic achievement, character, and leadership. Contact the address listed for further information.

IREM Foundation
Brooker Scholarship Coordinator
430 N. Michigan Ave.
Chicago, IL 60611

861
George H. McDonnell Scholarship

AMOUNT: None Specified **DEADLINE:** March 15
FIELDS/MAJORS: Civil Engineering

Open to graduating seniors of South Hadley High School who are town residents. Must be planning to attend a four-year college. Contact the address listed for further information.

Community Foundation of Western Massachusetts
PO Box 15769
1500 Main St.
Springfield, MA 01115

862
George M. Booker Scholarship for Minorities

AMOUNT: $1000-$2500 **DEADLINE:** March 15
FIELDS/MAJORS: Real Estate

Scholarships for minority students studying real estate. Must have a GPA of at least a 3.0 and be a U.S. citizen. Students should have completed at least two courses in real estate at the time of application. Two undergraduate and one graduate award offered annually. Recipients usually announced in June. Write to the address below for more information.

Institute of Real Estate Management Foundation
Attn: Booker Scholarship
430 North Michigan Ave.
Chicago, IL 60611

863
George T. Welsh Scholarship

AMOUNT: $1000-$1800 **DEADLINE:** April 1
FIELDS/MAJORS: All Areas of Study

Open to high school seniors and college freshmen who are residents of Walla Walla County, Washington, and have a minimum GPA of 2.0. Must have graduated from a Walla Walla high school and be unmarried. Contact the address listed for further information. Enclose a SASE.

Baker Boyer National Bank
George T. Welsh Scholarship
PO Box 1796
Walla Walla, WA 99362

864
George W. Frye Scholarship

AMOUNT: None Specified **DEADLINE:** None Specified
FIELDS/MAJORS: All Areas of Study

Awards for seniors at Narraguagus High School in Harrington, Maine, who plan to attend a two or four-year college or university. Based on financial need and academic standing. First priority will be given to a student from the town of Harrington. Contact the Narraguagus High School Guidance Office for more information.

Maine Community Foundation
245 East Maine St.
PO Box 148
Ellsworth, ME 04605

865
Georgia Beef Board Internship

AMOUNT: Maximum: $3000 **DEADLINE:** December 1
FIELDS/MAJORS: Agriculture, Animal Science, Agricultural Communications, Nutrition

A three-month internship is available with the Georgia Beef Board to assist with beef promotional and marketing activities. Recipient will be expected to relocate to the Macon area during the internship. Applicant must be a Georgia resident and at least a sophomore. Recipient will also receive a Georgia Cattlemen's/Cattlewomen's Association scholarship. Write to the address below for information.

Georgia Beef Board
Ms. Danette Amstein
PO Box 11347
Macon, GA 31212

866
Geoscience Scholarships for Ethnic Minorities

AMOUNT: $4000-$10000 **DEADLINE:** February 1
FIELDS/MAJORS: Earth, Space, Marine Sciences, Geology, Geophysics, Hydrology

Scholarships are available at the undergraduate and graduate level in the geosciences listed above. Applicants must be U.S. citizens and underrepresented minorities. For full-time study. Based on academic record and financial need. Approximately eighty awards offered annually. Write to the address below for details.

American Geological Institute
AGI Minority Geoscience Scholarships
4220 King St.
Alexandria, VA 22302

867
Gerald and Paul D'Amour Founders' Scholarship

AMOUNT: $500-$1000 DEADLINE: February 1
FIELDS/MAJORS: All Areas of Study

Awards open to high school seniors, undergraduates, graduates, non-traditional students, and Desert Storm veterans. Must be residents of or attending school in central and western Massachusetts and Connecticut. Based on academic merit and achievement, the awards may be applied to accredited two- or four-year or graduate schools. There are usually more than 120 awards offered annually. Contact the address listed for further information. Must have a GPA of at least 3.0.

Big Y Foods, Inc.
Ms. Katherine Hull Perkins
280 Chestnut St., PO Box 7840
Springfield, MA 01102

868
Gerber Foundation Scholarship

AMOUNT: Maximum: $1500 DEADLINE: February 28
FIELDS/MAJORS: All Areas of Study

Awards for full-time undergraduates who are dependents of an employee of the Gerber Company. Renewable with a GPA of 2.0 or better. Sixty awards are offered annually. Write to the address below for more information.

Gerber Companies Foundation
Dept. SC
445 State St.
Fremont, MI 49413

869
Gerber Prize for Excellence in Pediatrics

AMOUNT: Maximum: $2000 DEADLINE: August 31
FIELDS/MAJORS: Pediatric Medicine

Scholarships, fellowships, and awards for minority medical students in pediatrics. Minorities are defined here as African-American, American Indian (including Eskimos, Alaskan Aleuts, Hawaiian natives), Mexican-American, and mainland Puerto Rican. For study at Michigan medical schools. Academics is primary consideration; need is considered. Must be U.S. citizens. One award presented annually. There are two deadlines: May 31 deadline is for renewal applicants, and August 31 is for new applicants. Write to "special programs" at the address listed for details.

National Medical Fellowships, Inc.
110 West 32nd St. 8th Floor
New York, NY 10001

870
Geriatrics Clinician of the Year Award

AMOUNT: $2000 DEADLINE: December 8
FIELDS/MAJORS: Geriatrics

Awards are available for geriatrics clinicians whose primary focus is the delivery of patient care in the office, hospital, long-term care facility, or community. Must be AGS members who are maintaining a high level of professional competence through continuing medical education. Applicants must be nominated via a letter of nomination, at least one letter of support from colleagues, and the nominee's curriculum vitae. Write to the address listed for more information.

American Geriatrics Society
770 Lexington Ave., Suite 300
New York, NY 10021

871
Gerrish/FTE Fellowship

AMOUNT: Maximum: $2000
DEADLINE: June 13
FIELDS/MAJORS: Technology Education

Open to female graduate students with disabilities who are studying, researching, and writing on disability policy in an accredited college or university. Must be U.S. citizens with goals of careers in public policy or public information related to disabilities. An essay will be required. Contact the address below for further information.

ELA Foundation
Fellowship Program
1331 F St. NW
Washington, DC 20004-1107

872
Gerrish/FTE Scholarship Technology Education Graduate Study

AMOUNT: Maximum: $5000 DEADLINE: December 1
FIELDS/MAJORS: Technology Education

Scholarship for members (at least one year) of the International Technology Education Association who are technology teachers at any grade level, accepted into a graduate degree program in technology education, and beginning or continuing full-time graduate work. Write to the address listed for details.

International Technology Education Association
Tom Hughes
1914 Association Dr.
Reston, VA 22091

873

Gertrude and Harvey G. Fins Scholarship

AMOUNT: None Specified   DEADLINE: March 1
FIELDS/MAJORS: Law

Scholarships for Jewish men and women who are legal residents of the Chicago area. Must be attending/planning to attend DePaul University, Loyola University, IIT-Chicago/Kent, John Marshall, Southern Illinois University, or the University of Illinois at Urbana/Champaign for their law studies. Write to the address below for details after December 1.

Jewish Vocational Service
Attn: Academic Scholarship Program
One South Franklin St.
Chicago, IL 60606

874

Gertrude Botts-Saucier Scholarship

AMOUNT: None Specified   DEADLINE: None Specified
FIELDS/MAJORS: All Areas of Study

Scholarships for lineal descendants of worthy confederates or collateral descendants who are members of the children of the confederacy or the United Daughters of the Confederacy. This award is for students from Texas, Louisiana, or Mississippi. Write to the UDC chapter nearest you. If address is not known, write to the address below for further information and the address.

United Daughters of the Confederacy
Scholarship Coordinator
328 N. Boulevard
Richmond, VA 23220

875

Gertrude D. Curran Trust Scholarship

AMOUNT: None Specified   DEADLINE: March 31
FIELDS/MAJORS: Music

Open to music majors who are residents of Utica, New York. Contact the address listed for further information or call (315) 798-2233.

Gertrude D. Curran Trust FBO Curran Music School
C/O Trust Dept., Marine Midland Bank
PO Box 8203
Buffalo, NY 14240

876

GFWC of Massachusetts "Pennies for Art" Scholarship

AMOUNT: $500   DEADLINE: February 15
FIELDS/MAJORS: Art

Applicant must be a senior in a Massachusetts high school and present a letter of endorsement from a sponsoring Women's Club in your community. Write to the address below for details, be sure to include a SASE.

General Federation of Women's Clubs of Massachusetts
Chairperson, Art Division
245 Dutton Rd., PO Box 679
Sudbury, MA 01776

877

GHI Dissertation Scholarships

AMOUNT: Maximum: $1100   DEADLINE: May 15
FIELDS/MAJORS: German Studies, German History, German-American History

Awards for doctoral students working on topics related to the institute's general scope of interest. Twelve awards are offered annually. Write to the address below for more information.

German Historical Institute
1607 New Hampshire Ave. NW
Washington, DC 20009

878

Ghidotti Foundation

AMOUNT: None Specified   DEADLINE: None Specified
FIELDS/MAJORS: All Areas of Study

For students who have graduated from any public or private school located within the boundaries of Nevada County, California. Do not contact the bank for information. See a high school counselor for an application.

Wells Fargo Bank
PO Box 2511
Sacramento, CA 95812

879

Gibran Kahlil Gibran Educational Fund

AMOUNT: None Specified DEADLINE: June 1
FIELDS/MAJORS: All Areas of Study

Scholarships for Syrian and Lebanese peoples. Preference given to persons whose ancestors are from the town of Becherre or to other towns in Lebanon. Write to the address below for details.

Gibran Kahlil Gibran Educational Fund, Inc.
4 Longfellow Place, Suite 3802
Boston, MA 02114

880

Gilbert F. White Postdoctoral Fellowship Program

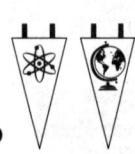

AMOUNT: None Specified DEADLINE: February 27
FIELDS/MAJORS: Natural Resources, Energy, Environmental Sciences

Fellowship is for researchers in social science or public policy programs in the areas of natural resources, energy, or the environment. Applicants must have completed doctoral requirements and preference will be given to those with teaching and/or research experience. This is a residential fellowship. Write to the address listed for details.

Resources for the Future
Coordinator for Academic Programs
1616 P St. NW
Washington, DC 20036

881

Gilbert Grant and Tuition Waiver

AMOUNT: $200-$2500 DEADLINE: None Specified
FIELDS/MAJORS: All Areas of Study

For permanent residents of Massachusetts. Must be enrolled in a Massachusetts undergraduate public institution. Be certain to file for a needs analysis (FAFSA, FAF, etc.), and contact your college financial aid office for further information.

Massachusetts Board of Regents of Higher Education
State Scholarship Office
330 Stuart St.
Boston, MA 02116

882

Gilbreth Memorial Fellowship

AMOUNT: Maximum: $2500 DEADLINE: November 15
FIELDS/MAJORS: Industrial Engineering

Scholarships are available for graduate industrial engineering majors who are enrolled on a full-time basis, members of the institute, and have a GPA of at least 3.4. Students must be nominated by their IIE department heads. Two awards offered annually. Contact your school's industrial engineering department head for information.

Institute of Industrial Engineers
Scholarship Program
25 Technology Park/Atlanta
Norcross, GA 30092

883

Gillian and Ellis Goodman Scholarship

AMOUNT: None Specified DEADLINE: March 1
FIELDS/MAJORS: Environmental Engineering

Open to students of junior level or above and legally domiciled in Cook County or the Chicago metro area. Preference given to career goals in engineering focusing on environmental concerns. Contact the address below for further information after December 1. Must have a GPA of at least 2.7.

Jewish Vocational Service
Academic Scholarship Program
1 S. Franklin St.
Chicago, IL 60606

884

Gilman Paper Company Foundation Scholarship Program

AMOUNT: None Specified DEADLINE: None Specified
FIELDS/MAJORS: All Areas of Study

Scholarships are available for children of employees of the Gilman Paper Company. Parent may check with the Human Resources Department where he/she works, or contact the address below.

Howard Gilman Foundation
Scholarship Program
111 West 50th St.
New York, NY 10020

885
Gina Finzi Memorial Student Summer Fellowships

AMOUNT: Maximum: $2000   DEADLINE: February 1
FIELDS/MAJORS: Medical Research

Awards for undergraduate, graduate, or medical students to foster an interest among young researchers in Lupus Erythematous through the conduct of basic, clinical, or psychosocial research under the supervision of an established investigator. Preference is given to students with a college degree. Five to ten awards offered annually. Write to the address below for more information.

Lupus Foundation of America, Inc.
1300 Piccard Dr., #200
Rockville, MD 20850-4303

886
Gladys C. Anderson Memorial Scholarship

AMOUNT: Maximum: $1000   DEADLINE: April 30
FIELDS/MAJORS: Religious Music, Classical Music

Open to legally blind women studying religious or classical music at the undergraduate level. Applicants must be U.S. citizens. Applicants must submit a sample performance tape of voice or instrumental selection (not to exceed thirty minutes). Write to the address listed for complete details or call (212) 502-7661.

American Foundation for the Blind
Scholarship Committee
11 Penn Plaza, # 300
New York, NY 10001

887
Glass, Molders, Pottery, Plastics, and Allied Workers Memorial Scholarship

AMOUNT: Maximum: $2500   DEADLINE: November 1
FIELDS/MAJORS: All Areas of Study

Dependent children of this union's members who rank in the top quarter of their senior class are eligible. Children of international union officers or employees are not eligible. Renewable if recipients maintain satisfactory progress toward requirements for a degree. Information and applications are available at local union offices, or write to address below for details. Must have a GPA of at least 3.4.

Glass, Molders, Pottery, Plastics, and Allied Workers
  Int'l Union
Memorial Scholarship Program
PO Box 6730
Princeton, NJ 08541

888
Glaxo Wellcome Opportunity Scholarship Program

AMOUNT: Maximum: $5000   DEADLINE: April 1
FIELDS/MAJORS: All Areas of Study

For any student who is a U.S. citizen and has lived in Durham, Orange, Wake, or Chatham counties for the past six months. Must be able to demonstrate the potential to succeed despite adversity as well as an exceptional desire to improve himself or herself through further education or training. Write to the address listed or call (919) 549-9840 for more information.

Triangle Community Foundation
Polly Guthrie, Program Officer
PO Box 12834
Research Triangle Pk., NC 27709

889
Glenn Moon Scholarship

AMOUNT: Maximum: $1000   DEADLINE: March 31
FIELDS/MAJORS: Education

Open to high school seniors who are Connecticut residents. Must be enrolling in four-year schools. Selections based on academics, financial need, and a career goal of education. Renewable for four years. This organization administers this award and two smaller awards. Contact your high school guidance counselor for further information and an application. Must have a GPA of at least 2.8.

Association of Retired Teachers of Connecticut
Glenn Moon Scholarship Fund, Inc.
405 W. Lakeside Blvd.
Waterbury, CT 06708

890
Gloria Fecht Memorial Scholarship

AMOUNT: $1000-$3000   DEADLINE: March 1
FIELDS/MAJORS: All Areas of Study

Scholarships are available for female Southern California residents enrolled at a four-year college or university, with a GPA of at least 3.0 and an interest in golf. Financial need is considered. Twenty to thirty awards are offered annually. Renewable for up to four years. Write to the address below for information.

Gloria Fecht Memorial Scholarships Fund
402 West Arrow Highway, Suite 10
San Dimas, CA 91773

891

GLSEN Scholarship

AMOUNT: Maximum: $500 DEADLINE: April 15
FIELDS/MAJORS: All Areas of Study

Open to gay, lesbian, bisexual, or transgendered students pursuing higher education. Must be between sixteen and twenty-one years of age, attending college in the fall, and Connecticut residents. Previous winners are not eligible to apply. Contact the address listed for further information.

Gay, Lesbian, and Straight Education Network,
  Ct. Chapter
Ronnie Kim, G.H. Robertson School
227 Cross St.
Coventry, CT 06238

892

Golden Gate Scholarships

AMOUNT: None Specified DEADLINE: March 31
FIELDS/MAJORS: Food Service, Restaurant/Hotel Management

Awards for students from the San Francisco Bay Area who have taken a food education and service training or other commercial food course approved by the GGRASF trustees. Preference is given to students enrolling full-time at the City College of San Francisco or Diablo Valley College. Must have a GPA of 2.75 or higher in hotel and restaurant courses. Write to the address listed for more information. Send a self-addressed postage paid envelope with at least $.90 postage in order to receive the full application package.

Golden Gate Restaurant Association Scholarship
  Foundation
Noah Andrew Froio, Scholarship Coordinator
720 Market St., Suite 200
San Francisco, CA 94102

893

Golden Key Scholar Awards

AMOUNT: Maximum: $10000 DEADLINE: February 15
FIELDS/MAJORS: All Areas of Study

Awards are available for graduate students who were members of the Golden Key National Honor Society. Applicants may be undergraduates or recent alumni, but they must hold the bachelor's degree by the time the scholarship is received. Based on academics, activities, and recommendations. Ten awards offered annually. Write to the address listed or call 1-800-377-2401 for more information.

Golden Key National Honor Society
1189 Ponce de Leon Ave.
Atlanta, GA 30306

894

Goldstein Scottish Rite Scholarships

AMOUNT: None Specified DEADLINE: May 15
FIELDS/MAJORS: All Areas of Study

Scholarships open to needy graduates of local Juneau, Alaska, high schools. The number and amount of awards varies. Contact the address listed for further information or call (907) 586-2849.

Goldstein Scottish Rite Trust
James H. Taylor, Manager
PO Box 021194
Juneau, AK 99802

895

Golf Course Superintendents Association of America Scholarship

AMOUNT: $500-$3500 DEADLINE: June 1
FIELDS/MAJORS: Turfgrass Management

Must have completed first year of a two-year program, or completed the second year of a four-year program, or be currently enrolled in a graduate program. Criteria: high scholastic capabilities, employee or former employee of a golf course, leadership, etc. Additional award for international students. Must be nominated. Scholarship applications may be obtained from your advisor or major professor. Write to address below for information if necessary.

Golf Course Superintendents Association of America
Scholarship and Research Committee
1421 Research Park Dr.
Lawrence, KS 66049

896

Golf Foundation Undergraduate Scholarships

AMOUNT: $2000 DEADLINE: March 1
FIELDS/MAJORS: All Areas of Study

Scholarships for graduating high school senior women who have been involved with the sport of golfing (skill or excellence in golf is not a criterion). Must be a U.S. citizen and have a minimum GPA of 3.0. Selection is made on the basis of academics, financial need, character, and an involvement with the sport of golf. Applications may be obtained by sending a request and a business-sized SASE to the address below.

Women's Western Golf Foundation
Mrs. Richard W. Willis
393 Ramsay Road
Deerfield, IL 60015

897
Gongoro Nakamura Memorial Scholarship

AMOUNT: None Specified DEADLINE: April 1
FIELDS/MAJORS: Debate, Public Speaking

Open to incoming freshmen who are members of Japanese ancestry and entering or enrolled at an accredited college or university. Applications and information may be obtained from local JACL chapters, district offices, and the national headquarters at the address listed or call (415) 921-5225. Please indicate your level of study and be certain to include a legal-sized SASE.

Japanese American Citizens League
National Scholarship and Award Program
1765 Sutter St.
San Francisco, CA 94115

898
Gordie Howe Scholarship

AMOUNT: Maximum: $1500 DEADLINE: March 1
FIELDS/MAJORS: All Areas of Study

Open to high school seniors who are Connecticut residents. To be used at a four-year school with a hockey program. Based on high academics and outstanding hockey ability. Must be planning to play hockey in college. Contact the address listed for further information. Must have a GPA of at least 3.0.

Hartford Whalers Foundation
Ms. Mary Lynn Gorman
242 Trumbull St.
Hartford, CT 06103

899
Gordon Scheer Scholarship

AMOUNT: Maximum: $1000 DEADLINE: June 30
FIELDS/MAJORS: Accounting

Open to Colorado residents who are enrolled as accounting majors in an accredited program at a Colorado college or university with a minimum GPA of 3.5. Must have completed intermediate accounting. Winners may reapply each time the scholarship is offered. Write to the address listed for details.

Colorado Society of Certified Public Accountants
Scholarship Coordinator
7979 E. Tufts Ave., #500
Denver, CO 80237

900
Government Scholars Program

AMOUNT: None Specified DEADLINE: January 13
FIELDS/MAJORS: Municipal Government

Summer program for New York sophomores, juniors, or seniors who are interested in pursuing a career in municipal government. The program combines work experience in the mayor's office with weekly seminars. Write to the address listed for more information.

New York City Department of Personnel
2 Washington St., 15th Floor
New York, NY 10004

901
Governor's Scholars Program

AMOUNT: Maximum: $4000 DEADLINE: March 1
FIELDS/MAJORS: All Areas of Study

Open to Arkansas high school seniors planning to attend an approved public or private school in Arkansas. Based on academic achievement and leadership qualities. One hundred awards per year. A minimum GPA of 3.6 is required. An ACT score of at least 27 or an SAT score of 1100 is required. Write to the address below for further information.

Arkansas Department of Higher Education
Financial Aid Division
114 East Capitol
Little Rock, AR 72201

902
Governor's Teaching Scholarship Program and Teacher Loan Program

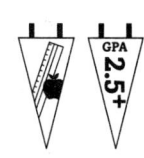

AMOUNT: Maximum: $5000 DEADLINE: None Specified
FIELDS/MAJORS: Education

Loans for South Carolina students intending to pursue a career in teaching. High school seniors must be in the top 40% of their high school class and have ACT/SAT scores equal to or better than the South Carolina average. Undergraduates must have passed the EEE exam and maintain a GPA of at least 2.7. Contact your school's financial aid office or the address below for more information.

South Carolina Student Loan Corporation
Suite 210
Interstate Center
Columbia, SC 29221

903

Governor's Work Force Development Grant

AMOUNT: Maximum: $1000   DEADLINE: April 15
FIELDS/MAJORS: All Areas of Study

Program for Delaware residents enrolled full-time in a degree program at a participating Delaware college and employed by a small business (one hundred or fewer employees). Selections based on financial need. Commission makes final awards July 1. Write to the address listed for more information.

Delaware Higher Education Commission
Carvel State Office Building
820 North French St., #4F
Wilmington, DE 19801

904

Grace Foundation Scholarship Fund

AMOUNT: Maximum: $2500
DEADLINE: January 31
FIELDS/MAJORS: Christian Service, Healthcare, Teaching, Theology, Welfare

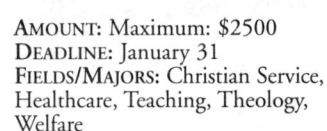

Scholarships for Southeast Asian Christian students with the intent of providing service in one of the above areas to the poor and uneducated in their own country. Must be able to express himself/herself in English and have financial need. Renewable with reapplication. Intended primarily for students from developing countries (including China). Minimum GPA of 3.0 or above. If interested, write to the address listed between September 1 and October 31 to request an application. Must indicate (in English) name/address of applicant, name and address of college (include beginning date), intended course of study, statement of financial need, and a brief background of Christian testimony.

Grace Foundation Scholarship Fund
PO Box 924
Menlo Park, CA 94026

905

Grace Whiting Myers— Malcolm T. Maceachern Student Loan Fund

AMOUNT: None Specified   DEADLINE: None Specified
FIELDS/MAJORS: Medical Record Administration/Medical Record Technology

Must have been accepted for enrollment in a program of medical record administration approved by the committee on allied health and accreditation. Must be in final year of program and a member of AHIMA and have a minimum GPA of 2.5. Graduate students must be a credentialed HIM professional (RRA, ART, or CCS) and an active AHIMA member. Must be a U.S. citizen. Write to address below for details. Please indicate your major field of study.

American Health Information Management Association
Fore Loan Program
919 N. Michigan Ave., Suite 1400
Chicago, IL 60611

906

Graduate and Postgraduate Research Grants

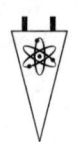

AMOUNT: Maximum: $2500   DEADLINE: February 1
FIELDS/MAJORS: Natural Resources Research

Graduate and postgraduate research grants for the support of research in which the natural resources of the Huyck Preserve are utilized. Must also work on the Preserve. Housing and lab space are provided at the Preserve. Please contact address below for complete information.

Edmund Niles Huyck Preserve
PO Box 189
Rensselaerville, NY 12147

907

Graduate Environmental Protection Scholarships

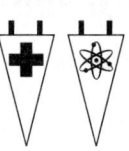

AMOUNT: None Specified   DEADLINE: February 15
FIELDS/MAJORS: Groundwater Hydrology, Toxicology, Public Health, Forestry

Contractual scholarships available for full-time students in graduate levels of study. Students must agree to work full-time for the Kentucky National Resources and Environmental Protection Cabinet after graduation. Must have good academic standing and a letter of recommendation from a faculty advisor. An essay will also be required. Write to the address listed for details.

Kentucky Water Resources Research Institute
Scholarship Program Coordinator
233 Mining and Mineral
Lexington, KY 40506

908

Graduate Fellowships

AMOUNT: $1000-$7000   DEADLINE: February 1
FIELDS/MAJORS: All Fields of Study

Fellowships are open to active members of Phi Kappa Phi who will be enrolling as first-year graduate students. Nomination by current chapter or the chapter in which you were initiated is required. Fifty awards per year. Thirty honorable mention awards of $1000 are awarded yearly. Application forms are available through the Chapter secretaries. Contact your Chapter's secretary to indicate your interest in becoming the Chapter's nominee, or contact the national office (504) 388-4917.

Phi Kappa Phi Honor Society
Louisiana State University
PO Box 16000
Baton Rouge, LA 70893

909
Graduate Fellowships

AMOUNT: None Specified DEADLINE: January 10
FIELDS/MAJORS: Graphic Communications

Open to graduate student in graphic communications with more than one year of study to complete and graduating college seniors who wish to pursue advanced training. Write to the address below for details. Please specify that you are interested in support for graduate studies. Applications available to print at the Web site: http://www.gatf.lm.com

National Scholarship Trust Fund of the Graphic Arts
4615 Forbes Ave.
Pittsburgh, PA 15213

910
Graduate Fellowships at National Laboratories and Cooperating Facilities

AMOUNT: None Specified DEADLINE: February 1
FIELDS/MAJORS: Science, Engineering

Program open to qualified college and university faculty members in science, mathematics, engineering, and technology. Awards open to qualified master's and doctoral degree candidates. Purpose is to provide the opportunity to conduct thesis or dissertation research or to explore research career options at a cooperating facility. Fellowships range from one to twelve months. Awards may include a monthly stipend of $1300, tuition assistance, and a travel allowance. Contact the dean of your department for further information.

Associated Western Universities, Inc.
4190 So. Highland Dr., Suite 211
Salt Lake City, UT 84124

911
Graduate Fellowships for Minorities and Women in the Physical Sciences

AMOUNT: $12500
DEADLINE: November 5
FIELDS/MAJORS: Astronomy, Chemistry, Computer Science, Geology, Materials/Mathematical Sciences, Physics

Six-year fellowship program for current college seniors with a minimum GPA of 3.0 or students completing a master's degree at an institution that does not have a Ph.D. program in your discipline. Applicants may also possess a degree and be out of school at least one year. Open to underrepresented minorities: African-, Hispanic-, Native-Americans, Eskimos, Aleutians, Pacific Islanders, or females. Must be U.S. citizens and have the ability to pursue graduate work at an NPSC member institution. Note: Students currently enrolled in a master's or Ph.D. program at an institution that offers a Ph.D. in the student's discipline are not eligible. The application period is August through November 5. Award announcements made at the end of January. Contact the address below for further information.

National Physical Science Consortium MSC 3NPS
New Mexico State University
Box 30001
Las Cruces, NM 88003

912
Graduate Fellowships for Study in Belgium

AMOUNT: Maximum: $12000 DEADLINE: January 31
FIELDS/MAJORS: Belgian Studies

Grant for students working toward a Ph.D. in an area of Belgian studies. Must be U.S. citizens, preferably under the age of thirty, with speaking and reading knowledge of Dutch, French, or German. The grant is for travel and expenses to Belgium for a period of ten months. Write to the address listed for more information.

Belgian American Educational Foundation, Inc.
195 Church St.
New Haven, CT 06510

913
Graduate Research Assistant Program

AMOUNT: None Specified
DEADLINE: None Specified
FIELDS/MAJORS: See Listing of Fields Below

Resident graduate assistantships are available at Los Alamos for students with a GPA of at least 2.5 who are looking to get paid relevant work experience while pursuing an advanced degree. Fields of study are Chemistry, Computer Science, Economics, Chemical, Electrical, Mechanical and Nuclear Engineering, Health, Environmental, Life, Earth, and Space Science. Other applicable fields include Materials Science, Metallurgy, Mathematics, Physics, and Optical Engineering. Write to the address below for information.

Los Alamos National Laboratory
Personnel Services Division
Mail Stop P282
Los Alamos, NM 87545

914
Graduate Research Fellowships (Viets Fellowship)

AMOUNT: $3000 DEADLINE: March 15
FIELDS/MAJORS: Neuromuscular Medicine

Fellowships are available for medical or graduate students involved in basic or clinical research related to Myasthenia Gravis (MG). Write to the address below for information.

Myasthenia Gravis Foundation of America
Fellowship Program
222 S. Riverside Plaza, Suite 1540
Chicago, IL 60606

915
Graduate Scholarships and Teaching Assistantships

AMOUNT: Maximum: $6000 DEADLINE: April 16
FIELDS/MAJORS: Fine Art

Open to graduate students at the School of the Museum of Fine Arts and Tufts University. Tuition scholarships are need-based grants and available for the first two years of the MFA program. Teaching assistantships are for second- and third-year students. Each school has slightly different criteria. Apply directly to the financial aid offices at Tufts or the School of the Museum of Fine Arts. Contact the financial aid offices of either school for the specific information regarding their programs.

School of the Museum of Fine Arts
Office of Financial Aid
230 The Fenway
Boston, MA 02115

916
Graduate Scholarship Program

AMOUNT: Maximum: $7200 DEADLINE: None Specified
FIELDS/MAJORS: All Areas of Study

Open to graduate students who are New Mexico residents. Expressly for underrepresented groups. Applicants must continue education in a New Mexico public university and serve ten hours per week in an unpaid internship or assistantship. Contact the Dean of Graduate Studies at a New Mexico four-year public postsecondary institution.

New Mexico Commission on Higher Education
Financial Aid and Student Services
PO Box 15910
Santa Fe, NM 87506

917
Graduate Scholarship Program

AMOUNT: None Specified DEADLINE: February 1
FIELDS/MAJORS: Counseling, Psychology, Mental Health, Mental Retardation, Speech Pathology

Scholarships for graduate students who intend to work directly with children in fields related to the areas above, as well as Exceptional Children, Remedial Skills Development, Hearing Impaired, Gifted and Talented. Based on commitment to children with special needs, scholarship, recommendations, and motivation and goals. Official application forms are available only between September 1st and November 15th. They are available from Junior Auxiliary Chapters, colleges and universities, and from the address below. Requests made at any other time will not be accepted.

National Association of Junior Auxiliaries
NAJA Scholarship Committee
PO Box 1873
Greenville, MS 38702

918
Graduate Scholarship Program

AMOUNT: None Specified DEADLINE: June 1
FIELDS/MAJORS: Dental Hygiene, Dental Research

Scholarships for students who have at least been accepted to a full-time master's or doctoral program. Minimum GPA of 3.0. Licensure as a dental hygienist is required. Write to the address below for more information.

American Dental Hygienists' Association Institute for Oral Health
444 N. Michigan Ave., Suite 3400
Chicago, IL 60611

919
Graduate Scholarships

AMOUNT: None Specified DEADLINE: January 31
FIELDS/MAJORS: Aerospace Education, Science

Applicants must be CAP members and majoring in aerospace education or science. For graduate study. Write to the address listed for details.

Civil Air Patrol
National Headquarters Cap (TT)
Maxwell AFB, AL 36112

920

Graduate Scholarships and Fellowships

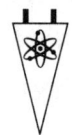

AMOUNT: $1250-$5000 DEADLINE: February 1
FIELDS/MAJORS: Food Science and Technology

Graduate fellowships to encourage and support research in food science and technology at accredited institutions in the U.S. or Canada. In addition, the Arthur T. Schramm Fellowship will provide tuition assistance for needy Ph.D. candidates. Thirty-nine awards offered annually. Write to the address below for details. Please specify your year in school or what degree you are pursuing. You may request information and an application via phone at (312) 782-8424 or "fax on demand" 1-800-234-0270. Graduates must request document #3440.

Institute of Food Technologists
Scholarship Department
221 North LaSalle St.
Chicago, IL 60601

921

Graduate Scholarships in the Marine Sciences

AMOUNT: Maximum: $3000 DEADLINE: March 1
FIELDS/MAJORS: Marine Sciences

Scholarships are available to qualified graduate students pursuing a degree in marine science. Qualifications considered include general aptitude and ability in area of study, character, previous academic accomplishments, and financial need. Only candidates approved as proper recipients for scholarship aid by the faculty of the university he/she attends (will attend) will be considered. Write to the address below for more information. Must have a GPA of at least 3.0.

International Women's Fishing Association Scholarship Trust
PO Drawer 3125
Palm Beach, FL 33480

922

Graduate Student Scholarships

AMOUNT: $2000-$4000 DEADLINE: June 21
FIELDS/MAJORS: Speech-Language Pathology, Communications Disorders

Awards for master's level studies in communication sciences and disorders programs. Four general awards per year. Also available are one award for a foreign or minority student and one award giving preference to a disabled student pursuing graduate studies in the field. (up to six awards total). Write to the address below for complete details.

American Speech-Language-Hearing Foundation
10801 Rockville Pike
Rockville, MD 20852

923

Graduate Student Scholarships

AMOUNT: Maximum: $1500 DEADLINE: April 1
FIELDS/MAJORS: Agricultural Engineering, Agronomy, Crop and Soil Sciences, Entomology, Food Sciences, Horticulture, Plant Pathology

Available to graduate students with high academic achievement and leadership abilities and who are enrolled in any field that may enhance the potato industry. A limited number of schools from across the country are participating chosen by structure of potato-related graduate programs. Contact the address listed for further information or (207) 379-2013. Must have a GPA of at least 2.5.

National Potato Council Auxiliary Scholarship Committee
Sheila Campbell
PO Box 26
Exeter, ME 04435

924

Graduate Study-Library Science Scholarship

AMOUNT: None Specified DEADLINE: May 15
FIELDS/MAJORS: Library Science, Information Science

Tuition and fee assistance for Pennsylvania residents enrolled in an ALA-approved program of graduate work in an institution located in Pennsylvania. Based on need, scholarship, motivation, and experience. Write to Ms. Margaret Bauer, Executive Director, at the address below for complete details.

Pennsylvania Library Association
1919 N. Front St.
Harrisburg, PA 17102

925

Graham-Fancher Scholarship Trust

AMOUNT: $200-$300 DEADLINE: May 1
FIELDS/MAJORS: All Areas of Study

For graduating seniors in northern Santa Cruz County, California, high schools. Must be resident of northern Santa Cruz, California. Contact your high school guidance counselor or write to the address below for details.

Graham-Fancher Scholarship Trust
C/O Robert H. Darrow, Attorney at Law
149 Josephine St., Suite A
Santa Cruz, CA 95060

926
Grain Sorghum Scholarship

AMOUNT: Maximum: $400 DEADLINE: February 1
FIELDS/MAJORS: Agriculture-Related Field

Open to a graduating high school senior or to a student currently enrolled in postsecondary education. The student must plan to pursue a course of study in preparation for a career in agriculture or an agricultural-related field. The applicants' parents or guardians must be members of the Association. Winners will be notified in May. Contact the address listed or call (402) 471-3552 for further information.

Nebraska Grain Sorghum Producers Association
Scholarship Coordinator
PO Box 94982
Lincoln, NE 68509

927
Grant and Programs for Theological Studies

AMOUNT: None Specified DEADLINE: None Specified
FIELDS/MAJORS: Theology, Religion

Grants for theology students at the graduate level of study who are members of the Presbyterian Church, USA Applicants must be U.S. citizens, demonstrate financial need, and be recommended by an academic advisor or church pastor. Write to the address below for more information.

Presbyterian Church, USA
Office of Financial Aid
100 Witherspoon St.
Louisville, KY 40202

928
Grant M. Mack Memorial Scholarships

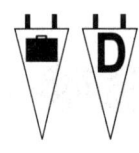

AMOUNT: Maximum: $2000 DEADLINE: March 1
FIELDS/MAJORS: Business

Two scholarships for graduate and undergraduate students. Must be legally blind and majoring in business. Write to the address listed or call (202) 467-5081 or 1-800-424-8666 for details.

American Council of the Blind
Scholarship Coordinator
1155 15th St. NW, Suite 720
Washington, DC 20005

929
Grant Program

AMOUNT: Maximum: $3000 DEADLINE: July 15
FIELDS/MAJORS: Parapsychology

Grants for research in parapsychology (ESP, psychic phenomena, psychokinesis). Not for travel, graduate, or undergraduate studies. For persons studying parapsychology directly (not those with merely a general interest in the subject). Write to the address below for details.

Parapsychology Foundation, Inc.
Eileen J. Garrett Library
228 E. 71st St.
New York, NY 10021

930
Grant Program for Dependents of Correctional Officers

AMOUNT: None Specified DEADLINE: None Specified
FIELDS/MAJORS: All Areas of Study

The Correctional Officer's Grant provides payment of tuition and mandatory fees for the spouse and children of Illinois correctional officers killed or 90% disabled in the line of duty. Recipients must be enrolled on at least half-time basis. Applicants must be U.S. citizens residing in Illinois and attending Illinois postsecondary institutions. Write to the address below for complete details.

Illinois Student Assistance Commission
1755 Lake Cook Road
Deerfield, IL 60015

931
Grant Program for Medical Studies

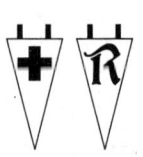

AMOUNT: $500-$1500 DEADLINE: None Specified
FIELDS/MAJORS: Medicine

Grants for medical students at the graduate level of study who are members of the Presbyterian Church, USA Applicants must be U.S. citizens, demonstrate financial need, and be recommended by an academic advisor or church pastor. Write to the address below for more information.

Presbyterian Church, USA
Office of Financial Aid
100 Witherspoon St.
Louisville, KY 40202

932
Grant Program for New Investigators

AMOUNT: Maximum: $12500   DEADLINE: None Specified
FIELDS/MAJORS: Pharmacy, Pharmacology

Fellowships for graduate students in pharmacy who are nearing the end of their last year of graduate study (earning Ph.D.). Information may be available from your pharmacy school. Write to the address below if necessary.

American Foundation for Pharmaceutical Education
One Church St.
Suite 202
Rockville, MD   20850

933
Grant-in-Aid for Graduate Students

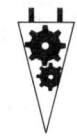

AMOUNT: $7500   DEADLINE: December 15
FIELDS/MAJORS: Air Conditioning/Refrigeration, HVAC Engineering

Grant for full-time graduate students in ASHRAE-related fields. Program is designed "to encourage the student to continue his/her preparation for service in the heating, ventilating, and air-conditioning industry." Relevance of proposed research is considered. Not renewable. Applications are made by your advisor on your behalf. Consult with your advisor, and write to the address below for further details and application forms. Please specify that your interest is in the graduate student Grant-in-Aid program.

American Society of Heating, Refrigerating, and
   Air-Conditioning Engineers
Manager of Research
1791 Tullie Circle, NE
Atlanta, GA   30329

934
Grant-in-Aid for Wildlife Research

AMOUNT: None Specified   DEADLINE: November 1
FIELDS/MAJORS: Wildlife, Large Game Animal Research

Awards for graduate students and more advanced investigators to support research on wildlife, and particularly North American big game animals and/or their habitat. Write to the address below for more information.

Boone and Crockett Club
Old Milwaukee Depot
250 Station Dr.
Missoula, MT   59801

935
Grant-in-Aid of Research

AMOUNT: $500-$2000   DEADLINE: January 31
FIELDS/MAJORS: American History, Political History

Grants for researchers of subjects that are addressed by the holdings of the LBJ Library. Research is done at the library. Twenty awards are offered annually. Interested applicants must contact the library at the address below (or call (512) 482-5137) to obtain information about materials available in the library on the proposed research topic.

Lyndon Baines Johnson Foundation
Archives, Lyndon B. Johnson Library
2313 Red River St.
Austin, TX   78705

936
Grants and Fellowships in Arthritis Research

AMOUNT: None Specified   DEADLINE: September 1
FIELDS/MAJORS: Arthritis Research

Various fellowship and grant programs open to doctors and scientists to further their training in patient care and research into arthritis. Doctoral dissertation awards are also available. Write to the address below for complete details.

Arthritis Foundation
Research Department
1314 Spring St., NW
Atlanta, GA   30309

937
Grants for Courses in German Language in Germany

AMOUNT: None Specified   DEADLINE: January 31
FIELDS/MAJORS: German Language

Grants to strengthen German language skills by studying in Germany. Open to full-time graduate students. Applicants must have completed three semesters of college-level German or equivalent. Must be between the ages of eighteen and thirty-two. Write to the address listed for more information.

Daad German Academic Exchange Service
New York Office
950 Third Ave., 19th Floor
New York, NY   10022

938
Grants for Field Research

AMOUNT: Maximum: $1200 DEADLINE: January 31
FIELDS/MAJORS: Science

Grants for graduate students in support of exploration and field research. Expeditions aided will be for specific scientific purposes, in accordance with the Club's stated objective, "to broaden our knowledge of the universe". Awards will be announced in April. Write to the address listed for more information.

Explorers Club Exploration Fund
Exploration Fund Committee
46 East 70th St.
New York, NY 10021

939
Grants for German Studies Programs-Sur Place Grants

AMOUNT: None Specified DEADLINE: May 1
FIELDS/MAJORS: German Studies

Grants to promote the study of German affairs from an inter- and multi-disciplinary perspective. Open to undergraduate juniors and seniors pursuing a German studies track or minor and to master's and Ph.D. candidates working on a certificate in German studies. Ph.D. candidates doing preliminary dissertation work are eligible. Must be U.S. or Canadian citizens. A second deadline date is November 1. Write to the address listed for additional information.

Daad German Academic Exchange Service
New York Office
950 Third Ave., 19th Floor
New York, NY 10022

940
Grants for Orchid Research

AMOUNT: $500-$12000 DEADLINE: January 1
FIELDS/MAJORS: Floriculture, Horticulture

Grants for experimental projects and fundamental and applied research on orchids. Qualified graduate students with appropriate interests may apply for grants in support of their research if it involves or applies to orchids. Purpose of award is to advance the scientific study of orchids in every aspect and to assist in the publication of scholarly and popular scientific literature on orchids. A second deadline date used is August 1 of each year. Post-graduates may only apply on behalf of the accredited institution or appropriate research institute they are associated with. Contact address listed for complete details.

American Orchid Society
Research Grants
6000 South Olive Ave.
West Palm Beach, FL 33405

941
Grants for Study, Research, and Information Visits to Germany

AMOUNT: None Specified DEADLINE: November 1
FIELDS/MAJORS: German Language and Studies

Grants to strengthen German language skills or knowledge of German culture to pursue research at universities and other institutions in Germany. Open to doctoral students and scientists for specific research projects. At least two years of teaching and/or research experience after the Ph.D. or equivalent and a research record in the proposed field are required. Write to the address listed for further information.

Daad German Academic Exchange Service
New York Office
950 Third Ave., 19th Floor
New York, NY 10022

942
Grants in Aid for Graduate Seminar

AMOUNT: Maximum: $2000 DEADLINE: March 1
FIELDS/MAJORS: Numismatics

Applicants must have completed one year of graduate study at a North American university. Recipients must attend the Society's annual graduate seminar in numismatics. Ten awards offered annually. Write to the address listed for details.

American Numismatic Society
Broadway at 155th St.
New York, NY 10032

943
Grants-in-Aid

AMOUNT: $650-$2400 DEADLINE: None Specified
FIELDS/MAJORS: History of Business, Technology, and Society

Grants-in-aid are available to scholars at all levels who are working within the Hagley's research collection topics. Stipends are for a minimum of two weeks and a maximum of two months at $1200 per month. Hagley offers three deadlines per year: March 31, June 30, and October 31. Write to Dr. Philip B. Scranton at the address shown below for details.

Hagley Museum and Library
PO Box 3630
Wilmington, DE 19807

944

Grants-in-Aid

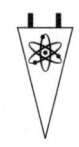

AMOUNT: Maximum: $2000   DEADLINE: January 15
FIELDS/MAJORS: Petroleum Geology, Geology, Geophysics, Paleontology

Grants are available to graduate students in studies relating to the earth science aspects of the petroleum industry. Several grant programs are offered by the AAPG. Write to the address listed for more details.

American Association of Petroleum Geologists
W.A. Morgan, Chairman/AAPG Grants CTME.
PO Box 979
Tulsa, OK 74101

945

Grants-in-Aid Program

AMOUNT: None Specified   DEADLINE: December 15
FIELDS/MAJORS: Twentieth Century American History, Public Policy, Political Science

These awards are for scholars investigating some aspect of the political, economic, and social development of the U.S. Principally between April 12, 1945, and January 20, 1953, or the public career of Harry S. Truman. Institute grant is for $1000. Research grant is for $12000. Dissertation fellowship is $20000 and is offered every other year. Interested persons should submit an informal proposal no later than December 15. Indicate what work has been done toward the completion of the project, what remains to be done, and the specific resources in the Truman Library that will be utilized. Applicants selected to continue in the second phase of the process will receive forms to be submitted by February 15.

Harry S. Truman Library Institute
Assistant Secretary-Treasurer
U.S. Highway 24 and Delaware St.
Independence, MO 64050

946

Grants-in-Aid Program in Support of Anthropological Research

AMOUNT: Maximum: $15000   DEADLINE: May 1
FIELDS/MAJORS: Anthropology

Open to qualified scholars affiliated with accredited institutions and organizations. Awards are for individual postdoctoral research or for dissertation thesis research. Write to the address below for details.

Wenner-Gren Foundation for Anthropological Research
Grants Programs
220 Fifth Ave.
New York, NY 10001

947

Grass Fellowships in Neurophysiology

AMOUNT: None Specified   DEADLINE: December 1
FIELDS/MAJORS: Neurophysiology

Summer fellowships for late predoctoral or early postdoctoral researchers who are academically prepared for independent research in neurophysiology. This is a resident fellowship at the Marine Biological Laboratory at Woods Hole, Massachusetts. Requires research proposal, budget, and recommendation. Interested persons should write to the address listed for further information. Request bulletin FA-298.

Grass Foundation
77 Reservoir Road
Quincy, MA 02170

948

Greater Bridgeport Area Foundation Scholarships

AMOUNT: None Specified   DEADLINE: May 1
FIELDS/MAJORS: All Areas of Study

Over fifty different scholarships are available for students who are residents of the greater Bridgeport Area Foundation service area, which includes: Bridgeport, Easton, Fairfield, Milford, Monroe, Selton, Stratford, Trumbull, and Wesport. Individual requirements will vary. Almost all awards for high school seniors. Write to the address below for information.

Greater Bridgeport Area Foundation
280 State St.
Bridgeport, CT 06604

949

Greater Hartford Interracial Scholarship

AMOUNT: Maximum: $750   DEADLINE: February 24
FIELDS/MAJORS: All Areas of Study

Open to high school seniors who are residents of Hartford or contiguous suburbs. May be used at two- or four-year schools. Must be in the upper third of class, be involved in community service, and be able to demonstrate financial need. This award may be renewable. Contact the address listed for further information. Must have a GPA of at least 3.0.

Greater Hartford Interracial Scholarship Fund, Inc.
Ellis Simpson
PO Box 320644
Hartford, CT 06132

950
Greater Hartford Jaycees Scholarship

AMOUNT: $1000-$2000 DEADLINE: February 14
FIELDS/MAJORS: Performing Arts, Technical Fields, All Areas of Study

Open to high school seniors who are residents of the Greater Hartford area. For use at an accredited four-year school. Must be able to demonstrate good academics, community service, and financial need. One scholarship is $2000, and the remaining four are for $1000 each. They are all renewable for four years if recipients maintain set standards of the donor. There is one award for performing arts, one award for technical fields, and the three remaining are for all other areas of study. Contact the address listed for further information. Must have a GPA of at least 3.0.

Greater Hartford Jaycees Foundation, Inc.
Vice President
1 Financial Plaza
Hartford, CT 06103

951
Greater Seattle Business Association Scholarships

AMOUNT: Maximum: $3500 DEADLINE: February 20
FIELDS/MAJORS: All Areas of Study

Awards open to undergraduate Washington residents who are self-identified gay/lesbian or children of gay/lesbian families. Must demonstrate significant financial need and potential leadership. Contact the address listed for further information.

Greater Seattle Business Association and Pride Foundation
2033 6th Ave., #804
Seattle, WA 98121

952
Grotefend Scholarship Fund

AMOUNT: None Specified DEADLINE: None Specified
FIELDS/MAJORS: All Areas of Study

For high school seniors who attended all four years of high school in Shasta County, California. Do not contact the bank. Please see your high school counselor for an application.

Wells Fargo Bank
PO Box 2511
Sacramento, CA 95812

953
Guggenheim Fellowship at the National Air and Space Museum

AMOUNT: $14000-$25000 DEADLINE: January 15
FIELDS/MAJORS: Aeronautics, Astronomy, Astrophysics, Space Research

Residential fellowships for predoctoral (all work completed except for dissertation) or postdoctoral researchers in the above areas. Persons holding Ph.D. must have received doctorate within seven years of the award. Fellowship is a six- to twelve-month, in-residence program. Notifications sent by April 15. Contact the address listed for further information.

National Air and Space Museum, Smithsonian Institution
Fellowship Coordinator
MRC 312
Washington, DC 20560

954
Guggenheim Foundation Dissertation Awards and Research Grants

AMOUNT: $15000-$35000 DEADLINE: August 1
FIELDS/MAJORS: Subspecialties Directly Related to Violence, Aggression, and Dominance

Fellowships supporting the writing (i.e., not the preliminary work) of Ph.D. dissertations and grants supporting advanced research in areas of concern to the Foundation. Priority given to research that can increase understanding and amelioration of urgent problems in the modern world related to these topics. Research area must be directly related to these topics. August 1 is the deadline for decisions announced in December. Write for details. Dissertation applicants are asked to take particular care in deciding to apply and in organizing and completing application.

Harry Frank Guggenheim Foundation
Research Grants and Dissertation Awards
527 Madison Ave.
New York, NY 10022

955
Guild Hall Summer Intern Program

AMOUNT: Maximum: $100 DEADLINE: March 1
FIELDS/MAJORS: Performing Arts, Theater

Internship for college students interested in working in theater. Possible housing is available, but transportation expenses are not provided. Three awards are offered annually. Write to the address below for more information.

Guild Hall
Ms. Brigitte Blachere, General Manager
158 Main St.
East Hampton, NY 11937

956
Guy D. and Mary Edith Halladay Scholarships

AMOUNT: $500-$2500　DEADLINE: April 14
FIELDS/MAJORS: All Areas of Study

Scholarships for graduate students of Kent County who are studying at a school in western Michigan. Based on academic ability and demonstrated financial need. Requires a minimum GPA of at least 3.0. Write to the address listed for details.

Grand Rapids Foundation
209-C Waters Bldg.
161 Ottawa Ave., NW
Grand Rapids, MI 49503

957
Guy M. Wilson, William D. Brewer, Jewell W. Brewer Scholarships

AMOUNT: Maximum: $500　DEADLINE: February 1
FIELDS/MAJORS: All Areas of Study

Scholarships available for Michigan residents who will be or are attending a college or university in Michigan. Applicants must be citizens of the U.S. and children of veterans. Twenty-eight awards offered annually. Write to the address below for additional information.

American Legion Auxiliary, Department of Michigan
212 North Verlinden
Lansing, MI 48915

958
H.B. Paul Lowenberg Lions Scholarship

AMOUNT: Maximum: $500　DEADLINE: May 15
FIELDS/MAJORS: All Areas of Study

Open to high school seniors who are residents of Hartford or bordering towns. May be used at two- or four-year schools. Preference to music and the arts majors. Based on academic success and financial need. Two to four awards offered annually. Contact the address listed for further information. Must have a GPA of at least 2.8.

Lions Club of Hartford, Inc.
Scholarship Chairman
PO Box 1175
Hartford, CT 06143

959
H. Fletcher Brown Fund Scholarships

AMOUNT: None Specified
DEADLINE: April 10
FIELDS/MAJORS: Medicine, Dentistry, Law, Engineering, or Chemistry

Scholarships for Delaware-born residents in the above areas of study. Based on career goals, grades, need, and character. For first-year undergraduate or first-year graduate study. Applicants must be in the upper 20% of graduating class with an SAT score of 1000 or above. The term "medicine" is limited to those preparing to practice as a Doctor of Medicine (M.D. degree) or a Doctor of Osteopathy (D.O. degree). Family income must be under $60,000 unless extenuating circumstances are demonstrated. Contact Mr. Gregg L. Landis at the address below for details. Must have a GPA of at least 3.2.

H. Fletcher Brown Fund
C/O Bank of Delaware, Trust Department
PO Box 791
Wilmington, DE 19899

960
H. Thomas Austern Memorial Writing Competition

AMOUNT: $1000-$3000　DEADLINE: May 16
FIELDS/MAJORS: Law

Writing competition open to law students interested in the areas of law that affect foods, drugs, devices, and biologics. Submitted papers are judged by a committee of practicing attorneys with relevant expertise on a variety of factors. Write to the address below for more information.

Food and Drug Law Institute
Director of Academic Programs
1000 Vermont Ave. NW, Suite 200
Washington, DC 20005

961
H.A. Miller Foundation Medical/Dental School Loans

AMOUNT: None Specified　DEADLINE: None Specified
FIELDS/MAJORS: Medicine, Dentistry

Low interest loans to graduates of Curry County, New Mexico, high schools who are attending medical or dental schools. Write to the address below for details.

H.A. Miller Foundation
C/O Rowley Law Firm, Attorneys at Law
PO Box 790, 305 Pile
Clovis, NM 88101

962
H.T. Ewald Foundation Scholarships

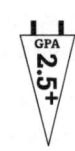

AMOUNT: $500-$3000 DEADLINE: April 1
FIELDS/MAJORS: All Areas of Study

Open to high school seniors who are residents of metropolitan Detroit. Based on financial need; however, letters of recommendation, grades and ACT/SAT scores, extracurricular and community activities will be considered. An autobiography (typed) of at least five hundred words concerning future aspirations will be required. Must be in the top half of class. Two to eighteen awards offered annually. Winners will be notified in late July. Write to the address listed for details. Must have a GPA of at least 2.5.

H.T. Ewald Foundation
Scholarship Coordinator
15175 E. Jefferson Ave.
Grosse Pointe, MI 48230

963
Hach Scientific Foundation Scholarship

AMOUNT: Maximum: $20000 DEADLINE: March 1
FIELDS/MAJORS: Chemistry or Chemical Engineering

Open to high school seniors who ranked in the upper 10% by the end of their junior year. Selection is based on scholarship, character, industry, and aspiration to make a contribution to his/her chosen discipline. Renewable with maintenance of a GPA of 3.0 on a 4.0 scale. Applicants must be residents of Colorado or Iowa. Write to the address below for information and application.

Hach Scientific Foundation
PO Box 389
Loveland, CO 80539

964
Hagley Winterthur Fellowships in Arts and Industries

AMOUNT: $1200-$7200 DEADLINE: December 1
FIELDS/MAJORS: History: Art, Industry, Economics

Open to all scholars who are researching in the fields above and interested in relationships between economic life and the arts. Stipends are for a period of one to six months at $1200 per month. Write to Dr. Philip B. Scranton at the address shown below for details.

Hagley Museum and Library
PO Box 3630
Wilmington, DE 19807

965
Haines Memorial Scholarship

AMOUNT: Maximum: $500 DEADLINE: February 18
FIELDS/MAJORS: Education: Elementary, Secondary

Must be full-time sophomore, junior, or senior in one of the public colleges or universities in South Dakota planning a career in elementary or secondary education. Applicant must have a cumulative GPA of at least 2.5. Apply through your college financial aid office.

South Dakota Board of Regents
Scholarship Committee
207 East Capitol Ave.
Pierre, SD 57501

966
Hal Connolly Scholar-Athlete Award

AMOUNT: Maximum: $1000 DEADLINE: January 30
FIELDS/MAJORS: All Areas of Study

Applicant must be a California resident who competed in high school varsity athletics, will be an incoming freshman under the age of twenty, and has a disability. Write to the address listed or call (916) 654-8055 for details. Must have a GPA of at least 2.8.

California Governor's Committee for Employment of
    Disabled Persons
Scholar-Athlete Awards Program
PO Box 826880, MIC 41
Sacramento, CA 94280

967
Hamilton Community Foundation Scholarships

AMOUNT: $400-$1000 DEADLINE: April 1
FIELDS/MAJORS: All Areas of Study

Open to residents of Hamilton County, Nebraska, attending schools in the U.S. Contact the address listed for further information or (402) 694-3200. Must have a GPA of at least 2.7.

Hamilton Community Foundation, Inc.
Scholarship Coordinator
PO Box 283
Aurora, NE 38818

968

Hampden Academy Fund

AMOUNT: None Specified DEADLINE: None Specified
FIELDS/MAJORS: All Areas of Study

Awards for graduating seniors from Hampden Academy in Bangor, Maine. Contact the Hampden Academy Guidance Office for more information.

Maine Community Foundation
245 East Maine St.
PO Box 148
Ellsworth, ME 04605

969

Handicapped Student Scholarships

AMOUNT: None Specified DEADLINE: December 31
FIELDS/MAJORS: All Areas of Study

Open to students with a physical disability who are between the ages of fifteen and forty. May be a current high school senior or undergraduate. Contact the address listed for further information. Must enclose a SASE for a reply.

Soroptimist Foundation, Inc.
Handicapped Students Awards Coordinator
2 Penn Center Plaza #1000
Philadelphia, PA 19102-1883

970

Hansen Foundation Scholarships

AMOUNT: $1500-$4000 DEADLINE: October 9
FIELDS/MAJORS: All Areas of Study

Hansen Leaders of Tomorrow, Hansen Merit Scholar, Hansen Student, and Vocational Education Student Scholarships for graduating high school students from schools in the twenty-six counties of northwest Kansas (as far southeast as Saline County). For use at a Kansas college, university, or technical school. Criteria for the different programs varies slightly. Information should be available from your high school guidance counselor or from the address below.

Dane G. Hansen Foundation
Hansen Foundation Scholarships
Dane G. Hansen Memorial Plaza
Logan, KS 67646

971

Harness Tracks of America Scholarships

AMOUNT: $3000 DEADLINE: June 15
FIELDS/MAJORS: All Areas of Study

Awards for children of licensed harness racing drivers, trainers, breeders, or caretakers. Applicants may also be young people actively engaged in harness racing. For any level of study. Five awards offered annually. Write to the address below for more information.

Harness Tracks of America
4640 East Sunrise, Suite 200
Tucson, AZ 85718

972

Harold Alfred Wyatt Scholarship (of the Oregon Community Foundation)

AMOUNT: None Specified DEADLINE: March 1
FIELDS/MAJORS: All Areas of Study

Open to graduating seniors of Baker County high schools. Preference given to seniors of Pine Eagle High School. Must be U.S. citizens. Students in middle range of high school GPA are encouraged to apply. For use at Oregon colleges only. This is a one time award. Contact the address listed for further information. Must have a GPA of at least 2.1.

Oregon State Scholarship Commission
Private Awards
1500 Valley River Dr., #100
Eugene, OR 97401-2130

973

Harold and Wilma Haller (of US Bank of Oregon)

AMOUNT: None Specified DEADLINE: March 1
FIELDS/MAJORS: All Areas of Study

Open to graduates of Wallowa County high schools who have not yet attended college. This is a one time award. Must be U.S. citizens or permanent residents to apply. U.S. Bancorp employees, their children, or near relatives are not eligible to apply for this award. Contact the address below for further information.

Oregon State Scholarship Commission
Private Awards
1500 Valley River Dr., #100
Eugene, OR 97401-2130

974
Harold E. Ennes Scholarship, Ennes Broadcast Technology Scholarship

AMOUNT: $1000   DEADLINE: July 1
FIELDS/MAJORS: Broadcast Technology and Engineering

Applicant must be an undergraduate student pursuing a career in the technical aspects of broadcasting. Harold Ennes Fund requires the recommendation of two members of SBE and preference is given to members of SBE. Write to the address below for details.

Society of Broadcast Engineers
Harold E. Ennes Scholarship Committee
8445 Keystone Crossing, Suite 140
Indianapolis, IN 46240

975
Harold Lancour Scholarship for Foreign Study

AMOUNT: $1000   DEADLINE: March 15
FIELDS/MAJORS: Library and Information Science

Applicants must be library students who plan to study abroad. For graduate study. Write to the executive secretary at the address below for details.

Beta Phi Mu International Library Science Honor Society
Executive Secretary, Beta Phi Mu
SLIS-Florida State University
Tallahassee, FL 32306

976
Harriett Barnhart Wimmer Scholarship

AMOUNT: Maximum: $1000   DEADLINE: March 31
FIELDS/MAJORS: Landscape Architecture/Design

Open to female undergraduates in their last year of study. Must demonstrate excellence in design ability and sensitivity to the environment. Contact the address listed for further information or call (202) 686-8337. Must have a GPA of at least 2.8.

Landscape Architecture Foundation
Scholarship Program
4401 Connecticut Ave. NW, #500
Washington, DC 20008

977
Harry A. Applegate Scholarship Award

AMOUNT: None Specified   DEADLINE: March 10
FIELDS/MAJORS: Marketing, Merchandising, Management, Marketing Education

Scholarships for active members of DECA who are furthering their education in marketing. For full-time study in a two- or four-year program. Obtain an application through the school guidance counselor, chapter advisor, state DECA advisor, or from the National DECA at the address listed.

Distributive Education Clubs of America, Inc.
1908 Association Dr.
Reston, VA 22091

978
Harry J. Donnelly Memorial Scholarship

AMOUNT: Maximum: $300   DEADLINE: June 2
FIELDS/MAJORS: Accounting, Law

Awards for undergraduates who are initiated members of Tau Kappa Epsilon and studying in the field of accounting. Graduate students in the field of law are also eligible. Applicants must be full-time students and have a GPA of at least 3.0. Write to the address listed for more information.

TKE Educational Foundation
8645 Founders Road
Indianapolis, IN 46268

979
Harry S. Truman Scholarship

AMOUNT: $3000-$27000   DEADLINE: January 27
FIELDS/MAJORS: Public Service/Government

Must be U.S. citizen or U.S. national from American Samoa or the Commonwealth of the Northern Marina Islands and at least a junior in the upper quarter of class, in an accredited institution. Must be committed to a career in public or government service. 136 awards offered to juniors for senior year. Must be nominated by your department. The foundation does not accept applications directly from students. Information should be available from your school's financial aid office. Must have a GPA of at least 3.0.

Harry S. Truman Scholarship Foundation
712 Jackson Place NW
Washington, DC 20006

980
Harry Shwachman Clinical Investigator Award

AMOUNT: Maximum: $60000 DEADLINE: August 1
FIELDS/MAJORS: Medical Research-Cystic Fibrosis

This three-year award provides the opportunity for clinically trained physicians to develop into independent biomedical research investigators who are actively involved in CF-related areas. It is also intended to facilitate the transition from postdoctoral training to a career in academic medicine. Support is available for up to $60000 per year plus up to $15000 for supplies. Must be U.S. citizen or permanent resident. Write to the address below for details.

Cystic Fibrosis Foundation
Office of Grants Management
6931 Arlington Rd.
Bethesda, MD 20814

981
Hartford County Retired Teachers Association Scholarship

AMOUNT: Maximum: $1500 DEADLINE: March 10
FIELDS/MAJORS: Teaching

Open to graduating seniors attending school in Hartford County who are planning a career in teaching. To be used at four-year schools. Based on leadership, character, academics, and financial need. Information and applications available from your high school guidance counselor. Must have a GPA of at least 3.0.

Hartford County Retired Teacher Association

982
Hartford Golf Club Foundation Scholarship

AMOUNT: $250-$2500 DEADLINE: June 1
FIELDS/MAJORS: All Areas of Study

Open to undergraduates and graduate students who have completed two years of work at the Club or are children of employees (for at least two years). Based on academics and financial need. Contact the address listed for further information. Must have a GPA of at least 3.0.

Hartford Golf Club Foundation
Ms. Wendy Zurstadt
134 Norwood Rd.
West Hartford, CT 06117

983
Harvey Fellows Program

AMOUNT: Maximum: $13000
DEADLINE: December 1
FIELDS/MAJORS: See Fields Listed Below

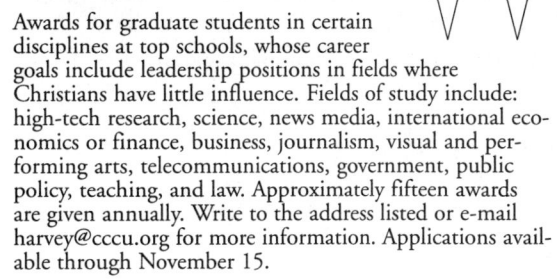

Awards for graduate students in certain disciplines at top schools, whose career goals include leadership positions in fields where Christians have little influence. Fields of study include: high-tech research, science, news media, international economics or finance, business, journalism, visual and performing arts, telecommunications, government, public policy, teaching, and law. Approximately fifteen awards are given annually. Write to the address listed or e-mail harvey@cccu.org for more information. Applications available through November 15.

Harvey Fellows Program
329 Eighth St. NE
Washington, DC 20002

984
Harvey Milk/Tom Homann Gay and Lesbian Scholarship

AMOUNT: $250-$1000 DEADLINE: June 25
FIELDS/MAJORS: All Areas of Study

Open to gay, lesbian, bisexual, and transgendered San Diego area students pursuing vocational, technical, or professional careers. Contact the address listed for further information. Be sure to include a SASE for a reply.

Imperial Court de San Diego
Scholarship Coordinator
PO Box 33915
San Diego, CA 92163

985
Haskell Awards

AMOUNT: $1000 DEADLINE: February 13
FIELDS/MAJORS: Architectural Writing

Awards given for fine writing on architectural subjects at an advanced level of study. Applicants may only submit unpublished works for consideration. Write to the address listed for details.

American Institute of Architects, New York Chapter
Arnold W. Brunner Grant
200 Lexington Ave.
New York, NY 10016

986
Hattie M. Strong Foundation Student Loans

AMOUNT: None Specified   DEADLINE: May 1
FIELDS/MAJORS: All Areas of Study

Interest free loans for students entering their final year of study at an accredited four-year college or graduate school. Must be a U.S. citizen or permanent resident. Applications are mailed January 1 through March 31 only. Write to the address below for details, and be sure to enclose a SASE.

Hattie M. Strong Foundation
1620 Eye St. NW, Suite 700
Washington, DC 20006

987
Hazel Corbin Assistance Fund Grants

AMOUNT: Maximum: $5000   DEADLINE: August 1
FIELDS/MAJORS: Nurse-Midwifery

Grants are available to registered nurses who are seeking nurse-midwifery certification and have been accepted into a nurse-midwifery program in the United States. Write to address below for details.

Maternity Center Association Foundation
Hazel Corbin Assistance Fund
281 Park Ave. South
New York, NY 10010

988
Hazel Hemphill Memorial Scholarship

AMOUNT: $500   DEADLINE: April 1
FIELDS/MAJORS: All Areas of Study

Scholarship for Rocky Mountain Farmers Union regular or associate members who plan on attending any college or vocational school conforming to GI Bill qualifications. One award given out per year. Write to the address listed for further information or an application.

Rocky Mountain Farmers Union/Morgan County Farmers Union
10800 E. Bethany Dr., 4th Floor
Aurora, CO 80014

989
Health Professional Scholarship

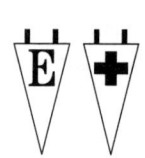

AMOUNT: None Specified   DEADLINE: None Specified
FIELDS/MAJORS: Health

Scholarships for Washington state residents who are studying a health profession. Recipients must agree to provide primary care in a state-defined shortage area for a period not less than three years or repay the scholarship with penalty. The scholarships are renewable for up to five years while the student is enrolled in an eligible health profession training program. Applications are available the January prior to the academic year for which the applicant wishes to be considered. Write to the address below for details.

Washington Higher Education Coordinating Board
917 Lakeridge Way
PO Box 43430
Olympia, WA 98504

990
Health Professionals Loan Repayment Program

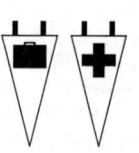

AMOUNT: None Specified   DEADLINE: December 1
FIELDS/MAJORS: See Below

A federal and state funded program to provide for incremental repayment of eligible outstanding student loans in return for service in a New Mexico health professional shortage area. The following areas of health are eligible: osteopathic and allopathic physician, physician assistants, advanced practice nursing, allied healthcare providers, podiatrists, optometrists, and dentists. Applicants must be New Mexico residents. Preference given to graduates of New Mexico public postsecondary institutions. A second deadline date is July 1. Contact the address below for more information.

New Mexico Commission on Higher Education
Financial Aid and Student Services
PO Box 15910
Santa Fe, NM 87506

991
Health Professions Scholarship Program

AMOUNT: None Specified   DEADLINE: None Specified
FIELDS/MAJORS: Healthcare and Related

Scholarships are available for junior, senior, and graduate Native American and Alaskan Native students pursuing a degree in a health related field. For this program, there are payback and service obligation requirements. Must have a GPA of at least 2.0. Contact your area Indian Health Service Office or write to the Scholarships Coordinator at the address below for complete information.

Indian Health Services, U.S. Department of Health and Human Services
Twinbrook Metro Plaza, Suite 100
12300 Twinbrook Parkway
Rockville, MD 20852

992
Health Sciences Scholarship Program

AMOUNT: $10000 DEADLINE: October 31
FIELDS/MAJORS: Allopathic, Osteopathic, Family, Internal, Pediatric Medicine, Nursing, Physician Assistant.

Twenty-five scholarships are available for fourth-year medical students in the areas above or students in the final year of a primary care education program for nurse practitioners, physician assistants, or nurse-midwives. Must have an interest in primary care in West Virginia. Recipients are obligated to sign a contract to practice in an underserved rural area for two years upon graduation. Applicants must attend Marshall University, West Virginia University, Alderson-Broaddus College, or College of West Virginia. Write to the address listed for more information.

University System of West Virginia
1018 Kanawha Blvd. E., Suite 901
Charleston, WV 25301

993
Health Valley Scholarship for Organic Agriculture and Nutrition

AMOUNT: Maximum: $1000 DEADLINE: September 1
FIELDS/MAJORS: Organic Agriculture, Human Nutrition

Open to juniors, seniors, and graduate students majoring in organic agriculture and/or nutrition. Based on academic performance, extracurricular excellence, and an essay demonstrating the applicant's commitment to the field. Winners will be notified by October 19. Contact the address listed for further information. Must have a GPA of at least 3.0.

Health Valley, Inc.
Health Valley Scholarship Program
16100 Foothill Blvd.
Irwindale, CA 91706-7811

994
Health Career Scholarship Program

AMOUNT: Maximum: $1000 DEADLINE: April 1
FIELDS/MAJORS: Health-Related Fields, Dentistry, Medicine

Scholarships are available for U.S. or Canadian citizens enrolled in a health-related program. RN candidates must be in their second year, and bachelor's candidates must be in their third year. Dental and medical students must be in their second year of dental or medical school. Write to the address listed for information, and include a statement as to your field and level of study and a SASE.

International Order of the King's Daughters and Sons
Mrs. Fred Cannon
PO Box 1310
Brookhaven, MS 39601

995
Hearlihy/FTE Grant Excellence in Teaching Technology Education

AMOUNT: Maximum: $2000 DEADLINE: January 1
FIELDS/MAJORS: Elementary/Secondary Technology Education

Applicant must be a teacher (elementary or secondary) who is successfully integrating technology education within the school curriculum and who is a member of the International Technology Education Association. Write to the address listed for details.

International Technology Education Association
Tom Hughes
1914 Association Dr.
Reston, VA 22091

996
Heartland Employee Trust Fund Scholarship

AMOUNT: None Specified DEADLINE: July 1
FIELDS/MAJORS: All Areas of Study

Scholarships for children of employees of the Heartland Health System (in northwest Missouri) who are seeking postsecondary educational experiences. Write to the address listed for details.

Heartland Health Foundation
801 Faraon St.
St. Joseph, MO 64501

997
Heath Education Fund Scholarships

AMOUNT: $750-$1000 DEADLINE: June 30
FIELDS/MAJORS: Ministry, Missionary, Social Work

Open to male high school graduates from schools in the southeastern U.S. The number of awards usually varies between eight and ten. Contact the address listed for further information or call 1-800-457-6417. Must have a GPA of at least 2.8.

Barnett Bank
Heath Education Fund C/O Donna Butcher
PO Box 40200
Jacksonville, FL 32203-0200

998

Hebrew Immigrant Aid Society Scholarships

AMOUNT: $1000 DEADLINE: April 15
FIELDS/MAJORS: All Areas of Study

Scholarships for students who were or whose parents were assisted in immigrating to the United States (after 1985) by the Hebrew Immigrant Aid Society. All applicants must be able to demonstrate two complete semesters of attendance at a U.S. high school, college, or graduate school. Based on financial need, academics, and community service. Seventy awards offered annually. Only scholarship winners will be notified. Write to the address below for details, and include a SASE.

Hebrew Immigrant Aid Society
Scholarship Awards
333 Seventh Ave.
New York, NY 10001

999

Hebrew Immigrant Aid Society Scholarships

AMOUNT: Maximum: $2000 DEADLINE: March 31
FIELDS/MAJORS: All Areas of Study

Open to beginning full-time postsecondary students at a college, university, or technical training school. Applicants must have immigrated to the U.S. with the assistance of HIAS, Chicago, and lived in the U.S. for at least two years. Must demonstrate academic excellence, community involvement, financial need, and a well thought out plan. Contact the address listed for further information or call (312) 357-4666. Must have a GPA of at least 3.2.

Hebrew Immigrant Aid Society
Scholarship Coordinator
1 S. Franklin St.
Chicago, IL 60606

1000

Helen James Brewer Scholarship

AMOUNT: None Specified DEADLINE: None Specified
FIELDS/MAJORS: English or Southern History and Literature

Awards for students enrolled in the study of English or Southern history and literature. Must be a member or dependent of a member of the United Daughters of the Confederacy who resides in Alabama, Florida, Georgia, South Carolina, Tennessee, or Virginia. Contact your local chapter of the UDC or write to the address below for more information.

United Daughters of the Confederacy
Education Committee
328 North Ave.
Richmond, VA 23220

1001

Helen L. Henderson Scholarship Loan Fund

AMOUNT: Maximum: $8000 DEADLINE: April 1
FIELDS/MAJORS: All Areas of Study

Loans open to all Benton County residents and to all Benton Central graduates regardless of county of residence. Loans based on academics and financial need. Loans are to be repaid within three years from graduation (or termination of education). No interest will be charged on loans during this period. Four awards are given annually. Write to the address below for more information.

Fowler State Bank
Attn: Anne Molter
PO Box 511
Fowler, IN 47944

1002

Helen M. Malloch and NFPW Scholarships

AMOUNT: $500-$1000 DEADLINE: May 1
FIELDS/MAJORS: Journalism, Communications

Scholarships for undergraduate women junior, senior, or graduate students majoring in journalism/communications at an accredited institution. Applicants do not have to be NFPW members. Write to the address listed for complete details.

National Federation of Press Women
C/O Jean Bormann
1163 320th Ave.
Charlotte, IA 52731

1003

Helen N. and Harold B. Shapira Scholarship

AMOUNT: $1000 DEADLINE: April 1
FIELDS/MAJORS: Medicine/Medical Research

Open to undergraduate and medical students who are enrolled at Minnesota schools and working in a curriculum with potential application to heart and blood vessel disease. Renewable. Two awards per year. Write to address below for details.

American Heart Association, Minnesota Affiliate Inc.
4701 West 77th St.
Minneapolis, MN 55435

1004
Helena Rubinstein Fellowship in Art History and Museum Studies

AMOUNT: None Specified DEADLINE: April 1
FIELDS/MAJORS: Art History/Museum Studies

Program is open to graduate students, postgraduate candidates, and undergraduates with the capacity for advanced scholarship. This is a residential program. Ten fellowships are available. Write to address below for details.

Whitney Museum of American Art Independent Study
  Program
384 Broadway, 4th Floor
New York, NY 10013

1005
Henry and Chiyo Kuwahara Creative Arts Scholarship

AMOUNT: None Specified DEADLINE: April 1
FIELDS/MAJORS: Creative Arts

Open to students to encourage creative projects, especially those that reflect Japanese-American culture and experience. Applicants must be members of the JACL. Professional artists are not eligible. Applications and information may be obtained from local JACL chapters, district offices, and the national headquarters at the address listed or call (415) 921-5225. Please indicate your level of study and be certain to include a legal-sized SASE.

Japanese-American Citizens League
National Scholarship and Award Program
1765 Sutter St.
San Francisco, CA 94115

1006
Henry and Chiyo Kuwahara Memorial Scholarships

AMOUNT: None Specified DEADLINE: April 1
FIELDS/MAJORS: All Areas of Study

Open to incoming freshmen and graduate students who are members of Japanese ancestry and entering or enrolled at an accredited college or university. Applications and information may be obtained from local JACL chapters, district offices, and the national headquarters at the address listed or call (415) 921-5225. Please indicate your level of study and be certain to include a legal-sized SASE.

Japanese-American Citizens League
National Scholarship and Award Program
1765 Sutter St.
San Francisco, CA 94115

1007
Henry Belin Du Pont Fellowship

AMOUNT: $6000 DEADLINE: November 15
FIELDS/MAJORS: History: Art, Industry, Economics, Museum Studies

Open to doctoral candidates who have completed all but the dissertation. This is a residential fellowship for four months and provides housing, use of computer, e-mail, Internet access, and an office, along with the stipend. Write to address below for details.

Hagley Museum and Library
PO Box 3630
Wilmington, DE 19807

1008
Henry G. Halladay Awards

AMOUNT: Maximum: $760 DEADLINE: August 31
FIELDS/MAJORS: Medicine

Five supplemental scholarships are presented annually to African-American men, enrolled in the first year of medical school, who have overcome significant obstacles to obtain a medical education. Must be U.S. citizens. There are two deadlines: May 31 deadline is for renewal applicants, and August 31 is for new applicants. Write to "special programs" at the address listed for details.

National Medical Fellowships, Inc.
110 West 32nd St., 8th Floor
New York, NY 10001

1009
Henry J. Reilly Memorial Scholarship

AMOUNT: $500 DEADLINE: April 10
FIELDS/MAJORS: All Areas of Study

Scholarships for children (or grandchildren) of members or associate members of the Reserve Officers Association. Must be accepted for full-time study at a four-year college or university, have a GPA of at least 3.3, and score a 1250 on the SAT or a 26 on the ACT. For incoming freshmen. Seventy-five awards offered annually. Write to the address below for details. Children, under the age of twenty-one, of deceased members (active and paid up in the ROA or ROAL at the time of their death) are also eligible. When requesting information, please specify your year in school.

Reserve Officers Association of the United States
Ms. Mickey Hagen, Scholarship Program
One Constitution Ave. NE
Washington, DC 20002

1010
Henry Luce Foundation/ ACLS Fellowship for Scholarship in American Art

AMOUNT: $18500 DEADLINE: November 15
FIELDS/MAJORS: American Art

Fellowships for dissertation research in visual art in America. Must be a U.S. citizen or permanent resident. Fellowships are for a one-year, non-renewable term beginning in the summer. Write to the address below for details.

American Council of Learned Societies
Office of Fellowships and Grants
228 E. 45th St.
New York, NY 10017

1011
Herbert Hoover Presidential Fellowships and Grants

AMOUNT: $500-$1200 DEADLINE: March 1
FIELDS/MAJORS: American History, Political Science, Public Policy

Scholarships are awarded to current graduate students, postdoctoral scholars, and qualified non-academic researchers. Priority given to proposals that have the highest probability of publication and use by educators and policy makers. Write to the address below for details.

Hoover Presidential Library Association
Ms. Patricia A. Hand
PO Box 696
West Branch, IA 52358

1012
Herbert Lehman Education Fund Scholarships

AMOUNT: $1400 DEADLINE: April 15
FIELDS/MAJORS: All Areas of Study

Scholarships for African-American high school seniors who will be entering a college in the South or a college that has a student population in which African-Americans are substantially underrepresented. Based on financial need and academics. Twenty to twenty-five awards offered per year. Renewable. All requests for application forms must be in writing and requested by the applicant. Write to the address below for details.

Herbert Lehman Education Fund
99 Hudson St., Suite 1600
New York, NY 10013

1013
Herbert Scoville Jr. Peace Fellowships

AMOUNT: $6000-$9000 DEADLINE: March 15
FIELDS/MAJORS: Arms Control, International Peace, Military Science

Fellowships available to outstanding graduate students. These are full-time, four- to six-month fellowships in Washington, DC. Scoville Fellows will be placed with one of the twenty-two organizations participating in the program where they may undertake a variety of activities, including research, writing, and organizing that support the goals of their host organization. Must have a baccalaureate degree by the time the Fellowship commences. Preference given to U.S. citizens. Awards are stipends of $1500 per month, health insurance, and travel expenses to Washington DC. March 15 is the deadline for fall semester. October 15 is the deadline for spring semester. Write to the address listed for further information.

Scoville Peace Fellowship Program
110 Maryland Ave. NE, #201
Washington, DC 20002

1014
Herman O. West Foundation Scholarship Program

AMOUNT: $2000 DEADLINE: February 28
FIELDS/MAJORS: All Areas of Study

Awards for high school seniors who are dependents of a full-time employees of the West Company. For two- or four-year colleges or universities. Extracurricular activities, motivation, and academic achievement will be considered. Information and applications are available in the Human Resource Departments at all West locations. Up to seven awards offered annually. Contact the Resource Department at the location where parent is employed.

Herman O. West Foundation
Human Resource Departments
PO Box 645
Lionville, PA 19341

1015
Herman Oscar Schumacher Scholarship Fund

AMOUNT: $500 DEADLINE: October 1
FIELDS/MAJORS: All Areas of Study

Awards for male residents of Spokane County, Washington, who have completed at least one year at an accredited college and demonstrate financial need. Applicants must be Christian, loyal to principles of democracy, and support the Constitution of the United States. Write to the address below for information. Applications will be accepted no earlier than the first day of class instruction and no later than October 1.

Washington Trust Bank
Trust Department
PO Box 2127
Spokane, WA 99210

1016
Hermione Grant Calhoun Scholarships

AMOUNT: $3000 DEADLINE: March 31
FIELDS/MAJORS: All Areas of Study

Award open to female full-time students who are legally blind. Contact the address below for complete details.

National Federation of the Blind
Mrs. Peggy Elliott, Chairman
805 Fifth Ave.
Grinnell, IA 50112

1017
Hermon Dunlap Smith Center for the History of Cartography

AMOUNT: Maximum: $2400 DEADLINE: March 2
FIELDS/MAJORS: History of Cartography

Fellowships for scholars in the study of cartography history are available through the Hermon Dunlap Smith Center for the History of Cartography. Fellowships usually last three months and the award is $800 per month. One or two awards offered annually. Write to the address below for details.

Newberry Library
The Smith Center Scholarship Committee
60 W. Walton St.
Chicago, IL 60610

1018
Herschel C. Price Foundation Scholarships

AMOUNT: $250-$2500 DEADLINE: April 1
FIELDS/MAJORS: All Areas of Study

Scholarships for West Virginia students who are or will be attending West Virginia institutions. For undergraduate and graduate study. Renewable. Grades are considered for these awards. Two hundred awards are given annually. Write to the address below for details. A SASE is required.

Herschel C. Price Educational Foundation
PO Box 412
Huntington, WV 25708

1019
Herzog August Bibliothek Wolfenbuttel Fellowship

AMOUNT: None Specified DEADLINE: None Specified
FIELDS/MAJORS: All Fields Relevant to Both Newberry and Wolfenbuttel Libraries

Open to doctorate students who receive fellowship awards from the Newberry Library, for a period in residence in Wolfenbuttel, Germany. Proposed project should link the collections of both libraries. Award is a monthly stipend and travel expenses and should be taken immediately following period of residency at Newberry. Contact the address listed for further information or call (312) 255-3666.

Newberry Library
Committee On Awards
60 W. Walton St.
Chicago, IL 60610

1020
HHMI-NIH Research Scholars Program

AMOUNT: $15000 DEADLINE: January 10
FIELDS/MAJORS: Medicine

This program is available at National Institutes of Health in Bethesda, Maryland, for medical students to spend a year doing intensive research in the following fields: cell biology and regulation, epidemiology and biostatistics, genetics, immunology, neuroscience, and structural biology. Write to the address listed for additional information.

Howard Hughes Medical Institute
HHMI-NIH Research Scholars Program
1 Cloister Court
Bethesda, MD 20814

1021
Hibernia Minority Youth Scholarship

AMOUNT: Maximum: $1500
DEADLINE: February 28
FIELDS/MAJORS: Business, Finance, Liberal Arts

Open to Ascension Parish high school seniors with a minimum GPA of 3.0 who are of African-American, Hispanic American, Native American, or Asian-American descent. Applicants must be accepted into an accredited college or university and be able to demonstrate financial need. Maximum family income may not exceed $40,000. Contact the address listed for further information or call Terrie Harris at 1-800-562-9007 ext. 33026.

Hibernia National Bank
Ken Bailey
PO Box 649
Donaldsonville, LA 70346

1022

Hiebler (Thomas and Jennie) Memorial Scholarship Fund

AMOUNT: Maximum: $1200 DEADLINE: None Specified
FIELDS/MAJORS: All Areas of Study

Applicants must be graduating from the Mancos or Montrose high school districts who plan to attend a college or university within the state of Colorado. Contact your guidance counselor or write to the address below for details.

Thomas and Jennie Hiebler Memorial Scholarship Fund
Union Bank, Trust Dept.
PO Box 109
San Diego, CA 92112

1023

Higgins-Quarles Award

AMOUNT: Maximum: $1000 DEADLINE: January 8
FIELDS/MAJORS: American History

Awards are available for minority graduate students at the dissertation stage of their Ph.D. programs. To apply, students should submit a brief two-page abstract of the dissertation project, along with a one-page budget explaining the travel and research plans for the funds requested. Write to the address listed for more information.

Organization of American Historians
Award and Prize Committee Coordinator
112 N. Bryan St.
Bloomington, IN 47408

1024

High School Research Program

AMOUNT: $250-$1500 DEADLINE: November 3
FIELDS/MAJORS: Health-Related Fields

Scholarships are available for submitting health-related research projects while in the senior year of high school. Typical subjects are: diseases of the elderly, cardiovascular exercise, air pollution attitudes, the effects of smoking on health, diseases of the lungs. For Indiana residents only. Prizes for this contest start at honorable mentions for $250 through 1st place for $1500. Write to the address below for information.

American Lung Association of Indiana
Communications Director
9410 Priority Way West Dr.
Indianapolis, IN 46240

1025

Higher Education and Employment Assistance Programs

AMOUNT: None Specified DEADLINE: October 1
FIELDS/MAJORS: All Areas of Study

Awards are available for members of the Zuni tribe who are enrolled in full-time study at a regionally-accredited institution of higher learning. Applicants must have GPAs of at least 2.0. Write to the address listed for more information.

Pueblo of Zuni Tribe
Higher Education
PO Box 339
Zuni, NM 87327

1026

Higher Education Loan Program (HELP)

AMOUNT: Maximum: $6000 DEADLINE: March 1
FIELDS/MAJORS: Obstetrics and Gynecology

Open to ACOG members (as Junior Fellows). Must be in an approved residency training program with at least one year completed. Must be a citizen of any country within the geographic confines of ACOG and be able to demonstrate financial need. Currently, the maximum loan is $6000 at 8% per annum, and repayment begins one year after training is completed. The second deadline date is October 1. Write to the address listed for more information.

American College of Obstetricians and Gynecologists
Attn: HELP, Kathy Bell
409 12th St. SW
Washington, DC 20024

1027

Hirsh Student Writing Competition

AMOUNT: Maximum: $1000 DEADLINE: February 1
FIELDS/MAJORS: Dentistry, Podiatry, Nursing, Pharmacy, Health Science, Healthcare Administration

Writing competition for students in one of the areas listed above who are currently attending an accredited school in the United States or Canada. Papers must be at least three thousand words in length, must contain only uncollaborated original work, and may relate to research done by the author. Write to the address listed for more information or call (414) 276-1881.

American College of Legal Medicine
Student Writing Competition
611 E. Wells St.
Milwaukee, WI 53202

1028
Hispanic Business College Fund

AMOUNT: Maximum: $1000   DEADLINE: January 31
FIELDS/MAJORS: Business

Ten awards for Hispanic students in the field of business. Must have GPAs of at least 3.0, be U.S. citizens, and show evidence of financial need. Write to the address listed for more information.

U.S. Hispanic Chamber of Commerce
Carmen Ortiz
1030 15th St. NW, Suite 206
Washington, DC 20005

1029
Holbrook Island Sanctuary Corp. Scholarship/ Internship Fund

AMOUNT: None Specified   DEADLINE: April 15
FIELDS/MAJORS: Natural History, Geology, Botany, Zoology, Ornithology, Science

Scholarship support to graduating seniors from a Hancock County High School or a resident of Hancock County who plans to continue education in an area such as the ones listed above. Applicants are required to submit a student proposal for a project to be completed in the sanctuary during the summer after senior year, a teacher recommendation, and an essay pertaining to the sanctuary. Write to Patti D'Angelo at the address listed for details.

Maine Community Foundation
245 East Maine St.
PO Box 148
Ellsworth, ME 04605

1030
Hollingworth Award

AMOUNT: Maximum: $2000   DEADLINE: January 15
FIELDS/MAJORS: Research: Education/Psychology Relating to Gifted/Talented Children

Research grants for graduate students, teachers, professors, educational administrator, psychologists, etc. Supports educational or psychological research of potential benefit to the gifted and talented. Research must be of publishable quality. Based on abstract and research proposal. Write to the address listed for more information.

Intertel Foundation, Hollingworth Award Committee
Dr. Roxanne Herrick Cramer, Chairman
4300 Sideburn Rd.
Fairfax, VA 22030

1031
Holmes Fund

AMOUNT: None Specified   DEADLINE: May 1
FIELDS/MAJORS: All Areas of Study

Awards for residents of Calais, Maine, wishing to pursue higher education. Contact the Calais High School Guidance Office for more information.

Maine Community Foundation
245 East Maine St.
PO Box 148
Ellsworth, ME 04605

1032
Homer Hatch Conservation Scholarship

AMOUNT: None Specified   DEADLINE: April 15
FIELDS/MAJORS: Conservation

Open to non-freshman undergraduate college students who are majoring in conservation or related fields of study. The applicants must submit a written statement of their career objective, provide a transcript, and maintain at least a 3.0 GPA. Contact the address listed or call (316) 364-2182 for further information.

Coffey County Conservation District
Scholarship Coordinator
313 Cross St.
Burlington, KS 66839

1033
Honorable Norman L. Utter Scholarship

AMOUNT: None Specified   DEADLINE: May 31
FIELDS/MAJORS: All Areas of Study

Scholarships for Nueces County residents attending Texas A&M at Corpus Christi or Del Mar College. Must have been a resident of the county for at least one year, be enrolled for at least 12 credit hours per semester, and have a GPA of at least 2.5. Selections based on merit and financial need. Write to the address below for complete information. Applicants are chosen by the Coastal Bend Community Foundation from candidates suggested by the colleges.

Coastal Bend Community Foundation
Mercantile Tower MT 276
615 N. Upper Broadway, #860
Corpus Christi, TX 78477

1034
Honored Scholars Program

AMOUNT: $1000 DEADLINE: None Specified
FIELDS/MAJORS: Visual, Performing Arts

These merit based scholarships are open to high school seniors, undergraduates, and graduate students. Must have a minimum GPA of 3.7 or excel in visual, performing arts. Applicants must also be U.S. citizens. The number of awards varies, and the amount starts at $1000. Contact the address listed for further information.

National Alliance for Excellence Honored Scholars Program
Linda Paras, President
55 Highway 35, #5
Red Bank, NJ 07701

1035
Honors Program and Tuition Grant

AMOUNT: $400-$2000 DEADLINE: April 1
FIELDS/MAJORS: All Areas of Study

Programs available to residents of Kansas who attend a Kansas independent or private institutions. Applicant must demonstrate financial need and maintain a 2.0 cumulative college GPA to renew grant. Grant is limited to four years unless recipient is enrolled in a designated five-year program. The tuition grant is limited to study at private institutions. Write to the address below for details.

Kansas Assn. of Student Financial Aid Administrators
C/O Kansas Board of Regents
700 SW Harrison, Suite 1410
Topeka, KS 66603

1036
Horace Mann Scholarship

AMOUNT: $1000-$20000 DEADLINE: February 28
FIELDS/MAJORS: All Areas of Study

Scholarships are available for graduating high school seniors who are children of public school employees. Applicants must have GPA of 3.0, an ACT score of at least 23, or 1100 on the SAT. May be entering a two- or four-year college or university full-time. Recipients will be notified by March 31. Awards may be renewed if recipients remain full-time students, maintain a minimum GPA of 2.0, and their parent(s) are still actively employed by a public school district or public college/university. Write to the address listed for further information or visit their Web site at http://www.horacemann.com.

Horace Mann Companies
Scholarship Program
PO Box 20490
Springfield, IL 62708

1037
Horace Wells Club Dental Scholarship

AMOUNT: Maximum: $1000 DEADLINE: None Specified
FIELDS/MAJORS: Dentistry

Open to citizens of the state of Connecticut. Applicants must be currently enrolled and in good academic standing in dental school. Must be able to demonstrate financial need and a commitment to providing care to the underserved. Contact your local Horace Wells Club, the address listed, or call (860) 886-1163 for further information.

Horace Wells Club
Dr. Jeremiah Lowney
100 Sherman St.
Norwich, CT 06360

1038
Housing Authority of the County of Contra Costa

AMOUNT: $400-$850 DEADLINE: May 8
FIELDS/MAJORS: All Areas of Study

For graduating high school seniors who are residents of housing authority of the county of Contra Costa public housing developments or who have received a section 8 rental housing voucher or certificate. Must be accepted by an accredited four-year college/university, community college, or technical/vocational school, or be currently enrolled in a school or college. Write to the address below for more information.

Housing Authority of the County of Contra Costa
Judy Hayes, Acting Admin. Svcs. Officer
3133 Estudillo St., PO Box 2759
Martinez, CA 94553

1039
Houston Advertising Federation Scholarship

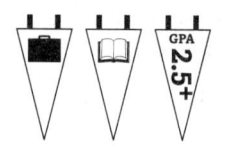

AMOUNT: Maximum: $2500 DEADLINE: March 13
FIELDS/MAJORS: Advertising, Marketing, Journalism, Communications

Scholarships for students studying in the fields above who are residents of or attending school in Houston, Texas. Applicants must have a GPA of at least 2.5 and be in their sophomore, junior, or senior year of undergraduate study. Write to the address listed for more information.

Houston Advertising Federation
PO Box 27592
Houston, TX 77227

1040

Howard A. Tribou Scholarship

AMOUNT: None Specified   DEADLINE: None Specified
FIELDS/MAJORS: All Areas of Study

Awards to support residents of Rockport or Camden, Maine, who graduated from Camden-Rockport High School. Contact the Camden-Rockport Guidance Office for more information.

Maine Community Foundation
245 East Maine St.
PO Box 148
Ellsworth, ME 04605

1041

Howard Brown Rickard Scholarship

AMOUNT: Maximum: $1000
DEADLINE: March 31
FIELDS/MAJORS: Architecture, Law, Medicine, Engineering, Natural Sciences

Open to full-time students who are legally blind, working toward a career in one of the areas listed above. Write to the address below for complete details.

National Federation of the Blind
Mrs. Peggy Elliott, Chairman
805 Fifth Ave.
Grinnell, IA 50112

1042

Howard F. Denise Scholarship Fund

AMOUNT: None Specified   DEADLINE: April 15
FIELDS/MAJORS: Agriculture Related

Scholarships for New York residents who are/will be undergraduates, have interest/membership in Grange, 4-H, or FFA, and are committed to a career in Agriculture. Contact your local Grange, 4-H, or FFA or write to the address listed for details.

New York State Grange
Scholarship Coordinator
100 Grange Place
Cortland, NY 13045

1043

Howard H. Hanks Jr. Scholarship in Meteorology

AMOUNT: $700   DEADLINE: June 16
FIELDS/MAJORS: Meteorology, Atmospheric Sciences, Ocean Science, Hydrology

Applicants must be entering their final year in one of the fields listed above. Must be enrolled full-time, have a minimum GPA of 3.0, and be U.S. citizens or permanent residents. Write to the address listed for details.

American Meteorological Society
45 Beacon St.
Boston, MA 02108

1044

Howard Hughes Predoctoral Fellowships in Biological Sciences

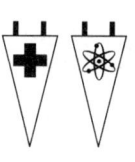

AMOUNT: Maximum: $15000   DEADLINE: November 12
FIELDS/MAJORS: See Listing of Fields Below

Fellowships for doctoral students in their first year of graduate study in one of these fields: biochemistry, biophysics, biostatistics, cell biology, developmental biology, epidemiology, mathematical biology, microbiology, neuroscience, molecular biology, pharmacology, physiology, structural biology, genetics, and virology. Eighty awards offered annually. Write to the address listed for further information.

Howard Hughes Medical Institute
Office of Grants and Special Programs
2101 Constitution Ave.
Washington, DC 20418

1045

Howard M. Soule Graduate Fellowships in Educational Leadership

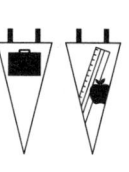

AMOUNT: $500-$1500   DEADLINE: May 1
FIELDS/MAJORS: Educational Administration

Open to Phi Delta Kappa members who are full-time students enrolled in a doctoral, master's, or specialist program. Write to the address below for complete details.

Phi Delta Kappa
International Headquarters
PO Box 789
Bloomington, IN 47402

1046
Howard Rock Foundation Scholarship Program

AMOUNT: $2500-$5000
DEADLINE: March 15
FIELDS/MAJORS: Economics, Education, Business, Public Administration

Scholarships are available for American Indian students majoring in one of the above fields. Applicants must be residents of Alaska. Four to six awards are offered annually. Write to the address below for information.

Howard Rock Foundation
1577 C St., Suite 304
Anchorage, AK 99501

1047
Howard S. Brembeck Scholarship

AMOUNT: Maximum: $5000   DEADLINE: April 1
FIELDS/MAJORS: Agricultural Engineering

Open to students with a degree in agricultural engineering, pursuing a graduate degree in a field that is related to the development of poultry equipment. (Specializing in any and all equipment that would be considered necessary to sustain the life of the animal during the production process.) Write to the address listed for more information. Must have a GPA of at least 2.9.

CTB, Inc.
Richard Gentry, Dir.of Corp. Relations
PO Box 2000
Milford, IN 46526

1048
Howard T. Orville Scholarship in Meteorology

AMOUNT: $2000   DEADLINE: June 16
FIELDS/MAJORS: Meteorology, Atmospheric Sciences, Ocean Sciences, Hydrology

Applicants must be entering their final year in one of the fields listed above. Must be enrolled full-time, have a minimum GPA of 3.0, and be U.S. citizens or permanent residents. Write to the address listed for details.

American Meteorological Society
45 Beacon St.
Boston, MA 02108

1049
Howard Vollum American Indian Scholarship

AMOUNT: None Specified   DEADLINE: March 1
FIELDS/MAJORS: Science, Computer Science, Engineering, Mathematics

Open to Native American residents of Clackamas, Multnomah, or Washington counties in Oregon or Clark County, Washington. Must submit certification of tribal enrollment or photocopy of the Johnson O'Malley student eligibility form or a letter from your tribe stating blood quantum and/or enrollment number of parent or grandparent. Awards may be received for a maximum of fifteen quarters. Contact the address listed for further information.

Oregon State Scholarship Commission
Private Awards
1500 Valley River Dr., #100
Eugene, OR 97401-2130

1050
Howard Young Medical Center Auxiliary Scholarship

AMOUNT: Maximum: $1000   DEADLINE: November 15
FIELDS/MAJORS: Medical or Medical-Related

Scholarships are available to residents of the area served by the Lakeland Union High School or the St. Germain School District located in the state of Wisconsin. Write to the address below for information.

Howard Young Medical Center Auxiliary
PO Box 470
Woodruff, WI 54568

1051
Hubbard Scholarship

AMOUNT: $3000   DEADLINE: May 1
FIELDS/MAJORS: Library Science

The scholarship's purpose is to recruit excellent librarians for Georgia and will be used to provide financial assistance to qualified candidates for a year's study in completing a master's degree in library science. Must be completing senior year in an accredited college or university or be a graduate of such an institution. Preference to Georgia residents. Write to the address below for complete details.

Georgia Library Association
Hubbard Scholarship Committee C/O SOLNET
1438 W. Peachtree St. NW, #200
Atlanta, GA 30309-2955

1052
Hubert Humphrey and Lincoln Foodservice Research Grants

AMOUNT: None Specified DEADLINE: April 30
FIELDS/MAJORS: Food Service/Management, Nutrition, Food Science

Grants to ASFSA members in graduate school. Must have a minimum GPA of 3.0, be currently enrolled in a graduate program, and be able to demonstrate research competency. The proposed research must be applicable to school foodservice and child nutrition and support the School Food Service Foundation's mission. Write to the address listed for details.

American School Food Service Association
Scholarship Committee
1600 Duke St., 7th Floor
Alexandria, VA 22314

1053
Huff Scholarships and CHHA/Rambling Willie Memorial Scholarships

AMOUNT: Maximum: $500 DEADLINE: April 30
FIELDS/MAJORS: Equine Studies (Horse-Related Fields)

Scholarships for students who have been accepted into a college or university and are pursuing a horse-related career. Students with harness racing experience will be given preference. For undergraduate study. Write to the address below for more information.

Harness Horse Youth Foundation
14950 Greyhound Court, Suite 210
Carmel, IN 46032

1054
Hugh Carcella Scholarship

AMOUNT: Maximum: $750 DEADLINE: March 15
FIELDS/MAJORS: All Areas of Study

Open to members and their children. Applicants must be incoming freshmen pursuing a four-year degree. Contact your local union first then the address listed for further information or call (610) 867-7524.

United Steel Workers of America-District 10
Program Director
53 Lehigh St. Lower Level
Bethlehem, PA 18018

1055
Hugh J. Andersen Memorial Scholarships

AMOUNT: Maximum: $2500 DEADLINE: August 31
FIELDS/MAJORS: Medicine

Scholarships, fellowships, and awards for minority medical students. Must be U.S. citizens. Minorities are defined here as African-American, American Indian (including Eskimos, Alaskan Aleuts, Hawaiian natives), Mexican-American, and mainland Puerto Rican. For study at Minnesota medical schools, or for Minnesota residents enrolled at any accredited medical school. Two awards are given annually. There are two deadlines: May 31 deadline is for renewal applicants, and August 31 deadline is for new applicants. Write to "special programs" at the address listed for details.

National Medical Fellowships, Inc.
110 West 32nd St.
New York, NY 10001

1056
Hughey "Crimp" and Mary Eddie Knight Memorial Scholarship

AMOUNT: None Specified DEADLINE: June 20
FIELDS/MAJORS: All Areas of Study

Award for an African-American graduate of the Sparkman public high schools. Applicant must be a sophomore, junior, or senior with a GPA of at least 2.5. Based on academics and an essay. For study at an Arkansas postsecondary institution. Write to the address below for more information.

Knight Homestead Estate
George Ann Stallings
PO Box 650
Sparkman, AR 71763-0650

1057
Huguenot Society of America Scholarships

AMOUNT: Maximum: $1400 DEADLINE: None Specified
FIELDS/MAJORS: All Areas of Study

Open to undergraduates who can submit written proof that they are from Huguenot ancestry. Ancestors must have migrated from France before 1787. Applicants must be U.S. citizens. Must be attending one of fifty select schools in the U.S. Apply to the financial aid office of your school for information and applications. Colleges submit applicants to the Society for approval.

Marie L. Rose Huguenot Society of America Scholarship
Office of the Scholarship Committee
122 East 58th St.
New York, NY 10022

1058
Hull Scholarships

AMOUNT: $1000 DEADLINE: March 15
FIELDS/MAJORS: All Areas of Study

Scholarships for students, under the age of twenty-three at initial application, who are children of employees of the Hull Pottery Company or a graduate of Crooksville High School (OH) (latter category: must have attended at least three and one-half years at CHS). Must have a GPA of at least 2.5. Eight awards are offered annually. Contact the superintendent's office of the Crooksville Exempted Village School District at the address below for details.

J. Brannon Hull Scholarship Fund, Inc.
C/O Superintendent's Office
91 S. Buckeye St.
Crooksville, OH 43731

1059
Hungarian Arts Club Scholarships

AMOUNT: $500-$2000 DEADLINE: December 1
FIELDS/MAJORS: Arts, Performing Arts

Open to students of Hungarian descent pursuing a degree in fine arts at a four-year institution. Proof of ancestry, portfolio, and references will be required. These awards are not renewable. Contact the address listed for further information or call (313) 459-5253. If you write, you must include a SASE for a reply.

Hungarian Arts Club
Jana Johnson
16580 Barrington
Plymouth, MI 48170-3404

1060
Hyland R. Johns Research Grants

AMOUNT: $5000 DEADLINE: April 1
FIELDS/MAJORS: Arboriculture

Grants are available for research in the field of arboriculture focusing on the biology and management and care of trees. Recipients must be qualified researchers for projects of interest and benefit to the arboriculture industry. Awards will be announced no later than September 30. Write to the address listed for more information. No phone calls please.

International Society of Arboriculture
ISA Research Trust
PO Box 3129, 1400 W. Anthony Dr.
Champaign, IL 61826

1061
IAPA-Inter-American Press Association Scholarships

AMOUNT: Maximum: $10000 DEADLINE: August 1
FIELDS/MAJORS: Journalism

Scholarships for Latin-American journalists under the age of thirty-five who are or will be studying in the U.S. or Canada. Must be a citizen of a Latin-American country. Reciprocal scholarships for citizens of the U.S. and Canada (to study in a Latin-American country) are also available. Fluency in the language of the country of study is required. Contact the address below for details.

Inter-American Press Association
2911 NW 39th St.
Miami, FL 33142

1062
IBD Foundation Graduate Fellowship

AMOUNT: Maximum: $5000 DEADLINE: April 8
FIELDS/MAJORS: Interior Design

Awards are available for individuals who have completed their undergraduate study and are practicing commercial interior design full- or part-time or are enrolled in or intending to continue graduate studies in interior design. Three or four awards are offered annually. Write to the address below for more information.

International Interior Design Association Headquarters
341 Merchandise Mart
Chicago, IL 60654

1063
Ice Skating Institute of America Education Foundation Scholarships

AMOUNT: $3000 DEADLINE: March 14
FIELDS/MAJORS: All Areas of Study

Awards are available for high school seniors or undergraduates with a GPA of at least 3.0 who are members of the ISIA. Must have held membership for at least four years and completed 240 hours of service. For full-time study. Five awards offered annually. Write to the address below for more information.

Ice Skating Institute of America
355 West Dundee Road
Buffalo Grove, IL 60089

1064
Ida and Benjamin Alpert Scholarships

AMOUNT: None Specified DEADLINE: May 14
FIELDS/MAJORS: Law

Scholarships for Michigan residents who are or will be attending law school. Attendance at a Michigan law school is not necessary. Based on essay (1000 to 1500 words). In addition to the amounts listed, honorable mention awards will be given as funds allow. Write to the address below for details.

Ida and Benjamin Alpert Foundation
C/O David J. Szymanksi
1303 City-County Building
Detroit, MI 48226

1065
Idaho Governor's Scholarship

AMOUNT: Maximum: $3000 DEADLINE: January 31
FIELDS/MAJORS: All Areas of Study

Awards for U.S. citizens who are Idaho residents first entering a vocational-technical program. Must plan on attending full-time and have had a high school GPA of 3.0 or better or provide evidence of ability to succeed in your chosen program. If a current high school senior, contact your high school counselor. If you have been out of school for more than a year, contact the address listed for further information.

Idaho State Board of Education
Caryl Smith
PO Box 83720
Boise, ID 83720

1066
Idaho Minority and "At-Risk" Student Scholarship

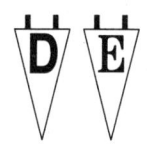

AMOUNT: Maximum: $2700 DEADLINE: January 31
FIELDS/MAJORS: All Areas of Study

Scholarships are available for Idaho residents who are U.S. citizens and graduates of Idaho high schools. One of the following must also apply: be migrant farm workers or children of migrant farm workers, first-generation college students, handicapped, or minorities. For use at Boise State University, Idaho State University, Lewis-Clark State College, University of Idaho, North Idaho College, College of Southern Idaho, or Albertson College of Idaho. Write to the address listed for information.

Idaho State Board of Education
PO Box 83720
Boise, ID 83720

1067
Idaho Student Incentive Grant

AMOUNT: Maximum: $5000 DEADLINE: January 31
FIELDS/MAJORS: All Areas of Study

Awards for students attending or planning to attend a college or university in Idaho. May be enrolled full- or part-time. Must demonstrate financial need. Contact the financial aid office of the school you are attending/plan to attend for information.

Idaho State Board of Education
PO Box 83720
Boise, ID 83720

1068
IFDA Educational Foundation Scholarships

AMOUNT: $1500 DEADLINE: October 15
FIELDS/MAJORS: All Areas of Study

Awards for student members of the IFDA who are enrolled at any level of study full-time. Based on an application, essay, and letter of recommendation. Write to the address below for more information.

International Furnishings and Design Association
1200 19th St. NW, Suite #300
Washington, DC 20036-2422

1069
IFEC Scholarships

AMOUNT: $1000-$2500 DEADLINE: March 17
FIELDS/MAJORS: Food Service, Food Service Communication

Scholarships for students in a postsecondary program in food service. Must have a background in or be studying a field related to communications as well. Communications here means some form of writing (recipe styling, food-related journalism, etc.) Write for complete information.

International Food Service Editorial Council
PO Box 491
Hyde Park, NY 12538

1070
Ildaura Murillo-Rhode Scholarship

AMOUNT: None Specified DEADLINE: June 1
FIELDS/MAJORS: Nursing

Open to outstanding Hispanic students at the diploma, associated, baccalaureate, or graduate levels. Must be currently enrolled in an accredited school of nursing and be citizens or legal residents of the United States. Applicants must have GPAs of 2.5 or above. Write to the address listed or call (512) 520-8026 for additional information.

National Association of Hispanic Nurses
Scholarship Chairperson
6905 Alamo Downs Pkwy.
San Antonio, TX 78238-4519

1071
Illinois Amvets Service Foundation

AMOUNT: $500   DEADLINE: March 1
FIELDS/MAJORS: All Areas of Study

Scholarships for children of veterans who served after September 15, 1940. All applicants must be high school seniors from Illinois, unmarried, and have taken the ACT. Also includes the Albert C. Reichter Memorial, Amvets Post #100, Post #235, Post #94, Post #51, Clarence E. Newlun Memorial, and Frank Tuman Scholarships. Write to the address below for more information.

Illinois Amvets Scholarship Program
Illinois Amvets State Headquarters
2200 South Sixth St.
Springfield, IL 62703

1072
Illinois CPA Society's Scholarships

AMOUNT: Maximum: $1000   DEADLINE: February 17
FIELDS/MAJORS: Accounting

Open to full-time students who are residents of Illinois. Applicants must have completed a minimum of 6 semester hours of accounting courses. Community college students must intend to transfer to a four-year school. Based on GPA, extracurricular activities, membership in Beta Alpha Psi or an accounting club, and work experience. Contact the address listed for further information or call (312) 993-0393. Must have a GPA of at least 2.8.

Illinois CPA Society
IL CPA Society's Scholarship Program
222 S. Riverside Plaza, #1600
Chicago, IL 60606-6098

1073
Illinois Funeral Directors Association Scholarships

AMOUNT: None Specified   DEADLINE: None Specified
FIELDS/MAJORS: Mortuary Science

Awards for Illinois residents studying mortuary science at any of the following three accredited Illinois schools: Southern Illinois University, Carl Sandburg (Galesburg), or Worsham's (Wheeling). Must be a second-year student. Selections based on GPAs. Write to the address below for more information. Must have a GPA of at least 3.0.

Illinois Funeral Directors Association
215 South Grand Ave. West
Springfield, IL 62704

1074
Illinois National Guard Grant Program

AMOUNT: None Specified   DEADLINE: September 15
FIELDS/MAJORS: All Areas of Study

Must be current member of Illinois National Guard having served at least one year. For study at a state-supported college on the undergraduate or graduate level. For enlisted personnel or officers up to the rank of Captain. Write to the address below for more details. Information is also available from National Guard units and Naval Militia Units in Illinois or from your college.

Illinois Student Assistance Commission
1755 Lake Cook Road
Deerfield, IL 60015

1075
Illinois NWSA Manuscript Prize

AMOUNT: $1000   DEADLINE: January 31
FIELDS/MAJORS: Women's Studies

Annual award for best book-length manuscript in women's studies. Along with the $1000 prize, the University of Illinois Press will publish the manuscript. Manuscripts can be on any subject in women's studies that expands our understanding of women's lives and gender systems. Interdisciplinary studies and discipline-specific studies are equally welcome. Write to the NWSA for details.

National Women's Studies Association
National Women's Studies Association
7100 Baltimore Ave., Suite 301
College Park, MD 20740

1076
Illinois Pork Quality Assurance Internship

AMOUNT: Maximum: $1500   DEADLINE: March 7
FIELDS/MAJORS: Food and Nutrition, Pork Production

Internships are available for juniors and seniors with an interest in pork production to work with the Illinois Pork Producers Association developing programs, seminars, incentives, and promotional materials through interactive networking and producer education that will assist with increasing enrollment in the pork quality assurance program. Requires a GPA of at least 2.5. Write to the address below for details.

Illinois Pork Producers Association
6411 South 6th St.
Frontage Road East
Springfield, IL 62707

1077
Illinois Sheriff's Association Scholarships

AMOUNT: None Specified DEADLINE: April 1
FIELDS/MAJORS: All Areas of Study

Open to students enrolled full-time at a certified institution of higher learning in Illinois, effective upcoming school year. Applicants must be permanent residents of Illinois. Contact your local County Sheriff's Department for information and applications. Must have a GPA of at least 2.5.

Illinois Sheriff's Association

1078
Illinois Sons of Italy Foundation

AMOUNT: None Specified DEADLINE: August 1
FIELDS/MAJORS: All Areas of Study

Scholarships for high school seniors who are residents of Illinois and are of Italian descent. Based on need, transcripts, and recommendation of principal or faculty advisor. Write to the scholarship committee at the address listed for details. Must have a GPA of at least 2.8.

George J. Spatuzza Scholarship Award Foundation
Order Sons of Italy in America, Illinois
7222 W. Cermack Rd, Suite 409
North Riverside, IL 60546

1079
Illinois State Library Training Grants

AMOUNT: $7500 DEADLINE: May 1
FIELDS/MAJORS: Library Science, Information Science

Up to fifteen scholarships for Illinois residents who are or will be attending an Illinois graduate school and pursuing a master's degree in library or information science. Must be a U.S. citizen and agree to work in an Illinois library after graduation. For full-time or part-time study. Write to the address below for details.

Illinois State Library
Training Grant Program
300 South Second St.
Springfield, IL 62701

1080
Illinois Veteran Grant Program

AMOUNT: None Specified DEADLINE: None Specified
FIELDS/MAJORS: All Areas of Study

Must be veteran who served honorably in the U.S. Armed Forces for at least one year. Applicants must have been residents of Illinois upon entering the service and must have returned to Illinois to reside within six months of leaving the service. Recipients are not required to enroll for a minimum number of credit hours each term. Contact any field office of the Department of Veteran's Affairs, college and university financial aid offices, or write to the address below for details.

Illinois Student Assistance Commission
1755 Lake Cook Road
Deerfield, IL 60015

1081
Image De Seattle Scholarship

AMOUNT: Maximum: $500 DEADLINE: April 15
FIELDS/MAJORS: All Areas of Study

Open to Hispanic high school seniors, undergraduates, and graduate students. Must be a resident of Washington for at least the past twelve months. Applications become available after mid-January. Recipients will be notified by June 30. Contact the address below for further information. Include a SASE for a reply.

Abraham Gonzalez Scholarship Committee
Chairperson, Image De Seattle
PO Box 21247
Seattle, WA 98111

1082
IMF Education Fund Loans

AMOUNT: Maximum: $8000 DEADLINE: May 30
FIELDS/MAJORS: Medicine

Loans for residents of Iowa studying toward becoming a doctor. Must be a junior or senior in medical school. Financial need is seriously considered. Write to the address below for details.

Iowa Medical Foundation
IMF Education Fund
1001 Grand Ave.
West Des Moines, IA 50265

1083
Independent Order of Odd Fellows Scholarship

AMOUNT: Maximum: $1000 DEADLINE: February 15
FIELDS/MAJORS: All Areas of Study

Scholarships are available to graduating high school seniors who reside in Rhode Island. Applicants must submit an essay of not more than two hundred words on the theme "Should the United States Assume the Role of Peacekeeper in the World?" Five awards are offered annually. Write to the address below for information.

Grand Lodge of Rhode Island, Independent Order of Odd Fellows
Ralph E. Peters, Grand Secretary
PO Box 296
Bristol, RI 02809

1084
Indian Nurse Scholarship

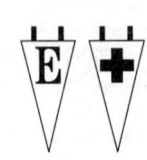

AMOUNT: $500-$1000 DEADLINE: None Specified
FIELDS/MAJORS: Nursing

Scholarships are available for Native American nursing students who are within two years of completing their nursing programs. Must be in good academic standing and enrolled in an accredited program. Write to the address below for information.

National Society of the Colonial Dames of America
Ms. H. Eugene Trotter, Consultant
3064 Luvan Blvd., Debordieu Colony
Georgetown, SC 29440

1085
Indiana Funeral Directors Association Scholarships

AMOUNT: Maximum: $500 DEADLINE: January 31
FIELDS/MAJORS: Mortuary Science

Awards for Indiana residents studying mortuary science. Applicants must intend to serve their internship in Indiana, and they must be admitted to or enrolled in an accredited program of mortuary science. Second deadline is April 30. Write to the address below for more information.

Indiana Funeral Directors Association
1311 West 96th St., Suite 120
Indianapolis, IN 46260

1086
Industrial Designers Society of America Scholarship

AMOUNT: Maximum: $2000 DEADLINE: May 1
FIELDS/MAJORS: Engineering Technologies

Open to student members at the junior and senior level. Must have a minimum GPA of 2.9 and be in the "next to the last year" of undergraduate work. Must be U.S. citizens. Requirements include a creative and original product design. Contact the address listed for further information or call (703) 759-0100.

Industrial Designers Society of America
Celia Weinstein, Marketing Director
142 Walker Rd.
Great Falls, VA 20165

1087
Industry Research Scholar Awards

AMOUNT: $50000 DEADLINE: September 10
FIELDS/MAJORS: Gastroenterology, Hepatomegaly, Related Fields

Awards for investigators who hold full-time faculty positions at universities or professional institutes. Those who have been at the assistant professor level or equivalent for more than five years are not eligible. Applicants goals must be research careers in gastroenterology and hepatomegaly. Contact the address below for further information or Web sites: http://www.gastro.org; http://www.asge.org; or http://hepar-sfgh.ucsf.edu.

American Digestive Health Foundation
Ms. Irene Kuo
7910 Woodmont Ave., 7th Floor
Bethesda, MD 20814

1088
Integrated Manufacturing Predoctoral Fellowships

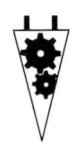

AMOUNT: $20000-$35000 DEADLINE: December 5
FIELDS/MAJORS: Manufacturing Engineering or Related Field

Fellowships are available for doctoral candidates who wish to further their education in a field directly related to integrated manufacturing. A cost-of-education allowance of up to $15000 is also available. Applicants must be U.S. citizens or nationals. Fellows must be enrolled full-time. Write to the address listed for additional information.

National Research Council, U.S. Department of Energy
Fellowship Office
2101 Constitution Ave.
Washington, DC 20418

1089
Interchange Fellowship and Martin McLaren Scholarship

AMOUNT: None Specified DEADLINE: November 15
FIELDS/MAJORS: Horticulture, Landscape Architecture, and Related Fields

Program for U.S. graduate students to spend a year in Great Britain studying horticulture or landscape architecture as well as working at American universities and botanical gardens in the U.K. Funds two graduate students annually. Send a SASE to the address listed for more information.

Garden Club of America
Ms. Shelley Burch
598 Madison Ave.
New York, NY 10022

1090
Interest-Free Loan Program

AMOUNT: Maximum: $3000 DEADLINE: April 15
FIELDS/MAJORS: All Areas of Study

Open to residents of the St. Louis area (St. Louis and the counties of St. Louis, St. Charles, and Jefferson) and Franklin, Missouri who are high school graduates and can demonstrate financial need. Loans are interest-free but will bear interest for any principal outstanding after the due date. Loans are for graduates, undergraduates, or vocational/tech study. Renewable to $15000. Write to the address below for details.

Scholarship Foundation of St. Louis
8215 Clayton Rd.
St. Louis, MO 63117

1091
Interest-Free Loans

AMOUNT: None Specified DEADLINE: None Specified
FIELDS/MAJORS: All Areas of Study

Interest-free loans for residents of Baltimore city or Baltimore County who have exhausted all other available avenues of funding. Aid is offered for study at any accredited vocational, undergraduate, or graduate institution. Referrals to other sources of financial aid and planning are also available from this nonprofit, private agency. Write to the address listed for details.

Central Scholarship Bureau
Pomona Square
1700 Reisterstown Rd., #220
Baltimore, MD 21208-2903

1092
International Affairs Scholarship

AMOUNT: $500 DEADLINE: March 1
FIELDS/MAJORS: International Affairs/International Relations

Students must be maintaining legal residence in Massachusetts and present a letter of endorsement from a sponsoring Women's Club in your community. Write to the address below for details, and be sure to include a SASE.

General Federation of Women's Clubs of Massachusetts
Scholarship Chairman, 245 Dutton Road
PO Box 679
Sudbury, MA 01776

1093
International Association of Fire Chiefs Scholarships

AMOUNT: $250-$4000
DEADLINE: August 1
FIELDS/MAJORS: Business and Urban Administration/Engineering/Fire Science

Open to members of a fire service of a state, county, provincial, municipal, community, industrial, or federal fire department. Based on high GPAs, number of years of service, (paid or volunteer), commitment to study, and financial need. Endorsement by a chief officer is most important. If applicant is the chief officer, the endorsement should come from the immediate superior. Contact the address below for further information.

International Association of Fire Chiefs Foundation
Scholarship Competition
11257 Wiltshire Rd.
York, PA 17403

1094
International Brotherhood of Boilermakers Scholarship

AMOUNT: $2500-$5000 DEADLINE: March 31
FIELDS/MAJORS: All Areas of Study

For children (includes legally adopted) of members in good standing (current, deceased, retired, or totally disabled) of the International Brotherhood of Boilermakers, Iron Ship Builders, Blacksmiths, Forgers, and Helpers (AFL-CIO, CLC). Awarded to high school seniors only. Based on academics, goals, and extracurricular activities. Fourteen awards offered annually. Applications may be obtained by writing to the address listed.

International Brotherhood of Boilermakers
Scholarship Program
753 State Ave., Suite 570
Kansas City, KS 66101

1095

International Brotherhood of Electrical Workers Scholarship Fund

AMOUNT: $2000-$5000 DEADLINE: None Specified
FIELDS/MAJORS: All Areas of Study

Scholarships for sons and daughters of members of local union #3 of the International Brotherhood of Electrical Workers (IBEW). For graduating high school seniors. Qualifying parent must have been employed (or available for employment) for at least five years by employer(s) who contribute to the educational and cultural fund. Twenty scholarships per year. Contact your parents local union #3 or write to the address below for details.

Educational and Cultural Fund of the Electrical Industry
158-11 Harry Van Arsdale Jr. Ave.
Flushing, NY 11365

1096

International Doctoral Scholarship for Jewish Studies

AMOUNT: $2000-$7500 DEADLINE: October 31
FIELDS/MAJORS: Jewish Studies

Any graduate student specializing in a Jewish field who is enrolled in a doctoral program at a recognized university is eligible to apply. For academic and religious leadership studies. Renewable for up to four years. Applicants are advised about decisions in August. Write to the address listed for details.

Memorial Foundation for Jewish Culture
15 East 26th St., Room 1703
New York, NY 10010

1097

International Fellowships

AMOUNT: Maximum: $15160 DEADLINE: December 2
FIELDS/MAJORS: All Areas of Study

Fellowships for one year of graduate study or advanced research in the U.S. To women of outstanding ability who are citizens of countries other than the United States. Applicants must hold the equivalent of a U.S. bachelor's degree. Forty-five awards offered annually. Also, six fellowships are available for members of International Federation of University Women to study in any country except their home county. Previous and current recipients of AAUW Fellowships are ineligible. Write to the address listed for more information.

American Association of University Women Educational Foundation
2201 N. Dodge St.
Iowa City, IA 52243

1098

International Fellowships in Jewish Studies

AMOUNT: $5000 DEADLINE: October 31
FIELDS/MAJORS: Jewish Studies

Applicants must be qualified scholars, researchers, or artists who process the knowledge and experience to formulate and implement a project in a field of Jewish specialization. Write to the address below for details.

Memorial Foundation for Jewish Culture
15 East 26th St., Room 1901
New York, NY 10010

1099

International Food Service Executives Association Scholarships

AMOUNT: $100-$500 DEADLINE: February 1
FIELDS/MAJORS: Foodservice, Hospitality

Open to students enrolled full-time at Johnson and Wales who are majoring in the above fields. Contact the address below for further information.

International Foodservice Executives Association
1100 S. State Rd. 7, #103
Margate, FL 33065

1100

International Reading Association Research Grants and Awards

AMOUNT: $500-$5000
DEADLINE: None Specified
FIELDS/MAJORS: Reading Research and Disabilities

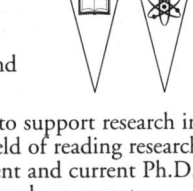

Grant and award programs designed to support research in and recognize contributions to the field of reading research and reading disabilities. Open to recent and current Ph.D. candidates (for dissertations) and to teachers, reporters, writers, and researchers. Some awards limited to IRA members. Write for complete details on membership and award programs. Information can also be found in the spring issues of Journal of Reading, Lectura Y Vida, Reading Research Quarterly, The Reading Teacher, and Reading Today.

International Reading Association
800 Barksdale Rd.
PO Box 8139
Newark, DE 19714

1101

International Scholarship Program for Community Service

AMOUNT: None Specified **DEADLINE:** November 30
FIELDS/MAJORS: Jewish Studies, Religious Studies, Social Work, Theology

Scholarships for persons who intend to pursue careers in the above fields. Recipients should agree to work for two to three years in a community with a shortage of persons in the recipients area of study. For study in any recognized Yeshiva school of social work, college, university, or seminary. Renewable. Write to the address below for details.

Memorial Foundation for Jewish Culture
15 E. 26th St., Room 1901
New York, NY 10010

1102

Iola Lioness Scholarship

AMOUNT: $500 **DEADLINE:** November 16
FIELDS/MAJORS: All Areas of Study

Awards for students from the Iola-Scandinavia school district who have been out of high school for at least five years and desire to return for further education. Two awards are offered annually. Write to the address below for more information.

Iola Lioness Club
Attn: Scholarship
170 Lafollette St.
Iola, WI 54945

1103

Irene and Daisy MacGregor Memorial and Alice W. Rooke Scholarship

AMOUNT: Maximum: $5000 **DEADLINE:** April 15
FIELDS/MAJORS: Medicine, Psychiatric Nursing

Scholarship available to students who have been accepted into an accredited school of medicine to pursue an M.D. or are studying in the field of psychiatric nursing (graduate level). All applicants must be sponsored by a local DAR chapter and be U.S. citizens. Contact your local DAR chapter or send a SASE to the address for more information.

National Society Daughters of the American Revolution
NSDAR Scholarship Committee
1776 D St. NW
Washington, DC 20006

1104

Irene E. Newman Scholarship

AMOUNT: None Specified **DEADLINE:** April 1
FIELDS/MAJORS: Dental Public Health

Scholarships for baccalaureate or graduate degree candidates in a full-time accredited program in Dental Public Health. Must have completed at least one year of program and have a GPA of at least 3.0. Write to the address below for more information.

American Dental Hygienists' Association Institute for Oral Health
444 N. Michigan Ave., Suite 3400
Chicago, IL 60611

1105

Irene Stambler Vocational Opportunities Grant Program

AMOUNT: Maximum: $2500 **DEADLINE:** None Specified
FIELDS/MAJORS: All Areas of Study

One-time grant for a female resident of the metropolitan Washington area who has recently undergone a separation, divorce, death, or serious illness of her spouse. To assist with realization of career plan. Write to the address below or call (301) 881-3700 for details.

Jewish Social Service Agency of Metropolitan Washington
6123 Montrose Road
Rockville, MD 20852

1106

Irene W. Hart Scholarship

AMOUNT: Maximum: $1000 **DEADLINE:** April 1
FIELDS/MAJORS: Education

Open to students of an accredited New Hampshire college or university who are graduates of a New Hampshire high school. Must demonstrate financial need, write an essay stating goals in the field of education, and have good academic standing. Contact the address listed for further information. Must have a GPA of at least 2.7.

New Hampshire Retired Educators Association (NHREA)
C/O Roland R. Boucher, Chair.
331 Mountain Rd.
Jaffrey, NH 03452

1107
Irma F. Rube Scholarship

AMOUNT: $500   DEADLINE: June 1
FIELDS/MAJORS: Cytotechnology

Scholarships are available for students enrolled in a cytotechnology program. Must have a GPA of at least 2.75. Write to the address below for information.

Southern Association of Cytotechnologists, Inc.
Education Committee
800 Madison Ave.
Memphis, TN 38163

1108
Irving W. Cook, WAOCGS Scholarship

AMOUNT: $1000   DEADLINE: February 1
FIELDS/MAJORS: Electronics, Communications, Related Fields

Scholarship available to students with any class amateur radio license who are residents of Kansas. For full-time study. Write to the address listed for information.

ARRL Foundation (American Radio Relay League)
Scholarship Program
225 Main St.
Newington, CT 06111

1109
Isabel M. Herson Scholarship in Education

AMOUNT: $500-$1000   DEADLINE: February 1
FIELDS/MAJORS: Elementary, Secondary Education

Open to high school seniors, undergraduates, and graduate students. Must be enrolled/planning to enroll in an elementary or secondary education program. For one full-time academic year. No affiliation with Zeta Phi Beta is required. Contact the address listed for further information or call (202) 387-3103. If writing, you must include a SASE for a reply. Must have a GPA of at least 2.8.

Zeta Phi Beta Sorority
National Educational Foundation
1734 New Hampshire Ave. NW
Washington, DC 20009

1110
ISCLT Scholarships

AMOUNT: None Specified   DEADLINE: None Specified
FIELDS/MAJORS: All Areas of Study

Scholarships for ISCLT registrants or regular class members or for children of ISCLT registrants or regular class members. Student class members are not eligible to apply. Write to the address below for details.

International Society for Clinical Laboratory Technology
917 Locust St., #1100
St. Louis, MO 63101

1111
ISI Scholarship Program

AMOUNT: Maximum: $1000   DEADLINE: October 31
FIELDS/MAJORS: Library and Information Science

The ISI scholarship will be granted only for beginning graduate study leading to a Ph.D. from a recognized program in library science, information science, or related fields of study. Applicants must be members of the Special Libraries Association and have worked in a special library. Applicants must submit evidence of financial need. One award is offered annually. Because ISI awards Medical Librarianship Scholarships through the Medical Library Association, persons planning careers in Medical Librarianship cannot be considered. Write to the address listed for more information.

Special Libraries Association
SLA Scholarship Committee
1700 Eighteenth St. NW
Washington, DC 20009

1112
Italian-American Chamber of Commerce Scholarships

AMOUNT: $1000   DEADLINE: May 31
FIELDS/MAJORS: All Areas of Study

Scholarships available to students of Italian ancestry who are residents of the following Illinois counties: Cook, DuPage, Kane, Lake, Will, and McHenry. Applicants may be high school seniors planning to attend a four-year school or current undergraduates. Must have a minimum GPA of 3.5. Write to the address below for details.

Italian American Chamber of Commerce of Chicago
30 S. Michigan Ave.
Chicago, IL 60603

1113
Italian-American Cultural Society Scholarships

AMOUNT: $750-$1000　DEADLINE: February 1
FIELDS/MAJORS: All Fields of Study

Scholarships offered to Ocean County senior high students of Italian descent. Applicants must submit an essay on Italian culture. Five awards given. Amount of the award depends upon the parents standing in the society. Write to the address below for details.

Italian-American Cultural Society of Ocean County, Inc.
PO Box 1602
Toms River, NJ 08754

1114
ITT Scholarship

AMOUNT: Maximum: $2000　DEADLINE: November 7
FIELDS/MAJORS: All Areas of Study

Open to sophomores and juniors who are residents of New York state with a minimum GPA of 3.0. Must be attending one of the ACI member schools and be recommended by the financial aid office. Do not write to the listed address, they cannot provide any additional information or forms. Contact your financial aid office at your school for further information. Applicants must be nominated by the financial aid office of their school. The school offices will have the information.

Associated Colleges of Illinois
ACI Program Administration
1735 N. Paulina Ave., Loft 401
Chicago, IL 60622

1115
Ittleson and Andrew W. Mellon Fellowships

AMOUNT: Maximum: $16000　DEADLINE: November 15
FIELDS/MAJORS: Visual Art, Art History and Theory, Architecture, and Related Areas

Two-year fellowship for doctoral student doing dissertation research in the fields of study above. Scholars are expected to spend half a year at the National Gallery of Art, half a year doing research anywhere in the U.S. or abroad, and the second year at the Center to complete the dissertation. Applicants must know two languages related to the topic of their dissertation. Fellowship is only available to U.S. citizens or legal residents. Contact the chairperson of the graduate department of art history at your school (or other appropriate department) or write to the address below for more information.

National Gallery of Art
Center for Study in the Visual Arts
Predoctoral Fellowship Program
Washington, DC 20565

1116
Iva W. and Roy Henry Scholarship

AMOUNT: Maximum: $1000　DEADLINE: May 15
FIELDS/MAJORS: All Areas of Study

Awards for students from Edgar County, Illinois. Applications are only accepted from April 1 through May 15. Seven awards are offered annually. Contact the Trust Department at the address below for more information.

Citizens National Bank of Paris
110-114 West Court St.
PO Box 790
Paris, IL 61944

1117
Ivan F. and Ina C. Legore Scholarship Fund

AMOUNT: None Specified　DEADLINE: April 15
FIELDS/MAJORS: All Areas of Study

Scholarship open to current seniors and graduates of Sarasota County high schools who have participated in at least one Sailor Circus performance. Student must submit application, transcript, two letters of recommendation, and SAT or ACT scores. Write to Lou Geller at the address listed for details.

Legore Scholarship Fund
PO Box 676
Venice, FL 34284

1118
Ivy Parker Memorial Scholarship

AMOUNT: Maximum: $2000　DEADLINE: February 1
FIELDS/MAJORS: Engineering

Scholarship for junior or senior woman majoring in engineering in an accredited program. Must have a GPA of at least 3.5. Based on financial need. Write to address listed for details. Please be certain to enclose a SASE. Information and applications for the SWE awards are also available from the deans of engineering schools.

Society of Women Engineers
Scholarship Selection Committee
120 Wall St., 11th Floor
New York, NY 10005

1119
J. Clawson Mills Scholarships

AMOUNT: None Specified   DEADLINE: November 7
FIELDS/MAJORS: Fine Arts

Award is generally given to mature scholars with demonstrated ability for one year of study or research at the Museum in any branch of the fine arts relating to the Museum's collections. Write to the address listed for further information.

Metropolitan Museum of Art
Fellowship Programs, Pia Quintano
1000 Fifth Ave.
New York, NY 10028

1120
J. Clifford Dietrich, Julie Y. Cross, John Hays Hanly Scholarships

AMOUNT: None Specified   DEADLINE: May 1
FIELDS/MAJORS: Law Enforcement, Police Administration

3 scholarships for students of Law Enforcement or Police Administration at an accredited college or university. Must have completed at least one year of study. No more than one scholarship is awarded to any one family. Students who are working toward an advanced degree are also eligible. Must be a U.S. citizen. Write to the address below for details. Include a SASE for an application.

Association of Former Agents of the U.S. Secret Service
PO Box 848
Annandale, VA 22003

1121
J. Desmond Slattery Professional Marketing Awards

AMOUNT: None Specified   DEADLINE: March 1
FIELDS/MAJORS: Marketing-Travel/Tourism

Open to professionals who submit any travel marketing related program, project, or activity that demonstrates an innovative and significant contribution to travel and tourism marketing. Appropriate supportive material such as cassettes, videotapes, posters, etc., should accompany each entry. Entries will be judged on originality, creativity, clarity of message results, and overall marketing excellence. Write to the address listed for further information.

Travel and Tourism Research Association
TTRA Awards Committee
546 E. Main St.
Lexington, KY 40508

1122
J. Desmond Slattery Undergraduate Student Award

AMOUNT: None Specified   DEADLINE: March 1
FIELDS/MAJORS: Travel/Tourism

Open to undergraduate university students enrolled in a degree-granting program. Applicants must submit a paper of a completed, original research study. Must be between five hundred and one thousand words clearly describing the rationale, methods, and results of research. Work should have been completed between March 1, 1997, and March 1, 1998, as an enrolled student. Write to the address listed for further information.

Travel and Tourism Research Association
TTRA Awards Committee
546 E. Main St.
Lexington, KY 40508

1123
J. Franklin Jameson Fellowship in American History

AMOUNT: Maximum: $10000   DEADLINE: January 15
FIELDS/MAJORS: American History

One semester fellowship is to support research at the Library of Congress by young historians. Applicants must hold the Ph.D. or equivalent, must have received this degree within the last five years, and must not have published or had accepted for publication a book-length historical work. Write to the address listed for details.

American Historical Association
Awards Administrator
400 A St. SE
Washington, DC 20003

1124
J. Hugh and Earle W. Fellows Memorial Fund Loans

AMOUNT: None Specified   DEADLINE: None Specified
FIELDS/MAJORS: Medicine, Nursing, Medical Technology, Theology

Low interest loans for residents of Escambia, Santa Rosa, Okaloosa, or Walton counties in Florida, who are studying in one of the above fields. Loans are interest free until graduation. Write to the address listed or call (904) 484-1706 for details.

J. Hugh and Earle W. Fellows Memorial Fund
C/O Pensacola Junior College, Exec. V. P.
1000 College Blvd.
Pensacola, FL 32504

1125
J. Waldo Smith Hydraulic Fellowship

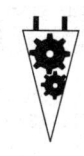

AMOUNT: $4000   DEADLINE: February 20
FIELDS/MAJORS: Civil Engineering/Hydraulics

Applicant must be a national ASCE member in good standing in a graduate program. Award is used for research in the field of experimental hydraulics. Write for complete details.

American Society of Civil Engineers
Student Services Department
1801 Alexander Bell Dr.
Reston, VA 20191

1126
J.D. Edsal Scholarship

AMOUNT: Maximum: $750   DEADLINE: April 15
FIELDS/MAJORS: Film Making, Advertising

Scholarships are available for Rhode Island residents enrolled in a film making or advertising program with career goals in one of these fields. For sophomore year and above. One award is given annually. Write to the address listed for information.

Rhode Island Advertising Club
18 Imperial Place
Providence, RI 02886

1127
J.E. Caldwell Centennial Scholarships

AMOUNT: Maximum: $2000   DEADLINE: February 15
FIELDS/MAJORS: Historical Preservation

Scholarships for graduate students in the area of historic preservation. Must be sponsored by a DAR chapter and be U.S. citizens. Contact your local or state DAR chapter or send a SASE to the address listed for details. Must have a GPA of at least 3.2.

National Society Daughters of the American Revolution
NSDAR Scholarship Committee
1776 D St. NW
Washington, DC 20006

1128
J.J. Barr Scholarship

AMOUNT: $5000   DEADLINE: April 1
FIELDS/MAJORS: Water Utility Industry

Scholarship for graduate students pursuing a degree in the Water Utility Industry. Must be a U.S. citizen. Write to the address below for more information.

National Association of Water Companies
Scholarship Committee
1725 K St. NW, Suite 1212
Washington, DC 20006

1129
Jack C. Nisbet Memorial Scholarship

AMOUNT: $750   DEADLINE: July 1
FIELDS/MAJORS: All Areas of Study

Scholarships available to members of the American Jersey Cattle Association who were participants in the last National Youth Achievement Contest. One award is offered annually. Write to the address below for details.

American Jersey Cattle Association
Scholarship Committee
6486 East Main St.
Reynoldsburg, OH 43068

1130
Jack E. Leisch Memorial National Scholarship

AMOUNT: Maximum: $1000   DEADLINE: February 20
FIELDS/MAJORS: Civil Engineering, Traffic Engineering, Geometric Design, Transportation Planning, Transportation Science, or Related Fields

Applicants must be ASCE members pursuing a graduate degree in civil engineering or a related field. Must be enrolled in a program approved by ABET, and the university must be a member of the Council of University Transportation Centers. Financial need, academic performance, and leadership capacity will be considered in selection. Award is to be used toward tuition fees only. Previous recipients are not eligible. Write to the address listed or call 1-800-548-ASCE for complete details.

American Society of Civil Engineers
Member Scholarships and Awards
1801 Alexander Bell Dr.
Reston, VA 20191-4400

1131
Jack Sebald Scholarship

AMOUNT: Maximum: $350   DEADLINE: March 1
FIELDS/MAJORS: All Areas of Study

Open to residents of Bay County who are children, (or grandchildren), of active, retired, or deceased Bay City police officers. Must be enrolled at an accredited college or university and have a minimum GPA of 2.5. Contact the address listed for further information.

Bay Area Community Foundation
Scholarship Director
703 Washington Ave.
Bay City, MI 48708-5670

1132
Jackie Robinson Foundation Scholarship

AMOUNT: Maximum: $5000   DEADLINE: April 1
FIELDS/MAJORS: All Areas of Study

Scholarships for minority high school seniors who have been accepted into a four-year college or university. Based on academic achievement, leadership, and financial need. Must be a U.S. citizen. Check with your high school guidance counselor to see if he or she has details on this program. Otherwise, write to the address below for details.

Jackie Robinson Foundation Scholarship Fund
Attn: Scholarship Program
3 West 35th St.
New York, NY 10011

1133
Jacob and Lewis Fox Scholarship

AMOUNT: Maximum: $2000   DEADLINE: December 15
FIELDS/MAJORS: All Areas of Study

Open to graduating seniors who attend HPHS, Bulkeley, or Weaver High Schools in Hartford. For use at a four-year school. Must be able to demonstrate academic ability, leadership, reverence, and financial need. Contact the address listed for further information. Must have a GPA of at least 3.0.

Jacob L. and Lewis Fox Foundation
William Saxton
PO Box 542
Farmington, CT 06034

1134
Jacob K. Javits Graduate Fellowships

AMOUNT: Maximum: $14400   DEADLINE: May 19
FIELDS/MAJORS: Arts, Social Science, Humanities

Doctoral fellowship in selected fields of study in arts, social science, and humanities. At the time of application, candidates must be eligible to begin to pursue study or research at the graduate level at an accredited institution of higher education. Applicants must be citizens of the U.S. Ninety individual fellowships are given annually. Write to the address listed for details.

U.S. Department of Education
600 Independence Ave. SW
Portals Building, Suite 600
Washington, DC 20024-5329

1135
Jacob Stump, Jr. and Clara Stump Memorial Fund Grants

AMOUNT: Maximum: $1000   DEADLINE: April 15
FIELDS/MAJORS: All Areas of Study

Open to graduating seniors who will attend state-supported Illinois schools. Must be from any of the following counties: Coles, Cumberland, Douglas, or Moultrie. Contact the address listed for further information or call (217) 234-6430.

Jacob Stump, Jr. and Clara Stump Memorial Scholarship Fund
Central National Bank of Mattoon
PO Box 685
Mattoon, IL 61938

1136
Jacobs Research Funds Small Grants Program

AMOUNT: Maximum: $1200   DEADLINE: February 15
FIELDS/MAJORS: Anthropology

Grants for students with any level of academic credentials who are doing research that supports the sociocultural or linguistic aspects of anthropology. The primary focus of study will be on indigenous peoples of Canada, the continental U.S. (especially the Pacific Northwest), and Mexico.

Whatcom Museum
Jacobs Funds Administrator
121 Prospect St.
Bellingham, WA 98225

1137
Jacqueline Donnee Vogt and Walter F. Wagner, Jr. Scholarships

AMOUNT: Maximum: $500   DEADLINE: May 15
FIELDS/MAJORS: Architecture

Open to Connecticut residents who have completed two years of a five-year bachelor's program. Selections based on academics and financial need. Both awards are renewable. Each scholarship offers one award yearly. Contact the address listed for further information. Must have a GPA of at least 3.0.

Connecticut Architecture Foundation
Judy Edwards, Exec. V. P.
87 Willow St.
New Haven, CT 06511

1138
Jaffe Family Foundation Research Award

AMOUNT: Maximum: $25000   DEADLINE: January 12
FIELDS/MAJORS: Allergy Research

Open to promising investigators involved in food allergy research and the immunopathogenic mechanisms associated with food allergic disorders. Must be fellow in training, resident, or postdoctoral scholar and an AAAAI member. Applicants must be nominated by program directors, deans, or department chairpersons. Program is intended to provide salary support, no overhead allowance may be charged by the sponsoring institution. Write to the address listed for more information or call (414) 272-6071.

American Academy of Allergy, Asthma, and Immunology
Chair, Committee to Grant Research Award
611 E. Wells St.
Milwaukee, WI 53202-3889

1139
Jake Gimbel Loan Program

AMOUNT: None Specified   DEADLINE: January 30
FIELDS/MAJORS: Education Certificate, Any Graduate Program

No interest loans are available for students enrolled in graduate or teaching credential programs in the state of California. Must have attended grades seven through twelve in Santa Barbara County and be recommended by the dean of graduate studies at your school. Applications are available from October 1 through January 26. Write to the address listed for further information.

Santa Barbara Foundation
Student Aid Director
15 East Carrillo St.
Santa Barbara, CA 93101

1140
James A. Finnegan Fellowship Contest

AMOUNT: $1000-$1500   DEADLINE: February 6
FIELDS/MAJORS: Political Science, Government

Summer fellowships for undergraduates attending accredited Pennsylvania colleges/universities or students from Pennsylvania attending any institution who have completed at least one semester of study. Paid internships last between eight and ten weeks. Interns are assigned positions in executive or legislative offices and will attend seminars with leading public officials and media figures. Students also receive financial awards. Contact the address listed for more information or call (610) 921-3070. To expedite the process, use their Web site for information http://members.aol.com/JAFINNEGAN. Must have a GPA of at least 2.8.

James A. Finnegan Fellowship Foundation
Contest Coordinator
3600 Raymond St.
Reading, PA 19605

1141
James and Mary Dawson Scholarship

AMOUNT: Maximum: $5000   DEADLINE: March 15
FIELDS/MAJORS: All Areas of Graduate Study

Scholarship available to a student from Scotland coming to America for graduate studies. Based on need, academics, and goals. Consideration is made for students who continue to enhance their knowledge of Scottish history or culture. Write to James S. McLeod, Chairman of the Charity and Education Committee, at the address listed for details.

St. Andrew's Society of Washington, D.C.
James McLeod, Chairman
7012 Arandale Rd.
Bethesda, MD 20817-4702

1142
James B. Carey Scholarships

AMOUNT: $1000   DEADLINE: April 15
FIELDS/MAJORS: All Areas of Study

Must be a child of an IUE member (including retired/deceased members). Must be accepted for admission or already enrolled as a full-time student at a college, university, nursing, or technical school. Undergraduates only. Nine awards offered annually. Write to the address below for details.

IUE International-Department of Social Action
Ms. Gloria T. Johnson, Director
1126 Sixteenth St. NW.
Washington, DC 20036

1143
James Butler Memorial and Nylcare Health Plans Mid-Atlantic Scholarships

AMOUNT: Maximum: $3000   DEADLINE: April 1
FIELDS/MAJORS: All Areas of Study

Awards for students who demonstrate financial need, as verified by parent's tax return for prior year or other suitable documents. Must be graduating high school senior or college student with a GPA of 2.5 or better. Also based upon three letters of reference, an essay on the challenge to American families today, and great involvement in school and community activities. Contact Nylcare customer service at 1-800-635-3121 for more information.

Nylcare/Mid-Atlantic Scholarship Foundation, Inc.
7617 Ora Glen Dr.
Greenbelt, MD 20770

1144
James Carlson Memorial Scholarship

AMOUNT: None Specified DEADLINE: March 1
FIELDS/MAJORS: Elementary, Secondary Education

Open to students pursuing a baccalaureate degree or in the fifty year of a five-year teaching certificate program. Priority for awards is as follows: 1. African, Asian, Hispanic, or Native Americans. 2. Dependents of Oregon Education Association members. 3. Students with a demonstrated commitment to teach autistic children. Must be U.S. citizens or permanent residents and residents of Oregon to apply. Contact the address below for further information.

Oregon State Scholarship Commission
Private Awards
1500 Valley River Dr., #100
Eugene, OR 97401-2130

1145
James D. Phelan Award in Literature

AMOUNT: $2000 DEADLINE: January 15
FIELDS/MAJORS: Creative Writing, Poetry, Playwriting

Awards for California-born authors of an unpublished work-in-progress who are between the ages of twenty and thirty-five. Work can be fiction, nonfictional prose, poetry, or drama. Write to the address listed for information.

San Francisco Foundation
Intersection for the Arts
446 Valencia St.
San Francisco, CA 94103

1146
James F. Lincoln Memorial Competition Awards

AMOUNT: $250-$2000 DEADLINE: June 16
FIELDS/MAJORS: Engineering

Contest open to undergraduate (enrolled in a four-year or longer curriculum leading to a bachelor's degree) and graduate engineering students. Based on submitted papers representing work on design, engineering, or fabrication problems relating to any type of building, bridge, or other stationary structure, machine, product, or apparatus. Approximately thirty-five awards offered annually. Write to the address below for more information. Must have a GPA of at least 2.8.

James F. Lincoln Arc Welding Foundation
PO Box 17035
Cleveland, OH 44117

1147
James F. Mulholland American Legion Scholarships

AMOUNT: $500 DEADLINE: May 1
FIELDS/MAJORS: All Areas of Study

Scholarships are available for high school seniors who are New York residents. Must be entering college the same year as graduation from high school. Applicant must be the child of a Legion or auxiliary member. Write to the address below for additional information.

American Legion-Department of New York
Department Adjutant
112 State St., Suite 400
Albany, NY 12207

1148
James Forsythe Milroy Foundation

AMOUNT: None Specified DEADLINE: None Specified
FIELDS/MAJORS: Agriculture or Related Fields

For high school seniors or recent graduates from Logan County, Ohio, high schools who have intentions of working in agriculture or an agriculturally-related field at the completion of college or equivalent training. Write to the address listed for more information.

James Forsythe Milroy Foundation
Citizens Federal Savings and Loan Assoc.
110 North Main St.
Bellefontaine, OH 43311

1149
James Francis Byrnes Scholarship

AMOUNT: Maximum: $2500 DEADLINE: February 15
FIELDS/MAJORS: All Areas of Study

Scholarships available to young South Carolinians who have lost one or both parents by death. Applicants should be average or above-average students with the potential, as evidenced by grades and college board scores, for earning a bachelor's degree. Awards for high school seniors through college sophomores. Write to the address listed for details. Must have a GPA of at least 2.0.

James F. Byrnes Foundation
PO Box 9596
Columbia, SC 29290

1150
James G. K. McClure Educational Scholarships

AMOUNT: $300-$1500   DEADLINE: May 15
FIELDS/MAJORS: All Areas of Study

Seventy-five to eighty awards for incoming freshmen who are residents of western North Carolina and plan to attend two- or four-year schools in that part of the state. Many schools are participants in the program and have additional information and applications in their financial aid offices. High school GPA, leadership, and financial need are considered. Contact your school's financial aid office for information. Do not contact the fund directly.

James G. K. McClure Educational and Development Fund
Sugar Hollow Farm
11 Sugar Hollow Land
Fairview, NC 28730

1151
James K. Rathmell, Jr. Memorial Scholarship

AMOUNT: $2000   DEADLINE: April 1
FIELDS/MAJORS: Horticulture

Scholarships for juniors, seniors, or graduate students pursuing a career in horticulture or floriculture, who wish to study abroad for six months or longer. Write to the address below for details. The BPFI also sponsors two awards through Future Farmers of America (check with your FFA advisor).

Bedding Plants Foundation, Inc.
Scholarship Program
PO Box 27241
Lansing, MI 48909

1152
James L. Goodwin Memorial Scholarship

AMOUNT: $1000-$3000   DEADLINE: April 1
FIELDS/MAJORS: Forestry

Open to high school seniors, undergraduates, and graduate students who are Connecticut residents. The college/university you attend must be accredited in forest management. Selections based on academics, enrollment in the forestry field of study, and financial need. Contact the address listed for further information, or call (860) 346-2372 to request an application. Must have a GPA of at least 3.0.

Connecticut Forest and Park Association, Inc.
16 Meriden Rd.
Rockfall, CT 06481

1153
James M. Hoffman Scholarship

AMOUNT: $500-$700   DEADLINE: March 31
FIELDS/MAJORS: All Areas of Study

Open to graduating seniors of Calhoun County high schools. Referral by your high school is required. Number of awards varies. Information and applications available ONLY in your high school.

James M. Hoffman Scholarship Trust
C/O SouthTrust Bank of Calhoun County, N.A.
PO Box 1000
Anniston, AL 36202

1154
James Madison Junior Fellowships

AMOUNT: None Specified   DEADLINE: March 1
FIELDS/MAJORS: Secondary Education-American History/American Government, Social Studies

Open to outstanding college seniors and graduates without teaching experience who intend to become secondary teachers in the fields listed above for grades seven through twelve. Must be a U.S. citizen or natural. Contact the address below for further information.

James Madison Memorial Fellowship Foundation
James Madison Fellowship Program
PO Box 4030, 2201 N. Dodge St.
Iowa City, IA 52243

1155
James V. Day Scholarship

AMOUNT: None Specified   DEADLINE: May 1
FIELDS/MAJORS: All Areas of Study

Open to residents of Maine entering their first year or higher of post-high school education or training. Must be U.S. citizens and parents must be current members of an American Legion Post in the department of Maine. Must be able to document financial need. Write to the address listed for additional information or application.

American Legion-Department of Maine
Department Adjutant, State Headquarters
PO Box 900
Waterville, ME 04903

1156
James W. Colgan Loan Fund

AMOUNT: $1500-$2000 DEADLINE: March 15
FIELDS/MAJORS: All Areas of Study

Applicants must be residents of Massachusetts (at least five years), enrolled, or planning to enroll in a college or technical school. Based on need. Interest free if repaid within the guidelines of Fleet Bank. For undergraduate study. Write to the address listed for details.

Community Foundation of Western Massachusetts
PO Box 15769
1500 Main St.
Springfield, MA 01115

1157
James Z. Naurison Scholarship Fund

AMOUNT: $400-$2000 DEADLINE: March 15
FIELDS/MAJORS: All Areas of Study

Open to undergraduate and graduate students who are residents of Hampden, Hampshire, Franklin, or Berkshire counties in Massachusetts, or Suffield or Enfield counties in Connecticut. Write to the address listed for complete details.

Community Foundation of Western Massachusetts
PO Box 15769
1500 Main St.
Springfield, MA 01115

1158
Jane A. Korzeniowski Memorial Scholarship

AMOUNT: $200 DEADLINE: March 15
FIELDS/MAJORS: All Areas of Study

One scholarship is available for a Chicopee resident. Based on financial need, academic merit, and extracurricular activities. Write to the address listed for information. Must have a GPA of at least 2.9.

Community Foundation of Western Massachusetts
PO Box 15769
1500 Main St.
Springfield, MA 01115

1159
Jane and Morgan Whitney Fellowships

AMOUNT: None Specified DEADLINE: November 7
FIELDS/MAJORS: Art Conservation, Art History, Decorative Arts, Fine Arts

Awarded for study, work, or research to students of the fine arts whose fields are related to the Museum's collections. Preference will be given to students in the decorative arts who are under the age of forty. Write to the address listed for further information.

Metropolitan Museum of Art
Fellowship Programs, Pia Quintano
1000 Fifth Ave.
New York, NY 10028

1160
Jane Coffin Childs Fund Postdoctoral Fellowships

AMOUNT: $26000 DEADLINE: February 1
FIELDS/MAJORS: Cancer Research, Oncology

Fellowship is for a three-year period with increases in stipend each year. Applicants must hold the M.D. or Ph.D. and submit a research proposal. For study into the causes, origins, and treatment of cancer. No restrictions on citizenship or institution. Recipients in general should not have more than one year of postdoctoral experience. Write to the address below for details.

Jane Coffin Childs Memorial Fund for Medical Research
Office of the Director
333 Cedar St., PO Box 3333
New Haven, CT 06510

1161
Janet Dziadulwicz Branden Awards

AMOUNT: $500-$1000 DEADLINE: March 2
FIELDS/MAJORS: Polish Studies

Scholarships are available for Polish-American students in Polish studies. Applicants must reside in Wisconsin, be U.S. citizens, and have a GPA of at least 3.0. Write to the address listed or call (414) 744-9029 for information.

Polanki, Polish Women's Cultural Club of Milwaukee
Ms. Valerie Lukaszewicz, Chairperson
4160 S. First St.
Milwaukee, WI 53207

1162
Janet M. Glasgow Essay Award

AMOUNT: $1500 DEADLINE: May 31
FIELDS/MAJORS: Medicine

This award is presented to an AMWA student member for the best essay of approximately one thousand words identifying a woman physician who has been a significant role model. Write to the address below for details.

American Medical Women's Association
Glasgow Essay Award
801 N. Fairfax St., Suite 400
Alexandria, VA 22314

1163

Janssen Pharmaceutical Research Award in Allergic Rhinitis

AMOUNT: Maximum: $25000　DEADLINE: January 12
FIELDS/MAJORS: Allergy/Immunology Medical Research

Grants for members of the American Academy of Allergy and Immunology (or persons who are awaiting acceptance into the academy) who are M.D.'s or Ph.D.'s. associated with an approved allergy and immunology training program. Write to the address listed or call (414) 272-6071 for details.

American Academy of Allergy and Immunology
Jerome Schultz
611 E. Wells St.
Milwaukee, WI 53202

1164

Japan-America Society of Washington Scholarships for Study in Japan

AMOUNT: $1500-$8000　DEADLINE: March 1
FIELDS/MAJORS: Japanese Study

Scholarships are open to graduate and undergraduate students currently enrolled full-time at an accredited college/university in the District of Columbia, Maryland, Virginia, or West Virginia. Applicants must have completed at least one year of college-level study in the United States before beginning study in Japan. Five awards are offered annually. Write to the address below for more information.

Japan-America Society of Washington
Chairman of the Scholarship Committee
1020 19th St. NW
Washington, DC 20036

1165

Japanese American Treaty Centennial Scholarship

AMOUNT: Maximum: $1000　DEADLINE: July 12
FIELDS/MAJORS: All Areas of Study

Scholarships for students graduating from a southern California high school who are of Japanese descent. Approximately twenty awards offered annually. Write to the address below for details. Please include a legal-sized SASE.

Japanese Chamber of Commerce of Southern California
244 S. San Pedro St., Room 504
Los Angeles, CA 90012

1166

Jay Murphy Scholarship

AMOUNT: $200-$1000　DEADLINE: April 1
FIELDS/MAJORS: Education

Open to entering or current college students or individuals who are in education and want to upgrade their skills. Individuals who are working and wish to go back to college to become teachers are also eligible. Applicants must have a 2.5 GPA. Transcripts and essay outlining career goals are required. Finalists will have a personal interview with the selection committee. Contact the address listed or call (334) 264-6223 for further information.

Central Alabama Community Foundation
412 N. Hull St.
PO Box 11587
Montgomery, AL 36111

1167

Jeanne Bray Scholarship Fund

AMOUNT: $2000　DEADLINE: None Specified
FIELDS/MAJORS: All Areas of Study

Open to adult or junior members of the NRA or children of law enforcement professionals who are members of the NRA, or who lost their lives, became disabled, or had to retire due to the performance of their duties and were NRA members at that time. Write to the address below for more information. Must have a GPA of at least 2.5.

National Rifle Association
Attn: Jeanne E. Bray Scholarship
11250 Waples Mill Road
Fairfax, VA 22030

1168

Jeannette Mowery Scholarship

AMOUNT: None Specified　DEADLINE: March 1
FIELDS/MAJORS: Law, Medicine, Dentistry

Open to graduate law, medicine, or dentistry students attending any school in Oregon. Must be U.S. citizens and residents of Oregon. Applicants may apply and compete annually. Contact the address below for further information.

Oregon State Scholarship Commission
Private Awards
1500 Valley River Dr., #100
Eugene, OR 97401-2130

1169
Jeannette Rankin Foundation Awards

AMOUNT: $1000   DEADLINE: March 1
FIELDS/MAJORS: All Areas of Study

Applicants must be women thirty-five years or older, United States citizens, and accepted or enrolled at a school to pursue an undergraduate degree or technical/vocational training course. Seven to ten awards given per year. Financial need is a primary factor. Send a business-sized SASE to the address below. In the lower, left-hand corner of the envelope, write "JRF 1998." Also, when applying, indicate your gender, age, and level of study or training. Requests for applications are only honored between September 1 and January 15.

Jeannette Rankin Foundation
PO Box 6653
Athens, GA 30604

1170
Jeffrey I. Glaser, M.D., Memorial Scholarship

AMOUNT: $400   DEADLINE: March 15
FIELDS/MAJORS: All Areas of Study

Scholarships are available for graduating seniors of Longmeadow High School, who have distinguished themselves academically and are on the swim team. Write to the address listed for information. Must have a GPA of at least 3.1.

Community Foundation of Western Massachusetts
PO Box 15769
1500 Main St.
Springfield, MA 01115

1171
Jenkins Scholarship (of U.S. Bank of Oregon)

AMOUNT: None Specified   DEADLINE: March 1
FIELDS/MAJORS: All Areas of Study

Open to high school seniors who are U.S. citizens and residents of Oregon and attending school in the Portland School District. (Preference given to Jefferson High School.) Minimum GPA required is 3.5. Continuing college students must have a minimum GPA of 3.0. Applicants may apply and compete annually. U.S. Bancorp employees, their children, or near relatives are not eligible to apply for this award. Contact the address below for further information.

Oregon State Scholarship Commission
Private Awards
1500 Valley River Dr., #100
Eugene, OR 97401-2130

1172
Jerome B. Steinbach Scholarship

AMOUNT: None Specified   DEADLINE: March 1
FIELDS/MAJORS: All Areas of Study

Scholarship for Oregon residents who are U.S. citizens and will be entering their sophomore (or above) year in the fall. Must have a GPA of at least 3.5. U.S. Bancorp employees, their children, or near relatives are not eligible to apply for this award. May apply and compete annually. Contact your college financial aid office or write to the address below for details.

Oregon State Scholarship Commission
Attn: Grant Department
1500 Valley River Dr., #100
Eugene, OR 97401

1173
Jerome L. Hauck Scholarship

AMOUNT: $1000   DEADLINE: June 1
FIELDS/MAJORS: All Areas of Study

Scholarship for a high school senior or graduate who is a son or daughter of either a full-time groom or a member of a Harness Horsemen Intl. member association. For full-time study, based on SAT/ACT scores, need, extra-curricular activities, academics, and citizenship. Renewable if student remains full-time and maintains a minimum GPA of 2.0. Applications will be available at all HHI member associations as well as from HHI at the address below.

Harness Horsemen International Foundation, Inc.
Jerome L. Hauck Scholarship
14 Main St.
Robbinsville, NJ 08691

1174
Jerome Playwright-In-Residence Fellowship

AMOUNT: $750   DEADLINE: January 15
FIELDS/MAJORS: Playwriting/Drama/Theater

Applicants must not have had more than two works produced by professional theaters and must spend the fellowship period as a member of the Playwrights' Center. Four to six scholarships are offered annually. Write to the address below for details.

Playwrights' Center
2301 Franklin Ave., East
Minneapolis, MN 55406

1175
Jerry Baker College Freshman Scholarship Program

AMOUNT: $1000 DEADLINE: April 1
FIELDS/MAJORS: Horticulture

Scholarships open to entering freshmen interested in careers in horticulture who will be attending a four-year college or university. Students must submit a letter of recommendation from a high school teacher or counselor; a letter of recommendation from a community leader; a copy of high school transcripts; and a copy of SAT and ACT scores. Students are also required to submit a copy of their acceptance letter from an accredited college. Write to the address below for more details.

Bedding Plants Foundation, Inc.
PO Box 27241
Lansing, MI 48909

1176
Jerry Clark Memorial Scholarship

AMOUNT: $10000 DEADLINE: July 1
FIELDS/MAJORS: Political Science

The Jerry Clark Memorial Scholarship will be awarded to a student majoring in political science for his/her junior and senior year of study. Applicant must be a child of an AFSCME member and have a GPA of 3.0 or above. Write to the address below for details.

American Federation of State, County, and Municipal
   Employees, AFL-CIO
Attn: Education Department
1625 L St., NW
Washington, DC 20036

1177
Jerry L. Pettis Memorial Scholarship

AMOUNT: $2500 DEADLINE: January 31
FIELDS/MAJORS: Medicine

Awards for junior or senior medical students with demonstrated interest in communication of science. Applicants must be nominated by the deans of AMA approved medical schools. Letters of application and recommendations will be required. Write to the address listed for more information. The scholarship recipient will be announced by May 1st.

American Medical Assn. Education and Research Foundation
Rita M. Palulonis
515 N. State St.
Chicago, IL 60610

1178
Jewel/Taylor C. Cotton Scholarship

AMOUNT: Maximum: $10000 DEADLINE: July 15
FIELDS/MAJORS: Business, Construction, Engineering, Architecture

Available for male or female high school graduate must be accepted in a four-year college or university with the intention of majoring in business or a field related to the business or construction industry. Must have a GPA of 2.5 or better and demonstrate financial need. For residents of the Chicago metropolitan area. Write to the address below for more information.

Chicago Urban League
Gina Blake, Scholarship Specialist
4510 South Michigan Ave.
Chicago, IL 60653

1179
Jewell Gardiner Memorial Fund Scholarship

AMOUNT: None Specified DEADLINE: August 1
FIELDS/MAJORS: Library Science

Candidate must be a Northern California resident enrolled in or accepted into an accredited graduate school of library science in California. Write for complete details.

California Media and Library Educators Association
Jewel Gardiner Memorial Fund Chairperson
1499 Old Bayshore Highway, Suite 142
Burlingame, CA 94010

1180
Jewelry Foundation Scholarship Fund Group

AMOUNT: $500-$1200 DEADLINE: May 11
FIELDS/MAJORS: Jewelry-Related Studies

Scholarships are available for residents of Rhode Island, who are pursuing a jewelry-related curriculum. Write to the address listed for information.

Rhode Island Foundation
70 Elm St.
Providence, RI 02903

1181
Jewish Braille Institute of America Scholarships

AMOUNT: None Specified   DEADLINE: None Specified
FIELDS/MAJORS: Religion/Theology, Community Service, Jewish Studies, Jewish Language

Scholarships for legally blind students studying toward a career in a field of Jewish endeavor (rabbi, cantor, communal service, Hebrew). Based on need. No formal application exists for this scholarship. Write to Gerald M. Kass at the address below for details.

Jewish Braille Institute of America
110 East 30th St.
New York, NY 10016

1182
Jewish Educational Loan Fund

AMOUNT: Maximum: $2000   DEADLINE: None Specified
FIELDS/MAJORS: All Areas of Study

Interest-free loans for residents of the Metropolitan Washington area who are within eighteen months of graduation (undergraduate or graduate). Repayment begins after graduation. Must be U.S. citizen (or permanent resident intending to apply for citizenship). For Jewish students. Write to the address below or call (301) 881-3700 for details.

Jewish Social Service Agency of Metropolitan Washington
6123 Montrose Road
Rockville, MD 20852

1183
Jewish Undergraduate Scholarship Fund

AMOUNT: Maximum: $3500   DEADLINE: May 30
FIELDS/MAJORS: All Areas of Study

Scholarships for Jewish residents of the Metropolitan Washington area who are currently enrolled as undergraduates. Must be less than thirty years old. Special consideration given to refugees. Based primarily on need. Write to the address below or call (301) 881-3700 for details.

Jewish Social Service Agency of Metropolitan Washington
6123 Montrose Road
Rockville, MD 20852

1184
JFCS Scholarships

AMOUNT: $5000   DEADLINE: None Specified
FIELDS/MAJORS: All Areas of Study

JFCS provides hundreds of grants and scholarships annually to help Jewish students with financial needs achieve their educational goals. Special scholarships are available for study in Israel. Eligibility requirements: acceptance to a college, vocational school, or university; residence in San Francisco, the Peninsula, Marin or Sonoma Counties; and a 3.0 GPA. Write to the address below for details.

Jewish Family and Children's Services
1600 Scott St.
San Francisco, CA 94115

1185
Jim Springer Memorial Scholarship

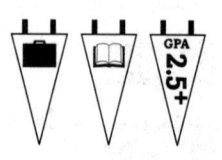

AMOUNT: Maximum: $500   DEADLINE: May 31
FIELDS/MAJORS: Marketing, Public Relations, Advertising, Communications

Scholarships for students from the Coastal Bend area of Texas majoring in one of the above areas. Must have a GPA of at least 2.5 and attend school full-time. Write to the address below for details.

Coastal Bend Community Foundation
Mercantile Tower MT276
615 N. Upper Broadway, #860
Corpus Christi, TX 78477

1186
Jimmie Ruth Picquet Scholarship

AMOUNT: None Specified   DEADLINE: None Specified
FIELDS/MAJORS: All Areas of Study

Open to students living in Bishop, Texas, who are attending or plan to attend college in pursuit of a degree. Must be able to demonstrate high academics and financial need. Contact the address below for further information.

Coastal Bend Community Foundation
Mercantile Tower MT276
615 N. Upper Broadway, #860
Corpus Christi, TX 78477

1187
Jimmie Ullery Charitable Trust

AMOUNT: Maximum: $1000   DEADLINE: June 1
FIELDS/MAJORS: Theology

Education for students in full-time Christian service. Scholarships have been awarded primarily for study at Presbyterian Theological Seminaries. Five to eight awards offered annually. For complete details write to Mr. R. Garvin Barry, Jr., at the address below.

Jimmie Ullery Charitable Trust, Scholarship Committee
First Presbyterian Church
709 S. Boston Ave.
Tulsa, OK 74119

1188
Jimmy A. Young Memorial Scholarship

AMOUNT: Maximum: $1000   DEADLINE: June 30
FIELDS/MAJORS: Respiratory Therapy

Open to minority students in an AMA-accepted respiratory care program. The foundation prefers that students be nominated by their schools, but "any student may initiate a request of sponsorship by the school." Must have a GPA of at least 3.0, provide a copy of a birth certificate, social security card, immigration visa, or evidence of citizenship. Recipient will be selected by September 1. Write to the address listed for additional information.

American Respiratory Care Foundation
11030 Ables Ln.
Dallas, TX 75229

1189
Joanne Grossnickle Scholarships

AMOUNT: None Specified   DEADLINE: June 15
FIELDS/MAJORS: All Areas of Study

Scholarships for graduates of Linganore, Francis Scott Key, or Walkersville high schools; members of the Union Bridge Church of the Brethren; or other persons whose heritage ties them to the Union Bridge Church. Based on need, ability, potential, and character. Preference given to first-time applicants and non-winners from previous years. Applicants must complete at least one year of college. Applicant must also have completed at least one successful year of postsecondary education. Write to the address below for more information.

Joanne Grossnickle Scholarship Fund Committee
C/O Union Bridge Church of the Brethren
PO Box 518
Union Bridge, MD 21791

1190
Joe Childs Scholarship

AMOUNT: Maximum: $500   DEADLINE: February 1
FIELDS/MAJORS: All Areas of Study

Open to members children who are high school seniors. For any course of study. Seven awards are offered annually. Contact the address listed for further information or call (216) 869-5374. If writing, you must include a SASE for a reply.

United Rubber Workers International Union
Scholarship Coordinator
570 White Pond Dr.
Akron, OH 44320

1191
Joel Garcia Memorial Scholarship

AMOUNT: $250-$2000   DEADLINE: April 3
FIELDS/MAJORS: Journalism

This scholarship is open to Latino high school seniors and undergraduate students pursuing a career in journalism. Must be a resident of California or attend an accredited school in California. Samples of applicants work, an essay, and transcripts are some of the attachments that will be required. For complete details, write to the address listed or call (213) 743-2440.

California Chicano News Media Association
USC School of Journalism
3716 S. Hope St., #301
Los Angeles, CA 90007-4344

1192
Joel Polsky-Fixtures Furniture Prizes and Academic Achievement Awards

AMOUNT: Maximum: $1000   DEADLINE: February 4
FIELDS/MAJORS: Interior Design

Awards for undergraduate and graduate students to aid research, thesis, or other academic projects. The furniture prize will be given for the discipline of interior design through literature or visual communication. The Academic Achievement Award is given for interior design research or thesis project. One award from each is offered annually. Send a legal-sized SASE to the address listed for more information.

American Society of Interior Designers Educational Foundation, Inc.
Scholarship and Awards Program
608 Massachusetts Ave., NE
Washington, DC 20002

1193

John A. Hartford/AFAR Medical Student Geriatric Grants

AMOUNT: $3000 DEADLINE: February 5
FIELDS/MAJORS: Clinical Geriatrics, Aging Research

Open to students who have completed at least one year of medical school. This grant is to attend an eight- to twelve-week intensive training session at selected training centers. If necessary, a travel and living stipend may be added to the award. Write to the address listed for more information or contact (212) 752-2327.

American Federation for Aging Research
Scholarships Coordinator
1414 Ave. of the Americas, 18th Floor
New York, NY 10019

1194

John and Bessie Adams Scholarship

AMOUNT: None Specified DEADLINE: May 1
FIELDS/MAJORS: All Areas of Study

Awards for students who are graduating seniors of Calais Memorial High School in Calais, Maine. Contact Calais High School Guidance Office for more information.

Maine Community Foundation
245 East Maine St.
PO Box 148
Ellsworth, ME 04605

1195

John and Elsa Gracik Scholarship

AMOUNT: Maximum: $1500 DEADLINE: None Specified
FIELDS/MAJORS: Mechanical Engineering

Open to high school seniors who will be entering college in an ABET accredited program or current undergraduate ASME members already in a program. Must be U.S. citizen and able to demonstrate financial need. Selections will be based on academics, character, leadership, and potential contribution to the mechanical engineering profession. Contact the address below for further information. Include a SASE for a reply. Must have a GPA of at least 2.8.

American Society of Mechanical Engineers
Nellie Malave
345 E. 47th St.
New York, NY 10017

1196

John B. and Brownie Young Memorial Fund Scholarship

AMOUNT: Maximum: $4500 DEADLINE: None Specified
FIELDS/MAJORS: All Areas of Study

Scholarships are available to graduating high school seniors from the city of Owensboro School District, Daviess County School Districts, or McLean County School Districts. Applicant must be unmarried and rank in the upper third of their graduating class. Write to the address below for information. Must have a GPA of at least 3.1.

Owensboro National Bank
Trust Department
230 Frederica St., PO Box 787
Owensboro, KY 42302

1197

John C. Chaffin Educational Fund Scholarship and Loan Programs

AMOUNT: $500-$4800 DEADLINE: May 1
FIELDS/MAJORS: All Areas of Study

Open to graduates of Newton North and Newton South High Schools. Eligible applicants will be high school seniors and students who have completed at least one year of higher education or successful work experience. For undergraduate study only. Contact your scholarship and loan advisor at your school. Graduates who have been out of school for one year or more may write the address below.

John C. Chaffin Educational Fund
Secretary
100 Walnut St.
Newtonville, MA 02160

1198

John C. Geilfuss Fellowship

AMOUNT: Maximum: $2000 DEADLINE: February 1
FIELDS/MAJORS: Business, Economic History of Wisconsin and/or the American Midwest

This fellowship is awarded for graduate level research in business and economics history of Wisconsin and the American midwest. Recipients generally will be ineligible for more than one award. Contact the address below for further information.

State Historical Society of Wisconsin
Dr. Michael E. Stevens, State Historian
816 State St.
Madison, WI 53706-1488

1199
John Carew Memorial Scholarship

AMOUNT: $1500 DEADLINE: April 1
FIELDS/MAJORS: Horticulture

Scholarships for graduate students who are pursuing a major in horticulture, with a specific interest in bedding plants or flowering potted plants. Write to the address below for details. The BPFI also sponsors two awards through Future Farmers of America (check with your FFA advisor).

Bedding Plants Foundation, Inc.
Scholarship Program
PO Box 27241
Lansing, MI 48909

1200
John Charles Wilson Scholarship

AMOUNT: $500-$3500 DEADLINE: February 15
FIELDS/MAJORS: Police Sciences, Fire Sciences

Scholarships for IAAI members (in good standing) or their immediate family members (students who are not IAAI members or family members may be nominated by a member of IAAI). For study in police or fire sciences including fire investigation and related subjects. Must be enrolled or accepted for enrollment in the next semester after application. Up to three awards per year. Write to the address below for details.

International Association of Arson Investigators, Inc.
Executive Secretary
300 South Broadway, Suite 300
St. Louis, MO 63102

1201
John Cornelius Memorial Scholarship

AMOUNT: $1500 DEADLINE: March 15
FIELDS/MAJORS: All Areas of Study

Scholarships are available for dependents of members of the Marine Corps Tankers Association or those who served in a Marine Tank Unit. For undergraduate study. Renewable. Active, discharged, and retired Marine tankers are also eligible to apply. Twelve awards per year. Write to the address below for details.

Marine Corps Tankers Association, Inc.
Phil Morell, Scholarship Chairman
1112 Alpine Heights Rd.
Alpine, CA 91901

1202
John D. and Catherine T. Macarthur Fellowships

AMOUNT: $17500-$37500 DEADLINE: November 15
FIELDS/MAJORS: Foreign Policy, International Relations, International Security, Etc.

Approximately six dissertation and six postdoctoral fellowships supporting research into the implications of recent changes in several countries on worldwide security issues. These fellowships require fellows to gain competence in skills not previously acquired; i.e., a significant departure from earlier works. Write to "Program on Peace and Security in a Changing World" at the below address for further information.

Social Science Research Council
Fellowship and Grant Coordinator
605 Third Ave., 17th Floor
New York, NY 10158

1203
John Dawe Scholarship

AMOUNT: Maximum: $950 DEADLINE: March 1
FIELDS/MAJORS: Dentistry, Dental Hygiene, Dental Assisting

Open to Hawaii residents. Applicants studying in other states may also apply as long as they have family residing in Hawaii. Any employee, volunteer, or board member of the Community Foundation is not eligible to apply. Contact the address below for further information.

Hawaii Community Scholarship Foundation
College Scholarships
900 Fort St. Mall, #1300
Honolulu, HI 96813

1204
John Dennis Scholarship

AMOUNT: Maximum: $1000 DEADLINE: January 31
FIELDS/MAJORS: Criminal Justice

Scholarships available to high school seniors who are Missouri residents planning to attend a Missouri college or university. Based on academics and financial need. Write to the address listed for details.

Missouri Sheriff's Association
229 Madison
Jefferson City, MO 65101

1205

John Edgar Thompson Foundation Grant

AMOUNT: None Specified   DEADLINE: None Specified
FIELDS/MAJORS: All Areas of Study

Grants are available for daughters of deceased railroad workers, who wish to pursue a postsecondary education. The father must have been in the active employ of a railroad at the time of death, although the cause need not be work-related. Assistance available until student reaches twenty-two years of age. Write to the address below for information. This grant may be used to assist in funding an education, although the primary purpose is to provide a monthly grant to daughters of deceased railroad workers from infancy to age eighteen or twenty-two.

John Edgar Thompson Foundation
Sheila Cohen, Director
201 South 18th St., Suite 318
Philadelphia, PA 19103

1206

John F. and Anna Lee Stacey Scholarship Fund

AMOUNT: Maximum: $5000   DEADLINE: February 1
FIELDS/MAJORS: Drawing and Painting

Grants for individuals who are devoted to a career in the classical or conservation tradition of Western Art. Must be U.S. citizens and between the age of eighteen and thirty-five years. Applicants must submit 35mm slides of their work to the judging committee. Write to the address listed for details.

National Cowboy Hall of Fame
Stacey Scholarship Fund
1700 Northeast 63rd St
Oklahoma City, OK 73111

1207

John F. Kennedy Scholars Award

AMOUNT: $1500   DEADLINE: April 4
FIELDS/MAJORS: Political Science

Scholarship for Massachusetts residents who are entering their junior or senior year of undergraduate study majoring in a field related to the study of American politics. Two awards per year, one to a male, one to a female. Registered Democrats preferred but not essential. Must have a minimum GPA of 3.0. Write to the address below for details.

Massachusetts Democratic State Committee
Scholarship Committee
133 Portland St.
Boston, MA 02114

1208

John Hebner Memorial Scholarship

AMOUNT: Maximum: $600   DEADLINE: March 1
FIELDS/MAJORS: All Areas of Study

Scholarships are available to legally blind students who are employed on a full-time basis and need additional funding for school while they are working. Write to the address listed or call (202) 467-5081 or 1-800-424-8666 for details.

American Council of the Blind
Scholarship Coordinator
1155 15th St. NW, Suite 720
Washington, DC 20005

1209

John L. Dales Scholarship Fund

AMOUNT: None Specified   DEADLINE: None Specified
FIELDS/MAJORS: All Areas of Study

Awards for students who are members of SAG (for a minimum of five years) or dependents of SAG members (membership for a minimum of eight years). Based on academics, essay, and recommendations. Write to the address below for more information.

Screen Actors Guild Foundation
5757 Wilshire Blvd.
Los Angeles, CA 90036

1210

John Lamar Cooper (of U.S. Bank of Oregon)

AMOUNT: None Specified   DEADLINE: March 1
FIELDS/MAJORS: All areas of study

Open to graduates or graduating seniors from a high school in Hood River County. Seniors must have a minimum GPA of 3.0, and undergraduates must have a minimum of 2.5. Must be U.S. citizens or permanent residents and residents of Oregon to apply. May be used at any Oregon college. U.S. Bancorp employees, their children, or near relatives are not eligible to apply for this award. Contact the address below for further information.

Oregon State Scholarship Commission
Private Awards
1500 Valley River Dr., #100
Eugene, OR 97401-2130

1211
John P. and James F. Mahoney Memorial Scholarship

AMOUNT: None Specified DEADLINE: March 15
FIELDS/MAJORS: All Areas of Study

Open to undergraduates and graduate students of Hampshire County, who will be or already are attending college or vocational school. Contact the address listed for further information.

Community Foundation of Western Massachusetts
PO Box 15769
1500 Main St.
Springfield, MA 01115

1212
John P. Hounsell Scholarship

AMOUNT: None Specified DEADLINE: March 1
FIELDS/MAJORS: All Areas of Study

Open to Oregon residents who graduated from a high school in Hood River County. Awards may be used at Oregon colleges only, unless recipients are accepted into an approved graduate level program at an institution that participates in the Western Regional Higher Education Compact. Applicants may apply and compete annually. Must be U.S. citizens or permanent residents. Contact the address below for further information.

Oregon State Scholarship Commission
Private Awards
1500 Valley River Dr., #100
Eugene, OR 97401-2130

1213
John Z. Duling Grant Program

AMOUNT: Maximum: $5000 DEADLINE: November 1
FIELDS/MAJORS: Arboriculture

Awards are available for research in the field of arboriculture. Award amount will depend upon the adjudged value of the project to the needs of the arboriculture industry. Write to the address below for more information.

International Society of Arboriculture
ISA Research Trust
PO Box GG
Savoy, IL 61874

1214
Johnson and Johnson Dissertation Grants

AMOUNT: Maximum: $2000 DEADLINE: November 3
FIELDS/MAJORS: Women's Health

Open to students in doctoral programs who have completed all predissertation requirements at graduate schools in the U.S. and expect to complete their dissertations by the summer of 1999. For original and significant research on issues related to women's health. Previous grants have concerned: smoking, estrogen and lung cancer, maternal and child health development in Africa, and AIDS awareness. Write to the address listed for details. The deadline to request an application is October 17.

Woodrow Wilson National Fellowship Foundation
Dept. WS
CN 5329
Princeton, NJ 08543-5281

1215
Johnson Controls Foundation Scholarship Program

AMOUNT: $1750-$7000 DEADLINE: February 15
FIELDS/MAJORS: All Areas of Study

Eligibility for scholarships limited to natural or legally adopted children of employees of Johnson Controls, Inc. Must be high school senior graduating in the current academic year and be in the upper 30% of class. Sixteen awards are given annually. Applications must be received by Corporate Human Resources, 5757 N. Green Bay Ave., X-34, Milwaukee, WI 53201. Must have a GPA of at least 2.8.

Johnson Controls Foundation
5757 N. Green Bay Ave.
PO Box 591
Milwaukee, WI 53201

1216
Johnson-Lasselle Scholarship

AMOUNT: None Specified DEADLINE: March 1
FIELDS/MAJORS: All Areas of Study

Open to high school seniors who are U.S. citizens and residents of Clackamas, Multnomah, or Washington counties in Oregon. Awards may be used at Oregon colleges only and may be received for a maximum of twelve quarters. Recipients may petition the State Scholarship Commission for an additional year of award if they are enrolled in a program with a normal undergraduate period of five years. Contact the address listed for further information.

Oregon State Scholarship Commission
Private Awards
1500 Valley River Dr., #100
Eugene, OR 97401-2130

1217

Johnston Lions Armand Muto Scholarship

AMOUNT: None Specified **DEADLINE:** April 15
FIELDS/MAJORS: All Areas of Study

Scholarships are available for high school seniors who are residents of Johnston, Rhode Island. One award is given annually. Contact the address listed for further information.

Rhode Island Foundation
David Nardolillo C/O R.I. Precision Co.
25 Dorr St.
Providence, RI 02908

1218

Jose Marti Scholarship Challenge Grant Fund

AMOUNT: $2000 **DEADLINE:** April 1
FIELDS/MAJORS: All Areas of Study

Applicant must be a U.S. citizen or legal resident, Hispanic-American, and a Florida resident, enrolled as a full-time undergraduate or graduate student at an eligible Florida institution. Renewable. A minimum 3.0 GPA is required. Contact the financial aid office at your college or write to the address below for details.

Florida Department of Education
Office of Student Financial Assistance
1344 Florida Education Center
Tallahassee, FL 32399

1219

Joseph Bonfitto Scholarship

AMOUNT: None Specified **DEADLINE:** March 15
FIELDS/MAJORS: Creative Design, Advertising, Art

One award is for a senior of Agawam High School who is pursuing an education in the above majors. Contact the address listed for further information.

Community Foundation of Western Massachusetts
PO Box 15769
1500 Main St.
Springfield, MA 01115

1220

Joseph Ehrenreich Scholarship

AMOUNT: $1000 **DEADLINE:** March 1
FIELDS/MAJORS: Photojournalism

There are five awards open to sophomores, juniors, and seniors at four-year schools. Seniors must have at least one-half year remaining. Based on academics and financial need. Write to Mike Smith at the address below for more information.

National Press Photographers Foundation
Detroit Free Press
321 W. Lafayette Blvd.
Detroit, MI 48231

1221

Joseph F. Dracup Scholarship

AMOUNT: Maximum: $2000 **DEADLINE:** November 10
FIELDS/MAJORS: Geodetic Surveying

Open to undergraduates to encourage and recognize students committed to a career in geodetic surveying. Contact the address below for further information.

American Cartographic Association
Lilly Matheson, ACSM Awards Program
5410 Grosvenor Ln., #100
Bethesda, MD 20814-2144

1222

Joseph F. Dracup Scholarship

AMOUNT: Maximum: $2000 **DEADLINE:** November 30
FIELDS/MAJORS: Surveying

Open to undergraduates studying surveying in a four-year degree program. Designed to encourage and recognize students committed to a career in geodetic surveying. It is provided by the American Association for Geodetic Surveying. Please contact address listed for complete information or call (301) 493-0200.

American Congress on Surveying and Mapping
Ms. Lilly Matheson
5410 Grosvenor Ln., #100
Bethesda, MD 20814-2144

1223

Joseph Henry Jackson Award

AMOUNT: $2000 **DEADLINE:** January 31
FIELDS/MAJORS: Creative Writing, Poetry

These awards are for authors of an unpublished work-in-progress fiction, nonfictional prose, or poetry. Applicants must be residents of northern California or Nevada for three years prior to the award year, and be between the ages of twenty and thirty-five. Write to the address listed for information.

San Francisco Foundation
Intersection for the Arts
446 Valencia St.
San Francisco, CA 94103

1224
Joseph L. Fisher Dissertation Award

AMOUNT: Maximum: $12000   DEADLINE: February 27
FIELDS/MAJORS: Natural Resources, Energy, Environmental Sciences

Fellowship is for doctoral candidate dissertation research in economics on issues relating to natural resources, energy, or the environment. Write to the address listed for details.

Resources for the Future
Coordinator for Academic Programs
1616 P St. NW
Washington, DC 20036

1225
Joseph R. Stone Scholarship

AMOUNT: $2400   DEADLINE: July 28
FIELDS/MAJORS: Travel and Tourism

Three awards are available for undergraduates in the field of travel and tourism. Must be a U.S. citizen or permanent resident and have a minimum GPA of 2.5. One parent must also be employed in the travel industry (car rental, airlines, hotel, etc.). Write to the address below for more information.

American Society of Travel Agents
Scholarship Committee
1101 King St., Suite 200
Alexandria, VA 22314

1226
Joseph Towner Scholarship

AMOUNT: Maximum: $1000   DEADLINE: June 15
FIELDS/MAJORS: All Areas of Study

Open to postsecondary students who have at least one gay or lesbian parent and are residents of any of the nine Bay Area counties: Alameda, Contra Costa, Marin, San Francisco, San Mateo, Santa Clara, Napa, Sonoma, and Solano. Must be twenty-five years of age or younger and be enrolled full-time with a minimum GPA of 2.5. Contact the address listed for further information.

Horizons Foundation
Scholarship Coordinator
870 Market St., #1155
San Francisco, CA 94102

1227
Journalism Awards Program

AMOUNT: $500-$2000   DEADLINE: None Specified
FIELDS/MAJORS: Journalism, Photojournalism, Broadcast News

Open to all undergraduate journalism majors who attend a journalism and mass communication accredited school (103 schools). Separate contests are held monthly during the school year. Contact the chair of the department to find out if your school is a participant in the program. If so, the department will have the applications/entry forms. Entry forms and information are available only through the journalism department offices of the participating schools. See your department for details. Do not write to address shown for more information, they will only refer you to your department office.

William Randolph Hearst Foundation
Journalism Awards, Jan Watten, Director
90 New Montgomery St., Suite 1212
San Francisco, CA 94105

1228
Journalism Foundation of Metropolitan St. Louis Scholarships

AMOUNT: None Specified   DEADLINE: March 23
FIELDS/MAJORS: Journalism, Communications, Advertising, Public Relations

Open to St. Louis metropolitan area residents. For juniors, seniors, or graduate students. Based on commitment to career in the above fields. Counties considered in the metro area are (Missouri) St. Louis, Franklin, Jefferson, Lincoln, St. Charles, or Warren, or the Illinois counties of Madison, St. Clair, Monroe, Clinton, Bond, and Jersey. Write to the address listed or call (314) 531-9700 for further information.

Journalism Foundation of Metropolitan St. Louis
Joseph Kenny or Jean M. Schildz
462 N. Taylor Ave.
St. Louis, MO 63108

1229
Jr. College Transfer Scholarship

AMOUNT: Maximum: $1000   DEADLINE: February 15
FIELDS/MAJORS: Chemical/Civil/Electrical/Industrial/Mechanical Engineering

Open to junior college students majoring in the fields listed above who are transferring to Florida A&M University. May be renewable for the second year. Applicant must have at least a 3.0 GPA and be recommended by an official of the college you are attending. Based on academics, work experience, extracurricular activities, essay, and recommendations. Write to the address listed for details.

Florida Engineering Society
Scholarship Coordinator
PO Box 750
Tallahassee, FL 32302

1230
Jr. College Transfer Scholarship

AMOUNT: Maximum: $1000 DEADLINE: February 15
FIELDS/MAJORS: Chemical/Civil/Electrical/Mechanical/Industrial Engineering

Open to junior college students majoring in the fields listed above who are transferring to Florida State University. May be renewable for the second year. Applicant must have at least a 3.0 GPA and be recommended by an official of the college you are attending. Based on academics, work experience, extracurricular activities, essay, and recommendations. Write to the address listed for details.

Florida Engineering Society
Scholarship Coordinator
PO Box 750
Tallahassee, FL 32302

1231
Jr. College Transfer Scholarship

AMOUNT: Maximum: $1000 DEADLINE: February 15
FIELDS/MAJORS: Civil/Computer/Electrical/Industrial/Mechanical/Chemical Engineering

Open to junior college students majoring in the fields listed above who are transferring to University of South Florida. May be renewable for the second year. Applicant must have at least a 3.0 GPA and be recommended by an official of the college you are attending. Based on academics, work experience, extracurricular activities, essay, and recommendations. Write to the address listed for details.

Florida Engineering Society
Scholarship Coordinator
PO Box 750
Tallahassee, FL 32302

1232
Jr. College Transfer Scholarship

AMOUNT: Maximum: $1500 DEADLINE: February 15
FIELDS/MAJORS: Chemical/Civil/Electrical/Industrial/Aerospace/Agricultural and Biological/Computer Engineering Environmental/Materials/Nuclear Science

Open to junior college students majoring in the fields listed above who are transferring to University of Florida. May be renewable for the second year. Applicant must have at least a 3.0 GPA and be recommended by an official of the college you are attending. Based on academics, work experience, extracurricular activities, essay, and recommendations. Write to the address listed for details.

Florida Engineering Society
Scholarship Coordinator
PO Box 750
Tallahassee, FL 32302

1233
Jr. College Transfer Scholarship

AMOUNT: Maximum: $2000 DEADLINE: February 15
FIELDS/MAJORS: Aerospace/Aircraft/Civil Engineering, Engineering Physics

Open to junior college students majoring in the fields listed above who are transferring to Embry-Riddle University. May be renewable for the second year. Applicant must have at least a 3.0 GPA and be recommended by an official of the college you are attending. Based on academics, work experience, extracurricular activities, essay, and recommendations. Write to the address listed for details.

Florida Engineering Society
Scholarship Coordinator
PO Box 750
Tallahassee, FL 32302

1234
Jr. College Transfer Scholarship

AMOUNT: Maximum: $2500 DEADLINE: February 15
FIELDS/MAJORS: Aerospace/Chemical/Civil/Computer/Electrical/Mechanical/Ocean Engineering

Open to junior college students majoring in the fields listed above who are transferring to Florida Institute of Technology. May be renewable for the second year. Applicant must have at least a 3.0 GPA and be recommended by an official of the college you are attending. Based on academics, work experience, extracurricular activities, essay, and recommendations. Write to the address listed for details.

Florida Engineering Society
Scholarship Coordinator
PO Box 750
Tallahassee, FL 32302

1235
Jr. College Transfer Scholarship

AMOUNT: Maximum: $750 DEADLINE: February 15
FIELDS/MAJORS: Aerospace/Civil/Computer/Electrical/Environmental/Industrial/Mechanical Engineering

Open to junior college students majoring in the fields listed above who are transferring to University of Central Florida. May be renewable for the second year. Applicant must have at least a 3.0 GPA and be recommended by an official of the college you are attending. Based on academics, work experience, extracurricular activities, essay, and recommendations. Write to the address listed for details.

Florida Engineering Society
Scholarship Coordinator
PO Box 750
Tallahassee, FL 32302

1236
Jr. College Transfer Scholarship

AMOUNT: None Specified DEADLINE: February 15
FIELDS/MAJORS: Civil/Computer/Electrical/Industrial/Mechanical/Audio/Aerospace/Architectural/Biomedical/Environmental/Manufacturing Engineering

Open to junior college students majoring in the fields listed above who are transferring to University of Miami. May be renewable for the second year. Applicant must have at least a 3.0 GPA and be recommended by an official of the college you are attending. Based on academics, work experience, extracurricular activities, essay, and recommendations. Award is half tuition per academic year. Write to the address listed for details.

Florida Engineering Society
Scholarship Coordinator
PO Box 750
Tallahassee, FL 32302

1237
Judicial Fellows Program

AMOUNT: None Specified DEADLINE: November 17
FIELDS/MAJORS: Law and Forensic Research

Highly competitive fellowship program in which selected individuals are placed in various national institutions of the federal judiciary. Must hold at least one advanced degree, have at least two years professional experience, and have multi-disciplinary training and familiarity with the judicial process. Application will be made with curriculum vitae, essay (less than seven hundred words) on interest in and qualifications for Judicial Fellows Program, and copies of no more than two publications or writing samples. Write to the address listed for more information.

Supreme Court of the United States
Judicial Fellows Program
Administrative Director, Room 5
Washington, DC 20543

1238
Judith Graham Poole Postdoctoral Research Fellowship

AMOUNT: $35000 DEADLINE: December 1
FIELDS/MAJORS: Hemophilia Research

Postdoctoral (M.D. or Ph.D.) fellowships for hemophilia-related research. Number of awards per year dependent on available funding. Topics that the NHF has expressed an interest in are clinical or basic research on biochemical, genetic, hematological, orthopedic, psychiatric, or dental aspects of hemophilia or Von Willebrand Disease. Contact the address below for complete details. The NHF has listed related topics of interest as rehabilitation, therapeutic modalities, psychosocial issues, and AIDS/HIV.

National Hemophilia Foundation
Karen O'Hagen
110 Greene St., Suite 303
New York, NY 10012

1239
Judith Resnik Memorial Scholarship

AMOUNT: Maximum: $2000 DEADLINE: February 1
FIELDS/MAJORS: Engineering (Space Related)

Open to female seniors studying engineering with a space-related major. Must be interested in a career in the space industry and have a minimum GPA of 3.5. Write to address listed for details. Please be certain to enclose a SASE. Information and applications for the SWE awards are also available from the deans of engineering schools.

Society of Women Engineers
Scholarship Selection Committee
120 Wall St., 11th Floor
New York, NY 10005

1240
Julius F. Neumueller Awards in Optics

AMOUNT: $500 DEADLINE: June 1
FIELDS/MAJORS: Optometry

Award for students pursuing a doctor of optometry degree. Based on paper (not to exceed three thousand words) on one of the following topics: geometrical optics, physical optics, ophthalmic optics, or optics of the eye. Cash award. Write to the address below for more information.

American Academy of Optometry
College of Optometry
University of Houston
Houston, TX 77204

1241
Junior and Community College Athletic Scholarship Program

AMOUNT: None Specified DEADLINE: None Specified
FIELDS/MAJORS: All Areas of Study

Awards available to students who participate in a sport. Must be full-time students enrolled in public junior and community colleges in Alabama. Awards may be renewed on the basis of continued participation in the designated sport or activity. Not based on financial need. Applicants should apply through the coach, athletic director, or financial aid officer at any public junior or community college in Alabama, rather than address below.

Alabama Commission on Higher Education
PO Box 302000
Montgomery, AL 36130

1242
Junior and Community College Performing Arts Scholarship Program

AMOUNT: None Specified DEADLINE: None Specified
FIELDS/MAJORS: Performing Arts

Applicants must demonstrate talent through competitive auditions. Awards are restricted to full-time students attending public junior and community colleges in Alabama. Not based on financial need. To apply, students should contact the financial aid office at any public junior or community college in Alabama, rather than address below. Auditions will also be scheduled as part of the application process.

Alabama Commission on Higher Education
PO Box 302000
Montgomery, AL 36130

1243
Junior Fellows Program

AMOUNT: Maximum: $3600 DEADLINE: March 1
FIELDS/MAJORS: See Fields Listed Below

Program for juniors, seniors, recent graduates, or graduate students in the areas of American history, literature, geography, cartography, graphic arts, architecture, history of photography, film, television, radio, music, rare books and arts, American popular culture, librarianship, preservation, and Asian, African, Middle Eastern, European, or Hispanic studies. This award has a time limit of ninety days at $300 per week. Write to the address listed or e-mail jrfell@loc.gov for more information.

Library of Congress
Program Coordinator, Library Services
Library of Congress, Lm-642
Washington, DC 20540

1244
Junior Show and Dairy Scholarship

AMOUNT: None Specified DEADLINE: July 1
FIELDS/MAJORS: All Areas of Study

Open to high school seniors and current college students who are West Virginia residents and have exhibited in the State Fair Junior Show within the past five years. Recommendations from a principal, counselor, or advisor will be considered along with academics. Contact the address below for further information.

State Fair of West Virginia
Manager, State Fair of West Virginia
PO Drawer 986
Lewisburg, WV 24901

1245
Junior Volunteer Scholarship

AMOUNT: Maximum: $1500 DEADLINE: April 1
FIELDS/MAJORS: Healthcare

Open to Southwest Washington Medical Center junior volunteers who are pursuing healthcare careers. Must be residents of Clark County or Skamania County. Contact the address listed or call (360) 256-2035 for further information.

Southwest Washington Medical Center
Scholarship Coordinator
400 N.E. Mother Joseph Pl.
Vancouver, WA 98668

1246
Justinian Society of Lawyers/DuPage County Chapter

AMOUNT: Maximum: $1000 DEADLINE: April 1
FIELDS/MAJORS: Law

Awarded to a student of Italian extraction who has completed at least one semester of law school. Write to address listed or call (630) 961-0225 for information and application.

Marsha H. Cellucci, Chairwoman-Scholarship
Cellucci, Yacobellis & Holman
1155 S. Washington St., #100
Naperville, IL 60540

1247
Juvenile Diabetes Foundation Awards

AMOUNT: None Specified DEADLINE: September 15
FIELDS/MAJORS: Medical Research (Juvenile Diabetes)

Postdoctoral grants and fellowships supporting basic and applied research on diabetes and related disorders. Includes research grants, career development awards, postdoctoral fellowships, and new training for established scientist awards. Write to the address below for more information.

Juvenile Diabetes Foundation International
Ruth Marsch, Grant Administrator
120 Wall St.
New York, NY 10005

1248
K2TEO Martin J. Green, Sr. Memorial Scholarship

AMOUNT: $1000 DEADLINE: February 1
FIELDS/MAJORS: All Areas of Study

Scholarships are available to students with a general class amateur radio license, who come from a "ham" family. For full-time study. Write to the address listed for information.

ARRL Foundation (American Radio Relay League)
Scholarship Program
225 Main St.
Newington, CT 06111

1249
Kaiser Permanente Dental Assistant Scholarship

AMOUNT: None Specified DEADLINE: March 1
FIELDS/MAJORS: Dental Assisting

Open to U.S. citizens who are residents of Oregon or Washington planning to enroll full-time in an accredited dental assistant training program in Oregon or southwest Washington. Awards may be used at any of the following schools: Blue Mountain Community College, Chemeketa Community College, Concorde Career Institute, Lane Community College, Linn-Benton Community College, or Portland Community College. This is a one-time award. Contact the address below for further information.

Oregon State Scholarship Commission
Private Awards
1500 Valley River Dr., #100
Eugene, OR 97401-2130

1250
Kalamazoo Chapter No. 116-Roscoe Douglas Scholarship

AMOUNT: Maximum: $1500 DEADLINE: March 1
FIELDS/MAJORS: Manufacturing Engineering, Manufacturing Engineering Technology

Open to full-time undergraduates enrolled in one of the following seven schools: Glen Oaks Community College, Jackson Community College, Kalamazoo Valley Community College, Kellogg Community College, Lake Michigan College, Southwestern Michigan College, or Western Michigan University. Recipients notified in June. Write to the address listed for more information. Must have a GPA of at least 3.5.

Society of Manufacturing Engineers Education Foundation
One SME Dr.
PO Box 930
Dearborn, MI 48121-0930

1251
Kankakee County Community Services Scholarships

AMOUNT: $1100 DEADLINE: April 16
FIELDS/MAJORS: All Areas of Study

Scholarships for students from income-qualifying families in Kankakee County, Illinois. For those who are or will be studying in a vocational/technical school or in a two- or four-year college/university in the state of Illinois. Based on need, academic potential, and commitment to civic affairs. For undergraduate study. Two to seven awards offered annually. Applications are available from your high school guidance office or from KCCSI at the address below.

Kankakee County Community Services
341 N. St. Joseph Ave.
PO Box 2216
Kankakee, IL 60901

1252
Kansas City Direct Marketing Association Scholarship

AMOUNT: Maximum: $2000 DEADLINE: March 1
FIELDS/MAJORS: Marketing

Scholarship established to promote and foster direct marketing education in the greater Kansas City metropolitan area. Must be enrolled or plan to enroll in a course or series of courses relating to the direct marketing industry. Must have a minimum GPA of 3.0 Contact your school's student advisory office or the address listed for further information.

Kansas City Direct Marketing Association Educational
    Foundation Fund
Advisory Committee
PO Box 419264
Kansas City, MO 64141-6264

1253
Kansas Educational Assistance Program

AMOUNT: None Specified DEADLINE: None Specified
FIELDS/MAJORS: All Areas of Study

Open to children of parents who entered military service as a resident of Kansas and whose status became POW, MIA, or killed in action in Vietnam. Applicants do not have to be residents of Kansas, but the award must be used at a Kansas school. Renewable. Write to the address listed for details.

Kansas Commission on Veterans' Affairs
Jayhawk Tower
700 SW Jackson, Suite 701
Topeka, KS 66603

1254
Kansas Funeral Association Scholarships

AMOUNT: None Specified   DEADLINE: March 15
FIELDS/MAJORS: Mortuary Science

Awards for Kansas residents studying mortuary science who have at least one but not more than two semesters of mortuary science school remaining. Write to the address below for more information.

Kansas Funeral Directors Association
1200 Kansas Ave.
Topeka, KS 66612

1255
Kappa Alpha Theta Foundation Scholarship

AMOUNT: $500-$10000   DEADLINE: February 1
FIELDS/MAJORS: All Areas of Study

Scholarships are available for Kappa Alpha Theta members. Applications available after October 1. Selections based on merit. Write to the address below for information. Must have a GPA of at least 3.0.

Kappa Alpha Theta, Sarasota Area-National Office
8740 Founders Road
Indianapolis, IN 46268

1256
Kappa Kappa Gamma Member Scholarships and Fellowships

AMOUNT: None Specified   DEADLINE: February 1
FIELDS/MAJORS: All Areas of Study

Graduate and undergraduate scholarships and grants for part-time study are available to members of Kappa Kappa Gamma. All applicants are requested to note their chapter membership on their requests. Graduates are asked to also note if they are full or part-time students. Send a SASE to the address below or contact your chapter for more information.

Kappa Kappa Gamma Foundation
Member Scholarships/Fellowships
PO Box 38
Columbus, OH 43216-0038

1257
Karen D. Carsel Memorial Scholarship

AMOUNT: Maximum: $500   DEADLINE: April 30
FIELDS/MAJORS: All Areas of Study

Scholarship open to full-time graduate students who present evidence of economic need. Student must submit evidence of legal blindness, three letters of recommendation, and transcripts of grades from the college he/she is attending. Write to the address listed for complete details or call (212) 502-7661.

American Foundation for the Blind
Scholarship Committee
11 Penn Plaza, #300
New York, NY 10001

1258
Karl "Pete" Furhmann IV Memorial Scholarship

AMOUNT: Maximum: $1000   DEADLINE: April 15
FIELDS/MAJORS: Horticulture

Scholarships for Ohio high school graduates studying horticulture at the associates or bachelor level. Must be an Ohio resident. Renewable. One award is offered annually. Write to the address below for details.

Fuhrmann Orchards
Karl "Pete" Fuhrmann IV Scholarship Fund
510 Hansgen-Morgan Rd.
Wheelersburg, OH 45694

1259
Karla Scherer Foundation Scholarships

AMOUNT: None Specified   DEADLINE: None Specified
FIELDS/MAJORS: Finance, Economics

Scholarship assistance for women attending accredited four-year colleges or universities to pursue undergraduate or graduate degrees in economics or finance. Must be preparing for careers in a manufacturing industry and be able to demonstrate financial need. Specifically for women who will become tomorrow's CEOs or CFOs. Applicants must request an application in writing by March 1 for the following academic year. When requesting information, applicants must include the school you are/will attend, major, and a carefully prepared, well written description of your career plans. Responses will only be mailed to those students whose written requests satisfy all requirements. If an applicant is a foreign student, you must also include that a U.S. visa has been issued. The financial aid offices of Stanford, Yale, and Georgetown have a history of not cooperating with the Foundation's aid policies and, consequently, applications for grants to study at those schools will not be considered. Contact the address listed for further detailed information. When writing for information, you must include a SASE for a reply.

Karla Scherer Foundation
737 N. Michigan Ave., Suite 2330
Chicago, IL 60611

1260
Kate B. and Hall J. Peterson, Stephen Botein Fellowships

AMOUNT: $5700-$11400 DEADLINE: January 15
FIELDS/MAJORS: American History, History of Publishing, Eighteenth Century Studies

Six to twelve month fellowships in support of research utilizing the collections of the American Antiquarian Society. Must hold Ph.D. or be involved in dissertation research. Write to the address listed for information about both awards. Please use the name of the award(s) when requesting information.

American Antiquarian Society
Director of Research and Publication
185 Salisbury St., Room 100
Worcester, MA 01609

1261
Katharine M. Grosscup Horticultural Scholarship

AMOUNT: Maximum: $2000 DEADLINE: February 15
FIELDS/MAJORS: Horticulture, Floriculture, Botany, Arboriculture, Landscape Design

Scholarships for juniors, seniors, or graduate students who are pursuing a degree in one of the fields listed above, or any related field. Preference is given to students from Ohio, Pennsylvania, West Virginia, Michigan, and Indiana. Several awards offered annually. Write to the address listed for information. Must have a GPA of at least 3.0.

Garden Club of America, Grosscup Scholarship Committee
Ms. Nancy Stevenson
11030 East Boulevard
Cleveland, OH 44106

1262
Katherine J. Schutze Memorial Scholarship

AMOUNT: None Specified DEADLINE: March 15
FIELDS/MAJORS: Theology

Applicants must be women members of the Christian Church (Disciples of Christ) who are preparing for the ordained ministry. For full-time study. Financial need is considered. Write to the address below for details. Must have a GPA of at least 2.3.

Christian Church (Disciples of Christ)
Attn: Scholarships
PO Box 1986
Indianapolis, IN 46206

1263
Katherine L. Rieger Scholarship

AMOUNT: Maximum: $1000 DEADLINE: February 15
FIELDS/MAJORS: Horticulture, Floriculture, Conservation, Forestry, Botany, Agronomy, Plant Pathology, Environmental Control, City Planning, Land Management

Open to juniors, seniors, and graduate students who are Pennsylvania residents. Must have a minimum GPA of 2.8. Must be sponsored by a Federated Garden Club in Pennsylvania and be able to demonstrate financial need. References, a personal letter (regarding goals, background, and commitment), an official transcript for the current period, and the application signed by the sponsoring club's president will be required. State winner will compete for one of the National Council Scholarships of $3500. A student may reapply if academics remain high and need is apparent. Contact a local club, the address listed, or (215) 643-0164 for details.

Garden Club Federation of Pennsylvania
Mrs. William A. Lamb, Scholarship Chair
925 Lorien Dr.
Gwynedd Valley, PA 19437-0216

1264
Katherine M. McKenna Scholarships

AMOUNT: Maximum: $1500 DEADLINE: June 1
FIELDS/MAJORS: Horticulture, Floriculture, Landscape Design, Landscape Architecture, conservation, Forestry, Botany, Ecology, or Allied Subjects

Scholarships for undergraduates (sophomores and up) and graduate students in any of the following areas of study. For students from Westmoreland and the seven contiguous counties in Pennsylvania. Renewable. Write to the address listed for details.

Greensburg Garden Center
Katherine M. McKenna Scholarship Fund
951 Old Salem Rd.
Greensburg, PA 15601

1265
Kathern F. Gruber Scholarships

AMOUNT: $1000-$2000 DEADLINE: April 17
FIELDS/MAJORS: All Areas of Study

Scholarships for children and spouses of blinded veterans. Veteran must be legally blind (from either service connected or non-service connected cause). Must be accepted or enrolled as a full-time student in an undergraduate or graduate program at an accredited institution. Twelve awards per year. Write to the address listed for details.

Blinded Veterans Association
Scholarship Coordinator
477 H St. NW
Washington, DC 20001

1266
Kathleen S. Anderson Award

AMOUNT: $1000   DEADLINE: December 1
FIELDS/MAJORS: Avian Research-Ornithology

Grants in support of projects in avian research in the following areas: migration, feeding ecology, habitat fragmentation, populations, competition, shorebirds, and endangered species. Projects must take place in the Americas. Work based at the Manomet Observatory is encouraged. Intended to support persons beginning a career in biology. Enrollment in academic program is desirable but not essential. Write to the address listed to request further information and proposal guidelines.

Manomet Observatory
Kathleeen S. Anderson Award
Box 1770
Manomet, MA 02345

1267
Kathryn M. Daugherty Scholarship for Education Majors

AMOUNT: Maximum: $500   DEADLINE: March 25
FIELDS/MAJORS: Education, Elementary Education

Available to undergraduate women with sophomore, junior, or senior standing who are pursuing education majors. Preference given to elementary education majors. Women must be studying full-time and maintain at least a 3.0 GPA. Recipient must demonstrate financial need. Send a SASE to the address listed for an application.

Business and Professional Women's Foundation of Maryland, Inc.
Scholarship Coordinator
282 New Mark Esplanade
Rockville, MD 20850

1268
KATU Thomas R. Dargan Minority Scholarship

AMOUNT: Maximum: $4000   DEADLINE: May 31
FIELDS/MAJORS: Any Broadcast Curriculum

Scholarships available to minority students residing in or attending a school in Oregon or Washington. Must be enrolled in the first, second, or third year of a broadcast curriculum at a four-year college, university, or an accredited community college. Must be U.S. citizens and have a minimum GPA of 3.0. Write to the address below for more information.

KATU Thomas R. Dargan Minority Scholarship
C/O Human Resources
PO Box 2
Portland, OR 97207-0002

1269
Kauai County Farm Bureau Scholarships

AMOUNT: $1000   DEADLINE: April 15
FIELDS/MAJORS: Agriculture and Remitted

Four scholarships for residents of Kauai studying in a field related to agriculture. Renewable. Preference given to undergraduates, but graduate students will also be considered. Based on academics and agriculture and aquaculture activities in school. Write to the address below for further information.

Kauai County Farm Bureau Scholarship
C/O Mr. Herbert Keamoai
PO Box 3895
Lihue, HI 96766

1270
KCPQ-TV/Ewing C. Kelly Scholarship

AMOUNT: Maximum: $2000   DEADLINE: February 15
FIELDS/MAJORS: All Areas of Study

Open to high school seniors located within the KCPQ viewing area (Seattle-Tacoma market as defined by Nielsen Station Index). Applicants must have been accepted to or have an application pending at an institution of higher learning. Based on academics and extracurricular activities. Finalists will be contacted by March 31 for interviews. Information and applications are available from your high school principal or counselor. Return completed applications to the address listed. Must have a GPA of at least 3.0.

KCPQ-TV
KCPQ-TV Scholarship
PO Box 98828
Tacoma, WA 98498

1271
Keepers Preservation Education Fund Fellowship

AMOUNT: Maximum: $500   DEADLINE: December 15
FIELDS/MAJORS: Historical Preservation

Awards are available for graduate students in the field of historical preservation to attend the annual meeting of the Society of Architectural Historians. Write to the address listed for more information.

Society of Architectural Historians
1365 North Astor St.
Chicago, IL 60610

1272
Kellie Cannon Memorial Scholarship

AMOUNT: Maximum: $1200   DEADLINE: March 1
FIELDS/MAJORS: Computer Science, Information Science, Data Processing

Scholarships are available to legally blind students majoring in computer science or a related field. Based on academic ability. Write to the address listed or call (202) 467-5081 or 1-800-424-8666 for details.

American Council of the Blind
Scholarship Coordinator
1155 15th St. NW, Suite 720
Washington, DC 20005

1273
Kemper Scholars Grant Program

AMOUNT: $1500-$7000   DEADLINE: None Specified
FIELDS/MAJORS: Business

Scholarships for enrolled freshmen at sixteen colleges and universities in the U.S. Must have potential to maintain a 3.0 GPA and have a career interest in the field of business. Contact the financial aid office at your school or write to the address below for details.

James S. Kemper Foundation
Kemper Scholars Grant Program
One Kemper Dr.
Long Grove, IL 60049

1274
Kenan T. Erim Award

AMOUNT: Maximum: $4000   DEADLINE: November 1
FIELDS/MAJORS: Archaeology/Classical Studies

This award will be given to an American or international research and/or excavating scholar working on Aphrodisias material. If the project involves work at Aphrodisias, candidates must submit written approval from the field director with their applications. Write to the address listed or call (617) 353-9361 for details.

Archaeological Institute of America-American Friends
   of Aphrodisias
Boston University
656 Beacon St., 4th Floor
Boston, MA 02215

1275
Kenji Kasai Memorial Scholarship

AMOUNT: None Specified   DEADLINE: April 1
FIELDS/MAJORS: All Areas of Study

Open to incoming freshmen who are members of Japanese ancestry and entering or enrolled at an accredited college or university. Applications and information may be obtained from local JACL chapters, district offices, and the national headquarters at the address listed or call (415) 921-5225. Please indicate your level of study and be certain to include a legal-sized SASE.

Japanese-American Citizens League
National Scholarship and Award Program
1765 Sutter St.
San Francisco, CA 94115

1276
Kennedy Center Internship Programs

AMOUNT: None Specified   DEADLINE: None Specified
FIELDS/MAJORS: Arts Administration

Various internships for juniors, seniors, graduates, and students who have graduated not more than two years ago. The internships are full-time (forty hours per week), held at the JFK center, and offer financial assistance of $650 per month. Write to the address below for details.

John F. Kennedy Center for the Performing Arts
Education Dept., Internship Coordinator
The Kennedy Center
Washington, DC 20566

1277
Kenneth Andrew Roe Scholarship

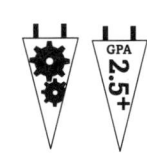

AMOUNT: Maximum: $5000   DEADLINE: None Specified
FIELDS/MAJORS: Mechanical Engineering

Open to ASME members for study in the junior or senior year. Selection will be based on scholastics, character, integrity leadership, potential contribution to the mechanical engineering profession, and financial need. Must be a U.S. citizen and resident of North America to apply. Contact the address below for further information. Include a SASE for a reply. Must have a GPA of at least 2.8.

American Society of Mechanical Engineers
Nellie Malave
345 E. 47th St.
New York, NY 10017

1278
Kenneth E. Schwartz Memorial Scholarship

AMOUNT: Maximum: $250 DEADLINE: May 31
FIELDS/MAJORS: Agriculture

Open to juniors and seniors at the University of Nebraska, Lincoln, who are members of currently paid Farm Bureau member families. Contact the address listed for further information or call (402) 421-4400.

Nebraska Farm Bureau Federation
Scholarship Coordinator
5225 S. 16th, PO Box 80299
Lincoln, NE 68501

1279
Kenneth W. Payne Student Prize Competition

AMOUNT: None Specified DEADLINE: September 1
FIELDS/MAJORS: Gay, Lesbian Topics

Open to lesbian, gay, bisexual, and transgendered students who are pursuing studies primarily in California. Prize is for excellence in a scholarly paper written by a student from an anthropological perspective about a gay or lesbian topic. Prize presented at the annual AAA annual meetings. Papers of fewer than forty double-spaced, typed pages on any lesbian or gay related subject for any world culture area are accepted. Contact the address listed for further information. Must have a GPA of at least 3.0.

American Anthropological Assn.-Society of Lesbian/
  Gay Anthropologists
Prof. Jennifer Robertson
1020 LS&A Bldg., 500 S. State St.
Ann Arbor, MI 48109-1382

1280
Kentucky Society of Certified Public Accountants Scholarships

AMOUNT: Maximum: $1000 DEADLINE: January 30
FIELDS/MAJORS: Accounting

Open to sophomores and above enrolled in a Kentucky college or university who plan a career as a CPA. Must have a minimum overall GPA of 2.75 and at least a 3.0 in accounting. Must have completed Principles of Accounting and be enrolled or completed Intermediate Accounting. Contact the address listed for further information.

Kentucky Society of Certified Public Accountants
Scholarship Coordinator
1735 Alliant Ave.
Louisville, KY 40299

1281
Kentucky Tuition Waiver Program for Veterans and Their Dependents

AMOUNT: None Specified DEADLINE: None Specified
FIELDS/MAJORS: All Areas of Study

Kentucky residents. For veterans/national guardsmen/and children (under age of twenty-three years)/ spouse/or non-remarried widow of a permanently and totally disabled war veteran who served during periods of federally recognized hostilities or was POW or MIA. For study at a community college, vocational-technical school, or four-year college. Please contact the address below for complete information.

Kentucky Division of Veterans Affairs
545 S. Third St.
Louisville, KY 40202

1282
Kepler Award

AMOUNT: Maximum: $2000 DEADLINE: April 1
FIELDS/MAJORS: Healthcare

Scholarship for students accepted into a medical school accredited in conjunction with the American Medical Association or the American Osteopathic Association. Recipient must establish a medical practice in the La Porte hospital service area and become a member of the medical staff. Option is to repay the award with interest at prime rate. Preference to local residents. Write the address listed or visit the Office of Development (State and Madison) for details, or call (219) 326-2471.

La Porte Hospital/La Porte Hospital Foundation
Office of Development, Sue Lawrence
PO Box 250
La Porte, IN 46352

1283
Kevin Child Scholarship

AMOUNT: $500-$1000 DEADLINE: July 10
FIELDS/MAJORS: All Areas of Study

Awards for students with a bleeding disorder pursuing a higher education. Applicants must be affiliated with or recommended by the NHF. Two awards are given annually. Write to the address listed for more information.

National Hemophilia Foundation
110 Greene St.
Suite 303
New York, NY 10012

1284
Key Bank New York Scholarship Program

AMOUNT: Maximum: $2000   DEADLINE: May 15
FIELDS/MAJORS: All Areas of Study

Scholarships for incoming freshmen who will attend a four- or five-year college or university in the New York State KeyBank District in which the student's reside. Must be graduating from a New York high school, have a minimum GPA of 2.5, be a full-time student, and be able to demonstrate financial need. The following are KeyBank areas by District: Albany, Buffalo, Hudson Valley, Long Island, Rochester, and Syracuse. Contact the financial aid office at your college or university for further information and applications. They are the only means from which to obtain the materials. Do not contact the bank(s).

Key Bank of New York

1285
Key Technology Scholarship

AMOUNT: None Specified   DEADLINE: March 1
FIELDS/MAJORS: Mechanical, Electrical, Agricultural Engineering, Food Technology

Open to high school seniors who are U.S. citizens and residents of Umatilla County, Oregon, or Walla Walla County, Washington. Must have a minimum GPA of 3.0. Preference may be given to dependents of Key Technology, Inc., employees. For undergraduate study. Contact the address below for further information.

Oregon State Scholarship Commission
Private Awards
1500 Valley River Dr., #100
Eugene, OR 97401-2130

1286
KGON/KFXX Scholarship (of the Oregon Community Foundation)

AMOUNT: None Specified   DEADLINE: March 1
FIELDS/MAJORS: Broadcasting, Journalism

Open to U.S. citizens who are residents of Clackamas, Multnomah, Washington, or Yamhill counties in Oregon or Clark County in Washington. Applicants may apply and compete annually. Contact the address listed for further information.

Oregon State Scholarship Commission
Private Awards
1500 Valley River Dr., #100
Eugene, OR 97401-2130

1287
Kimber Richter Family Scholarship

AMOUNT: $500   DEADLINE: March 15
FIELDS/MAJORS: All Areas of Study

One scholarship open to a student of Western Massachusetts who are of the Baha'i faith who are planning to/are attending college. Contact the address listed for further information.

Community Foundation of Western Massachusetts
PO Box 15769
1500 Main St.
Springfield, MA 01115

1288
King Koil Sleep Products Scholarships

AMOUNT: None Specified   DEADLINE: None Specified
FIELDS/MAJORS: Chiropractic Medicine

Open to student members of ICA. Awards based on academic achievement and service. The size and number of scholarships are determined annually. A GPA of at least 2.5 is required. Must be enrolled in an ICA member college. Individual criteria for each chapter may vary. Contact a SICA chapter officer or representative for applications and further information.

International Chiropractors Association
1110 N. Glebe Rd., Suite 1000
Arlington, VA 22201

1289
King Olav V Norwegian-American Heritage Fund

AMOUNT: $250-$3000   DEADLINE: March 1
FIELDS/MAJORS: Norwegian Studies/American Studies

Open to Americans of Norwegian heritage wanting to study their heritage and/or Norwegian students with American heritage wanting to study their heritage at a recognized institution. The Foundation decides the number and value of scholarships from year to year. Selections based on career goals, references, GPA, and participation in school and community activities. Write to the address listed for details.

Sons of Norway Foundation
Sons of Norway
1455 W. Lake St.
Minneapolis, MN 55408

1290
Kingsbury Fund Scholarships

AMOUNT: None Specified DEADLINE: None Specified
FIELDS/MAJORS: All Areas of Study

Awards for children of Kingsbury employees who can demonstrate financial need. Contact the address listed for further information.

Kingsbury Corporation
James E. O'Neil, Executive Trustee
80 Laurel St.
Keene, NH 03431

1291
Kingsley Alcid Brown Educational Fund

AMOUNT: None Specified DEADLINE: April 1
FIELDS/MAJORS: All Areas of Study

Awards for graduates of Washington County high schools to provide financial support for higher education at the graduate school level. Applicants must be accepted into an accredited graduate degree program to receive an award. Write to the address listed for more information.

Maine Community Foundation
PO Box 148
Ellsworth, ME 04605

1292
Kinko's/Eugene Graphic Arts Scholarship

AMOUNT: None Specified DEADLINE: March 1
FIELDS/MAJORS: Graphic Arts

Open to high school seniors who are U.S. citizens and residents of Lane County. An example of the applicants graphic art work will be required. This is a one-time award. Contact the address listed for further information.

Oregon State Scholarship Commission
Private Awards
1500 Valley River Dr., #100
Eugene, OR 97401-2130

1293
Kit C. King Graduate Scholarship Fund

AMOUNT: $500 DEADLINE: March 1
FIELDS/MAJORS: Photojournalism

Scholarship for a person pursuing an advanced degree in photojournalism. Must be accepted into a graduate program. Portfolio and a statement of goals and philosophy relating to documentary photojournalism will be required. Write to Scott C. Sines, Director of Photography and Graphics, at the address below for more information.

National Press Photographers Foundation
The Spokesman Review
West 999 Riverside Ave.
Spokane, WA 99210

1294
Knezevitch Grants

AMOUNT: $200 DEADLINE: November 30
FIELDS/MAJORS: All Areas of Study

Grants for students of Serbian descent. For both undergraduate or graduate study. Write to the address below for details. Be certain to enclose a SASE. Personal interview may be required.

Steven Knezevitch Trust
100 E. Wisconsin Ave., Suite 1020
Milwaukee, WI 53202

1295
Kodak Scholarship

AMOUNT: Maximum: $10000 DEADLINE: April 3
FIELDS/MAJORS: Engineering, Computer Science, Chemistry, Quantitative Business

Open to Latino students seeking engineering degrees with a GPA of 3.0 or better. Must be U.S. citizens majoring in computer science, quantitative business, chemistry, or engineering (chemical, electrical, industrial, or mechanical). Must be residents of Los Angeles City, Montebello, Commerce, Bell Gardens, or Monterey Park. One award is offered annually. Write to the address listed for more information.

Telacu Education Foundation
5400 East Olympic Blvd., Suite 300
Los Angeles, CA 90022

1296
Kohler Co. College Scholarship Program

AMOUNT: $500-$2500 DEADLINE: October 1
FIELDS/MAJORS: All Areas of Study

The foundation sponsors a scholarship program for graduating seniors who will be starting full-time study at an accredited two- or four-year school. Must be U.S. citizens. Applicants must be dependents of active or retired associates of Kohler Co. or its U.S. subsidiaries. Contact your school or write to the address below for complete details.

Kohler Foundation, Inc.
104 Orchard Rd.
Kohler, WI 53044

1297
Kopplemann Scholarship

AMOUNT: Maximum: $1000 DEADLINE: February 24
FIELDS/MAJORS: All Areas of Study

Open to high school seniors who are residents of Hartford County. For use at any four-year school. Based on academics, community service, and financial need. Preference to former newspaper carriers. These awards are renewable for $2500. Contact the address listed for further information. Must have a GPA of at least 2.8.

Greater Hartford Interracial Scholarship Fund, Inc.
Ellis Simpson
PO Box 32064
Hartford, CT 06132

1298
Kotzebue Higher Education Scholarship

AMOUNT: None Specified DEADLINE: August 1
FIELDS/MAJORS: All Areas of Study

Awards for individuals who are enrolled or eligible for enrollment to the Kotzebue IRA. Applicants must be enrolled in an accredited college or university before receiving funds. Amount of awards depends on yearly budget. Write to the address below for more information.

Kotzebue IRA Council
PO Box 296
Kotzebue, AK 99752

1299
KRAEF Foodservice Scholarships

AMOUNT: None Specified DEADLINE: July 1
FIELDS/MAJORS: Foodservice

Scholarships for Kentucky residents (or persons residing within twenty-five miles of Kentucky's boarders) enrolled in or accepted into a full-time college foodservice program. Renewable. Write to the address listed for details.

Kentucky Restaurant Association Educational Foundation
Scholarship Committee
512 Executive Park
Louisville, KY 40207

1300
Kuchler-Killian Memorial Scholarship

AMOUNT: $3000 DEADLINE: March 31
FIELDS/MAJORS: All Areas of Study

Open to full-time students who are legally blind from Connecticut or attending school in Connecticut. Write to the address below for details.

National Federation of the Blind
Mrs. Peggy Elliott, Chairman
805 Fifth Ave.
Grinnell, IA 50112

1301
Kyutaro and Yasuo Abiko Memorial Scholarships

AMOUNT: None Specified DEADLINE: April 1
FIELDS/MAJORS: Journalism, Agriculture

Applicants must be undergraduates of Japanese ancestry who are majoring in journalism or agriculture and are members of the JACL. Applications and information may be obtained from local JACL chapters, district offices, and the national headquarters at the address listed or call (415) 600-5225. Please indicate your level of study and be certain to include a legal-sized SASE.

Japanese-American Citizens League
National Scholarship and Award Program
1765 Sutter St.
San Francisco, CA 94115

1302
L. Phil Wicker Scholarship

AMOUNT: $1000 DEADLINE: February 1
FIELDS/MAJORS: Electronics, Communications, Related Fields

Scholarship available to students with a general class amateur radio license who are enrolled as full-time students in one of the above fields. Must be a resident of and attending school in: North Carolina, South Carolina, Virginia, or West Virginia. Write to the address listed for information.

ARRL Foundation (American Radio Relay League)
Scholarship Program
225 Main St.
Newington, CT 06111

1303
L.W. Frohlich Charitable Trust Fellowship

AMOUNT: None Specified DEADLINE: January 2
FIELDS/MAJORS: Art Conservation, Art History

Fellowship is for two years in the Department of Objects Conservation. Applicants should be conservators, art historians, or scientists who are at an advanced level in their training and who have demonstrated commitment to the physical examination and treatment of art objects. The next award will be given for a 1998-2000 fellowship. Write to the address listed for further information.

Metropolitan Museum of Art
Fellowship in Conservation, Pia Quintano
1000 Fifth Ave.
New York, NY 10028

1304
Ladies Auxiliary of the Fleet Reserve Association Scholarships

AMOUNT: None Specified   DEADLINE: April 15
FIELDS/MAJORS: All Areas of Study

Scholarships for sons and daughters (or grandchildren) of members of the Fleet Reserve Association (or deceased members) or active duty/retired/deceased Navy, Marine Corps, or Coast Guard. Write to the address listed for details. If parent is a member, include his or her FRA membership number.

Fleet Reserve Association, Ladies Auxiliary
LA FRA Scholarship Administrator, C/O FR
125 N. West St.
Alexandria, VA 22314

1305
Ladies Auxiliary, Bristol Volunteer Fire Dept. Scholarship

AMOUNT: Maximum: $1000   DEADLINE: May 5
FIELDS/MAJORS: All Areas of Study

Scholarships are available for children of Bristol, Rhode Island, firefighters and auxiliary members. Write to the address listed for information.

Bristol Volunteer Fire Department
Victoria Van Voast
359 Wood St.
Bristol, RI 02809

1306
LAF Class Fund Scholarships

AMOUNT: $500-$1500   DEADLINE: March 31
FIELDS/MAJORS: Landscape Architecture/Design

Open to juniors and seniors enrolled in landscape architecture or ornamental horticulture at any of the following schools: University of California, Irvine, Los Angeles, or Davis; Cal Poly at Pomona or San Louis Obispo. Write to the address listed for complete details or call (202) 686-8337. Must have a GPA of at least 2.7.

Landscape Architecture Foundation
Scholarship Program
4401 Connecticut Ave., #500
Washington, DC 20008

1307
Lakewood Medical Center Foundation Scholarship

AMOUNT: None Specified   DEADLINE: March 1
FIELDS/MAJORS: Medicine, Nursing, Pharmacy

Awards for students currently enrolled in an accredited school of medicine, nursing, or pharmacy who are from one of the following cities: Artesia, Bellflower, Cerritos, Compton, Cypress, Downey, Hawaiian Gardens, Lakewood, Long Beach, Norwalk, Paramount, or Signal Hill. Write to the address below for more information.

Lakewood Medical Center Foundation
PO Box 6070
Lakewood, CA 90712

1308
Lambda Alumni Association Gay, Lesbian, and Bi Scholarships

AMOUNT: Maximum: $1000   DEADLINE: December 31
FIELDS/MAJORS: Gay/Lesbian Studies, Women's Issues

Open to enrolled students who are openly lesbian, gay, or bisexual and have a minimum GPA of 3.0. Based on academics and application of studies to gay, lesbian, and bi concerns. Contact the address listed for further information.

University of Southern California
Lambda Alumni Association
830 Childs Way, Box 28
Los Angeles, CA 90089

1309
Lambda Alumni UCLA's Lesbian and Gay Association Scholarship

AMOUNT: Maximum: $1000   DEADLINE: March 10
FIELDS/MAJORS: All Areas of Study

Open to gay, lesbian, bisexual, or transgendered students with demonstrated service to the gay, lesbian, and bisexual community. Must be enrolled, with excellent academics, and be able to demonstrate financial need. Contact the address listed for further information. Must have a GPA of at least 3.1.

UCLA Lambda Alumni Association
Scholarship Coordinator
PO Box 24075
Los Angeles, CA 90024

1310
Lance Stafford Larson Student Scholarship Contest

AMOUNT: Maximum: $500 DEADLINE: October 31
FIELDS/MAJORS: Electrical/Computer Engineering, Computer Science

Open to all undergraduate IEEE Computer Society members. Award is for the best student paper concerning computer-related subjects are eligible. Based on technical content, writing skill, and overall presentation. Write to the address for details.

Institute of Electrical and Electronics Engineers, Inc.
IEEE Computer Society
1730 Massachusetts Ave. NW
Washington, DC 20036-1992

1311
Landscape Architecture Student Competition

AMOUNT: $600-$2000 DEADLINE: March 31
FIELDS/MAJORS: Landscape Architecture

Competition open to seniors and graduate students enrolled in a landscape engineering program. There will be a first, second, and third prize. Contact the address listed for further information or (202) 342-1100.

National Stone Association
Scholarship Administrator
1415 Elliot Pl. NW
Washington, DC 20007-2599

1312
Las Mujeres De Lulac Scholarships

AMOUNT: None Specified DEADLINE: June 1
FIELDS/MAJORS: All Areas of Study

Awards for Hispanics continuing education after interruption or single parents who can demonstrate financial need. Must submit most current transcript, proof of enrollment, letter of recommendation, and current financial verification. For undergraduate or graduate study. New Mexico residents only. Write to the address below for more details.

Las Mujeres De Lulac
Las Mujeres
PO Box 2203
Albuquerque, NM 87103

1313
Last Dollar Program

AMOUNT: None Specified DEADLINE: None Specified
FIELDS/MAJORS: All Areas of Study

Awards are available for minority Virginia residents who can be classified as first-time freshmen students and are enrolled at least half-time in a degree program at a Virginia public institution. Must demonstrate financial need as determined by the institution. Write to the address listed for more information.

Virginia Council of Higher Education
James Monroe Building
101 North 14th St.
Richmond, VA 23219

1314
Latin American and Caribbean Fellowship Program

AMOUNT: Maximum: $30000 DEADLINE: March 28
FIELDS/MAJORS: Social Sciences/Humanities

Fellowships for Latin-American and Caribbean practitioners and researchers whose work in grassroots development would benefit from advanced academic experience in the U.S. Fellowships are awarded to master's candidates and higher. Must demonstrate interest in the problems of poverty and development and be nominated by home institution. Up to forty fellowships are offered per year. Write to the address below for details.

Inter-American Foundation
IAF Fellowship Programs, Dept. 555
901 N. Stuart St., 10th Floor
Arlington, VA 22203

1315
Laura N. Dowsett Scholarship

AMOUNT: Maximum: $1000 DEADLINE: March 1
FIELDS/MAJORS: Occupational Therapy

Open to Hawaii residents and students attending school in another state, as long as they have family in Hawaii. Employees, volunteers, and board members of the Foundation are not eligible to apply. Contact the address below for further information.

Hawaii Community Scholarship Foundation
College Scholarships
900 Fort St. Mall, #1300
Honolulu, HI 96813

1316
Laura Woodman Memorial Scholarship

AMOUNT: None Specified DEADLINE: May 31
FIELDS/MAJORS: All Areas of Study

Scholarships for residents of Aransas, Bee, Jim Wells, Kleberg, Nueces, Refugio, and San Patricio counties. Preference given to members of the Texas Youth Rodeo Association. Must have a GPA of at least 2.5 and plan to attend school full-time. Write to the address below for complete information.

Coastal Bend Community Foundation
Mercantile Tower MT 276
615 N. Upper Broadway, #860
Corpus Christi, TX 78477

1317
Lauranne Sams Scholarship

AMOUNT: $500-$2500 DEADLINE: April 15
FIELDS/MAJORS: Nursing

Open to members enrolled in an undergraduate nursing program. Selections based on both academics, financial need, and community service. Write to the address below for information. You must enclose a SASE ($.55 postage) for a reply. Must have a GPA of at least 2.8.

National Black Nurses' Association
Scholarship Coordinator
PO Box 1823
Washington, DC 20013

1318
Law Enforcement Officers Dependent's Scholarship

AMOUNT: None Specified DEADLINE: August 1
FIELDS/MAJORS: All Areas of Study

Scholarships for Arkansas undergraduates who are dependent children or spouses of persons who were killed or permanently disabled in the line of duty as law enforcement officers in the state of Arkansas and certain highway and transportation department employees. Must be full-time students age twenty-three or under, at a state supported two- or four-year institution. Write to the address below for details.

Arkansas Department of Higher Education
Financial Aid Division
114 East Capitol
Little Rock, AR 72201

1319
Lawrence County Conservation District Scholarship Program

AMOUNT: Maximum: $500 DEADLINE: December 31
FIELDS/MAJORS: Environmental Science, Conservation, Agriculture

Scholarships are available to residents of Lawrence County, Pennsylvania, who are majoring in one of the above fields. Applicant must at least be in their first semester of schooling. Non-renewable. Write to the address listed for information.

Lawrence County Conservation District
Attn: Scholarship Committee
430 Court St.
New Castle, PA 16101

1320
Leather Art Scholarship Competition

AMOUNT: $500-$2000 DEADLINE: April 1
FIELDS/MAJORS: All Areas of Study

Prizes, to be used as scholarships, are available to graduating high school seniors who create art projects using leather. Winners may choose their own course of study. Write to the address listed or call (817) 281-7633 for information.

Tandy Leather Company
Art Scholarship Program
1400 Everman Parkway
Fort Worth, TX 76140

1321
Lebbeus F. Bissell Scholarship

AMOUNT: Maximum: $3000 DEADLINE: April 1
FIELDS/MAJORS: All Areas of Study

Open to high school seniors who are residents or attending school in any of the following: Rockville, Tolland, or Ellington, Connecticut. Based on academics, financial need, extracurricular activities, and community involvement. Awards are renewable up to four years. Contact the address listed for further information. Must have a GPA of at least 2.8.

Scholarship Advisory Committee
Thomas Mason, Chairman
PO Box 665
Rockville, CT 06066

1322

Lee-Jackson Foundation Scholarship

AMOUNT: $1000 DEADLINE: None Specified
FIELDS/MAJORS: All Areas of Study

Awards are available for high school juniors and seniors who plan to attend a college or university in Virginia. The three essays judged best (from each of the eight regions of the state) will win a $1000 award. Twenty-four awards are offered annually. Contact your principal or guidance department for more information.

Virginia Council of Higher Education
James Monroe Building
101 North 14th St.
Richmond, VA 23219

1323

Leica Inc. Photogrammetric Fellowship Award

AMOUNT: $1000 DEADLINE: None Specified
FIELDS/MAJORS: Photogrammetry

Applicants must be a member of the Society and have completed at least one undergraduate course in surveying or photogrammetry. Based on grades, recommendation, and statement of educational and career goals. For both undergraduate and graduate students. Write to the address below for more information.

American Society for Photogrammetry and Remote Sensing
ASPRS Awards Program
5410 Grosvenor Ln., Suite 210
Bethesda, MD 20814

1324

Leica Surveying Scholarships

AMOUNT: Maximum: $1000 DEADLINE: November 30
FIELDS/MAJORS: Surveying, Cartography

Open to undergraduates studying surveying at a school with a two- or four-year curriculum leading to a degree in surveying. Write to the address listed for complete details or call (301) 493-0200.

American Congress on Surveying and Mapping
Ms. Lilly Matheson
5410 Grosvenor Ln., #100
Bethesda, MD 20814

1325

Leica, Inc., Berntsen International, NSPS and Schonstedt Scholarships

AMOUNT: $1000-$1500 DEADLINE: November 10
FIELDS/MAJORS: Surveying

Open to undergraduates in either two- or four-year degree programs in surveying. Three of the four sponsors award two scholarships each. The fourth sponsor offers one award. Contact the address below for further information.

American Cartographic Association
Lilly Matheson, ACSM Awards Program
5410 Grosvenor Ln., #100
Bethesda, MD 20814-2144

1326

Leo J. Sexton Scholarship

AMOUNT: None Specified DEADLINE: None Specified
FIELDS/MAJORS: All Areas of Study

Awards to support residents of Machias, Maine, attending their first year of college. Contact the Machias High School Guidance Office for more information.

Maine Community Foundation
245 East Maine St.
PO Box 148
Ellsworth, ME 04605

1327

Leola W. and Charles Hugg Scholarship

AMOUNT: $200-$700 DEADLINE: May 1
FIELDS/MAJORS: All Areas of Study

Scholarships from this trust are available to students who have resided and attended high school in Williamson County, Texas, for at least two years or have been under the care of the Texas Baptist Children's Home in Round Rock, Texas. For undergraduate study. Must have and maintain a minimum GPA of 2.5. Applications are available at high schools in Williamson County, from the director of the Texas Baptist Children's Home or at the office of financial aid at Southwestern University in Georgetown.

Leola W. and Charles Hugg Trust
Texas Commerce Bank
PO Box 6033, S.U. Station
Georgetown, TX 78626

1328

Leonard M. Perryman Communications Scholarship for Minority Students

AMOUNT: $2500 DEADLINE: February 15
FIELDS/MAJORS: Religious Communications/Journalism

Applicants must be junior or senior communications minority students who intend to pursue a career in religious communications. Write to the scholarship committee at the address listed for details.

United Methodist Communications
Scholarship Committee, Public Media Div.
PO Box 320
Nashville, TN 37202

1329
Leopold Schepp Foundation Scholarships

AMOUNT: None Specified   DEADLINE: November 30
FIELDS/MAJORS: All Areas of Study

Scholarships for undergraduate students under thirty years of age. Based on character, ability in field of study, and financial need. Personal interview in New York city is required. Must be U.S. citizen or permanent resident. Eligible students are expected to apply also for institutional, state, and federal financial aid. Formal requests for application materials must be made after June 1 and before November 30, but the Foundation's list for consideration may close when a sufficient number of applications is received. Must have a GPA of at least 3.2.

Leopold Schepp Foundation
Executive Secretary
551 Fifth Ave., Suite 2525
New York, NY 10176

1330
Lerner-Scott Prize

AMOUNT: Maximum: $1000   DEADLINE: November 1
FIELDS/MAJORS: American and Women's History

Awards are available for the best doctoral dissertation submitted in U.S. women's history. Finalists will be asked to submit a complete copy of the dissertation. Write to the address listed for more information.

Organization of American Historians
Award and Prize Committee Coordinator
112 N. Bryan St.
Bloomington, IN 47408

1331
Leroy Matthews Physician/Scientist Award

AMOUNT: Maximum: $46000   DEADLINE: September 1
FIELDS/MAJORS: Medical Research-Cystic Fibrosis

Grants are available to newly trained pediatricians and internists (M.D.'s and M.D./Ph.D.'s) to complete subspecialty training, develop into independent investigators, and initiate a research program. Awards range from $36000 (stipend) plus $10000 (R&D) for one year to $60000 (stipend) plus $15000 (R&D) for year six. Write to the address below for details.

Cystic Fibrosis Foundation
Office of Grants Management
6931 Arlington Rd.
Bethesda, MD 20814

1332
Leslie T. Posey and Frances U. Posey Scholarships

AMOUNT: $1000-$4000   DEADLINE: March 1
FIELDS/MAJORS: Art, Painting, Sculpture

Applicants must be full-time graduate art majors in traditional painting or sculpture. If student is just starting their master's program, evidence of acceptance must be provided. Write to Robert E. Perkins, Administrator, at the address below for details.

Leslie T. Posey and Frances U. Posey Foundation
1800 Second St., Suite 905
Sarasota, FL 34236

1333
Leslie T. Posey and Frances U. Posey Scholarships

AMOUNT: None Specified   DEADLINE: March 1
FIELDS/MAJORS: Painting, Sculpture

Open to full-time graduate students in a program offering a recognized degree in painting or sculpture of the traditional kind. Must have a baccalaureate degree. Essay and slides of personal work will be required. Contact the address listed for further information or call (941) 957-0442.

Posey Foundation
Robert E. Perkins
1800 Second St., #905
Sarasota, FL 34236

1334
Lester J. Cappon Fellowships in Documentary Editing

AMOUNT: $800   DEADLINE: March 1
FIELDS/MAJORS: Editing, Proofreading

Fellowships available to doctoral candidates or postdoctoral scholars for residence at Newberry. Consists of editing scholarly projects on any subject relevant to the Library's collections. Stipends are $800 per month. Write to the address listed for details or call (312) 255-3666.

Newberry Library
Committee on Awards
60 W. Walton St.
Chicago, IL 60610

1335
Letourneau Student Writing Competition

AMOUNT: Maximum: $1000   DEADLINE: February 1
FIELDS/MAJORS: Law

Writing competition for students in the field of law who are currently attending an accredited school in the United States or Canada. Papers must be at least three thousand words in length, must contain only uncollaborated original work, and may relate to research done by the author. Write to the address listed for more information or call (414) 276-1881.

American College of Legal Medicine
Student Writing Competition
611 E. Wells St.
Milwaukee, WI 53202

1336
Library Education Scholarship, Continuing Education Scholarship

AMOUNT: None Specified   DEADLINE: September 15
FIELDS/MAJORS: Library/Information Sciences

Scholarship for Wisconsin residents who will be attending a master's level program in Wisconsin for the study of library or information science. Based on academic and professional accomplishments, as well as on financial need. Write to the address below for complete details.

Wisconsin Library Association
Chair, Library Careers Committee
4785 Hayes Rd.
Madison, WI 53704

1337
Lieutenant General Eugene F. Tighe, Jr., USAF Memorial Scholarship

AMOUNT: $1000   DEADLINE: January 10
FIELDS/MAJORS: Government, Political Science, Criminal Justice, and Related Areas

Open to full-time college undergraduate or postgraduate students in the U.S. or attending U.S. Institutions overseas. Must have GPAs of 3.0 or better. Based on an essay written by the applicant. Essay topic deals with an intelligence issue and a new topic is specified each year. Send a #10 SASE for information to the address listed.

Association of Former Intelligence Officers (AFIO)
  San Diego Chapter
Scholarship Administrator
1142 Miramonte Glen
Escondido, CA 92026

1338
Lifchez/Stronach Curatorial Internship

AMOUNT: Maximum: $12000   DEADLINE: January 30
FIELDS/MAJORS: Art History

Internships for recent college graduates or students who are enrolled in an art history M.A. program. Must demonstrate financial need or some other disadvantage that might jeopardize the continuance of their studies. Program runs for nine months, from September through June, and is full-time. Write to the address listed for additional information.

Metropolitan Museum of Art
Internship Programs
1000 Fifth Ave.
New York, NY 10028-0198

1339
Lighthouse Scholarship

AMOUNT: Maximum: $7000   DEADLINE: February 25
FIELDS/MAJORS: Journalism and Communications

Award for an outstanding junior in the field of journalism or communications. The scholarship is $15000 for junior and senior years. Applicants must demonstrate financial need and be U.S. citizens. For full-time study. Write to the address listed for more information. When requesting an application, students must state college major, career goals, and year of study. Deadline to request an application is December 20.

Scripps Howard Foundation
312 Walnut St., 28th Floor
PO Box 5380
Cincinnati, OH 45201

1340
Lights of the Jewish Special Needs Scholarships

AMOUNT: Maximum: $1000   DEADLINE: May 31
FIELDS/MAJORS: All Areas of Study

Grants for Jewish students in the St. Louis community. For study at a two- or four-year college or university in Missouri. Write to the address below for details.

Lights of the Jewish Special Needs Society
6 Sleepy Hollow Ln.
St. Louis, MO 63132

1341
Lillian and Arthur Dunn Scholarships

AMOUNT: Maximum: $1000 DEADLINE: February 15
FIELDS/MAJORS: All Areas of Study

Applicant must be a graduating high school senior whose mother is a current member of the DAR. Applicant must also be a United States citizen. Renewable. Contact your local DAR chapter or send a SASE to the address listed for more information.

National Society Daughters of the American Revolution
NSDAR Scholarship Committee
1776 D St. NW
Washington, DC 20006

1342
Lillian Grace Mahan Scholarship

AMOUNT: None Specified DEADLINE: April 1
FIELDS/MAJORS: Library Science

Open to graduate or undergraduate students who are Stark County residents studying library science. The awards will be presented after June 1. Write to the address listed for more information.

Canton Student Loan Foundation
Atrium South, Suite 204
4974 Higbee Ave. NW
Canton, OH 44718

1343
Lillian Moller Gilbreth Scholarship

AMOUNT: Maximum: $5000 DEADLINE: February 1
FIELDS/MAJORS: Engineering

Scholarship for junior or senior woman engineering major in an accredited program. Based on superior academic achievement and potential. Must have a GPA of at least 3.5. Write to address listed for details. Please be certain to enclose a SASE. Information and applications for the SWE awards are also available from the deans of engineering schools.

Society of Women Engineers
Scholarship Selection Committee
120 Wall St. 11th Floor
New York, NY 10005

1344
Lily and Catello Sorrentino Memorial Fund

AMOUNT: $350-$1000 DEADLINE: June 1
FIELDS/MAJORS: All Areas of Study

Scholarships are available for Rhode Island residents over forty-five years of age who are returning to school to complete an undergraduate degree. Must be able to demonstrate financial need. Write to the address listed for information.

Rhode Island Foundation
Special Funds Office
70 Elm St.
Providence, RI 02903

1345
Lincoln-Lane Foundation Scholarship

AMOUNT: None Specified DEADLINE: None Specified
FIELDS/MAJORS: All Areas of Study

Scholarships are available for residents of Tidewater, Virginia, for full-time study at any accredited college or university in the U.S. Based on academic ability, test scores, extracurricular activities, and demonstrated financial need. High potential for achievement in community service is also a consideration. Write to the address listed to request an application between October 1st and 15th, and return the required forms and materials "as soon as possible." Recipients are notified by the beginning of May.

Lincoln-Lane Foundation
112 Granby St.
Suite 300
Norfolk, VA 23510

1346
Linda Perry Touch the Future Scholarship

AMOUNT: Maximum: $1000 DEADLINE: January 31
FIELDS/MAJORS: Film/TV

Open to juniors, seniors, or graduate students who are residents of, or domiciled in Pinellas County. Students must show documentation that he/she has secured unpaid internships with film, commercial, or TV production company, studio, or other similar company within the television, film, and video production industries. Preference will be given to students in Florida colleges and universities. Contact the address listed or call (813) 464-7240 for further information.

St. Petersburg/Clearwater Area Film Commission
Scholarship Coordinator
14450 46th St. N, Suite 108
Clearwater, FL 33762

1347
Lionel Rocha Holmes and Edward A. Dutra Scholarships

AMOUNT: $500-$1000 DEADLINE: April 15
FIELDS/MAJORS: All Areas of Study

Open to students with a Portuguese heritage (within five generations). Must reside or attend school in any of the following six counties: El Dorado, Placer, Sacramento, San Joaquin, Solano, or Yolo. Must also have a minimum GPA of 3.0. Contact the address below for further information.

Portuguese Historical and Cultural Society
PHCS Scholarships
PO Box 161990
Sacramento, CA 95816

1348
LITA/GEAC-CLSI Scholarship

AMOUNT: Maximum: $2500 DEADLINE: April 1
FIELDS/MAJORS: Information Science

Applicants must be entering an ALA-accredited master's program with an emphasis on library automation. Previous experience will be considered. One award per year. Write to the address listed or call (312) 280-4269 for details.

American Library Association
Library and Information Technology Assn.
50 E. Huron St.
Chicago, IL 60611

1349
LITA/OCLC and LITA/LSSI Minority Scholarships

AMOUNT: Maximum: $2500 DEADLINE: April 1
FIELDS/MAJORS: Information Science

Applicants must be a Native American, Asian-American, African-American, Hispanic, Alaskan Native, or Pacific Islander graduate student who is entering or enrolled in an ALA-accredited master's program with an emphasis on library automation. Previous experience is considered, and U.S. or Canadian citizenship is required. Two awards per year. Write to the address listed or call (312) 280-4269 for details.

American Library Association
Library and Information Technology Assn.
50 E. Huron St.
Chicago, IL 60611

1350
Litherland/FTE Undergraduate Scholarship in Technology Education

AMOUNT: Maximum: $1000 DEADLINE: December 1
FIELDS/MAJORS: Technology Education

Scholarship for members (at least one year) of the International Technology Education Association who are preparing for a career in teaching. Applicant must not be a senior by application deadline. Must have a GPA of 2.5 or greater. Write to "Undergraduate Scholarship" at the address listed for details.

International Technology Education Association
Tom Hughes
1914 Association Dr.
Reston, VA 22091

1351
Littleton-Griswold Research Grant

AMOUNT: Maximum: $1000 DEADLINE: February 2
FIELDS/MAJORS: American Legal History

Grant available to American Historical Association members to support research in American legal history and the field of law and society. Eight awards are given annually. Write to the address listed for details.

American Historical Association
Award Administrator
400 A St., SE
Washington, DC 20003

1352
Liver Scholar Award Program

AMOUNT: Maximum: $30000 DEADLINE: January 15
FIELDS/MAJORS: Liver Research

Award open scientists with liver research training who hold an M.D., Ph.D., or M.D./Ph.D. degree and are wanting a career in liver disease research. Applicants must have three to four years of relevant postdoctoral experience prior to award and apply within the first three years of faculty appointment. Candidates must be sponsored by a non-federal public or private nonprofit institution engaged in healthcare and health-related research within the U.S. Must have institutional confirmation of a faculty appointment at the time the award commences and throughout its duration. At time of application, applicant cannot hold or have held any of the following awards: NIH R01, PO1, R29, K11, K08, Veterans Administration Merit Review, Associate Investigator, Research Associate, Clinical Investigator, AGA Industry Award, Glaxo Institute for

Digestive Health Award, or American Heart Association Awards. Contact the address listed for further information.

American Liver Foundation
Barbara Ramsthaler
1425 Pomton Ave.
Cedar Grove, NJ 07009

1353
Lloyd Lewis Fellowships in American History

AMOUNT: Maximum: $30000   DEADLINE: January 20
FIELDS/MAJORS: United States History

Fellowships for resident research program at Newberry. Must be established scholars in any field of United States history that is appropriate to the collections of the Library. Must hold a Ph.D. Must be a U.S. citizen or permanent resident. Write to the address listed for details or call (312) 255-3666.

Newberry Library
Committee on Awards
60 W. Walton St.
Chicago, IL 60610

1354
Lloyd M. Vanpeursem Scholarship

AMOUNT: None Specified   DEADLINE: March 1
FIELDS/MAJORS: All Areas of Study

Open to graduates of Lincoln County high schools, who are residents of the county and U.S. citizens. This award is usable at any two- or four-year nonprofit college in the U.S. Academic or vocational scholarships are also available. May be renewed if recipient reapplies each year, can document adequate progress toward a degree, remains in good academic standing, and has continued financial need. Contact the address below for further information.

Oregon State Scholarship Commission
Private Awards
1500 Valley River Dr., #100
Eugene, OR 97401-2130

1355
Lois Dupre Shuster Endowed Scholarship

AMOUNT: Maximum: $1000   DEADLINE: February 15
FIELDS/MAJORS: Horticulture, Floriculture, Landscape Architecture, Forestry, Botony, Plant Pathology, Environmental Control, City Planning, Land Management

Open to students from high school seniors to graduate level who are Pennsylvania residents. Must have a minimum GPA of 2.8. Must be sponsored by a Federated Garden Club in Pennsylvania and be able to demonstrate financial need. References, a personal letter, (regarding goals, background, and commitment), an official transcript for the current period, and the application signed by the sponsoring club's president will be required. A student may reapply if academics remain high and need is apparent. Contact a local club, the address listed, or (215) 643-0164 for details.

Garden Club Federation of Pennsylvania
Mrs. William A. Lamb, Scholarship Chair
925 Lorien Dr.
Gwynedd Valley, PA 19437-0216

1356
Lola B. Curry Scholarship

AMOUNT: None Specified   DEADLINE: None Specified
FIELDS/MAJORS: All Areas of Study

Awards for students who are from the state of Alabama and are members or dependents of members of the United Daughters of the Confederacy or the Children of the Confederacy. Contact your local chapter of the UDC or write to the address below for more information.

United Daughters of the Confederacy
Education Committee
328 North Ave.
Richmond, VA 23220

1357
Lone Star Employee Scholarships

AMOUNT: Maximum: $1000   DEADLINE: None Specified
FIELDS/MAJORS: All Areas of Study

Open to children of Lone Star employees who have a minimum GPA of 3.0 and rank in the top fifth of their class. Recipients must keep good grades for the award to be renewed each year. For undergraduate study. Contact the address listed for further information or (203) 969-8509.

Lone Star Industries
Personnel Representative
300 First Stamford Pl.
Stamford, CT 06912

1358
Long and Foster's Real Estate Scholarships

AMOUNT: Maximum: $1000   DEADLINE: March 2
FIELDS/MAJORS: All Areas of Study

Open to graduating high school seniors, with a minimum GPA of 3.0, planning on attending a four-year college or university. Applicants must be U.S. citizens and residents of specific counties in Delaware, Maryland, Pennsylvania,

Virginia, and Washington DC. Based on financial need, academic performance, leadership, and community/extracurricular activities. Information and applications are available from your high school guidance office or any of the Long and Foster's sales offices.

Long and Foster's Real Estate, Inc.
Scholarship Program, Corp., Mktg. Dept.
11351 Random Hills
Fairfax, VA 22030-6082

1359
Lonnie H. Carter Memorial Scholarship

AMOUNT: $1000-$2500 DEADLINE: February 6
FIELDS/MAJORS: Engineering

Awards are available for engineering juniors, seniors, or fifth-year students who are enrolled in an accredited Illinois engineering and technology program. Applicants must be interested in pursuing a career in consulting engineering, be U.S. citizens, and be in the upper half of their class. Eight awards per year. Write to the address listed or call Barb Dirks at (217) 528-7814 for more information. Must have a GPA of at least 2.0.

Consulting Engineers Council of Illinois
625 S. College
PO Box 1604
Springfield, IL 62705

1360
Lorain County Home Economics Scholarship

AMOUNT: Maximum: $300 DEADLINE: March 19
FIELDS/MAJORS: Home Economics

This scholarship is offered to a graduating high school senior who is pursuing the field of home economics at a college or two-year technical school. Must be a resident of Lorain County, Ohio. Write to the address listed or call (216) 934-6108 for more information.

Lorain County Home Economics Association
Kathie Resar
3952 Jaycox
Avon, OH 44011

1361
Lorain County Medical Scholarship Foundation Scholarships

AMOUNT: None Specified DEADLINE: May 15
FIELDS/MAJORS: Medicine, Nursing, and Related Health Fields

Scholarships for Lorain County, Ohio, students who are currently enrolled or formally admitted to medical school, (not pre-med), nursing students who have completed one year of study or are enrolled/admitted to courses in the health-related field. Must be able to demonstrate academic competence and financial need. Write to the address below for details.

Lorain County Medical Scholarship Foundation
5320 Hoag Dr., Suite D
Elyria, OH 44035

1362
Lord Post Freshman Scholarship

AMOUNT: Maximum: $2500 DEADLINE: February 24
FIELDS/MAJORS: All Areas of Study

Open to current undergraduates who are residents of the Greater Hartford area and attend two- or four-year schools. Based on academics and financial need. Preference for students who received a scholarship for freshman year. Contact the address listed for further information. Must have a GPA of at least 2.8.

Greater Hartford Interracial Scholarship Fund, Inc.
Ellis Simpson
PO Box 630644
Hartford, CT 06132

1363
Lottery Success Scholarships

AMOUNT: None Specified DEADLINE: None Specified
FIELDS/MAJORS: All Areas of Study

Open to full-time students enrolled at a New Mexico college or university, in the first regular semester immediately following your high school graduation. Must have graduated from a New Mexico public high school, accredited private high school, or obtained a New Mexico GED in May 1996 or later. Must obtain a minimum 2.5 GPA during the first college semester. Contact the financial aid office at any New Mexico public postsecondary institution for further information.

New Mexico Commission on Higher Education
Financial Aid and Student Services
PO Box 15910
Santa Fe, NM 87506

1364
Louis Pelzer Memorial Award

AMOUNT: Maximum: $500 DEADLINE: November 30
FIELDS/MAJORS: All Areas of Study

Award for the graduate student who submits the best essay in American history. Author must be enrolled in graduate program in any field. Write to the address listed for more information.

Organization of American Historians
Journal of American History
1125 E. Atwater, Indiana University
Bloomington, IN 47401

1365
Louise Dessureault Memorial Scholarship

AMOUNT: Maximum: $500 DEADLINE: April 15
FIELDS/MAJORS: Travel and Tourism, Hotel/Motel Management

Awards for Canadian juniors or seniors in one of the areas listed above who are enrolled in a four-year college in North America. Must have a GPA of 3.0 or better. Write to the address listed or call 1-800-682-8886 ext. 4251 for more information.

National Tourism Foundation
546 East Main St.
PO Box 3071
Lexington, KY 40596

1366
Louise Giles Minority Scholarships

AMOUNT: $3000 DEADLINE: April 1
FIELDS/MAJORS: Library Science

Applicants must be Native American, Asian-American, African-American, or Hispanic graduate students entering or enrolled in an ALA-accredited master's program. United States or Canadian citizenship is required. Must not have completed more than 12 semester hours toward master's degree. Write to the address shown for details.

American Library Association
Staff Liaison, ALA Scholarship Juries
50 E. Huron St.
Chicago, IL 60611

1367
Louise W. Dimmick Endowed Scholarship

AMOUNT: Maximum: $1000 DEADLINE: February 15
FIELDS/MAJORS: Horticulture, Floriculture, Landscape Architecture, Conservation, Forestry, Botony, Agronomy, Plant Pathology, Environmental Control, City Planning, Land Management

Open to students from high school seniors to graduate level who are Pennsylvania residents. Must have a minimum GPA of 2.8. Must be sponsored by a Federated Garden Club in Pennsylvania and be able to demonstrate financial need. References, a personal letter (regarding goals, background and commitment), an official transcript for the current period, and the application signed by the sponsoring club's president will be required. A student may reapply if academics remain high and need is apparent. Contact a local club, the address listed, or (215) 643-0164 for details.

Garden Club Federation of Pennsylvania
Mrs. William A. Lamb, Scholarship Chair
925 Lorien Dr.
Gwynedd Valley, PA 19437-0216

1368
Louisiana Honors Scholarship

AMOUNT: None Specified DEADLINE: June 1
FIELDS/MAJORS: All Areas of Study

Open to high school seniors and undergraduates who are Louisiana residents. Must be/have attended Louisiana high schools and are in/plan to be in Louisiana colleges. High school seniors must have a minimum GPA of 3.5, and current undergraduates must have a minimum of 3.0 Write to the address listed for details.

Louisiana Office of Student Financial Assistance
PO Box 91202
Baton Rouge, LA 70821-9202

1369
Louisiana Rockefeller State Wildlife Scholarships

AMOUNT: Maximum: $1000 DEADLINE: June 1
FIELDS/MAJORS: Wildlife, Forestry, Marine Science

Scholarships for Louisiana residents intending to obtain a degree in wildlife, forestry, or marine science. Must be repaid if degree is not obtained. Must have a GPA of at least 2.5 for undergraduate or master's level study. Renewable for up to six years. Write to the address below for details.

Louisiana Governor's Special Commission on Education Services
Attn: Director, Scholarship/Grant Div.
PO Box 91202
Baton Rouge, LA 70821

1370
Loyal Christian Benefit Association Scholarship

AMOUNT: Maximum: $1000　DEADLINE: October 15
FIELDS/MAJORS: All Areas of Study

Open to high school seniors who are enrolled in a technical institution or a four-year college. For undergraduate use only. Renewable based on continuing eligibility. Applicants must be members of the Loyal Christian Benefit Association. Contact the address listed for further information.

Loyal Christian Benefit Association
Eileen Jefferys, Branch Dev. Coordinator
PO Box 13005
Erie, PA 16514-1305

1371
Lucas V. Beau (Major General), Order of Daedalians, Flight Scholarship

AMOUNT: None Specified　DEADLINE: April 1
FIELDS/MAJORS: Aviation

Applicants must be CAP cadet members. Award is used for air and ground training toward a FAA private pilots license. Write to the address listed for details.

Civil Air Patrol
National Headquarters CAP (TT)
Maxwell AFB, AL 36112

1372
Lucile B. Kaufman Women's Scholarship

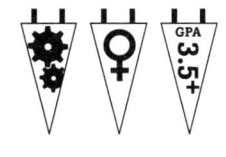

AMOUNT: Maximum: $1000　DEADLINE: March 1
FIELDS/MAJORS: Manufacturing Engineering, Manufacturing Engineering Technology

Open to full-time female undergraduates who have completed at least 30 credit hours in an ABET accredited degree program. Must have a minimum GPA of 3.5 and be planning a career in manufacturing engineering or manufacturing engineering technology. Recipients will be announced in June. Write to the address listed for more information.

Society of Manufacturing Engineers Education Foundation
One SME Dr.
PO Box 930
Dearborn, MI 48121-0930

1373
Lucille Keller Foundation Student Loan Program

AMOUNT: None Specified　DEADLINE: May 31
FIELDS/MAJORS: All Areas of Study

Interest-free loans are available for residents of Bartholomew County, Indiana. Applicants must be enrolled on a full-time basis and have a GPA of at least 2.0. Write to the address below for information.

Lucille Keller Foundation
Irwin Union Bank and Trust Company
Attn: Trust Department, PO Box 929
Columbus, IN 47202

1374
Lulac Scholarship Programs

AMOUNT: $100-$1000　DEADLINE: March 31
FIELDS/MAJORS: All Areas of Study

The Lulac National Scholarship Fund is a community-based scholarship program that awards over a half a million dollars each year to outstanding Hispanic students in communities served by participating councils of Lulac. To qualify, an applicant must be a U.S. citizen or legal resident and enrolled or planning to enroll in a two- or four-year college or university. Applicants must apply directly to a participating Lulac council in his/her community. A list of participating Lulac councils can be obtained by sending a SASE to the Lulac National Education Service Centers at the address below.

Lulac National Educational Service Centers, Inc.
Department of Scholarship Inquiries
1133 20th St. NW, #750
Washington, DC 20036

1375
Luling Foundation Scholarship

AMOUNT: Maximum: $1000　DEADLINE: May 1
FIELDS/MAJORS: Agriculture and Related Fields

Scholarship established at any agricultural college or university, trade, or vocational school with programs in agriculture within the state of Texas. Available to freshman pursuing a degree in agriculture or a related field. Students must be a permanent resident of Texas, residing in Caldwell, Gonzales, or Guadalupe counties, and have been active in 4-H or FFA. For further information and an application, write to the address below.

Luling Foundation
PO Drawer 31
Luling, TX 78648

1376
Luray Caverns Research Grant

AMOUNT: Maximum: $2500 DEADLINE: April 15
FIELDS/MAJORS: Travel, Tourism

Open to students conducting research on a thesis, dissertation, or terminal project relating to travel and tourism. Recipient will be required to submit an executive summary in addition to the completed project. Contact the address listed for further information.

National Tour Foundation
National Tour Foundation Research Grant
546 E. Main St.
Lexington, KY 40508

1377
Lyle Mamer, Julia Kiene Fellowship in Electrical Energy

AMOUNT: $1000-$2000 DEADLINE: March 1
FIELDS/MAJORS: Electrical-Related Fields

Open to women who are graduating seniors or those who have a degree from an accredited institution. The applications are judged on scholarship, character, financial need, and professional interest in electrical energy. The college or university selected by the recipient for advanced study must be accredited and approved by the EWRT Fellowship Committee. One award given for each fellowship. Write to the address below for further information.

Electrical Women's Round Table, Inc.
Executive Director
PO Box 292793
Nashville, TN 37229

1378
M. Geneva Gray Scholarship

AMOUNT: None Specified DEADLINE: March 1
FIELDS/MAJORS: All Areas of Study

Scholarships are available for Massachusetts residents who are undergraduates, come from families with several children to educate, with a family income in the $25,000 to $50,000 range. In September, write to the address below for information. Include a SASE with your request.

M. Geneva Gray Scholarship Fund
PNC Bank, New England, Trust Department
125 High St.
Boston, MA 02110

1379
Mabel E. Sherman Education Trust

AMOUNT: None Specified DEADLINE: None Specified
FIELDS/MAJORS: All Areas of Study

First preference is given to students who are residents of either Ida or Cherokee County, Iowa. Second preference is given to students who are residents of Iowa. Participation is limited to students who are attending one of the following four Iowa educational institutions: Buena Vista University, Cornell College, Morningside College, and Westmar University. Contact the financial aid offices of the four participating schools listed in the description.

Citizens 1st National Bank
Drawer 1227
Storm Lake, IA 50588

1380
Mabelle Wilhelmina Boldt Memorial Scholarship

AMOUNT: $2000 DEADLINE: March 4
FIELDS/MAJORS: Interior Design

Scholarship for graduate level students who have worked in the field for at least five years and are returning to school for further studies. Based on academic/creative accomplishment. Preference given to students with a focus on design research. One award per year. Send a SASE to the address listed for details.

American Society of Interior Designers Educational
    Foundation
Scholarship and Awards Program
608 Massachusetts Ave. NE
Washington, DC 20002

1381
MADD/Reliance Direct Essay Contest

AMOUNT: $2000-$5000 DEADLINE: July 15
FIELDS/MAJORS: All Areas of Study

Essay contest open to Connecticut residents who are undergraduates or graduate students in a Connecticut school. Essays must focus on the theme "The Effects of Drunk Driving on the Family" and be five hundred to one thousand words long. Winners will be notified by August 15. Contact the address listed for further information or call (203) 389-3595.

MADD State Office
MADD/Reliance Direct Essay Contest
131 Bradley Rd.
Woodbridge, CT 06525

1382
Madeline Pickett Cogswell Nursing Scholarships

AMOUNT: Maximum: $500 DEADLINE: February 15
FIELDS/MAJORS: Nursing

Applicants must be currently enrolled in an accredited school of nursing. Must be U.S. citizens and members, or related to a members, of NSDAR. A letter of sponsorship from your local DAR chapter will be required. A second deadline date is August 15. Contact your local DAR chapter or send a SASE to the address listed for more information.

National Society Daughters of the American Revolution
NSDAR Scholarship Committee
1776 D St. NW
Washington, DC 20006

1383
Madison Charitable Fund Scholarship

AMOUNT: None Specified DEADLINE: March 1
FIELDS/MAJORS: All Areas of Study

Open to high school seniors and undergraduates who are U.S. citizens and residents of Douglas County. Seniors must have a minimum GPA of 3.0, and undergraduates must have at least a 2.5. Preference given to students of Elkton High School. Awards may only be used at Oregon public colleges. Contact the address listed for further information.

Oregon State Scholarship Commission
Private Awards
1500 Valley River Dr., #100
Eugene, OR 97401-2130

1384
Madison County Hotel, Restaurant and Liquor Assn. Scholarships

AMOUNT: Maximum: $500 DEADLINE: None Specified
FIELDS/MAJORS: Culinary Arts, Restaurant/Hotel Management

Open to entering freshmen pursuing a career in culinary arts or restaurant/hotel management. Applicants must be residents of Madison County or attend school there. Based on primarily on academics, but financial need will be considered. Awards given after first semester if recipients hold a minimum GPA of 2.5. Contact the address listed for further information.

Madison County Hotel, Restaurant, and Liquor
 Association
Douglas M. Rusch, Scholarship Chairman
Colgate Inn I 5 Payne St.
Hamilton, NY 13346

1385
Mae Lasley Osage Scholarship Fund

AMOUNT: $250-$1000 DEADLINE: June 15
FIELDS/MAJORS: All Areas of Study

Scholarships are available for Osage Indians who are undergraduate students at any accredited university. Write to the address below for information.

Mae Lasley Osage Scholarship Fund
PO Box 2009
Tulsa, OK 74101

1386
Magazine Internship Program

AMOUNT: None Specified DEADLINE: December 15
FIELDS/MAJORS: Journalism

Summer internships are available with any of forty-two different magazines for journalism majors who will be entering their senior year and who plan to pursue a career in editorial journalism. Internships are available in New York and Washington, D.C. Write to the address below for information.

American Society of Magazine Editors
Marlene Kahan, Executive Director
919 Third Ave., 22nd Floor
New York, NY 10022

1387
Magoichi and Shizuko Kato Memorial Scholarship

AMOUNT: None Specified DEADLINE: April 1
FIELDS/MAJORS: Medicine, Theology, Religion

Open to graduate students of Japanese ancestry majoring in medicine or the ministry. Must be a member of the Japanese-American League to apply. Applications and information may be obtained from local JACL chapters, district offices, and the national headquarters at the address listed or call (415) 921-5225. Please indicate your level of study, and be certain to include a legal-sized SASE.

Japanese-American Citizens League
National Scholarship and Award Program
1765 Sutter St.
San Francisco, CA 94115

1388
Maine Campground Owners Association Scholarship

AMOUNT: Maximum: $500   DEADLINE: April 1
FIELDS/MAJORS: Outdoor Recreation

Awards are available for Maine residents who have completed at least one year of study in a program leading to a career in outdoor recreation. Must have a GPA of at least 2.5. Write to the address below for more information.

Maine Campground Owners Association
655 Main St.
Lewiston, ME 04240

1389
Maine Media Women Scholarship, Lee Agger Memorial Scholarship

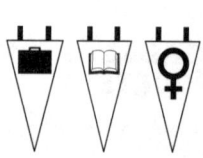

AMOUNT: None Specified   DEADLINE: April 1
FIELDS/MAJORS: Mass Communication-Journalism, Public Relations, Broadcasting, Advertising

Scholarships are available for female Maine residents enrolled in an area listed above. Preference will be given to an applicant who has already demonstrated motivation and ability in some aspect of mass communications. For more information, write to the address below.

Maine Media Women Scholarship
MMW Scholarship Committee
9 Middle St.
Hallowell, ME 04347

1390
Maine Rural Rehabilitation Fund Scholarship

AMOUNT: None Specified   DEADLINE: June 16
FIELDS/MAJORS: All Areas of Study

Scholarships for Maine citizens who are from farm families or from woods working families. Must be second generation farm/woods family, or child of deceased woods/farm worker, or 50% of family income from farm/woods work. FFA members majoring in agriculture are also eligible. Based on need. Must have a GPA of at least 2.7. Write to the address below for details.

Maine Department of Agriculture
Office of the Coordinator
State House Station 28
Augusta, ME 04333

1391
Maine Vietnam Veterans Scholarship

AMOUNT: None Specified   DEADLINE: May 1
FIELDS/MAJORS: All Areas of Study

Scholarships are available for Maine Vietnam veterans who served in the United States Armed Services in the Vietnam Theater or to their descendants. Preference will be given to veterans. Write to the address listed for more information.

Maine Community Foundation
245 East Maine St.
PO Box 148
Ellsworth, ME 04605

1392
Makarios Scholarship/ Theodore and Wally Lappas Award

AMOUNT: Maximum: $1000   DEADLINE: May 5
FIELDS/MAJORS: All Areas of Study

Ten scholarships for Greek Cypriots born in Cyprus and having permanent residence and citizenship there. For study in the United States. Must have financial need and high scholastic ability. Write to the address listed for details.

Cyprus Relief Fund of America, Inc.
Makarios Scholarship Fund, Inc.
13 E. 40th St.
New York, NY 10016

1393
Malcolm Baldrige Scholarships

AMOUNT: Maximum: $2000   DEADLINE: May 31
FIELDS/MAJORS: International Trade, Manufacturing

Awards for college sophomores or juniors who must be matriculated in either international trade or manufacturing. Must be fluent in (or have studied) a foreign language. Must also be able to demonstrate excellent academics and be a Connecticut resident. Preference given to students attending colleges in Connecticut. Contact the address listed for further information and an application. Must have a GPA of at least 3.0.

Malcolm Baldridge Scholarship Fund, CBIA
Brian V. Beaudin, President
370 Asylum St.
Hartford, CT 06103

1394
MALDEF Communications Scholarship Program

AMOUNT: None Specified DEADLINE: June 30
FIELDS/MAJORS: Communications, Journalism, Media Communications, Entertainment Law

Awards are available for Latino undergraduate or graduate students who seek a career in these fields upon graduation. Write to the address below for more information.

Mexican American Legal Defense and Education Fund
634 South Spring St.
11th Floor
Los Angeles, CA 90014

1395
MALDEF Law School Scholarship Program

AMOUNT: None Specified DEADLINE: June 30
FIELDS/MAJORS: Law

Open to full-time law students of Hispanic descent accepted to/enrolled in an accredited law school. Varying number of awards per year. Recipients must demonstrate a commitment to serve the Hispanic community after graduation. Write to the address below for details.

Mexican American Legal Defense and Educational Fund
MALDEF Law School Scholarship Program
634 S. Spring St., 11th Floor
Los Angeles, CA 90014

1396
Maley/FTE Scholarship Technology Teacher Professional Development

AMOUNT: Maximum: $1000 DEADLINE: December 1
FIELDS/MAJORS: Technology Education

Scholarship for members (at least one year) of the International Technology Education Association who are technology teachers at any grade level who are beginning or continuing graduate studies. Write to the address listed for details.

International Technology Education Association
Tom Hughes
1914 Association Dr.
Reston, VA 22091

1397
Manchester Scholarship Foundation Scholarships

AMOUNT: $500-$1500 DEADLINE: April 17
FIELDS/MAJORS: All Areas of Study

Open to high school seniors who are residents of Manchester. For use at four-year schools. Based on academics, school and community activities, and financial need. Contact the address listed for further information. Must have a GPA of at least 2.8.

Manchester Scholarship Foundation, Inc.
Kathleen F. Hedlund, President
PO Box 51
Manchester, CT 06045

1398
MAPA Safety Foundation Scholarship

AMOUNT: $1000 DEADLINE: August 1
FIELDS/MAJORS: Aviation Safety

Awards for juniors and seniors enrolled in a course of study that would promote general aviation safety. Must have a GPA of 3.0 or better and be a member of MAPA or sponsored by a MAPA member. Contact a local MAPA member or write to the address listed for more details.

Mooney Aircraft Pilot Association Safety Foundation
PO Box 460607
San Antonio, TX 78246

1399
Marcus and Theresa Levie Educational Scholarship

AMOUNT: None Specified DEADLINE: March 1
FIELDS/MAJORS: Helping Professions

Scholarships for Jewish men and women legally domiciled in Cook County, Illinois, who are identified as having promise for significant contributions in their chosen careers and are in need of financial assistance for full-time academic programs in one of the above fields. Must have completed at least the junior level of study or have started professional training. Write to the address below after December 1 for details.

Jewish Vocational Service
Attn: Scholarship Secretary
One South Franklin St.
Chicago, IL 60606

1400
Marcus Garvey Scholarship

AMOUNT: Maximum: $1000 DEADLINE: May 1
FIELDS/MAJORS: All Areas of Study

Open to high school seniors who are residents of Connecticut and are of West Indian parentage. Based on academics, community service, financial need, and an essay. Contact the address listed for further information. Must have a GPA of at least 3.0.

West Indian Foundation, Inc.
Scholarship Committee
PO Box 320394
Hartford, CT 06132

1401
Margaret and Charles E. Stewart Scholarship Fund

AMOUNT: $500 DEADLINE: April 30
FIELDS/MAJORS: Religion, Theology

Awards for African-American full-time seminary students enrolled as candidates for the master's of divinity degree, in preparation for the pastorate in the Black Church of any Protestant denomination. Write to the address below for more information.

Philadelphia Foundation
1234 Market St.
Suite 1900
Philadelphia, PA 19107

1402
Margaret E. Swanson Scholarship

AMOUNT: None Specified DEADLINE: April 1
FIELDS/MAJORS: Dental Hygiene

Scholarships for students who have completed at least one year in a full-time accredited program in Dental Hygiene. Based on need, organization, and leadership potential. Must have a GPA of at least 3.0. Write to the address below for more information.

American Dental Hygienists' Association Institute for Oral Health
444 N. Michigan Ave., Suite 3400
Chicago, IL 60611

1403
Margaret Hood Scholarship

AMOUNT: Maximum: $2000 DEADLINE: April 1
FIELDS/MAJORS: Healthcare

Open to upper-division students enrolled at accredited four-year colleges or universities and pursuing healthcare careers. Must be residents of Clark or Skamania counties. Contact the address listed or call (360) 256-2035 for further information.

Southwest Washington Medical Center
Scholarship Coordinator
400 N.E. Mother Joseph Pl.
Vancouver, WA 98668

1404
Margaret M. Prickett Scholarship

AMOUNT: Maximum: $1000 DEADLINE: March 31
FIELDS/MAJORS: All Areas of Study

Scholarships for daughters or granddaughters of Commissioned Officers or Warrant Officers in the U.S. Army who are on active duty, died on active duty, or retired after at least twenty years of service. For undergraduate study. Renewable. Write to the address listed for details. Specify the officers name, rank, social security number, and dates of active duty when requesting an application. Enclose a SASE.

Society of Daughters of the U.S. Army
Janet B. Otto, Scholarship Chairman
7717 Rockledge Court
West Springfield, VA 22152

1405
Margaret McNamara Memorial Fund Fellowships

AMOUNT: Maximum: $6000 DEADLINE: February 2
FIELDS/MAJORS: All Areas of Study

Fellowships are available to women from developing countries, with a record of service to women/children. Applicants must be twenty-five years of age or older and planning to return to their country of origin within two years of the grant date. Must be able to demonstrate financial need. Write to the address below for information.

Margaret McNamara Memorial Fund
1818 H St. NW, Room G-1000
Washington, DC 20433

1406
Margaret Sloggett Fisher Scholarships

AMOUNT: $1000 DEADLINE: April 15
FIELDS/MAJORS: History, Anthropology, Hawaiian Studies, Ethnic Studies

Scholarship for Hawaii residents studying in any of the above fields (studying in Hawaii or on the mainland). Must be junior, senior, or graduate student. Preference given to Kauai residents. Write to the address below for details.

Margaret Sloggett Fisher Scholarship Committee
PO Box 1631
Lihue
Kauai, HI 96766

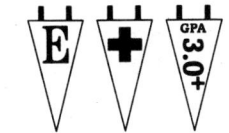

1407
Maria Borrero Scholarship

AMOUNT: Maximum: $500 DEADLINE: None Specified
FIELDS/MAJORS: Health Related Fields

Open to Hispanic high school seniors who are residents of Hartford, Connecticut. Must be in top 20% of the class with demonstrated leadership ability. Contact the address listed for further information. Must have a GPA of at least 3.4.

Hispanic Health Council
Victoria Barrera
175 Main St.
Hartford, CT 06106

1408
Maria Jackson/ General George A. White Scholarship

AMOUNT: None Specified DEADLINE: March 1
FIELDS/MAJORS: All Areas of Study

Scholarship for students who served in the Armed Forces, or whose parents served in the Armed Forces (U.S.). Must be able to provide documentation (DD93, DD214, discharge papers, etc.). Must have a GPA of at least 3.75 and be an Oregon resident. Contact your college financial aid office, contact your high school guidance department, or write to the address listed for details.

Oregon State Scholarship Commission
Attn: Grant Department
1500 Valley River Dr., #100
Eugene, OR 97401

1409
Marie Mahoney Egan, Anna Jones Scholarships

AMOUNT: None Specified DEADLINE: March 1
FIELDS/MAJORS: All Areas of Study

Scholarships for students who were graduated from a Lake County, Oregon, high school. The Jones scholarship is for Paisley High School graduates and must be used at Oregon public colleges. Egan scholarship requires graduation from a Lake County high school. Applicants must be U.S. citizens or permanent residents and residents of Lake County. Contact your college financial aid office, your high school guidance department, or write to the address listed for details.

Oregon State Scholarship Commission
Attn: Grant Department
1500 Valley River Dr., #100
Eugene, OR 97401

1410
Marin County American Revolution Bicentennial Scholarships

AMOUNT: $500-$2000 DEADLINE: March 31
FIELDS/MAJORS: All Areas of Study

Awards for high school seniors who have been residents of Marin County since September 1st of the year prior to submitting an application. Must be planning to attend an approved institution of higher education. Contact your high school counselor or address below for complete information.

Marin County American Revolution Bicentennial Committee
Beryl Buck Institute for Education
18 Commercial Blvd.
Novato, CA 94949

1411
Marine Corps Scholarship Foundation Scholarships

AMOUNT: $500-$2500 DEADLINE: April 1
FIELDS/MAJORS: All Areas of Study

Candidates must be the son/daughter of an active duty or reserve Marine in good standing, or the son/daughter of a Marine honorably and/or medically discharged or deceased. Must be a high school senior, high school graduate, or college undergraduate. Gross family income must not exceed $41,000 per year. Write to the address below for complete details.

Marine Corps Scholarship Foundation, Inc.
Scholarship Office
PO Box 3008
Princeton, NJ 08543

1412
Marion Barr Stanfield Art Scholarship

AMOUNT: None Specified   DEADLINE: February 15
FIELDS/MAJORS: Painting, Drawing, Sculpture, Photography

Applicants must be active Unitarian Universalist members who are majoring in painting, drawing, photography, and sculpture. Financial need must be demonstrated. Write to the address listed or call (617) 742-2100 for details.

Unitarian Universalist Association
Publications Department
25 Beacon St.
Boston, MA 02108

1413
Marion T. Weidman Scholarship

AMOUNT: None Specified   DEADLINE: None Specified
FIELDS/MAJORS: All Areas of Study

Awards to support high school graduates who are residents of Rockport, Maine. Contact the Camden-Rockport Guidance Office for more information.

Maine Community Foundation
245 East Maine St.
PO Box 148
Ellsworth, ME 04605

1414
Marjorie E. Hamblin Annual Endowed Scholarship

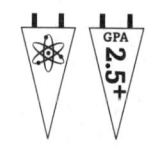

AMOUNT: Maximum: $1000   DEADLINE: February 15
FIELDS/MAJORS: Horticulture, Floriculture, Landscape Architecture, Conservation, Forestry, Botany, Plant Pathology, Environmental Control, Land Management

Open to students from high school seniors to graduate level who are Pennsylvania residents. Must have a minimum GPA of 2.8. Must be sponsored by a Federated Garden Club in Pennsylvania and be able to demonstrate financial need. References, a personal letter (regarding goals, background, and commitment), an official transcript for the current period, and the application signed by the sponsoring club's president will be required. A student may reapply if academics remain high and need is apparent. Contact a local club, the address listed, or (215) 643-0164 for details.

Garden Club Federation of Pennsylvania
Mrs. William A. Lamb, Scholarship Chair
925 Lorien Dr.
Gwynedd Valley, PA 19437-0216

1415
Marjorie Roy Rothermel Scholarship

AMOUNT: Maximum: $1500   DEADLINE: February 15
FIELDS/MAJORS: Mechanical Engineering

Applicants must be master's students in mechanical engineering and ASME members. Write to the address listed for details. Please be certain to enclose a SASE with your request.

American Society of Mechanical Engineers Auxiliary, Inc.
Mrs. Otto Prochaska
332 Valencia St.
Gulf Breeze, FL 32561

1416
Marjorie Sells Carter Trust Scholarship for New England Scouts

AMOUNT: Maximum: $1500   DEADLINE: April 15
FIELDS/MAJORS: All Areas of Study

Scholarships for boys from New England who have been Scouts for at least two years. Based on financial need, academics, and leadership potential. Award is renewable for one year. Details are available from any of the New England Scout Councils or write to the address listed.

Marjorie Sells Carter Scholarship Trust
Jeffrey McKee, Program Director
PO Box 280098 60 Darlin St.
East Hartford, CT 06128

1417
Mark and Catherine Winkler Foundation Grants

AMOUNT: None Specified   DEADLINE: None Specified
FIELDS/MAJORS: All Areas of Study

Awards available to single parents in any area of study who plan to attend or are enrolled in participating schools. These include Colorado College, George Mason University, Harvard University, and the University of Washington. Write to the address below for additional information.

Mark and Catherine Winkler Foundation
4900 Seminary Road
Alexandria, VA 22311

1418
Mark Hass Journalism Scholarship

AMOUNT: None Specified   DEADLINE: March 1
FIELDS/MAJORS: Journalism

Open to Oregon residents who are U.S. citizens or permanent residents. These are one time awards for high school seniors or current undergraduates. Contact the address below for further information.

Oregon State Scholarship Commission
Private Awards
1500 Valley River Dr., #100
Eugene, OR 97401-2130

1419
Mark J. Schroeder Scholarship in Meteorology

AMOUNT: $3000   DEADLINE: June 16
FIELDS/MAJORS: Meteorology, Atmospheric Science, Ocean Science, Hydrologic Science

Scholarships are for undergraduates entering their final year of study in meteorology, atmospheric science, oceanic science, or hydrologic science with a GPA of 3.0 or better. Must demonstrate financial need and be a U.S. citizen or permanent resident. Write to the address below for more information.

American Meteorological Society
45 Beacon St.
Boston, MA 02108

1420
Mark O. Hatfield Scholarship

AMOUNT: Maximum: $2000   DEADLINE: None Specified
FIELDS/MAJORS: Public Policy

Award for a scholar to do research in the fields above and produce a paper of publishable quality that will reflect the spirit and interests of Senator Mark Hatfield. Write to the address listed for more information.

Ripon Educational Fund
Executive Director
227 Massachusetts Ave. NE, Suite 201
Washington, DC 20002

1421
Mark Todd Hale Memorial Criminal Justice Scholarship

AMOUNT: Maximum: $1000   DEADLINE: May 31
FIELDS/MAJORS: Criminal Justice

Scholarships for students from the Coastal Bend area in Texas majoring in criminal justice. Must have a GPA of at least 3.0 and be attending school full-time. Write to the address below for details.

Coastal Bend Community Foundation
Mercantile Tower MT 276
615 N. Upper Broadway, #860
Corpus Christi, TX 78477

1422
Mark Ulmer Scholarship

AMOUNT: Maximum: $500   DEADLINE: June 1
FIELDS/MAJORS: All Areas of Study

Scholarship available for Native American sophomores, juniors, or seniors who attend one of the schools in the University of North Carolina system. Applicants must have a GPA of at least 2.0, be U.S. citizens, and North Carolina residents. Write to Ms. Lana T. Dial at the address below for more information.

Triangle Native American Society
PO Box 26841
Raleigh, NC 27611

1423
Marketing/Advertising Scholarship Awards

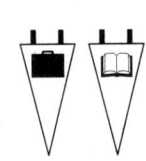

AMOUNT: $1000-$5000   DEADLINE: April 3
FIELDS/MAJORS: Marketing, Advertising, Communications, Commercial Art

Scholarships for students from Long Island, who are in one of the fields of study listed above. Based on transcripts, recommendations, personal statement, and samples of work. Write to the address listed or call (516) 944-0100 for more information.

Long Island Advertising Club, Inc.
Scholarship Committee
34 Richards Road, Suite 100
Port Washington, NY 11050

1424
Marshall A. Bristow Scholarship

AMOUNT: Maximum: $500   DEADLINE: April 1
FIELDS/MAJORS: Conservation/Environmental Science

Non-renewable scholarship given to freshmen enrolled at an accredited four-year college pursuing studies related to a career in agriculture, forestry, soil science, conservation, or environmental sciences. Applicants must be a resident of either Goochland or Powhatan counties. Please write to the address below for additional information.

Monacan Soil and Water Conservation District
PO Box 66
Goochland, VA 23063

1425
Martin Luther King, Jr. Scholarship

AMOUNT: None Specified   DEADLINE: February 1
FIELDS/MAJORS: All Areas of Study

Awards for African-American high school seniors who are residents of North Carolina. Priority will be given to children of NCAE members, but other selection criteria include: character, personality, and scholastic achievement. Write to the address listed for more details.

North Carolina Association of Educators
NCAE Minority Affairs Commission
PO Box 27347
Raleigh, NC 27611

1426
Maurice Yonover Scholarship

AMOUNT: None Specified   DEADLINE: March 1
FIELDS/MAJORS: Helping Professions

Open to master's and doctoral candidates with career goals in the "helping professions." Must be legally domiciled in Cook County, the Chicago metro area, or Northwest Indiana. Contact the address below for further information after December 1. Must have a GPA of at least 2.8.

Jewish Vocational Service
Academic Scholarship Program
1 S. Franklin St.
Chicago, IL 60606

1427
Mary Adeline Connor Professional Development Scholarship Program

AMOUNT: Maximum: $6000   DEADLINE: October 31
FIELDS/MAJORS: Library and Information Science

Scholarships for members of the Special Libraries Association who have worked in special libraries for at least five years. For post-M.L.S. study. Preference is given to persons who display an aptitude for special library work. One or more awards per year. Write to the address listed for details.

Special Libraries Association
SLA Scholarship Committee
1700 Eighteenth St. NW
Washington, DC 20009

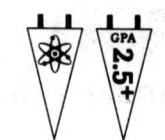

1428
Mary Alice Wheeler Endowed Scholarship

AMOUNT: Maximum: $1000   DEADLINE: February 15
FIELDS/MAJORS: Horticulture, Landscape Architecture, Conservation, Forestry, Botany, Plant Pathology, Environmental Control, Land Management

Open to students from high school seniors to graduate level who are Pennsylvania residents. Must have a minimum GPA of 2.8. Must be sponsored by a Federated Garden Club in Pennsylvania and be able to demonstrate financial need. References, a personal letter (regarding goals, background, and commitment), an official transcript for the current period, and the application signed by the sponsoring club's president will be required. A student may reapply if academics remain high and need is apparent. Contact a local club, the address listed, or (215) 643-0164 for details.

Garden Club Federation of Pennsylvania
Mrs. William A. Lamb, Scholarship Chair
925 Lorien Dr.
Gwynedd Valley, PA 19437-0216

1429
Mary Ann Reinert Nursing Scholarship

AMOUNT: None Specified   DEADLINE: July 1
FIELDS/MAJORS: Surgical Nursing

Scholarships for nursing students with a primary emphasis on the field of surgical nursing. For residents of Missouri and Kansas in areas served by Heartland Health Foundation (NW Missouri and NE Kansas). Write to the address listed for further information.

Heartland Health Foundation
801 Faraon St.
St. Joseph, MO 64501

1430
Mary Davis Fellowship

AMOUNT: $13000   DEADLINE: November 15
FIELDS/MAJORS: Western Art, Visual Art, and Related Areas

Two-year fellowship is available for doctoral scholars researching for the dissertation. One year will be spent in on research, and one year will be spent at the National Gallery of Art. Applicants must know two foreign languages related to the topic of their dissertation and be U.S. citizens or legal residents. Write to the address below for information.

National Gallery of Art
Center for Advanced Study in Visual Arts
Predoctoral Fellowship Program
Washington, DC 20565

1431
Mary E. Bivins Grants

AMOUNT: $200-$1200   DEADLINE: October 31
FIELDS/MAJORS: Theological Studies

Available to residents of the northern twenty-six counties of Texas who are majoring in theological studies at religious institutions. Contact the address listed for further information or call (806) 379-9400.

Mary E. Bivins Foundation
Scholarship Coordinator
1001 Wallace Blvd.
Amarillo, TX 79106

1432
Mary E. Hodges Fund Scholarships

AMOUNT: None Specified   DEADLINE: April 1
FIELDS/MAJORS: All Areas of Study

Open to students who have been Rhode Island residents for a minimum of five years and have family members in the Grand Lodge of Masons of Rhode Island. Based on financial need and academics. Contact the address listed for further information or call (401) 435-4650. Must have a GPA of at least 2.5.

Masonic Grand Lodge Charities of Rhode Island
John Fullhebron
222 Taunton Ave.
East Providence, RI 02914

1433
Mary Isabel Sibley Fellowship

AMOUNT: Maximum: $20000   DEADLINE: January 15
FIELDS/MAJORS: French Language and Literature

Fellowship is available to unmarried women between the ages of twenty-five and thirty-five who have demonstrated their ability to carry on original research. Must have completed or are at the dissertation stage of their Ph.D. and planning to devote full-time work to research during the fellowship year. Contact the address listed for further information.

Phi Beta Kappa Society
Mary Isabel Sibley Fellowship Committee
1811 Q St. NW
Washington, DC 20009

1434
Mary Lou Brown Scholarship

AMOUNT: $2500   DEADLINE: February 1
FIELDS/MAJORS: All Areas of Study

Scholarships are available to students with a general class amateur radio license, who reside in Alaska, Idaho, Montana, Oregon, or Washington. Must have a minimum GPA of 3.0 and attend school in their home state. For full-time study only. Applicants should have a demonstrated interest in promoting the Amateur Radio Service. Write to the address below for information.

ARRL Foundation (American Radio Relay League)
Scholarship Program
225 Main St.
Newington, CT 06111

1435
Mary McLeod Bethune Scholarship Challenge Grant Fund

AMOUNT: $3000   DEADLINE: None Specified
FIELDS/MAJORS: All Areas of Study

Applicants must be outstanding high school seniors who will attend the following schools full-time: Florida A&M, Bethune-Cookman College, Edward Waters College, or Florida Memorial College. Applicants must have a minimum 3.0 GPA, be able to demonstrate financial need, and be residents of Florida for at least one year. Information and applications available at the financial aid offices of the institutions listed.

Florida Department of Education
Office of Student Financial Assistance
1344 Florida Education Center
Tallahassee, FL 32399

1436

Mary Morrow-Edna Richards Scholarship

AMOUNT: Maximum: $1000 DEADLINE: January 12
FIELDS/MAJORS: Education

Awards for senior year of study at an accredited undergraduate institution in North Carolina. In return for funding, recipients agree to teach in North Carolina for at least two years after graduation. Must be residents of North Carolina. Based on character, scholastic achievement, promise as a teacher, and financial need. Application is made through your college or university. Contact the head of the education department for more information, or write to the address listed.

North Carolina Association of Educators
Mary Morrow-Edna Richards Scholarship
PO Box 27347
Raleigh, NC 27611

1437

Mary Moy Quan Ing Memorial Scholarship

AMOUNT: Maximum: $1200 DEADLINE: April 15
FIELDS/MAJORS: Journalism

Open to Asian-American high school seniors who are enrolling in college and pursuing a journalism career. Based on academics, sensitivity to Asian-American issues (as demonstrated by community involvement), and financial need. Contact your local AAJA chapter for further information, or request details from the address listed. Be sure to enclose a SASE with your request for information. Must have a GPA of at least 2.8.

Asian American Journalists Association
Scholarship Committee
1765 Sutter St., Suite 1000
San Francisco, CA 94115

1438

Mary Rowena Cooper Scholarship Fund

AMOUNT: None Specified DEADLINE: None Specified
FIELDS/MAJORS: All Fields of Study.

Scholarships are available for orphans of Vietnam war veterans. Write to the address below for details.

Winston-Salem Foundation
310 West Fourth St., Suite 229
Winston-Salem, NC 27101

1439

Mary Rubin and Benjamin M. Rubin Scholarship

AMOUNT: $500-$5000 DEADLINE: February 1
FIELDS/MAJORS: All Areas of Study

Scholarships for women from the state of Maryland who wish to attend or continue college (or any postsecondary school). Based on ability and need. Minimum GPA is 3.0. Renewable (by re-application). Write to the Mary Rubin and Benjamin M. Rubin Scholarship Fund in care of the address listed for details.

Central Scholarship Bureau
Bristol House Apartments, #108
4001 Clarks Ln.
Baltimore, MD 21215

1440

Maryland Association of Certified Public Accountants Scholarships

AMOUNT: $1000 DEADLINE: April 15
FIELDS/MAJORS: Accounting

Scholarship offered to residents of Maryland who are attending a Maryland college or university with the intent to pursue a career in accounting. Applicants must have a minimum GPA of 3.0 through completion of 15 credit hours, and demonstrate financial need. Write to the address below for further details.

Maryland Association of Certified Public Accountants, Inc.
PO Box 4417
Lutherville, MD 21094

1441

Maryland District 5 Scholarships

AMOUNT: None Specified DEADLINE: March 1
FIELDS/MAJORS: All Areas of Study

Awards are available for graduating high school seniors from Maryland district five who are planning to attend a school in Maryland. Awards are based on academic achievement, school participation, and financial need. To request further information, submit a letter of application indicating the plans for the scholarship, which school the applicant plans to attend and why, an official high school transcript, a copy of SAT scores, and a letter of recommendation to the address below.

Maryland Higher Education Commission
Maryland House of Delegates
16 Francis St.
Annapolis, MD 21401

1442
Mas Family Scholarships

AMOUNT: Maximum: $10000
DEADLINE: March 15
FIELDS/MAJORS: Engineering, Business, International Relations, Economics, Communications, Journalism

Open to Cuban-American undergraduates and graduates who are direct descendants of those who left Cuba (at least one parent or two grandparents) or were born in Cuba themselves. Must be financially in need and have a minimum GPA of 3.5. Selection based on academics, leadership qualities, and potential to contribute to the advancement of a free society. Applications may be requested in writing only after September 15. Contact the address listed or call (305) 592-7768 for further information.

Cuban American National Foundation
Mas Family Scholarships
7300 NW 35th Terrace
Miami, FL 33122

1443
Masao and Sumako Itano Memorial Scholarship

AMOUNT: None Specified   DEADLINE: April 1
FIELDS/MAJORS: All Areas of Study

Open to incoming freshmen who are members of Japanese ancestry and entering or enrolled at an accredited college or university. Applications and information may be obtained from local JACL chapters, district offices, and the national headquarters at the address listed or call (415) 921-5225. Please indicate your level of study and be certain to include a legal-sized SASE.

Japanese American Citizens League
National Scholarship and Award Program
1765 Sutter St.
San Francisco, CA 94115

1444
Masonic-Range Science Scholarship

AMOUNT: None Specified   DEADLINE: January 15
FIELDS/MAJORS: Range Science

Scholarships are available for graduating high school seniors and current freshmen who are majoring in range science. Applicants must be sponsored by a member of the Society for Range Management, the National Association of Conservation Districts, or the Soil and Water Conservation Society. Write to the address listed for more information.

Society for Range Management
Office of the Executive Vice President
1839 York St.
Denver, CO 80206

1445
Masquers Scholarships

AMOUNT: None Specified   DEADLINE: February 15
FIELDS/MAJORS: Performing Arts

Open to high school seniors, graduates, or prior recipients who plan to pursue or are pursuing an undergraduate degree leading to a career in the performing arts. Applications are available at all area high school counseling departments or by writing to the address listed or (414) 682-3760 for further information.

Masquers Coach House
Janet Schmidt
616 N. 8th St.
Manitowoc, WI 54220

1446
Mass Media Science and Engineering Fellows Program

AMOUNT: None Specified   DEADLINE: January 15
FIELDS/MAJORS: Engineering/Science

This program offers an opportunity for advanced students in the natural and social sciences and engineering to spend ten weeks during the summer working as reporters, researchers, or production assistants with media organizations nationwide. A modest stipend is included to help cover living expenses. Must be U.S. citizens and have a Ph.D. Write to the address listed for further information.

American Association for the Advancement of Science
Amie E. King, Coordinator
1200 New York Ave. NW
Washington, DC 20005

1447
Master's Scholarship

AMOUNT: None Specified   DEADLINE: February 4
FIELDS/MAJORS: Microelectronics

Scholarships are available to underrepresented minority students pursuing a master's degree in microelectronics. Must be enrolled in one of the forty-four participating universities. Awards pay tuition and fees up to $14000, a monthly stipend of $1400 for up to two years, a $2000 gift to the department in which the student is enrolled, and pays for travel expense to attend annual conference. Program also links students with industry advisors and possible internships. Must be a U.S. citizen or permanent resident. Contact your financial aid office to determine if your school is a participating member, for more information, and an application form. If they can provide no assistance, contact the address listed.

Semiconductor Research Corporation
Student Services
PO Box 12053
Research Triangle Pk., NC 27709

1448
Master's Thesis Fellowships

AMOUNT: Maximum: $2500 DEADLINE: May 1
FIELDS/MAJORS: U.S. Military and Naval History

Awards are available for master's degree thesis research in any area of history relevant to the Marine Corps (military and naval history, etc.). Applicants must be U.S. citizens or nationals. It is expected that part of the research will be undertaken at the Marine Corps Historical Archives in Washington, D.C. Write to the address listed for information.

Marine Corps Historical Center
Building 58
Washington Navy Yard
Washington, DC 20374

1449
MASWE Memorial Scholarships

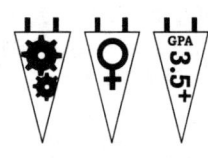

AMOUNT: Maximum: $2000 DEADLINE: February 1
FIELDS/MAJORS: Engineering

Scholarship for junior and senior woman engineering students in an accredited engineering program. Based on academics and financial need. Must have a GPA of at least 3.5. Two awards offered annually. Write to address listed for details. Be certain to enclose a SASE for a reply. Information is also available through the deans office of the school of engineering at your college.

Society of Women Engineers
Scholarship Selection Committee
120 Wall St., 11th Floor
New York, NY 10005

1450
Maury Ferriter Memorial Scholarship

AMOUNT: $400 DEADLINE: March 15
FIELDS/MAJORS: All Areas of Study

One scholarship is available for students who graduated from Holyoke Catholic High School and for students at Amherst College or Georgetown Law School. Write to the address listed for information.

Community Foundation of Western Massachusetts
PO Box 15769
1500 Main St.
Springfield, MA 01115

1451
Maxine Williams Scholarship Fund

AMOUNT: Maximum: $1000 DEADLINE: February 1
FIELDS/MAJORS: Medical Assisting

Applicants must be committed to a medical assisting career, hold a high school diploma or the equivalent, and be enrolled in a postsecondary medical assisting program. Scholarships awarded on the basis of interest, need, and aptitude. Write to the address listed for details. Deadlines are February 1 and June 1.

American Association of Medical Assistants Endowment
20 N. Wacker Dr., Suite 1575
Chicago, IL 60606

1452
Maylon-Smith Scholarship Award

AMOUNT: Maximum: $1000 DEADLINE: February 1
FIELDS/MAJORS: Psychological Research

Open to graduate students who are lesbian, gay, bisexual or transgendered, pursuing studies primarily in California, submitting proposals for research into psychological issues of importance to gay, lesbian, and bisexual individuals, groups or communities. Must be enrolled in a graduate program and research must be on a lesbian, gay, or bisexual topic. Contact the address listed for further information.

American Psychological Association Division 44
Susan Kashubeck, Ph.D., Psychology Dept.
222 Psychology Building
Lubbock, TX 79409-2051

1453
Maynard and Clara Eldridge Scholarship Fund

AMOUNT: None Specified DEADLINE: None Specified
FIELDS/MAJORS: Agriculture, Veterinary Science, Environmental Studies

Awards for graduating seniors of Hampden Academy who plan to pursue a postsecondary degree in one of the fields listed above. Contact the Hampden Academy Guidance Office for more information.

Maine Community Foundation
245 East Maine St.
PO Box 148
Ellsworth, ME 04605

1454
Maynard Jensen American Legion Memorial Scholarship

AMOUNT: Maximum: $500 DEADLINE: March 1
FIELDS/MAJORS: All Areas of Study

Scholarships are available for Nebraska students who are U.S. citizens and descendants of American Legion or auxiliary members, POW's, MIA's, KIA's, or deceased veterans. Based upon scholastic ability and financial need. Write to the address listed or call (402) 464-6338 for additional information.

American Legion-Department of Nebraska
Department Adjutant
PO Box 5205
Lincoln, NE 68505

1455
MBA Scholarships

AMOUNT: $2500-$10000 DEADLINE: March 31
FIELDS/MAJORS: All Areas of Business

Awards for minority students who are enrolled in full-time graduate or doctoral business programs. Based on financial need, activities, and GPA. Write to the address below for more information.

National Black MBA Association, Inc.
180 N. Michigan Ave., Suite 1515
Chicago, IL 60601

1456
MBNA Scholarship Program

AMOUNT: $1000 DEADLINE: July 15
FIELDS/MAJORS: Automotive Technology

Awards for minority high school graduates who have successfully completed at least two years in the high school auto mechanic program, or have aspirations to pursue a career in the automotive industry. For students in the Chicago metropolitan area with a GPA of 2.5 or greater. Write to the address below for more information.

Mercedes-Benz of North America
Ms. Gina Blake, Chicago Urban League
4510 South Michigan Ave.
Chicago, IL 60653

1457
McAllister Memorial, Donald Burnside Memorial Scholarships

AMOUNT: Maximum: $1000 DEADLINE: March 31
FIELDS/MAJORS: Aviation

Open to college juniors and seniors who are U.S. citizens enrolled in a non-engineering college curriculum leading to a degree in the field of aviation. Must have a minimum GPA of 3.25 and have at least one semester/quarter to be completed after September. Each scholarship is valued at $1000. Contact the address listed for further information about both awards. Be sure to include a SASE for a reply.

AOPA Air Safety Foundation
Ms. Mary Ann Eiff
314 Wildwood Ln.
Lafayette, IN 47905

1458
MCAP Scholarship Grant

AMOUNT: $500-$3000 DEADLINE: April 1
FIELDS/MAJORS: Construction, Civil Engineering, Construction Management

Scholarships for sophomores and juniors enrolled full-time in a civil engineering, construction, or construction management program at a Massachusetts college or university. Interested students must submit completed applications and transcripts of grades by the deadline date listed above. Write to the address below for details.

Massachusetts Construction Advancement Program
Scholarship Selection Board
888 Worcester St.
Wellesley, MA 02181

1459
McCurdy Memorial Scholarship

AMOUNT: Maximum: $1200 DEADLINE: March 31
FIELDS/MAJORS: All Areas of Study

Open to students who are residents of Calhoun County, Michigan. Contact Michael C. Jordan, Attorney, at the address listed for further information or call (616) 962-9591.

McCurdy Memorial Scholarship Foundation
Wagner and Jordan Law Offices
134 W. Van Buren St.
Battle Creek, MI 49017

1460
McDonnell Douglas Scholarship Program

AMOUNT: $1500   DEADLINE: March 5
FIELDS/MAJORS: All Areas of Study

Scholarships available to dependent children, step-children, and adopted children of employees of McDonnell Douglas Companies (or subsidiary or component company). Must be graduating high school senior and rank in the top third of graduating class. The actual deadline for this award is the first Friday in March. Number of awards vary from year to year. This year there will be thirty-two awards offered. Write to the address below for details, or have your parent contact the personnel office at his or her workplace. Must have a GPA of at least 3.0.

McDonnell Douglas Scholarship Foundation
Chairman Scholarship Committee
3855 Lakewood Blvd.
Long Beach, CA 90846

1461
McKnight Awards in Neuroscience

AMOUNT: None Specified   DEADLINE: None Specified
FIELDS/MAJORS: Neuroscience

Awards for students at the doctoral or postdoctoral level who are doing research in the area of neuroscience. Write to the address below for more information.

McKnight Endowment Fund for Neuroscience
600 TCF Tower
121 South Eighth St.
Minneapolis, MN 55402

1462
McKnight Black Doctoral Fellowship Program

AMOUNT: Maximum: $5000   DEADLINE: January 15
FIELDS/MAJORS: See Below

Fellowships for African-American doctoral students at participating Florida universities. For areas of study except: M.D., D.B.A., D.D.S., J.D., or D.V.M. The applicant must be a U.S. citizen. Write to the address below for details, or contact the academic department heads of your school.

Florida Endowment Fund for Higher Education
201 E. Kennedy Blvd., Suite 1525
Tampa, FL 33602

1463
Medical and Physician Assistant Student Loan for Service Program

AMOUNT: Maximum: $12000   DEADLINE: None Specified
FIELDS/MAJORS: Medicine

Loans open to New Mexico residents who are in medicine or studying in a physician assistants program in a New Mexico school. Loan may be forgiven by working in a medically underserved area of New Mexico. Must be U.S. citizens or legal residents who can demonstrate financial need. Write to the address listed for further information.

New Mexico Commission on Higher Education
Financial Aid and Student Services
PO Box 15910
Santa Fe, NM 87506

1464
Medical Scholarship Program

AMOUNT: Maximum: $2500   DEADLINE: May 15
FIELDS/MAJORS: Medicine (all Areas), Osteopathic Medicine

Scholarships for Georgia residents who have been accepted or matriculated into an M.D. or D.O. program. Recipient must agree to practice in a selected town in Georgia (all of the selected towns have populations of less than fifteen thousand) one year for each year of the award. Write to the address below for details.

Georgia State Medical Education Board
244 Washington St. SW, Room 574 J
Atlanta, GA 30334

1465
Medical Student Fellowships

AMOUNT: $2000   DEADLINE: March 1
FIELDS/MAJORS: Medicine-Epilepsy Research

Research grants for medical students to perform research projects related to epilepsy. A faculty advisor/preceptor must accept responsibility and supervision of the study. Write to the address below for details.

Epilepsy Foundation of America
Fellowship Programs
4351 Garden City Dr.
Landover, MD 20785

1466
Medical Student Loan Program

AMOUNT: None Specified DEADLINE: None Specified
FIELDS/MAJORS: Medicine

Loan for full-time medical students at an approved West Virginia school of medicine. Applicants must not be in default on any previous student loans, and they must meet any designated academic standards that have been set. Loans will be forgiven at a rate of $5000 for each period of twelve consecutive months of full-time practice in a medically underserved area in West Virginia. Write to the address listed for more information.

West Virginia Student and Educational Services
Loan Administrator
PO Box 4007
Charleston, WV 25364

1467
Medical/Science Research Grants

AMOUNT: Maximum: $35000 DEADLINE: March 1
FIELDS/MAJORS: Cancer Research

Grants for younger faculty or scientists beginning new projects. Must be investigators at Massachusetts institutions. A second deadline date is September 1. Contact the address below for further information.

American Cancer Society
30 Speen St.
Framingham, MA 01701

1468
Mel Larson Journalism Scholarship

AMOUNT: $1000-$2000 DEADLINE: April 1
FIELDS/MAJORS: Print Journalism

Scholarships for students majoring or minoring in print journalism or any form of Christian journalism. For study in religious and secular programs at U.S. and Canadian colleges. Must be a juniors or seniors and have a GPA of at least 3.0. Not for broadcast journalism studies. Write to the address below for details.

Evangelical Press Association, Inc.
Ronald E. Wilson, Exec Director
485 Panorama Rd.
Earlysville, VA 22936

1469
Mellon Fellowships in Humanistic Studies

AMOUNT: Maximum: $14000 DEADLINE: December 31
FIELDS/MAJORS: Humanities

Beginning graduate students only. Program is designed to attract and support fresh talent of outstanding ability enrolled in a program leading to a Ph.D. in one of the humanistic disciplines. Must be a U.S. citizen or permanent resident. Fellowships do not support the more quantifiable social sciences (law, library science, social work, education). Eighty awards offered annually. Write to the address listed for details. The deadline to request an application is December 8. Must have a GPA of at least 3.0.

Woodrow Wilson National Fellowship Foundation
CN 5329
Princeton, NJ 08543

1470
Mellon Postdoctoral Research Fellowships

AMOUNT: None Specified DEADLINE: January 20
FIELDS/MAJORS: History, Humanities, Linguistics

Six- to eleven-month fellowships for residential research program at Newberry. Available for postdoctoral research in any subject relevant to the Library. Award is for up to $2800 monthly. Applicants must be citizens of the U.S. or foreign nationals who have been residents in the U.S. for at least three years. Preference is given to applicants who have not held major fellowships or grants in the previous three years. Write to the address listed for details or call (312) 255-3666.

Newberry Library
Committee on Awards
60 W. Walton St.
Chicago, IL 60610

1471
Melva T. Owen Memorial Scholarship

AMOUNT: Maximum: $3000 DEADLINE: March 1
FIELDS/MAJORS: All Areas of Study

Scholarship for an undergraduate student. Must be legally blind. Three awards offered annually. Write to the address listed or call (202) 467-5081 or 1-800-424-8666 for details. Must have a GPA of at least 2.8.

American Council of the Blind
Scholarship Coordinator
1155 15th St. NW, Suite 720
Washington, DC 20005

1472
Memorial Conservation Scholarships

AMOUNT: $1000 DEADLINE: October 24
FIELDS/MAJORS: Conservation and Related Fields

One scholarship is offered to a New Jersey resident in their junior or senior year in college majoring in a field related to the conservation of natural resources. Based on financial need, academic ability, and involvement in extracurricular activities related to conservation. Write to the address below for details.

New Jersey Department of Agriculture
New Jersey Assoc. of Conservation Dists.
C/O NJDA-CN 330, Room 204
Trenton, NJ 08625

1473
Memorial Education Fellowship

AMOUNT: $2000 DEADLINE: March 1
FIELDS/MAJORS: Varies

Applicants must be women maintaining legal residence in Massachusetts for at least five years and present a letter of endorsement from the sponsoring Women's Club in your community. These awards are for graduate study. Write to the address below for details, be sure to include a SASE.

General Federation of Women's Clubs of Massachusetts
Chairman of Trustees, 245 Dutton Road
PO Box 679
Sudbury, MA 01776

1474
Mensa Essay Contest

AMOUNT: $200-$1000 DEADLINE: February 28
FIELDS/MAJORS: All Areas of Study

Contest open to high school seniors and college students who are members of Mensa. The essay's theme is educational plans. Scholarship applications with full contest details can be obtained from guidance counselors or financial aid officers, or by sending a SASE to the address below.

American Mensa Education and Research Foundation
Scholarship Chairman
3437 W. 7th St., #264
Ft. Worth, TX 76107

1475
Mental Health Minority Research Fellowship Program

AMOUNT: None Specified DEADLINE: February 28
FIELDS/MAJORS: Mental Health Research

Awards for minorities who have a master's degree in social work and will begin full-time study leading to a doctoral degree or are already in a doctoral social work program. Applicants must be U.S. citizens or permanent residents and be pursuing a career in mental health research. Write to the address below for more information.

National Institute of Mental Health
1600 Duke St., #300
Alexandria, VA 22314

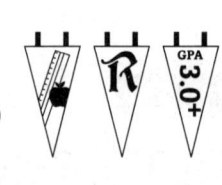

1476
Mental Retardation Scholastic Achievement Scholarship

AMOUNT: Maximum: $1000 DEADLINE: March 15
FIELDS/MAJORS: Mental Retardation (Special Education, Mental Health)

Scholarships for juniors and seniors who are communicant members of a Lutheran congregation and working toward a career in the field of mental retardation. Must have a GPA of at least 3.0. Write to the address listed for details.

Bethesda Lutheran Homes and Services, Inc.
National Christian Resource Center
700 Hoffmann Dr.
Watertown, WI 53094

1477
Mentor Graphics Scholarship

AMOUNT: None Specified DEADLINE: None Specified
FIELDS/MAJORS: Computer Science, Computer Engineering, Electrical Engineering

Open to Oregon residents who are U.S. citizens and entering junior or senior year at a four-year school. Preference to a female African or Hispanic-American. Recipients may reapply and compete annually. Contact the address below for further information.

Oregon State Scholarship Commission
Private Awards
1500 Valley River Dr., #100
Eugene, OR 97401-2130

1478
Mercer County Retired Teachers Scholarship

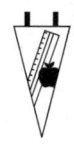

AMOUNT: $300-$500   DEADLINE: April 10
FIELDS/MAJORS: Teaching/Education

Scholarships for Mercer County residents who intend to pursue a career in teaching. Four awards per year. Based on need, academics, community activities, desire to enter field of education, and effort to help yourself. Applications are available from high school guidance counselors, area college scholarship counselors, or from the address below.

Mercer County Retired Teachers Association Scholarship
   Committee
Mrs. Elloise L. Lilliman, Chairperson
1202 Fourteenth St., Box 206
Viola, IL 61486

1479
Merck/AGS New Investigator Awards

AMOUNT: $2000   DEADLINE: December 8
FIELDS/MAJORS: Geriatrics

Awards are restricted to fellows-in-training and new, junior investigators holding an academic appointment not longer than five years post-fellowship. Awards will be chosen based on originality, scientific merit, relevance of the research, and overall academic accomplishments. Write to the address listed for more information.

American Geriatrics Society
770 Lexington Ave., Suite 300
New York, NY 10021

1480
Meridian Mutual Scholarships

AMOUNT: None Specified   DEADLINE: None Specified
FIELDS/MAJORS: All Areas of Study

Awards for children of employees or licensed agents of Meridian Mutual Insurance Company, its subsidiaries, and affiliates. Based primarily on academic achievements. Write to the address listed for more information.

Meridian Mutual Foundation, Inc.
2955 North Meridian St.
PO Box 1980
Indianapolis, IN 46206

1481
Merit Recognition Scholarship (MRS) Program

AMOUNT: $1000   DEADLINE: None Specified
FIELDS/MAJORS: All Areas of Study

Scholarship open to qualified students who rank in the top 5% of an accredited Illinois high school at the end of the seventh semester. Recipients must use the award within one year of high school graduation, and must be enrolled at least half-time. Must be a U.S. citizen or permanent resident and an Illinois resident. Contact your school's guidance counselor or principal for further information. Must have a GPA of at least 3.8.

Illinois Student Assistance Commission
1755 Lake Cook Road
Deerfield, IL 60015

1482
Mervin and Gena Leonard (of the Oregon Community Foundation)

AMOUNT: None Specified   DEADLINE: March 1
FIELDS/MAJORS: All Areas of Study

Open to high school seniors and undergraduates who are U.S. citizens and residents of Morrow or Umatilla counties. Students may apply and compete annually. Awards are to be used at Oregon public colleges. Contact the address listed for further information.

Oregon State Scholarship Commission
Private Awards
1500 Valley River Dr., #100
Eugene, OR 97401-2130

1483
MESBEC and NALE Programs

AMOUNT: None Specified   DEADLINE: September 15
FIELDS/MAJORS: All Areas of Study

Grants, loans, or combination awards awarded competitively to students who are at least one-quarter degree Native American. GPA of at least 3.0 required. Based on goals and potential for improving the lives of Indian peoples. For undergraduate or graduate study at any accredited college/university in the United States. Must have financial need and attend school full-time. Write to the address below for details.

Native American Scholarship Fund
Scholarship Programs
8200 Mountain Rd NE, Suite 203
Albuquerque, NM 87110

1484
Metropolitan Museum of Art Internship for Graduate Students

AMOUNT: $2500-$2750   DEADLINE: January 23
FIELDS/MAJORS: Art History, Art Conservation

Internships for individuals who have completed one year of graduate work in art history or a related field. Program runs for ten weeks from June through August and is full-time. Orientation required. Specific duties depend upon the needs of the Museum. Ethnically diverse students are encouraged to apply. Write to the address listed for additional information.

Metropolitan Museum of Art
Internship Programs
1000 Fifth Ave.
New York, NY 10028-0198

1485
Mexican American Grocers Association Scholarships

AMOUNT: None Specified   DEADLINE: July 31
FIELDS/MAJORS: Business

Open to sophomore or above college students of Hispanic descent studying a business-related field. Must show financial need. Renewable. Must have a GPA of at least 2.5. Write to the address below for more details. You must include a SASE for a reply.

Mexican American Grocers Association
Ms. Rosemarie Vega
405 N. San Fernando Rd.
Los Angeles, CA 90031

1486
MIA/KIA Dependents' Scholarship

AMOUNT: None Specified   DEADLINE: August 1
FIELDS/MAJORS: All Areas of Study

Scholarship open to all full-time undergraduate/graduate students and high school seniors who are dependent children or spouses of persons who were declared killed in action, missing in action, or prisoners of war in 1960 or after. Must attend an Arkansas school and be a state resident. Additional deadlines are: December 1 for the spring term, May 1 for the summer I term, and July 1 for the summer II term. Write to the address below for details.

Arkansas Department of Higher Education
Financial Aid Division
114 East Capitol
Little Rock, AR 72201

1487
Michael Curry Summer Internship

AMOUNT: Maximum: $1000   DEADLINE: November 1
FIELDS/MAJORS: Public Service

Internships. For Illinois residents who are at least a junior in college (graduate students are also eligible). Interns are placed with various state agencies in both Chicago and Springfield. Academic credit may be arranged. Must be a U.S. citizen. Write to the address below for details.

Illinois Governor's Office
Michael Curry Internship Program
2 1/2 State House
Springfield, IL 62706

1488
Michael J. Flosi Memorial Scholarship

AMOUNT: $500   DEADLINE: February 1
FIELDS/MAJORS: All Areas of Study

Scholarships available to high school seniors with at least a technician class amateur radio license who have been accepted at a two- or four-year college. Must be a resident of Indiana, Illinois, or Wisconsin. Must be U.S. citizens (or within three months of citizenship). Number of awards varies due to monetary considerations. Write to the address listed for information.

ARRL Foundation (American Radio Relay League)
Scholarship Program
225 Main St.
Newington, CT 06111

1489
Michael J. Quill Scholarship Fund

AMOUNT: $1200-$4800   DEADLINE: May 1
FIELDS/MAJORS: All Areas of Study

Applicants must be high school seniors and children of Transport Workers Union members (active, retired, disabled, or deceased). Must be/have been a member in good standing. Write to the address listed for more details.

Transport Workers Union of America, AFL-CIO
Michael J. Quill Scholarship Fund
80 West End Ave.
New York, NY 10023

1490
Michael Jewelers Foundation Scholarships

AMOUNT: Maximum: $1250   DEADLINE: March 1
FIELDS/MAJORS: Business

Open to incoming freshmen at the University of Connecticut who are Connecticut residents. Must be accepted/enrolled in a four-year program. Must also have played interscholastic athletics. Based on sports and community service. Renewable if recipients maintain preset standards. Contact your local Michael Jewelers for information and an application or call Mr. John Michaels, (203) 597-4905.

Michael Jewelers Foundation
Any Michaels Jewelers Store

1491
Michael Kraus Research Grants

AMOUNT: Maximum: $1000   DEADLINE: February 2
FIELDS/MAJORS: History-American Colonial

Three grants are available to American Historical Association members for research in American colonial history, with preference given to the intercultural aspects of American and European relations. Write to the address listed for details.

American Historical Association
Award Administrator
400 A St. SE
Washington, DC 20003

1492
Michael Masser Honoring Whitney Houston and Boosey/Hawkes Young Awards

AMOUNT: None Specified   DEADLINE: None Specified
FIELDS/MAJORS: Music

Awards to high school seniors graduating from Fiorello H. Laguardia High School of Music and Art in New York city. Based primarily on excellence in any area of music. Contact the office at Laguardia High School for more information.

American Society of Composers, Authors, and Publishers
One Lincoln Plaza
New York, NY 10023

1493
Michael Metcalf Memorial Fund

AMOUNT: $2000-$5000   DEADLINE: January 30
FIELDS/MAJORS: All Areas of Study

Two to four scholarships are available for sophomore and junior Rhode Island residents. Write to the address listed for information.

Rhode Island Foundation
Special Funds Office
70 Elm St.
Providence, RI 02903

1494
Michael Reese Women's Board Scholarship

AMOUNT: None Specified   DEADLINE: March 1
FIELDS/MAJORS: Medicine

Open to women medical students who have completed at least one year of medical school, accredited by the American Medical Association, with a minimum GPA of 3.0. Must be legally domiciled in Cook County or the Chicago metro area. Information and applications available after December 1 from the address below.

Jewish Vocational Service
Academic Scholarship Program
1 S. Franklin St.
Chicago, IL 60606

1495
Michigan Mortuary Science Foundation Grants

AMOUNT: $500-$2000   DEADLINE: December 8
FIELDS/MAJORS: Mortuary Science

Awards for full-time mortuary science students attending Wayne State University or a Michigan resident attending any accredited Michigan school, full-time, majoring in mortuary science. Write to the address below for more information.

Michigan Funeral Director Association
PO Box 27158
Lansing, MI 48909

1496
Michigan Scholarship Challenge Program

AMOUNT: Maximum: $1000   DEADLINE: April 15
FIELDS/MAJORS: Travel and Tourism, Hotel/Motel Management

Awards for Michigan residents in one of the areas listed above who are enrolled in a Michigan college full-time. Must have a GPA of 3.0 or better and be entering junior or senior year. Write to the address listed or call 1-800-682-8886 ext. 4251 for more information.

National Tourism Foundation
546 East Main St.
PO Box 3071
Lexington, KY 40596

1497
Midas Scholarships for Sons and Daughters

AMOUNT: Maximum: $1000   DEADLINE: May 31
FIELDS/MAJORS: All Areas of Study

Scholarships for students whose parents are employed by Midas International Corporation. Have your parent contact the human resources office at his or her workplace.

Midas International Corporation
Midas Scholarship Program
225 N. Michigan Ave.
Chicago, IL 60601

1498
Mildred Martignone Nurse Scholarship

AMOUNT: None Specified   DEADLINE: March 1
FIELDS/MAJORS: Nursing

Open to residents of District 7, Oregon Nurses Association, Umatilla County who are U.S. citizens. Must be entering final year of an accredited nursing program with a minimum GPA of 2.5. This is a one-time award. Contact the address below for further information.

Oregon State Scholarship Commission
Private Awards
1500 Valley River Dr., #100
Eugene, OR 97401-2130

1499
Miles and Shirley Fiterman Foundation Basic Research Awards

AMOUNT: $25000   DEADLINE: January 9
FIELDS/MAJORS: Gastrointestinal, Liver Function or Related Diseases

Applicants must be M.D.'s or Ph.D.'s holding full-time faculty positions at universities or institutions. Must be an individual member of any of the ADHF member organizations and below the level of assistant professor. Awards to those whose goal is a research career. Two awards are given annually. Contact the address below for further information or Web sites: http://www.gastro.org; http://www.asge.org; or http://hepar-sfgh.ucsf.edu.

American Digestive Health Foundation
Ms. Irene Kuo
7910 Woodmont Ave., 7th Floor
Bethesda, MD 20814

1500
Miles and Shirley Fiterman Foundation Clinical Research Awards

AMOUNT: $25000   DEADLINE: January 9
FIELDS/MAJORS: Clinical Research in hepatomegaly, nutrition, or gastroenterology

Applicants should be active investigators, with considerable achievements to date, but with on-going research. Must be an individual member of any of the ADHF member organizations. Young and mid-level investigators are encouraged to apply. Contact the address below for further information or Web sites: http://www.gastro.org; http://www.asge.org; or http://hepar-sfgh.ucsf.edu.

American Digestive Health Foundation
Ms. Irene Kuo
7910 Woodmont Ave., 7th Floor
Bethesda, MD 20814

1501
Miles Gray Memorial Scholarship

AMOUNT: Maximum: $350   DEADLINE: June 2
FIELDS/MAJORS: All Areas of Study

Scholarships are available to undergraduates who are members of Tau Kappa Epsilon. Must have demonstrated leadership capability within his chapter, on campus, or in the community. Must have a GPA of 2.5 or higher and be a full-time student in good standing. Write to the address listed for more information.

TKE Educational Foundation
8645 Founders Road
Indianapolis, IN 46268

1502
Milk Marketing Scholarship

AMOUNT: $500-$1000 DEADLINE: March 15
FIELDS/MAJORS: Dairy/Animal Science, Agriculture, Food/Nutrition Sciences

Scholarships for college sophomores, juniors, and seniors majoring in dairy sciences or food-related industry. Must have at least a 2.5 GPA. Six awards for $500 and one award for $1000 are offered annually. Dairy industry career is encouraged but not required. Write to at the address listed for details or call (614) 878-5333.

National Dairy Shrine Dairy Management, Inc.
Maurice Core
1224 Alton Darby Creek
Columbus, OH 43228-9792

1503
Millhollon Educational Trust Estate Loans

AMOUNT: Maximum: $1500 DEADLINE: July 1
FIELDS/MAJORS: All Areas of Study

Loans available to residents of Texas, under the age of twenty-five, planning to enroll in an accredited institution of higher education for the following term, with a minimum of 12 semester hours. A minimum GPA of 2.5 is required. The loan has a current interest rate of 8%. The payments and interest will begin ninety days after graduation or termination of school. Write to the address listed for details.

Millhollon Educational Trust Estate
309 West St. Anna
PO Box 643
Stanton, TX 79782

1504
Milton McKevett Teague Scholarships

AMOUNT: $1000-$2000 DEADLINE: April 8
FIELDS/MAJORS: Agriculture

Awards for graduating high school seniors, high school graduates, or holders of GED who are enrolled, or intending to enroll, as a candidate for a degree at a fully accredited college, vocation, trade, or business school. Applicants must have resided in Ventura County continuously for at least three years at the time of application. Write to the address listed or contact your high school counselor for more information.

Ventura County Community Fund
1355 Del Norte Road
Camarillo, CA 93010

1505
Minnesota Academic Excellence Scholarship

AMOUNT: None Specified
DEADLINE: None Specified
FIELDS/MAJORS: English, Writing, Fine Arts, Language, Math, Science, Social Science

Scholarships for students who have demonstrated outstanding ability, achievement, and potential in one of the fields listed above. Scholarship is renewable for up to three additional academic years if the student continues to meet the program's academic standards. Applicants must be residents of Minnesota attending a Minnesota institution. Write to the address listed, or contact the financial aid office for details.

Minnesota Higher Education Coordinating Board
Capitol Square, Suite 400
550 Cedar St.
Saint Paul, MN 55101

1506
Minnesota Gay/Lesbian/Bisexual/Transgender Scholarships

AMOUNT: $500-$1000 DEADLINE: April 1
FIELDS/MAJORS: All Areas of Study

Open to Minnesota residents who are gay, lesbian, bisexual, or transgendered planning to attend a postsecondary educational institution during the next academic year. Contact the address listed for further information.

Minnesota Gay/Lesbian/Bisexual/Transgender Educational Fund
MN GLBT Awards Committee
PO Box 7275
Minneapolis, MN 55407-0275

1507
Minnesota Indian Scholarship Program

AMOUNT: Maximum: $1850 DEADLINE: None Specified
FIELDS/MAJORS: All Areas of Study

Scholarship for Minnesota residents who are one-fourth or more Indian ancestry. Applicants must be a member of a federally-recognized Indian tribe or eligible for enrollment in a tribe. For full-time study in Minnesota. Contact your tribal education office, the Minnesota Indian Scholarship Program, or write to the address listed for details.

Minnesota Higher Education Coordinating Board
C/O Joe Aitken, Indian Education
1819 Bemidji Ave.
Bemidji, MN 56601

1508
Minnesota Legacy Scholarship

AMOUNT: MAXIMUM: $750   DEADLINE: APRIL 15
FIELDS/MAJORS: Travel and Tourism, Hotel/Motel Management

Awards for Minnesota residents in one of the areas listed above who are enrolled in any two- or four-year college full-time. Must have a GPA of 3.0 or better and be entering junior or senior year. Write to the address listed or call 1-800-682-8886 ext. 4251 for more information.

National Tourism Foundation
546 East Main St.
PO Box 3071
Lexington, KY 40596

1509
Minnesota Legionnaire Insurance Trust Scholarships

AMOUNT: $500   DEADLINE: March 15
FIELDS/MAJORS: All Areas of Study

Scholarships are available for Minnesota residents who are or will be enrolled at a Minnesota college or university. Applicant must be a U.S. citizen and the child of a veteran. For more information, contact the address below. Must have a GPA of at least 3.0.

American Legion-Department of Minnesota
State Veterans Service Bldg.
St. Paul, MN 55155

1510
Minnie Pearl Scholarship Program

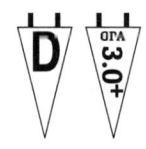

AMOUNT: $2000-$2500   DEADLINE: February 15
FIELDS/MAJORS: All Areas of Study

Scholarships for current high school seniors with significant bi-lateral hearing loss (must be mainstreamed) who have been accepted, but are not yet in attendance, at a junior college, college, university, or technical school. Must be a U.S. citizen and have a GPA of at least 3.0. Renewable with GPA of 3.0 ($500 renewal bonus with 3.5 GPA). Recipients will be notified in April. Write to the address listed for further information.

Ear Foundation at Baptist Hospital
Minnie Pearl Scholarship Program
1817 Patterson St.
Nashville, TN 37203

1511
Minorities in Government Finance Scholarship

AMOUNT: Maximum: $3500   DEADLINE: February 1
FIELDS/MAJORS: Public Administration, Accounting, Finance, Political Science, Economics, Business Administration

Open to upper division and graduate students who have a focus on government or nonprofit management. Applicants must be citizens or permanent residents of the U.S. or Canada and belong to one of the following groups: Black, Indian, Hispanic, Eskimo or Aleut, Asian, or Pacific Islander. Information may be available from the head of your department. If not, write to the address listed or call (312) 977-9700.

Government Finance Officers Association
Scholarship Committee
180 N. Michigan Ave., Suite 800
Chicago, IL 60601

1512
Minority Dental Laboratory Technician Scholarship

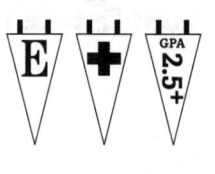

AMOUNT: $1000   DEADLINE: August 15
FIELDS/MAJORS: Dental Laboratory Technology

Applicants must be U.S. citizens and must be enrolled or planning to enroll in a dental lab technology program accredited by the Commission on Accreditation of the American Dental Association. Students must have a minimum GPA of 2.8 and demonstrate financial need. These awards are for minority students. Write to the address below for details.

ADA Endowment and Assistance Fund, Inc.
211 East Chicago Ave.
Chicago, IL 60611

1513
Minority Dental Student Scholarship Program

AMOUNT: $2000   DEADLINE: July 1
FIELDS/MAJORS: Dentistry

Awards for African-American, Hispanic, or Native American students entering their second year of a dental school accredited by the Commission on Dental Accreditation. Must demonstrate financial need and have a GPA of at least 2.5. Must be a U.S. citizens. Contact your school's financial aid office for more information.

ADA Endowment and Assistance Fund, Inc.
211 East Chicago Ave.
Chicago, IL 60611

1514
Minority Doctoral Assistance Loan-for-Service Program

AMOUNT: Maximum: $25000 DEADLINE: January 1
FIELDS/MAJORS: Education

Open to ethnic minorities and women to teach in an academic discipline in which ethnic minorities and women are demonstrably underrepresented in New Mexico public colleges and universities. Must have a bachelor's or master's from a New Mexico four-year college. Must have a sponsoring New Mexico four-year public institution and be approved by an academic committee of that sponsoring institution. Contact the graduate dean of a four-year public institution in New Mexico.

New Mexico Commission on Higher Education
Financial Aid and Student Services
PO Box 15910
Santa Fe, NM 87506

1515
Minority Doctoral Study Grant Program

AMOUNT: Maximum: $6000 DEADLINE: None Specified
FIELDS/MAJORS: Education, Education Administration

Grants are available for minority doctoral candidates studying at Oklahoma institutions. This program was created as an incentive to increase the number of minority faculty and staff in the Oklahoma State System of Higher Education. Recipients must agree to teach in a state system institution for a minimum of one year for each year of aid. Must be Oklahoma residents and nominated by the dean of your institution. Write to the address listed for information.

Oklahoma State Regents for Higher Education
Minority Doctoral Study Grant Program
500 Education Bldg. State Capitol Complex
Oklahoma City, OK 73105

1516
Minority Fellowship Program

AMOUNT: $8340-$10008 DEADLINE: January 15
FIELDS/MAJORS: Psychology

Fellowships for ethnic minority students pursuing doctoral degrees in APA-accredited doctoral programs in psychology. Must be a U.S. citizen or a permanent resident. Applicants must be in at least their second year of training. Fellowships are from ten to twelve months with a stipend of $834 per month. Write to the address below for more information.

American Psychological Association
Minority Fellowship Program
750 First St. NE
Washington, DC 20002

1517
Minority Fellowships

AMOUNT: $7800 DEADLINE: None Specified
FIELDS/MAJORS: Human Resource Management, Industrial Relations

Open to full-time minority students who are pursuing graduate degrees in Human Resource Management/Industrial Relations at one of thirteen consortium graduate schools. Must be a U.S. citizen. Write to the address below for more information.

Industrial Relations Council on Goals
PO Box 4363
East Lansing, MI 48826

1518
Minority Foundation Scholarship

AMOUNT: $2000-$4000 DEADLINE: February 1
FIELDS/MAJORS: All Areas of Study

For minority students who are full-time juniors, seniors, or graduate students and are Southern California residents. Must be attending the University of Southern California, have a minimum GPA of 3.0, and demonstrate involvement in community activities. Must not be employed more than twenty-eight hours per week. Based on academics and financial need. Contact the financial aid office, the address listed, or (213) 482-6300. If writing, you must include a SASE for a reply. The second deadline is April 1.

Golden State Minority Foundation
Scholarship Coordinator
1055 Wilshire Blvd., #1115
Los Angeles, CA 90017

1519
Minority Internship Program

AMOUNT: $2475-$3300
DEADLINE: February 15
FIELDS/MAJORS: Humanities, Art Studies, Anthropology, Astrophysics, Biology, History

Internships are available to minority undergraduate and graduate students at the Smithsonian, for research or museum-related activities. Programs range from nine to twelve weeks. Write to address below for details. Request the publication "Smithsonian Opportunities for Research and Study."

Smithsonian Institution
Office of Fellowships and Grants
955 L'enfant Plaza, Suite 7000
Washington, DC 20560

1520
Minority Master's Fellows Loan Program

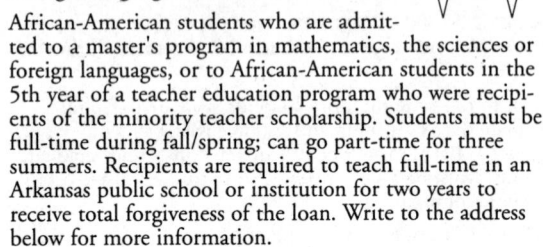

AMOUNT: $2500-$7500
DEADLINE: June 1
FIELDS/MAJORS: Mathematics, Science, Foreign Languages, Education

African-American students who are admitted to a master's program in mathematics, the sciences or foreign languages, or to African-American students in the 5th year of a teacher education program who were recipients of the minority teacher scholarship. Students must be full-time during fall/spring; can go part-time for three summers. Recipients are required to teach full-time in an Arkansas public school or institution for two years to receive total forgiveness of the loan. Write to the address below for more information.

Arkansas Department of Higher Education
Financial Aid Division
114 East Capitol
Little Rock, AR 72201

1521
Minority Medical Faculty Development Program

AMOUNT: $75000 DEADLINE: March 28
FIELDS/MAJORS: Medicine/Education

Applicants must be minority physicians who are U.S. citizens, have excelled in their education, are now completing or will have completed formal clinical training, and are committed to academic careers. Minorities here are African- and Mexican-Americans, Native Americans, and mainland Puerto Ricans who have completed college on the mainland. Fellowships aid research and last four years. Write to the address below for additional information.

Robert Wood Johnson Foundation
James R. Gavin III, M.D, Ph.D., Program
4733 Bethesda Ave, Suite 350
Bethesda, MD 20814

1522
Minority Physical Therapist Professional Scholarships

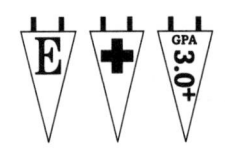

AMOUNT: Maximum: $2000 DEADLINE: March 1
FIELDS/MAJORS: Physical Therapy

Open to California residents who are currently enrolled in accredited physical therapy programs in a California school (accredited by the Commission of Accreditation of Physical Therapy Education-CAPTE). Must be members of groups including, but not limited to African-American, Asian/Pacific Islander, Native American, and Hispanic/Latino. Must be a U.S. citizen or permanent resident, completed one quarter/semester, have a minimum GPA of 3.0, and be a student member of the American Physical Therapy Association. Contact the address listed for further information or call (916) 929-2782. Applications may be requested between January 15 and February 15 of each year.

California Physical Therapy Fund, Inc.
Scholarship Coordinator
2295 Gateway Oaks Dr., #200
Sacramento, CA 95833

1523
Minority Professional Study Grant Program

AMOUNT: Maximum: $4000 DEADLINE: None Specified
FIELDS/MAJORS: Medicine, Dentistry, Law, Veterinary Medicine, Optometry

Grants are available for minority students studying at Oklahoma institutions. This program was created as an incentive to increase the number of minority groups in the programs listed above. Must be U.S. citizens to apply. Applicants are nominated annually by the deans of Oklahoma institutions. Write to the address listed for information.

Oklahoma State Regents for Higher Education
Minority Professional Study Program
500 Education Bldg. State Capitol Complex
Oklahoma City, OK 73105

1524
Minority Scholarship

AMOUNT: $1000 DEADLINE: April 11
FIELDS/MAJORS: Broadcasting, Journalism, Advertising, Communications (Graphic Etc.)

Applicants must be a minority and a resident of the following California counties: Santa Cruz, Santa Clara, Monterey, or San Benito. Must be enrolled at or accepted into an accredited California school studying a field related to broadcasting. Write to the address below for details.

KNTV Channel 11
Scholarship Board
645 Park Ave.
San Jose, CA 95110

1525
Minority Scholarship

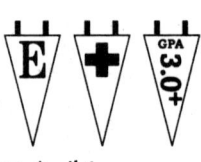

AMOUNT: None Specified DEADLINE: April 1
FIELDS/MAJORS: Dental Hygiene

Scholarships for students of underrepresented groups who have completed at lease one year of a full-time accredited program in Dental Hygiene. Must have a GPA of at least 3.0. Based on need and career goals. Males are also considered minorities for this award. Write to the address below for more information.

American Dental Hygienists' Association Institute for Oral Health
444 N. Michigan Ave., Suite 3400
Chicago, IL 60611

1526
Minority Scholarship Program

AMOUNT: $2500 DEADLINE: October 15
FIELDS/MAJORS: Psychology

Award for ethnic minority students accepted into a doctoral level psychology program in the state of California. Based on community involvement, leadership, knowledge of ethnic minority/cultural issues, career plans, and financial need. Scholarships are given to students in their first year of study. Write to the address below for more information.

California Psychological Association Foundation
1022 G St.
Sacramento, CA 95814

1527
Minority Scholarship Program

AMOUNT: Maximum: $2500 DEADLINE: October 15
FIELDS/MAJORS: Psychology

Scholarships open to minority students who have been accepted in a first year, full-time, doctoral level psychology program in a California school. Candidates must be considered a member of one or more of these established ethnic minority groups: African/Hispanic/Latino/Asian-American, Native American, Alaskan Native, or Pacific Islander. Scholarships are not made based solely on financial need, but it is taken into account. Winners will be announced in mid-December. Information and applications are sent to the financial aid offices of California graduate schools in early summer. Get the information from that source instead of writing to the address indicated.

California State Psychological Association Foundation
CSPA Scholarship Department
1022 G St.
Sacramento, CA 95814-0817

1528
Minority Scholarships

AMOUNT: $500-$2500 DEADLINE: January 15
FIELDS/MAJORS: Architecture

Twenty-five scholarships for minority high school seniors and college freshman who are entering degree programs at schools of architecture. Write to the address listed for more details.

American Architectural Foundation
AIA/AAF Scholarship Program Director
1735 New York Ave. NW
Washington, DC 20006

1529
Minority Teachers of Illinois and David A. Debolt Teacher Scholarships

AMOUNT: $5000 DEADLINE: None Specified
FIELDS/MAJORS: Preschool, Elementary, Secondary Education

Scholarships open to African-American, Native American, Hispanic, or Asian students who plan to become teachers. Must be full-time undergraduates, at sophomore level or above. Must sign a teaching commitment to teach one year for each year assistance is received. Must be U.S. citizens or permanent residents and Illinois residents. Contact the address below for further information about both scholarships.

Illinois Student Assistance Commission
1755 Lake Cook Road
Deerfield, IL 60015

1530
Minority Teachers Scholarship

AMOUNT: $5000 DEADLINE: June 1
FIELDS/MAJORS: Education

African-American college juniors enrolled full-time, admitted to an approved program resulting in teacher certification. Must have at least a 2.5 cumulative GPA. New awards are made to juniors only; continuing awards are made to seniors only. For Arkansas residents. Write to the address below for more information.

Arkansas Department of Higher Education
Financial Aid Division
114 East Capitol
Little Rock, AR 72201

1531
Minority Teaching Fellows Program

AMOUNT: $5000 DEADLINE: April 15
FIELDS/MAJORS: Education

For freshmen who are Tennessee residents, entering teaching education programs in Tennessee. Must have a GPA of 2.5 or better and agree to teach at a K-12 level in a Tennessee public school for one year. Contact your high school guidance office or the financial aid office for more information.

Tennessee Student Assistance Corporation
Suite 1950 Parkway Towers
404 James Robertson Parkway
Nashville, TN 37243

1532
Minority/Disadvantaged Scholarship Program

AMOUNT: $500-$3000 DEADLINE: January 17
FIELDS/MAJORS: Architecture

Applicants must be minority and/or disadvantaged high school seniors or current freshmen who are attending/plan to attend an NAAB school. Must be able to demonstrate financial need. Must be nominated by architect, counselor, pastor, dean of architectural school, etc. Nominations are due December 12, and the application and other paperwork is due January 17. Twenty awards per year. Renewable for up to three years. Students must be U.S. citizens and have a GPA of 2.0 or above. Write to "Minority/Disadvantaged Scholarship Program" at the address listed for details.

American Institute of Architects
American Architectural Foundation
1735 New York Ave., NW
Washington, DC 20006

1533
Minoru Yasui Memorial Scholarship

AMOUNT: Maximum: $1000 DEADLINE: April 15
FIELDS/MAJORS: Broadcasting

Open to Asian-American male students who show promise as broadcasters. Based on academics, sensitivity to Asian-American issues (as demonstrated by community involvement), and financial need. Contact your local AAJA chapter for further information, or request details from the address listed. Be sure to enclose a SASE with your request for information. Must have a GPA of at least 2.8.

Asian-American Journalists Association
Scholarship Committee
1765 Sutter St. Suite 1000
San Francisco, CA 94115

1534
Miriam A. Steel Scholarship

AMOUNT: Maximum: $1000 DEADLINE: February 15
FIELDS/MAJORS: Horticulture, Landscape Architecture, Forestry, Botany, Agronomy, Plant Pathology, Environmental Control, City Planning, Land Management

Open to high school seniors who are Pennsylvania residents. Must have a minimum GPA of 2.8. Must be sponsored by a Federated Garden Club in Pennsylvania and be able to demonstrate financial need. Preference given to a High School Gardener or member of the FFA or 4-H. References, a personal letter (regarding goals, background, and commitment), an official transcript for the current period, and the application signed by the sponsoring club's president will be required. A student may reapply if academics remain high and need is apparent. Contact a local club, the address listed, or (215) 643-0164 for details.

Garden Club Federation of Pennsylvania
Mrs. William A. Lamb, Scholarship Chair
925 Lorien Dr.
Gwynedd Valley, PA 19437-0216

1535
Miss Teenage America Contest

AMOUNT: Maximum: $10000 DEADLINE: September 15
FIELDS/MAJORS: All Areas of Study

Scholarships are available for young women under the age of nineteen with academic ability who are involved in school and community activities. The winner receives a $10,000 scholarship, a monthly column in Teen, and a year of travel and public appearances. Information and applications are available in the June and July issues of Teen. Must have a GPA of at least 3.2.

Teen Magazine
Peterson Publishing Company
6420 Wilshire Blvd.
Los Angeles, CA 90048

1536
Mississippi Funeral Directors Association Scholarships

AMOUNT: None Specified DEADLINE: September 15
FIELDS/MAJORS: Mortuary Science

Awards for Mississippi residents who have completed at least 15 credit hours in an accredited mortuary science school with no "D" in any required class and have a minimum GPA of 2.5. Must be a student member of the MFDA and recommended by a member of the MFDA. Second deadline date is May 15. Write to the address below for more information.

Mississippi Funeral Directors Association
PO Box 7576
Jackson, MS 39284

1537
Mississippi Resident Loans

AMOUNT: Maximum: $2000 DEADLINE: None Specified
FIELDS/MAJORS: All Areas of Study

Renewable loans offered to residents of Mississippi who demonstrate satisfactory academics, financial need, and a promise of financial responsibility. Must be U.S. citizens or permanent residents. Contact the address listed for further information or call (601) 939-9295. Must have a GPA of at least 2.5.

Field Co-Operative Association
Loan Committee
3560 Lakeland Dr., #607
Jackson, MS 39208

1538
Mississippi Scholarship

AMOUNT: $500 DEADLINE: February 1
FIELDS/MAJORS: Electronics, Communications, Related Fields

Scholarship available to students with any class amateur radio license, who are residents of and attend school in Mississippi. Must be less than thirty years of age. For full-time study only. Write to the address listed for information.

ARRL Foundation (American Radio Relay League)
Scholarship Program
225 Main St.
Newington, CT 06111

1539
Missouri Minority Teacher Education Scholarship

AMOUNT: Maximum: $3000
DEADLINE: February 15
FIELDS/MAJORS: Education, Math, Science

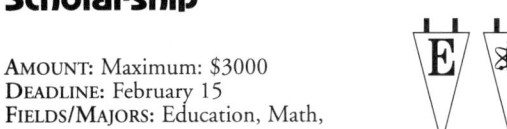

Open to minority Missouri students who are African/Asian/Hispanic or Native Americans. Freshmen and sophomores must be majoring in education and have ranked in the top quarter of high school class or completed 30 credit hours with a minimum GPA of 3.0. Adults returning to school or adults with a baccalaureate degree enrolled in an approved math or science education program are also eligible. Contact your high school guidance counselor, financial aid office, or college advisor to request an application.

Missouri Department of Elementary and Secondary Education
Scholarship Coordinator
PO Box 480
Jefferson City, MO 65102

1540
Missouri Minority Teacher Education Scholarship

AMOUNT: Maximum: $3000 DEADLINE: February 15
FIELDS/MAJORS: Math Education, Science Education

Open to students who are African-American, Asian-American, Hispanic-American, or Native American and are Missouri residents. Must rank in the top quarter of high school class and score at or above the 75th percentile on the ACT or SAT exams. Must be planning to teach in Missouri. Contact your high school counselor or the financial aid office or your college or university for further information. Must have a GPA of at least 3.0.

Missouri Department of Elementary and Secondary Education
Scholarship Coordinator
PO Box 480
Jefferson City, MO 65102

1541
Missouri Nurses Association Scholarship

AMOUNT: Maximum: $350 DEADLINE: March 31
FIELDS/MAJORS: Nursing

Open to nursing students in the final year of their programs. Applicants must be residents of the 15th district, which includes St. Charles, Lincoln, and Warren counties. A letter of introduction and a statement about their reasons for choosing nursing as a career will be required. Recipient will be notified by mail. Contact the address listed for further information.

Missouri Nurses Association, District 15
Marjory Wheeler
1345 W. Highway U
Troy, MO 63379

1542
Missouri Teacher Education Scholarship

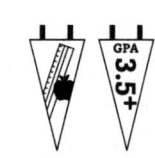

AMOUNT: Maximum: $2000 DEADLINE: February 15
FIELDS/MAJORS: Education

For Missouri high school seniors, college freshmen, or sophomores attending school in Missouri. Applicants must rank in the top 15% of their high school class or score in the top 15% on a college entry exam (ACT or SAT). Winners are notified in April of every year. Recipients must plan to be teachers in the state of Missouri. Contact your high school counselor, your financial aid office, or the address listed for more information. Must have a GPA of at least 3.6.

Missouri Department of Elementary and Secondary
  Education
Scholarship Coordinator
PO Box 480
Jefferson City, MO 65102

1543
Misty Wimberly Memorial Scholarship Fund

AMOUNT: Maximum: $1000 DEADLINE: May 31
FIELDS/MAJORS: All Areas of Study

Scholarships for graduating high school seniors from Nueces County. Must be past or present officer of FFA, FHA, 4-H, or Nueces County Council. Must have exhibited in Nueces County Junior Livestock Show. Write to the address below for complete information.

Coastal Bend Community Foundation
Mercantile Tower MT276
615 N. Upper Broadway, #860
Corpus Christi, TX 78477

1544
MLA Scholarship

AMOUNT: Maximum: $2000 DEADLINE: December 1
FIELDS/MAJORS: Medical Library Science

Graduate scholarship for students entering graduate school in medical librarianship or have at least half of the requirements to complete during the year following the granting of the scholarship. Must be studying in an ALA-accredited school. Grants support research, etc., into projects that will enhance the field of health science librarianship. Write to the address below for details.

Medical Library Association
Professional Development
6 N. Michigan Ave., Suite 300
Chicago, IL 60602

1545
Modesto Bee Minority Internship

AMOUNT: None Specified DEADLINE: December 31
FIELDS/MAJORS: Journalism, Photography, Graphics

Open to minority college students focusing on journalism, photography, and graphics. Write to the address listed for more information.

Modesto Bee
Sanders Lamont, Executive Editor
PO Box 5256
Modesto, CA 95352

1546
Modesto Bee Summer Internship

AMOUNT: None Specified DEADLINE: December 31
FIELDS/MAJORS: Journalism, Photography, Graphics

Open to college students focusing on journalism, reporting, editing, graphics, and photography. Write to the address listed for more information.

Modesto Bee
Sanders Lamont, Executive Editor
PO Box 5256
Modesto, CA 95352

1547
Montana Federation Scholarship

AMOUNT: Maximum: $1000 DEADLINE: May 1
FIELDS/MAJORS: Conservation, Horticulture, Park/Forestry, Floriculture, Related Areas

Open to Montana residents who are U.S. citizens and enrolled in the Montana university system. Must be at sophomore level or above, have a minimum GPA of 2.7, have potential for a successful future, and be able to demonstrate financial need. Contact the address listed for further information or call (406) 363-5693.

Montana Federation
Elizabeth Kehmeier
214 Wyant Ln.
Hamilton, MT 59840

1548
Montana Funeral Directors Association Scholarships

AMOUNT: $500-$1000 DEADLINE: June 1
FIELDS/MAJORS: Mortuary Science

One or two awards for residents of Montana studying mortuary science. Must be referred by a Montana FDA member and plan to return to Montana to work. Write to the address listed for more information.

Montana Funeral Directors Association
Steven C. Yeakel, Executive Director
PO Box 4267
Helena, MT 59604

1549
Montana Scholarship Challenge Program

AMOUNT: Maximum: $500 DEADLINE: April 15
FIELDS/MAJORS: Travel and Tourism, Hotel/Motel Management

Awards for Montana residents in one of the areas listed above who are enrolled in any two- or four-year college full-time. Must have a minimum GPA of 3.0 and be entering junior or senior year. Write to the address listed or call 1-800-682-8886 ext. 4251 for more information.

National Tourism Foundation
546 East Main St.
PO Box 3071
Lexington, KY 40596

1550
Monticello College Foundation Fellowship for Women

AMOUNT: Maximum: $12500 DEADLINE: January 20
FIELDS/MAJORS: Women's Studies, Literature, Humanities, History

Open to women with Ph.D. degrees. Preference will be given to applicants who are particularly concerned with the study of women, but study may be proposed in any field appropriate to Newberry's collections. Must be U.S. citizens. Fellowship is for six months work in residence at the Newberry Library. Write to the address listed or call (312) 255-3666 for complete details.

Newberry Library
Committee on Awards
60 W. Walton St.
Chicago, IL 60610

1551
Morris B. Ewing/ABS Scholarships

AMOUNT: Maximum: $1000 DEADLINE: July 1
FIELDS/MAJORS: All Fields of Study

Scholarships offered to members of the American Jersey Cattle Club who will be between sixteen and twenty-two years of age on January 1. This organization sponsors an essay contest as well as administers six other scholarship programs. Applicants may be high school seniors who are planning to enter college and current undergraduates. Write to the address below for details.

American Breeders Service/American Jersey Cattle Club
Sharon Abbott
6486 East Main St.
Reynoldsburg, OH 43068

1552
Morris Ewing Scholarship

AMOUNT: $500 DEADLINE: July 1
FIELDS/MAJORS: All Areas of Study

Scholarships are available to students involved in Jersey breeding who submit the best essays on the subject of breeding. Applicants must be age twenty-two or less. Write to the address below for details.

American Jersey Cattle Association/American Breeders Service
Scholarship Committee
6486 East Main St.
Reynoldsburg, OH 43068

1553
Morris K. Udall Dissertation Fellowships

AMOUNT: Maximum: $24000 DEADLINE: January 15
FIELDS/MAJORS: Public Policy

Open to doctoral candidates in the area of environmental public policy and conflict resolution who have the potential to make a significant contribution in the field. Must be full-time, in the final year of writing the dissertation, and anticipate receiving the doctoral degree at the end of the fellowship year. Must be U.S. citizens of permanent residents. Write to the address below for more information.

Morris K. Udall Dissertation Fellowship Program
Fellowship Coordinator
2201 N. Dodge St.
Iowa City, IA 52243-4030

1554
Morton A. Gibson Memorial Scholarships

AMOUNT: $2500 DEADLINE: May 30
FIELDS/MAJORS: All Areas of Study

Two grants for current high school seniors in the Metropolitan Washington area who have performed significant volunteer service in the local Jewish community or under the auspices of a Jewish organization. For full-time undergraduate study in the U.S. Based on volunteer service, need, and academics. Write to the address below or call (301) 881-3700 for details.

Jewish Social Service Agency of Metropolitan Washington
6123 Montrose Road
Rockville, MD 20852

1555
Morton B. Duggan, Jr. Memorial Scholarship

AMOUNT: Maximum: $1000 DEADLINE: June 30
FIELDS/MAJORS: Respiratory Therapy

Open to students who have completed at least one semester in an AMA-approved respiratory care program. Preference given to students from Georgia or South Carolina, but applications from students in all other states will be accepted. Must have a GPA of at least 3.0 and provide photocopy of birth certificate, social security card, immigration visa, or evidence of citizenship. Recipient will be selected by September 1. Write to the address listed for details.

American Respiratory Care Foundation
11030 Ables Ln.
Dallas, TX 75229

1556
Most Valuable Student Awards

AMOUNT: $1000-$5000 DEADLINE: January 10
FIELDS/MAJORS: All Areas of Study

Open to high school seniors who are U.S. citizens residing within the jurisdiction of a local Order of the Elks Lodge. Must be in the upper 5% of class with a 90% or better scholarship rating. Membership is not required. Based on academics, leadership, and financial need. Applications available after November 1. Applications must be filed with the local Lodge for entry into the judging process. Contact your local BPO Elks Lodge for details and an application. Their address may be found in your telephone directory. Information may also be obtained on the Elks' Web site: http://www.elks.org/enf/enf_scholar.cfm Applications are not available through the listed address, only from a local lodge or the Web site. Must have a GPA of at least 3.8.

Elks National Foundation
Scholarship Coordinator
2750 N. Lakeview Ave.
Chicago, IL 60614

1557
Mozelle and Willard Gold Memorial Scholarship

AMOUNT: Maximum: $3000 DEADLINE: March 31
FIELDS/MAJORS: All Areas of Study

Scholarship open to full-time students who are legally blind. Contact the address below for further information.

National Federation of the Blind
Mrs. Peggy Elliott, Chairman
814 Fifth Ave., #200
Grinnell, IA 50112

1558
Mr. and Mrs. Takashi Moriuchi Scholarship

AMOUNT: None Specified DEADLINE: April 1
FIELDS/MAJORS: All Areas of Study

Open to incoming freshmen who are members of Japanese ancestry and entering or enrolled at an accredited college or university. Applications and information may be obtained from local JACL chapters, district offices, and the national headquarters at the address listed, or call (415) 921-5225. Please indicate your level of study, and be certain to include a legal-sized SASE.

Japanese-American Citizens League
National Scholarship and Award Program
1765 Sutter St.
San Francisco, CA 94115

1559
Mr. Joseph P. Cunningham Memorial Scholarship

AMOUNT: None Specified DEADLINE: March 1
FIELDS/MAJORS: Business, Accounting

Two scholarships available to IIT juniors and seniors majoring in accounting or business administration. Applicants must be U.S. citizens and maintain at least a 2.0 GPA. Write to the address below for details.

Indiana Institute of Technology
Office of Scholarships and Financial Assistance
1600 East Washington Blvd.
Fort Wayne, IN 46803

1560
Mt. Pleasant Scholarship Foundation Awards

AMOUNT: $1000   DEADLINE: April 23
FIELDS/MAJORS: All Areas of Study

Scholarships for students residing in the east Cooper area. Based on academics and need. Write to the address below for details.

Mount Pleasant Scholarship Foundation
C/O J. Dodds
PO Box 745
Mount Pleasant, SC 29464

1561
Munson Auxiliary Scholarship

AMOUNT: $1500-$2500   DEADLINE: March 31
FIELDS/MAJORS: Health-Related Fields

Open to residents of Grand Traverse, Leelanau, Benzie, Kalkaska, Wexford, or Antrim counties. Must be residents for a period of at least six months. Applicants must be accepted into a health-related program of study in an accredited Michigan college. Winning applicants will be notified in writing by May 31. Contact the address listed for further information.

Munson Medical Center
Mary Frances James
2683 Green Meadows Dr.
Traverse City, MI 49684

1562
Munson Medical Center Auxiliary Scholarship

AMOUNT: $2300   DEADLINE: March 31
FIELDS/MAJORS: Health-Related

Awards for students from one of the following counties in a health-related field of study: Grand Traverse, Leelanau, Benzie, Kalkaska, Wexford, or Antrim, Michigan. Applicants must be undergraduates in a state-accredited college. Two or more awards per year. Write to the address below for more information.

Munson Medical Center Auxiliary
Ms. Mary Francis James
2683 Green Meadows Dr.
Traverse City, MI 49684

1563
Murphy Foundation Scholarships

AMOUNT: Maximum: $3000   DEADLINE: July 1
FIELDS/MAJORS: All Areas of Study

Open to residents of southern Arkansas who can demonstrate financial need. This need-based scholarship may be renewed if recipients maintain a minimum GPA of 3.0. Number and amount of awards vary, but the maximum amount is $3000. Contact the address listed for further information or (870) 862-4961.

Murphy Foundation
Ed Marsh, Union Building
200 N. Jefferson, #400
El Dorado, AR 71730

1564
Muscular Dystrophy Association Research Fellowship Program

AMOUNT: None Specified   DEADLINE: January 15
FIELDS/MAJORS: Medical Research, Neurology

Postdoctoral research fellowships for professionals or faculty members (in U.S. or abroad) who hold a Ph.D., M.D., or equivalent. Grants are from one to three years. Special consideration given to young investigators. Write to the address listed for complete details.

Muscular Dystrophy Association, Inc.
Research Department
3300 E. Sunrise Dr.
Tucson, AZ 85718

1565
Music Assistance Fund Scholarships

AMOUNT: $500-$2500   DEADLINE: December 16
FIELDS/MAJORS: Music, Instrumental

Scholarships for students of African-American descent (and similar heritage such as African-Caribbean, etc.) who are studying toward a career in this country's symphony orchestra. Must be a U.S. citizen. Based on auditions, recommendations, and need. Must be a student of orchestral instruments. (Note: voice, piano, saxophone, composition, and conducting are not included.) Write to the address below for details.

American Symphony Orchestra League
1156 Fifteenth St. NW
Suite 800
Washington, DC 20005

1566
Music Scholarships

AMOUNT: $500   DEADLINE: February 15
FIELDS/MAJORS: Music-Piano or Instrumental, Music Education, Music Therapy

Applicant must be a senior in a Massachusetts high school and present a letter of endorsement from a sponsoring Women's Club in your community. Auditions will be held to help determine recipients. Write to the address below for details, and be sure to include a SASE.

General Federation of Women's Clubs of Massachusetts
Chairman, Music Division
PO Box 679
Sudbury, MA 01776

1567
Myasthenia Gravis Foundation Fellowships

AMOUNT: None Specified   DEADLINE: November 1
FIELDS/MAJORS: Neuromuscular Medicine

Fellowships are available for postdoctoral scholars involved in clinical research related to Myasthenia Gravis (MG). Write to the address below for information.

Myasthenia Gravis Foundation of America
Fellowship Program
222 S. Riverside Plaza, Suite 1540
Chicago, IL 60606

1568
Myasthenia Gravis Foundation Nurses Research Fellowship

AMOUNT: None Specified   DEADLINE: February 1
FIELDS/MAJORS: Research Nursing

Award for currently licensed or registered professional nurses who are interested in research pertaining to problems faced by Myasthenia Gravis patients. Must be U.S. or Canadian citizens or permanent residents. Write to the address below for more information.

Myasthenia Gravis Foundation of America
222 S. Riverside Plaza
Suite 1540
Chicago, IL 60606

1569
Myron B. Foster Fund

AMOUNT: None Specified   DEADLINE: March 18
FIELDS/MAJORS: All Areas of Study

Awards for residents of Corinth pursuing postsecondary education. Contact the guidance office at Central High School for more details.

Maine Community Foundation
245 East Maine St.
PO Box 148
Ellsworth, ME 04605

1570
Myrtle and Earl Walker Scholarship

AMOUNT: Maximum: $500   DEADLINE: March 1
FIELDS/MAJORS: Manufacturing Engineering, Manufacturing Engineering Technology

Open to full-time undergraduates who have completed at least 30 credit hours in an ABET accredited degree program with a minimum GPA of 3.5. Write to the address listed for details.

Society of Manufacturing Engineering Education
    Foundation
One SME Dr.
PO Box 930
Dearborn, MI 48121

1571
NABWA Scholarships

AMOUNT: $5000-$10000   DEADLINE: February 15
FIELDS/MAJORS: Law

Scholarships for female minority law students in their first or second year of law school or those in their third year of a four-year program. Four to six awards offered annually. Write to the address below for information and an application.

National Association of Black Women Attorneys
Office of the President, Mabel D. Haden
3711 Macomb St. NW
Washington, DC 20016

1572
NAHJ Scholarships

AMOUNT: $1000-$2000   DEADLINE: February 27
FIELDS/MAJORS: Journalism, Print/Broadcast

For high school seniors, undergraduates, or graduate students majoring in journalism. Based on academic excellence, financial need, and interest in journalism as a career. Contact the address listed for further information. Must have a GPA of at least 2.5.

National Association of Hispanic Journalists
529 14th St. NW
1193 National Press Bldg.
Washington, DC 20045

1573
Namepa National Minority Scholarship Awards

AMOUNT: Maximum: $1000 DEADLINE: July 21
FIELDS/MAJORS: Engineering

Awards for minorities who are incoming freshmen and undergraduate transfer students. Freshmen must have a minimum GPA of 2.0 and an ACT score of 25 or SAT of 1000. Transfer students must have a minimum GPA of 3.0. Contact the address below for further information.

Namepa National Scholarship Fund
Namepa, Inc., Scholarship Chair
1133 W. Morse Blvd., #201
Winter Park, FL 32789

1574
Nancy Lorraine Jensen Memorial Scholarship Fund

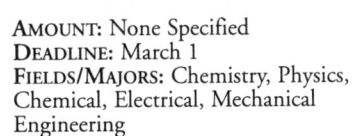

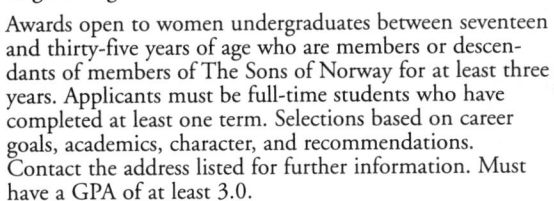

AMOUNT: None Specified
DEADLINE: March 1
FIELDS/MAJORS: Chemistry, Physics, Chemical, Electrical, Mechanical Engineering

Awards open to women undergraduates between seventeen and thirty-five years of age who are members or descendants of members of The Sons of Norway for at least three years. Applicants must be full-time students who have completed at least one term. Selections based on career goals, academics, character, and recommendations. Contact the address listed for further information. Must have a GPA of at least 3.0.

Sons of Norway Foundation
Sons Of Norway
1455 W. Lake St.
Minneapolis, MN 55408

1575
NASA Earth Science Graduate Student Research Program

AMOUNT: None Specified DEADLINE: March 12
FIELDS/MAJORS: Earth-Related Sciences

Fellowships for students enrolled full-time in a graduate program at a U.S. university and in a field supporting the study of earth as a system. Fifty awards per year. Additional information is available electronically via the Internet at: http://WWW.HQ.NASA.gov/office/MTPE/ or via anonymous FTP at: FTP.HP.NASA.gov/pub/MTPE. Paper copies of information received on-line will only be available to those who do not have access to the Internet.

NASA Earth System Science Fellowship Program
Code Ysp-44
Attn: Dr. Ghassem Asrar
Washington, DC 20546

1576
NASA Space Physiology Graduate Research Grant

AMOUNT: Maximum: $2500 DEADLINE: None Specified
FIELDS/MAJORS: Exercise Physiology, Musculoskeletal Physiology

Open to full-time graduate students for research in the areas of exercise, weightlessness, and musculoskeletal physiology. Contact the address listed for further information or call (317) 637-9200.

American College of Sports Medicine
Scholarship Coordinator
PO Box 1440
Indianapolis, IN 46206-1440

1577
Nate McKinney Memorial Scholarship

AMOUNT: $1000 DEADLINE: March 15
FIELDS/MAJORS: Music, Science, Athletics

Scholarships are available for graduating seniors of Gateway Regional High School in Huntington, Massachusetts, with an interest in two of the areas listed above. Must excel academically and demonstrate good citizenship. One award is given annually. Write to the address listed for information. Must have a GPA of at least 3.1.

Community Foundation of Western Massachusetts
PO Box 15769
1500 Main St.
Springfield, MA 01115

1578
Nathalie Rutherford Scholarship

AMOUNT: $1000 DEADLINE: March 27
FIELDS/MAJORS: Vocal Music

Scholarships for graduating high school seniors interested in pursuing a career in vocal music (Renaissance/Baroque, nineteenth, twentieth centuries songs or operatic arias). Must be from Port Chester, Rye, Rye Brook, Greenwich, Stamford, Darien, New Canaan, Norwalk, Westport, or Wilton. Write to the address below for details or call (203) 622-5136.

Greenwich Choral Society
PO Box 5
Greenwich, CT 06836-0005

1579
Nathan Cummings Scholarship Program, Sara Lee Corporation

AMOUNT: None Specified   DEADLINE: January 31
FIELDS/MAJORS: All Areas of Study

Scholarships for dependents of full-time employees of the Sara Lee Corporation. Students must be juniors in high school. Employees should contact their divisional human resources department for application procedures.

Sara Lee Corporation
Scholarship/Student Loan Administration
Three First National Plaza
Chicago, IL 60602

1580
National AAJA Internship Grant

AMOUNT: Maximum: $1000   DEADLINE: April 15
FIELDS/MAJORS: Journalism

Open to Asian-American students working as interns at a news organization. Based on academics, sensitivity to Asian-American issues (as demonstrated by community involvement), and financial need. Contact your local AAJA chapter for further information or request details from the address listed. Be sure to enclose a SASE with your request for information. Must have a GPA of at least 2.8.

Asian-American Journalists Association
Scholarship Committee
1765 Sutter St., Suite 1000
San Francisco, CA 94115

1581
National Alumni Fellowship

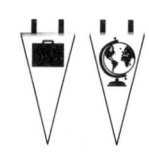

AMOUNT: $1000   DEADLINE: April 1
FIELDS/MAJORS: Home Economics, Related Fields

Applicants must be members of Kappa Omicron Nu and a master's candidate. Awards will be announced May 15. Write to the address below for details.

Kappa Omicron Nu Honor Society
4990 Northwind Dr., Suite 140
East Lansing, MI 48823

1582
National Amputation Foundation Scholarship

AMOUNT: Maximum: $125   DEADLINE: None Specified
FIELDS/MAJORS: All Areas of Study

Scholarships are available for entering freshmen who have had a major limb amputated and will be attending college to pursue their undergraduate degree. Write to the address listed or call (516) 887-3600 for information.

National Amputation Foundation
Scholarship Committee
38-40 Church St.
Malverne, NY 11565

1583
National Asian-American Journalists Association General Scholarships

AMOUNT: Maximum: $2000   DEADLINE: April 15
FIELDS/MAJORS: Print Journalism, Photojournalism, Broadcast Journalism

Applicants must be Asian-Americans who are pursuing careers in journalism (print, photo, or broadcast). Based on academics, sensitivity to Asian American issues (as demonstrated by community involvement), and financial need. Contact your local AAJA chapter for further information or request details from the address listed. Be sure to enclose a SASE with your request for information. Must have a GPA of at least 2.9.

Asian American Journalists Association
Scholarship Committee
1765 Sutter St., Suite 1000
San Francisco, CA 94115

1584
National Association of Black Journalists Scholarships

AMOUNT: Maximum: $2500   DEADLINE: March 20
FIELDS/MAJORS: Journalism

Open to African-American high school seniors who will be enrolled in a four-year school or are currently attending an accredited four-year university. All students must have a minimum GPA of 2.5. Must be/become a member of NABJ and cannot have previously won this award. Nomination by school advisor, dean or faculty member is required. Write to the address listed for further information.

National Association of Black Journalists Program
University of Maryland
3100 Taliaferro Hall
College Park, MD 20742-7717

1585

National Center for Atmospheric Research Postdoctoral Appointments

AMOUNT: $35000-$37000 DEADLINE: January 5
FIELDS/MAJORS: Atmospheric Sciences, or Any Related Area

Interested scientists just receiving a Ph.D. (or equivalent) and scientists with no more than four years applicable experience past the Ph.D. are eligible to apply. Primary criteria for selection are the applicants scientific capability and potential, originality and independence, and the ability to undertake research. Eight to ten awards offered annually. Write to the address listed for further information.

National Center for Atmospheric Research
Barbara Hansford, Advanced Study Program
PO Box 3000
Boulder, CO 80303

1586

National Council of Jewish Women, Rhode Island Section Scholarships

AMOUNT: Maximum: $750 DEADLINE: May 2
FIELDS/MAJORS: All Areas of Study

Scholarships available to Rhode island students attending college. Scholarships will be awarded based on financial need, evidence of involvement in community service, and academic worthiness. Checks for this award are made out to the recipients to do with as they deem necessary for their education. Several scholarships are offered yearly. Write to the address below for details. Must have a GPA of at least 2.8.

National Council of Jewish Women, Rhode Island Section
Attn: Seena Dittleman
93 Crestwood Rd
Cranston, RI 02920

1587

National Council of State Garden Clubs Scholarships

AMOUNT: Maximum: $1000 DEADLINE: July 1
FIELDS/MAJORS: Horticulture, Floriculture, Landscape Design, Conservation, Forestry, Botany, Agronomy, Plant Pathology, Environmental Control, City Planning, Land Management, and/or allied subjects

Awards for juniors, seniors, and graduate students who are Connecticut residents attending a Connecticut school and are studying in the above areas. Must have a minimum GPA of 3.0 and be able to demonstrate financial need. Write to the address listed or call (203) 248-0178 for details.

Federated Garden Clubs of Connecticut, Inc.
Headquarters
PO Box 854
Branford, CT 06405

1588

National Education Loan Fund

AMOUNT: None Specified DEADLINE: March 1
FIELDS/MAJORS: All Areas of Study

Interest-free loans for children of full paid life members of the Disabled American Veterans Auxiliary, children of full paid life members of the Disabled American Veterans (if mother is deceased), or full paid life members of the Disabled American Veterans Auxiliary. For full-time study in the U.S. Must have a GPA of 2.0 or better. Write to the address below for details.

Disabled American Veterans Auxiliary, National Headquarters
National Education Loan Fund Director
3725 Alexandria Pike
Cold Spring, KY 41076

1589

National Education Scholarship Awards

AMOUNT: None Specified DEADLINE: April 1
FIELDS/MAJORS: Fields Related to Materials Joining

Scholarships are available for students enrolled in programs related to materials joining at any college, university, or vocational/technical school in the U.S. Write to the address listed for information.

American Welding Society
National Education Scholarship Committee
550 NW LeJeune Road
Miami, FL 33126

1590

National Educational Grant

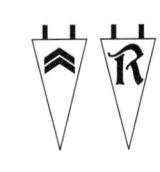

AMOUNT: None Specified DEADLINE: May 1
FIELDS/MAJORS: All Areas of Study

Scholarships for direct descendants (children, grandchildren, and great grandchildren) of members in good standing (or deceased members) of the Jewish War Veterans of the U.S.A. Must be accepted by a four-year college or a three-year nursing program. Application is made during senior year in high school. Application will have to be signed (sponsored) by a member of JWV. Winners will be announced August 24-31. Write to the address below for details.

Jewish War Veterans of the United States of America, Inc.
National Headquarters
1811 R St. NW
Washington, DC 20009

1591
National Endowment for the Humanities Fellowships

AMOUNT: Maximum: $30000 DEADLINE: December 15
FIELDS/MAJORS: Renaissance, Nineteenth and Twentieth Century Literature, Colonial America

Awards for established postdoctoral level scholars pursuing scholarship in a field appropriate to the Huntington's collection. Contact the address listed for further information.

Huntington Library, Art Collections and Botanical Gardens
Robert C. Ritchie, Director of Research
1151 Oxford Rd.
San Marion, CA 91108

1592
National Endowment for the Humanities Fellowships

AMOUNT: Maximum: $30000 DEADLINE: January 20
FIELDS/MAJORS: History, Humanities, Linguistics

Six- to eleven-month fellowships for residential research programs at Newberry. Available for postdoctoral research in any subject relevant to the Library. Applicants must be citizens of the U.S. or foreign nationals who have been residents in the U.S. for at least three years. Preference is given to applicants who have not held major fellowships or grants in the previous three years. Write to the address listed for details or call (312) 255-3666.

Newberry Library
Committee on Awards
60 W. Walton St.
Chicago, IL 60610

1593
National Federation of Music Clubs

AMOUNT: $400-$10000 DEADLINE: None Specified
FIELDS/MAJORS: Vocal/Instrumental Music

Open to students between the ages of sixteen and twenty-five. Based on musical ability and promise. Contact the address listed for further information. Include a SASE for a reply.

National Federation of Music Clubs
Scholarship Program
1336 N. Delaware
Indianapolis, IN 46202

1594
National Federation of Press Women Mini-grants

AMOUNT: $200 DEADLINE: May 1
FIELDS/MAJORS: Communication, Journalism

Small grants for members or student members to do research or attend a career-related course, seminar, or workshop. Must have been a member for at least two years. Paid after research or course. Write for mini-grant application at address listed.

National Federation of Press Women
C/O Jean Bormann
1163 320th Ave.
Charlotte, IA 52731

1595
National Federation of the Blind American Action Fund Scholarship

AMOUNT: $10000 DEADLINE: March 31
FIELDS/MAJORS: All Areas of Study

Award available to full-time students who are legally blind. Based on academic ability. One award offered annually. Write to the address below for details. Must have a GPA of at least 2.7.

National Federation of the Blind
Mrs. Peggy Elliott, Chairman
805 Fifth Ave.
Grinnell, IA 50112

1596
National Federation of the Blind Computer Science Scholarship

AMOUNT: $3000 DEADLINE: March 31
FIELDS/MAJORS: Computer Science

Open to legally blind full-time students studying in the computer science field. Write to the address below for more information.

National Federation of the Blind
Mrs. Peggy Elliot, Chairwoman
805 Fifth Ave.
Grinnell, IA 50112

1597
National Federation of the Blind Educator of Tomorrow Award

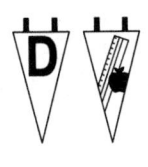

AMOUNT: $3000 DEADLINE: March 31
FIELDS/MAJORS: Education

Open to full-time students who are legally blind and are working toward a career in education at the primary, secondary, or postsecondary level. Write to the address below for details.

National Federation of the Blind
Mrs. Peggy Elliott, Chairman
805 Fifth Ave.
Grinnell, IA 50112

1598
National Federation of the Blind Humanities Scholarship

AMOUNT: $3000 DEADLINE: March 31
FIELDS/MAJORS: Humanities

Open to full-time students who are legally blind and majoring in any of the traditional humanities. Write to the address below for details.

National Federation of the Blind
Mrs. Peggy Elliott, Chairman
805 Fifth Ave.
Grinnell, IA 50112

1599
National Federation of the Blind Scholarships

AMOUNT: Maximum: $3000 DEADLINE: March 31
FIELDS/MAJORS: All Areas of Study

Scholarships for full-time students who are legally blind. Thirteen total scholarships available. Write to the address below for complete details.

National Federation of the Blind
Mrs. Peggy Elliott, Chairman
805 Fifth Ave.
Grinnell, IA 50112

1600
National Guard Educational Assistance Grant

AMOUNT: Maximum: $1000 DEADLINE: None Specified
FIELDS/MAJORS: All Areas of Study

Open to students who are active members of the Alabama National Guard. Maximum of $500 per semester to $1000 per year. Contact your unit commander for information and an application.

Alabama Commission on Higher Education
Office of Financial Aid
PO Box 30200
Montgomery, AL 36130

1601
National High School Oratorical Contest

AMOUNT: $14000-$18000 DEADLINE: December 1
FIELDS/MAJORS: All Areas of Study

Open to high school students. Undergraduate scholarships to the top three winning contestants of the competition. Each state winner receives $1500. For U.S. citizens. Oratory competition. Write to the American Legion State Headquarters in your state of residence for contest procedures. Write to the address below if you are unable to locate your local or state American Legion.

American Legion-National Headquarters
PO Box 1055
Indianapolis, IN 46206

1602
National Honor Society Scholarships

AMOUNT: $1000 DEADLINE: January 30
FIELDS/MAJORS: All Fields of Study

Scholarships for members of the National Honor Society. Two students from each participating chapter may be nominated (nomination required). To be used at any accredited two- or four-year college or university in the U.S. 250 awards per year. Contact your high school principal to express your interest in this award program. If your principal does not have information on this award, please ask him or her to write to the NASSP. Must have a GPA of at least 3.6.

National Association of Secondary School Principals
National Honor Society Awards
1904 Association Dr.
Reston, VA 22091

1603
National Institute of Health Scholarships

AMOUNT: Maximum: $20000 DEADLINE: None Specified
FIELDS/MAJORS: Health Sciences, Biomedical Research

Fifteen scholarships for students with disadvantaged backgrounds. Must demonstrate financial need or a statement indicating non-financial but other disadvantaged situation. Must have minimum GPA of 3.5. Recipients must serve as NIH employee for ten weeks (in summer) during sponsored year and after graduation for twelve months for each year scholarship was received (at Bethesda campus). Must be a U.S. citizen or permanent resident. Contact address listed for additional information.

U.S. Department of Health and Human Services
Public Health Service Institutes
7550 Wisconsin Ave., #604
Bethesda, MD 20892

1604
National Italian-American Foundation Scholarships

AMOUNT: Maximum: $5000 DEADLINE: May 25
FIELDS/MAJORS: All Areas of Study

The National Italian-American Foundation offers a wide variety of awards for qualified Italian-American students. Contact the address below for further information.

National Italian-American Foundation
Dr. Maria Lombardo, Education Director
1860 Nineteenth St. NW
Washington, DC 20009

1605
National Junior Classical League Scholarships

AMOUNT: None Specified DEADLINE: November 1
FIELDS/MAJORS: Classics

Scholarships for junior Classical League members who plan to study in the broad area of "classics." When requesting an application, please indicate the name of your local JCL chapter and your sponsor. Write to the address below for details. You should, however, be able to obtain application materials from your local JCL chapter.

National Junior Classical League
Miami University
Oxford, OH 45056

1606
National Medical Fellowships, Inc., Scholarships

AMOUNT: $200-$5000 DEADLINE: August 31
FIELDS/MAJORS: Medicine

Open to African-American, Native American, Mexican-American, and mainland Puerto Ricans who are U.S. citizens. Applicants must be first- or second-year students in an M.D. or D.O. program in U.S. accredited medical schools. Write to the address listed for additional information.

National Medical Fellowships, Inc.
Scholarship Coordinator
254 W. 31st St., 7th Floor
New York, NY 10001

1607
National Minority Scholarship Program

AMOUNT: $1500 DEADLINE: April 11
FIELDS/MAJORS: Public Relations, Communications

Applicants must be minority undergraduate students in public relations attending four-year accredited schools. Must have a GPA of at least 3.0. Public Relations Student Society of America membership and a major or minor of public relations is preferred. Students should have obtained at least junior status by the time the scholarship will be used. If your school does not offer a public relations degree, majors in communications or journalism are acceptable. Write to the address below for details.

Public Relations Society of America
Director, Educational Affairs
33 Irving Place
New York, NY 10003

1608
National Pathfinder Scholarship

AMOUNT: Maximum: $2000
DEADLINE: February 23
FIELDS/MAJORS: Chemistry, Sociology, Psychology, Pharmacology

Open to women currently enrolled in undergraduate or graduate programs such as chemistry, sociology, psychology, or pharmacology, with intended careers in chemical, biological, medical research, or counseling of addicts and their families. Contact your local Republican Women's Club state federation president or the address listed, or call (703) 548-9688 for further information.

National Federation of Republican Women
Scholarship Coordinator
124 North Alfred St.
Alexandria, VA 22314

1609
National Presbyterian College Scholarship

AMOUNT: $500-$1400 DEADLINE: December 1
FIELDS/MAJORS: All Areas of Study

Scholarships for high school seniors who are members of the Presbyterian Church (U.S.A.) and are U.S. citizens or permanent residents. Applicants must take the SAT/ACT prior to December 15 of their senior year. Write to the address listed for information and an application.

Presbyterian Church (U.S.A.)
Office of Financial Aid for Studies
100 Witherspoon St., Room M042-A
Louisville, KY 40202

1610
National Press Photographers Foundation Still Scholarship

AMOUNT: $1000   DEADLINE: March 1
FIELDS/MAJORS: Photojournalism, Photography

Scholarships are available to sophomores, juniors, and seniors in four-year schools. Based on need. Must have at least half of senior year remaining. Write to the address below for more information.

National Press Photographers Foundation
Bill Sanders
640 NW 100 Way
Coral Springs, FL 33071

1611
National Restaurant Association Industry Assistance Grants

AMOUNT: $1000   DEADLINE: January 1
FIELDS/MAJORS: All Areas of Study

Awards for restaurant industry professionals to further their education (but not as a student in food service/hospitality). Applicants must have a minimum of three years experience in a supervisory or management position in foodservice and currently be employed in the foodservice industry. Grants will include written materials, videos, and an examination. Contact the address below for further information.

National Restaurant Association Educational Foundation
250 S. Wacker Dr., #1400
Chicago, IL 60606

1612
National Restaurant Association Teacher Work-Study Grants

AMOUNT: $3000   DEADLINE: February 15
FIELDS/MAJORS: Foodservice, Hospitality

Awards available to foodservice/hospitality educators and administrators who wish to add hands-on work experience to gain a better understanding of day-to-day operations. Must currently be a full-time high school or college educator or administrator of a foodservice/hospitality program. Consulting work is not eligible for this program. Eight awards offered annually. Contact the address below for further information.

National Restaurant Association Educational Foundation
250 S. Wacker Dr., #1400
Chicago, IL 60606

1613
National Scholarship Trust Fund Scholarships

AMOUNT: $500-$1500   DEADLINE: March 1
FIELDS/MAJORS: Graphic Communications

Applicants must be interested in a graphic communications career and be high school seniors or college students. May be used for both two- and four-year schools. Renewable if recipients maintain a minimum GPA of 3.0. Approximately three hundred scholarships offered annually. Write to the address below for details. Deadline for college students is April 1; for high school students, March 1.

National Scholarship Trust Fund of the Graphic Arts
Ann Mayhew
200 Deer Run Rd.
Sowickley, PA 15143

1614
National Science Foundation Minority Graduate Research Fellowships

AMOUNT: Maximum: $24500   DEADLINE: November 6
FIELDS/MAJORS: Science, Mathematics, Engineering

Open to minorities who are U.S. citizens or permanent residents for graduate study leading to research based master's or doctoral degrees in the fields listed above. Based on all available documentation of ability, including academic records, recommendations regarding the applicant's qualifications, and GRE scores. Fellowships include a stipend of $15000 for twelve-month tenure and a cost of education allowance or $9500 per tenure year. Contact the address below for further information.

National Science Foundation
Oak Ridge Associated Universities
PO Box 3010
Oak Ridge, TN 37831

1615
National Sculpture Society Scholarship

AMOUNT: None Specified DEADLINE: May 31
FIELDS/MAJORS: Art-Sculpture

Scholarships are available for all levels of students enrolled in an art program with an emphasis in sculpture. Photos of work, a brief biography, and letters of recommendation will be required. Must be able to demonstrate financial need. Contact the address listed for further information, be sure to enclose a business-sized SASE.

National Sculpture Society
Attn: Scholarships
1177 Ave. of the Americas
New York, NY 10036

1616
National Sheriff's Association Law Enforcement Scholarships

AMOUNT: $1000 DEADLINE: March 1
FIELDS/MAJORS: Criminal Justice

Seven awards for undergraduates in the field of criminal justice. Applicants must be employed by a sheriff's office or the son or daughter of an individual employed by a sheriff's office. Write to the address listed for more information.

National Sheriff's Association
The Scholarship Fund
1450 Duke St.
Alexandria, VA 22314

1617
National Society of Professional Engineers Scholarship

AMOUNT: None Specified DEADLINE: December 1
FIELDS/MAJORS: Engineering

Open to high school seniors who are Connecticut residents planning to attend a four-year engineering school. There are one to five awards offered annually, and the scholarship amount varies. Selection for some awards is based on academics, and for others, demonstrated financial need is required. Contact the address listed for further information. Must have a GPA of at least 2.7.

Connecticut Society of Professional Engineers
Beverly Davidson
2600 Dixwell Ave.
Hamden, CT 06514

1618
National Society of Public Accountants Scholarship Foundation

AMOUNT: $500-$1000 DEADLINE: March 10
FIELDS/MAJORS: Accounting

For undergraduate accounting majors enrolled in accredited business schools, junior colleges, and universities. Must have a GPA of at least a 3.0. Must be a full-time student (evening program considered full-time if pursuing a degree in accounting). An additional stipend is awarded to the outstanding student of the competition. Must be a U.S. or Canadian citizen attending school in the U.S. Thirty awards per year. Applications and appraisal forms may be obtained from your school or by writing to the NSPA Scholarship Foundation at the address listed.

National Society of Public Accountants Scholarship Foundation
1010 N. Fairfax St.
Alexandria, VA 22314

1619
National Society to Prevent Blindness Grants-in-Aid

AMOUNT: $1000-$12000 DEADLINE: March 1
FIELDS/MAJORS: Ophthalmology

Grants are for the funding of studies that have limited or no research funding. They are used to help defray the costs of personnel, equipment, and supplies. Write to the address listed for details.

Fight for Sight Research Division
National Society to Prevent Blindness
500 E. Remington Rd.
Schaumburg, IL 60173

1620
National Society to Prevent Blindness Postdoctoral Research Fellowship

AMOUNT: Maximum: $28000 DEADLINE: March 1
FIELDS/MAJORS: Ophthalmology

Research fellowship for basic or clinical work at the early postdoctoral stage in ophthalmology, vision, or related sciences. Write to the address listed for details.

Fight for Sight Research Division
National Society to Prevent Blindness
500 E. Remington Rd.
Schaumburg, IL 60173

1621
National Society to Prevent Blindness Student Fellowships

AMOUNT: Maximum: $1500 DEADLINE: March 1
FIELDS/MAJORS: Ophthalmology

Fellowship is available to undergraduates, medical students, and graduate students interested in eye-related clinical or basic research. Award is given for up to three months of research. Write to the address listed for details.

Fight for Sight Research Division
National Society to Prevent Blindness
500 E. Remington Rd.
Schaumburg, IL 60173

1622
National Speakers Association Scholarship Program

AMOUNT: None Specified DEADLINE: June 2
FIELDS/MAJORS: Speech, Public Speaking

Awards for juniors, seniors, or graduate students studying in one of the fields above. For full-time study at any college or university. Four awards per year. Write to the address below for more information.

National Speakers Association
Attn: Scholarship Committee
1500 South Priest Dr.
Tempe, AZ 85281

1623
National Tour Foundation Internship

AMOUNT: $3000 DEADLINE: April 15
FIELDS/MAJORS: Travel, Tourism

Internship open to students who have excellent written oral and interpersonal skills. Includes travel to and accommodations at the annual convention as well as a stipend to offset travel and lodging in Kentucky. Internship is usually August through December and consists of working as part of the National Tour Foundation staff. National Tour Foundation maintains a list of almost two hundred internship positions. Contact the address listed for complete details. Must have a GPA of at least 3.2.

National Tour Foundation
Internship National Tour Foundation
546 E. Main St.
Lexington, KY 40508

1624
National University Scholarships

AMOUNT: $1000-$1500 DEADLINE: May 1
FIELDS/MAJORS: Jewish Spiritual, Cultural Values

Open to high school graduates, undergraduates, and graduate students accepted at one of the following universities in Israel: Bar-Ilan University, Ben Gurion University, Haifa University, The Hebrew University of Jerusalem, Technion, Tel Aviv University, and Weizmann Institute of Science. These awards are applied to one year's tuition. Purpose of award is to foster Jewish spiritual and cultural values through the experience of living in Israel and strengthen the ties that bind Jews in America and Israel. Contact the address listed for further information or call (501) 682-2952.

American Jewish League for Israel
Executive Director
130 E. 59th St., 14th Floor
New York, NY 10022

1625
National Wool Growers Memorial Fellowship

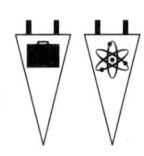

AMOUNT: $2500 DEADLINE: June 1
FIELDS/MAJORS: Sheep Industry

Fellowships are available for graduate students enrolled in sheep-related programs who wish to pursue a career in the sheep industry. Write to the address listed for information.

American Sheep Industry Association
Attn: Memorial Fellowship
6911 South Yosemite
Englewood, CO 80112

1626
National Zoo Research Traineeship Program

AMOUNT: Maximum: $2400 DEADLINE: December 31
FIELDS/MAJORS: Zoology, Animal Behavior, Veterinary, Exhibit Interpretation

All programs are at the National Zoological Park in Washington D.C. Programs last about twelve weeks, but time is determined mutually by trainee and sponsor. Based on scholastic achievement, relevant experience, and letters of reference. Preference is given to advanced undergraduates and recent graduates. Contact the address listed for complete information.

Friends of the National Zoo, Human Resource Office
Research Traineeship Program
National Zoological Park
Washington, DC 20008

1627
NationsBank Abilities Scholarships

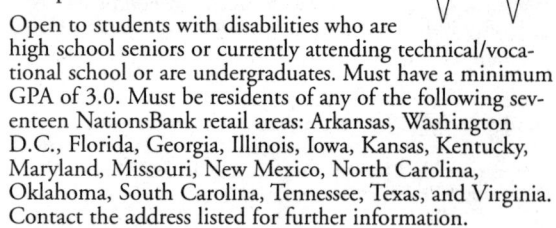

AMOUNT: None Specified
DEADLINE: March 31
FIELDS/MAJORS: Finance, Business, Computer Science

Open to students with disabilities who are high school seniors or currently attending technical/vocational school or are undergraduates. Must have a minimum GPA of 3.0. Must be residents of any of the following seventeen NationsBank retail areas: Arkansas, Washington D.C., Florida, Georgia, Illinois, Iowa, Kansas, Kentucky, Maryland, Missouri, New Mexico, North Carolina, Oklahoma, South Carolina, Tennessee, Texas, and Virginia. Contact the address listed for further information.

NationsBank Corp.
NationsBank Scholarship Program
PO Box 1465
Taylors, SC 29687

1628
Native American Education Grants

AMOUNT: $200-$1500   DEADLINE: June 1
FIELDS/MAJORS: All Areas of Study

Undergraduate grants for Alaska Natives and Native Americans pursuing college education. Must be U.S. citizens and have completed at least one semester of work at an accredited institution of higher education. Applicants must be members of the Presbyterian Church (U.S.A.) and demonstrate financial need. Write to address listed for details. Specify Native American Education Grants (NAEG).

Presbyterian Church (U.S.A.)
Office of Financial Aid for Studies
100 Witherspoon St.
Louisville, KY 40202

1629
Native American Internship Program

AMOUNT: $2500-$3000
DEADLINE: None Specified
FIELDS/MAJORS: Humanities, Art, Agriculture, Archeology, Anthropology, History

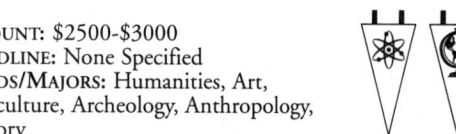

Internships available for Native American undergraduate and graduate students at the Smithsonian, for research or museum activities related to Native American studies. Program lasts for ten weeks. Write to address below for details. Request the publication "Smithsonian Opportunities for Research and Study."

Smithsonian Institution
Office of Fellowships and Grants
955 L'enfant Plaza, Suite 7000
Washington, DC 20560

1630
Native American Student Aid

AMOUNT: Maximum: $1550   DEADLINE: None Specified
FIELDS/MAJORS: All Areas of Study

Grants for Native Americans who are New York residents, on an official tribal roll of a New York state tribe (or children of), and attending an approved postsecondary institution in New York state. Renewable for up to four years. Write to the address below for complete details.

New York State Education Department
Attn: Native American Education Unit
478 Education Building Annex
Albany, NY 12234

1631
Native Daughters of the Golden West Scholarships

AMOUNT: Maximum: $1000   DEADLINE: None Specified
FIELDS/MAJORS: Nursing

Open to students who were born in and attend school in California. These scholarships are renewable if recipients maintain a minimum GPA of 3.0. Contact the address listed for further information or (408) 247-4881.

Native Daughters of the Golden West
Shirley Svindal, Chairman
3274 Victoria Ave.
Santa Clara, CA 95051

1632
Naturalist Intern Program

AMOUNT: None Specified   DEADLINE: None Specified
FIELDS/MAJORS: Environmental Education, Science Education, Natural Resources

Internship program for students who have completed at least two years of college study in one of the fields listed above. For students from or attending school in New York. Internships are approximately twelve weeks long. There is a stipend of $100 per week. Write to the address below for more information.

New York State Department of Environmental Conservation
Five Rivers Environmental Education Center
Game Farm Road
Delmar, NY 12054

1633
Navy League Scholarship Program

AMOUNT: Maximum: $2500 DEADLINE: April 1
FIELDS/MAJORS: Math and Science

Must be enrolled in freshman year at a college or university. Must be a direct dependent of sea personnel. Must be under the age of twenty-five and a U.S citizen. Based on academic and financial need. Twelve awards are given annually. Send a SASE to the address listed to the Scholarship Coordinator for more information.

Navy League of the United States
Attn: Scholarship Program
2300 Wilson Blvd.
Arlington, VA 22201

1634
Navy Supply Corps Foundation Scholarships

AMOUNT: None Specified DEADLINE: April 10
FIELDS/MAJORS: All Areas of Study

Sons/daughters of Navy Supply Corps Officers (including Warrant Officers) and Supply Corps Associated enlisted personnel on active duty, reserve, retired with pay, or deceased. For undergraduate study. Must have a GPA of at least 3.0. For a two- or four-year college. Several scholarships available. Write to the address listed or call (706) 354-4111 for details.

Navy Supply Corps Foundation
Navy Supply Corps School
1425 Prince Ave.
Athens, GA 30606

1635
NAWE Women's Research Awards

AMOUNT: $750 DEADLINE: October 1
FIELDS/MAJORS: Women's Studies

Supports research on any topic about the education, personal, and professional development of women and girls. Awards for graduate students and for persons at any career/professional level. Membership not required. Write to the address below for details. Please be certain to enclose a SASE with your request for information.

National Association for Women in Education
Anna Roman-Koller, Ph.D.
Dept. of Pathology, 701 Scaife Hall
Pittsburgh, PA 15261

1636
NAWIC Undergraduate Scholarships

AMOUNT: $500-$2000 DEADLINE: February 1
FIELDS/MAJORS: Construction, Architecture, Engineering Technology, Landscape Architecture

Scholarships are available for freshman, sophomore, and junior students who are enrolled in a construction-related program on a full-time basis. The applicant must desire a career in the construction industry. Based on application, financial need, interview, and transcripts. Contact the address listed for information or call 1-800-552-3506.

National Association of Women in Construction
NAWIC Scholarship Coordinator
327 S. Adams St.
Fort Worth, TX 76104

1637
NBAA Aviation Scholarships

AMOUNT: Maximum: $1000 DEADLINE: October 14
FIELDS/MAJORS: Aviation

Open to sophomores or above enrolled in an NBAA and University Aviation Association member institution (twenty-one member schools) who are planning a career in aviation. Applicants must have a minimum GPA of 3.0 and be U.S. citizens. Five awards are offered annually. Write to the address listed for details. Information may also be available in your department.

National Business Aircraft Association, Inc.
NBAA Scholarship Committee
1200 Eighteenth St. NW, Suite 400
Washington, DC 20036

1638
NCAR Graduate Research Assistantships

AMOUNT: $15695 DEADLINE: December 1
FIELDS/MAJORS: Atmospheric Sciences, Related Area

This program is designed to support university Ph.D. thesis research conducted in collaboration with NCAR scientists. Usually restricted to research projects that require facilities or expertise available at NCAR but not at the collaborating university. Renewal for a maximum tenure of two and one-half years is possible if reviews indicate that progress is satisfactory. Contact the address listed for further information.

National Center for Atmospheric Research
Barbara Hansford, Advanced Study Program
PO Box 3000
Boulder, CO 80303

1639
NCOA Scholarships

AMOUNT: $900-$1000 DEADLINE: March 31
FIELDS/MAJORS: All Areas of Study

Available to spouses and children of members. Children must be under twenty-five years of age. Based primarily on academics. Renewable. Thirty-five awards offered per year. For undergraduate study. Includes the Mary Barraco Scholarship, the William T. Green Scholarship, and the NCOA/Pentagon Federal Credit Union Grant (this last grant is not renewable). Write to the address listed for more information. Must have a GPA of at least 2.8.

Non-Commissioned Officers Association
Scholarship Administrator
PO Box 33610
San Antonio, TX 78265

1640
NCTE Grants-in-Aid

AMOUNT: Maximum: $12500 DEADLINE: February 15
FIELDS/MAJORS: English/Education

The grant program is for research in the field of English/reading education and is open to graduate students and educators. Must be member of NCTE. Write to the address below for details.

National Council of Teachers of English Research
    Foundation
Project Assistant
1111 W. Kenyon Road
Urbana, IL 61801

1641
NDSEG Fellowships

AMOUNT: $17500-$19500 DEADLINE: January 21
FIELDS/MAJORS: Mathematics, Engineering, Physics, Marine, and Biological Sciences

Research fellowships are available for students at the beginning of their graduate studies in one of the areas listed above. Applicants must be U.S. citizens. Minority, handicapped, and female candidates are encouraged to apply. Write to the address listed for information.

National Defense Science and Engineering Fellowship
    Program
Dr. George Outterson
200 Park Dr., Suite 211, PO Box 13444
Research Triangle, NC 27709

1642
Neal W. Munch and Marvin A. Clark Conservation Scholarship

AMOUNT: Maximum: $1000 DEADLINE: June 5
FIELDS/MAJORS: Conservation, Forestry, Soil Science, Environmental Studies, and Related

Three scholarships are available for junior and senior students who reside in either Middlesex or Monmouth County and are studying in a conservation-related field. Write to the address listed or call (908) 446-2300 for information.

Freehold Soil Conservation District
Education Coordinator
211 Freehold Road
Manalapan, NJ 07726

1643
Nebraska-Lois Johnson Scholarship Challenge Program

AMOUNT: Maximum: $500 DEADLINE: April 15
FIELDS/MAJORS: Travel and Tourism, Hotel/Motel Management

Awards for Nebraska residents in one of the areas listed above who are enrolled in any four-year college full-time. Must have a minimum GPA of 3.0 and be entering junior or senior year. Write to the address listed or call 1-800-682-8886 ext. 4251 for more information.

National Tourism Foundation
546 East Main St.
PO Box 3071
Lexington, KY 40596

1644
Ned McWherter Scholars Program

AMOUNT: $6000 DEADLINE: February 15
FIELDS/MAJORS: All Areas of Study

Scholarship open to Tennessee high school seniors who plan to enroll in a Tennessee higher education institution. Applicant must have a 3.5 GPA and have a 29 on the ACT or 1280 on the SAT. Contact your high school guidance office for more information.

Tennessee Student Assistance Corporation
Suite 1950, Parkway Towers
404 James Robertson Parkway
Nashville, TN 37243

1645
NEHA Education/Scholarship Foundation Award

AMOUNT: Maximum: $500 DEADLINE: January 10
FIELDS/MAJORS: All Areas of Study

Scholarship offered to members of the NEHA who are enrolled in a program of study leading to an undergraduate or associate degree. Application involves submitting an original manuscript on housekeeping within any industry segment. Write to the address listed for details.

National Executive Housekeepers Association
Educational Department
1001 Eastwind Dr., Suite 301
Westerville, OH 43081

1646
NEHA Scholarship Awards

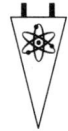

AMOUNT: Maximum: $1000 DEADLINE: February 1
FIELDS/MAJORS: Environmental Health

Scholarships available to students enrolled in an environmental health curriculum at an NEHA institutional/educational or sustaining member school or in an Environmental Health Accreditation Council accredited school. Must be junior, senior, or graduate students. Scholarships awarded at the Annual Educational Conference and Exhibition of the association each June/July. Write to the address listed for details.

National Environmental Health Association Scholarship
Veronica White, NEHA Liaison
720 S. Colorado Blvd., #970 S. Tower
Denver, CO 80246-1925

1647
NELA Scholarship Contest

AMOUNT: Maximum: $500 DEADLINE: April 1
FIELDS/MAJORS: All Areas of Study

Awards are available for immediate families of members or employees of the Northeastern Loggers Association. For high school seniors, students in an associate degree program or technical school, or juniors and seniors in four-year bachelor degree programs. Three awards offered annually. Write to the address listed or call (315) 369-3078 for more information.

Northeastern Loggers Association, Inc.
PO Box 69
Old Forge, NY 13420

1648
Nellie Martin Carman Scholarship Trust

AMOUNT: Maximum: $1000 DEADLINE: March 15
FIELDS/MAJORS: All Areas of Study

Scholarships available to high school seniors in the counties of King, Pierce, and Snohomish in the state of Washington. Must be U.S. citizens and plan to attend a Washington college or university. Based on financial need, school and community activities, and academics. Renewable if student maintains a minimum GPA of 3.0. Twenty-five to thirty awards offered annually. Information and applications are only available in the high schools. Applicants must be nominated by their high schools.

Nellie Martin Carman Scholarship Committee
C/O Barbara M. Scott Admin. Secretary
23825 15th Ave. SE, #128
Bothell, WA 98021

1649
Nemal Electronics Scholarship

AMOUNT: $500 DEADLINE: February 1
FIELDS/MAJORS: Electronics, Communications

Scholarship available to students with a general class amateur radio license pursuing a baccalaureate or higher degree. Must have a minimum GPA of 3.0 and be attending school full-time. Write to the address listed for information.

ARRL Foundation (American Radio Relay League)
Scholarship Program
225 Main St.
Newington, CT 06111

1650
Nevada Student Incentive Grant Program

AMOUNT: Maximum: $5000 DEADLINE: None Specified
FIELDS/MAJORS: All Areas of Study

Nevada residents attending approved Nevada postsecondary schools are eligible for these grants. Must be able to demonstrate substantial financial need. The Nevada Department of Education does not work with student eligibility, so you must contact the financial aid office at your school for information.

Nevada Department of Education
Nevada Student Incentive Grant Program
700 E. Fifth St.
Carson City, NV 89710

1651

New England Femara Scholarships

AMOUNT: $600   DEADLINE: February 1
FIELDS/MAJORS: All Areas of Study

Scholarships are available to students with a technician class amateur radio license who are residents of: Maine, Vermont, Connecticut, New Hampshire, Rhode Island, or Massachusetts. For full-time study. Write to the address listed for information.

ARRL Foundation (American Radio Relay League)
Scholarship Program
225 Main St.
Newington, CT 06111

1652

New England Regional Student Program

AMOUNT: None Specified   DEADLINE: None Specified
FIELDS/MAJORS: Varies by State

New England residents may attend public college and universities in other New England states at a reduced tuition rate for certain degree programs not available in their own state's schools. Write to address below to find out if your field of study is covered under this program. Information is also available at high school guidance offices and college financial aid offices.

New England Board of Higher Education
45 Temple Place
Boston, MA 02111

1653

New Hampshire Funeral Directors Association Scholarships

AMOUNT: Maximum: $500   DEADLINE: December 13
FIELDS/MAJORS: Mortuary Science

Awards for New Hampshire students who plan to return to work in New Hampshire. Write to the address below for more information.

New Hampshire Funeral Directors Association
62 Main St.
Pittsfield, NH 03263

1654

New Initiatives Grant

AMOUNT: Maximum: $3000   DEADLINE: February 15
FIELDS/MAJORS: Home Economics, Related Fields

Applicants must be Kappa Omicron Nu members. Awarded annually from the Kappa Omicron Nu, New Initiatives Fund. Awards announced April 15. Write to the address listed for details.

Kappa Omicron Nu Honor Society
4990 Northwind Dr., Suite 140
East Lansing, MI 48823

1655

New Jersey Funeral Service Education Corp. Scholarships

AMOUNT: Maximum: $1000   DEADLINE: June 30
FIELDS/MAJORS: Mortuary Science

Open to New Jersey residents currently enrolled in a mortuary school. Scholarships usable for any year and are not renewable. Write to the address below for more information or call (908) 974-9444.

New Jersey Funeral Service Education Corp.
Maryann Carroll, Community Relations
PO Box L
Manasquan, NJ 08736

1656

New Jersey I Scholarship Challenge Program

AMOUNT: Maximum: $1000   DEADLINE: April 15
FIELDS/MAJORS: Travel and Tourism, Hotel/Motel Management

Awards for New Jersey residents in one of the areas listed above who are enrolled in any four-year college full-time. Must have a GPA of 3.0 or better and be entering junior or senior year. Write to the address listed or call 1-800-682-8886 ext. 4251 for more information.

National Tourism Foundation
546 East Main St.
PO Box 3071
Lexington, KY 40596

1657

New Jersey II Scholarship Challenge Program

AMOUNT: Maximum: $500   DEADLINE: April 15
FIELDS/MAJORS: Travel and Tourism, Hotel/Motel Management

Awards for New Jersey residents in one of the areas listed above who are enrolled in any two-year college full-time. Must have a GPA of 3.0 or better. Write to the address listed or call 1-800-682-8886 ext. 4251 for more information.

National Tourism Foundation
546 East Main St.
PO Box 3071
Lexington, KY 40596

1658
New Jersey Medical Society Medical Student Loans

AMOUNT: Maximum: $6000   DEADLINE: None Specified
FIELDS/MAJORS: Medicine

Loans at 7% interest for medical students. Must be U.S. citizens and residents of New Jersey for at least five years. Must be (or become) member of MSNJ-Student Association and in the third or fourth year of medical school. Repayment begins two years after graduation from medical school. Write to the Chairman of the Committee on Medical Student Loan Fund at the address listed for details.

Medical Society of New Jersey
Committee on Medical Student Loan Fund
Two Princess Road
Lawrenceville, NJ 08648

1659
New Jersey Scholarship

AMOUNT: $5000-$10000   DEADLINE: April 1
FIELDS/MAJORS: See Below

Scholarships open to U.S. citizens residing in New Jersey pursuing a professional career in one of the following: natural resources, water utility, environmental science, biology, chemistry, business, engineering, computer science, communications, or law. Students who are officers or directors of NAWC, regular representatives of NAWC member companies, or members of their immediate families are not eligible. Write to the address below for details. Must have a GPA of at least 3.0.

National Association of Water Companies
Attn: Ms. Jean Lewis
1725 K St. NW
Washington, DC 20006

1660
New Mexico Scholars Program

AMOUNT: None Specified   DEADLINE: None Specified
FIELDS/MAJORS: All Areas of Study

Open to New Mexico high school graduates who plan to enroll in a New Mexico college full-time before their twenty-second birthdays. Must have graduated in the top 5% of high school class and have scored at least 25 on the ACT or 1140 on the SAT tests. Contact the financial aid office at your school for more information. Must have a GPA of at least 3.8.

New Mexico Commission on Higher Education
Financial Aid and Student Services
PO Box 15910
Santa Fe, NM 87506

1661
New Mexico Student Incentive Grant

AMOUNT: $200-$2500   DEADLINE: None Specified
FIELDS/MAJORS: All Areas of Study

Open to resident undergraduates attending New Mexico schools. Must be able to demonstrate extreme financial need. Must be U.S. citizens and residents of New Mexico. Contact the financial aid office at any New Mexico post-secondary institution for further information.

New Mexico Commission on Higher Education
Financial Aid and Student Services
PO Box 15910
Santa Fe, NM 87506

1662
New York Life Foundation Scholarships for Women in Health Professions

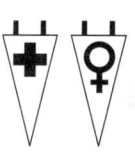

AMOUNT: $500-$1000   DEADLINE: April 15
FIELDS/MAJORS: Healthcare

Undergraduate women, twenty-five or older, seeking the necessary education for a career in a healthcare field and within twenty-four months of graduation. Must demonstrate need. Must be a U.S. citizen. The preapplication screening form is only available between October 1 and April 1. Up to one hundred scholarships are available. Not for graduate study, correspondence programs, or non-degree programs. Relatives of officers of New York Life Insurance Company are ineligible. Write to address below for details.

Business and Professional Women's Foundation
Scholarships
2012 Massachusetts Ave. NW
Washington, DC 20036

1663
New York Scholarship Challenge Program

AMOUNT: Maximum: $500   DEADLINE: April 15
FIELDS/MAJORS: Travel and Tourism, Hotel/Motel Management

Awards for New York residents in one of the areas listed above who are enrolled in any four-year New York school full-time. Must have a GPA of 3.0 or better and be entering junior or senior year. Write to the address listed or call 1-800-682-8886 ext. 4251 for more information.

National Tourism Foundation
546 East Main St.
PO Box 3071
Lexington, KY 40596

1664
New York State Assembly Session Internship

AMOUNT: $2800-$11500 DEADLINE: November 3
FIELDS/MAJORS: State Government

Awards for students from New York or who attend school in New York and are interested in a career in state government. For undergraduate juniors and seniors. Up to 150 positions are available. For graduates, ten positions are available. Contact a New York Assembly Campus Liaison or the address listed for more information.

Assembly State of New York, Albany
Assembly Intern Committee
Room 104A, Legislative Office Building
Albany, NY 12248

1665
New York State Grange Student Loan Fund

AMOUNT: None Specified DEADLINE: None Specified
FIELDS/MAJORS: All Areas of Study

Scholarships for members of a New York State Subordinate Grange. Must have been a member for at least six months at time of application. Renewable up to $5000. No repayment until after graduation. Interest: 5%. Application blanks are furnished by the fund secretary or may be obtained from Pomona secretaries.

New York State Grange
Scholarship Coordinator
100 Grange Place
Cortland, NY 13045

1666
Newberry-British Academy Fellowships

AMOUNT: None Specified DEADLINE: None Specified
FIELDS/MAJORS: Humanities

Open to scholars to pursue studies in any field in the humanities at the British Academy in Great Britain. Award is a daily stipend of 40 British pounds per day. Recipient's institution is expected to continue to pay his/her salary. Preference is given to those who have used the Newberry Library previously or are readers or staff of the Newberry. Contact the address listed for further information or call (312) 255-3666.

Newberry Library
Committee on Awards
60 W. Walton St.
Chicago, IL 60610

1667
Newhouse Scholarship

AMOUNT: Maximum: $2000 DEADLINE: April 15
FIELDS/MAJORS: Print Journalism

Applicants must be Asian-Americans who are pursuing careers in print journalism. May be graduating high school seniors through graduate students. Based on academics, sensitivity to Asian-American issues (as demonstrated by community involvement), and financial need. Contact your local AAJA chapter for further information, or request details from the address listed. Be sure to enclose a SASE with your request for information. Must have a GPA of at least 2.9.

Asian-American Journalists Association
Scholarship Committee
1765 Sutter St., Suite 1000
San Francisco, CA 94115

1668
Newhouse Scholarship/ Internship Program

AMOUNT: Maximum: $5000 DEADLINE: February 27
FIELDS/MAJORS: Print Journalism

For Hispanic college juniors and seniors majoring in print journalism. Recipients will have an opportunity to participate in a summer intern program following their junior year. Write to the address listed for more information.

National Association of Hispanic Journalists
529 14th St. NW
1193 National Press Building
Washington, DC 20045

1669
Newport Scholarship Fund Scholarships

AMOUNT: None Specified DEADLINE: May 10
FIELDS/MAJORS: All Areas of Study

Scholarships for graduating seniors and alumni of Newport, New Hampshire, high school. Applications are available from the high school's guidance office, or write to the address below for details.

Newport Scholarship Fund
PO Box 524
Newport, NH 03773

1670
News 4 Media Scholarship

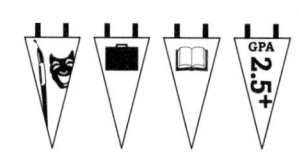

AMOUNT: None Specified   DEADLINE: May 2
FIELDS/MAJORS: Communications, Journalism, Advertising, Public Relations, Video, Film, Photography

Scholarships for Colorado residents majoring in the areas listed above. Must have a GPA of at least 2.5. Interview required. For graduating high school seniors or GED recipients. Write to the address below for details.

KCNC-TV NEWS 4
Media Scholarship
PO Box 5012
Denver, CO 80217

1671
News Photographer Scholarships

AMOUNT: Maximum: $1000   DEADLINE: April 30
FIELDS/MAJORS: Photojournalism

Applicants must be high school seniors, college freshmen, sophomores, or juniors who are residents of New Jersey. Must be enrolled in/accepted into a school to study photography as a major. Two awards offered annually. Write to the address listed for details.

Bob Baxter Scholarship Foundation
C/O New Jersey Newsphotos
Hemisphere Center, Route #1
Newark, NJ 07114

1672
Newspaper Editing Intern Program for Upperclassmen and Graduate Students

AMOUNT: None Specified   DEADLINE: November 15
FIELDS/MAJORS: Newspaper Journalism

Awards are available for juniors, seniors, or graduate students to work as interns to copy editors. Recipients are paid regular wages for their summer work, and upon returning to school, the students will receive a $1000 scholarship. Must be a U.S. citizen to apply. Applications are only available from August 15 through November 1. Contact the address listed for more information or call (609) 452-2820.

Dow Jones Newspaper Fund
PO Box 300
Princeton, NJ 08543

1673
Newtonville Woman's Club Scholarship

AMOUNT: $600   DEADLINE: March 1
FIELDS/MAJORS: Education

Applicants must be a senior in a Massachusetts high school who will enroll in a four-year accredited college or university in a teacher training program that leads to certification to teach. Letter of endorsement from a sponsoring Women's Club in your community is also required. Write to the address below for details, and be sure to include a SASE.

General Federation of Women's Clubs of Massachusetts
Scholarship Chairman
PO Box 679
Sudbury, MA 01776

1674
Nicaraguan and Haitian Scholarship Program

AMOUNT: $4000-$5000   DEADLINE: July 1
FIELDS/MAJORS: All Areas of Study

Scholarships for residents of Florida who were born in Nicaragua or Haiti or hold citizenship in either country. Applicant needs a cumulative high school GPA of 3.0 on a 4.0 scale and must have demonstrated community service. Write to the address below for details.

Florida Department of Education
Office of Student Financial Assistance
1344 Florida Education Center
Tallahassee, FL 32399

1675
Nicholas Van Slyck Scholarship

AMOUNT: $400   DEADLINE: May 1
FIELDS/MAJORS: Music

Scholarship for Merrimack Valley area graduating high school seniors who intend to pursue a career in music. Write to the address below for details.

Merrimack Valley Philharmonic Society, Inc.
Attn: Scholarship
PO Box 512
Lawrence, MA 01842

1676
NIGMS Predoctoral Fellowships

AMOUNT: Maximum: $1500 DEADLINE: November 15
FIELDS/MAJORS: Medical Science

Awards are available for minority graduate students working toward their Ph.D. in medical science. Must be U.S. citizens. Write to the address below for additional information.

National Institute of General Medical Sciences
National Institute of Health
45 Center Dr., MSC 6200, Room 2AS.43
Bethesda, MD 20892

1677
Nila Member, George M. Lamonte, and Sarah B. Askew Scholarships

AMOUNT: $500-$4000 DEADLINE: February 15
FIELDS/MAJORS: Library Science

Scholarships for New Jersey residents admitted to an ALA-accredited, graduate level library science program. Financial need is required. Three separate awards offered. Write to the address below for further information.

New Jersey Library Association
Scholarship Committee, Linda Defelice
1400 Tanyard Rd.
Sewell, NJ 08080

1678
NJSCPA Accounting Essay Contest

AMOUNT: Maximum: $1500 DEADLINE: February 1
FIELDS/MAJORS: Accounting

Contest sponsored in conjunction with New Jersey Business magazine to increase students' and the public's understanding of the CPA's role in business. The author of the winning essay receives a $1500 scholarship and the opportunity to have their work published in New Jersey Business magazine and newsletter. Write to the address listed for more information.

New Jersey Society of Certified Public Accountants
Scholarship Awards Committee
425 Eagle Rock Ave.
Roseland, NJ 07068

1679
NJSCPA College Scholarships

AMOUNT: Maximum: $1000 DEADLINE: None Specified
FIELDS/MAJORS: Accounting

Open to the top academically ranked juniors who are majoring in accounting at New Jersey colleges. Must be nominated by your accounting chairperson. Based on interviews conducted by the NJSCPA Scholarship Interview Committee. The awards are applied to the winner's senior year. Winners are selected in January. Contact your department chairperson for more information. Must have a GPA of at least 3.6.

New Jersey Society of Certified Public Accountants
Scholarship Awards Committee
425 Eagle Rock Ave.
Roseland, NJ 07068

1680
NJSCPA High School Scholarship Program

AMOUNT: $500-$2500 DEADLINE: October 31
FIELDS/MAJORS: Accounting

Open to New Jersey high school seniors who intend to major in accounting in college. Applications are mailed to all New Jersey guidance and business departments in September. Contact your high school guidance counselor or write to the address listed for more information. Must have a GPA of at least 2.8.

New Jersey Society of Certified Public Accountants
Scholarship Awards Committee
425 Eagle Rock Ave.
Roseland, NJ 07068

1681
Noble E. and Emma Belknap Lord Scholarship

AMOUNT: Maximum: $3000 DEADLINE: February 24
FIELDS/MAJORS: All Areas of Study

Open to high school seniors who are residents of the Greater Hartford area. For use at a four-year school. Based on community service and financial need. Must be in the top 40% of class. Contact the address listed for further information. Must have a GPA of at least 2.5.

Greater Hartford Interracial Scholarship Fund, Inc.
Ellis Simpson
PO Box 320644
Hartford, CT 06132

1682
Nobuko R. Kodama Fong Memorial Scholarships

AMOUNT: None Specified DEADLINE: April 1
FIELDS/MAJORS: All Areas of Study

Open to undergraduate members of Japanese ancestry who are entering or are enrolled at an accredited law school. Must be solely provided for by a single parent. Preference given to students from the Pacific Northwest District. Applications and information may be obtained from local JACL chapters, district offices, and the national headquarters at the address listed, or call (206) 623-5088. Please indicate your level of study, and be certain to include a legal-sized SASE.

Japanese-American Citizens League
National Scholarship and Award Program
671 S. Jackson St., # 206
Seattle, WA 98104

1683
Non-Commissioned Officers Association Auxiliary Scholarships

AMOUNT: $900-$1000 DEADLINE: March 31
FIELDS/MAJORS: All Areas of Study

Grants for children (under the age of twenty-five) and spouses of members of the Non-Commissioned Officers Association. Must be attending school full-time (undergraduate level), carrying 15 credit hours and maintaining a minimum GPA of 2.8. Contact your chapter or the address listed for details.

Non-Commissioned Officers Association Auxiliary
Scholarship Administrator
PO Box 33610
San Antonio, TX 78233-3610

1684
Nonprofit Sector Research Fund Grants

AMOUNT: $20000-$50000 DEADLINE: January 2
FIELDS/MAJORS: Public Policy, Political Science

Grants are available to encourage graduate students and scholars in the early stages of their careers to conduct research to expand understanding of nonprofit activities, including philanthropy and its underlying values. For dissertation and advanced research. Write to the address below for information.

Aspen Institute
Nonprofit Sector Research Fund
1333 New Hampshire Ave., Suite 1070
Washington, DC 20036

1685
Nordstrom Scholarships

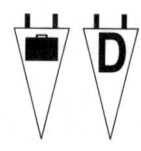

AMOUNT: $2000 DEADLINE: May 8
FIELDS/MAJORS: Business

Scholarships are available for undergraduate students with disabilities enrolled in or planning to enroll in a business program. Requires a four-part essay of not more than fifteen pages, and documentation of your handicap. Five awards are given annually. Write to the address below for information.

President's Committee on Employment of People with
  Disabilities
Scholarship Program
1331 F St. NW
Washington, DC 20004

1686
North American Loon Fund Grants

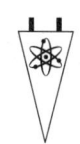

AMOUNT: None Specified DEADLINE: December 15
FIELDS/MAJORS: Ornithology-Loon Research

Grants to support specific research, management, and educational projects that may yield results useful to the NALF in furtherance of its goals and which will promote and enhance the conservation and management of loons in North America. Write to the address below for more information.

North American Loon Fund
Grant Committee
6 Lily Pond Road
Gilford, NH 03246

1687
North Carolina Division of Veterans Affairs Scholarships

AMOUNT: $1500-$4500 DEADLINE: May 31
FIELDS/MAJORS: All Areas of Study

Must be a son or daughter of deceased or disabled veterans or who were listed as POW/MIA. Veteran must have been a North Carolina resident at time of entry into service, or student must have been born in North Carolina and continuously resided in the state. Awards for both undergraduate and graduate students. Write to address listed for more details.

North Carolina Department of Admin., Div. of Veterans
  Affairs
Albemarle Bldg., Suite 1065
325 N. Salisbury St.
Raleigh, NC 27603

1688
North Carolina Police Graduate Program

AMOUNT: Maximum: $7500   DEADLINE: November 15
FIELDS/MAJORS: All Areas of Study

Open to college graduates who wish to work for four years and then attend graduate school. The students will attend a sixteen-week training program, work four years for the sponsoring law enforcement agency in North Carolina, and then is paid up to $7500 per year for education expenses, tuition, fees, books, supplies, room, and board. Contact the address listed or call (919) 715-5478 for further information.

North Carolina Police Corps
Neil Woodcock, Dir. of LESS
1950 Old Garner Rd.
Raleigh, NC 27610

1689
North Carolina Scholarship Challenge Program

AMOUNT: Maximum: $500   DEADLINE: April 15
FIELDS/MAJORS: Travel and Tourism, Hotel/Motel Management

Awards for North Carolina residents in one of the areas listed above who are enrolled in any four-year college full-time. Must have a GPA of 3.0 or better and be entering junior or senior year. Write to the address listed or call 1-800-682-8886 ext. 4251 for more information.

National Tourism Foundation
546 East Main St.
PO Box 3071
Lexington, KY 40596

1690
North Carolina Teaching Fellows Program

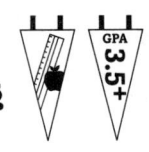

AMOUNT: Maximum: $20000   DEADLINE: October 31
FIELDS/MAJORS: Education

Scholarships are available for graduating high school seniors residing in North Carolina who plan to pursue a career in teaching. Recipients must commit to teaching in a public or government school in North Carolina for four years after graduation. The typical recipient will have a GPA of 3.6 or above and be in the top 10% of his/her class. Write to the address listed for information, and submit applications to your local counselor.

Public School Forum of North Carolina
3739 National Dr., Suite 210
Raleigh, NC 27612

1691
North Dakota Board of Nursing Education Loan Program

AMOUNT: Maximum: $1000   DEADLINE: None Specified
FIELDS/MAJORS: Nursing

Open to North Dakota residents who are U.S. citizens, have financial need, and have been accepted into a board approved nursing program. Write to the address listed for details.

North Dakota Board of Nursing
Chapter 54-04.1
919 S. 7th St., #504
Bismarck, ND 58504

1692
North Dakota Department of Transportation Scholarship Program

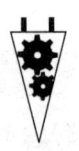

AMOUNT: $1000-$3000   DEADLINE: February 15
FIELDS/MAJORS: Civil Engineering, Construction, Related Fields

Applicants must have completed one year of study at any college but must be enrolled at a North Dakota school to receive the grant. Recipients must agree to work for the Department for a period of time at least equal to the time needed to complete the grant study period. Those who do not accept employment with the Department must repay grant on a prorated basis at 6%. Two to three awards are given annually. Write to the address listed for further information.

North Dakota Department of Transportation
Human Resources Division
608 E. Boulevard Ave.
Bismarck, ND 58505

1693
North Dakota Grain Dealers Educational Scholarship

AMOUNT: Maximum: $500   DEADLINE: September 30
FIELDS/MAJORS: Agriculture

Ten awards are available to students enrolled in an applicable North Dakota College who are majoring in agriculture. Preference is given to students pursuing a career in the grain marketing industry. Write to the address listed for further information.

North American Grain Dealers Educational Foundation
212 Black Building
Fargo, ND 58102

1694

North Dakota Physician Loan Repayment Program

AMOUNT: Maximum: $10000   DEADLINE: None Specified
FIELDS/MAJORS: Medicine

This program offers repayment of student loans for physicians and psychiatrists who agree to practice in specialized areas in North Dakota with limited access to medical care. Up to $10,000 per year for four years of student loan indebtedness may be canceled. Write to the address listed for information.

North Dakota Primary Care Cooperative-Center for Rural Health
Mary Amundson, Director
PO Box 9037
Grand Forks, ND 58202

1695

North Orange Tax District Scholarship

AMOUNT: None Specified   DEADLINE: March 31
FIELDS/MAJORS: Medicine, Dentistry, Medically Related Fields

Open to residents of the North Orange Tax District (for at least 1 year) prior to application. Boundary maps of the tax district, which encompasses portions of Apopka, north of Keene Rd, Plymouth, Zellwood and Tangerine are available at Florida Hospital. Contact the address listed for further information. You may pick up information and applications during normal business hours.

North Orange Tax District, Scholarship Committee
Florida Hospital Apopka, Exec. Offices
201 N. Park Ave.
Apopka, FL 32703

1696

North Port Business and Professional Women's Organization Scholarships

AMOUNT: $500-$1000   DEADLINE: April 15
FIELDS/MAJORS: All Areas of Study

Scholarships are available for female residents of North Port, Florida. Based on academic ability and financial need. Write to the address below for information.

North Port Area Business and Professional Women's Organization
C/O Arline Q. Reeves
PO Box 7085
North Port, FL 34287

1697

Northeastern Loggers' Association Scholarship

AMOUNT: $500   DEADLINE: April 1
FIELDS/MAJORS: All Areas of Study

Available to immediate families of individual members or the immediate families of employees of Industrial and Associate Members of the Northeastern Loggers' Association. Applicants must be seniors in high school, in a two-year associate degree/technical program, or juniors and seniors in a four-year school. Contact the address below for further information.

Northeastern Loggers' Association, Inc.
PO Box 69
Old Forge, NY 13420

1698

Northern New York City Community Foundation Scholarships

AMOUNT: $100-$2500   DEADLINE: April 1
FIELDS/MAJORS: All Areas of Study

Open to undergraduates who are residents of Lewis and Jefferson counties, New York. Must be enrolled in a college or university in the continental U.S. Based on academics and financial need. Contact the address listed for further information or call (315) 782-7110. Must have a GPA of at least 2.8.

Northern New York City Community Foundation
Alex C. Velto, Executive Director
120 Washington St.
Watertown, NY 13601

1699

Northrop Corporation Founders Scholarship

AMOUNT: Maximum: $1000   DEADLINE: February 1
FIELDS/MAJORS: Engineering

Scholarship for a sophomore SWE member. Must be an engineering major and a U.S. citizen. A GPA of at least 3.5 is required. Write to address listed for details. Please be certain to enclose a SASE. Information and applications for the SWE awards are also available from the Deans of Engineering Schools.

Society of Women Engineers
120 Wall St., 11th Floor
New York, NY 10005

1700
Northwest Danish Foundation Scholarships

AMOUNT: $250-$1000 DEADLINE: March 15
FIELDS/MAJORS: All Areas of Study

Open to students who are of Danish descent and are residents of Washington or Oregon. The scholarship may be used for study in Denmark. Preference given to applicants who can demonstrate active participation in their Danish communities. Contact the address below for further information.

Northwest Danish Foundation
1833 N. 105th St., #203
Seattle, WA 98133

1701
Novartis Pharmaceuticals/ Oncology Foundation Post-Master's Awards

AMOUNT: $3000 DEADLINE: February 1
FIELDS/MAJORS: Oncology Nursing

Awards available to students enrolled in, or applying to, a post-master's nurse practitioner certificate bearing program in an NLN-accredited school of nursing. Applicants must be currently licensed registered nurses and have a master's degree and a commitment to oncology nursing. Contact the address listed for further information about both awards.

Oncology Nursing Foundation
501 Holiday Dr.
Pittsburgh, PA 15220

1702
NPPF Television News Scholarship

AMOUNT: $1000 DEADLINE: March 1
FIELDS/MAJORS: Photojournalism

Scholarship for undergraduate in junior or senior year pursuing career in television news photojournalism. Sample of work, letter from advisor, and a biographical sketch will be required. Write to the address below for more information.

National Press Photographers Foundation
Ned Hockman
800 Hoover
Norman, OK 73072

1703
NRF/CRCA Scholarship Awards Program

AMOUNT: Maximum: $2000 DEADLINE: April 1
FIELDS/MAJORS: Liberal Arts and Sciences, Engineering, Architecture, Business

Scholarships for undergraduate students residing in Cook, Lake, DuPage, Kane, Kendall, DeKalb, McHenry, or Will counties in Illinois. Must be a U.S. citizen. For more information (or application forms), send a SASE ($.64 postage) to address below.

National Roofing Foundation
O'Hare International Center
10255 W. Higgins Rd., Suite 600
Rosemont, IL 60018

1704
NRF/NERCA Scholarship Awards Program

AMOUNT: Maximum: $1000 DEADLINE: January 9
FIELDS/MAJORS: Engineering, Architecture, Construction

Scholarships for undergraduate study in an area related to roofing for residents of Connecticut, Maine, Massachusetts, New Hampshire, New Jersey, New York, Pennsylvania, Rhode Island, or Vermont. One award is offered annually. For more information (or application forms), send a SASE ($.64 postage) to the address listed.

National Roofing Foundation
O'Hare International Center
10255 W. Higgins Rd., Suite 600
Rosemont, IL 60018

1705
NSA Undergraduate Training Program

AMOUNT: None Specified
DEADLINE: November 30
FIELDS/MAJORS: Computer Science, Electrical or Computer Engineering, Languages, Math

Program for high school seniors (particularly minorities) who are interested in studying one of the fields above. Program offers full tuition, books, and a salary during the undergraduate years, as well as a job in the summer. Applicants must have a minimum GPA of 3.0, an ACT score of 27 or SAT score of 1200, and be U.S. citizens. Write to the address listed for additional details.

National Security Agency
Kelly Freeman-Garrett
9800 Savage Rd., Suite 6840
Ft. George Meade, MD 20755

1706
NSDAR Occupational Therapy Scholarships

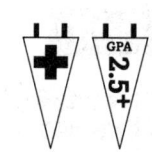

AMOUNT: $333-$500 DEADLINE: September 1
FIELDS/MAJORS: Occupational Therapy, Physical Therapy

Scholarships are available for first-year undergraduate students enrolled in an accredited therapy program. Affiliation with the DAR is not required. Based on academics, financial need, and recommendations. Applicants must be U.S. citizens. Write to the address listed for information or call (202) 628-1776. Must have a GPA of at least 2.6.

Daughters of the American Revolution
NSDAR Occupational Therapy Scholarships
1776 D St. NW
Washington, DC 20006

1707
NSF Graduate Research Fellowships

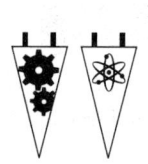

AMOUNT: Maximum: $24500 DEADLINE: November 6
FIELDS/MAJORS: Mathematics, Science, Engineering

Fellowships for graduate study leading to research based master's or doctoral degrees in the fields listed above. Applicants must be U.S. citizens or permanent residents. Based on all available documentation of ability, including academic records, recommendations regarding the applicant's qualifications, and GRE scores. Fellowships include a stipend of $15,000 for twelve-month tenure and a cost of education allowance of $9,500 per tenure year. Write to the address listed for details. Information is also available from departmental offices at many colleges and universities.

National Science Foundation
Oak Ridge Associated Universities
PO Box 3010
Oak Ridge, TN 37831

1708
NSPS Scholarships

AMOUNT: Maximum: $1000 DEADLINE: November 30
FIELDS/MAJORS: Surveying

Open to undergraduates studying surveying in a four-year degree program. Please contact address listed for complete information or call (301) 493-0200.

American Congress on Surveying and Mapping
Ms. Lilly Matheson
5410 Grosvenor Ln., #100
Bethesda, MD 20814-2144

1709
Nursing Economics Foundation Scholarships

AMOUNT: Maximum: $5000 DEADLINE: May 1
FIELDS/MAJORS: Nursing

Scholarships open to students matriculated or matriculating into an accredited master's or doctoral nursing program. Must be pursuing a degree in the field of nursing science with an emphasis on nursing administration or management. Must be a registered nurse. Write to the address listed for complete details.

Nursing Economics Foundation
East Holly Ave., Box 56
Pitman, NJ 08701

1710
Nursing Grants for Persons of Color

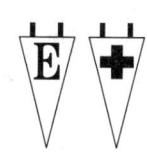

AMOUNT: $2000-$4000 DEADLINE: None Specified
FIELDS/MAJORS: Nursing

Awards are available for Minnesota students of color in a nursing program in the state of Minnesota. Must be U.S. citizens or permanent residents. Write to the address listed for more information.

Minnesota Higher Education Services Office
400 Capital Square
550 Cedar St.
Saint Paul, MN 55101

1711
Nursing Incentive Scholarship

AMOUNT: $1000-$2000 DEADLINE: June 1
FIELDS/MAJORS: Nursing

Scholarships for Kentucky residents who have been admitted to a nursing school in Kentucky. Preference is given to applicants with financial need who have agreed to work in a sponsoring hospital. Write to the address listed for more information.

Kentucky Board of Nursing
Nursing Incentive Scholarship Fund
312 Whittington Parkway, Suite 300
Louisville, KY 40222

1712
Nursing Scholarship

AMOUNT: Maximum: $5000 DEADLINE: None Specified
FIELDS/MAJORS: Nursing

Award for Indiana students who have been admitted to attend an Indiana school as a full-time or part-time nursing student. Applicants must have a GPA of 2.0 or better and demonstrate financial need. Recipients are required to agree, in writing, to work in any type of healthcare setting in Indiana for at least two years after graduation. Write to the address below for more information.

Indiana Student Assistance Commission
150 W. Market St.
Suite 500
Indianapolis, IN 46204

1713
Nursing Scholarships

AMOUNT: $1000-$2000 DEADLINE: None Specified
FIELDS/MAJORS: Nursing

Awards for students who have attained the clinical level of their nursing education and are interested in continuing with their education. Applicants must attend a nursing school in Texas and be U.S. citizens or permanent residents. Eight hundred awards are offered annually. Write to the address below for more information.

Good Samaritan Foundation
Scholarship Coordinator
5615 Kirby Dr., Suite 308
Houston, TX 77005

1714
Nursing Scholastic Achievement Scholarships

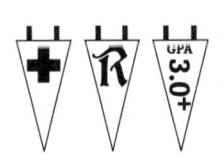

AMOUNT: Maximum: $1000 DEADLINE: March 15
FIELDS/MAJORS: Nursing

Scholarships for communicant members of Lutheran congregations who are juniors or seniors in a school of nursing. Must have a GPA of at least 3.0 and be able to demonstrate past or present involvement (a minimum of one hundred hours) in a community or church activity that benefits people who are mentally retarded. Write to the address listed for details.

Bethesda Lutheran Homes and Services, Inc.
National Christian Resource Center
700 Hoffmann Dr.
Watertown, WI 53094

1715
Nursing, Physical Therapy, or Respiratory Therapy Scholarships

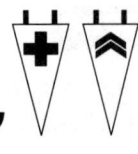

AMOUNT: $500 DEADLINE: March 15
FIELDS/MAJORS: Nursing, Physical Therapy, or Respiratory Therapy

Scholarships available for Michigan residents who will be or are attending a college or university in Michigan. Applicants must be citizens of the U.S. and children of veterans, enrolled or accepted in one of the above programs. Write to the address below for additional information.

American Legion Auxiliary-Department of Michigan
212 North Verlinden
Lansing, MI 48915

1716
NWSA Graduate Scholarship in Lesbian Studies

AMOUNT: $500 DEADLINE: February 15
FIELDS/MAJORS: Women's Studies, Lesbian Studies

Scholarship for graduate student researching for master's thesis or Ph.D. dissertation. Write to the address below for information and an application.

National Women's Studies Association
University of Maryland
7100 Baltimore Ave., Suite 301
College Park, MD 20740

1717
NWSA Graduate Scholarships in Lesbian Studies

AMOUNT: None Specified DEADLINE: April 5
FIELDS/MAJORS: Lesbian Studies

Open to gay, lesbian, bisexual, and transgendered students who are attending/plan to attend a college or university in Orange County. An essay and personal references will be required. Contact the address listed for further information. Be sure to include a SASE for a reply.

Orange County Imperial Court, Inc.
Scholarship Coordinator
12922 Harbor Blvd., #338
Garden Grove, CA 92640

1718
NWSA Scholarship in Jewish Women's Studies

AMOUNT: $500 DEADLINE: February 15
FIELDS/MAJORS: Jewish Women's Studies

Scholarship for graduate student whose area is Jewish Women's Studies. Write to the address below for details.

National Women's Studies Association
University of Maryland
7100 Baltimore Ave., Suite 301
College Park, MD 20740

1719
O'Meara Foundation Scholarship

AMOUNT: $400-$3000 DEADLINE: June 1
FIELDS/MAJORS: All Areas of Study

Open to high school seniors and undergraduates who are residents of Hartford County. Must be able to demonstrate financial need. These awards are renewable. Contact the address listed for further information.

O'Meara Foundation, Inc.
Elaine J. Boyd, Executive Director
4 Grimes Rd.
Rocky Hill, CT 06067

1720
O.V. McDaniel Scholarship

AMOUNT: Maximum: $300 DEADLINE: March 25
FIELDS/MAJORS: Education

One scholarship is offered to an Angleton High School graduate who has completed at least 60 hours of college or university work and who desires a degree in an education related field. Write to address listed for more details.

Westside Elementary School Scholarship Fund
C/O Pat Tasa
300 South Walker St.
Angleton, TX 77515

1721
O.H. Ammann Fellowship

AMOUNT: Maximum: $5000 DEADLINE: February 20
FIELDS/MAJORS: Structural Engineering

Applicant must be a National ASCE member in good standing in any grade. Award is used for purposes of encouraging the creation of new knowledge in the field of structural design and construction. Write to the address listed or call 1-800-548-ASCE for complete details.

American Society of Civil Engineers
Member Scholarships and Awards
1801 Alexander Bell Dr.
Reston, VA 20191

1722
Occupational Therapy Scholarships

AMOUNT: $500-$1000 DEADLINE: February 15
FIELDS/MAJORS: Occupational Therapy, Physical Therapy, Art or Music Therapy

Students must be enrolled in an accredited school of occupational, physical, art, or music therapy. United States citizenship is required. For undergraduate study. Contact your local DAR chapter or send a SASE to the address listed for details.

National Society Daughters of the American Revolution
NSDAR Scholarship Committee
1776 D St. NW
Washington, DC 20006

1723
Ohio Academic Scholarship Program

AMOUNT: Maximum: $2000 DEADLINE: None Specified
FIELDS/MAJORS: All Areas of Study

Scholarships are available to graduating Ohio high school seniors who plan to attend a college or university in Ohio. Based on GPA and ACT test scores. At least one scholarship per high school is awarded. Contact your school guidance counselor for further information. Must have a GPA of at least 3.0.

Ohio Student Aid Commission
Customer Service
PO Box 16610
Columbus, OH 43216

1724
Ohio American Legion Auxiliary Continuing Education Fund Grants

AMOUNT: $200 DEADLINE: January 1
FIELDS/MAJORS: All Areas of Study

Grants open to upperclassmen who are spouses or descendants of a veteran who served during these time frames: 4/6/17-11/11/18, 12/7/41-12/31/46, 6/25/50-1/31/55, 12/22/61-5/7/75, 8/24/82-7/31/84, 12/20/89-1/31/90, or 8/2/90 to cessation. Must be Ohio residents and be able to demonstrate financial need. Fifteen grants awarded annually. Contact the address below for further information.

American Legion Auxiliary-Dept. of Ohio
C. Baughman-Underwood
804 Summit Gardens
Kent, OH 44240

1725
Ohio Bicentennial Legacy Scholarships

AMOUNT: $9000-$12000 DEADLINE: February 13
FIELDS/MAJORS: Ohio History

Open to master and doctoral level research projects in Ohio's past. Based on the relative quality of the project in terms of historical significance and the appropriateness of the proposed research methodology. Also considered is the relevance and usefulness of the anticipated results to the Commission and the people of Ohio in terms of helping them to understand the state's past. Contact the address listed for further information or call Maureen Damiani at (614) 752-0578.

Ohio Bicentennial Commission
Stephen C. George, Executive Director
Statehouse, Room 021 North
Columbus, OH 43215

1726
Ohio Instructional Grant, Ohio Student Choice Grant

AMOUNT: $288-$4296 DEADLINE: October 1
FIELDS/MAJORS: All Areas of Study

Scholarships are available to full-time undergraduates who are Ohio residents attending or planning to attend a college or university in Ohio. See your high school counselor or financial aid office, or contact the address listed for further information.

Ohio Student Aid Commission
Customer Service
PO Box 16610
Columbus, OH 43216

1727
Ohio League for Nursing Student Aid

AMOUNT: $500-$1000 DEADLINE: April 30
FIELDS/MAJORS: Nursing

Grants, loans, and combination grant/loans for students pursuing initial RN or LPN licensure. Renewable. Must live and attend school in the greater Cleveland area. Expected to join OLN after graduation and work as a nurse in the Cleveland area after graduation (Cuyahoga, Geauga, Lake, Lorain, Medina, Portage, or Summit counties). Write to the address below for details.

Ohio League for Nursing
Student Aid for Greater Cleveland Area
2800 Euclid Ave., Suite 235
Cleveland, OH 44115

1728
Ohio National Guard Tuition Program

AMOUNT: None Specified DEADLINE: None Specified
FIELDS/MAJORS: All Areas of Study

Open to members of the Ohio National Guard enlisted or re-enlisted for six years. Must be enrolled as an undergraduate in eligible higher education institution. Must be a U.S. citizen. Renewable for four years. Grant covers 60% of tuition and fees at state-supported schools. Applications are available at Ohio National Guard Recruiting Centers. Write to the address below for further details.

Ohio Adjutant General's Department
Office of Tuition Grant
2825 W. Granville Rd.
Columbus, OH 43235

1729
Ohio Pork Council Women Scholarship

AMOUNT: $500 DEADLINE: April 16
FIELDS/MAJORS: All Areas of Study

Scholarships for Ohio residents who are sons or daughters of members of a local and/or state Pork Producers Council. For junior, senior, or graduate study. Must have a GPA of at least 2.5. Write to the address below for more information.

Ohio Pork Council Women Scholarship
Ohio Pork Producers Council
5930 Sharon Woods Blvd., Suite 101
Columbus, OH 43229

1730
Ohio Safety Officers College Memorial Fund

AMOUNT: None Specified DEADLINE: None Specified
FIELDS/MAJORS: All Areas of Study

Scholarships are available to undergraduate Ohio residents who are children of peace officers or firefighters who were killed in the line of duty. Applicants must be under twenty-six years of age. Contact your school financial aid office or the address listed.

Ohio Student Aid Commission
Customer Service
PO Box 16610
Columbus, OH 43216

1731
Ohio Scholarship Challenge Program

AMOUNT: Maximum: $1000 DEADLINE: April 15
FIELDS/MAJORS: Travel and Tourism, Hotel/Motel Management

Awards for Ohio residents in one of the areas listed above who are enrolled in any two- or four-year college full-time. Must have a minimum GPA of 3.0 and be entering junior or senior year. Write to the address listed or call 1-800-682-8886 ext. 4251 for more information.

National Tourism Foundation
546 East Main St.
PO Box 3071
Lexington, KY 40596

1732
Ohio War Orphan Scholarships

AMOUNT: None Specified DEADLINE: July 1
FIELDS/MAJORS: All Areas of Study

Scholarships are available to undergraduate Ohio residents who are children of deceased or severely disabled veterans. Applicants must be under the age of twenty-one. Contact your school's financial aid office, your high school guidance counselor, or the address listed for further information.

Ohio Student Aid Commission
Customer Service
PO Box 16610
Columbus, OH 43216

1733
Oklahoma Area Higher Education Grant Program

AMOUNT: None Specified DEADLINE: None Specified
FIELDS/MAJORS: All Areas of Study

Open to members of the Seneca-Cayuga, Ottawa, Eastern Shawnee, Miami, Quapaw, Modoc, and Iowa of Kansas and Nebraska Indian tribes that are recognized federally. All students must be full-time and have a GPA of at least a 2.0. Submit applications for the fall quarter by June 1, spring (winter quarter) October 15, spring quarter January 15, and summer quarter April 15. For more information, write to the address below.

Bureau of Indian Affairs
Oklahoma Area Education Office
4149 Highline Blvd., Suite 380
Oklahoma City, OK 73108

1734
Oklahoma State Regents' Academic Scholars Program

AMOUNT: Maximum: $5500 DEADLINE: None Specified
FIELDS/MAJORS: All Areas of Study

Available to Oklahoma residents who score in the 99.5 percentile on the ACT or SAT exams. It is also awarded to residents and nonresidents who have been designated as a finalist or scholar in the National Merit, National Achievement, or National Hispanic Scholarship Competitions. Write to the address listed or call (405) 524-9153 for further details. Must have a GPA of at least 3.3.

Oklahoma State Regents for Higher Education
Academic Scholars Program
500 Education Bldg. State Capitol Complex
Oklahoma City, OK 73105

1735
Oklahoma Tuition Aid Grants

AMOUNT: Maximum: $1000 DEADLINE: None Specified
FIELDS/MAJORS: All Areas of Study

This is a need-based program that offers grants to students enrolled for a minimum of 6 credit hours. Family size and income are considered in determining the degree of financial need. The maximum award is 75% of enrollment costs or $1000, whichever is less. Must be Oklahoma residents attending an eligible Oklahoma school. Contact your high school or college financial aid office or write to the address listed for more information.

Oklahoma State Regents for Higher Education
Oklahoma Tuition Aid Grant Program
PO Box 3020
Oklahoma City, OK 73101-3020

1736
Olean Business Institute Scholarships

AMOUNT: $1000-$2800 DEADLINE: December 1
FIELDS/MAJORS: Business and Related Fields

Scholarships to Olean Business Institute given to freshmen based upon a competitive exam held on the first Saturdays of December and March. Second deadline date is March 7. Write to the address listed for further information.

Olean Business Institute
301 North York Union St.
Olean, NY 14760

1737
Olfactory Research Fund

AMOUNT: None Specified   DEADLINE: January 15
FIELDS/MAJORS: Otolaryngology

Fund is to support research which seeks to integrate the study of olfaction with current issues in developmental, perceptual, social, and cognitive psychology, and related disciplines. For those who are currently specializing in olfaction or those who wish to redirect their research. Applicant must possess a doctoral degree in a related field. Contact the address listed for additional information.

Olfactory Research Fund, Ltd.
145 E. 32nd St.
New York, NY 10016

1738
Olga Paul Scholarship Fund

AMOUNT: None Specified   DEADLINE: None Specified
FIELDS/MAJORS: Secondary Education

Scholarships for residents of Bishop, Texas (must have Bishop mailing address) who plan to enter the field of teaching. Preference given to those wanting to teach secondary English or other secondary level subject. Financial need and scholastic ability may be considered. Write to the address below for complete information.

Coastal Bend Community Foundation
Mercantile Tower MT276
615 N. Upper Broadway, #860
Corpus Christi, TX 78477

1739
Olin Fellowships

AMOUNT: $1000-$3000   DEADLINE: March 15
FIELDS/MAJORS: Fisheries, Marine Biology, and Related Areas

ASF Fellowships are offered annually to individuals seeking to improve their knowledge or skills in advanced fields related to Atlantic Salmon (Biology, Management, or Conservation). For use at any accredited university, research laboratory, or active management program. Must be U.S. or Canadian citizen. Application forms may be obtained from the Atlantic Salmon Federation at the address below or from Box 429, St. Andrews, N.B., E0G 2X0, Canada.

Atlantic Salmon Federation
PO Box 807
Calais, ME 04619

1740
Olive B. O'Conner Annual Music Award

AMOUNT: Maximum: $500   DEADLINE: January 25
FIELDS/MAJORS: Music

Scholarships for high school seniors planning on studying music who are from one of the following New York counties: Allegany, Cattaraugus, Chautauqua, Erie, Niagara, Orleans, or Wyoming. Write to the address listed for more information.

New York State Federation of Women's Clubs
8th District Music Chairman, D. Blakely
155 Seneca St.
Gowanda, NY 14070

1741
Olympus Advanced Endoscopic Training Scholarship

AMOUNT: $40000   DEADLINE: September 3
FIELDS/MAJORS: Gastroenterology, Endoscopic Procedures

Candidates must have completed (or currently completing) a minimum of eighteen months of formal accredited gastroenterology training or equivalent endoscopic training within an accredited surgical training program. The physician should be committed to assuming a faculty position at an academic center. Two awards are given annually. Contact the address below for further information or Web sites: http://www.gastro.org; http://www.asge.org; or http://hepar-sfgh.ucsf.edu.

American Digestive Health Foundation
Ms. Irene Kuo
7910 Woodmont Ave., 7th Floor
Bethesda, MD 20814

1742
Omar Stang Academic Scholarship

AMOUNT: None Specified   DEADLINE: April 20
FIELDS/MAJORS: All Areas of Study

Scholarships for high school seniors whose parents are employees of South Miami Hospital. Based on academics, civic involvement, and financial need. Must be going full-time to a four-year college or university. Recipients must maintain a minimum GPA of 2.8. Write to the address below for details.

Omar Stang Family/South Miami Health Systems, Inc.
Noelene Westman
7400 SW 62nd Ave.
Miami, FL 33143

1743
Omicron Nu Research and Maude Gilchrist Fellowships

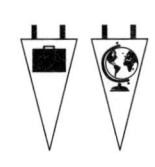

AMOUNT: Maximum: $2000 DEADLINE: January 15
FIELDS/MAJORS: Home Economics/Related Fields

Applicants must be members of Kappa Omicron Nu and enrolled in a Ph.D. program in home economics. Awards will be announced April 1. Write to the address listed for details.

Kappa Omicron Nu Honor Society
4990 Northwind Dr., Suite 140
East Lansing, MI 48823

1744
On-Line Editing Program

AMOUNT: $1000 DEADLINE: November 15
FIELDS/MAJORS: News Editing, Reporting

Summer jobs open to juniors, seniors, and graduate students as editors and reporters for on-line newspapers publishing on the World Wide Web. Interns are paid regular wages by the on-line newspapers for which they work. Students returning to school will receive a $1000 scholarship to continue their education. Contact the address listed for further information or (609) 452-2820. Applications available from August 15 through November 1.

Dow Jones News Foundation
PO Box 300
Princeton, NJ 08543

1745
Oncological Research Awards

AMOUNT: None Specified DEADLINE: March 1
FIELDS/MAJORS: Oncology

The American Cancer Society provides support for junior investigators as well as established researchers into areas related to cancer. Both basic and applied research is supported. Must hold Ph.D. at the time application for funding is made. Write to the address below or call (404) 329-7558 for details and policies.

American Cancer Society, Inc.
Extramural Grants and Awards
1599 Clifton Rd., NE
Atlanta, GA 30329

1746
Oncology Nursing Certification Corporation Master's Scholarships

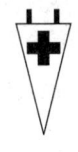

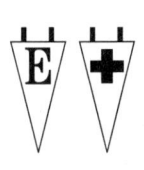

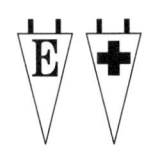

AMOUNT: $3000 DEADLINE: February 1
FIELDS/MAJORS: Oncology Nursing

Scholarships available to master's students in the field of oncology nursing. All applicants must be currently licensed registered nurses. For full-time or part-time studies at an NLN-accredited school of nursing. Write to the address listed for more information.

Oncology Nursing Foundation
501 Holiday Dr.
Pittsburgh, PA 15220

1747
Oncology Nursing Ethnic Minority Bachelor's Scholarships

AMOUNT: $2000 DEADLINE: February 1
FIELDS/MAJORS: Oncology Nursing

Scholarships available to minority bachelor's students in the field of oncology nursing. All applicants must be currently licensed registered nurses. For full- or part-time students in an NLN-accredited school of nursing. Write to the address listed for more information.

Oncology Nursing Foundation
501 Holiday Dr.
Pittsburgh, PA 15220

1748
Oncology Nursing Ethnic Minority Master's Scholarships

AMOUNT: $3000 DEADLINE: February 1
FIELDS/MAJORS: Oncology Nursing

Scholarships available to ethnic minority master's students enrolled in the field of oncology nursing. All applicants must be currently licensed registered nurses. For full-time or part-time students. Write to the address listed for more information.

Oncology Nursing Foundation
501 Holiday Dr.
Pittsburgh, PA 15220

1749
Oncology Nursing Foundation and Glaxo Wellcome Master's Scholarships

AMOUNT: $3000 DEADLINE: February 1
FIELDS/MAJORS: Oncology Nursing

Scholarships available to master's students in the field of oncology nursing. All applicants must be currently licensed registered nurses and currently enrolled, full- or part-time in a degree program in an NLN accredited school of nursing. Write to the address listed for more information about both these awards.

Oncology Nursing Foundation
501 Holiday Dr.
Pittsburgh, PA 15220

1750
Oncology Nursing Foundation Research Grants

AMOUNT: $3000-$10000 DEADLINE: November 1
FIELDS/MAJORS: Oncology Nursing

Research grants available to students and scholars in the field of oncology nursing. The individual criteria for each award may vary. All applicants must be registered nurses actively involved in some aspect of care of patients with cancer. The awards include: Oncology Nursing Foundation Research Grant, Oncology Nursing Society Research Grant, Ortho Biotech Research Grant, Pharmacia and Upjohn, Inc. Research Grant, Purdue Frederick Research Grant, Rhone-Poulenc Rorer Pharmaceuticals, Inc. New Investigators Research Grants, Sigma Theta Tau International/ONS Research Grant, and the SmithKline Beecham Oncology Research Grants. These seven awards offer a total of ten grants annually. Write to the address listed for more information about all eight awards.

Oncology Nursing Foundation
501 Holiday Dr.
Pittsburgh, PA 15220

1751
Oncology Nursing, Immunex and Roberta Scofield Bachelor's Scholarships

AMOUNT: Maximum: $2000 DEADLINE: February 1
FIELDS/MAJORS: Oncology Nursing

Scholarships available to nurses enrolled in a bachelor program in the field of oncology nursing. All applicants must be currently licensed registered nurses and be able to demonstrate a commitment to oncology nursing. For full- or part-time students in an NLN-accredited School of Nursing. The awards include: Immunex Bachelor's Scholarships, Oncology Nursing Certification Corporation Bachelor's Scholarships, and Roberta Pierce Scofield Bachelor's Scholarships. Combined, fifteen awards are offered annually. Write to the address listed for more information about all three awards.

Oncology Nursing Foundation
501 Holiday Dr.
Pittsburgh, PA 15220

1752
Opal Dancey Memorial Foundation

AMOUNT: $2500 DEADLINE: June 15
FIELDS/MAJORS: Theology

Grants awarded primarily in the Midwest. Preference given to McCormick, United, Garrett, Trinity, Asbury, and Methodist Theological School in Ohio. Given to students seeking a master of divinity degree only from accredited theological schools and seminaries. Renewable if recipients maintain satisfactory scholastic work. Applications sent January through May 31. Write to the address below for more information.

Opal Dancey Memorial Foundation
Rev. Gary R. Imms, Chairman
45 South St.
Croswell, MI 48422

1753
Oppenheim Student's Fund, Inc. Scholarships

AMOUNT: $250-$1500 DEADLINE: May 1
FIELDS/MAJORS: All Areas of Study

Open to high school seniors who are residents of Niagara County or seniors in a Niagara County high school. Contact the address listed for further information or (716) 286-4243.

Oppenheim Students Fund, Inc.
Anne Lascelle, Board of Education
607 Walnut Ave.
Niagara Falls, NY 14303

1754
Oregon AFL-CIO Graduating Seniors Scholarships

AMOUNT: None Specified DEADLINE: March 1
FIELDS/MAJORS: All Areas of Study

Open to Oregon high school seniors. In addition to required essays, applicants must also submit an essay of five hundred words or less in response to the question, "In recent months, there has been a lot of debate on both the state and federal level about raising the minimum wage. What kind of wage or salary is needed to support a family?" For more information about minimum wage, call Amy Klare (503) 585-6320. Preference may be given to applicants from union families. Must be a U.S. citizen or permanent resident to apply. This is a one time award. Contact the address below for further information.

Oregon State Scholarship Commission
Private Awards
1500 Valley River Dr., #100
Eugene, OR 97401-2130

1755
Oregon Associated Loggers (OAL) Scholarship Grant

AMOUNT: Maximum: $1200   DEADLINE: April 11
FIELDS/MAJORS: Forestry and Related

Grant for Oregon high school seniors who intend to pursue a college education at a four-year institution majoring in forest resource and/or related field(s). Based on application, transcripts, and an essay (less than two pages). Currently offers three awards annually. Write to the address below for details.

Oregon Associated Loggers, Inc.
1127 25th St., SE
PO Box 12339
Salem, OR 97309

1756
Oregon Association of Public Accountants Scholarships

AMOUNT: Maximum: $1000   DEADLINE: April 1
FIELDS/MAJORS: Accounting

Scholarships for Oregon residents who will be incoming freshmen in Oregon schools pursuing a career in accounting. Ten to fifteen awards offered annually. The sponsor urges applicants to pay close attention to the instructions on the application form (or else be disqualified). Mail your request for an application to the address below and enclose a #10 SASE envelope.

Oregon Association of Public Accountants
Scholarship Foundation
1804 NE 43rd Ave.
Portland, OR 97213

1757
Oregon Private 150 Scholarship

AMOUNT: None Specified   DEADLINE: March 1
FIELDS/MAJORS: Business

Open to Oregon residents who are U.S. citizens and entering junior or senior year or graduate school. Must have a minimum GPA of 3.0 and be enrolled full-time. For use at any school in Oregon. Contact the address below for further information.

Oregon State Scholarship Commission
Private Awards
1500 Valley River Dr., #100
Eugene, OR 97401-2130

1758
Oregon Sheep Growers Association Scholarship

AMOUNT: $1000   DEADLINE: July 15
FIELDS/MAJORS: Animal Husbandry, Agriculture, Pre-Veterinary Medicine, Animal Science

Two scholarships for students in the areas of animal husbandry and agriculture, with an interest in the sheep industry. For sophomore, junior, senior, or graduate students. Applicant must be a resident of Oregon but does not need to attend an Oregon school. Write to the address below for details.

Oregon Sheep Growers Association
Scholarship Committee
1270 Chemeketa St., NE
Salem, OR 97301

1759
Oregon State Home Builders Scholarships

AMOUNT: None Specified   DEADLINE: March 1
FIELDS/MAJORS: Construction Engineering, Architectural Engineering, Building Construction

Scholarships for students of construction engineering, housing studies, or interior merchandising at Oregon State University; building inspection at Chemeketa Community College; construction technology at Lane College or Portland Community College; architectural engineering at Mt. Hood Community College; or building construction at Clackamas Community College. Contact the financial aid office at your college for details.

Oregon State Scholarship Commission
Attn: Grant Department
1500 Valley River Dr., #100
Eugene, OR 97401

1760
Ornamental Horticulture Scholarship

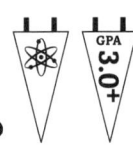

AMOUNT: Maximum: $1000   DEADLINE: March 31
FIELDS/MAJORS: Ornamental Horticulture

Open to juniors and seniors enrolled in ornamental horticulture at any of the following three schools: University of California, Davis, Cal Poly-Pomona, and Cal Poly-San

Luis Obispo. Demonstrated involvement in academics, community, and professional activities will be required. Write to the address listed for details or call (202) 686-8337. Must have a GPA of at least 3.0.

Landscape Architecture Foundation
Scholarship Program
4401 Connecticut Ave. NW, #500
Washington, DC 20008

1761
Osage Tribal Education Committee Program

AMOUNT: None Specified   DEADLINE: None Specified
FIELDS/MAJORS: All Areas of Study

Open to Osage Indians enrolled in accredited postsecondary educational institutions including college, university, technical, and vocational schools. Submit applications by the fall semester July 1, spring semester December 31, and summer term May 1. For more information write to the address below.

Osage Tribal Education Committee
Oklahoma Area Education Office
4149 Highline Blvd., Suite 380
Oklahoma City, OK 73108

1762
Oscar W. Rittenhouse Memorial Scholarship

AMOUNT: Maximum: $2500   DEADLINE: June 15
FIELDS/MAJORS: Law, Law Enforcement

Open to New Jersey residents who are enrolled in or accepted into law school and who have an interest in pursuing a career in law enforcement. One-year scholarship grant. Recipients may reapply in succeeding years. Write to the address listed for details. Be sure to use the award name on the envelope.

County Prosecutors Association of New Jersey Foundation
Scholarship Coordinator
25 Market St., CN-085
Trenton, NJ 08625

1763
Oshkosh Foundation Grants

AMOUNT: None Specified   DEADLINE: None Specified
FIELDS/MAJORS: All Areas of Study

Scholarships are offered by the Oshkosh Foundation for the benefit of residents of Oshkosh, Wisconsin. Must be graduating high school senior from one of the six schools in the Oshkosh school district and be a resident of Oshkosh or of Winnebago County. Write to the address listed for further information. Must have a GPA of at least 3.0.

Oshkosh Foundation
404 N. Main St.
PO Box 1726
Oshkosh, WI 54902

1764
Osteopathic Medical Student Loan for Service Program

AMOUNT: Maximum: $12000   DEADLINE: July 1
FIELDS/MAJORS: Osteopathic Medicine

Loans open to New Mexico residents who are students in osteopathic medicine or a physician assistant program in New Mexico. Must be U.S. citizens or permanent residents and be able to demonstrate financial need. Loan may be forgiven by working in a medically underserved area of New Mexico. Write to the address listed for further information.

New Mexico Commission on Higher Education
Financial Aid and Student Services
PO Box 15910
Santa Fe, NM 87506

1765
Oswald Boehme Scholarship

AMOUNT: Maximum: $250   DEADLINE: March 1
FIELDS/MAJORS: Manufacturing Engineering, Manufacturing Engineering Technology

Open to full-time undergraduates enrolled in a degree program at one of the following institutions: Marquette University or Valparaiso University. Must have a minimum GPA of 3.0. One award is offered annually. Write to the address listed for more information.

Society of Manufacturing Engineers Education Foundation
One SME Dr.
PO Box 930
Dearborn, MI 48121-0930

1766
Ottis Lock Scholarships

AMOUNT: $250-$500   DEADLINE: May 1
FIELDS/MAJORS: American History-East Texas

One scholarship for a student pursuing the study of history or social studies at a college or university in east Texas. The association supports studies relating to east Texas. Award is not renewable. Research grants for study of east Texas history are also available. Write to the address below for details.

East Texas Historical Association
Ottis Lock Scholarship
PO Box 6223, SFA Station
Nacogdoches, TX 75962

1767
Otto M. Stanfield Legal Scholarship

AMOUNT: None Specified DEADLINE: February 15
FIELDS/MAJORS: Law

Open to active Unitarian Universalist members who are entering law school and have financial need. Write to the address listed or call (617) 742-2100 for details.

Unitarian Universalist Association
Publication Department
25 Beacon St.
Boston, MA 02108

1768
Outboard Marine Foundation Scholarships

AMOUNT: $500-$4000 DEADLINE: February 1
FIELDS/MAJORS: All Areas of Study

Awards for students who are children of Outboard Marine Corporation employees. High school seniors and undergraduates may apply. Contact the address below for further information.

Outboard Marine Corporation
Mr. Laurin M. Baker, Secretary
100 Sea Horse Dr.
Waukegan, IL 60085

1769
Outcomes Research Training Award

AMOUNT: Maximum: $100000 DEADLINE: September 10
FIELDS/MAJORS: Gastroenterology Medicine

Applicants must be M.D.'s who are committed to academic careers and who have completed the clinical training necessary for board eligibility in gastroenterology (twelve months) at an accredited North American institution. Write to the address below for more information or Web sites: http://www.gastro.org; http://www.asge.org; or http://hepar-sfgh.uscf.edu.

American Digestive Health Foundation
Ms. Irene Kuo
7910 Woodmont Ave., 7th Floor
Bethesda, MD 20814

1770
Overseas Press Club Foundation Scholarships

AMOUNT: Maximum: $1000 DEADLINE: December 8
FIELDS/MAJORS: Journalism

Awards open to students studying in the U.S. who aspire to careers as foreign correspondents. Must submit a cover letter and essay of approximately five hundred words, concentrates on an area of the world or an international issue that is in keeping with the applicant's interest. May be in the form of a story, news analysis, or traditional essay. The cover letter should be autobiographical in nature illustrating how you developed your interest in a particular part of the world or issue or how you would use your scholarship. Inquiries can be made by mail at the address listed, by phone at (212) 983-4655 or by fax at (212) 983-4692. Judges will be looking for strong reporting skills, color, and understanding or passion. All entries must be typed.

Overseas Press Club Foundation
William J. Holstein, President
320 E. 42nd St.
New York, NY 10017

1771
Owen Electric Cooperative Scholarship Program

AMOUNT: Maximum: $2000 DEADLINE: February 1
FIELDS/MAJORS: All Areas of Study

Scholarships are available for students living in Owen Electric's service area, who are U.S. citizens, juniors, or seniors, with a GPA of at least 3.0. For full-time study. Service area covers Boone, Campbell, Carroll, Gallatin, Grant, Kenton, Owen, Pendleton, and Scott counties in Kentucky. Write to the address below for information.

Owen Electric Cooperative
Scholarship Program
510 South Main St.
Owenton, KY 40359

1772
P.L.A.Y. Corps Awards

AMOUNT: Maximum: $500 DEADLINE: None Specified
FIELDS/MAJORS: Sports Coaching

Open to college students who are athletic, service oriented, like kids, and participated in sports while growing up. This sponsor first offers a training clinic then affords an opportunity to coach a team (in the sport of the students choice) for eighty to one hundred hours. At the end of the "season," the coaches receive $500 towards tuition. Sports involved include: baseball, basketball, cheerleading, football, softball, swimming, tennis, track and field, and ice hockey. Contact the address below for further information.

P.L.A.Y. Corps
NIKE, Inc.
1 Bowerman Dr.
Beaverton, OR 97005

1773

Pennsylvania Association of Conservation District Auxiliary Scholarships

AMOUNT: Maximum: $200 DEADLINE: None Specified
FIELDS/MAJORS: Agriculture, Agribusiness, Biology, Horticulture, Floriculture, Natural Resources

Open to juniors and seniors who are Pennsylvania residents and U.S. citizens. Must be able to demonstrate financial need. For use at two- or four-year Pennsylvania schools. These awards are not renewable. Contact the address listed for further information and deadline dates or call (814) 696-0877.

Pennsylvania Assn. of Conservation Dist. Auxiliary
Donna Fisher
1407 Blair St.
Hollidaysburg, PA 16648

1774

Pacific Printing and Imaging Association Scholarships

AMOUNT: $500-$2500 DEADLINE: April 1
FIELDS/MAJORS: Printing, Graphic Arts

Open to residents of Washington, Oregon, Alaska, Idaho, Montana, or Hawaii who plan careers in printing, print management, or graphic arts technology. An essay and references will be required. May be renewed. Contact the address listed for further information. Must have a GPA of at least 2.9.

Pacific Printing and Imaging Association
Jim Olsen, President
180 Nickerson, #102
Seattle, WA 98109

1775

Padgett Business Services Scholarships

AMOUNT: $500-$4000 DEADLINE: March 1
FIELDS/MAJORS: All Areas of Study

Open to high school seniors planning to attend an accredited college or university. Applicants, parent(s), or guardian(s) must own and operate (be active in the day-to-day operations) a small business (fewer than twenty employees). Must own at least 10% of the stock or capital of the business. Based on GPAs, test scores, and educational and career plans. All regional winners will become eligible for the grand prize scholarship of $4000. Local winners will be announced in May, and the grand prize will be awarded in July. Contact the local Padgett Business Services in your area (425 locations) for additional information and applications. Addresses and phone numbers are in phone directories or call 1-800-723-4388 in the U.S., 1-800-363-3123 in Canada, or 1-888-723-4388 in Quebec/The Maritimes.

Padgett Business Services

1776

Palmetto Fellows Scholarship

AMOUNT: Maximum: $5000 DEADLINE: None Specified
FIELDS/MAJORS: All Areas of Study

Scholarships for South Carolina residents who will be entering freshmen. Based on demonstrated academic ability and SAT test scores. For use at a South Carolina institution. Write to the address below for additional information. Must have a GPA of at least 3.5.

South Carolina Commission on Higher Education
1333 Main St., Suite 200
Columbia, SC 29201

1777

PAMA Scholarship

AMOUNT: None Specified DEADLINE: October 31
FIELDS/MAJORS: Aviation-Maintenance

Scholarships for students working toward a license in airframe and powerplant (A & P). Must have completed at least 25% of course and have a GPA of at least 3.0. Financial need and recommendation are also considered. Applications are accepted and given priority in the order of Pama Chapters, institutions, and individuals. Applications accepted July 1 through October 31. Recipients will be notified by end of December. Write to the address below for details.

Professional Aviation Maintenance Association, Inc.
PAMA Headquarters
1200 Eighteenth St. NW, #401
Washington, DC 20036

1778

Panasonic and Itzhak Perlman Young Soloists Award

AMOUNT: None Specified DEADLINE: November 3
FIELDS/MAJORS: Vocal Music, Instrumental Music

Scholarship is available to applicants who are vocalist or instrumentalist and are twenty-five years of age and under and disabled. Write to the address below for more information.

Very Special Arts
Education Office
J.F. Kennedy Center for the Performing Art
Washington, DC 20566

1779
Parkersburg Zonta Club Scholarship

AMOUNT: $500 DEADLINE: May 9
FIELDS/MAJORS: All Areas of Study

Open to female full-time juniors and seniors. Must be current residents of Wood County, West Virginia, or Belpre, Ohio, and graduated from a high school in either of those areas. Must have a minimum GPA of 3.0. Based on application, financial need, and a well-defined career objective. Write to the address listed for details.

Zonta Club of Parkersburg
PO Box 184
Parkersburg, WV 26102

1780
Parking Industry Institute Scholarship

AMOUNT: $500-$2000 DEADLINE: March 1
FIELDS/MAJORS: All Areas of Study

Thirteen scholarships for students who are members, or whose parents are members, of the National Parking Association. Based on service, "good" grades, and financial need. May be renewed. Write to the address below for details. Must have a GPA of at least 2.8.

National Parking Association
Mr. David Cotter
1112-16th St. NW
Washington, DC 20036

1781
Parrett Scholarship

AMOUNT: None Specified DEADLINE: None Specified
FIELDS/MAJORS: Engineering, Science, Medicine, or Dentistry

Open to residents of Washington who have completed their first year of college. Must be enrolled full-time. Contact the address listed for further information.

Parrett Scholarship Foundation
U.S. Bank of Washington, Trustee
PO Box 720
Seattle, WA 98111-0720

1782
Past President's Parley Nurses Scholarships

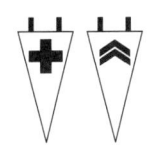

AMOUNT: None Specified DEADLINE: June 1
FIELDS/MAJORS: Nursing

Five scholarships are available to Ohio residents pursuing a career in nursing who are U.S. citizens and children of veterans (living, deceased or disabled) who served during the following time frames: 4/6/17-11/11/18, 12/7/41-12/31/46, 6/25/50-1/31/55, 12/22/61-5/7/75, 8/24/82-7/31/84, 12/20/89-1/31/90, 8/2/90 to cessation. Write to the address below for additional information.

American Legion Auxiliary-Department of Ohio
Department Secretary
1100 Brandywine Blvd., Bldg. D, Box 2279
Zanesville, OH 43702

1783
Past Presidents' Parley Health Occupation Scholarships

AMOUNT: Maximum: $300 DEADLINE: May 15
FIELDS/MAJORS: Nursing Assistant, Dental Assistant, L.P.N., Lab Technician, Therapy

Scholarships are available for Arizona residents who are U.S. citizens pursuing a degree in a health-related field. Must be enrolled/accepted into an accredited institution in Arizona that offers a certificate or degree program in healthcare occupations. Immediate family members of veterans will be given priority. Based on character, academics, initiative, and financial need. Write to the address listed for information. Must have a GPA of at least 2.5.

American Legion Auxiliary-Department of Arizona
Past Presidents' Parley Chairman
4701 N. 19th Ave., #100
Phoenix, AZ 85015

1784
Patricia and Gail Ishimoto Memorial Scholarships

AMOUNT: None Specified DEADLINE: April 1
FIELDS/MAJORS: All Areas of Study

Open to incoming freshmen who are members of Japanese ancestry and entering or enrolled at an accredited college or university. Applications and information may be obtained from local JACL chapters, district offices, and the national headquarters at the address listed or call (415) 921-5225. Please indicate your level of study and be certain to include a legal-sized SASE.

Japanese-American Citizens League
National Scholarship and Award Program
1765 Sutter St.
San Francisco, CA 94115

1785
Paul A. Greebler Scholarship

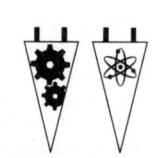

AMOUNT: Maximum: $2000 DEADLINE: March 1
FIELDS/MAJORS: Nuclear Engineering/Nuclear Science

Applicants must have completed two or more years in a nuclear science or nuclear engineering program. Sponsorship by a branch, division, local section, or member of the American Nuclear Society is required. Must be a U.S. citizen. Write to address shown for details. With your application request, please include the name of the university you will be attending, year you will be in, and major course of study.

American Nuclear Society
H&A Scholarship Program
555 N. Kensington Ave.
La Grange Park, IL 60525

1786
Paul and Helen Grauer Scholarship

AMOUNT: $1000 DEADLINE: February 1
FIELDS/MAJORS: Electronics, Communications, Related Fields

Scholarship available to students with a novice class amateur radio license, who are enrolled as full-time students in one of the above fields and reside in and attend school in Iowa, Kansas, Missouri, or Nebraska. Write to the address listed for information.

ARRL Foundation (American Radio Relay League)
Scholarship Program
225 Main St.
Newington, CT 06111

1787
Paul and Mary Haas Foundation Scholarship Grant

AMOUNT: Maximum: $1500 DEADLINE: August 30
FIELDS/MAJORS: All Areas of Study

Scholarships are available to graduating high school seniors who reside within thirty miles of Corpus Christi, have above average grades, and can demonstrate financial need. Write to the address listed for information. Must have a GPA of at least 3.0.

Paul and Mary Haas Foundation
Scholarship Program
PO Box 2928
Corpus Christi, TX 78403

1788
Paul Arnold Memorial Scholarship

AMOUNT: Maximum: $3500 DEADLINE: February 20
FIELDS/MAJORS: Interior Design, Fashion Design, Graphic Design

Awards open to gay/lesbian students who can demonstrate financial need, originality of vision, and aptitude. Contact the address listed for further information.

Greater Seattle Business Association and Pride Foundation
2033 6th Ave., #804
Seattle, WA 98121

1789
Paul Fowler Scholarship

AMOUNT: Maximum: $2830 DEADLINE: None Specified
FIELDS/MAJORS: All Areas of Study

Scholarship program for high school seniors in Washington state who are designated as Washington scholars. Nonrenewable. Must demonstrate "outstanding ability and willingness to work for an education." Write to the address below for information. Must have a GPA of at least 2.8.

Washington Higher Education Coordinating Board
917 Lakeridge Way
PO Box 43430
Olympia, WA 98504

1790
Paul H. Kutschenreuter Scholarship

AMOUNT: $5000 DEADLINE: June 16
FIELDS/MAJORS: Meteorology, Atmospheric Science

Scholarships for students entering their last year of study toward a degree in meteorology. Based on academics and financial need. Must have a minimum GPA of 3.0, be enrolled full-time, and be U.S. citizens or permanent residents. Application forms and further information may be obtained through the AMS headquarters at the address listed.

American Meteorological Society
45 Beacon St.
Boston, MA 02108

1791
Paul Jackson Memorial Scholarship, V.L. Peterson Scholarship

AMOUNT: None Specified DEADLINE: July 1
FIELDS/MAJORS: All Areas of Study

Scholarships available to members of the American Jersey Cattle Association who are of sophomore standing or above. This award also includes the William A. Russell Scholarship. Write to the address listed for details.

American Jersey Cattle Association
Scholarship Committee
6486 East Main St.
Reynoldsburg, OH 43068

1792
Paul L. Fowler Memorial Scholarship

AMOUNT: Maximum: $3000   DEADLINE: January 31
FIELDS/MAJORS: All Areas of Study

Scholarships are available for Idaho residents graduating high school seniors who demonstrate outstanding academic ability. For full-time undergraduate study at any accredited U.S. college or university. Two awards are offered annually. Must be U.S. citizens. Write to the address listed for information. Must have a GPA of at least 3.0.

Idaho State Board of Education
PO Box 83720
Boise, ID 83720

1793
Paumanauke Native American Indian Scholarship

AMOUNT: $500   DEADLINE: July 1
FIELDS/MAJORS: All Areas of Study

Scholarships are available for tribally-enrolled Native American attending colleges, universities, or accredited postsecondary institutions on a full-time basis. Write to the address below for information.

Paumanauke Pow-Wow and Native American Living Arts Festival, Inc.
333 Lagoon Dr. South
Copiague, NY 11726

1794
Pawtucket East High School Class of '42 Scholarship

AMOUNT: Maximum: $500   DEADLINE: April 1
FIELDS/MAJORS: All Areas of Study

Scholarships are available for graduating seniors of Tolman High School in Pawtucket, Rhode Island. One award is given annually. Write to the address listed for information.

Rhode Island Foundation
Special Funds Office
70 Elm St.
Providence, RI 02903

1795
PCT&S and Presidential Scholarships

AMOUNT: None Specified   DEADLINE: April 15
FIELDS/MAJORS: All Areas of Study

Must be high school seniors in top 20% of class. Must submit SAT score. Must maintain GPA of 3.0 (or better) to continue scholarship. Residents of OH, MA, DE, CT, or VT are also eligible. Renewable. Contact address listed for complete information. Scholarships for continuing students and students who do not meet the criteria for the above awards are also available: check the PCT&S catalog for information on these awards.

Philadelphia College of Textiles and Science
Schoolhouse Ln. and Henry Ave.
Attn: Scholarship Programs
Philadelphia, PA 19144

1796
Peace Scholar Dissertation Fellowships

AMOUNT: $14000   DEADLINE: November 17
FIELDS/MAJORS: Areas Related to International Peace and Conflict Management

Fellowships are available for doctoral candidates who have demonstrated a clear interest in issues of international peace and conflict management, who have completed all required work except the dissertation. Dissertation study must reflect a topic that advances the state of knowledge about international peace and conflict management. Write to the address listed for information.

U.S. Institute of Peace
Jennings Randolph Fellowship Program
1550 M St. NW, Suite 700
Washington, DC 20005

1797
Pearl Harbor-Honolulu Branch 46 Fleet Reserve Association Scholarship

AMOUNT: None Specified   DEADLINE: April 15
FIELDS/MAJORS: All Areas of Study

Scholarships for sons, daughters, and spouses of members in good standing (alive or deceased) of the Pearl Harbor-Honolulu Branch 46 of the Fleet Reserve Association. Based on academics, character, leadership, and financial need. Write to the address below for additional information.

Fleet Reserve Association
Pearl Harbor-Honolulu Branch 46
PO Box 6067
Honolulu, HI 96818

1798
Pendleton Community Memorial Health Corporation Scholarships

AMOUNT: Maximum: $1500   DEADLINE: June 20
FIELDS/MAJORS: Health/Medicine, Dentistry

Scholarships for residents of the following areas: Pendleton, Pilot Rock, Athena, Weston, Adams, Helix, and Ukiah (Umatilla County, Oregon). For study in a healthcare-related field. For full-time study. Applicants must maintain a 2.0 GPA. Write to the address listed or call Norman Vorvick at (503) 276-1260 ext. 209 for more information.

Pendleton Community Memorial Health Corporation
PO Box 786
Pendleton, OR 97801

1799
Pennsylvania Association of Conservation Districts Auxiliary Scholarships

AMOUNT: Maximum: $500   DEADLINE: June 30
FIELDS/MAJORS: Agriculture, Conservation, Environmental Studies

Scholarships for Pennsylvania residents studying in one of the above fields in Pennsylvania. For junior or senior students in four-year programs and second year students in associate degree programs. Based on need. Write to "Scholarship" at the address below for details.

PACD Auxiliary
Blair County Conservation District
1407 Blair St.
Holidaysburg, PA 16648

1800
Peoria Journal Star Scholarships

AMOUNT: Maximum: $1000   DEADLINE: May 1
FIELDS/MAJORS: Journalism

Scholarships for graduating high school seniors living in the Peoria Journal Star's circulation area. Renewable for up to four years. Write to address below for details.

Peoria Journal Star
Director, Educational Services
1 News Plaza
Peoria, IL 61643

1801
Pepper Family Foundation Scholarship

AMOUNT: Maximum: $1000   DEADLINE: November 7
FIELDS/MAJORS: All Areas of Study

Open to students attending any one of twelve ACI member schools. Each school sets its own criteria, but the candidates must be nominated by their financial aid offices. If this information is in your profile, you have indicated that you attend one of the member schools. Verify your school's membership with the financial aid office. Do not write to the listed address, they cannot provide any additional information or forms. Contact your financial aid office for further information. Applicants must be recommended by the financial aid office of their school. The school offices will have the information.

Associated Colleges of Illinois
ACI Program Administration
1735 N. Paulina Ave., Loft 401
Chicago, IL 60622

1802
Pergamon-NWSA Graduate Scholarship in Women's Studies

AMOUNT: $500-$1000   DEADLINE: February 15
FIELDS/MAJORS: Women's Studies

Award available for a woman researching for a master's thesis or Ph.D. dissertation in women's studies. Preference will be given to NWSA members and to those whose research projects focus on "color" or "class." Two awards per year. Write to the address below for details.

National Women's Studies Association
/100 Baltimore Ave., Suite 301
University of Maryland
College Park, MD 20740

1803
Perry F. Hadlock Memorial Scholarship

AMOUNT: $1000   DEADLINE: February 1
FIELDS/MAJORS: Electrical Engineering

Scholarship available to students with a general class amateur radio license, who are enrolled as full-time electrical engineering students. Preference will be given to students at Clarkson University. Write to the address listed for information.

ARRL Foundation (American Radio Relay League)
Scholarship Program
225 Main St.
Newington, CT 06111

1804
Peter Connacher Scholarships

AMOUNT: None Specified   DEADLINE: March 1
FIELDS/MAJORS: All Areas of Study

Scholarships for Oregon residents who were prisoners of war or who are descendants of prisoners of war. Must be able to provide documentation. Renewable. Must be U.S. citizens or permanent residents to apply. Contact your high school guidance department, your college financial aid office, or the address listed for details.

Oregon State Scholarship Commission
Attn: Grant Department
1500 Valley River Dr., #100
Eugene, OR 97401

1805
Peter D. Courtois Concrete Construction Scholarships

AMOUNT: Maximum: $1000   DEADLINE: January 15
FIELDS/MAJORS: Engineering, Construction, Material Science

Open to upcoming seniors majoring in any of the fields listed above. Selections based on demonstrated interest and ability to work in the field of concrete construction. Must have a course load of six or more credit hours each semester during the period for which the awards are made. Write to the address below for details. Must have a GPA of at least 2.8.

American Concrete Institute
ACI ConREF
PO Box 9094
Farmington Hills, MI 48333

1806
Peter Doctor Memorial Indian Scholarship Foundation

AMOUNT: None Specified   DEADLINE: May 31
FIELDS/MAJORS: All Areas of Study

Open to students who are enrolled members of New York State Indian tribes after one full year of college. Applicants must contact their representative according to what Reservation they are enrolled with. Write to the address below for more information.

Peter Doctor Memorial Indian Scholarship Foundation, Inc.
Clara Hill, Treasurer
PO Box 731
Basom, NY 14013

1807
Peter J. Derosier Memorial Scholarship

AMOUNT: None Specified   DEADLINE: March 15
FIELDS/MAJORS: All Areas of Study

Open to students from western Massachusetts who are at least twenty-four years of age and entering college for the first time. Contact the address listed for further information.

Community Foundation of Western Massachusetts
PO Box 15769
1500 Main St.
Springfield, MA 01115

1808
Peter Kaufman Memorial Scholarship

AMOUNT: Maximum: $1000   DEADLINE: June 15
FIELDS/MAJORS: All Areas of Study

Open to high school seniors who are lesbian, gay, bisexual, or transgendered, pursuing studies primarily in California. Based on involvement/work with the gay community. Contact the address listed for further information. If you write for information, include a SASE for a reply.

Gay and Lesbian Education Commission
Kathy J. Gill, L.A. Unified School Dist.
450 N. Grand Ave.
Los Angeles, CA 90012

1809
PG&E, LGBEA, and GLSEN Scholarship

AMOUNT: $500-$1000   DEADLINE: None Specified
FIELDS/MAJORS: All Areas of Study

Open to gay, lesbian, or bisexual high school seniors from the San Francisco Bay area. Must be in good academic standing and reside in any of the following nine counties: Alameda, Contra Costa, Marin, Napa, San Francisco, San Mateo, Santa Clara, Sonoma, and Solano. Must also be able to provide proof of enrollment in an institution of higher learning. Contact the address listed for further information. If writing, be sure to enclose a SASE for a reply. Must have a GPA of at least 3.0.

PG&E/LGBEA and GLSEN
PG&E/LGBEA and GLSEN Scholarship Comm.
PO Box 70554
Point Richmond, CA 94807

1810
Pharmacia and Upjohn Master's Scholarship

AMOUNT: $3000 DEADLINE: February 1
FIELDS/MAJORS: Oncology Nursing

Awards to students who are registered nurses with an interest in and commitment to oncology nursing. Must be enrolled in a graduate nursing degree program with an application to oncology nursing, in an NLN-accredited school of nursing. May be attending school full- or part-time. Contact the address listed for further information.

Oncology Nursing Foundation
501 Holiday Dr.
Pittsburgh, PA 15220

1811
PHD ARA Scholarship

AMOUNT: $500 DEADLINE: February 1
FIELDS/MAJORS: Electronic Engineering, Computer Sciences, Journalism

Scholarships are available to students with any class amateur radio license, who are residents of: Iowa, Kansas, Missouri, or Nebraska, and are children of deceased amateur radio operators. Write to the address below for information.

ARRL Foundation (American Radio Relay League)
Scholarship Program
225 Main St.
Newington, CT 06111

1812
Phi Delta Kappa Scholarship Grants

AMOUNT: $1000-$5000 DEADLINE: January 31
FIELDS/MAJORS: Education

Candidates must be high school seniors who are planning to pursue careers in education. The criteria involved in the selection include academic records, recommendations, school and community activities, and written expression. Forty-seven awards are offered annually. Contact the address listed for further information. You must include a SASE for a reply. You may also use their Web site for more information. Must have a GPA of at least 3.0.

Phi Delta Kappa International
Scholarship Coordinator
PO Box 789
Bloomington, IN 47402

1813
Phi Sigma Iota Member Scholarships

AMOUNT: None Specified DEADLINE: February 1
FIELDS/MAJORS: Foreign Languages

Open to active members of Phi Sigma Iota (Foreign Languages Honor Society) who meet standards of excellence in scholarship in any of the foreign languages. Eight award programs per year. Contact your faculty advisor, or write to the address below for complete details.

Phi Sigma Iota
Office of the Executive Director
5211 Essen Ln., Suite 2
Baton Rouge, LA 70809

1814
Phil Shanline Scholarship

AMOUNT: $500
DEADLINE: None Specified
FIELDS/MAJORS: Sciences, Engineering, Health, Education, Business

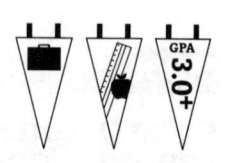

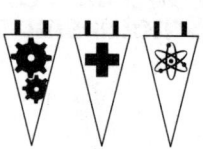

Awards open to sophomores and above attending an accredited school in Nebraska. (By the North Central Association of Colleges and Schools). Must have a minimum GPA of 3.0, ability to demonstrate leadership in quality and community service, and quality assurance technologies. Four awards offered annually. Contact the address listed for further information.

American Society for Quality Control
Al Schrader, 1998 Scholarship Chair
6141 Morrill Ave.
Lincoln, NE 68507

1815
Philadelphia/South Jersey District Council, U.N.I.T.E

AMOUNT: $500-$1000 DEADLINE: April 15
FIELDS/MAJORS: All Areas of Study

Applicants must be children of two-year members only of the Philadelphia South Jersey District Council and be graduates of an accredited high school within two calendar years preceding the award year, or graduate within the award year. Write to the address below for more information.

Knitted Outerwear Manufacturers' Association
35 South Fourth St.
Philadelphia, PA 19106

1816
Philip D. Reed Undergraduate Award

AMOUNT: Maximum: $5000   DEADLINE: None Specified
FIELDS/MAJORS: Environmental Engineering

Open to sophomores who have a minimum GPA of 3.0 and a demonstrated interest in environmental engineering. Renewable if recipients maintain a minimum GPA of 3.0. Applicants must be enrolled in any of seventy-nine participating colleges/universities in the U.S and be nominated by the dean. Applicants must also be of African-American, Puerto Rican-American, Mexican-American, or Native American descent. Contact the dean's office of your college for further information. If this information is in your profile, you have indicated that you are attending one of the participating schools. Please do not contact the Council. They will be unable to respond.

National Action Council for Minorities in Engineering
Scholarship Coordinator
3 W. 35th St.
New York, NY 10001-2281

1817
Philip Morris Companies Scholarship Program

AMOUNT: None Specified   DEADLINE: None Specified
FIELDS/MAJORS: All Areas of Study

Available to children of Kraft Foods employees. For study at college, university, or trade/vocational school. Children of employees at all Philip Morris business units (including Philip Morris, PM International, PM Capital, PM Companies, Miller Brewing, and Kraft General Foods) are eligible for these awards. Contact your parents' workplace (human resources department) for details.

Kraft Foods
PO Box 7188
Madison, WI 53707

1818
Philip Pearlman Scholarship Fund

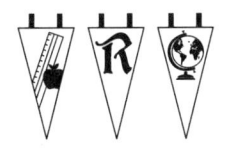

AMOUNT: $500   DEADLINE: June 15
FIELDS/MAJORS: Social Service, Rabbinics, Education, Jewish Studies

Scholarships for Jewish residents of New Jersey who are studying toward a career in the Jewish field, whether in the Rabbinate, Cantorate, Education, Administration, or Social Work. For undergraduate or graduate studies in the U.S. or Israel. Recipients or a family member must be present at the Jewish Festival (on September 7th) to accept the award. Write to the address below for details.

Jewish Festival of the Arts
C/O Ms. Simi Pearlman, Committee Chairman
34 Wellington Rd.
East Brunswick, NJ 08816

1819
Philip, David and Stephen Kelley Scholarship Fund

AMOUNT: None Specified   DEADLINE: May 1
FIELDS/MAJORS: Vocational/Technical

Awards for graduating seniors from Winthrop High School who plan to pursue a postsecondary education at the vocational or technical college level. Contact the Winthrop High School Guidance Office for more information.

Maine Community Foundation
245 East Maine St.
PO Box 148
Ellsworth, ME 04605

1820
Philippines Subic Bay/ Cubi Point Scholarship

AMOUNT: $2500   DEADLINE: April 1
FIELDS/MAJORS: All Areas of Study

Scholarships for dependents of U.S. Navy sea service personnel, who were stationed at the U.S. Naval facility, Philippines (Subic Bay, Cubi Point and/or San Miguel) or permanently homeported at a U.S. Naval facility. Applicants must be high school graduates or equivalent and U.S. citizens. Must have (or have had) a minimum GPA of 2.0. Write to the address below for more information.

Navy League of the United States
Attn: Scholarship Program
2300 Wilson Boulevard
Arlington, VA 22201

1821
Phillips Family Scholarship

AMOUNT: None Specified   DEADLINE: May 1
FIELDS/MAJORS: All Areas of Study

Awards for residents of Shirley who have completed at least one year of postsecondary education. Academics and personal goals will be considered. Contact Goldie Phillips, PO Box 40, Shirley, ME, 04485 for more information.

Maine Community Foundation
245 East Maine St.
PO Box 148
Ellsworth, ME 04605

1822
Phipps Scholarship

AMOUNT: None Specified DEADLINE: February 1
FIELDS/MAJORS: All Areas of Study

Open to Connecticut female college juniors and above, who have a minimum GPA of 3.0 and are matriculating for either a bachelor's or master's degree. Based on future promise, academics, and financial need. Contact the address listed for further information.

West Hartford Women's Club
Ms. Catherine Davidson
109 S. Main St., #A3
West Hartford, CT 06107

1823
Phoenix Scholarship

AMOUNT: $1000 DEADLINE: May 2
FIELDS/MAJORS: Creative Arts

Scholarships for residents of Livingston County who have an interest in the creative arts. Based on need and exceptional creativity. Applicants must be high school seniors or first- or second-year college students. Write to the address below for more information.

Psychological Services for Youth
Dr. Patricia Carpenter
121 West North St.
Brighton, MI 48116

1824
Photographers' Fund Fellowships

AMOUNT: Maximum: $1000 DEADLINE: May 12
FIELDS/MAJORS: Photography

Two fellowships are available for part-time students in the field of photography. Applicants may be from the following counties in New York: Albany, Clinton, Columbia, Delaware, Dutchess, Essex, Franklin, Fulton, Greene, Hamilton, Montgomery, Orange, Otsego, Rensselaer, Saratoga, Schnectady, Schoharie, Sullivan, Ulster, Warren, or Washington. Write to the address listed for more information.

Center for Photography at Woodstock
59 Tinker St.
Woodstock, NY 12498

1825
Physical Therapist Professional and Assistant Scholarships

AMOUNT: Maximum: $2000 DEADLINE: March 1
FIELDS/MAJORS: Physical Therapy

Open to California residents who are currently enrolled in accredited physical therapy programs in a California school. (accredited by the Commission of Accreditation of Physical Therapy Education). Must have completed one quarter/semester, have a minimum GPA of 3.0, and be student members of the American Physical Therapy Association. The professional scholarship is for therapists, and the assistant scholarship is for therapists' assistants. Contact the address listed for further information or call (916) 929-2782. Applications may be requested between January 15 and February 15 of each year.

California Physical Therapy Fund, Inc.
Scholarship Coordinator
2295 Gateway Oaks Dr., #200
Sacramento, CA 95833

1826
Physical/Occupational Therapy Contractual Scholarship

AMOUNT: $3000-$4000 DEADLINE: None Specified
FIELDS/MAJORS: Physical Therapy, Occupational Therapy

Contractual scholarships available for physical therapy or occupational therapy majors entering their last two years of study. Recipients must allow the resource group to place them in their first professional job after graduation. May apply before senior year (but funds are not disbursed until senior year.) Based on academics, leadership, and career potential. Must be U.S. citizens. Information and applications are available from your department chairman, financial aid officer, or by writing to the address listed. If you write, you must include a business-sized SASE for a reply.

Allied Resources
Scholarship Coordinator
810 Regal Dr., Suite H
Huntsville, AL 35801

1827
Physician Assistant Foundation Awards Program

AMOUNT: $2000-$5000 DEADLINE: February 1
FIELDS/MAJORS: Physician Assisting

Various scholarships to undergraduates and graduates in a physician assistant program. Based on academic record, activities, community involvement, and financial need. Applicants must be attending a CAAHEP-accredited program and be student members of the AAPA. Between forty and fifty awards offered annually. Write to the address below for more information.

Physician Assistant Foundation of American Academy of Physician Assistants
Undergraduate of Graduate Education Program
950 N. Washington St.
Alexandria, VA 22314

1828
Physio-Control Advanced Practice Scholarship

AMOUNT: Maximum: $2000 DEADLINE: June 1
FIELDS/MAJORS: Nursing

Open to nurses pursuing an advanced clinical practice degree to become a nurse practitioner or clinical nurse specialist. Preference given to nurses focusing on cardiac nursing, including cardiac resuscitation. Write to the address below for more information.

Emergency Nurses Association (ENA) Foundation
Funding Program
216 Higgins Rd.
Park Ridge, IL 60068

1829
Pi Gamma Mu Scholarship

AMOUNT: $1000-$2000 DEADLINE: January 30
FIELDS/MAJORS: Social Science, Sociology, Anthropology, Political Science, History

Open to Pi Gamma Mu members who are full-time graduate students with financial need. Letters of recommendation are required. Intended primarily for first-year graduate study. Ten awards offered annually. Write to the address below for details.

Pi Gamma Mu International Honor Society in Social Science
Executive Director
1001 Millington, Suite B
Winfield, KS 67156

1830
PIF/Lifeline Scholarship Program

AMOUNT: Maximum: $1000 DEADLINE: March 1
FIELDS/MAJORS: See Listing of Fields Below

Scholarships available for adult students who are enrolled in one of the following programs: physical therapy, occupational therapy, speech/hearing therapy, mental health, or rehabilitation. Recipients must be preparing for, or already involved in, careers working with people with disabilities/brain-related disorders. Send a SASE to the address below for information. All applicants must be sponsored by a Pilot Club in their hometown or college/university town.

Pilot International Foundation
PO Box 5600
244 College St.
Macon, GA 31208

1831
Pillsbury Creative Writing Scholarship Program

AMOUNT: None Specified DEADLINE: October 31
FIELDS/MAJORS: Creative Writing

For students majoring in or planning to major in writing. Must have lived in Santa Barbara County for a minimum of two years prior to the application deadline. Must be able to demonstrate unusual aptitude or potential in the filed of writing and financial need. Applications available from October 1. Applications available at high school counselor's offices in Santa Barbara County, at the address listed, and at some English or writing departments.

Santa Barbara Foundation
Student Aid Director
15 East Carrillo St.
Santa Barbara, CA 93101

1832
Pillsbury Music Scholarship Program

AMOUNT: None Specified DEADLINE: May 15
FIELDS/MAJORS: Music

Open to music majors who demonstrate unusual aptitude or potential in the field of music. Financial need is the primary consideration. Must have lived in Santa Barbara County for at least two years prior to the application. Applications available from April 1. Contact Dan Oh for an application or more information at dano@shfoundation.org

Santa Barbara Foundation
Student Aid Director
15 East Carrillo St.
Santa Barbara, CA 93101

1833
Pilot International Foundation Scholarships

AMOUNT: Maximum: $1500 DEADLINE: April 1
FIELDS/MAJORS: All Areas of Study

Scholarships for undergraduates enrolled in one of the following programs: physical therapy, occupational therapy, speech/hearing therapy, mental health, or rehabilitation. Must be preparing for, or already involved in, careers working with people with disabilities/brain-related disorders. All applicants must be sponsored by their Pilot Club (in your hometown or town in which you attend college). Information and applications are available directly from your sponsoring Pilot Club. Must have a minimum GPA of 3.5 and be full-time students. If you need to contact the Foundation, include a SASE and write to the address listed for a reply.

Pilot International Foundation
PO Box 5600
244 College St.
Macon, GA 31208-5600

1834
Pioneers of Flight Scholarship-Academic/Flight Training

AMOUNT: $2500   DEADLINE: November 15
FIELDS/MAJORS: Aviation Related Fields

For juniors and seniors who are at least eighteen years old and are working toward a career in general aviation. Renewable one time. Nomination by a member (regular or associate) of the National Air Transportation Association is required. Based on academics, potential, and leadership. Six awards per year. Write the address listed or call (703) 845-9000 to obtain a National Air Transportation Association member listing by state if you are unaware of members with whom you would pursue nomination. Must have a GPA of at least 2.9.

National Air Transportation Foundation
Pioneers of Flight Scholarship Programs
4226 King St.
Alexandria, VA 22302

1835
Piscataquis County Area Scholarships-Foxcroft Academy

AMOUNT: None Specified   DEADLINE: March 18
FIELDS/MAJORS: All Areas of Study

Awards for graduates of Foxcroft Academy in Piscataquis County, Maine. Includes the Walter H. and Eva L. Burgess, Harry M. and Lillian R. Bush, Howard T. Clark Foxcroft Academy, and Jeffrey A. Kilpatrick scholarships. At least four scholarships per year are awarded. Contact the Foxcroft Academy Registrar for more details.

Maine Community Foundation
245 East Maine St.
PO Box 148
Ellsworth, ME 04605

1836
Piscataquis County Area Scholarships-Piscataquis Community High School

AMOUNT: None Specified   DEADLINE: April 1
FIELDS/MAJORS: All Areas of Study

Awards for graduates of Piscataquis Community High School in Piscataquis County, Maine. Includes the Crockett, Guilford High School Memorial, Charles D. Shaw, and Richmond D. Pearson scholarship funds. At least four scholarships are awarded yearly. Contact the Piscataquis High School guidance office for more details.

Maine Community Foundation
245 East Maine St.
PO Box 148
Ellsworth, ME 04605

1837
Pitney Bowes Scholarships for Dependents of Employees

AMOUNT: None Specified   DEADLINE: None Specified
FIELDS/MAJORS: All Areas of Study

Scholarships for graduating high school seniors who are dependent children of current, retired, or deceased Pitney Bowes employees. If your parents have not received information about this award, write to the address below. Indicate where (and when) your parent worked for Pitney Bowes.

Pitney Bowes, Inc.
Scholarship Committee
World Headquarters
Stamford, CT 06926

1838
Piton Foundation/Charter Fund Scholarships

AMOUNT: None Specified   DEADLINE: May 9
FIELDS/MAJORS: All Areas of Study

Scholarships for graduating high school seniors from Colorado. Based upon financial need. Write to the address below, or call Cindy Kennedy at (303) 572-1727 for details.

Charter Fund
the Charter Fund
370 17th St., Suite 5300
Denver, CO 80202

1839
Plastic Surgery Educational Foundation Essay Contest

AMOUNT: None Specified   DEADLINE: March 2
FIELDS/MAJORS: Plastic Surgery, Otolaryngology

Awards for students based on the best essay written about plastic surgery. The program offers eight cash awards in four categories: basic science, clinical research, essay scholarship, and investigator. Write to the address listed for more information.

Plastic Surgery Educational Foundation
444 East Algonquin Road
Arlington Heights, IL 60005

1840
Pleasant Hawaiian Holidays Scholarship

AMOUNT: $1500   DEADLINE: July 28
FIELDS/MAJORS: Travel and Tourism

Awards are available for students from southern California whose parents are employed in the travel industry and who have career goals in the travel industry as well. Applicants must submit an essay explaining their future plans, have a GPA of 3.0 or greater, and be a U.S. citizen or legal resident. One award is given annually. The second award is for a school anywhere else in U.S. Write to the address below for more information.

American Society of Travel Agents
Scholarship Committee
1101 King St., Suite 200
Alexandria, VA 22314

1841
Plenum Scholarship Program

AMOUNT: Maximum: $1000 DEADLINE: October 31
FIELDS/MAJORS: Library and Information Science

Scholarships for members of the Special Libraries Association who have worked in special libraries. For doctoral study. Preference is given to persons who display an aptitude for special library work. One award per year. Based on academic achievement, evidence of financial need, and dissertation topic approval. Write to the address listed for details.

Special Libraries Association
SLA Scholarship Committee
1700 Eighteenth St. NW
Washington, DC 20009

1842
Plumas-Sierra County Farm Bureau Scholarships

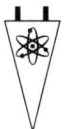

AMOUNT: Maximum: $1000 DEADLINE: May 15
FIELDS/MAJORS: Agriculture

Scholarships for graduating seniors from Plumas or Sierra County high schools who are from farm families. Must be a family member of a Plumas-Sierra County Farm Bureau in good standing. For study of agriculture and related fields. Applications may be obtained from Plumas and Sierra County high schools, or write to the address below for details.

Plumas-Sierra County Farm Bureau
PO Box 35
Loyalton, CA 96118

1843
Polaire Weissman Fund

AMOUNT: None Specified DEADLINE: November 7
FIELDS/MAJORS: Fine Arts, Costume History

Applicants should be graduate students who preferably will have completed studies in the fine arts or costume history and would like to pursue costume history in a museum, teaching, or other area related to the field of costume history. Award is available in alternate years and is generally awarded for nine month terms. Write to the address listed for further information.

Metropolitan Museum of Art
Fellowship Programs, Pia Quintano
1000 Fifth Ave.
New York, NY 10028

1844
Police Officer/Fire Officer Survivor Grant Program

AMOUNT: None Specified DEADLINE: None Specified
FIELDS/MAJORS: All Areas of Study

The Police Officer/Fire Officer Grant provides payment of tuition and mandatory fees for the spouse and children (ages twenty-five and under) of Illinois police/fire officers killed in the line of duty. Recipients must be enrolled on at least a half-time basis. Applicants must be U.S. citizens or permanent residents and Illinois residents. Write to the address below for details.

Illinois Student Assistance Commission
1755 Lake Cook Road
Deerfield, IL 60015

1845
Police Officers and Firefighters Survivors Educational Grant

AMOUNT: None Specified DEADLINE: None Specified
FIELDS/MAJORS: All Areas of Study

This program awards tuition, fees, books, and supplies to students who are dependents or spouses of police officers or firefighters killed in the line of duty in Alabama. Students must be enrolled in an undergraduate program at a public, postsecondary educational institution in Alabama. Write to the address listed for details or call (334) 281-1921.

Alabama Commission on Higher Education
Office of Financial Aid
PO Box 30200
Montgomery, AL 36130

1846
Polingaysi Qoyawayma Teaching Program

AMOUNT: None Specified DEADLINE: None Specified
FIELDS/MAJORS: Math/Science Education

Scholarships for student members of the American Indian Science and Engineering Society. Must be able to prove tribal enrollment. For graduate studies toward teaching certificate. Program is designed to support teachers who will work in teaching math and sciences to Native American students. Write to the address listed or call (303) 939-0023 for details.

American Indian Science and Engineering Society
Scholarship Coordinator
5661 Airport Blvd.
Boulder, CO 80301-2339

1847
Pollard and A.J. (Andy) Spielman Scholarships

AMOUNT: $2000-$3000 DEADLINE: July 28
FIELDS/MAJORS: Travel and Tourism

Four awards are available for students in the field of travel and tourism who are attending school for the purpose of re-entering the work force in the field of travel. Must be U.S. citizens or legal residents and have a GPA of at least 2.5. Must be enrolled (enrolling) in a proprietary travel school or two-year junior college. Write to the address below for more information.

American Society of Travel Agents
Scholarship Committee
1101 King St., Suite 200
Alexandria, VA 22314

1848
Population Council Fellowships in the Social Sciences

AMOUNT: None Specified DEADLINE: January 2
FIELDS/MAJORS: Population Studies and Related Fields

Doctoral, postdoctoral, and midcareer research fellowships for advanced training in population studies or for study plans in population in combination with a social science discipline. Doctoral applicants should have completed all coursework requirements. Applicants requesting support for either the dissertation fieldwork or the dissertation writing period will be considered. Postdoctoral awards open to Ph.D.'s or holders of equivalent degrees who wish to undertake training and research at an institution other than the one at which they received their Ph.D. Midcareer awards open to persons with a minimum of five years of professional experience in the population field. No M.P.H. or M.A. candidates will be considered. Applicants will be notified about the results of the competition in March. Contact the address listed, and include a brief description of your academic and professional qualifications and a short statement about your research or study plans.

Population Council
Manager, Fellowship Prog., Research Div.
One Dag Hammarskjold Plaza
New York, NY 10017

1849
Porter McDonnell Memorial Award

AMOUNT: Maximum: $1000 DEADLINE: November 10
FIELDS/MAJORS: Surveying

Open to women students pursuing a bachelor's degree who have the potential for leadership in the surveying and mapping profession. Contact the address below for further information.

American Cartographic Association
Lilly Matheson, ACSM Awards Program
5410 Grosvenor Ln., #100
Bethesda, MD 20814-2144

1850
Porter McDonnell Memorial Award

AMOUNT: Maximum: $1000 DEADLINE: November 30
FIELDS/MAJORS: Surveying, Cartography

Award is open to female students enrolled in a surveying or mapping program in any accredited college or university in the U.S. Must demonstrate potential for leadership in the mapping and surveying profession. Write to the address listed for more information or call (301) 493-0200. Must have a GPA of at least 3.0.

American Congress On Surveying and Mapping
Ms. Lilly Matheson
5410 Grosvenor Ln., #100
Bethesda, MD 20814

1851
Portland Area Scholarships

AMOUNT: None Specified DEADLINE: April 1
FIELDS/MAJORS: All Areas of Study

Awards for students who reside and have graduated from the Portland area. Includes Jessica Ann Herrick, Misty Renee Cote and Michaela Lee Herrick Memorial, The Chet Jordan, The Kenneth Jordan, and The Connie Davis Memorial Scholarships. Contact the address listed for further information.

Maine Community Foundation
245 East Maine St.
PO Box 148
Ellsworth, ME 04605

1852

Portuguese Continental Union Scholarships

AMOUNT: $250-$500 DEADLINE: February 15
FIELDS/MAJORS: All Areas of Study

Scholarships for members of Portuguese Continental Union (for at least one year). Must have good character and meet entrance (or continuing) requirements for college or university of your choice. For full-time, undergraduate study. Scholarship is paid directly to your school. Write to the union at the address below for details. Must have a GPA of at least 2.0.

Portuguese Continental Union
Scholarship Committee
899 Boylston St.
Boston, MA 02115

1853

Portuguese Foundation, Inc. Scholarships

AMOUNT: Maximum: $1000 DEADLINE: March 1
FIELDS/MAJORS: All Areas of Study

Awards are available for high school seniors of Portuguese ancestry. Must be residents of Connecticut, demonstrate academic success, community service, financial need, and be U.S. citizens or permanent residents. Eight to ten awards offered annually. Write to the address listed for more details. Must have a GPA of at least 3.0.

Portuguese Foundation, Inc.
Gabriel R. Serrano
86 New Park Ave.
Hartford, CT 06106

1854

Post-Graduate Scholarship Program

AMOUNT: None Specified DEADLINE: February 15
FIELDS/MAJORS: All Areas of Study

Must be nominated by the faculty athletic representative or director of athletics of an NCAA member institution. Eligibility is restricted to student athletes attending NCAA member institutions. 125 awards per year. Must be U.S. citizens and ethnic minorities. Selections are made in the academic year in which the student completes his or her final season of eligibility for intercollegiate athletics under NCAA legislation. Write to the address below for details.

National Collegiate Athletic Association
6201 College Blvd.
Overland Park, KS 66211

1855

Postdoctoral Fellowship Program

AMOUNT: $24000-$30000 DEADLINE: September 1
FIELDS/MAJORS: Biology, Medicine Relevant to Cancer Research

Fellowships are available for postdoctoral research at California institutions in the biological or medical sciences relevant to cancer research. There are no citizenship requirements, but the applicant must already hold the Ph.D. Write to the address below for information.

American Cancer Society, California Division
Research Fellowship Program
PO Box 2061
Oakland, CA 94604

1856

Postdoctoral Fellowship, AHA California Affiliate

AMOUNT: $20300-$32300 DEADLINE: October 1
FIELDS/MAJORS: Cardiovascular Research

Postdoctoral fellowships for California residents or students at California institutions to support beginning investigators in areas relating to cardiovascular research. Must be a U.S. citizen or hold a current visa. Write to the address below for more information. Deadline to request applications is July 1.

American Heart Association, California Affiliate
Research Department
1710 Gilbreth Road
Burlingame, CA 94010

1857

Postdoctoral Fellowship, Physician Research Training, Scholar Awards

AMOUNT: None Specified DEADLINE: March 1
FIELDS/MAJORS: Cancer Research and Related Fields

The American Cancer Society provides support to new investigators to qualify for an independent career in cancer research. Both basic and applied research is supported. Must hold Ph.D. at the time application is made. Write to the address below or call (404) 329-7558 for details and policies.

American Cancer Society, Inc.
Extramural Grants and Awards
1599 Clifton Road, NE
Atlanta, GA 30329

1858

Postdoctoral Fellowships

AMOUNT: Maximum: $29000   DEADLINE: None Specified
FIELDS/MAJORS: Toxicology and Related Disciplines

Postdoctoral research fellowships for recent recipients of D.V.M., M.D., or Ph.D. (biochemical, pharmacology, cell/molecular biology, genetics, immunology, chemistry, biophysics, mathematics, etc.). Supports original research related to chemical toxicity at CIIT's laboratory. Up to twenty-five awards per year. Write to the address below for details.

Chemical Industry Institute of Toxicology
6 Davis Dr.
PO Box 12137
Research Triangle Pk., NC 27709

1859

Postdoctoral Fellowships in Law and Social Science

AMOUNT: $30000   DEADLINE: February 2
FIELDS/MAJORS: Law, Social Science

Available to scholars who have completed all requirements for their Ph.D. within the past two years or are currently in the final stages of completing their dissertation. Research must be in the areas of: social scientific approaches to law, sociolegal studies, the legal profession, or legal institutions. Held in residence at the ABF. Minorities encouraged to apply. Write to the address listed for information.

American Bar Foundation
Ann Tatalovich, Assistant Director
750 N. Lake Shore Dr.
Chicago, IL 60611

1860

Postdoctoral Research Fellow Program Award

AMOUNT: Maximum: $10000   DEADLINE: January 15
FIELDS/MAJORS: Liver Research, Liver Physiology

Award open to M.D., Ph.D., and M.D./Ph.D. postdoctoral fellows to enter an academic career in liver disease research. Candidates must be sponsored by a non-federal public or private nonprofit institution engaged in healthcare and health-related research within the U.S. and its possessions. Must be in the first or second year of appointment as a postdoctoral research fellow or trainee. Individuals with more than two years of postdoctoral research training or who are already well established in the field of hepatology are ineligible for this award. Contact the address listed for further information.

American Liver Foundation
Barbara Ramsthaler
1425 Pomton Ave.
Cedar Grove, NJ 07009

1861

Postdoctoral Research Fellowships

AMOUNT: $30000   DEADLINE: November 30
FIELDS/MAJORS: Mathematics

Awards for scholars who have earned their Ph.D. in the field of mathematics in 1993 or later. Most fellowships last for a year, but a shorter period is possible, and in exceptional cases, two-year awards may be made. Awards will be announced by spring. Preference is given to U.S. citizens. Write to the address below for more information.

Mathematical Sciences Research Institute
1000 Centennial Dr., #5070
Berkeley, CA 94720

1862

Postdoctoral Research Fellowships

AMOUNT: $30000-$33000   DEADLINE: September 1
FIELDS/MAJORS: Medical Research-Cystic Fibrosis

Fellowships for M.D.'s and Ph.D.'s interested in conducting basic or clinical research related to cystic fibrosis. Stipends are $30000 (first year), $31000 (second year), and $33000 (optional third year). Must be a U.S. citizen or permanent resident. Write to the address below for details.

Cystic Fibrosis Foundation
Office of Grants Management
6931 Arlington Rd.
Bethesda, MD 20814

1863

Postdoctoral Research Fellowships for Basic and Physician Scientists

AMOUNT: $100000   DEADLINE: None Specified
FIELDS/MAJORS: Cancer Research (Oncology)

Open to the following degree holders: M.D., Ph.D., D.D.S., or D.V.M. who are involved in cancer research. Sponsorship by a senior member of the research community is required. The proposed investigation must be conducted at a university, hospital, or research institution. Write to the address below for details. The deadlines are August 15, December 15, and March 15.

Damon Runyon-Walter Winchell Cancer Fund
131 E. 36th St.
New York, NY 10016

1864
Pre-Veterinary Scholarships

AMOUNT: None Specified DEADLINE: April 15
FIELDS/MAJORS: Veterinary Medicine

Open to undergraduate or graduate students from New Mexico pursuing a career in animal/veterinary sciences. Minimum 3.0 GPA required. Send a SASE with application, and write to the address listed for more information.

Albuquerque Veterinary Association
Ms. Mary H. Hume, D.V.M.
3601 Eubank NE
Albuquerque, NM 87111

1865
Predoctoral Fellowship, AHA California Affiliate

AMOUNT: $16500 DEADLINE: October 1
FIELDS/MAJORS: Cardiovascular Research

Predoctoral fellowships for California residents or students at California institutions to support doctoral dissertation projects in areas relating to cardiovascular research. Must be a U.S. citizen or hold a current visa. Write to the address below for more information. Deadline to request applications is July 1.

American Heart Association, California Affiliate
Research Department
1710 Gilbreth Road
Burlingame, CA 94010

1866
Prepharmacy Scholarship

AMOUNT: None Specified DEADLINE: May 1
FIELDS/MAJORS: Pharmacy

Scholarship for African-American students from the state of Washington who are studying to become a pharmacist. Based on academics, an essay, and an interview with the coalition scholarship committee in the Seattle area. Write to the address below for more information.

Northwest Pharmacists Coalition
PO Box 22975
Seattle, WA 96122

1867
Presbyterian Ethnic Leadership Supplemental Grant

AMOUNT: $500-$1000 DEADLINE: None Specified
FIELDS/MAJORS: Ministry

Open to full-time students who are African, Asian, Hispanic, Native Americans, or Alaska Natives. Must be enrolled in a PC seminary or theological institution approved by the students' Committee on Preparation for Ministry. Must be studying for the first professional degree for a church occupation or a position within one of the ecumenical agencies in which the PC participates. Contact the address listed for further information.

Presbyterian Church (U.S.A.)
Office of Financial Aid for Studies
100 Witherspoon St.
Louisville, KY 40202-1396

1868
Presbyterian Study Grant

AMOUNT: $500-$1500 DEADLINE: None Specified
FIELDS/MAJORS: Preparation for Ministry

Open to full-time students in a PC seminary or theological institution approved by the students' Committee on Preparation for Ministry. Must be studying for the first professional degree for a church occupation or a position within one of the ecumenical agencies in which the PC participates. Contact the address listed for further information.

Presbyterian Church (U.S.A.)
Office of Financial Aid for Studies
100 Witherspoon St.
Louisville, KY 40202-1396

1869
President Francesco Cossiga Fellowships

AMOUNT: None Specified DEADLINE: None Specified
FIELDS/MAJORS: History, Cartography, Humanities

Fellowships for research program at Newberry. Available to scholars to research any subject relevant to the Library's collections. Preference is given to applicants who have studied the history of cartography. Write to the address listed for details, or contact the Ministero degli Affari Esteri, Direzione General delle relazioni culturali, Ufficio IX, Roma, Italia for an application.

Newberry Library
Committee on Awards
60 W. Walton St.
Chicago, IL 60610

1870
President's Grant-in-Aid

AMOUNT: None Specified   DEADLINE: January 6
FIELDS/MAJORS: Medical Research (Allergy/Immunology)

Grants for members of the American Academy of Allergy and Immunology. To support a wide range of scholarly activities. Applicant must be an M.D., Ph.D., or D.O. and be sponsored by an AAAI Fellow. Write to the address listed or call (414) 272-6071 for details.

American Academy of Allergy and Immunology
Jerome Schultz, Continuing Med. Educ. Mgr.
611 E. Wells St.
Milwaukee, WI 53202

1871
Press Club of Houston Educational Foundation Scholarship

AMOUNT: Maximum: $40000   DEADLINE: March 1
FIELDS/MAJORS: Journalism, Communications, Broadcasting

Scholarship offered to a college junior or senior with good overall scholastic standing. Must reside in Harris County or one of the surrounding counties, or be attending school in one of those counties. Write to the address listed or call (713) 867-8847 for more details. Must have a GPA of at least 2.7.

Press Club of Houston Educational Foundation
PO Box 541038
Houston, TX 77254

1872
Primary Care Service Corps Scholarship Program

AMOUNT: Maximum: $15000   DEADLINE: April 6
FIELDS/MAJORS: Physician Assistant, Nurse Practitioner, Midwife

Open to New York residents who are enrolled or accepted in an approved graduate, undergraduate, or certificate course of study and be within twenty-four months of completion of professional training if attending full-time. Applicants attending part-time must be within forty-eight months of completion. Must then be eligible to practice in New York State. Recipients must fulfill a service obligation by providing primary care (at least thirty-five hours per week) in an underserved area of a facility serving high need populations for eighteen months (for full-time award) and nine months (for part-time award). Contact the address listed for further information.

New York State Department of Health
Primary Care Service Corps
Corning Tower, #1084-Empire State Plaza
Albany, NY 12237-0053

1873
Prince George's Chamber of Commerce Foundation Scholarship

AMOUNT: Maximum: $1000   DEADLINE: May 15
FIELDS/MAJORS: All Areas of Study

Open to residents of Prince George's County, Maryland, who graduated from county schools. Preference given to business-related majors. Must be able to demonstrate financial need. Contact the address listed for further information or call (301) 731-5000.

Prince George's Chamber of Commerce Foundation
Administer
4640 Forbes Blvd., #200
Lanham, MD 20706

1874
Printing Industry of Minnesota Scholarships

AMOUNT: Maximum: $1000   DEADLINE: February 15
FIELDS/MAJORS: Print Communications

Open to graduating high school seniors and persons who have graduated within the last five years who are accepted as full-time students by accredited technical schools, colleges, or universities that offer one-, two-, and four-year programs leading to a degree or graphic arts diploma. Applicants must have a minimum GPA of 3.0, be Minnesota residents or children of employees of Minnesota graphic arts firms, and pursuing careers in graphic arts. Preference given to children of full-time employees of a member of the Printing Industry of Minnesota. Awards will be announced in May. Recipients are eligible to compete for a second-year scholarship. Contact the address listed for further information or call (612) 379-3360.

Printing Industry of Minnesota Education Foundation
Scholarship Coordinator
2829 University Ave. SE, #750
Minneapolis, MN 55414-3222

1875
Priscilla Maxwell Endicott Scholarship Fund

AMOUNT: $500-$1000   DEADLINE: April 20
FIELDS/MAJORS: All Areas of Study

Award for female high school seniors or women enrolled in college. Must have a standing as an amateur woman golfer, demonstrate financial need, scholastic achievement, and provide letters of recommendation from a teacher and a golf pro or coach. Must also be a resident of Connecticut. May be used for two- or four-year schools. Contact your high school guidance counselor for further information and an application or write to the address listed.

Connecticut Women's Golf Association
Ms. Julie Keggi, Scholarship Chairwoman
1321 Whittemore Rd.
Middlebury, CT 06762

1876
Pro-Therapy Student Advance Program

AMOUNT: Maximum: $5000   DEADLINE: None Specified
FIELDS/MAJORS: Physical or Occupational Therapy

Awards for students in their final year of physical/occupational therapy school. In return for receiving the award, the student makes a commitment to become a member of the pro-therapy traveling team, upon graduation, for a period of one year. Write to the address listed for more information.

Pro-Therapy of America, Inc.
PO Box 1600
Birmingham, MI 48012

1877
Proctor and Gamble Oral Health/ADHA Institute Scholarship Program

AMOUNT: Maximum: $1000   DEADLINE: May 1
FIELDS/MAJORS: Dental Hygiene

Applicants must have a minimum GPA of 3.0 in high school or natural science courses or pre-dental hygiene courses. Student must be planning to major in dental hygiene. Twenty-five awards of $1000 each offered in nationwide competition. Application will be available in guidance offices, or students may write for an application packet. Applicants will be notified in fall as to whether or not they have been selected as recipients. Write to Beatrice H. Pedersen, associate administrator, at the address below for more details.

ADHA Institute for Oral Health
444 N. Michigan Ave, Suite 3400
Chicago, IL 60611

1878
Proctor and Gamble, Sons and Daughters Scholarships

AMOUNT: None Specified   DEADLINE: November 15
FIELDS/MAJORS: All Areas of Study

Scholarships for graduating high school seniors who are children (natural, adopted, stepchildren), employees, or retirees of Proctor and Gamble companies (or its U.S. or Puerto Rico subsidiaries). Must submit ACT/SAT scores. 125 awards per year. Program is administered by the College Scholarship Service. Information should be available from your parent's workplace. If not available there, write to the address listed.

Procter and Gamble Fund Scholarship Program
Sons and Daughters Scholarships
PO Box 599
Cincinnati, OH 45201

1879
Professional Development Fellowship for Artists and Art Historians

AMOUNT: $5000   DEADLINE: January 31
FIELDS/MAJORS: Art, Art History

Fellowships are available for minority art and art history majors in the final year of graduate study. Applicants must be U.S. citizens or permanent residents and be able to demonstrate financial need. Write to the address listed for information.

College Art Association
Fellowship Program
275 Seventh Ave.
New York, NY 10001

1880
Professional Education Scholarship for Graduate Study

AMOUNT: Maximum: $1000   DEADLINE: May 1
FIELDS/MAJORS: Journalism

Must be women members of NFPW with a bachelor's degree and two years' membership. Based on academic and professional performance, career potential, and financial need. Write to the address listed for complete details.

National Federation of Press Women
C/O Jean Bormann
1163 320th Ave.
Charlotte, IA 52731

1881
Professional Growth Scholarship

AMOUNT: None Specified   DEADLINE: April 15
FIELDS/MAJORS: Food Service/Management

Open to graduate students who meet all five of the following criteria: 1) proof of acceptance as a graduate student in a food science and nutrition or food service management program at an accredited institution, 2) be a current ASFSA member for a minimum of two years -or- dependent of an ASFSA member, 3) have a minimum GPA of 2.7, 4) provide a transcript showing completion of at least one course of the planned program, 5) submit application with all required attachments postmarked no later than April 15. Write to the address listed for additional information.

American School Food Service Association
Scholarship Committee
1600 Duke St., 7th Floor
Alexandria, VA 22314

1882
Professional Land Surveyors of Oregon Scholarships

Amount: None Specified **Deadline:** March 1
Fields/Majors: Surveying

Scholarships for Oregon residents who are majoring in surveying. Must intend to pursue a career in land surveying. Must be entering junior or senior year in the fall at an Oregon college. Contact your financial aid office or write to the address below for details.

Oregon State Scholarship Commission
Attn: Grant Department
1500 Valley River Dr., #100
Eugene, OR 97401

1883
Program in Public Policy and International Affairs

Amount: $1500-$15000 **Deadline:** March 14
Fields/Majors: Public Policy/International Affairs

Minority program for undergraduates and graduate students interested in careers in public policy and international affairs. Must be a U.S. citizen or permanent resident. Awards start at $1500 for freshmen, $3000 for seniors, and $15000 for graduates. Write to the address below for details.

Woodrow Wilson National Fellowship Foundation
Dr. Richard O. Hope, VP, WWNFF
CN 5281
Princeton, NJ 08543

1884
Project 21 Poster and Essay Scholarship

Amount: $1000 **Deadline:** June 21
Fields/Majors: Commercial Art, Creative Writing

Scholarships are available to the ten winners of the Project 21 Poster and Essay Contest. Applicants must submit a poster, which must have been displayed in their school, or an essay, which must have been published in the school newspaper on the issue of underage casino gambling. Must reside in New York, Connecticut, Delaware, Washington D.C., Maryland, New Jersey, or Pennsylvania. Write to the address below for information. Students who are high school as well as college undergraduates attending school in the states listed above are eligible.

Harrah's Casino Hotel
Jerry Boone
777 Harrah's Blvd.
Atlantic City, NJ 08401

1885
Project Grants

Amount: $3000-$10000 **Deadline:** November 1
Fields/Majors: Byzantine Studies, Pre-Columbian Studies, Archaeological Research

Grants available to assist with scholarly projects in the above fields. Support is generally for archaeological research, as well as for the recovery, recording, and analysis of materials that would otherwise be lost. Other eligible projects may include materials analysis of works of art and/or excavated materials and a systematic campaign to survey or photograph monuments and objects that are at risk. Write to the address listed for details.

Dumbarton Oaks
Office of the Director
1703 32nd St. NW
Washington, DC 20007

1886
Project: Delta Plumber Scholarships

Amount: None Specified **Deadline:** July 1
Fields/Majors: All Areas of Study

Scholarships for participants, or children of participants, in project: Delta Plumber. Membership in NAPHCC not required. Renewable with 2.0 GPA. Six awards are offered per year. Write to the address below for details.

National Association of Plumbing Heating Cooling
   Contractors
Delta Faucet Scholarship Program
PO Box 6808
Falls Church, VA 22040

1887
Prospective Teacher Scholarship Loan

Amount: Maximum: $2500 **Deadline:** February 10
Fields/Majors: Education

Any North Carolina resident enrolled in an education program at a North Carolina school is eligible to apply. High school seniors with an SAT score of at least 900 and a minimum GPA of 3.0 are also eligible. College students must have a minimum GPA of 3.0. Two to five hundred awards are given annually. Write to the address listed for complete details.

North Carolina Department of Public Instruction
Division of Teacher Education Services
301 North Wilmington St.
Raleigh, NC 27601

1888
PSEF Basic Research Grant

AMOUNT: $5000-$10000 DEADLINE: January 12
FIELDS/MAJORS: Plastic Surgery

Awards for students to do research on the basic science related to plastic and reconstructive surgery. Thirty to forty grants up to $5000, and up to fifteen grants of $10,000 are awarded annually. Write to the address listed for more information. Applications are also available on their Web site address listed.

Plastic Surgery Educational Foundation
444 East Algonquin Road
Arlington Heights, IL 60005

1889
PSEF Combined Research Grant Program

AMOUNT: $10000 DEADLINE: January 1
FIELDS/MAJORS: Plastic Surgery, Otolaryngology

Open to investigators who wish to pursue a collaborative research project involving the two specialties of plastic surgery and otolaryngology. Write to the address listed for more information.

Plastic Surgery Educational Foundation
444 East Algonquin Road
Arlington Heights, IL 60005

1890
PTC Research Prizes

AMOUNT: $2000 DEADLINE: June 30
FIELDS/MAJORS: Telecommunications Research

Awards are available for the authors of the best research papers concerning telecommunications concerns of the Pacific region. Must hold at least a bachelor's degree. One to three awards offered annually. Write to the address below for more information.

Pacific Telecommunications Council
2454 Beretania St., Suite 302
Honolulu, HI 96826

1891
Public Employee Retirement Research/ Administration Scholarship

AMOUNT: Maximum: $3500 DEADLINE: February 1
FIELDS/MAJORS: Finance, Business Administration, Social Sciences, Public Administration

Open to full- or part-time graduate students intending to pursue a career in state and local government finance with a focus on public sector retirement benefits. Applicants must be citizens of the U.S. or Canada. Recommendation from academic advisor or dean of the program will be required. Information may be available from the head of your department. If not, write to the address listed or call (312) 977-9700. Applications are available in November for awards in the following spring.

Government Finance Officers Association
Scholarship Committee
180 N. Michigan Ave., Suite 800
Chicago, IL 60601

1892
Public Investor Scholarship

AMOUNT: Maximum: $3000 DEADLINE: None Specified
FIELDS/MAJORS: Public, Business Administration, Finance, Social Sciences

Open to full- or part-time graduate students who are planning to pursue a career in state or local government finance. Applicants must be citizens or permanent residents of the U.S. or Canada. Recommendation from academic advisor or dean of the graduate program will be required. Information may be available from the head of your department. If not, write to the address listed or call (312) 977-9700. Applications are available in November for awards in the following spring.

Government Finance Officers Association
Scholarship Committee
180 N. Michigan Ave., Suite 800
Chicago, IL 60601

1893
Public Service Scholarships

AMOUNT: $500-$1000 DEADLINE: May 14
FIELDS/MAJORS: All Areas of Study

Scholarships for full-time undergraduate or full- or part-time graduate students who intend to pursue careers in government service. Preference is given to students with some work experience in public service. Number of awards per year varies. Must have a GPA of at least 3.5. Send a SASE to the address below for details.

Public Employees Roundtable
Public Service Scholarships
PO Box 14270
Washington, DC 20044

1894
Public Service Scholarships

AMOUNT: None Specified DEADLINE: None Specified
FIELDS/MAJORS: Government

Open to full-time sophomores through seniors and full- or part-time graduate students. All applicants must have a minimum GPA of 3.5. Preference given to those with previous public service work or community service experience. A two page essay will be required. Contact the address listed for further information or see their Web site: http://patriot.net/~permail/

Public Employees Roundtable
Public Service Scholarship Program
PO Box 14270
Washington, DC 20044-4270

1895
Purina Mills Research Fellowship

AMOUNT: Maximum: $12500 DEADLINE: February 2
FIELDS/MAJORS: Animal/Poultry/Dairy Science

Fellowships for graduate students conducting research relating to the field of nutrition and companion animal sciences. For full-time study. Based on application, transcripts, grade reports, recommendations, and research proposal. Write to the address listed to request an application packet.

Purina Research Awards Committee
Anne Witzofsky, Purina Mills, Inc.
PO Box 66812
St. Louis, MO 63166

1896
Quarton-McElroy/ Iowa Broadcasters Association Scholarships

AMOUNT: Maximum: $2500 DEADLINE: April 15
FIELDS/MAJORS: Broadcast Production/Journalism, Telecommunications

Awards for Iowa high school seniors who plan on attending an Iowa four-year college or university full-time. Based on academics, leadership skills, and extracurricular activities. Must maintain a 2.5 GPA for renewal up to four years. Four awards are given annually. Contact the address below for further information.

Iowa Broadcasters Association
PO Box 71186
Des Moines, IA 50325

1897
Quebec Scholarship

AMOUNT: Maximum: $500 DEADLINE: April 15
FIELDS/MAJORS: Travel and Tourism, Hotel/Motel Management

Awards for Canadian juniors or seniors in one of the areas listed above who are enrolled in a two- or four-year college. Must have a GPA of 3.0 or better. Graduate students are also eligible to apply. Write to the address listed or call 1-800-682-8886 ext. 4251 for more information.

National Tourism Foundation
546 East Main St.
PO Box 3071
Lexington, KY 40596

1898
Quota International of Springfield Scholarship

AMOUNT: Maximum: $1000 DEADLINE: February 1
FIELDS/MAJORS: Hearing Impaired

Scholarship available to a resident of the greater Springfield area who is either hearing impaired or studying a field pertaining to working with the hearing impaired. Write to the address listed for details.

Quota Club of Springfield
219 North Main St.
East Longmeadow, MA 01028

1899
R. Robert and Sally D. Funderburg Research Scholar Award

AMOUNT: $25000 DEADLINE: September 10
FIELDS/MAJORS: Gastric Biology, Pathobiology

Awards for established investigators in the field of gastric biology, who hold faculty positions at accredited institutions. Women and minorities are encouraged to apply. Individual members of the ADHF member societies will be given preference. One award is given annually. Contact the address below for further information or Web sites: http://www.gastro.org; http://www.asge.org; or http://hepar-sfgh.ucsf.edu.

American Digestive Health Foundation
Ms. Irene Kuo
7910 Woodmont Ave., 7th Floor
Bethesda, MD 20814

1900
R.L. Gillette Scholarship

AMOUNT: Maximum: $2500
DEADLINE: April 30
FIELDS/MAJORS: Music, Literature

Open to legally blind female undergraduates enrolled in a four-year degree program. Applicants must be U.S. citizens. Write to the address listed for complete details or call (212) 502-7661.

American Foundation for the Blind
Scholarship Committee
11 Penn Plaza # 300
New York, NY 10001

1901
R.W. Bob Holden Scholarship

AMOUNT: $250-$500 DEADLINE: May 1
FIELDS/MAJORS: Hotel Management

Scholarships for Hawaii residents studying hotel management. Must have a GPA of at least 3.0. Write to the address below for details.

Hawaii Hotel Association
Ms. Susan Haramoto
2250 Kalakaua Ave., #404-4
Honolulu, HI 96815

1902
Rain Bird Company Scholarship

AMOUNT: Maximum: $1000 DEADLINE: March 31
FIELDS/MAJORS: Landscape Architecture/Design

Open to students in their final two years of undergraduate study (third, fourth or fifth years). Based on financial need, demonstrated commitment to the profession through participation in extracurricular activities, and exemplary scholastic achievements. Write to the address listed for details or call (202) 686-8337. Must have a GPA of at least 3.2.

Landscape Architecture Foundation
Scholarship Program
4401 Connecticut Ave. NW, #500
Washington, DC 20008

1903
Ralph J. Rossignuolo and Bill Menster Scholarships

AMOUNT: Maximum: $1500 DEADLINE: April 1
FIELDS/MAJORS: All Areas of Study

Open to students who are Iowa residents and children or grandchildren of an Iowa AMVET. Awards will be announced on or before May 15. Contact the address listed or call (515) 284-4257 for more information.

Iowa Department of AMVETS
Iowa AMVET Scholarships
PO Box 77
Des Moines, IA 50301

1904
Ramona P. Jordan Memorial Scholarship

AMOUNT: Maximum: $1000 DEADLINE: April 1
FIELDS/MAJORS: All Areas of Study

Open to graduating seniors of Elmore County High School based on academic ability and need. GPAs must be at least a 2.5 or above. High school transcript and essay outlining career goals are required. Contact the address listed or call (334) 264-6223 for further information.

Central Alabama Community Foundation
412 N. Hull St.
PO Box 11587
Montgomery, AL 36111

1905
Ramona's Mexican Food Products Scholarship

AMOUNT: None Specified
DEADLINE: June 1
FIELDS/MAJORS: Medicine, Law, Business, Engineering, or Journalism

The Ramona's Mexican Food Products Scholarship is available to students of Hispanic descent wishing to pursue a career in one of the fields listed above. Student must have a 3.5 GPA or better, be planning to attend a school in the state of California, and be currently enrolled in Lincoln, Garfield, or Roosevelt high school. Student must remain single while on scholarship. No student is allowed to change their major field of study without first notifying the foundation. Any change outside the fields specified by the foundation would result in the loss of the scholarship. Write to the address below for details.

Ramona's Mexican Food Products, Inc.
Scholarship Foundation
13633 South Western Ave.
Gardena, CA 90249

1906
Ray Kageler

AMOUNT: None Specified DEADLINE: March 1
FIELDS/MAJORS: All Areas of Study

Open to graduate students who are U.S. citizens, residents of Oregon, and members of a credit union affiliated with the Oregon Credit Union League. Applicants may apply and compete annually. Contact the address below for further information.

Oregon State Scholarship Commission
Private Awards
1500 Valley River Dr., #100
Eugene, OR 97401-2130

1907
Raymond A. and Ina C. Best Scholarship

AMOUNT: $10000 DEADLINE: January 15
FIELDS/MAJORS: Business Administration

Award open to member studying for his/her master's degree at Rensselaer Polytechnic Institute. Contact the address listed for further information.

Tau Beta Pi-Alabama Power Company
D. Stephen Pierre, Jr. P.E., Director
150 St. Joseph St., PO Box 2247
Mobile, AL 36652

1908
Raymond Davis Scholarship

AMOUNT: $1000 DEADLINE: December 15
FIELDS/MAJORS: Imaging Science/Photogrammetry

Scholarships for juniors, seniors, or full-time graduate students in imaging technology sciences. Write to the address below for complete details.

Society for Imaging Science and Technology
Membership Office
7003 Kilworth Ln.
Springfield, VA 22151

1909
Raymond E. Page Scholarship

AMOUNT: Maximum: $1000 DEADLINE: March 31
FIELDS/MAJORS: Landscape Architecture/Design

Open to undergraduates who are in need of financial assistance regardless of scholastic ability. A two page description of how the money is to be used and a recommendation from a current professor will be required. Write to the address listed for details or call (202) 686-8337.

Landscape Architecture Foundation
Scholarship Program
4401 Connecticut Ave. NW, #500
Washington, DC 20008

1910
Raymond H. Trott Scholarship Fund

AMOUNT: $500 DEADLINE: May 1
FIELDS/MAJORS: Banking

Scholarships are available for residents of Rhode Island who are preparing for a career in banking. Write to the address below for information.

Rhode Island Foundation
Special Funds Office
70 Elm St.
Providence, RI 02903

1911
Real-Time Intern Program for Upperclassmen and Graduate Students

AMOUNT: $1000 DEADLINE: November 15
FIELDS/MAJORS: Electronic Media (Not Including Broadcasting)

Awards are available for juniors, seniors, or graduate students to work as interns in electronic media. Recipients are paid regular wages for their summer work, which includes jobs as editors and reporters for financial news services. Must be U.S. citizens to apply. Applications are only available from August 1 through November 1. Contact the address listed for more information or call (609) 452-2820.

Dow Jones Newspaper Fund
PO Box 300
Princeton, NJ 08543

1912
Realty Foundation of New York Scholarships

AMOUNT: None Specified DEADLINE: None Specified
FIELDS/MAJORS: All Areas of Study

Open to undergraduates who are active employees (or their dependent children) of New York City Real Estate Industry E151. Contact the address listed for further information.

Realty Foundation of New York
Scholarship Aid Committee
551 Fifth Ave., #1105
New York, NY 10017

1913
Reedsburg Bank Webb High School Scholarships

AMOUNT: Maximum: $500   DEADLINE: None Specified
FIELDS/MAJORS: All Areas of Study

Two scholarships for graduating seniors from Webb High School in Reedsburg, Wisconsin. Write to the address listed for more information.

Reedsburg Bank
201 Main St.
PO Box 90
Reedsburg, WI 53959

1914
Reference Service Press Fellowship

AMOUNT: $2000   DEADLINE: May 30
FIELDS/MAJORS: Library Science

Awards for college seniors or graduates who have been accepted into an accredited MLS program. Must be a California resident attending school anywhere in the U.S. or a student from any other state attending school in California. Request an application form and further information from the address below.

California Library Association
Scholarship Committee
717 K St., Suite 300
Sacramento, CA 95814

1915
Regents Graduate/Professional Fellowships

AMOUNT: Maximum: $3500   DEADLINE: March 1
FIELDS/MAJORS: All Areas of Study

Scholarships are available to academically strong graduate students who are residents of Ohio and are continuing their education in an Ohio school. Must be nominated by your undergraduate college/university. Based upon academic ability. Contact a college financial aid administrator, the college/university graduate school, or the address listed for further information. Must have a GPA of at least 3.0.

Ohio Student Aid Commission
Customer Service
PO Box 16610
Columbus, OH 43216

1916
Regular Membership Fellowships

AMOUNT: Maximum: $7840   DEADLINE: January 6
FIELDS/MAJORS: Classical Studies

Awards are available for graduate students in classical studies in the U.S. or Canada. Based on transcripts, recommendations, and examinations in Greek language, history, archaeology, or literature. Applicants may have taken one year of graduate work but not completed the Ph.D. Six awards offered annually. Write to the address listed for more information.

American School of Classical Studies at Athens
Committee on Admissions and Fellowships
6-8 Charlton St.
Princeton, NJ 08540

1917
Renate W. Chasman Scholarship for Women

AMOUNT: $2000   DEADLINE: May 1
FIELDS/MAJORS: Natural Sciences, Engineering, Mathematics

Scholarships are available for women who are continuing their education after an interruption. Applicant must be a resident of Long Island and be enrolled as a junior, senior, or graduate student in one of the fields listed above. Must be a U.S. citizen or permanent resident. Write to the address below for information.

Brookhaven Women in Science
PO Box 183
Upton, NY 11973

1918
Rene Mansho Scholarship

AMOUNT: Maximum: $500   DEADLINE: None Specified
FIELDS/MAJORS: All Areas of Study

Scholarships for graduating high school seniors on the Island of Oahu. Eligible schools are Pearl City H.S., Waipahu H.S., Mililani H.S., Leilehua H.S., Waialua H.S., and Kahuku H.S. Private high school seniors in the Council 1 District are also eligible. Contact your high school guidance office or write to the address listed for details.

Rene Mansho Charity Fund
C/O Michelle Kidani
94-134 Keahilele St.
Mililani, HI 96789

1919

Research and Education Grant

AMOUNT: Maximum: $5000 DEADLINE: January 31
FIELDS/MAJORS: Science, Horticulture

Graduate and postdoctoral grants are available for scholars with a proposed program of scientific, academic, or artistic investigation of herbal plants. Write to the address listed for information.

Herb Society of America, Inc.
Research and Education Grants
9019 Kirtland Chardon Road
Kirtland, OH 44094

1920

Research Assistance

AMOUNT: Maximum: $500 DEADLINE: October 1
FIELDS/MAJORS: Japanese Studies

Small grants are available for a variety of scholarly needs that are not covered by other funding sources, such as research assistance and manuscript typing. Applicants must clearly explain what the funds would be used for. Write to the address below for more information.

Northeast Asia Council Association for Asian Studies
1 Ln. Hall
University of Michigan
Ann Arbor, MI 48109

1921

Research Awards and Grants Program

AMOUNT: Maximum: $35000 DEADLINE: January 1
FIELDS/MAJORS: Respiratory Disease, Medical Research, Epidemiology

Awards for scholars with two years of research experience or for doctoral candidates. Programs for funding include research training, pediatric pulmonary research, nursing research, Dalsemer Scholar, career investigator research grant, and behavioral science dissertation grants. Must be a Canadian citizen or a U.S. citizen or permanent resident. Write to the address below for information.

American Lung Association
Medical Affairs Division
1740 Broadway
New York, NY 10019

1922

Research Fellowship

AMOUNT: None Specified DEADLINE: November 1
FIELDS/MAJORS: Japanese Studies

Fellowships available to scholars who hold an academic position in a research institution and have substantial experience in research, teaching, or writing in their respective fields of study. Write to the address listed for additional information.

Japan Foundation
New York Office
152 West 57th St.
New York, NY 10019

1923

Research Fellowships and Young Investigator Grant Program

AMOUNT: Maximum: $25000 DEADLINE: September 5
FIELDS/MAJORS: Nephrology, Urology

Research fellowships for clinical and basic research into understanding and curing of kidney and urologic diseases. Must be sponsored by member of NKF. At award activation, research candidates may not have completed more than four and one-half years of research training beyond a doctoral degree. No more than ten years can have elapsed between last doctoral degree and this award. Young investigators candidate must be holding a position on a faculty or staff of a research institution. Awarded no later than three and one-half years after initial appointment to position. Contact the address below for further information.

National Kidney Foundation
Research Fellowship Committee
30 East 33rd St.
New York, NY 10016

1924

Research Fellowships in New England History and Culture

AMOUNT: $1500 DEADLINE: January 31
FIELDS/MAJORS: History-New England

Research fellowships are available for graduate and postgraduate scholars conducting research into the history of New England, at the Peabody Essex Museum. Stipends will be awarded for up to two months. Write to the address below for information.

Peabody Essex Museum
Fellowship Program, Phillips Library
East India Square
Salem, MA 01970

1925
Research Grants

AMOUNT: $15000-$20000 DEADLINE: None Specified
FIELDS/MAJORS: Geography, Geology, Anthropology, Archaeology, Astronomy, Biology

Investigators who hold doctor's degrees and are associated with institutions of higher learning or other scientific and educational nonprofit organizations, such as museums, are eligible to apply. For field research. Scholars in the fields of Botany, Oceanography, Paleontology, and Zoology are also encouraged to apply. 250 grants are awarded per year. Address inquiries to Secretary, Committee for Research and Exploration, at the address below.

National Geographic Society
Committee for Research and Exploration
PO Box 98249
Washington, DC 20090

1926
Research Grants

AMOUNT: $400-$2000 DEADLINE: None Specified
FIELDS/MAJORS: U.S. Military History and Related Areas

Graduate-level and advanced study research grants for individuals who have demonstrated ability and special aptitude for advanced study in American military history and related fields. Six awards per year. Write to "Research Grants" at the address listed for further information.

U.S. Marine Corps Historical Center
Building 58
Washington Navy Yard
Washington, DC 20374

1927
Research Grants

AMOUNT: Maximum: $2000 DEADLINE: February 1
FIELDS/MAJORS: Geology

Open to any master's or doctoral student at universities in the U.S.A, Canada, Mexico, or Central America. Award is intended to help support thesis research. GSA membership is not required. Approximately 250 awards per year. Write for complete details. Application forms should be available from your department or from the campus GSA representative. If necessary, write to the Research Grants Administrator at the address listed.

Geological Society of America
3300 Penrose Place
PO Box 9140
Boulder, CO 80301

1928
Research in the Biology of Aging

AMOUNT: Maximum: $5500 DEADLINE: February 26
FIELDS/MAJORS: Geriatrics

Open to predoctoral Ph.D. and M.D. students to undertake a three-month research project in an area of biomedical research in aging under the auspices of a mentor. The scholarships consist of $4000 for the student and $1500 for the mentor. Write to the address listed or call (212) 752-2327 for more information.

American Federation for Aging Research/Glenn Foundation
1414 Ave. of the Americas
New York, NY 10019

1929
Research Professorships

AMOUNT: Maximum: $40000 DEADLINE: September 30
FIELDS/MAJORS: Mathematics

Awards for midcareer mathematicians who have earned their Ph.D. in the field of mathematics no later than 1992. The award is limited to a ceiling of $30000 and normally will not exceed half of the applicants salary. Awards will be announced mid-December. Write to the address below for more information.

Mathematical Sciences Research Institute
1000 Centennial Dr., #5070
Berkeley, CA 94720

1930
Research Scholarships in Geriatric Pharmacology

AMOUNT: Maximum: $4000 DEADLINE: January 21
FIELDS/MAJORS: Medicine, Pharmacology

Open to medical or pharmaceutical doctoral students who are interested in geriatrics or geriatric pharmacology. The award allows the recipient to undertake an eight- to twelve-week, full-time research project conducted under the supervision of a faculty mentor. Student must show academic ability, statement of purpose, and letters of reference. Write to the address listed for more information or contact (212) 752-2327.

Merck Co. Foundation/American Federation for Aging Research
Scholarships Coordinator
1414 Ave. of the Americas, 18th Floor
New York, NY 10019

1931
Research Support Grants

AMOUNT: $18000-$22000 DEADLINE: December 15
FIELDS/MAJORS: Humanities, Arts, Social Sciences

Fellowships are available from the Getty Center Scholar Program. These are two-year pre and postdoctoral residential fellowships. Evaluated in terms of how the dissertation or book bears upon the theme. Research projects that lead from the passions to issues about the nature and history of the humanities will be of special interest. Write to the address below for information.

Getty Research Institute for the History of Art and the
   Humanities
Scholars and Seminars Program
1200 Getty Center Dr., #1100
Los Angeles, CA 90049-1688

1932
Research Training Fellowships for Medical Students

AMOUNT: $14500 DEADLINE: None Specified
FIELDS/MAJORS: Medicine

Fellowships for doctoral candidates enrolled in medical school, to encourage more M.D.'s to pursue a career in biological research. Forty-four awards offered annually. Write to address below for further information.

Howard Hughes Medical Institute
Office of Grants and Special Programs
4000 Jones Bridge Road
Chevy Chase, MD 20815

1933
Research Travel Grant— North America

AMOUNT: $1000 DEADLINE: October 1
FIELDS/MAJORS: Korean Research

Available to scholars engaged in research on Korea who wish to use museum, library, or other archival materials in the United States or Canada. Primarily intended to support postdoctoral research. Contact the address below for further information.

Association for Asian Studies, Inc.
University of Michigan
1 Lane Hall
Ann Arbor, MI 48109

1934
Research Travel within the U.S.A.

AMOUNT: Maximum: $1500 DEADLINE: October 1
FIELDS/MAJORS: Japanese Studies

Awards for graduate students who are engaged in scholarly research on Japan and wish to use museum, library, or other archival materials located in the U.S.A. Applicants must be U.S. citizens or permanent residents. Though primarily to support postdoctoral research on Japan, Ph.D. candidates may also apply. Second deadline date is February 1 for the spring awards. Write to the address below for more information.

Northeast Asia Council Association for Asian Studies
1 Lane Hall
University of Michigan
Ann Arbor, MI 48109

1935
Respiratory Diseases Research Award

AMOUNT: Maximum: $25000 DEADLINE: January 12
FIELDS/MAJORS: Allergy/Immunology Medical Research

Available to members who are fellows in training, residents, or postdoctoral scholars associated with an approved allergy and immunology or clinical and laboratory immunology training program. A research proposal must accompany application. Write to the address listed for details.

American Academy of Allergy and Immunology/ Glaxo
   Wellcome
Committee Chair to Grant Research Awards
611 E. Wells St.
Milwaukee, WI 53202-3889

1936
Retired Officers Association Student Loans

AMOUNT: None Specified DEADLINE: March 1
FIELDS/MAJORS: All Areas of Study

Interest-free loans for dependent sons and daughters (under twenty-four years old) of members of the Retired Officers Association. For undergraduate study. Renewable. Applicants must never have been married and must have a GPA of at least 3.0. Write to the address below for details. Persons applying for these loans are automatically considered for special grant programs.

Retired Officers Association
Educational Assistance Program
201 N. Washington St.
Alexandria, VA 22314

1937
Reuben Trane Scholarships

AMOUNT: Maximum: $5000 DEADLINE: December 1
FIELDS/MAJORS: Engineering Technology, Heating, Air-Conditioning

Open to students who have completed at least one semester with a minimum GPA of 3.0 at an ABET accredited school. Must have at least two full years of school remaining. Must be able to demonstrate financial need. These are two-year scholarships. To remain eligible for the second year, recipients must remain full-time with satisfactory academic standing. Contact the address listed for further information.

American Society of Heating, Refrigerating, and
    Air-Conditioning Engineers
Scholarship Program
1791 Tullie Circle NE
Atlanta, GA 30329

1938
Reverend Frederick V. Slota Scholarship

AMOUNT: Maximum: $500 DEADLINE: February 15
FIELDS/MAJORS: All Areas of Study

One award is given to a high school senior who is a Rhode Island resident of Polish-American descent with outstanding academic excellence. The award is irrespective of financial need Write to the address listed or call (401) 831-7177 for more information. Must have a GPA of at least 3.7.

Rhode Island Polonia Scholarship Foundation
Foundation Office
866 Atwells Ave.
Providence, RI 02909

1939
Rhode Island Higher Education Assistance Authority Scholarships

AMOUNT: $250-$700 DEADLINE: March 1
FIELDS/MAJORS: All Areas of Study

Rhode Island resident who is enrolled or plans to enroll at least half-time at an eligible postsecondary institution. Must demonstrate financial need. For study at a vocational-technical school, community college, or four-year college. U.S. citizen, national, or permanent resident. Renewable. Write to the address listed or call (401) 736-1170 for complete details.

Rhode Island Higher Education Assistance Authority
560 Jefferson Blvd.
Warwick, RI 02886

1940
Rhode Island Polonia Undergraduate Scholarships

AMOUNT: Maximum: $500 DEADLINE: February 15
FIELDS/MAJORS: All Areas of Study

Three awards for high school seniors who are Rhode Island students of Polish-American descent accepted in a two or four-year postsecondary school. Must be U.S. citizens, have a minimum GPA of "B", and be able to demonstrate financial need. Write to the address listed or call (401) 831-7177 for more information. Must have a GPA of at least 2.8.

Rhode Island Polonia Scholarship Foundation
Foundation Office
866 Atwells Ave.
Providence, RI 02909

1941
Rice-Cullimore Scholarship

AMOUNT: Maximum: $2000 DEADLINE: February 15
FIELDS/MAJORS: Mechanical Engineering

Grants for foreign students studying mechanical engineering at a U.S. school on the graduate level. Applications are made through the Institute of International Education. Write to the address listed for details.

American Society of Mechanical Engineers Auxiliary, Inc.
345 E. 47th St.
New York, NY 10017

1942
Richard B. Irvine, M.D. Memorial Scholarship Award

AMOUNT: None Specified DEADLINE: October 15
FIELDS/MAJORS: Medicine

Scholarships for medical students who were graduated from high schools in, or live in, one of the following cities: Clayton, Concord, Pleasant Hill, Pacheco, or Martinez (Contra Costa County, California). Based on financial need. Contact the address below for further information.

Mt. Diablo Medical Center, Richard B. Irvine, M.D.
    Scholarship
2540 East St.
PO Box 4110
Concord, CA 94524-4110

1943

Richard E. Merwin Scholarship

AMOUNT: Maximum: $3000   DEADLINE: May 31
FIELDS/MAJORS: Electrical/Computer Engineering, Computer Science

Scholarship open to juniors through graduate level students in the fields listed above. Must be active members of a Computer Society student branch chapter at their institution. Applicants must have a minimum overall GPA of 2.5 for all undergraduate course work and be enrolled as a full-time student as defined by his or her academic institution during the course of the award. Write to the address listed for details.

Institute of Electrical and Electronics Engineers, Inc.
IEEE Computer Society
1730 Massachusetts Ave. NW
Washington, DC 20036-1992

1944

Richard F. Walsh/Alfred W. Di Tolla Foundation Scholarship

AMOUNT: $1750   DEADLINE: December 31
FIELDS/MAJORS: All Areas of Study

Scholarship for sons and daughters of members in good standing of the International Alliance of Theatrical Stage Employees and Moving Picture Technicians, Artists, and Allied Crafts of the U.S. and Canada (IATSE). Applicant must be a high school senior planning to enroll in a full-time program at any accredited college or university. Renewable. Two awards offered annually. Write to the address listed for complete details.

Richard F. Walsh/Alfred W. Di Tolla Foundation
Foundation Office
1515 Broadway, Suite 601
New York, NY 10036

1945

Richard Klutznick Scholarship Fund

AMOUNT: Maximum: $2500   DEADLINE: April 1
FIELDS/MAJORS: Social Work

Applicants must be Jewish graduate students attending accredited schools studying social work and have records of good scholarship. Award recipients must agree to accept a two-year position with BBYO upon graduation. Write to the address below for details.

B'nai Brith Youth Organization
1640 Rhode Island Ave. NW
Washington, DC 20036

1946

Richard M. Weaver Fellowship and Salvatori Fellowship Awards Programs

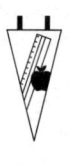

AMOUNT: None Specified   DEADLINE: February 15
FIELDS/MAJORS: Teaching-College Level

One-year fellowship to encourage graduate work in preparation for college teaching. Must be a U.S. citizen and ISI member. For study at any school in the U.S. or abroad. Write to the address listed or call 1-800-526-7022 for complete details.

Intercollegiate Studies Institute
Fellowship Awards Programs
3901 Centerville Rd., PO Box 4431
Wilmington, DE 19807

1947

Richard W. and Florence B. Irwin Law Scholarship

AMOUNT: None Specified   DEADLINE: August 31
FIELDS/MAJORS: Law

Scholarships are available for Northampton residents who are attending or have been accepted into law school. Must have been a resident of Northampton for at least five years. Write to the address listed for information.

Community Foundation of Western Massachusetts
PO Box 15769
1500 Main St.
Springfield, MA 01115

1948

Risk Assessment Science and Engineering Fellowships

AMOUNT: Maximum: $42000   DEADLINE: January 15
FIELDS/MAJORS: Engineering, Food, Drug, or Agricultural Sciences, Economics

Applicants must have Ph.D. or equivalent degrees. Persons with master's degrees in engineering and three years' professional experience also qualify. Recipients spend one year working as special assistants to the offices of the USDA or the FDA. Program begins in September. Must demonstrate exceptional competence in the areas of science, engineering, or economics and have some interest in applying personal knowledge toward the solution of health, agriculture, or environmental problems. Minority and disabled students encouraged to apply. Must be U.S. citizens. Federal employees are not eligible. Contact address listed or call (202) 326-6760 for more details.

American Association for the Advancement of Science
Fellowship Program
1200 New York Ave, NW
Washington, DC 20005

1949
Rita G. Rudel Award

AMOUNT: $20000   DEADLINE: May 31
FIELDS/MAJORS: Behavioral Neurology, Developmental Neuropsychology

Applicants must hold a Ph.D. or M.D. degree and should be in the early to middle stage of their postdoctoral careers. Must be doing research in the field of Developmental Neuropsychology or Developmental Behavioral Neurology. Write to the address below for more information.

Rita G. Rudel Foundation
PO Box 674
Chappaqua, NY 10514

1950
Riverside County Physicians Memorial Foundation Scholarship

AMOUNT: None Specified   DEADLINE: None Specified
FIELDS/MAJORS: Medicine

Award open to residents of Riverside County, California, who have been accepted by or currently enrolled (in good standing) in an accredited medical or osteopathic school. Must be able to demonstrate financial need. Contact the address listed for further information.

Riverside County Physicians Memorial Foundation
3993 Jurupa Ave.
Riverside, CA 92506

1951
Robert "Aqqaluk" Newlin, Sr. Memorial Trust Scholarship

AMOUNT: None Specified   DEADLINE: September 1
FIELDS/MAJORS: All Areas of Study

Scholarships available to Alaska natives who are residents of or associated with the Northwest Arctic Borough of the state of Alaska. Based on academics, financial need, and Inupiaq cultural activities. For students in vocational training through postgraduate level. Contact the address below for further information.

Robert "Aqqaluk" Newlin, Sr. Memorial Trust
Martha Siikauraq, Executive Director
PO Box 509
Kotzebue, AK 99752

1952
Robert B. Bailey, III, Minority Student Scholarships

AMOUNT: $250-$1000   DEADLINE: November 1
FIELDS/MAJORS: Foreign Studies

Awards are available for minority students interested in study abroad. The stipend is intended for use in the cost of travel or the program fee. Must be U.S. citizens or permanent residents and be able to demonstrate financial need. November 1 is the deadline for the winter/spring program and April 1 is the deadline for the summer/fall program. Notification is about three weeks after the deadlines. Write to the address below for more information.

Council on International Educational Exchange
Scholarship Committee
205 East 42nd St.
New York, NY 10017

1953
Robert Bosch Foundation Fellowship

AMOUNT: $3500   DEADLINE: October 15
FIELDS/MAJORS: All Areas of Study

Fellowships are available for postdoctoral scholars to study in Germany. Applicant must be fluent in German and be available to work in a government assignment for nine months and in the private sector for four months. Twenty awards are given annually. Write to the address below for information.

CDS International, Inc.
330 7th Ave., 19th Floor
New York, NY 10001

1954
Robert Browning and Lee S. Burke Scholarships

AMOUNT: Maximum: $3500   DEADLINE: February 20
FIELDS/MAJORS: All Areas of Study

Awards open to gay/lesbian students who are residents of any of the following states: Washington, Oregon, Idaho, Montana, or Alaska. Must be able to demonstrate financial need, community involvement, and have clear educational goals. Contact the address listed for further information.

Greater Seattle Business Association and Pride Foundation
2033 6th Ave., #804
Seattle, WA 98121

1955
Robert D. Watkins Minority Graduate Fellowship

AMOUNT: $12000   DEADLINE: May 1
FIELDS/MAJORS: Microbiological Sciences

One-year fellowship for students who are African-American, Hispanic-American, Native American, or Native Pacific Islander. Must have completed first year of doctoral studies in microbiological science, be ASM student members, and U.S. citizens or permanent residents. Project's mentor must also be an ASM member. Write to the address below for additional information.

American Society for Microbiology
Office of Education and Training
1325 Massachusetts Ave. NW
Washington, DC 20005

1956
Robert E. Altenhofen Memorial Scholarship

AMOUNT: $1000   DEADLINE: None Specified
FIELDS/MAJORS: Photogrammetry

Applicant must be a student or active member of the Society. For undergraduate or graduate study. Based on interest and potential in the theoretical aspects of photogrammetry and remote sensing. Write to the address below for more information.

American Society for Photogrammetry and Remote Sensing
ASPRS Awards Program
5410 Grosvenor Ln., Suite 210
Bethesda, MD 20814

1957
Robert E. Thunen Memorial Educational Scholarships

AMOUNT: Maximum: $2500   DEADLINE: March 1
FIELDS/MAJORS: Architecture, Electrical Engineering, Interior Decorating and Design

Scholarships are available to those in the above fields who wish to study illumination as a career. Applicants must be juniors, seniors, or graduate students who are enrolled in a four-year school located in one of the following areas: northern California, Nevada, Oregon, or Washington state. Letters of recommendation are required. At least two awards are given annually. Write to the address listed for details.

Illuminating Engineering Society of North America
460 Brannen St.
PO Box 77527
San Francisco, CA 94107

1958
Robert H. and Clarice Smith Fellowship

AMOUNT: $16000   DEADLINE: None Specified
FIELDS/MAJORS: Art History-Dutch or Flemish

One-year fellowships are available for doctoral scholars researching for the dissertation. The Smith Fellow may use the grant to study either in the U.S. or abroad. Applicants must know two foreign languages related to the topic of their dissertation and be U.S. citizens or legal residents. Write to the address below for information.

National Gallery of Art
Center for Advanced Study in Visual Arts
Predoctoral Fellowship Program
Washington, DC 20565

1959
Robert H. Goddard Space Science and Engineering Scholarship

AMOUNT: $10000   DEADLINE: December 4
FIELDS/MAJORS: Engineering

Must be a U.S. citizen in at least the junior year of college. Must have scholastic plans leading to future participation in the Aerospace Sciences and Technology. Write for complete details.

National Space Club
Goddard Scholarship
655 15th St. NW, Suite 300
Washington, DC 20005

1960
Robert Kaufman Memorial Scholarship Fund

AMOUNT: $250-$5000   DEADLINE: March 1
FIELDS/MAJORS: Accounting

Scholarships are available for students who are pursuing or planning to pursue an education in accounting at an accredited college or university in the U.S. Applicants must be third year students or above and have a 3.5 GPA or equivalent in accounting. Write to the address below for an application, and enclose a SASE.

Independent Accountants International Educational Foundation, Inc.
9200 South Dadeland Boulevard, Suite 510
Miami, FL 33156

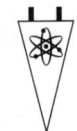

1961
Robert L. Baker Graduate Student Scholarship

AMOUNT: None Specified DEADLINE: None Specified
FIELDS/MAJORS: Ornamental Horticulture/Garden Design

Open to graduate students in ornamental horticulture or garden design. Must be a Maryland resident. Write to the address listed for details.

Federated Garden Clubs of Maryland, Robert Baker
   Scholarship
Mrs. Pauline Vollmer, Chairperson
6405 Murray Hill Rd.
Baltimore, MD 21212

1962
Robert M. Lawrence, M.D. Scholarship

AMOUNT: Maximum: $2500 DEADLINE: June 30
FIELDS/MAJORS: Respiratory Therapy

Open to third- and fourth-year students in an accredited respiratory therapy program. Must have a GPA of at least 3.0. Also based on recommendations and an essay. Must provide copy of birth certificate, social security card, immigration visa, or other evidence of citizenship. Recipient will selected by September 1. Write to the address listed for more information.

American Respiratory Care Foundation
Scholarship Committee
11030 Ables Ln.
Dallas, TX 75229

1963
Robert R. Robinson Memorial Scholarship

AMOUNT: $500 DEADLINE: May 31
FIELDS/MAJORS: Public Administration, Urban Management/Planning, and Related

Scholarships for students enrolled in Michigan colleges and universities as a junior, senior, or graduate student. Competitively awarded based on academics, community involvement, and a commitment to a career in local government administration. Write to the address below for details.

Robert R. Robinson Memorial Scholarship Fund
Michigan Townships Association
PO Box 80078
Lansing, MI 48909

1964
Robert S. Morison Fellowship

AMOUNT: $40000 DEADLINE: November 1
FIELDS/MAJORS: Neurology, Neurosurgery

Fellowships for medical doctors who have been accepted into or completed residence in neurology or neurosurgery and in need of two years intensive research or training preparation for a career in academic neurology or neurosurgery. Write to the address below for complete details.

Grass Foundation
PO Box 850250
Braintree, MA 02185-0250

1965
Robert Schreck Memorial Fund

AMOUNT: None Specified DEADLINE: July 15
FIELDS/MAJORS: Medicine, Engineering, Veterinary Medicine, Physics, Chemistry, Architecture

Grants for El Paso County residents (for at least two years). Open to juniors, seniors, and graduate students. A second deadline date of November 15 is for the spring semester. Write for complete details.

Texas Commerce Bank, Trust Department
Robert Schreck Memorial Fund
PO Drawer 140
El Paso, TX 79980

1966
Rock Sleyster Memorial Scholarship

AMOUNT: $2500 DEADLINE: May 1
FIELDS/MAJORS: Psychiatry

Candidates must be high achieving seniors with demonstrated interest in psychiatry, scholarship, and financial need. Must be nominated by your medical school. Letters from the Office of the Dean outlining basis of nomination, the applicant outlining career goals, and a member of the Department of Psychiatry will be required. For U.S. citizens studying in the U.S. or Canada. Approximately twenty awards offered annually. Write to the address listed for further information. Recipients will be announced by September 1st.

American Medical Assn. Education and Research Foundation
Harry S. Jonas, M.D., Director
515 North State St.
Chicago, IL 60610

1967
Rockefeller Foundation Residential Fellowships

AMOUNT: Maximum: $30000   DEADLINE: January 20
FIELDS/MAJORS: Gender Studies in Medieval or Early Modern Europe

Eleven-month residential research fellowships are available for postdoctoral scholars wishing to pursue extensive research in gender studies of medieval or early modern European studies (c.1200-1750). Write to the address listed or call (312) 255-3666 for more information.

Newberry Library
Committee on Awards
60 W. Walton St.
Chicago, IL 60610

1968
Rockefeller State Wildlife Scholarship

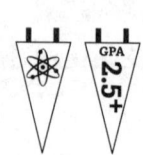

AMOUNT: Maximum: $1000   DEADLINE: June 1
FIELDS/MAJORS: Forestry, Wildlife Studies, Marine Science

Scholarships offered to Louisiana residents who are or will be full-time students at a college or university in Louisiana. Applicants must be U.S. citizens with a minimum GPA of 2.5. For undergraduates and two years of graduate studies. Write to the address listed for details.

Louisiana Office of Student Financial Assistance
PO Box 91202
Baton Rouge, LA 70821-9202

1969
Rocky Mountain Coal Mining Institute Scholarships

AMOUNT: Maximum: $1000   DEADLINE: February 2
FIELDS/MAJORS: Engineering-Mining, Geology, Mineral Processing, Metallurgy.

Open to sophomores enrolled in the above areas of study who are pursuing degree in a mining-related field or engineering discipline. For U.S. citizens who are residents of Arizona, Colorado, Montana, New Mexico, North Dakota, Texas, Utah, or Wyoming. Must have interest in Western coal as a possible career path. Applications are available at the offices of department heads of engineering colleges approved by RMCMI, or contact the address listed for more information.

Rocky Mountain Coal Mining Institute
Office of Admissions
3000 Youngfield St., Suite 324
Lakewood, CO 80215

1970
Roger Revelle Fellowship in Global Stewardship

AMOUNT: Maximum: $45000   DEADLINE: January 15
FIELDS/MAJORS: Engineering, Sciences, Especially Environmental and Conservational

Applicants must have Ph.D. or equivalent degrees and three years' postdoctoral experience. Persons with master's degrees in engineering and six years professional experience also qualify. Recipients spend one year working as special assistant for the Congress or an executive branch agency. Program begins in September. Must demonstrate exceptional competence in the areas of environmental sciences, engineering, and have some interest in applying personal knowledge toward the solution of global conservation efforts. Minority and disabled students encouraged to apply. Must be U.S. citizens. Federal employees are not eligible. Contact the address listed or call (202) 326-6760 for more details.

American Association for the Advancement of Science
Fellowship Program
1200 New York Ave. NW
Washington, DC 20005

1971
Ronald McDonald Children's Charities Health and Medical Scholars Program

AMOUNT: $1000   DEADLINE: January 31
FIELDS/MAJORS: Pre-Medical or Healthcare

Awards for African-American college sophomores in one of the fields above. Applicants must have a GPA of at least 3.0, have unmet financial need, and be involved in community service in the area of healthcare. Sixty awards are given annually. Write to the address below for more information.

United Negro Scholarship Fund
8260 Willow Oaks Corporate Dr.
PO Box 10444
Fairfax, VA 22031

1972
Ronald Reagan Leadership Award

AMOUNT: Maximum: $1000   DEADLINE: June 2
FIELDS/MAJORS: All Areas of Study

Leadership awards for Tau Kappa Epsilon members given in recognition of outstanding leadership as demonstrated by activities and accomplishments on campus, in the community, and within the chapter. All initiated undergraduate members of Tau Kappa Epsilon are eligible. Contact the address listed for complete information.

TKE Educational Foundation
8645 Founders Rd.
Indianapolis, IN 46268

1973
Roofing Industry Scholarship

AMOUNT: Maximum: $1000 DEADLINE: January 9
FIELDS/MAJORS: All Areas of Study

Two scholarships for undergraduate study in any field for children of members or employees of the National Roofing Contractors Association. For more information (or application forms), send a SASE ($.64 postage) to address below.

National Roofing Foundation
O'Hare International Center
10255 W. Higgins Rd., Suite 600
Rosemont, IL 60018

1974
Roothbert Fund Scholarships

AMOUNT: $500-$2000 DEADLINE: February 1
FIELDS/MAJORS: All Areas of Study

Scholarships for undergraduates and graduates of ability and character, especially those whose daily actions seem prompted by spiritual motives. Preference given to those considering teaching as a career. For applicants in New York, Connecticut, Pennsylvania, Washington, D.C., Massachusetts, Vermont, New Jersey, New Hampshire, Delaware, Maryland, Virginia, and West Virginia. Write to the address below for information. Enclose a SASE to receive a reply.

Roothbert Fund
Scholarships
475 Riverside Dr., Room 252
New York, NY 10115

1975
Rosa Ponselle Fund Scholarship

AMOUNT: Maximum: $500 DEADLINE: March 15
FIELDS/MAJORS: Music-Vocal/Opera

Scholarship for a Connecticut resident who is in junior year of a four-year college or music school. Students studying independently are also encouraged to apply. Applicants must be prepared to perform a twenty-minute classical program and must include a letter of recommendation from their teachers. Selection based on training and background of ten operatic arias. Write to the address listed for details.

Rosa Ponselle Fund
Scholarship Chairman
PO Box 1672
Meriden, CT 06450

1976
Rosann S. Berry Annual Meeting Fellowship

AMOUNT: Maximum: $500 DEADLINE: December 15
FIELDS/MAJORS: Architectural History

Awards are available for architectural history students engaged in advanced graduate study to attend the annual meeting of the Society of Architectural Historians. Write to the address listed for more information.

Society of Architectural Historians
1365 North Astor St.
Chicago, IL 60610

1977
Roswell Artist-in-Residence Program

AMOUNT: $500 DEADLINE: August 15
FIELDS/MAJORS: Painting, Drawing, Sculpture, Printmaking, Other Fine Art Media

Residence program for professional studio artists to provide the unique opportunity to concentrate on their work in a supportive, communal environment for periods of six months to one year. Five awards are offered annually. Write to the address listed for more information.

Roswell Museum and Art Center Foundation
100 West 11th St.
Roswell, NM 88201

1978
Roswell L. Gilpatric Internship

AMOUNT: $2500-$2750 DEADLINE: January 30
FIELDS/MAJORS: Art History, Art Conservation

Internships for college juniors, seniors, recent graduates, and graduate students who have interest in museum careers, art history, or a related field. Program runs for ten weeks, from June through August, and includes orientation to the Museum. Internship is full-time, thirty-five hours per week. Ethnically diverse students are encouraged to apply. Write to the address listed for additional information.

Metropolitan Museum of Art
Internship Programs
1000 Fifth Ave.
New York, NY 10028-0198

1979
Rotary International Foundation Scholarships

AMOUNT: $10000-$23000 DEADLINE: March 1
FIELDS/MAJORS: International and Cultural Studies

Scholarships are available for students interested in a period of study abroad. Scholarship terms are for the academic year, two to three full years or three to six months. Applicants must have completed at least two years of university or college coursework and be citizens of a country in which there is a Rotary club. Contact your local Rotary club or call (847) 866-3000 for information.

Rotary International Foundation
One Rotary Center
1560 Sherman Ave.
Evanston, IL 60201

1980
ROTC Scholarships

AMOUNT: None Specified DEADLINE: November 1
FIELDS/MAJORS: All Areas of Study

The Air Force offers full tuition plus a monthly allowance of $100 to high school seniors who will be enrolling/have enrolled full-time in a college or university. Applicants must be U.S. citizens with a minimum 2.5 GPA, in the top 25% of their class, and have a 24 ACT score or 1000 SAT. Contact your local Air Force Recruiter for information and an application. Do not write to the address shown for the material.

Air Force
Headquarters Air Force ROTC Recruiting Division
Building 500
Maxwell AFB, AL 36112

1981
Rowley/Ministerial Education Scholarship

AMOUNT: None Specified DEADLINE: March 15
FIELDS/MAJORS: Theology

Applicants must be members of the Christian Church (Disciples of Christ) who are preparing for the ordained ministry. Must be a full-time student. Financial need is considered. Write to the address below for details. Must have a GPA of at least 2.3.

Christian Church (Disciples of Christ)
Attn: Scholarships
PO Box 1986
Indianapolis, IN 46206

1982
Roy and Roxie Campanella Physical Therapist Scholarships

AMOUNT: Maximum: $2000 DEADLINE: March 1
FIELDS/MAJORS: Physical Therapy

Open to currently enrolled students in the next to last year of study. Must be a program accredited by the Commission of Accreditation of Physical Therapy Education (CAPTE). Must be student members of the Association. A statement from a physical therapist will be required regarding the student's potential as a physical therapist, character, leadership, clinical education, and "how the student has demonstrated sensitivity to peoples of different cultures." Contact the address listed for further information or call (916) 929-2782. Applications may be requested between January 15 and February 15 of each year. Must have a GPA of at least 3.0.

California Physical Therapy Fund, Inc.
Scholarship Coordinator
2295 Gateway Oaks Dr., #200
Sacramento, CA 95833

1983
Royal Neighbors of America Fraternal Scholarships

AMOUNT: $500-$8000 DEADLINE: December 1
FIELDS/MAJORS: All Areas of Study

Applicants must be high school seniors who have been beneficial members of the Royal Neighbors for at least two years preceding the date of the application and be in the upper third of graduating class. Must be pursuing a bachelor's degree full-time. Write to the address below for details. Must have a GPA of at least 2.7.

Royal Neighbors of America
Fraternal Scholarship Committee
230 16th St.
Rock Island, IL 61201

1984
RTKL Traveling Fellowship

AMOUNT: Maximum: $2500 DEADLINE: February 14
FIELDS/MAJORS: Architecture

Applicants must be in the last two years of an architecture program and planning to travel for school credit outside the United States in an established school program. Winner selected from proposals outlining foreign travel directly relevant to education goals. Information and applications are available only from the deans (or department heads) of accredited architecture schools in the U.S. and Canada.

American Institute of Architects
American Architectural Foundation
1735 New York Ave. NW
Washington, DC 20006

1985
RTNDF Abe Schecter Graduate Scholarship

AMOUNT: Maximum: $1000   DEADLINE: March 2
FIELDS/MAJORS: Broadcast, Electronic Journalism

Open to full-time graduate students whose career objective is electronic journalism. An essay will be required. Write to the address listed for details.

Radio and Television News Directors Foundation, Inc.
RTNDF Scholarships
1000 Connecticut Ave. NW, #615
Washington, DC 20036

1986
RTNDF Len Allen Award for Radio News Management

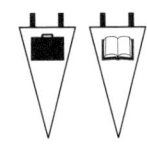

AMOUNT: Maximum: $2000   DEADLINE: March 2
FIELDS/MAJORS: News Management

Open to full-time undergraduate and graduate students who have a career objective of radio news management. An essay will be required. Write to the address listed for details.

Radio and Television News Directors Foundation, Inc.
RTNDF Scholarships
1000 Connecticut Ave. NW, #615
Washington, DC 20036

1987
RTNDF President's Award for Television News Management

AMOUNT: Maximum: $2000   DEADLINE: March 2
FIELDS/MAJORS: News Management

Open to full-time undergraduate and graduate students who have a career objective of television news management. An essay will be required. Write to the address listed for details.

Radio and Television News Directors Foundation, Inc.
RTNDF Scholarships
1000 Connecticut Ave. NW, #615
Washington, DC 20036

1988
RTNDF Summer and Entry-Level Internships

AMOUNT: $3000-$7800
DEADLINE: March 2
FIELDS/MAJORS: News Management, Electronic Journalism

Three summer internship programs and three six-month, entry-level internships in television or radio news management are available to juniors, seniors, and graduate minority students. Must have career objectives of radio and television news management. Applicants must be willing to relocate. Write to the address listed for more information. Must have a GPA of at least 3.0.

Radio and Television News Directors Foundation
RTNDF Internship Coordinator
1000 Connecticut Ave. NW, #615
Washington, DC 20036

1989
RTNDF Undergraduate Scholarships

AMOUNT: Maximum: $1000   DEADLINE: March 2
FIELDS/MAJORS: Broadcast, Electronic Journalism

Open to full-time sophomores, juniors, and seniors seeking a career in broadcast journalism. Must be officially enrolled in college and be in good standing. Based on examples of reporting and/or photographic skills. Write to the address listed for details. Must have a GPA of at least 2.5.

Radio and Television News Directors Foundation, Inc.
RTNDF Scholarships
1000 Connecticut Ave. NW, #615
Washington, DC 20036

1990
Ruby Marsh Eldred Scholarship Fund

AMOUNT: None Specified   DEADLINE: March 1
FIELDS/MAJORS: All Areas of Study

Scholarship open to high school seniors who have been residents of central or western Crawford County, Pennsylvania, for at least one year. Must rank in the top 25% of class and plan to enroll in a regionally accredited two- or four-year college. Write to the address below for further information and an application. Must have a GPA of at least 3.2.

Ruby Marsh Eldred Scholarship Fund
C/O Mary Ann Kirkpatrick, Esquire
Old Post Bldg., 941 Federal Court
Meadville, PA 16335

1991
Rudolph Dillman Memorial Scholarship

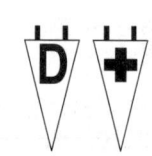

AMOUNT: Maximum: $2500 DEADLINE: April 30
FIELDS/MAJORS: Rehabilitation, Education of Visually Impaired and Blind Persons

Open to legally blind graduates and undergraduates who are studying in the field of rehabilitation and/or education of visually impaired and blind persons. Must be U.S. citizens. One of the four awards is for applicants who can demonstrate financial need. Write to the address listed for complete details or call (212) 502-7661.

American Foundation for the Blind
Scholarship Committee
11 Penn Plaza, #300
New York, NY 10001

1992
Rural Nurse Practitioner Scholarship

AMOUNT: None Specified DEADLINE: May 1
FIELDS/MAJORS: Nurse Practitioner

Open to Illinois residents who are registered nurses accepted or enrolled in an accredited nurse practitioners program. Purpose of awards is to develop the pool of rural health practitioners to help meet primary care needs in rural Illinois. Recipients agree to practice for two years in an approved rural Illinois county. Contact the Macoupin County Farm Bureau office, the address listed, or call (217) 854-2571 for more information.

Illinois Farm Bureau
Greg Carney, Asst. Dir. of Local Gvt.
PO Box 2901
Bloomington, IL 61702-2901

1993
Ruritan National Foundation Awards

AMOUNT: None Specified DEADLINE: April 1
FIELDS/MAJORS: All Areas of Study

Educational grants and loans are offered by Ruritan. Requires reference of two Ruritan members. Grades and need are considered. Re-application is permitted to continue the award into subsequent years of study. Some degree of preference is given to freshmen and sophomores. Write to the address below for details.

Ruritan National Foundation
PO Box 487
Dublin, VA 24084

1994
Ruth Good and Louis C. Stearns, III, Scholarship Fund

AMOUNT: None Specified DEADLINE: None Specified
FIELDS/MAJORS: All Areas of Study

Awards for graduating seniors from Hampden Academy in Bangor, Maine. Contact the Hampden Academy Guidance Office for more information.

Maine Community Foundation
245 East Maine St.
PO Box 148
Ellsworth, ME 04605

1995
Ruth O. Dority Fund

AMOUNT: None Specified DEADLINE: None Specified
FIELDS/MAJORS: All Areas of Study

Awards for residents of Sedgwick pursuing postsecondary education. Contact the guidance offices at George Stevens Academy or Deer Isle-Stonington High School.

Maine Community Foundation
245 East Maine St.
PO Box 148
Ellsworth, ME 04605

1996
Ruth S. Widener— Honoring the Late Mrs. Ralph Widener Scholarships

AMOUNT: None Specified
DEADLINE: None Specified
FIELDS/MAJORS: History, English, Business Administration, Computer Science

Scholarships for students at Washington and Lee University who are direct descendants of confederate soldiers. History major is preferred. Must be able to prove lineage. Write to the UDC chapter nearest you. If address is not known, write to the address below for further information and address.

United Daughters of the Confederacy
Scholarship Coordinator
328 North Boulevard
Richmond, VA 23220

1997
Ruth Satter Memorial Award

AMOUNT: $500-$1000 DEADLINE: January 15
FIELDS/MAJORS: All Areas of Study

Scholarship for women pursuing their doctorate who have taken at least three years off to raise children. Applications available after October 1. Write to the address below for more details.

Association for Women in Science Educational Foundation
National Headquarters
1200 New York Ave. NW, #650
Washington, DC 20005

1998
Ruth Taylor Scholarship

AMOUNT: None Specified DEADLINE: June 15
FIELDS/MAJORS: Medicine, Social Work

Scholarships for Westchester County, New York, residents who are graduate students in social work or medicine. Based on need, ability, and interest in public service. Write to the commissioner's office at the address below for details.

Westchester County Department of Social Services
Ruth Taylor Award Fund Committee
112 E. Post Road
White Plains, NY 10601

1999
S. Frank "Bud" Raftery Scholarship Competition

AMOUNT: Maximum: $2000 DEADLINE: November 15
FIELDS/MAJORS: All Areas of Study

Essay contest open to natural children or legally adopted dependents of IBPAT members in good standing. Essay topic is chosen annually, and details and application forms are carried in the July/August issue of the "Painters and Allied Trades Journal". Winners are notified in March. Contact the address listed for further information.

International Brotherhood of Painters and Allied Trades
IBPAT Scholarship Committee
1750 New York Ave. NW, United Unions
Washington, DC 20006

2000
S.D. Bechtel, Jr. Foundation Fellows Scholarship

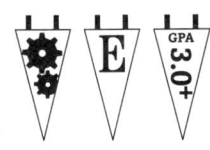

AMOUNT: Maximum: $5000 DEADLINE: None Specified
FIELDS/MAJORS: Engineering

Open to sophomores with a minimum GPA of 3.0. Renewable if recipients maintain a minimum GPA of 3.0. Applicants must be enrolled in any of seventy-nine participating colleges/universities in the U.S and be nominated by the dean. Applicants must be of African-American, Puerto Rican-American, Mexican-American, or Native American descent. Contact the dean's office of your college for further information. Please do not contact the Council. They will be unable to respond.

National Action Council for Minorities in Engineering
Scholarship Coordinator
3 W. 35th St.
New York, NY 10001-2281

2001
Sabina Farmers Exchange Scholarships

AMOUNT: Maximum: $500 DEADLINE: April 30
FIELDS/MAJORS: Agriculture

Scholarships for graduating high school seniors in southwestern Ohio who will be studying agriculture. Three awards per year; two of these awards are limited to students who will be attending OSU-Wooster. Based on character, need, and citizenship. Must maintain a GPA of at least 2.0 in college. Write to the address below for details.

Sabina Farmers Exchange
Scholarship Committee
PO Box 7, 292 N. Howard St.
Sabina, OH 45169

2002
Saburo Kido Memorial Scholarship

AMOUNT: None Specified DEADLINE: April 1
FIELDS/MAJORS: All Areas of Study

Open to undergraduates who are members of Japanese ancestry and entering or enrolled at an accredited college or university. Applications and information may be obtained from local JACL chapters, district offices, and the national headquarters at the address listed or call (415) 921-5225. Please indicate your level of study and be certain to include a legal-sized SASE.

Japanese-American Citizens League
National Scholarship and Award Program
1765 Sutter St.
San Francisco, CA 94115

2003
Sachs Foundation Scholarship

AMOUNT: $3500-$4500 DEADLINE: March 1
FIELDS/MAJORS: All Areas of Study

Open to African-American high school seniors who are residents of Colorado. (For a minimum of five years).

Applicants must demonstrate financial need. Based on academics and need. Renewable if recipients maintain a minimum GPA of 2.5 and complete at least 12 credit hours per term. Applications available from January 1 to February 15 of each year. Contact your high school counselor, write to the address listed, or call (719) 633-2353 for more information. Must have a GPA of at least 2.9.

Sachs Foundation
Scholarship Coordinator
90 S. Cascade Ave., #1410
Colorado Springs, CO 80903

2004
Sage Scholarships

AMOUNT: $500-$1500 DEADLINE: April 8
FIELDS/MAJORS: All Areas of Study

Awards for graduating high school seniors from Ventura County who have shown initiative and improvement in his/her academic accomplishments. Must show financial need with maximum parent income of no more than $65,000 per year and be intending to enroll as a degree candidate at a vocational, trade, community or accredited college, or university. Must have a minimum GPA of 3.0. Three awards offered annually. Write to the address listed or contact your high school counselor for more information.

Ventura County Community Fund
1355 Del Norte Road
Camarillo, CA 93010

2005
Sally Kress Tompkins Fellowship

AMOUNT: Maximum: $7500 DEADLINE: January 13
FIELDS/MAJORS: Architectural History

Summer internships for students studying architectural history to work as an intern on a historic American buildings survey summer project. Based primarily on academic records and recommendations. Write to the address listed for more information.

Society of Architectural Historians
1365 North Astor St.
Chicago, IL 60610

2006
Sally Pike Memorial Fund

AMOUNT: None Specified DEADLINE: None Specified
FIELDS/MAJORS: Music

Awards for graduating seniors from Cony High School who are pursuing degrees in music at the college level. Based on character and musical achievement and aptitude. Contact the Cony High School Guidance Office for more information.

Maine Community Foundation
245 East Maine St.
PO Box 148
Ellsworth, ME 04605

2007
Sam S. Kuwahara Memorial Scholarship

AMOUNT: None Specified DEADLINE: April 1
FIELDS/MAJORS: Agriculture

Available to undergraduate students of Japanese ancestry who are studying agriculture and are members of the Japanese-American Citizens League. Write to the address listed for more details or call (415) 921-5225. Please be sure to include a SASE with your request.

Japanese-American Citizens League
National Headquarters
1765 Sutter St.
San Francisco, CA 94115

2008
Samuel Fletcher Tapman Student Chapter Scholarships

AMOUNT: Maximum: $1500 DEADLINE: February 20
FIELDS/MAJORS: Civil Engineering

Must be a member in good standing of an American Society of Civil Engineers Student Chapter and a freshman, sophomore, or junior. Must continue undergraduate education in a recognized educational institution. Twelve awards offered annually. Write to the address listed or call 1-800-548-ASCE for more details.

American Society of Civil Engineers
Member Scholarships and Awards
1801 Alexander Bell Dr.
Reston, VA 20191

2009
Samuel H. Kress Joint Athens-Jerusalem Fellowship

AMOUNT: $5500 DEADLINE: November 15
FIELDS/MAJORS: Classical Studies, Art History, Architecture, Archaeology

Awards are available for Ph.D. candidates in the areas of study above. Must be U.S. citizens or permanent residents. Write to the address listed for more information.

American School of Classical Studies at Athens
Committee on Admissions and Fellowships
6-8 Charlton St.
Princeton, NJ 08540

2010
Samuel Huntington Public Service Award

AMOUNT: $10000   DEADLINE: February 15
FIELDS/MAJORS: Public Service

Two awards are available to graduating seniors from accredited colleges who would like to pursue public service anywhere in the world. The stipend allows students to engage in a meaningful public service activity for up to one year before proceeding on to graduate school or a career. Write to the address listed for more information.

Samuel Huntington Fund
Attn: D.F. Goodwin
25 Research Dr.
Westborough, MA 01582

2011
Samuel Robinson Award

AMOUNT: $1000   DEADLINE: April 1
FIELDS/MAJORS: All Areas of Study

Scholarships for juniors or seniors at a Presbyterian college. Applicants must be U.S. citizens and members of the Presbyterian Church (U.S.A.). Must be a full-time student. Write to the address listed for information and an application.

Presbyterian Church (U.S.A.)
Office of Financial Aid for Studies
100 Witherspoon St.
Louisville, KY 40202

2012
San Jose GI Forum Scholarships

AMOUNT: $500-$2000   DEADLINE: March 21
FIELDS/MAJORS: All Areas of Study

Scholarships for Hispanic students who are graduating from Santa Clara County, California, high schools. Must have a GPA of at least 2.5 and plan to enroll in an accredited college or university in an associate's or bachelor's degree program. Write to address below for details.

San Jose GI Forum Scholarship Foundation Inc.
1680 Alum Rock Ave.
San Jose, CA 95116

2013
San Pedro Peninsula Hospital Auxiliary Health Grants

AMOUNT: $600-$1000   DEADLINE: November 22
FIELDS/MAJORS: Healthcare-Related

Scholarships for students who reside in the San Pedro Peninsula Hospital service area who plan to enter a healthcare profession. Renewable once. For two- or four-year study. Must have completed at least two semesters of study. Service area includes cities of San Pedro, Palos Verdes Peninsula, Lomita, Harbor City, and Wilmington. Write to the address listed for more details.

San Pedro Peninsula Hospital Auxiliary
Healthcareers Committee
1386 W. Seventh St.
San Pedro, CA 90732

2014
Santee Family Scholarship

AMOUNT: Maximum: $1000   DEADLINE: April 1
FIELDS/MAJORS: Education

Open to residents or former residents of the Alabama Sheriffs' Boys and Girls Ranches. Applicants must be sponsored by a Ranch staff person and must be under the age of twenty-five. Copy of high school transcript is required. Applicants must submit a biographical sketch and an essay outlining career goals. Contact the address listed or call (334) 264-6223 for further information.

Central Alabama Community Foundation
412 N. Hull St.
PO Box 11587
Montgomery, AL 36111

2015
Sarah and Abraham Milstein Scholarship

AMOUNT: None Specified   DEADLINE: March 15
FIELDS/MAJORS: All Areas of Study

Scholarships are available for the valedictorian and salutatorian of Westfield High School. Write to the address listed for information.

Community Foundation of Western Massachusetts
PO Box 15769
1500 Main St.
Springfield, MA 01115

2016
Sarah Bradley Tyson Memorial Fellowships

AMOUNT: $500   DEADLINE: April 15
FIELDS/MAJORS: Home Economics, Horticulture, Conservation Sciences, and Related

Fellowships for advanced study at an educational institution of recognized standing in the U.S. Awards have been made in recognition of leadership in cooperative extension work and initiative in scientific research. Write to the address below for complete details.

Woman's National Farm and Garden Association
Mrs. Elmer Braun
13 Davis Dr.
Saginaw, MI 48602

2017
Sarasota Jazz Club Scholarships

AMOUNT: None Specified   DEADLINE: April 1
FIELDS/MAJORS: All Areas of Study

Scholarships for residents of Sarasota or Manatee counties in Florida. Based on musical (jazz) audition. Write to the address listed or call (941) 366-1552 for details.

Jazz Club of Sarasota
Scholarship Committee
290 Coconut Ave., Bldg. 3
Sarasota, FL 34236

2018
Sarina Slaid Memorial Scholarship

AMOUNT: Maximum: $2500   DEADLINE: April 1
FIELDS/MAJORS: All Areas of Study

Open to Southwest Washington Medical Center junior volunteers based on financial need and overall excellence. Must be residents of Clark or Skamania counties. Contact the address listed or call (360) 256-2035 for further information.

Southwest Washington Medical Center
Scholarship Coordinator
400 N.E. Mother Joseph Pl.
Vancouver, WA 98668

2019
Sawyer Scholarship Fund

AMOUNT: None Specified   DEADLINE: May 1
FIELDS/MAJORS: All Areas of Study

Awards for sons, daughters, and spouses of employees of the Sawyer Group of Companies. The scholarship can be used for any advanced educational studies beyond high school. Contact Mr. Kerry Woodbury, Sawyer Management Services, for more information.

Maine Community Foundation
245 East Maine St.
PO Box 148
Ellsworth, ME 04605

2020
Schechter Foundation Grants

AMOUNT: $1250   DEADLINE: July 1
FIELDS/MAJORS: Physical, Occupational Therapy

Grants for graduate students enrolled in one of the above programs at New York, Columbia, or Hahnemann universities. Twenty-five to thirty awards offered annually. Must be a U.S. citizens to apply. Contact the address below for further information.

Schechter Foundation
535 Madison Ave., 28th Floor
New York, NY 10022

2021
Scholar Athlete Milk Mustache of the Year Award

AMOUNT: Maximum: $7500   DEADLINE: April 10
FIELDS/MAJORS: All Areas of Study

Open to high school students who excel in varsity level sports. Applicants must also have a history of academic achievement and be considered leaders by peers, teachers, and coaches. A letter of reference describing a significant contribution, an act of citizenship, or an act of community service made within the past twelve months will also be required. Entries will be judged by the Sports Illustrated staff, former Sportsmen of Year, and previous Milk Mustache Athletes. Contact the address listed for further information. Must have a GPA of at least 2.8.

National Fluid Milk Processor Promotion Board
Scholar Athlete Milk Mustache of Year
PO Box 9249
Medford, NY 11763-9249

2022
Scholars in Residence Program Fellowships

AMOUNT: Maximum: $30000   DEADLINE: January 12
FIELDS/MAJORS: Black Culture, History, Museum Administration

To assist scholars and professionals whose research in the black experience will benefit from extended access to the Center's collections. Allows fellows to spend six months to a year in residence and includes seminars, forums, and conferences. Candidates for advanced degrees must have received the degree or completed all the requirements for it by the center's deadline. Contact the address listed for further information and an application.

Schomburg Center for Research in Black Culture
515 Malcolm X Boulevard
New York, NY 10037

2023
Scholarship Awards and Achievement Awards

AMOUNT: $100-$1000   DEADLINE: May 14
FIELDS/MAJORS: All Areas of Study

The prospective candidate must have been a member of the Sons of Poland for at least two years and be insured by the Association. You must be entering an accredited college in September of the year of graduation from high school. Write to the address below for complete details.

Association of the Sons of Poland
Scholarship Committee
333 Hackensack St.
Carlstadt, NJ 07072

2024
Scholarship Program

AMOUNT: $250-$2000   DEADLINE: June 30
FIELDS/MAJORS: Automotive Technology

Students must be active in automotive curricula in two- or four-year schools, or interested in pursuing an automotive career. Must be at the sophomore level of study or higher the year the scholarship is granted. Twenty-six to thirty awards per year. Write to the address below for complete details. The Hall of Fame also has a resume bank to help graduates locate jobs.

Automotive Hall of Fame
3225 Cook Road
PO Box 1727
Midland, MI 48641

2025
Scholarship Program for Advanced Study and Research

AMOUNT: $1000-$3000   DEADLINE: February 16
FIELDS/MAJORS: Architecture

Applicants must be in the final year of a professional degree program or have received a professional degree in architecture. Applicants must present a project proposal related to their continuing education goals. Work to be conducted under the direction of a U.S. university. Ten to twenty awards are offered annually. Write to address listed for details.

American Institute of Architects
American Architectural Foundation
1735 New York Ave., NW
Washington, DC 20006

2026
Scholarship Program for Professional Degree Candidates

AMOUNT: $500-$2500   DEADLINE: February 2
FIELDS/MAJORS: Architecture

Assists students who are in the last two years of a professional degree program in architecture (including bachelor's). Applicants must be in the final two years of study in a professional degree program. Students are nominated by their schools for this award. For study at schools with programs accredited by the National Architecture Accrediting Board. Award recipients are announced in April. Write to address listed if details are needed. Applications are available only from your architecture school.

American Institute of Architects
American Architectural Foundation
1735 New York Ave. NW
Washington, DC 20006

2027
Scholarships for Children of Deceased or Disabled Veterans

AMOUNT: None Specified   DEADLINE: April 1
FIELDS/MAJORS: All Areas of Study

Open to children of deceased or 100% disabled veterans or servicemen classified as POW/MIA. Must be U.S. citizens, Florida residents, and enrolled in a college, university, or vo-tech school. Parent must have entered military from Florida and have served during one of the defined conflict periods included on the application Information is available at the school you attend/plan to attend, or write to the Department of Veterans' Affairs or to the address below for details.

Florida Department of Education
Office of Student Financial Assistance
1344 Florida Education Center
Tallahassee, FL 32399

2028
Scholarships for Children of Deceased/Disabled Oregon Peace Officers

AMOUNT: None Specified   DEADLINE: March 1
FIELDS/MAJORS: All Areas of Study

Scholarships for study at Oregon public colleges. Must be child of an Oregon peace officer (police/law enforcement, prison guard/correction officer) who was killed or severely disabled in the line of duty. Your college financial aid office should have information about this scholarship. If not, write to the address listed for more information.

Oregon State Scholarship Commission
Attn: Grant Department
1500 Valley River Dr., #100
Eugene, OR 97401

2029
Scholarships for Children of Missionaries

AMOUNT: None Specified DEADLINE: November 1
FIELDS/MAJORS: All Areas of Study

Scholarships for children of missionaries (active, retired, or deceased) from the Episcopal Church. Available for undergraduate or graduate level study. Write to the address listed or call (212) 867-8400 or 1-800-334-7626 for more details.

Episcopal Church Center
815 Second Ave.
New York, NY 10017

2030
Scholarships for Dependents of Blind Parents

AMOUNT: None Specified DEADLINE: None Specified
FIELDS/MAJORS: All Areas of Study

Available to students who apply within two years of graduation to Alabama state institutions of higher learning. Must come from families in which the head of the family is blind and whose family income is insufficient to provide educational benefits. The program is restricted to students who are Alabama residents. Write to the address listed for details or call (334) 281-1921.

Alabama Commission on Higher Education
Office of Financial Aid
PO Box 30200
Montgomery, AL 36130

2031
Scholarships for Foreign Students

AMOUNT: None Specified DEADLINE: November 1
FIELDS/MAJORS: Church-Related Studies, Theology

Scholarships for students from developing countries who are in some type of theological training within the Anglican Communion. Preference is given to students pursuing a master's degree, but it is open for all levels of study. Write to the address listed or call (212) 867-8400 or 1-800-334-7626 for more details. Applications must be authorized or approved by the diocesan Bishop, the Archbishop, or another provincial authority.

Episcopal Church Center
815 Second Ave.
New York, NY 10017

2032
Scholarships for Graduate Study in Scotland

AMOUNT: Maximum: $16000 DEADLINE: March 15
FIELDS/MAJORS: All Areas of Study

Graduate scholarship for a year's study in Scotland is available for seniors of Scottish descent who demonstrate academic excellence and leadership skills. Applicants must be endorsed by their institutions regarding character and probable future development. Must live within two hundred miles of Washington, D.C. This is defined as D.C. and the states of Delaware, Maryland, North Carolina, New Jersey, Pennsylvania, Virginia, and West Virginia. Write to the address listed or call (301) 656-5130 for information. Must have a GPA of at least 3.4.

St. Andrew's Society of Washington
James S. McLeod, Chairman
7012 Arandale Rd.
Bethesda, MD 20817-4702

2033
Scholarships for Minority Ministries

AMOUNT: None Specified DEADLINE: November 1
FIELDS/MAJORS: Church-Related Studies, Theology

Scholarships for Asian-American, African-American, Hispanic, and Native American students for assistance in pursuing theological education or a graduate-level degree at a church-approved seminary or in an Episcopal studies program. Write to the address listed or call (212) 867-8400 or 1-800-334-7626 for more details.

Episcopal Church Center
815 Second Ave.
New York, NY 10017

2034
Scholarships for Science, Math and Engineering

AMOUNT: $1000-$40000 DEADLINE: December 1
FIELDS/MAJORS: Math, Science, Engineering

Open to senior high school students. Based on an independent research project and high school record. Forty awards per year. (All awards larger than $1000 are four-year awards.) Request official rules and entry form from your high school. If they are not available there, write to the address below. Must have a GPA of at least 3.3.

Westinghouse Science Talent Search
Youth Dept. Science Service
1719 N St. NW
Washington, DC 20036

2035
Scholastic Achievement Grant

AMOUNT: $300-$2000   DEADLINE: February 15
FIELDS/MAJORS: All Areas of Study.

Open to high school seniors who are Connecticut residents. Must be in the top 20% of class and have a minimum SAT of 1200. Must be able to demonstrate financial need. For information and applications contact your high school guidance office or the address listed. Must have a GPA of at least 2.8.

Connecticut Department of Higher Education
John Siegrist
61 Woodland St.
Hartford, CT 06105

2036
Scholastic Art or Writing Awards

AMOUNT: $100-$5000   DEADLINE: None Specified
FIELDS/MAJORS: Creative Writing, Art, Photography

Open to high school juniors and seniors who can demonstrate accomplishments in creative writing, art, or photography. Contact the address listed for further information. Include a SASE for a reply.

Scholastic, Inc.
Scholastic Art or Writing Awards
555 Broadway
New York, NY 10012

2037
Scholastic Sports America Scholarship

AMOUNT: $2500   DEADLINE: March 15
FIELDS/MAJORS: All Areas of Study

Grants for graduating high school seniors (in this school year). Eight awards per year (half to males, half to females). Based on academics and school/community service. Not based on athletics (but they may be considered toward school service). Must be U.S. citizen or permanent resident. These are one-time grants. Competitive. Write to the address below for complete details and application (information may also be available in your high school guidance office). Applications are only accepted until March 15. Employees (and their immediate family members) of ESPN, Inc., Capital Cities/ABC, Inc., the Hearst Corporation, or their subsidiaries are not eligible. Must have a GPA of at least 2.9.

ESPN Scholarship
ESPN Plaza
PO Box 986
Bristol, CT 06011

2038
Schonstedt Scholarship in Surveying

AMOUNT: Maximum: $1500   DEADLINE: November 30
FIELDS/MAJORS: Surveying

Open to undergraduates studying surveying in a four-year degree program. Must have completed the first two years. A magnetic locator will be donated to the Survey Program at the school of each of the winners of this scholarship. Please contact address listed for complete information or call (301) 493-0200.

American Congress on Surveying and Mapping
Ms. Lilly Matheson
5410 Grosvenor Ln., #100
Bethesda, MD 20814-2144

2039
School Librarians Workshop Scholarship

AMOUNT: Maximum: $2500   DEADLINE: February 2
FIELDS/MAJORS: Library Science, Children's or Young Adult

Applicants must be entering an ALA-accredited master's program or a school library media program that meets ALA curriculum guidelines for an NCATE-accredited unit. Based on interest in working with children or young adults in a school library setting. Write to the address listed or call (312) 280-4384 for details.

American Library Association
American Assn. of School Librarians
50 E. Huron St.
Chicago, IL 60611

2040
Schuyler M. Meyer, Jr. Scholarship Fund

AMOUNT: Maximum: $1000   DEADLINE: June 15
FIELDS/MAJORS: All Areas of Study

Scholarships are available for Native American Indians who demonstrate financial need, academic ability, and potential for success. Applicants must be single parents, full-time students, and have GPAs of 2.0 or better. Write to the address listed or call (303) 939-0023 for information.

American Indian Science and Engineering Society
Scholarship Coordinator
5661 Airport Blvd.
Boulder, CO 80301-2339

2041
Schwalenberg Medical School Loan Program-Rollo P. Bourbon, M.D., Scholarship

AMOUNT: None Specified   DEADLINE: January 30
FIELDS/MAJORS: Medicine

Interest free loans available for students in medical school. Repayment begins eighteen months after student receives an M.D. or otherwise leaves school. Must have attended a Santa Barbara school, grades seven through twelve, and graduated from a Santa Barbara high school. When 50% of the loan has been repaid, the loan is considered paid in full. Must be U.S. citizens and residents of Santa Barbara County, California. Financial need is the primary consideration. Applications available from October 1. One Rollo P. Bourbon, M.D., Scholarship will be awarded to a Schwalenberg loan applicant. Write to the address listed for details. Applicants who do not meet the residency guidelines but have demonstrated strong ties to Santa Barbara County will be considered.

Santa Barbara Foundation
Student Aid Director
15 East Carrillo St.
Santa Barbara, CA 93101

2042
Schwartz Writing Competition

AMOUNT: Maximum: $1000   DEADLINE: February 1
FIELDS/MAJORS: Medicine

Writing competition for medical students who are currently enrolled in an accredited school in the United States or Canada. Papers must be no less than three thousand words in length, contain only uncollaborated original work, and may deal with any aspect of legal medicine or relate to research done by the author. Write to the address listed for more information or call (414) 276-1881.

American College of Legal Medicine
Student Writing Competition
611 E. Wells St.
Milwaukee, WI 53202

2043
Schwing America, Inc. Concrete Scholarship

AMOUNT: $2000-$3000   DEADLINE: January 15
FIELDS/MAJORS: Architecture, Construction, Technology, Engineering

Open to upcoming seniors majoring in any of the fields listed above. Must be attending school full-time. Based on academics and demonstrated interest and ability to work in any concrete-related field. These awards are for specific schools. Contact the address listed for further information. Must have a GPA of at least 3.0.

Concrete Research and Education Foundation of ACI International
ACI ConREF
PO Box 9094
Farmington Hills, MI 48333

2044
Screaming Politicians Essay Contest

AMOUNT: Maximum: $1000   DEADLINE: July 4
FIELDS/MAJORS: All Areas of Study

Essay contest open to all college students and college-bound high school students. Essays must be five hundred to one thousand words on the topic of "The Pros and Cons of a Cashless Society" and be returned with an official completed application, available only at the Screaming Politicians Web site: http://www.screamingpoliticians.com. Essays must be original and factually accurate and must not infringe upon any material protected by copyright. Winner will be announced in August on the Screaming Politicians Web site. Please do not write to this organization. They will be unable to respond. You may access their information only by visiting their Web site: http://www.screamingpoliticians.com for further information and an official entry form.

Screaming Politicians and Topical Discussions
Screaming Politicians Essay Contest
4720 Vineland Ave., #300
North Hollywood, CA 91602

2045
SCWU Scholarship

AMOUNT: Maximum: $500   DEADLINE: October 17
FIELDS/MAJORS: All Areas of Study

Scholarships to provide financial assistance to lesbians currently residing in Orange County or the greater Long Beach area. Must have completed at least 12 college units with a minimum GPA of 2.0 and be currently enrolled in an accredited college or trade school. Contact the address listed for further information.

Southern California Women for Understanding
Long Beach/Orange County Chapter
PO Box 91091
Long Beach, CA 90809

2046
Sealaska Scholarship Program

AMOUNT: None Specified   DEADLINE: April 1
FIELDS/MAJORS: All Areas of Study

Scholarships for either Alaska Natives (as defined by the Alaska Native Claims Settlement Act (43usca,1602(b)) who are (or are dependents of) shareholders or stockholders of Sealaska Corporation or Native Americans who reside in southeastern Alaska. Write to the address below for details.

Sealaska Heritage Foundation
Scholarship Program
One Sealaska Plaza, Suite 201
Juneau, AK 99802

2047
Seaspace Scholarship Program

AMOUNT: None Specified DEADLINE: February 1
FIELDS/MAJORS: Marine and Aquatic Sciences

Awards for juniors, seniors, and graduate students studying in the fields listed above. Juniors and seniors must have GPA of 3.5 or better, and graduate students must have at least a 3.0 GPA. For study in the U.S. Must demonstrate financial need. Write to the address listed for more information.

Houston Underwater Club, Inc.
Seaspace Scholarship Committee
PO Box 3753
Houston, TX 77253

2048
Second Effort Scholarship

AMOUNT: $1000 DEADLINE: None Specified
FIELDS/MAJORS: All Areas of Study

Applicants must be Arkansas residents who achieved one of the top ten scores on their general education diploma. The GED test must have been taken in Arkansas. For approved Arkansas two- or four-year public or private school. ADHE will contact those individuals who are eligible.

Arkansas Department of Higher Education
Financial Aid Division
114 East Capitol
Little Rock, AR 72201

2049
Second Marine Division Association Memorial Scholarship

AMOUNT: Maximum: $700 DEADLINE: April 1
FIELDS/MAJORS: All Areas of Study

Scholarships for children of current or former Second Marine Division officers or enlisted men. Based on need (yearly family earnings must be less than $30,000). Renewable. For undergraduate studies as long as student remains an unmarried dependent. Write to the address listed for details. Requests for applications must be in the form of a handwritten letter by the applicant with a SASE to Darrel B. Albers, Board of Trustees, SMDA Memorial Scholarship Fund, 20082 Fernglen Dr., Yorba Linda, CA 92886-6016. Must have a GPA of at least 2.5.

Second Marine Division Association
Memorial Scholarship Fund
PO Box 8180
Camp Lejeune, NC 28542

2050
SEG Foundation Scholarship Program

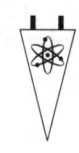

AMOUNT: $500-$3000 DEADLINE: March 1
FIELDS/MAJORS: Geophysics

Scholarships are available for students who intend to pursue careers in exploration geophysics. For undergraduate or graduate study. Based on academic ability. Eighty-one awards offered annually. Write to the address below for complete details.

Society of Exploration Geophysicists Foundation
Scholarship Committee
PO Box 702740
Tulsa, OK 74170

2051
SEIU Scholarship Program

AMOUNT: Maximum: $3000 DEADLINE: March 15
FIELDS/MAJORS: All Areas of Study

Applicants must be union members or the children of members in good standing for at least three years and have not completed more than one year of college. Automatically renewable for up to four years. Based on academics and leadership ability. Three different regions give three awards for a total of nine awards given annually. Contact your parent's local SEIU or write to the address listed for more details.

Service Employees International Union
Scholarship Committee
1313 L St. NW
Washington, DC 20005

2052
Selby Foundation Undergraduate Scholarships

AMOUNT: None Specified DEADLINE: None Specified
FIELDS/MAJORS: All Areas of Study

Open to full-time students who are residents of DeSoto, Manatee, or Sarasota counties. Must have a minimum GPA of 3.0 and be able to demonstrate financial need. Must be attending one of twenty-one participating Florida institutions. University of South Florida at Sarasota is the only school where applicants may be attending for as little as six semester hours. Contact the financial aid officer at your school to determine if your school is a participant and to obtain further information.

Selby Foundation
Undergraduate Scholarship Program
1800 Second St., #905
Sarasota, FL 34236

2053
Selected Professions Fellowship

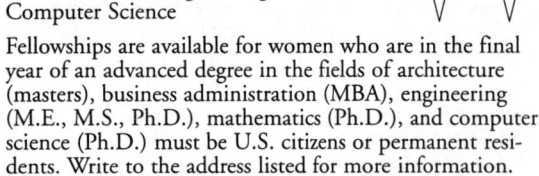

AMOUNT: $5000-$12000
DEADLINE: January 6
FIELDS/MAJORS: Architecture, Business Administration, Engineering, Math, Computer Science

Fellowships are available for women who are in the final year of an advanced degree in the fields of architecture (masters), business administration (MBA), engineering (M.E., M.S., Ph.D.), mathematics (Ph.D.), and computer science (Ph.D.) must be U.S. citizens or permanent residents. Write to the address listed for more information.

American Association of University Women
Fellowship Programs
2201 N. Dodge St., Department 67
Iowa City, IA 52243

2054
Sema Scholarship Fund Awards

AMOUNT: Maximum: $2000 DEADLINE: April 15
FIELDS/MAJORS: Automotive Aftermarket and Related

Scholarships for students currently enrolled in an accredited college, university, or vocational/technical school in a course of study leading to a career in the automotive aftermarket or related fields. Based on career intentions, GPA (not specified), "rigor of curriculum," and recommendations. Write to the address listed for additional information. Must have a GPA of at least 2.8.

Specialty Equipment Market Association
Jerry Forster, Sema Scholarship Fund
PO Box 4910
Diamond Bar, CA 91765

2055
Semantics Project Grants

AMOUNT: $30-$4500 DEADLINE: None Specified
FIELDS/MAJORS: Semantics

Grants to support research in general semantics. Projects must be specifically in or explicitly related to the field of general semantics. Applicants must have knowledge of general semantics and present evidence to that effect. Interested applicants may wish to review the books: Science and Sanity: An Introduction to Non-Aristotelian Systems and General Semantics, by Alfred Korzybski, and Graduate Research in General Semantics, by Kenneth G. Johnson (the latter available for $5 from the Institute of General Semantics, 163 Engle St., Englewood, NJ 07631).

General Semantics Foundation
Project Grants in Semantics
14 Charcoal Hill
Westport, CT 06880

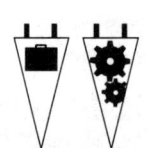

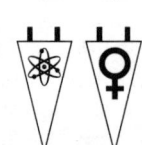

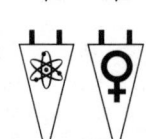

2056
Seminars on Teaching about Japan

AMOUNT: Maximum: $3000 DEADLINE: October 1
FIELDS/MAJORS: Japanese Studies

Grants are available for scholars to design seminars or courses to improve the teaching of the Japanese studies at the college or pre-college level. Applicants should be prepared to explain the character or rationale of their seminar and be able to prepare a budget estimate. Write to the address below for more information.

Northeast Asia Council Association for Asian Studies
1 Lane Hall
University of Michigan
Ann Arbor, MI 48109

2057
Seminole/Miccosukee Indian Scholarships

AMOUNT: None Specified DEADLINE: None Specified
FIELDS/MAJORS: All Areas of Study

Applicants must be Florida residents and members of the Seminole or the Miccosukee tribes. Can be either full- or part-time undergraduate or graduate students. Must demonstrate financial need. Write for further information. Details and application forms are available from your tribal office.

Florida Department of Education
Office of Student Financial Assistance
1344 Florida Education Center
Tallahassee, FL 32399

2058
Senator George J. Mitchell Scholarship

AMOUNT: None Specified DEADLINE: April 26
FIELDS/MAJORS: All Areas of Study

Awards for Maine high school graduates who plan to attend a college or university in Maine. Based on academics, financial need, community service, and public service. Scholarships are awarded on a rotational basis. No high school will qualify for a second scholarship until each high school in Maine has received one scholarship. Write to the address listed for more details.

Maine Community Foundation
245 East Maine St.
PO Box 148
Ellsworth, ME 04605

2059
Senior Adult Scholarship Program

AMOUNT: None Specified DEADLINE: None Specified
FIELDS/MAJORS: All Areas of Study

Scholarships for Alabama residents sixty years of age or above who are attending an accredited two-year college in Alabama. Contact the financial aid office at your college for details.

Alabama Commission on Higher Education
PO Box 30200
Montgomery, AL 36130

2060
Senior Citizens Reduced Tuition Act

AMOUNT: None Specified DEADLINE: None Specified
FIELDS/MAJORS: All Areas of Study

Award for senior citizens (age sixty-five and over) from New Mexico who are attending any public postsecondary institution in New Mexico. This enables senior citizens to pay the reduced tuition rate of $5.00 per credit hour (up to six credit hours per semester.) Enrollment is on a space-available basis. Contact the financial aid office at any institution at any New Mexico public postsecondary institution.

New Mexico Commission on Higher Education
Financial Aid and Student Services
PO Box 15910
Santa Fe, NM 87506

2061
Senior Health Scholarship for Students in the Greater St. Louis Area

AMOUNT: None Specified DEADLINE: April 10
FIELDS/MAJORS: Health, Medicine

Awards are available for high school seniors in the St. Louis metropolitan area who intend to enter a four-year college in the field of health studies. Must demonstrate financial need. Contact your guidance counseling office for applications and information. The foundation does not send out any information.

Combined Health Appeal of Greater St. Louis
Mr. Philip D. Carlock, Executive Dir.
50 Crestwood Executive Center, #201
St. Louis, MO 63126-1945

2062
Senior in Education

AMOUNT: Maximum: $250 DEADLINE: May 1
FIELDS/MAJORS: Education

Applicant must be a senior in education and graduated from a Geauga County high school. Must have two college/university references and a fifty-word paragraph on why you should be chosen for this award. For more information, write the address below. This award may not be given every year.

Geauga County Retired Teachers Association
Bill Flinta, Scholarship Chairman
14680 Maplewood Dr.
Burton, OH 44021

2063
Senior Merit Awards

AMOUNT: None Specified DEADLINE: August 31
FIELDS/MAJORS: Medicine

Awards given to senior medical students in recognition of outstanding academic achievement, leadership, and community service. Includes the Irving Graef Memorial Scholarship, William and Charlotte Cadbury Award, Franklin C. McLean Award, and James H. Robinson Memorial Prize. There are two deadlines: May 31 deadline is for renewal applicants, and August 31 deadline is for new applicants. Send a SASE ($.55 postage) to the address below for additional information.

National Medical Fellowships, Inc.
110 West 32nd St.
New York, NY 10001

2064
Sequoyah Graduate Fellowships

AMOUNT: None Specified DEADLINE: October 1
FIELDS/MAJORS: All Areas of Study

Fellowships are available for American Indian or Native Alaskan graduate students. All applicants must be enrolled full-time and provide a class schedule. Must be minimally one-quarter degree Indian blood from a federally recognized tribe. Write to the address below for details.

Association on American Indian Affairs, Inc.
Box 268
Sisseton, SD 57262

2065
Sertoma Communicative Disorders Scholarships

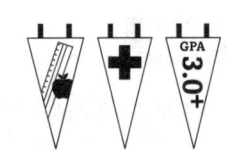

AMOUNT: $2500 DEADLINE: March 27
FIELDS/MAJORS: Audiology, Speech Pathology

Open to master's level students in audiology or speech pathology. Applicants must be citizens of the U.S., Mexico, or Canada and enrolled full-time in a U.S. institution accredited by ASHA's Council on academic accreditation. Must have a minimum GPA of 3.2 in college coursework. Thirty awards are offered annually. Information is available from the address listed or from NSSLHA chapters, universities, Sertoma Affiliates, and speech and hearing organizations. Must include a business-sized SASE for a reply.

Sertoma International
Leslie Freese
1912 E. Meyer Blvd.
Kansas City, MO 64132

2066
Sertoma Scholarships for Students with Hearing Loss

AMOUNT: $1000 DEADLINE: May 1
FIELDS/MAJORS: All Areas of Study

Scholarships are available for full-time students enrolled in or planning to enroll in any accredited four-year program. Applicants must have a documented hearing loss and a GPA of at least 3.2. Based on academic ability. Thirteen scholarships are offered annually. Write to the address listed for information.

Sertoma International
Leslie Freese
1912 E. Meyer Blvd.
Kansas City, MO 64132

2067
Service Loan

AMOUNT: Maximum: $1500 DEADLINE: April 1
FIELDS/MAJORS: All Areas of Study

Provides undergraduate students with an opportunity to pay a portion of their educational debt through service in various school, church, and community projects. Applicants must be full-time sophomore or junior students and must serve three hundred hours in a campus-related project, church-related project, community organization, or as a volunteer in a mission. Contact the financial aid office at your school for information and forms. If they are not available there, write to address listed.

Presbyterian Church (U.S.A.)
Office of Financial Aid for Studies
100 Witherspoon St.
Louisville, KY 40202

2068
Service Merchandise Scholarships

AMOUNT: Maximum: $500 DEADLINE: January 15
FIELDS/MAJORS: Business, Merchandising, Marketing, Economics, and Accounting

Applicant must be a current high school senior or recent graduate planning to attend a four-year college on a full-time basis. Approximately one hundred awards offered annually. Do not mail requests for information anywhere; information and applications must be picked up from catalog showrooms only. Please stop by your local Service Merchandise store after October 15 to pick up an application/brochure or call 1-800-251-1212 for stores nearest you. Although the deadline date is January 15, only the first 2500 applications are processed, so mail early.

Service Merchandise Company, Inc.
Scholarship Program

2069
SETAC Program for Minority Students and Mentors in Environmental Chemistry

AMOUNT: None Specified DEADLINE: September 8
FIELDS/MAJORS: Environmental Chemistry and Toxicology

Awards are available for minority students and faculty mentors in the areas of environmental chemistry or toxicology. Selected individuals will receive a one-year membership to the Society of Environmental Toxicology and Chemistry and funds to travel and attend the SETAC world conference in Canada. Write to the address below for more information.

Society of Environmental Toxicology and Chemistry
Mr. Rodney Parrish, Executive Director
1010 North 12th Ave.
Pensacola, FL 32501

2070
Seth R. Brooks and Corrine H. Brooks Scholarship Fund

AMOUNT: None Specified DEADLINE: April 15
FIELDS/MAJORS: All Areas of Study

Applicants must be undergraduate or graduate children of Beta Theta Pi members. No limitation is placed on marital status. One award per year. Write to the address below for details. Must have a GPA of at least 2.8.

Beta Theta Pi Administrative Office
208 E. High St.
PO Box 6277
Oxford, OH 45056

2071
Shaver-Hitchings Scholarship

AMOUNT: Maximum: $1500 DEADLINE: March 15
FIELDS/MAJORS: Physician's Assistant, Medicine, Allied Health

Award open to graduate students in the above areas who wish to help others. Applicants must be residents of Durham, Orange, Chatham, or Wake counties in North Carolina. Students need not be pursuing a degree in addictive disorders but must show a demonstrated commitment to working with others in that field. Contact the address listed or call (919) 549-9840 for further information.

Triangle Community Foundation
Polly Guthrie, Program Officer
PO Box 12834
Research Triangle Pa, NC 27709

2072
Shaw-Worth Scholarship Award

AMOUNT: Maximum: $1000 DEADLINE: March 15
FIELDS/MAJORS: Animal Rights

Awards for New England high school seniors who have made meaningful contributions to animal protection over a significant period of time. Contact the address listed for more information.

Humane Society of the United States
New England Regional Office
PO Box 619
Jacksonville, VT 05342

2073
Sheet Metal Workers' International Scholarship

AMOUNT: $2500 DEADLINE: March 1
FIELDS/MAJORS: All Areas of Study

Scholarships for members or immediate family of members of the Sheet Metal Workers International Association. For full-time undergraduate study. Write to the address below for more information.

Sheet Metal Workers International Association
Scholarship Fund
1750 New York Ave. NW, 6th Floor
Washington, DC 20006

2074
Sheriffs' Association of Indiana Scholarships

AMOUNT: None Specified DEADLINE: April 1
FIELDS/MAJORS: Law, Law Enforcement, Criminology, and Related

Scholarships for members and children of members of the Indiana Sheriffs' Association. Must be Indiana resident, high school senior, or full-time undergraduate at an Indiana college or university working toward a career related to law enforcement. Must be between seventeen and twenty-three years old and be in top half of high school or college class. Thirty-two awards per year. Applications are available through your local sheriff's office, the financial aid or admissions office at your college, or the guidance office of your high school. Please obtain application from one of those sources. Must have a GPA of at least 2.5.

Indiana Sheriffs' Association, Inc.
PO Box 19127
Indianapolis, IN 46219

2075
Sheryl A. Horak Law Enforcement Explorer Memorial Scholarship

AMOUNT: $1000 DEADLINE: March 31
FIELDS/MAJORS: Law Enforcement

Any law enforcement explorer who is at least a high school senior may apply. Candidates will be evaluated according to their academic record, leadership ability, and extracurricular activities. Must be under twenty-one years of age. One award is given annually. Write to the address below for more information.

Boy Scouts of America
Exploring Division, S210
1325 West Walnut Hill Ln., PO Box 152079
Irving, TX 75015

2076
Shields-Gillespie Scholarship

AMOUNT: Maximum: $700 DEADLINE: January 1
FIELDS/MAJORS: Preschool Education, Kindergarten Education

Applicants must be a current member of the American Orff-Schulwerk Association and must have been an AOSA member in good standing for two years. Must be a U.S. citizen or have resided in the U.S. for the past five years. Must be able to demonstrate financial need and present evidence of low-income populations he/she teaches. Write to the address below for more information.

American Orff-Schulwerk Association
Music and Movement Education
PO Box 391089
Cleveland, OH 44139

2077
Sho Sato Memorial Scholarships

AMOUNT: None Specified DEADLINE: April 1
FIELDS/MAJORS: Law

Applicants must be of Japanese ancestry and entering or enrolled at an accredited law school. Must also be members of the Japanese-American Citizens League. Applications and information may be obtained from local JACL chapters, district offices, and the national headquarters at the address listed, or call (415)921-5225. Please indicate your level of study and be certain to include a legal-sized SASE.

Japanese-American Citizens League
National Scholarship and Award Program
1765 Sutter St.
San Francisco, CA 94115

2078
Short-Term Fellowships

AMOUNT: Maximum: $1000 DEADLINE: December 1
FIELDS/MAJORS: Bibliography, History of Printing and Publishing

Graduate research fellowships for one or two months. Supports inquiry into research focusing on books or manuscripts (the physical objects themselves). Approximately eight awards per year. Three letters of recommendation are required. Award amount is per month. Write to the address listed for details.

Bibliographical Society of America
BSA Executive Secretary
PO Box 397, Grand Central Station
New York, NY 10163

2079
Short-Term Research Fellowships

AMOUNT: $2000-$4000 DEADLINE: January 15
FIELDS/MAJORS: Humanities/Social Science

Two- to four-month research fellowships are available for pre or postdoctoral study. Open to American citizens and foreign nationals. For study in any area in which the Library has holdings. Write to address listed for details.

John Carter Brown Library
Attn: Director
Box 1894, Brown University
Providence, RI 02912

2080
Short-Term Resident Fellowships for Individual Research

AMOUNT: None Specified DEADLINE: March 1
FIELDS/MAJORS: History (American and Western), Humanities, Literature

Scholars who hold a Ph.D. may apply for residential fellowships. Applicants must be working on a specific research project in a field appropriate to the Newberry's collection. Doctoral candidates who have completed all requirements except the dissertation are also invited to apply. Preference given to scholars from outside the Chicago area. Fellowships can be two weeks to two months (three months for foreign scholars). Write to the address listed or call (312) 255-3666.

Newberry Library
Committee on Awards
60 W. Walton St.
Chicago, IL 60610

2081
Short-Term Travel To Japan for Professional Purposes

AMOUNT: None Specified DEADLINE: October 1
FIELDS/MAJORS: Japanese Studies

Awards for scholars who have a Ph.D. (or comparable professional qualification) and need time in Japan to complete their work. These grants are intended for short-term research trips by scholars who are already familiar with Japan and with their topic. Second deadline date is February 1 for the spring awards. Ph.D. candidates are not eligible to apply. Write to the address below for more information.

Northeast Asia Council Association for Asian Studies
1 Lane Hall
University of Michigan
Ann Arbor, MI 48109

2082
SHPE Engineering and Science Scholarships

AMOUNT: $500-$7000
DEADLINE: April 15
FIELDS/MAJORS: Engineering, Science

Scholarships for Hispanic students seeking careers in science or engineering. For undergraduate or graduate study. Based on potential, character, need, involvement, and scholastic aptitude. Must be attending school full-time. Write to the address listed for details. Must have a GPA of at least 2.7.

Society of Hispanic Professional Engineers Foundation
SHPE Scholarships, Kathy Borunda
5400 E. Olympic Blvd., Suite 210
Los Angeles, CA 90022

2083
Shula Scholars Awards

AMOUNT: $500-$1500   DEADLINE: None Specified
FIELDS/MAJORS: Sports Management

Five to seven scholarships for graduates of St. Thomas who were varsity players and will be majoring in sports management. Minimum GPA: 2.5. Financial need considered. Write to the address listed for details.

Shula Scholars Program
Mr. Al Avila
16400 NW 32nd Ave.
Miami, FL 33043

2084
Sickle Cell (Sybil Fong Sam) Scholarship Contest

AMOUNT: $200-$500   DEADLINE: March 30
FIELDS/MAJORS: All Areas of Study

Open to high school seniors who are Connecticut residents. One award is for $200, one for $300, and the third for $500. Recipients are selected through an evaluation process of written essays. The Sickle Cell Disease Association of America will select the topic(s) for the essays. Contact the address listed for further information.

Sickle Cell Disease Association of America
Garey E. Coleman
114 Woodland St., #2101
Hartford, CT 06105

2085
Sico Foundation Scholarships

AMOUNT: Maximum: $4000   DEADLINE: February 15
FIELDS/MAJORS: All Areas of Study

Applicants must be high school seniors who reside in the state of Delaware or the following counties in Pennsylvania: Adams, Berks, Chester, Cumberland, Dauphin, Delaware, Lancaster, Lebanon, or York. Residents of Cecil County in Maryland are also eligible. Award must be used at selected schools. Write to the address below for details.

Sico Foundation
Scholarships Coordinator
Mount Joy, PA 17552

2086
Sid Richardson Memorial Fund

AMOUNT: None Specified   DEADLINE: March 29
FIELDS/MAJORS: All Areas of Study

Awards for children of persons who are or were employed by one of these Sid Richardson Companies: Sid Richardson Carbon and Gas, Richardson Products II, SRGG Aviation, Inc., Leapartners, L.P. (DBA Sid Richardson Gasoline Co., Jal), Bass Enterprises Production, Bass Brothers Enterprises, Inc., Richardson Oils, Inc., Perry R. Bass, Inc., Sid W. Richardson Foundation, San Jose Cattle, City Center Development, and Richard Aviation. Write to address listed for details. Please include the name, social security number, and dates of employment of the qualifying employee.

Sid Richardson Memorial Fund
Jo Helen Rosacker
309 Main St.
Fort Worth, TX 76102

2087
Sigma Theta Tau American Nurses' Foundation Grant

AMOUNT: $6000   DEADLINE: May 1
FIELDS/MAJORS: Nursing

Grant for nurses who have completed master's degree study. Supports research of a clinical nature. One award per year. Request application forms for the ANF Grant Program from the address below.

Sigma Theta Tau International/American Nurses
  Foundation
American Nurses Foundation
600 Maryland Ave. SW, Suite 100 West
Washington, DC 20024

2088
Sigma Theta Tau Int'l/ American Association of Diabetes Educators Grant

AMOUNT: Maximum: $6000   DEADLINE: October 1
FIELDS/MAJORS: Nursing

Grant for nurses who have completed master's degree study to encourage them to contribute to the enhancement of quality and increase the availability of diabetes education and care research. One grant is offered annually. Request application forms for the AADE Grant Program from the address below.

Sigma Theta Tau International Honor Society of
  Nursing/AADE
AADE Education and Research Foundation
444 North Michigan Ave., Suite 1240
Chicago, IL 60611

2089
Sigma Theta Tau Int'l/ Emergency Nursing Foundation Grant

AMOUNT: Maximum: $6000   DEADLINE: March 1
FIELDS/MAJORS: Nursing

Grant for nurses who have completed master's degree study that will advance the specialized practice of emergency nursing. One grant is offered annually. Request application forms for the AADE Grant Program from the address below.

Sigma Theta Tau International/Emergency Nursing Foundation
Emergency Nursing Foundation
216 Higgins Road
Park Ridge, IL 60068

2090
Sigma Theta Tau Int'l/ Mead Johnson Nutritionals Perinatal Grants

AMOUNT: $10000   DEADLINE: June 1
FIELDS/MAJORS: Nursing

Grant for nurses who have completed master's degree study. Supports research relating to perinatal issues (up to one year old). One award per year. Must be a U.S. citizen. Request application forms for the Mead Johnson Grant Program from the below address.

Sigma Theta Tau International Honor Society of Nursing
Program Department
550 West North St.
Indianapolis, IN 46202

2091
Sigma Theta Tau International/Glaxo Wellcome Research Grant

AMOUNT: Maximum: $5000   DEADLINE: October 1
FIELDS/MAJORS: Nursing

Grant for nurses who have completed master's degree study. Supports research relating to the prescribing practices of advanced practicing nurses. One award is offered annually. Request application forms for the Glaxo Grant Program from the address below.

Sigma Theta Tau International Honor Society of Nursing/Glaxo Wellcome,
Program Department
550 West North St.
Indianapolis, IN 46202

2092
Sigma Theta Tau International Small Research Grants

AMOUNT: $3000   DEADLINE: March 1
FIELDS/MAJORS: Nursing

Grants for nurses who have completed master's degree study. There is no specific focus of this program; but pilot, multidisciplinary, and international research is encouraged. Ten to fifteen awards per year. Request application forms for the Small Grants Program from the address below.

Sigma Theta Tau International Honor Society of Nursing
Program Department
550 West North St.
Indianapolis, IN 46202

2093
Sigma Theta Tau International/Oncology Nursing Society Grant

AMOUNT: $10000   DEADLINE: December 1
FIELDS/MAJORS: Nursing

Grant for nurses who have completed master's degree study. Supports research of an oncology clinically-oriented topic. One award per year. Request application forms for the ONS Grant Program from the address below.

Sigma Theta Tau International Honor Society of Nursing
Oncology Nursing Foundation
501 Holiday Dr.
Pittsburgh, PA 15220

2094
Sigma Theta Tau Nursing

AMOUNT: $3000-$10000   DEADLINE: March 1
FIELDS/MAJORS: Nursing

Grant for nurses who have completed master's degree study. Supports research relating to caregiving issues for HIV-positive persons. One award per year. Write to the address listed for more information.

Sigma Theta Tau International Honor Society of Nursing
Program Department
550 West North St.
Indianapolis, IN 46202

2095
Sigma Theta Tau/American Association of Critical Care Nurses Grant

AMOUNT: $10000 DEADLINE: October 1
FIELDS/MAJORS: Nursing

Grant for nurses who have completed master's degree study. Supports research relating to critical care nursing practice. One award per year. Request application forms for the AACN Grant Program from the address below.

Sigma Theta Tau International/AACN
Department of Research
101 Columbia
Alison Viejo, CA 92656

2096
Simmons Scholarships

AMOUNT: $2000 DEADLINE: July 28
FIELDS/MAJORS: Travel and Tourism

Awards are available for master's or doctoral students of travel and tourism at a recognized college, university, or proprietary travel school. Must be U.S. citizens or legal residents and have a GPA of at least 2.5. Two awards per year are given. Write to the address below for more information.

American Society of Travel Agents
Scholarship Committee
1101 King St., Suite 200
Alexandria, VA 22314

2097
Sinfonia Foundation Research Assistance Grants

AMOUNT: Maximum: $1000 DEADLINE: May 1
FIELDS/MAJORS: Music Research

Grants supporting research on American music or music in America. Must show history of scholarly writing in music or show unusual knowledge in area to be researched. Write to the address below for details.

Sinfonia Foundation
10600 Old State Rd.
Evansville, IN 47711

2098
Singles Association of Florida Scholarship

AMOUNT: Maximum: $1000 DEADLINE: February 1
FIELDS/MAJORS: All Areas of Study

Scholarship limited to children of single parent household. Applicants must have minimum test scores of 1000 on the SAT or a composite of 24 on ACT. Selection based on academic achievement, activities, leadership, and financial need. Recipients must be planning to attend a Florida college or university on a full-time basis and be U.S. citizens. Write to the address listed for more details.

Singles Association of Florida
335 Avocado St.
Bradenton, FL 34207

2099
Six Meter Club of Chicago Scholarship

AMOUNT: $500 DEADLINE: February 1
FIELDS/MAJORS: All Areas of Study

Scholarship available to undergraduates with any class amateur radio license who are residents of Illinois. Must be attending an Illinois school full-time. Write to the address listed for information. Must have a GPA of at least 2.5.

ARRL Foundation (American Radio Relay League)
Scholarship Program
225 Main St.
Newington, CT 06111

2100
Six-Month Internships

AMOUNT: Maximum: $8000 DEADLINE: January 30
FIELDS/MAJORS: Art History, Art Conservation, or Related Fields

Internships for seniors, recent graduates, or graduate students who have demonstrated financial need. For work at the museum, full-time (thirty-five hour week), June 8 through December 4. Must attend orientation. Preference given to ethnically diverse applicants. Essay must accompany application. Write to the address listed for additional information.

Metropolitan Museum of Art
Internship Programs
1000 Fifth Ave.
New York, NY 10028-0198

2101
SLA Scholarship Program

AMOUNT: Maximum: $6000 DEADLINE: October 31
FIELDS/MAJORS: Library/Information Science

For study in librarianship leading to a master's degree at a recognized school of library or information science. Preference will be given to those who display an aptitude for and interest in special library work. Up to three awards given per year. Write to the address listed for complete details.

Special Libraries Association
SLA Scholarship Committee
1700 Eighteenth St., NW
Washington, DC 20009

2102
Slocum-Lunz Foundation

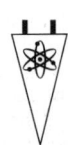

AMOUNT: Maximum: $700 DEADLINE: April 1
FIELDS/MAJORS: Marine Biology/Natural Sciences

The foundation provides scholarship and/or grant monies to be used in the support of scholars and educational institutions in the fields of marine biology and closely related natural sciences. Applications from beginning graduate students and advanced undergraduates will also be considered. Academic work does not have to be performed in South Carolina. Ten to fifteen awards are given annually. Contact address below for complete information.

Slocum-Lunz Foundation
Marine Resources Research Institute
PO Box 12559
Charleston, SC 29412

2103
Smithsonian Fellowship Program

AMOUNT: $3000-$25000 DEADLINE: January 15
FIELDS/MAJORS: Humanities, Art Studies, Anthropology, Astrophysics, Biology, History

Fellowships are available to pre and postdoctoral scholars for research in one of the above fields or any field of interest to the Smithsonian. Write to the address below for details. Request the publication "Smithsonian Opportunities for Research and Study."

Smithsonian Institution
Office of Fellowships and Grants
955 L'enfant Plaza, Suite 7000
Washington, DC 20560

2104
Smithsonian Marine Station at Link Port Fellowships

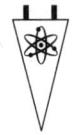

AMOUNT: None Specified DEADLINE: February 15
FIELDS/MAJORS: Marine Sciences

Fellowships are available for pre and postdoctoral scholars to support research in Marine Science at Link Port. Three levels of fellowships are offered: ten-week periods for graduate students, two- to twelve-month periods for recent Ph.D.'s and for senior scholars who have held the Ph.D. for more than seven years. Write to the address below for information.

Smithsonian Institution
Smithsonian Marine Station at Link Port
Old Dixie Highway
Fort Pierce, FL 34946

2105
Society of Certified Public Accountants, Wyoming Society, Scholarships

AMOUNT: $300 DEADLINE: April 1
FIELDS/MAJORS: Accounting

Scholarships for graduates of Wyoming high schools who are considering majoring in accounting and will be attending the University of Wyoming or any junior/community college in Wyoming. Two awards per year. Write to the society at the address listed for details.

Wyoming Society of Certified Public Accountants
1721 Warren Ave.
Cheyenne, WY 82001

2106
Society of Naval Architects and Marine Engineers Awards

AMOUNT: None Specified DEADLINE: None Specified
FIELDS/MAJORS: Naval Architecture, Marine, Ocean Engineering

Undergraduate and graduate scholarships for students studying naval architecture or marine or ocean engineering. Applicants must be U.S. or Canadian citizens and attending or plan to attend one of twenty-four ABET or CEAB-accredited schools. Write to the address listed for further information.

Society of Naval Architects and Marine Engineers
Executive Director of the Society
601 Pavonia Ave., #400
Jersey City, NJ 07306

2107
Society of Physics Students Scholarships

AMOUNT: $1000-$4000 DEADLINE: February 15
FIELDS/MAJORS: Physics

Awards are available for juniors who are members of the Society of Physics Students. Based on scholarship, dedication to physics, and activity in SPS. Write to the address listed for more information.

Sigma Pi Sigma Trust Endowment Fund
American Institute of Physics
One Physics Ellipse
College Park, MD 20740

2108
Society of Plastics Engineers Scholarship Fund

AMOUNT: $3000-$4000   DEADLINE: December 15
FIELDS/MAJORS: Plastics/Chemical/Mechanical/Industrial Engineering, Physics, Chemistry

Nine to ten awards are available for high school graduates who are full-time students in a four-year college or two-year technical program in engineering with a focus on plastics. Preference is given to advanced students. Must be in good academic standing with your school and be able to demonstrate financial need. Write to the address listed for more information.

Society of Plastics Engineers
PO Box 403
Brookfield, CT 06804

2109
Society of Satellite Professionals International Scholarships

AMOUNT: $1000-$4000   DEADLINE: December 12
FIELDS/MAJORS: Aeronautical/Aerospace Engineering, Communications, Related Fields

Scholarships for undergraduate or graduate students in the above areas of study who are committed to the field of satellite communications. Includes the SSPI Scholarship, the A.W. Perigard Scholarship, the Phillips Publishing, Inc., Scholarship, the Hughes Communications Scholarships, and the SSPI Mid-Atlantic Chapter Scholarship. Applications available at your department. If they do not have the information, write to the address below. Must include a legal-sized SASE for a reply.

Society of Satellite Professionals International
Educational Award Programs
2200 Wilson Blvd., Suite 102-258
Arlington, VA 22201

2110
Soil and Water Conservation Scholarship

AMOUNT: $250   DEADLINE: March 1
FIELDS/MAJORS: Natural Resources, Conservation (Soil and Water), and Related

Scholarships for students enrolled in or accepted into a two- or four-year program, who are from Benton County, Iowa, and studying in the area of natural resources. Contact the SWCD office at the address listed for details.

Soil and Water Conservation District-Benton County Commissioners Sponsor Scholarship
1705 W. D St.
Vinton, IA 52349

2111
Sons of the American Revolution Oratorical Contest

AMOUNT: Maximum: $1500   DEADLINE: September 1
FIELDS/MAJORS: All Areas

Scholarships open to high school juniors and seniors and college freshmen and sophomores. Based on a five hundred word essay on applicants' Revolutionary heritage. Winners may advance to national competitions. Write to the address below for details.

Miami Chapter, Florida Society of Sons of the American Revolution
Dr. Arthur E. Chapman
1239 Mariposa Ave., #7
Coral Gables, FL 33146

2112
Soroptomist International of Hays Training Award

AMOUNT: None Specified   DEADLINE: January 15
FIELDS/MAJORS: All Areas of Study

Scholarships open to women completing undergraduate programs or entering vocational or technical training programs. Must be head of household. Write to the address below for information.

Soroptomist International of Hays
Jolene Moore
1921 Whittier
Hays, KS 67601

2113
Soroptomist International of Hays Youth Citizenship Award

AMOUNT: None Specified   DEADLINE: January 15
FIELDS/MAJORS: All Areas of Study

Scholarships open to high school seniors who have made outstanding contributions to home, school, or community. Write to the address below for information.

Soroptomist International of Hays
Jolene Moore
1921 Whittier
Hays, KS 67601

2114
South Carolina "Other Race" Program

AMOUNT: Maximum: $1000 DEADLINE: None Specified
FIELDS/MAJORS: All Areas of Study

Scholarships for South Carolina residents who are members of a minority group attending a South Carolina public college or university. Write to the address below for additional information.

South Carolina Commission on Higher Education
1333 Main St., Suite 200
Columbia, SC 29201

2115
South Carolina Graduate Incentive Fellowship Program

AMOUNT: Maximum: $10000 DEADLINE: None Specified
FIELDS/MAJORS: All Areas of Study

Fellowships for South Carolina residents who are members of a minority group attending a South Carolina public college or university. For graduate and doctoral study. Write to the address below for additional information.

South Carolina Commission On Higher Education
1333 Main St., Suite 200
Columbia, SC 29201

2116
South Carolina National Guard Tuition Assistance

AMOUNT: Maximum: $500 DEADLINE: None Specified
FIELDS/MAJORS: All Areas of Study

Scholarships for South Carolina National Guard or Air National Guard who are attending an in-state school in a program approved by the Veterans Education Division. Renewable. Write to the local National Guard or to Adjutant General of S.C., 1 National Guard Road, Columbia, S.C., 29201 for more information.

South Carolina Commission on Higher Education
1333 Main St., Suite 200
Columbia, SC 29201

2117
South Carolina Optometric Association Student Loan Fund

AMOUNT: $1000 DEADLINE: July 1
FIELDS/MAJORS: Optometry

Residents of South Carolina enrolled in an accredited school of optometry. Must have GPAs of 2.5 or better. Recommendation by SCOA member will be required. Write for complete details.

South Carolina Optometric Association
Financial Aid Program
2730 Devine St.
Columbia, SC 29205

2118
South Carolina Press Association Foundation Scholarships

AMOUNT: $2000-$2500 DEADLINE: June 1
FIELDS/MAJORS: Newspaper-Related

Scholarships for students entering their junior year in a South Carolina college or university program and preparing for a career in the newspaper industry. Must agree to work in the newspaper field in the United States for at least two years. Renewable. Usually three awards are given annually. Write to the address below for details.

South Carolina Press Association Foundation, Inc.
William C. Rogers, Secretary
PO Box 11429
Columbia, SC 29211

2119
South Carolina Tuition Grants

AMOUNT: $3320 DEADLINE: None Specified
FIELDS/MAJORS: All Areas of Study

Scholarships available to undergraduate students who are residents of South Carolina attending a private in-state institution. Based primarily on financial need. Contact your financial aid office or the following address for more information: Tuition Grants Commission, 1310 Lady St., Suite 811, Keenan Bldg. PO Box 12159, Columbia, S.C. 29211.

South Carolina Commission on Higher Education
1333 Main St., Suite 200
Columbia, SC 29201

2120
South Central Modern Languages Association Fellowships

AMOUNT: $800-$2400 DEADLINE: March 1
FIELDS/MAJORS: History (American and European), Humanities, Literature, Linguistics, Semantics

Fellowships are available to doctoral candidates or postdoctoral scholars who are members of the South Central Modern Language Association at time of application.

Applicants from outside the Chicagoland region must have been members for three continuous years. Stipends are for $800 monthly for up to three months. Contact the address listed or call (312) 255-3666 for more information.

Newberry Library
Committee on Awards
60 W. Walton St.
Chicago, IL 60610

2121
South Dakota Retailers Association

AMOUNT: $1000 DEADLINE: May 13
FIELDS/MAJORS: Retail

Scholarships are available for students enrolled in a retail-related course of study at a university, college, or vocational school located in South Dakota. Applicants must intend to pursue a career in the retail field. Must have completed one quarter of study at time of application. Write to the address below for more information.

South Dakota Retailers Association
PO Box 638
Pierre, SD 57501

2122
Southern Building Code Congress International Education Fund

AMOUNT: None Specified DEADLINE: May 31
FIELDS/MAJORS: All Areas of Study

Awards for dependents of members of the Southern Building Code Congress International. Based on financial need, character, integrity, and scholastic ability. Write to the address below for more information.

Southern Building Code Congress International
Educational Services
900 Montclair Road
Birmingham, AL 35213

2123
Southern Scholarship Foundation Scholars

AMOUNT: $4800 DEADLINE: March 1
FIELDS/MAJORS: All Areas of Study

Need-based awards for students at FSU, University of Florida, Bethune-Cookman College, or Florida A&M University that provides housing at no cost. Must maintain a GPA of least 2.85. Based on need, academic promise, and character. 450 awards are given annually. Write to the address below for details.

Southern Scholarship Foundation
322 Stadium Dr.
Tallahassee, FL 32304

2124
Southern States Scholarship Program

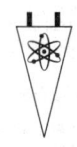

AMOUNT: $600-$800 DEADLINE: None Specified
FIELDS/MAJORS: Agriculture

Awards for students accepted at one of the following schools: University of Delaware, University of Kentucky, University of Maryland, North Carolina State, Virginia Polytechnic Institute, Virginia State, or West Virginia State. Applicant must be a resident of the state in which the school he/she plans to attend is located. Must be the son or daughter of a producer of agriculture products. Renewable with good academic record. Awards are $800 for the first year and $600 for any years thereafter. Write to the address below for more information or apply directly to your university's college of agriculture.

Southern States Cooperative, Inc.
PO Box 26234
Richmond, VA 23260

2125
Southington Woman's Club Scholarships

AMOUNT: None Specified DEADLINE: February 10
FIELDS/MAJORS: All Areas of Study

Open to women who have completed two or more years of undergraduate work in accredited institutions of higher learning with a 3.0 average or better and are matriculating for a bachelor's or postgraduate degree. Contact the address listed for further information.

General Federation of Women's Clubs, Southington Chapter
Vivian Petz
44 Cloverdale Rd.
Southington, CT 06489

2126
Special Education Teacher Tuition Waiver Program

AMOUNT: None Specified DEADLINE: February 15
FIELDS/MAJORS: Special Education

Awards for current teachers and talented students to pursue careers in special education in elementary or secondary schools in Illinois. Must be a U.S. citizen or permanent resident and a resident of Illinois and agree to take courses to prepare for teaching children with handicaps and learning disabilities. For graduate or undergraduate students who already hold a valid teaching certificate that is not in the discipline of special education. Contact the address below for further information.

Illinois Student Assistance Commission
1755 Lake Cook Road
Deerfield, IL 60015

2127
Speech Language Pathologist Incentive Program

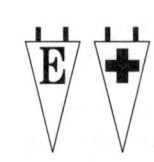

AMOUNT: None Specified DEADLINE: March 31
FIELDS/MAJORS: Speech Pathology

Scholarship for students who meet academic requirements and enroll in a graduate speech pathology program. Commission makes final awards July 1. Write to the address listed for more information.

Delaware Higher Education Commission
Carvel State Office Building
820 North French St., #4F
Wilmington, DE 19801

2128
Spence Reese Scholarship

AMOUNT: Maximum: $2000 DEADLINE: May 15
FIELDS/MAJORS: Medicine/Law/Engineering/Political Science

Male high school seniors. Preference to applicants who are within a 250 mile radius of San Diego. Criteria: academic standing, ability, need, and citizenship. Four awards are given annually. Renewable for four years. Write to the address listed for details. Be certain to enclose a SASE when requesting information. Must have a GPA of at least 2.8.

Boys and Girls Clubs of San Diego
1761 Hotel Circle South, Suite 123
San Diego, CA 92108

2129
Spencer Dissertation Year Fellowships for Research in Education

AMOUNT: Maximum: $17000 DEADLINE: October 22
FIELDS/MAJORS: Education

Fellowships are available for doctoral students who have completed all program requirements except the dissertation. Dissertation topics must concern education, and all pre-dissertation requirements must be completed by June 1, 1998. To encourage research relevant to the improvement of education. Approximately thirty awards offered annually. Write to the address listed for information.

Spencer Foundation, Inc.
Dissertation Fellowship Program
900 N. Michigan Ave., Suite 2800
Chicago, IL 60611-1542

2130
Spencer Foundation Fellowships

AMOUNT: Maximum: $35000 DEADLINE: January 20
FIELDS/MAJORS: History of Instruction, Philosophy of Education, History of Literacy

Six- to eleven-month residential fellowships are available for postdoctoral scholars wishing to pursue extensive research in the areas listed above. Applicants must be at the early stages of their careers. Both a junior and senior fellow will be awarded. Award amounts vary. Write to the address listed or call (312) 255-3666 for more information.

Newberry Library
Committee on Awards
60 W. Walton St.
Chicago, IL 60610

2131
SPIE Educational Scholarships and Grants in Optical Engineering

AMOUNT: $500-$7000 DEADLINE: April 6
FIELDS/MAJORS: Optics, Optical Engineering

Scholarships for students majoring in optics or a related field: optical engineering, photonics, imaging, electronic, and optoelectronic technologies. Committee places special emphasis on the long-range contribution of potential recipients. Write to the address listed for details.

International Society for Optical Engineering
SPIE Scholarship Committee
PO Box 10
Bellingham, WA 98227

2132
SPJST Scholarship Program

AMOUNT: Maximum: $750 DEADLINE: None Specified
FIELDS/MAJORS: All Areas of Study

Open to graduating high school seniors and college undergraduates who have been members of the SPJST Society for one year or more. Based on test scores, academic records, recommendations, and SPJST involvement. Write to the address listed for additional information.

SPJST Society of Texas
Supreme Lodge SPJST
PO Box 100
Temple, TX 76503

2133
Sports Journalism Scholarship

AMOUNT: Maximum: $600 DEADLINE: June 7
FIELDS/MAJORS: Sports Journalism

Scholarship for incoming freshmen at Louisiana schools who are interested in pursuing a career in sports journalism. Based on academics, experience in journalism, and financial need. Contact the address below for further information. Must have a GPA of at least 2.9.

Louisiana Sports Writers Association
Daily Iberian, Glenn Quebedeaux, Sports
PO Box 1290
New Iberia, LA 70560

2134
Sports Medicine Scholarship

AMOUNT: Maximum: $250 DEADLINE: May 15
FIELDS/MAJORS: Physical Therapy, Athletic Training

Open to high school seniors who are residents of any of the following: Avon, Bloomfield, Bristol, East Hartford, Farmington, Glastonbury, Hartford, Manchester, New Britain, Simsbury, West Hartford, Windsor, or Wethersfield. Must be entering a four-year school. Based on academics and interest in these two fields as careers. Contact the address listed for further information. Must have a GPA of at least 2.7.

Physical Therapy and Sports Medicine Associates
Ms. Jill Lipson
270 Farmington Ave., #367
Farmington, CT 06032

2135
SREB Doctoral Scholars Program

AMOUNT: $12000 DEADLINE: April 1
FIELDS/MAJORS: All Areas of Study

Awards are available for the purpose of encouraging ethnic minority students to pursue doctoral degrees and become college-level teachers. Preference is given to Science, Engineering, and Mathematics students. For residents of Alabama, Arkansas, Florida, Georgia, Kentucky, Louisiana, Maryland, Virginia, Mississippi, North/South Carolina, Oklahoma, Texas, Tennessee, W. Virginia. Write to the address below for information.

Southern Regional Education Board
592 Tenth St., NW
Atlanta, GA 30318

2136
St. Andrew's Society Scholarships

AMOUNT: None Specified DEADLINE: March 15
FIELDS/MAJORS: All Fields of Study

Available to students enrolled in U.S. or Scottish institutions who are residents of Delaware, Maryland, North Carolina, New Jersey, Pennsylvania, Virginia, West Virginia, or Washington D.C. Based on need, academics, and goals. Amount and number of scholarships vary depending on availability of funds. Write to James S. McLeod, Chairman of the Charity and Education Committee, at the address listed for details or call (301) 229-6140.

St. Andrew's Society of Washington, D.C.
James McLeod, Chairman
7012 Arandale Rd.
Bethesda, MD 20817-4702

2137
St. Louis Chapter No. 17 Scholarship

AMOUNT: Maximum: $1000 DEADLINE: March 1
FIELDS/MAJORS: Manufacturing Engineering, Industrial Technology

Open to full-time undergraduates enrolled in one of the six following schools: Jefferson College, Mineral Area College, St. Louis Community College-at Florissant Valley, University of Missouri-Rolla, Southeast Missouri State University, or Southern Illinois University. Must have a minimum GPA of 3.5 and maintain an overall 3.0 to continue eligibility through the academic year. Write to the address listed for more information.

Society of Manufacturing Engineers Education Foundation
One SME Dr.
PO Box 930
Dearborn, MI 48121-0930

2138
St. Mary's Medical Center Auxiliary Scholarships

AMOUNT: Maximum: $1000 DEADLINE: None Specified
FIELDS/MAJORS: Health-Related

Scholarship available for graduates of Racine County, Wisconsin, high schools who have a GPA of at least 3.0 and will be attending an accredited college or school in a health-related field. Must demonstrate financial need. Contact your high school guidance counselor (notice is mailed to area counselors) or write for details.

St. Mary's Medical Center Auxiliary
Scholarship Committee
3801 Spring St.
Racine, WI 53405

2139
Stanley F. and Helen Balcerzak Award

AMOUNT: Maximum: $1000 DEADLINE: March 2
FIELDS/MAJORS: Polish Studies

Scholarships are available for Polish-American students majoring in any field and non-Polish students majoring in Polish studies. Applicants must reside in Wisconsin, be U.S. citizens, and have a GPA of at least 3.0. Write to the address listed or call (414) 744-9029 for information.

Polanki, Polish Women's Cultural Club of Milwaukee
Ms. Valerie Lukaszewicz, Chairperson
4160 S. First St.
Milwaukee, WI 53207

2140
Stanley K. Bansen Memorial Scholarship

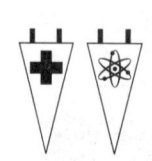

AMOUNT: None Specified DEADLINE: July 1
FIELDS/MAJORS: Dairy Science, Animal Science, Dairy Manufacturing, Agriculture Business, or Veterinary Medicine

Scholarships available to members of the American Jersey Cattle Association who are enrolled in post-baccalaureate studies in dairy or animal science, dairy manufacturing, agriculture business, or veterinary science. Write to the address listed for details.

American Jersey Cattle Association
Scholarship Committee
6486 East Main St.
Reynoldsburg, OH 43068

2141
Star Supporter Scholarship/Loan

AMOUNT: None Specified DEADLINE: March 15
FIELDS/MAJORS: Theology, Church-Related Studies

Applicants must be African-American members of the Christian Church who are preparing to enter the ordained ministry and can demonstrate financial need. Full-time enrollment is mandatory. Write to the address below for details. Must have a GPA of at least 2.3.

Christian Church (Disciples of Christ)
Attn: Scholarships
PO Box 1986
Indianapolis, IN 46206

2142
Starr Fellowship for Training in Asian Painting

AMOUNT: None Specified DEADLINE: None Specified
FIELDS/MAJORS: Asian Art Conservation

Fellowship is for training in the conservation and mounting of Asian paintings and is designed as an apprenticeship. Experience is neither anticipated nor expected. However, it is intended for a person who might pursue this field as a lifetime career. The stipend amount depends on available funds. Write to the address listed for further information.

Metropolitan Museum of Art-Asian Art Conservation
Ms. Sondra M. Castile
1000 Fifth Ave.
New York, NY 10028

2143
State Association of the Daughters of Pioneers of Washington Scholarships

AMOUNT: Maximum: $600 DEADLINE: April 1
FIELDS/MAJORS: History, Education, English

Open to juniors, seniors, and graduate full-time students who are Washington residents attending school in Washington. Applicants must be descendants of a person establishing residence in one of the following: Washington state, during/prior to 1870; Oregon state, during/prior to 1853; Idaho state, during/prior to 1863; Montana state (west of the crest of the Rocky Mountains), during/prior to 1863. Contact the address listed for further information.

State Association of the Daughters of Pioneers of Washington
Ms. Kathleen Garbe, Administrator
Rt. 1 Box 106
Touchet, WA 99360-9726

2144
State Farm Foundation Exceptional Student Fellowship

AMOUNT: Maximum: $3000 DEADLINE: February 15
FIELDS/MAJORS: Business

Scholarships for employees or agents of State Farm Insurance Companies or children of employees or agents of State Farm. Must be juniors or seniors. At least seventy-five awards per year. Write to the address below for details. Information may also be available at your/your parent's workplace. Must have a GPA of at least 3.2.

State Farm Companies Foundation
One State Farm Plaza
Bloomington, IL 61710

2145
State of Idaho Scholarship Program

AMOUNT: Maximum: $2700   DEADLINE: January 31
FIELDS/MAJORS: All Areas of Study

Scholarships are available for Idaho resident graduating high school seniors who are planning to enroll at an Idaho college or university. Twenty-five awards are offered annually, with one-quarter of these awards for students who will be attending a vocational school. Must be U.S. citizens. Write to the address listed or contact your high school counselor for more information.

Idaho State Board of Education
Ms. Caryl Smith
PO Box 83720
Boise, ID 83720

2146
State St. BPW Club Scholarship

AMOUNT: Maximum: $1000   DEADLINE: March 31
FIELDS/MAJORS: All Areas of Study

Open to women who are twenty-five years of age or older and are residents of any of the following counties: Albany, Schenectady, Rensselaer, Saratoga, Columbia, Schoharie, Greene, or Washington. Must be enrolled or accepted into a program leading to an academic, technical, or vocational degree or certificate. Contact the address listed for further information. Be sure to include a SASE for a reply.

National Federation of Business and Professional
   Women's Clubs
State St. Chapter, Kathy Macri
PO Box 491
Voorheesville, NY 12186

2147
STC Scholarships in Technical Communication

AMOUNT: $2000   DEADLINE: February 15
FIELDS/MAJORS: Technical Communication

Scholarships for students in established degree programs studying some area of technical communication. Must be full-time student and either have advanced standing in a two- or four-year program (including students who will be sophomores) or be a full-time master's or doctoral student. Fourteen awards given per year (seven undergraduate, seven graduate). Write to the address below or contact your department of study for application forms or additional information.

Society for Technical Communication
901 N. Stuart St., Suite 904
Arlington, VA 22203

2148
Steele-Reese Foundation Scholarships

AMOUNT: Maximum: $5000   DEADLINE: February 1
FIELDS/MAJORS: All Areas of Study

Scholarships are available to the students of Lemhi and Custer counties in Idaho. Students must attend one of the following colleges and universities: Brigham Young, Albertson College of Idaho, College of Southern Idaho, Idaho State, University of Idaho, Western Montana, Gonzaga, Pacific Lutheran, Lewis and Clark, and the University of Montana. For entering freshmen. Students must contact their college or university financial aid office for further information.

Steele-Reese Foundation
C/O Davidson, Dawson and Clark
330 Madison Ave.
New York, NY 10017

2149
Steven Hume Memorial Scholarship

AMOUNT: Maximum: $500   DEADLINE: May 1
FIELDS/MAJORS: All Areas of Study, with Preference Given to Science-Related Studies

Scholarship started in 1994 to honor Tustin High School teacher Steven Hume. One scholarship will be awarded to Tustin High School's outstanding graduating science student. Write to the address listed for further information.

Tustin Public Schools Foundation
642-B South B St.
Tustin, CA 92680

2150
Stone Bridge Volunteer Fire Dept. Scholarship

AMOUNT: Maximum: $500   DEADLINE: April 20
FIELDS/MAJORS: All Areas of Study

Scholarships are available for residents of Tiverton, Rhode Island. Three to five awards offered annually. Write to the address listed for information.

Stone Bridge Fire Department
Jenny Rapoport, Advisory Committee Chair
49 Leonard Dr.
Tiverton, RI 02878

2151
Stoody-West Fellowship

AMOUNT: $6000   DEADLINE: February 15
FIELDS/MAJORS: Journalism (religious)

Awards for Christian graduate students enrolled in journalism at accredited schools who plan a career in religious journalism. Write to the fellowship committee at the address listed for details.

United Methodist Communications
Fellowship Committee, Public Media Div.
PO Box 320
Nashville, TN 37202

2152
Strawberry Scholarships

AMOUNT: $500-$1500   DEADLINE: April 1
FIELDS/MAJORS: All Areas of Study

Awards are available for children of workers employed for at least two consecutive seasons since 1991 in the California strawberry harvest. Must be sponsored by a legitimate California strawberry grower for verification of eligibility in the program and reside in one of the following growing regions: Watsonville/Salinas; Santa Maria; Oxnard; Orange County/San Diego, or Fresno. Contact your academic advisor or write to the address below for more information.

California Strawberry Commission
PO Box 269
Watsonville, CA 95077

2153
Student Aid Scholarship Funds

AMOUNT: $100-$2500   DEADLINE: April 25
FIELDS/MAJORS: All Areas of Study

For U.S. citizens or legal residents accepted at or enrolled in an accredited two- or four-year college located in the U.S. Applicants must be residents of New Hampshire. Five hundred awards are offered annually. Some are grants. Some are low-cost loans. Some are a combination of both. Write address below for complete program(s) information.

New Hampshire Charitable Fund Student Aid Program
37 Pleasant St.
Concord, NH 03301

2154
Student Assistance Grant

AMOUNT: Maximum: $624   DEADLINE: January 2
FIELDS/MAJORS: All Areas of Study

Applicants must be Arkansas residents who are full-time undergraduates or high school seniors. Awarded on a first-come, first-served basis by financial need. Student must be attending or planning to attend an approved Arkansas public or private postsecondary institution. Write to the address below for details.

Arkansas Department of Higher Education
Financial Aid Division
114 East Capitol
Little Rock, AR 72201

2155
Student Associate Membership Fellowships

AMOUNT: Maximum: $7840   DEADLINE: January 31
FIELDS/MAJORS: Anthropology, Art History, Classics

Six awards are available for graduate students who have passed their qualifying examinations for the Ph.D. and do not intend to follow the regular program of the school. Write to the address listed for more information.

American School of Classical Studies at Athens
Committee on Admissions and Fellowships
6-8 Charlton St.
Princeton, NJ 08540

2156
Student Award Program

AMOUNT: $3000   DEADLINE: April 30
FIELDS/MAJORS: Healthcare, Health Policy, Medicine (M.D., D.O., Ph.D.)

Stipends for doctoral (M.D. and Ph.D.) students interested in the improvement of health and medical care in the state of Michigan. Supports a wide range of activities including research, pilot projects, intervention/demonstration projects, feasibility studies, proposal development, and critical literature reviews. Must be a Michigan resident attending a Michigan school. Projects must address quality of care, cost containment, healthcare access, or a major public health/medical issue. Must focus (geographically) on the state of Michigan. Proposal required. Program announcement may be found in your department office or financial aid office. If unavailable, write to the address below.

Blue Cross Blue Shield of Michigan Foundation
Margie Nagel, Program Officer
600 Lafayette East, B243
Detroit, MI 48226

2157
Student Choice Grants

AMOUNT: None Specified   DEADLINE: None Specified
FIELDS/MAJORS: All Areas of Study

Open to undergraduates who have completed at least 6 credit hours at one of the following: College of Santa Fe, St. Johns College in Santa Fe, or the College of the Southwest in Hobbs. Applicants must be residents of New Mexico. Contact the financial aid office at one of the schools listed for more information.

New Mexico Commission on Higher Education
Financial Aid and Student Services
PO Box 15910
Santa Fe, NM 87506

2158
Student Financial Aid—Loans

AMOUNT: $1000-$5000   DEADLINE: May 15
FIELDS/MAJORS: Medicine, Dentistry, Allied Health Fields

Delaware resident. Not for undergraduate study. In selecting applicants, the academy considers academic record and need. The academy also administers the Delaware state "Delaware Institute of Medical Education and Research" program at the Jefferson Medical College. For full-time study. Write for complete details.

Delaware Academy of Medicine
1925 Lovering Ave.
Wilmington, DE 19806

2159
Student Internship Program

AMOUNT: None Specified   DEADLINE: March 31
FIELDS/MAJORS: Television and Film-Related Fields

Summer internships for full-time students pursuing degrees at a college or university in the United States. Those who have graduated fifteen months prior to the deadline to apply are also eligible. Twenty-eight positions are available. Use the e-mail address: internships@emmys.org or Web site address: http://www.emmys.org to receive more information.

Academy of Television Arts and Sciences

2160
Student Loan Fund

AMOUNT: Maximum: $3000   DEADLINE: None Specified
FIELDS/MAJORS: Mechanical Engineering

Loans available for juniors, seniors, and graduate mechanical engineering students. Must be a member of ASME and a U.S. citizen. Loans are interest-free until graduation. Write to the address listed for details.

American Society of Mechanical Engineers Auxiliary, Inc.
Mrs. Robert B. Watson, Chairman
623 N Valley Forge Rd
Devon, PA 19333

2161
Student Loan Funds

AMOUNT: $2200-$3000   DEADLINE: June 1
FIELDS/MAJORS: All Areas of Study

Loans are available for residents of Saginaw County, Michigan, for full-time study at any accredited U.S. school. Applicant must have a GPA of at least 2.0 and be able to demonstrate financial need. Includes the C.K. Eddy Family Memorial Fund, Michael Jeffers Memorial Fund, C.M. and A.A. Reid Fund, and Anthony and Elizabeth Brenske Fund. Two hundred awards are offered annually. Write to the address below for information.

Citizens Bank
Trust Department
101 N. Washington Ave.
Saginaw, MI 48607

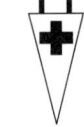

2162
Student Loan Program

AMOUNT: Maximum: $5000   DEADLINE: February 1
FIELDS/MAJORS: Periodontology

Applicants must be postdoctoral candidates in periodontology. Must have completed at least four months of study in a periodontal specialty training program approved by the council on dental education (ADA). Renewable. Twenty-two loans were made in 1992 (out of thirty-seven applications). Contact the address below for further information.

American Academy of Periodontology
Meeting and Membership Services Dept.
737 N. Michigan Ave., #800
Chicago, IL 60611

2163
Student Loan-for-Nursing Program

AMOUNT: Maximum: $12000   DEADLINE: July 1
FIELDS/MAJORS: Nursing

Loans open to New Mexico residents accepted/enrolled in an accredited program at a New Mexico public postsecondary institution. Must be U.S. citizens or legal residents. Recipients serve in one of the designated shortage areas of the state. Loan principal and interest may be forgiven. Applies to licensed practical nurses, A.D./B.S./M.S. in nursing. Write to the address listed for additional information.

New Mexico Commission on Higher Education
Financial Aid and Student Services
PO Box 15910
Santa Fe, NM 87506-5910

2164
Student Loans

AMOUNT: $2625-$5000 DEADLINE: March 1
FIELDS/MAJORS: All Areas of Study

Open to undergraduates who are Desert Schools Federal Credit Union members, U.S. citizens, enrolled at least half-time at an educational institution approved by the U.S. Department of Education and Desert Schools Federal Credit Union, and free of default on any other education loan programs. Variable interest rate subject to change July 1 of every year. Repayment begins within sixty days of the final loan disbursement. Contact the address listed for further information. Must have a GPA of at least 2.0.

Desert Schools Federal Credit Union
Attn: Marketing
PO Box 11350
Phoenix, AZ 85061-1350

2165
Student Opportunity Scholarships

AMOUNT: $100-$1400 DEADLINE: April 1
FIELDS/MAJORS: All Areas of Study

Open to high school seniors who are African-American, Hispanic-American, Asian-American, Native American, and Alaskan Natives and are Presbyterian Church members and U.S. citizens or permanent residents. Must be able to demonstrate financial need. Write to address listed for details. Specify Student Opportunity Scholarships (SOS).

Presbyterian Church (U.S.A.)
Office of Financial Aid for Students
100 Witherspoon St.
Louisville, KY 40202

2166
Student Paper Competition

AMOUNT: $250-$1000 DEADLINE: February 1
FIELDS/MAJORS: Water Conservation

Prizes given for best papers on water pollution control, water quality problems, water-related concerns, or hazardous wastes. Semi-finalists will present papers at the annual WPCF conference. Categories are 1)operations students, 2)bachelor's students, 3)master's students, and 4)Ph.D. students. Initial judging is based on a five hundred to one thousand word abstract. Write to the address below for details.

Water Environment Federation
Program Specialist, Bryan M. Fuhs
601 Wythe St.
Alexandria, VA 22314

2167
Student Research Award

AMOUNT: $500 DEADLINE: December 8
FIELDS/MAJORS: Geriatrics

Awards will be given to the student presenting the most outstanding paper or poster at the AGS annual meeting. Awardee will be chosen based on originality, scientific merit, and relevance of the research. All abstracts must be submitted on the official AGS abstract form. Write to the address listed for more information. You may call AGS at (212) 308-1414 to obtain copies of the abstract form.

American Geriatrics Society
770 Lexington Ave., Suite 300
New York, NY 10021

2168
Student Research Fellow Award

AMOUNT: Maximum: $2500 DEADLINE: January 15
FIELDS/MAJORS: Liver Research

Research fellowships for M.D. and Ph.D. students to encourage them to gain exposure in the research laboratory, and possibly consider liver research as a career option. Fellowships are for three months. Must be full-time student at a graduate or medical school. Not for terminal Ph.D. funding. Write to the address listed for further information.

American Liver Foundation
Barbara Ramsthaler
1425 Pompton Ave.
Cedar Grove, NJ 07009

2169
Student Research Fellowships

AMOUNT: $2100 DEADLINE: January 15
FIELDS/MAJORS: Dental Research

For students enrolled in an accredited DDS/DMD or hygiene program at an accredited dental school within the U.S. Must be sponsored by a faculty member at that school. Should not be due to receive their degree in the year the award is given. Applicants may have an advanced degree in a basic science subject. Twenty-six awards offered annually. Contact the address below for complete information.

American Association for Dental Research
Patricia J. Reynolds
1619 Duke St.
Alexandria, VA 22314

2170
Student Research Grants in Sexuality

AMOUNT: Maximum: $750   DEADLINE: September 1
FIELDS/MAJORS: Sexuality Studies

Three grants for students doing scholarly research on sexuality. Applicants must be enrolled in a degree-granting program. Write to the address listed for more information. Deadlines for the submission of applications are February 1, September 1.

Society for the Scientific Study of Sexuality
Ilsa L. Lottes, Ph.D.
PO Box 208
Mount Vernon, IA 52314-0208

2171
Student Research Program, AHA California Affiliate

AMOUNT: $2500   DEADLINE: January 15
FIELDS/MAJORS: Heart or Stroke Research

Program for California students or students at California institutions to work in an assigned laboratory in California under the direction and supervision of experienced scientists. Must be a junior or senior and have completed one year of organic chemistry and biological sciences and one quarter of physics or calculus. Write to the address below for more information. Deadline to request applications is December 15.

American Heart Association, California Affiliate
Research Department
1710 Gilbreth Road
Burlingame, CA 94010

2172
Student Traineeship Research Grants

AMOUNT: $1500   DEADLINE: None Specified
FIELDS/MAJORS: Cystic Fibrosis Research

Doctoral (M.D. or Ph.D.) research grants for students who plan a career in research and have a lab project that can be completed in less than one year. Award intended to interest student in cystic fibrosis research and offset costs of the project. Contact the foundation for further information on application procedure.

Cystic Fibrosis Foundation
Medical/Research Programs
6931 Arlington Rd.
Bethesda, MD 20814

2173
Sub-Saharan Africa Dissertation Internship Awards

AMOUNT: $20000   DEADLINE: March 2
FIELDS/MAJORS: All Areas of Study

Fellowships are available to African scholars who have completed all the Ph.D. requirements except the dissertation. Award is to increase the quality of overseas advanced studies for outstanding African scholars and to enhance the relevance of their training to the process of economic development in Africa. Priority is given to agricultural and environmental majors. Write to the address listed for information.

Rockefeller Foundation
African Dissertation Internships
420 Fifth Ave.
New York, NY 10018

2174
Suburban Hospital Scholarship Program

AMOUNT: Maximum: $5000   DEADLINE: April 30
FIELDS/MAJORS: Nursing, Medical Technology, Medical Therapy, Physician Assistant

Program for juniors or seniors in the fields of study listed above who are from the Washington, D.C. metropolitan area. Applicants must have a GPA of at least a 2.5. Two awards are offered annually. Write to the address listed for more details.

Suburban Hospital
Department of Human Resources
8600 Old Georgetown Rd.
Bethesda, MD 20814

2175
Successful Farming Scholarship

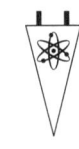

AMOUNT: Maximum: $2000   DEADLINE: None Specified
FIELDS/MAJORS: Agriculture

Scholarships for graduating high school seniors from farming families (parents or guardians derive majority of income from farming) who will be studying agriculture in an approved curriculum at a two- or four-year college. Must be in top 50% of high school class and in test scores. Strong consideration given to extracurricular activities and work. Write to the address listed for details. Must have a GPA of at least 2.0.

Successful Farming-Bayer Corporation
1716 Locust St.
Des Moines, IA 50309

2176
Sue Kay Lay Memorial Scholarship

AMOUNT: Maximum: $1500   DEADLINE: None Specified
FIELDS/MAJORS: All Areas of Study

Open to high school seniors graduating at the end of spring semester with a minimum GPA of 3.2. Must be a resident of the Coastal Bend area, planning to attend college full-time, and be able to demonstrate financial need. Contact the address below for further information.

Coastal Bend Community Foundation
Mercantile Tower MT276
615 N. Upper Broadway, #860
Corpus Christi, TX 78477

2177
Sumitomo Bank of California Scholarships

AMOUNT: None Specified   DEADLINE: April 1
FIELDS/MAJORS: Business, Banking, Accounting, Economics, International Trade

Applicants must be California residents attending California schools and members of the Japanese-American Citizens League. For both undergraduate and graduate studies. Applications and information may be obtained from local JACL chapters, district offices, and the national headquarters at the address listed or call (415) 921-5225. Please indicate your level of study and be certain to include a legal-sized SASE.

Japanese-American Citizens League
National Scholarship and Award Program
1765 Sutter St.
San Francisco, CA 94115

2178
Summer Fellowship Grants

AMOUNT: Maximum: $2000   DEADLINE: May 15
FIELDS/MAJORS: Medical Research (allergy/immunology)

Grants for medical students pursuing a career in the fields of allergy and immunology. Grants support summer research. Must be a full-time medical student who has successfully completed at least eight months of medical school. Must be U.S. or Canadian residents. Write to the address listed or call (414) 272-6071 for details.

American Academy of Allergy, Asthma, and Immunology
Summer Fellowship Grant
611 E. Wells St.
Milwaukee, WI 53202

2179
Summer Fellowship Intern Program

AMOUNT: None Specified   DEADLINE: November 21
FIELDS/MAJORS: Communications, Radio, Television

Internships available for juniors or seniors in a four-year college or university who are interested in the fields of communication, radio, or television. Internship includes a one-week orientation prior to the eight-week internship. Write to the address listed for more information.

International Radio and Television Society Foundation
420 Lexington Ave.
Suite 1714
New York, NY 10170

2180
Summer Fellowships of the Electrochemical Society, Inc.

AMOUNT: None Specified   DEADLINE: January 1
FIELDS/MAJORS: Electrochemistry and Related Fields

Awards are available for graduate students enrolled in a college or university in the U.S. or Canada. Applicants must be studying a field related to the objectives of the Electrochemical Society. Renewable. Write to the address below for more information.

Electrochemical Society, Inc.
10 South Main St.
Pennington, NJ 08534

2181
Summer Internship Program

AMOUNT: None Specified   DEADLINE: April 1
FIELDS/MAJORS: All Areas of Study

Ten-week summer internship program to provide valuable work experience for a blind postsecondary student. Duties include activities in the areas of public information and education, membership assistance, communications, legislative monitoring, and publications. Write to the address listed or call (202) 467-5081 or 1-800-424-8666 for details.

American Council of the Blind
Oral Miller, Executive Director
1155 15th St. NW, Suite 720
Washington, DC 20005

2182
Summer Internships

AMOUNT: $2500-$2750 DEADLINE: January 16
FIELDS/MAJORS: Art History, Art Conservation

Summer internships at the Museum for juniors, seniors, or recent graduates who have not yet entered graduate school. Must have background in art history or a related field. Programs last ten weeks, from June through August and are full-time. Current freshmen and sophomores are not eligible. Availability varies. Ethnically diverse students encouraged to apply. Write to the address listed for additional information.

Metropolitan Museum of Art
Attn: Internship Programs
1000 Fifth Ave.
New York, NY 10028-0198

2183
Summer Medical Student Fellowship

AMOUNT: $2200 DEADLINE: February 1
FIELDS/MAJORS: Urology

Fellowships allowing highly qualified medical students to work in urology research laboratories for two months in the summer. Write to the address below for additional information. Must have a GPA of at least 2.8.

American Foundation for Urologic Disease, Inc.
Research Scholar Division
300 West Pratt St., Suite 401
Baltimore, MD 21201

2184
Summer Research Fellowships in Law and Social Science

AMOUNT: Maximum: $3500
DEADLINE: March 2
FIELDS/MAJORS: Social Science, Humanities

Fellowships available for minority students who have completed sophomore year. Applicants must have a minimum GPA of 3.0 and intend to pursue graduate studies in the above fields. Must be U.S. citizens or permanent residents. The program lasts ten weeks, and the recipients will work at the ABF offices for thirty-five hours per week. Awards will be announced by April 15. Write to the address listed for information.

American Bar Foundation
Assistant Director
750 N. Lake Shore Dr.
Chicago, IL 60611

2185
Summer Scholarships in Epidemiology

AMOUNT: $2000 DEADLINE: April 1
FIELDS/MAJORS: Medical Research-Cystic Fibrosis

Scholarships are available for M.D.'s currently working in cystic fibrosis to increase skills in epidemiology. Awards cover tuition and expenses of up to $2000 for selected summer epidemiology programs. Coursework should include biostatics and epidemiology, particularly clinical epidemiology and/or clinical trials. Write to the address below for details.

Cystic Fibrosis Foundation
Office of Grants Management
6931 Arlington Rd.
Bethesda, MD 20814

2186
Super Valu Stores Scholarships

AMOUNT: $1000 DEADLINE: None Specified
FIELDS/MAJORS: Food Distribution

Scholarships for employees and children of employees of Super Valu supermarkets and affiliated retailers. For study at either Michigan State University and Western Michigan University. Renewable once. For certificate, undergraduate, or graduate study. Contact the regional personnel department of your or your parent's workplace for details. If necessary, write to the address below.

Super Valu Stores, Inc.
Corporate Offices, Attn: Jon Seltzer
PO Box 990
Minneapolis, MN 55440

2187
Surflant Scholarship

AMOUNT: None Specified DEADLINE: April 15
FIELDS/MAJORS: All Areas of Study

Scholarships for dependent children of a military sponsor who has spent a minimum of three years in a command (ship) under the control of Commander, Naval Surface Forces, Atlantic Fleet. For undergraduate study only. When writing for information, you must include your military sponsor's name, rank, and SSN; dependent's name and SSN; list of Surflant commands and dates onboard. Write for more information and an application form to the address below. Be sure to include the information requested above.

Surflant Scholarship Foundation
1628 Pocahontas St.
Norfolk, VA 23511

2188
Susan W. Freestone Vocational Education Award

AMOUNT: $500-$1000 DEADLINE: April 15
FIELDS/MAJORS: Agriculture

Scholarships for graduating high school seniors who were members of a Junior Grange and are now members of a New York Subordinate Grange. For use at one of New York's agricultural and technical colleges. Contact the financial aid office at the college you will be attending, or write to the address listed for details.

New York State Grange
Scholarship Coordinator
100 Grange Place
Cortland, NY 13045

2189
Sussman-Miller Educational Assistance Fund

AMOUNT: None Specified DEADLINE: July 10
FIELDS/MAJORS: All Areas of Study

Open to full-time undergraduates who have been New Mexico residents for at least one year. Must have a minimum GPA of 2.5, completed one full semester, and be able to demonstrate financial need. Contact the address listed for further information, and be sure to include a SASE for a reply.

Albuquerque Community Foundation
PO Box 36960 Dept. 7197
Albuquerque, NM 87176

2190
Sustaining Fellows Award

AMOUNT: Maximum: $5000 DEADLINE: None Specified
FIELDS/MAJORS: Engineering

Open to students completing first year. Renewable if recipients maintain a minimum GPA of 3.0. Applicants must be enrolled in any of seventy-nine participating colleges/universities in the U.S and be nominated by the dean. Applicants must also be of African-American, Latino-American, or Native American descent. Contact the dean's office of your college for further information. If this information is in your profile, you have indicated that you are attending one of the participating schools. Please do not contact the Council. They will be unable to respond.

National Action Council for Minorities in Engineering
Scholarship Coordinator
3 W. 35th St.
New York, NY 10001-2281

2191
Swedish Community Scholarships

AMOUNT: $600-$1250 DEADLINE: April 1
FIELDS/MAJORS: All Areas of Study

Scholarships for graduating high school seniors residing in King County, Washington. Based on academics and need. Interview required. Five awards per year. Write to the address below for details. Must have a GPA of at least 2.8.

Seattle Swedish Community Scholarships
1416 N. 55th St.
Seattle, WA 98103

2192
Sylvia W. Farny Scholarship

AMOUNT: Maximum: $1500 DEADLINE: February 15
FIELDS/MAJORS: Mechanical Engineering

Scholarships for mechanical engineering students entering their final year of undergraduate study. Application must be made in junior year (students enrolled in a five-year program would apply in the fourth year). Must be a student member of ASME and a U.S. citizen. Information sheets are forwarded to the colleges and universities in the fall of each year. If necessary to write for more details, please be certain to enclose a SASE.

American Society of Mechanical Engineers Auxiliary, Inc.
Mrs. Harry E. Flanders, Jr.
3556 Stevens Way
Martinez, GA 30907

2193
Symee R. Feinberg Memorial Scholarship

AMOUNT: Maximum: $1000 DEADLINE: February 24
FIELDS/MAJORS: Human Services

Open to graduating high school seniors who are residents of Hartford. Must be able to demonstrate financial need and paid or volunteer experience helping others. Contact the address below for further information.

State of Connecticut Dept. of Children and Families
Ellis Simpson
PO Box 320644
Hartford, CT 06132

2194
T.J. Schmitz Scholarship

AMOUNT: Maximum: $600 DEADLINE: June 2
FIELDS/MAJORS: All Areas of Study

Scholarships are available to undergraduates who are members of Tau Kappa Epsilon. Must have demonstrated leadership capability within his chapter, on campus, or in the community. Must have a GPA of 2.5 or higher and be a full-time student in good standing. Write to the address listed for more information.

TKE Educational Foundation
8645 Founders Road
Indianapolis, IN 46268

2195
T.R.H. Development Foundation Scholarships

AMOUNT: None Specified **DEADLINE:** April 10
FIELDS/MAJORS: Medicine, Nursing

Scholarships for students in health-related fields. Most funds are designed to support nursing. Must live in one of Webster, Hamilton, Wright, Humboldt, Pocahontas, or Calhoun counties in Iowa. Write to the address listed or call (515) 573-6509 or (515) 574-6753 for more information.

T.R.H. Development Foundation
802 Kenyon Rd.
Fort Dodge, IA 50501

2196
Ta Liang Memorial Award

AMOUNT: $500 **DEADLINE:** None Specified
FIELDS/MAJORS: Photogrammetry, Remote Sensing

Applicant must be a student member of the Society who is currently pursuing graduate level studies. Based on scholastic record, research plans, recommendations, and community service activities. Write to the address below for more information.

American Society for Photogrammetry and Remote Sensing
ASPRS Awards Program
5410 Grosvenor Ln., Suite 210
Bethesda, MD 20814

2197
Talbert Abrams Civil Engineering Scholarship

AMOUNT: Maximum: $3000 **DEADLINE:** February 15
FIELDS/MAJORS: Civil Engineering

Open to junior college students majoring in the field listed above who are transferring to a Florida college or university. Applicant must have at least a 3.0 GPA and be recommended by an official of the college you are attending. Based on academics, work experience, extracurricular activities, essay, and recommendations. Write to the address listed for details.

Florida Engineering Society
Scholarship Coordinator
PO Box 750
Tallahassee, FL 32302

2198
Talbert Family Memorial Scholarship

AMOUNT: Maximum: $2000 **DEADLINE:** None Specified
FIELDS/MAJORS: Accounting

Open to full-time juniors attending school in Texas, with a minimum GPA of 3.25. Must be a resident of the Coastal Bend area and graduated from a Coastal Bend high school. Five or more awards may be offered. Contact the address below for further information.

Coastal Bend Community Foundation
Mercantile Tower MT276
615 N. Upper Broadway, #860
Corpus Christi, TX 78477

2199
Talent Scholarships

AMOUNT: None Specified **DEADLINE:** None Specified
FIELDS/MAJORS: Music, Theater, Forensics

Scholarships available at Central Methodist for full-time undergraduate students majoring in the fields listed above. Applicants may be required to audition with faculty from the area of interest. It is recommended that auditions and interviews be scheduled and completed by April 1. You may call the Admissions Office, 1-888-262-1854, to schedule an audition or interview. Scholarship amounts may vary and may not exceed tuition. Write to the address listed for details.

Central Methodist College
Financial Aid Office
411 Central Methodist Square
Fayette, MO 65248

2200
Tandy Technology Scholars

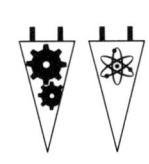

AMOUNT: $1000 **DEADLINE:** October 15
FIELDS/MAJORS: Mathematics, Science, Computer Science

Scholarships are available for graduating high school seniors who plan to enroll in a full-time, four-year program in one of the above fields. Must be nominated by your high school. Based on grades, test scores, and extracurricular and community service activities. Approximately one hundred awards given per year. Write to the address below for information.

Tandy Corporation
Tandy Technology Scholars Program
TCU Box 298990
Fort Worth, TX 76129

2201
Target All-Around Scholarships

AMOUNT: $1000-$10000   DEADLINE: December 15
FIELDS/MAJORS: All Areas of Study

Open to high school seniors who are U.S. citizens or permanent residents. For use at vocational, technical, two- or four-year schools. Applications will be accepted from September 1 through December 15. Primarily based on applicants community volunteer hours and volunteer leadership awards and honors. Must have a minimum GPA of 2.0. Recipients will be notified on or about April 2. Employees of Target, Dayton Hudson Corp., Citizens' Scholarship Foundation of America, their subsidiaries, affiliates, advertising and promotion agencies, and their spouses, parents, children, siblings (and their spouses), and persons living in the same households of employees are not eligible to apply. Applications and information is available at the Target All-Around Scholarship Program display, located near the front of Target stores.

Target Stores

2202
Tau Beta Pi— Deuchler Fellowship

AMOUNT: $10000   DEADLINE: January 15
FIELDS/MAJORS: Water Supply, Waste-Water Treatment, Ecological Disciplines

Award open to graduate members in any of the above fields. Contact the address listed for further information.

Tau Beta Pi-Alabama Power Company
D. Stephen Pierre, Jr. P.E., Director
150 St. Joseph St., PO Box 2247
Mobile, AL 36652

2203
Tau Beta Pi— King Fellowship

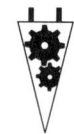

AMOUNT: $10000   DEADLINE: January 15
FIELDS/MAJORS: Engineering

Award open to graduate members whose leadership and participation in his/her national technical society's branch are judged outstanding. Contact the address listed for further information.

Tau Beta Pi-Alabama Power Company
D. Stephen Pierre, Jr. P.E., Director
150 St. Joseph St., PO Box 2247
Mobile, AL 36652

2204
Tau Beta Pi— Spencer Fellowship

AMOUNT: $10000   DEADLINE: January 15
FIELDS/MAJORS: Engineering

Award open to graduate members of Tau Beta Pi. Based on contributions made to applicant's undergraduate chapter and college. Contact the address listed for further information.

Tau Beta Pi-Alabama Power Company
D. Stephen Pierre, Jr. P.E., Director
150 St. Joseph St., PO Box 2247
Mobile, AL 36652

2205
Tau Beta Pi— Stark Fellowship

AMOUNT: $10000   DEADLINE: January 15
FIELDS/MAJORS: Fluid Power

Award open to Tau Beta Pi members who plan graduate study in the field of fluid power. Contact the address listed for further information.

Tau Beta Pi-Alabama Power Company
D. Stephen Pierre, Jr. P.E., Director
150 St. Joseph St., PO Box 2247
Mobile, AL 36652

2206
Tau Beta Pi— Williams Fellowship

AMOUNT: $10000   DEADLINE: January 15
FIELDS/MAJORS: Education, Engineering

Award open to graduate member who possesses outstanding cultural and ethical attributes and plans to earn a doctoral degree and become an engineering teacher. Contact the address listed for further information.

Tau Beta Pi-Alabama Power Company
D. Stephen Pierre, Jr. P.E., Director
150 St. Joseph St., PO Box 2247
Mobile, AL 36652

2207
TBA Scholarships

AMOUNT: Maximum: $6400   DEADLINE: March 28
FIELDS/MAJORS: All Areas of Study

Eight awards for graduating high school seniors with a good academic record who plan on attending one of the following universities: Harvard, William and Mary,

Virginia Tech, Virginia, Johns Hopkins, East Carolina, M.I.T., Old Dominion, Virginia Commonwealth, Richmond, Norfolk State, or James Madison. Applicants must demonstrate financial need and reside in the TBA service area. Contact your guidance counselor for more information or call the Tidewater Builders Association at (757) 420-2434. Must have a GPA of at least 2.5.

Tidewater Builders Association Scholarship Foundation
2117 Smith Ave.
Chesapeake, VA 23320

2208
Teacher Education Tuition Scholarships

AMOUNT: None Specified   DEADLINE: March 1
FIELDS/MAJORS: Education

Scholarships for one year to outstanding students preparing to teach in the Oregon school system. The scholarships may be used to attend any Oregon public college. Applicants must be Oregon residents. Write for complete details.

Oregon Congress of Parents and Teachers
Teacher Education Scholarship Committee
531 SE 14th Ave.
Portland, OR 97214

2209
Teachers' Loan-for-Service Program

AMOUNT: Maximum: $4000   DEADLINE: July 1
FIELDS/MAJORS: Education

Loans for minority or physically disabled students from New Mexico who attend a New Mexico institution and are studying to be teachers of grades K-12. Open to undergraduates and graduate students. Loan will be forgiven if recipient agrees to serve at a public institution in Lea, Otero, Eddy, Chaves, or Roosevelt counties in New Mexico following graduation. Write to the address listed for more information.

New Mexico Commission on Higher Education
Financial Aid and Student Services
PO Box 15910
Santa Fe, NM 87506

2210
Teaching Projects Grants

AMOUNT: Maximum: $1000   DEADLINE: October 1
FIELDS/MAJORS: Korean Education

Grant supports planning, workshops, and material related to teaching about Korea or integrating Korean studies topics in broader categories of instruction. Contact the address below for further information.

Association for Asian Studies, Inc.
University of Michigan
1 Lane Hall
Ann Arbor, MI 48109

2211
TechForce Pre-Engineering Minority Prize

AMOUNT: None Specified   DEADLINE: None Specified
FIELDS/MAJORS: Pre-Engineering

Open to high school seniors with outstanding academics, records of achievement in community service, and involvement in precollege math and science programs. Must be nominated by directors of university-related precollege programs or those recognized by the National Association of Precollege Directors. Available for use at seventy-nine colleges/universities in the U.S. Applicants must be of African-American, Puerto Rican-American, Mexican-American, or Native American descent. Contact program directors at your high schools for further information about being nominated for this prize. Please do not contact the Council. They will be unable to respond. Must have a GPA of at least 3.3.

National Action Council for Minorities in Engineering
Scholarship Coordinator
3 W. 35th St.
New York, NY 10001-2281

2212
Technical Vocational Grants

AMOUNT: None Specified   DEADLINE: January 31
FIELDS/MAJORS: Aerospace Studies (Vocational/Technical)

Candidates must be CAP Cadets and seniors who are qualified and want to continue their education in special aerospace courses at an accredited trade, technical, or vocational school. Write to the address listed for details.

Civil Air Patrol
National Headquarters CAP (TT)
Maxwell AFB, AL 36112

2213
Technology Policy Science and Engineering Fellowship

AMOUNT: None Specified   DEADLINE: January 15
FIELDS/MAJORS: Industrial Studies, Engineering, Science, Manufacturing, Technology, and Related Areas

Applicants must have a minimum of five years' industrial management experience and a Ph.D. or equivalent degrees. Persons with master's degrees in engineering and six years' experience also qualify. Recipients spend one year at the

RAND Critical Technologies Institute. Must demonstrate exceptional competence in the areas of engineering, science, or technology. Minorities and disabled are encouraged to apply. Must be U.S. citizens. Federal employees are not eligible. Write to the address listed or call (202) 326-6700.

American Association for the Advancement of Science
Fellowship Programs
1200 New York Ave. NW
Washington, DC 20005

2214
Technology Scholarship for Alabama Teachers

AMOUNT: None Specified   DEADLINE: None Specified
FIELDS/MAJORS: Teaching

Available to full-time, certified Alabama public school teachers. Award is graduate tuition for attendance at a public college or university. The purpose of this award is to provide computer technology. First priority given to teachers in the fields of English, science, math, social science, history, and those teaching kindergarten to grade six. Write to the address listed or call (334) 281-1921.

Alabama Commission on Higher Education
Office of Financial Aid
PO Box 30200
Montgomery, AL 36130

2215
Tennessee Student Assistance Award

AMOUNT: $3042   DEADLINE: May 1
FIELDS/MAJORS: All Areas of Study

Nonrepayable grant for undergraduate students currently attending eligible Tennessee institutions. Recipients must be a resident of Tennessee and be eligible for a federal Pell grant. This grant is given on the basis of need. Write to the address below for further information.

Tennessee Student Assistance Corporation
Suite 1950 Parkway Towers
404 James Robertson Parkway
Nashville, TN 37243

2216
Tennessee Teaching Scholars Forgivable Loan Program

AMOUNT: None Specified   DEADLINE: April 15
FIELDS/MAJORS: Education

Forgivable loans for college juniors, seniors, and post-baccalaureate students admitted to state-approved teacher education programs in Tennessee. Must be U.S. citizens and residents of Tennessee with a minimum GPA of 2.75 and pledge to teach at the preschool, elementary, or secondary level one year for each year the award was received. Contact the financial aid office at your school or the address below for further information.

Tennessee Student Assistance Corporation
Suite 1950, Parkway Towers
404 James Robertson Parkway
Nashville, TN 37243

2217
Texas AFL-CIO Scholarships

AMOUNT: Maximum: $1000   DEADLINE: January 31
FIELDS/MAJORS: All Areas of Study

Scholarships for members or children (high school seniors) of members of the AFL-CIO (Texas Chapter) U102. Children of members of affiliated AFL-CIO unions may also apply. Contact your local Central Labor council for further information. Applicants must be U.S. citizens. Information should be available from your Central Labor Council, the address listed, or (512) 477-6195. If writing, please specify your (your parent's) local union.

Texas AFL-CIO
Scholarship Program
PO Box 12727
Austin, TX 78711

2218
Texas Association of Nurserymen Scholarship

AMOUNT: $1000   DEADLINE: June 1
FIELDS/MAJORS: Horticulture

Open to high school seniors or returning college students who are Texas residents and enrolled full-time in a TAN-approved school (fourteen approved schools). Must be majoring in horticulture or other fields involved in the horticulture industry. Write to the address listed for more information.

Texas Association of Nurserymen Education and Research
   Foundation
Scholarship Coordinator
7730 S. IH-35
Austin, TX 78745

2219
Texas Association of Private Schools Scholarships

AMOUNT: None Specified
DEADLINE: January 1
FIELDS/MAJORS: See Below

Scholarships for Texas graduating high school seniors. Based on academic record, recommendation, and a short essay. Program is designed to encourage vocational or technical skills. Fields include computer science, accounting, cosmetology, drafting, medical/dental assisting, welding, and court reporting. Scholarship is tuition. Contact your high school counselor or write to the address below for details.

Texas Association of Private Schools
PO Box 13481
Austin, TX 78711

2220
Texas Farm Bureau Youth Foundation Scholarship

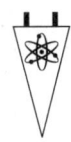

AMOUNT: Maximum: $1000   DEADLINE: March 15
FIELDS/MAJORS: Agriculture

Open to graduating high school seniors whose families have been Texas Farm Bureau members since at least March 15, 1996. Based on academics, extracurricular activity, involvement, recommendations, and financial need. Renewable up to four years. Winner selected by committee from Baylor University and McLennan Community College. Scholarship will be awarded in May. Contact the address listed for further information.

Texas Farm Bureau Youth Foundation
Scholarship Coordinator
PO Box 2689
Waco, TX 76702-2689

2221
Texas Library Association Research Grant/DEMCO, Inc.

AMOUNT: Maximum: $2000   DEADLINE: January 31
FIELDS/MAJORS: Library Science

Grants for Texas students to support research involving library use, resource sharing, administrative study, etc. Pilot studies and experimental programs are encouraged. Write to the address below for more information.

Texas Library Association Briscoe Library
Daniel H. Jones, Chair
7703 Floyd Curl Dr.
San Antonio, TX 78284

2222
Texas Library Association Scholarships

AMOUNT: $500-$2000   DEADLINE: January 31
FIELDS/MAJORS: Library Science

Awards are for Texas graduate students to study at an ALA-accredited school in Texas leading to a library science degree. Write to the address below for more information.

Texas Library Association Briscoe Library
Daniel H. Jones, Chair
7703 Floyd Curl Dr.
San Antonio, TX 78284

2223
Texas Minority Leaders in Education Scholarship Program

AMOUNT: $1000-$2000   DEADLINE: None Specified
FIELDS/MAJORS: Education

Minority students must be planning to pursue a career in education in Texas upon graduation. Must be accepted or enrolled as full-time students in one of the public universities affiliated with this program. Must have a GPA of at least a 3.0. Write to the address listed for more information.

Southwestern Bell Foundation
Pearl Garza Fracchia, Area Manager
One Bell Plaza, Room 3040
Dallas, TX 75202

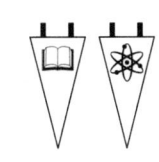

2224
Texas Outdoor Writers Association Scholarships

AMOUNT: Maximum: $1000   DEADLINE: November 1
FIELDS/MAJORS: Outdoor/Environmental Conservation/Wildlife Management Communications

Scholarships open to juniors, seniors, graduate students, and active professionals who are seeking further training. Must be planning to enroll/enrolled in communications-related courses incorporating the fields listed above through visual, oral, or print media. For use at an accredited Texas college or university. Winners announced at the TOWA annual meeting, February 21, in Waco, Texas. Contact the address or e-mail listed for further information: steve.lightfoot@tpwd.state.tx.us.

Texas Outdoor Writers Association
TOWA Scholarship
1715 Chamois Knoll
Round Rock, TX 78664

2225
Textron Sponsored Scholarship Program

AMOUNT: $250-$1000   DEADLINE: December 1
FIELDS/MAJORS: All Areas of Study

Twenty awards for children of employees of Textron or its divisions who plan to attend a vocational/technical school, junior college, college, or university. High school seniors as well as enrolled undergraduates are eligible. Write to the address listed for more information.

Textron Charitable Trust
College Scholarship Service
PO Box 6730
Princeton, NJ 08541

2226
Thanks Be to Grandmother Winifred Foundation

AMOUNT: Maximum: $5000 DEADLINE: March 21
FIELDS/MAJORS: All Areas of Study

Grants are available to women who are least fifty-four years of age and U.S. citizens with a social security number. Applicants must submit a grant proposal that benefits adult women. (Those who are twenty-one years of age or above.) A second deadline date for these awards is September 21. Write to the address below for more information.

Thanks Be to Grandmother Winifred Foundation
PO Box 1449
Wainscott, NY 11975

2227
The ASCAP Raymond Hubbell Music Scholarship Awards

AMOUNT: None Specified DEADLINE: None Specified
FIELDS/MAJORS: Music Composition

Awards to music composition students at various colleges, universities, or conservatories across the country. Contact the office of financial aid at your school for more details.

American Society of Composers, Authors, and Publishers
One Lincoln Plaza
New York, NY 10023

2228
Theo Dykes Memorial Scholarship

AMOUNT: None Specified DEADLINE: April 1
FIELDS/MAJORS: All Areas of Study

Award for an African-American male with demonstrated economic need, as verified by parent's tax return for prior year or other suitable documents. Must be a graduating high school senior or college student with a GPA of 2.5 or better. Also based upon three letters of reference, an essay on the challenge to American families today, and involvement in school and community activities. This award is available for students in the metropolitan Washington D.C. area. Contact Nylcare customer service at 1-800-635-3121 for more information.

Nylcare/Mid-Atlantic Scholarship Foundation, Inc.
7617 Ora Glen Dr.
Greenbelt, MD 20770

2229
Theodore Roosevelt Memorial Fund

AMOUNT: $200-$2000 DEADLINE: February 15
FIELDS/MAJORS: Natural History

Eighty grants for study of North American fauna including field research, study of the collections at the American Museum of Natural History, or for work at any of the Museum's field stations. Write to the address listed for complete information.

American Museum of Natural History
Central Park West at 79th St.
New York, NY 10024

2230
Theodore Rousseau Fellowships

AMOUNT: None Specified DEADLINE: November 7
FIELDS/MAJORS: Fine Arts, Art History, Art Conservation

Fellowships awarded for the training of students whose goal is to enter museums as curators of painting. Applicants should have been enrolled for at least one year in an advanced degree program in the field of art history. Fellowships will support examination of paintings in major European collections rather than supporting library research. Fellowships must take place between September 1 and August 31. Write to the address listed for further information.

Metropolitan Museum of Art
Fellowship Programs, Pia Quintano
1000 Fifth Ave.
New York, NY 10028

2231
Theta Delta Chi Educational Foundation

AMOUNT: Maximum: $1000 DEADLINE: April 30
FIELDS/MAJORS: All Areas of Study

Scholarships are available to members of the Theta Delta Chi fraternity. Applications will be judged on the basis of the candidates history of service to Theta Delta Chi, scholastic achievements, promise, and financial need. Primarily for undergraduate study (but graduate students will be considered). Ten to twenty awards offered annually. Contact address below for complete information.

Theta Delta Chi Educational Foundation
Scholarship Committee
135 Bay State Road
Boston, MA 02215

2232
ThinkQuest Scholarships Contest

AMOUNT: $3000-$25000
DEADLINE: February 28
FIELDS/MAJORS: Arts and Literature, Interdisciplinary Studies, Science and Mathematics, Social Sciences, or Sports and Health

Available to students between the ages of twelve to nineteen who are not enrolled in any postsecondary institution. Students must form a team with one or two other students (headed by one) and may have one to three coaches (teachers, mentors, etc.) Teams collaborate in the "Internet Style" of learning, interactive and participatory, that encourages exploration of the Internet's timely resources and creates new relationships that broaden their communities. Approximately thirty-five teams will be named finalists. Five awards are presented in each of the five categories. Applicants interested in joining or forming a team can find each other in a ThinkQuest electronic meeting place or find additional information on all other aspects of ThinkQuest by contacting their Web site at http://www.advanced.org/thinkquest.

ThinkQuest

2233
Thomas "Bear" Mangino Scholarships

AMOUNT: Maximum: $750   DEADLINE: April 21
FIELDS/MAJORS: All Areas of Study

Nine awards for high school seniors who are from Lawrence County, Pennsylvania. Based on personal statement, grades, need, etc. Write to the address listed for more information.

Thomas "Bear" Mangino Foundation
Scholarship Screening Committee
PO Box 347
New Castle, PA 16103

2234
Thomas Ewing Memorial Educational Grants for Carriers

AMOUNT: $1000-$2000   DEADLINE: February 14
FIELDS/MAJORS: All Areas of Study

Open to anyone who is currently a Washington Post carrier for at least two years. Must plan to continue being a post carrier through the current school year. Must be a high school senior, a high school graduate, or hold a G.E.D. and anticipating of attending college or vocational school in the near future. Thirty-six grants are given annually. Write to the address listed for complete details.

Washington Post
Thomas Ewing Memorial Educational Grants
1150 15th St. NW
Washington, DC 20071

2235
Thomas F. Seay Scholarship

AMOUNT: Maximum: $2000   DEADLINE: April 1
FIELDS/MAJORS: Real Estate

Scholarship for Illinois residents who are U.S. citizens and enrolled in a degree program with an emphasis on real estate. Based on career interest, GPA, and need. GPAs of at least 3.5 on a 5.0 point scale (2.8 on a 4.0 scale) and have completed thirty college credit hours. Write to the address listed for details.

Illinois Real Estate Educational Foundation
3180 Adloff Ln.
PO Box 19451
Springfield, IL 62794

2236
Thomas Jordan Doctoral Scholarships

AMOUNT: $3000   DEADLINE: February 1
FIELDS/MAJORS: Oncology Nursing

Grants available to doctoral students in the field of oncology nursing. All applicants must be currently licensed registered nurses. Write to the address listed for more information.

Oncology Nursing Foundation
501 Holiday Dr.
Pittsburgh, PA 15220

2237
Thomas L., Myrtle R., Arch, and Eva Alexander Fund Scholarships

AMOUNT: $560-$2000   DEADLINE: None Specified
FIELDS/MAJORS: All Areas of Study

Open to graduating seniors of Posey County high schools. Based on academic achievement. First year awards are $2000, and the second year awards range from $560 to $750. Deadlines vary by high school. Contact the address listed for further information or your high school guidance office. Must have a GPA of at least 2.9.

Thomas L., Myrtle R., Arch, and Eva Alexander
   Scholarship Fund
Citizens National Bank
PO Box 719
Evansville, IN 47705

2238
Thomas S. Morgan Scholarship and William E. Parrish Scholarship

AMOUNT: Maximum: $750 DEADLINE: March 15
FIELDS/MAJORS: History

Grants are available to members of Phi Alpha Theta who are entering graduate school for the first time. Two awards (one from each of the above named scholarships) offered annually. Write to address listed or call 1-800-394-8195 for details. Please indicate the name of your chapter. Information may be available from your chapter officers.

Phi Alpha Theta-International Honor Society in History
Headquarters Office
50 College Dr.
Allentown, PA 18104

2239
Thomas T. Hayashi Memorial Scholarships

AMOUNT: None Specified DEADLINE: April 1
FIELDS/MAJORS: Law

Applicants must be of Japanese ancestry and entering or enrolled at an accredited law school. Must also be members of the Japanese-American Citizens League. Applications and information may be obtained from local JACL chapters, district offices, and the national headquarters at the address listed, or call (415) 921-5225. Please indicate your level of study and be certain to include a legal-sized SASE.

Japanese-American Citizens League
National Scholarship and Award Program
1765 Sutter St.
San Francisco, CA 94115

2240
Three Percent Scholarship Program

AMOUNT: None Specified DEADLINE: None Specified
FIELDS/MAJORS: All Areas of Study

Scholarships available to students who are New Mexico residents, possess good moral character, satisfactory initiative, and good scholastic standing. One-third of awards are based upon financial need. Applicants must attend a New Mexico postsecondary institution. Contact the financial aid office at any New Mexico public institution.

New Mexico Commission on Higher Education
Financial Aid and Student Services
PO Box 15910
Santa Fe, NM 87501

2241
Thurgood Marshall Scholarships

AMOUNT: None Specified DEADLINE: None Specified
FIELDS/MAJORS: All Areas of Study

Awards for entering freshman who are pursuing a bachelor's degree full-time at one of the thirty-seven historically black public colleges and universities. Applicants must be U.S. citizens, have a GPA of at least 3.0, and have a score of 1000 or more on the SAT or 24 or higher on the ACT. Renewable for four years. Write to the address below or contact the on-campus TMSF coordinator for more information.

Thurgood Marshall Scholarship Fund
Scholarship Coordinator
100 Park Ave.
New York, NY 10017

2242
Tibor T. Polgar Fellowships

AMOUNT: $3500 DEADLINE: March 4
FIELDS/MAJORS: Environmental Studies, Restoration, Hydrology

Fellowships are available to undergraduate and graduate students for research projects conducted on the Hudson River. The program seeks information that contributes to physical, chemical, or biological understanding of the patterns, processes, and relationships that exist in the estuary. Fellowship amounts are summer salaries. Write to the address below for information.

Hudson River Foundation
Polgar Fellowship Com., Hudson River
40 W. 20th St., 9th Fl.
New York, NY 10011

2243
Tilles Charity Fund

AMOUNT: None Specified DEADLINE: None Specified
FIELDS/MAJORS: All Areas of Study

Open to residents of St. Louis city or St. Louis County who are attending colleges and universities in Missouri. Approximately eight awards offered annually. See the financial aid office at the school you are/plan on attending for further information.

Rosalie Tilles Non-Sectarian Charity Fund
C/O Mercantile Bank
PO Box 387
St. Louis, MO 63166

2244
Timothy Bigelow Scholarship

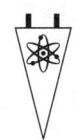

AMOUNT: $2500 DEADLINE: May 15
FIELDS/MAJORS: Landscape Horticulture or Any Related Discipline

Awards for seniors in a two-year program or juniors in a four-year program studying horticulture. Applicants must be from one of the six New England states and have a minimum GPA of at least 2.25. Preference is given to students who want to work in the nursery industry following graduation. Two awards are offered annually. Write to the address below for more information.

Horticultural Research Institute
1250 I St. NW, Suite 500
Washington, DC 20005

2245
TMS Presidential Scholarship

AMOUNT: Maximum: $4000 DEADLINE: June 30
FIELDS/MAJORS: Metallurgy, Material Science Engineering, Minerals Processing/Extraction

Available to full-time student members studying subjects in relation to metallurgy, material science engineering, or minerals processing at a college or university. Based on academic achievement, activities in and out of school, leadership abilities, personal profile statement, and letters of recommendation. A travel stipend to attend the annual banquet and receive the award is also included. Write to the address listed or call (412) 776-9000 ext. 213 for more information.

Minerals, Metals, and Materials Society
TMS Student Awards Program
420 Commonwealth Dr.
Warrendale, PA 15086

2246
TMS/International Symposium on Superalloys Scholarships

AMOUNT: Maximum: $1000 DEADLINE: June 30
FIELDS/MAJORS: Metallurgy, Material Science Engineering, Materials Processing/Extracting

Available to full-time undergraduate and graduate student members majoring in metallurgy and material science engineering with an emphasis or career objective in studying Superalloys. Based on academic achievement, activities in and out of school, leadership abilities, personal profile statement, and letters of recommendation. Write to the address listed or call (412) 776-9000 ext. 213 for more information.

Minerals, Metals, and Materials Society
TMS Student Awards Program
420 Commonwealth Dr.
Warrendale, PA 15086

2247
TMS/EMPMD Gilbert Chin Scholarship Program

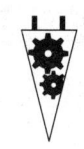

AMOUNT: Maximum: $2000 DEADLINE: June 30
FIELDS/MAJORS: Photonic, Electronic, Magnetic Material Science and Engineering

Available to full-time junior or senior members. Must be studying subjects in relation to electronic, magnetic, and/or photonic materials at a college or university. Based on academic achievement, activities in and out of school, leadership abilities, personal profile statement, and letters of recommendation. Write to the address listed or call (412) 776-9000 ext. 213 for more information.

Minerals, Metals, and Materials Society
TMS Student Awards Program
420 Commonwealth Dr.
Warrendale, PA 15086

2248
TMS/EPD Scholarships

AMOUNT: $2000 DEADLINE: June 30
FIELDS/MAJORS: Extracting/Processing of Materials, Mining

Available to full-time seniors who are members. Must be studying subjects in relation to the extraction and processing of materials. Based on academic achievement, activities in and out of school, leadership abilities, personal profile statement, and letters of recommendation. An addition, a travel stipend of up to $500 is available for recipients to attend the annual meeting and receive the award. A non-monetary donation will also be made to the student's library in his or her name. Write to the address listed or call (412) 776-9000 ext. 213 for more information.

Minerals, Metals, and Materials Society
TMS Student Awards Program
420 Commonwealth Dr.
Warrendale, PA 15086

2249
TMS/LMD Scholarship

AMOUNT: Maximum: $2000 DEADLINE: June 30
FIELDS/MAJORS: Non-Ferrous Metallurgy, Material Science Engineering

Available to full-time junior or senior students who are members. Must be studying subjects in relation to non-ferrous metallurgy or light metals at a college or university. Based on academic achievement, activities in and out of school, leadership abilities, personal profile statement, and letters of recommendation. A travel stipend of up to $500 will be given for recipient to attend annual luncheon and receive award. Write to the address listed or call (412) 776-9000 ext. 213 for more information.

Minerals, Metals, and Materials Society
TMS Student Awards Program
420 Commonwealth Dr.
Warrendale, PA 15086

2250
TMS/SMD Scholarships

AMOUNT: Maximum: $2500 DEADLINE: June 30
FIELDS/MAJORS: Physical Metallurgy, Material Science Engineering

Available to full-time senior students who are members. Must be studying subjects in relation to physical metallurgy or material science engineering at a college or university. Based on academic achievement, activities in and out of school, leadership abilities, personal profile statement, and letters of recommendation. A travel stipend is also awarded to attend the annual banquet to receive award. Write to the address listed or call (412) 776-9000 ext. 213 for more information.

Minerals, Metals, and Materials Society
TMS Student Awards Program
420 Commonwealth Dr.
Warrendale, PA 15086

2251
Together We Can Scholarship

AMOUNT: $2000 DEADLINE: None Specified
FIELDS/MAJORS: All Areas of Study

Available to new freshmen who attended Chattanooga public schools from sixth grade through senior year. Students must have at least a "C" average, though most recipients have a "B" average. Family income must be less than $35000, though most recipients' family incomes average just $10000. Award numbers and amounts vary. Must fill out FAFSA form. Contact the address listed for further information. Must have a GPA of at least 2.5.

Community Foundation of Greater Chattanooga
Scholarship Program
736 Market St.
Chattanooga, TN 37402-4803

2252
Tom and Judith Comstock Scholarship

AMOUNT: $500 DEADLINE: February 1
FIELDS/MAJORS: All Areas of Study

Scholarship available to high school seniors with a general class amateur radio license who have been accepted at a two or four-year college. Must be a resident of Texas or Oklahoma and an ARRL member. Write to the address listed for information.

ARRL Foundation (American Radio Relay League)
Scholarship Program
225 Main St.
Newington, CT 06111

2253
Tony's Foodservice Scholarship

AMOUNT: Maximum: $1000 DEADLINE: April 15
FIELDS/MAJORS: Foodservice/Management

Open to undergraduates who meet all six of the following criteria: 1) be enrolled/plan to enroll in an institution that has a program designed to improve school food service, 2) be an active ASFSA member for a minimum of one year with a history of employment in school foodservice, or a dependent of an ASFSA member, 3) have a satisfactory academics, 4) all coursework must include real-time interactive classroom instruction, 5) desire to make school foodservice a career, 6) submit application with all required attachments postmarked no later than April 15. Write to the address listed for details. Must have a GPA of at least 2.8.

American School Food Service Association
SFS Foundation Scholarship Committee
1600 Duke St., 7th Floor
Alexandria, VA 22314

2254
Tourette Syndrome Association Research and Training Grants

AMOUNT: $5000-$40000 DEADLINE: December 19
FIELDS/MAJORS: Tourette Syndrome-Related (Biochemistry, Epidemiology, Psychology, Etc.)

Postdoctoral training fellowships and basic or clinical research grants for researchers whose areas of study are specifically relevant to Gilles de la Tourette Syndrome. To receive an application packet and a review of TSA literature (includes areas of interest to TSA), interested persons should call (718) 224-2999 or Fax (718) 279-9596. Preliminary screening based on letter of intent, which should include a brief description of the scientific basis of the proposed project and approximate level of funding sought.

Tourette Syndrome Association, Inc.
Research and Training Grants
42-40 Bell Blvd.
Bayside, NY 11361

2255
Tower Hill Botanic Garden Scholarship

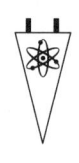

AMOUNT: $500-$2000 DEADLINE: May 1
FIELDS/MAJORS: Horticulture or Related Field

Scholarship available to juniors or seniors or graduate students majoring in horticulture or a related field. Applicants must be residents of New England or enrolled in a college or university in New England. Based on academic ability, interest in horticulture, and financial need. Notification of the award will be June 15. Write to the address listed for further information.

Worcester County Horticultural Society, Tower Hill Botanic Garden
Tower Hill Botanic Garden
PO Box 598
Boylston, MA 01505-0598

2256
Township Officials of Illinois Scholarship

AMOUNT: Maximum: $2000   DEADLINE: March 1
FIELDS/MAJORS: History, Government, and Related

Six scholarships for graduating seniors from Illinois high schools who have maintained at least a 3.0 GPA and will be attending an Illinois college, majoring in history or government related areas. Based on school and community activities and a five hundred word essay. Write to the address listed for details.

Township Officials of Illinois
Scholarship Program
PO Box 455
Astoria, IL 61501

2257
Tracy Scholarship

AMOUNT: None Specified   DEADLINE: None Specified
FIELDS/MAJORS: All Areas of Study

Open to students who will graduate from El Dorado High School, Placerville, El Dorado County, CA. Must have been a resident of El Dorado County for two years prior to graduation. Contact your guidance counselor for information and an application. Do not contact the bank.

Wells Fargo Bank
PO Box 2511
Sacramento, CA 95812

2258
Training in the Neurosciences for Minorities

AMOUNT: $10000-$18000
DEADLINE: January 15
FIELDS/MAJORS: Neurosciences

Fellowships for ethnic minority students pursuing doctoral degrees in APA-accredited doctoral programs in psychology or neuroscience. Must be a U.S. citizen or permanent resident. Write to the address below or call (202) 336-6027 for more information.

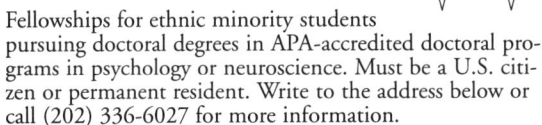

American Psychological Association
Minority Fellowship Program/Neuroscience
750 First St. NE
Washington, DC 20002

2259
Travel Research Grant

AMOUNT: Maximum: $1000   DEADLINE: March 1
FIELDS/MAJORS: Travel and Tourism

Open to individuals or organizations for the development of a research technique or methodology in a particularly creative manner. Entries judged on their ability to improve measurement, decrease costs, and improve information for better application and understanding by management. Contact the address listed for further information.

Travel and Tourism Research Association
TTRA Awards Committee
546 E. Main St.
Lexington, KY 40508

2260
Trent R. Dames and William W. Moore Fellowships

AMOUNT: $2000-$6000   DEADLINE: February 20
FIELDS/MAJORS: Civil Engineering

Awards for practicing engineers or earth scientists, professors, or graduate students. To be used for postgraduate research to aid in the creation of new knowledge for the benefit and advancement of the profession of civil engineering. Contact your local ASCE Chapter, write to the address listed, or call 1-800-548-ASCE for details.

American Society of Civil Engineers
Member Scholarships and Awards
1801 Alexander Bell Dr.
Reston, VA 20191

2261
Truman D. Picard Scholarship Program

AMOUNT: Maximum: $1500   DEADLINE: February 20
FIELDS/MAJORS: Natural Resources

Awards for high school seniors and undergraduates who are Native American or Alaskan students. Must be able to show academic merit, financial need, and be a member of a federally recognized tribe or Native Alaska Corporation. Four awards offered annually. Contact the address listed or call (503) 282-4296 for further information.

Intertribal Timber Council
Attn: Education Committee
4370 NE Halsey St.
Portland, OR 97213

2262

Tschudy Family Scholarship

AMOUNT: Maximum: $2000 DEADLINE: January 31
FIELDS/MAJORS: All Areas of Study

Scholarships are available for graduates of Emmett High School who plan to enroll or are currently enrolled, full-time, at Boise State University, Idaho State University, University of Idaho, or Lewis-Clark State College. Must be U.S. citizens and residents of Idaho. Five awards are offered annually. Write to the address listed for information.

Idaho State Board of Education
PO Box 83720
Boise, ID 83720

2263

Tuition Credit for Active Reservists

AMOUNT: None Specified DEADLINE: None Specified
FIELDS/MAJORS: All Areas of Study

Applicants must be Nebraska residents who are enlisted members at a Nebraska-based unit of the active selected reserve of the armed forces. Tuition credit for 50% of the charges is for use at Nebraska schools only. Write to address below for details.

Nebraska Department of Veterans Affairs
PO Box 95083
Lincoln, NE 68509

2264

Tuition Grants Program

AMOUNT: Maximum: $2800 DEADLINE: None Specified
FIELDS/MAJORS: All Areas of Study

Applicant must be a child of a Michigan veteran who was killed in action or died from another cause during a war or war condition and as a result of service-connected injury. Other criteria includes Michigan residency for preceding twelve months and student must be between the ages of sixteen and twenty-six. Grants are for Michigan tax-supported schools only. Write for complete details.

Michigan Veterans Trust Fund
611 W. Ottawa
PO Box 30026
Lansing, MI 48909

2265

Tuition Incentive Program

AMOUNT: None Specified DEADLINE: None Specified
FIELDS/MAJORS: All Areas of Study

Tuition incentive program open for applicants before graduation or receipt of GED. Must be receiving (or have received) Medicaid from the Family Independence Agency. Must be under the age of twenty at the time of high school graduation or GED completion and be enrolled in college within four years of graduation. For use at any Michigan public community college, nonprofit associate degree-granting college/university, or public university. Write to the address below for details.

Michigan Department of Social Services
Suite 1318
PO Box 30037
Lansing, MI 48909

2266

Tuition Opportunity Program for Students Award

AMOUNT: None Specified DEADLINE: December 15
FIELDS/MAJORS: All Areas of Study

Open to Louisiana residents who are applying as first-time freshmen within four semesters of graduation from an approved Louisiana high school. Must have/have had a minimum GPA of 2.5 and completed 16.5 units of the core curriculum. Must be U.S. citizens to apply. Awards are tuition waivers. December 15 is the deadline for new high school graduates and June 1 is the deadline for other incoming freshmen. Write to the address listed for details.

Louisiana Office of Student Financial Assistance
PO Box 91202
Baton Rouge, LA 70821-9202

2267

Tuition Opportunity Program Performance Award

AMOUNT: None Specified DEADLINE: June 1
FIELDS/MAJORS: All Areas of Study

Open to Louisiana residents who are incoming freshmen or current undergraduates. If a high school senior, a minimum GPA of 3.5 is required. Undergraduates must have at least a 3.0. Must be U.S. citizens to apply. Awards are tuition waivers plus $400 per year. Write to the address listed for details.

Louisiana Office of Student Financial Assistance
PO Box 91202
Baton Rouge, LA 70821-9202

2268
Tuition Opportunity Program Teachers Award

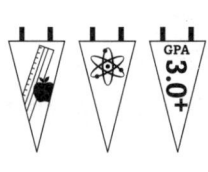

AMOUNT: $4000-$6000 DEADLINE: June 1
FIELDS/MAJORS: Education, Mathematics, Chemistry

Scholarships offered to residents of Louisiana who are/will be attending college in Louisiana, planning a teaching career. A minimum GPA of 3.25 is required from high school seniors and undergraduates. The award is a $4000 year loan for education majors or a $6000 loan for math and chemistry majors. The loans are forgiven by working as a certified teacher in Louisiana one year for each year the loan is received. Must be U.S. citizens to apply. Contact the financial aid office of the school you plan to attend for details, or contact the address listed.

Louisiana Office of Student Financial Assistance
PO Box 91202
Baton Rouge, LA 70821-9202

2269
Tuition Scholarships

AMOUNT: $300-$500 DEADLINE: March 15
FIELDS/MAJORS: All Areas of Study

Open to any Catholic Aid Association member of at least two years who is a high school graduate and is now entering their freshman or sophomore year in a college, university, or technical school. Write to the address below for complete details. Applications are accepted after January 10.

Catholic Aid Association
3499 N. Lexington Ave.
Saint Paul, MN 55126

2270
Tuition Waiver for Children of Deceased or Disabled Law Officers

AMOUNT: None Specified DEADLINE: None Specified
FIELDS/MAJORS: All Areas of Study

Tuition waivers are available for South Carolina dependents of deceased or disabled firemen, law officers, and members of Civil Air Patrol or organized rescue squad. Students must attend public institutions located in South Carolina. Children of deceased or totally disabled veterans are also eligible. Contact your school's financial aid office or the address below for more information.

South Carolina Commission on Higher Education
1333 Main St.
Suite 200
Columbia, SC 29201

2271
Tuition Waiver for Senior Citizens

AMOUNT: None Specified DEADLINE: None Specified
FIELDS/MAJORS: All Areas of Study

Tuition waivers are available for South Carolina residents, age sixty and over, attending South Carolina public colleges. Contact your school's financial aid office or the address below for more information.

South Carolina Commission on Higher Education
1333 Main St.
Suite 200
Columbia, SC 29201

2272
Tuition Waiver Program for North American Indians

AMOUNT: None Specified DEADLINE: None Specified
FIELDS/MAJORS: All Areas of Study

Open to any Michigan resident who is at least one-quarter North American Indian (certified by their Tribal Nation) and willing to attend any public Michigan college, university, or community college. Award is for all levels of study. Renewable. Write to the address below for further information (including procedures for certification of ancestry, if necessary). Bureau of Indian Affairs also provides funds for persons who are at least one-eighth American Indian. Information on BIA awards may also be obtained from the address below.

Michigan Commission on Indian Affairs
611 West Ottawa St.
Lansing, MI 48913

2273
Tulsa Legacy Scholarships

AMOUNT: Maximum: $500 DEADLINE: April 15
FIELDS/MAJORS: Travel and Tourism, Hotel/Motel Management

Awards for Oklahoma juniors or seniors in one of the areas listed above who are enrolled in a four-year college in Oklahoma. Must have a GPA of 3.0 or better. Write to the address listed or call 1-800-682-8886 ext. 4251 for more information.

National Tourism Foundation
546 East Main St.
PO Box 3071
Lexington, KY 40596

2274
Two Scholarships for Edward County

AMOUNT: None Specified   DEADLINE: None Specified
FIELDS/MAJORS: All Areas of Study

Are awarded to Edward County residents. One award is given to a student with a 3.5 GPA or above. The second award is given to a student with a 2.5 to 3.45 GPA. All recipients must be attending an accredited educational facility within the state of Kansas. Contact the address listed for further information.

Chamber of Commerce-Kinsley Area
Eula I. Westphal, Scholarship Chair
110 Marsh
Kinsley, KS 67547

2275
Two-Year College Academic Scholarship Program

AMOUNT: None Specified   DEADLINE: None Specified
FIELDS/MAJORS: All Areas of Study

This program is limited to students who are accepted for enrollment at public, two-year institutions in Alabama. Based on academics. Renewable if students demonstrate academic excellence. Priority given to in-state residents. Apply through the financial aid office at any public, two-year, postsecondary educational institution, rather than address listed below.

Alabama Commission on Higher Education
PO Box 302000
Montgomery, AL 36130

2276
Two/Ten International Footwear Foundation Scholarship Program

AMOUNT: $200-$2000   DEADLINE: January 15
FIELDS/MAJORS: All Areas of Study

Applicants must be worker or a dependent of a worker whose work is related to the footwear, leather, or allied industries. Based on need and academics. 200 to 250 awards offered annually. Must have been graduated from high school within the last four years or currently be a high school senior. Write to the address below for details and a preliminary application form.

Two/Ten International Footwear Foundation
56 Main St.
Watertown, MA 02172

2277
Tylenol Scholarship

AMOUNT: $1000-$10000   DEADLINE: November 15
FIELDS/MAJORS: All Areas of Study

Must be an incoming freshman or current undergraduate attending any college or vocational or technical school. Based on leadership responsibilities in community/school activities and GPAs. 510 awards offered annually. Information and applications will be available, starting in September, in stores where Tylenol products are sold. Please check the stores first, as that will be fastest way to obtain a form. If they are out of forms, you may call the following number and leave your name and address. A form will be mailed to you. 1-800-676-8437.

McNeilab, Inc.
Scholarship Office
Fort Washington, PA 19034

2278
U. Magazine Scholarship Awards

AMOUNT: $1000   DEADLINE: June 27
FIELDS/MAJORS: All Areas of Study

Scholarship available to students demonstrating outstanding academic excellence. 3.2 GPA required. Must be able to demonstrate financial need and cocurricular and extracurricular activities. Write to "U. Scholarships for excellence, achievement, and leadership" at the address below for details.

U. the National College Magazine
1800 Century Park East, Suite 820
Los Angeles, CA 90067

2279
U. Magazine Scholarship Awards

AMOUNT: $1000   DEADLINE: June 27
FIELDS/MAJORS: Journalism

Scholarship available to students demonstrating outstanding academic excellence. 3.0 GPA required. Must be able to demonstrate financial need. Write to "U. Scholarships for excellence, achievement, and leadership" at the address below for details.

U. the National College Magazine
1800 Century Park East, Suite 820
Los Angeles, CA 90067

2280

U. Magazine Scholarship Awards

AMOUNT: $1000 DEADLINE: June 27
FIELDS/MAJORS: Liberal Arts, Humanities

Scholarship available to students demonstrating outstanding academic excellence. 3.0 GPA required. Must be able to demonstrate financial need. Write to "U. Scholarships for excellence, achievement, and leadership" at the address below for details.

U. the National College Magazine
1800 Century Park East, Suite 820
Los Angeles, CA 90067

2281

U. Magazine/Chevrolet Scholarships

AMOUNT: $1000 DEADLINE: June 27
FIELDS/MAJORS: Social Sciences

Awards open to undergraduates with a minimum GPA of 3.2 and ability to demonstrate financial need. Contact the address below for further information.

U. Magazine and Chevrolet
1800 Century Park East, Suite 820
Los Angeles, CA 90067

2282

U. Magazine/Discover Card Scholarships

AMOUNT: $1000 DEADLINE: June 27
FIELDS/MAJORS: Marketing

Awards open to undergraduates who are marketing majors with a minimum GPA of 3.2. Must be able to demonstrate financial need and be involved in activities that benefit others. Contact the address below for further information.

U. Magazine and Discover Card
1800 Century Park East, Suite 820
Los Angeles, CA 90067

2283

U. Magazine/General Motors Acceptance Corporation Scholarships

AMOUNT: $1000 DEADLINE: June 27
FIELDS/MAJORS: Finance

Scholarship available to undergraduates studying the above field. Minimum 3.2 GPA required. Must be able to demonstrate financial need. Write to "U. Scholarships for excellence, achievement, and leadership" at the address below for details.

U. Magazine and General Motors Acceptance Corporation
1800 Century Park East, Suite 820
Los Angeles, CA 90067

2284

U. Magazine/ Scholarships

AMOUNT: $1000 DEADLINE: June 27
FIELDS/MAJORS: Business Administration

Scholarship available to students studying the above field. Minimum 3.2 GPA required. Must be able to demonstrate financial need. Write to "U. Scholarships for excellence, achievement, and leadership" at the address below for details.

U. Magazine and Mastercard
1800 Century Park East, Suite 820
Los Angeles, CA 90067

2285

U. Magazine/Nike Scholarships

AMOUNT: $1000 DEADLINE: June 27
FIELDS/MAJORS: All Areas of Study

Scholarship available to undergraduates. Minimum 3.0 GPA required. Must be able to demonstrate financial need and be a participant in outdoor sports. Write to "U. Scholarships for excellence, achievement, and leadership" at the address below for details.

U. Magazine and Nike
1800 Century Park East, Suite 820
Los Angeles, CA 90067

2286

U. Magazine/Plymouth Scholarships

AMOUNT: $1000 DEADLINE: June 27
FIELDS/MAJORS: Technology, Computer Science

Scholarship available to students studying the above fields. Minimum 3.2 GPA required. Must be able to demonstrate financial need. Write to "U. Scholarships for excellence, achievement, and leadership" at the address below for details.

U. Magazine and Plymouth
1800 Century Park East, Suite 820
Los Angeles, CA 90067

2287
U. Magazine/Texas Instruments Scholarships

AMOUNT: $1000 DEADLINE: June 28
FIELDS/MAJORS: Computer Science

Open to undergraduate students with a minimum GPA of 3.2. Must be able to demonstrate financial need. Contact the address below for further information.

U. Magazine and Texas Instruments
1800 Century Park East, Suite 820
Los Angeles, CA 90067

2288
U. Magazine/Warner Brothers Scholarships

AMOUNT: $1000 DEADLINE: June 27
FIELDS/MAJORS: Communications

Scholarship available to students studying the above field. Minimum 3.0 GPA required. Must be able to demonstrate financial need. Write to "U. Scholarships for excellence, achievement, and leadership" at the address below for details.

U. Magazine and Warner Brothers
1800 Century Park East, Suite 820
Los Angeles, CA 90067

2289
U. Scholarship/Chrysler Scholarships

AMOUNT: $1000 DEADLINE: June 27
FIELDS/MAJORS: Marketing

Scholarship available to students studying the above field. A minimum 3.0 GPA is required. Must be able to demonstrate financial need. Write to "U. Scholarships for excellence, achievement, and leadership" at the address below for details.

U. Magazine and Chrysler
1800 Century Park East, Suite 820
Los Angeles, CA 90067

2290
U.S. Environmental Protection Agency Scholarship

AMOUNT: Maximum: $4000 DEADLINE: June 15
FIELDS/MAJORS: Chemistry, Chemical Engineering, Environmental Sciences, Biology, and Related

Scholarship for students with junior status or higher enrolled full-time. Must agree to work at the Environmental Protection Agency, a tribal location, or an environmental facility during the summers, if a job is offered. Students may reapply every year. Write to the address listed or call (303) 939-0023 for more information. Must have a GPA of at least 2.0.

American Indian Science and Engineering Society
Scholarship Coordinator
5661 Airport Blvd.
Boulder, CO 80301-2339

2291
U.S. Junior Chamber International Senate Scholarships

AMOUNT: Maximum: $1000 DEADLINE: January 8
FIELDS/MAJORS: All Areas of Study

Open to high school seniors only who display academic success, community and school service, and positions of leadership. Must be able to demonstrate financial need. Contact the address listed for further information. Must have a GPA of at least 2.8.

U.S. Junior Chamber International Senate Scholarship Committee
Robert Barron
466 Ash St., #110
Willimantic, CT 06226

2292
U.S. Olympic Committee Student Intern Program

AMOUNT: None Specified
DEADLINE: February 15
FIELDS/MAJORS: See Listing Below

Internships are available for juniors, seniors, and graduate students in Lake Placid, New York, Colorado Springs, Colorado, and Chula Vista, California. Program is conducted on a year-round basis. Applicants must be in a degree-bearing program in relevant academic fields to the USOC and its member organizations. These include, but are not limited to: journalism, sports administration, broadcasting, exercise physiology, computer science, sports science, and coaching. Job descriptions and work expectations will be reviewed and explained by the intern's supervisor on the first day of the internship. Approximately twenty-eight openings are offered annually. The deadline dates are: February 15 for the summer session, June 1 for the fall semester, and October 1 for the winter/spring semester. Every attempt will be made to complete the selection process within six to eight weeks after the application deadline. Write to the address listed for an application packet. Must have a GPA of at least 2.8.

U.S. Olympic Committee
Educational Programs
One Olympic Plaza
Colorado Springs, CO 80909

2293
UCT Retarded Citizens Teacher Scholarship

AMOUNT: Maximum: $750   DEADLINE: None Specified
FIELDS/MAJORS: Education, Mentally Handicapped

Scholarships for juniors, seniors, and graduate students in education of the mentally retarded or current teachers who require additional course work to be certified to teach people with mental retardation. Prime consideration is given to UCT members. Recipients must plan to be of service in the United States or Canada. Applicants teaching in areas of special education other than mental retardation are not eligible. When requesting an application, list a brief history of your experience with the mentally handicapped, an indication of your current standing in college, and a statement of your educational or career plans. Application is made through the local UCT contact person, whose name may be received from the home office at the address listed.

Order of United Commercial Travelers of America
632 N. Park St. Scholarship Director
PO Box 159019
Columbus, OH 43215

2294
UFCW Scholarship Program

AMOUNT: $1000-$2000   DEADLINE: December 31
FIELDS/MAJORS: All Areas of Study

Applicants must be members or children of members of the UFCW who are high school seniors and will be enrolling in a college or university as a full-time student. Automatically renewable for four years, at $1000 per year. Applicants must be less than age twenty. Seven awards offered each year. Write to the address listed for details. Information is also available in editions of "UFCW Action," the bimonthly magazine of the union.

United Food and Commercial Workers International Union
Education Office
1775 K Street NW
Washington, DC 20006

2295
Ullery Charitable Trust Fund Scholarship

AMOUNT: None Specified   DEADLINE: June 1
FIELDS/MAJORS: All Areas of Study

Scholarships open to members of the Presbyterian Church in Oklahoma. Preference given to members of the First Presbyterian Church of Tulsa, Presbytery of eastern Oklahoma, or the Synod of the Sun. Must be accepted or enrolled at an accredited college or seminary and be pursuing a career in Christian ministry. Cumulative GPA of 2.5 is required. Write to the address listed for details.

First Presbyterian Church
Scholarship Fund Program
709 S. Boston Ave.
Tulsa, OK 74119

2296
UNCF/Merck Dissertation Fellowships

AMOUNT: Maximum: $25000   DEADLINE: January 15
FIELDS/MAJORS: Biomedical Life, Physical Science

Open to African-Americans enrolled full-time in a Ph.D. or equivalent doctoral program. Must be within two years of completing dissertation research. Contact Jerry L. Bryant, Ph.D., at the address listed or the Web site: www.uncf.org for further information.

United Negro College Fund
Scholarship Program
PO Box 10444
Fairfax, VA 22031

2297
UNCF/Merck Postdoctoral Fellowships

AMOUNT: Maximum: $40000   DEADLINE: January 15
FIELDS/MAJORS: Biomedical Life, Physical Science

Open to African-Americans who hold a Ph.D. or equivalent degree in biomedical life or physical science. Must be appointed as a postdoctoral fellow at an academic or non-academic research institution (private industrial laboratories are excluded.) Contact Jerry L. Bryant, Ph.D., at the address listed or the Web site: www.uncf.org for further information.

United Negro College Fund
Scholarship Program
PO Box 10444
Fairfax, VA 22031

2298
UNCF/Merck Undergraduate Scholarships

AMOUNT: Maximum: $25000   DEADLINE: January 15
FIELDS/MAJORS: Life, Physical Science

Open to African-American juniors with a minimum GPA of 3.3. Two summer internships are also offered. Contact Jerry L. Bryant, Ph.D., at the address listed or the Web site: www.uncf.org for further information.

United Negro College Fund
Scholarship Program
PO Box 10444
Fairfax, VA 22031

2299
Undergraduate/ Graduate Loans

AMOUNT: $200-$1500 DEADLINE: None Specified
FIELDS/MAJORS: All Areas of Study

Loans for full-time undergraduate or graduate students who are U.S. citizens and members of the Presbyterian Church (U.S.A.). Based upon academic ability and demonstrated financial need. Write to the address listed for details.

Presbyterian Church (U.S.A.)
Office for Financial Aid for Studies
100 Witherspoon St.
Louisville, KY 40202

2300
Undergraduate and Graduate Scholarships

AMOUNT: $350-$1000 DEADLINE: April 1
FIELDS/MAJORS: All Areas of Study

Applicants must be students of Armenian ancestry enrolled at an accredited college or university. Based on financial need. Involvement with the Armenian community is considered. Renewable once. Scholarships available for both undergraduates and graduate students. Write to the address below for details.

Armenian Relief Society of North America, Inc.
Ms. Seda Aghamianz
80 Bigelow Ave.
Watertown, MA 02172

2301
Undergraduate Fellowships and Graduate Fellowships

AMOUNT: $4000 DEADLINE: March 1
FIELDS/MAJORS: Art, Fine Arts, Photography, Drawing, Sculpture, Filmmaking, Video

Twelve fellowships are shared between undergraduates and graduates who are enrolled, or are planning to be enrolled, full-time for the entire academic year at an accredited school of arts, college, or university. Must be a Virginia resident. $4,000 is for undergraduates, and $5000 is for graduates. Write to the address listed for more information.

Virginia Museum of Fine Arts
Office of Education and Outreach
2800 Grove Ave.
Richmond, VA 23221

2302
Undergraduate Research Fellowship

AMOUNT: $2500 DEADLINE: February 1
FIELDS/MAJORS: Microbiological Sciences

Fellowships available to second- or third-year undergraduates planning to attend graduate school and study the microbiological sciences. Must be a U.S. citizen or permanent resident. Must be a joint application with an ASM member scientist. Write to the address below or visit http://WWW.ASMU.S.A.org/edusrc/edu2.HTM.

American Society for Microbiology
Office of Education and Training
1325 Massachusetts Ave. NW
Washington, DC 20005

2303
Undergraduate Research Fellowships in Pharmaceutics

AMOUNT: $5000 DEADLINE: October 1
FIELDS/MAJORS: Pharmaceutics

Fellowships to encourage undergraduate students to pursue advanced degrees and enter the field of pharmaceuticals. Fellowships are for one or two years. Must be a U.S. citizen and have a GPA of 3.0 or better. Write to the address below for details.

Pharmaceutical Manufacturers Association Foundation, Inc.
1100 15th St. NW
Washington, DC 30005

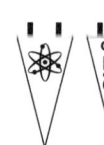

2304
Undergraduate Scholarships

AMOUNT: $1000-$2000 DEADLINE: February 1
FIELDS/MAJORS: Food Science, Technology

Scholarships open to undergraduates enrolled in a food service and technology curriculum. Applicant must have a GPA of at least 2.5. Ninety-four awards per year. February 1 is the deadline for juniors and seniors, February 15 is the deadline for freshmen, and March 1 is the deadline for sophomores. Must be enrolled/planning to enroll in an IFT-approved food science/technology program. When requesting an application by phone or fax, you will automatically receive a list of IFT-approved programs. Write to the address below for details, specifying your year in school. You may request information via phone at (312) 782-8424 or "fax on demand" 1-800-234-0270. Freshmen request document #3410, Sophomores request document #3420, Juniors and Seniors request document #3430.

Institute of Food Technologists
Scholarship Department
221 North LaSalle St.
Chicago, IL 60601

2305
Undergraduate Scholarships

AMOUNT: $1000-$5000 DEADLINE: March 1
FIELDS/MAJORS: Food Service, Hospitality, Food Management, Culinary Arts

Scholarships available to full-time students. Must have one thousand hours of industry-related work experience and a GPA of at least 3.0. Applicants must have completed their first year of study and must be pursuing an associates or bachelor's degree. May be used at a foreign institution. Recipient will be notified after July 15. Scholarship is renewable. Contact the address listed or call 1-800-765-2122 for more information. Applications available after December 31 for next fall.

National Restaurant Association Education Foundation
Scholarship Department
250 South Wacker Dr., Suite 1400
Chicago, IL 60606

2306
Undergraduate Scholarships

AMOUNT: $500-$5000 DEADLINE: June 15
FIELDS/MAJORS: Metallurgy, Materials Science

Scholarships are for undergraduates. Selection is based on interest in metallurgy and materials science, motivation, achievement, potential, and scholarship. Thirty-four $500 awards, three $2000 awards, two full tuition awards, and seven $5000 awards. Must be a sophomore, junior, or senior. Must be U.S., Canadian, or Mexican citizens. Application forms are available in the offices of the university departments of metallurgy/materials, from faculty advisors of ASM student chapters, from local ASM chapters, or by writing to the address listed.

ASM Foundation for Education and Research
Scholarship Program
Materials Park, OH 44073

2307
Undergraduate Scholarships

AMOUNT: Maximum: $10000 DEADLINE: October 31
FIELDS/MAJORS: All Areas of Study

Must be Indiana high school senior in good standing who has never attended college. Must have faith in a divine being and a firm belief in the free enterprise system and the American way of life. Must exhibit outstanding scholastic achievement and leadership potential. Awards are limited to certain Indiana colleges. Financial need not a factor. Six to eleven awards are given annually. Unspecified number of scholarships. Renewable. Write to the address below for complete details.

Eisenhower Memorial Scholarship Foundation, Inc.
223 South Pete Ellis Dr., Suite 27
Bloomington, IN 47408

2308
Undergraduate Scholarships

AMOUNT: None Specified DEADLINE: February 15
FIELDS/MAJORS: All Areas of Study

Scholarship applicant's permanent residence or high school must be located within thirty miles of a Potlatch Corp. facility. The majority of scholarships are awarded to students residing near company facilities in Idaho, Minnesota, Arkansas, and Washington. Write to the address listed for further information. A return envelope is not necessary. Applications must be requested between October 1 and December 15.

Potlatch Foundation for Higher Education
Corporate Programs Administrator
PO Box 193591
San Francisco, CA 94119

2309
Undergraduate Scholarships and Grants

AMOUNT: Maximum: $6000 DEADLINE: March 16
FIELDS/MAJORS: Fine Art

Open to students at the School of the Museum of Fine Arts and Tufts University. March 16 is the deadline for new students, and April 16 is the deadline for returning students. Contact the financial aid offices of either school for the specific information regarding their programs. GPA must be at least 2.8.

School of the Museum of Fine Arts
Office of Financial Aid
230 The Fenway
Boston, MA 02115

2310
Undergraduate, Curriculum, and Postgraduate Scholarships

AMOUNT: $2000 DEADLINE: February 1
FIELDS/MAJORS: Athletic Trainer

For student members of the National Athletic Trainers' Association. Must be an upperclass undergraduate or graduate student pursuing an academic program leading to a career in athletic training. A GPA of at least 3.0 is expected. Write to the address below for details.

National Athletic Trainers' Association
Grants and Scholarship Foundation, Inc.
2952 Stemmons Freeway
Dallas, TX 75247

2311
Undergraduate/Advanced Undergraduate College Scholarships

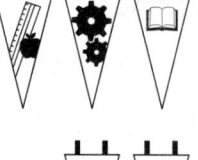

AMOUNT: None Specified
DEADLINE: January 31
FIELDS/MAJORS: All Areas of Study

Applicants must be CAP cadets or senior members who have received the Billy Mitchell Award or the Senior Rating in Level II of the senior training program. Scholarships will be offered in each of the four disciplines: engineering, science, education, humanities. Write to the address listed for details.

Civil Air Patrol
National Headquarters CAP (TT)
Maxwell AFB, AL 36112

2312
Underwood-Smith Teacher Scholarships

AMOUNT: Maximum: $5000
DEADLINE: April 15
FIELDS/MAJORS: Education

Undergraduate and graduate students from West Virginia having outstanding academic credentials. Applicant's academic performance must be in the top 10% of their class. The intention is for a recipient to obtain a teaching certificate and to commit to an elementary or secondary teaching career in West Virginia. Must have a GPA of 3.5 and attend a school in West Virginia. Write to the address listed for more details.

State College and University Systems of West Virginia
University Systems
PO Box 4007
Charleston, WV 25364

2313
Union Bank of California Scholarship

AMOUNT: None Specified
DEADLINE: April 1
FIELDS/MAJORS: Business, Accounting, Economics, International Trade

Applicants must be California residents majoring in the above fields. Must also be members of the Japanese-American Citizen League. Applications and information may be obtained from local JACL chapters, district offices, and the national headquarters at the address listed, or call (415) 921-5225. Please indicate your level of study and be certain to include a legal-sized SASE.

Japanese-American Citizens League
National Scholarship and Award Program
1765 Sutter St.
San Francisco, CA 94115

2314
Union Camp Corporation Scholarship Program

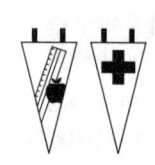

AMOUNT: None Specified
DEADLINE: None Specified
FIELDS/MAJORS: Health, Education, Human Services

Open to students that have focused on the areas of health, education, and human services. Only open to the children of Union Camp employees at all of the company's facilities. Write to the address below for more information.

Union Camp Corporation
1600 Valley Rd.
Wayne, NJ 07470

2315
Union County Cattlewomen Scholarship (of Oregon Community Foundation)

AMOUNT: None Specified
DEADLINE: March 1
FIELDS/MAJORS: Agriculture

Open to residents of Union County who are U.S. citizens and at least a sophomores. Awards may be renewable, provided that the recipient reapplies each year, can document adequate progress toward a degree, and remains in good academic standing. Contact the address below for further information.

Oregon State Scholarship Commission
Private Awards
1500 Valley River Dr., #100
Eugene, OR 97401-2130

2316
Union Pacific Railroad Employee Dependent Scholarship Program

AMOUNT: $750
DEADLINE: February 1
FIELDS/MAJORS: All Areas of Study

Scholarships for sons and daughters of employees of the Union Pacific Railroad (for at least one year by September 1 of year scholarship starts). Must be senior in high school and rank in upper 25% of class. Dependents of retired or deceased employees are also eligible. Sons and daughters of elected officers are not eligible. Contact the address below for further information. Must have a GPA of at least 3.0.

Union Pacific Railroad
Scholarship Administrator
1416 Dodge St., Room 320
Omaha, NE 68179

2317
Union Plus Credit Card Scholarship Program

AMOUNT: $500-$4000 DEADLINE: January 31
FIELDS/MAJORS: All Areas of Study

Scholarships for members and their children of AFL-CIO Unions that participate in the Union Plus Program. Having a Union Plus Card is not necessary for this scholarship. For undergraduate study only. Contact (or have your parent contact) your local union to get more information on this program. Write to the address below (on a postcard) if necessary.

Union Privilege Scholarship Program
Mrs. Wade
1125 15th St. NW, #300
Washington, DC 20005

2318
Unite Scholarship

AMOUNT: $325 DEADLINE: June 30
FIELDS/MAJORS: All Areas of Study

Scholarships for incoming freshmen. Parent must be member of UNITE, Union of Needletrade Industry and Textile Employees, in good standing for at least two years. Children of employees of UNITE itself are not eligible. Three awards per year. Renewable up to four years. Write to the address below for more information.

Union of Needletrade Industries and Textile Employees
UNITE Scholarship Program
15 Union Square
New York, NY 10003

2319
United Daughters of the Confederacy Scholarships

AMOUNT: None Specified DEADLINE: None Specified
FIELDS/MAJORS: Nursing

Scholarships for lineal descendants of worthy confederates or collateral descendants who are members of the Children of the Confederacy or the United Daughters of the Confederacy. The Ship Island award is reserved for graduate studies. Includes the Phoebe Pember Memorial Scholarship, Ship Island, and the Mrs. J.O. Jones Memorial Scholarship. Write to the UDC chapter nearest you. If address is not known, write to the address below for further information and the address.

United Daughters of the Confederacy
Scholarship Coordinator
328 North Boulevard
Richmond, VA 23220

2320
United Paperworkers International Union Scholarship Awards

AMOUNT: Maximum: $1000 DEADLINE: March 15
FIELDS/MAJORS: All Areas of Study

Open to high school seniors who are sons or daughters of paid union members. Awards can be used at accredited undergraduate colleges and universities. Applicants must be U.S. or Canadian citizens. Financial need is a consideration. Write to the address listed for more information.

United Paperworkers International Union
Scholarship Awards Program
PO Box 1475
Nashville, TN 37202

2321
UPS Foundation Education Endowment Fund Scholarships

AMOUNT: Maximum: $3000 DEADLINE: November 7
FIELDS/MAJORS: All Areas of Study

Open to students attending any one of ACI member schools. Each institution determines the criteria for the award. Candidates must be recommended by the financial aid office. Applications are processed in September for the next academic year. Do not write to the listed address, they cannot provide any additional information or forms. Contact your financial aid office for further information. Applicants must be recommended by the financial aid office of their school. The school offices will have the information.

Associated Colleges of Illinois
ACI Program Administration
1735 N. Paulina Ave. Loft 401
Chicago, IL 60622

2322
UPS Scholarships for Female and Minority Students

AMOUNT: Maximum: $2500
DEADLINE: November 15
FIELDS/MAJORS: Industrial Engineering

Scholarships are available for undergraduate industrial engineering majors who are enrolled on a full-time basis, members of the institute, with a GPA of at least 3.4, and of junior standing or below. Applicants must be minority or female students and be nominated by their school's IIE department head. Contact your school's

Industrial Engineering Department Head for information. Must have a GPA of at least 3.4.

Institute of Industrial Engineers
Scholarship Program
25 Technology Park/Atlanta
Norcross, GA 30092

2323
Urban Fellows Program

AMOUNT: Maximum: $18000   DEADLINE: January 20
FIELDS/MAJORS: Urban Government, Public Administration, Planning, Public Service

Full-time program lasting nine months that combines work in mayoral offices and city agencies with an intensive seminar component that explores key issues facing New York city government. For recent bachelor's degree holder (must have received degree within past two years). Must be New York residents. Write to the address listed for complete details.

New York City Department of Personnel
Urban Fellows Program
2 Washington St., 15th Floor
New York, NY 10004

2324
Urban League of Greater Hartford Scholarships for African-Americans

AMOUNT: Maximum: $1000   DEADLINE: May 15
FIELDS/MAJORS: All Areas of Study

Open to African-American high school graduates or GED recipients who are residents of the greater Hartford area. Must be enrolled or accepted to an accredited college or university. Based on community involvement, grades, SAT scores, and financial need. Contact the address listed for further information. Must have a GPA of at least 2.8.

Urban League of Greater Hartford Scholarship
Ms. Beverly LeConche
1229 Albany Ave.
Hartford, CT 06112

2325
USF&G Foundation Scholarship

AMOUNT: $500-$5000   DEADLINE: March 15
FIELDS/MAJORS: All Areas of Study

Open only to USF&G foundation family members of its employees. Awarded on the basis of financial need. Write to the address listed for more information.

USF&G Foundation, Inc.
Sue Lovell. Corp. Foundation Admin.
100 Light St.
Baltimore, MD 21201

2326
Utah Career Teaching Scholarship Program

AMOUNT: None Specified   DEADLINE: March 31
FIELDS/MAJORS: Education/Teaching

Scholarships for Utah residents who plan to pursue a career in teaching. Recipients must attend an accredited Utah public or private college or university. Scholarship is valid for up to four years of full-time equivalent enrollment or until teacher certification requirements are met, whichever is shorter. Program covers full tuition and fees. Recipients are subject to payback regulations if the student does not fulfill his/her promise to teach in Utah schools following completion of training. Write to the address below for details.

Utah State Office of Education
Certification
250 East 500 South
Salt Lake City, UT 84111

2327
Utah State Student Incentive Grant

AMOUNT: Maximum: $2500   DEADLINE: None Specified
FIELDS/MAJORS: All Areas of Study

Scholarships for residents of Utah who demonstrate financial need. For undergraduate study in a Utah college or university. Information and applications available at high school guidance counselor offices and financial aid offices or colleges. Completed forms must be returned to the financial aid offices. Information is available from your high school guidance counselor, the financial aid office of your college, or you can write to the address listed.

Utah State Board of Regents
355 W. North Temple
3 Triad Center, Suite 550
Salt Lake City, UT 84180

2328
Utility Workers Union of America Merit Scholarships

AMOUNT: $500-$2000   DEADLINE: December 31
FIELDS/MAJORS: All Areas of Study

Open to high school students whose parent(s) are members of the Utility Workers Union of America, AFL-CIO. Must be graduating high school in spring of 1999 and enter college in the fall of 1999. Applicants must take the Preliminary SAT/National Merit Scholarship Qualifying Test (PSAT/NMSQT). Write to the address listed for details.

Utility Workers Union of America, AFL-CIO
Scholarship Program Coordinator
815 16th St. NW, #605
Washington, DC 20006

2329
UTUIA Scholarships

AMOUNT: $500 DEADLINE: March 31
FIELDS/MAJORS: All Areas of Study

For U.S. citizens who are high school graduates under twenty-five years of age. Must be UTU members or children/grandchildren of UTU members. Must maintain satisfactory academic record. For full-time study at a community college, vocational-technical school, or four-year college/university. Fifty awards offered each year. Renewable for up to three more years. Write to the address below for additional information.

United Transportation Union Insurance Association
UTUIA Scholarship Program
14600 Detroit Ave.
Cleveland, OH 44107

2330
Velma Flies Anderson Scholarship

AMOUNT: None Specified DEADLINE: July 1
FIELDS/MAJORS: Registered Nursing

Award for students in the senior year of a registered nursing program and reside within the Heartland Service region (northwest Missouri or northeast Kansas). Primarily based on excellence in GPA and clinical performance evaluations. Write to the address listed for more information. Must have a GPA of at least 3.0.

Heartland Health Foundation
801 Faraon
St. Joseph, MO 64501

2331
Ventura County Minority Business Group Scholarships

AMOUNT: Maximum: $4000 DEADLINE: April 8
FIELDS/MAJORS: Business

Applicants must be high school graduating seniors. They must be minority students who are enrolled, or intending to enroll, as a candidate for a business-related degree at a fully accredited college, university, vocation, trade, or business school. Must have a GPA of 3.0 or better and be a resident of Ventura County, California. Write to the address listed or call (805) 988-0196 for more information.

Ventura County Community Foundation
1355 Del Norte Rd.
Camarillo, CA 93010

2332
Vera McKenzie Nursing Scholarship

AMOUNT: Maximum: $500 DEADLINE: April 1
FIELDS/MAJORS: Nursing

Open to high school seniors accepted into the nursing program at Clark College. Must be residents of Clark County or Skamania County. Contact the address listed or call (360) 256-2035 for further information.

Southwest Washington Medical Center
Scholarship Committee
400 N.E. Mother Joseph Pl.
Vancouver, WA 98668

2333
Verne Catt McDowell Corporation Scholarship

AMOUNT: None Specified DEADLINE: None Specified
FIELDS/MAJORS: Theology/Religion

Applicants must be members of the Christian Church (Disciples of Christ) seeking to become ministers and accepted into a graduate program at an approved institution of theological education. Preference given to students from Oregon. Four students are supported at a time. Write to the address shown below for details.

Verne Catt McDowell Corporation
PO Box 1336
Albany, OR 97321-0440

2334
Vernon County Cooperative Association Scholarship

AMOUNT: Maximum: $500 DEADLINE: March 31
FIELDS/MAJORS: Agriculture or Related Field

One scholarship is available to a high school senior to continue studies in agriculture or a related field. Applicant must be enrolled in a Vernon County School System. Write to Judy Neuerburg, chairperson, at the address listed for more details.

Vernon County Cooperative Association
C/O Vernon Electric Cooperative
110 North Main
Westby, WI 54667

2335
Very Special Arts Wisconsin—Earl and Eugenia Quirk Scholarships

AMOUNT: Maximum: $750 DEADLINE: March 27
FIELDS/MAJORS: Fine Art, Music, Dance, Drama, Visual Art, Creative Writing

Open to Wisconsin residents with disabilities who have been accepted to an accredited college or university of fine arts or a related arts oriented program. Entering freshmen must have a minimum high school GPA of 2.5. Purpose is to provide programming in the arts, listed above, for disabled adults and children who can serve as role models for others. Contact the address listed for further information or call (608) 241-2131 Voice/TTY.

Very Special Arts Wisconsin
Heather Dumke
4785 Hayes Rd.
Madison, WI 53704

2336
Veterans Dependents Educational Assistance Program

AMOUNT: $7000 DEADLINE: None Specified
FIELDS/MAJORS: All Areas of Study

Applicants must be surviving children, widows, or spouses of California veterans who are service connected disabled or died of service-related causes. The veteran must have served during a "qualifying war period." Award must be used at California state universities: University of California campuses, and California community colleges. Contact the address listed or their Web site for further information.

California Department of Veterans Affairs
Division of Veterans Services
1227 O St., #101
Sacramento, CA 95814

2337
Veterans Dependents Educational Benefits

AMOUNT: None Specified DEADLINE: None Specified
FIELDS/MAJORS: All Areas of Study

Open to undergraduate Maine residents who are children (not yet twenty-one years old) or spouses of veterans who are totally disabled due to service or who died in service. Write to the address listed for details.

Maine Bureau of Veteran Services
117 State House Station
Augusta, ME 04333

2338
Vice Admiral E.P. Travers Scholarships and Loans

AMOUNT: $500-$3000 DEADLINE: March 1
FIELDS/MAJORS: All Areas of Study

Scholarships for undergraduate children of active duty and retired service members (USN, USMC). Based primarily on need, with academic progress also considered. Must be enrolled full-time and have a GPA of at least 2.0. The Travers loans are interest-free for the parent or spouse of the student. Write to the address listed for information. Please indicate the name of the award program when requesting information.

Navy-Marine Corps Relief Society
Education Programs
801 N. Randolph St., Suite 1228
Arlington, VA 22203

2339
Vicki Carr Scholarship Fund for Texas Students

AMOUNT: None Specified DEADLINE: March 1
FIELDS/MAJORS: All Areas of Study

Awards for Texas residents of Latino heritage. Must be between the ages of seventeen and twenty-two. Must be a U.S. citizen or permanent resident. Send a SASE to the address below for an official application. Applications will only be accepted between January 1 and March 1.

Vicki Carr Scholarship Foundation
PO Box 780968
San Antonio, TX 78278

2340
Vicki Howard Community Service Award

AMOUNT: Maximum: $500 DEADLINE: April 8
FIELDS/MAJORS: All Areas of Study

Awards for graduating high school seniors from the Simi Valley/Moorpark area who have shown outstanding dedication to his/her community through community service. Applicants must have a GPA of 3.0 or greater and be enrolled or intending to enroll as a degree candidate at a fully accredited college, vocation, trade, or business school. Write to the address listed or contact your high school counselor for more information.

Ventura County Community Fund
1355 Del Norte Road
Camarillo, CA 93010

2341
Victor Sikevitz and The Janet and Samuel A. Goldsmith Scholarships

AMOUNT: None Specified DEADLINE: March 1
FIELDS/MAJORS: Communal Service

Open to juniors or above who are legally domiciled in Cook County or the Chicago metro area. For students with career goals in Jewish communal service. Contact the address below for further information after December 1. Must have a GPA of at least 2.7.

Jewish Vocational Service
Academic Scholarship Program
1 S. Franklin St.
Chicago, IL 60606

2342
Vietnam Era Veteran's Children Scholarship

AMOUNT: None Specified DEADLINE: March 1
FIELDS/MAJORS: All Areas of Study

Open to Oregon residents who are children of U.S. Armed Forces veterans who served any portion of their military service between February 28, 1961 and May 7, 1975. Documentation verifying this time frame will be required. This is a one-time award for use at any Oregon college. Contact the address below for further information.

Oregon State Scholarship Commission
Private Awards
1500 Valley River Dr., #100
Eugene, OR 97401-2130

2343
Vietnam Veteran's Scholarship Program

AMOUNT: None Specified DEADLINE: None Specified
FIELDS/MAJORS: All Areas of Study

Vietnam veterans are eligible for scholarships to attend New Mexico schools. Must be a resident of New Mexico, and eligibility must be certified by the New Mexico Veteran's Service Commission. Write to the address below or contact the financial aid office at the New Mexico school of your choice. Information may also be obtained by calling the Veterans Service Commission at (505) 827-6300.

New Mexico Veterans' Service Commission
PO Box 2324
Santa Fe, NM 87503

2344
Vincent K. Derscheid Scholarship Fund

AMOUNT: $2000 DEADLINE: November 29
FIELDS/MAJORS: Accounting

Scholarships are available for junior accounting majors enrolled in a regionally accredited accounting program at a Wisconsin college or university. Based on academic achievement, extracurricular activities, community service, and recommendations from educators. Write to the address below for information.

WICPA Educational Foundation, Inc.
235 N. Executive Dr., Suite 200
PO Box 1010
Brookfield, WI 53008

2345
Virginia Student Financial Aid Program

AMOUNT: None Specified DEADLINE: None Specified
FIELDS/MAJORS: All Areas of Study

Available for undergraduates who are Virginia residents enrolled at least half-time and are able to demonstrate financial need. Must have graduated from a Virginia high school with a minimum GPA of 2.5. For use at any Virginia public college or university. Write to the address listed for more information.

Virginia Council of Higher Education
James Monroe Building
101 North 14th St.
Richmond, VA 23219

2346
Vocational Gold Seal Endorsement Scholarship Program

AMOUNT: $2000 DEADLINE: April 1
FIELDS/MAJORS: Vocational and Technical Fields

Grants for outstanding high school graduates who are Florida residents. Award is given to students who have been awarded the gold seal and will be enrolled in college full-time. Contact your high school guidance office for details.

Florida Department of Education
Office of Student Financial Assistance
1344 Florida Education Center
Tallahassee, FL 32399

2347
Vocational Horticulture Scholarships

AMOUNT: $500-$1000 DEADLINE: April 1
FIELDS/MAJORS: Horticulture, Floriculture

Scholarships for students enrolled in one- or two-year vocational or technical horticulture or floriculture programs. Up to four awards per year. Minimum GPA of 3.0 required. Must be U.S. or Canadian citizen. Write to the address below for details. Please specify your interest in the vocational scholarships program.

Bedding Plants Foundation, Inc.
Scholarship Program
PO Box 27241
Lansing, MI 48909

2348
Vocational Rehabilitation Benefits

AMOUNT: Maximum: $2000 DEADLINE: None Specified
FIELDS/MAJORS: All Areas of Study

Grants for physically or mentally handicapped South Carolina residents who are attending a South Carolina college or university. Based on financial need. Contact the nearest Vocational Rehabilitation Office or the Vocational Rehabilitation Dept., 1410 Boston Ave., PO Box 15, W. Columbia, S.C. 29171.

South Carolina Commission on Higher Education
1333 Main St., Suite 200
Columbia, SC 29201

2349
Vocational Training Grants

AMOUNT: $200-$3000 DEADLINE: None Specified
FIELDS/MAJORS: Vocational/Technical Programs

Must be continuous resident of Marin County for at least one year prior to application. Must be a U.S. citizen and demonstrate financial need. Must be accepted for full- or part-time enrollment in a state licensed or industry sanctioned training program. Write to the address below for details.

Marin Educational Foundation
1010 B St., Suite 300
San Rafael, CA 94901

2350
W. Allen Herzog Scholarship

AMOUNT: Maximum: $400 DEADLINE: June 2
FIELDS/MAJORS: Accounting, Finance

Scholarship is available to undergraduate Tau Kappa Epsilon members who are full-time students pursuing a degree in accounting or finance. Must have a minimum GPA of 2.75. Applicants should have a record of leadership within their chapters and campus organizations. Preference will first be given to members of Nu Chapter, but if no qualified candidate applies, the award will be open to any member of TKE. Write to the address listed for more information.

TKE Educational Foundation
8645 Founders Road
Indianapolis, IN 46268

2351
W. Lincoln Hawkins Undergraduate Research Fellowship

AMOUNT: Maximum: $5000 DEADLINE: None Specified
FIELDS/MAJORS: Chemical Engineering

Open to sophomores who have a minimum GPA of 3.0 and are involved in university supported research. Renewable if recipients maintain a minimum GPA of 3.0. Applicants must be enrolled in any of seventy-nine participating colleges/universities in the U.S and be nominated by the dean. Applicants must also be of African-American, Puerto Rican-American, Mexican-American, or Native American descent. Contact the dean's office of your college for further information. Please do not contact the Council. They will be unable to respond.

National Action Council for Minorities in Engineering
Scholarship Coordinator
3 W. 35th St.
New York, NY 10001-2281

2352
W.H. "Howie" McClennan Scholarship

AMOUNT: $2500 DEADLINE: February 1
FIELDS/MAJORS: All Areas of Study

Awards for high school seniors or undergraduates with a parent who was a firefighter and died in the line of duty. Students must have a minimum GPA of 2.0 and be able to demonstrate financial need. Contact the address below for further information.

International Association of Fire Fighters
Office of the President
1750 New York Ave. NW
Washington, DC 20006

2353
W.M. Keck Foundation Fellowships

AMOUNT: $2300 DEADLINE: December 15
FIELDS/MAJORS: Renaissance, Nineteenth and Twentieth Century Literature, Colonial America

Awards for research to complete a dissertation or to begin a new project. Contact the address listed for further information.

Huntington Library, Art Collections and Botanical Gardens
Robert C. Ritchie, Director of Research
1151 Oxford Rd.
San Marion, CA 91108

2354
Waiver of Tuition

AMOUNT: None Specified DEADLINE: July 1
FIELDS/MAJORS: All Areas of Study

Applicants must be undergraduate students and the child, spouse, widow, or widower of a member of the armed forces who was killed, disabled, or missing in action. Nebraska residency is required, and award is for use at Nebraska schools only. One hundred awards are given annually. Write to the address below for details.

Nebraska Department of Veterans Affairs
PO Box 95083
Lincoln, NE 68509

2355
Wakefield Citizens' Scholarship

AMOUNT: $300-$1450 DEADLINE: None Specified
FIELDS/MAJORS: All Areas of Study

Scholarships for graduating high school seniors who reside in Wakefield, Massachusetts. For full-time study. Financial need is a primary consideration. Write to the address listed for details. Information may also be available from you high school guidance office.

Citizens Scholarship Foundation of Wakefield, Inc.
PO Box 321
Wakefield, MA 01880

2356
Wallace S. and Wilma K. Laughlin Foundation Trust Scholarship Fund

AMOUNT: $1000 DEADLINE: June 15
FIELDS/MAJORS: Mortuary Science

Awards for graduates of a Nebraska high school who meet all the premortuary educational requirements of the Nebraska Bureau of Examining Boards, are recommended by a Nebraska FDA member, and are residents of Nebraska. Write to the address below for more information.

Nebraska Funeral Directors Association
2727 West 2nd St.
PO Box 2118
Hastings, NE 68902

2357
Walter and Marie Schmidt Scholarship (of US Bank Oregon)

AMOUNT: None Specified DEADLINE: March 1
FIELDS/MAJORS: Registered Nursing

Open to Oregon residents who are U.S. citizens enrolled or planning to enroll at least half-time in a training program to become registered nurses. Must have a desire to pursue a career in geriatric healthcare. May apply and compete annually. U.S. Bancorp employees, their children, or near relatives are not eligible to apply for this award. Contact the address listed for further information.

Oregon State Scholarship Commission
Private Awards
1500 Valley River Dr., #100
Eugene, OR 97401-2130

2358
Walter Byers Postgraduate Scholarship

AMOUNT: Maximum: $12500 DEADLINE: January 20
FIELDS/MAJORS: All Areas of Study

Two scholarships for students who have participated in varsity level sports at an NCAA institution. Must be nominated, have a GPA of at least 3.5, and be within 30 semester hours of receiving degree. Write to address below for details.

National Collegiate Athletic Association
6201 College Blvd.
Overlaod Park, KS 66211

2359
Walter Davies (of U.S. Bank of Oregon)

AMOUNT: None Specified DEADLINE: March 1
FIELDS/MAJORS: All Areas of Study

Open to high school seniors and undergraduates who are Oregon residents and are employees or children (natural or adopted) of employees of U.S. Bancorp. Must have graduated from an Oregon high school. Applicants may apply and compete annually. Contact the address below for further information.

Oregon State Scholarship Commission
Private Awards
1500 Valley River Dr., #100
Eugene, OR 97401-2130

2360
Walter Reed Smith Scholarship

AMOUNT: None Specified
DEADLINE: None Specified
FIELDS/MAJORS: Home Economics, Nutrition, Nursing

Scholarships for students in Home Economics who are direct descendants of worthy confederates. Must be able to prove lineage. For women over the age of thirty. Contact the UDC nearest you. If the address is not known, write to the below address for further information and an address.

United Daughters of the Confederacy
Scholarship Coordinator
328 North Boulevard
Richmond, VA 23220

2361
Walter S. Barr Graduate Fellowships

AMOUNT: None Specified   DEADLINE: February 1
FIELDS/MAJORS: All Areas of Study

Fellowships available to Hampden County residents who are furthering their education as full-time graduate students. Write to the executive secretary at the address below for details.

Horace Smith Fund
Executive Secretary
1441 Main St.
Springfield, MA 01102

2362
Walter S. Barr Scholarships and Horace Smith Fund Loans

AMOUNT: None Specified   DEADLINE: December 31
FIELDS/MAJORS: All Areas of Study

Barr Scholarships are for high school seniors who are residents of: Agawam, Chicopee, East Longmeadow, Longmeadow, Ludlow, Springfield, West Springfield, and Wilbraham. Smith loans are for all full-time undergraduate students. If the loans are repaid within one year after graduation, no interest is charged. Write to address below for further details.

Horace Smith Fund
PO Box 3034
Springfield, MA 01101

2363
War Orphans Educational Aid

AMOUNT: Maximum: $600   DEADLINE: None Specified
FIELDS/MAJORS: All Areas of Study

Resident of Iowa for at least two years prior to application. Child of parent who died in, or as a result of, military service during any of the following periods: 4/6/17-6/2/21, 9/16/40-12/31/46, 6/25/50-1/31/55, 8/5/64-5/7/75, and the Persian Gulf Conflict. Must attend a college or university in Iowa. Write to the address below for complete details.

Iowa Division of Veteran Affairs
Camp Dodge
7700 NW Beaver Dr.
Johnston, IA 50131

2364
War Orphans Educational Program

AMOUNT: None Specified   DEADLINE: None Specified
FIELDS/MAJORS: All Areas of Study

Awards for West Virginia students who are children of war veterans who died during active duty or died as a result of active duty. Applicants must be between the ages of sixteen and twenty-three and planning to attend a school within the state of West Virginia. Renewable with a GPA of at least 2.0. For undergraduate study. Write to the address below for complete details.

State of West Virginia, WV Division of Veterans Affairs
Administrative Office of the Division
1321 Plaza East, Suite 101
Charleston, WV 25301

2365
Warren Weaver Fellows Program

AMOUNT: $40000-$55000   DEADLINE: February 28
FIELDS/MAJORS: All Areas of Study

Postdoctoral, one-year, resident fellowships are available at the Rockefeller Foundation in a variety of program areas. (For information about current programs, visit the Foundation's Web site at http://www.rockfound.org). Applicants are strongly encouraged to visit the Foundation's Web site prior to requesting further information. Contact the address listed for complete information.

Rockefeller Foundation
Warren Weaver Fellowship Program
420 Fifth Ave.
New York, NY 10018-2702

2366
Washington Apple Commission Farmworker Education Program

AMOUNT: None Specified DEADLINE: April 15
FIELDS/MAJORS: All Areas of Study

Scholarships available for farmworkers, spouses, or children of farmworkers who have worked as laborers in the apple orchards of Washington state. Applicants must be or will be full-time students in a two- or four-year accredited school. Write to the address listed for additional information.

Washington Apple Commission
PO Box 18
Wenatchee, WA 98807

2367
Washington Crossing Foundation Scholarship

AMOUNT: $5000-$10000 DEADLINE: January 15
FIELDS/MAJORS: Government Service

Applicants must be high school seniors and U.S. citizens who are planning careers in government service at the local, state, or federal level. Award is based on essay, scholarship, and recommendation of high school principal. Write to the address below for details. Must have a GPA of at least 2.8.

Washington Crossing Foundation, Eugene C. Fish, Esquire
1280 General DeFermoy Rd.
PO Box 17
Washington Crossing, PA 18977

2368
Washington Crossing Foundation Scholarships

AMOUNT: $1000-$10000 DEADLINE: January 15
FIELDS/MAJORS: Government Service

Open to high school seniors who are enrolled in or accepted to a four-year school. Selections are based on academics, community service, purpose in and preparation for career choice, historical perspective, and leadership. Contact the address listed for further information. Must have a GPA of at least 2.8.

Washington Crossing Foundation
Eugene C. Fish
PO Box 17
Washington Crossing, PA 18977

2369
Washington Printing Guild Scholarships

AMOUNT: $600-$1000 DEADLINE: February 28
FIELDS/MAJORS: Graphic Arts Education

Open to students accepted into a graphic arts education program and who are residents of the District of Columbia, Maryland, or Virginia. Must be U.S. citizens, have a minimum GPA of 2.5, and be nominated by a supervisor, counselor, or Printing and Graphic Communications Association member employer. Based on financial need and references. Contact the address listed for more information or call (202) 682-3001.

Washington Printing Guild
Scholarship Coordinator
7 West Tower, 1333 H St. NW
Washington, DC 20005-4707

2370
Washington Scholars Program

AMOUNT: None Specified DEADLINE: None Specified
FIELDS/MAJORS: All Areas of Study

Scholarship program for outstanding students in Washington state high schools. Must be nominated by high school principal. Supports study at public or private colleges. Based on academic achievements, leadership, and community service activities. May be renewed if recipients maintain a minimum GPA of 3.3 Contact your counselor or principal for details. Must have a GPA of at least 3.5.

Washington Higher Education Coordinating Board
917 Lakeridge Way
PO Box 43430
Olympia, WA 98504

2371
Wasie Foundation Scholarships

AMOUNT: $1000-$14000 DEADLINE: April 15
FIELDS/MAJORS: All Areas of Study

Awards open to U.S. citizens of Polish ancestry who are full-time students at one of the following Minnesota institutions: College of St. Benedict, College of St. Catherine, College of St. Scholastica, Dunwoody Institute, Hamline University Law School, St. John's University, St. Mary's University of Minnesota, University of Minnesota, Twin Cities, University of St. Thomas, or William Mitchell College of Law. Based on academic ability, leadership, responsibility, career goals, extracurricular activities, and financial need. Write to the address listed for more information.

Wasie Foundation
First Bank Place, Suite 4700
601 Second Ave. South
Minneapolis, MN 55402

2372
Wax Scholarship

AMOUNT: Maximum: $1000 DEADLINE: October 15
FIELDS/MAJORS: Agriculture

Scholarships are available for Georgia residents who are members or children of members of the Georgia Cattlemen's Association. Applicant must be enrolled in an agriculture program at any accredited school of agriculture. Three awards are offered annually. Write to the address below for information.

Georgia Cattlemen's Association/The Wax Company, Inc.
100 Cattlemen's Dr.
Macon, GA 31210

2373
Wayne Kay Graduate Fellowships

AMOUNT: Maximum: $5000 DEADLINE: March 1
FIELDS/MAJORS: Manufacturing Engineering, Industrial Engineering

Open to graduate students who are enrolled in an ABET approved graduate program. Must have a minimum GPA of 3.5. Based on academics, exemplary character, and leadership capability and demonstrated potential for future leadership in the profession. Write to the address listed for details.

Society of Manufacturing Engineering Education Foundation
One SME Dr.
PO Box 930
Dearborn, MI 48121

2374
Wayne Kay Scholarship

AMOUNT: Maximum: $2500 DEADLINE: March 1
FIELDS/MAJORS: Manufacturing Engineering, Manufacturing Technology

Open to full-time undergraduates who have completed at least 30 credit hours in an ABET-accredited program. Applicants must have a minimum GPA of 3.5. Ten awards are offered annually. Write to the address listed for details.

Society of Manufacturing Engineering Education
  Foundation
One SME Dr.
PO Box 930
Dearborn, MI 48121

2375
Weeta F. Colebank and Mississippi Challenge Scholarship

AMOUNT: Maximum: $1000 DEADLINE: April 15
FIELDS/MAJORS: Travel and Tourism, Hotel/Motel Management

For Mississippi residents who are juniors or seniors and enrolled in a four-year college in Mississippi. Must have a GPA of 3.0 or better. Write to the address listed or call 1-800-682-8886 ext. 4251 for more information.

National Tourism Foundation
546 East Main St.
PO Box 3071
Lexington, KY 40596

2376
Welsh Society Scholarships

AMOUNT: $500-$1000 DEADLINE: None Specified
FIELDS/MAJORS: All Areas of Study

Open to high school seniors who are of Welsh descent. Must be residents of Philadelphia, Pennsylvania, and live and be planning to attend any institution within a 150 mile radius of Philadelphia. Based on ACT/SAT scores, potential, goals, extracurricular activities, recommendations, and membership in Welsh organizations. Contact the address listed for further information. Must have a GPA of at least 2.8.

Welsh Society of Philadelphia
Daniel E. Williams
450 Broadway
Camden, NJ 08103

2377
West Hartford Women's Club Scholarship

AMOUNT: Maximum: $1000 DEADLINE: April 1
FIELDS/MAJORS: All Areas of Study

Open to high school seniors who are West Hartford residents. Selections based on academics, school involvement, community service, and financial need. Contact the address listed for further information. Must have a GPA of at least 3.0.

West Hartford Women's Club
Ms. Catherine Davidson
109 S. Main St., #3
West Hartford, CT 06107

2378
West Indian Migrant Farm Workers Memorial Scholarship

AMOUNT: Maximum: $1000 DEADLINE: March 31
FIELDS/MAJORS: All Areas of Study

Open to high school seniors of West Indian heritage. Selections based on academics and financial need. Contact the address listed for further information. Must have a GPA of at least 3.0.

West Indian Foundation, Inc.
Scholarship Committee
PO Box 320394
Hartford, CT 06132-0394

2379
West Virginia Higher Education Grant Program

AMOUNT: $350-$2348 DEADLINE: March 1
FIELDS/MAJORS: All Areas of Study

Applicant must be a U.S. citizen and a resident of West Virginia for one year prior to application. Must enroll as a full-time undergraduate in an approved educational institution in West Virginia or Pennsylvania. Must be able to demonstrate financial need. Contact your high school guidance counselor, your college financial aid office, or the address listed for details.

West Virginia Higher Education Grant Program
State College/University Systems of W.V.
PO Box 4007
Charleston, WV 25364

2380
Western Massachusetts Pharmacists Association Awards

AMOUNT: None Specified DEADLINE: July 31
FIELDS/MAJORS: Pharmacy

Awards open to students who are at least in the third year of a pharmacy program. Must be residents of Hampden, Hampshire, Franklin, or Berkshire counties in Massachusetts. Contact the address listed for further information.

Western Mass. Pharmaceutical Association
Scholarship Committee
PO Box 268
Springfield, MA 01101

2381
Western Sunbathing Association Scholarship Program

AMOUNT: Maximum: $1000 DEADLINE: April 1
FIELDS/MAJORS: All Areas of Study

Scholarships for children of members (for at least three years) of the Western Sunbathing Association. Must be less than twenty-seven years old and have a GPA of at least 2.5. Part-time students will be considered. Two awards per year. Write to the address listed for details.

Western Sunbathing Association, Inc.
WSA Scholarship Committee
PO Box 1168-107
Studio City, CA 91604

2382
Westinghouse/CBS Career Horizons Scholarship

AMOUNT: None Specified
DEADLINE: None Specified
FIELDS/MAJORS: Electrical/Industrial/Mechanical Engineering, Computer Science, Accounting, Business, Finance, Marketing, Communications, Journalism

Open to sophomores and juniors who have a minimum GPA of 3.0 and are enrolled at any of the following historically black colleges or universities: Atlanta University Center, Florida A&M, Howard University, North Carolina A&T University, Prairie View A&M University, Southern University A&M College, Tennessee State University, and Tuskegee University. Contact the financial aid office at your school for information and an application.

United Negro College Fund
Scholarship Program
PO Box 10444
Fairfax, VA 22031-4511

2383
Westmoreland/Penn Virginia Corporation Foundation

AMOUNT: None Specified DEADLINE: December 1
FIELDS/MAJORS: All Areas of Study

Grants to students residing within communities in which Westmoreland and Penn Virginia have any extractive industry operations. Children of employees of Westmoreland and Penn Virginia who are employed within a Westmoreland Mining Division area or by a mining or extractive industry subsidiary are also eligible.

For undergraduate study. Applications are available at your high school. Write to the address listed for more information.

Westmoreland Coal Company and Penn Virginia
    Corporation Foundation
2 North Cascade Ave.
Holly Sugar Building, 14th Floor
Colorado Springs, CO 80903

2384
Westwood Merit Scholarship

AMOUNT: Maximum: $1000 DEADLINE: February 20
FIELDS/MAJORS: All Areas of Study

Open to high school seniors who are residents of Westwood and plan to attend a college or university in the fall. Based on academics, honors, test scores, extracurricular activities, achievements, and employment experience. May be renewable for a total of four years. Contact your high school guidance counselor or the address listed for further information. Must have a GPA of at least 3.0.

Westwood Foundation
Westwood City Hall
4700 Rainbow Blvd.
Westwood, KS 66205

2385
Westwood Vocational/Technical Scholarship

AMOUNT: Maximum: $1000 DEADLINE: February 20
FIELDS/MAJORS: All Areas of Study

Open to high school seniors who are residents of Westwood and plan to attend a Kansas area vocational/technical school in the fall. Based on academics, honors, test scores, extracurricular activities, achievements, and employment experience. Renewable for a total of two years. Contact your high school guidance counselor or the address listed for further information. Must have a GPA of at least 2.4.

Westwood Foundation
Westwood City Hall
4700 Rainbow Blvd.
Westwood, KS 66205

2386
Wexner Graduate Fellowship Program

AMOUNT: None Specified DEADLINE: February 1
FIELDS/MAJORS: Jewish Studies

Awards for North American students who are college graduates and plan to enter a graduate program in preparation for a career in Jewish Education, communal service, the Rabbinate, the Cantorate, or Jewish Studies. Write to the address below for more information.

Wexner Foundation
158 W. Main St.
PO Box 668
New Albany, OH 43054

2387
WFLA National Scholarships

AMOUNT: $1000 DEADLINE: February 1
FIELDS/MAJORS: All Areas of Study

Scholarships are available to full-time students who have been members of the Western Fraternal Life Association for at least two years prior to application. Five awards per year. Write to the address below for information.

Western Fraternal Life Association
1900 First Ave., NE
Cedar Rapids, IA 52402

2388
Wheatland Township Scholarship

AMOUNT: Maximum: $1000 DEADLINE: May 1
FIELDS/MAJORS: All Areas of Study

Open to high school seniors who have been residents of Wheatland Township, Will County, for at least one year. Applicants must have a minimum GPA of 3.0 and demonstrate local government and community service activities. A five hundred word essay will also be required. Contact your high school administrator or the address listed for further information.

Wheatland Township Republican Organization
Donald Raue, Treasurer
28 W. 118 Plainview Dr.
Naperville, IL 60564

2389
Whitney M. Young Memorial Scholarship

AMOUNT: $500-$800 DEADLINE: July 15
FIELDS/MAJORS: All Areas of Study

Available for male or female minority students who are currently enrolled in a postsecondary institution. Students must maintain a GPA of 2.5 or better. Must demonstrate financial need and live in the Chicago area. Write to the address below for more information.

Chicago Urban League
Gina Blake, Scholarship Specialist
4510 South Michigan Ave.
Chicago, IL 60653

2390
Wiche Professional Student Exchange Program

AMOUNT: None Specified DEADLINE: None Specified
FIELDS/MAJORS: See Listing Below

The student exchange program helps Alaska residents obtain access to eight fields of graduate education not available in Alaska but made available at participating institutions in other western states at reduced tuition rate. Fields include dentistry, medicine, occupational therapy, optometry, podiatry, osteopathy, physical therapy, and veterinary medicine. Write to the address listed or call 1-800-441-2962 for information.

Alaska Commission on Postsecondary Education
Wiche Certifying Office
3030 Vintage Blvd.
Juneau, AK 99801

2391
WICI, Seattle Professional Chapter Communications Scholarships

AMOUNT: None Specified DEADLINE: March 3
FIELDS/MAJORS: Communications

Awards for Washington residents and/or students at a four-year institution in the state of Washington. For female juniors, seniors, or graduate students. Three awards offered annually. Applications are available at many financial aid offices and schools or departments of communication, or write to the address below for details and an application.

Women in Communications, Inc., Seattle Professional
  Chapter
WICI Scholarship Chair
8310 SE 61st St.
Mercer Island, WA 98040

2392
WICPA Accounting Scholarships

AMOUNT: $1000 DEADLINE: November 29
FIELDS/MAJORS: Accounting

Scholarships are available for high school seniors who are residents of Wisconsin and are planning to enroll in an accounting program at an accredited Wisconsin college or university. Applicant must have a GPA of at least 3.0. Write to the address below for information.

WICPA Educational Foundation, Inc.
235 N. Executive Dr., Suite 200
PO Box 1010
Brookfield, WI 53008

2393
WICPA Minority Accounting Program

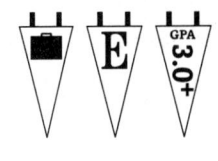

AMOUNT: $4000 DEADLINE: November 29
FIELDS/MAJORS: Accounting

Scholarships are available for high school seniors who are residents of Wisconsin and are planning to enroll in an accredited accounting program at an accredited Wisconsin college or university. Applicant must have a GPA of at least 3.0 and be of Hispanic, African-American, Native-American, or Asian descent. Write to the address below for information.

WICPA Educational Foundation, Inc.
235 N. Executive Dr., Suite 200
PO Box 1010
Brookfield, WI 53008

2394
WICPA North Central Chapter Scholarships

AMOUNT: $1500 DEADLINE: November 29
FIELDS/MAJORS: Accounting

Scholarships are available for junior accounting majors enrolled in a regionally accredited accounting program at a Wisconsin college or university. Based on academic achievement, extracurricular activities, community service, and recommendations from educators. Applicant must have graduated from a high school in the North Central area of Wisconsin. Write to the address below for information.

WICPA Educational Foundation, Inc.
235 N. Executive Dr., Suite 200
PO Box 1010
Brookfield, WI 53008

2395
WICPA Northeast Chapter Scholarships

AMOUNT: $1000 DEADLINE: November 29
FIELDS/MAJORS: Accounting

Scholarships are available for junior accounting majors enrolled in a regionally accredited accounting program at a Wisconsin college or university. Based on academic achievement, extracurricular activities, community service, and recommendations from educators. Applicant must reside in the northeast area of Wisconsin. Write to the address below for information.

WICPA Educational Foundation, Inc.
235 N. Executive Dr., Suite 200
PO Box 1010
Brookfield, WI 53008

2396

Widdy Neale Scholarship

AMOUNT: $1000-$1500 DEADLINE: June 25
FIELDS/MAJORS: All Areas of Study

Open to high school seniors who are Connecticut residents. Must be used at a four-year school. Applicants must have worked at a member golf club and demonstrate good academics and financial need. Contact the address listed for further information. Must have a GPA of at least 2.7.

Connecticut State Golf Association
Mr. Herbert Emanuelson, Scholarship Chair
129 Samson Rock Dr.
Madison, CT 06443

2397

Wilbur C. Stauble Trust Scholarship

AMOUNT: $500-$1500 DEADLINE: January 31
FIELDS/MAJORS: All Areas of Study

Open to dependent children or step children of Veeder Industries, Inc., employees. For use at any two- or four-year college or graduate school. Based on academics, school activities, community service, goals, and personal references. Write to the address listed for more information. Must have a GPA of at least 2.8.

Citizens' Scholarship Foundation of America, Inc.
Citizens Scholarship Foundation
PO Box 297
St. Peter, MN 56082

2398

Wildlife Leadership Awards

AMOUNT: Maximum: $1500 DEADLINE: March 1
FIELDS/MAJORS: Wildlife Science

Awards for full-time undergraduate juniors or seniors enrolled in a wildlife science program. Recipients must have at least one semester or two quarters remaining in their degree program. Write to the address listed for more information.

Rocky Mountain Elk Foundation
Wildlife Leadership Awards-Jodi Bishop
PO Box 8249
Missoula, MT 59807

2399

Wilhelm-Frankowski Medical Education Scholarship

AMOUNT: $3500-$5000 DEADLINE: April 30
FIELDS/MAJORS: Medicine, Osteopathic Medicine

Open to student members in the first, second, or third year of medical or osteopathic medical school. Criteria include: community service and participation in women's health issues and student medical groups other than AMWA. Contact the address below for further information.

American Medical Women's Association Foundation
Maria Glanz
801 N. Fairfax St., #400
Alexandria, VA 22314

2400

Will-South Cook Soil and Water District Scholarships

AMOUNT: Maximum: $750 DEADLINE: April 1
FIELDS/MAJORS: Horticulture, Wildlife, Natural Resources

Open to students attending an accredited college or accredited school of higher learning and live within Will County or in South Cook County (south of 22nd Street). Not based on financial need. Recipients announced in May. Contact the address listed for further information or call (815) 462-3106.

Soil and Water Conservation District, Will-South Cook
District Office, Scholarship Coordinator
1201 S. Gouger Rd.
New Lenox, IL 60451

2401

William A. Fischer Memorial Scholarship

AMOUNT: $2000 DEADLINE: None Specified
FIELDS/MAJORS: Remote Sensing

Award is to facilitate graduate-level studies and career goals adjudged to address new and innovative uses of remote sensing data/techniques that relate to natural, cultural, or agricultural resources. Awards are restricted to members of ASPRS. Write to the address below for more information.

American Society for Photogrammetry and Remote Sensing
ASPRS Awards Program
5410 Grosvenor Ln., Suite 210
Bethesda, MD 20814

2402
William and Ruth Cozard Educational Trust

AMOUNT: None Specified DEADLINE: June 1
FIELDS/MAJORS: All Areas of Study

Students must have graduated from Chamberlain High School, Chamberlain, South Dakota, in order to apply. Must have a minimum GPA of 3.0 These are interest-free loans for students. Write to the address below for information and application.

Norwest Bank South Dakota N.A.
201 S. Main
Chamberlain, SD 57325

2403
William B. Keeling Dissertation Award

AMOUNT: None Specified DEADLINE: March 1
FIELDS/MAJORS: Hotel-Restaurant Administration, Travel and Tourism

This award for Ph.D. dissertations in tourism is given every three years. The next year it will be given is 1999. Submissions are welcomed in the year the award is given. Contact the address listed for further information.

Travel and Tourism Research Association
TTRA Scholarship Committee
546 E. Main St.
Lexington, KY 40508

2404
William B. Rice Aid Fund Inc.

AMOUNT: None Specified DEADLINE: None Specified
FIELDS/MAJORS: All Areas of Study

Applicants must be residents of Hudson, Massachusetts. Demonstrate financial need. Awards are loans and scholarships. Write to the address below for details.

William B. Rice Aid Fund Inc.
C/O Hudson Savings Bank, Attn: Treasure
PO Box 190
Hudson, MA 01749

2405
William B. Ruggles Right to Work Scholarship

AMOUNT: Maximum: $2000 DEADLINE: March 31
FIELDS/MAJORS: Journalism

Scholarships are available for students majoring in journalism. Applicants must submit a five hundred word essay that demonstrates their understanding of the "Right to Work" principle. Write to the address listed for complete details.

National Right to Work Committee
Attn: William B. Ruggles Scholarship
8001 Braddock Road
Springfield, VA 22160

2406
William C. Doherty Scholarship

AMOUNT: Maximum: $800 DEADLINE: December 31
FIELDS/MAJORS: All Areas of Study

Must be natural or legally adopted child of a letter carrier (active, retired, or deceased). Parent must have been a member of the National Association of Letter Carriers for at least one year. Applicant must be a high school senior. Applications and information are available only through The Postal Record (periodical).

National Association of Letter Carriers
Scholarship Committee
100 Indiana Ave. NW
Washington, DC 20001

2407
William C. Ezell Fellowship

AMOUNT: Maximum: $6000 DEADLINE: May 15
FIELDS/MAJORS: Optometry

Fellowships are available for master's or doctoral candidates in optometry who are pursuing a degree on a full-time basis. Write to the address below or contact your department of optometry for information.

American Optometric Foundation
Ezell Fellowship
6110 Executive Blvd., Suite 506
Rockville, MD 20852

2408
William C. Stokoe Scholarship

AMOUNT: Maximum: $1000 DEADLINE: March 15
FIELDS/MAJORS: Deaf Education, Sign Language

Must be a deaf student who is pursuing part-time or full-time graduate studies in a field related to sign language or the deaf community or is developing a special project on one of these topics. Write to the address listed for details.

National Association of the Deaf
Stokoe Scholarship Secretary
814 Thayer Ave.
Silver Spring, MD 20910

2409
William E. Weisel Scholarship

AMOUNT: Maximum: $1000   DEADLINE: March 1
FIELDS/MAJORS: Manufacturing Engineering, technology

Open to full-time undergraduates who have completed at least 30 credit hours and are planning a career in robotics/automated systems. Must be enrolled in an ABET-accredited program, have a GPA of at least 3.5, and be a U.S. or Canadian citizen. One award is given annually. Write to the address listed for details.

Society of Manufacturing Engineering Education Foundation
One SME Dr.
PO Box 930
Dearborn, MI 48121

2410
William F. Miller, M.D. Postgraduate Award

AMOUNT: Maximum: $1000   DEADLINE: June 30
FIELDS/MAJORS: Respiratory Therapy

Scholarship for a respiratory care practitioner who has already earned a bachelor's degree with a minimum GPA of 3.0. Must provide proof of acceptance into an advanced degree program at a fully accredited school. Recipient will be selected by September 1. Write to the address listed for details.

American Respiratory Care Foundation
11030 Ables Ln.
Dallas, TX 75229

2411
William Fairburn, Jr. and Cynthia Fairburn Memorial Scholarships

AMOUNT: Maximum: $2000   DEADLINE: April 8
FIELDS/MAJORS: Liberal Arts, Humanities

Applicants must be graduating high school seniors in Ventura County who intend to pursue studies in liberal arts/humanities at an accredited college or university. Must have a GPA of 3.0 or better. Based on letters of recommendation, essay, and a possible personal interview. Write to the address listed or call (805) 988-0196 for more information.

Ventura County Community Foundation
1355 Del Norte Road
Camarillo, CA 93010

2412
William G. Corey Memorial Scholarship

AMOUNT: Maximum: $3000   DEADLINE: March 1
FIELDS/MAJORS: All Areas of Study

Scholarship awarded to the top applicant from Pennsylvania. Must be legally blind. Write to the address listed or call (202) 467-5081 or 1-800-424-8666 for details.

American Council of the Blind
Scholarship Coordinator
1155 15th St. NW, Suite 720
Washington, DC 20005

2413
William Heath Educational Fund for Ministers, Priests, Missionaries

AMOUNT: $500-$1000   DEADLINE: June 30
FIELDS/MAJORS: Religion, Theology, Social Work

Scholarships for graduates of a high school in the southeastern U.S. who are studying ministry, missionary, or social work. Applicants must be thirty-five years of age or less. Based on character, academic ability, and financial need. Write to the address below for details.

First Florida Bank
William Heath Educational Fund
PO Box 40200
Jacksonville, FL 32203

2414
William J. and Marijane E. Adams, Jr. Scholarship

AMOUNT: $1000   DEADLINE: April 15
FIELDS/MAJORS: Agricultural and Biological Engineering

Available for sophomores, juniors, and seniors in agricultural or biological engineering. Must have a minimum GPA of 2.5 and be a student member of ASAE and your curriculum accredited by ABET or CEAB. Must be able to demonstrate financial need. Award announcement made in September. Write to the address below for more information.

American Society of Agricultural Engineers
The ASAE Foundation
2950 Niles Rd.
St. Joseph, MI 49085

2415
William J. and Marijane E. Adams, Jr. Scholarship

AMOUNT: Maximum: $1000 DEADLINE: April 15
FIELDS/MAJORS: Biological Engineering, Agricultural Engineering

Scholarships are available for undergraduates majoring in biological engineering or agricultural engineering accredited by ABET or CEAB with a GPA of 2.5 or better. Must be student members of ASAE. Winner will be announced in September. Write to the address listed for more information.

Adams Scholarship Fund
ASAE Foundation
2950 Niles Rd.
St. Joseph, MI 49085

2416
William J. and Marijane E. Adams, Jr. Scholarship

AMOUNT: Maximum: $1000 DEADLINE: None Specified
FIELDS/MAJORS: Mechanical Engineering

Open to ASME members attending school in California, Hawaii, or Nevada. Must be at least in second year of study in an ABET-accredited school and have a minimum GPA of 2.5. Must be able to demonstrate financial need and have a special interest in product development and design. Contact the address below for further information. Include a SASE for a reply.

American Society of Mechanical Engineers
Nellie Malave
345 E 47th St.
New York, NY 10017

2417
William J. Locklin Scholarship

AMOUNT: Maximum: $1000 DEADLINE: March 31
FIELDS/MAJORS: Landscape Architecture/Design

Award was initiated to stress the importance of twenty-four hour lighting in landscape designs. Open to students pursuing a program in lighting design or those landscape architectural students focusing on lighting design in studio projects. Write to the address listed for details or call (202) 686-8337. Must have a GPA of at least 2.8.

Landscape Architecture Foundation
Scholarship Program
4401 Connecticut Ave. NW, #500
Washington, DC 20008

2418
William P. Willis Scholarship

AMOUNT: Maximum: $2600 DEADLINE: March 1
FIELDS/MAJORS: All Areas of Study

Scholarships available for low-income, full-time undergraduates attending a public college or university in Oklahoma. Must be Oklahoma residents having an effective gross income of less than $20,000. One award per public institution. Requires nomination by college/university president. Contact your school's financial aid office for further information. Must have a GPA of at least 2.5.

Oklahoma State Regents for Higher Education
William P. Willis Scholarship Program
500 Education Bldg. State Capitol Complex
Oklahoma City, OK 73105-4503

2419
William Randolph Hearst Minority Scholarships

AMOUNT: Maximum: $2500 DEADLINE: None Specified
FIELDS/MAJORS: Pre-Engineering, Engineering

Open to high school seniors with demonstrated academic excellence, leadership skills, and a commitment to a career in engineering. Renewable if recipients maintain a minimum GPA of 3.0. Available for use at seventy-nine colleges/universities in the U.S. Applicants must be of African-American, Puerto Rican-American, Mexican-American, or Native American descent. Contact counselors at your high schools or the financial aid office of the college you plan to attend for further information. If this information is in your profile, you have indicated that you will be attending one of the participating schools. Please do not contact the Council. They will be unable to respond. Must have a GPA of at least 3.3.

National Action Council for Minorities in Engineering
Scholarship Coordinator
3 W. 35th St.
New York, NY 10001-2281

2420
William Tasse Alexander Scholarship

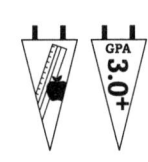

AMOUNT: $1000-$3500 DEADLINE: March 1
FIELDS/MAJORS: Teaching/Education

Scholarships for residents of Mecklenberg County, North Carolina, who plan to pursue teaching as a career. For junior and senior undergraduates. Must have at least a 3.0 GPA. Write to the address below for details on this and other scholarships administered by the foundation.

Foundation for the Carolinas
301 S. Brevard St.
Charlotte, NC 28202

2421
William W. Burgin, Jr., Medical Scholarship

AMOUNT: Maximum: $2500 DEADLINE: June 30
FIELDS/MAJORS: Respiratory Therapy

Award for a second-year student in an accredited respiratory therapy program. Must have a GPA of at least 3.0. Based on recommendations and an essay. Must provide copies of birth certificate, social security card, immigration visa, or other evidence of citizenship. Write to the address listed for more information.

American Respiratory Care Foundation
Scholarship Committee
11030 Ables Ln.
Dallas, TX 75229

2422
William Wilson Memorial and Wallace G. McCauley Memorial Scholarships

AMOUNT: Maximum: $600 DEADLINE: June 2
FIELDS/MAJORS: All Areas of Study

Awards for members of Tau Kappa Epsilon who are full-time students at the junior or senior level of study. Applicants should have demonstrated exceptional understanding of the importance of good alumni relations to the Chapter and its members and have excelled in the development, promotion, and execution of effective programs that have increased alumni contact, awareness, and participation in Fraternity activities. Two awards offered annually. Write to the address listed for more information.

TKE Educational Foundation
8645 Founders Road
Indianapolis, IN 46268

2423
Wilma Hoyle-Maxine Chilton Memorial Scholarships

AMOUNT: $400 DEADLINE: May 15
FIELDS/MAJORS: Political Science, Public Programs, Special Education

Scholarships are available for Arizona residents who are U.S. citizens. Applicants must be at least sophomores enrolled at the University of Arizona, Arizona State University, or Northern Arizona University. Honorably discharged veterans or immediate family members of veterans will be given preference. Write to the address listed for information.

American Legion Auxiliary-Department of Arizona
Scholarship Coordinator
4701 N. 19th Ave., #100
Phoenix, AZ 85015

2424
Wilson-Cook Endoscopic Research Scholar Award

AMOUNT: $36000 DEADLINE: January 9
FIELDS/MAJORS: Endoscopic Research

Applicants must hold full-time faculty positions at universities or professional institutes. Young faculty, reaching the level of assistant professor or equivalent, are eligible. Candidates must devote at least 30% of their effort in research related to gastrointestinal endoscopy. Five awards are given annually. Contact the address below for further information or Web sites: http://www.gastro.org; http://www.asge.org; or http://hepar-sfgh.ucsf.edu.

American Digestive Health Foundation
Ms. Irene Kuo
7910 Woodmont Ave., 7th Floor
Bethesda, MD 20814

2425
Winnie C. Davis—Children of the Confederacy Scholarship

AMOUNT: None Specified DEADLINE: None Specified
FIELDS/MAJORS: All Areas of Study

Scholarships for members of the Children of the Confederacy. Must be approved by the third vice president general. Write to the UDC chapter nearest you. If address is not known, write to the address below for further information and the address.

United Daughters of the Confederacy
Scholarship Coordinator
328 North Boulevard
Richmond, VA 23220

2426
Winston E. Parker Scholarship

AMOUNT: $2000-$3000 DEADLINE: May 1
FIELDS/MAJORS: Forestry, Arboriculture, Ornamental Horticultural, or Related Fields

Scholarships available to college students in their junior, senior, or graduate years of study in one of the fields listed above. Applicant must reside in central or southern New Jersey. Write to the address below for details.

Moorestown Rotary Charities Inc.
Winston E. Parker Scholarship Committee
PO Box 105
Moorestown, NJ 08057

2427
Winterthur Museum Fellowships

AMOUNT: $1000-$30000
DEADLINE: January 15
FIELDS/MAJORS: See Listing Below

Fellowships are available for doctoral and postdoctoral research at the Winterthur Museum and Library in African-American history, cultural history, historic preservation, folklore, anthropology, archaeology, art history, decorative arts, material culture, preindustrial technology, women's history, architectural history, and urban studies. Generally, stipends are $1000 to $2000 per month, and the fellowships range from one to six months. Must be U.S. citizens to apply. Write to the address listed for information.

Winterthur Museum and Library
Advanced Studies Office
Research Fellowship Program
Winterthur, DE 19735

2428
Wisconsin Coulee Region Community Action Scholarships

AMOUNT: Maximum: $100 DEADLINE: April 1
FIELDS/MAJORS: Human Services

Open to high school seniors who are residents of Crawford, LaCrosse, Monroe, or Vernon counties, Wisconsin. Applicants must be interested in careers in the human services field. Contact your high school guidance counselor for further information, the address listed, or the second CAP office at 106 N. Main in Viroqua.

Wisconsin Coulee Region Community Action Program, Inc.
Scholarship Coordinator
201 Melby
Westby, WI 54667

2429
Wisconsin League for Nursing Scholarship Program

AMOUNT: Maximum: $500 DEADLINE: None Specified
FIELDS/MAJORS: Nursing

Twelve scholarships for students in National League for Nursing accredited programs in Wisconsin. Must be U.S. citizens and Wisconsin residents. Must be at least halfway through an academic program. Categories include RN seeking a BSN, student seeking RN (ADN diploma or BSN), and BSN/RN seeking MSN. Must have GPAs of at least 3.0. Contact the office of the dean at your nursing school for details, or write to the address listed for more details.

Wisconsin League for Nursing, Inc.
2121 E. Newport Ave.
Milwaukee, WI 53211

2430
Wisconsin PTA Scholarship Program

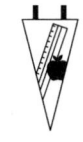

AMOUNT: $1000 DEADLINE: February 15
FIELDS/MAJORS: Education

Wisconsin resident. Open to seniors in public high schools. Awarded to high school graduate who intends to pursue a career in the field of education. Write for complete details.

Wisconsin PTA
4797 Hayes Rd, Suite 2
Madison, WI 53704

2431
Wisconsin Restaurant Association Scholarships

AMOUNT: $750-$1500 DEADLINE: March 4
FIELDS/MAJORS: Foodservice, Culinary Arts, Hospitality Management

Scholarships open to Wisconsin residents. They are available for full-time students in two-year technical programs in Wisconsin schools and students enrolled full-time in four-year programs in any school in the U.S. Non-traditional students are encouraged to apply. Students must be employed at a Wisconsin foodservice establishment to apply. Recipients may reapply each year of their programs. Contact the address below for further information or call (608) 251-3663.

Wisconsin Restaurant Association Education Foundation
Carrianne Wolfe
31 S. Henry St., #300
Madison, WI 53703-3110

2432
WISE Internships

AMOUNT: $1750 DEADLINE: December 19
FIELDS/MAJORS: Engineering

A ten-week summer program competition open to seniors majoring in engineering. Recipients will be under the guidance of a nationally prominent engineering professor and can earn three transferable credit hours. Additionally, students will interact with leaders in Congress, administration, industry, and non-government organizations. There is a stipend of $1750, and lodging and travel expenses are paid. Must have a GPA of at least 3.0.

Washington Internships for Students of Engineering
Anne Hickox, WISE Program
400 Commonwealth Dr.
Warrendale, PA 15096-0001

2433

Woman's Club of Lake Geneva Scholarships

AMOUNT: None Specified DEADLINE: June 20
FIELDS/MAJORS: All Areas of Study

Scholarships for residents of the badger high school district (in Walworth County, Wisconsin). Based on grades, course of study, and need. For upperclass students. Applications are available from Annie's ice cream parlor, or write to the address below for details.

Lake Geneva Woman's Club
C/O Mrs. Dora Halsey
1032 Bonnie Brae Ln.
Lake Geneva, WI 53147

2434

Women in Management Scholarship

AMOUNT: None Specified DEADLINE: April 1
FIELDS/MAJORS: Management, Business

Open to students enrolled in a degree program planning to pursue a management or business career. One undergraduate award and one award for graduates. Contact the address listed for further information.

Women in Management, Inc.
Scholarship Chairperson
PO Box 1334
Dubuque, IA 52004-1334

2435

Women on Books Scholarship

AMOUNT: Maximum: $1000 DEADLINE: June 12
FIELDS/MAJORS: English, Journalism, Creative Writing

Open to African-American students who have a minimum GPA of 2.5. Must be currently attending a four-year school and pursuing a writing career (creative or journalism). Must also be able to demonstrate financial need. Contact the address below for further information.

Women on Books
Scholarship Committee
879 Rainier Ave. N, #A105
Renton, WA 98055

2436

Women's Auxiliary Scholarship Loan Fund

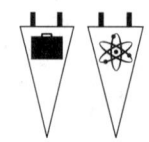

AMOUNT: None Specified DEADLINE: March 15
FIELDS/MAJORS: Mining, Metallurgy, Material Science, Earth Science, Geology

Loans available for full-time junior or senior college or university students and graduate students for a degree in earth sciences or related fields. Other fields recognized include petroleum and mining economics. Preference given to undergraduates, and each recipient commits to repaying 50% of the money lent with no interest charge. Repayment begins no later than six months after graduation. Contact the chapter of WAAIME at your college or university for details. If necessary to find out the address of your local scholarship loan fund chairman, write to the address listed. Application forms are not sent until after the interview.

WAAIME Headquarters
Scholarship Loan Fund
345 E. 47th St., 14th Floor
New York, NY 10017

2437

Women's Opportunity Award

AMOUNT: $3000-$5000 DEADLINE: December 1
FIELDS/MAJORS: All Areas of Study

Open to mature women who are heads of households, who need additional skills, training, and education to upgrade their employment status. Only women working toward a vocational or undergraduate degree are eligible. Application is made through participating Soroptimist Clubs. Club addresses can be found in your local telephone directory, chamber of commerce, or city hall. If you cannot find a Club nearby, you may write to the address listed. Include a SASE for a reply.

Soroptimist International of the Americas, Inc.
Women's Opportunity Awards Coordinator
2 Penn Center Plaza, #1000
Philadelphia, PA 19102-1883

2438

Women's Research and Education Institute Congressional Fellowship

AMOUNT: None Specified DEADLINE: February 15
FIELDS/MAJORS: Women and Public Policy Issues

Annual fellowship program that places women graduate students in congressional offices and on strategic committee staffs, encouraging more effective participation by women in the formation of policy at all levels. Must be currently enrolled in a graduate degree program. Award is tuition and a living stipend for an academic year. Write to the address below for details, and enclose a SASE.

Women's Research and Education Institute
Shari Miles, Director
1750 New York Ave. NW, #350
Washington, DC 20006

2439
Women's Resource Center of Sarasota Scholarship

AMOUNT: None Specified DEADLINE: None Specified
FIELDS/MAJORS: All Areas of Study

Scholarships are available for female residents of Sarasota County who are single, divorced (or in the process of divorce), legally separated, widowed, or have a disabled spouse. Must be twenty-one years of age or older, a high school graduate, and accepted into their program of choice. Applications available January 5 at area school financial aid offices and at the Center. Write to the address listed for further information.

Women's Resource Center of Sarasota
Scholarship Coordinator
340 S. Tuttle Ave.
Sarasota, FL 34237

2440
Women's Studies Research Grants

AMOUNT: Maximum: $1500 DEADLINE: November 3
FIELDS/MAJORS: Women's Studies

For doctoral candidates in the above fields who will soon complete all doctoral requirements except the dissertation. These grants are to be used for research expenses connected with the dissertation. The purpose is to encourage original and significant research on topics about women. Approximately twenty awards per year. Write to the attention of Women's Studies Department for further information. Application request deadline is October 17.

Woodrow Wilson National Fellowship Foundation
Women's Studies Research Grants
CN 5281
Princeton, NJ 08543

2441
Woodie and Mabel Best Scholarships (of U.S. Bank of Oregon)

AMOUNT: None Specified DEADLINE: March 1
FIELDS/MAJORS: All Areas of Study

Open to Oregon residents who are U.S. citizens or permanent residents and who are graduating (or have graduated) from a high school in Harney County. Minimum GPA for high school seniors is 3.0, and current undergraduates must have a minimum of 2.75. U.S. Bancorp employees, their children, or near relatives are not eligible for the award. Contact the address below for further information.

Oregon State Scholarship Commission
Private Awards
1500 Valley River Dr., #100
Eugene, OR 97401-2130

2442
Woodrow Wilson Fellowships

AMOUNT: $43000 DEADLINE: October 1
FIELDS/MAJORS: Research in Humanities, Social Sciences

Residential fellowships for postdoctoral scholars for advanced research in the fields above. Selection primarily based on scholarly promise, importance and originality of project proposal, and the likelihood that the work will advance basic understanding of the topic of study. Applicants must hold a doctorate or have equivalent professional accomplishments. Write to the address listed for more information.

Woodrow Wilson International Center
Fellowships Office
1000 Jefferson Dr. SW, SI MRC 022
Washington, DC 20560

2443
Work/Learn Program Internships

AMOUNT: None Specified DEADLINE: November 1
FIELDS/MAJORS: Environmental Research

Internships available to undergraduates and graduate students in the field of environmental research. November 1 is the deadline for full-time internships offered in spring (January-May), and March 1 is the deadline for the internships offered in summer (May-August) each year. Dormitory space is available on the premises. There is a stipend offered of $190 through $250 per week. Write to the address listed for further information.

Smithsonian Environmental Research Center
Work/Learn Program
PO Box 28
Edgewater, MD 21037

2444
Workshops and Courses to Improve Language Teaching and Pedagogy

AMOUNT: Maximum: $5000 DEADLINE: October 1
FIELDS/MAJORS: Japanese Language

Grants are available for scholars to design workshops or courses to improve the teaching of the Japanese language at the college or pre-college level. Applicants should be prepared to explain the character or rationale of their project and be able to prepare a budget estimate. Write to the address below for more information.

Northeast Asia Council Association for Asian Studies
1 Lane Hall
University of Michigan
Ann Arbor, MI 48109

2445
Writers of the Future Contest

AMOUNT: $500-$4000 DEADLINE: None Specified
FIELDS/MAJORS: Science Fiction or Fantasy Writing

Contest for amateur science fiction writers. Entries must be works of prose (short stories or novels) that have not been previously published. Write to the address below for more details.

L. Ron Hubbard
PO Box 1630
Los Angeles, CA 90078

2446
WTA Scholarship Fund

AMOUNT: None Specified DEADLINE: March 6
FIELDS/MAJORS: Transportation

Scholarships are available for Wyoming high school graduates enrolled at or planning to enroll at a Wyoming college, university, or trade school, who plan to pursue a career in transportation. Write to the address listed for information.

Wyoming Trucking Association
PO Box 1909
Casper, WY 82602

2447
WTOL-TV Broadcast and Communications Scholarship

AMOUNT: $3000 DEADLINE: None Specified
FIELDS/MAJORS: Broadcast Communications

Awards open to African-American and Hispanic-American undergraduates from the Toledo, Ohio, area. Must be at least a junior with a minimum GPA of 3.0. Contact the address below for further information.

Fifty Men and Women of Toledo and Image, NW
   Ohio Chapter
J.C. Caldwell
PO Box 80056
Toledo, OH 43608

2448
Wyeth Fellowship

AMOUNT: $16000 DEADLINE: November 15
FIELDS/MAJORS: American Art

Two-year fellowships are available for doctoral scholars researching for the dissertation. One year will be spent on research, and one year will be spent at the National Gallery of Art. Applicants must know two foreign languages related to the topic of the dissertation and be U.S. citizens or legal residents. One fellowship is given annually. Write to the address below for information.

National Gallery of Art
Center for Advanced Study in Visual Arts
Predoctoral Fellowship Program
Washington, DC 20565

2449
Wyeth-Ayerst Scholarships

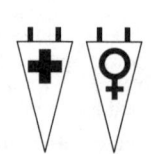

AMOUNT: $2000 DEADLINE: April 15
FIELDS/MAJORS: Bio/Medical Research and Technology, Pharmaceuticals, Public Health

Scholarships are open to women twenty-five years of age or older who are U.S. citizens studying in one of the fields above. Applicants must be graduating within twelve to twenty-four months from September 1, demonstrate need for financial assistance, and be accepted into an accredited program of course study at a U.S. institution. Student must have a plan to use the training to upgrade skills for career advancement, to train for a new career field, or to enter or re-enter the job market. Write to the address below for details.

Business and Professional Women's Foundation
Scholarships
2012 Massachusetts Ave. NW
Washington, DC 20036

2450
Wyoming Scholarship Challenge Program

AMOUNT: Maximum: $1000 DEADLINE: April 15
FIELDS/MAJORS: Travel and Tourism, Hotel/Motel Management

Awards for Wyoming residents in one of the areas listed above who are enrolled in a two- or four-year college full-time. Must have a GPA of 3.0 or better. Write to the address listed or call 1-800-682-8886 ext. 4251 for more information.

National Tourism Foundation
546 East Main St.
PO Box 3071
Lexington, KY 40596

2451
Yale Center for British Art Fellowships

AMOUNT: None Specified   DEADLINE: January 15
FIELDS/MAJORS: British Art, History, or Literature

Visiting fellowships enable scholars engaged in postdoctoral or equivalent research in British art, history, or literature to study the center's holdings of paintings, drawings, prints, and rare books and to make use of its research facilities. Grants cover travel and per diem and normally run for a period of four weeks. Contact address listed or call (203) 432-2822 for complete information.

Yale Center for British Art
1080 Chapel St.
PO Box 208280
New Haven, CT 06520

2452
Yale New Haven Hospital Minority Nursing/Allied Health Scholarship

AMOUNT: Maximum: $1500   DEADLINE: March 1
FIELDS/MAJORS: Nursing, Allied Health

Open to high school seniors who are Connecticut residents and enrolled or accepted into a four-year school with an accredited nursing or allied health program. Based on financial need and academics. Contact the address listed for further information. Must have a GPA of at least 2.7.

Yale New Haven Hospital
C/O Human Resources
20 York St.
New Haven, CT 06504

2453
Yanmar/Society of Automotive Engineers Scholarship

AMOUNT: $1000-$2000   DEADLINE: April 1
FIELDS/MAJORS: Engineering, Natural Resources, Nuclear Science, Mathematics

Open to North American citizens at college senior or graduate level. Studies must be related to the conservation of energy in transportation, agriculture, construction ,and power generation. Special emphasis is placed on study or research related to the internal combustion engine. Contact the address listed for further information or call (724) 772-8534.

Yanmar/Society of Automotive Engineers
Lori Pail, Scholarship Coordinator
400 Commonwealth Dr.
Warrendale, PA 15096-0001

2454
Yellow Ribbon Scholarship

AMOUNT: Maximum: $500   DEADLINE: April 15
FIELDS/MAJORS: Travel and Tourism, Hotel/Motel Management

Open to students with disabilities who are residents of North America and enrolled in a college in North America. High school seniors must have a GPA of 3.0 or better, and continuing students must have a GPA of at least 2.5. Write to the address listed or call 1-800-682-8886 ext. 4251 for more information.

National Tourism Foundation
546 East Main St.
PO Box 3071
Lexington, KY 40596

2455
YMA Scholarship Program

AMOUNT: Maximum: $4000   DEADLINE: August 31
FIELDS/MAJORS: Men's Apparel/Textile Industry Related Fields

Ten scholarships for students attending Fashion Institute of Technology, Pratt Institute, Philadelphia College of Textiles and Sciences, or North Carolina State University. Based on need and merit. The individual colleges determine the winners of the awards. Application for these awards is made through the financial aid office at your college (not the YMA).

Young Menswear Association
YMA Scholarship Program
1328 Broadway
New York, NY 10001

2456
York Foundation Scholarships

AMOUNT: $500-$2000   DEADLINE: April 1
FIELDS/MAJORS: All Areas of Study

Open to high school juniors, with preference given to students attending schools in the Spring Grove area. Contact the address listed for further information or call (717) 843-8651.

York Foundation
Mrs. Cline
20 W. Market St.
York, PA 17401

2457
Yoshiko Tanaka Memorial Scholarship

AMOUNT: None Specified DEADLINE: April 1
FIELDS/MAJORS: Japanese Language and Culture

Available to undergraduate students of Japanese ancestry who have an interest in Japanese language, culture, or enhancing U.S. Japanese relations. Applicants must be members of the Japanese-American Citizens League. Write to the address listed for more details or call (415) 921-5225. Please be sure to include a SASE with your request.

Japanese-American Citizens League
National Headquarters
1765 Sutter St.
San Francisco, CA 94115

2458
Yoshiyama Award for Exemplary Service to the Community

AMOUNT: $5000 DEADLINE: April 1
FIELDS/MAJORS: All Areas of Study

Awards are available for graduating high school seniors in the United States and territories engaged in extraordinary community service. Ten to fifteen awards offered annually. Submit nomination packages to the Yoshiyama Award, PO Box 19247, Washington, DC 20036-9247. Must have a GPA of at least 2.7.

Hitachi Foundation
1509 22nd St. NW
Washington, DC 20037

2459
You've Got a Friend in Pennsylvania Scholarship

AMOUNT: $1000 DEADLINE: February 1
FIELDS/MAJORS: All Areas of Study

Scholarship available to students with a general class amateur radio license who are residents of Pennsylvania and members of AARL. For full-time study in a program leading to a baccalaureate or higher degree. Write to the address listed for information.

ARRL Foundation (American Radio Relay League)
Scholarship Program
225 Main St.
Newington, CT 06111

2460
Young Arts Scholarship Competition

AMOUNT: $500-$1000 DEADLINE: February 1
FIELDS/MAJORS: Arts

Students enrolled as a seniors in accredited Texas high schools are eligible to enter the competition. Students may enter in the following categories: fiber, glass, graphics/drawing, jewelry, leather, metal works, painting, photography, pottery, sculpture, or wood craft. Contact the address listed for further information.

Texas Arts and Crafts Educational Foundation
Official Texas State Arts and Crafts Fair
PO Box 1527
Kerrville, TX 78029-1527

2461
Young Lawyers Program

AMOUNT: None Specified DEADLINE: March 15
FIELDS/MAJORS: Law

Grants to lawyers who hold the JD or LLB degree, have passed the bar exam, and who are under the age of thirty-two. This program offers young lawyers the chance to gain unique insight into the structure and function of German law through ten months of taking legal courses and interning in Germany. Applicants must be fluent in German and be U.S. or Canadian citizens. Write to the address listed for further information.

Daad German Academic Exchange Service
New York Office
950 Third Ave., 19th Floor
New York, NY 10022

2462
Young Manufacturer of the Year Scholarships

AMOUNT: Maximum: $2500 DEADLINE: February 15
FIELDS/MAJORS: Computer Science, Chemical/Biological Science, Agriculture/Food Processing, Mechanical/Manual

Open to California high school seniors as part of California Manufacturing Week, March 15-21. Awards will be presented that week. Information and applications have already been sent to all the high schools throughout the state. Contact your high school guidance office for further information. If they are out of materials, they may contact Mr. Jeff Gorell, Communications Director, at (916) 498-3315. Must have a GPA of at least 2.9.

California Manufacturers Association

2463
Young Printer's Executive Club Scholarship

AMOUNT: Maximum: $2500   DEADLINE: June 1
FIELDS/MAJORS: Printing Management

Open to residents of New York, New Jersey, and Connecticut who are enrolled at the Rochester Institute of Technology. Must have a minimum GPA of 3.0 and be committed to one interview in the tri-state area. May be renewed. Contact the address listed for further information or (212) 685-2995.

Young Printer's Executive Club
Jim Printergash
220 E. 42nd St., #402
New York, NY 10017

2464
Youth Activity Grants

AMOUNT: None Specified   DEADLINE: April 1
FIELDS/MAJORS: Natural Sciences

Open to high school seniors and undergraduates to help them participate in field research, under the supervision of a qualified scientist, anywhere in the world. Applicants must be U.S. citizens. Awards will be announced about the end of May. Write to the address listed for complete details. Must have a GPA of at least 2.9.

Explorers Club
Youth Activity Fund
46 East 70th St.
New York, NY 10021

2465
Youth Automobile Safety Essay Competition

AMOUNT: Maximum: $500   DEADLINE: March 15
FIELDS/MAJORS: All Areas of Study

This essay contest is open to high school seniors who are California residents. Must have a minimum GPA of 3.0 and be accepted to an accredited two- or four-year college, university, or trade school in the U.S. Must be intending to enroll as a full-time freshman by fall, 1998. Applicant's parent or legal guardian must be currently employed full-time by a government entity. If parent or guardian is retired or deceased, they must have been employed full-time. Winners will be notified by May 15, 1998. Contact the address below for further information.

Civil Service Employees Insurance Company
Scholarship Contest
PO Box 7764
San Francisco, CA 94120-7764

2466
Yutaka Nakazawa Memorial Scholarship

AMOUNT: None Specified   DEADLINE: April 1
FIELDS/MAJORS: Judo

Applicants must be Japanese-American Citizen League members studying judo at the college level. Applications and information may be obtained from local JACL chapters, district offices, and the national headquarters at the address listed, or call (415) 921-5225. Please indicate your level of study and be certain to include a legal-sized SASE.

Japanese-American Citizens League
National Scholarship and Award Program
1765 Sutter St.
San Francisco, CA 94115

2467
Zola N. and Lawrence R. Nell Educational Trust Scholarship Program

AMOUNT: None Specified   DEADLINE: May 1
FIELDS/MAJORS: Medicine, Dentistry, or Related Fields

Applicants must be graduates of a high school in Segdwick County, Kansas (Wichita, Kansas area). Must be qualified students who have been accepted for the study of medicine, dentistry, or other health practitioners programs at the post-baccalaureate level and return to Kansas for practice. All applicants should provide the address and phone number where they may be reached from April through June. Write to the address listed for more information.

Commerce Bank, N.A.
Attn: Judy Quick, IMG Dept.
PO Box 637
Wichita, KS 67201

2468
Zonta Scholarship

AMOUNT: Maximum: $1000   DEADLINE: May 15
FIELDS/MAJORS: All Areas of Study

Scholarships for area women who are returning to school after an interruption, with the intention of returning to the work force afterwards. Awards will be one for $1000 or two awards for $500 each. Awards dependent on number and types of applications received. Write to the address below for details.

Zonta Club of Green Bay
Scholarship Program
PO Box 97
Green Bay, WI 54305

School Specific Awards

ABILENE CHRISTIAN UNIVERSITY

2469
Leadership Award

AMOUNT: Maximum: $4000 DEADLINE: February 15
FIELDS/MAJORS: All Areas of Study

For incoming undergraduates who scored 20 to 24 on the ACT and 820 to 1020 on the SAT and have fewer than 25 credit hours. Must be affiliated with the churches of Christ and a resident of campus-owned housing. Write to the address below or call 1-800-460-6228 or (915) 674-2643 for more information. GPA must be at least 2.5.

Abilene Christian University
Leadership Scholarship Committee
ACU Box 6000
Abilene, TX 79699

2470
National Merit Finalist Scholarship

AMOUNT: $8116 DEADLINE: March 1
FIELDS/MAJORS: All Areas of Study

Students entering ACU who are National Merit Finalists with fewer than 25 credit hours. Write to the address below or call 1-800-460-6228 or (915) 674-2643 for more information. GPA must be at least 3.5.

Abilene Christian University
Office of Admissions
ACU Box 6000
Abilene, TX 79699

2471
Presidential Full-Tuition Scholar Award

AMOUNT: None Specified DEADLINE: March 15
FIELDS/MAJORS: All Areas of Study

Awards are available for entering freshmen who have a minimum GPA of 3.5 in high school, an ACT score of at least 28 or an SAT score of at least 1240, who have no more than 14 credit hours. Must reside on campus and be enrolled for a minimum of 15 semester hours. Write to the address below or call 1-800-460-6228 or (915) 674-2643 for more information.

Abilene Christian University
Mr. Don King, Director of Admissions
ACU Box 6000
Abilene, TX 79699

2472
Transfer Scholarship

AMOUNT: $1000-$2000 DEADLINE: March 1
FIELDS/MAJORS: All Areas of Study

Awards open to transfer students with a minimum of 24 credit hours and a minimum GPA of 3.25. Contact the address below or call 1-800-460-6228 or (915) 674-2643 for further information.

Abilene Christian University
Student Financial Services
ACU Box 29007
Abilene, TX 79699

2473
Trustee Scholarships

AMOUNT: $500-$4500 DEADLINE: March 1
FIELDS/MAJORS: All Areas of Study

Scholarships for undergraduates entering with fewer than 25 credit hours. Must have received a minimum of 22 on the ACT or 910 or above on the SAT. Write to the address below or call 800-460-6228 or (915) 674-2643 for more information. GPA must be at least 2.5.

Abilene Christian University
Office of Admissions
ACU Box 6000
Abilene, TX 79699

ACADEMY OF BUSINESS COLLEGE

2474
Academy of Business College Scholarships

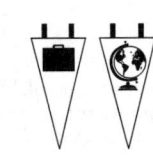

AMOUNT: $2000 DEADLINE: April 18
FIELDS/MAJORS: Business, Computer, Legal Field

Scholarships are awarded to outstanding high school seniors interested in careers in business, computer, or the legal field. Must have a minimum GPA of 2.2 during junior and senior years and be involved in extracurricular school activities or community service activities. Effective writing skills are a plus. Three awards are offered annually. Write to the address below for more information.

Academy of Business College
2525 W. Beryl Ave.
Phoenix, AZ 85021-1641

ACADEMY OF NATURAL SCIENCES OF PHILADELPHIA

2475
Jessup/McHenry Awards

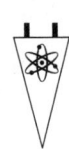

AMOUNT: None Specified DEADLINE: March 1
FIELDS/MAJORS: Botany

Grants for pre- and postdoctoral students who require the resources of the Academy of Natural Sciences of Philadelphia. Studies are performed under the supervision of a member of the curatorial staff of the Academy. The studies are to be conducted at the Academy. The McHenry fund is limited to the study of botany. A second deadline date for this award is October 1. Students commuting within the Philadelphia area are ineligible. Contact the address below for further information.

Academy of Natural Sciences of Philadelphia
Dr. A.E. Schuyler, Jessup-McHenry Fund
1900 Benjamin Franklin Parkway
Philadelphia, PA 19103-1195

ADAMS STATE COLLEGE

2476
Adams State College Alumni Scholarships

AMOUNT: None Specified DEADLINE: March 15
FIELDS/MAJORS: All Areas of Study

Scholarships for students attending Adams State College given by the Alumni Department. Contact the alumni office at the address below for details.

Adams State College
Alumni Office
Alamosa, CO 81102

2477
Adams State College Private Scholarships

AMOUNT: None Specified DEADLINE: March 15
FIELDS/MAJORS: All Areas of Study

Scholarships, administered by the Adams State College financial aid office, are available for students attending ASC. Criteria for each program varies. Contact the financial aid office at the address below for details. Request the publication: "Adams State College Private Scholarship Directory." Also, be certain to inquire at your high school guidance office and, if you have participated in high school athletics, your high school coach.

Adams State College
Financial Aid Office
Alamosa, CO 81102

2478
National Scholarships and Activity Grants

AMOUNT: $100-$2800 DEADLINE: March 15
FIELDS/MAJORS: All Areas of Study

Awards for undergraduate students at Adams State. Must have a GPA of at least a 2.5. The National Scholarship is for residents of states other than Colorado. Write to the address below for more details.

Adams State College
Financial Aid Office
Alamosa, CO 81102

2479
President's and Adams Scholarships

AMOUNT: $400-$2020 DEADLINE: March 15
FIELDS/MAJORS: All Areas of Study

Scholarships for incoming freshman or transfer students at Adams State. Must have a GPA of at least a 3.2. For President's Award must have an ACT score of at least 21 or an SAT score of 970. Write to the address below for more information.

Adams State College
Financial Aid Office
Alamosa, CO 81102

2480
Woodward Memorial Scholarship Program

AMOUNT: $3500 DEADLINE: March 15
FIELDS/MAJORS: All Areas of Study

Scholarships for students at Adams State College. For full-time study. Thirty awards offered annually. Based on leadership, academics, and character. "Must not have appeared on any list published…indicating…membership in any organization that is subversive to the interest of the United States of America." Contact the Woodward Scholarship committee through the financial aid office for complete details.

Adams State College
Financial Aid Office
Alamosa, CO 81102

ADELPHI UNIVERSITY

2481
Adelphi University Scholarship

AMOUNT: Maximum: $5000 DEADLINE: January 1
FIELDS/MAJORS: All Areas of Study

Adelphi University Scholarship is offered to new, full-time students who demonstrate high academic achievement. For new freshmen, SAT score must be 1100. Transfer students must have a transfer GPA of at least 3.2. Write to the address below for more information.

Adelphi University
Office of Student Financial Services
Garden City, NY 11530

2482
Athletic Grants

AMOUNT: $2000-$13000 DEADLINE: January 1
FIELDS/MAJORS: Athletics

Adelphi University Athletic Award is offered to full-time students who demonstrate exceptional ability in the area of athletics. Student's athletic performance/record is a consideration. Write to the address below for more information.

Adelphi University
Office of Student Financial Services
Garden City, NY 11530

2483
Financial Grant

AMOUNT: None Specified DEADLINE: January 1
FIELDS/MAJORS: All Areas of Study

Adelphi University Financial Grant is offered to full-time undergraduate students who demonstrate financial need. Write to the address below for more information.

Adelphi University
Office of Student Financial Services
Garden City, NY 11530

2484
Presidential Scholarship

AMOUNT: Maximum: $13500 DEADLINE: January 1
FIELDS/MAJORS: All Areas of Study

Adelphi University Presidential Scholarship is offered to new, full-time students enrolled in the University's Honor College who demonstrate exceptional academic achievement. Must have a SAT score of 1300. Write to the address below for more information.

Adelphi University
Office of Student Financial Services
Garden City, NY 1153

2485
Restricted Scholarships

AMOUNT: None Specified DEADLINE: January 1
FIELDS/MAJORS: All Areas of Study

These scholarships are offered to full- and part-time students on a competitive basis, with consideration given to students whose individual profiles coincide with specific donor requirements. Write to the address below for more information.

Adelphi University
Office of Student Financial Services
Garden City, NY 11530

2486
Scholarship for Honors

AMOUNT: Maximum: $10000 DEADLINE: January 1
FIELDS/MAJORS: All Areas of Study

Adelphi University Scholarship for Honors is offered to new, full-time students enrolled in the University's Honors College who demonstrate outstanding academic achievement. Must have a SAT score of 1200. Write to the address below for more information.

Adelphi University
Office of Student Financial Services
Garden City, NY 11530

2487
Talent Awards

AMOUNT: $1000-$6000 DEADLINE: January 1
FIELDS/MAJORS: Theater, Dance, Art, or Music

Adelphi University Talent Scholarships are offered to full-time students who demonstrate exceptional talent in the areas of theater, dance, art, or music. Students must submit a portfolio to, or audition with, the department of their concentration. Write to the address below for more information.

Adelphi University
Office of Student Financial Services
Garden City, NY 11530

ALASKA PACIFIC UNIVERSITY

2488
National Methodist Foundation Scholarships at APU

AMOUNT: $2000-$3000 DEADLINE: April 1
FIELDS/MAJORS: All Areas of Study

Scholarship for students at Alaska Pacific University who are members of the United Methodist Church. Must meet criteria determined by their conference and have proven record of academic accomplishment. Financial need is considered. Three to four awards offered annually. Contact the financial aid office and your department for further information.

Alaska Pacific University
APU Scholarships
4101 University Dr.
Anchorage, AK 99508

ALFRED UNIVERSITY

2489
Art Portfolio Review Scholarship

AMOUNT: $2500-$3600 DEADLINE: February 15
FIELDS/MAJORS: Art and Design

Award based on portfolio review of entering full-time freshmen in the School of Art and Design in the New York State College of Ceramics. Renewable for four years. Write to the address below for details.

Alfred University
Student Financial Aid Office
26 N. Main St.
Alfred, NY 14802

ALLEGHENY COLLEGE

2490
Dean's Achievement Awards

AMOUNT: Maximum: $5000 DEADLINE: February 15
FIELDS/MAJORS: All Areas of Study

Open to high school seniors who are in the top 20% of their graduating class. Based on strong academic record and achievement in activities. Contact the address below for further information. GPA must be at least 3.4.

Allegheny College
Office of Financial Aid
Meadville, PA 16335

2491
Presidential Scholar Awards

AMOUNT: Maximum: $7500 DEADLINE: February 15
FIELDS/MAJORS: All Areas of Study

Open to high school seniors who are in the top 10% of their graduating class. Contact the address below for further information. GPA must be at least 3.7.

Allegheny College
Office of Financial Aid
Meadville, PA 16335

ALLENTOWN COLLEGE OF SAINT FRANCIS DE SALES

2492

Allentown College Need Based Grants

AMOUNT: None Specified DEADLINE: February 1
FIELDS/MAJORS: All Areas of Study

Awards for incoming freshmen at Allentown College who demonstrate financial need. Renewable each year based on satisfactory academic progress and continuing need. Write to the address below for more information or call (610) 282-1100. GPA must be at least 2.4.

Allentown College of Saint Francis De Sales
Financial Aid Office
2755 Station Ave.
Center Valley, PA 18034

2493

Departmental Scholarships

AMOUNT: None Specified DEADLINE: February 1
FIELDS/MAJORS: All Areas of Study

Departmental awards for incoming freshmen at Allentown College who are interested in a specific major. Based on academic achievement, demonstrated talent in the pertinent field, and participation in a special scholarship day held annually in December/January. Some of these awards may depend on financial need. Renewable. Write to the address below for more information or call (610) 282-1100. GPA must be at least 2.8.

Allentown College of Saint Francis De Sales
Financial Aid Office
2755 Station Ave.
Center Valley, PA 18034

2494

De Sales Scholarships

AMOUNT: Maximum: $3500 DEADLINE: February 1
FIELDS/MAJORS: All Areas of Study

Open to accepted incoming freshmen at Allentown College. Applicants must be in the top 30% of their class. Renewable if recipients achieve at least a 2.5 GPA at the end of freshman year and a minimum GPA of 2.7 at the end of the other academic years. Write to the address below for more information or call (610) 282-1100.

Allentown College of Saint Francis De Sales
Financial Aid Office
2755 Station Ave.
Center Valley, PA 18034

2495

Family Tuition Reduction Plans

AMOUNT: None Specified DEADLINE: February 1
FIELDS/MAJORS: All Areas of Study

Awards are available at Allentown College for families with two or more dependents in attendance as full-time undergraduates. The second and succeeding children will be eligible for a tuition reduction up to a maximum of 15% of tuition. Forms and additional information may be obtained in the Treasurer's Office. Write to the address below for more information or call (610) 282-1100.

Allentown College of Saint Francis De Sales
Financial Aid Office
2755 Station Ave.
Center Valley, PA 18034

2496

High School Teaching Scholarships

AMOUNT: None Specified DEADLINE: February 1
FIELDS/MAJORS: Education

Scholarship competition for entering students who are in the teaching certification program. Accepted students with at least a B average and minimum SAT scores of 1100 are invited to compete for these awards. Renewable. Write to the address below for more information. GPA must be at least 3.0.

Allentown College of Saint Francis De Sales
Financial Aid Office
2755 Station Ave.
Center Valley, PA 18034

2497

Presidential Scholarships

AMOUNT: None Specified DEADLINE: February 1
FIELDS/MAJORS: All Areas of Study

Available to accepted incoming freshmen at Allentown College. Applicants must be in the top 5% of their class and have a combined SAT score of at least 1300 or an ACT score of 30. Renewable if recipients achieve a GPA of 3.0 at the end of freshman year and at least a 3.3 at the end of the other academic years. Write to the address below for more information or call (610) 282-1100.

Allentown College of Saint Francis De Sales
Financial Aid Office
2755 Station Ave.
Center Valley, PA 18034

2498
Student Activities Scholarship Awards

AMOUNT: None Specified
DEADLINE: February 1
FIELDS/MAJORS: All Areas of Study

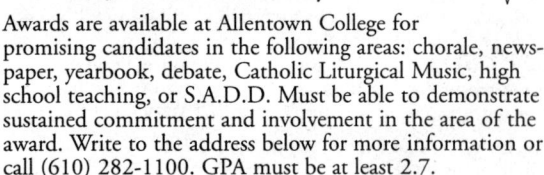

Awards are available at Allentown College for promising candidates in the following areas: chorale, newspaper, yearbook, debate, Catholic Liturgical Music, high school teaching, or S.A.D.D. Must be able to demonstrate sustained commitment and involvement in the area of the award. Write to the address below for more information or call (610) 282-1100. GPA must be at least 2.7.

Allentown College of Saint Francis De Sales
Financial Aid Office
2755 Station Ave.
Center Valley, PA 18034

2499
Trustee Scholarships

AMOUNT: Maximum: $5000   DEADLINE: February 1
FIELDS/MAJORS: All Areas of Study

Awards for incoming freshmen accepted at Allentown College. Applicants must be in the top 15% of their class and have a combined SAT score of at least 1200 or an ACT score of 28. Renewable if recipients achieve at least a 2.7 GPA at the end of freshman year and a minimum GPA of 3.0 at the end of the other academic years. Write to the address below for more information or call (610) 282-1100.

Allentown College of Saint Francis De Sales
Financial Aid Office
2755 Station Ave.
Center Valley, PA 18034

ALMA COLLEGE

2500
Alma College Merit Scholarships and Distinguished Scholar Award

AMOUNT: $500-$2000   DEADLINE: None Specified
FIELDS/MAJORS: All Areas of Study

Scholarships for National Merit Scholarship Finalists. Renewable based on maintaining a "B" average. Students must be accepted at Alma to be eligible to apply. Contact the address below or call 1-800-321-ALMA for further information.

Alma College
Office of Admissions
Alma, MI 48801

2501
Alma College Religious Leadership Award

AMOUNT: Maximum: $1000   DEADLINE: None Specified
FIELDS/MAJORS: All Areas of Study

This award is for membership in any religious denomination. Based on financial need, recommendations, and essay. Renewable based on a "B" average at Alma. Students must be accepted at Alma to be eligible. Contact the address below or call 1-800-321-ALMA for further information.

Alma College
Office of Admissions
Alma, MI 48801

2502
Community College Scholarship

AMOUNT: Maximum: $4500   DEADLINE: None Specified
FIELDS/MAJORS: All Areas of Study

Scholarships for students who have received their associate's degree and demonstrate superior academic achievement. Renewable based on a "B" average while at Alma. Must be accepted at Alma to be eligible. Contact the address below or call 1-800-321-ALMA for further information. GPA must be at least 2.9.

Alma College
Office of Admissions
Alma, MI 48801

2503
Dow Chemical Company Foundation Scholarship

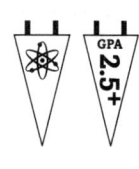

AMOUNT: Maximum: $2000   DEADLINE: None Specified
FIELDS/MAJORS: Chemistry

Awards for students planning a career in chemistry or biochemistry. Renewable based on maintaining a "B" average. Students must be accepted at Alma to be eligible. Contact the address listed or call 1-800-321-ALMA for further information. Must have a GPA of at least 2.8.

Alma College
Office of Admissions
Alma, MI 48801

2504

Performance Scholarship

AMOUNT: Maximum: $1500 DEADLINE: April 1
FIELDS/MAJORS: Vocal/Instrumental Music, Dance, Art and Design, Theater

Awards for a high level of accomplishment in any of the fields listed above. Renewable based on participation at Alma College. Students must apply and be accepted before auditioning. Auditions must be completed by April 1. Contact the address below or call 1-800-321-ALMA for further information.

Alma College
Office of Admissions
Alma, MI 48801

2505

Phi Theta Kappa Scholarship

AMOUNT: Maximum: $2000 DEADLINE: None Specified
FIELDS/MAJORS: All Areas of Study

Scholarship to recognize students who have been inducted into the Phi Theta Kappa honorary society. Renewable based on a "B" average at Alma. Students must be accepted at Alma to be eligible. Contact the address below for further information.

Alma College
Office of Admissions
Alma, MI 48801

2506

Presidential Scholarship

AMOUNT: Maximum: $5500 DEADLINE: None Specified
FIELDS/MAJORS: All Areas of Study

Scholarship for incoming freshmen with a minimum ACT score of 25, SAT of 1140, and a GPA of 3.25. High school performance in English, science, math, social science, and foreign language is used to determine the recomputed GPA. Renewable if recipients maintain a minimum "B" average at Alma. Must be accepted at Alma to be eligible to apply. Contact the address below or call 1-800-321-ALMA for further information.

Alma College
Office of Admissions
Alma, MI 48801

2507

Tartan Award

AMOUNT: Maximum: $4500 DEADLINE: None Specified
FIELDS/MAJORS: All Areas of Study

Awards for high school seniors with at least a 25 ACT score or ranked in the top 20% of the class. High school performance in English, science, math, social science, and foreign language is used to determine the recomputed GPA. Must be accepted into Alma. Renewable if recipients maintain a "B" average. Contact the Office of Admissions or call 1-800-321-ALMA for further information. GPA must be at least 3.5.

Alma College
Office of Admissions
Alma, MI 48801

2508

Transfer Student Scholarship

AMOUNT: Maximum: $4000 DEADLINE: None Specified
FIELDS/MAJORS: All Areas of Study

Scholarships for students who have demonstrated superior academic achievement at their previous undergraduate institution or in high school. Renewable based on maintaining a "B" average at Alma. Must be accepted to be eligible. Contact the address below or call 1-800-321-ALMA for further information. GPA must be at least 2.7.

Alma College
Office of Admissions
Alma, MI 48801

2509

Trustees Honors Scholarship

AMOUNT: Maximum: $7000 DEADLINE: None Specified
FIELDS/MAJORS: All Areas of Study

Scholarship for incoming freshmen who have been accepted at Alma. High school performance in English, science, math, social science, and foreign language is used to determine the recomputed GPA. Renewable if recipients maintain a "B" average. Contact the address below or call 1-800-321-ALMA for further information. GPA must be at least 3.8.

Alma College
Office of Admissions
Alma, MI 48801

ALVERNO COLLEGE

2510

Alverno Scholarships

AMOUNT: None Specified DEADLINE: March 21
FIELDS/MAJORS: All Areas of Study

Alverno College administers many scholarship programs for students attending Alverno. Most require participation in scholarship opportunity days. Contact the admissions office or financial aid office for details.

Alverno College
3401 S. 29th St.
PO Box 343922
Milwaukee, WI 53234

ARCHAEOLOGICAL INSTITUTE OF AMERICA

2511
Helen M. Woodruff Fellowship

AMOUNT: None Specified DEADLINE: November 15
FIELDS/MAJORS: Archaeology and Classical Studies

A predoctoral or postdoctoral fellowship for study of the fields listed above has been established by the Institute at the Academy of Rome. This fellowship, combined with other funds from the American Academy in Rome, will support a Rome prize fellowship that will be open to citizens or permanent residents of the U.S. Write to the address below or call (617) 353-9361 for details.

Archaeological Institute of America
American Academy in Rome
7 East 60th St.
New York, NY 10022

AMERICAN COLLEGE FOR THE APPLIED ARTS

2512
Emilio Pucci Scholarship

AMOUNT: Maximum: $1800 DEADLINE: March 15
FIELDS/MAJORS: Design

Scholarships for graduating high school seniors who will be entering the American College for the Applied Arts (Los Angeles, Atlanta, or London). Based on interest and ability in the areas relating to design. Write to the address below for more information.

American College for the Applied Arts
Scholarship Admissions Committee
3330 Peachtree Road, NE
Atlanta, GA 30326

2513
Founders Scholarship Award at American College for the Applied Arts

AMOUNT: None Specified
DEADLINE: March 15
FIELDS/MAJORS: Visual Communication, Fashion Design, Interior Design

Scholarship for high school juniors and seniors at the American College for the Applied Arts (Los Angeles, Atlanta, or London). Must have a minimum GPA of 3.2. Contact the address below for further information.

American College for the Applied Arts-Atlanta
Office of the Director of Education
3330 Peachtree Rd., NE
Atlanta, GA 30326

AMERICAN COLLEGE OF MUSICIANS

2514
American College of Musicians Scholarships

AMOUNT: $100 DEADLINE: November 15
FIELDS/MAJORS: Music Performance, Piano

Must have entered guild auditions with a national or International program for at least ten years, received the Paderewski Medal, and performed in the high school diploma program. Winners are selected by auditions. 150 awards per year. Applications are available from your teacher, or write to the address below for details.

American College of Musicians
808 Rio Grande
Box 1807
Austin, TX 78767

AMERICAN INSTITUTE FOR ECONOMIC RESEARCH

2515
Summer Fellowship Program

AMOUNT: None Specified DEADLINE: March 31
FIELDS/MAJORS: Economics and Related (Banking, Finance)

Summer fellowships in economic science at the Institute open to undergraduates who have completed their junior year and are applying to doctoral programs or to graduate students already enrolled in a doctoral program. Approximately one dozen fellowships are awarded per year. Write to the address below for complete details.

American Institute for Economic Research
Pamela P. Allard, Asst. to the Director
Division Street
Great Barrington, MA 01230

ANGELO STATE UNIVERSITY

2516

Aileen B. Trimble Memorial Scholarship

AMOUNT: None Specified DEADLINE: November 1
FIELDS/MAJORS: Communication, Journalism

Open to students majoring in communication, particularly journalism. Second deadline is June 1. Contact the Communications, Drama, and Journalism Department for further information.

Angelo State University
Financial Aid Office
PO Box 11015
San Angelo, TX 76909

2517

Air Force Sergeants Association/Coors Distributing Co. Scholarship

AMOUNT: None Specified DEADLINE: November 1
FIELDS/MAJORS: All Areas of Study

Available to dependent children or spouses of U.S. Air Force active duty, retired, or deceased personnel who meet academic requirements. Must demonstrate financial need. Contact the address below for further information.

Angelo State University
Financial Aid Office
PO Box 11015
San Angelo, TX 76909

2518

Amoco Production Co. and San Angelo Human Resources Association Scholarships

AMOUNT: None Specified DEADLINE: November 1
FIELDS/MAJORS: Business Administration

Open to juniors and seniors majoring in business with a minimum GPA of 3.0. Second deadline is June 1. Contact the business administration department for further information about both awards.

Angelo State University
Financial Aid Office
PO Box 11015
San Angelo, TX 76909

2519

Annette Dominguez and Xander Guy Briones Memorial Scholarship

AMOUNT: None Specified DEADLINE: November 1
FIELDS/MAJORS: Nursing

Open to nursing majors. Second deadline is June 1. Contact the Nursing Department about both awards.

Angelo State University
Financial Aid Office
PO Box 11015
San Angelo, TX 76909

2520

Arlen Lohse Scholarship

AMOUNT: None Specified DEADLINE: November 1
FIELDS/MAJORS: Journalism

Open to deserving students who have at least 30 hours at ASU. Second deadline is June 1. Contact the Communications, Drama, and Journalism Department for further information.

Angelo State University
Financial Aid Office
PO Box 11015
San Angelo, TX 76909

2521

ASU Valedictorian Scholarships

AMOUNT: None Specified DEADLINE: November 1
FIELDS/MAJORS: All Areas of Study

Open to the valedictorians of any affiliated Texas high school. Contact the address below for further information.

Angelo State University
Financial Aid Office
PO Box 11015
San Angelo, TX 76909

2522
Berne Enslin Memorial Scholarship

AMOUNT: Maximum: $200   DEADLINE: November 1
FIELDS/MAJORS: Communications, Drama

Open to deserving communications or drama majors. Second deadline is June 1. Contact the Communications, Drama, and Journalism Department for further information.

Angelo State University
Financial Aid Office
PO Box 11015
San Angelo, TX 76909

2523
Bertha B. Becton, Ola Fay Bettesworth Memorial Scholarships

AMOUNT: None Specified   DEADLINE: November 1
FIELDS/MAJORS: All Areas of Study

Open to deserving students with high academic standing. Second deadline date is June 1. Contact the address below for further information about both awards. Must have a GPA of at least 3.2.

Angelo State University
Financial Aid Office
PO Box 11015
San Angelo, TX 76909

2524
Carlton Ivy White Memorial Scholarship

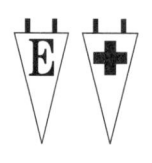

AMOUNT: None Specified   DEADLINE: November 1
FIELDS/MAJORS: Nursing

Open to deserving students majoring in nursing. Special consideration given to minorities and males. Second deadline is June 1. Contact the Nursing Department for further information.

Angelo State University
Financial Aid Office
PO Box 11015
San Angelo, TX 76909

2525
Claude Collins, Jr., Virginia Lea Carson Harris Memorial Scholarships

AMOUNT: None Specified   DEADLINE: November 1
FIELDS/MAJORS: Nursing

Open to deserving students pursuing a BS in nursing. Second deadline date is June 1. Contact the Nursing Department for further information.

Angelo State University
Financial Aid Office
PO Box 11015
San Angelo, TX 76909

2526
Concho Valley Medical Alliance, Ruth A. Decuir Memorial Scholarships

AMOUNT: None Specified   DEADLINE: November 1
FIELDS/MAJORS: Nursing

Open to nursing majors with high academic standing and demonstrated financial need. Second deadline is June 1. Contact the Nursing Department for further information about both awards. Must have a GPA of at least 2.8.

Angelo State University
Financial Aid Office
PO Box 11015
San Angelo, TX 76909

2527
David Fennell Memorial and Minnie H. Mayer Memorial Scholarships

AMOUNT: None Specified   DEADLINE: November 1
FIELDS/MAJORS: Music

Open to talented instrumental majors. Minnie H. Mayer Memorial Scholarship gives preference to piano students. Second deadline is June 1. Contact the Music Department for further information.

Angelo State University
Financial Aid Office
PO Box 11015
San Angelo, TX 76909

2528
Dean Chenoweth Scholarship

AMOUNT: None Specified　DEADLINE: November 1
FIELDS/MAJORS: Journalism

Open to deserving students, with preference to graduates from Tom Green County high schools. Academic requirements must be met, and financial need may be considered. Contact the Communications, Drama, and Journalism Department for further information.

Angelo State University
Financial Aid Office
PO Box 11015
San Angelo, TX 76909

2529
Dr. Eldon U. Black Vocal Scholarship

AMOUNT: None Specified　DEADLINE: November 1
FIELDS/MAJORS: Voice

Open to enrolled/accepted voice majors. Second deadline date is June 1. Contact the Music Department for further information.

Angelo State University
Financial Aid Office
PO Box 11015
San Angelo, TX 76909

2530
Dr. Gerald L. Richards Memorial Scholarship

AMOUNT: None Specified　DEADLINE: November 1
FIELDS/MAJORS: Business

Open to undergraduates and graduate students pursuing a degree in a business-related field. Second deadline is June 1. Contact the Business Administration Department for further information. Must have a GPA of at least 2.7.

Angelo State University
Financial Aid Office
PO Box 11015
San Angelo, TX 76909

2531
Dr. Merril W. Everhart Memorial Scholarship

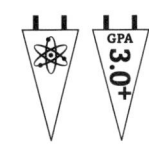

AMOUNT: None Specified　DEADLINE: November 1
FIELDS/MAJORS: Natural Science

Open to juniors majoring in one of the natural sciences with a minimum GPA of 3.0. Second deadline is June 1. Contact the Biology Department for further information.

Angelo State University
Financial Aid Office
PO Box 11015
San Angelo, TX 76909

2532
Dr. Verna Mae Crutchfield, Amy Pettit Scholarships

AMOUNT: None Specified　DEADLINE: November 1
FIELDS/MAJORS: Special Education

Open to juniors and seniors majoring in special education. Second deadline date is June 1. Contact the Education Department for further information about both awards.

Angelo State University
Financial Aid Office
PO Box 11015
San Angelo, TX 76909

2533
E.F. Noelke Memorial Scholarship

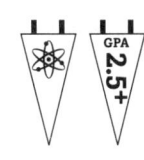

AMOUNT: None Specified　DEADLINE: November 1
FIELDS/MAJORS: Range Management, Sheep Raising

Open to deserving agriculture students. Preference given to candidates pursuing an education in range management or sheep raising. Contact the Department of Agriculture for further information. Must have a GPA of at least 2.7.

Angelo State University
Financial Aid Office
PO Box 11015
San Angelo, TX 76909

2534
Elizabeth Boren Eaton Memorial, Olson-Buttery Memorial Scholarships

AMOUNT: None Specified　DEADLINE: November 1
FIELDS/MAJORS: Education

Open to deserving students majoring in education. Second deadline is June 1. Contact the Education Department for further information.

Angelo State University
Financial Aid Office
PO Box 11015
San Angelo, TX 76909

2535
Elizabeth Ward Memorial Scholarship

AMOUNT: None Specified　DEADLINE: November 1
FIELDS/MAJORS: Home Economics

Open to deserving home economics students. Second deadline is June 1. Contact the Department of Agriculture for further information. Must have a GPA of at least 2.6.

Angelo State University
Financial Aid Office
PO Box 11015
San Angelo, TX 76909

2536
Frank Junell Scholarship in Business

AMOUNT: Maximum: $2500　DEADLINE: November 1
FIELDS/MAJORS: Business

Open to deserving juniors and seniors with outstanding academic records. Second deadline date is June 1. Contact the Business Administration Department for further information. Must have a GPA of at least 3.1.

Angelo State University
Financial Aid Office
PO Box 11015
San Angelo, TX 76909

2537
Harold W. "Brookie" Broome and John C. Coleman Scholarships

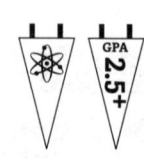

AMOUNT: None Specified　DEADLINE: November 1
FIELDS/MAJORS: Agriculture

Open to deserving students pursuing a bachelor's degree in agriculture. Second deadline date is June 1. Contact the Department of Agriculture for further information. Must have a GPA of at least 2.6.

Angelo State University
Financial Aid Office
PO Box 11015
San Angelo, TX 76909

2538
Head-of-the-River Ranch Scholarship

AMOUNT: None Specified　DEADLINE: November 1
FIELDS/MAJORS: Biological Science

Open to enrolled/accepted students majoring in the biological sciences. Second deadline is June 1. Contact the Biology Department for further information. Must have a GPA of at least 2.7.

Angelo State University
Financial Aid Office
PO Box 11015
San Angelo, TX 76909

2539
Houston Livestock Show and Rodeo Scholarship

AMOUNT: Maximum: $1000　DEADLINE: November 1
FIELDS/MAJORS: Agriculture

Open to undergraduates majoring in an agricultural field, who can demonstrate financial need. Second deadline date is June 1. Contact the Department of Agriculture for further information. Must have a GPA of at least 2.7.

Angelo State University
Financial Aid Office
PO Box 11015
San Angelo, TX 76909

2540
Isla Mils Eckert Memorial Scholarship

AMOUNT: Maximum: $500　DEADLINE: November 1
FIELDS/MAJORS: Business

Open to female students in the field of business. Second deadline is June 1. Contact the Business Administration Department for further information.

Angelo State University
Financial Aid Office
PO Box 11015
San Angelo, TX 76909

2541
James W. Keller Memorial Scholarship

AMOUNT: Maximum: $500　DEADLINE: November 1
FIELDS/MAJORS: All Areas of Study

Open to Hispanic males who are enrolled/accepted into ASU. Second deadline is June 1. Contact the address below for further information.

Angelo State University
Financial Aid Office
PO Box 11015
San Angelo, TX 76909

2542
J.E. Henderson Memorial, Mary and Sharon Stringer Memorial Scholarships

Amount: None Specified **Deadline:** November 1
Fields/Majors: Business Administration

Open to business majors enrolled/accepted into ASU. Second deadline is June 1. Contact the Business Administration Department about both awards.

Angelo State University
Financial Aid Office
PO Box 11015
San Angelo, TX 76909

2543
John Henry McCommon, III, Memorial Scholarship

Amount: Maximum: $1000 **Deadline:** November 1
Fields/Majors: Nursing

Open to sophomore nursing majors with a minimum GPA of 3.0. Second deadline is June 1. Contact the Nursing Department for further information.

Angelo State University
Financial Aid Office
PO Box 11015
San Angelo, TX 76909

2544
John L. Bishop Memorial, Hauztenc Cox Jackson Memorial Scholarship

Amount: $300 **Deadline:** November 1
Fields/Majors: Education

Open to juniors and seniors majoring in education. Second deadline date is June 1. Contact the Education Department for further information about both awards.

Angelo State University
Financial Aid Office
PO Box 11015
San Angelo, TX 76909

2545
Josephine Bell Fine Arts Scholarship

Amount: Maximum: $400 **Deadline:** November 1
Fields/Majors: Fine Arts

Open to fine arts majors enrolled/accepted by ASU. Second deadline date is June 1. Contact the Communications, Drama, and Journalism Department for further information.

Angelo State University
Financial Aid Office
PO Box 11015
San Angelo, TX 76909

2546
Josephine Morris Ballard, Alan Davis Memorial Scholarship

Amount: None Specified **Deadline:** November 1
Fields/Majors: All Areas of Study

Open to deserving students from any Coleman County high school. Second deadline date is June 1. Contact the address below for further information about both awards.

Angelo State University
Financial Aid Office
PO Box 11015
San Angelo, TX 76909

2547
Karen Holt Copes Memorial Scholarship

Amount: None Specified **Deadline:** November 1
Fields/Majors: Kinesiology

Open to juniors and seniors majoring in kinesiology with a minimum GPA of 2.75. Second deadline date is June 1. Contact the Kinesiology Department for further information.

Angelo State University
Financial Aid Office
PO Box 11015
San Angelo, TX 76909

2548
Long Memorial Scholarship

Amount: Maximum: $400 **Deadline:** November 1
Fields/Majors: Journalism

Open to journalism majors preferably from Eldorado, Texas. Second deadline is June 1. Contact the

Communications, Drama, and Journalism Department for further information.

Angelo State University
Financial Aid Office
PO Box 1115
San Angelo, TX 76909

2549
Louis Cellum Memorial Scholarship

AMOUNT: None Specified DEADLINE: November 1
FIELDS/MAJORS: Pre-engineering

Open to deserving students majoring in pre-engineering. Second deadline is June 1. Contact the Physics Department for further information.

Angelo State University
Financial Aid Office
PO Box 11015
San Angelo, TX 76909

2550
Marthas of the First United Methodist Church, Juanita Norris Memorial

AMOUNT: None Specified DEADLINE: November 1
FIELDS/MAJORS: Drama

Open to deserving drama majors. Second deadline is June 1. Contact the Communications, Drama, and Journalism Department for further information.

Angelo State University
Financial Aid Office
PO Box 11015
San Angelo, TX 76909

2551
Millard Cope Trust Scholarship

AMOUNT: None Specified DEADLINE: November 1
FIELDS/MAJORS: Journalism

Open to outstanding junior and senior journalism majors planning careers in newspaper work. Second deadline is June 1. Contact the Communications, Drama, and Journalism Department for further information. Must have a GPA of at least 3.1.

Angelo State University
Financial Aid Office
PO Box 11015
San Angelo, TX 76909

2552
Mobile Oil Corporation Scholarship

AMOUNT: Maximum: $250 DEADLINE: November 1
FIELDS/MAJORS: Accounting

Open to seniors majoring in accounting. June 1 is the second deadline date. Contact the address below for further information. Must have a GPA of at least 2.7.

Angelo State University
Financial Aid Office
PO Box 11015
San Angelo, TX 76909

2553
Modern Languages Scholarship

AMOUNT: None Specified DEADLINE: November 1
FIELDS/MAJORS: Foreign Languages: French, Spanish, German

Open to undergraduates majoring in French, Spanish, or German. Second deadline is June 1. Contact the Modern Languages Department for further information.

Angelo State University
Financial Aid Office
PO Box 11015
San Angelo, TX 76909

2554
Music Endowment, Charles Van Pelt Memorial, and Sean W. Vick Endowment

AMOUNT: None Specified DEADLINE: November 1
FIELDS/MAJORS: Music

Open to deserving music majors. Second deadline is June 1. Contact the Music Department about all three awards. Must have a GPA of at least 2.5.

Angelo State University
Financial Aid Office
PO Box 11015
San Angelo, TX 76909

2555
Norwest Scholarship in Business

AMOUNT: Maximum: $2500 DEADLINE: November 1
FIELDS/MAJORS: Business

Open to juniors who intend to complete senior year at ASU. Second deadline is June 1. Contact the Business Administration Department for further information. Must have a GPA of at least 2.8.

Angelo State University
Financial Aid Office
PO Box 11015
San Angelo, TX 76909

2556
Olson-Buttery Memorial Scholarship

AMOUNT: None Specified DEADLINE: November 1
FIELDS/MAJORS: Pre-pharmacy, Pre-medicine, Nursing

Open to deserving students majoring in any of the fields listed above. Second deadline is June 1. Contact the Biology Department for further information.

Angelo State University
Financial Aid Office
PO Box 11015
San Angelo, TX 76909

2557
Olson-Buttery Memorial Scholarship

AMOUNT: None Specified DEADLINE: November 1
FIELDS/MAJORS: Pre-Pharmacy, Pre-Medicine, Nursing

Open to students majoring in the above listed fields. Second deadline date is June 1. Contact the Nursing Department for further information.

Angelo State University
Financial Aid Office
PO Box 11015
San Angelo, TX 76909

2558
Omar E. Hunter Memorial, Edwin S. Mayer, Sr. Memorial Scholarships

AMOUNT: $200 DEADLINE: None Specified
FIELDS/MAJORS: Computer Science

Open to enrolled undergraduates. Second deadline is June 1. Contact the Computer Science Department for information about both awards.

Angelo State University
Financial Aid Office
PO Box 11015
San Angelo, TX 76909

2559
Opal Stockard Memorial Scholarship

AMOUNT: Maximum: $500 DEADLINE: November 1
FIELDS/MAJORS: Nursing

Open to junior and senior nursing majors from Coleman County. Second deadline is June 1. Contact the Nursing Department for further information.

Angelo State University
Financial Aid Office
PO Box 11015
San Angelo, TX 76909

2560
Robert G. Carr and Nona K. Carr Scholarships (Graduate)

AMOUNT: Maximum: $4500 DEADLINE: February 1
FIELDS/MAJORS: All Areas of Study

Scholarships for graduate students at Angelo State University who are academically accomplished and have high GRE/GMAT scores (GPA of at least 3.5). Write to the address below for details.

Angelo State University
Carr Academic Scholarship Program
Box 11007-C, ASU Station
San Angelo, TX 76909

2561
University Theater Scholarships

AMOUNT: None Specified DEADLINE: November 1
FIELDS/MAJORS: Performing Arts

Scholarships are available to students in the performing arts. Contact the head of the Department of Communications, Drama, and Journalism.

Angelo State University
Director of Student Financial Aid
PO Box 11015
San Angelo, TX 76909

2562
Owen Kyle Aylor Memorial Scholarship

AMOUNT: None Specified DEADLINE: November 1
FIELDS/MAJORS: Music Education, Vocal

Open to vocal music education majors. Second deadline is June 1. Contact the Music Department for further information. Must have a GPA of at least 2.6.

Angelo State University
Financial Aid Office
PO Box 11015
San Angelo, TX 76909

2563
Pat Baker Memorial Scholarship

AMOUNT: None Specified DEADLINE: November 1
FIELDS/MAJORS: Education

Open to juniors and seniors who graduated from a high school in Tom Green County. Second deadline is June 1. Contact the Education Department for further information.

Angelo State University
Financial Aid Office
PO Box 11015
San Angelo, TX 76909

2564
Robert Junell Scholarship

AMOUNT: None Specified DEADLINE: November 1
FIELDS/MAJORS: Education

Open to freshmen from Tom Green, Sterling Coke, and Mitchell counties who plan to teach. Second deadline is June 1. Contact the address below for further information.

Angelo State University
Financial Aid Office
PO Box 11015
San Angelo, TX 76909

2565
Robert Stephen Archer Agricultural Scholarship

AMOUNT: None Specified DEADLINE: November 1
FIELDS/MAJORS: Agriculture

Open to juniors, seniors, and graduate students majoring in agriculture. Second deadline date is June 1. Contact the Department of Agriculture for further information.

Angelo State University
Financial Aid Office
PO Box 11015
San Angelo, TX 76909

2566
San Angelo Police Association, Bernard P. Taylor Memorial Scholarships

AMOUNT: None Specified DEADLINE: November 1
FIELDS/MAJORS: Government

Open to government majors. Police award also requests applicants have a criminal justice option. Bernard P. Taylor award gives preference to applicants who are conservatives. Contact the Government Department for further information about both awards.

Angelo State University
Financial Aid Office
PO Box 11015
San Angelo, TX 76909

2567
San Angelo Retired Teachers Association Scholarship

AMOUNT: None Specified DEADLINE: November 1
FIELDS/MAJORS: Education

Open to juniors and seniors who intend to teach. Second deadline date is June 1. Contact the Education Department for further information.

Angelo State University
Financial Aid Office
PO Box 1015
San Angelo, TX 76909

2568
State Farm Insurance Companies Scholarship

AMOUNT: None Specified DEADLINE: November 1
FIELDS/MAJORS: Insurance

Open to minority and female students interested in careers in the insurance industry. Second deadline date is June 1. Contact the Business Administration Department for further information. Must have a GPA of at least 2.7.

Angelo State University
Financial Aid Office
PO Box 11015
San Angelo, TX 76909

2569
Susan Miles History Scholarship

AMOUNT: Maximum: $1000   DEADLINE: November 1
FIELDS/MAJORS: History

Open to enrolled/accepted history majors. Second deadline date is June 1. Contact the History Department for further information.

Angelo State University
Financial Aid Office
PO Box 11015
San Angelo, TX 76909

2570
Texas Society of Certified Public Accountants-San Angelo Chapter

AMOUNT: None Specified   DEADLINE: November 1
FIELDS/MAJORS: Accounting

Open to juniors and seniors who can demonstrate financial need. June 1 is the second deadline date. Contact the address below for further information. Must have a GPA of at least 2.7.

Angelo State University
Financial Aid Office
PO Box 11015
San Angelo, TX 76909

2571
Walton A. Foster Memorial Scholarship

AMOUNT: Maximum: $500   DEADLINE: November 1
FIELDS/MAJORS: Communications, Journalism

Open to juniors and seniors who have a minimum GPA of 2.8 overall and 3.0 in the major. Second deadline is June 1. Contact the Communications, Drama, and Journalism Department for further information.

Angelo State University
Financial Aid Office
PO Box 11015
San Angelo, TX 76909

2572
Wayland Yates Memorial, Harrison Youngren Scholarships

AMOUNT: None Specified   DEADLINE: November 1
FIELDS/MAJORS: Journalism

Open to students who plan to pursue a journalism degree at ASU. Second deadline is June 1. Contact the Communications, Drama, and Journalism Department for further information about both awards.

Angelo State University
Financial Aid Office
PO Box 11015
San Angelo, TX 11015

2573
Wilton J. Brown Memorial, Olson-Buttery Memorial Scholarships

AMOUNT: None Specified   DEADLINE: November 1
FIELDS/MAJORS: Physics, Geology

Open to students majoring in the above areas. Second deadline is June 1. Contact the Physics Department about both awards.

Angelo State University
Financial Aid Office
PO Box 11015
San Angelo, TX 76909

ANNA MARIA COLLEGE

2574
Catholic High School Scholarship

AMOUNT: Maximum: $1000   DEADLINE: None Specified
FIELDS/MAJORS: All Areas of Study

Open to incoming freshmen who will be graduating from a Catholic high school. Write to the address below for more information or call (508) 849-3366.

Anna Maria College
Office of Financial Aid
50 Sunset Lane
Paxton, MA 01612-1198

2575
Graduate Alumni Scholarship

AMOUNT: Maximum: $500   DEADLINE: None Specified
FIELDS/MAJORS: All Areas of Study

Open to incoming freshmen and transfer students who have a parent who received a graduate degree from Anna Maria College. Write to the address below for more information or call (508) 849-3366.

Anna Maria College
Office of Financial Aid
50 Sunset Lane
Paxton, MA 01612-1198

2576
Music Performance Scholarship

AMOUNT: None Specified   DEADLINE: None Specified
FIELDS/MAJORS: Piano, Voice, Guitar, Orchestral Music

This scholarship is awarded to full-time freshman applicants based on results of a performance competition that is held annually. Categories include piano, voice, guitar, and orchestral instruments. Contact the Music Department for more information at (508) 849-3450.

Anna Maria College
Office of Financial Aid
50 Sunset Lane
Paxton, MA 01612-1198

2577
Paxton Regional Scholarship

AMOUNT: Maximum: $1000   DEADLINE: None Specified
FIELDS/MAJORS: All Areas of Study

Available to all freshmen and transfer students who live or attend school in Paxton, Worcester, Holden, Leicester, Spencer, or Rutland, Massachusetts. Write to the address below for more information or call (508) 849-3366.

Anna Marie College
Office of Financial Aid
50 Sunset Lane
Paxton, MA 01612-1198

2578
Recognition Scholarships

AMOUNT: Maximum: $2000   DEADLINE: None Specified
FIELDS/MAJORS: All Areas of Study

These scholarships are awarded to all freshman and transfer students accepted into the full-time undergraduate day division regardless of financial need. Must have at least a 2.5 GPA. Renewable in subsequent years providing recipients maintain full-time status and a minimum GPA of 2.5. Write to the address below for more information or call (508) 849-3366.

Anna Maria College
Office of Financial Aid
50 Sunset Lane
Paxton, MA 01612-1198

2579
Service Grants

AMOUNT: Maximum: $1500   DEADLINE: None Specified
FIELDS/MAJORS: All Areas of Study

Anna Maria College offers a number of service grants based on leadership and extracurricular activities performed during high school. Write to the address below for more information.

Anna Maria College
Office of Financial Aid
Paxton, MA 01612-1198

2580
Sibling Scholarship

AMOUNT: Maximum: $1000   DEADLINE: None Specified
FIELDS/MAJORS: All Areas of Study

Open to incoming freshmen and transfer students who have a sibling enrolled in the full-time undergraduate day program on the Paxton campus. Automatically renewed as long as the sibling is enrolled. Write to the address below for more information or call (508) 849-3366.

Anna Maria College
Office of Financial Aid
50 Sunset Lane
Paxton, MA 01612-1198

2581
Trustee Bronze Academic Achievement Scholarships

AMOUNT: Maximum: $2000   DEADLINE: None Specified
FIELDS/MAJORS: All Areas of Study

Scholarships are available to all full-time freshmen accepted into the undergraduate day division with GPAs of 2.9 or above. Must have SAT scores ranging from 1000 to 1049. Write to the address below for more information or call (508) 849-3366.

Anna Maria College
Office of Financial Aid
50 Sunset Lane
Paxton, MA 01612-1198

2582

Trustee Bronze Transfer Students Merit Scholarships

GPA 3.0+

AMOUNT: Maximum: $2000 DEADLINE: None Specified
FIELDS/MAJORS: All Areas of Study

These scholarships are available to all transfer students accepted into the full-time undergraduate day division with GPAs of 3.25 to 3.49. Transfer students must have earned a minimum of 24 credit hours prior to enrollment. Write to the address below for more information or call (508) 849-3366.

Anna Maria College
Office of Financial Aid
50 Sunset Lane
Paxton, MA 01612-1198

2583

Trustee Gold Academic Achievement Scholarships

AMOUNT: Maximum: $5000 DEADLINE: None Specified
FIELDS/MAJORS: All Areas of Study

Scholarships available to all full-time freshmen accepted into the undergraduate day division with minimum SAT scores of 1150. Renewable if recipients remain full-time and maintain a minimum 2.0 GPA at the end of freshman year. Write to the address below for more information or call (508) 849-3366.

Anna Maria College
Office of Financial Aid
50 Sunset Lane
Paxton, MA 01612-1198

2584

Trustee Gold Transfer Students Merit Scholarships

GPA 3.5+

AMOUNT: Maximum: $5000 DEADLINE: None Specified
FIELDS/MAJORS: All Areas of Study

Available to all transfer students accepted into the full-time undergraduate day division with GPAs of 3.7 or above. Must have completed a minimum of 24 credit hours prior to enrollment. Write to the address below more information or call (508) 849-3366.

Anna Maria College
Office of Financial Aid
50 Sunset Lane
Paxton, MA 01612-1198

2585

Trustee Silver Academic Achievement Scholarships

GPA 3.0+

AMOUNT: Maximum: $3000 DEADLINE: None Specified
FIELDS/MAJORS: All Areas of Study

Scholarships are available to all full-time freshmen accepted into the undergraduate day division with GPAs of 3.0 or above. Must have SAT scores ranging from 1050 to 1149. Write to the address below for more information or call (508) 849-3366.

Anna Maria College
Office of Financial Aid
50 Sunset Lane
Paxton, MA 01612-1198

2586

Trustee Silver Transfer Students Merit Scholarships

GPA 3.5+

AMOUNT: Maximum: $3000 DEADLINE: None Specified
FIELDS/MAJORS: All Areas of Study

These scholarships are available to all transfer students accepted into the full-time undergraduate day division with GPAs of 3.5 to 3.69. Transfer students must have earned a minimum of 24 credit hours prior to enrollment. Write to the address below for more information or call (508) 849-3366.

Anna Maria College
Office of Financial Aid
50 Sunset Lane
Paxton, MA 01612-1198

2587

Undergraduate Alumni Scholarship

AMOUNT: Maximum: $1000 DEADLINE: None Specified
FIELDS/MAJORS: All Areas of Study

Open to incoming freshmen and transfer students who have a parent who received an undergraduate degree from Anna Maria College. Write to the address below for more information or call (508) 849-3366.

Anna Maria College
Office of Financial Aid
50 Sunset Lane
Paxton, MA 01612-1198

ANTIOCH UNIVERSITY

2588
Arthur Morgan Public Service Scholarships

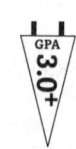

AMOUNT: Maximum: $6000 DEADLINE: February 1
FIELDS/MAJORS: All Areas of Study

Scholarships are available at Antioch for admitted entering freshmen who show academic promise and demonstrate an interest in a career in public/community service. Renewable if recipients maintain a minimum GPA of 3.2. Participation in volunteer and community service, work experience, and leadership qualities will be considered along with the GPA. Contact the address below for further information.

Antioch University
Office of Admissions
795 Livermore Street
Yellow Springs, OH 45387

2589
Dean's Transfer Scholarships

AMOUNT: Maximum: $4000 DEADLINE: February 1
FIELDS/MAJORS: All Areas of Study

Scholarships are available at Antioch for admitted transfer students who demonstrate outstanding academic ability and potential. Involvement in volunteer and community service, work experience, and leadership qualities will be considered along with the GPA. Renewable if recipients maintain a minimum GPA of 3.2. Write to the address below for information.

Antioch University
Office of Admissions
795 Livermore Street
Yellow Springs, OH 45387

2590
Horace Mann Presidential Scholarships

AMOUNT: Maximum: $8000 DEADLINE: February 1
FIELDS/MAJORS: All Areas of Study

Scholarships are available for admitted entering freshmen at Antioch. Must have a minimum GPA of 3.5. Selections based on high school curriculum, volunteer and community service involvement, work experience, and leadership qualities along with the GPA. Available for use on the Yellow Springs campus. Contact the address below for further information or call 1-800-543-9436.

Antioch University
Office of Admissions
795 Livermore Street
Yellow Springs, OH 45387

2591
Presidential Transfer Scholarships

AMOUNT: Maximum: $6000 DEADLINE: February 1
FIELDS/MAJORS: All Areas of Study

Scholarships are available at Antioch for admitted transfer students who demonstrate outstanding academic ability and potential. Involvement in volunteer and community service, work experience, and leadership qualities will be considered along with the GPA. Renewable if recipients maintain a minimum GPA of 3.5. Write to the address below for information.

Antioch University
Office of Admissions
795 Livermore Street
Yellow Springs, OH 45387

APPALACHIAN STATE UNIVERSITY

2592
Alumni Memorial Scholarship

AMOUNT: None Specified DEADLINE: January 15
FIELDS/MAJORS: All Areas of Study

Scholarships awarded to students at Appalachian State University whose parent or parents also attended Appalachian State. Contact the office of admissions for details.

Appalachian State University
Office of Admissions
Scholarship Section
Boone, NC 28608

2593
Appalachian College Scholars Program

AMOUNT: $1000
DEADLINE: December 12
FIELDS/MAJORS: Arts and Sciences

Scholarships awarded to incoming freshmen and transfer students enrolling in the following. Requires a minimum GPA of 3.3. For students in psychology, anthropology, biology, chemistry, English, foreign language, social work, literature, geography, planning, geology, history, math, philosophy, sociology, religious studies, physics, astronomy, political science, and criminology. Contact the office of admissions for details.

Appalachian State University
Office of Admissions
Scholarship Section
Boone, NC 28608

2594
Army ROTC Graduate Scholarships

AMOUNT: None Specified DEADLINE: None Specified
FIELDS/MAJORS: All Areas of Study

Two-year scholarships available to graduate students at Appalachian State University who plan to participate in the Army ROTC program. Awards include a maximum of $3000 toward tuition and fees, $225 per semester for textbooks, and $150 per month tax-free subsistence. Contact the Department of Military Science for further information or call 1-800-ASU-0012.

Appalachian State University
Office of Admissions
Department of Military Science
Boone, NC 28608

2595
Army ROTC Scholarships

AMOUNT: None Specified DEADLINE: None Specified
FIELDS/MAJORS: All Areas of Study

Two- and three-year scholarships available to students at Appalachian State University who plan to participate in the Army ROTC program. Applicants must have a minimum GPA of 2.5. The three-year scholarships require applicants have taken the SAT/ACT tests. Awards include tuition, fees, $225 per semester for textbooks, and $150 per month tax-free subsistence. Contact the Department of Military Science for further information or call 1-800-ASU-0012.

Appalachian State University
Office of Admissions
Department of Military Science
Boone, NC 28608

2596
Bob Allen Scholarship

AMOUNT: None Specified DEADLINE: December 12
FIELDS/MAJORS: All Areas of Study

Scholarships awarded to students at Appalachian State University who reside in Mecklenburg County. Applicant must be a graduating high school senior. Contact your high school counselor for more information.

Appalachian State University
Office of Admissions
Scholarship Section
Boone, NC 28608

2597
College of Fine and Applied Arts Scholarships

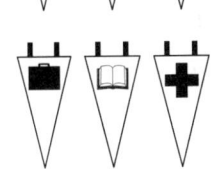

AMOUNT: $1000
DEADLINE: December 12
FIELDS/MAJORS: Fine and Applied Arts

Scholarships awarded to incoming freshmen and transfer students enrolling in the College of Fine and Applied Arts. Requires a minimum GPA of 3.25. For students in art, communications, health, leisure, exercise science, home economics, military science, theater, and dance. Entering freshmen must be in the top 25% of their class with an SAT score of 1100 or better. Contact the office of admissions for details.

Appalachian State University
Office of Admissions
Scholarship Section
Boone, NC 28608

2598
Forensics Talent Awards

AMOUNT: None Specified DEADLINE: None Specified
FIELDS/MAJORS: Forensics

Scholarships are available to students at Appalachian State University who plan to participate in the forensics program. Write to the address below for information.

Appalachian State University
Department of Communications
Boone, NC 28608

2599
Geology Scholarships

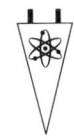

AMOUNT: $1000-$1600 DEADLINE: March 14
FIELDS/MAJORS: Geology

Scholarships awarded to students at Appalachian State University who are geology majors. Contact the office of admissions for details.

Appalachian State University
Department of Geology
Boone, NC 28608

2600

Governor James G. Martin Scholarship

AMOUNT: None Specified DEADLINE: December 12
FIELDS/MAJORS: All Areas of Study

Scholarships awarded to students at Appalachian State University who display outstanding academic ability, leadership qualities, and participation in community activities. Must be a resident of North Carolina to apply. Contact the office of admissions for details. GPA must be at least 3.5.

Appalachian State University
Office of Admissions
Scholarship Section
Boone, NC 28608

2601

Ida Belle Ledbetter and William Hubbard Memorial Scholarships

AMOUNT: None Specified DEADLINE: February 21
FIELDS/MAJORS: Biology

Scholarships awarded to students at Appalachian State University who are biology majors. Write to the address below for information.

Appalachian State University
Department of Biology
Boone, NC 28608

2602

James G.K. McClure Scholarship

AMOUNT: None Specified DEADLINE: December 12
FIELDS/MAJORS: All Areas of Study

Scholarships awarded to students at Appalachian State University who reside in Western North Carolina. Contact the office of admissions for details.

Appalachian State University
Office of Admissions
Scholarship Section
Boone, NC 28608

2603

New River Light & Power Company Scholarships

AMOUNT: $1000-$2000 DEADLINE: December 12
FIELDS/MAJORS: All Areas of Study

Scholarships awarded to students at Appalachian State University who graduated from Watauga High School. Based on merit and financial need. Fifteen awards offered annually. Contact the office of admissions for details.

Appalachian State University
Office of Admissions
Scholarship Section
Boone, NC 28608

2604

Paul B. Patterson Scholarship

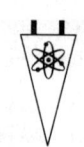

AMOUNT: None Specified DEADLINE: December 12
FIELDS/MAJORS: Mathematics

Scholarships awarded to students at Appalachian State University who are mathematics majors. Write to the address below for information.

Appalachian State University
Department of Mathematics
Boone, NC 28608

2605

Pershing Rifle Drill Team Scholarships

AMOUNT: None Specified DEADLINE: December 12
FIELDS/MAJORS: All Areas of Study

Scholarships awarded to students at Appalachian State University who plan to participate in the Pershing Rifle Drill Team. Contact the office of admissions for details.

Appalachian State University
Department of Military Science
Boone, NC 28608

2606

Physics Merit Scholarships

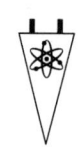

AMOUNT: None Specified DEADLINE: December 12
FIELDS/MAJORS: Physics

Scholarships awarded to students at Appalachian State University who are physics majors. Write to the address below for information.

Appalachian State University
Department of Physics
Boone, NC 28608

2607
Prospective Teacher Scholarship Loan

AMOUNT: None Specified   DEADLINE: None Specified
FIELDS/MAJORS: Education

Loans are available to students at Appalachian State University who plan to enter the teaching profession. Write to the address below for information.

Appalachian State University
Financial Aid Office
Scholarship Section
Boone, NC 28608

2608
School of Music Scholarships

AMOUNT: None Specified   DEADLINE: None Specified
FIELDS/MAJORS: Music

Scholarships are available to students at Appalachian State University who are music majors. Includes the Cratis Williams Scholarship, Dorothy Frazee Thomas Scholarship in Strings, Elsie Erneston Music Scholarship in Voice, Music Talent Awards, Pedrigo Music Scholarship in Voice, and A.J. Fletcher Scholarships. Write to the address below for information.

Appalachian State University
School of Music
Boone, NC 28608

2609
Seby Jones Scholarships

AMOUNT: None Specified   DEADLINE: December 12
FIELDS/MAJORS: All Areas of Study

Scholarships awarded to high school seniors in Wake County, North Carolina. Contact your high school counselor for more information.

Appalachian State University
Office of Financial Aid
Scholarship Section
Boone, NC 28608

2610
Teaching Fellows Scholarship

AMOUNT: None Specified   DEADLINE: None Specified
FIELDS/MAJORS: Education

Available to high school seniors planning to attend Appalachian State University and enter the teaching profession. Applicant must be a resident of North Carolina. Contact your high school counselor for information.

Appalachian State University
Financial Aid Office
Scholarship Section
Boone, NC 28608

2611
Theater Faculty Freshman Scholarship, Talent/Participation Award

AMOUNT: $250-$500   DEADLINE: March 14
FIELDS/MAJORS: Drama

Scholarships are available to students at Appalachian State University who are drama majors. Write to the address below for information.

Appalachian State University
Department of Theater and Dance
Boone, NC 28608

2612
W.H. Plemmons Leadership Fellows Program

AMOUNT: $1000   DEADLINE: December 12
FIELDS/MAJORS: All Areas of Study

Scholarships awarded to students at Appalachian State University who have demonstrated outstanding academic ability and participation in community service activities. Must have a minimum GPA of 3.0 and be able to demonstrate financial need. Contact the office of admissions for details.

Appalachian State University
Office of Admissions
Scholarship Section
Boone, NC 28608

ARIZONA STATE UNIVERSITY

2613
AG Communications Systems Corporation Scholarship

AMOUNT: Maximum: $2000   DEADLINE: February 1
FIELDS/MAJORS: Electrical Engineering, Computer Science

Open to ASU juniors and seniors majoring in the above with an emphasis in telecommunications. Must have a minimum GPA of 3.0 and be full-time students. Refer to School of Construction for deadline date, and write to the address below for more information.

Arizona State University
Vern Hastings, ASU Del E. Webb
PO Box 870204
Tempe, AZ 85287

2614
Arizona Broadcasters Association Scholarship

AMOUNT: Maximum: $2000   DEADLINE: April 1
FIELDS/MAJORS: Broadcasting

Open to enrolled full-time ASU undergraduates majoring in broadcasting. Contact the address below for further information or call (602) 965-1034 (voice mail).

Arizona State University
Cheryl Herrera
Wilson, #203
Tempe, AZ 85287-0803

2615
Arizona CPA Foundation Outstanding Senior Award

AMOUNT: Maximum: $2000   DEADLINE: December 15
FIELDS/MAJORS: Accounting

Open to ASU accounting majors who are entering seniors. Based on outstanding achievement, extracurricular activities, and an overall GPA that places the applicant in the top 10% of ASU accounting majors. Write to the address below for more information or call (602) 965-8710. GPA must be at least 3.4.

Arizona State University
Keith Zaborski
PO Box 873506 BAC 226
Tempe, AZ 85287-3506

2616
Arizona Public Service Scholarships

AMOUNT: Maximum: $1000
DEADLINE: March 30
FIELDS/MAJORS: Engineering, Business

Open to full-time undergraduates who are Arizona residents. There are three categories to this scholarship for business or engineering majors with a minimum GPA of 3.0: business majors, dependents of APS employees, and minorities in engineering who are members of the following student groups: American Indian Science and Engineering Society, Society of Hispanic Professional Engineers, Arizona Council of Black Engineers and Scientists, and the Society of Women Engineers. Contact the address below for further information.

Arizona State University
Scholarship Office Main Campus
PO Box 870412
Tempe, AZ 85287

2617
Associated Highway Patrolmen of Arizona Scholarship

AMOUNT: Maximum: $1500   DEADLINE: June 30
FIELDS/MAJORS: All Areas of Study

Open to students who are Arizona residents and dependents of active or retired regular members of the Associated Highway Patrolmen of Arizona. Must be between the ages of sixteen and twenty-three. Selections based on GPA, community leadership, and financial need. Preference will be given to students who have received this award in the past. Contact the address below for further information. Must have a GPA of at least 2.7.

Arizona State University
Scholarship Office Main Campus
PO Box 870412
Tempe, AZ 85287

2618
ASU President's Club Scholarships

AMOUNT: Maximum: $2000   DEADLINE: None Specified
FIELDS/MAJORS: All Areas of Study

This includes three separate awards: 1) Heather Farr Award, 2) Merit-based undergraduate award, and 3) Need-based graduate award. All applicants must be Arizona residents. (1) Farr award: for undergraduates or graduates with a minimum GPA of 2.75, demonstrated financial need, and a high level of personal achievement. (2) Merit-based undergraduate award: applicants must have a minimum GPA of 3.0. Selections based on exceptional achievement. (3) Need-based graduate student award: applicants must have a minimum GPA of 3.5 and be able to demonstrate financial need. Contact the address below for further information.

Arizona State University
Scholarship Office Main Campus
PO Box 870412
Tempe, AZ 85287

2619
ASU Teacher Incentive Program

AMOUNT: Maximum: $3000   DEADLINE: April 1
FIELDS/MAJORS: Education

Open to ASU students admitted to the Professional Teacher Preparation Program. Must have a minimum GPA of 2.5. Undergraduates may receive $3000 per year for a maximum of $9000. Graduates may receive $3000 for a maximum of $18,000. Must be enrolled in the Professional Teacher Preparation Program or the Post/Bac/ITC and have successfully completed the PTPP exams. Contact the address below for further information.

Arizona State University
Richard Daniel
PO Box 871211
Tempe, AZ 85287-1211

2620
Bechtel Foundation

AMOUNT: Maximum: $1750 DEADLINE: None Specified
FIELDS/MAJORS: Construction

Scholarship is awarded to a ASU senior with a GPA of 3.0 or above. Must have completed a minimum of 15 credit hours per semester. Refer to School of Construction for deadline date, and write to the address below for more information.

Arizona State University
Vern Hastings, ASU Del E. Webb
PO Box 870204
Tempe, AZ 85287

2621
Boeing Company Scholarship

AMOUNT: Maximum: $2000 DEADLINE: February 1
FIELDS/MAJORS: Mechanical/Electrical Engineering, Computer/Aerospace Systems

Open to ASU full-time juniors with a minimum GPA of 3.0. Along with the scholarship, there is a possibility of future employment with the Boeing Company. Write to the address below for more information.

Arizona State University
Manuel Aroz
CEAS/SAS 7006
Tempe, AZ 85287

2622
Carl Weingartner Memorial Scholarship

AMOUNT: Maximum: $2600 DEADLINE: February 1
FIELDS/MAJORS: Mechanical Engineering

Open to ASU full-time sophomores, juniors, and seniors with a minimum GPA of 3.0. Must be able to demonstrate financial need. Write to the address below for more information.

Arizona State University
Manuel Aroz
CEAS/SAS 7006
Tempe, AZ 85287

2623
Duncan Jennings Memorial Scholarship

AMOUNT: Maximum: $1700 DEADLINE: December 15
FIELDS/MAJORS: Marketing

Scholarship is awarded to a ASU junior or senior professional business student with an interest in advertising and a GPA of 3.0 or better. Must be an Arizona resident. Write to the address below or call (602) 965-8710 for more information.

Arizona State University
Keith Zaborski
PO Box 873506 BAC 226
Tempe, AZ 85287-3506

2624
FISCM Doctoral Research and Gene Gallup Fellowship

AMOUNT: $500-$3500 DEADLINE: December 15
FIELDS/MAJORS: Marketing

Scholarships are awarded to ASU doctoral-level graduates majoring in marketing. Write to the address below or call (602) 965-8710 for more information.

Arizona State University
Keith Zaborski
PO Box 873506
Tempe, AZ 85287-3506

2625
Gage Davus Travel Scholarship

AMOUNT: $500-$3000 DEADLINE: April 15
FIELDS/MAJORS: Architecture

Open to full-time upper year and graduate ASU students enrolled in Landscape Architecture, Planning Architecture program. Must be U.S. citizens and have a minimum GPA of 3.2. Applicants for the $500 awards must be signed up for one of the SOA or SPLA summer travel programs. One $3000 award and four $500 awards are offered annually. Contact the address below for further information.

Arizona State University
Anna West
PO Box 871905
Tempe, AZ 85287-1905

2626
Graphic Arts Technical Foundation Scholarship

AMOUNT: Maximum: $4500 DEADLINE: None Specified
FIELDS/MAJORS: Agribusiness

Open to ASU full-time students enrolled in Agribusiness. Refer to the School of Agribusiness for the deadline date. GPA must be at least 2.6.

Arizona State University
Dr. Julie Stanton
6001 S. Power Rd.
Mesa, AZ 85206

2627
Hugh L. Hamilton Scholarship

AMOUNT: Maximum: $2000 DEADLINE: December 15
FIELDS/MAJORS: Finance

Open to finance majors who have completed FIN 300, 331, and 361 by end of spring semester with a minimum overall GPA of 3.0 and at least a 3.25 in business. Must be able to demonstrate financial need and leadership abilities. Candidates will be interviewed by the Finance Department Scholarship Committee. Write to the address below for more information or call (602) 965-8710.

Arizona State University
Keith Zaborski
PO Box 873506 BAC 226
Tempe, AZ 85287-3506

2628
Ilene Peggylamb Scholarship

AMOUNT: Maximum: $3000 DEADLINE: None Specified
FIELDS/MAJORS: Music

Open to full-time ASU outstanding graduate students. Must be able to demonstrate financial need. Contact the School of Music for information regarding the deadline date. Contact the address below for further information or call (602) 965-9861. GPA must be at least 2.6.

Arizona State University
Margaret Jaconelli, School of Music
PO Box 870405
Tempe, AZ 85287-0405

2629
Kaibab Industries Scholarship

AMOUNT: Maximum: $1700 DEADLINE: April 15
FIELDS/MAJORS: All Areas of Study

Open to incoming freshmen who are Arizona residents and first-time freshmen. In February of each year, Kaibab Industries announces the scholarships to high schools and employees. Schools and employees send in nominations for the scholarship by March 31. Applications are then mailed to each nominated student. Contact the address below for further information. Must have a GPA of at least 2.9.

Arizona State University
Scholarship Office Main Campus
PO Box 870412
Tempe, AZ 85287

2630
Krueger Family Foundation Scholarship

AMOUNT: Maximum: $2000 DEADLINE: December 15
FIELDS/MAJORS: Finance

Open to ASU full-time juniors or seniors majoring in finance with GPAs of 3.0 or higher. Must be residents of Arizona. Write to the address below for more information or call (602) 965-810.

Arizona State University
Keith Zaborski
PO Box 873506 BAC 226
Tempe, AZ 85287-3506

2631
Marty Zajac Memorial Scholarship

AMOUNT: Maximum: $1500 DEADLINE: September 30
FIELDS/MAJORS: Business

Open to full-time ASU undergraduates with a minimum GPA of 3.0. The Zajac family committee makes the final selection in the fall semester of each year. Application deadline is August through September. Contact the address listed or call (602) 965-8710 for further information.

Arizona State University
Keith Zaborski
PO Box 873506 BAC 226
Tempe, AZ 85287-3506

2632
Native American Justice Studies Scholarship

AMOUNT: Maximum: $2000   DEADLINE: None Specified
FIELDS/MAJORS: Justice Studies

Open to full-time ASU Native American undergraduates enrolled in the American Indian Justice Studies Program. Must be in the top third of class and be of Native American descent. Application deadline date is spring semester. Contact the Department below for further information or call (602) 965-1034 (voice mail). GPA must be at least 2.6.

Arizona State University
Cheryl Herrera
Wilson, #203
Tempe, AZ 85287-0803

2633
Oscar A. and Joyce B. Shiell Scholarship

AMOUNT: None Specified   DEADLINE: March 30
FIELDS/MAJORS: All Areas of Study

Open to undergraduates who are seeking their first degree and are Arizona residents. Must have a minimum GPA of 3.0. Based primarily on financial need. Contact the address below for further information.

Arizona State University
Scholarship Office Main Campus
PO Box 870412
Tempe, AZ 85287

2634
Pepsico Scholarship

AMOUNT: $6000   DEADLINE: December 15
FIELDS/MAJORS: Business

Scholarships are open to ASU first-year minority graduate students in business. Award is $6000 plus tuition waiver. Recipients selected on the basis of GMAT scores, undergraduate performance, and evidence of leadership and community service. Write to the address below or call (602) 965-8710 for more information. GPA must be at least 3.0.

Arizona State University
Keith Zaborski
PO Box 873506 BAC 226
Tempe, AZ 85287-3506

2635
Pimalco/Gila River Indian Community Scholarship

AMOUNT: None Specified   DEADLINE: July 30
FIELDS/MAJORS: All Areas of Study

Open to residents of the Gila River Indian Community and/or on the tribal registry of the Maricopa or Pima Indian Tribes. Must be admitted to ASU as full-time students. Renewable up to five years as long as academic standards are met. Contact the address below for further information.

Arizona State University
Scholarship Office Main Campus
PO Box 870412
Tempe, AZ 85287

2636
Registrar's Scholarship

AMOUNT: None Specified   DEADLINE: July 30
FIELDS/MAJORS: Journalism, Justice Studies, Communication, Recreation, Broadcasting

Open to full-time sophomores, juniors, and seniors who are Arizona residents. Must have a minimum GPA of 3.0. This is a non-renewable award. Award is in-state tuition. Contact the address below for further information.

Arizona State University, College of Liberal Arts and Sciences
Kay Dingman, Administrative Assistant
PO Box 870302
Tempe, AZ 85287-2602

2637
Rod J. McMullin, Salt River Project Water Resources Scholarship

AMOUNT: Maximum: $1778   DEADLINE: February 1
FIELDS/MAJORS: Civil Engineering

Open to ASU full-time juniors, seniors, and graduate students in civil engineering with an emphasis in water resources. Must have a minimum GPA of 3.0. Applicants must be U.S. citizens and residents of Arizona. Write to the address below for more information.

Arizona State University
Manuel Aroz
CEAS/SAS 7006
Tempe, AZ 85287

2638
School of Construction Scholarship

AMOUNT: Maximum: $1500 DEADLINE: None Specified
FIELDS/MAJORS: Construction

Open to ASU sophomores, juniors, and seniors who have completed at least 15 credit hours per semester with a minimum GPA of 3.0. Incoming freshmen must be in the top 5% of graduating class. Refer to School of Construction for deadline date, and write to the address below for more information.

Arizona State University
Vern Hastings, ASU Del E. Webb
PO Box 870204
Tempe, AZ 85287

2639
Seymour L. Rosen Scholarship

AMOUNT: Maximum: $3000 DEADLINE: None Specified
FIELDS/MAJORS: Music

Open to full-time ASU undergraduates and graduate students who have a minimum GPA of 3.0 and are U.S. citizens. Must demonstrate outstanding artistic ability and financial need. Preference given to Arizona residents. Contact the School of Music for information regarding the deadline date. Contact the address below for further information or call (602) 965-9861.

Arizona State University
Margaret Jaconelli, School of Music
PO Box 870405
Tempe, AZ 85287-0405

2640
Superior Companies Scholarship

AMOUNT: Maximum: $800 DEADLINE: March 15
FIELDS/MAJORS: All Areas of Study

Open to full-time undergraduates who are Arizona residents with a minimum GPA of 3.0. Preference given to children of Superior Co. employees. Financial need may be considered. May be renewed if a minimum GPA of 3.0 is maintained. Contact the address below for further information.

Arizona State University
Scholarship Office Main Campus
PO Box 870412
Tempe, AZ 85287

2641
Thomas P. Papandrew Scholarship

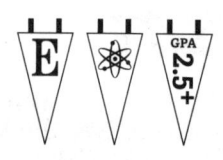

AMOUNT: Maximum: $1000 DEADLINE: March 31
FIELDS/MAJORS: Landscape Architecture/Design

Open to minority students enrolled full-time at Arizona State University who are Arizona residents. Must be able to demonstrate financial need. Renewable as long as recipient continues to demonstrate financial need and other criteria are also met or exceeded. Write to the address listed for additional information or call (202) 686-8337. Must have a GPA of at least 2.8.

Landscape Architecture Foundation
Scholarship Program
4401 Connecticut Ave. NW, #500
Washington, DC 20008

2642
Valley Paving Association Scholarship

AMOUNT: Maximum: $1000 DEADLINE: October 30
FIELDS/MAJORS: Civil Engineering, Construction

Open to juniors and seniors who are Arizona residents and U.S. citizens. Must be full-time students and able to demonstrate financial need. Contact the address below for further information.

Arizona State University
Scholarship Office Main Campus
PO Box 870412
Tempe, AZ 85287

2643
Vinnell Foundation Scholarship

AMOUNT: Maximum: $1600 DEADLINE: None Specified
FIELDS/MAJORS: Construction

Open to ASU sophomores, juniors, and seniors who have completed at least 15 credit hours per semester with a minimum GPA of 3.0. Incoming freshmen must be in the top 5% of graduating class. Refer to School of Construction for deadline date, and write to the address below for more information.

Arizona State University
Vern Hastings, ASU Del E. Webb
PO Box 870204
Tempe, AZ 85287

ARKANSAS STATE UNIVERSITY

2644
Academic Distinction Scholarship

GPA 3.0+

AMOUNT: None Specified DEADLINE: April 1
FIELDS/MAJORS: All Areas of Study

Open to high school seniors who are Arkansas residents. Must have an ACT of 24-25, SAT of 1010, or a minimum GPA of 3.0. Recipients must enter ASU, Jonesboro, full-time within one year of graduation. Renewable if recipients complete 12 credit hours per semester with a minimum GPA of 3.0 for the first three semesters and a minimum GPA of 3.25 for the remaining five semesters. Award is tuition. Contact the address below or your high school counselor for further information.

Arkansas State University, Jonesboro
Financial Aid Office
PO Box 1620
State University, AR 72467

2645
Trustee's Scholarship

GPA 3.5+

AMOUNT: None Specified DEADLINE: April 1
FIELDS/MAJORS: All Areas of Study

Open to high school seniors who are Arkansas residents or high school age GED recipients (with a minimum score of 48). Must enter ASU, Jonesboro, within one year of graduation. Renewable if recipients complete at least 12 credit hours per semester with a minimum GPA of 3.5 and participates in the Honors Program. Award is tuition, double occupancy room in the residence hall, and $1200 per semester. Contact the address below or your high school counselor for further information.

Arkansas State University
Financial Aid Office
PO Box 1620
State University, AR 72467

ARMENIAN BIBLE COLLEGE

2646
Armenian Bible College Scholarships

AMOUNT: Maximum: $2000 DEADLINE: June 30
FIELDS/MAJORS: All Areas of Study

Scholarships for students attending Armenian Bible College in any area of study who have pledged to work as a minister, evangelist, missionary, or youth director after graduation. Write to the address below for more details.

Armenian Bible College
Dr. Yeghia Babikian, Director
1605 E. Elizabeth St.
Pasadena, CA 91104

ASHLAND UNIVERSITY

2647
Alumnus Grant

AMOUNT: $1000 DEADLINE: None Specified
FIELDS/MAJORS: All Areas of Study

Sons and daughters of Ashland University alumni are eligible for this grant. The grant is renewable by maintaining satisfactory academic progress. Write to the address below for more information.

Ashland University
401 College Ave.
Ashland, OH 44805

2648
Amstutz Endowed Scholarship

AMOUNT: $2000 DEADLINE: None Specified
FIELDS/MAJORS: All Areas of Study

The award is made annually to a full-time student of Ashland University on the basis of merit and promise. Write to the address below for more information.

Ashland University
401 College Ave.
Ashland, OH 44805

2649
Ashland Symphony Orchestra

AMOUNT: $600 DEADLINE: None Specified
FIELDS/MAJORS: Orchestra Music

Scholarships to Ashland University student string players, regardless of their majors. Scholarships are granted on the basis of an audition and the student's agreement to participate in all orchestra performances and rehearsals. Write to the address below for more information.

Ashland University
401 College Ave.
Ashland, OH 44805

2650

Ashland University Faculty Women's Club Memorial Scholarship

AMOUNT: $400 DEADLINE: None Specified
FIELDS/MAJORS: All Areas of Study

Awarded to a woman at the end of her sophomore year. The recipient must be high or superior in leadership, character, promise, and scholastic ability. Write to the address below for more information.

Ashland University
401 College Ave.
Ashland, OH 44805

2651

Brethren Grant

AMOUNT: $1000 DEADLINE: None Specified
FIELDS/MAJORS: All Areas of Study

Students who are members of the Ashland-based Brethren Church are eligible for this grant. A letter verifying membership is required from the student's minister. Write to the address below for more information.

Ashland University
401 College Ave.
Ashland, OH 44805

2652

Cindy Barr Memorial Scholarship

AMOUNT: $1000 DEADLINE: None Specified
FIELDS/MAJORS: All Areas of Study

Awarded to a female freshmen athlete at Ashland University. Write to the address below for more information.

Ashland University
401 College Ave.
Ashland, OH 44805

2653

Dr. William R. Zaffiro Memorial Endowed Scholarship

AMOUNT: None Specified DEADLINE: None Specified
FIELDS/MAJORS: Psychology

Awarded annually to a deserving student majoring in psychology with a 3.0 GPA. Write to the address below for more information.

Ashland University
401 College Ave.
Ashland, OH 44805

2654

Emil H. Ritter Endowed Scholarship

AMOUNT: $1000 DEADLINE: None Specified
FIELDS/MAJORS: All Areas of Study

Awarded to a second-year Ashland County student demonstrating scholastic achievement, community involvement, and promise of leadership. Write to the address below for more information.

Ashland University
401 College Ave.
Ashland, OH 44805

2655

Hugo H. and Mabel B. Young Scholarship

AMOUNT: None Specified DEADLINE: None Specified
FIELDS/MAJORS: All Areas of Study

Available to full-time students who have exhibited financial need and scholastic achievement. Preference will be given to residents of Loudonville, Ohio. Write to the address below for more information.

Ashland University
401 College Ave.
Ashland, OH 44805

2656

John M. Ashbrook Scholarship

AMOUNT: $2000 DEADLINE: None Specified
FIELDS/MAJORS: Political Science or Public Affairs

The Ashbrook Scholarship is awarded to full-time Ashland University students interested in public affairs. All Ashbrook Scholars are required to maintain a 3.0 GPA and to major or minor in political science or minor in public affairs. Write to the address below for more information.

Ashland University
401 College Ave.
Ashland, OH 44805

2657
Joseph R. Benden Jr. Memorial Scholarship

AMOUNT: $5000   DEADLINE: None Specified
FIELDS/MAJORS: All Areas of Study

Scholarship is a one-time award to incoming freshmen from Wayne County who demonstrate financial need. Write to the address below for more information.

Ashland University
401 College Ave.
Ashland, OH 44805

2658
Kappa Omicron Phi Scholarship

AMOUNT: $150   DEADLINE: None Specified
FIELDS/MAJORS: Human Services or Home Economics

$150 from the human services-home economics honor society to a human services-home economics sophomore major for use in the junior year at Ashland University, based on financial need and academic standing. Write to the address below for more information.

Ashland University
401 College Ave.
Ashland, OH 44805

2659
Lubrizol Corporation Award

AMOUNT: $500   DEADLINE: None Specified
FIELDS/MAJORS: Chemistry

The Lubrizol Corporation of Cleveland, Ohio, awards a $500 scholarship to a junior or senior majoring in chemistry, who plans a career in pure chemistry or related fields. The award is given solely on the basis of academic excellence. Write to the address below for more information.

Ashland University
401 College Ave.
Ashland, OH 44805

2660
Mabel Zehner Award

AMOUNT: None Specified   DEADLINE: None Specified
FIELDS/MAJORS: Organ Music

Awarded to a student interested in the study of organ. Write to the address below for more information.

Ashland University
401 College Ave.
Ashland, OH 44805

2661
Oakville, Indiana, Brethren Church Scholarship

AMOUNT: $500   DEADLINE: None Specified
FIELDS/MAJORS: Ministry, Christian Work

Given to a student from the Oakville Brethren Church preparing for the ministry or full-time Christian work. Write to the address below for more information.

Ashland University
401 College Ave.
Ashland, OH 44805

2662
Pennsylvania District Women's Missionary Society Award

AMOUNT: $200   DEADLINE: None Specified
FIELDS/MAJORS: Missionary

Award given to a woman who is a member of the Ashland-based Brethren Church. Write to the address below for more information.

Ashland University
401 College Ave.
Ashland, OH 44805

2663
Pi Alpha Gamma Award

AMOUNT: $200   DEADLINE: None Specified
FIELDS/MAJORS: All Areas of Study

Awarded to a woman at the close of her junior year. Write to the address below for more information.

Ashland University
401 College Ave.
Ashland, OH 44805

2664
Presidential, Achievement, and Transfer Scholarship

AMOUNT: $1000-$6000   DEADLINE: None Specified
FIELDS/MAJORS: All Areas of Study

These scholarships are given to freshman and transfer students according to high school or college GPAs and ACT scores. The Presidential is worth $4000 to $6000 per year. The Transfer Scholarship is worth $1000 to $4000 per year, while the Achievement Scholarship is worth $2000 per year. Write to the address below for more information.

Ashland University
401 College Ave.
Ashland, OH 44805

2665
Sisterhood of Mary and Martha Award

AMOUNT: $200 DEADLINE: None Specified
FIELDS/MAJORS: All Areas of Study

Given to a woman in her freshman year. Write to the address below for more information.

Ashland University
401 College Ave.
Ashland, OH 44805

2666
Southeast Laymen's Scholarship

AMOUNT: $200 DEADLINE: None Specified
FIELDS/MAJORS: All Areas of Study

The scholarship is awarded each year to a seminary or pre-seminary student of the Southeast District of the Ashland-based Brethren Church. If there are no eligible candidates, the scholarship is given to a worthy student of the Brethren Church. Write to the address below for more information.

Ashland University
401 College Ave.
Ashland, OH 44805

2667
William and Hattie Vachon Memorial Scholarship

AMOUNT: $1000 DEADLINE: None Specified
FIELDS/MAJORS: All Areas of Study

Available to qualified full-time students with an average of B or better. Must be a residents of Ashland County. Write to the address below for more information. GPA must be at least 3.0.

Ashland University
401 College Ave.
Ashland, OH 44805

AUGSBURG COLLEGE

2668
Center for Global Education Scholarships for Students of Color

AMOUNT: Maximum: $2500 DEADLINE: October 15
FIELDS/MAJORS: Foreign Study

Scholarships are available to enable students of color, who otherwise may not have sufficient funding, to participate in semester abroad programs. Priority will be given to U.S. citizens and permanent residents. Must be a currently enrolled undergraduate. The second deadline date is May 15 for the fall program. Write to the address below for more information.

Center for Global Education at Augsburg College
2211 Riverside Ave.
Minneapolis, MN 55454

AVILA COLLEGE

2669
Athletic Grant

AMOUNT: None Specified DEADLINE: April 15
FIELDS/MAJORS: All Areas of Study

Awarded on basis of talent in men's soccer, basketball, baseball; women's soccer, volleyball, basketball, and softball. Write to the address below for more information.

Avila College
11901 Wornall Rd.
Kansas City, MO 64145

2670
Family Grant

AMOUNT: $500 DEADLINE: April 15
FIELDS/MAJORS: All Areas of Study

$500 per year for each student of the same immediate family concurrently attending Avila College on a full-time basis. Eligibility continues as long as two or more members remain enrolled full-time. Write to the address below for more information.

Avila College
11901 Wornall Rd.
Kansas City, MO 64145

2671
Focus Grant

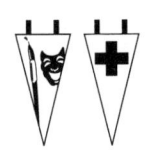

AMOUNT: $1500 DEADLINE: April 15
FIELDS/MAJORS: Pre-Medicine or Art

Awarded to students interested in pre-medicine or art on a competitive basis. Write to the address below for more information.

Avila College
11901 Wornall Rd.
Kansas City, MO 64145

2672
Missouri Grant

AMOUNT: Maximum: $1500 DEADLINE: April 15
FIELDS/MAJORS: All Areas of Study

For Missouri residents with demonstrated need. Write to the address below for more information.

Avila College
11901 Wornall Rd.
Kansas City, MO 64145

2673
Performance Grant

AMOUNT: None Specified DEADLINE: April 15
FIELDS/MAJORS: Music or Theater

Awarded to students based on talent in music or theater. Write to the address below for more information.

Avila College
11901 Wornall Rd.
Kansas City, MO 64145

2674
President's Scholarships

AMOUNT: $1500-$5000 DEADLINE: April 15
FIELDS/MAJORS: All Areas of Study

For freshman students based on their GPAs of 3.2 or higher and their ACT scores of 21-22 award is $1500, 23-24 award is $3000, 25-26 award is $4000, and 27+ award is $5000. For transfer students with GPAs of 3.2-3.49 award is $500, 3.5-3.69 award is $1000, and for 3.7-4.0 award is $1500. Write to the address below for more information.

Avila College
11901 Wornall Rd.
Kansas City, MO 64145

2675
Saint Teresa of Avila Award

AMOUNT: $1000-$1500 DEADLINE: April 15
FIELDS/MAJORS: All Areas of Study

$1500 awarded annually to any first-time, full-time freshman who has graduated from a Catholic high school and lives in one of Avila's residence halls. The award is available to both Catholic and non-Catholic students regardless of need. $1000 for commuter students. Write to the address below for more information.

Avila College
11901 Wornall Rd.
Kansas City, MO 64145

2676
Sisters of St. Joseph of Carondelet Grant

AMOUNT: $1000 DEADLINE: April 15
FIELDS/MAJORS: All Areas of Study

$1000 grants awarded to new freshmen or sophomore students who demonstrate exceptional need. Write to the address below for more information.

Avila College
11901 Wornall Rd.
Kansas City, MO 64145

BALDWIN-WALLACE COLLEGE

2677
Alumni Scholarships

AMOUNT: Maximum: $1000 DEADLINE: None Specified
FIELDS/MAJORS: All Areas of Study

Awarded annually to children and grandchildren of B-W alumni. Write to the address below for more information.

Baldwin-Wallace College
275 Eastland Rd.
Berea, OH 44017

2678
B-W Founders Scholarships

AMOUNT: Maximum: $3500 DEADLINE: None Specified
FIELDS/MAJORS: All Areas of Study

Awarded to incoming freshmen whose outstanding academic skills and diverse personal qualities will enrich campus life, foster community spirit, and advance the mission of the College. Write to the address below for more information.

Baldwin-Wallace College
275 Eastland Rd.
Berea, OH 44017

2679
B-W Multicultural Scholarships

AMOUNT: $2000 DEADLINE: None Specified
FIELDS/MAJORS: All Areas of Study

Awarded to incoming freshman students who show academic promise and have demonstrated participation in high school activities coupled with leadership skills. Write to the address below for more information.

Baldwin-Wallace College
275 Eastland Rd.
Berea, OH 44017

2680
Laurels Scholarships

AMOUNT: Maximum: $5000 DEADLINE: None Specified
FIELDS/MAJORS: All Areas of Study

Awarded to incoming freshman students who demonstrate academic skills, extracurricular, and community involvement, leadership qualities, and the commitment to overcome obstacles. Write to the address below for more information.

Baldwin-Wallace College
275 Eastland Rd.
Berea, OH 44017

2681
Margaret Rusk Griffiths Music Scholarships

AMOUNT: $200-$3000 DEADLINE: None Specified
FIELDS/MAJORS: Music

Awarded to students on the basis of their musical and general academic ability. Students must have GPAs of 3.0 or above. Write to the address below for more information.

Baldwin-Wallace College
275 Eastland Rd.
Berea, OH 44017

2682
Presidential Honorary Scholarships

AMOUNT: Maximum: $6000 DEADLINE: None Specified
FIELDS/MAJORS: All Areas of Study

Awarded to student who rank in the upper 15% of their graduating class with outstanding academic ability and potential as revealed by their ACT or SAT scores. Write to the address below for more information. GPA must be at least 3.6.

Baldwin-Wallace College
275 Eastland Rd.
Berea, OH 44017

2683
Talent Honorary Scholarships

AMOUNT: $500 DEADLINE: None Specified
FIELDS/MAJORS: Theater or Art

Awarded to new students who possess outstanding talent in such areas as theater and art. Write to the address below for more information.

Baldwin-Wallace College
275 Eastland Rd.
Berea, OH 44017

2684
Trustees Honor Scholarships

AMOUNT: Maximum: $4000 DEADLINE: None Specified
FIELDS/MAJORS: All Areas of Study

Awarded to students who have strong academic potential. Must have at least a 3.2 GPA. Write to the address below for more information.

Baldwin-Wallace College
275 Eastland Rd.
Berea, OH 44017

BARRY UNIVERSITY

2685
Athletic Grants

AMOUNT: None Specified DEADLINE: February 15
FIELDS/MAJORS: Athletics or Sports

Awarded to students who show outstanding athletic ability. Contact the appropriate head coach or the Athletic Department for more information.

Barry University
11300 N.E. Second Ave.
Miami Shores, FL 33161-6695

2686
Barry Grants

AMOUNT: $500-$7000 DEADLINE: February 15
FIELDS/MAJORS: All Areas of Study

Awarded to students who demonstrate academic promise and financial need. Awards are made on a first come, first serve basis. Write to the address below for more information.

Barry University
11300 N.E. Second Ave.
Miami Shores, FL 33161-6695

BARTON COLLEGE

2687
40 and 8 Voiture 930 of American Legion Post 13 Scholarship

AMOUNT: None Specified DEADLINE: March 15
FIELDS/MAJORS: Nursing

Open to junior and senior nursing majors. Must have a minimum GPA of 2.5. Selection made by the faculty of the School of Nursing. Contact the address below for further information.

Barton College
Financial Aid Office
Wilson, NC 27893

2688
Anne Harrison Ruffin Memorial Scholarship

AMOUNT: Maximum: $3000 DEADLINE: March 15
FIELDS/MAJORS: All Areas of Study

Open to incoming freshmen who are residents of Wilson County, can demonstrate financial need, and have a minimum GPA of 2.0. Renewable. Contact the address below for further information.

Barton College
Financial Aid Office
Wilson, NC 27893

2689
Bertha R. Brewer Memorial Scholarship

AMOUNT: None Specified DEADLINE: March 15
FIELDS/MAJORS: History, Social Sciences

Open to juniors and seniors majoring in the above areas. Faculty of the Department of History and Social Sciences makes the selection. Contact the address below for further information.

Barton College
Financial Aid Office
Wilson, NC 27893

2690
Bethany Rose Joyner Scholarship

AMOUNT: None Specified DEADLINE: March 15
FIELDS/MAJORS: All Areas of Study

Open to high school seniors who have demonstrated above average academics, participated in worthwhile school and community activities, and have financial need. Renewable if recipient maintains a minimum GPA of 2.5. Contact the address below for further information.

Barton College
Financial Aid Office
Wilson, NC 27893

2691
Buster and Kitty Bell Scholarship

AMOUNT: None Specified DEADLINE: March 15
FIELDS/MAJORS: All Areas of Study

Open to students of above average academic ability who can demonstrate financial need. Must have a minimum GPA of 2.5 to apply. Contact the address below for further information.

Barton College
Financial Aid Office
Wilson, NC 27893

2692
C.B. Mashburn Scholarship

AMOUNT: None Specified DEADLINE: March 15
FIELDS/MAJORS: Religion

Open to students majoring in religion with preference given to members of Disciples of Christ. Selection made by Department of Religion and Philosophy, Chaplain of the College, and the Office of Financial Aid. Contact the address below for further information.

Barton College
Financial Aid Office
Wilson, NC 27893

2693

Dr. and Mrs. W. Raleigh Parker, Sr. Scholarship

AMOUNT: None Specified
DEADLINE: March 15
FIELDS/MAJORS: Education, Nursing, Pre-med., Psychology

Open to students majoring in any of the fields listed above. Selection based on financial need and recommendation of the respective concerned departments. Contact the address below for further information. Must have a GPA of at least 2.8.

Barton College
Financial Aid Office
Wilson, NC 27893

2694

Emma Wiggs Riley Memorial Scholarship

AMOUNT: None Specified   DEADLINE: March 15
FIELDS/MAJORS: Nursing

Open to juniors and seniors who demonstrate financial need and scholastic merit. Priority is given to registered nurses working toward the baccalaureate degree in nursing. Contact the address below for further information. Must have a GPA of at least 3.0.

Barton College
Financial Aid Office
Wilson, NC 27893

2695

George H. Adams Memorial Scholarship

AMOUNT: None Specified   DEADLINE: March 15
FIELDS/MAJORS: All Areas of Study

Open to entering or continuing students. First preference given to residents of Wilson County. Second preference given to a resident of North Carolina. Contact the address below for further information.

Barton College
Financial Aid Office
Wilson, NC 27893

2696

Greater Wilson Rotary Club and TPA Scholarships

AMOUNT: None Specified   DEADLINE: March 15
FIELDS/MAJORS: All Areas of Study

Open to students who can demonstrate financial need. Preference given to residents of Wilson County, North Carolina. Contact the address below for further information about both awards.

Barton College
Financial Aid Office
Wilson, NC 27893

2697

Gretchen B. Boyette Scholarship

AMOUNT: None Specified   DEADLINE: March 15
FIELDS/MAJORS: Business

Open to full-time students who are enrolled in the School of Business and can demonstrate financial need. Renewable if recipients make satisfactory progress toward graduation.

Barton College
Financial Aid Office
Wilson, NC 27893

2698

Groves L. Herring Memorial Scholarship

AMOUNT: None Specified   DEADLINE: March 15
FIELDS/MAJORS: Music Composing

Scholarship is available to an outstanding senior composer majoring in music. Contact the address below for further information. Must have a GPA of at least 3.0.

Barton College
Financial Aid Office
Wilson, NC 27893

2699

Herman and Dell W. Bowen Scholarship

AMOUNT: None Specified   DEADLINE: March 15
FIELDS/MAJORS: All Areas of Study

Open to entering freshmen with first preference given to residents of Martin County and second preference given to North Carolina residents. Contact the address below for further information.

Barton College
Financial Aid Office
Wilson, NC 27893

2700
High Honors Scholarship Program

AMOUNT: None Specified DEADLINE: March 15
FIELDS/MAJORS: All Areas of Study

Open to high school seniors with a minimum GPA of 3.4 and at least a score of 1100 on the SAT. Renewable if recipients remain full-time students and maintain a minimum GPA of 3.0. Award is 25% of tuition. Contact the address below for further information.

Barton College
Financial Aid Office
Wilson, NC 27893

2701
Honors Scholarship

AMOUNT: None Specified DEADLINE: March 15
FIELDS/MAJORS: All Areas of Study

Open to high school seniors in the top 10% of their class. Must have a minimum GPA of 3.2 and at least a score of 1000 of the SAT. Renewable for four years if recipients remain full-time and maintain a minimum GPA of 3.0. Award is 20% of tuition. Contact the address below for further information.

Barton College
Financial Aid Office
Wilson, NC 27893

2702
Hugh Ange Memorial and Dr. John Barclay Scholarships

AMOUNT: None Specified DEADLINE: March 15
FIELDS/MAJORS: Ministry

Open to students preparing for the ministry. Contact the address below for further information about both awards.

Barton College
Financial Aid Office
Wilson, NC 27893

2703
J.P. Tyndall Scholarship

AMOUNT: None Specified DEADLINE: March 15
FIELDS/MAJORS: Natural Science

Open to outstanding seniors. Based on academics, involvement in departmental activities, and potential for future contributions in science. Selected by the faculty of the Department of Biological and Physical Sciences. Contact the address below for further information. Must have a GPA of at least 3.1.

Barton College
Financial Aid Office
Wilson, NC 27893

2704
John and Cassie Cowell Memorial Scholarship

AMOUNT: None Specified DEADLINE: March 15
FIELDS/MAJORS: All Areas of Study

Open to students from Pamlico County, North Carolina. Contact the address below for further information.

Barton College
Financial Aid Office
Wilson, NC 27893

2705
Joseph Bryan and Jane Wilson O'Neal Fellowship

AMOUNT: None Specified DEADLINE: March 15
FIELDS/MAJORS: Science

Open to undergraduates pursuing careers in science or science-related field. Contact the address below for further information.

Barton College
Financial Aid Office
Wilson, NC 27893

2706
Larry W. Staley Memorial Scholarship

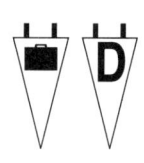

AMOUNT: None Specified DEADLINE: March 15
FIELDS/MAJORS: Business, Accounting

First preference of this award given to students with disabilities in financial need. Second preference given to business or accounting majors with financial need. Selection made by office of financial aid. (When applicable, in conjunction with the School of Business). Contact the address below for further information.

Barton College
Financial Aid Office
Wilson, NC 27893

2707
Leadership/Activities Scholarship

AMOUNT: None Specified DEADLINE: March 15
FIELDS/MAJORS: All Areas of Study

Open to high school seniors in the top 15% of class. Must have a minimum GPA of 2.5 and at least a score of 920 on the SAT. Renewable if recipients remain full-time and maintain a minimum GPA of 2.5. Award is 15% of tuition. Contact the address below for further information.

Barton College
Financial Aid Office
Wilson, NC 27893

2708
Leona Boswell Smith Scholarship

AMOUNT: None Specified DEADLINE: March 15
FIELDS/MAJORS: Nursing

Open to nursing majors. Based on academics, achievement, and financial need. Selection made by the School of Nursing, Offices of Financial Aid and Admissions. Contact the address below for further information. Must have a GPA of at least 2.9.

Barton College
Financial Aid Office
Wilson, NC 27893

2709
Lill Chapman Tomlinson and George W. Tomlinson Scholarship

AMOUNT: None Specified DEADLINE: March 15
FIELDS/MAJORS: Music, History, Social Science.

Open to full-time juniors and seniors who are residents of North Carolina and have a minimum GPA of 2.5. First preference given to piano majors. Second preference given to students with a major in the Department of History and Social Sciences. Contact the address below for further information.

Barton College
Financial Aid Office
Wilson, NC 27893

2710
Lottie Ellis Tuition Scholarship

AMOUNT: None Specified DEADLINE: March 15
FIELDS/MAJORS: Pre-nursing, Pre-medicine

Scholarship to be used to aid in funding tuition expenses. First preference given to a pre-nursing student. Second preference given to a pre-med. student. Selection made by Department of Nursing faculty with the financial aid and admissions offices. Contact the address below for further information.

Barton College
Financial Aid Office
Wilson, NC 27893

2711
Mary Alice and Howard B. Chapin Scholarship

AMOUNT: Maximum: $1500 DEADLINE: March 15
FIELDS/MAJORS: Elementary, Secondary Education

Open to students planning to teach in North Carolina schools, from Kindergarten through twelfth grade. Contact the address below for further information.

Barton College
Financial Aid Office
Wilson, NC 27893

2712
Ruth Patton Grady Scholarship

AMOUNT: None Specified DEADLINE: March 15
FIELDS/MAJORS: Elementary Education

Open to entering freshmen who will be majoring in elementary education. First preference given to minorities, second preference to all other entering freshmen, and third preference to transfer students. Must have a minimum GPA of 3.0 and at least a score of 920 on the SAT. Renewable if recipient maintains a minimum GPA of 2.75 and continues as an elementary education major. Contact the address below for further information.

Barton College
Financial Aid Office
Wilson, NC 27893

2713
Selah Morton Nursing Scholarship

AMOUNT: None Specified DEADLINE: March 15
FIELDS/MAJORS: Nursing

Open to students preparing for a career in nursing. Contact the address below for further information.

Barton College
Financial Aid Office
Wilson, NC 27893

2714
Ted C. Foy, Mildred E. Hartsock, and Mamie Jennings Lucas Scholarships

AMOUNT: None Specified **DEADLINE:** March 15
FIELDS/MAJORS: English

Open to English majors. Selection made by the English Department. Contact the address below for further information about all three awards. Must have a GPA of at least 2.9.

Barton College
Financial Aid Office
Wilson, NC 27893

2715
Transfer Honors Scholarships

AMOUNT: None Specified **DEADLINE:** March 15
FIELDS/MAJORS: All Areas of Study

Open to transfer students with a minimum of 27 semester hours and at least a 3.25 GPA. Renewable if recipients remain full-time and maintain a minimum GPA of 3.0. Contact the address below for further information.

Barton College
Financial Aid Office
Wilson, NC 27893

2716
Undergraduate Fellowship Program

AMOUNT: Maximum: $1000 **DEADLINE:** March 15
FIELDS/MAJORS: All Areas of Study

Open to high school seniors with demonstrated leadership abilities and excellent academic records. Must rank in the upper 25% of class and have a minimum SAT score of 1100. Must be accepted at the College. Renewable up to four years if recipients maintain a minimum GPA of 3.25. Contact the address below for further information.

Barton College
Financial Aid Office
Wilson, NC 27893

2717
W.R. and Rosa W. Robertson Fellowship

AMOUNT: None Specified **DEADLINE:** March 15
FIELDS/MAJORS: Christian Ministry

Open to students pursuing a career in Christian ministry or in a church vocation. Contact the address below for further information.

Barton College
Financial Aid Office
Wilson, NC 27893

2718
Will and Sarah Condon Rodgers Scholarship

AMOUNT: None Specified **DEADLINE:** March 15
FIELDS/MAJORS: All Areas of Study

Open to students who demonstrate financial need and academic promise. Preference given to residents of Wilson and Greene counties in North Carolina. Award is approximately two-thirds tuition, room, board, books, and fees. Contact the address below for further information.

Barton College
Financial Aid Office
Wilson, NC 27893

2719
Wilson Evening Lions Club Scholarship

AMOUNT: Maximum: $500 **DEADLINE:** March 15
FIELDS/MAJORS: Education of the Deaf and Hard of Hearing

Open to rising seniors. Recipient is selected by the School of Education. Contact the address below for further information. Must have a GPA of at least 2.9.

Barton College
Financial Aid Office
Wilson, NC 27893

2720
Wilson Sertoma Club Scholarship

AMOUNT: Maximum: $500 **DEADLINE:** March 15
FIELDS/MAJORS: Education of the Deaf and Hard of Hearing

Open to students who are deaf or hard of hearing or students majoring in the education of the deaf and hard of hearing. First preference given to residents of Wilson County. Selection made by the School of Education. Contact the address below for further information.

Barton College
Financial Aid Office
Wilson, NC 27893

2721
Wilson Woman's Club Nursing Scholarship

AMOUNT: None Specified DEADLINE: March 15
FIELDS/MAJORS: Nursing

Open to juniors and seniors based on academics and financial need. Preference given to residents of Wilson County. Selection is made by the School of Nursing and offices of financial aid and admissions. Contact the address below for further information. Must have a GPA of at least 2.8.

Barton College
Financial Aid Office
Wilson, NC 27893

BEAVER COLLEGE

2722
Beaver College Achievement Award

AMOUNT: $4000-$24000 DEADLINE: None Specified
FIELDS/MAJORS: All Areas of Study

Awarded to students who participate in school activities, community service, volunteer work, or special talents. Write to the address below for more information.

Beaver College
450 S. Easton Rd.
Glenside, PA 19038

2723
Beaver College Grant

AMOUNT: $100-$8500 DEADLINE: None Specified
FIELDS/MAJORS: All Areas of Study

Awarded to students on the basis of financial need. Write to the address below for more information.

Beaver College
450 S. Easton Rd.
Glenside, PA 19038

2724
Departmental Competitions

AMOUNT: $1000-$6000 DEADLINE: None Specified
FIELDS/MAJORS: All Areas of Study

Students can compete in the area of their intended major at a one-day event. Achievement Awards awarded to those who excel in their major. Write to the address below for more information.

Beaver College
450 S. Easton Rd.
Glenside, PA 19038

2725
Distinguished Scholarship

AMOUNT: $8000-$62240 DEADLINE: None Specified
FIELDS/MAJORS: All Areas of Study

Awarded to students who demonstrate academic excellence, outstanding leadership, and community and volunteer service. Write to the address below for more information.

Beaver College
450 S. Easton Rd.
Glenside, PA 19038

2726
Gate Loan

AMOUNT: $1000-$3000 DEADLINE: None Specified
FIELDS/MAJORS: All Areas of Study

This is a low-interest loan partially subsidized by the College. The loans are distributed to those students who have demonstrated the greatest financial need. Write to the address below for more information.

Beaver College
450 S. Easton Rd.
Glenside, PA 19038

2727
Open House Essay Contest

AMOUNT: Maximum: $3000 DEADLINE: None Specified
FIELDS/MAJORS: All Areas of Study

Students who attend a Beaver College Open House in the fall may submit an essay that they have written on a topic presented by the Enrollment Management Office. Write to the address below for more information.

Beaver College
450 S. Easton Rd.
Glenside, PA 19038

2728

Philadelphia Scholar Award

AMOUNT: Maximum: $8000   DEADLINE: None Specified
FIELDS/MAJORS: All Areas of Study

Awarded to five students from one of Philadelphia's comprehensive high schools on the basis of academic talent and promise. Write to the address below for more information.

Beaver College
450 S. Easton Rd.
Glenside, PA 19038

BELLARMINE COLLEGE

2729

Academic Scholarships *GPA 3.0+*

AMOUNT: None Specified   DEADLINE: January 15
FIELDS/MAJORS: All Areas of Study

Applicants must be in the top 25% of their high school class with a GPA of at least 3.4 and an ACT score of 24 or an SAT score of 1000. For undergraduate study. Contact the financial aid office at the address below for details.

Bellarmine College
Financial Aid Office
2001 Newburg Road
Louisville, KY 40205

2730

Bellarmine Scholars Program *GPA 3.5+*

AMOUNT: None Specified   DEADLINE: January 15
FIELDS/MAJORS: All Areas of Study

Scholarships are available at Bellarmine for incoming freshmen who are in the top 5% of their high school class, with a minimum 3.9 GPA, and ACT of at least 30 (or SAT of 1300 or more). An essay and interview are also required. Three to five awards offered annually. Awards are full tuition for school. Contact the financial aid office at the address below for details.

Bellarmine College
Financial Aid Office
2001 Newburg Road
Louisville, KY 40205

2731

McDonough Service Grants *GPA 2.5+*

AMOUNT: $1000-$2500   DEADLINE: January 15
FIELDS/MAJORS: All Areas of Study

Scholarships are available at Bellarmine College for full-time students who participate in community activities, have a GPA of at least 2.5, and are in the top half of their graduating high school class. For undergraduate study. Contact the financial aid office at the address below for details.

Bellarmine College
Financial Aid Office
2001 Newburg Road
Louisville, KY 40205

BEMIDJI STATE UNIVERSITY

2732

Abe Patterson Memorial Scholarship *GPA 3.0+*

AMOUNT: None Specified   DEADLINE: None Specified
FIELDS/MAJORS: All Areas of Study

Open to entering freshmen from Beltrami County who have a minimum GPA of 3.0. Must be able to demonstrate financial need. Contact the address below for further information.

Bemidji State University
Office of Admissions and Scholarships
102 Deputy Hall, Scholarship Officer
Bemidji, MN 56601-2699

2733

Alumni Relative Scholarship

AMOUNT: Maximum: $600   DEADLINE: None Specified
FIELDS/MAJORS: All Areas of Study

Open to new and returning students who are relatives of active BSU alumni. Application forms are available from any active alumnus or the Alumni office. Deadline for consideration is March 1 for new freshmen and May 1 for transfer/returning students. Contact the Alumni office for further information.

Bemidji State University
Office of Admissions and Scholarships
102 Deputy Hall, Scholarship Officer
Bemidji, MN 56601-2699

2734
Campus Honors Scholarships

GPA 3.0+

Amount: Maximum: $600 **Deadline:** April 1
Fields/Majors: All Areas of Study

Open to graduating seniors who are in the top 15% of class. Application for admission serves as the application for this scholarship. Must be admitted by April 1 to be eligible. Contact the address below for further information or call (218) 755-2040. GPA must be at least 3.3.

Bemidji State University
Office of Admissions and Scholarships
102 Deputy Hall, Scholarship Officer
Bemidji, MN 56601-2699

2735
Fred and Mabel Hamm Scholarship

GPA 3.5+

Amount: None Specified **Deadline:** None Specified
Fields/Majors: All Areas of Study

Open to sophomores, juniors, and seniors who have a minimum GPA of 3.5. Must demonstrate high level of reading and writing competence and financial need. Contact the Vice President for Academic Affairs for further information.

Bemidji State University
Office of Admissions and Scholarships
102 Deputy Hall, Scholarship Officer
Bemidji, MN 56601-2699

2736
Full Tuition Scholarships

GPA 3.5+

Amount: $3000 **Deadline:** February 1
Fields/Majors: All Areas of Study

Open to graduating seniors who are in the top 10% of class. Renewable based on completion of at least 30 semester hours with a minimum GPA of 3.5. Contact the address below for further information or call (218) 755-2040.

Bemidji State University
Office of Admissions and Scholarships
102 Deputy Hall, Scholarship Officer
Bemidji, MN 56601-2699

2737
Harding Scholarship

GPA 2.5+

Amount: None Specified **Deadline:** None Specified
Fields/Majors: All Areas of Study

Open to sophomores, juniors, and seniors who have a minimum GPA of 2.5. Must be able to demonstrate financial need. Contact the address below for further information.

Bemidji State University
Office of Admissions and Scholarships
102 Deputy Hall, Scholarship Officer
Bemidji, MN 56601-2699

2738
Hartz Scholarship

GPA 3.0+

Amount: None Specified **Deadline:** None Specified
Fields/Majors: All Areas of Study

Open to entering freshmen who are in the top 20% of graduating class. Contact the address below for further information. GPA must be at least 3.0.

Bemidji State University
Office of Admissions and Scholarships
102 Deputy Hall, Scholarship Officer
Bemidji, MN 56601-2699

2739
James and Janet Love Scholarship

GPA 3.0+

Amount: None Specified **Deadline:** None Specified
Fields/Majors: All Areas of Study

Open to sophomores, juniors, and seniors who have a minimum GPA of 3.0 and are eligible for financial aid. Contact the address below for further information.

Bemidji State University
Office of Admissions and Scholarships
102 Deputy Hall, Scholarship Officer
Bemidji, MN 56601-2699

2740
John Glas Memorial Scholarship

GPA 3.0+

Amount: None Specified **Deadline:** None Specified
Fields/Majors: All Areas of Study

Open to juniors and seniors from Minnesota who have a minimum GPA of 3.0. Must be able to demonstrate financial need. Contact the address below for further information.

Bemidji State University
Office of Admissions and Scholarships
102 Deputy Hall, Scholarship Officer
Bemidji, MN 56601-2699

2741
Les Duly Scholarship

AMOUNT: None Specified **DEADLINE:** None Specified
FIELDS/MAJORS: All Areas of Study

Open to students of color who are U.S. citizens. Must have a GPA between 2.5 and 3.25. Preference given to females. Contact the address below for further information.

Bemidji State University
Office of Admissions and Scholarships
102 Deputy Hall, Scholarship Officer
Bemidji, MN 56601-2699

2742
National Space Grant Scholarships

AMOUNT: None Specified **DEADLINE:** None Specified
FIELDS/MAJORS: Space Studies

Open to students majoring in space studies. Contact Dr. John Annexstad, Space Studies, for additional information. GPA must be at least 2.8.

Bemidji State University
Office of Admissions and Scholarships
102 Deputy Hall, Scholarship Officer
Bemidji, MN 56601-2699

2743
Naylor Electric Scholarship

AMOUNT: None Specified **DEADLINE:** None Specified
FIELDS/MAJORS: All Areas of Study

Open to entering freshmen who are in the top 15% of graduating class and transfer students with a minimum GPA of 3.25. Contact the address below for further information.

Bemidji State University
Office of Admissions and Scholarships
102 Deputy Hall, Scholarship Officer
Bemidji, MN 56601-2699

2744
Peoples Natural Gas Scholarship

AMOUNT: None Specified **DEADLINE:** None Specified
FIELDS/MAJORS: All Areas of Study

Open to students who will be enrolled in their second year at BSU, received a scholarship during their first year but are without continuing scholarship support. Must have a minimum GPA of 3.25. Contact the address below for further information.

Bemidji State University
Office of Admissions and Scholarships
102 Deputy Hall, Scholarship Officer
Bemidji, MN 56601-2699

2745
Presidential Scholarships

AMOUNT: Maximum: $1500 **DEADLINE:** March 15
FIELDS/MAJORS: All Areas of Study

Open to incoming freshmen who are in the top 10% of their high school class. Based on academics and extracurricular leadership activities in school, community, and the arts. Contact the address below for further information or call (218) 755-2040. GPA must be at least 3.6.

Bemidji State University
Office of Admissions and Scholarships
102 Deputy Hall, Scholarship Officer
Bemidji, MN 56601-2699

2746
Residential Life/Dining Services Scholarship

AMOUNT: None Specified **DEADLINE:** None Specified
FIELDS/MAJORS: All Areas of Study

Open to students who are campus residents, on the campus food plan, and in good academic standing. Must be active contributors to the residential community. Contact the Director of Residential Life for further information. GPA must be at least 2.5.

Bemidji State University
Office of Admissions and Scholarships
102 Deputy Hall, Scholarship Officer
Bemidji, MN 56601-2699

2747
Rick Maynard Scholarship

AMOUNT: None Specified **DEADLINE:** None Specified
FIELDS/MAJORS: All Areas of Study

Open to Theta Tau Epsilon members with proven leadership skills and a minimum GPA of 2.5. Contact the Theta Tau Epsilon advisor for additional information.

Bemidji State University
Office of Admissions and Scholarships
102 Deputy Hall, Scholarship Officer
Bemidji, MN 56601-2699

2748
Special Situation Scholarships

AMOUNT: None Specified DEADLINE: None Specified
FIELDS/MAJORS: All Areas of Study

Open to new and returning students who are at least twenty-five years of age and have a GPA of 2.5 or higher. Preference given to single parents. Contact the address below for further information.

Bemidji State University
Office of Admissions and Scholarships
102 Deputy Hall, Scholarship Officer
Bemidji, MN 56601-2699

2749
Star Tribune-Cowles Media Scholarship

AMOUNT: None Specified DEADLINE: None Specified
FIELDS/MAJORS: Mass Communications (Journalism)

Open to Native American freshmen or new transfer students majoring in mass communications (journalism). Contact the Mass Communications Department for additional information.

Bemidji State University
Office of Admissions and Scholarships
102 Deputy Hall, Scholarship Officer
Bemidji, MN 56601-2699

2750
Sullivan International Student Scholarship

AMOUNT: None Specified DEADLINE: None Specified
FIELDS/MAJORS: All Areas of Study

Open to international students who are juniors and seniors with a minimum GPA of 3.0. Must give evidence of leadership skills, be involved in campus or community activities and be able to demonstrate financial need. Contact the address below for further information.

Bemidji State University
Office of Admissions and Scholarships
102 Deputy Hall, Scholarship Officer
Bemidji, MN 56601-2699

2751
Transfer Student Scholarships

AMOUNT: Maximum: $600 DEADLINE: April 1
FIELDS/MAJORS: All Areas of Study

Open to students transferring from a Minnesota community college to Bemidji State University. Must have completed an associates degree with a GPA of at least 3.5. Contact the address below for further information or call (218) 755-2040.

Bemidji State University
Office of Admissions and Scholarships
102 Deputy Hall, Scholarship Officer
Bemidji, MN 56601-2699

2752
Winston and Irene Naylor Scholarship

AMOUNT: None Specified DEADLINE: None Specified
FIELDS/MAJORS: All Areas of Study

Open to sophomores, juniors, and seniors who have a minimum GPA of 3.0. Must be able to demonstrate financial need. Contact the address below for further information.

Bemidji State University
Office of Admissions and Scholarships
102 Deputy Hall, Scholarship Officer
Bemidji, MN 56601-2699

BENEDICTINE COLLEGE

2753
Griffis Memorial Scholarship

AMOUNT: None Specified DEADLINE: None Specified
FIELDS/MAJORS: Art, Drama

Awards for women studying for a bachelor's degree in art or drama at Benedictine College in Atchinson, Kansas. Applicants must have a GPA of 3.0 or above for the scholarship and 2.5 or better for an achievement award. Write to the address below for more information.

Benedictine Sisters
Mount St. Scholastica
801 South 8th St.
Atchinson, KS 66002

BETHUNE-COOKMAN COLLEGE

2754
Selby Foundation Minority Scholarships

AMOUNT: None Specified   DEADLINE: None Specified
FIELDS/MAJORS: All Areas of Study

Awards for students who will be attending Bethune-Cookman College full-time. Must be a resident of Sarasota or Manatee counties before entering college and have a minimum GPA of 3.0. Write to address below for further information.

Selby Foundation
Bethune-Cookman-Financial Aid Officer
640 Second St.
Daytona Beach, FL 32015

BLACK HILLS STATE UNIVERSITY

2755
Betty Richey Scholarship

AMOUNT: $1000   DEADLINE: February 15
FIELDS/MAJORS: Elementary Education

One award is available to a junior or senior who is majoring in elementary education. Student must be a West River/South Dakota resident. Write to the address below for more information.

Black Hills State University
1200 University St.
Spearfish, SD 57783

2756
Clarkson Memorial Scholarships

AMOUNT: $1500   DEADLINE: February 15
FIELDS/MAJORS: All Areas of Study

One scholarship for a sophomore at Black Hills State University with a GPA of 3.0 or better. Write to the address below for more information.

Black Hills State University
1200 University St.
Spearfish, SD 57783

2757
College of Education Alumni Scholarship

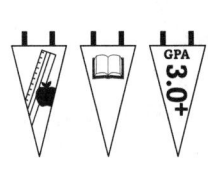

AMOUNT: $500   DEADLINE: February 15
FIELDS/MAJORS: Elementary Education, Middle School Education, Special Education, or Library Media

Three awards are available to students who are majoring in elementary education, middle school education, special education, or library media, with a minimum 3.0 GPA. Write to the address below for more information.

Black Hills State University
1200 University St.
Spearfish, SD 57783

2758
College of Education Departmental Scholarship

AMOUNT: $500   DEADLINE: February 15
FIELDS/MAJORS: Elementary Education, Middle School Education, Special Education, or Library Media

One award is given to a new freshman and one or more award(s) to upperclassmen. They are available to students who are majoring in elementary education, middle school education, special education, or library media, with a minimum 3.0 GPA. Write to the address below for more information.

Black Hills State University
1200 University St.
Spearfish, SD 57783

2759
Crazy Horse Memorial-Jonas Scholarships

AMOUNT: $1000   DEADLINE: February 15
FIELDS/MAJORS: All Areas of Study

One scholarship for a Native American student at Black Hills State University who has a GPA of 3.0 or better and is in their third or fourth year of study. Write to the address below for more information.

Black Hills State University
1200 University St.
Spearfish, SD 57783

2760
Darleen Young Scholarship

AMOUNT: $500   DEADLINE: February 15
FIELDS/MAJORS: Administrative Assistant, Business Administration, or Office Administration

One award is available to sophomore, junior, or senior students majoring in administrative assistance, business education, or office administration. Write to the address below for more information.

Black Hills State University
1200 University St.
Spearfish, SD 57783

2761
Gladys Holst McFarland Memorial Scholarship

AMOUNT: $500   DEADLINE: February 15
FIELDS/MAJORS: Elementary Education, Secondary Education, Special Education

One award is available to a sophomore, junior, or senior who is majoring in elementary, secondary, or special education with a minimum 3.0 GPA. He/she must be a full-time student and show outstanding leadership ability. Write to the address below for more information.

Black Hills State University
1200 University St.
Spearfish, SD 57783

2762
Hatterschiedt Foundation, Inc. Educational Scholarships

AMOUNT: $1000   DEADLINE: February 15
FIELDS/MAJORS: All Areas of Study

Four scholarships for incoming freshmen at Black Hills State University who are South Dakota residents, have a GPA of 3.0 or better, and demonstrate financial need. Write to the address below for more information.

Black Hills State University
1200 University St.
Spearfish, SD 57783

2763
John Edward Hess Memorial Scholarships

AMOUNT: $1000   DEADLINE: February 15
FIELDS/MAJORS: All Areas of Study

Two scholarships for Native American students at Black Hills State University who are residents of a South Dakota reservation with a GPA of 2.0 or better. Students must enroll for 16 hours each semester. Write to the address below for more information.

Black Hills State University
1200 University St.
Spearfish, SD 57783

2764
John T. Vucurevich Scholarships

AMOUNT: $1000   DEADLINE: February 15
FIELDS/MAJORS: All Areas of Study

Scholarships for third- or fourth-year students at Black Hills State University who are in good standing and have financial need. Write to the address below for more information. GPA must be at least 2.0.

Black Hills State University
1200 University St.
Spearfish, SD 57783

2765
Marc Boesen Memorial Scholarships

AMOUNT: $1000   DEADLINE: February 15
FIELDS/MAJORS: All Areas of Study

Scholarships for continuing students at Black Hills State University who demonstrate strong leadership qualities through extensive participation in extracurricular activities in the school and community. Applicants should have a GPA of 3.0 or better. One award is offered annually. Write to the address below for more information.

Black Hills State University
1200 University St.
Spearfish, SD 57783

2766
McDaniel Family Scholarship

AMOUNT: $1000   DEADLINE: February 15
FIELDS/MAJORS: Accounting, Business Administration, Human Resource Management, Marketing, or Office Administration

One award is available to an incoming freshman accounting, business administration, human resource management, marketing, or office administration major. The recipient must be a South Dakota resident, preferable, but not necessarily, from Hughes, Sully, or Hyde counties. Must maintain a 2.5 GPA or better. Write to the address below for more information.

Black Hills State University
1200 University St.
Spearfish, SD 57783

2767
Michael Schlimgen Memorial Scholarship

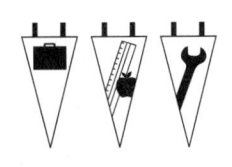

AMOUNT: $500 DEADLINE: February 15
FIELDS/MAJORS: Accounting, Business Administration, Business Education, Human Resource Management, Marketing, Office Administration, or Tourism and Hospitality Management

One award is available to a sophomore, junior, or senior majoring in accounting, business administration, business education, human resource management, marketing, office administration, or tourism and hospitality management. Write to the address below for more information.

Black Hills State University
1200 University St.
Spearfish, SD 57783

2768
Mr. L.R. and Mrs. Nellie Pike Chiesman Memorial Scholarship

AMOUNT: $1000 DEADLINE: February 15
FIELDS/MAJORS: All Areas of Study

Award is available to a high school graduate who has not previously attended a postsecondary institution. Must have a minimum 3.0 GPA and must be admitted to Black Hills State University. One award is offered annually. Write to the address below for more information.

Black Hills State University
1200 University St.
Spearfish, SD 57783

2769
Patricia Romkema Memorial and South Dakota Innkeepers Association Scholarship

AMOUNT: $500 DEADLINE: February 15
FIELDS/MAJORS: Tourism and Hospitality Management

One award for each scholarship is available to a sophomore, junior, or senior tourism and hospitality management major. Write to the address below for more information.

Black Hills State University
1200 University St.
Spearfish, SD 57783

2770
Presidential Scholarship

AMOUNT: $1000 DEADLINE: February 15
FIELDS/MAJORS: All Areas of Study

Available to high school graduates who have not previously attended a postsecondary institution, have a minimum 3.0 GPA, and have been admitted to Black Hills State University. Write to the address below for more information.

Black Hills State University
1200 University St.
Spearfish, SD 57783

2771
Richard Price Memorial Scholarship

AMOUNT: $500 DEADLINE: February 15
FIELDS/MAJORS: Tourism and Hospitality Management

One award is available to a junior or senior tourism and hospitality management major with a minimum GPA of 3.0. Write to the address below for more information.

Black Hills State University
1200 University St.
Spearfish, SD 57783

2772
Ronald Dolly Loyalty Scholarship

AMOUNT: $1000 DEADLINE: February 15
FIELDS/MAJORS: All Areas of Study

One award is available to a junior or senior who has maintained a 2.75 or better GPA. The student must be enrolled in at least 15 credit hours per semester to be eligible. Applicants must provide three letters of recommendation and write a short essay on their interest in economic development and/or creation of quality job opportunities for the state of South Dakota or work out of state, but for the state of South Dakota. Write to the address below for more information.

Black Hills State University
1200 University St.
Spearfish, SD 57783

2773
Taco John's Scholarship

AMOUNT: $500 DEADLINE: February 15
FIELDS/MAJORS: Accounting, Business Administration, Human Resource Management, Marketing, Office Administration, or Tourism and Hospitality Management

One award is available to an incoming freshman accounting, business administration, business education, human resource management, marketing, office administration, or tourism and hospitality management major. Write to the address below for more information.

Black Hills State University
1200 University St.
Spearfish, SD 57783

2774
Walter Higbee and Borcile Fowler Memorial Scholarship

AMOUNT: $1000 DEADLINE: February 15
FIELDS/MAJORS: Elementary Education or Special Education

Each award is for $1000 and is available to a new freshman majoring in elementary or special education with a minimum 3.0 GPA, minimum ACT of 22, full-time enrollment, and a South Dakota resident. Write to the address below for more information.

Black Hills State University
1200 University St.
Spearfish, SD 57783

2775
Yvonne Weyrich Business Award

AMOUNT: $500 DEADLINE: February 15
FIELDS/MAJORS: Business Administration

One award is available to a student who is of senior status at the time of the award and is majoring in business administration. Write to the address below for more information.

Black Hills State University
1200 University St.
Spearfish, SD 57783

BLUFFTON COLLEGE

2776
Leadership/Service Grants

AMOUNT: Maximum: $3000 DEADLINE: April 15
FIELDS/MAJORS: All Areas of Study

Scholarships available at Bluffton College for freshmen who demonstrate strong leadership skills and service at the high school level-in church, school, or the community. Applicants must rank in the top 50% of their graduating class. Write to the address below for details. GPA must be at least 2.7.

Bluffton College
Office of Admissions
280 W. College Ave.
Bluffton, OH 45817

ARCHAEOLOGICAL INSTITUTE OF AMERICA, BOSTON UNIVERSITY

2777
Anna C. and Oliver C. Colburn Fellowship

AMOUNT: Maximum: $11000 DEADLINE: February 1
FIELDS/MAJORS: All Areas of Study

One fellowship will be awarded to an applicant contingent upon his or her acceptance as an incoming Associate Member or Student Associate Member of the American School of Classical Studies at Athens. Competition is open to U.S. or Canadian citizens or permanent residents who are at the predoctoral stage or who have received the Ph.D. degree within the last five years. Write to the address below or call (617) 353-9361 for details.

Archaeological Institute of America
Boston University
656 Beacon Street, 4th Floor
Boston, MA 02215

2778
Harriet and Leon Pomerance Fellowship

AMOUNT: Maximum: $3000 DEADLINE: November 1
FIELDS/MAJORS: Aegean Bronze Age Archaeology

Applicants must be working on a project of a scholarly nature relating to Aegean Bronze Age Archaeology. Preference will be given to candidates whose project requires travel to the Mediterranean for purposes stated above. Must be U.S. or Canadian citizens. Write to the address below or call (617) 353-9361 for details.

Archaeological Institute of America
Boston University
656 Beacon Street, 4th Floor
Boston, MA 02215

2779
Olivia James Traveling Fellowship

AMOUNT: Maximum: $15000   DEADLINE: November 1
FIELDS/MAJORS: Classics, Sculpture, Architecture, Archaeology, and History

Competition is open to students who are citizens or permanent residents of the United States. The award is to be used for travel and study in: Greece, the Aegean Islands, Sicily, Southern Italy, Asia Minor, or Mesopotamia. Preference will be given to individuals engaged in dissertation research or to recent recipients of the Ph.D. Write to the address below or call (617) 353-9361 for details.

Archaeological Institute of America
Boston University
656 Beacon Street, 4th Floor
Boston, MA 02215

BRADLEY UNIVERSITY

2780
Bradley Legacy Scholarships

AMOUNT: Maximum: $1500   DEADLINE: March 1
FIELDS/MAJORS: All Areas of Study

Awards for full-time incoming freshmen and transfer students (beginning on, or after, August 1998) whose parent(s) or grandparent(s) are Bradley graduates. Write to the address below for more information.

Bradley University
Office of Financial Assistance
Peoria, IL 61625

2781
Caterpillar, Inc., Employee Dependents Scholarships

AMOUNT: Maximum: $2500   DEADLINE: March 1
FIELDS/MAJORS: All Areas of Study

Open to full-time undergraduate dependents of eligible employees of Caterpillar, Inc., who are attending Bradley University. Write to the address below for more information.

Bradley University
Office of Financial Assistance
Peoria, IL 61625

2782
Deans-Valedictorian Scholarship

AMOUNT: $5000   DEADLINE: March 1
FIELDS/MAJORS: All Areas of Study

Open to entering freshmen who rank in the top 10% of their class and have a combined SAT score of at least 1240 or an ACT of 28. Award amounts vary from $5000 to one-half of tuition. Entering freshmen who rank first in their graduating class receive one-half tuition. Write to the address below for more information. GPA must be at least 3.7.

Bradley University
Office of Financial Assistance
Peoria, IL 61625

2783
Fine Art Scholarships

AMOUNT: $1000-$2500   DEADLINE: March 1
FIELDS/MAJORS: All Areas of Study

Award for applicants with particular talent in the fine and performing arts, including art, music, theater, and forensics. Selection is competitive and, with the exception of forensics, requires applicants to declare a major in the specialty area. Auditions and/or portfolio submissions are required. Write to the address below for more information.

Bradley University
Office of Financial Assistance
Peoria, IL 61625

2784
Garrett-Provost Scholars

AMOUNT: $2500-$8000   DEADLINE: March 1
FIELDS/MAJORS: All Areas of Study

Through this program, Bradley recognizes outstanding academic achievement of entering freshmen from multicultural or ethnically diverse backgrounds. Applicants must be in the top 15% of their graduating class. Awards vary from $2500 to $8000 per year. Write to the address below for more information. GPA must be at least 3.6.

Bradley University
Office of Financial Assistance
Peoria, IL 61625

2785
Phi Theta Kappa Scholarship

AMOUNT: Maximum: $4000 DEADLINE: May 1
FIELDS/MAJORS: All Areas of Study

Open to members who are transfer students with the last 12 hours of transferable course work coming from an accredited community college. Must be enrolled for full-time study at Bradley. Write to the address below for more information.

Bradley University
Office of Financial Assistance
Peoria, IL 61625

2786
Presidential Scholarships

AMOUNT: None Specified DEADLINE: April 1
FIELDS/MAJORS: All Areas of Study

Full tuition awards for the first forty National Merit, National Hispanic, or National Achievement finalists who commit to Bradley University by April 1. Write to the address below for more information.

Bradley University
Office of Financial Assistance
Peoria, IL 61625

2787
Transfer Excellence Scholarship

AMOUNT: Maximum: $5000 DEADLINE: May 1
FIELDS/MAJORS: All Areas of Study

Open to transfer students with a minimum GPA of 3.5, who have acquired 45 hours of transferable coursework, the last 24 hours of credit having been earned at a community college. Must be enrolled for full-time study at Bradley. Write to the address below for more information.

Bradley University
Office of Financial Assistance
Peoria, IL 61625

BRANDEIS UNIVERSITY

2788
Annenberg Scholarships

AMOUNT: Maximum: $17500 DEADLINE: None Specified
FIELDS/MAJORS: All Areas of Study

Open to the most accomplished and academically gifted high school graduates in the nation who have distinguished themselves in studies and in the breadth of their intellectual pursuits. Must also have demonstrated initiative and commitment to a variety of activities beyond the classroom. Contact the address below for further information. GPA must be at least 4.0.

Brandeis University
Office of Financial Aid
PO Box 9110
Waltham, MA 02254-9110

2789
Brandeis-Waltham Scholarships

AMOUNT: None Specified DEADLINE: None Specified
FIELDS/MAJORS: All Areas of Study

Open to the four top graduating seniors from Waltham High School, in Waltham, Massachusetts. Scholarships are full tuition for four years. Contact the address below for further information. GPA must be at least 3.8.

Brandeis University
Office of Financial Aid
PO Box 9110
Waltham, MA 02254-9110

2790
Hiatt Challenger Memorial Scholarships

AMOUNT: None Specified DEADLINE: None Specified
FIELDS/MAJORS: All Areas of Study

Open to incoming freshmen who meet the Justice Brandeis Scholar criteria, including peerless class rank, standardized test scores, and demonstrated scholarly achievement. A one thousand word essay will also be required. Award is 75% of tuition. Renewable for four years if recipients maintain preset standards. Contact the address below for further information. GPA must be at least 4.0.

Brandeis University
Office of Financial Aid
PO Box 9110
Waltham, MA 02254-9110

2791

Justice Brandeis and Norman S. Rabb Scholarships, Gilbert Grants

AMOUNT: Maximum: $17500 DEADLINE: None Specified
FIELDS/MAJORS: All Areas of Study

Scholarships for incoming freshmen who demonstrate exceptional academic promise. Recipients usually rank at the top of their classes, earn standardized test scores in the top 2% nationally, and have participated in intellectual activities beyond the traditional high school curriculum. Renewable if recipients maintain preset standards. The Rabb Scholarship may be used for study abroad. Contact the address below for further information.

Brandeis University
Office of Financial Aid
PO Box 9110
Waltham, MA 02254-9110

2792

Presidential Awards

AMOUNT: Maximum: $10000 DEADLINE: None Specified
FIELDS/MAJORS: All Areas of Study

Open to incoming freshmen demonstrating unusual academics. Recipients generally rank in the top portion of their classes, earn high standardized test scores, and have participated in a wide range of high school and community activities. Renewable if recipients maintain preset standards. Contact the address below for further information. GPA must be at least 3.8.

Brandeis University
Office of Financial Aid
PO Box 9110
Waltham, MA 02254-9110

BRIGHAM YOUNG UNIVERSITY

2793

Brigham Young University Multicultural Program

AMOUNT: None Specified DEADLINE: None Specified
FIELDS/MAJORS: All Areas of Study

Scholarships available at Brigham Young University for undergraduates who are African-American, Latino, Asian, Polynesian, and Native American. Applicants must be at least one-quarter of one of the listed ethnicities. Write to the address below for information.

Brigham Young University
199 Ernest L. Wilkinson Center
PO Box 27908
Provo, UT 84602

2794

Departmental Financial Aid for Graduate Students at BYU

AMOUNT: None Specified DEADLINE: None Specified
FIELDS/MAJORS: All Areas of Study

Teaching/research assistantships, internships, and supplementary awards for graduate students at BYU. These are administered by the individual departments. Applicants must be admitted into a graduate program and have a minimum GPA of 3.0. You must contact your department at least several weeks in advance of the start of graduate studies to be considered for financial aid.

Brigham Young University
Graduate School
B-336, ASB
Provo, UT 84602

BROOKLYN COLLEGE

2795

Abraham S. Goodhartz Memorial Scholarship

AMOUNT: Maximum: $500 DEADLINE: March 1
FIELDS/MAJORS: Judaic Culture, History, Tradition

Open to a student of the areas listed above. Contact the address listed for further information.

Brooklyn College
Office of the V.P. for Student Life
2113 Boylan Hall
Brooklyn, NY 11210

2796

Abram Klotzman Memorial Scholarship

AMOUNT: Maximum: $1000 DEADLINE: March 1
FIELDS/MAJORS: Music

Open to an outstanding student in the Conservatory of Music. Contact the address listed for further information. Must have a GPA of at least 3.5.

Brooklyn College
Office of the V.P. for Student Life
2113 Boylan Hall
Brooklyn, NY 11210

2797
Alfred M. Peiser Memorial Scholarship

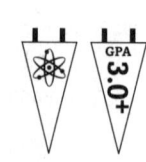

AMOUNT: Maximum: $1000   DEADLINE: March 1
FIELDS/MAJORS: Mathematics

Open to an outstanding student for senior year of study. Contact the address listed for further information. Must have a GPA of at least 3.1.

Brooklyn College
Office of the V.P. for Student Life
2113 Boylan Hall
Brooklyn, NY 11210

2798
Anne Margulies Newman '33 and Herbert Newman Scholarship

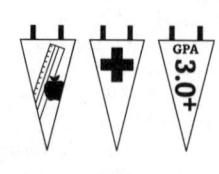

AMOUNT: Maximum: $300   DEADLINE: March 1
FIELDS/MAJORS: Education, Health Science

Open to two outstanding undergraduates; one in the School of Education, and the second for a major in health science. Contact the address listed for further information. Must have a GPA of at least 3.1.

Brooklyn College
Office of the V.P. for Student Life
2113 Boylan Hall
Brooklyn, NY 11210

2799
Anne Touger Memorial Scholarship

AMOUNT: None Specified   DEADLINE: March 1
FIELDS/MAJORS: English

Open to outstanding students for use in senior year. Must be an English major with a commitment to the pursuit of social justice. Contact the address listed for further information. Must have a GPA of at least 3.1.

Brooklyn College
Office of the V.P. for Student Life
2113 Boylan Hall
Brooklyn, NY 11210

2800
Barbara Gerber '62 Scholarship

AMOUNT: Maximum: $300   DEADLINE: March 1
FIELDS/MAJORS: Comparative Literature

Open to outstanding undergraduates majoring in comparative literature. Contact the address listed for further information. Must have a GPA of at least 3.2.

Brooklyn College
Office of the V.P. for Student Life
2113 Boylan Hall
Brooklyn, NY 11210

2801
Bernard Cole Memorial Scholarship

AMOUNT: Maximum: $350   DEADLINE: March 1
FIELDS/MAJORS: Photography

Open to undergraduates who have been recognized in the discipline of photography. Contact the address listed for further information. Must have a GPA of at least 2.7.

Brooklyn College
Office of the V.P. for Student Life
2113 Boylan Hall
Brooklyn, NY 11210

2802
Brooklyn College Dance Theater Scholarship

AMOUNT: None Specified   DEADLINE: March 1
FIELDS/MAJORS: Dance

Open to outstanding dance majors. Award is partial or full tuition. Contact the address listed for further information. Must have a GPA of at least 3.0.

Brooklyn College
Office of the V.P. for Student Life
2113 Boylan Hall
Brooklyn, NY 11210

2803
Brooklyn College Faculty Circle International Student Scholarship

AMOUNT: None Specified   DEADLINE: March 1
FIELDS/MAJORS: All Areas of Study

Open to registered international students who can demonstrate academic merit and financial need. Must be making reasonable progress toward a degree. Contact the address listed for further information. Must have a GPA of at least 2.9.

Brooklyn College
Office of the V.P. for Student Life
2113 Boylan Hall
Brooklyn, NY 11210

2804
Brooklyn Women's Club Scholarship

AMOUNT: Maximum: $400 DEADLINE: March 1
FIELDS/MAJORS: All Areas of Study

Open to juniors for outstanding contributions made to the college during the freshman and sophomore years. Contact the address listed for further information. Must have a GPA of at least 2.9.

Brooklyn College
Office of the V.P. for Student Life
2113 Boylan Hall
Brooklyn, NY 11210

2805
Carl Altman Scholarship

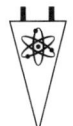

AMOUNT: Maximum: $800 DEADLINE: March 1
FIELDS/MAJORS: Chemistry

Open to chemistry majors for the junior and/or senior year of study. Contact the address listed for further information.

Brooklyn College
Office of the V. P. for Student Life
2113 Boylan Hall
Brooklyn, NY 11210

2806
Chancy Foundation Scholarship

AMOUNT: None Specified DEADLINE: March 1
FIELDS/MAJORS: Music

Open to undergraduates in the Conservatory of Music. Must be able to demonstrate achievement and potential. Award is partial to full tuition. Contact the address listed for further information. Must have a GPA of at least 2.9.

Brooklyn College
Office of the V.P. for Student Life
2113 Boylan Hall
Brooklyn, NY 11210

2807
Charles A. Mastronardi Scholarship

AMOUNT: None Specified DEADLINE: March 1
FIELDS/MAJORS: Special Education

Open to outstanding students in the School of Education preparing for a career in special education. Contact the address listed for further information.

Brooklyn College
Office of the V.P. for Student Life
2113 Boylan Hall
Brooklyn, NY 11210

2808
Conservatory of Music Scholarship

AMOUNT: None Specified DEADLINE: March 1
FIELDS/MAJORS: Music

Open to outstanding students in the Conservatory of Music. Award is partial to full tuition. Contact the address listed for further information. Must have a GPA of at least 2.7.

Brooklyn College
Office of the V.P. for Student Life
2113 Boylan Hall
Brooklyn, NY 11210

2809
Daniel E. Mayers Memorial Scholarship

AMOUNT: Maximum: $300 DEADLINE: March 1
FIELDS/MAJORS: All Areas of Study

Open to juniors and seniors who have performed service to the African-American community and who are able to demonstrate academic merit. Contact the address listed for further information. Must have a GPA of at least 3.0.

Brooklyn College
Office of the V.P. for Student Life
2113 Boylan Hall
Brooklyn, NY 11210

2810
David and Ruth Buchalter Memorial Scholarship

AMOUNT: None Specified DEADLINE: March 1
FIELDS/MAJORS: Economics

Open to economic majors who can demonstrate outstanding academic merit. Contact the address listed for further information. Must have a GPA of at least 3.2.

Brooklyn College
Office of the V.P. for Student Life
2113 Boylan Hall
Brooklyn, NY 11210

2811
David M. Sharefkin Memorial Scholarship

AMOUNT: Maximum: $600   DEADLINE: March 1
FIELDS/MAJORS: Chemistry

Open to chemistry majors who have a minimum GPA of 3.0. Contact the address listed for further information.

Brooklyn College
Office of the V.P. for Student Life
2113 Boylan Hall
Brooklyn, NY 11210

2812
Fanny Gerber Scholarship

AMOUNT: Maximum: $250   DEADLINE: March 1
FIELDS/MAJORS: Liberal Studies

Open to outstanding students at the completion of one year's study in the Master of Liberal Studies Program. Contact the address listed for further information. Must have a GPA of at least 3.2.

Brooklyn College
Office of the V.P. for Student Life
2113 Boylan Hall
Brooklyn, NY 11210

2813
Fanny Singer Memorial Scholarship

AMOUNT: Maximum: $500   DEADLINE: March 1
FIELDS/MAJORS: Education

Open to outstanding juniors in the School of Education who are preparing to teach elementary school. Contact the address listed for further information. Must have a GPA of at least 3.1.

Brooklyn College
Office of the V.P. for Student Life
2113 Boylan Hall
Brooklyn, NY 11210

2814
Flatbush Federal Savings and Loan Association Scholarship

AMOUNT: Maximum: $250   DEADLINE: March 1
FIELDS/MAJORS: Economics, Accounting

Open to graduating seniors who have shown excellence in economics or accounting. For graduate study and planned teaching. Contact the address listed for further information. Must have a GPA of at least 3.1.

Brooklyn College
Office of the V.P. for Student Life
2113 Boylan Hall
Brooklyn, NY 11210

2815
Florence English Scholarship

AMOUNT: None Specified   DEADLINE: March 1
FIELDS/MAJORS: Vocal Music

Open to outstanding vocal students in the Conservatory of Music. Award is partial to full tuition. Contact the address listed for further information.

Brooklyn College
Office of the V.P. for Student Life
2113 Boylan Hall
Brooklyn, NY 11210

2816
Frances Goodman Memorial Scholarship

AMOUNT: Maximum: $1000   DEADLINE: March 1
FIELDS/MAJORS: Education

Open to juniors, for the senior year of study, who are planning a career in public school teaching. Contact the address listed for further information.

Brooklyn College
Office of the V.P. for Student Life
2113 Boylan Hall
Brooklyn, NY 11210

2817
Freda Len '75 Memorial Scholarship

AMOUNT: None Specified   DEADLINE: March 1
FIELDS/MAJORS: Law, Paralegal

Open to graduating seniors who intend to become paralegals or who have been accepted by a law school. Contact the address listed for further information.

Brooklyn College
Office of the V.P. for Student Life
2113 Boylan Hall
Brooklyn, NY 11210

2818
George Investment Foundation Team Scholarship

AMOUNT: Maximum: $2200   DEADLINE: March 1
FIELDS/MAJORS: All Areas of Study

Open to incoming freshmen who can demonstrate academic ability and have a parent who is a veteran of the U.S. Armed Forces. Contact the address listed for further information. Must have a GPA of at least 3.1.

Brooklyn College
Office of the V.P. for Student Life
2113 Boylan Hall
Brooklyn, NY 11210

2819
Graduate Scholarship

AMOUNT: Maximum: $250   DEADLINE: March 1
FIELDS/MAJORS: Arts, Social Sciences, Physical Sciences

Open to graduating seniors for graduate study. Contact the address listed for further information.

Brooklyn College
Office of the V.P. for Student Life
2113 Boylan Hall
Brooklyn, NY 11210

2820
Greater New York Savings Bank Scholarship

AMOUNT: Maximum: $500   DEADLINE: March 1
FIELDS/MAJORS: Economics

Open to a graduating senior majoring in economics. Contact the address listed for further information.

Brooklyn College
Office of the V.P. for Student Life
2113 Boylan Hall
Brooklyn, NY 11210

2821
Harvey L. Young Family Scholarship

AMOUNT: Maximum: $1000   DEADLINE: March 1
FIELDS/MAJORS: Accounting

Available for senior year of study. Must be able to demonstrate academic merit. Contact the address listed for further information. Must have a GPA of at least 3.0.

Brooklyn College
Office of the V.P. for Student Life
2113 Boylan Hall
Brooklyn, NY 11210

2822
Helen Biren Scholarship in Geology

AMOUNT: Maximum: $1000   DEADLINE: March 1
FIELDS/MAJORS: Geology

Open to qualified junior and senior geology majors. Contact the address listed for further information. Must have a GPA of at least 2.8.

Brooklyn College
Office of the V.P. for Student Life
2113 Boylan Hall
Brooklyn, NY 11210

2823
Helen Brell Honors Scholarship

AMOUNT: None Specified   DEADLINE: March 1
FIELDS/MAJORS: English

Open to junior and senior English majors with an English index of at least 3.6. Award is partial or full tuition. Contact the address listed for further information.

Brooklyn College
Office of the V.P. for Student Life
2113 Boylan Hall
Brooklyn, NY 11210

2824
Ida F. Gold Memorial Scholarship

AMOUNT: Maximum: $250   DEADLINE: March 1
FIELDS/MAJORS: Political Science

Open to a talented, deserving political science major. Contact the address listed for further information. Must have a GPA of at least 3.0.

Brooklyn College
Office of the V.P. for Student Life
2113 Boylan Hall
Brooklyn, NY 11210

2825
Irving and Dorothy Lazar Scholarship

AMOUNT: Maximum: $350   DEADLINE: March 1
FIELDS/MAJORS: Biology

Open to an outstanding student in the Department of Biology. Contact the address listed for further information. Must have a GPA of at least 3.5.

Brooklyn College
Office of the V.P. for Student Life
2113 Boylan Hall
Brooklyn, NY 11210

2826
Jack and Estelle Rapaport '37 Scholarship

AMOUNT: Maximum: $2500   DEADLINE: March 1
FIELDS/MAJORS: All Areas of Study

Open to a meritorious minority student. Contact the address listed for further information. Must have a GPA of at least 3.0.

Brooklyn College
Office of the V.P. for Student Life
2113 Boylan Hall
Brooklyn, NY 11210

2827
Jack Devine Memorial Scholarship

AMOUNT: Maximum: $1000   DEADLINE: March 1
FIELDS/MAJORS: Language/Culture/Traditions, Caribbean

Open to students who have demonstrated an interest in the language, culture, and traditions of the Caribbean. Contact the address listed for further information.

Brooklyn College
Office of the V.P. for Student Life
2113 Boylan Hall
Brooklyn, NY 11210

2828
Jay E. Greene '32 Memorial Scholarship

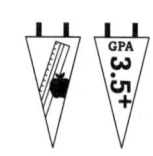

AMOUNT: Maximum: $500   DEADLINE: March 1
FIELDS/MAJORS: Education

Open to an outstanding undergraduate majoring in education. Contact the address listed for further information. Must have a GPA of at least 3.5.

Brooklyn College
Office of the V.P. for Student Life
2113 Boylan Hall
Brooklyn, NY 11210

2829
Jeanette Trum Granoff '35 Graduate Scholarship

AMOUNT: Maximum: $1250   DEADLINE: March 1
FIELDS/MAJORS: Science

Open to an outstanding graduating senior entering a master's program in science. Contact the address listed for further information. Must have a GPA of at least 3.5.

Brooklyn College
Office of the V.P. for Student Life
2113 Boylan Hall
Brooklyn, NY 11210

2830
Jeffrey Chanin '62 Scholarship

AMOUNT: Maximum: $2500   DEADLINE: March 1
FIELDS/MAJORS: Political Science, History

Open to undergraduates who are able to demonstrate a high level of scholastic achievement and a potential for future success in graduate study. Contact the address listed for further information. Must have a GPA of at least 3.2.

Brooklyn College
Office of the V.P. for Student Life
2113 Boylan Hall
Brooklyn, NY 11210

2831
Jerome J. Viola Memorial Scholarship

AMOUNT: Maximum: $250   DEADLINE: March 1
FIELDS/MAJORS: Art History, Studio Art

Open to outstanding students in art history or studio art. Preference given to students enrolled in the School of General Studies. Contact the address listed for further information. Must have a GPA of at least 3.1.

Brooklyn College
Office of the V.P. for Student Life
2113 Boylan Hall
Brooklyn, NY 11210

2832
Jonathan Marc Zimmering Memorial Prize in Pre-engineering

AMOUNT: Maximum: $300 DEADLINE: March 1
FIELDS/MAJORS: Engineering

Open to the most gifted student completing two years of pre-engineering and continuing studies for the bachelor's degree in engineering. Contact the address listed for further information. Must have a GPA of at least 3.3.

Brooklyn College
Office of the V.P. for Student Life
2113 Boylan Hall
Brooklyn, NY 11210

2833
Jonas Salk Scholarship

AMOUNT: Maximum: $3500 DEADLINE: March 1
FIELDS/MAJORS: Medicine

Open to students enrolled/accepted into medical school. Contact the address listed for further information.

Brooklyn College
Office of the V.P. for Student Life
2113 Boylan Hall
Brooklyn, NY 11210

2834
Joseph G. Cohen Memorial Scholarship

AMOUNT: Maximum: $600 DEADLINE: March 1
FIELDS/MAJORS: Secondary Education.

Open to students preparing to teach in junior or senior high schools. Contact the address listed for further information. Must have a GPA of at least 2.7.

Brooklyn College
Office of the V.P. for Student Life
2113 Boylan Hall
Brooklyn, NY 11210

2835
Lado Scholarship and Siegmund Levarie Scholarship

AMOUNT: None Specified DEADLINE: March 1
FIELDS/MAJORS: Music

Open to outstanding students in the Conservatory of Music. Awards up to partial or full tuition. Contact the address listed for further information about both awards.

Brooklyn College
Office of the V.P. for Student Life
2113 Boylan Hall
Brooklyn, NY 11210

2836
Lester D. Crow Scholarship

AMOUNT: Maximum: $450 DEADLINE: March 1
FIELDS/MAJORS: Education

Open to education majors for outstanding academics and good college citizenship. Contact the address listed for further information. Must have a GPA of at least 3.2.

Brooklyn College
Office of the V.P. for Student Life
2113 Boylan Hall
Brooklyn, NY 11210

2837
Libby Kohl Banks '41 Memorial Scholarship

AMOUNT: Maximum: $800 DEADLINE: March 1
FIELDS/MAJORS: Biology

Open to biology majors who can demonstrate achievement and motivation. Contact the address listed for further information. Must have a GPA of at least 2.8.

Brooklyn College
Office of the V.P. for Student Life
2113 Boylan Hall
Brooklyn, NY 11210

2838
Louis Goodman Creative Writing Scholarship

AMOUNT: Maximum: $250 DEADLINE: March 1
FIELDS/MAJORS: Creative Writing

Open to students showing creative writing talent. Contact the address listed for further information.

Brooklyn College
Office of the V.P. for Student Life
2113 Boylan Hall
Brooklyn, NY 11210

2839
Louis P. Goldberg Memorial Scholarship

AMOUNT: Maximum: $500   DEADLINE: March 1
FIELDS/MAJORS: Political Science, Economics, Sociology

Open to a graduating senior enrolling in a master's degree program. Contact the address listed for further information.

Brooklyn College
Office of the V.P. for Student Life
2113 Boylan Hall
Brooklyn, NY 11210

2840
Mae Rimmer and Jack Rimmer '46 Scholarship

AMOUNT: Maximum: $1000   DEADLINE: March 1
FIELDS/MAJORS: Science

Open to juniors who can demonstrate an outstanding academic record. Contact the address listed for further information. Must have a GPA of at least 3.2.

Brooklyn College
Office of the V.P. for Student Life
2113 Boylan Hall
Brooklyn, NY 11210

2841
Margaret Ann Kneller Scholarship

AMOUNT: Maximum: $500   DEADLINE: March 1
FIELDS/MAJORS: All Areas of Study

Open to a senior with a physical disability who can demonstrate academic achievement, leadership in student affairs, and a commitment to community service. Contact the address listed for further information.

Brooklyn College
Office of the V.P. for Student Life
2113 Boylan Hall
Brooklyn, NY 11210

2842
Martin L. Rosenthal Memorial Scholarship

AMOUNT: Maximum: $250   DEADLINE: March 1
FIELDS/MAJORS: Political Science

Open to outstanding students majoring in political science. Contact the address listed for further information. Must have a GPA of at least 3.1.

Brooklyn College
Office of the V.P. for Student Life
2113 Boylan Hall
Brooklyn, NY 11210

2843
Maurice Lieberman Scholarship

AMOUNT: Maximum: $1000   DEADLINE: March 1
FIELDS/MAJORS: Music, History, Theory, Composition

Open to students in the Conservatory of Music majoring in any of the listed fields. Contact the address listed for further information.

Brooklyn College
Office of the V.P. for Student Life
2113 Boylan Hall
Brooklyn, NY 11210

2844
Merit Scholarship for Excellence in Philosophy

AMOUNT: Maximum: $400   DEADLINE: March 1
FIELDS/MAJORS: Philosophy

Open to an outstanding philosophy major who has completed at least forty-five credits. Contact the address listed for further information. Must have a GPA of at least 3.0.

Brooklyn College
Office of the V.P. for Student Life
2113 Boylan Hall
Brooklyn, NY 11210

2845
Michael Bruce Duchin Memorial Scholarship

AMOUNT: Maximum: $1000   DEADLINE: March 1
FIELDS/MAJORS: Geology

Open to juniors and seniors who are qualified geology majors. Contact the address listed for further information. Must have a GPA of at least 3.0.

Brooklyn College
Office of the V.P. for Student Life
2113 Boylan Hall
Brooklyn, NY 11210

2846
Mildred L. Lipkin Memorial Scholarship

AMOUNT: Maximum: $250   DEADLINE: March 1
FIELDS/MAJORS: Elementary, Mathematics Education

Open to students in the School of Education preparing to teach mathematics at the elementary school level. Contact the address listed for further information.

Brooklyn College
Office of the V.P. for Student Life
2113 Boylan Hall
Brooklyn, NY 11210

2847
Mobile Foundation Scholarship

AMOUNT: Maximum: $500   DEADLINE: March 1
FIELDS/MAJORS: Computer/Information Science

Open to students majoring in the fields listed above. Contact the address listed for further information.

Brooklyn College
Office of the V.P. for Student Life
2113 Boylan Hall
Brooklyn, NY 11210

2848
Mordecai Gabriel Scholarship

AMOUNT: Maximum: $800   DEADLINE: March 1
FIELDS/MAJORS: Biology

Open to undergraduates who can demonstrate superior scholarship. Contact the address listed for further information. Must have a GPA of at least 3.5.

Brooklyn College
Office of the V.P. for Student Life
2113 Boylan Hall
Brooklyn, NY 11210

2849
Morris Charney Memorial Scholarship

AMOUNT: Maximum: $300   DEADLINE: March 1
FIELDS/MAJORS: Chemistry

Open to graduating seniors for excellence in chemistry. Contact the address listed for further information. Must have a GPA of at least 3.2.

Brooklyn College
Office of the V.P. for Student Life
2113 Boylan Hall
Brooklyn, NY 11210

2850
Paul J. and Angela H. Salvatore Memorial Scholarship

AMOUNT: Maximum: $1000   DEADLINE: March 1
FIELDS/MAJORS: Romance Language

Open to undergraduates majoring in a romance language. For continued study at Brooklyn College. Contact the address listed for further information.

Brooklyn College
Office of the V.P. for Student Life
2113 Boylan Hall
Brooklyn, NY 11210

2851
Paul Taylor Scholarship

AMOUNT: None Specified   DEADLINE: March 1
FIELDS/MAJORS: Philosophy

Open to outstanding students who have completed at least two electives in the Department of Philosophy. Contact the address listed for further information. Must have a GPA of at least 3.1.

Brooklyn College
Office of the V.P. for Student Life
2113 Boylan Hall
Brooklyn, NY 11210

2852
Pearl Gross Brickner '40 Scholarship

AMOUNT: Maximum: $1000   DEADLINE: March 1
FIELDS/MAJORS: Nutrition

Open to outstanding undergraduates majoring in nutrition. Contact the address listed for further information. Must have a GPA of at least 3.0.

Brooklyn College
Office of the V.P. for Student Life
2113 Boylan Hall
Brooklyn, NY 11210

2853
Professor Nathan Schmukler Scholarship

AMOUNT: Maximum: $2500   DEADLINE: March 1
FIELDS/MAJORS: Accounting

Open to juniors and seniors who have achieved, or show promise of achieving, an outstanding academic record.

Contact the address listed for further information. Must have a GPA of at least 3.1.

Brooklyn College
Office of the V.P. for Student Life
2113 Boylan Hall
Brooklyn, NY 11210

2854
Professor Stanley Zimmering Prize in Biology

AMOUNT: Maximum: $300   DEADLINE: March 1
FIELDS/MAJORS: Biology

Open to graduating seniors who plan an academic career in research and teaching biology and who have been accepted by graduate school. Contact the address listed for further information.

Brooklyn College
Office of the V.P. for Student Life
2113 Boylan Hall
Brooklyn, NY 11210

2855
Rich Relative Scholarship

AMOUNT: Maximum: $1000   DEADLINE: March 1
FIELDS/MAJORS: All Areas of Study

Open to students who have completed freshman year. Contact the address listed for further information. Must have a GPA of at least 3.0.

Brooklyn College
Office of the V.P. for Student Life
2113 Boylan Hall
Brooklyn, NY 11210

2856
Robert Namoli Memorial Scholarship

AMOUNT: Maximum: $500   DEADLINE: March 1
FIELDS/MAJORS: Education

Open to outstanding undergraduates in the School of Education. Contact the address listed for further information. Must have a GPA of at least 3.1.

Brooklyn College
Office of the V.P. for Student Life
2113 Boylan Hall
Brooklyn, NY 11210

2857
Sam Beller '59 Scholarship

AMOUNT: Maximum: $2000   DEADLINE: March 1
FIELDS/MAJORS: Business

Open to junior and senior business majors who can demonstrate developed goals and displayed entrepreneurial skills. Contact the address listed for further information. Must have a GPA of at least 2.8.

Brooklyn College
Office of the V.P. for Student Life
2113 Boylan Hall
Brooklyn, NY 11210

2858
Seymour Richman Memorial Scholarship

AMOUNT: Maximum: $1000   DEADLINE: March 1
FIELDS/MAJORS: Biology

Open to incoming freshmen who can demonstrate outstanding achievement and significant potential for study in the Department of Biology. Contact the address listed for further information. Must have a GPA of at least 3.0.

Brooklyn College
Office of the V.P. for Student Life
2113 Boylan Hall
Brooklyn, NY 11210

2859
Sheldon J. Korchin Memorial Scholarship

AMOUNT: None Specified   DEADLINE: March 1
FIELDS/MAJORS: Psychology

Open to a senior planning to pursue graduate study in psychology at Brooklyn College. Contact the address listed for further information.

Brooklyn College
Office of the V.P. for Student Life
2113 Boylan Hall
Brooklyn, NY 11210

2860
Sheldon L. Smith Scholarship

AMOUNT: None Specified   DEADLINE: March 1
FIELDS/MAJORS: Instrumental Music

Open to students majoring in instrumental music in the Conservatory of Music. Award is partial tuition. Contact the address listed for further information.

Brooklyn College
Office of the V.P. for Student Life
2113 Boylan Hall
Brooklyn, NY 11210

2861
Special Training Scholarship

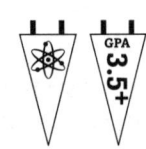

AMOUNT: Maximum: $250   DEADLINE: March 1
FIELDS/MAJORS: Geology

Open to qualified students majoring in geology, to be used for field studies. Contact the address listed for further information. Must have a GPA of at least 2.9.

Brooklyn College
Office of the V.P. for Student Life
2113 Boylan Hall
Brooklyn, NY 11210

2862
Spikol-Luskin Scholarship

AMOUNT: Maximum: $350   DEADLINE: March 1
FIELDS/MAJORS: Liberal Arts

Open to liberal arts majors who plan on completing requirements for state certification and entering teaching as a career. Contact the address listed for further information.

Brooklyn College
Office of the V.P. for Student Life
2113 Boylan Hall
Brooklyn, NY 11210

2863
Stanley Schiff Memorial Scholarship

AMOUNT: Maximum: $250   DEADLINE: March 1
FIELDS/MAJORS: Judaic Studies

Open to a graduating senior who plans to continue Judaic studies in graduate school. Contact the address listed for further information.

Brooklyn College
Office of the V.P. for Student Life
2113 Boylan Hall
Brooklyn, NY 11210

2864
Stewart M. Monchik Memorial Scholarship

AMOUNT: Maximum: $1000   DEADLINE: March 1
FIELDS/MAJORS: Computer/Information Science

Open to students (for junior year of study), majoring in the fields listed above. Contact the address listed for further information.

Brooklyn College
Office of the V.P. for Student Life
2113 Boylan Hall
Brooklyn, NY 11210

2865
Susan Solomon and Zachary Solomon '57 Scholarship

AMOUNT: Maximum: $1000   DEADLINE: March 1
FIELDS/MAJORS: Economics

Open to undergraduates majoring in economics. Based on academic merit. Contact the address listed for further information. Must have a GPA of at least 3.0.

Brooklyn College
Office of the V.P. for Student Life
2113 Boylan Hall
Brooklyn, NY 11210

2866
Susan Zisselman Memorial Scholarship

AMOUNT: Maximum: $1000   DEADLINE: March 1
FIELDS/MAJORS: Arts, Humanities

Open to a deserving disabled student. Must be able to demonstrate financial need and a commitment to the arts or humanities. Contact the address listed for further information.

Brooklyn College
Office of the V.P. for Student Life
2113 Boylan Hall
Brooklyn, NY 11210

2867
Treasury Management Association Scholarship

AMOUNT: None Specified   DEADLINE: March 1
FIELDS/MAJORS: Business

Open to full-time juniors and seniors majoring in business who have a strong record of academic achievement. Award is full tuition. Contact the address listed for further information. Must have a GPA of at least 3.1.

Brooklyn College
Office of the V.P. for Student Life
2113 Boylan Hall
Brooklyn, NY 11210

2868
Violet Klein Memorial Scholarship

AMOUNT: Maximum: $1000　DEADLINE: March 1
FIELDS/MAJORS: Health, Nutrition Sciences

Open to an outstanding undergraduate who plans to enter graduate studies in the area of gerontology. Contact the address listed for further information. Must have a GPA of at least 3.5.

Brooklyn College
Office of the V.P. for Student Life
2113 Boylan Hall
Brooklyn, NY 11210

2869
Walter W. Gerboth, Richard Franco Goldman, Rubin Goldmark Scholarships

AMOUNT: Maximum: $500　DEADLINE: March 1
FIELDS/MAJORS: Music

Open to outstanding students in the Conservatory of Music. Contact the address listed for further information about all three awards. Must have a GPA of at least 3.2.

Brooklyn College
Office of the V.P. for Student Life
2113 Boylan Hall
Brooklyn, NY 11210

2870
Warren Schuyler Dean Scholarship

AMOUNT: Maximum: $1000　DEADLINE: March 1
FIELDS/MAJORS: Music, Violin

Open to outstanding violin students in the Conservatory of Music. Contact the address listed for further information. Must have a GPA of at least 3.0.

Brooklyn College
Office of the V.P. for Student Life
2113 Boylan Hall
Brooklyn, NY 11210

BROWN UNIVERSITY

2871
Champlin Foundations Scholarship

AMOUNT: None Specified　DEADLINE: April 1
FIELDS/MAJORS: All Areas of Study

Scholarships open to students of Brown University who graduated from a Rhode Island public high school. Funds are awarded to Brown. The University selects the recipients, awards the scholarship, and administers the program. Contact the financial aid office for further information.

Champlin Foundations
David A. King, Executive Director
300 Centerville Rd., #300S
Warwick, RI 02886-0203

2872
Long-Term Research Fellowships

AMOUNT: $13375　DEADLINE: January 15
FIELDS/MAJORS: Humanities/Social Science

Five-month research fellowships are available for postdoctoral study. Must be United States citizens or residents for at least three years preceding the fellowship term. Residency at the John Carter Brown Library is required. Write to address below for details.

John Carter Brown Library
Attn: Director
Box 1894, Brown University
Providence, RI 02912

BRYN MAWR GRADUATE SCHOOL OF ARTS AND SCIENCES

2873
Alice McGuffey Laughlin Fellowship

AMOUNT: None Specified　DEADLINE: January 2
FIELDS/MAJORS: Literature, Art

Awards open to graduate students in either of the above fields. Contact the address below for further information.

Bryn Mawr Graduate School of Arts and Sciences
101 N. Merion Ave.
Bryn Mawr, PA 19010

2874
Annemarie Bettmann Holborn and Jack T. and Janice N. Holmes Awards

AMOUNT: None Specified DEADLINE: January 2
FIELDS/MAJORS: Classics, Classical/Near Eastern Archaeology

Holborn award open to graduate and undergraduate students in any of the above fields. Holmes Fellowship for graduates only. Contact the address below for further information.

Bryn Mawr Graduate School of Arts and Sciences
101 N. Merion Ave.
Bryn Mawr, PA 19010

2875
Barbara Cooley McNamee Dudley Fund Scholarship

AMOUNT: None Specified DEADLINE: January 2
FIELDS/MAJORS: All Areas of Study

Award open to international students for both undergraduate and graduate study. Contact the address below for further information.

Bryn Mawr Graduate School of Arts and Sciences
101 N. Merion Ave.
Bryn Mawr, PA 19010

2876
Bob and Audrey Conner Fund Scholarship

AMOUNT: None Specified DEADLINE: January 2
FIELDS/MAJORS: Biology

Award open for summer support to graduate students in biology. Contact the address below for further information.

Bryn Mawr Graduate School of Arts and Sciences
101 N. Merion Ave.
Bryn Mawr, PA 19010

2877
Emma and Fritz Guggenbuhl Fund in Mathematics

AMOUNT: None Specified DEADLINE: January 2
FIELDS/MAJORS: Mathematics

Awards open to graduate students in mathematics. Contact the address below for further information.

Bryn Mawr Graduate School of Arts and Sciences
101 N. Merion Ave.
Bryn Mawr, PA 19010

2878
Grace Frank Fellowship Fund

AMOUNT: None Specified DEADLINE: January 2
FIELDS/MAJORS: Humanities

Award open to graduate students in humanities. Contact the address below for further information.

Bryn Mawr Graduate School of Arts and Sciences
101 N. Merion Ave.
Bryn Mawr, PA 19010

2879
Henry Joel Cadbury Fellowship Fund

AMOUNT: None Specified DEADLINE: January 2
FIELDS/MAJORS: Humanities

Award open to advanced graduate students in humanities. Contact the address below for further information.

Bryn Mawr Graduate School of Arts and Sciences
101 N. Merion Ave.
Bryn Mawr, PA 19010

2880
Howard Lehman Goodhart Fellowship Fund

AMOUNT: None Specified DEADLINE: January 2
FIELDS/MAJORS: Medieval Studies

Award open to graduate students in medieval studies. Contact the address below for further information.

Bryn Mawr Graduate School of Arts and Sciences
101 N. Merion Ave.
Bryn Mawr, PA 19010

2881

Margaret Gilman and Anne Cutting Jones and Edith Melcher Fund Awards

AMOUNT: None Specified   DEADLINE: January 2
FIELDS/MAJORS: French

Award open to graduate students studying French. Contact the address below for further information about both awards.

Bryn Mawr Graduate School of Arts and Sciences
101 N. Merion Ave.
Bryn Mawr, PA 19010

2882

Marguerite Bartlett Hamer and Bertha Haven Putman Fellowships

AMOUNT: None Specified   DEADLINE: January 2
FIELDS/MAJORS: History

Awards open to graduate students in history. Contact the address below for further information about both awards.

Bryn Mawr Graduate School of Arts and Sciences
101 N. Merion Ave.
Bryn Mawr, PA 19010

2883

Max Richter Fellowship Fund

AMOUNT: None Specified   DEADLINE: January 2
FIELDS/MAJORS: International Affairs

Awards open to advanced graduate students. May be used to fund dissertation overseas. Applicants must be U.S. citizens. Contact the address below for further information.

Bryn Mawr Graduate School of Arts and Sciences
101 N. Merion Ave.
Bryn Mawr, PA 19010

2884

Melodee Siegel Kornacker Fellowship

AMOUNT: None Specified   DEADLINE: January 2
FIELDS/MAJORS: Biology, Chemistry, Geology, Physics, Psychology

Awards open to graduate students in any of the above fields. Contact the address below for further information.

Bryn Mawr Graduate School of Arts and Sciences
101 N. Merion Ave.
Bryn Mawr, PA 19010

2885

Mildred Clarke Ressinger/ Mildred and Carl Otto Von Kienbusch Fellowship

AMOUNT: None Specified   DEADLINE: January 2
FIELDS/MAJORS: All Areas of Study

Awards open to students working toward the doctorate. Contact the address below for further information about both awards.

Bryn Mawr Graduate School of Arts and Sciences
101 N. Merion Ave.
Bryn Mawr, PA 19010

2886

Nora M. and Patrick J. Healy Scholarship Fund

AMOUNT: None Specified   DEADLINE: January 2
FIELDS/MAJORS: Arts and Sciences, Social Work, Social Research

Awards open to graduate students in any of the above fields. Contact the address below for further information.

Bryn Mawr Graduate School of Arts and Sciences
101 N. Merion Ave.
Bryn Mawr, PA 19010

2887

Theodore N. Ely Fund Scholarship

AMOUNT: None Specified   DEADLINE: January 2
FIELDS/MAJORS: Archaeology, Art History

Award open to graduate students in either of the above fields. Contact the address below for further information.

Bryn Mawr Graduate School of Arts and Sciences
101 N. Merion Ave.
Bryn Mawr, PA 19010

2888

Wheeler and Florence Jenkins Scholarship Fund

AMOUNT: None Specified   DEADLINE: January 2
FIELDS/MAJORS: Mathematics, Physics

Awards open to graduate and undergraduate students in either of the above fields. Contact the address below for further information.

Bryn Mawr Graduate School of Arts and Sciences
101 N. Merion Ave.
Bryn Mawr, PA 19010

CALIFORNIA COLLEGE OF ARTS AND CRAFTS

2889
CCAC Scholarships and Creative Achievement Scholarships

AMOUNT: None Specified   DEADLINE: March 1
FIELDS/MAJORS: All Areas of Study

Scholarships for students at the California College of Arts and Crafts. Most scholarships are need based; some, talent based. Five to six hundred awards offered annually. Contact the school at the address below for details.

California College of Arts and Crafts
Office of Enrollment Services
5212 Broadway at College
Oakland, CA 94618

2890
Todd Master's' Scholarship

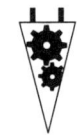

AMOUNT: Maximum: $500   DEADLINE: October 1
FIELDS/MAJORS: Architecture

Open to gay students with a commitment to the field of architecture and drawing. Must be enrolled at California College of Arts and Crafts. Contact the address below for further information.

California College of Arts and Crafts
Anita Kermes, Director of Financial Aid
415 Irwin St.
San Francisco, CA 94107-2206

CALIFORNIA STATE POLYTECHNIC UNIVERSITY, POMONA

2891
Kellogg Scholars Program

AMOUNT: Maximum: $7200   DEADLINE: November 30
FIELDS/MAJORS: Ornamental Horticulture

Kellogg Scholars are among the best and brightest that high schools have to offer, often in the top 5% of their class and demonstrating outstanding leadership skills. Applicants must have a minimum GPA of 3.75 and plan to enroll as a first-time freshman at Cal Poly, Pomona, full-time. Write to the address below or call (909) 869-3702 for more information.

California State Polytechnic University, Pomona
College of Agriculture
Building 7, Room 110
Pomona, CA 91768

CALIFORNIA STATE UNIVERSITY AT FRESNO

2892
Bureau of Indian Affairs (BIA) Grant

AMOUNT: None Specified   DEADLINE: February 1
FIELDS/MAJORS: All Areas of Study

Scholarships for students who are at least one-quarter American Indian, Eskimo, or Aleut. Contact your tribal agency for more information.

California State University at Fresno
Financial Aid Office
5150 North Maple Ave.
Fresno, CA 93740

2893
Undergraduate Scholarships

AMOUNT: $100-$2000   DEADLINE: February 1
FIELDS/MAJORS: All Areas of Study

Scholarships for undergraduates at California State University at Fresno who have a minimum GPA of 3.0 (exception of 2.5 GPA is made for special grants). Involvement in campus and community activities is required. Students studying for a second bachelor's or master's degree are not eligible. Write to the address below for more information.

California State University at Fresno
Financial Aid Office
5150 North Maple Ave.
Fresno, CA 93740

CALIFORNIA STATE UNIVERSITY, LONG BEACH

2894

CSU Forgivable Loan-Doctoral Incentive Program

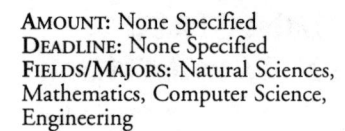

AMOUNT: None Specified
DEADLINE: None Specified
FIELDS/MAJORS: Natural Sciences, Mathematics, Computer Science, Engineering

Doctoral program initiated to increase the number of minority, female, and handicapped educators in underrepresented fields in California. Recipients must commit to return to California to teach after completion of degree at a participating institution. Write to the address below for information.

California State University, Long Beach
Office of the Chancellor
400 Golden Shore, Suite 222
Long Beach, CA 90802

CALIFORNIA STATE UNIVERSITY, NORTHRIDGE

2895

Continuing Graduate Scholarships

AMOUNT: None Specified   DEADLINE: March 2
FIELDS/MAJORS: All Areas of Study

For need-based awards, applicants must be pursuing first master's degree or first credential and have a minimum GPA of 3.0. Must be Classified, Conditionally Classified, or P.B. Credential (PBU students are not eligible). Must be enrolled full-time unless preapproved for three-quarter time based on extenuating circumstances. Merit-based awards for students pursuing first master's degree or credential, who have a minimum GPA of 3.75 (or 3.6 undergraduate GPA if applying as an entering graduate student). Must be Classified, Conditionally Classified, or P.B. Credential (PBU students are not eligible). Must be enrolled full-time. Contact the address below for further information.

California State University, Northridge
Office of Financial Aid
18111 Nordhoff St.
Northridge, CA 91330-8307

2896

Continuing Undergraduate Scholarships

AMOUNT: None Specified   DEADLINE: March 2
FIELDS/MAJORS: All Areas of Study

Applicants must have declared a major by junior class level and have a minimum GPA of 3.0 to be considered for most University need-based scholarships. Must be enrolled full-time, unless preapproved for three-quarter time, based on extenuating circumstances. Must file the FAFSA by March 2. Applicants for merit-based awards must be pursuing first bachelor's degree and have a declared major by time of application and be enrolled full-time and have a minimum GPA of 3.6. Contact the address below for further information.

California State University, Northridge
Office of Financial Aid
18111 Nordhoff St.
Northridge, CA 91330-8307

2897

First-time Freshmen and Transfer Student Scholarship

AMOUNT: None Specified   DEADLINE: March 2
FIELDS/MAJORS: All Areas of Study

Open to transfer students and incoming freshmen from high school. Must have a minimum GPA of 3.0 (as determined by the CSUN Admissions Office) and be enrolled full-time. Must demonstrate financial need and file a FAFSA. The University Scholarship Program requires one application to be considered for the more than three hundred scholarships available. Contact the address below for further information.

California State University, Northridge
Office of Financial Aid
18111 Nordhoff St.
Northridge, CA 91330-8307

CAPITOL COMMUNITY COLLEGE

2898

Martin Luther King, Jr., Youth Foundation Scholarships

AMOUNT: Maximum: $2000   DEADLINE: April 15
FIELDS/MAJORS: All Areas of Study

Open to Hartford residents who are graduating high school seniors or second-year students at Capitol Community College. Based on community service, academics, and financial need. For use at four-year schools. Contact the address listed for further information.

Martin Luther King, Jr., Youth Foundation, Inc.
Ms. Valerie Bolden-Barrett
Box F
Hartford, CT 06103

CARSON-NEWMAN COLLEGE

2899

Bonner Scholarships

AMOUNT: $1100-$1950 DEADLINE: None Specified
FIELDS/MAJORS: All Areas of Study

Awards for students who demonstrate financial need and community service. Must apply through the C-N Bonner office. Renewable for three years. $1950 during school year, and $1100 during summer. Contact the address below or call 1-800-678-9061 or (423) 471-3247 for further information.

Carson-Newman College
Office of Financial Aid
Jefferson City, TN 37760

2900

Carson-Newman College Academic Scholarships

AMOUNT: None Specified DEADLINE: None Specified
FIELDS/MAJORS: All Areas of Study

Awards for entering freshmen with an ACT score of 24 or SAT score of 1100 and a GPA of 3.0 or higher. Must demonstrate financial need. Renewable if GPA of 3.0 is maintained. Contact the address below or call 1-800-678-9061 or (423) 471-3247 for further information.

Carson-Newman College
Office of Financial Aid
Jefferson City, TN 37760

2901

Honors Program Scholarship

AMOUNT: $500 DEADLINE: None Specified
FIELDS/MAJORS: All Areas of Study

Awards for students who have been accepted to the Honors Program. Renewable for three additional years if participating in the Honors Program. Contact the address below for further information.

Carson-Newman College
Office of Financial Aid
Jefferson City, TN 37760

2902

Minister's Dependent Grant

AMOUNT: Maximum: $1000 DEADLINE: None Specified
FIELDS/MAJORS: All Areas of Study

Awards for students who are dependents of full-time Southern Baptist ministers. Renewable for three additional years. Contact the address below or call 1-800-678-9061 or (423) 471-3247 for further information.

Carson-Newman College
Office of Financial Aid
Jefferson City, TN 37760

2903

Performance Scholarships

AMOUNT: None Specified DEADLINE: None Specified
FIELDS/MAJORS: Music, Debate

Awards based on skill and performance in music, debate, and band. Contact the director of your performance specialty or call 1-800-678-9061 or (423) 471-3247 for further information.

Carson-Newman College
Office of Financial Aid
Jefferson City, TN 37760

2904

Phi Theta Kappa

AMOUNT: Maximum: $2500 DEADLINE: None Specified
FIELDS/MAJORS: All Areas of Study

Awards for members who have completed an associates degree before enrollment. Must have a minimum GPA of 3.0. A recommendation is also required. Contact the address below or call 1-800-678-9061 or (423) 471-3247 for further information.

Carson-Newman College
Office of Financial Aid
Jefferson City, TN 37760

2905

Presidential Excellence Scholarship

AMOUNT: None Specified DEADLINE: December 31
FIELDS/MAJORS: All Areas of Study

Awards for high school seniors who achieved a minimum of 30 as their ACT score or higher than 1350 on the SAT. Must also have a minimum GPA of 3.6 or higher to qualify. Up to five awards are offered annually. The awards are full tuition. Contact the address below or call 1-800-678-9061 or (423) 471-3247 for further information.

Carson-Newman College
Office of Financial Aid
Jefferson City, TN 37760

2906
Presidential Honors Scholarship

AMOUNT: None Specified   DEADLINE: None Specified
FIELDS/MAJORS: All Areas of Study

Awards for high school seniors with an ACT score of 29 or higher, a minimum of 1300 on the SAT, and a GPA of 3.3. Awards also for transfer students with a minimum of 32 credit hours and a GPA of 3.5 or higher. Based on academic performance and demonstrated financial need. Renewable if GPA of 3.0 is maintained. Contact the address below or call 1-800-678-9061 or (423) 471-3247 for further information.

Carson-Newman College
Office of Financial Aid
Jefferson City, TN 37760

2907
Presidential Incentive Scholarship

AMOUNT: $500   DEADLINE: None Specified
FIELDS/MAJORS: All Areas of Study

Awards for upperclassmen not currently receiving a scholarship. Must have a minimum GPA of 3.5. Renewable if GPA of 3.0 or higher is maintained. The award is anywhere from $500 to one-half of tuition. Contact the address below or call 1-800-678-9061 or (423) 471-3247 for further information.

Carson-Newman College
Office of Financial Aid
Jefferson City, TN 37760

CASE WESTERN RESERVE UNIVERSITY

2908
Accountancy Scholarships at Case Western

AMOUNT: $1000   DEADLINE: February 1
FIELDS/MAJORS: Accounting

Two scholarships for freshmen who intend to major in accounting at Case Western Reserve University. Scholarships are renewable for a second year if high academic achievement is maintained. Write to the address below for details.

Case Western Reserve University
Office of Financial Aid, 109 Pardee Hall
10900 Euclid Ave.
Cleveland, OH 44106

2909
Albert W. Smith Scholarships and the Alexander Treuhaft Scholarships

AMOUNT: $16430   DEADLINE: February 1
FIELDS/MAJORS: Science and Engineering

Four full-tuition scholarships offered to qualified applicants for admission as freshmen. Awards are renewable for each of the four years of undergraduate study, provided high academic achievement is maintained. Students must already be accepted into a science or engineering program at CWRU. Write to the address below for details.

Case Western Reserve University
Office of Financial Aid, 109 Pardee Hall
10900 Euclid Ave.
Cleveland, OH 44106

2910
Alden Undergraduate Fellowships in Systems Engineering

AMOUNT: $3500   DEADLINE: February 1
FIELDS/MAJORS: Systems Engineering (Computer Science)

Scholarships for junior or senior undergraduates majoring in systems engineering at Case Western Reserve University. Applicants must have a minimum GPA of 3.2 for the last three semesters preceding the application. Two awards per year. Write to the Department of Systems Engineering at the address below for additional information and application procedures.

Case Western Reserve University
Office of Financial Aid, 109 Pardee Hall
10900 Euclid Ave.
Cleveland, OH 44106

2911
Andrew Squire Scholarships and the Adelbert Alumni Scholarships

AMOUNT: $17800   DEADLINE: February 1
FIELDS/MAJORS: All Areas of Study

Five full-tuition scholarships offered to qualified applicants for admission as freshmen. Awards are renewable for each of the four years of undergraduate study, provided high academic achievement is maintained. Awards range from $17800 to full tuition. Write to the address below for details. GPA must be at least 2.8.

Case Western Reserve University
Office of Financial Aid, 109 Pardee Hall
10900 Euclid Ave.
Cleveland, OH 44106

2912
Case Alumni Association Junior and Senior Scholarships

AMOUNT: None Specified   DEADLINE: February 1
FIELDS/MAJORS: All Areas of Study

A number of scholarships funded by the Case Alumni Association of the Case School of Engineering are awarded to juniors and seniors on the basis of academic achievement, financial need, and participation in extracurricular activities. Write to the address below for details.

Case Western Reserve University
Office of Financial Aid, 109 Pardee Hall
10900 Euclid Ave.
Cleveland, OH 44106

2913
Creative Achievement Award at Case Western

AMOUNT: $8900   DEADLINE: February 1
FIELDS/MAJORS: Art, Drama/Theater, Music

Scholarships offered to entering freshmen at Case Western Reserve University. Must demonstrate outstanding creative ability and achievement. Awards are renewable for four years, provided there is continued evidence of outstanding creative achievement and satisfactory academic achievement. Three awards per year. Write to the address below for additional information.

Case Western Reserve University
Office of Financial Aid, 109 Pardee Hall
10900 Euclid Ave.
Cleveland, OH 44106

2914
Curtis Lee Smith Scholarship and the Elizabeth Walker Scholarship

AMOUNT: $10000-$13000   DEADLINE: February 1
FIELDS/MAJORS: All Areas of Study

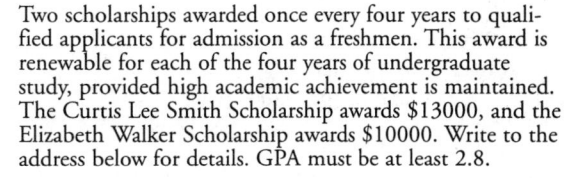

Two scholarships awarded once every four years to qualified applicants for admission as a freshmen. This award is renewable for each of the four years of undergraduate study, provided high academic achievement is maintained. The Curtis Lee Smith Scholarship awards $13000, and the Elizabeth Walker Scholarship awards $10000. Write to the address below for details. GPA must be at least 2.8.

Case Western Reserve University
Office of Financial Aid, 109 Pardee Hall
10900 Euclid Ave.
Cleveland, OH 44106

2915
Materials Science and Engineering Scholarships at Case Western

AMOUNT: $3000   DEADLINE: February 1
FIELDS/MAJORS: Materials Science and Engineering

Five scholarships offered to entering freshmen at Case Western Reserve University who intend to major in materials science and engineering. Scholarships are renewable for each of the four years of undergraduate study if high academic achievement is maintained. Write to the address below for details.

Case Western Reserve University
Office of Financial Aid, 109 Pardee Hall
10900 Euclid Ave.
Cleveland, OH 44106

2916
Minority Scholars Program

AMOUNT: None Specified   DEADLINE: February 1
FIELDS/MAJORS: All Areas of Study

The minority scholars program is a program of career counseling, academic preparation, internships, and mentoring for selected minority students from underrepresented groups. Students must be entering as freshmen at Case Western Reserve University. Write to the address below for details.

Case Western Reserve University
Office of Financial Aid, 109 Pardee Hall
10900 Euclid Ave.
Cleveland, OH 44106

2917
National Merit Scholarships at Case Western

AMOUNT: $500-$2000   DEADLINE: February 1
FIELDS/MAJORS: All Areas of Study

At least twenty-five four-year scholarships for National Merit Scholarship Corporation finalists who have listed

Case Western Reserve University as their first-choice institution. Write to the address below for details.

Case Western Reserve University
Office of Financial Aid, 109 Pardee Hall
10900 Euclid Ave.
Cleveland, OH 44106

2918
Physics Scholarship at Case Western

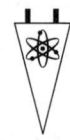

AMOUNT: $2000   DEADLINE: February 1
FIELDS/MAJORS: Physics

Four scholarships offered to entering freshmen at Case Western Reserve who intend to major in physics. Criteria for selection include high school grades, college entrance examination scores, and extracurricular activities. Scholarship is renewable for one additional year provided high academic achievement is maintained. May not be offered every year. Write to the address below for details.

Case Western Reserve University
Office of Financial Aid, 109 Pardee Hall
10900 Euclid Ave.
Cleveland, OH 44106

2919
Plain Dealer Charities Scholarship

AMOUNT: $1000   DEADLINE: February 1
FIELDS/MAJORS: Business Management, Print Journalism

Scholarships for entering freshmen at Case Western who are studying business management or print journalism. Must have graduated in the top 20% of high school class in Cuyahoga, Lake, Geauga, Portage, Summit, Medina, or Lorain counties in Ohio. Applicants must have genuine financial need to be determined by the CWRU office of financial aid. Two awards per year. Write to the address below for details. GPA must be at least 3.2.

Case Western Reserve University
Office of Financial Aid, 109 Pardee Hall
10900 Euclid Ave.
Cleveland, OH 44106

2920
Presidents Scholarships at Case Western

AMOUNT: $13800   DEADLINE: February 1
FIELDS/MAJORS: All Areas of Study

Scholarships are awarded to entering freshmen who rank in the top 10% of their high school graduating class and who have composite SAT scores of at least 1400 or a composite ACT score of 33. A cumulative GPA of 3.0 is required for renewal. Write to the address below for details.

Case Western Reserve University
Office of Financial Aid, 109 Pardee Hall
10900 Euclid Ave.
Cleveland, OH 44106

2921
Provost's Scholarships at Case Western

AMOUNT: Maximum: $9200   DEADLINE: February 1
FIELDS/MAJORS: All Areas of Study

Provost's Scholarships are awarded to entering freshmen who rank in the top 15% of their high school graduating class and who have composite SAT scores of 1300 or a composite ACT score of 31. Student must maintain a 3.0 GPA to renew scholarship. Write to the address below for details.

Case Western Reserve University
Office of Financial Aid, 109 Pardee Hall
10900 Euclid Ave.
Cleveland, OH 44106

2922
University Grants-in-Aid, University Loans (at CWRU)

AMOUNT: $100-$5000   DEADLINE: April 30
FIELDS/MAJORS: All Areas of Study

A Case Western Reserve University Grant-in-Aid is a tuition allowance awarded to a student who exhibits a combination of academic success and financial need. A University Loan is a low interest (8%) long-term loan to a student to assist with educational expenses. Grants-in-Aid range from $100 to full tuition. University Loans grants range from $200-$5000. Write to the address below for details.

Case Western Reserve University
Office of Financial Aid, 109 Pardee Hall
10900 Euclid Ave.
Cleveland, OH 44106

CATHOLIC UNIVERSITY OF AMERICA

2923
Archdiocesan Scholarships

AMOUNT: $15062   DEADLINE: February 15
FIELDS/MAJORS: All Areas of Study

Scholarships are available at the Catholic University of America for Catholic members of high school graduating classes. Based on aptitude and achievement. Not restricted to Catholic high schools. Write to the address below for details. GPA must be at least 2.8.

Catholic University of America
Office of Admissions and Financial Aid
Washington, DC 20064

2924
Board of Trustee Scholarships

AMOUNT: Maximum: $16500 DEADLINE: February 1
FIELDS/MAJORS: All Areas of Study Except Law

Seven to nine graduate scholarships are available at the Catholic University of America in any school except law. Contact the financial aid office at the address listed for details.

Catholic University of America
Office of Admissions and Financial Aid
Washington, DC 20064

2925
Cardinal Gibbons Scholarships

AMOUNT: None Specified DEADLINE: None Specified
FIELDS/MAJORS: All Areas of Study

Scholarships are available at the Catholic University of America for freshmen students who have demonstrated outstanding academic ability. Students must also have exhibited strong leadership qualities in school, church, and community activities. Renewable up to four years if recipients maintain preset standards and it is transferable between different undergraduate programs. Write to the address below for more information.

Catholic University of America
Office of Admissions and Financial Aid
Washington, DC 20064

2926
Clyde C. Cowan Scholarships

AMOUNT: Maximum: $6000 DEADLINE: None Specified
FIELDS/MAJORS: Physics

Scholarships are available at the Catholic University of America for full-time entering freshmen. May be renewed an additional three years. Contact the financial aid office at the address below for details.

Catholic University of America
Office of Admissions and Financial Aid
Washington, DC 20064

2927
Family Scholarships

AMOUNT: $2000 DEADLINE: None Specified
FIELDS/MAJORS: All Areas of Study

Scholarships are available at the Catholic University of America for full-time undergraduate students who have one or more siblings also attending this school. Contact the financial aid office at the address below for details.

Catholic University of America
Office of Admissions and Financial Aid
Washington, DC 20064

2928
Francis Owen Rice Scholarship

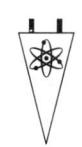

AMOUNT: Maximum: $6000 DEADLINE: February 1
FIELDS/MAJORS: Chemistry

Scholarships are available at the Catholic University of America for full-time entering freshmen. May be renewed for an additional three years. Write to the address below for information.

Catholic University of America
Office of Admissions and Financial Aid
Washington, DC 20064

2929
Graduate Fellowships

AMOUNT: None Specified DEADLINE: None Specified
FIELDS/MAJORS: All Areas of Study

Applicants must be graduate students who have been accepted to the Catholic University of America. Knights of Columbus members as well as their dependents are eligible. Write to address below for details.

Knights of Columbus
Catholic University of America
Attn: Director of Financial Aid
Washington, DC 20064

2930
John M. Cooper Scholarships

AMOUNT: Maximum: $6000 DEADLINE: February 1
FIELDS/MAJORS: Anthropology

Scholarships are available at the Catholic University of America for full-time entering freshmen. May be renewed an additional three years. Write to the address below for information.

Catholic University of America
Office of Admissions and Financial Aid
Washington, DC 20064

2931
Justine Bayard Ward Scholarships

AMOUNT: Maximum: $6000 DEADLINE: None Specified
FIELDS/MAJORS: Music

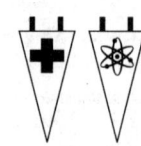

Scholarships are available at the Catholic University of America for full-time entering freshmen. May be renewed for an additional three years. Contact the financial aid office at the address below for details.

Catholic University of America
Office of Admissions and Financial Aid
Washington, DC 20064

2932
Knights of Columbus Scholarships

AMOUNT: $1000-$1500 DEADLINE: None Specified
FIELDS/MAJORS: All Areas of Study

Scholarships are available at the Catholic University of America for sons and daughters of living or deceased members of Knights of Columbus. These awards are for incoming freshmen. Usually, more than ten scholarships are offered. Write to the address below for more information.

Catholic University of America
Office of Admissions and Financial Aid
Washington, DC 20064

2933
Martin R.P. McGuire Scholarship

AMOUNT: Maximum: $6000 DEADLINE: February 15
FIELDS/MAJORS: Classics

Scholarships are available at the Catholic University of America for full-time entering freshmen. May be renewed an additional three years. Write to the address below for information.

Catholic University of America
Office of Admissions and Financial Aid
Washington, DC 20064

2934
Music Scholarships

AMOUNT: None Specified DEADLINE: None Specified
FIELDS/MAJORS: Music

Scholarships are available at the Catholic University of America for students studying music. Includes the John Paul Music Scholarship, the David Burchuk Memorial Scholarship, the Clifford E. Brown Scholarship, the William Masselos Scholarship, and the Benjamin T. Rome Endowment Scholarship. Individual award requirements may vary. For graduate study. Contact the financial aid office at the address below for details.

Catholic University of America
Office of Admissions and Financial Aid
Washington, DC 20064

2935
Program Scholarships

AMOUNT: None Specified
DEADLINE: None Specified
FIELDS/MAJORS: Engineering, Nursing, Music, Chemistry, Classics, Physics

Scholarships are available at the Catholic University of America for incoming freshmen pursuing studies in engineering, nursing, music, chemistry, classics, and physics. For full-time students. Write to the address below for more information.

Catholic University of America
Office of Admissions and Financial Aid
Washington, DC 20064

2936
Sister Olivia Gowan Scholarships

AMOUNT: Maximum: $12000 DEADLINE: None Specified
FIELDS/MAJORS: Nursing

Scholarships are available at the Catholic University of America for full-time entering freshmen. May be renewed for an additional three years. Contact the financial aid office at the address below for details.

Catholic University of America
Office of Admissions and Financial Aid
Washington, DC 20064

CENTER FOR HELLENIC STUDIES

2937
Resident Junior Fellowships

AMOUNT: Maximum: $22000 DEADLINE: October 15
FIELDS/MAJORS: Greek Classical Studies

Fellowships are available for classical Greek studies to those who hold a Ph.D. and can demonstrate professional competence in ancient Greek. Preference will be shown to applicants in the early stages of their careers. Eleven resident fellowships are available. Write to the address below for details.

Center for Hellenic Studies
The Director
3100 Whitehaven St., NW
Washington, DC 20008

CENTRAL CONNECTICUT STATE UNIVERSITY

2938
Alvin B. Wood Scholarship Fund

AMOUNT: None Specified   DEADLINE: None Specified
FIELDS/MAJORS: All Areas of Study

Awarded to a minority student with a minimum 24 credits completed, who demonstrated leadership and service to Central Connecticut State University. Write to the address below for complete details.

Central Connecticut State University
CCSU Foundation, Inc.
PO Box 612
New Britain, CT 06050

2939
Business Education Alumni Award

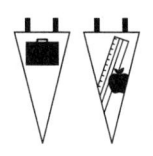

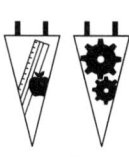

AMOUNT: None Specified   DEADLINE: None Specified
FIELDS/MAJORS: Business Education

Award made annually to an alumnus who has completed bachelor's degree requirements in business education at Central Connecticut State University. Write to the address below for more information.

Central Connecticut State University
CCSU Foundation, Inc.
PO Box 612
New Britain, CT 06050

2940
CCSU Technology Scholarships

AMOUNT: None Specified   DEADLINE: None Specified
FIELDS/MAJORS: Technology

Scholarships available for CCSU students studying technology or with a career interest in a technological field. Includes the Paul K. Rogers, Raymond D. and Ellen N. Martinsen, Litton Industries, and the Stephen and Marie Burg and Family Scholarships. Write to the address below for more information. Individual criteria for each award may vary.

Central Connecticut State University
CCSU Foundation, Inc.
PO Box 612
New Britain, CT 06050

2941
Frank D. Cannata Scholarship Fund

AMOUNT: None Specified   DEADLINE: None Specified
FIELDS/MAJORS: Accounting or Business Education

Scholarships awarded to undergraduate seniors with the highest GPA in accounting and business education. Write to the address below for additional information.

Central Connecticut State University
CCSU Foundation, Inc.
PO Box 612
New Britain, CT 06050

2942
Geary Memorial Fund

AMOUNT: None Specified   DEADLINE: None Specified
FIELDS/MAJORS: Elementary Education, Engineering Technology, Special Education

Awarded to junior level students majoring in elementary education, special education, or engineering technology. Write to the address below for additional information.

Central Connecticut State University
CCSU Foundation, Inc.
PO Box 612
New Britain, CT 06050

2943
James A. and Mary Hayes Lord Scholarship

AMOUNT: None Specified   DEADLINE: None Specified
FIELDS/MAJORS: Education, Professional Studies, Technology

This scholarship is available to a full-time junior or senior in either the School of Education and Professional Studies or the School of Technology. Write to the address below for more details.

Central Connecticut State University
CCSU Foundation, Inc.
PO Box 612
New Britain, CT 06050

2944
Jerome Vigor Memorial Fund

AMOUNT: None Specified DEADLINE: None Specified
FIELDS/MAJORS: Economics

Awarded to a graduating senior majoring in economics who has been accepted for graduate studies at an accredited college or university. Write to the address below for more information.

Central Connecticut State University
CCSU Foundation, Inc.
PO Box 612
New Britain, CT 06050

2945
John Huntington Athletic Training Scholarship

AMOUNT: None Specified DEADLINE: None Specified
FIELDS/MAJORS: Athletic Training

Awarded to a senior completing requirements for athletic training certification at Central Connecticut State University. Write to the address below for additional information.

Central Connecticut State University
CCSU Foundation, Inc.
PO Box 612
New Britain, CT 06050

2946
Ki Hoon Kim Scholarship

AMOUNT: None Specified DEADLINE: None Specified
FIELDS/MAJORS: All Areas of Study

Awarded to Korean students attending Central Connecticut State University and university faculty and students who want to study or do research in Korea. Write to the address below for additional information.

Central Connecticut State University
CCSU Foundation, Inc.
PO Box 612
New Britain, CT 06050

2947
Koh Scholarship

AMOUNT: None Specified DEADLINE: None Specified
FIELDS/MAJORS: Korean Studies

Scholarship for students of Korean descent or United States citizens studying in the Republic of Korea. Write to the address below for additional information.

Central Connecticut State University
CCSU Foundation, Inc.
PO Box 612
New Britain, CT 06050

2948
Martin and Sophie Grzyb Memorial Fund

AMOUNT: None Specified DEADLINE: None Specified
FIELDS/MAJORS: Polish Studies

Awarded to a student of American birth who excels in Polish studies at Central Connecticut State University. Write to the address below for additional information.

Central Connecticut State University
CCSU Foundation, Inc.
PO Box 612
New Britain, CT 06050

2949
Miano Memorial Fund

AMOUNT: None Specified DEADLINE: None Specified
FIELDS/MAJORS: Science, Mathematics, Arts, Humanities

An award to a junior-level CCSU student chosen alternately from science or mathematics majors and arts or humanities majors. Write to the address below for additional information.

Central Connecticut State University
CCSU Foundation, Inc.
PO Box 612
New Britain, CT 06050

2950
Michael J. Witty Scholarship Fund

AMOUNT: None Specified DEADLINE: None Specified
FIELDS/MAJORS: Accounting

Award given to students in the School of Business majoring in accounting, with preference given to a student who demonstrates special ability and interest in taxation. Write to the address below for additional information.

Central Connecticut State University
CCSU Foundation, Inc.
PO Box 612
New Britain, CT 06050

2951
Middlesex Mutual Assurance Company Scholarship

AMOUNT: None Specified DEADLINE: None Specified
FIELDS/MAJORS: Business, Insurance

This scholarship is awarded to a CCSU junior in the School of Business expressing a commitment to a career in the insurance field. Write to the address below for additional information.

Central Connecticut State University
CCSU Foundation, Inc.
PO Box 612
New Britain, CT 06050

2952
Paul Vouras Award

AMOUNT: None Specified DEADLINE: None Specified
FIELDS/MAJORS: Social and Political Science, Geography, Sociology, Economics, History

Presented to a graduating CCSU senior with the highest cumulative GPA of a student majoring in social science, geography, sociology, political science, economics, or history. Write to the address below for more information.

Central Connecticut State University
CCSU Foundation, Inc.
PO Box 612
New Britain, CT 06050

2953
Pauline M. Alt Re-entry Scholarship

AMOUNT: None Specified DEADLINE: None Specified
FIELDS/MAJORS: All Areas of Study

Awarded to matriculated undergraduates with preference given to women who have returned to higher education following an absence of three or more years. Write to the address below for additional information.

Central Connecticut State University
CCSU Foundation, Inc.
PO Box 612
New Britain, CT 06050

2954
Pauline M. Alt Teacher Education Scholarship

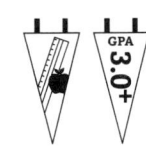

AMOUNT: None Specified DEADLINE: None Specified
FIELDS/MAJORS: Elementary Education

Awarded to full-time undergraduates with GPAs of 3.25 or better. Preference given to elementary education majors. Write to the address below for additional information.

Central Connecticut State University
CCSU Foundation, Inc.
PO Box 612
New Britain, CT 06050

2955
Richard Judd Scholarship

AMOUNT: None Specified DEADLINE: None Specified
FIELDS/MAJORS: All Areas of Study

Awarded annually to a CCSU student from greater New Britain who has demonstrated outstanding community service. Write to the address below for more information.

Central Connecticut State University
CCSU Foundation, Inc.
PO Box 612
New Britain, CT 06050

2956
Thomas F. Martucci Scholarship Fund

AMOUNT: None Specified DEADLINE: None Specified
FIELDS/MAJORS: All Areas of Study

Awarded to an incoming first-year student with a demonstrated record of participation and leadership in extracurricular activities who has graduated from Newington High School. Write to the address below for complete details.

Central Connecticut State University
CCSU Foundation, Inc.
PO Box 612
New Britain, CT 06050

2957
Tomestic Scholarship

AMOUNT: None Specified DEADLINE: None Specified
FIELDS/MAJORS: Theater

Awarded to a student who has made outstanding contributions to the Theater Department at Central Connecticut State University. Write to the address below for additional information.

Central Connecticut State University
CCSU Foundation, Inc.
PO Box 612
New Britain, CT 06050

2958
Undergraduate Education Scholarships

AMOUNT: None Specified DEADLINE: None Specified
FIELDS/MAJORS: Education

Scholarships for undergraduate students pursuing degrees in different areas of education. Includes the Valle P. Lattanzio, Florence Widger Lohse, William and Josephine (Bertino) Tansey, and Stella Willins scholarships. The individual criteria for each of these awards may vary. Write to the address below for more information.

Central Connecticut State University
CCSU Foundation, Inc.
PO Box 612
New Britain, CT 06050

CENTRAL METHODIST COLLEGE

2959
Athletic Scholarships

AMOUNT: None Specified DEADLINE: None Specified
FIELDS/MAJORS: All Areas of Study

Scholarships available at Central Methodist for full-time undergraduate students. These athletic scholarships are offered in football, basketball, baseball, softball, volleyball, soccer, track, tennis, and golf. The maximum award is full tuition. Amounts vary and are awarded by the head coach. Write to the address below for details.

Central Methodist College
Financial Aid Office
411 Central Methodist Square
Fayette, MO 65248

2960
United Methodist Student Grant

AMOUNT: Maximum: $1000 DEADLINE: None Specified
FIELDS/MAJORS: All Areas of Study

Awards available at Central Methodist for full-time undergraduate students who are active members of a United Methodist Church. Applicants must be residents of Missouri. Renewable with a 2.5 GPA. Write to the address below for details.

Central Methodist College
Financial Aid Office
411 Central Methodist Square
Fayette, MO 65248

CENTRAL MISSOURI STATE UNIVERSITY

2961
Achievement Awards

AMOUNT: $100-$300 DEADLINE: February 15
FIELDS/MAJORS: All Areas of Study

Open to high school seniors who demonstrate potential or outstanding performance in a given academic area. Each department determines its own award value and selects its own recipients. Applicants must indicate their anticipated degree program on the scholarship application. Contact the address below for further information or call (660) 543-4541. GPA must be at least 2.7.

Central Missouri State University
Scholarship Officer, Admissions Office
Administration, #104
Warrensburg, MO 64093

2962
Distinguished Scholars Award

AMOUNT: None Specified DEADLINE: February 15
FIELDS/MAJORS: All Areas of Study

Open to high school seniors who rank in the upper 5% of graduating class or have a minimum GPA of 3.5. Applicants must participate in the Distinguished Scholar Award Competition. Award is tuition, room, board, and book allowance. Contact the address below for further information or call (660) 543-4541.

Central Missouri State University
Scholarship Officer, Admissions Office
Administration, #104
Warrensburg, MO 64093

2963
High School Recognition Scholarship

AMOUNT: Maximum: $500 DEADLINE: None Specified
FIELDS/MAJORS: All Areas of Study

Open to high school seniors who are ranked in the upper 25% of graduating class. May not be receiving the Distinguished Scholar, University Scholar, Presidents, or National Merit Scholarships. May be renewable. Contact the address below for further information or call (660) 543-4541. GPA must be at least 2.7.

Central Missouri State University
Scholarship Officer, Admissions Office
Administration, #104
Warrensburg, MO 64093

2964
National Merit Finalists Scholarship

AMOUNT: None Specified DEADLINE: None Specified
FIELDS/MAJORS: All Areas of Study

Open to high school seniors who have been designated as National Merit Finalists. Award is tuition, room, board, and book allowance. Contact the address below for further information or call (660) 543-4541.

Central Missouri State University
Scholarship Officer, Admissions Office
Administration, #104
Warrensburg, MO 64093

2965
Presidents Scholarship

GPA 2.5+

AMOUNT: Maximum: $1000 DEADLINE: None Specified
FIELDS/MAJORS: All Areas of Study

Open to high school seniors who are ranked in the upper 25% of graduating class. May not be receiving the Distinguished Scholar, University Scholar, or National Merit Scholarships. Contact the address below for further information or call (660) 543-4541. GPA must be at least 2.7.

Central Missouri State University
Scholarship Officer, Admissions Office
Administration, #104
Warrensburg, MO 64093

2966
Regents Scholarship

GPA 2.5+

AMOUNT: Maximum: $1500 DEADLINE: None Specified
FIELDS/MAJORS: All Areas of Study

Open to high school seniors who have been admitted to CMSU. Must be ranked in the upper 25% of graduating class or be the valedictorian or salutatorian. May not be receiving the Distinguished Scholar, University Scholar, or National Merit Scholarships. Contact the address below for further information or call (660) 543-4541. GPA must be at least 2.7.

Central Missouri State University
Scholarship Officer, Admissions Office
Administration, #104
Warrensburg, MO 64093

2967
University Scholar Award

GPA 3.5+

AMOUNT: None Specified DEADLINE: February 15
FIELDS/MAJORS: All Areas of Study

Open to high school seniors who rank in the upper 5% of graduating class or have a minimum GPA of 3.75. Applicants must participate in the Distinguished Scholar Award Competition. Award is tuition and nonresident fees. Recipients of this award may not be receiving the Distinguished Scholar Award. Contact the address below for further information or call (660) 543-4541.

Central Missouri State University
Scholarship Officer, Admissions Office
Administration, #104
Warrensburg, MO 64093

CENTRAL WYOMING COLLEGE

2968
Advertiser Scholarship

AMOUNT: None Specified DEADLINE: December 8
FIELDS/MAJORS: All Areas of Study

Open to recent Riverton High School graduates. Contact the address below or call (307) 855-2150 or 1-800-865-0195 for further information.

Central Wyoming College
Financial Aid Office
2660 Peck Ave.
Riverton, WY 82501-1520

2969
David Usher Memorial Fund Scholarship

E

AMOUNT: Maximum: $250 DEADLINE: December 8
FIELDS/MAJORS: All Areas of Study

Open to Native American full-time students who are nineteen or under, have a 2.25 GPA, and participate in community service activities. Contact the address below or call (307) 855-2150 or 1-800-865-0195 for further information.

Central Wyoming College
Financial Aid Office
2660 Peck Ave.
Riverton, WY 82501-1520

2970
Dennis George Scholarship

AMOUNT: None Specified DEADLINE: December 8
FIELDS/MAJORS: All Areas of Study

Open to a native Fremont County resident who has participated in an RHS rodeo. Contact the address below or call (307) 855-2150 or 1-800-865-0195 for further information.

Central Wyoming College
Financial Aid Office
2660 Peck Ave.
Riverton, WY 82501-1520

2971
First Interstate Scholarship

AMOUNT: None Specified DEADLINE: December 8
FIELDS/MAJORS: All Areas of Study

Open to full-time students with a 2.5 GPA or above. Contact the address below or call (307) 855-2150 or 1-800-865-0195 for further information. GPA must be at least 2.5.

Central Wyoming College
Financial Aid Office
2660 Peck Ave.
Riverton, WY 82501-1520

2972
Ida and Homer Fike Memorial Scholarship

AMOUNT: None Specified DEADLINE: December 8
FIELDS/MAJORS: All Areas of Study

Open to full-time students with a 3.0 GPA or above. Contact the address below or call (307) 855-2150 or 1-800-865-0195 for further information.

Central Wyoming College
Financial Aid Office
2660 Peck Ave.
Riverton, WY 82501-1520

2973
Wind River Tribal Endowment Scholarship

AMOUNT: Maximum: $1980 DEADLINE: December 8
FIELDS/MAJORS: All Areas of Study

Open to Native American full-time students who are nineteen or under, have a 2.5 GPA, and participate in community service activities. Contact the address below or call (307) 855-2150 or 1-800-865-0195 for further information.

Central Wyoming College
Financial Aid Office
2660 Peck Ave.
Riverton, WY 82501-1520

2974
Wyoming Department of Commerce

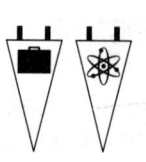

AMOUNT: Maximum: $1500 DEADLINE: December 8
FIELDS/MAJORS: Business, Technology, or Agriculture

Open to high school graduates or residents of a rural Wyoming community who demonstrate financial need and are enrolled in a degree or certificate program in business, technology, or agriculture. Contact the address below or call (307) 855-2150 or 1-800-865-0195 for further information.

Central Wyoming College
Financial Aid Office
2660 Peck Ave.
Riverton, WY 82501-1520

CENTRE COLLEGE

2975
Centre College Scholarships

AMOUNT: $2500 DEADLINE: February 1
FIELDS/MAJORS: All Areas of Study

Renewable scholarships for entering freshmen at Centre College in Kentucky. Some based on academics only, others consider financial need. Includes the Centre Honor, Academic Recognition, President's, Trustee, Dean's, Faculty, Day, and Heritage Scholarships. Contact the address below for further information. GPA must be at least 2.5.

Centre College
Elaine Larson, Dir. of Student Fin. Plan
600 West Walnut Street
Danville, KY 40422

CHADRON STATE UNIVERSITY

2976
Abbott Foundation Endowed Scholarship

AMOUNT: None Specified DEADLINE: None Specified
FIELDS/MAJORS: Business Administration

Open to students majoring in business administration. Applicants must have graduated from a high school located in any of the following areas: Chadron, Alliance, Bridgeport, Cody, Hemingford, Gordon, Merriman, Valentine, Thedford, Hyannis, or Mullen. Write to the address listed for more information.

Chadron State University
Financial Aid Office
1000 Main St.
Chadron, NE 69337

2977
Al Beguin Memorial Scholarship

AMOUNT: None Specified   DEADLINE: None Specified
FIELDS/MAJORS: Chemistry

Open to chemistry majors who can demonstrate scholastic ability and financial need. Contact the Dean of the School of Mathematics and Science. Must have a GPA of at least 3.0.

Chadron State University
Financial Aid Office
1000 Main St.
Chadron, NE 69337

2978
American Legion Vocal Music Scholarship

AMOUNT: None Specified   DEADLINE: None Specified
FIELDS/MAJORS: Vocal Music

Open to full-time undergraduates who are members of Versatility, the choir or vocal music group. Must have a minimum GPA of 2.5 or be in the upper one-half of their graduating classes. Contact the Versatility director for an application and information.

Chadron State University
Financial Aid Office
1000 Main St.
Chadron, NE 69337

2979
Arthur G. Peterson Family Memorial Scholarship

AMOUNT: None Specified   DEADLINE: None Specified
FIELDS/MAJORS: Education

Open to juniors and seniors who are Nebraska residents. Based on good character, leadership, and exceptional potential for teaching as evidenced by GPA. Contact the address listed for further information. Must have a GPA of at least 3.1.

Chadron State University
Financial Aid Office
1000 Main St.
Chadron, NE 69337

2980
Board of Trustees Scholarship

AMOUNT: None Specified   DEADLINE: January 10
FIELDS/MAJORS: All Areas of Study

Open to students graduating from Nebraska high schools. Renewable each year if recipients maintain a minimum GPA of 3.25. Scholarships are for full tuition (up to 16 hours per semester). Contact your high school guidance counselor or the address below for further information.

Chadron State University
Financial Aid Office
1000 Main St.
Chadron, NE 69337

2981
Bruce Furniture, Inc., Scholarship

AMOUNT: None Specified   DEADLINE: None Specified
FIELDS/MAJORS: Business

Open to seniors with a minimum GPA of 2.5 from Scotts Bluff, Box Butte, Grant, or Sheridan County high schools majoring in business. Second priority given to students of the above high schools regardless of major. Contact the address listed for further information.

Chadron State University
Financial Aid Office
1000 Main St.
Chadron, NE 69337

2982
Carl Horst Accounting Scholarship

AMOUNT: None Specified   DEADLINE: None Specified
FIELDS/MAJORS: Accounting

Open to full-time undergraduates majoring in accounting. Must have a minimum GPA of 3.0. Contact the Dean of the School of Business and Applied Science.

Chadron State University
Financial Aid Office
1000 Main St.
Chadron, NE 69337

2983
Charles and Doris Harrington Family Scholarship

AMOUNT: None Specified DEADLINE: None Specified
FIELDS/MAJORS: Music Education, Instrumental Music

Open to music education majors with an emphasis in instrumental music. Must have a minimum GPA of 3.0. Contact the Music Department Chairperson.

Chadron State University
Financial Aid Office
1000 Main St.
Chadron, NE 69337

2984
Cliff Johnson Endowed Scholarship

AMOUNT: None Specified DEADLINE: None Specified
FIELDS/MAJORS: Education

Open to freshmen and transfer students who are from: Cheyenne, Deuel, Garden, or Keith counties in Nebraska, or Sedgewick County in Colorado. Preference given to education majors. Must have a minimum GPA of 3.0. Contact the address listed for further information.

Chadron State University
Financial Aid Office
1000 Main St.
Chadron, NE 69337

2985
Community First Bank Scholarship

AMOUNT: None Specified DEADLINE: None Specified
FIELDS/MAJORS: All Areas of Study

Open to freshmen. Based on scholastic ability, leadership, and financial need. Write to the address listed for more information. Must have a GPA of at least 3.0.

Chadron State University
Financial Aid Office
1000 Main St.
Chadron, NE 69337

2986
Cook Family Endowed Scholarship

AMOUNT: None Specified DEADLINE: None Specified
FIELDS/MAJORS: All Areas of Study

Open to freshmen and transfer students from Wyoming. First preference to students from: Niobrara, Goshen, Platte, or Laramie counties. Must have a minimum GPA of 3.0. Contact the address listed for further information.

Chadron State University
Financial Aid Office
1000 Main St.
Chadron, NE 69337

2987
Count C. Cruea Memorial "Exit" Scholarship

AMOUNT: None Specified DEADLINE: None Specified
FIELDS/MAJORS: Agribusiness, Marketing

Open to graduating seniors who have exhibited outstanding dedication and understanding in the fields of marketing and agribusiness. Contact the Dean of the School of Business and Applied Science. Must have a GPA of at least 3.2.

Chadron State University
Financial Aid Office
1000 Main St.
Chadron, NE 69337

2988
Crites-Shaffer Family Scholarship

AMOUNT: None Specified DEADLINE: None Specified
FIELDS/MAJORS: All Areas of Study

Open to seniors who are residents of: Dawes, Sheridan, Box Butte, or Sioux counties, graduating from an accredited high school. Renewable if recipients maintain a minimum GPA of 3.0. Contact the address listed for further information.

Chadron State University
Financial Aid Office
1000 Main St.
Chadron, NE 69337

2989
Crow Butte Annual Scholarship

AMOUNT: None Specified DEADLINE: None Specified
FIELDS/MAJORS: Science

Open to students majoring in a science discipline. Does not include health professions. Preference to graduates of a Dawes or Sioux County high school. Must have a minimum GPA of 3.0. Financial need is a consideration. Contact the address listed for further information.

Chadron State University
Financial Aid Office
1000 Main St.
Chadron, NE 69337

2990
Delores Irelan Endowed Scholarship

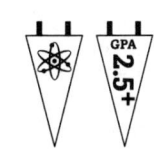

AMOUNT: None Specified   DEADLINE: None Specified
FIELDS/MAJORS: Mathematics, Science

Open to students majoring in mathematics and/or science. Contact the address listed for further information. Must have a GPA of at least 2.5.

Chadron State University
Financial Aid Office
1000 Main St.
Chadron, NE 69337

2991
Dora V. Taylor Endowed Scholarship

AMOUNT: None Specified   DEADLINE: None Specified
FIELDS/MAJORS: All Areas of Study

Preference for this award is given to international students. The scholarship, however, is not restricted to international students. Contact the address listed for further information. Must have a GPA of at least 2.8.

Chadron State University
Financial Aid Office
1000 Main St.
Chadron, NE 69337

2992
Doris Gates Memorial Scholarship

AMOUNT: None Specified   DEADLINE: None Specified
FIELDS/MAJORS: Science

Open to juniors who have maintained a minimum GPA of 3.0 through freshman and sophomore years. Must be majoring in the science field and show an interest in the study of plants, animals, birds, and their habitat, including the problem of conservation. Contact the address listed for further information.

Chadron State University
Financial Aid Office
1000 Main St.
Chadron, NE 69337

2993
Dorothy Post Memorial Scholarship

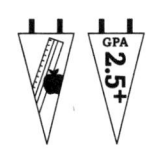

AMOUNT: None Specified   DEADLINE: None Specified
FIELDS/MAJORS: Education

Open to full-time undergraduates from Sheridan County. Must have a minimum GPA of 2.5. Contact the address listed for further information.

Chadron State University
Financial Aid Office
1000 Main St.
Chadron, NE 69337

2994
Dr. Alfred Blinde Memorial Scholarship

AMOUNT: None Specified   DEADLINE: None Specified
FIELDS/MAJORS: Vocal Music

Open to juniors and seniors pursuing a career in vocal music. Contact the Music Department Chairperson.

Chadron State University
Financial Aid Office
1000 Main St.
Chadron, NE 69337

2995
Dr. Dan Johnson Endowed Scholarship

AMOUNT: None Specified   DEADLINE: None Specified
FIELDS/MAJORS: Pre-Dentistry

Open to students enrolled in the allied health field. Preference given to those enrolled in pre-dentistry. May be renewable. Contact the address listed for further information. Must have a GPA of at least 2.8.

Chadron State University
Financial Aid Office
1000 Main St.
Chadron, NE 69337

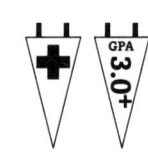

2996
Dr. Leo and Eunice Hoevet Scholarship

AMOUNT: None Specified   DEADLINE: None Specified
FIELDS/MAJORS: Pre-Medicine

Open to students who have demonstrated ability and interest in the field of medicine. Contact the Dean of the School of Mathematics and Science. Must have a GPA of at least 3.0.

Chadron State University
Financial Aid Office
1000 Main St.
Chadron, NE 69337

2997
Dr. Richard L. David Memorial Scholarship

AMOUNT: None Specified   DEADLINE: None Specified
FIELDS/MAJORS: Optometry

Open to juniors and seniors planning to pursue a career in optometry. Based on academics. Contact the address listed for further information. Must have a GPA of at least 3.0.

Chadron State University
Financial Aid Office
1000 Main St.
Chadron, NE 69337

2998
Dr. William and Jean Boehle Music Scholarship

AMOUNT: None Specified   DEADLINE: None Specified
FIELDS/MAJORS: Music

Open to music majors who have a minimum GPA of 2.5 or graduated in the upper half of their class. Contact the Music Department Chairperson.

Chadron State University
Financial Aid Office
1000 Main St.
Chadron, NE 69337

2999
Ed and Marian Hollstein Educational Endowment Scholarship

AMOUNT: None Specified   DEADLINE: None Specified
FIELDS/MAJORS: All Areas of Study

Open to full-time students who are residents of Sioux, Box Butte, Dawes, and Sheridan counties. Based on scholastic ability and financial need. Contact the address listed for further information. Must have a GPA of at least 3.0.

Chadron State University
Financial Aid Office
1000 Main St.
Chadron, NE 69337

3000
Edna B. Drummond Memorial Scholarship

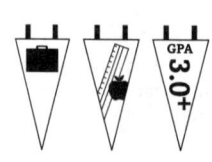

AMOUNT: None Specified   DEADLINE: None Specified
FIELDS/MAJORS: Business Education

Open to full-time students majoring in business education. Based on academic merit. Contact the address listed for further information. Must have a GPA of at least 3.0.

Chadron State University
Financial Aid Office
1000 Main St.
Chadron, NE 69337

3001
Edwin C. and Avis A. Nelson Scholarship

AMOUNT: None Specified   DEADLINE: None Specified
FIELDS/MAJORS: Education

Open to freshmen pursuing a career in teaching. May be renewed. Contact the address listed for further information. Must have a GPA of at least 2.5.

Chadron State University
Financial Aid Office
1000 Main St.
Chadron, NE 69337

3002
Elizabeth and Bertha Braddock Memorial Scholarship

AMOUNT: $500-$1000   DEADLINE: None Specified
FIELDS/MAJORS: All Areas of Study

Numerous scholarships open to sophomores and above who are residents of western Nebraska. Based on scholarship, activities, and character. Contact the address listed for further information. Must have a GPA of at least 3.0.

Chadron State University
Financial Aid Office
1000 Main St.
Chadron, NE 69337

3003
Ethel Delzell Memorial Scholarship

AMOUNT: None Specified   DEADLINE: None Specified
FIELDS/MAJORS: Family and Consumer Science

Open to sophomores and juniors. Based on academics and the completion of at least one semester of classes. Contact the Dean of the School of Business and Applied Science prior to the first of April. Must have a GPA of at least 3.0.

Chadron State University
Financial Aid Office
1000 Main St.
Chadron, NE 69337

3004
F. Clark and Norma T. Elkins Endowed Scholarship

AMOUNT: None Specified
DEADLINE: None Specified
FIELDS/MAJORS: History, Social Science, Elementary Education

Open to full-time juniors and seniors majoring in any of the areas listed above. Must have a minimum GPA of 3.0. Contact the address listed for further information.

Chadron State University
Financial Aid Office
1000 Main St.
Chadron, NE 69337

3005
Frances Burnham Hunt Education Scholarship

AMOUNT: None Specified   DEADLINE: None Specified
FIELDS/MAJORS: Education

Open to full-time undergraduates, majoring in education and having a minimum GPA of 2.5. Contact the address listed for further information.

Chadron State University
Financial Aid Office
1000 Main St.
Chadron, NE 69337

3006
Frances Hess and Wilbur "Eby" Richards Endowed Scholarship

AMOUNT: None Specified   DEADLINE: None Specified
FIELDS/MAJORS: Education

Open to education majors. First preference given to an elementary education major. Second preference to any education major. Contact the address listed for further information.

Chadron State University
Financial Aid Office
1000 Main St.
Chadron, NE 69337

3007
Gary Bunner Business Scholarship

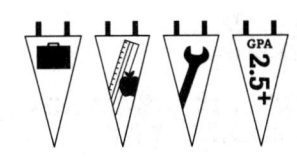

AMOUNT: None Specified   DEADLINE: None Specified
FIELDS/MAJORS: Business, Business Education, Real Estate, Office Management, Economics, Finance

Open to full-time undergraduates majoring in any of the fields listed above. Must have a minimum GPA of 2.5 or rank in the upper half of their high school graduating class. Contact the Dean of the School of Business and Applied Science.

Chadron State University
Financial Aid Office
1000 Main St.
Chadron, NE 69337

3008
Giggling Gals 4-H Scholarship

AMOUNT: None Specified   DEADLINE: None Specified
FIELDS/MAJORS: All Areas of Study

Open to freshmen involved in at least five years of 4-H, including their high school senior year. Five home economics 4-H projects are a prerequisite for consideration. Preference given to a Dawes County resident. Applicants need to complete a CSC scholarship application and attach a letter from their county agent verifying eligibility. Contact the address listed for further information.

Chadron State University
Financial Aid Office
1000 Main St.
Chadron, NE 69337

3009
Glenn O. and Evelyn F. Emick Scholarship

AMOUNT: None Specified   DEADLINE: None Specified
FIELDS/MAJORS: Pre-Medicine

A number of scholarships for incoming students majoring in pre-med. Should applicants not be available, then students in other science and/or teaching fields may be considered. Contact the Dean of the School of Mathematics and Science.

Chadron State University
Financial Aid Office
1000 Main St.
Chadron, NE 69337

3010
Gramberg Endowed Scholarship

AMOUNT: None Specified DEADLINE: None Specified
FIELDS/MAJORS: Industrial Technology

Open to full-time freshmen in industrial technology. Must be enrolled in 6 hours of industrial technology courses each semester and have a minimum GPA of 2.5. Contact the address listed for further information.

Chadron State University
Financial Aid Office
1000 Main St.
Chadron, NE 69337

3011
Harold and Kenneth Thompson Memorial Scholarship

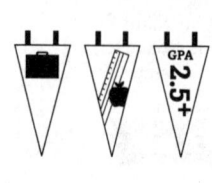

AMOUNT: None Specified DEADLINE: None Specified
FIELDS/MAJORS: Education, Business Administration

Open to majors in education or business administration. Preference given to business administration major who has an emphasis in real estate. Contact the address listed for further information. Must have a GPA of at least 2.8.

Chadron State University
Financial Aid Office
1000 Main St.
Chadron, NE 69337

3012
Harold E. Willey Memorial Scholarship

AMOUNT: None Specified DEADLINE: None Specified
FIELDS/MAJORS: All Areas of Study

Open to full-time undergraduates of sophomore level or above. Applicants must be children of Nebraska farmers/ranchers or children of their employees. Must have a minimum GPA of 3.0. Contact the address listed for further information.

Chadron State University
Financial Aid Office
1000 Main St.
Chadron, NE 69337

3013
Hazel Beckwith Morgan Memorial Scholarship

AMOUNT: None Specified DEADLINE: None Specified
FIELDS/MAJORS: Music, Music Education

Open to students majoring in music or music education. Contact the address listed for further information.

Chadron State University
Financial Aid Office
1000 Main St.
Chadron, NE 69337

3014
J. Lewis and Helen J. Hammitt Annual Music Scholarship

AMOUNT: None Specified DEADLINE: None Specified
FIELDS/MAJORS: Keyboard, Vocal Music

Open to music majors with first preference given to keyboard and second preference to vocal. Contact the Music Department Chairperson. Must have a GPA of at least 2.5.

Chadron State University
Financial Aid Office
1000 Main St.
Chadron, NE 69337

3015
Jacque and Dorothy Schmiedt Scholarship

AMOUNT: None Specified DEADLINE: None Specified
FIELDS/MAJORS: English, Library Media

Open to seniors who are Wyoming high school graduates. Payment will be made when the recipient is enrolled in the Professional Education Semester (the Block). Contact the address listed for further information. Must have a GPA of at least 3.0.

Chadron State University
Financial Aid Office
1000 Main St.
Chadron, NE 69337

3016
James T. Bentley Scholarship

AMOUNT: None Specified DEADLINE: None Specified
FIELDS/MAJORS: Education

Open to students majoring in education. Must be residents of Illinois. Based on academics and financial need. Write to the address listed for more information. Must have a GPA of at least 3.0.

Chadron State University
Financial Aid Office
1000 Main St.
Chadron, NE 69337

3017
Jennie Bennett and Emma Steckleberg Memorial Scholarship

AMOUNT: None Specified   DEADLINE: None Specified
FIELDS/MAJORS: Elementary Education, English, Spanish

Open to students from Sheridan County. Based on academics, commendable activities, and financial need. Write to the address listed for more information. Must have a GPA of at least 3.0.

Chadron State University
Financial Aid Office
1000 Main St.
Chadron, NE 69337

3018
John Castek Memorial Scholarship

AMOUNT: None Specified   DEADLINE: None Specified
FIELDS/MAJORS: All Areas of Study

Open to students who have attended a rural Dawes County school. Based on scholastic ability. Contact the address listed for further information. Must have a GPA of at least 3.0.

Chadron State University
Financial Aid Office
1000 Main St.
Chadron, NE 69337

3019
Kathryn Knapp Memorial Scholarship

AMOUNT: None Specified   DEADLINE: None Specified
FIELDS/MAJORS: Education

Open to education majors who have a minimum GPA of 2.5. May be renewed. Contact the Dean of the School of Business and Applied Science.

Chadron State University
Financial Aid Office
1000 Main St.
Chadron, NE 69337

3020
Knights of Columbus Scholarship

AMOUNT: None Specified   DEADLINE: None Specified
FIELDS/MAJORS: Special Education, Human Services

Open to students majoring in special education. Second preference to majors in human services. Contact the address listed for further information. Must have a GPA of at least 2.8.

Chadron State University
Financial Aid Office
1000 Main St.
Chadron, NE 69337

3021
Leland Houder Memorial Scholarship

AMOUNT: None Specified   DEADLINE: None Specified
FIELDS/MAJORS: Secondary Mathematics Education

Open to undergraduates who have a minimum GPA of 2.5. Contact the address listed for further information.

Chadron State University
Financial Aid Office
1000 Main St.
Chadron, NE 69337

3022
Leon Rittenhouse Scholarship

AMOUNT: None Specified   DEADLINE: None Specified
FIELDS/MAJORS: All Areas of Study

Open to seniors who have sound academic records. Must be able to demonstrate financial need. Contact the address listed for further information. Must have a GPA of at least 3.0.

Chadron State University
Financial Aid Office
1000 Main St.
Chadron, NE 69337

3023
Lloyd and Lora Fackelman Memorial Scholarship

AMOUNT: None Specified   DEADLINE: None Specified
FIELDS/MAJORS: All Areas of Study

Open to sophomores and above who are single parents. Contact the address listed for further information.

Chadron State University
Financial Aid Office
1000 Main St.
Chadron, NE 69337

3024
Lyle Kime Memorial Scholarship

AMOUNT: None Specified DEADLINE: None Specified
FIELDS/MAJORS: Business Education, Business Administration

Open to married students majoring in either of the fields listed above. Contact the address listed for further information. Must have a GPA of at least 2.8.

Chadron State University
Financial Aid Office
1000 Main St.
Chadron, NE 69337

3025
Magowan Agricultural Scholarships

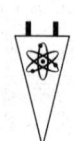

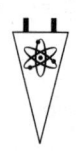

AMOUNT: None Specified DEADLINE: None Specified
FIELDS/MAJORS: Agriculture

A number of scholarships are available for first-time enrollees. Contact the Dean of the School of Business and Applied Science.

Chadron State University
Financial Aid Office
1000 Main St.
Chadron, NE 69337

3026
Mary Carpenter Paulson Memorial Scholarship

AMOUNT: None Specified DEADLINE: None Specified
FIELDS/MAJORS: Fine Arts, Vocal Music

Open to fine arts majors with preference given to students majoring in voice. Contact the Music Department Chairperson.

Chadron State University
Financial Aid Office
1000 Main St.
Chadron, NE 69337

3027
Minority Music Endowed Scholarship

AMOUNT: None Specified DEADLINE: None Specified
FIELDS/MAJORS: Music

Open to African/Asian/Hispanic/Native Americans who are majoring in music or participating in instrumental/vocal ensembles. Applicants will need to supply an audition tape with the application. Contact the Music Department Chairperson.

Chadron State University
Financial Aid Office
1000 Main St.
Chadron, NE 69337

3028
Myrtle Stickney/Perry Moody Memorial Scholarship

AMOUNT: None Specified DEADLINE: None Specified
FIELDS/MAJORS: Agriculture, Agribusiness

A number of scholarships are available for first-time enrollees. Contact the Dean of the School of Business and Applied Science.

Chadron State University
Financial Aid Office
1000 Main St.
Chadron, NE 69337

3029
Nebraska Federal Women's Program Annual Scholarship

AMOUNT: None Specified DEADLINE: None Specified
FIELDS/MAJORS: Natural Resources

Open to female nontraditional students of sophomore level or above. Must be able to demonstrate financial need. Contact the address listed for further information.

Chadron State University
Financial Aid Office
1000 Main St.
Chadron, NE 69337

3030
Nebraska Society of Certified Public Accountants Scholarship

AMOUNT: None Specified DEADLINE: None Specified
FIELDS/MAJORS: Accounting

Open to juniors, to be awarded for senior year. Applicants must have the interest and capabilities of becoming successful accountants and must be considering accounting careers. Contact the Dean of the School of Business and Applied Science. Must have a GPA of at least 3.0.

Chadron State University
Financial Aid Office
1000 Main St.
Chadron, NE 69337

3031
Otunhan Native American Scholarship

Amount: None Specified **Deadline:** None Specified
Fields/Majors: All Areas of Study

Open to full-time undergraduates who are at sophomore level or above. Must have a minimum GPA of 2.5 and be able to document Native American heritage. Contact the address listed for further information.

Chadron State University
Financial Aid Office
1000 Main St.
Chadron, NE 69337

3032
Paul Dannacher Memorial Scholarship

Amount: None Specified **Deadline:** None Specified
Fields/Majors: Business

Open to students majoring in the area of business. Financial need is a consideration. Contact the address listed for further information. Must have a GPA of at least 2.8.

Chadron State University
Financial Aid Office
1000 Main St.
Chadron, NE 69337

3033
Paul Hefti Memorial Scholarship

Amount: None Specified **Deadline:** None Specified
Fields/Majors: All Areas of Study

Open to full-time students who are residents of Nebraska. Based on scholastic ability and character. Contact the address listed for further information. Must have a GPA of at least 3.0.

Chadron State University
Financial Aid Office
1000 Main St.
Chadron, NE 69337

3034
Paula Jo Connell Memorial Scholarship

Amount: None Specified **Deadline:** None Specified
Fields/Majors: Preschool, Elementary Education

Open to students pursuing preschool education with a second preference given to majors in elementary education. Based on academics and character. Contact the address listed for further information. Must have a GPA of at least 2.8.

Chadron State University
Financial Aid Office
1000 Main St.
Chadron, NE 69337

3035
Pepper Creek Outdoor Learning Scholarship

Amount: None Specified **Deadline:** None Specified
Fields/Majors: Natural Resources

Open to students majoring in natural science or outdoor recreation. Contact the address listed for further information. Must have a GPA of at least 2.5.

Chadron State University
Financial Aid Office
1000 Main St.
Chadron, NE 69337

3036
P.O. and Grace Gaylord Family Memorial Scholarship

Amount: None Specified **Deadline:** None Specified
Fields/Majors: Pre-Engineering

Open to students in pre-engineering. Based on scholastic ability. Contact the address listed for further information. Must have a GPA of at least 3.0.

Chadron State University
Financial Aid Office
1000 Main St.
Chadron, NE 69337

3037
Ralph D. and Claire M. (Baker) Shipp Scholarship

Amount: None Specified **Deadline:** January 15
Fields/Majors: All Areas of Study

Open to graduates from Sheridan or Cherry county high schools. May be renewed. Contact the address listed for further information. Must have a GPA of at least 2.8.

Chadron State University
Financial Aid Office
1000 Main St.
Chadron, NE 69337

3038
Reta King Memorial Scholarship

AMOUNT: None Specified   DEADLINE: None Specified
FIELDS/MAJORS: Library Science

Open to sophomores majoring in library science. Based on scholastic ability. Contact the Director of Library Services for further information. Must have a GPA of at least 3.0.

Chadron State University
Financial Aid Office
1000 Main St.
Chadron, NE 69337

3039
Rolland and Deloris Dewing History Scholarship

AMOUNT: None Specified   DEADLINE: None Specified
FIELDS/MAJORS: History, Social Science

Open to full-time students with a minimum GPA of 2.5 or an ACT score of at least 18. Contact the address listed for further information.

Chadron State University
Financial Aid Office
1000 Main St.
Chadron, NE 69337

3040
Royce Vathauer Memorial Scholarship

AMOUNT: None Specified   DEADLINE: None Specified
FIELDS/MAJORS: Elementary Education

Open to majors in elementary education. Selection made by the Chadron State College Scholarship Committee. Contact the address listed for further information. Must have a GPA of at least 2.8.

Chadron State University
Financial Aid Office
1000 Main St.
Chadron, NE 69337

3041
Sandra Moreland Channer Memorial Scholarship

AMOUNT: None Specified   DEADLINE: None Specified
FIELDS/MAJORS: Elementary Education

Open to sophomores or above majoring in elementary education. First preference given to graduates of Cherry or Sheridan county high schools. Contact the address listed for further information. Must have a GPA of at least 2.8.

Chadron State University
Financial Aid Office
1000 Main St.
Chadron, NE 69337

3042
Ted Galusha Memorial Scholarship

AMOUNT: None Specified   DEADLINE: None Specified
FIELDS/MAJORS: Music, Drama, Art

Open to full-time freshmen, sophomores, and juniors majoring in the areas listed above. Contact the address listed for further information.

Chadron State University
Financial Aid Office
1000 Main St.
Chadron, NE 69337

3043
Tom and Kathy Bass Endowed Scholarship

AMOUNT: None Specified   DEADLINE: None Specified
FIELDS/MAJORS: Business

Open to juniors and seniors majoring in business. Write to the address listed for more information.

Chadron State University
Financial Aid Office
1000 Main St.
Chadron, NE 69337

3044
Vida Mackey Memorial Scholarship

AMOUNT: None Specified   DEADLINE: None Specified
FIELDS/MAJORS: All Areas of Study

Open to senior women students who are able to demonstrate financial need. Contact the address listed for further information.

Chadron State University
Financial Aid Office
1000 Main St.
Chadron, NE 69337

CHAPMAN UNIVERSITY

3045
Carrie Cooper Scholarship

AMOUNT: None Specified   DEADLINE: None Specified
FIELDS/MAJORS: Education

Scholarships are awarded to needy students majoring in education and interested in pursuing a career in teaching. Contact the address below for further information.

Chapman University
333 N. Glassell
Orange, CA 92866

3046
Children of Chapman Grants

AMOUNT: $1000   DEADLINE: None Specified
FIELDS/MAJORS: All Areas of Study

Each year $1,000 grants will be awarded to the children of those who hold undergraduate or graduate degrees from Chapman. Full-time United States or international students are eligible to receive the award for a total of four years or 130 cumulative credits. Contact the address below for further information.

Chapman University
333 N. Glassell
Orange, CA 92866

3047
Disciples Fellowship Award

AMOUNT: $2000   DEADLINE: None Specified
FIELDS/MAJORS: All Areas of Study

Awards are available to students who are members of the Christian Church (Disciples of Christ) with GPAs of 3.0 or higher. Contact the address below for further information.

Chapman University
333 N. Glassell
Orange, CA 92866

3048
Gail C. Fong Scholarship

AMOUNT: None Specified   DEADLINE: None Specified
FIELDS/MAJORS: All Areas of Study

Scholarships are awarded to worthy and needy students. Also includes the following scholarships: Margaret Hashinger Trust Scholarship and Hashinger/Carroll Scholarship, Hoskings Memorial, Ellsworth Lewis, William T. Salmon and Jennie Salmon, and Gamma Beta Phi Honor Society. Contact the address below for further information.

Chapman University
333 N. Glassell
Orange, CA 92866

3049
Gerald R. and Kay Ryer Scholarship

AMOUNT: None Specified   DEADLINE: None Specified
FIELDS/MAJORS: Physical Therapy

Scholarships are awarded to physical therapy graduate students. Contact the address below for further information.

Chapman University
333 N. Glassell
Orange, CA 92866

3050
Guy B. Mize, Jr. Scholarship

AMOUNT: None Specified   DEADLINE: None Specified
FIELDS/MAJORS: Business

Scholarships are awarded to students with financial need who are planning careers in business. Contact the address below for further information.

Chapman University
333 N. Glassell
Orange, CA 92866

3051
Hugo and Helen Pensanti Endowed Scholarship

AMOUNT: None Specified   DEADLINE: None Specified
FIELDS/MAJORS: Pre-Medicine

Scholarships are awarded to students majoring in pre-medicine. Contact the address below for further information.

Chapman University
333 N. Glassell
Orange, CA 92866

3052
Jim Dean Scholarship

AMOUNT: None Specified DEADLINE: None Specified
FIELDS/MAJORS: Journalism

Scholarships are awarded to needy and worthy students with preference given to those planning a career in journalism. Contact the address below for further information.

Chapman University
333 N. Glassell
Orange, CA 92866

3053
Martin M. and Esther H. Kennedy Scholarship

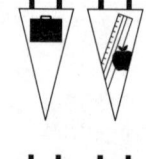

AMOUNT: None Specified
DEADLINE: None Specified
FIELDS/MAJORS: Communications, Teaching, Business, or Physical Therapy

Scholarships are awarded to graduate students in communications, teaching, business, and physical therapy. Contact the address below for further information.

Chapman University
333 N. Glassell
Orange, CA 92866

3054
Mary S. and W. Bradford Hellis Scholarship

AMOUNT: None Specified DEADLINE: None Specified
FIELDS/MAJORS: All Areas of Study

Scholarships are awarded, with preference given to students who are residents of Orange County. Contact the address below for further information.

Chapman University
333 N. Glassell
Orange, CA 92866

3055
Mayr/Anderson Scholarship

AMOUNT: None Specified DEADLINE: None Specified
FIELDS/MAJORS: All Areas of Study

Scholarships are awarded to needy students from California. Contact the address below for further information.

Chapman University
333 N. Glassell
Orange, CA 92866

3056
Merrill Miller Scholarship

AMOUNT: None Specified DEADLINE: None Specified
FIELDS/MAJORS: Environmental Science

Scholarships are awarded to students majoring in environmental science. Contact the address below for further information.

Chapman University
333 N. Glassell
Orange, CA 92866

3057
Muth Family and Orco Block Company Scholarship

AMOUNT: None Specified DEADLINE: None Specified
FIELDS/MAJORS: Liberal Arts or Business/Economics

Scholarships are awarded to students, with one-third going to liberal arts students and two-thirds to business/economics students. Contact the address below for further information.

Chapman University
333 N. Glassell
Orange, CA 92866

3058
Ojai First Christian Church Scholarship

AMOUNT: None Specified DEADLINE: None Specified
FIELDS/MAJORS: Theology (Ministry)

Scholarships are awarded to Disciples student planning to enter the ministry. Contact the address below for further information.

Chapman University
333 N. Glassell
Orange, CA 92866

3059
Philosophy Scholarship for Religious Studies

AMOUNT: None Specified DEADLINE: None Specified
FIELDS/MAJORS: Philosophy

Scholarships are awarded to students of academic excellence, personal religious commitment, and exemplary moral character who have an interest in undergraduate study of philosophy and a commitment to pursuing graduate work in religious studies. Contact the address below for further information.

Chapman University
333 N. Glassell
Orange, CA 92866

3060
Robert Fahey Memorial Scholarship

AMOUNT: None Specified   DEADLINE: None Specified
FIELDS/MAJORS: Mathematics or Science

Scholarships are awarded to a student teacher candidate with emphasis in mathematics or science. Contact the address below for further information.

Chapman University
333 N. Glassell
Orange, CA 92866

3061
Susan Reynard Dedischew Memorial Scholarship

AMOUNT: None Specified   DEADLINE: None Specified
FIELDS/MAJORS: Counseling Psychology

Scholarships are awarded to re-entry women students majoring in counseling psychology. Contact the address below for further information.

Chapman University
333 N. Glassell
Orange, CA 92866

3062
Timothy O'Brien Memorial Scholarship

AMOUNT: None Specified   DEADLINE: None Specified
FIELDS/MAJORS: All Areas of Study

Scholarships are awarded with preference given to hard-working students. Contact the address below for further information.

Chapman University
333 N. Glassell
Orange, CA 92866

3063
Vaughan R. Harlan Scholarship

AMOUNT: None Specified   DEADLINE: None Specified
FIELDS/MAJORS: All Areas of Study

Scholarships are awarded with preference given to children of Chapman graduates. Contact the address below for further information.

Chapman University
333 N. Glassell
Orange, CA 92866

3064
Will Green Harton and General Will S. Green Scholarship

AMOUNT: None Specified   DEADLINE: None Specified
FIELDS/MAJORS: Journalism

Scholarships are awarded to deserving students studying journalism. Contact the address below for further information.

Chapman University
333 N. Glassell
Orange, CA 92866

3065
Women's Campus Club Scholarship

AMOUNT: None Specified   DEADLINE: None Specified
FIELDS/MAJORS: All Areas of Study

Scholarships are awarded to students who have a 3.0 GPA, leadership abilities, goals, character, and evidence of need. Contact the address below for further information.

Chapman University
333 N. Glassell
Orange, CA 92866

CHARLESTON SOUTHERN UNIVERSITY

3066
Brewer Scholarship

AMOUNT: Maximum: $1000   DEADLINE: None Specified
FIELDS/MAJORS: All Areas of Study

Recipient must exemplify Christian values in lifestyle and commitment, be a resident of Lancaster, Kershaw, or Chesterfield counties of South Carolina, or other deserving students. Must be enrolled a minimum of 12 semester hours and have a GPA of at least 2.0. Contact the address below for further information.

Charleston Southern University
PO Box 118087
Charleston, SC 29423

3067
Business Student Scholarship

AMOUNT: $500 DEADLINE: None Specified
FIELDS/MAJORS: Business

Awarded to a worthy and deserving student majoring in business. Contact the address below for further information.

Charleston Southern University
PO Box 118087
Charleston, SC 29423

3068
Dantzler Family Teacher Education Scholarship

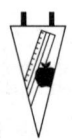

AMOUNT: Maximum: $500 DEADLINE: None Specified
FIELDS/MAJORS: Education

Recipient must be a teacher education major, worthy, deserving, and in need of financial assistance. Priority will be given to Chester or Lancaster counties residents. Contact the address below for further information.

Charleston Southern University
PO Box 118087
Charleston, SC 29423

3069
Diamond Hill Plywood Scholarship

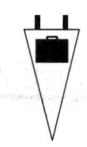

AMOUNT: $1000 DEADLINE: None Specified
FIELDS/MAJORS: Business Administration

Awarded to a senior business administration major. Priority given to students living in Darlington or Florence counties and deserving financial aid. Five awards are given annually. Contact the address below for further information.

Charleston Southern University
PO Box 118087
Charleston, SC 29423

3070
Dr. David W. Cuttino Music Scholarship

AMOUNT: None Specified DEADLINE: None Specified
FIELDS/MAJORS: Music

Awarded to music majors enrolled a minimum of 12 semester hours with an overall GPA of 2.0. If other than an entering freshman, GPA must be a 3.0. Contact the address below for further information.

Charleston Southern University
PO Box 118087
Charleston, SC 29423

3071
Gamble Givens & Moody P.A. CPA Scholarship

AMOUNT: $250 DEADLINE: None Specified
FIELDS/MAJORS: Business Administration, Accounting

Must be a rising senior, business administration major (accounting emphasis) major, overall GPA of at least 2.5 and GPA of at least 3.0 in accounting-related course work, and must be enrolled a minimum of 12 semester hours. Contact the address below for further information.

Charleston Southern University
PO Box 118087
Charleston, SC 29423

3072
George H. Newton Christian Scholarship

AMOUNT: $1000 DEADLINE: None Specified
FIELDS/MAJORS: All Areas of Study

Recipient must exemplify Christian values and morals in his/her personal lifestyle. Must be enrolled a minimum of 12 semester hours and demonstrate financial need. Contact the address below for further information.

Charleston Southern University
PO Box 118087
Charleston, SC 29423

3073
Hankinson Scholarship

AMOUNT: Maximum: $500 DEADLINE: None Specified
FIELDS/MAJORS: All Areas of Study

Awarded to worthy and deserving students. Contact the address below for further information.

Charleston Southern University
PO Box 118087
Charleston, SC 29423

3074
Harold and Vivian Rowell Scholarship

AMOUNT: Maximum: $500 DEADLINE: None Specified
FIELDS/MAJORS: All Areas of Study

Recipient must exemplify Christian values in his/her lifestyle and commitment. First priority to a resident of Lancaster County, South Carolina, enrolled a minimum of 12 semester hours. If other than a freshman, recipient must have at least a 2.0 GPA. Contact the address below for further information.

Charleston Southern University
PO Box 118087
Charleston, SC 29423

3075
Horton Family Scholarship

AMOUNT: $500-$1000 DEADLINE: None Specified
FIELDS/MAJORS: Music Therapy

Awarded to music therapy majors enrolled a minimum of 12 semester hours. If other than an entering first-time freshman, student must have a minimum of 2.5 GPA. Contact the address below for further information.

Charleston Southern University
PO Box 118087
Charleston, SC 29423

3076
James H. Outz Memorial Scholarship

AMOUNT: None Specified DEADLINE: None Specified
FIELDS/MAJORS: Music

Awarded to music majors with financial need. Contact the address below for further information.

Charleston Southern University
PO Box 118087
Charleston, SC 29423

3077
Lisa Sineath Nursing Scholarship

AMOUNT: None Specified DEADLINE: None Specified
FIELDS/MAJORS: Nursing

Awarded to a nursing degree student enrolled a minimum of 12 semester hours with financial need. If other than entering first-time freshmen, students must have at least a 2.5 GPA. Contact the address below for further information.

Charleston Southern University
PO Box 118087
Charleston, SC 29423

3078
Mason Family Scholarship

AMOUNT: $1000 DEADLINE: None Specified
FIELDS/MAJORS: All Areas of Study

Awarded to a student of Florence or Marion counties, South Carolina. Must be enrolled a minimum of 12 semester hours and be worthy and deserving. Contact the address below for further information.

Charleston Southern University
PO Box 118087
Charleston, SC 29423

3079
One Accord Gospel Choir Scholarship

AMOUNT: Maximum: $500 DEADLINE: None Specified
FIELDS/MAJORS: All Areas of Study

Recipient must exemplify Christian values in his/her lifestyle and commitment. Must be a sophomore, junior, or senior with a cumulative GPA of at least 2.5 or above. Contact the address below for further information.

Charleston Southern University
PO Box 118087
Charleston, SC 29423

3080
Parish Scholarship

AMOUNT: $1000 DEADLINE: None Specified
FIELDS/MAJORS: Business Administration, Accounting, Finance, Mathematics, Computer Science, or Information Systems

Two awards are given to a rising junior or senior enrolled in a minimum of 12 semester hours. One award is given to a student majoring in business administration with an emphasis in accounting or finance. Second award is given to a student majoring in mathematics, computer science, or business administration with emphasis in information systems with an overall GPA of at least 3.0. Contact the address below for further information.

Charleston Southern University
PO Box 118087
Charleston, SC 29423

3081
Payne Family Scholarship

AMOUNT: Maximum: $500   DEADLINE: None Specified
FIELDS/MAJORS: All Areas of Study

Recipient must be a profession Christian and have financial need. Contact the address below for further information.

Charleston Southern University
PO Box 118087
Charleston, SC 29423

3082
Strom Thurmond Scholarship

AMOUNT: $1000   DEADLINE: None Specified
FIELDS/MAJORS: Political Science

Awarded to needy and deserving student(s) to continue education in a way that would promote individual incentive and liberty as opposed to socialism and communism. Preference given to political science majors. Contact the address below for further information.

Charleston Southern University
PO Box 118087
Charleston, SC 29423

3083
Thaddeus John Bell, II, Memorial Scholarship

AMOUNT: $500   DEADLINE: None Specified
FIELDS/MAJORS: Sports

Awarded to a African-American student athlete who is enrolled full-time, participates in varsity football, basketball, or track, and has the highest GPA of all candidates applying, with a minimum GPA of 2.5. Contact the address below for further information.

Charleston Southern University
PO Box 118087
Charleston, SC 29423

3084
Wal-Mart Scholarship

AMOUNT: $5000   DEADLINE: None Specified
FIELDS/MAJORS: Technology

Recipient must be a U.S. citizen, incoming freshman, who demonstrates community service and leadership and high academic achievement: ACT score of 27 or above; SAT score of 1100 or above; high school GPA of 3.5 or above; high school rank of 90% or above. Student must be enrolled full-time and declare a major in technology. Contact the address below for further information.

Charleston Southern University
PO Box 118087
Charleston, SC 29423

3085
Walter Charles Cecil and Christine Steinberg Drowota Scholarship

AMOUNT: $1000   DEADLINE: None Specified
FIELDS/MAJORS: All Areas of Study

Recipient must be a new freshman who is one of the top three in their high school graduating class in Charleston, Berkeley, or Dorchester counties. Must be enrolled for at least 15 semester hours. Contact the address below for further information.

Charleston Southern University
PO Box 118087
Charleston, SC 29423

3086
Whittington Family Scholarship

AMOUNT: None Specified   DEADLINE: None Specified
FIELDS/MAJORS: Church Music

Awarded to church music majors enrolled 12 or more semester hours. Must be residents of South Carolina with financial need. Contact the address below for further information.

Charleston Southern University
PO Box 118087
Charleston, SC 29423

CHATHAM COLLEGE

3087
Minna Kaufmann Ruud Fund

AMOUNT: $3500   DEADLINE: January 30
FIELDS/MAJORS: Vocal Music

Scholarships for promising female singers at Chatham College. One award is given annually. Contact the dean of admissions address below for details.

Chatham College
Office of Admissions
Woodland Rd.
Pittsburgh, PA 15232

CHRISTIAN HERITAGE COLLEGE

3088
Freshman Academic Scholarships

AMOUNT: Maximum: $3000   DEADLINE: None Specified
FIELDS/MAJORS: All Areas of Study

Awards for freshmen who have been admitted to CHC and have a GPA of 3.0 or better from high school. The amount of the award varies depending mainly on GPA. Renewable with a GPA of at least 3.4. Forty-five to fifty awards are offered annually. Write to the address below for more information.

Christian Heritage College
Financial Aid Office
2100 Greenfield Dr.
El Cajon, CA 92019

CHRISTOPHER NEWPORT UNIVERSITY

3089
1st Lt. Jeffery Spengler Memorial History Scholarship

AMOUNT: Maximum: $300   DEADLINE: April 1
FIELDS/MAJORS: History

Awarded to a junior majoring in history with a GPA of at least 2.5. Write to the address below or call (757) 594-7170 for more information.

Christopher Newport University
Office of Financial Aid
50 Shoe Lane
Newport News, VA 23606

3090
Alumni Society of Christopher Newport University Graduate Scholarship

AMOUNT: Maximum: $1000   DEADLINE: April 1
FIELDS/MAJORS: All Areas of Study

Awarded to all students enrolled in graduate studies at the University. Write to the address below or call (757) 594-7170 for more information.

Christopher Newport University
Office of Financial Aid
50 Shoe Lane
Newport News, VA 23606

3091
Art, Music, Theater Scholarships

AMOUNT: $200-$2000   DEADLINE: April 1
FIELDS/MAJORS: Art, Music, or Theater

Awarded to CNU students majoring in music, art, or theater. Contact the Chairman of the Arts and Communications Department or call (757) 594-7170 for more information.

Christopher Newport University
Office of Financial Aid
50 Shoe Lane
Newport News, VA 23606

3092
Daisy Garland and Sidney Harmon Scholarship

AMOUNT: $500-$2300   DEADLINE: April 1
FIELDS/MAJORS: All Areas of Study

The recipients must be rising seniors with a minimum GPA of 3.0, who have contributed significantly to the student life at CNU and will still be involved during his/her senior year. Write to the address below or call (757) 594-7170 for more information.

Christopher Newport University
Office of Financial Aid
50 Shoe Lane
Newport News, VA 23606

3093
Daughters of Penelope Scholarship

AMOUNT: Maximum: $500   DEADLINE: April 1
FIELDS/MAJORS: All Areas of Study

Open to full-time, degree-seeking students with a GPA of 3.0 or higher and financial need. Preference is given to females. Amount of scholarship is dependent on the annual donation but is expected to be $500. Write to the address below or call (757) 594-7170 for more information.

Christopher Newport University
Office of Financial Aid
50 Shoe Lane
Newport News, VA 23606

3094
Dr. William T. Patrick, Jr., Scholars in Science

AMOUNT: None Specified DEADLINE: April 1
FIELDS/MAJORS: Biology or Physics

The recipients will be the senior student with the highest GPA majoring in biology and the senior student with the highest GPA majoring in physics. Write to the address below or call (757) 594-7170 for more information.

Christopher Newport University
Office of Financial Aid
50 Shoe Lane
Newport News, VA 23606

3095
G. Keith McMurran Memorial Endowment Scholarship

AMOUNT: Maximum: $500 DEADLINE: April 1
FIELDS/MAJORS: Business

Awarded to a full-time student, with junior status, financial need, a GPA of 2.75 or better, and a major in one of the business disciplines. Write to the address below or call (757) 594-7170 for more information.

Christopher Newport University
Office of Financial Aid
50 Shoe Lane
Newport News, VA 23606

3096
Helen Mugler White Scholarship

AMOUNT: $500-$600 DEADLINE: April 1
FIELDS/MAJORS: All Areas of Study

The recipient must be female between the ages of twenty-four and forty-five years old, be enrolled as a classified student, have a GPA of 3.0 or higher, and have substantial financial need. Preference will be given to eligible students attending on a part-time basis taking a minimum of nine credit hours per semester and showing participation in some community activity or organization. Write to the address below or call (757) 594-7170 for more information.

Christopher Newport University
Office of Financial Aid
50 Shoe Lane
Newport News, VA 23606

3097
James City County Rotary Club Scholarship

AMOUNT: Maximum: $250 DEADLINE: April 1
FIELDS/MAJORS: All Areas of Study

Awarded to an entering freshman with a 3.0 high school GPA, who is a graduate of Bruton High School, Lafayette High School, or Walsingham Academy. Write to the address below or call (757) 594-7170 for more information.

Christopher Newport University
Office of Financial Aid
50 Shoe Lane
Newport News, VA 23606

3098
Leon Hodge Memorial Scholarship

AMOUNT: $100-$500 DEADLINE: April 1
FIELDS/MAJORS: All Areas of Study

The scholarship is awarded to a student with financial need. All students applying for need-based aid will be considered for this scholarship. Write to the address below or call (757) 594-7170 for more information.

Christopher Newport University
Office of Financial Aid
50 Shoe Lane
Newport News, VA 23606

3099
Lion Douglas C. Petty Memorial Scholarship

AMOUNT: Maximum: $1000 DEADLINE: April 1
FIELDS/MAJORS: All Areas of Study

Awarded to a student who is a resident of Newport News, has a GPA of at least 2.0, and has financial need. Write to the address below or call (757) 594-7170 for more information.

Christopher Newport University
Office of Financial Aid
50 Shoe Lane
Newport News, VA 23606

3100
Mary K. Stern CPA PC Accounting Scholarship

AMOUNT: Maximum: $500 DEADLINE: April 1
FIELDS/MAJORS: Accounting

Awarded to a junior or senior accounting major with at least a 3.0 GPA. Write to the address below or call (757) 594-7170 for more information.

Christopher Newport University
Office of Financial Aid
50 Shoe Lane
Newport News, VA 23606

3101
Nancy Gonzales Turner Memorial Scholarship

AMOUNT: None Specified DEADLINE: April 1
FIELDS/MAJORS: English

The recipient must be a full- or part-time student majoring in English with a 3.0 high school GPA, or a current CNU transfer student with a 3.0 GPA. Write to the address below or call (757) 594-7170 for more information.

Christopher Newport University
Office of Financial Aid
50 Shoe Lane
Newport News, VA 23606

3102
Newport News Shipbuilding Employees' Credit Union Scholarship

AMOUNT: Maximum: $1500 DEADLINE: April 1
FIELDS/MAJORS: All Areas of Study

The student must be a member of the Newport News Shipbuilding Employees' Credit Union and be a full-time student at CNU. The scholarship is awarded to a student with financial need; academic achievement will determine the recipient if all other factors are equal. Write to the address below or call (757) 594-7170 for more information.

Christopher Newport University
Office of Financial Aid
50 Shoe Lane
Newport News, VA 23606

3103
Oyster Point Kiwanis David Petersen Scholarship

AMOUNT: Maximum: $1000 DEADLINE: April 1
FIELDS/MAJORS: All Areas of Study

Awarded to a CNU full-time sophomore (or higher) with at least a 3.0 GPA and demonstrated financial need. Write to the address below or call (757) 594-7170 for more information.

Christopher Newport University
Office of Financial Aid
50 Shoe Lane
Newport News, VA 23606

3104
Patrick Henry Mall and Mall Merchants Scholarship

AMOUNT: Maximum: $500 DEADLINE: April 1
FIELDS/MAJORS: Business Administration

Awarded to a sophomore, junior, or senior majoring in business administration. The student may be part-time or full-time and have a GPA of 3.0 or higher. Write to the address below or call (757) 594-7170 for more information.

Christopher Newport University
Office of Financial Aid
50 Shoe Lane
Newport News, VA 23606

3105
Peninsula Council of Garden Clubs Scholarship

AMOUNT: $200-$500 DEADLINE: April 1
FIELDS/MAJORS: Horticulture

The recipient must be a resident of the Peninsula (Newport News, Hampton, Poquoson, York County) and a junior or senior whose field of concentration is horticulture. Write to the address below or call (757) 594-7170 for more information.

Christopher Newport University
Office of Financial Aid
50 Shoe Lane
Newport News, VA 23606

3106
Peninsula Estate Planning Scholarship

AMOUNT: Maximum: $1000 DEADLINE: April 1
FIELDS/MAJORS: Business or Economics

The recipient is a junior or senior with a GPA of at least 3.5, enrolled in the College of Business and Economics and who has at least 30 credits earned at CNU. Write to the address below or call (757) 594-7170 for more information.

Christopher Newport University
Office of Financial Aid
50 Shoe Lane
Newport News, VA 23606

3107
Peninsula Rotary Club Endowment Scholarship

AMOUNT: None Specified DEADLINE: April 1
FIELDS/MAJORS: All Areas of Study

Open to full-time juniors who are Peninsula residents. Must have a minimum GPA of 3.0 and financial need. The amount of the award varies. Write to the address listed or call (757) 594-7170 for more information.

Christopher Newport University
Office of Financial Aid
50 Shoe Ln.
Newport News, VA 23606

3108
Sears Business Scholarship

AMOUNT: Maximum: $500 DEADLINE: April 1
FIELDS/MAJORS: Business

Awarded to a declared business major enrolled for a minimum of six credit hours and in need of financial assistance. Write to the address below or call (757) 594-7170 for more information.

Christopher Newport University
Office of Financial Aid
50 Shoe Lane
Newport News, VA 23606

3109
Teresa Van Dover Memorial Scholarship

AMOUNT: Maximum: $1100 DEADLINE: April 1
FIELDS/MAJORS: English, Creative Writing, Journalism

Awarded to a student majoring in English with concentration in writing or journalism. Write to the address below or call (757) 594-7170 for more information.

Christopher Newport University
Office of Financial Aid
50 Shoe Lane
Newport News, VA 23606

3110
Warwick Kiwanis Scholarship

AMOUNT: Maximum: $500 DEADLINE: April 1
FIELDS/MAJORS: All Areas of Study

Awarded to a full-time sophomore, junior, or senior with financial need and academic achievement, with a minimum academic average of 2.5. Write to the address below or call (757) 594-7170 for more information.

Christopher Newport University
Office of Financial Aid
50 Shoe Lane
Newport News, VA 23606

AMERICAN SOCIETY OF COMPOSERS, AUTHORS, AND PUBLISHERS

3111
The ASCAP Dreyfus/ Warner-Chappell, City College Scholarship

AMOUNT: None Specified DEADLINE: None Specified
FIELDS/MAJORS: Music or Lyrics

Awards to music or lyrics students at the City College of New York. Contact the office of financial aid at the school for more details.

American Society of Composers, Authors, and Publishers
One Lincoln Plaza
New York, NY 10023

CITY COLLEGE OF SAN FRANCISCO

3112
Allen (Dan) Memorial Scholarship

AMOUNT: Maximum: $600 DEADLINE: April 1
FIELDS/MAJORS: All Areas of Study

Open to lesbian, gay, bisexual, and transgendered students demonstrating service to the gay/lesbian community and/or creative, academic, or other achievements of benefit to the gay/lesbian communities. Must be enrolled at City College of San Francisco in at least 6 units, have completed 16 units with a minimum GPA of 2.5, and be publicly identified as a lesbian or gay man. Must be able to demonstrate personal and financial hardship. April 1 deadline is for spring term and October 1 is deadline for fall term. Contact the address below for further information.

City College of San Francisco
Elaine Mannon, Scholarship Office
50 Phelam Ave., Box L230
San Francisco, CA 94112

3113
Bisexual, Gay, and Lesbian Alliance Scholarship

AMOUNT: Maximum: $200   DEADLINE: March 6
FIELDS/MAJORS: All Areas of Study

Open to lesbian, gay, bisexual, and transgendered students demonstrating service to the gay/lesbian community and/or creative, academic, or other achievements of benefit to the gay/lesbian communities. Must be enrolled at City College of San Francisco in at least 6 units and have completed 16 units with a minimum GPA of 3.0. Must be able to demonstrate personal and financial hardship. March 1 deadline is for spring term and October 3 is deadline for fall term. Contact the address below for further information.

City College of San Francisco
Elaine Mannon, Scholarship Office
50 Phelam Ave., Box L230
San Francisco, CA 94112

3114
Tim Wolfred Scholarship

AMOUNT: Maximum: $50   DEADLINE: None Specified
FIELDS/MAJORS: Gay, Lesbian Studies

Open to lesbian, gay, bisexual, and transgendered students with financial need who are taking at least one class in gay/lesbian studies. Deadline is second week of both fall and spring semesters. Based exclusively on need. Contact the address below for further information.

City College of San Francisco
Elaine Mannon, Scholarship Office
50 Phelam Ave., Box L230
San Francisco, CA 94112

CITY UNIVERSITY OF NEW YORK

3115
Margot Karle Scholarship

AMOUNT: $200-$400   DEADLINE: August 15
FIELDS/MAJORS: All Areas of Study

Scholarship available to full-time female students in the City University of New York undergraduate system who have demonstrated both financial need and a high degree of community involvement. Write to the address below for more information.

Astraea National Lesbian Action Foundation
Program Director
116 E. 16th St., 7th Floor
New York, NY 10003

CLARION UNIVERSITY

3116
Clarence and Janet Lesser Scholarships

AMOUNT: None Specified   DEADLINE: April 15
FIELDS/MAJORS: Art, Music, Athletics

Scholarships are awarded to both men and women who are studying art, music, and intercollegiate athletics. High school students are encouraged to apply. Based on talent, academic promise, and leadership potential. Write to the address below for more information.

Clarion University
104 Egbert Hall
Office of Financial Aid
Clarion, PA 16214

CLEMSON UNIVERSITY

3117
Alumni Past Presidents Scholarship

AMOUNT: Maximum: $3500   DEADLINE: March 1
FIELDS/MAJORS: All Areas of Study

Open to accepted/enrolled students at Clemson who are South Carolina residents. Contact the financial aid office at the address below for details or call (864) 656-2280.

Clemson University
Financial Aid Office
G01 Sikes Hall, Box 345123
Clemson, SC 29634

3118
Amick Farms Honorary Annual Scholarship

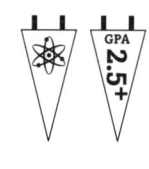

AMOUNT: Maximum: $4000   DEADLINE: None Specified
FIELDS/MAJORS: Poultry Science

Open to entering freshmen admitted to Clemson. Preference given (in descending order) to a resident of Saluda, Lexington, Edgefield, or Newberry counties. Write to the address below for further information or call (864) 656-2280. GPA must be at least 2.5.

Clemson University
Financial Aid Office
G01 Sikes Hall, Box 345123
Clemson, SC 29634

3119
Bill Hudson Family Endowment Scholarship

AMOUNT: $5300   DEADLINE: February 1
FIELDS/MAJORS: All Areas of Study

Award open to undergraduates with a minimum GPA of 2.5. Must be South Carolina residents and be able to demonstrate financial need. Award is renewable. Contact the address below for further information or call (864) 656-2280.

Clemson University
Office of Student Financial Aid
G01 Sikes Hall, Box 345123
Clemson, SC 29634

3120
CIBA-Geigy Annual Prestige Scholarship

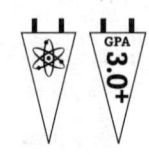

AMOUNT: Maximum: $6000   DEADLINE: March 1
FIELDS/MAJORS: Textile Chemistry

Scholarship for accepted/enrolled students at Clemson majoring in chemistry. Must have a minimum GPA of 3.0. Contact the financial aid office at the address below for details or call (864) 656-2280.

Clemson University
Financial Aid Office
G01 Sikes Hall, Box 345123
Clemson, SC 29634

3121
Fieldcrest Foundation Scholarships

AMOUNT: Maximum: $2500   DEADLINE: February 1
FIELDS/MAJORS: Textiles, Industrial Management

Awards open to juniors and seniors at Clemson with a minimum GPA of 2.5. Must be able to demonstrate financial need. Two awards offered annually. Contact the address below for further information or call (864) 656-2280.

Clemson University
Office of Student Financial Aid
G01 Sikes Hall, Box 345123
Clemson, SC 29634

3122
Frank J. Jervey Alumni Scholarships

AMOUNT: Maximum: $2500   DEADLINE: March 1
FIELDS/MAJORS: All Areas of Study

Several scholarships available to enrolled/admitted students at Clemson with outstanding academic potential. Contact the financial aid office at the address below for details or call (864) 656-2280. GPA must be at least 2.8.

Clemson University
Financial Aid Office
G01 Sikes Hall, Box 345123
Clemson, SC 29634

3123
Horace M. and Maybelle M. Kinsey Scholarship

AMOUNT: None Specified   DEADLINE: March 1
FIELDS/MAJORS: Agriculture

Awarded to outstanding students in agricultural sciences who are South Carolina residents. Criteria includes: scholarship, character, leadership, and dedication to agriculture. Preference is given to Colleton County residents. Four awards offered annually. Write for complete details.

Clemson University
Financial Aid Office
G01 Sikes Hall
Clemson, SC 29634

3124
Howard Eugene Hord Endowed Scholarship

AMOUNT: $1400-$14000   DEADLINE: February 1
FIELDS/MAJORS: Engineering

Awards open to undergraduates with a minimum GPA of 2.5. Contact the address below for further information or call (864) 656-2280.

Clemson University
Office of Student Financial Aid
G01 Sikes Hall, Box 345123
Clemson, SC 29634

3125
IPTAY Academic Scholarship

AMOUNT: Maximum: $2500   DEADLINE: March 1
FIELDS/MAJORS: All Areas of Study

Open to enrolled/admitted students at Clemson who do not participate in intercollegiate athletics. Several scholarships offered annually. Contact the financial aid office at the address below for details or call (864) 656-2280. GPA must be at least 2.8.

Clemson University
Financial Aid Office
G01 Sikes Hall, Box 345123
Clemson, SC 29634

3126
James A. "Shine" Milling Presidential Scholarships

AMOUNT: Maximum: $5500 DEADLINE: March 1
FIELDS/MAJORS: Engineering, Industrial Management

Several scholarships available to enrolled/admitted students at Clemson majoring in engineering or industrial management. Must have a minimum GPA of 3.0. Contact the financial aid office at the address below for details or call (864) 656-2280.

Clemson University
Financial Aid Office
G01 Sikes Hall, Box 345123
Clemson, SC 29634

3127
James Roy Carter, Jr., Presidential Scholarships

AMOUNT: Maximum: $3700 DEADLINE: February 1
FIELDS/MAJORS: Agriculture, Engineering, Forestry

Awards open to undergraduates who are residents of Chester, York, and Lancaster counties in South Carolina. Must have a minimum GPA of 2.5. Two awards offered annually. Contact the address below for further information or call (864) 656-2280.

Clemson University
Office of Student Financial Aid
G01 Sikes Hall, Box 345123
Clemson, SC 29634

3128
Jim and DeeGee Bannon Scholarship

AMOUNT: Maximum: $5800 DEADLINE: February 1
FIELDS/MAJORS: All Areas of Study

Awards open to all undergraduates enrolled/admitted to Clemson who have a minimum GPA of 2.5. This award is renewable. Contact the address below for further information or call (864) 656-2280.

Clemson University
Office of Student Financial Aid
G01 Sikes Hall, Box 345123
Clemson, SC 29634

3129
J.W. Jones Endowed Agricultural Scholarship

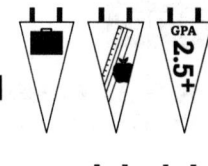

AMOUNT: $4000
DEADLINE: February 1
FIELDS/MAJORS: Agriculture, Agricultural Economics, Education, Engineering, Mechanization, Business, Agronomy

Award open to undergraduates majoring in the fields listed. Must have a minimum GPA of 2.5. Contact the address below for further information or call (864) 656-2280.

Clemson University
Office of Student Financial Aid
G01 Sikes Hall, Box 345123
Clemson, SC 29634

3130
Lillie Hawkins Floyd Trust Scholarships

AMOUNT: Maximum: $2500 DEADLINE: February 1
FIELDS/MAJORS: All Areas of Study

Award open to unmarried undergraduates at Clemson with a minimum GPA of 2.5. Must be able to demonstrate financial need. Renewable if students remain single. Three awards offered annually. The Call of the Enoree, available in the Clemson library, provides information about this award. You may also contact the address below for further information or call (864) 656-2280.

Clemson University
Office of Student Financial Aid
G01 Sikes Hall, Box 345123
Clemson, SC 29634

3131
Palmetto Fellows Scholarships

AMOUNT: Maximum: $5000 DEADLINE: March 1
FIELDS/MAJORS: All Areas of Study

Open to accepted entering freshmen who are residents of South Carolina. Must be ranked in the top 5% of class and score well the ACT/SAT. Renewable if recipients maintain a minimum GPA of 3.0 Contact your high school guidance counselor for application procedures.

Clemson University
Financial Aid Office
G01 Sikes Hall, Box 345123
Clemson, SC 29634

3132

Pickens County Scholars Program

AMOUNT: Maximum: $7500 **DEADLINE:** March 1
FIELDS/MAJORS: All Areas of Study

Scholarships open to enrolled/admitted students at Clemson who graduated from a high school in Pickens County. Preference given to graduates of Pickens and Easley High Schools. Contact the financial aid office at the address below for details or call (864) 656-2280.

Clemson University
Financial Aid Office
G01 Sikes Hall, Box 345123
Clemson, SC 29634

3133

Robert C. Edwards Scholarships

AMOUNT: None Specified **DEADLINE:** March 1
FIELDS/MAJORS: All Areas of Study

Scholarship for entering freshmen with outstanding academic potential. Several awards offered each year. Renewable. Contact the financial aid office at the address below for details. Must have a GPA of at least 2.8.

Clemson University
Financial Aid Office
G01 Sikes Hall
Clemson, SC 29634

3134

Sanford and Irene Loef Scholarship

AMOUNT: $2500 **DEADLINE:** February 1
FIELDS/MAJORS: Industrial Education

Award open to sophomores, juniors, and seniors majoring in industrial education. Must have a minimum GPA of 2.5. Contact the address below for further information.

Clemson University
Office of Student Financial Aid
G01 Sikes Hall, Box 345123
Clemson, SC 29634

3135

Speck Farrar Scholarships

AMOUNT: Maximum: $3000 **DEADLINE:** February 1
FIELDS/MAJORS: All Areas of Study

Awards open to undergraduates at Clemson with a minimum GPA of 2.5. Must demonstrate financial need. Five scholarships offered annually. Contact the address below for further information or call (864) 656-2280.

Clemson University
Office of Student Financial Aid
G01 Sikes Hall, Box 345123
Clemson, SC 29634

3136

Thelma and Harry Hair Scholarship

AMOUNT: $3800 **DEADLINE:** February 1
FIELDS/MAJORS: All Areas of Study

Award open to undergraduates who are residents of Calhoun County, South Carolina. Must have a minimum GPA of 2.5. Contact the address below for further information or call (864) 656-2280.

Clemson University
Office of Student Financial Aid
G01 Sikes Hall, Box 345123
Clemson, SC 29634

3137

Thomas M. Hunter Endowed Scholars Scholarships

AMOUNT: Maximum: $2500 **DEADLINE:** March 1
FIELDS/MAJORS: Engineering

Scholarships for enrolled/admitted students at Clemson majoring in engineering. Does not include a waiver of out-of-state tuition and fee differential. Contact the financial aid office at the address below for details or call (864) 656-2280. GPA must be at least 3.5.

Clemson University
Financial Aid Office
G01 Sikes Hall, Box 345123
Clemson, SC 29634

3138

Walter T. Cox Presidential Scholarship

AMOUNT: Maximum: $6000 **DEADLINE:** March 1
FIELDS/MAJORS: All Areas of Study

Open to accepted/enrolled students at Clemson. Contact the financial aid office at the address below for details or call (864) 656-2280. GPA must be at least 3.8.

Clemson University
Financial Aid Office
G01 Sikes Hall, Box 345123
Clemson, SC 29634

3139
William A. Kenyon Scholarships

AMOUNT: Maximum: $2500 DEADLINE: March 1
FIELDS/MAJORS: All Areas of Study

Scholarships available to enrolled/admitted students at Clemson with outstanding academic potential. Four awards offered annually. Contact the financial aid office at the address below for details or call (864) 656-2280. GPA must be at least 2.8.

Clemson University
Financial Aid Office
G01 Sikes Hall, Box 345123
Clemson, SC 29634

CLEVELAND INSTITUTE OF ART

3140
Institute of Art Scholarships for Entering Students

AMOUNT: $2500-$12500 DEADLINE: March 1
FIELDS/MAJORS: All Areas of Study

Scholarships for students in their first year of study at the Cleveland Institute of Art. Contact the financial aid office at the address below for details.

Cleveland Institute of Art
Financial Aid Office
11141 East Blvd.
Cleveland, OH 44106

CLEVELAND STATE UNIVERSITY

3141
Allen B. Curtis Scholarship

AMOUNT: None Specified DEADLINE: April 15
FIELDS/MAJORS: Chemical Engineering

Awarded to an entering freshman in the field of chemical engineering. Preference given to graduates of Glenville High School. Applicant must demonstrate financial need. Contact the address below for further information.

Cleveland State University
Office of Student Financial Assistance
2344 Euclid Ave.
Cleveland, OH 44115

3142
Curtis Wilson Scholarship for New Freshmen

AMOUNT: $1000 DEADLINE: May 1
FIELDS/MAJORS: All Areas of Study

Recipient must be a Cleveland or East Cleveland high school graduate of African-American descent. Applicants must demonstrate financial need and have a 2.5 GPA or higher. Contact the address below for further information.

Cleveland State University
Office of Student Financial Assistance
2344 Euclid Ave.
Cleveland, OH 44115

3143
Dance Scholarships

AMOUNT: None Specified DEADLINE: May 15
FIELDS/MAJORS: Dance

Dance scholarships are given for recognition and commitment to the Modern Dance Company. The student must exhibit talent and desire to dance either by establishing a minor in dance or personally designing a dance major. Contact Lynn Deering in the Dance Department for audition schedule and more information.

Cleveland State University
Office of Student Financial Assistance
2344 Euclid Ave.
Cleveland, OH 44115

3144
Engineering Merit Awards

AMOUNT: $1000 DEADLINE: May 1
FIELDS/MAJORS: Engineering

Awarded annually to six CSU freshmen engineering applicants based on ACT/SAT scores. Renewable for three years contingent upon a minimum 3.25 GPA each year. Contact the College of Engineering for more details.

Cleveland State University
Office of Student Financial Assistance
2344 Euclid Ave.
Cleveland, OH 44115

3145
Frank J. Ambrose Scholarship

AMOUNT: None Specified DEADLINE: February 15
FIELDS/MAJORS: Engineering

Awarded to three graduating seniors from Ohio high schools. Qualified applicant must rank in the upper 10% of his/her graduating class or have a minimum 3.5 GPA. Students must submit a typed essay of no more than one thousand words stating the reasons the student chose engineering as a major and three letters of recommendation, one must be from a science or mathematics teacher. Contact the address below for further information.

Cleveland State University
Office of Student Financial Assistance
2344 Euclid Ave.
Cleveland, OH 44115

3146
Industrial Engineering

AMOUNT: $1500 DEADLINE: June 1
FIELDS/MAJORS: Industrial Engineering or Manufacturing Engineering

Student's must submit an essay indicating their interest in industrial or manufacturing engineering. An interview with the scholarship committee is required. Contact the Industrial Engineering Department for more details.

Cleveland State University
Office of Student Financial Assistance
2344 Euclid Ave.
Cleveland, OH 44115

3147
Link Program Scholarship

AMOUNT: $2000 DEADLINE: April 1
FIELDS/MAJORS: Business, Engineering, or Computer and Information Sciences.

Awarded to an incoming minority freshman student interested in the field of business, engineering, or computer and information sciences. Must have a minimum high school GPA of 2.5 or higher. Contact the Career Services Center for further information.

Cleveland State University
Office of Student Financial Assistance
2344 Euclid Ave.
Cleveland, OH 44115

3148
Mary A. Spisak Scholarship

AMOUNT: None Specified DEADLINE: April 15
FIELDS/MAJORS: All Areas of Study

Awarded to a National Achievement or National Merit Scholarship recipient. Renewable based on a minimum 3.0 GPA. Contact the address below for further information.

Cleveland State University
Office of Student Financial Assistance
2344 Euclid Ave.
Cleveland, OH 44115

3149
Music Talent Scholarships

AMOUNT: None Specified DEADLINE: April 1
FIELDS/MAJORS: Music

Awarded to a music major who had a successful audition. Must have a 2.5 GPA or higher. Contact the Department of Music for further information.

Cleveland State University
Office of Student Financial Assistance
2344 Euclid Ave.
Cleveland, OH 44115

3150
Plain Dealer Charities Scholarship

AMOUNT: $1000 DEADLINE: April 15
FIELDS/MAJORS: All Areas of Study

Awarded to two entering freshmen who are residents and graduates of a high school in Cuyahoga, Lake, Geauga, Portage, Summit, Medina, or Lorain counties and who rank in the upper 20% on SAT or ACT scores. Contact the address below for further information.

Cleveland State University
Office of Student Financial Assistance
2344 Euclid Ave.
Cleveland, OH 44115

3151
Presidential Scholarship

AMOUNT: None Specified DEADLINE: February 15
FIELDS/MAJORS: All Areas of Study

Open to new students entering Cleveland State University in fall 1998. Must rank in the top 10% of his/her class or maintained a 3.5 GPA. Students must submit an essay of one thousand words that critiques a book, an autobiographical essay, three letters of recommendation, and a personal interview. Contact the address below for further information. GPA must be at least 3.5.

Cleveland State University
Office of Student Financial Assistance
2344 Euclid Ave.
Cleveland, OH 44115

3152
Richard Eaton Foundation Grant

AMOUNT: None Specified   DEADLINE: April 15
FIELDS/MAJORS: Communications

Awarded to a new freshman interested in the field of communications. Contact the address below for further information.

Cleveland State University
Office of Student Financial Assistance
2344 Euclid Ave.
Cleveland, OH 44115

3153
Ruth Ann Moyer Scholarship

AMOUNT: None Specified   DEADLINE: June 1
FIELDS/MAJORS: All Areas of Study

Awarded to adult students who demonstrate career and personal ambition, financial need, and ability to overcome personal hardship or challenge. Students must be Ohio residents. An autobiographical essay and a personal interview are required. Contact the address below for further information.

Cleveland State University
Office of Student Financial Assistance
2344 Euclid Ave.
Cleveland, OH 44115

3154
Theater Arts Scholarship

AMOUNT: None Specified   DEADLINE: May 10
FIELDS/MAJORS: Theater

Awarded to students majoring in theater who have GPAs of 2.5 or higher. Contact the Department of Theater Arts for further information.

Cleveland State University
Office of Student Financial Assistance
2344 Euclid Ave.
Cleveland, OH 44115

3155
Visual Art Merit Scholarship

AMOUNT: None Specified   DEADLINE: February 1
FIELDS/MAJORS: Art

Must be a declared art major and be enrolled in at least one art course for each quarter. Attach a typed sheet that lists and describes participation in art events and activities. 2.5 GPA overall and 3.0 in Art Department. Contact the Art Department for further information.

Cleveland State University
Office of Student Financial Assistance
2344 Euclid Ave.
Cleveland, OH 44115

CLOVIS COMMUNITY COLLEGE

3156
Clovis Rotary Scholarship

AMOUNT: None Specified   DEADLINE: July 30
FIELDS/MAJORS: All Areas of Study

Awards open to residents of Curry County, New Mexico. Must be a full-time student with a minimum GPA of 2.75. Must also be able to demonstrate financial need. One award is given annually. Contact the address below for further information.

Clovis Community College
Financial Aid Office
417 Schepps Blvd.
Clovis, NM 88101

COASTAL CAROLINA UNIVERSITY

3157
Burroughs Foundation Scholarship

AMOUNT: None Specified   DEADLINE: None Specified
FIELDS/MAJORS: All Areas of Study

Awarded to undergraduate students who are residents of Horry County. Contact the address below for further information.

Coastal Carolina University
PO Box 261954
Conway, SC 29528-6054

3158
Carrie Sue Urbush Memorial Scholarship

AMOUNT: None Specified DEADLINE: None Specified
FIELDS/MAJORS: Accounting

Awarded to a junior level accounting major based on academic merit. It is renewable for the senior year. Contact the address below for further information.

Coastal Carolina University
PO Box 261954
Conway, SC 29528-6054

3159
Charles and JoAnne Dickinson Fellowship

AMOUNT: None Specified DEADLINE: None Specified
FIELDS/MAJORS: Religion or Philosophy

Awarded to students interested in religion or philosophy. Financial need is an award consideration. Contact the address below for further information.

Coastal Carolina University
PO Box 261954
Conway, SC 29528-6054

3160
Georgetown County Higher Education Commission Scholarship

AMOUNT: None Specified DEADLINE: None Specified
FIELDS/MAJORS: All Areas of Study

Awarded to a graduating senior from Georgetown County who demonstrates academic merit and school and community involvement. Contact the address below for further information.

Coastal Carolina University
PO Box 261954
Conway, SC 29528-6054

3161
Grand Strand Chapter of Certified Public Accountants Scholarship

AMOUNT: None Specified DEADLINE: None Specified
FIELDS/MAJORS: Accounting

Awarded to a senior from South Carolina who is an accounting major. Financial need is an award consideration. Contact the address below for further information.

Coastal Carolina University
PO Box 261954
Conway, SC 29528-6054

3162
Greater Horry Board of Realtors Scholarship

AMOUNT: None Specified DEADLINE: None Specified
FIELDS/MAJORS: Real Estate

Awarded to an outstanding real estate student. To be eligible, students must have a minimum 3.0 GPA and 60 earned credit hours. Contact the address below for further information.

Coastal Carolina University
PO Box 261954
Conway, SC 29528-6054

3163
GTE Mathematics Scholarships

AMOUNT: None Specified DEADLINE: None Specified
FIELDS/MAJORS: Mathematics

This scholarship is awarded to the entering freshman achieving the highest overall score in the mathematics contest for high school students held annually at Coastal. The recipient must major in mathematics. Contact the address below for further information.

Coastal Carolina University
PO Box 261954
Conway, SC 29528-6054

3164
Horry County Higher Education Commission Mathematics Scholarship

AMOUNT: None Specified DEADLINE: None Specified
FIELDS/MAJORS: Mathematics

This scholarship is awarded to the Horry County resident achieving the highest overall score in the mathematics contest for high school students held annually at Coastal. The recipient must major in mathematics and maintain a minimum 3.0 GPA. Contact the address below for further information.

Coastal Carolina University
PO Box 261954
Conway, SC 29528-6054

3165
Horry County Higher Education Commission Scholarships

AMOUNT: None Specified **DEADLINE:** None Specified
FIELDS/MAJORS: All Areas of Study

These scholarships are awarded to the top ranking high school seniors in Horry County high schools who enroll at Coastal. Recipients must maintain a minimum 3.0 GPA. Contact the address below for further information.

Coastal Carolina University
PO Box 261954
Conway, SC 29528-6054

3166
Institute of Management Accountants Scholarship

AMOUNT: None Specified **DEADLINE:** None Specified
FIELDS/MAJORS: Accounting

Awarded to a junior or senior majoring in accounting. Contact the address below for further information.

Coastal Carolina University
PO Box 261954
Conway, SC 29528-6054

3167
Lucille Cicero Memorial Scholarship

AMOUNT: None Specified **DEADLINE:** None Specified
FIELDS/MAJORS: Theater

Awarded to full-time students enrolled in one or more theater courses. Preference will be given to members of the Upstage Company. Contact the address below for further information.

Coastal Carolina University
PO Box 261954
Conway, SC 29528-6054

3168
Mitch Skipper Memorial Scholarship

AMOUNT: None Specified **DEADLINE:** None Specified
FIELDS/MAJORS: All Areas of Study

Awarded to residents of Horry, Georgetown, or Marion counties who demonstrate financial need. Contact the address below for further information.

Coastal Carolina University
PO Box 261954
Conway, SC 29528-6054

3169
Moser Scholarship

AMOUNT: None Specified **DEADLINE:** None Specified
FIELDS/MAJORS: Music

Awarded to a student interested in music. Contact the address below for further information.

Coastal Carolina University
PO Box 261954
Conway, SC 29528-6054

3170
Myrtle Beach Garden Club Scholarship

AMOUNT: None Specified **DEADLINE:** None Specified
FIELDS/MAJORS: Horticulture

Awarded to a student in horticulture-related studies. Contact the address below for further information.

Coastal Carolina University
PO Box 261954
Conway, SC 29528-6054

3171
Nelson Scholarship Fund

AMOUNT: None Specified **DEADLINE:** None Specified
FIELDS/MAJORS: Marine Science or Art

Awarded to students in marine science and the arts. Special preference is given to students form Myrtle Beach. Contact the address below for further information.

Coastal Carolina University
PO Box 261954
Conway, SC 29528-6054

3172
Rebecca Thomas Jones Memorial Scholarship

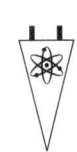

AMOUNT: None Specified **DEADLINE:** None Specified
FIELDS/MAJORS: Marine Science

Awarded to a junior or senior marine science major. Financial need is an award consideration. Contact the address below for further information.

Coastal Carolina University
PO Box 261954
Conway, SC 29528-6054

3173
Richard A. and Karen W. Spivey Scholarship

AMOUNT: None Specified   DEADLINE: None Specified
FIELDS/MAJORS: All Areas of Study

This merit scholarship is made to residents of Horry County who demonstrate financial need. Contact the address below for further information.

Coastal Carolina University
PO Box 261954
Conway, SC 29528-6054

3174
T. Alec Black Scholarship

AMOUNT: None Specified   DEADLINE: None Specified
FIELDS/MAJORS: Business

Awarded to a business major who is a resident of South Carolina. Contact the address below for further information.

Coastal Carolina University
PO Box 261954
Conway, SC 29528-6054

3175
Thomas J. Trout Scholarship

AMOUNT: None Specified   DEADLINE: None Specified
FIELDS/MAJORS: English

Awarded to full-time junior or senior students who are majoring in English. Contact the address below for further information.

Coastal Carolina University
PO Box 261954
Conway, SC 29528-6054

3176
Vera Barger Memorial Scholarship

AMOUNT: None Specified   DEADLINE: None Specified
FIELDS/MAJORS: Music

Awarded to full-time students of exceptional talent in the area of music. Financial need is an award consideration. Contact the address below for further information.

Coastal Carolina University
PO Box 261954
Conway, SC 29528-6054

3177
William A. and L. Maud Kimbel and D. L. Scurry and Jacie Hyatt Scholarships

AMOUNT: None Specified   DEADLINE: None Specified
FIELDS/MAJORS: All Areas of Study

Awarded to students who demonstrate academic merit and financial need. Contact the address below for further information.

Coastal Carolina University
PO Box 261954
Conway, SC 29528-6054

COLLEGE MISERICORDIA

3178
Honor Scholarships

AMOUNT: None Specified   DEADLINE: March 1
FIELDS/MAJORS: All Areas of Study

Honor scholarships are to demonstrate commitment to academic excellence, and the College awards financial assistance to incoming freshmen and transfer students who have attained outstanding academic records. Contact the address below for further information.

College Misericordia
301 Lake St.
Dallas, TX 18612-1098

3179
Presidential Scholarships

AMOUNT: None Specified   DEADLINE: March 1
FIELDS/MAJORS: Pre-Law or Humanities

Scholarships are awarded to incoming freshmen intending to enroll in pre-law or the humanities. High school senior applicants should rank in the upper 20% of their class and have achieved SAT or ACT scores in the eightieth percentile or better. Full, half, and honorary tuition awards are made. Contact the address below for further information. GPA must be at least 3.5.

College Misericordia
301 Lake St.
Dallas, TX 18612-1098

COLLEGE OF MARIN

3180
Gay and Lesbian Student Scholarship

AMOUNT: Maximum: $250 DEADLINE: March 4
FIELDS/MAJORS: All Areas of Study

Open to gay and lesbian students currently enrolled at College of Marin. Scholarship was established in memory of Ned Tuck and Bill Peters by their friends and co-workers. Get applications from the financial aid office. Contact the address below for further information.

College of Marin,
Foundation Development Office
Margaret Elliot
PO Box 446
Kentfield, CA 94914

COLLEGE OF ST. CATHERINE

3181
Abigail Associates Research Grants

AMOUNT: $1000-$3000 DEADLINE: April 17
FIELDS/MAJORS: Women's Studies

Awards are available at the College of St. Catherine for preparation and presentation of publishable quality research in women's studies. Grants are awarded in two categories-contribution of women from the Catholic tradition to public policy and/or services, and self-esteem among women and girls. For female researchers. Does not require residency at the center. Write to Sharon Doherty at the address below for information.

College of St. Catherine
Abigail Quigley McCarthy Center
2004 Randolph Ave.
St. Paul, MN 55105

3182
St. Caecelia Scholarship for Excellence in Music

AMOUNT: Maximum: $5000 DEADLINE: March 1
FIELDS/MAJORS: Music

Awards for high school seniors planning to study music full-time. Renewable up to three years if recipients maintain a minimum GPA of 3.0. Write to the address below for more information.

College of St. Catherine
2004 Randolph Ave.
St. Paul, MN 55105

COLLEGE OF THE CANYONS

3183
Clete Roberts Memorial Scholarship

AMOUNT: Maximum: $1500 DEADLINE: December 12
FIELDS/MAJORS: Broadcast Journalism

Open to students majoring in broadcast journalism who have broadcast experience. Applications available in the Financial Aid Office, C-110. Contact the address below for further information or call (805) 259-7800. GPA must be at least 2.0.

College of the Canyons
Office of Student Financial Aid
26455 Rockwell Canyon Rd.
Santa Clarita, CA 91355-1899

3184
EMI/Selena Scholarship

AMOUNT: Maximum: $2500 DEADLINE: December 1
FIELDS/MAJORS: All Areas of Study

Open to full-time sophomores who are U.S. citizens and of Hispanic descent. Must be at a two-year or technical school, planning to transfer in fall. Must have a minimum GPA of 3.0. Applications available in the Financial Aid Office, C-110. Contact the address below for further information or call (805) 259-7800.

College of the Canyons
Office of Student Financial Aid
26455 Rockwell Canyon Rd.
Santa Clarita, CA 91355-1899

3185
Real Estate Endowment Fund Scholarship

AMOUNT: Maximum: $800 DEADLINE: April 15
FIELDS/MAJORS: Real Estate

Open to full- or part-time students who have completed at least one real estate course. Must have a minimum GPA of 2.0 and be able to demonstrate financial need. Applications available in the Financial Aid Office, C-110. Contact the address below for further information or call (805) 259-7800.

College of the Canyons
Office of Student Financial Aid
26455 Rockwell Canyon Rd.
Santa Clarita, CA 91355-1899

COLLEGE OF THE SISKIYOUS

3186
Associated Chambers of Commerce Harry Crebbin Memorial Scholarship

AMOUNT: $1000 DEADLINE: None Specified
FIELDS/MAJORS: Business

Award for a student graduating from COS and planning to attend a four-year university. Applicants must be from northern California. Write to the address below for more information.

College of the Siskiyous
Financial Aid Office
800 College Ave.
Weed, CA 96094

3187
Beta Sigma Phi-Xi Upsilon Chi Chapter

AMOUNT: $200 DEADLINE: May 1
FIELDS/MAJORS: All Areas of Study

Scholarships for female freshmen who attend the College of the Siskiyous full-time and are residents of Siskiyou County. Applicants must demonstrate financial need, have a minimum GPA of 3.0, and have graduated from a Siskiyou County high school. One award is given annually. Write to the address below for details.

College of the Siskiyous
Financial Aid Office
800 College Ave.
Weed, CA 96094

3188
California Retired Teachers Association Scholarships

AMOUNT: $250 DEADLINE: May 1
FIELDS/MAJORS: Education

Scholarships for students who intend to enroll at the College of the Siskiyous and pursue a career in education. Must be a graduate of a Siskiyou County high school and have a GPA of at least 3.0. Write to the address below for details.

College of the Siskiyous
Financial Aid Office
800 College Ave.
Weed, CA 96094

3189
Chapter VV of P.E.O. Scholarship

AMOUNT: $600 DEADLINE: None Specified
FIELDS/MAJORS: All Areas of Study

Scholarships are available for female students over age eighteen from Siskiyou County who currently attend the College of the Siskiyous. For undergraduate study, not intended for freshmen. Must have a GPA of at least a 3.0. Write to the address below for additional information.

College of the Siskiyous
Office of Financial Aid
800 College Ave.
Weed, CA 96094

3190
Cliff Bearden Memorial Scholarship

AMOUNT: $125 DEADLINE: None Specified
FIELDS/MAJORS: All Areas of Study

Scholarships are available for African-American students of Siskiyou County to attend the College of the Siskiyous. For undergraduate study. Write to the address below for additional information.

College of the Siskiyous
Office of Financial Aid
800 College Ave.
Weed, CA 96094

3191
COS Vocational Nursing Scholarship

AMOUNT: None Specified DEADLINE: May 1
FIELDS/MAJORS: Nursing

Scholarships for students at the College of the Siskiyous who are majoring in nursing. Must have a GPA of 3.0 in classroom theory and clinical performance. Must be enrolled in the third semester of the vocational nursing program. Two awards per year. Write to the address below for details.

College of the Siskiyous
Financial Aid Office
800 College Ave.
Weed, CA 96094

3192
COS Faculty Scholarships

AMOUNT: None Specified DEADLINE: May 1
FIELDS/MAJORS: All Areas of Study

Scholarships for academically promising freshmen entering the College of the Siskiyous. Must have a GPA of at least 3.4 and be enrolling for full-time study. Renewable with a GPA of 3.0. Write to the address below for details.

College of the Siskiyous
Financial Aid Office
800 College Ave.
Weed, CA 96094

3193
Eric Clem Memorial Scholarship

AMOUNT: $100-$300 DEADLINE: May 1
FIELDS/MAJORS: Drama

Scholarships for freshmen at the College of the Siskiyous who are majoring in drama. $100 award is for beginning students; $300 award is for returning students. Contact the Drama Department or write to the address below for details.

College of the Siskiyous
Financial Aid Office
800 College Ave.
Weed, CA 96094

3194
Gertrude Horn Condrey Memorial Scholarship

AMOUNT: None Specified DEADLINE: None Specified
FIELDS/MAJORS: Nursing

Scholarships are available for nursing students from Siskiyou County who are enrolled in the LVN program at the College of the Siskiyous. Based primarily on financial need. Write to the address below for additional information.

College of the Siskiyous
Office of Financial Aid
800 College Ave.
Weed, CA 96094

3195
Harry Crebbin Memorial Scholarship

AMOUNT: $1000 DEADLINE: May 1
FIELDS/MAJORS: Business and Related

Scholarships for students at the College of the Siskiyous who graduated from Siskiyou County high schools, are enrolled (or planning to enroll) at the College of the Siskiyous for full-time study, and intend to transfer to a four-year college in a business-related major. Write to the address below for details.

College of the Siskiyous
Financial Aid Office
800 College Ave.
Weed, CA 96094

3196
Music Performance Scholarships

AMOUNT: $100-$200 DEADLINE: None Specified
FIELDS/MAJORS: Music

Scholarships for students at COS who are performing artists-vocalists and/or instrumentalists. Applicants must perform in a minimum of three groups and be enrolled in music theory each semester to qualify for the $200 scholarships. For the $100 scholarships, the student must perform at least twice each semester and is encouraged to enroll in music theory. Twelve awards are given annually. Contact the Music Department for deadlines and other information, or write to the address below for details.

College of the Siskiyous
Financial Aid Office
800 College Ave.
Weed, CA 96094

3197
Patricia K. Thompson Memorial Scholarship

AMOUNT: $150 DEADLINE: May 1
FIELDS/MAJORS: Drama, English, Creative Writing

Scholarships for students at the College of the Siskiyous who have demonstrated a proficiency in creative writing. For second-year study. Must have a GPA of at least 3.0. Based on sample of work (may be poetry, fiction, drama, etc.). Write to the address below for details.

College of the Siskiyous
Financial Aid Office
800 College Ave.
Weed, CA 96094

3198
Penny Ordway Memorial Scholarship

AMOUNT: $1000 DEADLINE: April 1
FIELDS/MAJORS: Art

Award for an art major at COS who has demonstrated scholastic achievement and has completed at least 30 units of study. Write to the address below for more information.

College of the Siskiyous
Financial Aid Office
800 College Ave.
Weed, CA 96094

3199
Scroggins Memorial Scholarship

AMOUNT: $100   DEADLINE: May 1
FIELDS/MAJORS: History

Scholarships for freshman students at the College of the Siskiyous who have plans to continue as a sophomore at COS in the fall. Applicants must have a minimum of six units in history with a grade of B or better and the intent of continuing in history or debate. Students must demonstrate financial need and have a minimum GPA of 3.0. Write to the address below for details.

College of the Siskiyous
Financial Aid Office
800 College Ave.
Weed, CA 96094

3200
Soroptimists International of Yreka

AMOUNT: $575   DEADLINE: May 1
FIELDS/MAJORS: All Areas of Study

Scholarships are open to female freshmen who are enrolled full-time at the College of the Siskiyous. Applicant must be a resident of Siskiyou County, be able to demonstrate financial need, and be twenty-five years of age or older. This scholarship is renewable for a maximum of two years. Write to the address below for details.

College of the Siskiyous
Financial Aid Office
800 College Ave.
Weed, CA 96094

3201
Whetstine Memorial Scholarship

AMOUNT: $300   DEADLINE: January 1
FIELDS/MAJORS: Mathematics

Scholarships for students at the College of the Siskiyous who are majoring in mathematics. Grades and need are considered. Recommendation of instructor is required. One award is given annually. Write to the address below for details.

College of the Siskiyous
Financial Aid Office
800 College Ave.
Weed, CA 96094

COLORADO COLLEGE

3202
Athletic Scholarships

AMOUNT: None Specified   DEADLINE: January 15
FIELDS/MAJORS: All Areas of Study

Scholarships are available at Colorado College for male students who will be participating in the intercollegiate ice hockey program and female students who will be participating in the intercollegiate soccer program. Write to the address below for information.

Colorado College
Office of Financial Aid
14 East Cache La Poudre
Colorado Springs, CO 80903

3203
Colorado College National Merit Scholarship

AMOUNT: $750-$2000   DEADLINE: January 15
FIELDS/MAJORS: All Areas of Study

Scholarships are available at Colorado College for national merit scholarship finalists who indicate their intention to attend Colorado College. Write to the address below for information.

Colorado College
Office of Financial Aid
14 East Cache La Poudre
Colorado Springs, CO 80903

3204
Margaret T. Barnes Scholarship

AMOUNT: $19026   DEADLINE: January 15
FIELDS/MAJORS: Biology, Geology, Mathematics, Physics, Psychology, Biochemistry, Environmental Sciences, or Neuroscience

Scholarships are available at Colorado College for new students majoring in one of the areas listed above. Renewable for three additional years. Contact the Barnes Selection Committee at the address below for information.

Colorado College
Office of Financial Aid
14 East Cache La Poudre
Colorado Springs, CO 80903

3205
Otis A. Barnes Scholarship

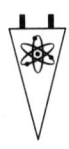

AMOUNT: $19026 DEADLINE: January 15
FIELDS/MAJORS: Chemistry

Scholarships are available at Colorado College for new students majoring in chemistry. Renewable for three additional years. Contact the Chemistry Department or write to the address below for information.

Colorado College
Office of Financial Aid
14 East Cache La Poudre
Colorado Springs, CO 80903

COLORADO INSTITUTE OF ART

3206
Colorado Institute of Art Scholarships for High School Seniors

AMOUNT: $12000-$24000 DEADLINE: March 30
FIELDS/MAJORS: All Areas of Study

Awards for graduating high school seniors planning to attend the Colorado Institute of Art who submit the best slides or original work that follows the requirements of the scholarship bulletin sent to high school guidance counselors each year. Write to the address below for more information.

Colorado Institute of Art
Financial Aid Office
200 E. 9th Ave.
Denver, CO 80203

COLORADO STATE UNIVERSITY

3207
Academic Achievement Awards

AMOUNT: Maximum: $1000 DEADLINE: December 1
FIELDS/MAJORS: All Areas of Study

Open to incoming freshmen who demonstrate academic achievement. Must submit completed Application for Admission. Funding is limited and is given on a first come, first serve basis; therefore, early application is encouraged. Historically, funds are exhausted by January 1. Write to the address below for details or call (970) 491-6321. GPA must be at least 3.0.

Colorado State University
Office of Admissions
Spruce Hall
Fort Collins, CO 80523

3208
Advocacy Diversity Award

AMOUNT: Maximum: $1000 DEADLINE: March 20
FIELDS/MAJORS: All Areas of Study

Scholarships for students who exhibit a commitment to advance diversity at Colorado State. Must be U.S. citizens, Colorado residents, have a minimum GPA of 2.0, and be pursuing a first bachelor's degree. Based on contributions to multicultural awareness through leadership activities and continuing contributions. Write to the address below for details or call (970) 491-6321.

Colorado State University
Financial Aid Office
103 Administration Annex
Fort Collins, CO 80523-8024

3209
Alexander D. Dotzenko Memorial Scholarship

AMOUNT: $500 DEADLINE: February 7
FIELDS/MAJORS: Soil Science, Crop Science

Open to juniors and seniors majoring in soil and crop sciences. One award per year. Write to the address below for more information.

Colorado State University
College of Agricultural Sciences
121 Shepardson
Ft. Collins, CO 80523

3210
Animal Science Memorial Scholarships

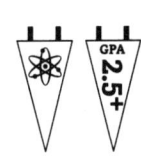

AMOUNT: $500-$1500 DEADLINE: February 7
FIELDS/MAJORS: Animal Science, Equine Science

Open to undergraduates majoring in the above fields. Based on academic ability, need, and potential for professional development. Must be full-time students and U.S. citizens. Write to the address below for more information. GPA must be at least 2.7.

Colorado State University
College of Agricultural Sciences
121 Shepardson
Ft. Collins, CO 80523

3211
Beau Mitchell Memorial Scholarship

AMOUNT: Maximum: $1050 DEADLINE: March 3
FIELDS/MAJORS: All Areas of Study

Scholarships are available at CSU for undergraduate students who were former Boy Scouts or possess a strong orientation for outdoor life. Must be able to demonstrate financial need. Write to the address below for details.

Colorado State University
Financial Aid Office
108 Student Services
Fort Collins, CO 80523

3212
Bob Appleman/Arkansas Valley Seeds Scholarship

AMOUNT: $500 DEADLINE: February 7
FIELDS/MAJORS: Seed Science or Related Field

Two scholarships are available for sophomore or junior students enrolled in seed science or a related major. Awards are $500 per year for two years. Must be full-time and a U.S. citizen. Write to the address below for more information.

Colorado State University
College of Agricultural Sciences
121 Shepardson
Ft. Collins, CO 80523

3213
Class of '56 Alumni Scholarship

AMOUNT: Maximum: $325 DEADLINE: March 1
FIELDS/MAJORS: All Areas of Studies

Scholarships for entering full-time freshmen at Colorado State University. Based on scholastics, need, leadership, and extracurricular activities. Not renewable. Contact the alumni center for details. GPA must be at least 2.8.

Colorado State University
Alumni Center
Ft. Collins, CO 80523

3214
College of Agricultural Sciences Scholarships

AMOUNT: None Specified DEADLINE: February 2
FIELDS/MAJORS: Agriculture and Related

Scholarships for undergraduate students at CSU enrolled in the College of Agriculture. Includes the Denver Agricultural and Livestock Club Scholarship, Diversity Scholarship in Agriculture, Edward Reid Graves Family Scholarship, and the National By-Products, Inc., Agricultural Scholarship. Must be U.S. citizens to apply. Contact the college dean for details and application form.

Colorado State University,
College of Agricultural Sciences
Office of the Dean
121 Shepardson
Ft. Collins, CO 80523

3215
Colorado Farm Bureau Scholarships

AMOUNT: Maximum: $2000 DEADLINE: February 7
FIELDS/MAJORS: Agriculture and Related Fields

Scholarships are available at CSU for freshmen and transfer students majoring in any agriculture-related field. Applicants must be children of Colorado Farm Bureau members, Colorado residents, and U.S. citizens. Five awards per year. Write to the address below for details. GPA must be at least 2.5.

Colorado State University
College of Agricultural Sciences
121 Shepardson
Fort Collins, CO 80523

3216
Colorado National Bank Scholarship

AMOUNT: Maximum: $2000 DEADLINE: March 2
FIELDS/MAJORS: Business Administration, Economics, Finance, Accounting, Marketing

Open to high school seniors who are Colorado residents and U.S. citizens. Must demonstrate school or community activities and financial need. Must have (and maintain) a minimum GPA of 2.5. May be renewed if recipients maintain preset standards. Contact the address below for further information or call (970) 491-6321.

Colorado State University
Financial Aid Office
103 Administration Annex
Ft. Collins, CO 80523-8024

3217
Colorado Seed Industry Scholarship

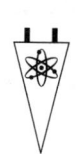

AMOUNT: $1000 DEADLINE: February 7
FIELDS/MAJORS: Seed Science

Must be a junior or senior enrolled in the seed option or majoring in one of the programs involved in the seed science option or having work experience in the seed industry. Must be a U.S. citizen to apply. One award per year. Write to the address below for more information.

Colorado State University
College of Agricultural Sciences
121 Shepardson
Ft. Collins, CO 80523

3218
CSU Animal Science Scholarships

AMOUNT: $500-$2500   DEADLINE: February 7
FIELDS/MAJORS: Animal Science

Scholarships are available at CSU for undergraduate students enrolled in an animal science program. Includes the Colonel Arthur C. Allen, Thomas R. Blackburn, Equine Science Achievement, National Western Stock Show, Wilbur W. Smith Memorial, and Dean Sherman S. Wheeler Scholarships. Requirements vary. Some awards require Colorado residence, all require U.S. citizenship. Together, these five sponsors offer a minimum of sixteen awards annually. Write to the address below for details. GPA must be at least 2.7.

Colorado State University
Financial Aid Office
108 Student Services
Fort Collins, CO 80523

3219
Distinguished Scholars Awards

AMOUNT: Maximum: $2000   DEADLINE: December 1
FIELDS/MAJORS: All Areas of Study

Open to incoming freshmen who demonstrate academic achievement. Participation in Honors Program is required. To be considered, a completed Application for Admission must be submitted. Funding is limited and is given on a first come, first serve basis; therefore, early application is encouraged. Historically, funds are exhausted by January 1. Write to the address below for details or call (970) 491-6321. GPA must be at least 3.0.

Colorado State University
Office of Admissions
Spruce Hall
Fort Collins, CO 80523

3220
Dorothy and Roy Malone Scholarship

AMOUNT: Maximum: $1650   DEADLINE: March 3
FIELDS/MAJORS: All Areas of Study

Scholarships are available at CSU for undergraduates who graduated from Pueblo County high schools in the top one-third of their class. Applicants must demonstrate financial need and participation in extracurricular activities. Must be a U.S. citizen to apply. Write to the address below for details. GPA must be at least 2.8.

Colorado State University
Financial Aid Office
108 Student Services
Fort Collins, CO 80523

3221
Dude Ranchers' Educational Trust Scholarship

AMOUNT: $2000   DEADLINE: February 7
FIELDS/MAJORS: Equine Science, Agribusiness, Agricultural Economics

Must be a sophomore or junior majoring in equine science, agribusiness, agricultural and resource economics, or farm and ranch management with sincere interest in a career in dude ranch employment, management, or ownership. Must have a GPA of 3.0 or better. Must be a U.S. citizen to apply. Two awards per year. Write to the address below for more information.

Colorado State University
College of Agricultural Sciences
121 Shepardson
Ft. Collins, CO 80523

3222
Evelyn Jones Alumni Scholarships

AMOUNT: Maximum: $1220   DEADLINE: March 3
FIELDS/MAJORS: All Areas of Study

Scholarships are available at CSU for freshmen who are children of CSU alums. Based on academic ability, leadership, and financial need. Write to the address below for details.

Colorado State University
Financial Aid Office
108 Student Services
Fort Collins, CO 80523

3223
Farm Credit Scholarship

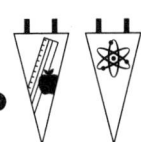

AMOUNT: $500   DEADLINE: February 7
FIELDS/MAJORS: Agribusiness, Agricultural Education, Animal Science

Open to sophomores, juniors, and seniors with an interest in Farm Credit employment or career as a producer. Preference given to Farm Credit members or children of members. Must be U.S. citizens to apply. Three awards per year. Write to the address below for more information.

Colorado State University
College of Agricultural Sciences
121 Shepardson
Ft. Collins, CO 80523

3224
Flack Family Scholarship

AMOUNT: None Specified   DEADLINE: March 3
FIELDS/MAJORS: All Areas of Study

Open to students who are residents of Elbert County, Colorado, and U.S. citizens. Must be in good academic standing and able to demonstrate financial need. Contact the address below for further information. Must have a GPA of at least 2.5.

Colorado State University
Financial Aid Office
103 Administration Annex
Ft. Collins, CO 80523-8024

3225
Orville S. Johnson Memorial Agricultural Scholarships

AMOUNT: Maximum: $500   DEADLINE: February 7
FIELDS/MAJORS: Agricultural or Civil Engineering, Range Science, Water Resources

Scholarships are available at CSU for freshman students majoring in one of the above fields, who graduated from Sterling High School in Logan County, or Akron, Arickaree, Lone Star, Otis, or Woodlin high schools in Washington County. Must be Colorado residents and U.S. citizens. Write to the address below for details.

Colorado State University
College of Agricultural Sciences
121 Shepardson
Fort Collins, CO 80523

3226
Private Scholarships at Colorado State University

AMOUNT: $250-$1500   DEADLINE: March 2
FIELDS/MAJORS: All Areas of Study

Scholarships are available at CSU for all class levels and majors. Approximately twenty donors, combined, offer 150 scholarships annually. Applicants must be able to demonstrate financial need and complete the FAFSA. Request only one "Private Scholarship Application," as one form is used for all these scholarships. Applications available at the Financial Aid Office at the address below.

Colorado State University
Financial Aid Office
103 Administration Annex
Fort Collins, CO 80523-8024

3227
Richard and Shirley Blake Scholarship

AMOUNT: Maximum: $1000   DEADLINE: February 7
FIELDS/MAJORS: Agricultural Economics, Resource Economics

One scholarship is available to a sophomore, junior, or senior in agricultural and resource economics. Must have a GPA of 3.0 or better and be a U.S. citizen. Write to the address below for more information.

Colorado State University
College of Agricultural Sciences
121 Shepardson
Ft. Collins, CO 80523

3228
Robinson A. McWayne Memorial Scholarship

AMOUNT: Maximum: $1500   DEADLINE: March 3
FIELDS/MAJORS: All Areas of Study

Scholarships are available at CSU for undergraduate students who are residents of Hawaii. Based on academics and financial need. Write to the address below for details.

Colorado State University
Financial Aid Office
108 Student Services
Fort Collins, CO 80523

3229
Wyoming Colorado State University Alumni Scholarship

AMOUNT: $500   DEADLINE: March 3
FIELDS/MAJORS: All Areas of Study

Scholarships for entering freshmen at Colorado State University who are from Wyoming. Based on merit and financial need. Not renewable. Must be U.S. citizens to apply. Contact the alumni center for further information.

Colorado State University
Alumni Center
Ft. Collins, CO 80523

COLUMBIA UNIVERSITY

3230
Aura E. Severinghaus Award

AMOUNT: Maximum: $2000 DEADLINE: August 31
FIELDS/MAJORS: Medicine

For senior minority medical students attending Columbia University, College of Physicians and Surgeons. Must be a U.S. citizen. Minorities are defined as African-American, American Indian (including Eskimos, Alaskan Aleuts, Hawaiian natives), Mexican-American, and mainland Puerto Rican. Based on academics and leadership. One award is presented annually. There are two deadlines: May 31 deadline is for renewal applicants, and August 31 is for new applicants. Send a SASE to the address listed for additional information.

National Medical Fellowships, Inc.
110 West 32nd St., 8th Floor
New York, NY 10001

3231
Joseph H. Bearns Prize in Music

AMOUNT: None Specified DEADLINE: March 15
FIELDS/MAJORS: Music Composition

Two annual prizes for music composition are offered in this contest. Applicants must be American citizens. Based on manuscript. Attendance at Columbia University is not necessary. Write to the address below for further information.

Columbia University
Dept. of Music Bearns Prize Committee
2960 Broadway MC 1813
New York, NY 10027

3232
Predissertation Fellowship Program

AMOUNT: Maximum: $3000 DEADLINE: February 3
FIELDS/MAJORS: History, Sociology, Political Science, Anthropology, Economics, Geography

Research grants are available to those studying in the above fields and specializing in European studies. Must have completed a minimum of two years of graduate study. These are non-residential fellowships and are not for students in advanced stages of dissertation research. Must be a U.S. citizen or legal resident of the U.S. or Canada. Write to address below for details.

Council for European Studies
Columbia University
Box 44, Schermerhorn Hall
New York, NY 10027

3233
Taraknath Das Grants

AMOUNT: $3000-$3500 DEADLINE: August 1
FIELDS/MAJORS: All Areas of Study

Five grants for Indian nationals (holding Indian passports) who are enrolled in graduate studies in the United States. Applicants must have completed at least one year of graduate study. Write to the address listed for more information.

Taraknath Das Foundation, Southern Asian Institute
Columbia University
420 West 118th St.
New York, NY 10027

COLUMBUS COLLEGE OF ART AND DESIGN

3234
Columbus College of Art and Design Scholarships

AMOUNT: $8000-$30000 DEADLINE: March 1
FIELDS/MAJORS: Art

Awards for undergraduate students at CCAD based on artistic ability. Must have GPAs of 2.0 or better. Write to the address below for complete details.

Columbus College of Art and Design
Financial Aid Office
107 North Ninth St.
Columbus, OH 43215

COLUMBUS STATE UNIVERSITY

3235
American Association of University Women

AMOUNT: None Specified DEADLINE: None Specified
FIELDS/MAJORS: All Areas of Study

Available to a female adult re-entry program student. Contact the address below for further information.

Columbus State University
Financial Aid Office
4225 University Ave.
Columbus, GA 31907

3236
Art Scholarships

AMOUNT: None Specified **DEADLINE:** None Specified
FIELDS/MAJORS: Art, Art Education, or Visual Arts

Scholarships are available to art and art education majors who demonstrate a high aptitude in the visual arts. Contact the address below for further information.

Columbus State University
Financial Aid Office
4225 University Ave.
Columbus, GA 31907

3237
Columbus Junior Women's Club Scholarship Endowment Fund

AMOUNT: None Specified **DEADLINE:** None Specified
FIELDS/MAJORS: Art, Music, or Theater Arts

Available to students majoring in art, music, or theater arts. Contact the address below for further information.

Columbus State University
Financial Aid Office
4225 University Ave.
Columbus, GA 31907

3238
Columbus State University Honor Scholarship

AMOUNT: $3300 **DEADLINE:** None Specified
FIELDS/MAJORS: All Areas of Study

Ten scholarships are available to academically talented entering freshmen. Contact the address below for further information.

Columbus State University
Financial Aid Office
4225 University Ave.
Columbus, GA 31907

3239
Columbus State University Presidential Scholarship

AMOUNT: None Specified **DEADLINE:** None Specified
FIELDS/MAJORS: All Areas of Study

Scholarships are available to the top five graduates of Chattahoochee Valley Community State University. Contact the address below for further information.

Columbus State University
Financial Aid Office
4225 University Ave.
Columbus, GA 31907

3240
Dwight Curtis Floyd Memorial Fine Arts Scholarship

AMOUNT: None Specified **DEADLINE:** None Specified
FIELDS/MAJORS: Fine Arts

Available to students majoring in fine arts. Contact the address below for further information.

Columbus State University
Financial Aid Office
4225 University Ave.
Columbus, GA 31907

3241
Edward Shorter Endowment

AMOUNT: None Specified **DEADLINE:** None Specified
FIELDS/MAJORS: Art

Available to students majoring in art. Contact the address below for further information.

Columbus State University
Financial Aid Office
4225 University Ave.
Columbus, GA 31907

3242
Georgia Lung Association Health Science Scholarship

AMOUNT: None Specified **DEADLINE:** None Specified
FIELDS/MAJORS: Respiratory Therapy

Available to students pursuing studies in respiratory therapy. Contact the address below for further information.

Columbus State University
Financial Aid Office
4225 University Ave.
Columbus, GA 31907

3243
Judge Averill Graduate Fellowship

AMOUNT: None Specified **DEADLINE:** None Specified
FIELDS/MAJORS: Business Administration

Available to outstanding full-time students pursuing a master of business administration degree. Contact the address below for further information.

Columbus State University
Financial Aid Office
4225 University Ave.
Columbus, GA 31907

3244
Louise B. and F. L. Griffin Nursing Scholarship

AMOUNT: None Specified DEADLINE: None Specified
FIELDS/MAJORS: Nursing

Scholarship awarded annually to a nursing student based on demonstrated leadership and scholastic achievement. Also includes: Kenneth Nance Nursing Scholarship and Lucy Q. Page Nursing Scholarship. Contact the address below for further information.

Columbus State University
Financial Aid Office
4225 University Ave.
Columbus, GA 31907

3245
Maude Flournoy Dixon Piano Scholarship

AMOUNT: None Specified DEADLINE: None Specified
FIELDS/MAJORS: Piano Music

Available to students majoring in music with a concentration in piano. Also includes: Alma Taliaferro McGee Piano Endowment Fund. Contact the address below for further information.

Columbus State University
Financial Aid Office
4225 University Ave.
Columbus, GA 31907

3246
Norman Illges Medical Technology Scholarship

AMOUNT: None Specified DEADLINE: None Specified
FIELDS/MAJORS: Medical Technology

Scholarship is awarded annually to a medical technology major on the basis of scholastic achievement and commitment to a career in the health field. Contact the address below for further information.

Columbus State University
Financial Aid Office
4225 University Ave.
Columbus, GA 31907

3247
Patrons of Music Scholarships

AMOUNT: None Specified DEADLINE: None Specified
FIELDS/MAJORS: Music

Available to students majoring in music. Also includes: Gerald B. and Charlotte A. Saunders Music Scholarship Endowment. Contact the address below for further information.

Columbus State University
Financial Aid Office
4225 University Ave.
Columbus, GA 31907

3248
Paul Amos Scholarship

AMOUNT: None Specified DEADLINE: None Specified
FIELDS/MAJORS: All Areas of Study

Available to undergraduate students who are employed full-time in the Columbus and Phoenix City area. Contact the address below for further information.

Columbus State University
Financial Aid Office
4225 University Ave.
Columbus, GA 31907

3249
Regents' Opportunity Scholarship

AMOUNT: None Specified DEADLINE: None Specified
FIELDS/MAJORS: Public Administration or Business Administration

Awarded to Georgia residents who are economically disadvantaged and enrolled in the master of public administration or the master of business administration degree programs. Contact the address below for further information.

Columbus State University
Financial Aid Office
4225 University Ave.
Columbus, GA 31907

3250
Regents' Scholarship

AMOUNT: None Specified DEADLINE: None Specified
FIELDS/MAJORS: All Areas of Study

Scholarships are available to full-time freshmen degree-seeking students who are residents of the state of Georgia.

Applicants must be in the upper 25% of their class to qualify. Students must demonstrate financial need. Contact the address below for further information. GPA must be at least 3.2.

Columbus State University
Financial Aid Office
4225 University Ave.
Columbus, GA 31907

3251
Retired Officers Association Scholarships

AMOUNT: None Specified   DEADLINE: None Specified
FIELDS/MAJORS: All Areas of Study

Scholarships are available to ROTC cadets. Contact the address below for further information.

Columbus State University
Financial Aid Office
4225 University Ave.
Columbus, GA 31907

3252
Rotary Club of Columbus Scholarships

AMOUNT: None Specified   DEADLINE: None Specified
FIELDS/MAJORS: All Areas of Study

These awards are given to outstanding junior and senior students at Columbus State University. Contact the address below for further information.

Columbus State University
Financial Aid Office
4225 University Ave.
Columbus, GA 31907

3253
Virginia Cook Lee and Katie Lou Cook Memorial Scholarship Endowment

AMOUNT: None Specified   DEADLINE: None Specified
FIELDS/MAJORS: Music or Music Education

Available to students majoring in music and music education. Also includes: Ruth S. Schwob Music Scholarship Endowment and Simon Schwob Foundation Music Endowment. Contact the address below for further information.

Columbus State University
Financial Aid Office
4225 University Ave.
Columbus, GA 31907

3254
William Howard Memorial Scholarship

AMOUNT: None Specified   DEADLINE: None Specified
FIELDS/MAJORS: All Areas of Study

This scholarship is available annually to an incoming freshman on the basis of scholastic achievement. Contact the address below for further information.

Columbus State University
Financial Aid Office
4225 University Ave.
Columbus, GA 31907

CONCORDIA COLLEGE, MOORHEAD MINNESOTA

3255
Cord Scholarship

AMOUNT: None Specified   DEADLINE: August 15
FIELDS/MAJORS: All Areas of Study

Concordia will match any amount received by students through congregational scholarships. Write to the address below for details.

Concordia College, Moorhead Minnesota
901 S. Eighth St.
Moorhead, MN 56562

3256
Performing Arts Scholarship

AMOUNT: None Specified   DEADLINE: March 15
FIELDS/MAJORS: Drama/Theater, Music, Forensics

Open to incoming freshmen who will be majoring in music, drama, or forensics at Concordia College (Moorhead, Minnesota). Renewable. Write to the address below for details.

Concordia College, Moorhead Minnesota
901 S. Eighth St.
Moorhead, MN 56562

CONCORDIA COLLEGE, ST. PAUL

3257

Music Scholarship

AMOUNT: None Specified DEADLINE: May 31
FIELDS/MAJORS: Music

Scholarships for undergraduates at Concordia College-St. Paul who intend to major, minor, or take a concentration in music. Based on a five to ten minute tape. Renewable for one year. Write to address below for additional information.

Concordia College, St. Paul
Office of Admission
275 North Syndicate
St. Paul, MN 55104

CONCORDIA COLLEGE, NEBRASKA

3258

Academic Division Scholarships

AMOUNT: None Specified DEADLINE: None Specified
FIELDS/MAJORS: All Areas of Study

Awards for full-time undergraduates who demonstrate excellence in academic work in a particular department or division. Renewable at the discretion of the division chair and as funds allow. Write to the address below for more information.

Concordia College, Nebraska
Office of Financial Aid
800 N. Columbia Ave.
Seward, NE 68434

3259

Board of Regents Scholarship

AMOUNT: None Specified DEADLINE: None Specified
FIELDS/MAJORS: All Areas of Study

Awards for first-time, full-time freshmen. Amount of award depends on GPA (must be over 3.0) and if the applicant was a National Merit finalist. Renewable if applicant maintains a GPA of at least 3.0. Write to the address below for more information. GPA must be at least 3.0.

Concordia College, Nebraska
Office of Financial Aid
800 N. Columbia Ave.
Seward, NE 68434

3260

Concordia Alumni Grant

AMOUNT: $400 DEADLINE: None Specified
FIELDS/MAJORS: All Areas of Study

Awards given to full-time undergraduates who are dependents of Concordia alumni. Renewable upon conditions set by the dean of students. Write to the address below for more information.

Concordia College, Nebraska
Office of Financial Aid
800 N. Columbia Ave.
Seward, NE 68434

3261

Concordia Private Donor Aid

AMOUNT: None Specified DEADLINE: None Specified
FIELDS/MAJORS: All Areas of Study

Awards for full-time undergraduates that are based on unmet financial eligibility as determined by the FAFSA you must file. Write to the address below for more information.

Concordia College, Nebraska
Office of Financial Aid
800 N. Columbia Ave.
Seward, NE 68434

3262

NACCC Grant

AMOUNT: $700 DEADLINE: None Specified
FIELDS/MAJORS: All Areas of Study

Awards for full-time undergraduates and graduates whose congregation is a member of the NACCC (Nebraska Association of Congregations for Concordia College). Applicants pastor must sign the application. Renewable. Write to the address below or contact the office of church relations for more information.

Concordia College, Nebraska
Office of Financial Aid
800 N. Columbia Ave.
Seward, NE 68434

3263
Presidential Scholarship

AMOUNT: $750   DEADLINE: None Specified
FIELDS/MAJORS: All Areas of Study

Awards for full-time undergraduate transfer students and freshmen. Based on financial need, personal essay, and recommendation from high school faculty or administration. Renewable if a GPA of at least 2.75 is maintained. Write to the address below for more information.

Concordia College, Nebraska
Office of Financial Aid
800 N. Columbia Ave.
Seward, NE 68434

3264
Professional Churchwork Grant

AMOUNT: $750   DEADLINE: None Specified
FIELDS/MAJORS: Religious Work

Awards for full-time undergraduates who are members of the Lutheran Church, Missouri Synod, who declare their intent and commitment to enter full-time professional church work. Renewable upon conditions set by the dean. Write to the address below for more information.

Concordia College, Nebraska
Office of Financial Aid
800 N. Columbia Ave.
Seward, NE 68434

3265
Seward County Grant

AMOUNT: $700   DEADLINE: None Specified
FIELDS/MAJORS: All Areas of Study

Awards for graduating high school seniors from a Seward County high school. Write to the address below for more information.

Concordia College, Nebraska
Office of Financial Aid
800 N. Columbia Ave.
Seward, NE 68434

3266
Talent Awards

AMOUNT: None Specified   DEADLINE: None Specified
FIELDS/MAJORS: Art, Music, Speech/Drama

Awards for full-time undergraduates upon initial admission to Concordia. Awards are renewable. Write to the address below for more information.

Concordia College, Nebraska
Office of Financial Aid
800 N. Columbia Ave.
Seward, NE 68434

3267
Tower Scholarship

AMOUNT: None Specified   DEADLINE: None Specified
FIELDS/MAJORS: All Areas of Study

Awards for undergraduate transfer students. Amount of award depends on GPA (must be over 3.0) and if the applicant was a National Merit finalist. Renewable if applicant maintains a GPA of at least 3.0. Write to the address below for more information.

Concordia College, Nebraska
Office of Financial Aid
800 N. Columbia Ave.
Seward, NE 68434

CONCORDIA UNIVERSITY, IRVINE

3268
Activity Awards for Athletics, Drama, Music

AMOUNT: None Specified   DEADLINE: None Specified
FIELDS/MAJORS: Athletics, Drama, Music

Awards for Concordia students who demonstrate special ability in one of these three areas: athletic, music, or drama. Must be U.S. citizens and have GPAs of at least 2.5. Write to the address below for more information.

Concordia University, Irvine
Financial Aid Office
1530 Concordia West
Irvine, CA 92715

3269
C.F.W. Walther Grant

AMOUNT: Maximum: $1000   DEADLINE: None Specified
FIELDS/MAJORS: Religion, Theology

Awards for Concordia students who are children of full-time LCMS church professionals in the areas of parish pastor, directors of Christian education and evangelism, missionaries, or social workers in a church-sponsored agency. Must have GPAs of 2.5, be U.S. citizens, and have financial need. Write to the address below for more information.

Concordia University, Irvine
Financial Aid Office
1530 Concordia West
Irvine, CA 92715

3270
Christ College Grant

Amount: $1000-$3000 **Deadline:** None Specified
Fields/Majors: Religion, Theology

Awards for Concordia students who intend to enter full-time church careers in the Lutheran Church, Missouri Synod. Must have GPAs of at least 2.5 and be U.S. citizens. Renewable. Write to the address below for more information.

Concordia University, Irvine
Financial Aid Office
1530 Concordia West
Irvine, CA 92715

3271
Concordia University Academic Scholarships

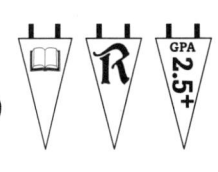

Amount: None Specified **Deadline:** None Specified
Fields/Majors: All Areas of Study

Awards for freshman students who have achieved high school GPAs of at least 3.0. Must be a full-time student and a U.S. citizen. Renewable. Write to the address below for more information.

Concordia University, Irvine
Financial Aid Office
1530 Concordia West
Irvine, CA 92715

3272
Concordia University Lutheran Awards

Amount: None Specified **Deadline:** None Specified
Fields/Majors: All Areas of Study

Awards for Concordia students who graduated from a Lutheran high school or who are members of the Aid Association for Lutherans or the Lutheran Brotherhood. Must have GPAs of at least 2.5 and be enrolled in full-time study. For U.S. citizens. Write to the address below for more information.

Concordia University, Irvine
Financial Aid Office
1530 Concordia West
Irvine, CA 92715

3273
Endowment Grants

Amount: None Specified **Deadline:** None Specified
Fields/Majors: Theology, Religion

Awards for Concordia students preparing for full-time church careers in the LCMS and/or as specified by the donor. Must have GPAs of at least 2.5 and be enrolled in full-time study. For U.S. citizens. Write to the address below for more information.

Concordia University, Irvine
Financial Aid Office
1530 Concordia West
Irvine, CA 92715

3274
Grants-in-Aid

Amount: None Specified **Deadline:** None Specified
Fields/Majors: All Areas of Study

Awards for Concordia students who are in good standing and can demonstrate financial need. Must be U.S. citizens and have GPAs of at least 2.5. Write to the address below for more information.

Concordia University, Irvine
Financial Aid Office
1530 Concordia West
Irvine, CA 92715

3275
Home Congregation Grants and Matching Grants

Amount: None Specified **Deadline:** None Specified
Fields/Majors: Religion, Theology

Awards for Concordia students who intend to enter full-time church careers in the Lutheran Church, Missouri Synod. Must have GPAs of at least 2.5 and be U.S. citizens. These awards are funded by the student's home congregation. Write to the address below for more information.

Concordia University, Irvine
Financial Aid Office
1530 Concordia West
Irvine, CA 92715

3276
Lutheran Church, Missouri Synod District Grants

Amount: $100-$1000 **Deadline:** None Specified
Fields/Majors: Religion, Theology

Awards for Concordia students who intend to enter full-time church careers in the Lutheran Church, Missouri Synod. Must have GPAs of at least 2.5 and be U.S. citizens. Renewable. Write to the address below for more information.

Concordia University, Irvine
Financial Aid Office
1530 Concordia West
Irvine, CA 92715

3277
Successor Grant

AMOUNT: Maximum: $1000   DEADLINE: None Specified
FIELDS/MAJORS: Religion, Theology

Awards for Concordia students who are eligible LCMS young men named by their pastor. Applicants must plan to enter the seminary after graduation from Concordia. Must be U.S. citizens and have GPAs of at least 2.5. Renewable. Write to the address below for more information.

Concordia University, Irvine
Financial Aid Office
1530 Concordia West
Irvine, CA 92715

3278
Trustees' Award

AMOUNT: None Specified   DEADLINE: None Specified
FIELDS/MAJORS: All Areas of Study

Awards for Concordia students from underrepresented ethnic backgrounds. Must have a GPA of at least 2.5 and be a U.S. citizen. Write to the address below for more information.

Concordia University, Irvine
Financial Aid Office
1530 Concordia West
Irvine, CA 92715

CONCORDIA UNIVERSITY, OREGON

3279
F.W.J. Sylwester, Church Work Family Award

AMOUNT: Maximum: $1500   DEADLINE: None Specified
FIELDS/MAJORS: All Areas of Study

Awards for students at Concordia University, Oregon, who are either married to or children of professional church workers in the Lutheran Church, Missouri Synod. Write to the address below for more information.

Concordia University, Oregon
Office of Admissions
2811 NE Holman St.
Portland, OR 97211

3280
Lutheran High School Graduate

AMOUNT: Maximum: $1500   DEADLINE: None Specified
FIELDS/MAJORS: All Areas of Study

Awards for students at Concordia University, Oregon, who graduated from a Lutheran high school. Write to the address below for more information.

Concordia University, Oregon
Office of Admissions
2811 NE Holman St.
Portland, OR 97211

3281
Presidential Scholarships for Freshmen

AMOUNT: $1290-$12900   DEADLINE: None Specified
FIELDS/MAJORS: All Areas of Study

Awards for entering freshmen at Concordia University, Oregon. Based on high school GPA and SAT or ACT scores. Renewable for four years. Write to the address below for more information. GPA must be at least 3.5.

Concordia University, Oregon
Office of Admissions
2811 NE Holman St.
Portland, OR 97211

3282
Presidential Scholarships for Transfers

AMOUNT: $1290-$6450   DEADLINE: None Specified
FIELDS/MAJORS: All Areas of Study

Awards for transfer students at Concordia University, Oregon. Based on high school GPA and SAT or ACT scores. Renewable for four years. Write to the address below for more information. GPA must be at least 3.5.

Concordia University, Oregon
Office of Admissions
2811 NE Holman St.
Portland, OR 97211

3283
Professional Church Work Grant

AMOUNT: Maximum: $4500　DEADLINE: None Specified
FIELDS/MAJORS: Christian Service, Education, Social Work

Awards for students at Concordia University, Oregon, who indicate an intent to serve the Lord Jesus Christ in a Lutheran Church, Missouri Synod ministry, i.e., Pastor, Teacher, Director of Christian Education, or Social Worker. You will receive guaranteed $4500 per year as part of your financial assistance. Write to the address below for more information.

Concordia University, Oregon
Office of Admissions
2811 NE Holman St.
Portland, OR 97211

CORNELL UNIVERSITY

3284
Harold Moore Memorial Award

AMOUNT: $500-$1500　DEADLINE: April 1
FIELDS/MAJORS: Botany, Plant Taxonomy, and Related Fields

Fellowships are available at Cornell for graduate students to support research in plant science. Four awards are given annually. Write to the address below for information.

Cornell University
Director, L.H. Bailey Hortorium
467 Mann Library
Ithaca, NY 14853

3285
Mellon Postdoctoral Fellowship Program

AMOUNT: Maximum: $30000　DEADLINE: January 3
FIELDS/MAJORS: Asian Studies, Classics, German Studies, Romance Studies, Russian Literature

Fellowships for scholars and nontenured teachers in the above fields who completed their Ph.D. requirements in the last five years. U.S. citizenship, Canadian citizenship, or permanent residency required. These are residential fellowships at Cornell. Three or four fellows per year. Write to address below for details. Must have Ph.D. in hand at time of application.

Cornell University
Agnes Sirrine, Program Administrator
27 East Ave., A.D. White Center
Ithaca, NY 14853

3286
New York State Grange Cornell Fund

AMOUNT: None Specified　DEADLINE: None Specified
FIELDS/MAJORS: Agriculture/Life Sciences-Related

Scholarships for students in the College of Agriculture and Life Sciences at Cornell University. Preference given to students from Grange families. Further preference given to students who transfer from a New York A&T College. Contact the financial aid office or write to the address listed for details.

New York State Grange
Scholarship Coordinator
100 Grange Place
Cortland, NY 13045

3287
Society for the Humanities Postdoctoral Fellowships

AMOUNT: $32000　DEADLINE: October 21
FIELDS/MAJORS: Humanities

Six to ten fellowships for Ph.D. applicants with at least one year of college teaching experience. Ph.D. must have been awarded before applying. This fellowship program seeks to bring scholars from a wide variety of disciplines in the study of one topic. Write to the address below for details. Must have Ph.D. in hand at time of application.

Cornell University
Agnes Sirrine, Program Administrator
27 East Ave. A.D. White Center
Ithaca, NY 14853

3288
Telluride Association Scholarships

AMOUNT: $4000-$16000　DEADLINE: February 15
FIELDS/MAJORS: All Areas of Study

Scholarships for full-time undergraduate and graduate students at Cornell University. Not a cash award; rather, these awards provide room and board at Telluride House, a self-governing intellectual community for selected students at Cornell. Twenty-five awards are given annually. If you write for information, you must include a SASE for a reply.

Telluride Association
Attn: Administrative Director
217 West Ave.
Ithaca, NY 14850

CREIGHTON UNIVERSITY

3289
Linn Scholarship

AMOUNT: $2500 DEADLINE: February 1
FIELDS/MAJORS: All Areas of Study

Awarded to students based on factors including involvement, leadership, and academic performance. Contact the address below for further information.

Creighton University
Office of Financial Aid
2500 California Plaza
Omaha, NE 68178

3290
Presidential Scholarship

AMOUNT: None Specified DEADLINE: February 1
FIELDS/MAJORS: All Areas of Study

A three-quarters tuition award is given to top applicants, to Creighton (any undergraduate school or college). Based on high test scores and class rank, as well as involvement and leadership skills. Twenty awards are given annually. Contact the address below for further information.

Creighton University
Office of Financial Aid
2500 California Plaza
Omaha, NE 68178

3291
Reinert Scholarship

AMOUNT: $5000 DEADLINE: February 1
FIELDS/MAJORS: All Areas of Study

Awarded to students scoring a minimum of 30 on the ACT and 1340 on the SAT. Students must have 3.8 GPAs and rank in the top 7.5% of their high school class and demonstrate involvement and leadership skills. Contact the address below for further information.

Creighton University
Office of Financial Aid
2500 California Plaza
Omaha, NE 68178

3292
Scott Scholarship

AMOUNT: None Specified DEADLINE: February 1
FIELDS/MAJORS: Business Administration

A full-tuition award is given to top applicants to Creighton's College of Business Administration. Based on high test scores and class rank. Three awards are given annually. Contact the address below for further information.

Creighton University
Office of Financial Aid
2500 California Plaza
Omaha, NE 68178

CURTIS INSTITUTE OF MUSIC

3293
Tuition Waivers at Curtis Institute

AMOUNT: $19000-$24000 DEADLINE: March 3
FIELDS/MAJORS: All Areas of Study Offered at Curtis

Renewable scholarships, for accepted students, covering full tuition, at the Curtis Institute of Music. Based on merit and financial need. The undergraduate awards are for $19,000, and the graduate awards are for $24,000. Write to the address below for complete details.

Curtis Institute of Music
1726 Locust St.
Philadelphia, PA 19103

DAEMEN COLLEGE

3294
Athletic Scholarship

AMOUNT: None Specified DEADLINE: December 1
FIELDS/MAJORS: Sports

Awarded to full-time freshmen and transfers accepted for admission with recommendation of the appropriate coach. Must maintain player eligibility. Contact the address below for further information.

Daemen College
4380 Main St.
Amherst, NY 14226

3295
Dean's Scholarship

AMOUNT: $500-$2000 DEADLINE: December 1
FIELDS/MAJORS: All Areas of Study

Awarded annually to freshmen or transfers of proven academic ability, as verified by college or high school average, rank in class, and/or SAT/ACT scores. Renewable upon maintaining a 3.3 GPA. Contact the address below for further information.

Daemen College
4380 Main St.
Amherst, NY 14226

3296

Departmental Scholarship

AMOUNT: $300-$1500 DEADLINE: December 1
FIELDS/MAJORS: All Areas of Study

Available in each academic area offered at the College. Award is based upon above average academic qualifications and an indicated financial need, as determined by the Financial Aid Form (FAF). Freshmen and transfers who apply must also submit the recommendation form signed by teacher/faculty in the appropriate area of study. Renewable upon maintaining a 2.0 GPA. Contact the address below for further information.

Daemen College
4380 Main St.
Amherst, NY 14226

3297

Full Tuition Scholarship

AMOUNT: None Specified DEADLINE: December 1
FIELDS/MAJORS: All Areas of Study

This prestigious scholarship is awarded to students who meet two or the three criteria: have a minimum cumulative high school average of 95%, rank in the top 1% of their graduating class, or scored at least 1250 on their SATs. Renewable upon maintaining a 3.5 cumulative average as a full-time registrant. Contact the address below for further information.

Daemen College
4380 Main St.
Amherst, NY 14226

3298

Medical Technology Scholarship

AMOUNT: $2000 DEADLINE: December 1
FIELDS/MAJORS: Medical Technology

This scholarship is for freshmen and transfers accepted to Daemen's Medical Technology Department. Renewable upon maintaining departmental eligibility. Contact the address below for further information.

Daemen College
4380 Main St.
Amherst, NY 14226

3299

Presidential Scholarship

AMOUNT: $1000 DEADLINE: December 1
FIELDS/MAJORS: All Areas of Study

Awarded to entering freshmen who have maintained a minimum high school average of 85% and who demonstrate a high potential for success at the college level. Consideration is based solely on academic criteria. Contact the address below for further information. GPA must be at least 3.7.

Daemen College
4380 Main St.
Amherst, NY 14226

3300

Visual Arts Scholarship

AMOUNT: $5000 DEADLINE: December 1
FIELDS/MAJORS: Visual Arts

Awarded to freshmen art students whose portfolio reflects outstanding talent as determined by a portfolio review by the Art Department faculty. Renewable upon maintaining departmental standards. Contact the address below for further information.

Daemen College
4380 Main St.
Amherst, NY 14226

DALLAS BAPTIST UNIVERSITY

3301

Academic Excellence Scholarship

AMOUNT: None Specified DEADLINE: March 15
FIELDS/MAJORS: All Areas of Study

Awarded to new students who have demonstrated exceptional academic ability in their prior high school or college academic work. A student must have made a minimum score of 30 on the ACT or 1310 on the SAT. To remain in good standing for the scholarship, the student must live on campus, maintain at least a 3.0 GPA, enroll as a full-time student, complete the Christian Leadership Course during the first year of enrollment, submit an annual renewal form, and complete the Free Application for Federal Student Aid and all other required financial aid applications. Contact the address below for further information.

Dallas Baptist University
3000 Mountain Creek Pkwy.
Dallas, TX 75211-9299

3302
Alumni Dependent Scholarship

AMOUNT: $25 DEADLINE: March 15
FIELDS/MAJORS: All Areas of Study

Awarded to full-time students who are the dependent children or spouses of a Dallas Baptist University or Decatur Baptist College alumnus/alumna. The alumnus must be a graduate of Dallas Baptist University or Decatur Baptist College and must be attending full-time during the fall and/or spring to receive the scholarship. Contact the address below for further information.

Dallas Baptist University
3000 Mountain Creek Pkwy.
Dallas, TX 75211-9299

3303
Alumni Family Scholarship

AMOUNT: $30 DEADLINE: March 15
FIELDS/MAJORS: All Areas of Study

Awarded to full-time students who have a brother, sister, parent, or grandparent who is currently attending Dallas Baptist University or who graduated from Dallas Baptist University or Decatur Baptist College. The student must be attending concurrently to receive the scholarship. Only one family member is eligible to receive the scholarship. Contact the address below for further information.

Dallas Baptist University
3000 Mountain Creek Pkwy.
Dallas, TX 75211-9299

3304
Athletic Scholarship

AMOUNT: None Specified DEADLINE: March 15
FIELDS/MAJORS: All Areas of Study

Awarded for participation on the men's baseball team and the women's volleyball and soccer teams. Students must be exceptionally well-qualified, athletically-gifted on a competitive basis. Contact the athletic office at (214) 333-5327 for further information.

Dallas Baptist University
3000 Mountain Creek Pkwy.
Dallas, TX 75211-9299

3305
Christian Leadership Scholarship

AMOUNT: None Specified DEADLINE: March 15
FIELDS/MAJORS: All Areas of Study

Awarded to new students who have demonstrated exceptional Christian character and leadership abilities as well as proven academic skills. Awarded to students who have demonstrated servant-leadership by giving their lives to serving God and His people. To remain in good standing for the scholarship, the student must live on campus, maintain at least a 2.5 GPA, enroll as a full-time student, complete the Christian Leadership Course during the first year of enrollment, be involved in a volunteer or service activity on campus, have a positive influence on the Dallas Baptist University campus, submit an annual renewal form, and complete the Free Application for Federal Student Aid and all other required financial aid applications. Contact the address below for further information.

Dallas Baptist University
3000 Mountain Creek Pkwy.
Dallas, TX 75211-9299

3306
Dallas Federation of Music Clubs Music Scholarship

AMOUNT: None Specified DEADLINE: March 15
FIELDS/MAJORS: Music

Awarded to music majors who are pursuing any area of applied music. Contact the Dean of the College of Fine Arts at (214) 333-5316 for further information.

Dallas Baptist University
3000 Mountain Creek Pkwy.
Dallas, TX 75211-9299

3307
Dr. Elliott Mendenhall Pre-Med Scholarship

AMOUNT: None Specified DEADLINE: March 15
FIELDS/MAJORS: Pre-Med

Awarded to students who are preparing for a medical career and rank in the upper one-third of their class. Contact the Dean of the College of Natural Sciences and Mathematics for further information. GPA must be at least 3.0.

Dallas Baptist University
3000 Mountain Creek Pkwy.
Dallas, TX 75211-9299

3308
Dr. Paul Storm Scholarship

AMOUNT: None Specified DEADLINE: March 15
FIELDS/MAJORS: Pre-Med

Awarded to students who are preparing for a medical career. Contact the Dean of the College of Natural Sciences and Mathematics for further information.

Dallas Baptist University
3000 Mountain Creek Pkwy.
Dallas, TX 75211-9299

3309
Edmund F. Boettcher Vocal Scholarship

AMOUNT: None Specified DEADLINE: March 15
FIELDS/MAJORS: Vocal Music

Awarded to music majors who are pursuing vocal studies as their major area of applied music. Contact the Dean of the College of Fine Arts at (214) 333-5316 for further information.

Dallas Baptist University
3000 Mountain Creek Pkwy.
Dallas, TX 75211-9299

3310
Southwestern Bell Foundation Texas Leaders in Education Scholarship

AMOUNT: None Specified DEADLINE: March 15
FIELDS/MAJORS: Education

Awarded to economically disadvantaged junior and senior education majors planning to pursue a teaching career. Contact the address below for further information.

Dallas Baptist University
3000 Mountain Creek Pkwy.
Dallas, TX 75211-9299

DANIEL WEBSTER COLLEGE

3311
Alumni Award

AMOUNT: None Specified DEADLINE: February 1
FIELDS/MAJORS: All Areas of Study

Awards for juniors at Daniel Webster. Based on academic achievement and financial need. Write to the address below for more details. Must have a GPA of at least 2.9.

Daniel Webster College
Financial Assistance Office
20 University Dr.
Nashua, NH 03063

3312
Claude Goodrich Scholarship

AMOUNT: None Specified DEADLINE: February 1
FIELDS/MAJORS: Aviation, Flight Training

Open to continuing flight training students who have demonstrated maturity, responsibility, and an avid interest in aviation. Write to the address below for more details.

Daniel Webster College
Financial Assistance Office
20 University Dr.
Nashua, NH 03063

3313
Curtis J. Riendeau, Helen Nixon, Gerald Hardy II Memorial Scholarships

AMOUNT: None Specified DEADLINE: February 1
FIELDS/MAJORS: All Areas of Study

Awards for sophomores in the baccalaureate program. To be used in junior year. Based on contribution to student life on campus, financial need, and good academic standing. Write to the address below for more details. Must have a GPA of at least 2.9.

Daniel Webster College
Financial Assistance Office
20 University Dr.
Nashua, NH 03063

3314
Daniel Webster College Merit Grant

AMOUNT: None Specified DEADLINE: February 1
FIELDS/MAJORS: All Areas of Study

Open to incoming students based on prior academic achievement. Renewable for all four years if recipients maintain a minimum GPA of 2.0. Contact the address below for further information.

Daniel Webster College
Financial Assistance Office
20 University
Nashua, NH 03063-1300

3315
Daniel Webster College Trustee Scholarship

AMOUNT: None Specified DEADLINE: February 1
FIELDS/MAJORS: All Areas of Study

Open to returning students with outstanding academic records at DWC. Must have successfully completed at least 12 credits as a full-time day student, be in good social standing, and have a minimum GPA of 3.65. Contact the address below for further information.

Daniel Webster College
Financial Assistance Office
20 University
Nashua, NH 03063-1300

3316
Karen Janice Maloney and Michael J. Keating Scholarship Funds

AMOUNT: None Specified DEADLINE: February 1
FIELDS/MAJORS: Flight Operations

Awards for freshmen in the flight operations program at Daniel Webster. Based on academic promise and financial need. Maloney Scholarship gives preference to women, and the Keating Scholarship is for both entering freshmen and transfer students. Transfer students must have a minimum GPA of 2.0. Write to the address below for more details.

Daniel Webster College
Financial Assistance Office
20 University Dr.
Nashua, NH 03063

3317
Louise J. Levesque-Hills Scholarship

AMOUNT: None Specified DEADLINE: February 1
FIELDS/MAJORS: Creative Writing

Award for a freshman in the associate program or a junior in the baccalaureate program who is majoring in creative writing. Based primarily on the improvement of writing skills. Write to the address below for more details.

Daniel Webster College
Financial Assistance Office
20 University Dr.
Nashua, NH 03063

3318
Peter Damian Covich Memorial Scholarship

AMOUNT: None Specified DEADLINE: February 1
FIELDS/MAJORS: Flight Operations

Awards for students entering senior year in the flight operations program at Daniel Webster. Based on flight performance, academics, and financial need. Write to the address below for more details. Must have a GPA of at least 2.9.

Daniel Webster College
Financial Assistance Office
20 University Dr.
Nashua, NH 03063

3319
Sidney W. Clarkson Jr. Scholarship

AMOUNT: None Specified DEADLINE: February 1
FIELDS/MAJORS: Aviation, Flight Training

Award for a junior in the Flight Division who is maintaining a minimum GPA of 3.0 at the end of the fall semester of the junior year. Write to the address below for more details.

Daniel Webster College
Financial Assistance Office
20 University Dr.
Nashua, NH 03063

DARTMOUTH COLLEGE

3320
Charles A. Eastman Dissertation Fellowship for Native American Scholar

AMOUNT: $25000 DEADLINE: March 15
FIELDS/MAJORS: Arts and Sciences

Fellowships are available for U.S. citizens of Native American descent who plan careers in college or university teaching. Write to the address below for information.

Dartmouth College
Office of Graduate Studies
6062 Clement, Room 305
Hanover, NH 03755

3321
Charles Zimmerman Scholarship

AMOUNT: $2000-$2500 DEADLINE: None Specified
FIELDS/MAJORS: All Areas of Study

Open to freshmen entering Dartmouth College who are greater Hartford residents. Applicants must contact the Financial Aid Office at Dartmouth. Contact the Financial Aid Office at Dartmouth for further information.

Dartmouth Alumni Club of Hartford
Allen Collins
61 Stoner Dr.
West Hartford, CT 06107

DELAWARE STATE UNIVERSITY

3322
Herman H. Holloway, Sr., Memorial Scholarship

AMOUNT: None Specified DEADLINE: March 14
FIELDS/MAJORS: All Areas of Study

Scholarship for high school seniors who have a GPA of at least 3.25, an 850 or better on the SAT or 20 or better on the ACT, and are enrolled full-time at a Delaware State University. Commission makes final awards July 1. Write to the address listed for more information.

Delaware Higher Education Commission
Carvel State Office Building
820 North French St., #4F
Wilmington, DE 19801

DEL MAR COLLEGE

3323
Harry Porter Memorial Scholarship

AMOUNT: None Specified DEADLINE: May 31
FIELDS/MAJORS: Foodservice Management, Restaurant Management

Scholarships for students at Del Mar College who are majoring in restaurant management. Write to the address below for complete information.

Coastal Bend Community Foundation
Mercantile Tower MT 276
615 N. Upper Broadway, #860
Corpus Christi, TX 78477

DENISON UNIVERSITY

3324
Alumni Scholarship

AMOUNT: $5000 DEADLINE: February 1
FIELDS/MAJORS: All Areas of Study

Scholarships for students at Denison University. Based on superior academic performance and potential. Open to all incoming freshmen who are deemed to be high achievers. Contact the office of admissions or the financial aid office at the address below for details.

Denison University
Financial Aid Office
Box M
Granville, OH 43023

3325
Batelle Memorial Institute Foundation Scholarship

AMOUNT: None Specified DEADLINE: January 1
FIELDS/MAJORS: All Areas of Study

Scholarships for students at Denison University. Based on potential for superior academic work and outstanding leadership qualities. Must be residents of Franklin or contiguous counties in Ohio. Up to two awards offered per year. Each award is one-half tuition. Awards are renewable. Contact the admissions office for details. GPA must be at least 2.8.

Denison University
Financial Aid Office
Box M
Granville, OH 43023

3326
Black Achievers Scholarship

AMOUNT: None Specified DEADLINE: January 1
FIELDS/MAJORS: All Areas of Study

Applicants must be African-American students who are outstanding participants in the YMCA's Black Achievers Program. Based on academic accomplishment. Renewable if recipients maintain preset standards. Awards are one-half tuition. Write to the address below for details. GPA must be at least 2.7.

Denison University
Financial Aid Office
Box M
Granville, OH 43023

3327
Faculty Scholarship for Achievement and Trustee Scholarship

AMOUNT: None Specified DEADLINE: January 1
FIELDS/MAJORS: All Areas of Study

Scholarships for students who are valedictorians or salutatorians of their high school classes. Must meet criteria of the honors program; must have interview or attend a campus visitation program. Renewable for four years. Denison Faculty Scholarships are full tuition, and the Trustee Scholarships are three-quarters tuition. Based on academics, extracurricular achievements, test scores, and recommendations by counselors and teachers. Write to the address below for details. GPA must be at least 2.9.

Denison University
Financial Aid Office
Box M
Granville, OH 43023

3328
Heritage Scholarship

AMOUNT: None Specified   DEADLINE: January 1
FIELDS/MAJORS: All Areas of Study

Applicants must show outstanding academic performance and potential. Must meet the criteria for honors program, have recommendations from a counselor and teachers, and demonstrate extracurricular achievements. Awards are half tuition. Renewable if recipients maintain preset standards. Write to the address below for details. GPA must be at least 2.9.

Denison University
Financial Aid Office
Box M
Granville, OH 43023

3329
I Know I Can Scholarship

AMOUNT: $2000   DEADLINE: January 1
FIELDS/MAJORS: All Areas of Study

Scholarships for seniors in Columbus high schools who participated in the I Know I Can Program. Must be able to demonstrate financial need. Renewable if recipients maintain preset standards. Write to the address below for details.

Denison University
Financial Aid Office
Box M
Granville, OH 43023

3330
Jonathan Everett Dunbar Scholarship in the Humanities

AMOUNT: None Specified   DEADLINE: January 1
FIELDS/MAJORS: Humanities

Award for a freshman intending a humanities major showing outstanding academic performance and potential. Successful candidates normally will have a high school rank in the top 10% of their graduating class and combined SAT scores of at least 1300 or ACT composite of 30. Must meet the criteria for the honors program, have recommendations from teachers, and interview with a Denison representative on campus or in students' home area. Award is full tuition. Write to the address below for details. GPA must be at least 3.0.

Denison University
Financial Aid Office
Box M
Granville, OH 43023

3331
Marimac Scholarship

AMOUNT: $1000-$2500   DEADLINE: None Specified
FIELDS/MAJORS: Performing or Visual Art

Applicants required to submit art portfolio or audition (auditions on campus). Available for freshmen only. Selection based on special aptitude in this field. Application is made to the Fine Arts Department. Write to the address below for more details.

Denison University
Financial Aid Office
Box M
Granville, OH 43023

3332
National Merit Founders Scholarship

AMOUNT: $500-$2000   DEADLINE: January 1
FIELDS/MAJORS: All Areas of Study

Applicant must show outstanding performance on college board PSAT/NMSQT. Selection by National Merit Scholarship Corporation. National Merit finalists invited into the Denison honors program will automatically be given the award. Scholarship renewable for four years. Write to the address below for details.

Denison University
Financial Aid Office
Box M
Granville, OH 43023

3333
Parajon, HLA Scholarships

AMOUNT: None Specified   DEADLINE: January 1
FIELDS/MAJORS: All Areas of Study

Scholarships for Hispanic, Asian, and Native American freshmen at Denison University. Strong academic performance and potential is required. Based on academics, extracurricular achievements, and recommendations from counselors and teachers. Renewable if recipients maintain preset standards. Thirty awards offered annually from each of the two sponsors. Awards are one-half tuition. Contact the office of admissions or the financial aid office at the address below for details. GPA must be at least 2.5.

Denison University
Financial Aid Office
Box M
Granville, OH 43023

3334
Park National Bank Scholarship

AMOUNT: $6000 DEADLINE: January 1
FIELDS/MAJORS: All Areas of Study

Scholarships for freshmen at Denison University from Licking County, Ohio, who have superior academic records or potential. Renewable up to four years if recipients maintain preset standards. One or two awards per year. A 3.0 GPA required. Write to the address below for details.

Denison University
Financial Aid Office
Box M
Granville, OH 43023

3335
Tyree, Fisher and Meredith, and Bob and Nancy Good Scholarships

AMOUNT: None Specified DEADLINE: January 1
FIELDS/MAJORS: All Areas of Study

Scholarships for African-American students at Denison University. Based on strong academic performance and potential. The Tyree and Fisher/Meredith awards are renewable if recipients maintain preset standards. Awards range from one-third to one-half tuition. Contact the office of admissions or the financial aid office at the address below for details. GPA must be at least 2.7.

Denison University
Financial Aid Office
Box M
Granville, OH 43023

3336
Wells Scholarship in Science

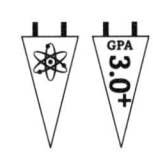

AMOUNT: None Specified DEADLINE: January 1
FIELDS/MAJORS: Math and Science

For freshman mathematics or science major. Successful candidates normally will have a high school class rank in the top 5% of their graduating class and combined SAT scores of approximately 1300 or above or an ACT composite score in the range of 30 or above. Applicant must meet the criteria for the honors program, have recommendations from teachers, and interview with a Denison representative on campus or in the students' home area. Renewable if recipient maintains preset standards. Award is full tuition. Write to the address below for details. GPA must be at least 3.0.

Denison University
Financial Aid Office
Box M
Granville, OH 43023

DEPAUW UNIVERSITY

3337
Holton Memorial Scholarship

AMOUNT: $5000-$23500 DEADLINE: February 15
FIELDS/MAJORS: All Fields of Study

Open to Putnam County high school seniors who demonstrate substantial leadership and/or a commitment to community service. This scholarship is merit based. Contact your high school guidance counselor for further information, write to the address below, or call 1-800-447-2495. GPA must be at least 3.0.

DePauw University
Office of Admissions
Greencastle, IN 46135

DEVRY INSTITUTES OF TECHNOLOGY

3338
Dean's Scholarships

AMOUNT: $1000-$1500 DEADLINE: January 23
FIELDS/MAJORS: All Areas of Study

Open to high school graduates. Applicants with minimum ACT scores of 24/SAT scores 1100 are eligible for $1000 per term tuition awards. Students with ACT scores of 28 or above/SAT scores of 1240 or higher are eligible for $1500 per term tuition awards. Contact your high school counselor, the Director of Admissions at the Devry Campus you wish to attend, or write to the address below for details or 1-800-73DEVRY ext. 2089. November 19 is the deadline for awards made in December, January, and February. December 24 is the deadline for awards made in January and February. GPA must be at least 3.1.

Devry Institutes of Technology
1 Tower Lane, #1000
Villa Park, IL 60181

3339
President's Scholarships

AMOUNT: None Specified DEADLINE: March 16
FIELDS/MAJORS: All Areas of Study

Competition for full-tuition scholarships. Local selection committees will determine winners based on ACT/SAT scores, class rank, GPA, leadership, and extracurricular/community services. Must have a minimum GPA of 3.0. Renewable if recipients maintain the 3.0 GPA. Winners and alternates selected by April 30. Contact your high school counselor, the Director of Admissions at the Devry Campus you wish to attend, write to the address listed for details, or call 1-800-73DEVRY ext. 2089.

Devry Institutes of Technology
1 Tower Ln., #1000
Villa Park, IL 60181

DOWLING COLLEGE

3340
Dowling College Awards

AMOUNT: $5000-$10000 DEADLINE: January 31
FIELDS/MAJORS: Aviation Technology

Awards for CAP members studying aviation technology at Dowling College. Four awards offered annually. Contact the address below for further information.

Dowling College
Financial Aid Office
Oakdale, NY 11769

DREW UNIVERSITY

3341
Drew Need-Based Scholarships

AMOUNT: $100-$7000 DEADLINE: March 1
FIELDS/MAJORS: All Areas of Study

Scholarships are available at Drew University for students in good standing with financial need and academic ability. Write to the address below for information, or contact your school guidance counselor.

Drew University
Elisa Joy Seibert, Administrative Asst.
Office of Financial Assistance
Madison, NJ 07940

3342
Drew Recognition Award

AMOUNT: $6000-$10000 DEADLINE: March 1
FIELDS/MAJORS: All Areas of Study

Scholarships available at Drew University for first-year students who do not qualify for the Drew Scholars Program but have academic credentials above the median of the entering class. Write to the address below for information, or contact your school guidance counselor. GPA must be at least 3.0.

Drew University
Elisa Joy Seibert, Administrative Asst.
Office of Financial Assistance
Madison, NJ 07940

3343
Drew Scholars Program

AMOUNT: None Specified DEADLINE: March 1
FIELDS/MAJORS: All Areas of Study

Scholarships available at Drew for first-year students who graduate in the top 1% of their high school graduating class, with minimum test scores of 1450 SAT or 34 ACT for category one awards. Students in top 5% with 1400 SAT or higher and 33 ACT or higher may apply for category two awards. Write to the address below for information, or contact your school guidance counselor. GPA must be at least 3.7.

Drew University
Elisa Joy Seibert, Administrative Asst.
Office of Financial Assistance
Madison, NJ 07940

3344
Educational Opportunity Fund Scholars Grants

AMOUNT: Maximum: $2100 DEADLINE: March 1
FIELDS/MAJORS: All Areas of Study

Scholarships available at Drew University for full-time students who demonstrate exceptional financial need. Applicants must be New Jersey residents. Write to the address below for information, or contact your school guidance counselor.

Drew University
Elisa Joy Seibert, Administrative Asst.
Office of Financial Assistance
Madison, NJ 07940

3345
Edward Bloustein Distinguished Scholars Program

AMOUNT: Maximum: $1000 DEADLINE: March 1
FIELDS/MAJORS: All Areas of Study

Scholarships are available at Drew University for entering freshmen who demonstrate superior academic achievement. Candidates are nominated by their high school. Applicants must be New Jersey residents. Write to the address below for information, or contact your school guidance counselor. GPA must be at least 3.0.

Drew University
Elisa Joy Seibert, Administrative Asst.
Office of Financial Assistance
Madison, NJ 07940

3346
Elsie Fisher Scholars

AMOUNT: None Specified   DEADLINE: March 1
FIELDS/MAJORS: All Areas of Study

Scholarships available at Drew University for first-year students with financial need and academic ability who participate in community activities. Write to the address below for information, or contact your school guidance counselor. GPA must be at least 3.0.

Drew University
Elisa Joy Seibert, Administrative Asst.
Office of Financial Assistance
Madison, NJ 07940

3347
Garden State Scholars Program

AMOUNT: Maximum: $500   DEADLINE: March 1
FIELDS/MAJORS: All Areas of Study

Scholarships are available at Drew University for entering freshmen who demonstrate superior academic achievement. Candidates are nominated by their high school. Applicants must be New Jersey residents. Write to the address below for information, or contact your school guidance counselor. GPA must be at least 3.0.

Drew University
Elisa Joy Seibert, Administrative Asst.
Office of Financial Assistance
Madison, NJ 07940

3348
Named Scholarships

AMOUNT: None Specified   DEADLINE: March 1
FIELDS/MAJORS: All Areas of Study

Scholarships available at Drew University for students who fit the criteria specified by the donors. Several different awards are offered. These awards are listed in the Drew University Catalog. Write to the address below for information, or contact your school guidance counselor. GPA must be at least 3.0.

Drew University
Elisa Joy Seibert, Administrative Asst.
Office of Financial Assistance
Madison, NJ 07940

3349
Presidential Scholarships

AMOUNT: Maximum: $10000   DEADLINE: March 1
FIELDS/MAJORS: Art, Music

Scholarships available at Drew University for first-year students who graduate in the top 25% of their high school graduating class and show superior artistic or creative talents. Write to the address below for information, or contact your school guidance counselor. GPA must be at least 2.5.

Drew University
Elisa Joy Seibert, Administrative Asst.
Office of Financial Assistance
Madison, NJ 07940

3350
Rose Annual Scholarship

AMOUNT: None Specified   DEADLINE: March 1
FIELDS/MAJORS: All Areas of Study

Scholarships available at Drew University for junior or senior students who demonstrate exceptional financial need and academic ability. Write to the address below for information, or contact your school guidance counselor.

Drew University
Elisa Joy Seibert, Administrative Asst.
Office of Financial Assistance
Madison, NJ 07940

3351
Thomas H. Kean Minority Student Scholarships

AMOUNT: $1000-$10000   DEADLINE: March 1
FIELDS/MAJORS: All Areas of Study

Scholarships available at Drew University for first-year minority students who do not qualify for the drew scholars program. Write to the address below for information, or contact your school guidance counselor. GPA must be at least 3.0.

Drew University
Elisa Joy Seibert, Administrative Asst.
Office of Financial Assistance
Madison, NJ 07940

DREXEL UNIVERSITY

3352

A.J. Drexel Scholarship

GPA 3.0+

AMOUNT: Maximum: $8000   DEADLINE: February 1
FIELDS/MAJORS: All Areas of Study

Awarded to freshman applicants with strong academic records (usually with a GPA of 3.0 or better), high SAT scores, and involvement in extracurricular activities. Transfer students with strong academic records (usually with a GPA of 3.2 or better), with at least 30 credits of college coursework. Contact the address below for further information.

Drexel University
32 and Chestnut St.
Philadelphia, PA 19104

DRURY COLLEGE

3353

Academic Honor Scholars Scholarships

GPA 2.5+

AMOUNT: $1500-$3500   DEADLINE: March 1
FIELDS/MAJORS: All Areas of Study

Scholarships are based on ACT or SAT composite scores and GPAs. Renewable if recipients maintain a 2.75 GPA during the first year of school and a minimum 3.0 for the remaining three years. Contact the address below for further information.

Drury College
Financial Aid Office
900 N. Benton Ave.
Springfield, MO 65802-9977

3354

Drury College Dean Scholarships

GPA 3.5+

AMOUNT: $1000   DEADLINE: May 1
FIELDS/MAJORS: All Areas of Study

Open to high school seniors selected as National Merit finalists and semi-finalists, valedictorians, salutatorians, or rank in the top 2% of their graduating classes. Contact your high school guidance counselor or write to the address below for further information. GPA must be at least 3.6.

Drury College
Financial Aid Office
900 N. Benton Ave.
Springfield, MO 65802

3355

Drury College Leadership Awards

GPA 2.5+

AMOUNT: $500   DEADLINE: March 1
FIELDS/MAJORS: All Areas of Study

Open to undergraduates who are active in church, civic, or school activities. Preference for class officers, association officers, newspaper/yearbook editors, and church/civic youth leaders. Renewable if students maintain a minimum GPA of 2.5. Contact your high school guidance counselor or write to the address below for further information.

Drury College
Financial Aid Office
900 N. Benton Ave.
Springfield, MO 65802

3356

Drury College Scholars Scholarship

GPA 3.0+

AMOUNT: $5000   DEADLINE: February 20
FIELDS/MAJORS: All Areas of Study

Open to high school seniors who scored a 29 or higher on the ACT or a 1300 on the SAT and have a 3.5 GPA. Renewable if student maintains a minimum GPA of 3.0 throughout school. Fifteen awards offered annually. Contact your high school guidance counselor or write to the address below for further information.

Drury College
Financial Aid Office
900 N. Benton Ave.
Springfield, MO 65802

3357

Drury Trustee Scholarships

GPA 3.0+

AMOUNT: None Specified   DEADLINE: February 20
FIELDS/MAJORS: All Areas of Study

Open to high school seniors with a minimum GPA of 3.5. Leadership, community, and church activities will be considered. Renewable if recipients maintain a minimum GPA of 3.0. Seven awards offered annually. Award is full tuition. Contact the address below for further information.

Drury College
Financial Aid Office
900 N. Benton Ave.
Springfield, MO 65802-9977

3358

Missouri High Education Academic Scholarships

AMOUNT: Maximum: $2000   DEADLINE: July 15
FIELDS/MAJORS: All Areas of Study

Open to high school seniors who are Missouri residents and are enrolled/accepted in a participating institution. Must have ACT/SAT scores in the top 3% of all students taking the tests. This is renewable. Contact the your high school counselor or the address below. Must have a GPA of at least 3.5.

Drury College
Financial Aid Office
900 N. Benton Ave.
Springfield, MO 65802-9977

3359

Presidential Scholarship

AMOUNT: $6000   DEADLINE: February 20
FIELDS/MAJORS: All Areas of Study

Open to high school seniors who scored a 29 or higher on the ACT or a 1300 on the SAT and have a 3.5 GPA. Renewable if student maintains a minimum GPA of 3.0 throughout school. Thirteen awards offered annually. Contact your high school guidance counselor or write to the address below for further information.

Drury College
Financial Aid Office
900 N. Benton Ave.
Springfield, MO 65802

DUKE UNIVERSITY

3360

Angier B. Duke Memorial Scholarships

AMOUNT: None Specified   DEADLINE: None Specified
FIELDS/MAJORS: All Areas of Study

Awarded competitively to incoming freshman on the basis of academic merit and leadership abilities. Candidates are selected on the basis of intellectual performance, creative talent, and promise of being eventual leaders in whatever field of endeavor they choose. Award is full tuition for four years plus other bonuses. Contact the address below for further information. GPA must be at least 3.5.

Duke University
Angier B. Duke Memorial Scholarships
104A W. Duke Bldg., Box 90736
Durham, NC 27708-0736

3361

Athletic Scholarships

AMOUNT: None Specified   DEADLINE: None Specified
FIELDS/MAJORS: All Areas of Study

Awarded in football, baseball, field hockey, volleyball, men's and women's basketball, men's and women's golf, men's and women's soccer, men's and women's lacrosse, and men's and women's tennis. Contact the appropriate coach at (919) 684-2120 for further information.

Duke University
Office of Undergraduate Financial Aid
2106 Campus, Box 90397
Durham, NC 27708-6225

3362

Merit Scholarships with Conditions

AMOUNT: None Specified   DEADLINE: None Specified
FIELDS/MAJORS: All Areas of Study

Awarded to National Merit Finalist or Semi-finalist students who are residents of North and South Carolina. Contact the address below for further information.

Duke University
Office of Undergraduate Financial Aid
2106 Campus, Box 90397
Durham, NC 27708-6225

DUMBARTON OAKS

3363

Bliss Prize Fellowship in Byzantine Studies

AMOUNT: None Specified   DEADLINE: November 1
FIELDS/MAJORS: Byzantine Studies

Open to outstanding college seniors who intend to enter the field of Byzantine studies. Must have completed at least one year of ancient or medieval Greek by January. Students must be nominated by their advisors by October 15. Fellows are usually offered a Junior Fellowship at Dumbarton Oaks after completing two years of the Bliss Fellowship. These awards cover graduate school tuition and living expenses for two years. Write to the address below for details.

Dumbarton Oaks
Office of the Director
1703 32nd St. NW
Washington, DC 20007

3364
Fellowships and Junior Fellowships

AMOUNT: $17600-$37700 DEADLINE: November 1
FIELDS/MAJORS: Byzantine Studies, Pre-Columbian Studies, Landscape Architecture

Applicants must hold a Ph.D. or have established themselves in their field and wish to pursue their own research at the Harvard University Dumbarton Oaks Research Facilities (residential fellowships). Scholars who have fulfilled all preliminary requirements for a Ph.D. (or other terminal degree) are eligible for the junior fellowships. All Fellows are expected to be able to communicate satisfactorily in English. Awards will be announced in February. Write to the address below for details.

Dumbarton Oaks
Office of the Director
1703 32nd Street NW
Washington, DC 20007

3365
Summer Fellowships

AMOUNT: $1050-$1575 DEADLINE: November 1
FIELDS/MAJORS: Byzantine Studies, Landscape Architecture

Fellowships are available for a period of six to nine weeks and are open to all scholars at any graduate level. Awards provide a maintenance allowance of $175 per week, housing, lunches, and possible travel reimbursement. Write to the address below for details.

Dumbarton Oaks
Office of the Director
1703 32nd St. NW
Washington, DC 20007

EAST-WEST CENTER

3366
East-West Center Scholarships and Basic Grants

AMOUNT: None Specified DEADLINE: March 1
FIELDS/MAJORS: All Areas of Study

Scholarships are awarded for students at the East-West Center. Based on academics, abilities, potential, and/or need. Write to the address below for more information.

East-West Center
Office of Student Affairs and Open Grants
1777 East-West Rd.
Honolulu, HI 96848

EASTERN NEW MEXICO UNIVERSITY

3367
Baron M. Stuart Endowed Scholarship

AMOUNT: $1000 DEADLINE: March 1
FIELDS/MAJORS: Business

Award for a full-time undergraduate business student who has a GPA of at least 3.0 and has successfully completed 60 credit hours by the effective date of the award. One award per year. Write to the address below for more information.

Eastern New Mexico University
ENMU College of Business
Station 49
Portales, NM 88130

3368
Christian Rojas Memorial Scholarship

AMOUNT: Maximum: $500 DEADLINE: March 1
FIELDS/MAJORS: All Areas of Study

Open to juniors and seniors who have a minimum GPA of 3.25 and have completed 60 hours. Financial need is a factor. Preference given to students who are actively involved in extracurricular activities. Contact the address below for further information.

Eastern New Mexico University
Office of Development
Station 8
Portales, NM 88130

3369
Dabbs Merit Endowed Scholarship

AMOUNT: $1000 DEADLINE: March 1
FIELDS/MAJORS: Nursing

Must be a resident of New Mexico with an ACT score of 26 or above. Must be pursuing a bachelor of science degree in nursing and admitted in the nursing program. Financial need may be a factor. Write to the address below for more information. GPA must be at least 2.6.

Eastern New Mexico University
College of Liberal Arts and Sciences
Station 19
Portales, NM 88130

3370
Dobbs-Burke Memorial Scholarship

AMOUNT: Maximum: $500 DEADLINE: March 1
FIELDS/MAJORS: All Areas of Study

Open to full-time students who demonstrate scholarship, leadership, and citizenship. Preference will be given to New Mexico residents. Financial need is a determining factor. Contact the address below for further information. GPA must be at least 2.9.

Eastern New Mexico University
Office of Development
Station 8
Portales, NM 88130

3371
Dr. and Mrs. Ira C. Ihde Endowed Scholarship Award in History

AMOUNT: $800 DEADLINE: March 1
FIELDS/MAJORS: History

Open to juniors and seniors majoring in history with a GPA of 3.5 or better in history courses and a minimum cumulative GPA of 3.3. Financial need is a factor. Write to the address below for more information.

Eastern New Mexico University
College of Liberal Arts and Sciences
Station 19
Portales, NM 88130

3372
Farmers Insurance Group of Companies Scholarship

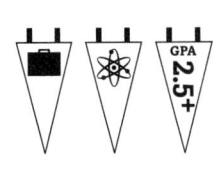

AMOUNT: Maximum: $500 DEADLINE: March 1
FIELDS/MAJORS: Insurance, Mathematics, Business Administration, Personnel

Open to students majoring in the fields listed above. Must have a minimum GPA of 2.7 and be able to demonstrate financial need. Contact the address below for further information.

Eastern New Mexico University
Office of Development
Station 8
Portales, NM 88130

3373
First Savings Bank Scholarship

AMOUNT: Maximum: $300 DEADLINE: March 1
FIELDS/MAJORS: All Areas of Study

Open to high school seniors who are residents of Curry or Roosevelt counties, New Mexico. Must be a freshman during the effective year of the award. Contact the address below for further information. Must have a GPA of at least 2.5.

Eastern New Mexico University
Office of Development
Station 8
Portales, NM 88130

3374
Garland Tillery Memorial Scholarship in Business

AMOUNT: $600 DEADLINE: March 1
FIELDS/MAJORS: Business

Award for a full-time undergraduate business student who has a GPA of at least 3.0 and will be a sophomore by the effective date of the award. Must be a New Mexico resident with a family history of New Mexico residency. One award per year. Write to the address below for more information.

Eastern New Mexico University
ENMU College of Business
Station 49
Portales, NM 88130

3375
Gilbert May Endowed Scholarship

AMOUNT: $1000 DEADLINE: March 1
FIELDS/MAJORS: Accounting

Award for a full-time undergraduate accounting student who has a cumulative GPA of at least 3.0 and has successfully completed 12 credit hours by the effective date of the award. One award per year. Write to the address below for more information.

Eastern New Mexico University
ENMU College of Business
Station 49
Portales, NM 88130

3376
Gordon and Margaret Thomas Honor Scholarship

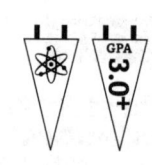

AMOUNT: Maximum: $500 DEADLINE: March 15
FIELDS/MAJORS: Chemistry

Open to high school seniors with a GPA of 3.25, a minimum ACT score of 26, and a demonstrated interest in and aptitude for chemistry. Current freshmen may also apply if they have completed a minimum of 16 hours with a 3.25 GPA. Other undergraduates may also apply if they have a minimum GPA of 3.25. Contact the address below for further information.

Eastern New Mexico University
Dept. of Physical Sciences/Chemistry
Station 33
Portales, NM 88130

3377
Harold Runnels Memorial Scholarship

AMOUNT: Maximum: $500 DEADLINE: March 1
FIELDS/MAJORS: All Areas of Study

Open to full-time students who are New Mexico residents. Must have a minimum GPA of 3.0. Financial need may be a factor. Renewable if recipient maintains preset standards. Contact the address below for further information.

Eastern New Mexico University
Office of Development
Station 8
Portales, NM 88130

3378
I.V. Payne Endowed Scholarship

AMOUNT: $600-$1000 DEADLINE: March 1
FIELDS/MAJORS: Education Administration

Award for a graduate student in the master of education program with an emphasis on education administration. Must have at least one year of successful teaching experience in a public school. Financial need is a consideration. Write to the address below for more information.

Eastern New Mexico University
College of Education and Technology
Station 25
Portales, NM 88130

3379
June West Scholarship in American Studies

AMOUNT: $500 DEADLINE: March 1
FIELDS/MAJORS: American Studies, English, History, Sociology, Anthropology

Must be a junior or senior majoring in any of the above fields with a GPA of 3.0 or better. Three or four awards per year. Write to the address below for more information.

Eastern New Mexico University
College of Liberal Arts and Sciences
Station 19
Portales, NM 88130

3380
Lorraine Schula Endowed Scholarship in Art

AMOUNT: $1500 DEADLINE: March 1
FIELDS/MAJORS: Art

Open to full-time students who are declared art majors. Applicants will need to submit slides along with the forms and application. Write to the address below for more information.

Eastern New Mexico University
College of Fine Arts
Station 16
Portales, NM 88130

3381
Lorraine Schula Scholarship in Music

AMOUNT: Maximum: $700 DEADLINE: March 1
FIELDS/MAJORS: Music

Award for a student at Eastern New Mexico University who is majoring in music and is a participant in ensemble. Applicants must be at the sophomore level or above and have a GPA of 3.0 or better. Financial need is a consideration. Approximately four awards per year. Write to the address below for more information.

Eastern New Mexico University
College of Fine Arts
Station 16
Portales, NM 88130

3382
Mary L. Peed Scholarship

AMOUNT: $1500-$3000　DEADLINE: March 1
FIELDS/MAJORS: Music

Award for full-time students at Eastern New Mexico University who are majoring in music and can demonstrate financial need. Applicants must be New Mexico residents and have a GPA of at least 3.0. One award per year. Write to the address below for more information.

Eastern New Mexico University
College of Fine Arts
Station 16
Portales, NM 88130

3383
Myrtle Moore Women in Business Scholarship

AMOUNT: None Specified　DEADLINE: March 1
FIELDS/MAJORS: Business

Award for a full-time female undergraduate business student who has a GPA of at least 3.0 and has successfully completed 27-40 credit hours by the effective date of the award. Award is in-state tuition, fees, room, board, and books. Write to the address below for more information.

Eastern New Mexico University (Noble Foundation)
ENMU College of Business
Station 49
Portales, NM 88130

3384
New Broadcasters Association/Harold Runnels Memorial Scholarship

AMOUNT: $1000-$2000　DEADLINE: March 1
FIELDS/MAJORS: Communication (Radio/TV emphasis)

Must be a communication major with radio/TV emphasis and a GPA of 3.0 or higher. Write to the address below for more information.

Eastern New Mexico University
College of Liberal Arts and Sciences
Station 19
Portales, NM 88130

3385
New Mexico Society of Public Accountants, A.J. Groebner Scholarship

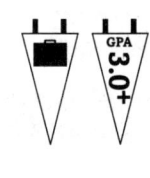

AMOUNT: $600　DEADLINE: March 1
FIELDS/MAJORS: Accounting

Award for a full-time undergraduate accounting student who has a GPA of at least 3.0, has successfully completed 60 credit hours, and is a graduate of a New Mexico high school. One award per year. Write to the address below for more information.

Eastern New Mexico University
ENMU College of Business
Station 49
Portales, NM 88130

3386
New Mexico State Police Association Scholarship

AMOUNT: Maximum: $750　DEADLINE: January 1
FIELDS/MAJORS: All Areas of Study

Open to full-time students who are dependents of an active or retired member of the New Mexico State Police Association. Must be between the ages of sixteen and twenty-five. High school seniors must have a minimum GPA of 3.0, and current undergraduates must have a GPA of 2.5 or better. A second deadline date is July 1. Contact the address below for further information.

Eastern New Mexico University
Office of Development
Station 8
Portales, NM 88130

3387
Physics Scholarship

AMOUNT: Maximum: $500　DEADLINE: March 1
FIELDS/MAJORS: Physics

Open to junior and senior physics majors. (May apply in sophomore year for the following fall). Must have a cumulative GPA of 3.2 or higher in physics and a minimum GPA of 3.0 in other studies. Contact the address below for further information.

Eastern New Mexico University
College of Liberal Arts and Sciences
Station 19
Portales, NM 88130

3388
PNM Native American Scholarship

AMOUNT: None Specified DEADLINE: March 1
FIELDS/MAJORS: All Areas of Study

Open to Native Americans who are residents of New Mexico. Must be affiliated with a recognized New Mexico tribe or pueblo. Each level of school has its own minimum GPA requirement: freshmen must have at least a 2.0; sophomores a minimum of 2.3; juniors and seniors at least a 2.5: and graduate students must have a minimum of 3.0. Preference given to undergraduates. Contact the address below for further information.

Eastern New Mexico University
Vice President for Student Affairs
Station 34
Portales, NM 88130

3389
Portales Kiwanis Scholarship

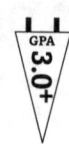

AMOUNT: Maximum: $400 DEADLINE: March 1
FIELDS/MAJORS: All Areas of Study

Open to students who will be juniors or seniors at the effective date of the award. Must have a minimum GPA of 3.0, be a graduate of a Roosevelt County high school, and have evidence of community service activities. Recipient may reapply for this award. Contact the address below for further information.

Eastern New Mexico University
Office of Development
Station 8
Portales, NM 88130

3390
Portales Rotary Club Freshman Award

AMOUNT: Maximum: $500 DEADLINE: March 1
FIELDS/MAJORS: All Areas of Study

Open to graduating seniors of a Roosevelt County high school. Must be a freshman at effective date of award. Based on academic achievement and financial need. Contact your high school counselor for information and an application.

Eastern New Mexico University
Portales, NM 88130

3391
Presser Foundation Scholarship

AMOUNT: $2250 DEADLINE: March 1
FIELDS/MAJORS: Music

Award for a student at Eastern New Mexico University who is majoring in music and completing junior year of study. Must have at least one-third of accumulated credit hours in subjects outside the field of music. One award per year. Write to the address below for more information.

Eastern New Mexico University
College of Fine Arts
Station 16
Portales, NM 88130

3392
Ronald K. Payne/KMPG Peat Marwick Scholarship Fund

AMOUNT: $750 DEADLINE: March 1
FIELDS/MAJORS: Accounting

Awards for full-time undergraduate accounting students who have a GPA of at least 3.0. Must have completed both semesters of intermediate accounting. Two awards per year. Write to the address below for more information.

Eastern New Mexico University
ENMU College of Business
Station 49
Portales, NM 88130

3393
Ruth Carden Stuart Scholarship

AMOUNT: Maximum: $500 DEADLINE: March 1
FIELDS/MAJORS: English

Open to full-time students enrolled in a bachelor's or master's degree program. Undergraduates must have a minimum GPA of 3.0, and graduates must have a GPA of 3.5 or higher. Must be pursuing a career in teaching. Contact the address below for further information.

Eastern New Mexico University
College of Liberal Arts and Sciences
Station 19
Portales, NM 88130

3394
Steven R. Hudson Scholarship

AMOUNT: Maximum: $1000 DEADLINE: March 1
FIELDS/MAJORS: Accounting

Open to full-time accounting majors who have completed a minimum of 50 hours by the effective date of the award. Must demonstrate academic excellence. Contact the address below for further information.

Eastern New Mexico University
College of Business
Station 49
Portales, NM 88130

3395
Tremewan Family Scholarship

AMOUNT: Maximum: $500 DEADLINE: March 1
FIELDS/MAJORS: Business

Open to students who will be full-time undergraduates by the effective date of the award. Must demonstrate academic excellence and financial need. Contact the address below for further information. GPA must be at least 2.9.

Eastern New Mexico University
College of Business
Station 49
Portales, NM 88130

3396
University Symphony League Scholarship

AMOUNT: $600-$1200 DEADLINE: March 1
FIELDS/MAJORS: All Areas of Study

Award for a student at Eastern New Mexico University who is active in the University Symphony Orchestra in the string section. Must be recommended by the orchestra director and approved by the members of the University Symphony League Board. Must enroll in private lessons on the major instrument each semester. Write to the address below for more information.

Eastern New Mexico University
College of Fine Arts
Station 16
Portales, NM 88130

EASTERN WASHINGTON UNIVERSITY

3397
Athletic Scholarships

AMOUNT: None Specified DEADLINE: None Specified
FIELDS/MAJORS: All Areas of Study

Awarded to students who participate in men's football, women's volleyball, men's and women's basketball, golf, tennis, and indoor and outdoor track/cross country. Contact the Athletic Office for further information.

Eastern Washington University
Financial Aid and Scholarship Office
526 5th St., MS 66
Cheney, WA 99004-2431

3398
National Merit Finalists and Semi-Finalist

AMOUNT: $2500 DEADLINE: None Specified
FIELDS/MAJORS: All Areas of Study

Awarded to students who are named National Merit Finalist or Semi-finalists if they enter Eastern as freshmen. The scholarship is renewable for an additional three years as long as a 3.5 GPA is maintained. Contact the Office of Admissions for further information.

Eastern Washington University
Financial Aid and Scholarship Office
526 5th St., MS 142
Cheney, WA 99004-2431

3399
U.S. Army ROTC Scholarships

AMOUNT: $1500 DEADLINE: February 14
FIELDS/MAJORS: All Areas of Study

Army ROTC offers two- and three-year scholarships to freshmen and sophomores with a minimum 2.5 GPA.

Eastern Washington University
Financial Aid and Scholarship Office
526 5th St., MS 142
Cheney, WA 99004-2431

ECKERD COLLEGE

3400
Church and Campus Scholarships

AMOUNT: Maximum: $7000   DEADLINE: None Specified
FIELDS/MAJORS: All Areas of Study

Open to entering Presbyterian students who show leadership and academic abilities. Must be nominated and recommended by their pastor and show promise to become outstanding Christian citizens. Based partially on financial need. Write to the address below for details or call (813) 864-8334. GPA must be at least 2.8.

Eckerd College
Director of Financial Aid
4200 54th Ave. South
St. Petersburg, FL 33711

3401
Florida Residents Scholarship

AMOUNT: $5000-$11400   DEADLINE: None Specified
FIELDS/MAJORS: All Areas of Study

Available to all students who have been Florida residents for one year. Amount awarded depends partially on financial need and academic record. Contact the address below for details or call (810) 864-8334.

Eckerd College
Director of Financial Aid
4200 54th Ave. South
St. Petersburg, FL 33711

3402
Freshman Research Associateships

AMOUNT: Maximum: $1500   DEADLINE: February 15
FIELDS/MAJORS: All Areas of Study

Available to entering freshmen with outstanding overall high school record. Awards also consist of the opportunity to work closely with a faculty member on a research project of mutual interest. Nonrenewable. Write to the address below for details or call (813) 864-8334. GPA must be at least 2.8.

Eckerd College
Director of Financial Aid
4200 54th Ave. South
St. Petersburg, FL 33711

3403
Honors Scholarships

AMOUNT: Maximum: $5000   DEADLINE: None Specified
FIELDS/MAJORS: All Areas of Study

Open to outstanding incoming freshmen and transfer students. Recipients may receive up to $5000. Renewable yearly. Amount of award is determined in part by financial need. Write to the address below for details. GPA must be at least 3.4.

Eckerd College
Director of Financial Aid
4200 54th Ave. South
St. Petersburg, FL 33711

3404
Junior Achievement Scholarships

AMOUNT: $5000-$6000   DEADLINE: March 1
FIELDS/MAJORS: All Areas of Study

Scholarships for junior achievement students who will attend Eckerd College. Up to fifteen awards per year. Renewable. Additional information is available from the college. Contact Richard R. Hallin, dean of admissions, for details.

Eckerd College
Director of Financial Aid
PO Box 12560
St. Petersburg, FL 33733

3405
Presidential Scholarships

AMOUNT: $8000-$10000   DEADLINE: February 15
FIELDS/MAJORS: All Areas of Study

Offered to entering freshmen with excellent academic achievement and demonstrated leadership. Write to the address below for details. GPA must be at least 3.2.

Eckerd College
Director of Financial Aid
4200 54th Ave. South
St. Petersburg, FL 33711

3406
Special Honors Scholarships

AMOUNT: Maximum: $16450   DEADLINE: February 15
FIELDS/MAJORS: All Areas of Study

Open to entering freshmen who have been named finalists or semi-finalists in the National Merit Scholarship, the National Achievement, or the National Hispanic Scholarship programs. Contact the address below for details.

Eckerd College
Director of Financial Aid
4200 54th Ave. South
St. Petersburg, FL 33711

3407
Special Talent Scholarships

GPA 3.0+

AMOUNT: None Specified   DEADLINE: None Specified
FIELDS/MAJORS: All Areas of Study

Available to incoming students who have shown remarkable leadership, service, or talent in a curricular or extracurricular activity (math, English, sports, music, theater, art, community service, etc.). Amount and number of awards varies. Separate application and audition/tapes/slides/etc. required for the creative arts fields. Students should submit a letter of recommendation. Contact the address below for details or call (810) 864-8334. GPA must be at least 3.0.

Eckerd College
Director of Financial Aid
4200 54th Ave. South
St. Petersburg, FL 33711

EDGEWOOD COLLEGE

3408
Cray Research Foundation Award

AMOUNT: $1000   DEADLINE: March 15
FIELDS/MAJORS: Science, Computer Science, Mathematics

Applicants must be full-time Edgewood undergraduate students majoring in science, mathematics, or computer science. Minorities and women are encouraged to apply. Write to the address below for details.

Edgewood College
Office of Admissions
855 Woodrow Street
Madison, WI 53711

3409
Dane County High School Award

GPA 2.5+

AMOUNT: $250-$1000   DEADLINE: March 15
FIELDS/MAJORS: All Areas of Study

Applicants must be first-time freshmen who have graduated from Dane County, Wisconsin, high schools. Applicants must have at least 2.5 GPAs. Renewable. Write to the address below for details.

Edgewood College
Office of Admissions
855 Woodrow Street
Madison, WI 53711

3410
Dominican Honor Scholarship

GPA 3.0+

AMOUNT: $500-$3500   DEADLINE: March 15
FIELDS/MAJORS: All Areas of Study

Applicants must be incoming freshmen who meet two of the three requirements for eligibility: minimum 3.0 GPA, ACT score of 20 (SAT 1000), or rank in the top 25% of their graduating class. Renewable. Write to the address below for details.

Edgewood College
Office of Admissions
855 Woodrow Street
Madison, WI 53711

3411
Ebben Family Scholarship

AMOUNT: $500-$3000   DEADLINE: March 15
FIELDS/MAJORS: All Areas of Study

Applicants must be incoming freshmen who have been involved in co-curricular activities and have displayed academic promise. Preference will be given to Wisconsin residents from the Fox River Valley area. Write to the address below for details.

Edgewood College
Office of Admissions
855 Woodrow Street
Madison, WI 53711

3412
Edgewood Employment Work Program

AMOUNT: $200-$1600   DEADLINE: March 15
FIELDS/MAJORS: All Areas of Study

Students in this program work an average of ten hours per week on campus. A limited number of positions are available for those without financial need. Write to the address below for details.

Edgewood College
Office of Admissions
855 Woodrow Street
Madison, WI 53711

3413

Edgewood Grant

AMOUNT: $200-$2000   DEADLINE: March 15
FIELDS/MAJORS: All Areas of Study

Grants for Edgewood College students, with preference given to students with financial need. For undergraduate study. Write to the address below for details.

Edgewood College
Office of Admissions
855 Woodrow Street
Madison, WI 53711

3414

Fine Arts Grants in Art, Music, Drama, and Writing

AMOUNT: $250-$1500   DEADLINE: March 15
FIELDS/MAJORS: All Areas of Study

Open to incoming freshmen who are interested, but not necessarily majoring in art, music, drama, or English and plan to continue their participation in the arts at Edgewood. Transfer students are also eligible. Financial need must be demonstrated. Renewable. Write to the address below for details.

Edgewood College
Office of Admissions
855 Woodrow Street
Madison, WI 53711

3415

Leadership Incentive Award

AMOUNT: $250   DEADLINE: March 15
FIELDS/MAJORS: All Areas of Study

Open to first-time freshmen who have shown leadership in high school and who will make a commitment to continue involvement in co-curricular activities at Edgewood. Award is designed to meet the cost of a room on campus. Renewable. Write to the address below for details.

Edgewood College
Office of Admissions
855 Woodrow Street
Madison, WI 53711

3416

Mazzuchelli Catholic High School Enrichment Award

AMOUNT: None Specified   DEADLINE: March 15
FIELDS/MAJORS: All Areas of Study

Applicants must be incoming freshmen who graduated from a Catholic-sponsored high school. Students who have been involved in community service projects are encouraged to apply. Write to the address below for details.

Edgewood College
Office of Admissions
855 Woodrow St.
Madison, WI 53711

3417

Neviaser Ahana Student Achievement Award

AMOUNT: $2000   DEADLINE: March 15
FIELDS/MAJORS: All Areas of Study

Awards for incoming freshmen who are African-American, Asian, Hispanic, or Native American with GPAs of at least 2.5 and ranking in the upper 50% of their graduating class. Preference will be given to Dane County residents. Renewable. Write to the address below for details. GPA must be at least 2.5.

Edgewood College
Office of Admissions
855 Woodrow Street
Madison, WI 53711

3418

O'Connor Memorial Scholarship

AMOUNT: $200-$800   DEADLINE: March 15
FIELDS/MAJORS: All Areas of Study

Applicants must be students from Columbus, Wisconsin, with preference given to those from St. Jerome's Parish. Other criteria include academic excellence and financial need. Write to the address below for details.

Edgewood College
Office of Admissions
855 Woodrow Street
Madison, WI 53711

3419

Presidential Scholarship

AMOUNT: None Specified   DEADLINE: March 15
FIELDS/MAJORS: All Areas of Study

Open to incoming freshmen with at least 3.5 GPAs, ACT minimum of 25 (SAT of 1100), and rank in the top 15% of their graduating class. Extracurricular activities are considered. Renewable. Write to the address below for details.

Edgewood College
Office of Admissions
855 Woodrow St.
Madison, WI 53711

3420
St. Catherine Moran Foreign Language Scholarship

AMOUNT: $500-$1500 DEADLINE: March 15
FIELDS/MAJORS: Foreign Languages: French or Spanish

Applicants must be incoming freshmen who are interested in majoring in a foreign language. Applicants will arrange for an oral audition and submit a written essay. Edgewood offers majors in French and Spanish. Write to the address below for details.

Edgewood College
Office of Admissions
855 Woodrow St.
Madison, WI 53711

3421
Todd Wehr Edgedome Grant

AMOUNT: $250-$1500 DEADLINE: March 15
FIELDS/MAJORS: All Areas of Study.

Awards for freshmen, particularly those with an interest in intercollegiate athletics. Grant recipients will be required to spend two to three hours a week doing a service project for the Athletic Department. Applicant need not be on a team for consideration. Write to the address below for details.

Edgewood College
Office of Admissions
855 Woodrow Street
Madison, WI 53711

3422
Transfer Honor Scholarship

AMOUNT: $500-$1500 DEADLINE: December 1
FIELDS/MAJORS: All Areas of Study

Applicants must be transferring to Edgewood from another school with a minimum of 15 credits and a minimum 3.0 GPA. Renewable. For undergraduate study. Write to the address below for details.

Edgewood College
Office of Admissions
855 Woodrow Street
Madison, WI 53711

3423
Wisconsin Rural Rehabilitation Grant

AMOUNT: $500 DEADLINE: March 15
FIELDS/MAJORS: Nursing/Medical Technology

Applicants must be from Wisconsin farm families who have enrolled or are continuing study in nursing or medical technology at Edgewood. Write to the address below for details.

Edgewood College
Office of Admissions
855 Woodrow Street
Madison, WI 53711

ELIZABETH CITY STATE UNIVERSITY

3424
Dr. A.P. and Frances Dickson Scholarship

AMOUNT: None Specified DEADLINE: November 1
FIELDS/MAJORS: All Areas of Study

Awarded annually to a full-time undergraduate student who currently resides in Hoke County, North Carolina. Recipients are chosen by the Financial Aid Office on the basis of academic standing and financial need. Contact the address below for further information. There are three deadline dates: June 1 (academic year), November 1 (spring semester), and April 1 (summer).

Elizabeth City State University
Financial Aid Office
Parkview Dr.
Elizabeth City, NC 27909

3425
Incentive Scholarship and Grant Program For Native Americans

AMOUNT: $700-$3000 DEADLINE: November 1
FIELDS/MAJORS: All Areas of Study

Available to American Indian students who are residents of North Carolina. The need-based program provides awards of $700 per year to students with substantial need, and the merit-based provides awards of $3,000 per year to qualifying students. Contact the address below for further information. There are three deadline dates: June 1 (academic year), November 1 (spring semester), and April 1 (summer).

Elizabeth City State University
Financial Aid Office
Parkview Dr.
Elizabeth City, NC 27909

3426
James Lee Scholarship

AMOUNT: None Specified   DEADLINE: November 1
FIELDS/MAJORS: All Areas of Study

Awarded annually to a full-time North Carolina resident undergraduate student. Recipients are chosen by the Financial Aid Office on the basis of academic standing and financial need. Contact the address below for further information. There are three deadline dates: June 1 (academic year), November 1 (spring semester), and April 1 (summer).

Elizabeth City State University
Financial Aid Office
Parkview Dr.
Elizabeth City, NC 27909

3427
North Carolina Non-Service Scholarships

AMOUNT: None Specified   DEADLINE: November 1
FIELDS/MAJORS: All Areas of Study

Scholarships are available to qualified students with GPAs of at least 3.0 and demonstrated financial need. Contact the address below for further information. There are three deadline dates: June 1 (academic year), November 1 (spring semester), and April 1 (summer).

Elizabeth City State University
Financial Aid Office
Parkview Dr.
Elizabeth City, NC 27909

3428
North Carolina Sheriffs' Association Undergraduate Criminal Justice

AMOUNT: None Specified   DEADLINE: November 1
FIELDS/MAJORS: Criminal Justice

Awarded annually to a North Carolina resident undergraduate who is majoring in criminal justice. Recipients are chosen by the Financial Aid Office on the basis of academic standing and financial need. First preference is given to a son or daughter of any law enforcement officer killed in the line of duty. Second preference is given to a son or daughter of any sheriff or deputy sheriff who is deceased, retired (regular or disability), or currently active in North Carolina law enforcement. Third preference is given to any criminal justice student meeting the academic and financial need criteria. Contact the address below for further information. There are three deadline dates: June 1 (academic year), November 1 (spring semester), and April 1 (summer).

Elizabeth City State University
Financial Aid Office
Parkview Dr.
Elizabeth City, NC 27909

3429
Thurgood Marshall Scholarship

AMOUNT: $4000   DEADLINE: November 1
FIELDS/MAJORS: All Areas of Study

Awarded to an entering freshman. Applicant must be a U.S. citizen; be a full-time student pursuing a bachelor's degree in any discipline and maintain full-time status for the duration of the scholarship; have a high school GPA of not less than 3.0; have a combined score 1000 or more on the SAT or a score of 24 or more on the ACT; and have a letter of recommendation from a high school principal, counselor, teacher, or community service organization. Contact the address below for further information. There are three deadline dates: June 1 (academic year), November 1 (spring semester), and April 1 (summer).

Elizabeth City State University
Financial Aid Office
Parkview Dr.
Elizabeth City, NC 27909

3430
Vocational Rehabilitation Grants

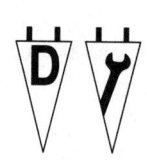

AMOUNT: None Specified   DEADLINE: November 1
FIELDS/MAJORS: All Areas of Study

Grants are available to students with any type of impairment/disability (speech, hearing, sight, rheumatic heart, missing limbs, crippling disabilities, etc.) Contact the local Vocational Rehabilitation Center for counseling, evaluation, and determination of their eligibility for these grants. There are three deadline dates: June 1 (academic year), November 1 (spring semester), and April 1 (summer).

Elizabeth City State University
Financial Aid Office
Parkview Dr.
Elizabeth City, NC 27909

ELIZABETHTOWN COLLEGE

3431
A.L.B. and Ellen R. Martin Memorial Scholarship

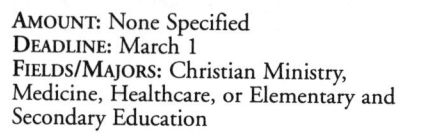

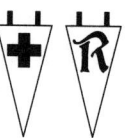

AMOUNT: None Specified
DEADLINE: March 1
FIELDS/MAJORS: Christian Ministry, Medicine, Healthcare, or Elementary and Secondary Education

Awarded to students who are preparing for full-time service in the Christian ministry, medicine, healthcare, or elementary and secondary education. Preference is given in the order of the career fields mentioned. Contact the address below for further information.

Elizabethtown College
M. Clarke Paine, Dir. of Financial Aid
One Alpha Dr.
Elizabethtown, PA 17022

3432
Alice L. Knouse Scholarship

AMOUNT: None Specified DEADLINE: March 1
FIELDS/MAJORS: Business

Awarded to a junior business major who possesses a high degree of academic achievement, service to the business department and the campus in general, and demonstrates financial need. The award will be used for the senior year. Contact the address below for further information.

Elizabethtown College
M. Clarke Paine, Dir. of Financial Aid
One Alpha Dr.
Elizabethtown, PA 17022

3433
Annette Mumma Nation Scholarship

AMOUNT: None Specified DEADLINE: March 1
FIELDS/MAJORS: All Areas of Study

Awarded to outstanding Elizabethtown College women who have balanced academics with their extracurricular activities and contributions to college life. Contact the address below for further information.

Elizabethtown College
M. Clarke Paine, Dir. of Financial Aid
One Alpha Dr.
Elizabethtown, PA 17022

3434
Benjamin G. and Vera B. Musser Pre-Medical Scholarship

AMOUNT: None Specified DEADLINE: March 1
FIELDS/MAJORS: Medical Profession

Awarded to a junior or senior student who evidences a sincere desire to pursue a career in the medical profession, and who is chosen on the basis of academic performance, financial need, and faculty letters of recommendation. Contact the address below for further information.

Elizabethtown College
M. Clarke Paine, Dir. of Financial Aid
One Alpha Dr.
Elizabethtown, PA 17022

3435
Cyrus B. Krall Memorial Scholarship

AMOUNT: None Specified DEADLINE: March 1
FIELDS/MAJORS: Religion, Philosophy, or Education

Awarded to students who are members of the Church of the Brethren and who are preparing for a career in the fields of religion and philosophy or education. Contact the address below for further information.

Elizabethtown College
M. Clarke Paine, Dir. of Financial Aid
One Alpha Dr.
Elizabethtown, PA 17022

3436
Edgar Lerr Ministerial Scholarship

AMOUNT: None Specified DEADLINE: March 1
FIELDS/MAJORS: Ministry

Awarded to a worthy student preparing for the ministry. Contact the address below for further information.

Elizabethtown College
M. Clarke Paine, Dir. of Financial Aid
One Alpha Dr.
Elizabethtown, PA 17022

3437
Elizabethtown College Presidential Scholarships

AMOUNT: $9000 DEADLINE: March 1
FIELDS/MAJORS: All Areas of Study

Awarded to academically superior entering freshmen. Students must rank in the top 2% of their secondary school class and must have taken a very challenging curriculum, have combined recentered SAT score of at least 1300 or ACT score of 29, plan to enroll in the College full-time (12 credit hours or more), and display good academic promise, citizenship, and extracurricular achievement. Contact the address below for further information. GPA must be at least 3.8.

Elizabethtown College
M. Clarke Paine, Dir. of Financial Aid
One Alpha Dr.
Elizabethtown, PA 17022

3438

Elizabethtown College Provost Scholarship

AMOUNT: $3000-$7000 DEADLINE: March 1
FIELDS/MAJORS: All Areas of Study

Awarded to entering students. Students must rank in the upper 10% of their secondary school class and must have taken a challenging curriculum, have combined recentered SAT score of at least 1150 or ACT score of 25, plan to enroll in the College full-time (12 credit hours or more), and display good academic promise, citizenship, and extracurricular achievement. Contact the address below for further information. GPA must be at least 3.0.

Elizabethtown College
M. Clarke Paine, Dir. of Financial Aid
One Alpha Dr.
Elizabethtown, PA 17022

3439

Fund for the Advancement of Ethnic Understanding

AMOUNT: None Specified DEADLINE: March 1
FIELDS/MAJORS: All Areas of Study

Awarded to underprivileged ethnic minorities in the form of scholarship aid or program aid. Contact the address below for further information.

Elizabethtown College
M. Clarke Paine, Dir. of Financial Aid
One Alpha Dr.
Elizabethtown, PA 17022

3440

Harold E. Smith Company Occupational Therapy Scholarship

AMOUNT: None Specified DEADLINE: March 1
FIELDS/MAJORS: Occupational Therapy

Awarded to a full-time sophomore (for the junior year) majoring in occupational therapy. The award is based upon academic achievement, scientific aptitude, personal character, and financial need. Contact the address below for further information.

Elizabethtown College
M. Clarke Paine, Dir. of Financial Aid
One Alpha Dr.
Elizabethtown, PA 17022

3441

Hazel Knappenberger Goddwin Memorial Elementary Education Scholarship

AMOUNT: None Specified DEADLINE: March 1
FIELDS/MAJORS: Elementary Education

Awarded to deserving students studying for a degree in elementary education. Contact the address below for further information.

Elizabethtown College
M. Clarke Paine, Dir. of Financial Aid
One Alpha Dr.
Elizabethtown, PA 17022

3442

Jenny Shinn Memorial Scholarship

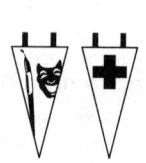

AMOUNT: None Specified DEADLINE: March 1
FIELDS/MAJORS: Music Therapy

Awarded to an upper-class music therapy major (or majors) who demonstrates the potential for outstanding service as a music therapist. Contact the address below for further information.

Elizabethtown College
M. Clarke Paine, Dir. of Financial Aid
One Alpha Dr.
Elizabethtown, PA 17022

3443

John P. Shepard, Jr. Scholarship

AMOUNT: None Specified DEADLINE: March 1
FIELDS/MAJORS: All Areas of Study

Awarded to a full-time upper-class student who shows excellence in academic achievement, extracurricular activities, and personal character. Contact the address below for further information.

Elizabethtown College
M. Clarke Paine, Dir. of Financial Aid
One Alpha Dr.
Elizabethtown, PA 17022

3444

John W. Hess Scholarship

AMOUNT: None Specified DEADLINE: March 1
FIELDS/MAJORS: Business, Education, or Music

Awarded to students demonstrating financial need majoring in business, education, or music with good academic standing. Contact the address below for further information.

Elizabethtown College
M. Clarke Paine, Dir. of Financial Aid
One Alpha Dr.
Elizabethtown, PA 17022

3445
Layser Scholarship

AMOUNT: None Specified   DEADLINE: March 1
FIELDS/MAJORS: Christian Ministry

Awarded to a deserving student demonstrating academic ability, citizenship, and financial need, and planning a career in Christian ministry. Contact the address below for further information.

Elizabethtown College
M. Clarke Paine, Dir. of Financial Aid
One Alpha Dr.
Elizabethtown, PA 17022

3446
Non-Traditional Occupational Therapy Scholarship

AMOUNT: None Specified   DEADLINE: March 1
FIELDS/MAJORS: Occupational Therapy

Awarded to a non-traditional student majoring in occupational therapy with financial need and academic promise. Contact the address below for further information.

Elizabethtown College
M. Clarke Paine, Dir. of Financial Aid
One Alpha Dr.
Elizabethtown, PA 17022

3447
Religion Scholarship

AMOUNT: None Specified   DEADLINE: March 1
FIELDS/MAJORS: Religion

Awarded to a deserving religion major who demonstrates financial need. Contact the address below for further information.

Elizabethtown College
M. Clarke Paine, Dir. of Financial Aid
One Alpha Dr.
Elizabethtown, PA 17022

3448
Ressler Mill Foundation Scholarship

AMOUNT: None Specified   DEADLINE: March 1
FIELDS/MAJORS: Occupational Therapy

Awarded to a full-time junior (for the senior year) majoring in occupational therapy. The award is based upon academic achievement, scientific aptitude, personal character, and financial need. Contact the address below for further information.

Elizabethtown College
M. Clarke Paine, Dir. of Financial Aid
One Alpha Dr.
Elizabethtown, PA 17022

3449
Rettew Associates, Inc. Scholarship

AMOUNT: None Specified   DEADLINE: March 1
FIELDS/MAJORS: Environmental Science

Awarded to an environmental science major with an overall GPA of 3.0 or higher who demonstrates financial need. Contact the address below for further information.

Elizabethtown College
M. Clarke Paine, Dir. of Financial Aid
One Alpha Dr.
Elizabethtown, PA 17022

3450
Sallie K. and Charles D. Schaeffer Chemistry Scholarship

AMOUNT: None Specified   DEADLINE: March 1
FIELDS/MAJORS: Chemistry

Awarded to a chemistry major with a 3.0 GPA or greater in the major as well as cumulative. Contact the address below for further information.

Elizabethtown College
M. Clarke Paine, Dir. of Financial Aid
One Alpha Dr.
Elizabethtown, PA 17022

3451
Sheldon S. R. Madeira Scholarship

AMOUNT: None Specified   DEADLINE: March 1
FIELDS/MAJORS: Education

Awarded to a student or students preparing for a career in education who exhibits ability for college study, shows need for financial aid, and displays strong campus citizenship qualities. Contact the address below for further information.

Elizabethtown College
M. Clarke Paine, Dir. of Financial Aid
One Alpha Dr.
Elizabethtown, PA 17022

ELON COLLEGE

3452
Athletic Scholarships

AMOUNT: None Specified   DEADLINE: February 15
FIELDS/MAJORS: All Areas of Study

Available to students who are participating in the Intercollegiate Athletics Program. These awards are based on performance in compliance with NCAA regulations. Amount of awards varies. Contact the athletics department at Elon for information.

Elon College
Athletic Department
2700 Campus Box
Elon College, NC 27244

3453
Fine Arts Scholarships

AMOUNT: $200-$7500   DEADLINE: February 15
FIELDS/MAJORS: Music, Theater

Available to outstanding incoming freshmen who will be pursuing a major in theater or music. Based upon an audition. Write to the address below for details.

Elon College
Fine Arts Department
2700 Campus Box
Elon College, NC 27244

3454
Honors Fellowships

AMOUNT: $2000-$5000   DEADLINE: February 15
FIELDS/MAJORS: All Areas of Study

Available to incoming freshmen with a high school record of academic excellence and high test scores. Competition is held in the spring of each year. Award includes one $500 travel grant. Write to the address below for details. GPA must be at least 3.5.

Elon College
Office of Financial Planning
2700 Campus Box
Elon College, NC 27244

3455
Isabella Cannon Leadership Fellows Scholarships

AMOUNT: Maximum: $2000   DEADLINE: February 1
FIELDS/MAJORS: All Areas of Study

Available to full-time students who demonstrate a high school record of academic excellence, high test scores, and leadership abilities. Write to the address below for details. GPA must be at least 3.0.

Elon College
Office of Financial Planning
2700 Campus Box
Elon College, NC 27244

3456
Jefferson-Pilot Business Fellows Scholarships

AMOUNT: Maximum: $2000   DEADLINE: February 1
FIELDS/MAJORS: Business, Economics, Accounting

Open to incoming Fellows, admitted to Elon College, who are majoring or minoring in either business administration, economics, or accounting. Write to the address below for details. GPA must be at least 3.0.

Elon College
Office of Financial Planning
2700 Campus Box
Elon College, NC 27244

3457
North Carolina Teaching Fellowships

AMOUNT: $10000   DEADLINE: February 15
FIELDS/MAJORS: Education

Awards are available to students pursuing a career in teaching. Recipients must teach for four years in a North Carolina public school after graduation. Award consists of up to $10,000 for four years plus air fare to London for one semester and program-related expenses for two winter term courses. Write to the address below for details.

Elon College
Office of Financial Planning
2700 Campus Box
Elon College, NC 27244

3458
Presidential Scholarships

AMOUNT: $1000-$3000 DEADLINE: February 15
FIELDS/MAJORS: All Areas of Study

Available to incoming freshmen with superior academics and ACT or SAT test scores. Based on class rank and/or GPA and SAT/ACT scores. No separate application is needed. Scholarships are automatically awarded to students who meet the necessary criteria. Renewable. Write to the address below for details. GPA must be at least 3.0.

Elon College
Office of Financial Planning
2700 Campus Box
Elon College, NC 27244

3459
ROTC Scholarships

AMOUNT: None Specified DEADLINE: February 15
FIELDS/MAJORS: All Areas of Study

Available to students who will be participating in the Army ROTC program. Award is full tuition, books, and $100 per month. Elon provides all four-year ROTC scholarship recipients free room and board. Write to the address below for details.

Elon College
Office of Financial Planning
2700 Campus Box
Elon College, NC 27244

3460
Science Fellows Scholarship

AMOUNT: Maximum: $2000 DEADLINE: February 1
FIELDS/MAJORS: Biology, Chemistry, Computer Science, Mathematics, Physics

Awards are available for incoming freshmen, admitted to Elon College, in the areas of study listed above. Based on academics, recommendations, and an on-campus interview. Renewable. Nominations to compete for a Science Fellows Scholarship are made by the Office of Admissions. Write to the address listed for details.

Elon College
Office of Financial Aid
2700 Campus Box
Elon College, NC 27244

3461
UCC Ministerial Discount

AMOUNT: $500-$1000 DEADLINE: February 15
FIELDS/MAJORS: All Areas of Study

Available to full-time students who are dependent children of full-time ministers in the United Church of Christ. Write to the address below for details.

Elon College
Office of Financial Planning
2700 Campus Box
Elon College, NC 27244

EMBRY-RIDDLE UNIVERSITY

3462
Colonel Louisa Spruance Morse CAP Scholarships

AMOUNT: None Specified DEADLINE: April 1
FIELDS/MAJORS: Aeronautics/Aviation

Applicants must be CAP members or former CAP members currently enrolled in Air Force ROTC at Embry-Riddle University. Contact your ROTC instructor for details.

Civil Air Patrol
National Headquarters Cap (TT)
Maxwell AFB, AL 36112

EMERSON COLLEGE

3463
Emerson Grants

AMOUNT: None Specified DEADLINE: March 1
FIELDS/MAJORS: All Areas of Study

Awarded to enrolled, full-time students who demonstrate financial need. Students must apply for aid each year. Write to the address below for complete details.

Emerson College
Office of Financial Aid
100 Beacon St.
Boston, MA 02116

3464

President's Awards

AMOUNT: None Specified   DEADLINE: March 1
FIELDS/MAJORS: All Areas of Study

President's awards are for students admitted to the honors program who show a demonstrated financial need. Students must be enrolled full-time and must apply for aid each year. For undergraduate study. Write to the address below for complete details.

Emerson College
Office of Financial Aid
100 Beacon St.
Boston, MA 02116

3465

State Scholarship Programs

AMOUNT: None Specified   DEADLINE: March 1
FIELDS/MAJORS: All Areas of Study

The following states currently allow their grants/scholarships to be used at Emerson: Connecticut, Delaware, District of Columbia, Maine, Maryland, Massachusetts, New Hampshire, Pennsylvania, Rhode island, and Vermont. If you are a resident of one of these states, you should contact your state scholarship agency for application procedures and deadlines. Write to the address below for more information.

Emerson College
Office of Financial Aid
100 Beacon St.
Boston, MA 02116

EMORY UNIVERSITY

3466

Alben W. Barkley Debate Scholars

AMOUNT: None Specified   DEADLINE: None Specified
FIELDS/MAJORS: All Areas of Study

Awards are available at Emory University for freshman students who are outstanding debaters. Write to the address below or call (404) 727-6036 or 1-800-727-6036 for information.

Emory University
Melissa Wade, Director of Barkley Forum
Drawer U
Atlanta, GA 30322

3467

Charles and Ann Duncan Scholars

AMOUNT: None Specified   DEADLINE: None Specified
FIELDS/MAJORS: All Areas of Study

Awards are available at Emory University for undergraduate students who demonstrate academic excellence and leadership potential. Preference is given to students from Texas and the Southwest. Write to the address below or call (404) 727-6036 or 1-800-727-6036 for information. GPA must be at least 3.0.

Emory University
Office of Admission
200 Boisfeuillet Jones Center
Atlanta, GA 30322

3468

Chris A. Yannopoulos Scholars

AMOUNT: None Specified   DEADLINE: None Specified
FIELDS/MAJORS: Classical Studies

Awards are available at Emory University for undergraduate students who demonstrate academic excellence and leadership potential. Write to the address below or call (404) 727-6036 or 1-800-727-6036 for information. GPA must be at least 3.0.

Emory University
Office of Admission
200 Boisfeuillet Jones Center
Atlanta, GA 30322

3469

Courtesy Scholarships

AMOUNT: None Specified   DEADLINE: None Specified
FIELDS/MAJORS: All Areas of Study

Awards are available at Emory University for children of Emory faculty and staff. Write to the address below or call (404) 727-6039 or 1-800-727-6039 for information.

Emory University
Office of Human Resources
Atlanta, GA 30322

3470

D. Abbott Turner Scholars

AMOUNT: None Specified   DEADLINE: None Specified
FIELDS/MAJORS: All Areas of Study

Awards are available at Emory University for undergraduate students who demonstrate academic excellence and leadership potential. Preference is given to students who graduated from Brookstone School in Columbus, then to students from the Chattahoochee Valley area. Write to the address below or call (404) 727-6036 or 1-800-727-6036 for information. GPA must be at least 3.0.

Emory University
Office of Admission
200 Boisfeuillet Jones Center
Atlanta, GA 30322

3471
Emory College Scholarships

AMOUNT: None Specified DEADLINE: None Specified
FIELDS/MAJORS: All Areas of Study

Awards are available at Emory University for undergraduate students who demonstrate academic excellence and leadership potential. Includes the Flora Glenn Candler, Ignatius Alphonso Few, Augustus Baldwin Longstreet, Dumas Malone, Kemp Malone, David M. Potter, and Alexander Means Scholarships. Requirements vary. Write to the address below or call (404) 727-6036 or 1-800-727-6036 for information. GPA must be at least 3.0.

Emory University
Office of Admission
200 Boisfeuillet Jones Center
Atlanta, GA 30322

3472
Emory National Merit Scholarships

AMOUNT: $750-$2000 DEADLINE: None Specified
FIELDS/MAJORS: All Areas of Study

Awards are available at Emory University for entering freshmen who were National Merit finalists that listed Emory University as their first college of choice. Recipients with demonstrated financial need will receive up to $2000, while all others will receive $750. Write to the address below or call (404) 727-6039 or 1-800-727-6039 for information.

Emory University
Office of Financial Aid
300 Boisfeuillet Jones Center
Atlanta, GA 30322

3473
Henry L. Bowden, Edward D. Smith, Pollard Turman Leadership Scholars

AMOUNT: None Specified DEADLINE: None Specified
FIELDS/MAJORS: All Areas of Study

Awards are available at Emory University for undergraduate students who demonstrate academic excellence and leadership potential. Preference is given to students from Atlanta, then Georgia, then the southeastern U.S. Write to the address below or call (404) 727-6036 or 1-800-727-6036 for information. GPA must be at least 3.0.

Emory University
Office of Admission
200 Boisfeuillet Jones Center
Atlanta, GA 30322

3474
Martin Luther King, Jr., Scholars

AMOUNT: None Specified DEADLINE: None Specified
FIELDS/MAJORS: All Areas of Study

Awards are available at Emory University for undergraduate students who graduated from Atlanta public schools. Write to the address below or call (404) 727-6036 or 1-800-727-6036 for information.

Emory University
Office of Admission
200 Boisfeuillet Jones Center
Atlanta, GA 30322

3475
Methodist Ministerial Scholarships

AMOUNT: None Specified DEADLINE: None Specified
FIELDS/MAJORS: All Areas of Study

Awards are available at Emory University for children of active United Methodist ministers or missionaries. Write to the address below or call (404) 727-6039 or 1-800-727-6039 for information.

Emory University
Office of Financial Aid
300 Boisfeuillet Jones Center
Atlanta, GA 30322

3476
Robert W. Woodruff Scholars

AMOUNT: None Specified DEADLINE: None Specified
FIELDS/MAJORS: All Areas of Study

Awards are available at Emory University for undergraduate students with clearly demonstrated outstanding academic ability, leadership skills, unselfish character, and intellectual and personal vigor. Write to the address below or call (404) 727-6036 or 1-800-727-6036 for information. GPA must be at least 3.6.

Emory University
Office of Admission
200 Boisfeuillet Jones Center
Atlanta, GA 30322

EVANGEL COLLEGE

3477
Assembly of God 50% Tuition Discount

AMOUNT: $3650 DEADLINE: February 15
FIELDS/MAJORS: All Areas of Study

Scholarships are available at Evangel for full-time students who are legal dependents of nationally appointed full-time Assemblies of God foreign or home missionaries, active duty chaplains, Assembly of God College faculty members, or employees of General Council of the Assemblies of God. Write to the address below for information.

Evangel College
Office of Enrollment
1111 N. Glenstone
Springfield, MO 65802

3478
Athletic Scholarships

AMOUNT: None Specified DEADLINE: February 15
FIELDS/MAJORS: All Areas of Study

Scholarships are available at Evangel for full-time students who plan to participate in the intercollegiate athletics program. Write to the address below for information.

Evangel College
Director of Athletics
Springfield, MO 65802

3479
Behavioral Science Endowed and Private Scholarships

AMOUNT: None Specified DEADLINE: February 15
FIELDS/MAJORS: Behavioral Sciences

Scholarships are available at Evangel for full-time students who will be or are pursuing a degree in the behavioral sciences. Applicants must have GPAs of at least 3.0. Other requirements vary. Includes the Mary Ann McCorcle Memorial Scholarship, the Dr. Billie Davis Sociology Scholarship, the Behavioral Science Alumni Scholarship, and Amy Dawn Marks Memorial Scholarship. Write to the address below for information.

Evangel College
Office of Enrollment
1111 N. Glenstone
Springfield, MO 65802

3480
Biblical Studies Endowed and Private Scholarships

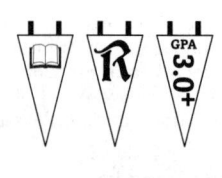

AMOUNT: None Specified DEADLINE: February 15
FIELDS/MAJORS: Biblical Studies

Scholarships are available at Evangel for full-time students who will be or are pursuing a degree in Biblical studies. Applicants must have GPAs of at least 3.0. Includes the Glen and Ann Ahlf, Julia LaBruto, L.L. Jack and Alma Mae Thornton Memorial, Denny Duron Evangelistic, Phi Sigma Tau Philosophy Honor Society, the Biblical Studies Alumni, Mel Blakeney Memorial Scholarship, and Alexander A. Vazakas Memorial Scholarships. Write to the address below for information.

Evangel College
Office of Enrollment
1111 N. Glenstone
Springfield, MO 65802

3481
Business and Economics Endowed and Private Scholarships

AMOUNT: None Specified DEADLINE: February 15
FIELDS/MAJORS: Business, Economics

Scholarships are available at Evangel for full-time students who will be or are pursuing a degree in business or economics. Applicants must have GPAs of at least 3.0. Includes the Troy and Marjorie Compton, Charles W. Elmendorf Memorial, Max and Audrey Phraim, Allen and Udell Lawrence, Phi Beta Lambda Club, the Business and Economics Alumni, and Baird, Kurtz, and Dobson Scholarships. Write to the address below for information.

Evangel College
Office of Enrollment
1111 N. Glenstone
Springfield, MO 65802

3482
Communications Endowed and Private Scholarships

AMOUNT: None Specified DEADLINE: February 15
FIELDS/MAJORS: Communications

Scholarships are available at Evangel for full-time students who will be or are pursuing a degree in communications. Applicants must have GPAs of at least 3.0. Includes the Dr. Nonna D. Dalan Memorial Speech Scholarship, the Society for Collegiate Journalists Scholarship, the Inez H. Spence Memorial Scholarship, and the Communications Alumni Scholarship. Write to the address below for information.

Evangel College
Office of Enrollment
1111 N. Glenstone
Springfield, MO 65802

3483
David M. Webb Computer Science Scholarship

AMOUNT: None Specified DEADLINE: February 15
FIELDS/MAJORS: Computer Science, Information Technology

Scholarships are available at Evangel for full-time students who will be or are pursuing a career in computer science. Applicants must have GPAs of at least 3.0. Write to the address below for information.

Evangel College
Office of Enrollment
1111 N. Glenstone
Springfield, MO 65802

3484
Education Endowed and Private Scholarships

AMOUNT: None Specified DEADLINE: February 15
FIELDS/MAJORS: Education

Scholarships are available at Evangel for full-time students who will be or are pursuing a degree in education. Applicants must have GPAs of at least 3.0. Includes the Thomas and Laura Ardovino Memorial, John Dickinson Memorial, Harland A. Kingsriter Memorial, Bessye Hillin Memorial, Rev. and Mrs. T.H. Spence, Jan Sylvester Memorial, and the Education Alumni Scholarships. Write to the address below for information.

Evangel College
Office of Enrollment
1111 N. Glenstone
Springfield, MO 65802

3485
Forensics Scholarships

AMOUNT: None Specified DEADLINE: February 15
FIELDS/MAJORS: All Areas of Study

Scholarships are available at Evangel for full-time students who plan to participate in the forensics (debate) program. Write to the address below for information.

Evangel College
Chairperson
Communications Department
Springfield, MO 65802

3486
Gene L. Mills Engineering Scholarship

AMOUNT: None Specified DEADLINE: February 15
FIELDS/MAJORS: Engineering

Scholarships are available at Evangel for full-time students who will be or are pursuing a career in engineering. Applicants must have GPAs of at least 3.0. Write to the address below for information.

Evangel College
Office of Enrollment
1111 N. Glenstone
Springfield, MO 65802

3487
Health, Physical Education, and Recreation Endowed and Private Scholarships

AMOUNT: None Specified DEADLINE: February 15
FIELDS/MAJORS: Health, Physical Education, Recreation

Scholarships are available at Evangel for full-time students who will be or are pursuing a degree in the above fields. Applicants must have GPAs of at least 3.0. Includes the Holsinger Athletic Academic Excellence Scholarship, Stair Family Athletic Scholarship, Dr. Donald Pearson Physical Education Scholarship, and the HPER Alumni Scholarship. Write to the address below for information.

Evangel College
Office of Enrollment
1111 N. Glenstone
Springfield, MO 65802

3488
Humanities Endowed and Private Scholarships

AMOUNT: None Specified DEADLINE: February 15
FIELDS/MAJORS: Humanities

Scholarships are available at Evangel for full-time students pursuing a degree in the humanities. Applicants must have GPAs of at least 3.0. Includes the Ira J. Bixler Memorial, Leland and Avis DeSpain Endowed, Elsie M. Elmendorf Memorial, Ben Messick F.R.S.A. Memorial, Christopher L. Moore, Dorothy Mae Riepma Memorial, the Sara Mudd Drama, and the Humanities Alumni Scholarships. Write to the address below for information.

Evangel College
Office of Enrollment
1111 N. Glenstone
Springfield, MO 65802

3489
Music Endowed and Private Scholarships

AMOUNT: None Specified DEADLINE: February 15
FIELDS/MAJORS: Music

Scholarships are available at Evangel for full-time students pursuing a degree in music. Applicants must have GPAs of at least 3.0. Includes eighteen different awards. Requirements vary. Write to the address below for information.

Evangel College
Office of Enrollment
1111 N. Glenstone
Springfield, MO 65802

3490
Music Scholarships

AMOUNT: None Specified DEADLINE: February 15
FIELDS/MAJORS: Music

Scholarships are available at Evangel for full-time students who are pursuing or plan to pursue a degree in music. Write to the address below for information.

Evangel College
Chairperson
Music Department
Springfield, MO 65802

3491
Presidential, Academic Achievement, College Honor Scholarships

AMOUNT: $1000-$2000 DEADLINE: February 15
FIELDS/MAJORS: All Areas of Study

Scholarships are available at Evangel for freshmen/transfer students who demonstrate academic achievement in high school. Based upon a combination of GPA and test scores. Write to the address below for information. GPA must be at least 3.0.

Evangel College
Office of Enrollment
1111 N. Glenstone
Springfield, MO 65802

3492
ROTC Scholarship

AMOUNT: None Specified DEADLINE: February 15
FIELDS/MAJORS: All Areas of Study

Scholarships are available at Evangel for full-time students who will be participating in the ROTC program. Write to the address below for information. GPA must be at least 3.0.

Evangel College
Office of Enrollment
1111 N. Glenstone
Springfield, MO 65802

3493
Science and Technology Private and Endowed Scholarships

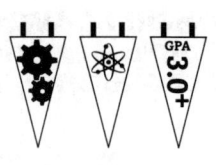

AMOUNT: None Specified DEADLINE: February 15
FIELDS/MAJORS: Science and Technology Related Fields

Scholarships are available at Evangel for full-time students who will be or are pursuing a science and technology-related career. Applicants must have GPAs of at least 3.0. Includes the Herbert S. Killen Memorial Scholarship, the David M. Webb Scholarships, the Science and Technology Alumni Scholarships, and the Virginia E. Pinckney Memorial Scholarships. Write to the address below for information.

Evangel College
Office of Enrollment
1111 N. Glenstone
Springfield, MO 65802

3494
Social Science Endowed and Private Scholarships

AMOUNT: None Specified DEADLINE: February 15
FIELDS/MAJORS: Social Sciences

Scholarships are available at Evangel for full-time students pursuing a degree in the social sciences. Applicants must have GPAs of at least 3.0. Includes fourteen different awards. Requirements vary. Write to the address below for information.

Evangel College
Office of Enrollment
1111 N. Glenstone
Springfield, MO 65802

3495
Thomas F. Zimmerman Ministerial Grant

AMOUNT: $730 DEADLINE: February 15
FIELDS/MAJORS: All Areas of Study

Scholarships are available at Evangel for full-time students who are legal dependents of nationally appointed full-time Assemblies of God ministers who can demonstrate great financial need. Write to the address below for information.

Evangel College
Office of Enrollment
1111 N. Glenstone
Springfield, MO 65802

3496

Valedictorian Scholarships

AMOUNT: $500 DEADLINE: February 15
FIELDS/MAJORS: All Areas of Study

Scholarships are available at Evangel for full-time freshman students who graduated at the top of their high school class. Write to the address below for information.

Evangel College
Office of Enrollment
1111 N. Glenstone
Springfield, MO 65802

3497

Wanda Cuthbertson Nursing Memorial Scholarship

AMOUNT: None Specified DEADLINE: February 15
FIELDS/MAJORS: Nursing

Scholarships are available at Evangel for full-time students pursuing a degree in nursing. Applicants must have GPAs of at least 3.0. Write to the address below for information.

Evangel College
Office of Enrollment
1111 N. Glenstone
Springfield, MO 65802

EVERGREEN STATE COLLEGE

3498

Bennett/Roussos Scholarship

AMOUNT: $2000 DEADLINE: February 3
FIELDS/MAJORS: All Areas of Study

Offered to a new or returning student who is enrolled full-time and demonstrates a genuine and continuing passion for a particular area of study or interest. The applicant must demonstrate focus in the area identified, as well as a sense of curiosity and commitment to learning. Contact the address below for further information.

Evergreen State College
Office of the Dean of Enrollment Service
2700 Evergreen Parkway
Olympia, WA 98505-0002

3499

Byron Youtz Memorial Scholarship

AMOUNT: $1000 DEADLINE: February 3
FIELDS/MAJORS: Natural Sciences or Humanities/Art

Offered to a returning Evergreen student enrolled full-time with junior or senior standing for the academic year. Applicants must demonstrate a commitment to study in either the natural sciences or humanities/arts and must give evidence of strong personal interest in the alternate discipline. Contact the address below for further information.

Evergreen State College
Office of the Dean of Enrollment Service
2700 Evergreen Parkway
Olympia, WA 98505-0002

3500

Carleton Morris Cooley Scholarship

AMOUNT: $500 DEADLINE: February 3
FIELDS/MAJORS: English

Offered to a currently enrolled Evergreen student who will have senior standing for the academic year, demonstrates excellence in writing in the English language, and has accumulated the equivalent of 48 quarter hour credits in English courses. Preference will be given to students who participate in college governance. Contact the address below for further information.

Evergreen State College
Office of the Dean of Enrollment Service
2700 Evergreen Parkway
Olympia, WA 98505-0002

3501

Charles J. McCann Scholarship

AMOUNT: $750 DEADLINE: February 3
FIELDS/MAJORS: All Areas of Study

Offered to an Evergreen student with senior standing for the academic year who will be attending full-time and has completed at least three quarters at Evergreen at the time of application. The applicant must show the capacity to work well with others and demonstrate the ability to successfully carry out a plan of study. Preference will be given to students demonstrating financial need. Contact the address below for further information.

Evergreen State College
Office of the Dean of Enrollment Service
2700 Evergreen Parkway
Olympia, WA 98505-0002

3502
Clearwood Scholarship

AMOUNT: $350   DEADLINE: February 3
FIELDS/MAJORS: All Areas of Study

Offered to a currently enrolled student of ethnic background attending Evergreen full-time who can demonstrate a commitment to enhancing multiculturalism at the college. Student must demonstrate financial need. Contact the address below for further information.

Evergreen State College
Office of the Dean of Enrollment Service
2700 Evergreen Parkway
Olympia, WA 98505-0002

3503
Ethel MacPhail Scholarship

AMOUNT: $2000   DEADLINE: February 3
FIELDS/MAJORS: Business Management, Business Administration, Management Science, or Economics

Offered to an upper-division (junior or senior) female student who is attending full-time, with strong academic standing concentrating in a field related to business management (business administration, management science, economics, etc.), and with demonstrated financial need. Contact the address below for further information.

Evergreen State College
Office of the Dean of Enrollment Service
2700 Evergreen Parkway
Olympia, WA 98505-0002

3504
Evergreen State College Alumni Association Scholarship

AMOUNT: $1000   DEADLINE: February 3
FIELDS/MAJORS: All Areas of Study

Offered to an undergraduate student enrolled full-time who has completed at least 40 credits at Evergreen (at the time of application) and is at least twenty-five years of age. The applicant must also demonstrate financial need. Contact the address below for further information.

Evergreen State College
Office of the Dean of Enrollment Service
2700 Evergreen Parkway
Olympia, WA 98505-0002

3505
Evergreen State College Foundation Scholarship

AMOUNT: None Specified   DEADLINE: February 3
FIELDS/MAJORS: Music, Art, Journalism, or Science

Offered to new students entering Evergreen in the fall quarter as full-time undergraduate students. Scholarships are awarded to students who have distinguished themselves in a wide range of areas, e.g., high academic achievement, community service, music, art, journalism, science, etc. Contact the address below for further information.

Evergreen State College
Office of the Dean of Enrollment Service
2700 Evergreen Parkway
Olympia, WA 98505-0002

3506
First Peoples' Scholarship

AMOUNT: None Specified   DEADLINE: February 3
FIELDS/MAJORS: Music, Art, Journalism, or Science

Offered to a new students of ethnic background (Asian, African-American, Hispanic, Native American) entering Evergreen in the fall quarter as full-time undergraduate students. Scholarships are awarded to students who have distinguished themselves in a wide range of areas, e.g., high academic achievement, community service, music, art, journalism, science, etc. Contact the address below for further information.

Evergreen State College
Office of the Dean of Enrollment Service
2700 Evergreen Parkway
Olympia, WA 98505-0002

3507
Jackie Robinson Memorial Scholarship

AMOUNT: $500   DEADLINE: February 3
FIELDS/MAJORS: All Areas of Study

Offered to a currently enrolled junior or senior student of ethnic background (Asian, African-American, Hispanic, Native American) attending Evergreen full-time. This scholarship seeks to recognize a student for academic achievement and outstanding commitment to community involvement and social justice. Contact the address below for further information.

Evergreen State College
Office of the Dean of Enrollment Service
2700 Evergreen Parkway
Olympia, WA 98505-0002

3508
Juno Scholarship

AMOUNT: $3000 DEADLINE: None Specified
FIELDS/MAJORS: Drawing, Painting, or Printmaking

Awarded annually to a continuing student who shows great promise as an artist in drawing, painting, or printmaking, who can demonstrate financial need, and who will be a full-time student for the academic year. Contact the address below for further information. There are two deadline dates Part One is due April 1, and Part Two is due May 10.

Evergreen State College
Office of the Dean of Enrollment Service
2700 Evergreen Parkway
Olympia, WA 98505-0002

3509
Mark Blakley Memorial Award

AMOUNT: $750 DEADLINE: February 3
FIELDS/MAJORS: Fine Arts

Offered to a new or currently enrolled student attending Evergreen full-time who is pursuing the fine arts (including writing, painting, sculpture, photography, etc.). Award will go to a student who shows talent, potential, and creativity. Contact the address below for further information.

Evergreen State College
Office of the Dean of Enrollment Service
2700 Evergreen Parkway
Olympia, WA 98505-0002

3510
Merv Cadwallader Scholarship

AMOUNT: $500 DEADLINE: February 3
FIELDS/MAJORS: All Areas of study

Offered to a new or currently enrolled Evergreen student with junior or senior standing for the academic year who will be attending full-time. The applicant must demonstrate, through previous academic work and extracurricular activities, a personal commitment to the betterment of society through good citizenship and community involvement. Preference will be given to students demonstrating financial need. Contact the address below for further information.

Evergreen State College
Office of the Dean of Enrollment Service
2700 Evergreen Parkway
Olympia, WA 98505-0002

3511
Microsoft Alumni Scholarship

AMOUNT: $1000 DEADLINE: February 3
FIELDS/MAJORS: Computers

Offered to a new or returning student with sophomore, junior, or senior standing for the academic year who has demonstrated the goal of applying technology (use of computers, computer software, electron communications, or digital media) to their discipline of study through past individual or academic projects. Financial need must be demonstrated. Contact the address below for further information.

Evergreen State College
Office of the Dean of Enrollment Service
2700 Evergreen Parkway
Olympia, WA 98505-0002

3512
Non Sequitur Scholarship

AMOUNT: $1900 DEADLINE: February 3
FIELDS/MAJORS: All Areas of Study

Offered to a currently enrolled student attending Evergreen full-time for the academic year. Contact the address below for further information.

Evergreen State College
Office of the Dean of Enrollment Service
2700 Evergreen Parkway
Olympia, WA 98505-0002

3513
Roger F. Camp Memorial Scholarship

AMOUNT: $100 DEADLINE: February 3
FIELDS/MAJORS: All Areas of Study

Offered to a full-time, second-year Evergreen student demonstrating exceptional financial need. Contact the address below for further information.

Evergreen State College
Office of the Dean of Enrollment Service
2700 Evergreen Parkway
Olympia, WA 98505-0002

3514
Shauna May Memorial Scholarship

AMOUNT: $1000 DEADLINE: February 3
FIELDS/MAJORS: Humanities, Literature, History, Philosophy, Anthropology, Psychology, or Religion

Offered to a new or currently enrolled student, with junior or senior standing, attending Evergreen full-time, who is pursuing studies in the humanities: literature, history, philosophy, anthropology, psychology, or religion. Contact the address below for further information.

Evergreen State College
Office of the Dean of Enrollment Service
2700 Evergreen Parkway
Olympia, WA 98505-0002

3515
Soroptimist International of Olympia Endowment Scholarship

AMOUNT: $500 DEADLINE: February 1
FIELDS/MAJORS: All Areas of Study

Offered to a new or currently enrolled Evergreen female student who has completed a minimum of 45 credits at the time of application, with demonstrated involvement in community activities/services. The successful applicant must enroll as a full-time student. Contact the address below for further information.

Evergreen State College
Office of the Dean of Enrollment Service
2700 Evergreen Parkway
Olympia, WA 98505-0002

3516
Steven Gibson Memorial Scholarship

AMOUNT: $800 DEADLINE: February 3
FIELDS/MAJORS: All Areas of Study

Offered to a currently enrolled student who has completed at least one quarter at Evergreen and plans to attend full-time for the academic year. The applicant must demonstrate financial need. Contact the address below for further information.

Evergreen State College
Office of the Dean of Enrollment Service
2700 Evergreen Parkway
Olympia, WA 98505-0002

3517
Ward Bowden Memorial Scholarship

AMOUNT: $250 DEADLINE: February 3
FIELDS/MAJORS: Journalism or Political Science

Offered to a new or currently enrolled student attending Evergreen full-time who demonstrates an interest in journalism or political science. Contact the address below for further information.

Evergreen State College
Office of the Dean of Enrollment Service
2700 Evergreen Parkway
Olympia, WA 98505-0002

3518
Zonta Club of Olympia Scholarship

AMOUNT: $500 DEADLINE: February 3
FIELDS/MAJORS: All Areas of Study

Offered to a currently enrolled female Evergreen student attending at least half-time, who is twenty-three years or older as of March 15, 1997, and who has at that date been a resident of Thurston County for at least twelve consecutive months. Applicants should demonstrate an interest in business or the professions (legal, medical, etc.) and personal commitment to improving the legal, political, economic, and professional status of women. Contact the address below for further information.

Evergreen State College
Office of the Dean of Enrollment Service
2700 Evergreen Parkway
Olympia, WA 98505-0002

FALMOUTH UNIVERSITY

3519
Falmouth Institute Scholarships

AMOUNT: Maximum: $1000 DEADLINE: May 1
FIELDS/MAJORS: All Areas of Study

Scholarships are available for American Indian graduating high school seniors. One award is offered annually. Write to the address below for information.

Falmouth Institute
3918 Prosperity, Suite 302
Fairfax, VA 22031

FASHION INSTITUTE OF TECHNOLOGY

3520

FIT Scholarships, FIT Grants

AMOUNT: Maximum: $2500   DEADLINE: None Specified
FIELDS/MAJORS: All Areas of Study

Available to full-time undergraduates who can demonstrate financial need. Some scholarships require maintaining GPAs of at least 3.0. Contact the office of financial aid at the address below for further information or call (212) 217-7684.

Fashion Institute of Technology
Scholarship Chairman
27th and 7th Ave.
New York, NY 10001

FAULKNER UNIVERSITY

3521

Academic Excellence Award

AMOUNT: None Specified   DEADLINE: None Specified
FIELDS/MAJORS: All Areas of Study

Open to valedictorians or salutatorians of Alabama high schools who are Alabama residents. Must be admitted to Faulkner. Awards consist of tuition and room and board. Applicants must be Alabama residents. Other top scholars in a school of more than one hundred students may qualify. A minimum GPA of 3.4 is required to maintain the award. Contact the address below for further information or call (334) 260-6200.

Faulkner University
Office of Admissions
5345 Atlanta Highway
Montgomery, AL 36109

3522

Bible Award

AMOUNT: Maximum: $2000   DEADLINE: None Specified
FIELDS/MAJORS: Biblical Studies

Open to enrolled students who have completed at least 60 hours toward a Bible degree. Renewable if recipients demonstrate satisfactory academic progress. Applicants must be Alabama residents. Maximum award from all University sources cannot exceed $3000. Contact the address below for further information or call (334) 260-6200.

Faulkner University
Office of Admissions
5345 Atlanta Highway
Montgomery, AL 36109

3523

Bible Bowl Award

AMOUNT: Maximum: $500   DEADLINE: None Specified
FIELDS/MAJORS: All Areas of Study

Open to admitted incoming freshmen who are/were Bible Bowl team members. Renewable if recipients demonstrate satisfactory academic progress. Applicants must also be Alabama residents. Contact the address below for further information or call (334) 260-6200.

Faulkner University
Office of Admissions
5345 Atlanta Highway
Montgomery, AL 36109

3524

Minister's Child Award

AMOUNT: Maximum: $500   DEADLINE: None Specified
FIELDS/MAJORS: All Areas of Study

Open to incoming freshmen, admitted to Faulkner, who are Alabama residents. Must have a parent who is a minister who derives at least 50% of his income from church work. Contact the address below for further information or call (334) 260-6200.

Faulkner University
Office of Admissions
5345 Atlanta Highway
Montgomery, AL 36109

3525

President's List Scholarship

AMOUNT: Maximum: $500   DEADLINE: None Specified
FIELDS/MAJORS: All Areas of Study

Open to students enrolled at Faulkner with a minimum GPA of 3.96 for two consecutive semesters. The 3.96 must have been earned at Faulkner and maintained to keep the award. Contact the address below for further information or call (334) 260-6200.

Faulkner University
Office of Admissions
5345 Atlanta Highway
Montgomery, AL 36109

FISHER COLLEGE

3526
Fisher College Scholarship

AMOUNT: $600 DEADLINE: March 1
FIELDS/MAJORS: All Areas of Study

Applicants must be young women high school graduates with credits acceptable to admittance committee of school as well as indication of financial need. For study at Fisher College. Not renewable. Write to the address below for details, and be sure to include a SASE.

General Federation of Women's Clubs of Massachusetts
118 Beacon St.
Boston, MA 02116

FLAGLER COLLEGE

3527
Bruce Arthur Appel Memorial Scholarship

AMOUNT: None Specified DEADLINE: April 1
FIELDS/MAJORS: Law

Open to juniors and seniors who intend to pursue a career in law. Must have a minimum GPA of 3.0 and be accepted into the pre-law program. Contact the Office of Academic Affairs for further information.

Flagler College
Director of Financial Aid
PO Box 1027
St. Augustine, FL 32085

3528
Florida Bankers Education Foundation Scholarship/Loan

AMOUNT: None Specified DEADLINE: April 1
FIELDS/MAJORS: Banking

Open to juniors and seniors who are Florida residents and intend to pursue a career in Florida banking. Must have a minimum GPA of 2.5. Students are required to take out a loan through a Florida bank with the loan being canceled if the student works at least twelve continuous months after graduation in Florida commercial banking after graduation. Contact the Business Administration Department for further information.

Flagler College
Director of Financial Aid
PO Box 1027
St. Augustine, FL 32085

3529
Lewis Scholar Awards

AMOUNT: None Specified DEADLINE: April 1
FIELDS/MAJORS: All Areas of Study

Awards for high school seniors who have demonstrated exceptional academic achievement and leadership. Based on merit, without regard to financial need. Award includes tuition, fees, and room and board for four years of study. Recipients are selected following personal interviews. Contact the address listed for details. Must have a GPA of at least 3.8.

Flagler College
Director of Financial Aid
PO Box 1027
St. Augustine, FL 32085

3530
Samuel M. Proctor Memorial Scholarship

AMOUNT: None Specified DEADLINE: April 1
FIELDS/MAJORS: Law

Open to juniors and seniors who intend to pursue a career in law. Must have a minimum GPA of 3.2 and be accepted into the pre-law program. Contact the Office of Academic Affairs for further information.

Flagler College
Director of Financial Aid
PO Box 1027
St. Augustine, FL 32085

3531
Sophie S. Laval Memorial Scholarship

AMOUNT: None Specified DEADLINE: April 1
FIELDS/MAJORS: Business Administration, Economics, Social Science, Religion

Open to junior and senior women who are residents of Florida. Must have a minimum GPA of 2.4 and be able to demonstrate financial need. Contact the address listed for details.

Flagler College
Director of Financial Aid
PO Box 1027
St. Augustine, FL 32085

FLORIDA INTERNATIONAL UNIVERSITY

3532
Academic Opportunity Program Scholarship

AMOUNT: Maximum: $1200 DEADLINE: January 31
FIELDS/MAJORS: All Areas of Study

Award for African-American high school seniors. Must have a minimum GPA of 3.0 and a recommendation from a counselor or faculty member. Renewable by maintaining a minimum GPA of 2.5. Write to address below for information and an application.

Florida International University
Office of Minority Student Services
University Park
Miami, FL 33199

3533
American Bankers Insurance Group Scholarship

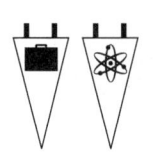

AMOUNT: $750 DEADLINE: June 1
FIELDS/MAJORS: Actuarial Science

Award open to juniors enrolled in the actuarial certificate program. Write to the address below for more information.

Florida International University
Statistics Department-DM 404
University Park Campus
Miami, FL 33199

3534
Anne Ackerman Scholarship

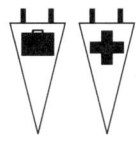

AMOUNT: $2000
DEADLINE: March 5
FIELDS/MAJORS: Criminal Justice, Health Service. Administration, Public Administration, Social Work

Scholarship is available to full-time undergraduate or graduate level students in any of the colleges four disciplines: criminal justice, health services administration, public administration, or social work. Students must be residents of Dade County, fully committed to FIU, and have a 3.5 GPA or above. Essay on civic leadership and public service required. Write to the address below for more information.

Florida International University
College of Urban and Public Affairs
Office of the Dean-AC1 200
North Miami, FL 33181

3535
Army ROTC Scholarship

AMOUNT: None Specified DEADLINE: None Specified
FIELDS/MAJORS: All Areas of Study

Scholarship from the U.S. Army for entering freshmen under twenty-five years of age. Applicants will have choice between active or reservist duty upon completion of schooling. Must be a U.S. citizen. Scholarships include full tuition, stipend for books, and fees. Those interested in further information MUST write to the following:

ARMY ROTC,
Scholarship Management Division, ATCC-PS,
Florida International University
Army ROTC Office
Miami, FL 33199

3536
Bertha Margaret Diaz Health Services Scholarship Fund

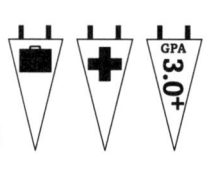

AMOUNT: $1500 DEADLINE: March 5
FIELDS/MAJORS: Health Service Administration

Scholarship is available to a deserving health services administration graduate student who maintains a 3.1 GPA or better and is of Hispanic descent. Write to the address below for more information.

Florida International University
College of Urban and Public Affairs
Office of the Dean-AC1 200
North Miami, FL 33181

3537
Delores Auzenne Fellowship

AMOUNT: $5000 DEADLINE: February 1
FIELDS/MAJORS: All Areas of Study

Fellowships available for African-American graduate students attending school full-time. Must have a minimum GPA of 3.0 and be U.S. citizens or permanent residents. Write to the address below for more information.

Florida International University
Equal Opportunity Program, PC 215
University Park
Miami, FL 33199

3538
Faculty Scholars

AMOUNT: Maximum: $1600 DEADLINE: February 15
FIELDS/MAJORS: All Areas of Study

Awards for high school seniors with a minimum GPA of 3.5 and combined SAT of 1270 or ACT of 28. Award is renewable by maintaining a minimum GPA of 3.0. Write to address below for information and application.

Florida International University
Office of Admissions
PC 140 University Park
Miami, FL 33199

3539
FIU/Community College Honors Scholarship

AMOUNT: Maximum: $2000 DEADLINE: February 15
FIELDS/MAJORS: All Areas of Study

Awards for transfer students from transfer-approved Florida Community Colleges, or students who have achieved an A.A. degree. Special attention paid to honors courses, extracurricular activities, and letters of recommendation. Renewable with full-time enrollment and maintaining a minimum GPA of 3.3. Write to the address below for information and application.

Florida International University
Honors College-DM 368
University Park
Miami, FL 33199

3540
Focus Scholarship

AMOUNT: None Specified DEADLINE: May 1
FIELDS/MAJORS: Education

Scholarships available to attract minority students to the field of education. Scholarship is for junior year. Renewable for senior year. Recipients receive full tuition and books. Write to the address below for information and application.

Florida International University
College of Education, ACI 140
3000 NE 145th St.
N. Miami, FL 33181

3541
George J. Berlin Urban Planning and Policy Scholarship

AMOUNT: $2500 DEADLINE: March 5
FIELDS/MAJORS: Urban Planning, Policy Issues

Scholarship is available to a graduate student who demonstrates financial need and academic excellence in urban planning and/or policy issues. Write to the address below for more information.

Florida International University
College of Urban and Public Affairs
Office of the Dean, ACI 200
North Miami, FL 33181

3542
Krell Scholarship

AMOUNT: $500 DEADLINE: January 31
FIELDS/MAJORS: International Relations

Scholarships are available to juniors, seniors, and graduate students in international relations. Must have a minimum 3.3 GPA, demonstrated financial need and completed at least 9 credit hours in international relations courses. Write to the address below for more information.

Florida International University
International Relations Dept., DM 499
University Park
Miami, FL 33199

3543
Manpower Access-To-Community Health (MATCH Program)

AMOUNT: Maximum: $38000 DEADLINE: January 15
FIELDS/MAJORS: Public Health

Must be a public health graduate student. To qualify as a candidate for the program, an individual must complete a written application, essay, resume, minimum of three references, and undergo a formal interview. Approximately twenty fellows will be selected each year. Write to the address below for more information.

Florida International University
M.S., Ches, Match Program Coordinator
1330 New Hampshire NW, #122
Washington, DC 20036

3544
Music Scholarship

AMOUNT: None Specified DEADLINE: None Specified
FIELDS/MAJORS: Music

Awards to students recommended by the FIU music department after auditions. The music department will provide audition dates. Write to the address below for more information.

Florida International University
School of Music PA 141
University Park
Miami, FL 33199

3545
National Achievement Scholarship

AMOUNT: Maximum: $5000   DEADLINE: February 15
FIELDS/MAJORS: All Areas of Study

Open to high school seniors who are National Merit Finalists with a GPA of 3.0 or better. Must have taken PSAT/NMSQT in junior year. Write to the address below for information and application.

Florida International University
Office of Admissions
PC 140 University Park
Miami, FL 33199

3546
National Hispanic Scholarship

AMOUNT: Maximum: $5000   DEADLINE: February 15
FIELDS/MAJORS: All Areas of Study

Entering freshman must be recognized as a National Hispanic Scholar, with a minimum GPA of 3.0. Award is renewable by maintaining GPA. Honorable mention recipients and semi-finalists may qualify for a partial scholarship. Write to address below for information and application.

Florida International University
Office of Admissions
PC 140 University Park
Miami, FL 33199

3547
National Hispanic Scholarship Fund

AMOUNT: $500-$1000   DEADLINE: June 5
FIELDS/MAJORS: All Areas of Study

Scholarships are available to U.S. citizens or permanent residents of Hispanic background who have completed at least 15 units of college work prior to submission of application. Must be enrolled in college in the fall and be in attendance through the spring (every year). Write to the address below for more information.

Florida International University
Financial Aid Office
University Park, PC 125
Miami, FL 33199

3548
Phi Theta Kappa Scholarship

AMOUNT: $2000   DEADLINE: February 15
FIELDS/MAJORS: All Areas of Study

Awards for juniors who will be transferring to FIU from a community college. Students must be members of Phi Theta Kappa and should submit a letter of recommendation from their PTK advisor. Write to the address below for additional information.

Florida International University
Honors College, DM 368
University Park
Miami, FL 33199

3549
Professional Opportunities for African-American Students and Graduates

AMOUNT: $1300   DEADLINE: April 15
FIELDS/MAJORS: All Areas of Study

Students must be admitted to graduate school for the first time in the spring or summer semester. Must be U.S. citizens or permanent residents. This is a one-time award for students of African-American descent. Write to the address below for more information.

Florida International University
Division of Graduate Studies, PC 520
University Park
Miami, FL 33199

3550
Rozenwaig Single Mothers Scholarship Fund

AMOUNT: $2000   DEADLINE: March 5
FIELDS/MAJORS: Social Work

Scholarship is available to a graduate student in good academic standing in the School of Social Work. The student must be a single mother, over the age of thirty-five, and demonstrate financial need. Essay on family life required. Write to the address below for more information.

Florida International University
College of Urban and Public Affairs
Office of the Dean, ACI 200
North Miami, FL 33181

3551
Scholarships for Disadvantaged Students (SDS)

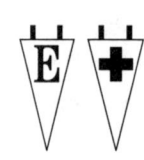

AMOUNT: None Specified   DEADLINE: August 15
FIELDS/MAJORS: Public Health

Scholarships are available to students from disadvantaged backgrounds, including racial and ethnic minorities. Must be a U.S. citizen, meet the definition of an "individual from a disadvantaged background," and be enrolled as a full-time student in the public health program at FIU. A second deadline date every year is December 4. Write to the address below for more information.

Florida International University
Department of Public Health, ACI 394
3000 NE 145th St.
North Miami, FL 33181

3552
Theater and Dance

AMOUNT: None Specified   DEADLINE: April 30
FIELDS/MAJORS: Theater and Dance

The theater and dance department will hold auditions and recommend talented students for the awards. They also will provide the audition dates, times, etc. Write to the address below for additional information.

Florida International University
Theater and Dance Dept., PAC 131
University Park
Miami, FL 33199

3553
Valedictorian and Salutatorian Scholarships

AMOUNT: $1000-$2000   DEADLINE: January 31
FIELDS/MAJORS: All Areas of Study

Awards for high school seniors who are first or second in their class. Applicants' high school counselor will be required to submit confirmation of class rank. Write to address below for information and an application.

Florida International University
Office of Admissions, PC 140
University Park
Miami, FL 33199

FORDHAM UNIVERSITY

3554
Amy Reiss Blind Student Scholarship

AMOUNT: None Specified   DEADLINE: February 1
FIELDS/MAJORS: Law

Scholarship for a blind student admitted or matriculated in the Fordham University School of Law (studying toward JD). Award is based on financial need. Write to the address below for details.

Morrison, Cohen, Singer & Weinstein
Amy Reiss
750 Lexington Ave.
New York, NY 10022

3555
Joseph P. Fitzpatrick S.J. Doctoral Fellowship

AMOUNT: $14000   DEADLINE: February 1
FIELDS/MAJORS: All Areas of Study

Fellowships open to exceptionally qualified minority students seeking a doctoral degree. Contact the address below for further information. GPA must be at least 3.1.

Fordham University
Graduate Admissions Office, Keating 216
Fordham University
Bronx, NY 10458

3556
Luce Fellowship

AMOUNT: None Specified   DEADLINE: February 1
FIELDS/MAJORS: Biological Sciences

Fellowships open to female graduates. Fellowship includes a stipend and tuition remission. Contact the address below for further information.

Fordham University
Graduate Admissions Office, Keating 216
Fordham University
Bronx, NY 10458

3557
Presidential Scholarship

AMOUNT: None Specified   **DEADLINE:** February 1
FIELDS/MAJORS: Psychology

Scholarships open to minority students enrolled in a psychology degree program. These awards may be given in concert with other awards or separately. Contact the address below for further information.

Fordham University
Graduate Admissions Office, Keating 216
Fordham University
Bronx, NY 10458

3558
Schering-Plough Dissertation Fellowship

AMOUNT: None Specified   **DEADLINE:** February 1
FIELDS/MAJORS: Biological Sciences

Fellowships open to doctoral candidates in the form of stipends to allow students to complete their dissertations during the tenure of the fellowship. Contact the address below for further information.

Fordham University
Graduate Admissions Office, Keating 216
Fordham University
Bronx, NY 10458

3559
Seix-Dow Fellowship

AMOUNT: None Specified   **DEADLINE:** February 1
FIELDS/MAJORS: Economics, International Development, International Economics

Fellowships open to Hispanic students enrolled in any of the above areas. Contact the address below for further information.

Fordham University
Graduate Admissions Office, Keating 216
Fordham University
Bronx, NY 10458

FORT HAYS STATE UNIVERSITY

3560
Alice McFarland Scholarship

AMOUNT: $1000   **DEADLINE:** January 15
FIELDS/MAJORS: English

Award open to English majors who plan to teach in secondary school. One award is offered annually. Contact the address below for further information.

Fort Hays State University
Office of Student Financial Aid
600 Park St.
Hays, KS 67601

3561
American Women's Business Association Scholarship

AMOUNT: None Specified   **DEADLINE:** January 15
FIELDS/MAJORS: All Areas of Study

Scholarships available at Fort Hays State University for juniors and seniors who have a minimum GPA of 2.5. Write to the address below for information.

American Women's Business Association
Ms. Martha Smith
1101 Downing
Hays, KS 67601

3562
English Honor Award Scholarships

AMOUNT: $200-$400   **DEADLINE:** January 15
FIELDS/MAJORS: English

Award open to high school seniors and transfer students who declare an English major. Contact the address below for further information.

Fort Hays State University
Office of Student Financial Aid
600 Park St.
Hays, KS 67601

3563
Freshman Political Science Awards

AMOUNT: $100-$400 DEADLINE: January 15
FIELDS/MAJORS: Political Science

Awards from Fort Hayes State open to beginning freshmen majoring in political science. Fifteen to twenty-five scholarships offered annually. Contact the address below for further information.

Fort Hays State University
Office of Student Financial Aid
600 Park St.
Hays, KS 67601

3564
Gas Capital Scholarship

AMOUNT: None Specified DEADLINE: February 15
FIELDS/MAJORS: Petroleum

Scholarships to Fort Hays State University for students pursuing a petroleum-related career. Must be a resident of any of the following Kansas counties: Finney, Grant, Greeley, Hamilton, Haskell, Kearny, Morton, Seward, Stanton, or Stevens. Write to the address below for information.

Gas Capital Scholarship Committee
630 S. Main
Hugoton, KS 67951

3565
Geosciences Award of Excellence

AMOUNT: $200 DEADLINE: January 15
FIELDS/MAJORS: Geology, Earth Science Education

Awards open to first-time incoming freshmen who have demonstrated superior academics. Contact the address below for further information. GPA must be at least 2.7.

Fort Hays State University
Office of Student Financial Aid
600 Park St.
Hays, KS 67601

3566
Graduate Student English Awards

AMOUNT: $1000 DEADLINE: January 15
FIELDS/MAJORS: English

Award open to beginning and returning graduate students who are enrolled full-time (9 hours or more). Must have a minimum GPA of 3.0 overall and at least a 3.5 in English. Contact the address below for further information.

Fort Hays State University
Office of Student Financial Aid
600 Park St.
Hays, KS 67601

3567
Health and Human Performance Award of Excellence

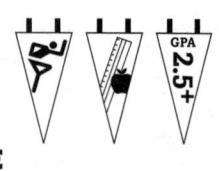

AMOUNT: $200 DEADLINE: January 15
FIELDS/MAJORS: Athletic Training, Teaching, Recreation/Sports Management

Awards open to first-time incoming freshmen who have demonstrated superior academics. Contact the address below for further information. GPA must be at least 2.7.

Fort Hays State University
Office of Student Financial Aid
600 Park St.
Hays, KS 67601

3568
History Award of Excellence

AMOUNT: $200 DEADLINE: January 15
FIELDS/MAJORS: History

Awards open to first-time incoming freshmen who have demonstrated superior academics. Contact the address below for further information. GPA must be at least 2.7.

Fort Hays State University
Office of Student Financial Aid
600 Park St.
Hays, KS 67601

3569
Information Networking, Telecommunications Award of Excellence

AMOUNT: $200 DEADLINE: January 15
FIELDS/MAJORS: Information Networking, Telecommunications

Awards open to first-time incoming freshmen who have demonstrated superior academics. Contact the address below for further information. GPA must be at least 2.7.

Fort Hays State University
Office of Student Financial Aid
600 Park St.
Hays, KS 67601

3570
Jack L. Tangeman Memorial Scholarship

AMOUNT: $200 DEADLINE: January 15
FIELDS/MAJORS: Elementary Education

Award open to seniors majoring in elementary education who exhibit academic potential and financial need. Contact the address below for further information. GPA must be at least 2.7.

Fort Hays State University
Office of Student Financial Aid
600 Park St.
Hays, KS 67601

3571
Jennie G. and Pearl Abell Scholarship

AMOUNT: None Specified DEADLINE: January 15
FIELDS/MAJORS: All Areas of Study

Scholarships available at Fort Hays State University for residents of Clark County, Kansas. Must be able to demonstrate good moral character, motivation, and financial need. Write to the address below for information.

Abell Educational Trust
Mrs. Willis Shattuck
Box 487
Ashland, KS 67831

3572
Kansas Farm Bureau Scholarship

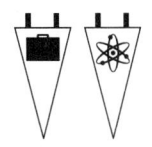

AMOUNT: $1000 DEADLINE: January 15
FIELDS/MAJORS: Agribusiness

Award open to juniors and seniors majoring in agribusiness or a closely related field. Applicants parents must be voting members of the Kansas Farm Bureau. Two awards offered annually. Contact the address below for further information.

Fort Hays State University
Office of Student Financial Aid
600 Park St.
Hays, KS 67601

3573
Kansas Nurses' Foundation Scholarships

AMOUNT: None Specified DEADLINE: January 15
FIELDS/MAJORS: Nursing

Scholarships open to Fort Hays State University students with a minimum GPA of 3.0, attending at least 6 credit hours per semester and able to demonstrate financial need. Open to both undergraduate and graduate students. Five awards are offered annually. Write to the address below for information.

Kansas State Nurses Association
700 SW Jackson, #601
Topeka, KS 66603

3574
Lawrence V. Gould, Sr. Memorial Award

AMOUNT: $100-$400 DEADLINE: January 15
FIELDS/MAJORS: Political Science, International Relations

Award to open juniors and seniors who have a minimum GPA of 2.5. Must have completed two courses in international relations and commit to completion of one additional course. Contact the address below for further information.

Fort Hays State University
Office of Student Financial Aid
600 Park St.
Hays, KS 67601

3575
Mathematics, Computer Science Award of Excellence

AMOUNT: $200 DEADLINE: January 15
FIELDS/MAJORS: Mathematics, Computer Science

Awards open to first-time incoming freshmen who have demonstrated superior academics. Contact the address below for further information. GPA must be at least 2.7.

Fort Hays State University
Office of Student Financial Aid
600 Park St.
Hays, KS 67601

3576
Michael Marks Literature, Roberta Stout Memorial Scholarships

AMOUNT: $500-$1000 DEADLINE: January 15
FIELDS/MAJORS: English

Awards open to sophomores, juniors, and seniors who are English majors. Must have a minimum GPA of 3.0. Contact the address below for further information about both awards.

Fort Hays State University
Office of Student Financial Aid
600 Park St.
Hays, KS 67601

3577
Modern Language Award of Excellence

AMOUNT: $200 DEADLINE: January 15
FIELDS/MAJORS: French, German, Spanish

Awards open to first-time incoming freshmen who have demonstrated superior academics. Contact the address below for further information. GPA must be at least 2.7.

Fort Hays State University
Office of Student Financial Aid
600 Park St.
Hays, KS 67601

3578
Nursing Award of Excellence

AMOUNT: $200 DEADLINE: January 15
FIELDS/MAJORS: Nursing

Awards open to first-time incoming freshmen who have demonstrated superior academics. Applicants will need to submit a paragraph explaining reasons for wanting to become a nurse. Contact the address below for further information. GPA must be at least 2.7.

Fort Hays State University
Office of Student Financial Aid
600 Park St.
Hays, KS 67601

3579
Philosophy Award of Excellence

AMOUNT: $200 DEADLINE: January 15
FIELDS/MAJORS: Philosophy, Pre-Theology

Awards open to first-time incoming freshmen who have demonstrated superior academics. Contact the address below for further information. GPA must be at least 2.7.

Fort Hays State University
Office of Student Financial Aid
600 Park St.
Hays, KS 67601

3580
Physics Award of Excellence

AMOUNT: $200 DEADLINE: January 15
FIELDS/MAJORS: Physics, Pre-Engineering, Physics Engineering, Physical Science Education

Awards open to first-time incoming freshmen who have demonstrated superior academics. Contact the address below for further information. GPA must be at least 2.7.

Fort Hays State University
Office of Student Financial Aid
600 Park St.
Hays, KS 67601

3581
Political Science Award of Excellence

AMOUNT: $200 DEADLINE: January 15
FIELDS/MAJORS: American Government, Political Science, Public Administration, Pre-Law

Awards open to first-time incoming freshmen who have demonstrated superior academics. Contact the address below for further information. GPA must be at least 2.7.

Fort Hays State University
Office of Student Financial Aid
600 Park St.
Hays, KS 67601

3582
Psychology Award of Excellence

AMOUNT: $200 DEADLINE: January 15
FIELDS/MAJORS: Psychology

Awards open to first-time incoming freshmen who have demonstrated superior academics. Contact the address below for further information. GPA must be at least 2.7.

Fort Hays State University
Office of Student Financial Aid
600 Park St.
Hays, KS 67601

3583
Sociology and Social Work Award of Excellence

AMOUNT: $200 DEADLINE: January 15
FIELDS/MAJORS: Sociology, Social Work

Awards open to first-time incoming freshmen who have demonstrated superior academics. Contact the address below for further information. GPA must be at least 2.7.

Fort Hays State University
Office of Student Financial Aid
600 Park St.
Hays, KS 67601

3584
Teacher Education Award of Excellence

AMOUNT: $200 DEADLINE: January 15
FIELDS/MAJORS: Elementary, Secondary Education

Awards open to first-time incoming freshmen who have demonstrated superior academics. Applicants should include any experiences involving working with children or youth. (Teaching Sunday school, helping with scouting programs, etc.) Contact the address below for further information. GPA must be at least 2.7.

Fort Hays State University
Office of Student Financial Aid
600 Park St.
Hays, KS 67601

FRANKLIN COLLEGE

3585
Pullman Journalism Scholarship

AMOUNT: $1000-$8500 DEADLINE: February 1
FIELDS/MAJORS: Journalism

Scholarships are available at Franklin College for full-time undergraduate students who are journalism majors that demonstrate superior academic potential. Fifteen to twenty awards are offered annually. Write to the address below for details.

Franklin College
Financial Aid Office
501 East Monroe Street
Franklin, IN 46131

GENEVA COLLEGE

3586
Bakke Law School Scholarship

AMOUNT: None Specified DEADLINE: None Specified
FIELDS/MAJORS: Law

Awards for top Geneva graduates who go on to attend a nationally prominent law school. Recipients could be eligible for a full-tuition law school scholarship. Write to the address below for more information.

Geneva College
Center for Law and Public Policy
Beaver Falls, PA 15010

3587
Clergy and Synod Grants

AMOUNT: None Specified DEADLINE: None Specified
FIELDS/MAJORS: All Areas of Study

Renewable scholarships for dependent, unmarried children of ordained ministers or missionaries. For full-time study. Contact the office of admissions for details.

Geneva College
Office of Admissions
Beaver Falls, PA 15010

3588
C.M. Lee Distinguished Scholar Award

AMOUNT: None Specified DEADLINE: None Specified
FIELDS/MAJORS: All Areas of Study

Two scholarships available for incoming freshmen at Geneva College. Based upon grades, test scores, a written essay, an interview, and commitment to the Christian religion. Contact the office of admissions for further information.

Geneva College
Office of Admissions
Beaver Falls, PA 15010

3589
Geneva Athletic Grants

AMOUNT: None Specified DEADLINE: None Specified
FIELDS/MAJORS: All Areas of Study

Grants for undergraduate students at Geneva College who will be participating in intercollegiate athletics. Contact the coach of your sport or the office of admissions for further information.

Geneva College
Office of Admissions
Beaver Falls, PA 15010

3590
Geneva Grants

AMOUNT: None Specified   DEADLINE: None Specified
FIELDS/MAJORS: All Areas of Study

Grants for students at Geneva College. Based on need and academics. Renewable as necessary. Must be a full-time student. Contact the financial aid office or the office of admissions for details.

Geneva College
Office of Admissions
Beaver Falls, PA 15010

3591
Geneva Scholar Award

AMOUNT: None Specified   DEADLINE: None Specified
FIELDS/MAJORS: All Areas of Study

Scholarships available for full-time freshmen at Geneva College who have a GPA of at least 3.0 from high school and a minimum score of 1000 on the SAT or a 24 on the ACT. Scholarships are renewable if 3.0 GPA is maintained. Transfer students are also eligible for this award. Contact the office of admissions for further information.

Geneva College
Office of Admissions
Beaver Falls, PA 15010

3592
Humane Studies Fellowships

AMOUNT: Maximum: $12000   DEADLINE: December 31
FIELDS/MAJORS: Individual Rights, Market Economies

Fellowships at the IHS for junior, senior, and graduate students who have a clearly demonstrated interest in the classical liberal/libertarian tradition of individual rights and market economies. Based on academic and/or professional performance, relevance of one's work to the advancement of a free society and potential for success. Final decisions are reached in March or April. Contact the address below for further information.

Institute for Humane Studies at George Mason University
Fellowship Coordinator
4084 University Dr., #101
Fairfax, VA 22030

3593
Merit Awards

AMOUNT: None Specified   DEADLINE: None Specified
FIELDS/MAJORS: All Areas of Study

Scholarships available for undergraduate students at Geneva College who are National Merit Finalists or Semifinalists. Contact the office of admissions for further information.

Geneva College
Office of Admissions
Beaver Falls, PA 15010

3594
Presidential Scholarships

AMOUNT: None Specified   DEADLINE: None Specified
FIELDS/MAJORS: All Areas of Study

Scholarships available for students at Geneva College who demonstrate high academic achievement and financial need. Contact the office of admissions for further information.

Geneva College
Office of Admissions
Beaver Falls, PA 15010

3595
RPCNA Grants at Geneva

AMOUNT: None Specified   DEADLINE: None Specified
FIELDS/MAJORS: All Areas of Study

Renewable scholarships for students at Geneva College who are communicant members of the reformed Presbyterian Church of North America (RPCNA). For full-time study. Contact the office of admissions for further information.

Geneva College
Office of Admissions
Beaver Falls, PA 15010

GEORGE MASON UNIVERSITY

3596
Mary Roberts Rinehart Awards

AMOUNT: Maximum: $900   DEADLINE: November 30
FIELDS/MAJORS: Creative Writing, Poetry

Awards are available for unpublished writers who need financial assistance to complete works of fiction, poetry, drama, biography, autobiography, or history with strong narrative quality. Applicants must be nominated by a program faculty member, a sponsoring writer, agent, or editor. Submit writing samples of up to thirty pages. Write to the address below for information.

George Mason University
Department of English
Mary Roberts Rinehart Fund
4400 University Dr.
Fairfax, VA 22030

GEORGETOWN UNIVERSITY LAW CENTER

3597
Public Interest Law Graduate Fellow/Staff Attorney Fellowships

AMOUNT: $29000 DEADLINE: November 15
FIELDS/MAJORS: Law (Public Policy, Communications)

Two-year, postgraduate (i.e., post-JD/LLB) residential fellowships for law students. Provides extensive training and experience in public interest advocacy in the federal courts, administrative agencies, and legislative bodies. Fellows receive an LLM in advocacy at the end of the fellowship term. Four fellowships per year (two to three available for the 1993-95 term). Write to the address below for details.

Georgetown University Law Center
Institute for Public Representation
600 New Jersey Ave. NW, Suite 312
Washington, DC 20001

GEORGE WASHINGTON UNIVERSITY

3598
Felix Morley Journalism Competition

AMOUNT: $750-$2500 DEADLINE: December 1
FIELDS/MAJORS: Writing

Competition open to students (under the age of twenty-five) who demonstrate appreciation of a free society. Applicants must submit articles published in student newspapers or other publications between July 1, 1996, and December 1, 1997. First place wins $2500, second place wins $1000, and third place is $750. Contact the address below for further information.

Institute for Humane Studies at George Washington University
Scholarship Coordinator
4084 University Dr., #101
Fairfax, VA 22030

3599
Film and Fiction Scholarship

AMOUNT: Maximum: $10000 DEADLINE: January 15
FIELDS/MAJORS: Film, Fiction Writing, Playwriting

Scholarships open to students currently pursuing a Master of Fine Arts degree in the fields listed above. Must be able to demonstrate an interest in classical liberalism. Decisions made in the beginning of March. Contact the address below for further information.

Institute for Humane Studies at George Washington University
Scholarship Coordinator
4084 University Dr., #101
Fairfax, VA 22030

3600
Wolcott Foundation Fellowships

AMOUNT: $1800 DEADLINE: February 1
FIELDS/MAJORS: Business Administration, Public Management, International Affairs

Fellowships for master's degree students at George Washington University. Award is considered a grant if for four years after graduation, recipients work in federal, state, or local government or in select private international business. Some preference given to persons active in Masonic activities (Demolay, Job's Daughters, Rainbow, etc.). Must be a U.S. citizen. Information is available from the address below.

High Twelve International
Wolcott Foundation Fellowships at GWU
402 Beasley St.
Monroe, LA 71203

GEORGIA INSTITUTE OF TECHNOLOGY

3601
Atlanta Power Engineering Society Scholarship

AMOUNT: None Specified DEADLINE: None Specified
FIELDS/MAJORS: Electrical Engineering

Open to deserving undergraduates pursuing a career in electrical engineering. Selection made by the scholarship committee of the School of Electrical and Computer Engineering. Contact the department for further information. GPA must be at least 2.9.

Georgia Institute of Technology
Financial Aid Office
225 North Ave.
Atlanta, GA 30332

3602
Babcock and Wilcox Scholarships

AMOUNT: None Specified   DEADLINE: None Specified
FIELDS/MAJORS: Mechanical Engineering

Open to juniors and seniors who have strong academic records and are in need of financial assistance. The junior award may be renewed for the senior year. Preference given to children of Babcock and Wilcox employees and students who reside near a Babcock and Wilcox facility. May be offered part-time summer employment. Contact the address below for further information. GPA must be at least 3.3.

Georgia Institute of Technology
Financial Aid Office
225 North Ave.
Atlanta, GA 30332

3603
Blount Endowed Scholarship

AMOUNT: Maximum: $5000   DEADLINE: None Specified
FIELDS/MAJORS: Civil, Environmental, Mechanical, Industrial Engineering

Open to enrolled students who are Georgia residents. Award may be renewed for up to four consecutive years based on sustained outstanding performance and a minimum GPA of 3.0. Write to the address below for further information.

Georgia Institute of Technology
Financial Aid Office
225 North Ave.
Atlanta, GA 30332

3604
Chevron U.S.A., Inc. Scholarships

AMOUNT: None Specified   DEADLINE: None Specified
FIELDS/MAJORS: Electrical Engineering

Open to juniors and seniors seeking a degree in electrical engineering. Must be U.S. citizens or permanent residents. Based on financial need and academics. Awarded by the School of Electrical and Computer Engineering. Contact the department for further information. GPA must be at least 3.3.

Georgia Institute of Technology
Financial Aid Office
225 North Ave.
Atlanta, GA 30332

3605
Damar, Inc., Scholarship

AMOUNT: None Specified   DEADLINE: None Specified
FIELDS/MAJORS: All Areas of Study

Open to students who are residents of Cobb County, Georgia. Based on financial need and academic ability. Selection made by the Office of Student Financial Planning and Services. Contact the address below for further information. GPA must be at least 3.0.

Georgia Institute of Technology
Financial Aid Office
225 North Ave.
Atlanta, GA 30332

3606
Engineering Minority Scholarship

AMOUNT: None Specified   DEADLINE: None Specified
FIELDS/MAJORS: Engineering

Open to minority students who are pursuing a career in various engineering disciplines. Coordinated through the Office of Minority and Special Programs. Contact the address below for further information.

Georgia Institute of Technology
Financial Aid Office
225 North Ave.
Atlanta, GA 30332

3607
Framatome Technologies Scholarship

AMOUNT: None Specified   DEADLINE: None Specified
FIELDS/MAJORS: Mechanical, Electrical, Chemical Engineering

Open to seniors who are pursuing a degree in mechanical, electrical, or chemical engineering. Must maintain a minimum GPA of 3.0. Contact the address below for further information.

Georgia Institute of Technology
Financial Aid Office
225 North Ave.
Atlanta, GA 30332

3608
General Motors Endowed Scholarship

AMOUNT: Maximum: $2500   DEADLINE: None Specified
FIELDS/MAJORS: All Areas of Study

Open to undergraduate minority and female students enrolled at Georgia Tech. Preference given to minority General Motors employees, spouses, and children. May be renewed for up to three years. Recipients selected by the Office of Student Financial Planning and Services. Write to the address below for further information.

Georgia Institute of Technology
Financial Aid Office
225 North Ave.
Atlanta, GA 30332

3609
Guy R. Bastain Memorial Scholarship

AMOUNT: Maximum: $5000   DEADLINE: None Specified
FIELDS/MAJORS: All Areas of Study

Open to enrolled students who show strong academic promise. Preference give to residents of Georgia. Based on financial need. Write to the address below for further information. GPA must be at least 3.0.

Georgia Institute of Technology
Financial Aid Office
225 North Ave.
Atlanta, GA 30332

3610
IHS Group, Inc. Scholarship

AMOUNT: None Specified   DEADLINE: None Specified
FIELDS/MAJORS: Mechanical, Electrical, Civil Engineering

Open to juniors and seniors who are majoring in civil, mechanical, or electrical engineering. Must be U.S. citizens and have a minimum GPA of 3.5. Contact the address below for further information.

Georgia Institute of Technology
Financial Aid Office
225 North Ave.
Atlanta, GA 30332

3611
Jack Phinizy Educational and Charitable Foundation Scholarship

AMOUNT: None Specified   DEADLINE: None Specified
FIELDS/MAJORS: Engineering

Open to qualified students in their first or second year. Strictly for the residents of Florida, Georgia, and North Carolina. Preference given to residents of Richmond County, Georgia. Based on academics, engineering aptitude, and financial need. Contact the address below for further information. GPA must be at least 2.8.

Georgia Institute of Technology
Financial Aid Office
225 North Ave.
Atlanta, GA 30332

3612
John Houston Wear, Jr. Scholarship

AMOUNT: None Specified   DEADLINE: None Specified
FIELDS/MAJORS: Architecture

Open to deserving students majoring in architecture. Recipients selected by the College of Architecture. Contact the department for further information. GPA must be at least 2.8.

Georgia Institute of Technology
Financial Aid Office
225 North Ave.
Atlanta, GA 30332

3613
Lubrizol Foundation Scholarship

AMOUNT: None Specified   DEADLINE: None Specified
FIELDS/MAJORS: Chemistry, Biochemistry, Chemical Engineering

Open to students enrolled in the School of Chemistry and Biochemistry and the School of Chemical Engineering. Awards are distributed through the respective schools. Contact the schools indicated for further information. GPA must be at least 2.9.

Georgia Institute of Technology
Financial Aid Office
225 North Ave.
Atlanta, GA 30332

3614
McDermott, Inc., Scholarship

AMOUNT: None Specified DEADLINE: None Specified
FIELDS/MAJORS: Civil Engineering

Open to juniors and seniors majoring in civil engineering. Must be U.S. citizens or permanent residents. Based on outstanding academics and financial need. Contact the address below for further information. GPA must be at least 3.3.

Georgia Institute of Technology
Financial Aid Office
225 North Ave.
Atlanta, GA 30332

3615
Merck and Co., Inc. Scholarship

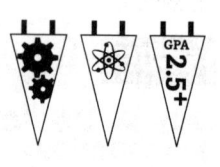

AMOUNT: None Specified DEADLINE: None Specified
FIELDS/MAJORS: Chemical Engineering

Open to students majoring in chemical engineering. Recipients selected by Merck and Co., Inc. Contact the address below for further information. GPA must be at least 2.8.

Georgia Institute of Technology
Financial Aid Office
225 North Ave.
Atlanta, GA 30332

3616
NACME Incentive Grant Program Scholarship

AMOUNT: None Specified DEADLINE: None Specified
FIELDS/MAJORS: Engineering

Open to minority students enrolled full-time making satisfactory academic progress. Must have a minimum GPA of 2.5 and complete at least 36 quarter hours during the academic year. Based on academics and financial need. Renewable for three additional years based on continued qualifications. Contact the address below for further information.

Georgia Institute of Technology
Financial Aid Office
225 North Ave.
Atlanta, GA 30332

3617
National Starch and Chemical Scholarship

AMOUNT: None Specified DEADLINE: None Specified
FIELDS/MAJORS: Chemical Engineering

Open to students majoring in chemical engineering. Recipients selected by the School, based on scholastic performance and financial need. Contact the address below for further information. GPA must be at least 2.8.

Georgia Institute of Technology
Financial Aid Office
225 North Ave.
Atlanta, GA 30332

3618
Occidental Chemical Company Scholarship

AMOUNT: None Specified DEADLINE: None Specified
FIELDS/MAJORS: Chemical Engineering

Open to students enrolled in the School of Chemical Engineering. Funds awarded through the School. Contact the school for further information. GPA must be at least 2.8.

Georgia Institute of Technology
Financial Aid Office
225 North Ave.
Atlanta, GA 30332

3619
Richard C. Kessler Scholarship

AMOUNT: Maximum: $5000 DEADLINE: None Specified
FIELDS/MAJORS: Industrial, Systems Engineering

Open to freshmen and sophomores who are residents of Effingham County, Georgia (for at least one year). Recipients chosen on basis of merit, with financial need being a secondary factor. Recipients will be requested to perform two weeks of volunteer work during the year of the scholarship at New Ebenezer Retreat and Conference Center in Rincon, Georgia. Freshmen candidates must demonstrate service activities, leadership, academic, and performance records. Sophomores must have a GPA equal to or greater than the sophomore class average. Awards are made by the Office of Student Financial Planning and Services. Write to the address below for further information. GPA must be at least 3.0.

Georgia Institute of Technology
Financial Aid Office
225 North Ave.
Atlanta, GA 30332

3620
S.H. Wilkinson Memorial Scholarship

AMOUNT: None Specified DEADLINE: None Specified
FIELDS/MAJORS: Engineering

Open to students majoring in engineering. Selections based on strong academics and financial need. Contact the address below for further information. GPA must be at least 3.2.

Georgia Institute of Technology
Financial Aid Office
225 North Ave.
Atlanta, GA 30332

3621
William Rhodes Technology Scholarship

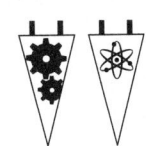

AMOUNT: Maximum: $12000 DEADLINE: None Specified
FIELDS/MAJORS: Engineering, Science

Open to students who graduated from high schools in Collier County, Florida. Awards made by the Office of Student Financial Planning and Services. Write to the address below for further information.

Georgia Institute of Technology
Financial Aid Office
225 North Ave.
Atlanta, GA 30332

GOLDEN GATE UNIVERSITY

3622
AIDS Awareness Scholarship

AMOUNT: None Specified DEADLINE: April 4
FIELDS/MAJORS: All Areas of Study

Open to lesbian, gay, bisexual, and transgendered students enrolled at Golden Gate University. Must have a commitment/involvement in AIDS awareness and be able to demonstrate financial need. Students having direct involvement with an AIDS-related community service provider are encouraged to apply. Contact the address below for further information.

Golden Gate University
Financial Aid Office
536 Mission St.
San Francisco, CA 94105

GRAND RAPIDS COMMUNITY COLLEGE

3623
Polish Heritage Scholarship

AMOUNT: $500 DEADLINE: March 15
FIELDS/MAJORS: All Areas of Study

Scholarships for students of Polish descent attending Grand Rapids Junior College. Write to the address below for details.

Grand Rapids Community College Foundation
  Scholarships
Director of Financial Aid
143 Bostwick, NE
Grand Rapids, MI 49503

GREAT LAKES CHRISTIAN COLLEGE

3624
Alumni Scholarship

AMOUNT: None Specified DEADLINE: May 1
FIELDS/MAJORS: All Areas of Study

Scholarships for juniors; one for a male, one for a female, one for a vocational ministry major, and one for a non-vocational ministry major. Contact the financial aid office at the address below for details.

Great Lakes Christian College
Financial Aid Office
6211 W. Willow Highway
Lansing, MI 48901

3625
College Grants and Scholarships

AMOUNT: None Specified DEADLINE: May 1
FIELDS/MAJORS: All Areas of Study

Open to any student or prospective student who has expressed intent to study for vocational ministry may apply. Contact the financial aid office at the address below for details.

Great Lakes Christian College
Financial Aid Office
6211 W. Willow Highway
Lansing, MI 48901

3626
Detro Scholarship

AMOUNT: None Specified   DEADLINE: None Specified
FIELDS/MAJORS: All Areas of Study

Open to prospective or current students with financial need. Contact the address below for further information.

Great Lakes Christian College
Financial Aid Office
6211 W. Willow Highway
Lansing, MI 48917

3627
Great Lakes Christian College Endowed Scholarships

AMOUNT: None Specified   DEADLINE: May 1
FIELDS/MAJORS: All Areas of Study

Scholarships for students at GLBC who intend to enter the ministry. Includes the Good Samaritan Trust, the Deryll B. Sprunger Tuition Scholarship, and the Buchanan Church of Christ Scholarships. Contact the financial aid office at the address below for details.

Great Lakes Christian College
Financial Aid Office
6211 W. Willow Highway
Lansing, MI 48901

3628
Great Lakes Christian College Music Scholarship

AMOUNT: None Specified   DEADLINE: May 1
FIELDS/MAJORS: Music

Applicants for this award should submit a twenty-minute audition tape that best displays their talent. Write to address below for additional information.

Great Lakes Christian College
Financial Aid Office
6211 W. Willow Highway
Lansing, MI 48901

3629
New York Christian Institute Scholarship

AMOUNT: None Specified   DEADLINE: None Specified
FIELDS/MAJORS: All Areas of Study

Open to students from the Northeastern states. Contact the address below for further information.

Great Lakes Christian College
Financial Aid Office
6211 W. Willow Highway
Lansing, MI 48917

GREENVILLE COLLEGE

3630
Presidential Scholarship

AMOUNT: $4500-$6000   DEADLINE: None Specified
FIELDS/MAJORS: All Areas of Study

Available to incoming freshmen with the minimum ACT/SAT and a minimum 3.3 GPA. Must demonstrate leadership qualities and participate in on-campus competition on one of the designated days. Participants receive $4500. Ten winners receive $6000 awards, which are renewable for up to four years. Competition dates are 11/15, 12/13, 01/17, 02/07, and 03/14. Contact the address below for further information or call 1-800-345-4440.

Greenville College
Office of Admissions
315 East College Ave.
Greenville, IL 62246

3631
Provost Scholarship

AMOUNT: $3500-$5000   DEADLINE: None Specified
FIELDS/MAJORS: All Areas of Study

Available to incoming freshmen with the minimum ACT/SAT and a 3.3 minimum GPA. Must demonstrate leadership qualities and participate in on-campus competition on one of the designated days. All participants receive $3500. Five winners receive $5000 awards, which are renewable. Competition dates are in November through March. Contact the address below for further information or call 1-800-345-4440.

Greenville College
Office of Admissions
315 East College Ave.
Greenville, IL 62246

3632
Snyder Science Scholarship

AMOUNT: $4500-$6000   DEADLINE: None Specified
FIELDS/MAJORS: All Areas of Study

Available to incoming freshmen who plan to major in chemistry, engineering, math, or physics and participate in an on-campus competition on January 17. Must have the minimum ACT/SAT and a 3.3 minimum GPA. Student must demonstrate leadership qualities. Participants receive $4500. Two winners receive $6000 awards, which are renewable for up to four years. Contact the address below for further information or call 1-800-345-4440.

Greenville College
Office of Admissions
315 East College Ave.
Greenville, IL 62246

HAMPSHIRE COLLEGE

3633
Lemelson Fellowships

AMOUNT: $5500-$21000 DEADLINE: November 15
FIELDS/MAJORS: All Areas of Study

Fellowships are available at Hampshire College for undergraduate students who are sophomores or above, who wish to be part of a team that will strive to create or refine specific programs, devices, and concepts that address contemporary problems. Must have a strong academic record. Write to the address below for details. Must have a GPA of at least 3.0.

Lemelson National Program in Invention, Innovation, and Creativity
Hampshire College
Amherst, MA 01002

HARDING UNIVERSITY

3634
Transfer Scholarship

AMOUNT: None Specified DEADLINE: None Specified
FIELDS/MAJORS: All Areas of Study

Award for transfer students who have a GPA of 3.25 or higher. Write to the address listed for more information.

Harding University
Director of Student Financial Services
Box 2282
Searcy, AR 72149

HAROLD WASHINGTON COLLEGE

3635
Anheuser-Busch Foundation

AMOUNT: $500-$800 DEADLINE: July 15
FIELDS/MAJORS: All Areas of Study

Available for male or female minority students who are heads of households and currently enrolled in Harold Washington College. Write to the address below for more information.

Chicago Urban League
Gina Blake, Scholarship Specialist
4510 South Michigan Ave.
Chicago, IL 60653

HARVARD UNIVERSITY

3636
Villa I Tatti Fellowships

AMOUNT: Maximum: $30000 DEADLINE: October 15
FIELDS/MAJORS: Italian Renaissance

Fellowship program for postdoctoral scholars in the field of Italian Renaissance studies. Based on applicant's scholarly excellence and promise and the importance of the proposed research topic. Program includes a period of study in Florence, Italy. Write to the address below for more information.

Harvard University Center for Italian Renaissance Studies
University Place
124 Mt. Auburn St.
Cambridge, MA 02138

HAVERFORD COLLEGE

3637
Haverford College Scholarships

AMOUNT: None Specified DEADLINE: November 15
FIELDS/MAJORS: All Areas of Study

Financial aid is available to students planning to attend Haverford College. The assistance is based on financial need. For more information see the school's Web site: www.Haverford.edu or contact the address below.

Haverford College
Financial Aid Office
370 Lancaster Ave.
Haverford, PA 19041

HUDSON INSTITUTE

3638
Herman Kahn Resident Fellowships

AMOUNT: Maximum: $18000 DEADLINE: April 1
FIELDS/MAJORS: Political Science, Economics, International Relations, Education

Residential fellowships for candidates who have completed all requirements for Ph.D. except dissertation. Fellows are expected to spend 50% of their time on projects the Institute assigns in their general area. Areas of fellowship are in education, domestic political economy, international political economics, political theory, and in national security studies. Postdoctoral fellowships also available. Application is made with vitae, three letters of recommendation (two academic, one non-academic), recent publications and theses proposal, and graduate school transcripts. Contact the Institute at the address below for details.

Hudson Institute
Herman Kahn Center
PO Box 26-919
Indianapolis, IN 46226

HUNTER COLLEGE – CITY UNIVERSITY OF NEW YORK

3639
Intercambio Fellowships

AMOUNT: None Specified DEADLINE: None Specified
FIELDS/MAJORS: Puerto Rican Studies

These awards are designed to support dissertation-related research on Puerto Rican themes by advanced students at the CUNY graduate school. Write to the address listed for information.

Hunter College-City University of New York
Floyd Moreland, Graduate Center 1501
695 Park Ave., Box 548
New York, NY 10021

HUSSON COLLEGE

3640
Ruth Milan-Altrusa Scholarship Fund

AMOUNT: None Specified DEADLINE: None Specified
FIELDS/MAJORS: Nursing

Awards for graduating seniors from the Bangor, Maine, area who plan to pursue a bachelor's degree in nursing at EMMC/Husson College. Contact the Husson College Financial Aid Office for more information.

Maine Community Foundation
245 East Maine St.
PO Box 148
Ellsworth, ME 04605

IDAHO STATE UNIVERSITY

3641
Snake River Section Scholarship

AMOUNT: $250-$500 DEADLINE: February 1
FIELDS/MAJORS: Geology, Mining, and Related

Scholarships for Idaho undergraduates studying in a minerals-related area. Not need-based. One award per year. Write to the address below for details.

Society for Mining, Metallurgy, and Exploration, Snake River Section
Idaho State University
Dept. of Geology, Paul Link
Pocatello, ID 83209

ILLINOIS INSTITUTE OF TECHNOLOGY

3642
Armour Scholarship

AMOUNT: None Specified DEADLINE: January 15
FIELDS/MAJORS: Chemical, Computer, Electrical, Mechanical Engineering, Computer Science

Open to admitted incoming freshmen who are in the top 25% of graduating class with a minimum GPA of 3.5. A supplemental application, interview, and portfolio will be required. This scholarship is awarded to finalists for ITT's Honors Program in engineering and medicine. Award is half tuition for four years. Contact the address below for further information or call (312) 567-3025. ITT offers an online application that can be found at www.iit.edu/admission/undergrad/application.

Illinois Institute of Technology
Office of Admissions
10 W. 33rd St.
Chicago, IL 60616

3643
Crown Scholarship

AMOUNT: None Specified   DEADLINE: February 16
FIELDS/MAJORS: Architecture

Open to admitted incoming freshmen who are in the top 10% of graduating class with a minimum GPA of 3.5. A supplemental application, interview, and portfolio will be required. Contact the address below for further information or call (312) 567-3025. ITT offers an online application that can be found at www.iit.edu/admission/undergrad/application.

Illinois Institute of Technology
Office of Admissions
10 W. 33rd St.
Chicago, IL 60616

3644
Gunsaulus Scholarship

AMOUNT: None Specified   DEADLINE: May 1
FIELDS/MAJORS: All Areas of Study

Open to admitted freshmen who are in the top 25% of graduating class and are of Native American, Latin-American, or African-American descent. A separate application and interview will be required. Admitted students are automatically reviewed for this scholarship. Award is half tuition and renewable for four or five years. Contact the address below for further information or call (312) 567-3025. ITT offers an online application that can be found at www.iit.edu/admission/undergrad/application. GPA must be at least 3.2.

Illinois Institute of Technology
Office of Admissions
10 W. 33rd St.
Chicago, IL 60616

3645
Heald Scholarship

AMOUNT: None Specified
DEADLINE: May 1
FIELDS/MAJORS: Architecture, Pre-Law, Pre-Med

Open to admitted outstanding freshmen who are in the top 25% of graduating class with a minimum GPA of 3.5, who wish to pursue a math or science based profession. All admitted students are automatically reviewed for this scholarship. Award is half tuition renewable for four or five years. Contact the address below for further information or call (312) 567-3025. ITT offers an online application that can be found at www.iit.edu/admission/undergrad/application.

Illinois Institute of Technology
Office of Admissions
10 W. 33rd St.
Chicago, IL 60616

3646
ITT Athletic Scholarships

AMOUNT: None Specified   DEADLINE: May 1
FIELDS/MAJORS: All Areas of Study

Open to admitted incoming freshmen who are in the top 25% of graduating class. Scholarships awarded at the coaches discretion. The following sports are available: men's and women's swimming, basketball, and cross country; men's baseball and women's volleyball. Contact the appropriate coach for further information or call (312) 567-3025. GPA must be at least 2.5.

Illinois Institute of Technology
Office of Admissions
10 W. 33rd St.
Chicago, IL 60616

3647
Purnell Scholarship

AMOUNT: None Specified   DEADLINE: February 16
FIELDS/MAJORS: All Areas of Study

Open to admitted freshmen who are in the top 25% of graduating class and are of Native American, Latin-American, or African-American descent. A separate application and interview will be required. Admitted students are automatically reviewed for this scholarship. Award is full tuition and renewable for four or five years. Contact the address below for further information or call (312) 567-3025. ITT offers an online application that can be found at www.iit.edu/admission/undergrad/application. GPA must be at least 3.2.

Illinois Institute of Technology
Office of Admissions
10 W. 33rd St.
Chicago, IL 60616

3648
ROTC Supplemental Scholarships

AMOUNT: None Specified DEADLINE: May 1
FIELDS/MAJORS: All Areas of Study

Open to admitted incoming freshmen who are in the top 25% of graduating class. These scholarships supplement the Air Force, Army, or Naval ROTC scholarships awarded by the military. Award amounts vary, up to full tuition and room and board. Renewable. Contact the address below for further information or call (312) 567-3025. ITT offers an online application that can be found at www.iit.edu/admission/undergrad/application. GPA must be at least 2.5.

Illinois Institute of Technology
Office of Admissions
10 W. 33rd St.
Chicago, IL 60616

3649
Women in Science and Engineering Scholarship

AMOUNT: None Specified DEADLINE: May 1
FIELDS/MAJORS: All Areas of Study

Open to admitted women freshmen who are in the top 25% of graduating class. This merit-based scholarship is to support women pursuing math and science based professions at ITT. Admitted students are automatically reviewed for this scholarship. Award is half tuition and renewable for four or five years. Contact the address below for further information or call (312) 567-3025. ITT offers an online application that can be found at www.iit.edu/admission/undergrad/application GPA must be at least 3.2.

Illinois Institute of Technology
Office of Admissions
10 W. 33rd St.
Chicago, IL 60616

ILLINOIS STATE UNIVERSITY

3650
Agriculture Faculty Scholarship

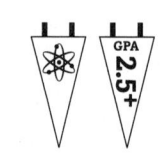

AMOUNT: $400-$1000 DEADLINE: February 6
FIELDS/MAJORS: Agriculture

Two scholarships awarded to incoming freshmen, transfer students enrolling in an agricultural curriculum, and continuing students at Illinois State University. Applicants must have participated in FFA as an officer or section president. Concurrent participation in a Departmental club or serving as an Agriculture Associate is required. Must maintain a minimum GPA of 2.5. For more information, contact your high school guidance counselor, write to the address below, or call (309) 438-5654.

Illinois State University, Dept. of Agriculture
Turner Hall 150
Campus Box 5020
Normal, IL 61761

3651
Benton K. Bristol Scholarship

AMOUNT: $400-$1000 DEADLINE: February 6
FIELDS/MAJORS: Agriculture

Open to incoming freshmen or transfer students enrolling in an agricultural curriculum at ISU. Based on demonstrated academic achievement and leadership. Contact the address listed, call (309) 438-5654, or contact your high school counselor for further information. Must have a GPA of at least 2.8.

Illinois State University, Dept. of Agriculture
Turner Hall 150
Campus Box 5020
Normal, IL 61761

3652
Clarence and Mabel Ropp Scholarship

AMOUNT: $400-$1000 DEADLINE: February 6
FIELDS/MAJORS: Agriculture

Open to transfer students who have graduated from community college within the top 25% of their graduating class. Based on academics and extracurricular activities. Preference given to those with farm backgrounds and/or leadership experience in FFA or 4-H. Contact the address listed or call (309) 438-5654 for further information. Must have a GPA of at least 3.2.

Illinois State University, Dept. of Agriculture
Turner Hall 150
Campus Box 5020
Normal, IL 61761

3653
Clarence L. Moore Scholarship

AMOUNT: $1000 DEADLINE: February 7
FIELDS/MAJORS: Dairy Science

Scholarship awarded to an incoming freshman or transfer student enrolling full-time in an agricultural curriculum at Illinois State University. Selection will be based on demonstrated academic achievement, leadership abilities, and activities. Financial need will be considered. Preference given to students with an interest in or background in dairy science. For more information, contact your high school guidance counselor or write to the address below. Must have a GPA of at least 2.9.

Illinois State University, Dept. of Agriculture
Turner Hall 150
Campus Box 5020
Normal, IL 61761

3654
John W. Green, Sr. Scholarship

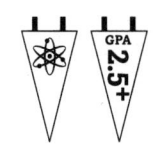

AMOUNT: $400-$1000 DEADLINE: February 6
FIELDS/MAJORS: Agriculture

Open to incoming freshmen enrolling in the Department of Agriculture at ISU. Based on academic excellence, leadership, GPA, and high school and civic activities. Contact the address listed or call (309) 438-5654 or your high school counselor for further information. Must have a GPA of at least 2.9.

Illinois State University, Dept. of Agriculture
Turner Hall 150
Campus Box 5020
Normal, IL 61761

3655
McLean County Farm Bureau Scholarship

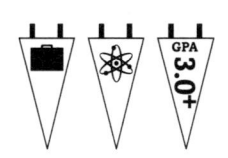

AMOUNT: $400-$1000 DEADLINE: February 6
FIELDS/MAJORS: Agriculture or Agribusiness

Scholarship awarded to an incoming freshmen enrolling in an agricultural curriculum at Illinois State University. Selection will be based on demonstrated high academic achievement, leadership abilities, and activities. Financial need will be considered. Applicant must be a resident of McLean County. For more information, contact your high school guidance counselor, write to the address listed, or call (309) 438-5654. Must have a GPA of at least 3.0.

Illinois State University, Dept. of Agriculture
Turner Hall 150
Campus Box 5020
Normal, IL 61761

3656
Paul A. Funk Foundation Incoming Freshman Scholarship

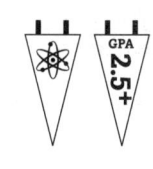

AMOUNT: $1000 DEADLINE: February 7
FIELDS/MAJORS: Agriculture

Scholarships available for incoming freshmen. Based on academic achievement, leadership, citizenship, and dedication to agriculture during high school. Write to the address below for more information. GPA must be at least 2.8.

Illinois State University, Dept. of Agriculture
Turner Hall 150
Campus Box 5020
Normal, IL 61761

3657
Paul V. Whalen Scholarship

AMOUNT: $400-$1000 DEADLINE: February 6
FIELDS/MAJORS: Agriculture

Scholarship awarded to an incoming freshman enrolling in an agriculture curriculum at Illinois State University. Selection will be based on demonstrated academic achievement and leadership abilities. Applicants must be residents of Colchester or the surrounding area. For more information, contact your high school guidance counselor, write to the address below, or call (309) 438-5654. GPA must be at least 2.9.

Illinois State University, Dept. of Agriculture
Turner Hall 150
Campus Box 5020
Normal, IL 61761

3658
Reg and Edith Henry Leadership Scholarship

AMOUNT: $400-$1000 DEADLINE: February 6
FIELDS/MAJORS: Agriculture

Open to incoming freshmen or transfer students accepted at ISU. Based on leadership. Preference given to a current or former State FFA officer or Section president. Concurrent participation in a Departmental club or serving as an Agriculture Associate is required. Must maintain a minimum GPA of 2.5. Contact the address listed or call (309) 438-5654 for further information.

Illinois State University, Dept. of Agriculture
Turner Hall 150
Campus Box 5020
Normal, IL 61761

3659
State of Illinois Director of Agriculture Scholarship

AMOUNT: $400-$1000 DEADLINE: February 6
FIELDS/MAJORS: Agriculture or Agribusiness

Scholarship awarded to an incoming freshman or transfer student enrolling in an agricultural curriculum at Illinois State University. Selection will be based on demonstrated academic achievement and leadership abilities. Financial need will be considered. Applicants must be Illinois farmers or children of Illinois farmers. Five awards offered per year. For more information, contact your high school guidance counselor, write to the address below, or call (309) 438-5654. GPA must be at least 2.9.

Illinois State University, Dept. of Agriculture
Turner Hall 150
Campus Box 5020
Normal, IL 61761

INDIANA STATE UNIVERSITY

3660
Alumni Scholarships and ISU Academic Scholarships

AMOUNT: $1500 DEADLINE: February 1
FIELDS/MAJORS: All Areas of Study

Scholarships are available at Indiana State University for incoming full-time freshmen who rank in the top 10% of their graduating class or have a GPA of at least 3.7. Based on academic ability, scope, and nature of extracurricular activities and any awards, recognitions, or citations received. Awards range from $1500 to full in-state tuition. Write to the address below for details.

Indiana State University
Office of Admissions
Terre Haute, IN 47809

3661
Creative and Performing Arts Award

AMOUNT: None Specified DEADLINE: None Specified
FIELDS/MAJORS: Art, Drama, Music

Scholarships are available at Indiana State University for full-time incoming freshmen who exhibit talent in the areas listed above. These scholarships require a separate application and audition, portfolio review, or interview. Contact the department of the area for which you are applying. Contact the individual departments, at the address below, for specific information. Several departments schedule auditions, competitions, and interviews in the fall and winter. Early contact is highly recommended.

Indiana State University
Office of Admissions
Terre Haute, IN 47809

3662
Dean's Scholarship

AMOUNT: Maximum: $1200 DEADLINE: February 1
FIELDS/MAJORS: All Areas of Study

Scholarships are available at Indiana State University for full-time incoming freshmen who rank in the top 25% of their graduating class or have a GPA of at least 3.5. Based on potential for success in chosen major. Write to the address below for details.

Indiana State University
Office of Admissions
Terre Haute, IN 47809

3663
President's Merit Scholarship

AMOUNT: None Specified DEADLINE: February 1
FIELDS/MAJORS: All Areas of Study

Available to incoming full-time freshmen at Indiana State University who rank in the top 10% of their graduating class or have a GPA of at least 3.7. Based on academic ability, potential, test scores, leadership potential, extracurricular activities, and community service. An interview will be required. Award is full in-state tuition, room and board, and a stipend for books and supplies. Write to the address below for details.

Indiana State University
Office of Admissions
Terre Haute, IN 47809

3664
Summer Honors Scholarship

AMOUNT: Maximum: $1100 DEADLINE: February 1
FIELDS/MAJORS: All Areas of Study

Scholarships are available at Indiana State University for full-time incoming freshmen who participate in the summer honors program. Based on class rank, GPA, standardized test scores, and school curriculum. Write to the address below for details. GPA must be at least 3.5.

Indiana State University
Office of Admissions
Terre Haute, IN 47809

3665
Warren M. Anderson Scholarship

AMOUNT: Maximum: $1200 DEADLINE: February 1
FIELDS/MAJORS: All Areas of Study

Scholarships are available at Indiana State University for incoming full-time freshmen who rank in the top 30% of their graduating class or have a GPA of at least 3.0. Based on school and community service accomplishments and a letter of recommendation from a counselor, civic leader, principal, or minister will be required. Ethnicity is a consideration for this award. Write to the address below for details.

Indiana State University
Office of Admissions
Terre Haute, IN 47809

INDIANA UNIVERSITY

3666
Dr. Gombojab Hangin Scholarship

AMOUNT: Maximum: $2500 DEADLINE: January 1
FIELDS/MAJORS: All Areas of Study

Scholarships are available for students of Mongolian heritage. Preference given to citizens of Mongolia, People's Republic of China, or the former Soviet Union. Write to the address listed for information.

Mongolia Society, Inc.
Hangin Scholarship Committee
322 Goodbody Hall, Indiana University
Bloomington, IN 47405

INSTITUTE FOR ADVANCED STUDY

3667
Postdoctoral Fellowships at the Institute for Advanced Study

AMOUNT: None Specified DEADLINE: None Specified
FIELDS/MAJORS: Historical Studies, Social Sciences, Natural Sciences, Mathematics

The Institute has four separate schools as below by the fields above. Competition is open, and the major consideration is the expectation that each fellow's period of residence will result in work of significance and individuality. 160 fellowships are awarded per year. Write to the address or each school's e-mail for further information. School of Historical Studies, deadline November 15, e-mail mzelazny@ias.edu. School of Mathematics, deadline December 1, e-mail math.ias.edu. School of Natural Science, deadline December 1, e-mail michelle@sns.ias.edu. School of Social Science, deadline November 15, e-mail dlk@ias.edu.

Institute for Advanced Study
Postdoctoral Fellowships
Olden Lane
Princeton, NJ 08540

INSTITUTE OF AMERICAN INDIAN ARTS

3668
Institute of American Indian Arts Scholarships

AMOUNT: $300-$10000 DEADLINE: April 15
FIELDS/MAJORS: Art, Museum Studies

Scholarships are available for undergraduate Native American students at the Institute of American Indian Art. Based on financial need. Must be from a federally recognized Native American tribe and members of Alaskan Native Corps. Write to the address below for information.

Institute of American Indian Art
PO Box 20007
Santa Fe, NM 87504

INSTITUTE OF CURRENT WORLD AFFAIRS

3669
John Miller Musser Memorial Forest and Fellowship

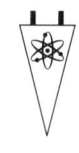

AMOUNT: None Specified DEADLINE: September 1
FIELDS/MAJORS: Forestry, Environmental Science

Fellowships are available to postdoctoral scholars to support research, outside of the U.S., in an area of interest to the foundation, including those areas mentioned above. Tenure is two years. Applicants must be age thirty-six or less and have a good command of written/spoken English. Second deadline date is April 1 for a June decision. Write to the address below for information.

Institute of Current World Affairs
Gary L. Hansen, Program Administrator
4 West Wheelock Street
Hanover, NH 03755

3670
John O. Crane Memorial Fellowship

AMOUNT: None Specified DEADLINE: September 1
FIELDS/MAJORS: International Studies-Middle East, Eastern Europe

Fellowships are available to postdoctoral scholars to support research, outside the U.S., in an area of interest to the foundation, including those areas mentioned above. Tenure is two years. Applicants must be age thirty-six or less and have a good command of written/spoken English. Second deadline date is April 1 for a June decision. Write to the address below for information.

Institute of Current World Affairs
Gary L. Hansen, Program Administrator
4 West Wheelock Street
Hanover, NH 03755

INSTITUTE OF EARLY AMERICAN HISTORY AND CULTURE

3671
Postdoctoral Fellowship

AMOUNT: $30000 DEADLINE: November 1
FIELDS/MAJORS: Early American History and Culture

Postdoctoral residential fellowship. Must meet requirements for Ph.D. before beginning fellowship (ABD). Must have potential for eventual publication. Residence is maintained at the College of William and Mary. Applicants may not have previously published a book. Ph.D. holders who have begun careers in the field are welcome to apply. Tenure is for two years. Includes appointment as Assistant Professor. Write to the address below for more information.

Institute of Early American History and Culture
Office of the Director
PO Box 8781
Williamsburg, VA 23187

IOWA STATE UNIVERSITY

3672
Alice McCarthy Commons Memorial Scholarship

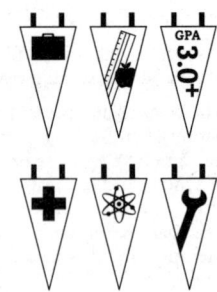

AMOUNT: None Specified
DEADLINE: January 2
FIELDS/MAJORS: Apparel Merchandising/Design, Dietetics, Early Childhood Education, Food Science, Nutritional Science, Hotel/Restaurant Management

Open to incoming freshmen who rank in the top 10% of high school graduating class. Qualified applicants will receive a letter outlining the procedure for application. Contact the address below for further information. GPA must be at least 3.0.

Iowa State University-College of Family/Consumer Sciences
Letha DeMoss
122A MacKay Hall
Ames, IA 50011-1120

3673
American Indian Scholarship

AMOUNT: None Specified DEADLINE: May 1
FIELDS/MAJORS: All Areas of Study

Open to incoming freshmen, admitted to ISU, who are at least 25% Native American and demonstrate financial need. Contact the address below or call (515) 294-2223 for further information.

Iowa State University-Special Population Unit
Office of Student Financial Aid
12 Beardshear Hall
Ames, IA 50011

3674
Animal Science Scholarship

AMOUNT: Maximum: $500 DEADLINE: March 15
FIELDS/MAJORS: Animal Science

Open to entering freshmen, admitted to ISU, majoring in animal science or animal science-pre-veterinary medicine. Based on academics, leadership, and interest in the animal industry. Two to four awards offered annually. Contact the address below or call (515) 294-6614 for further information.

Iowa State University-College of Agriculture
Scholarship Committee
119 Kildee Hall
Ames, IA 50011

3675
Austin and Isabel Dowell Scholarship

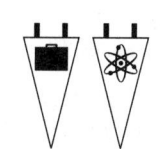

AMOUNT: Maximum: $500   DEADLINE: March 1
FIELDS/MAJORS: Agribusiness/Economics, Consumer Science

Open to full-time undergraduate students attending ISU. Based on academic achievement and financial need. Contact the address below or call (515) 294-2223 for further information.

Iowa State University
Office of Student Financial Aid
12 Beardshear Hall
Ames, IA 50011

3676
Barbara Nelson Eddy Scholarship for Excellence

AMOUNT: Maximum: $2500
DEADLINE: January 2
FIELDS/MAJORS: Apparel Merchandising/Design, Dietetics, Early Childhood Education, Food Science, Nutritional Science, Hotel/Restaurant Management

Open to incoming freshmen who are ranked number one or two or rank in the top 5% of high school graduating class. Based on outstanding achievement, extracurricular activities, or other personal activities outside the classroom. Must show promise of ability and inclination to make a significant contribution to society. Qualified applicants will receive a letter outlining the procedure for application. Contact the address below for further information. GPA must be at least 3.5.

Iowa State University-College of Family/Consumer Sciences
Letha DeMoss
122A MacKay Hall
Ames, IA 50011-1120

3677
Charles Blaul and Mary G. Whiting Scholarships

AMOUNT: Maximum: $1000   DEADLINE: March 1
FIELDS/MAJORS: All Areas of Study

Open to undergraduates attending ISU, based on academics and financial need. Contact the address below or call (515) 294-2223 for further information about both awards.

Iowa State University
Office of Student Financial Aid
12 Beardshear Hall
Ames, IA 50011

3678
Charles W. Schafer Scholarships

AMOUNT: None Specified   DEADLINE: March 1
FIELDS/MAJORS: Civil Engineering

Open to entering freshmen, admitted to ISU, who are U.S. citizens. Based on academics and financial need. Renewable up to four years if student maintains a minimum GPA of 3.0. Contact the address below or call (515) 294-2223 for further information.

Iowa State University-College of Engineering
Scholarship Coordinator
116 Marston Hall-Engineering Student Svc.
Ames, IA 50011

3679
Charlotte Gustafson Akins Home Economics Scholarship

AMOUNT: None Specified
DEADLINE: January 2
FIELDS/MAJORS: Apparel Merchandising/Design, Dietetics, Early Childhood Education, Food Science, Nutritional Science, Hotel/Restaurant Management

Open to incoming freshmen who rank in the top 10% of high school graduating class. Based on academics, financial need, professional potential, and involvement in professional and extracurricular activities. Qualified applicants will receive a letter outlining the procedure for application. Contact the address below for further information. GPA must be at least 3.3.

Iowa State University-College of Family/Consumer Sciences
Letha DeMoss
122A MacKay Hall
Ames, IA 50011-1120

3680
Christina Hixson Opportunity Awards

AMOUNT: Maximum: $2500   DEADLINE: February 15
FIELDS/MAJORS: All Areas of Study

Open to incoming freshmen accepted at ISU, who are Iowa residents. Awards recognize the obstacles and adversity some students face. Based on financial need, family circumstances, and potential for success. One hundred awards are offered annually. Contact the address below for further information or call (515) 294-6545.

Iowa State University
Christina Hixson Opt'y Awards
314 Alumni Hall
Ames, IA 50011

3681
Clair B. Watson Design Scholarship

AMOUNT: Maximum: $1000   DEADLINE: February 10
FIELDS/MAJORS: Architecture, Regional Planning, Graphic Design, Interior Design, Landscape Architecture

Open to entering freshmen enrolled/admitted to the College of Design at ISU. Based on high school rank, ACT scores, and a self-authored essay. A portfolio may be submitted for consideration but is not required. Contact the address below for further information. GPA must be at least 3.0.

Iowa State University
Roger Baer, Assistant Dean
134 College of Design
Ames, IA 50011-3091

3682
Clyde Black and Son Agriculture Award

AMOUNT: Maximum: $400   DEADLINE: May 1
FIELDS/MAJORS: Agronomy

Open to entering freshmen, admitted to ISU, based on extracurricular activities, leadership, scholarship, work/community experience, and financial need. Three to four awards are given annually. Contact the Chair of Undergraduate Scholarship and Recognition Committee at the address below or call (515) 294-3846 for further information.

Iowa State University-Department of Agronomy
Department of Agronomy
1126C Agronomy
Ames, IA 50011

3683
College of Agriculture Freshman Scholarship

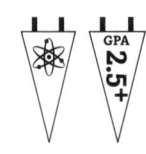

AMOUNT: Maximum: $300   DEADLINE: None Specified
FIELDS/MAJORS: Agriculture

Open to full-time freshmen, admitted to Iowa State University, majoring in agricultural education. Must have GPAs of 2.5 or higher during the first semester, and the award will be received second semester. Contact the address below for further information.

Iowa State University-College of Agriculture
Agricultural Education and Studies Dept.
201 Curtiss Hall
Ames, IA 50011

3684
Computational Science Fellowship Program

AMOUNT: None Specified   DEADLINE: January 24
FIELDS/MAJORS: Life or Physical Science, Engineering, Mathematics

Fellowships are available at Iowa State for graduate students in their second year of graduate studies (or above). For science or engineering students with career objectives in computational science. Must be a U.S. citizen or permanent resident. The awards are $1500 per month, and the deadline date to apply is the third Wednesday of every January. Write to the address below for information.

Iowa State University
Ames Laboratory
125 S. Third St., Sherman Place
Ames, IA 50010

3685
Computer Science Freshman Scholarship

AMOUNT: $500-$1000   DEADLINE: December 15
FIELDS/MAJORS: Computer Science

Open to incoming freshmen, admitted to ISU, who were in the top 5% of their graduating classes and had an ACT composite of 29 or above. Consideration will be given to high school preparation in Math and Science. Renewable if student earns 12 or more graded credits with a minimum GPA of 2.75 in the first semester. Contact the address below or call (515) 294-2223 for further information.

Iowa State University
Computer Science Advising
223 Atanasoff Hall
Ames, IA 50011

3686
Dairy Science Freshman Scholarship

AMOUNT: Maximum: $400   DEADLINE: April 1
FIELDS/MAJORS: Dairy Science

Open to students who are enrolled or admitted to Iowa State University and majoring in dairy science or dairy science, pre-vet. Leadership and dairy-related activities are the primary criteria. Contact the address below for further information. GPA must be at least 2.5.

Iowa State University-College of Agriculture
Dairy Science Cur. Scholarship Committee
123 Kildee Hall
Ames, IA 50011

3687
Delta Chi Memorial Scholarship

AMOUNT: Maximum: $100   DEADLINE: March 1
FIELDS/MAJORS: All Areas of Study

Open to enrolling freshmen at Iowa State University. Based on ACT scores, academics, and leadership. For further information, send a SASE to the address listed. Must have a GPA of at least 3.0.

Delta Chi Fraternity
Scholarship Committee
405 Hayward Ave.
Ames, IA 50014

3688
Department of Music Scholarships

AMOUNT: None Specified   DEADLINE: None Specified
FIELDS/MAJORS: Music, Voice, Woodwinds, Brasses, Percussion, Keyboard, Strings

Open to music majors in voice, woodwinds, brasses, percussion, keyboard; music majors and non-music majors in strings and piano accompanying. Applicants must complete ISU admission process, submit Department of Music Scholarship application and two recommendation forms, and perform an audition. Auditions are held in late January and early February. Information may be obtained from the Department of Music at the address below or call (515) 294-2223.

Iowa State University, Department of Music
Scholarship and Admission Committee
149 Music Hall
Ames, IA 50011

3689
Devries Scholarship

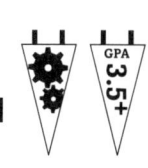

AMOUNT: None Specified   DEADLINE: March 1
FIELDS/MAJORS: Pre-Business

Open to full-time entering freshmen, admitted to ISU, who are Iowa residents. Renewable by maintaining a 3.2 GPA. One award offered annually. Contact the address below or call (515) 294-2223 for further information.

Iowa State University-College of Business
Ann Coppernoll Farni
204 Carver Hall
Ames, IA 50011

3690
Dewild Grant Reckert Scholarship

AMOUNT: Maximum: $1000   DEADLINE: March 1
FIELDS/MAJORS: Engineering

Open to entering freshmen, admitted to ISU, who graduated from a Lyon County, Iowa, high school with a minimum GPA of 3.0. Relevant work experience, courses taken, leadership, and extracurricular activities will be considered. One award offered annually. Contact the address below or call (515) 294-2223 for further information.

Iowa State University-College of Engineering
Scholarship Coordinator
116 Marston Hall-Engineering Student Svc.
Ames, IA 50011

3691
Distinguished Scholar

AMOUNT: Maximum: $2500   DEADLINE: March 1
FIELDS/MAJORS: All Areas of Study

Open to entering freshmen accepted at ISU. Based on academic excellence as determined by high school class rank, cumulative GPA, and ACT or SAT scores. Finalists selected on basis of academic information from admission files. Contact the address below for further information or call (515) 294-2223. GPA must be at least 3.0.

Iowa State University Foundation
Office of Admissions
100 Alumni Hall
Ames, IA 50011

3692
Don P. Shafer Memorial Scholarship

AMOUNT: None Specified   DEADLINE: March 1
FIELDS/MAJORS: Engineering

Open to entering freshmen, admitted to ISU, with a minimum high school GPA of 3.5. Based on academics. Preference will be given to Iowa residents then students from the midwest. Contact the address below or call (515) 294-2223 for further information.

Iowa State University-College of Engineering
Scholarship Coordinator
116 Marston Hall-Engineering Student Svc.
Ames, IA 50011

3693
Dorothy Klindt Memorial Scholarship

AMOUNT: Maximum: $1000
DEADLINE: December 1
FIELDS/MAJORS: Agriculture, Consumer Science

Open to incoming freshmen in the colleges of Agriculture or Family and Consumer Sciences. Based on above average academics and involvement in school/community/work activities. Preference to female students from rural areas and small towns in the Iowa counties of: Scott, Cedar, Clinton, or Muscatine. Four awards offered annually. Contact the address below or call (515) 294-2223 for further information. GPA must be at least 2.7.

Iowa State University
M. Porter, Alumni Suite, Memorial Union
2229 W. Lincoln Way
Ames, IA 50014

3694
Dow Chemical Company Scholarships

AMOUNT: Maximum: $1000 DEADLINE: March 1
FIELDS/MAJORS: Chemical Engineering

Open to entering freshmen, admitted to ISU, who are U.S. citizens or permanent residents. Based on academic achievement. One award offered annually. Contact the address below or call (515) 294-2223 for further information.

Iowa State University-College of Engineering
Scholarship Coordinator
116 Marston Hall-Engineering Student Svc.
Ames, IA 50011

3695
Dow-Goetz and Noble Hines Scholarships

AMOUNT: $1000-$4000 DEADLINE: February 15
FIELDS/MAJORS: Chemistry

Open to incoming freshmen, admitted to ISU, who have had a minimum of one year of Chemistry in high school. Must have a minimum GPA of 3.5 and an ACT composite of 27 or higher. One award offered annually. Contact the address below or call (515) 294-2223 for further information about both scholarships.

Iowa State University-Department of Chemistry
Chemistry Undergraduate Office
1608 Gilman Hall
Ames, IA 50011

3696
Edalene Stohr Brown Scholarship

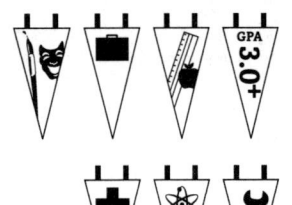

AMOUNT: None Specified
DEADLINE: January 2
FIELDS/MAJORS: Apparel Merchandising/Design, Dietetics, Early Childhood Education, Food Science, Nutritional Science, Hotel/Restaurant Management

Open to incoming freshmen who rank in the top 10% of high school graduating class and are interested in business careers. Based on academics and demonstrated leadership qualities. Qualified applicants will receive a letter outlining the procedure for application. Contact the address below for further information. GPA must be at least 3.0.

Iowa State University-College of Family/Consumer Sciences
Letha DeMoss
122A MacKay Hall
Ames, IA 50011-1120

3697
Eda Lord Demarest Scholarship

AMOUNT: None Specified
DEADLINE: January 2
FIELDS/MAJORS: Apparel Merchandising/Design, Dietetics, Early Childhood Education, Food Science, Nutritional Science, Hotel/Restaurant Management

Open to incoming freshmen who rank in the top 10% of high school graduating class. Qualified applicants will receive a letter outlining the procedure for application. Contact the address below for further information. GPA must be at least 3.0.

Iowa State University-College of Family/Consumer Sciences
Letha DeMoss
122A MacKay Hall
Ames, IA 50011-1120

3698
Edward F. and Phoebe H. Knipling Scholarships

AMOUNT: None Specified DEADLINE: December 1
FIELDS/MAJORS: Agriculture

Open to enrolled or admitted students pursuing degrees in agriculture. Award is renewable. Contact the address below or call (515) 294-6614 for further information. GPA must be at least 2.8.

Iowa State University-College of Agriculture
Assoc. Dean for Academic Programs
134 Curtiss Hall
Ames, IA 50011-1050

3699
Erben A. and Margaret H. Hunziker Scholarship

AMOUNT: None Specified DEADLINE: March 1
FIELDS/MAJORS: Engineering

Open to incoming freshmen, admitted to ISU, based on academics and financial need. Must have graduated from a high school in Iowa. Renewable for one year if student maintains a minimum GPA of 2.75. One award offered annually. Contact the address below or call (515) 294-2223 for further information.

Iowa State University-College of Engineering
Scholarship Coordinator
116 Marston Hall-Engineering Student Svc.
Ames, IA 50011

3700
Ethel McKinley Bliss Scholarship

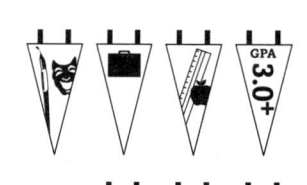

AMOUNT: None Specified
DEADLINE: January 2
FIELDS/MAJORS: Apparel Merchandising/Design, Dietetics, Early Childhood Education, Food Science, Nutritional Science, Hotel/Restaurant Management

Open to incoming freshmen who rank in the top 10% of high school graduating class and are Iowa residents. Based on academics, leadership potential, and financial need. Qualified applicants will receive a letter outlining the procedure for application. Contact the address below for further information. GPA must be at least 3.3.

Iowa State University-College of Family/Consumer Sciences
Letha DeMoss
122A MacKay Hall
Ames, IA 50011-1120

3701
Evered Ihrig Memorial Scholarships

AMOUNT: Maximum: $1000 DEADLINE: January 31
FIELDS/MAJORS: Animal Science

Open to entering freshmen, admitted to ISU, who will be graduating from high schools in any of the following counties: Benton, Cedar, Iowa, Johnson, Louisa, Linn, Muscatine, or Washington. Persons having some degree of family relationship to the late Charles Leslie Ihrig or Wenona Ihrig are also eligible. Based on academics, extracurricular activities, and interest in forestry. Contact the address below or call (515) 294-6614 for further information. GPA must be at least 2.8.

Iowa State University-College of Agriculture
Dept. of Forestry, Dr. J. Michael Kelly
251 Bessey Hall
Ames, IA 50011-1021

3702
Excellence in Agriculture Scholarship

AMOUNT: None Specified DEADLINE: December 1
FIELDS/MAJORS: Agriculture

Open to entering freshmen, admitted to ISU, with a minimum GPA of 3.5 and an ACT composite of 28 or higher or SAT score of 1160 or higher. Must have potential to make a significant contribution to society as demonstrated by extracurricular activities or employment experiences. Contact the address below or call (515) 294-6614 for further information.

Iowa State University-College of Agriculture
Associate Dean for Academic Programs
134 Curtiss Hall
Ames, IA 50011

3703
Family and Consumer Undergraduate Scholarships

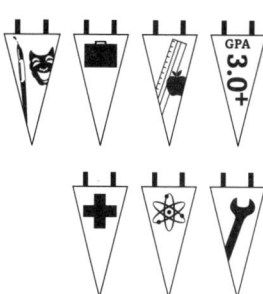

AMOUNT: None Specified
DEADLINE: January 2
FIELDS/MAJORS: Apparel Merchandising/Design, Dietetics, Early Childhood Education, Food Science, Nutritional Science, Hotel/Restaurant Management

Open to incoming freshmen who are ranked in the top 10% of high school graduating class. Qualified applicants will receive a letter outlining the procedure for application. Includes the Judy Hintzman Furgason, Helen Geertz Memorial, Helen Green Grieve, Carol Critzman Hansen, George E. and Nellie Stromer Heald, Elizabeth Helser and the Edith A. and Louis W. Herdlicka, Hazel Hermanson Lawrence, Irene Beavers, Iva and Stephen Inman, and the Iowa Farm Bureau Scholarships. Contact the address below for further information. GPA must be at least 3.3.

Iowa State University-College of Family/Consumer Sciences
Letha DeMoss
122A MacKay Hall
Ames, IA 50011-1120

3704
Floyd Andre Scholarship

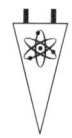

AMOUNT: None Specified DEADLINE: December 1
FIELDS/MAJORS: Agriculture

Open to entering Iowa resident freshmen, admitted to ISU, based on extracurricular activities and leadership potential. One award is given annually. Contact the address below or call (515) 294-6614 for further information.

Iowa State University-College of Agriculture
Associate Dean for Academic Programs
134 Curtiss Hall
Ames, IA 50011

3705
Forestry Scholarship

AMOUNT: $500-$1000   DEADLINE: January 31
FIELDS/MAJORS: Forestry

Open to entering freshmen, admitted to ISU, based on academic achievement and extracurricular activities. Two awards offered annually. Contact the address below or call (515) 294-2223 for further information.

Iowa State University-Department of Forestry
Dr. Steven Jungst
251 Bessey Hall
Ames, IA 50011

3706
Francis V. Kirkpatrick Scholarships

AMOUNT: Maximum: $1000   DEADLINE: March 1
FIELDS/MAJORS: All Areas of Study

Open to incoming freshmen, admitted to ISU, from Keokuk County, Iowa. One award offered annually. Contact the address below or call (515) 294-2223 for further information.

Iowa State University
Office of Student Financial Aid
12 Beardshear Hall
Ames, IA 50011

3707
Fred Schleiter Scholarship

AMOUNT: None Specified   DEADLINE: March 1
FIELDS/MAJORS: All Areas of Study

Open to non-resident minority students, admitted to ISU, who have a high financial need. Contact the address below or call (515) 294-2223 for further information.

Iowa State University-Special Population Unit
Office of Student Financial Aid
12 Beardshear Hall
Ames, IA 50011

3708
Gene C. Meyer Scholarship

AMOUNT: $500   DEADLINE: January 31
FIELDS/MAJORS: Forestry

Open to students admitted to ISU, majoring in forestry with an emphasis of forest products and industrial forest management. Applicants must be enrolled in or have already completed courses in business, economics, or agribusiness. Based on academics and financial need. Award ranges from $500 to full in-state tuition. Contact the address below for further information. GPA must be at least 2.8.

Iowa State University
Dr. J. Michael Kelly, Dept. of Forestry
251 Bessey Hall
Ames, IA 50011-1021

3709
General Engineering Scholarships

AMOUNT: None Specified   DEADLINE: March 1
FIELDS/MAJORS: Engineering

Open to incoming freshmen, admitted to ISU, based on academic achievement. Contact the address below or call (515) 294-2223 for further information.

Iowa State University-College of Engineering
Scholarship Coordinator
116 Marston Hall-Engineering Student Svc.
Ames, IA 50011

3710
George and Dorothy Thomson Scholarship

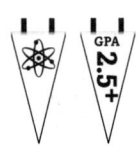

AMOUNT: Maximum: $1000   DEADLINE: January 31
FIELDS/MAJORS: Forestry

Open to students admitted to ISU, majoring in forestry. Based on academics, extracurricular activities, and demonstrated interest in forestry. Preference given to students transferring from the community college system. Contact the address below for further information. GPA must be at least 2.8.

Iowa State University
Dr. J. Michael Kelly, Dept. of Forestry
251 Bessey Hall
Ames, IA 50011-1021

3711
George Washington Carver Project Excellence Scholarship

AMOUNT: None Specified DEADLINE: None Specified
FIELDS/MAJORS: All Areas of Study

Open to African-American seniors, attending ISU, who reside in the Washington D.C. area. Based on academics and ability to communicate. Must be nominated by your high school. Awards vary to pay for tuition, fees, room and board, and a stipend. Contact your high school guidance counselor or call (515) 294-2223 for further information.

Iowa State University-Special Populations Unit
Office of Student Financial Aid
12 Beardshear Hall
Ames, IA 50011

3712
Harry J. and Nellie B. Griffith Memorial Scholarship

AMOUNT: $500 DEADLINE: March 1
FIELDS/MAJORS: All Areas of Study

Open to incoming freshmen, admitted to ISU, who are graduates of Wilton High School and Durant High School. Students who earn at least a 2.5 GPA may have their scholarship renewed, but amounts may vary, depending on availability of funds. Contact the address below or call (515) 294-2223 for further information.

Iowa State University
Office of Student Financial Aid
12 Beardshear Hall
Ames, IA 50011

3713
Harvey Louis Dunker Scholarship

AMOUNT: None Specified DEADLINE: March 1
FIELDS/MAJORS: Engineering

Open to incoming freshmen, admitted to ISU, based on academics and financial need. Renewable up to four years if student maintains a minimum GPA of 2.75. Contact the address below or call (515) 294-2223 for further information.

Iowa State University-College of Engineering
Scholarship Coordinator
116 Marston Hall-Engineering Student Svc.
Ames, IA 50011

3714
Henning H. Henningson Memorial Scholarships

AMOUNT: Maximum: $1000 DEADLINE: March 1
FIELDS/MAJORS: Electrical Engineering

Open to incoming freshmen, admitted to ISU, who come from a rural Iowa background. Based on academic achievement. Two awards offered annually. Contact the address below or call (515) 294-2223 for further information.

Iowa State University-College of Engineering
Scholarship Coordinator
116 Marston Hall-Engineering Student Svc.
Ames, IA 50011

3715
Hoechst Celanese Scholarships

AMOUNT: None Specified
DEADLINE: March 1
FIELDS/MAJORS: Chemical Engineering

Open to incoming African-American, Hispanic, or women freshmen, admitted to ISU, who are U.S. citizens or Native American students. Renewable up to four years based on student's GPA. Contact the address below or call (515) 294-2223 for further information.

Iowa State University-College of Engineering
Scholarship Coordinator
116 Marston Hall-Engineering Student Svc.
Ames, IA 50011

3716
H. Stuart Kuyper Scholarships

AMOUNT: None Specified DEADLINE: March 1
FIELDS/MAJORS: Engineering

Open to entering freshmen, admitted to ISU, based on academic achievement. Contact the address below or call (515) 294-2223 for further information.

Iowa State University-College of Engineering
Scholarship Coordinator
116 Marston Hall-Engineering Student Svc.
Ames, IA 50011

3717
ISU Agriculture Foundation Scholarships

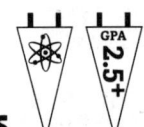

AMOUNT: Maximum: $1000 DEADLINE: December 1
FIELDS/MAJORS: Agriculture

Open to enrolled or admitted students in the College of Agriculture who have an interest in farming as careers. Applicants must be Iowa residents and be able to demonstrate good academics and leadership. Contact the address below or call (515) 294-6614 for further information. GPA must be at least 2.8.

Iowa State University-College of Agriculture
Assoc. Dean for Academic Programs
134 Curtiss Hall
Ames, IA 50011-1050

3718
I. W. Arthur Memorial Scholarship

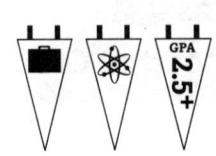

AMOUNT: Maximum: $750 DEADLINE: May 1
FIELDS/MAJORS: Economics, Agribusiness

Open to incoming freshmen for their second semester at ISU. Based on a minimum GPA of 2.5 for the first semester's work. Six awards offered annually. Contact the address below or call (515) 294-2223 for further information.

Iowa State University-Department of Economics
Professor-in-Charge, Undergrad Economics
280 Heady Hall
Ames, IA 50011

3719
John and Helen Wessman Scholarships

AMOUNT: None Specified DEADLINE: March 1
FIELDS/MAJORS: Agricultural Engineering

Open to incoming freshmen, admitted to ISU, based on academic achievement. Leadership and extracurricular activities will also be considered. Renewable for one year if student maintains a minimum GPA of 2.75. Contact the address below or call (515) 294-2223 for further information.

Iowa State University-Department of Agriculture and
  Biosystems Engineering
Chair, Scholarship Committee
102 Davidson Hall
Ames, IA 50011

3720
Johnie Christian Scholarship

AMOUNT: None Specified
DEADLINE: January 2
FIELDS/MAJORS: Apparel Merchandising/Design, Dietetics, Early Childhood Education, Food Science, Nutritional Science, Hotel/Restaurant Management

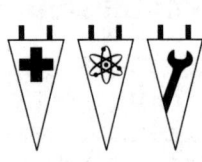

Open to incoming freshmen who rank in the top 10% of high school graduating class. Preference given to minority and underprivileged students. Qualified applicants will receive a letter outlining the procedure for application. Contact the address below for further information. GPA must be at least 2.8.

Iowa State University-College of Family/Consumer Sciences
Letha DeMoss
122A MacKay Hall
Ames, IA 50011-1120

3721
John F. Stevens Scholarship

AMOUNT: None Specified DEADLINE: March 1
FIELDS/MAJORS: Chemical Engineering

Open to incoming freshmen, admitted to ISU, based on academic achievement. One award offered annually. Contact the address below or call (515) 294-2223 for further information.

Iowa State University-College of Engineering
Scholarship Coordinator
116 Marston Hall-Engineering Student Svc.
Ames, IA 50011

3722
J.S. Latta, Jr. Pre-Business Scholarship

AMOUNT: Maximum: $500 DEADLINE: March 1
FIELDS/MAJORS: Pre-Business

Open to entering freshmen, admitted to ISU, who demonstrates academic achievement, character, and financial need. Two awards offered annually. Contact the address below or call (515) 294-2223 for further information.

Iowa State University-College of Business
Ann Coppernoll Farni
204 Carver Hall
Ames, IA 50011

3723
Katherine Burnlett Annin Scholarship

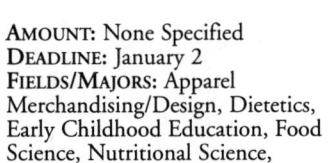

AMOUNT: None Specified
DEADLINE: January 2
FIELDS/MAJORS: Apparel Merchandising/Design, Dietetics, Early Childhood Education, Food Science, Nutritional Science, Hotel/Restaurant Management

Open to incoming female freshmen who rank in the top 10% of high school graduating class. Based on academics and demonstrated interest in politics or public service. Applicants must be U.S. citizens. Contact the address below for further information. GPA must be at least 3.3.

Iowa State University-College of Family/Consumer Sciences
Letha DeMoss
122A MacKay Hall
Ames, IA 50011-1120

3724
Kim Bailey Memorial Scholarship

AMOUNT: Maximum: $500 DEADLINE: March 15
FIELDS/MAJORS: All Areas of Study

Open to seniors whose schools are in the Kansas City metropolitan area. Must be in the top 25% of their classes and plan to attend Iowa State after graduation. Based on leadership, academics, character, and financial need. One award offered annually. Contact the address below or call (913) 829-1384 for further information. GPA must be at least 2.5.

Iowa State Club of Kansas City
Joe Chandler
16605 W 132nd St.
Olathe, KS 66062

3725
Larry J. McComber Scholarship

AMOUNT: None Specified DEADLINE: March 1
FIELDS/MAJORS: Engineering

Open to incoming freshmen, admitted to ISU, based on academics and financial need. One award offered annually. Contact the address below or call (515) 294-2223 for further information.

Iowa State University-College of Engineering
Scholarship Coordinator
116 Marston Hall-Engineering Student Svc.
Ames, IA 50011

3726
Leland and Cora Allbaugh Scholarship

AMOUNT: None Specified
DEADLINE: January 2
FIELDS/MAJORS: Apparel Merchandising/Design, Dietetics, Early Childhood Education, Food Science, Nutritional Science, Hotel/Restaurant Management

Open to incoming freshmen who rank in the top 10% of high school graduating class. Based on academics and demonstrated financial need. Qualified applicants will receive a letter outlining the procedure for application. Contact the address below for further information. GPA must be at least 3.3.

Iowa State University-College of Family/Consumer Sciences
Letha DeMoss
122A MacKay Hall
Ames, IA 50011-1120

3727
Leonard Hermanson Family Scholarship

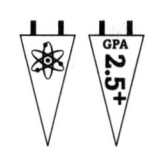

AMOUNT: None Specified   DEADLINE: December 1
FIELDS/MAJORS: Agriculture

Open to enrolled or admitted students in the College of Agriculture. Award may be renewed. Contact the address below or call (515) 294-6614 for further information. GPA must be at least 2.5.

Iowa State University-College of Agriculture
Assoc. Dean for Academic Programs
134 Curtiss Hall
Ames, IA 50011-1050

3728
Lualis Uthoff Dumenil Scholarship

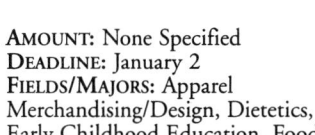

AMOUNT: None Specified
DEADLINE: January 2
FIELDS/MAJORS: Apparel Merchandising/Design, Dietetics, Early Childhood Education, Food Science, Nutritional Science, Hotel/Restaurant Management

Open to current undergraduates and incoming freshmen who rank in the top 10% of high school graduating class. Preference given to students in consumer sciences education or textiles and clothing. Qualified applicants will receive a letter outlining the procedure for application. Contact the address below for further information. GPA must be at least 2.9.

Iowa State University-College of Family/Consumer Sciences
Letha DeMoss
122A MacKay Hall
Ames, IA 50011-1120

3729
Margaret and Barton Morgan Scholarship

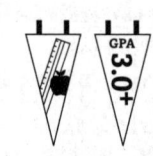

AMOUNT: Maximum: $600 DEADLINE: January 30
FIELDS/MAJORS: Education, School Administration

Open to full-time undergraduates, admitted to ISU, with minimum GPAs of 3.0. Must demonstrate financial need. Two awards offered annually. Contact the address below or call (515) 294-2223 for further information.

Iowa State University
Education Student Services
E105 Lagomarcino Hall
Ames, IA 50011

3730
Maria Roberts Scholarship

AMOUNT: Maximum: $500 DEADLINE: March 1
FIELDS/MAJORS: All Areas of Study

Open to ISU full-time freshmen and sophomores based on academics and financial need. One or two awards offered annually. Contact the address below or call (515) 294-2223 for further information.

Iowa State University
Office of Student Financial Aid
12 Beardshear Hall
Ames, IA 50011

3731
Marian Daniels Mathematics Scholarships

AMOUNT: $500-$1000 DEADLINE: February 15
FIELDS/MAJORS: Mathematics

Open to incoming freshmen, admitted to ISU, based on academics and mathematical interests and abilities. Applicants must submit high school transcript, one or two letters of recommendation (one from a mathematics teacher), ACT or SAT scores, and scores from American High School Mathematics Contest, if available. Contact the address below or call (515) 294-2223 for further information.

Iowa State University-Mathematics Department
Richard Tondra, Undergrad Coordinator
490 Carver
Ames, IA 50011

3732
Mary K. Alexander Scholarship and Hazel Hatcher Memorial Scholarship

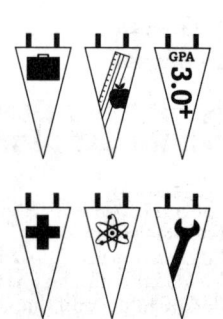

AMOUNT: Maximum: $2000
DEADLINE: January 2
FIELDS/MAJORS: Apparel Merchandising/Design, Dietetics, Early Childhood Education, Food Science, Nutritional Science, Hotel/Restaurant Management

Open to incoming freshmen who rank in the top 10% of high school graduating class. Based on academics, financial need, professional potential, and involvement in professional and extracurricular activities. Qualified applicants will receive a letter outlining the procedure for application. Contact the address below for further information. GPA must be at least 3.3.

Iowa State University-College of Family/Consumer Sciences
Letha DeMoss
122A MacKay Hall
Ames, IA 50011-1120

3733
Max and Adele Levine Scholarship

AMOUNT: Maximum: $500 DEADLINE: March 1
FIELDS/MAJORS: Chemistry, Engineering, Microbiology

Open to graduates of an Iowa high school admitted to Iowa State. Academic achievement and financial need are considered. One award offered annually. Contact the address below or call (515) 294-2223 for further information.

Iowa State University
Office of Student Financial Aid
12 Beardshear Hall
Ames, IA 50011

3734
Mildred D. Bradbury Memorial Scholarship

AMOUNT: None Specified
DEADLINE: January 2
FIELDS/MAJORS: Apparel Merchandising/Design, Dietetics, Early Childhood Education, Food Science, Nutritional Science, Hotel/Restaurant Management

Open to incoming freshmen who rank in the top 10% of high school graduating class and are top academic achievers. Qualified applicants will receive a letter outlining the procedure for application. Contact the address below for further information. GPA must be at least 3.3.

Iowa State University-College of Family/Consumer Sciences
Letha DeMoss
122A MacKay Hall
Ames, IA 50011-1120

3735
Minnie E. Kruckenburg/Walter Wells and Nathaniel Howard Scholarships

AMOUNT: Maximum: $1000   DEADLINE: March 1
FIELDS/MAJORS: All Areas of Study

Open to full-time undergraduate students attending Iowa State. Based on academic achievement and financial need. Contact the address below or call (515) 294-2223 for further information about all three awards.

Iowa State University
Office of Student Financial Aid
12 Beardshear Hall
Ames, IA 50011

3736
Melvin R. Van Winkle Scholarship

AMOUNT: Maximum: $500   DEADLINE: March 1
FIELDS/MAJORS: Electrical Engineering, Computer Engineering

Open to incoming freshmen, admitted to ISU, based on academic achievement. Applicants must be residents of Lee County, Iowa, and be able to demonstrate financial need. One award offered annually. Contact the address below or call (515) 294-2223 for further information. GPA must be at least 2.7.

Iowa State University-College of Engineering
Scholarship Coordinator
116 Marston Hall-Engineering Student Svc.
Ames, IA 50011

3737
Monsanto Company Scholarships

AMOUNT: None Specified   DEADLINE: March 1
FIELDS/MAJORS: Chemical, Electrical, Mechanical, or Civil Engineering

Open to incoming minority freshmen, admitted to ISU, who are from Iowa, Illinois, Missouri, Kansas, or Nebraska. Must have ranked in upper 10% of their high school class and demonstrate financial need. Awards are for resident tuition, room, board, books, supplies, and computer fees. One or two awards are offered annually. Contact the address below or call (515) 294-2223 for further information. GPA must be at least 3.3.

Iowa State University-College of Engineering
Scholarship Coordinator
116 Marston Hall-Engineering Student Svc.
Ames, IA 50011

3738
Orscheln Farm and Home Supply Scholarships

AMOUNT: Maximum: $5000   DEADLINE: December 1
FIELDS/MAJORS: Agriculture

Open to students admitted to ISU, who are Iowa residents living south of U.S. Highway 30. Preference given to students living in Orscheln trade areas who have four years of FFA experience, leadership potential, good character, and moral traits. Must be able to demonstrate financial need, interest in family farm, and service orientation. Award ranges from $500 to full state tuition. Contact the address below for further information or call (515) 294-6614. GPA must be at least 2.8.

Iowa State University-College of Agriculture
Assoc. Dean for Academic Programs
134 Curtiss Hall
Ames, IA 50011-1050

3739
Outstanding Freshman Scholarship

AMOUNT: Maximum: $750   DEADLINE: January 30
FIELDS/MAJORS: Industrial Education/Technology

Open to entering freshmen enrolled in the Department of Industrial Education and Technology at ISU. Based on academic performance. One award offered annually. Contact the address below or call (515) 294-2223 for further information.

Iowa State University
Dr. John Dugger
114I Ed. II
Ames, IA 50011

3740
Paul E. Morgan Scholarships

AMOUNT: None Specified   DEADLINE: March 1
FIELDS/MAJORS: Engineering

Open to incoming freshmen who are women, Native Americans, Hispanic, or African-Americans attending ISU. Based on academic achievement. Contact the address below or call (515) 294-2223 for further information.

Iowa State University-College of Engineering
Scholarship Coordinator
116 Marston Hall-Engineering Student Svc.
Ames, IA 50011

3741
Philip Jennings Memorial Scholarship

AMOUNT: None Specified DEADLINE: March 1
FIELDS/MAJORS: Engineering

Open to incoming freshmen, admitted to ISU, based on academics and financial need. One award offered annually. Contact the address below or call (515) 294-2223 for further information.

Iowa State University-College of Engineering
Scholarship Coordinator
116 Marston Hall-Engineering Student Svc.
Ames, IA 50011

3742
President's Leadership Class

AMOUNT: Maximum: $1000 DEADLINE: May 1
FIELDS/MAJORS: All Areas of Study

Open to entering freshmen, admitted to ISU, based on exceptional leadership involvement and citizenship during high school. Academic ability, minimum ACT score of 25, and motivation toward continuance of leadership activities are required. Thirty awards are offered annually. Contact the address below or call (515) 294-3445 for further information.

Iowa State University
Office of Admissions
100 Alumni Hall
Ames, IA 50011

3743
Presidential Scholarship for Excellence

AMOUNT: Maximum: $2500 DEADLINE: March 1
FIELDS/MAJORS: All Areas of Study

Open to entering freshmen accepted at ISU. Based on academic excellence as determined by high school class rank, cumulative GPA, and ACT or SAT scores. Recipients must maintain a minimum GPA of 3.0 for full-time study to renew the awards. Finalists selected from information on admission files. Contact the address below for further information or call (515) 294-2223.

Iowa State University Foundation
Office of Admissions
100 Alumni Hall
Ames, IA 50011

3744
Ralph W. Williams Scholarships

AMOUNT: Maximum: $500 DEADLINE: July 15
FIELDS/MAJORS: Agriculture, Pomology

Open to entering freshman, admitted to ISU, who is a former 4-H member and is twenty-five years of age or older. Contact the address below or call (515) 294-2223 for further information.

Iowa State University-Department of Horticulture
Chair, Scholarship Committee
106 Horticulture Hall
Ames, IA 50011

3745
Reverend Joseph B. Rognlien Scholarship

AMOUNT: Maximum: $4750 DEADLINE: March 15
FIELDS/MAJORS: All Areas of Study

Open to full-time undergraduate students, attending ISU, who are children or grandchildren of Christian ministers. One award offered annually. Contact the address below or call (515) 294-2223 for further information.

Iowa State University
Office of Student Financial Aid
12 Beardshear Hall
Ames, IA 50011

3746
Rex Beresford and Animal Science Freshman Scholarships

AMOUNT: Maximum: $500 DEADLINE: March 15
FIELDS/MAJORS: Animal Science, Pre-Vet

Open to entering freshmen, admitted to ISU, who show academic excellence and financial need. Must be nominated by the county extension director or vocational agriculture teacher. One to four awards are awarded annually. Contact Department of Animal Science Scholarship Committee at the address below or call (515) 294-2223 for further information.

Iowa State University-College of Agriculture
119 Kildee Hall
Ames, IA 50011

3747
Robert E. and Patricia A. Jester Scholarship

AMOUNT: None Specified DEADLINE: December 1
FIELDS/MAJORS: Agronomy, Animal Ecology/Science, Biochemistry, Biophysics, Zoology

Open to entering freshmen majoring in entomology, food science, human nutrition, forestry, genetics, horticulture, microbiology, or plant pathology at Iowa State. Must have a GPA of 3.0 or higher. One award offered annually. Contact the address below or call (515) 294-6614 for further information.

Iowa State University-College of Agriculture
Associate Dean for Academic Programs
124 Curtiss Hall
Ames, IA 50011

3748
Roger and Marie Feldman Endowed Scholarship

AMOUNT: Maximum: $2500 DEADLINE: March 1
FIELDS/MAJORS: All Areas of Study

Open to incoming freshmen, admitted to ISU, who are Iowa residents and graduated from Iowa high schools. One award offered annually. Contact the address below or call (515) 294-2223 for further information.

Iowa State University
Office of Student Financial Aid
12 Beardshear Hall
Ames, IA 50011

3749
R.S. Latta, Jr. Education Scholarships

AMOUNT: Maximum: $1000 DEADLINE: January 30
FIELDS/MAJORS: Education

Open to full-time undergraduates majoring in a program of teacher education at ISU. Renewable if recipients maintain a minimum GPA of 3.0, remain full-time, and are able to demonstrate financial need. Contact the address below or call (515) 294-2223 for further information.

Iowa State University
Education Student Services
E105 Lagomarcino
Ames, IA 50011-3192

3750
Ruth G. English Home Economics Excellence

AMOUNT: None Specified
DEADLINE: January 2
FIELDS/MAJORS: Apparel Merchandising/Design, Dietetics, Early Childhood Education, Food Science, Nutritional Science, Hotel/Restaurant Management

Open to incoming freshmen who are ranked in the top 10% of high school graduating class. Qualified applicants will receive a letter outlining the procedure for application. Contact the address below for further information. GPA must be at least 3.3.

Iowa State University-College of Family/Consumer Sciences
Letha DeMoss
122A MacKay Hall
Ames, IA 50011-1120

3751
State of Iowa Scholarships

AMOUNT: None Specified DEADLINE: December 1
FIELDS/MAJORS: All Areas of Study

Open to Iowa high school seniors who have been designated a State of Iowa Scholar and list Iowa State as their college of choice. Must be in the upper 15% of high school class. Contact your guidance counselor or address for complete details. Must have a GPA of at least 3.4.

Iowa College Student Aid Commission
200 10th St., 4th Floor
Des Moines, IA 50309-3609

3752
Stephen E. Simon Scholarships

AMOUNT: None Specified DEADLINE: March 1
FIELDS/MAJORS: Engineering

Open to incoming freshmen, admitted to ISU, based on academic achievement. Contact the address below or call (515) 294-2223 for further information.

Iowa State University-College of Engineering
Scholarship Coordinator
116 Marston Hall-Engineering Student Svc.
Ames, IA 50011

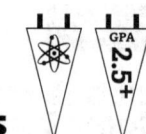

3753
Sterling E. Ainsworth Freshman Scholarships

AMOUNT: Maximum: $500 DEADLINE: July 15
FIELDS/MAJORS: Horticulture

Open to entering freshmen accepted at ISU who are horticulture majors. Must have an interest in floriculture, ornamental fruits, or vegetables. Based on academic record and financial need. Two awards are offered annually. Contact the address below for further information or call (515) 294-2223. GPA must be at least 2.5.

Iowa State University-Department of Horticulture
Chair, Scholarship Committee
106 Horticulture Hall
Ames, IA 50011

3754
Ted Ness Memorial Scholarship

AMOUNT: Maximum: $1000 DEADLINE: March 1
FIELDS/MAJORS: Engineering

Open to incoming freshmen, admitted to ISU, based on academic achievement. One award offered annually. Contact the address below or call (515) 294-2223 for further information.

Iowa State University-College of Engineering
Scholarship Coordinator
116 Marston Hall-Engineering Student Svc.
Ames, IA 50011

3755
Tom and Corrine Lonegran Scholarship

AMOUNT: Maximum: $500 DEADLINE: March 1
FIELDS/MAJORS: All Areas of Study

Open to full-time incoming freshmen admitted to Iowa State. Based on academics and demonstration of financial need. One award offered annually. Contact the address below or call (515) 294-2223 for further information.

Iowa State University
Office of Student Financial Aid
12 Beardshear Hall
Ames, IA 50011

3756
Undergraduate Scholarships for Family and Consumer Sciences

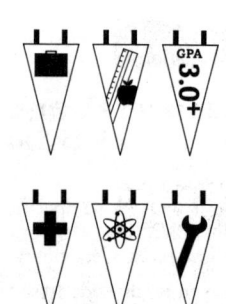

AMOUNT: None Specified
DEADLINE: January 2
FIELDS/MAJORS: Apparel Merchandising/Design, Dietetics, Early Childhood Education, Food Science, Nutritional Science, Hotel/Restaurant Management

Open to incoming freshmen who are ranked in the top 10% of high school graduating class. Qualified applicants will receive a letter outlining the procedure for application. Includes the Keo Anderson Minert, Ruth Morrison, Letitia Jones Olson, Louise M. Rosenfeld, Naomi Wilkinson Scott, Hazel M. Stokes, Lulu L. Tregoning, Jeanne Verne Blahnik, Beverly J. and Jewell Crabtree, Charlotte A. and Charles M. Fullgraf, Catherin Landreth Memorial, and the Lisa K. Mack Scholarships. Contact the address below for further information. GPA must be at least 3.2.

Iowa State University-College of Family/Consumer Sciences
Letha DeMoss
122A MacKay Hall
Ames, IA 50011-1120

3757
Vincent V. Malcolm Scholarship

AMOUNT: None Specified DEADLINE: December 1
FIELDS/MAJORS: Agriculture

Open to worthy enrolled or admitted students pursuing degrees in agriculture. Contact the address below or call (515) 294-6614 for further information. GPA must be at least 2.8.

Iowa State University-College of Agriculture
Assoc. Dean for Academic Programs
134 Curtiss Hall
Ames, IA 50011-1050

3758
Virgil and Dorothy Lagomarcino Scholarship

AMOUNT: Maximum: $500 DEADLINE: January 30
FIELDS/MAJORS: Education

Open to full-time undergraduates enrolled in at least 12 credit hours per semester in the College of Education at ISU. Based on outstanding academics and financial need. Must have a minimum GPA of 3.0. A minimum of two awards are offered annually. Contact the address below or call (515) 294-2223 for further information.

Iowa State University
Education Student Services
E105 Lagomarcino
Ames, IA 50011-3192

3759
Wayne Gross Memorial Scholarship

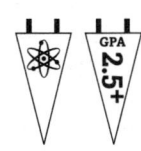

AMOUNT: Maximum: $400   DEADLINE: December 1
FIELDS/MAJORS: Animal Science

Open to entering freshmen, admitted to ISU, majoring in agriculture. Based on demonstrated academics, leadership, and financial need. Preference given to graduates of Carroll and adjacent county high schools. Contact the address below or call (515) 294-6614 for further information. GPA must be at least 2.8.

Iowa State University-College of Agriculture
Assoc. Dean for Academic Programs
134 Curtiss Hall
Ames, IA 50011-1050

3760
Winton Etchen Agronomy Scholarships

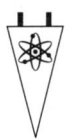

AMOUNT: Maximum: $500   DEADLINE: June 1
FIELDS/MAJORS: Agronomy

Open to freshmen at Iowa State University, who are studying agronomy. Based on high school rank and achievements, national test scores, work experiences, leadership, and interpersonal skills. Two awards offered annually. Write to the address listed or call (515) 262-8323 for more information.

Agribusiness Association of Iowa
900 Des Moines St.
Des Moines, IA 50309

3761
Women in Science and Engineering Scholarship

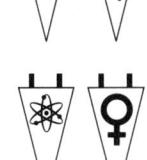

AMOUNT: Maximum: $1000
DEADLINE: December 31
FIELDS/MAJORS: Agriculture/Biological/Physical/Computer Sciences, Math, Engineering

Open to entering women freshmen, admitted to ISU, who are/were in the top 5% of their graduating classes or have an ACT composite score of 30 or higher. Contact the address below or call (515) 294-2223 for further information. GPA must be at least 3.5.

Iowa State University-Women in Science and Engineering Program
Krishna S. Athreya
210 Lab of Mechanics
Ames, IA 50011

3762
Younkers Farm Aid Scholarship

AMOUNT: Maximum: $1000   DEADLINE: December 1
FIELDS/MAJORS: Agriculture

Open to entering freshman, admitted to ISU, who are residents of Iowa, Nebraska, Illinois, Minnesota, or South Dakota. Must rank in upper half of class, have high ACT/SAT scores, display leadership qualities, and demonstrate financial need. At least half of family income must come from farming. Contact the address below or call (515) 294-6614 for further information. GPA must be at least 2.5.

Iowa State University-College of Agriculture
Assoc. Dean for Academic Programs
134 Curtiss Hall
Ames, IA 50011-1050

JACKSONVILLE UNIVERSITY

3763
Charles J. and Edna S. Williams Memorial Scholarship

AMOUNT: None Specified   DEADLINE: March 15
FIELDS/MAJORS: All Areas of Study

Applicants must be Florida or Georgia residents with excellent leadership and academic qualities. Must have a minimum GPA of 3.5. Scholarships are for full tuition and room and board. Contact your high school guidance office or the financial aid office at the address below for details.

Jacksonville University
Financial Aid Office
Jacksonville, FL 32211

3764
Fine Arts and Fine Arts Service Awards

AMOUNT: Maximum: $1000   DEADLINE: March 15
FIELDS/MAJORS: Performing Arts

Scholarships are available to students of outstanding achievement in art, dance, music, and theater at

Jacksonville University. Audition or portfolio review will be required from admitted incoming students. Current students must be participating in art, band, chorus, orchestra, dance, and theater. Write to the address below for details.

Jacksonville University
William J. McNeiland
College of Fine Arts, Division of Music
Jacksonville, FL 32211

3765
Phillips fine Arts Scholarships

AMOUNT: None Specified DEADLINE: March 15
FIELDS/MAJORS: Fine Arts

Open to artistically talented incoming freshmen who have a minimum GPA of 3.0. Applicants will need to arrange for an audition or portfolio review if a visual art major. Based on financial need and ability. Contact the address below for further information.

Jacksonville University
Financial Aid Office
2800 University Blvd. North
Jacksonville, FL 32211-3394

3766
Presidents and University Scholarship

AMOUNT: None Specified DEADLINE: February 1
FIELDS/MAJORS: All Areas of Study

Tuition is available to graduating Florida seniors from high schools in the following counties: Clay, Duval, Baker, St. Johns, and Nassau. Minimum 3.5 GPA and an SAT of at least 1150 are required. Renewable for four years if recipients meet preset standards. Contact your high school guidance counselor or the financial aid office at the address below for details.

Jacksonville University
Financial Aid Office
Jacksonville, FL 32211

3767
Service Awards at Jacksonville University

AMOUNT: None Specified DEADLINE: March 15
FIELDS/MAJORS: All Areas of Study

Awards for students at Jacksonville University who participate in various campus activities. Write to the address below for details.

Jacksonville University
Financial Aid Office
Jacksonville, FL 32211

3768
Trustee Scholarship Program

AMOUNT: $3500-$6000 DEADLINE: March 15
FIELDS/MAJORS: All Areas of Study

Open to incoming freshmen with minimum GPA of 3.2. Transfer students qualify based on their college GPA. These awards are renewable up to four years if recipients maintain preset standards. Write to the address below for information.

Jacksonville University
Financial Aid Office
Jacksonville, FL 32211

JOE KUBERT SCHOOL OF CARTOON AND GRAPHIC ART

3769
Marvel Scholarship

AMOUNT: None Specified DEADLINE: July 18
FIELDS/MAJORS: Cartooning, Graphic Arts

A full three-year tuition scholarship is available for students who are accepted into the Joe Kubert School. Based upon submitted portfolio. Write to the address below for information.

Joe Kubert School of Cartoon and Graphic Art
37 Myrtle Ave.
Dover, NJ 07801

JOHN BROWN UNIVERSITY

3770
Athletic Scholarship

AMOUNT: None Specified DEADLINE: None Specified
FIELDS/MAJORS: All Areas of Study

Available to full-time students who are recommended by a coach. Award amounts vary but cannot exceed tuition, room, and board costs. Contact the Athletic Department at (501) 524-7305.

John Brown University
Office of Financial Aid
2000 West University Dr.
Siloam Springs, AR 72761

3771
Divisional Scholarship

AMOUNT: Maximum: $3000 DEADLINE: January 15
FIELDS/MAJORS: All Areas of Study

Available to freshmen who demonstrate superior academic and leadership potential with a GPA of at least 3.5. Must be in the top 10% of their graduating class and placed in the top 90 percentile on the ACT/SAT exams. Award is renewable by maintaining an appropriate GPA. Write to the address below for details.

John Brown University
Office of Financial Aid
2000 West University Dr.
Siloam Springs, AR 72761

3772
Engineering Achievement Award

AMOUNT: Maximum: $3000 DEADLINE: May 1
FIELDS/MAJORS: Engineering

Available to incoming full-time freshmen enrolled as engineering majors and placed in the top 80 percentile on the ACT/SAT exams. Award is renewable by maintaining appropriate GPA and continuing as an engineering major. Write to the address below for details. GPA must be at least 2.8.

John Brown University
Office of Financial Aid
2000 West University Dr.
Siloam Springs, AR 72761

3773
Missionary Children's Scholarship

AMOUNT: None Specified DEADLINE: None Specified
FIELDS/MAJORS: All Areas of Study

Available to students with at least one parent who is a full-time minister or missionary or are themselves employed as a minister or missionary. Award amounts vary. Write to the address below for details.

John Brown University
Office of Financial Aid
2000 West University Dr.
Siloam Springs, AR 72761

3774
Music/Choral Scholarships

AMOUNT: None Specified DEADLINE: None Specified
FIELDS/MAJORS: Music

Available to full-time students who are pursuing a degree in the music field. Audition is required. Award amounts vary. Contact address below for details.

John Brown University
Office of Financial Aid
2000 West University Dr.
Siloam Springs, AR 72761

3775
Presidential Scholarship

AMOUNT: None Specified DEADLINE: December 15
FIELDS/MAJORS: All Areas of Study

Available to entering freshmen who demonstrate superior academic and leadership potential with a high school GPA of at least 3.9. Must be in the top 5% of their graduating class and placed in the top 95 percentile on the ACT/SAT exams. Award is up to full tuition. Write to the address below for details.

John Brown University
Office of Financial Aid
2000 West University St.
Siloam Springs, AR 72761

JOHNS HOPKINS UNIVERSITY

3776
Beneficial-Hodson Scholarship

AMOUNT: $13000 DEADLINE: January 1
FIELDS/MAJORS: All Areas of Study

Awards for full-time accepted freshmen. Renewable if 3.0 GPA is maintained. Nominations by high school guidance counselors are required by January 1. Approximately eighteen awards are offered annually. Write to the address below for more information.

Johns Hopkins University
3400 N. Charles Street
Baltimore, MD 21218

3777
Hackerman Loan

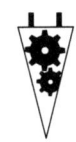

AMOUNT: $1000-$4000 DEADLINE: February 1
FIELDS/MAJORS: Engineering

No interest loans offered to undergraduate Johns Hopkins students enrolled in the G.W.C. Whiting School of Engineering. Students are given up to eight years to repay. Write to the address below for details.

Johns Hopkins University
3400 N. Charles Street
Baltimore, MD 21218

3778
Hodson Achievement Scholarship

AMOUNT: None Specified DEADLINE: January 1
FIELDS/MAJORS: All Areas of Study

Scholarship available to full-time freshmen who are members of underrepresented minority groups from mid-Atlantic states. This is a full grant to meet the student's need (minus work obligation in upper-class years). Nominations by high school guidance counselors are due January 1. Write to the address below for details.

Johns Hopkins University
3400 N. Charles Street
Baltimore, MD 21218

3779
Johns Hopkins Grants

AMOUNT: None Specified DEADLINE: February 1
FIELDS/MAJORS: All Areas of Study

The Johns Hopkins grant is available each year to full-time matriculated undergraduate students who are able to demonstrate financial need. Renewable each year. Write to the address below for details.

Johns Hopkins University
3400 N. Charles Street
Baltimore, MD 21218

JUNIATA COLLEGE

3780
Juniata College Scholarships

AMOUNT: None Specified DEADLINE: March 1
FIELDS/MAJORS: All Areas of Study

Need-based and merit-based scholarships are available to entering, transfer, and continuing students at Juniata. Includes the Juniata Annual, Endowed, Merit Recognition, and Transfer Scholarships. Write to the address below for details.

Juniata College
Office of Student Financial Planning
Huntingdon, PA 16652

KANSAS STATE UNIVERSITY

3781
Buzzard Scholarship, Gamma Theta Upsilon

AMOUNT: None Specified DEADLINE: August 1
FIELDS/MAJORS: Geography/Geophysics

Scholarship for students entering graduate school. Based on GPA, activities in GTU chapters, service to Geography Department, and recommendations. Awarded after first term of enrollment in graduate school. One may apply for only one GTU scholarship. Write to Mr. Lawrence R. Handley, first vice president, at the U.S. Fish and Wildlife Service, National Wetlands Research Center, at the address below. Information may be available from your local chapter or in the current issue of The Geographical Bulletin. Must have a GPA of at least 3.0.

Gamma Theta Upsilon, International Geographical
  Honor Society
Office of the Dean
Eisenhower Hall, Kansas State University
Manhattan, KS 66506-0801

KANSAS WESLEYAN UNIVERSITY

3782
Abbott Memorial Scholarship

AMOUNT: None Specified DEADLINE: March 15
FIELDS/MAJORS: All Areas of Study

Scholarships are available to Osage Indian students. Write to the address below for more details.

Kansas Wesleyan University
Office of Financial Assistance
100 E. Claflin
Salina, KS 67401

3783
A.B. Mackie Scholarship

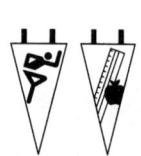

AMOUNT: None Specified DEADLINE: March 15
FIELDS/MAJORS: Physical Education

Scholarships are available to men majoring in physical education. Write to the address below for more details.

Kansas Wesleyan University
Office of Financial Assistance
100 E. Claflin
Salina, KS 67401

3784
Alvah Rock Memorial Scholarship

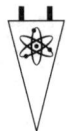

AMOUNT: None Specified   DEADLINE: March 15
FIELDS/MAJORS: All Areas of Study

Scholarships are available to any member of the United Methodist Church of Hope, Kansas, or a Methodist from Dickinson County, Kansas, who desires to attend Kansas Wesleyan University. Write to the address below for more details.

Kansas Wesleyan University
Office of Financial Assistance
100 E. Claflin
Salina, KS 67401

3785
Alvin G. Burton Memorial Scholarship and Rooney Elvin Buford Memorial Trust

AMOUNT: None Specified   DEADLINE: March 15
FIELDS/MAJORS: United Methodist Ministry

Scholarships are available to junior or senior men entering the United Methodist ministry. Write to the address below for more details.

Kansas Wesleyan University
Office of Financial Assistance
100 E. Claflin
Salina, KS 67401

3786
Bruno and Emma Meyer Scholarship

AMOUNT: None Specified   DEADLINE: March 15
FIELDS/MAJORS: Church Missionary

Scholarships are available to students entering church missionary work. Write to the address below for more details.

Kansas Wesleyan University
Office of Financial Assistance
100 E. Claflin
Salina, KS 67401

3787
Charles and Tressa Corsaut Scholarship

AMOUNT: None Specified   DEADLINE: March 15
FIELDS/MAJORS: Religion (Christian)

Scholarships are available to students training in religious and Christian fields. Write to the address below for more details.

Kansas Wesleyan University
Office of Financial Assistance
100 E. Claflin
Salina, KS 67401

3788
Cora Stephan McFadden Scholarship

AMOUNT: None Specified   DEADLINE: March 15
FIELDS/MAJORS: Philosophy, Religion

Scholarships are available to students majoring in philosophy and religion. Write to the address below for more details.

Kansas Wesleyan University
Office of Financial Assistance
100 E. Claflin
Salina, KS 67401

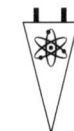

3789
Dr. Albert Robinson, Jr. Endowed Scholarship

AMOUNT: None Specified   DEADLINE: March 15
FIELDS/MAJORS: Biology

Scholarships are available to students majoring in biology. Write to the address below for more details.

Kansas Wesleyan University
Office of Financial Assistance
100 E. Claflin
Salina, KS 67401

3790
Dr. and Mrs. Glen Eaton Nursing Scholarship

AMOUNT: None Specified   DEADLINE: March 15
FIELDS/MAJORS: Nursing

Scholarships are available to nursing students who can demonstrate financial need. Write to the address below for more details.

Kansas Wesleyan University
Office of Financial Assistance
100 E. Claflin
Salina, KS 67401

3791
Eisenhower Scholarships

AMOUNT: $2500 DEADLINE: March 15
FIELDS/MAJORS: All Areas of Study

Awards for high school seniors who have GPAs of at least 3.5, minimum ACT scores of 22, and SAT scores of 1030. Transfer students are also eligible for this award based on their transferring GPA. Write to the address below for more details.

Kansas Wesleyan University
Office of Financial Assistance
100 E. Claflin
Salina, KS 67401

3792
Harris L. and Anna M. Hart Partners in Education Scholarship

AMOUNT: None Specified DEADLINE: March 15
FIELDS/MAJORS: Art, Literature

Scholarships are available to students with an interest in the arts or literature. Must be able to demonstrate financial need. Write to the address listed for more details.

Kansas Wesleyan University
Office of Financial Assistance
100 E. Claflin
Salina, KS 67401

3793
Homer E. Jewell Scholarship

AMOUNT: None Specified DEADLINE: March 15
FIELDS/MAJORS: Nursing

Scholarship available to students entering the nursing profession. Write to the address listed for more details.

Kansas Wesleyan University
Office of Financial Assistance
100 E. Claflin
Salina, KS 67401

3794
Johanna Rinker Endowed Scholarship

AMOUNT: None Specified DEADLINE: March 15
FIELDS/MAJORS: All Areas of Study

Scholarships are available to students with GPAs of at least 3.5 and ACT scores of at least 20. Write to the address below for more details.

Kansas Wesleyan University
Office of Financial Assistance
100 E. Claflin
Salina, KS 67401

3795
John D. Isaacson Scholarship

AMOUNT: None Specified DEADLINE: March 15
FIELDS/MAJORS: All Areas of Study

Scholarships are available to students currently enrolled in KWU who graduated from Kansas high schools. Must have a minimum GPA of 2.5. Write to the address listed for more details.

Kansas Wesleyan University
Office of Financial Assistance
100 E. Claflin
Salina, KS 67401

3796
Kansas Wesleyan University Awards

AMOUNT: $200-$4000 DEADLINE: March 15
FIELDS/MAJORS: All Areas of Study

Need-based awards for KWU students with outstanding ability in academics or athletics. Write to the address below for more details.

Kansas Wesleyan University
Office of Financial Assistance
100 E. Claflin
Salina, KS 67401

3797
Lillian R. Toothaker Scholarship

AMOUNT: None Specified DEADLINE: March 15
FIELDS/MAJORS: All Areas of Study

Scholarships are available to students from Sheridan County, Kansas. Write to the address below for more details.

Kansas Wesleyan University
Office of Financial Assistance
100 E. Claflin
Salina, KS 67401

3798
Marjorie Jennings Endowed Scholarship

AMOUNT: None Specified   DEADLINE: March 15
FIELDS/MAJORS: All Areas of Study

First preference for this scholarship is a female student who is a resident of Kansas. Second preference is for a student with a strong belief in Christian higher education values. Write to the address listed for more details.

Kansas Wesleyan University
Office of Financial Assistance
100 E. Claflin
Salina, KS 67401

3799
Maude Wiltse Dupree and Dr. Glen L. Gish Scholarships

AMOUNT: None Specified   DEADLINE: March 15
FIELDS/MAJORS: Music, Fine Arts

Scholarships are available to students involved within the Music Department. If not possible, students who are interested in the fine arts are accepted. Write to the address below for more details about both awards.

Kansas Wesleyan University
Office of Financial Assistance
100 E. Claflin
Salina, KS 67401

3800
Memorial Scholarships

AMOUNT: $2000   DEADLINE: March 15
FIELDS/MAJORS: All Areas of Study

Awards for high school seniors who have GPAs of at least 3.0, minimum ACT scores of 20, and SAT scores of 950. Transfer students are also eligible for this award based on their transferring GPA. Write to the address below for more details.

Kansas Wesleyan University
Office of Financial Assistance
100 E. Claflin
Salina, KS 67401

3801
Orland and Ilah B. Hazen Scholarship

AMOUNT: None Specified   DEADLINE: March 15
FIELDS/MAJORS: All Areas of Study

Scholarships are available to students who are residents of Beloit or Mitchell counties, Kansas. Write to the address listed for more details.

Kansas Wesleyan University
Office of Financial Assistance
100 E. Claflin
Salina, KS 67401

3802
Otto A. Karl Endowment Scholarship

AMOUNT: None Specified   DEADLINE: March 15
FIELDS/MAJORS: Christian Ministry

Scholarship available to juniors and seniors who have committed themselves to the Christian ministry. Write to the address listed for more details.

Kansas Wesleyan University
Office of Financial Assistance
100 E. Claflin
Salina, KS 67401

3803
Presidential Scholarships

AMOUNT: $4500   DEADLINE: March 1
FIELDS/MAJORS: All Areas of Study

Awards for high school seniors who have GPAs of at least 3.75, minimum ACT scores of 25, and SAT scores of 1140. Scholar candidates must be nominated by their high school principal, counselor, pastor, or Wesleyan representative, and then are selected for on-campus interviews. Renewable with GPAs of at least 3.3. Write to the address below for more details.

Kansas Wesleyan University
Office of Financial Assistance
100 E. Claflin
Salina, KS 67401

3804
Rev. R.G. and Elizabeth Trent Endowed Scholarship

AMOUNT: None Specified   DEADLINE: March 15
FIELDS/MAJORS: Music, Art

Scholarships are available to a female student studying music and art. Write to the address below for more details.

Kansas Wesleyan University
Office of Financial Assistance
100 E. Claflin
Salina, KS 67401

3805
Roland P. Dodds and Bob Dole Endowed Scholarships

AMOUNT: None Specified DEADLINE: March 15
FIELDS/MAJORS: All Areas of Study

Scholarships are available to students with disabilities. Write to the address below for more details about both awards.

Kansas Wesleyan University
Office of Financial Assistance
100 E. Claflin
Salina, KS 67401

3806
Tuthill Scholarship

AMOUNT: None Specified DEADLINE: March 15
FIELDS/MAJORS: Family Living or Home Economics

Scholarships are available to students who have preference in the fields of family living or home economics. Write to the address below for more details.

Kansas Wesleyan University
Office of Financial Assistance
100 E. Claflin
Salina, KS 67401

3807
Vanier Trust Scholarship

AMOUNT: None Specified DEADLINE: March 15
FIELDS/MAJORS: All Areas of Study

Scholarships are available to Kansas students. Write to the address below for more details.

Kansas Wesleyan University
Office of Financial Assistance
100 E. Claflin
Salina, KS 67401

3808
Vivian Kochanoski Endowed Scholarship

AMOUNT: None Specified DEADLINE: March 15
FIELDS/MAJORS: Nursing

Scholarships are awarded to nursing students on basis of merit. Write to the address below for more details.

Kansas Wesleyan University
Office of Financial Assistance
100 E. Claflin
Salina, KS 67401

KENDALL COLLEGE OF ART AND DESIGN

3809
Kendall College Merit Scholarships

AMOUNT: None Specified DEADLINE: February 15
FIELDS/MAJORS: Art, Design

This is one of the nation's largest merit scholarship programs for art and design students. Write to the address below for additional information, or call the Admissions Office at (616) 451-2787 for details and an application. GPA must be at least 2.5.

Kendall College of Art and Design
111 Division Ave. North
Grand Rapids, MI 49503

KENT STATE UNIVERSITY

3810
Amy Weaver Memorial Scholarship

AMOUNT: $100-$600 DEADLINE: June 15
FIELDS/MAJORS: Music

Available to entering freshmen pursuing a bassoon major. Audition and Music Theory placement test required. Amounts vary according to recommendation of bassoon instructor and coordinator of admissions and scholarships. Renewable if student fulfills service requirements. Write to the address below for details or contact the music director at (330) 672-2172.

Kent State University
Hugh A. Glausser School of Music
PO Box 5190
Kent, OH 44242

3811
Arthur Wallach Scholarship

AMOUNT: Maximum: $1000 DEADLINE: June 1
FIELDS/MAJORS: Music Education

Available to incoming freshman pursuing a music education major. High school GPA of 3.0 required. Woodwinds and percussions are area of performance. Audition and

Music Theory placement test required. Renewable if service requirements are fulfilled and student develops artistically. Write to the address below for details or contact the music director at (330) 672-2172.

Kent State University
Hugh A. Glauser School of Music
PO Box 5190
Kent, OH 44242

3812
Delta Omicron-Zeta Omicron

AMOUNT: $100-$150   DEADLINE: None Specified
FIELDS/MAJORS: Music

Available to students who demonstrate an excellence in music and outstanding service in the School of Music. Write to the address below for details or contact the music director at (330) 672-2172. GPA must be at least 2.5.

Kent State University
Hugh A. Glauser School of Music
PO Box 5190
Kent, OH 44242

3813
Delta Omicron-Zeta Sigma

AMOUNT: Maximum: $200   DEADLINE: None Specified
FIELDS/MAJORS: Music

Available to students with junior or senior standing who demonstrate excellence in music and outstanding service in the School of Music. Amount of scholarship varies. Write to the address below for details or contact the music director at (330) 672-2172. GPA must be at least 3.0.

Kent State University
Hugh A. Glauser School of Music
PO Box 5190
Kent, OH 44242

3814
Dolores Parker Morgan Scholarship

AMOUNT: Maximum: $1000   DEADLINE: March 1
FIELDS/MAJORS: Music

Offered to entering freshmen with a high school GPA of at least 3.0 and pursuing a music major. Preference given to minority students. Audition and Music Theory placement test required. Renewable if service requirements are fulfilled and student develops artistically. Write to the address below for details or contact the music director at (330) 672-2172.

Kent State University
Hugh A. Glauser School of Music
PO Box 5190
Kent, OH 44242

3815
Eddie Teener Calabrese Memorial Scholarship

AMOUNT: Maximum: $250   DEADLINE: April 15
FIELDS/MAJORS: Music

Offered to students with sophomore, junior, or senior standing and pursuing a music major. Minimum 2.5 overall GPA and 3.0 music GPA. Must demonstrate financial need. Write to the address below for details or contact the music director at (330) 672-2172.

Kent State University
Hugh A. Glauser School of Music
PO Box 5190
Kent, OH 44242

3816
Floy O. Barthel Scholarship Competition

AMOUNT: None Specified   DEADLINE: None Specified
FIELDS/MAJORS: Piano

Awarded to outstanding piano solo performance competitor. Write to the address below for details or contact the music director at (330) 672-2172.

Kent State University
Hugh A. Glauser School of Music
PO Box 5190
Kent, OH 44242

3817
Frances Crawford Memorial Award

AMOUNT: None Specified   DEADLINE: None Specified
FIELDS/MAJORS: Music, Vocal

Offered to an outstanding senior voice major. Write to the address below for details or contact the music director at (330) 672-2172.

Kent State University
Hugh A. Glauser School of Music
PO Box 5190
Kent, OH 44242

3818
Irene Beamer Memorial Scholarships

AMOUNT: Maximum: $800 DEADLINE: April 1
FIELDS/MAJORS: Music, Vocal

Offered to graduate student voice major. Amount of scholarship varies. Write to the address below for details or contact the music director or voice coordinator at (330) 672-2172.

Kent State University
Hugh A. Glausser School of Music
PO Box 5190
Kent, OH 44242

3819
Jonas Lipson Scholarship

AMOUNT: $100-$600 DEADLINE: June 15
FIELDS/MAJORS: Music, Orchestral String

Open to orchestral string instrument freshmen. Audition and Music Theory placement test required. Performance ability needed. Renewal based on artistic development and fulfillment of service responsibilities. Write to the address below for details or contact the music director at (330) 672-2172.

Kent State University
Hugh A. Glausser School of Music
PO Box 5190
Kent, OH 44242

3820
Kappa Kappa Psi Scholarships

AMOUNT: Maximum: $100 DEADLINE: None Specified
FIELDS/MAJORS: Wind, Percussion majors

Offered to students pursuing a wind or percussion major and based on performance ability. Selected by wind and percussion faculty, director of band, and officers of local chapters. Write to the address below for details or contact the band director at (330) 672-2515.

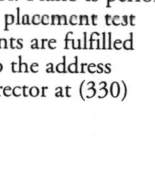

Kent State University
Hugh A. Glausser School of Music
PO Box 5190
Kent, OH 44242

3821
Kent State University Orchestra Society Scholarships

AMOUNT: $100-$400 DEADLINE: September 1
FIELDS/MAJORS: All Fields of Study

Awarded on performance ability and financial need. Renewal based on artistic development and fulfillment of service responsibilities. Amount varies. Write to the address below for details or contact the orchestra director at (330) 672-2636.

Kent State University
Hugh A. Glausser School of Music
PO Box 5190
Kent, OH 44242

3822
Lee and Floy Barthel Scholarship

AMOUNT: None Specified DEADLINE: None Specified
FIELDS/MAJORS: Music, Piano

Offered to piano music student with sophomore, junior, or senior standing. Write to the address below for details or contact the music director at (330) 672-2172.

Kent State University
Hugh A. Glausser School of Music
PO Box 5190
Kent, OH 44242

3823
Lilly-Christine Wallach Scholarship

AMOUNT: Maximum: $1000 DEADLINE: June 1
FIELDS/MAJORS: Music Education

Offered to entering freshman with a high school GPA of 3.0 and pursuing a music education major. Piano is performance area. Audition and Music Theory placement test required. Renewable if service requirements are fulfilled and student develops artistically. Write to the address below for details or contact the music director at (330) 672-2172.

Kent State University
Hugh A. Glausser School of Music
PO Box 5190
Kent, OH 44242

3824
Marching Band Scholarships

AMOUNT: $75-$200 DEADLINE: None Specified
FIELDS/MAJORS: Marching Band

Open for members of marching band, audition required. Write to the address below for details or contact the band director at (330) 672-2515.

Kent State University
Hugh A. Glausser School of Music
PO Box 5190
Kent, OH 44242

3825
McGinnis Sinfonia Scholarships

AMOUNT: None Specified DEADLINE: None Specified
FIELDS/MAJORS: Orchestra

Open for outstanding students in the School of Music Orchestra with sophomore, junior, senior, or graduate standing. Amount of awards vary. Write to the address below for details or contact the orchestra director at (330) 672-2636.

Kent State University
Hugh A. Glausser School of Music
PO Box 5190
Kent, OH 44242

3826
Miles Vending Machine Scholarship

AMOUNT: Maximum: $50 DEADLINE: None Specified
FIELDS/MAJORS: Music

Available to outstanding music student for excellence in music and service in the School of Music. Non-renewable. Write to the address below for details or contact the music director at (330) 672-2172. GPA must be at least 2.5.

Kent State University
Hugh A. Glausser School of Music
PO Box 5190
Kent, OH 44242

3827
Music Scholarships

AMOUNT: $500-$3000 DEADLINE: June 15
FIELDS/MAJORS: Music

Offered to music majors. Audition and Music Theory placement test required. Renewal based on artistic development and fulfillment of service requirements. Number of awards varies. Write to the address below for details or contact the music director at (330) 672-2172.

Kent State University
Hugh A. Glausser School of Music
PO Box 5190
Kent, OH 44242

3828
School of Music Special Scholarships

AMOUNT: $100-$1000 DEADLINE: June 15
FIELDS/MAJORS: Music

Awarded to outstanding music students who have been recommended by the scholarship committee. Renewal based on artistic development and fulfillment of service requirements. Write to the address below for details or contact the music director at (330) 672-2172.

Kent State University
Hugh A. Glausser School of Music
PO Box 5190
Kent, OH 44242

3829
Tau Beta Sigma Scholarship

AMOUNT: Maximum: $100 DEADLINE: None Specified
FIELDS/MAJORS: Music, Wind, and Percussion Majors

Open to freshmen wind and percussion majors only, based on performance ability. Selected by Director of Bands and officers of local Chapter Tau Beta Sigma sorority. Write to the address below for details or contact the band director at (330) 672-2515.

Kent State University
Hugh A. Glausser School of Music
PO Box 5190
Kent, OH 44242

KENT STATE UNIVERSITY, TUSCARAWAS CAMPUS

3830
Bank One Book Scholarship

AMOUNT: Maximum: $500 DEADLINE: April 1
FIELDS/MAJORS: All Areas of Study

Open to full or part-time students at Kent State who are Tuscarawas County residents. Must be able to demonstrate financial need and not have won this award previously. Contact the financial aid office at your campus for details. GPA must be at least 2.8.

Kent State University, Tuscarawas Campus
Financial Aid Office
University Dr., NE
New Philadelphia, OH 44663

3831
Chestnut Society Scholarships

AMOUNT: $100-$200 DEADLINE: April 1
FIELDS/MAJORS: All Areas of Study

The Chestnut Society seeks to provide funds for non-traditional students who have prior college experience and a high GPA. Must be Tuscarawas County resident, completed at least 12 hours of coursework, with a minimum GPA of 3.0, and be at least twenty-one years old. Must be able to demonstrate financial need. Up to four awards offered annually. Contact the financial aid office at KSU (either campus).

Kent State University, Tuscarawas Campus
Financial Aid Office
330 University Dr., NE
New Philadelphia, OH 44663

3832
Citizenship Scholarship

AMOUNT: Maximum: $1000   DEADLINE: April 1
FIELDS/MAJORS: All Areas of Study

Scholarships for returning students at Kent State who display excellent citizenship through community activities or social awareness activities and have a superior academic record. One award per year. Contact the financial aid office at your campus for details. GPA must be at least 3.3.

Kent State University, Tuscarawas Campus
Financial Aid Office
University Dr., NE
New Philadelphia, OH 44663

3833
Daniel J. Steiner Scholarship

AMOUNT: Maximum: $1000   DEADLINE: April 1
FIELDS/MAJORS: Nursing

Scholarship available for female students in a nursing program, who were graduates of either New Philadelphia High School or Tuscarawas Central Catholic High School. Applicants must demonstrate financial need. Contact the financial aid office for details. GPA must be at least 3.0.

Kent State University, Tuscarawas Campus
Financial Aid Office
University Dr., NE
New Philadelphia, OH 44663

3834
Errington Memorial Scholarship

AMOUNT: $200   DEADLINE: April 1
FIELDS/MAJORS: Nursing

Scholarships for Tuscarawas County, Ohio, residents enrolled in the nursing program at Kent State. Academic record is considered. One award per year. Contact the financial aid office for details.

Kent State University, Tuscarawas Campus
Financial Aid Office
University Dr., NE
New Philadelphia, OH 44663

3835
Foundation Scholarships and General Scholarships

AMOUNT: Maximum: $1500   DEADLINE: April 1
FIELDS/MAJORS: All Areas of Study

Scholarships for new students at Kent State University. Awards are based on superior academic record. Includes Preston Memorial Scholarship, William Mellor Scholarship, Richard Demuth Scholarship, Mary Hanhart Scholarship, and General Foundation Scholarship. Nine awards per year. Contact the financial aid office at your campus for details. GPA must be at least 3.0.

Kent State University, Tuscarawas Campus
Financial Aid Office
University Dr., NE
New Philadelphia, OH 44663

3836
General Scholarship

AMOUNT: Maximum: $1000   DEADLINE: April 1
FIELDS/MAJORS: All Areas of Study

Scholarships for students at Kent State who have a superior academic record and are at least in their sophomore year. Nine awards per year. Contact the financial aid office at your campus for details. GPA must be at least 3.0.

Kent State University, Tuscarawas Campus
Financial Aid Office
University Dr., NE
New Philadelphia, OH 44663

3837
Hannah Pittis Schoenbrunn Grange Scholarship

AMOUNT: $200   DEADLINE: April 1
FIELDS/MAJORS: Nursing, Agriculture

Scholarships for female students at KSU pursuing a degree in nursing and for male students studying agriculture. At least three awards are offered annually. Contact the financial aid office for details.

Kent State University, Tuscarawas Campus
Financial Aid Office
University Dr., NE
New Philadelphia, OH 44663

3838
Mabel Hammersley Nursing Scholarships

AMOUNT: Maximum: $1500   DEADLINE: April 1
FIELDS/MAJORS: Nursing

Two scholarships for entering students in nursing. Must have a superior academic record. Contact the financial aid office for details. GPA must be at least 3.0.

Kent State University, Tuscarawas Campus
Financial Aid Office
University Dr., NE
New Philadelphia, OH 44663

3839
Lillian Stollar Memorial and Gertrude Kederly Memorial Scholarships

AMOUNT: $1000   DEADLINE: April 1
FIELDS/MAJORS: All Areas of Study

Scholarships for students at Kent State University, Tuscarawas Campus, who are residents of Tuscarawas County, Ohio, and graduated from a public school in the county. Must demonstrate financial need. Four awards offered annually. Contact the financial aid office for details. GPA must be at least 3.0.

Tuscarawas Antique Club
Kent State University, Fin. Aid Office
330 University Dr., NE
New Philadelphia, OH 44663

3840
Manley Scholarship

AMOUNT: None Specified   DEADLINE: April 1
FIELDS/MAJORS: All Areas of Study

Open to full- or part-time freshmen at Kent State who are residents of Tuscarawas County. Must be in the top 15% of graduating class with a minimum GPA of 3.5 and an ACT score of at least 25. Renewable without reapplication if a minimum GPA of 3.3 is maintained. Award is full tuition. Contact the financial aid office at your campus for details.

Kent State University, Tuscarawas Campus
Financial Aid Office
University Dr., NE
New Philadelphia, OH 44663

3841
Minority Scholarships

AMOUNT: $1000-$1500   DEADLINE: April 1
FIELDS/MAJORS: All Areas of Study

Scholarships for minority students at Kent State who have a superior academic record and are returning students or new transfer students. Must be at least in sophomore year. One award offered annually. Contact the financial aid office at your campus for details. GPA must be at least 3.0.

Kent State University, Tuscarawas Campus
Financial Aid Office
University Dr., NE
New Philadelphia, OH 44663

3842
New Philadelphia Rotary Club Scholarship

AMOUNT: $250-$500   DEADLINE: April 1
FIELDS/MAJORS: All Areas of Study

Open to full- or part-time students at Kent State who are residents of New Philadelphia or the New Philadelphia school district. Must be able to demonstrate financial need and have a superior academic record. Renewable if recipients maintain a minimum GPA of 3.0 and meet the financial need requirements. Contact the financial aid office at your campus for details.

Kent State University, Tuscarawas Campus
Financial Aid Office
University Dr., NE
New Philadelphia, OH 44663

3843
Office Technology Scholarship

AMOUNT: Maximum: $1500   DEADLINE: April 1
FIELDS/MAJORS: Business Technology

Scholarships for new students at Kent State who are majoring in business technology. Must have a superior academic record. One award per year. Contact the financial aid office for details. GPA must be at least 3.0.

Kent State University, Tuscarawas Campus
Financial Aid Office
University Dr., NE
New Philadelphia, OH 44663

3844
Roy A. Wilson and Ruth A. Wilson Memorial Fund Award

AMOUNT: None Specified DEADLINE: April 1
FIELDS/MAJORS: All Areas of Study

Scholarships for full-time students at Kent State who were residents of the Claymont School District when they graduated from high school. Preference is given to incoming freshmen. Applicants must demonstrate financial need. Contact the financial aid office at your campus for details.

Kent State University, Tuscarawas Campus
Financial Aid Office
University Dr., NE
New Philadelphia, OH 44663

3845
Samuel H. Winston Memorial Scholarship

AMOUNT: Maximum: $1000 DEADLINE: April 1
FIELDS/MAJORS: Sciences

Scholarships for students at Kent State University who graduated from Tuscarawas High School and are studying any of the sciences. Must have a GPA at least 3.0. At least two awards are offered annually. Contact the financial aid office for details.

Kent State University, Tuscarawas Campus
Financial Aid Office
330 University Dr., NE
New Philadelphia, OH 44663

3846
Willie P. Morrow Memorial Scholarship

AMOUNT: Maximum: $500 DEADLINE: April 1
FIELDS/MAJORS: All Areas of Study

Scholarships for African-American students at Kent State who are residents of Tuscarawas County. Based upon financial need and academic potential. One award per year. Contact the financial aid office at your campus for details. GPA must be at least 2.8.

Kent State University, Tuscarawas Campus
Financial Aid Office
University Dr., NE
New Philadelphia, OH 44663

KENTUCKY WESLEYAN COLELGE

3847
Presidential Scholarship, James Graham Brown Scholarship

AMOUNT: None Specified DEADLINE: March 1
FIELDS/MAJORS: All Areas of Study

Scholarships are available at Kentucky Wesleyan College for undergraduate students, based upon academic excellence and school and community service. Write to the address below for details.

Kentucky Wesleyan College
Financial Aid Office
3000 Frederica Street
Owensboro, KY 42303

KENYON COLLEGE

3848
Kenyon Honor and Science Scholarships

AMOUNT: $11000-$22000 DEADLINE: February 15
FIELDS/MAJORS: All Areas of Study

Scholarships available to undergraduate students at Kenyon College who demonstrate exceptional scholastic achievement, outstanding leadership skills, and spirited community service. Write to the address below for more details. GPA must be at least 3.8.

Kenyon College
Gregory A. Buckles
Office of Admissions, Ransom Hall
Gambier, OH 43022

KNOX COLLEGE

3849
Colorado Alumni Scholarships

AMOUNT: Maximum: $1500 DEADLINE: February 15
FIELDS/MAJORS: All Areas of Study

Open to admitted first-year Colorado students who academically rank high in high school. Selections made based on competitive interviews and reviews of the candidates applications. Contact the address below for further information or call (309) 341-7100. GPA must be at least 3.2.

Knox College
Office of Admission
Galesburg, IL 61401

3850
Dow Chemical Company Foundation Scholarships

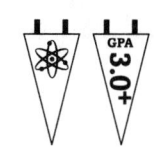

AMOUNT: Maximum: $4000 DEADLINE: February 15
FIELDS/MAJORS: Chemistry

Open to outstanding high school seniors in science. Applicants must be U.S. citizens and plan to pursue a chemistry degree at Knox. Preference given to students who are inclined to pursue their education through the Ph.D. level. Contact the address below for further information or call (309) 341-7100. GPA must be at least 3.0.

Knox College
Office of Admission
Galesburg, IL 61401

3851
Ellen Browning Scripps Scholarships

AMOUNT: Maximum: $6000 DEADLINE: February 15
FIELDS/MAJORS: All Areas of Study

Open to admitted first-year students who are in the top 10% of senior class. Must be able to demonstrate strong academics and potential. Renewable if recipients achieve a minimum GPA of 2.8 at the end of the first year and at least a 3.0 thereafter. Contact the address below for further information or call (309) 341-7100.

Knox College
Office of Admission
Galesburg, IL 61401

3852
Hermann Muelder Scholarships

AMOUNT: Maximum: $8000 DEADLINE: February 15
FIELDS/MAJORS: All Areas of Study

Open to admitted first-year students at Knox who rank in the top 5% of graduating class. Must demonstrate excellence in the classroom and contributions to their communities. Renewable with achievement of a minimum GPA of 2.8 at the end of the first year and at least a 3.0 thereafter. Contact the address below for further information or call (309) 341-7100.

Knox College
Office of Admission
Galesburg, IL 61401

3853
Knox Creative Arts Scholarships

AMOUNT: $1500-$3000 DEADLINE: February 15
FIELDS/MAJORS: Creative Writing, Drama, Theater, Music, Art

Open to first-year students who are academically qualified and have special abilities in the above fields. Selections based on auditions, interviews, examination of work completed, and academics. Auditions/interviews must be scheduled to take place before February 15. Contact the address below for further information or call (309) 341-7100. GPA must be at least 2.8.

Knox College
Office of Admission
Galesburg, IL 61401

3854
Lincoln Presidential Scholarships

AMOUNT: Maximum: $17500 DEADLINE: February 15
FIELDS/MAJORS: All Areas of Study

Open to admitted first-year students at Knox. Applicants must excel in academics, ranking in the top percentage points of class, and contribute significantly to their schools and communities. Renewable if recipients achieve a minimum GPA of 3.0 at the end of the first year and at least a 3.3 thereafter. Contact the address below for further information or call (309) 341-7100.

Knox College
Office of Admissions
Galesburg, IL 61401

3855
National Hispanic Scholars Scholarships

AMOUNT: $6000-$8000 DEADLINE: February 15
FIELDS/MAJORS: All Areas of Study

Open to admitted first-year students who received Scholar or Honorable Mention status in the National Hispanic Scholar Recognition Program sponsored by the College Board. Renewable annually. Contact the address below for further information or call (309) 341-7100.

Knox College
Office of Admission
Galesburg, IL 61401

3856
Rothwell Stephens Scholarship

AMOUNT: Maximum: $4000 DEADLINE: February 15
FIELDS/MAJORS: Mathematics

Open to admitted first-year students interested in pursuing mathematics and score among the highest on the Department of Mathematics two-hour examination. The test is preferably given on campus prior to February 15. If applicants are unable to come to campus, other arrangements are possible. Contact the address below for further information or call (309) 341-7100. GPA must be at least 2.8.

Knox College
Office of Admission
Galesburg, IL 61401

3857
Transfer Student Scholarships

AMOUNT: Maximum: $8000 DEADLINE: April 1
FIELDS/MAJORS: All Areas of Study

Open to members of the honorary society Phi Theta Kappa and other transfer students who have completed an associates degree from an accredited community college. Must have a minimum GPA of 3.5 in a demanding liberal arts curriculum and complete an application for admission by April 1. Contact the address below for further information or call (309) 341-7100.

Knox College
Office of Admission
Galesburg, IL 61401

LABAN/BARTENIEFF INSTITUTE OF MOVEMENT

Laban/Bartenieff Institute of Movement Studies Aid Programs

AMOUNT: $1000-$3000 DEADLINE: April 30
FIELDS/MAJORS: Movement Studies

Various aid programs are available for students at the institute of movement studies. Must be an American citizen or permanent resident. Four awards are offered annually. Write to the address below for more information.

Laban/Bartenieff Institute of Movement Studies
Financial Aid Office
11 East 4th St.
New York, NY 10003

LAKE ERIE COLLEGE

3859
Catherine L. Gates Scholarship

AMOUNT: None Specified DEADLINE: March 1
FIELDS/MAJORS: All Areas of Study

Award for a promising female sophomore to be used in her junior year. One award is offered annually. Write to the address below for more information.

Lake Erie College
Financial Aid Office
391 W. Washington St.
Painesville, OH 44077

LEO BAECK INSTITUTE

3860
Daad Fellowships in German-Jewish History and Culture

AMOUNT: $2000 DEADLINE: November 1
FIELDS/MAJORS: Jewish Studies

Research fellowships available at the Leo Baeck Institute for postdoctoral scholars who are studying the social, communal, and intellectual history of German-speaking Jewry. Applicants must be less than thirty-six years of age and citizens of the U.S. Write to the address below for information.

Leo Baeck Institute
Fellowship Programs
129 East 73rd Street
New York, NY 10021

3861
Fritz Halbers Fellowship

AMOUNT: $3000 DEADLINE: November 1
FIELDS/MAJORS: Jewish Studies

Fellowships are available for research at the Leo Baeck institute for current predoctoral scholars who are studying the social, communal, and intellectual history of German-speaking Jewry. Applicants must be U.S. citizens. Write to the address below for information.

Leo Baeck Institute
Fellowship Programs
129 East 73rd Street
New York, NY 10021

LEWIS AND CLARK COLLEGE

3862
Babara Hirschi Neely and Trustee Scholarships

AMOUNT: $16820   DEADLINE: February 1
FIELDS/MAJORS: Science, Intercultural, International Studies

Awards for entering freshmen interested in science, natural systems, intercultural, or international issues. Must have outstanding academic credentials. Renewable for three years if recipient maintains academic excellence. Write to the address below for complete details. GPA must be at least 2.8.

Lewis and Clark College
Office of Admissions
Portland, OR 97219

3863
Cheney Foundation Scholarships

AMOUNT: $1000   DEADLINE: February 1
FIELDS/MAJORS: All Areas of Study

Five awards for currently enrolled freshmen to use in their sophomore year. There are an additional five awards to be given to seniors. Must demonstrate academic excellence and community and college service. Renewable. Ten awards offered annually. Write to the address below for complete details.

Lewis and Clark College
Office of Admissions
Portland, OR 97219

3864
Chevron Corporation, U.S.A., Scholarships

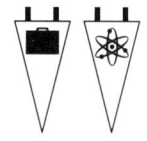

AMOUNT: $2000   DEADLINE: February 1
FIELDS/MAJORS: Business, Science, Mathematics

Awards for first-year students seeking a future in one of the fields listed above. Must be an Oregon resident. Recipients must declare a business, math, or science major by junior year. Renewable. Contact your high school guidance counselor or write to the address below for further information.

Lewis and Clark College
Office of Admissions
Portland, OR 97219

3865
Dr. Robert B. Pamplin, Jr., Society of Fellows

AMOUNT: $16820   DEADLINE: February 1
FIELDS/MAJORS: All Areas of Study

Recipients chosen from freshmen (may be extended to transfer students) who have demonstrated academic achievement. Students named to the society of fellows are guaranteed full tuition and fees without the use of loan programs as well as a $500 stipend each year for books, computers, travel expenses, etc. Renewable. Write to the address below for complete details.

Lewis and Clark College
Office of Admissions
Portland, OR 97219

3866
Forensics Scholarship

AMOUNT: $1000-$2500   DEADLINE: February 1
FIELDS/MAJORS: Forensics, Debate

Awards for Lewis and Clark students who have outstanding records of achievement in debate and forensics. Write to the address below for more information.

Lewis and Clark College
Director of Forensics
0615 SW Palatine Hill Road
Portland, OR 97219

3867
Helen Sanders Scholarship

AMOUNT: $2250-$4500   DEADLINE: February 1
FIELDS/MAJORS: History, Ethnohistory

Awards for entering students who are Native Americans with first priority to descendants of any of the original allottees of the Quinault reservation. Based on financial need and academic performance. Write to the address below for more information.

Lewis and Clark College
Office of Admissions
Portland, OR 97219

3868
Herbert Templeton Merit Scholarships for National Merit Finalists

AMOUNT: $750-$2000   DEADLINE: February 1
FIELDS/MAJORS: All Areas of Study

Awards for freshmen who are National Merit Finalists and have named Lewis and Clark as their first choice college with the National Merit Corporation. Must demonstrate financial need. Write to the address below for more information.

Lewis and Clark College
Office of Admissions
Portland, OR 97219

3869
Multicultural Grants

AMOUNT: Maximum: $1500   DEADLINE: February 1
FIELDS/MAJORS: All Areas of Study

Awards for African-American, Native American, and Hispanic-American students who can demonstrate financial need. Write to the address below for more information.

Lewis and Clark College
Office of Admissions
Portland, OR 97219

3870
Music Scholarships

AMOUNT: $1000-$2500   DEADLINE: February 1
FIELDS/MAJORS: Music

Awards for Lewis and Clark students who have outstanding talent in music. Application will include an audition. Write to the address below for complete details.

Lewis and Clark College
Department of Music
0615 SW Palatine Hill Road
Portland, OR 97219

3871
Portland General Electric Scholarships

AMOUNT: $2250   DEADLINE: February 1
FIELDS/MAJORS: All Areas of Study

Awards for entering freshmen who are from Oregon and demonstrate academic excellence. Renewable with continued academic merit. Information and applications are available through the high schools. GPA must be at least 2.7.

Lewis and Clark College
Office of Admissions
Portland, OR 97219

3872
R.B. Pamplin Corporation Scholarships

AMOUNT: $2500   DEADLINE: February 1
FIELDS/MAJORS: All Areas of Study

Awards for current sophomores who have demonstrated academic achievement as well as community and college service. To be used for junior year. Renewable for senior year with continued academic merit. Write to the address below for complete details.

Lewis and Clark College
Office of Admissions
Portland, OR 97219

3873
Sheryl Reed Smith Scholarship

AMOUNT: Maximum: $5000   DEADLINE: February 1
FIELDS/MAJORS: All Areas of Study

Awards for entering Oregon students who will graduate from a Wallowa County high school. Write to the address below for more information.

Lewis and Clark College
Office of Admissions
Portland, OR 97219

LINCOLN TECHNICAL INSTITUTE

3874
Drafting, CAD Technology

AMOUNT: None Specified   DEADLINE: None Specified
FIELDS/MAJORS: Drafting, CAD Technology

Open to applicants who are residents of Union County, U.S. citizens, and possess a high school diploma or GED equivalent. Applicants will be screened by Lincoln's standard entrance exam, and the top finishers will be interviewed by an independent committee who will make the final selection. Contact the address listed or call (908) 964-7800 for further information.

Lincoln Technical Institute
Linda Stender, Chairman
2299 Vauxhall Rd.
Union, NJ 07083-5032

LINCOLN UNIVERSITY

3875
LASER (Lincoln Advanced Science and Engineering Reinforcement) Program

AMOUNT: None Specified DEADLINE: March 15
FIELDS/MAJORS: Science, Engineering

Awards are available to undergraduate students at Lincoln University who are pursuing a science or engineering degree. Write to the address below for details.

Lincoln University
Financial Aid Office
Lincoln Hall, Room 101
Lincoln University, PA 19352

3876
Lincoln University Scholarships

AMOUNT: $4000 DEADLINE: March 15
FIELDS/MAJORS: All Areas of Study

Awards are available to undergraduate students at Lincoln University who demonstrate academic excellence (3.0 GPA or above) and high SAT scores (900+). Award size ranges from $1000 (alumni merit, honors merit), $1000 (presidential) $2000 (W.W. Smith) to full tuition (founders). Write to the address below for details.

Lincoln University
Financial Aid Office
Lincoln Hall, Room 101
Lincoln University, PA 19352

3877
MARC (Minority Access to Research Career) Scholarship

AMOUNT: None Specified DEADLINE: March 15
FIELDS/MAJORS: Science

Awards are available to junior minority students at Lincoln University who are pursuing a science degree. Applicants must have a GPA of at least 3.0 or above. Write to the address below for details.

Lincoln University
Financial Aid Office
Lincoln Hall, Room 101
Lincoln University, PA 19352

LOGAN COLLEGE OF CHIROPRACTIC

3878
Logan-Scharnhorst Scholarships

AMOUNT: Maximum: $500 DEADLINE: July 25
FIELDS/MAJORS: All Areas of Study (Chiropractic)

Several scholarships awarded each trimester at Logan College. Must have a GPA of at least 2.8. Financial need is considered. Contact the financial aid office at the address below for details.

Logan College of Chiropractic
Financial Aid Office
PO Box 1065
Chesterfield, MO 63006

LORAS COLLEGE

3879
Academic Scholarships

AMOUNT: $5500-$7000 DEADLINE: April 15
FIELDS/MAJORS: All Areas of Study

Open to high school seniors who have a minimum GPA of 3.3, an ACT score of at least 25, and a minimum SAT score of 1140. Must be enrolling/accepted by Loras full-time. Extracurricular activities will also be considered. Renewable if recipients maintain a minimum GPA of 3.2. Write to the address below for details.

Loras College
Office of Financial Planning
1450 Alta Vista St., PO Box 178
Dubuque, IA 52004

3880
American Council of the Blind Scholarships

AMOUNT: $1000-$3000 DEADLINE: March 1
FIELDS/MAJORS: All Areas of Study

Open to full-time enrolled students who are legally blind. Write to the address below for details.

Loras College
Office of Financial Planning
1450 Alta Vista St., PO Box 178
Dubuque, IA 52004

3881
Angelfire Scholarship

AMOUNT: $500-$1500   DEADLINE: February 15
FIELDS/MAJORS: All Areas of Study

Open to full- and part-time enrolled students who are military veterans of the Vietnam War or refugees from Vietnam, Laos, or Cambodia. Write to the address below for details.

Loras College
Office of Financial Planning
1450 Alta Vista St., PO Box 178
Dubuque, IA 52004

3882
Carver Scholarship

AMOUNT: Maximum: $7200   DEADLINE: March 14
FIELDS/MAJORS: All Areas of Study

Open to full-time second semester sophomores who have a minimum GPA of 2.8 and graduated from a high school in Iowa. Write to the address below for details.

Loras College
Office of Financial Planning
1450 Alta Vista St., PO Box 178
Dubuque, IA 52004

3883
Charles E. Fahrney Foundation Scholarship

AMOUNT: Maximum: $2000   DEADLINE: February 15
FIELDS/MAJORS: All Areas of Study

Open to full-time students who are residents of Wapello County. Contact the address below for more information.

Loras College
Office of Financial Planning
1450 Alta Vista St., PO Box 178
Dubuque, IA 52004

3884
Corrigan Scholarship

AMOUNT: None Specified   DEADLINE: None Specified
FIELDS/MAJORS: All Areas of Study

Open to juniors and seniors. Must be able to demonstrate financial need, involvement, and commitment to Loras and the community. Contact Pat Flanagan at the address below for more information.

Loras College
Office of Financial Planning
1450 Alta Vista St., PO Box 178
Dubuque, IA 52004

3885
Datatel Scholarship

AMOUNT: $500-$1500   DEADLINE: February 15
FIELDS/MAJORS: All Areas of Study

Open to full- and part-time enrolled students. Based on academic merit, external activities, and letters of recommendation. Award amounts are based on tuition costs. Write to the address below for details. GPA must be at least 2.9.

Loras College
Office of Financial Planning
1450 Alta Vista St., PO Box 178
Dubuque, IA 52004

3886
Des Moines Chapter Iowa Council of the United Blind

AMOUNT: $1000-$1500   DEADLINE: April 15
FIELDS/MAJORS: All Areas of Study

Open to full-time enrolled students who are legally blind. Write to the address below for details.

Loras College
Office of Financial Planning
1450 Alta Vista St., PO Box 178
Dubuque, IA 52004

3887
Des Moines Women's Club Memorial Scholarship

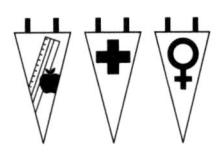

AMOUNT: Maximum: $1000   DEADLINE: February 1
FIELDS/MAJORS: Education, Health

Open to female students who are residents of any of the following Iowa counties: Polk, Boone, Dallas, Jasper, Madison, Marion, Story, or Warren. Contact the address below for more information.

Loras College
Office of Financial Planning
1450 Alta Vista St., PO Box 178
Dubuque, IA 52004

3888
Goldwater Scholarship

AMOUNT: None Specified DEADLINE: January 15
FIELDS/MAJORS: Mathematics, Science

Open to current full-time sophomores and juniors. Contact the address listed for more information.

Loras College
Office of Financial Planning
1450 Alta Vista St., PO Box 178
Dubuque, IA 52004

3889
Hormel Foods Scholarship

AMOUNT: None Specified
DEADLINE: None Specified
FIELDS/MAJORS: All Areas of Study

Open to students who are children of full-time Hormel employees. Write to the address below for details.

Loras College
Office of Financial Planning
1450 Alta Vista St., PO Box 178
Dubuque, IA 52004

3890
Homeland Minorities in Banking Scholarships

AMOUNT: Maximum: $2000
DEADLINE: April 15
FIELDS/MAJORS: Accounting, Finance, Computer Science, Business

Open to high school seniors, college freshmen, and sophomores who are Iowa residents, admitted to Loras, and of African-American, Asian, Hispanic, or Native American descent. Must have a minimum GPA of 2.5. Contact the address listed for more information.

Loras College
Office of Financial Planning
1450 Alta Vista St., PO Box 178
Dubuque, IA 52004

3891
Iowa College Foundation Minority Scholarship

AMOUNT: Maximum: $5000 DEADLINE: March 14
FIELDS/MAJORS: All Areas of Study

Open to minority high school seniors who are enrolling into/accepted by Loras College. Write to the address below for details.

Loras College
Office of Financial Planning
1450 Alta Vista St., PO Box 178
Dubuque, IA 52004

3892
Morris Scholarship

AMOUNT: $750-$1250 DEADLINE: February 1
FIELDS/MAJORS: All Areas of Study

Open to undergraduates and graduate students who are minority Iowa residents. Contact the address listed for more information.

Loras College
Office of Financial Planning
1450 Alta Vista St., PO Box 178
Dubuque, IA 52004

3893
Teachers for Catholic Schools Program Scholarship

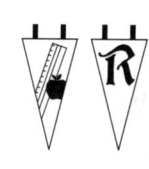

AMOUNT: None Specified DEADLINE: April 1
FIELDS/MAJORS: Education

Open to students of the Catholic faith. Must provide a letter of support from your pastor or clergyman capable of judging your potential for teaching in a Catholic school and a statement of why you wish to teach in a Catholic school. Contact the address listed for more information.

Loras College
Office of Financial Planning
1450 Alta Vista St., PO Box 178
Dubuque, IA 52004

LOYOLA UNIVERSITY (CHICAGO)

3894
Damen Scholarships

AMOUNT: Maximum: $7000 DEADLINE: February 14
FIELDS/MAJORS: All Areas of Study

Open to admitted incoming freshmen at Loyola University. These awards are based on academics and talent, not financial need. Typical recipient has a minimum GPA of 3.5. Renewable up to three years if recipients maintain at least a 3.0 GPA and continues full-time status. Contact your high school guidance office, the address below, or call (773) 508-3155 for further information.

Loyola University
Financial Aid Office
6525 N. Sheridan Road
Chicago, IL 60626

3895
Loyola Freshman Scholarships

AMOUNT: Maximum: $5000 DEADLINE: February 14
FIELDS/MAJORS: All Areas of Study

Open to admitted incoming freshmen at Loyola University. These awards are based on academics and talent, not financial need. Typical recipient has a minimum GPA of 3.5. Renewable up to three years if recipients maintain at least a 3.0 GPA and continues full-time status. Contact your high school guidance office, the address below, or call (773) 508-3155 for further information.

Loyola University
Financial Aid Office
6525 N. Sheridan Road
Chicago, IL 60626

3896
Presidential Scholarships

AMOUNT: Maximum: $10000 DEADLINE: February 14
FIELDS/MAJORS: All Areas of Study

Open to admitted incoming freshmen at Loyola University. These awards are based on academics and talent, not financial need. Typical recipient has a minimum GPA of 3.5. Renewable up to three years if recipients maintain at least a 3.0 GPA and continues full-time status. Contact your high school guidance office, the address below, or call (773) 508-3155 for further information.

Loyola University
Financial Aid Office
6525 N. Sheridan Road
Chicago, IL 60626

3897
Transfer Academic Scholarships

AMOUNT: Maximum: $5000 DEADLINE: February 14
FIELDS/MAJORS: All Areas of Study

Open to admitted transfer students who have completed at least 30 semester hours (or 45 quarter hours) of transferable credit with an outstanding GPA. Renewable for a second year if recipients maintain a minimum GPA of 3.0 and continue full-time status. Contact the address below for further information or call (773) 508-3155.

Loyola University
Financial Aid Office
6525 N. Sheridan Road
Chicago, IL 60626

LOYOLA UNIVERSITY (NEW ORLEANS)

3898
Business Scholarship for Academic Excellence

AMOUNT: None Specified DEADLINE: December 1
FIELDS/MAJORS: Business

Open to high school seniors who have a minimum GPA of 3.2 and will be attending Loyola full-time. Renewable if recipients remain business majors for four years and maintain a minimum GPA of 3.0. Contact the address below for further information or call (504) 865-3240.

Loyola University, New Orleans
Office of Admissions, Box 18
6363 St. Charles Ave.
New Orleans, LA 70118

3899
College of Music Scholarships

AMOUNT: None Specified DEADLINE: April 1
FIELDS/MAJORS: Music

Open to incoming freshmen and transfer students in a music degree program. Based on talent and needs of the College. Audition days are in February and March. Contact the College of Music at (504) 865-3037 for more information.

Loyola University, New Orleans
Office of Admissions
6363 St. Charles Ave.
New Orleans, LA 70118

3900
Dean's Academic Excellence Scholarships

AMOUNT: None Specified DEADLINE: December 1
FIELDS/MAJORS: All Areas of Study

Open to incoming full-time freshmen who have a minimum GPA of 3.5, an ACT score of at least 29, or a minimum SAT of 1300. Write to the address below for details or call (504) 865-3240.

Loyola University, New Orleans
Office of Admissions
6363 St. Charles Ave.
New Orleans, LA 70118

3901
Drama Scholarship

AMOUNT: None Specified **DEADLINE:** February 7
FIELDS/MAJORS: Drama

Open to high school seniors with a minimum GPA of 2.5 who plan to attend Loyola full-time. Audition with the Department of Drama and Speech will be required in December and February. Contact the Department of Drama and Speech at (504) 865-3840 for further information.

Loyola University, New Orleans
Office of Admissions, Box 18
6363 St. Charles Ave.
New Orleans, LA 70118

3902
Ignatian Scholarships for Academic Excellence

AMOUNT: None Specified **DEADLINE:** December 1
FIELDS/MAJORS: All Areas of Study

Award open to incoming freshmen who will be attending school full-time. Must have a minimum 29 ACT or 1300 SAT with a minimum GPA of 3.5. Renewable if student remains full-time and maintains a minimum GPA of 3.3. Write to the address below for details or call (504) 865-3240.

Loyola University, New Orleans
Attn: Coordinator of Scholarship Programs
6363 St. Charles Ave., Campus Box 18
New Orleans, LA 70118

3903
Loyola Academic Excellence Scholarships

AMOUNT: None Specified **DEADLINE:** December 1
FIELDS/MAJORS: All Areas of Study

Scholarships for incoming full-time freshmen who have a minimum GPA of 3.2. Based on competitive test scores. Award renewable if recipients maintain a minimum GPA of 3.0. Write to the address below for details or call (504) 865-3240.

Loyola University, New Orleans
Office of Admissions
6363 St. Charles Ave.
New Orleans, LA 70118

3904
Loyola Transfer Scholarships

AMOUNT: None Specified **DEADLINE:** June 1
FIELDS/MAJORS: All Areas of Study

Open to incoming transfer students who have completed at least 12 academic credits with a minimum GPA of 3.2. Write to the address below for details or call (504) 865-3240.

Loyola University, New Orleans
Office of Admissions
6363 St. Charles Ave.
New Orleans, LA 70118

3905
Social Justice Scholarships

AMOUNT: None Specified **DEADLINE:** December 1
FIELDS/MAJORS: Sociology

Open to incoming full-time freshmen majoring in sociology. Must have a minimum GPA of 3.0 and demonstrate significant community involvement. Renewable if student completes forty-five hours of community service each semester. Write to the address below for details.

Loyola University, New Orleans
Attn: Coordinator of Scholarship Programs
6363 St. Charles Ave., Campus Box 18
New Orleans, LA 70118

3906
Visual Arts Scholarship

AMOUNT: None Specified **DEADLINE:** February 15
FIELDS/MAJORS: Visual Arts

Open to undergraduates who will be entering visual arts full-time. An audition and portfolio review will be required. Contact the Visual Arts Department at (504) 861-5456 for further information.

Loyola University, New Orleans
Office of Admissions, Box 18
6363 St. Charles Ave.
New Orleans, LA 70118

LURLEEN WALLACE COLLEGE OF NURSING

3907
Alabama Nursing Scholarship

AMOUNT: Maximum: $600   DEADLINE: None Specified
FIELDS/MAJORS: Nursing

Available to students with at least junior standing who are residents of Alabama and are enrolled in the Lurleen Wallace College of Nursing. Certain requirements must be met or the scholarship must be repaid. Contact the College of Nursing at (205) 782-5425 for details.

Alabama Commission on Higher Education
Office of Financial Aid
PO Box 30200
Montgomery, AL 36130

MARQUETTE UNIVERSITY

3908
Burke Scholarships

AMOUNT: None Specified   DEADLINE: February 17
FIELDS/MAJORS: All Areas of Study

Open to high school seniors who are Wisconsin residents and will be attending Marquette full-time. Must be in the top 10% of class. Demonstrated financial need and volunteerism will be considered. Five awards are offered. Each award is full tuition. Information and applications will be available after November 1. Contact the address below for further information. GPA must be at least 3.3.

Marquette University
Office of Admissions
1217 W. Wisconsin Ave.
Milwaukee, WI 53233

3909
College of Arts and Sciences Scholarships

AMOUNT: Maximum: $7500   DEADLINE: None Specified
FIELDS/MAJORS: Biology, English, Foreign Languages, History, Mathematics

Open to high school seniors who will be attending school full-time. Selections based on tests given at Marquette, February 8. There will be two first-place awards. Contact the address below for further information. GPA must be at least 2.8.

Marquette University
Office of Admissions
1217 W. Wisconsin Ave.
Milwaukee, WI 53233

3910
College of Business Administration Scholarships

AMOUNT: Maximum: $7500   DEADLINE: None Specified
FIELDS/MAJORS: Business Administration

Open to high school seniors who will be attending school full-time. Must be enrolled in the College of Business Administration for the first semester. Contact Admissions after December 1 for information regarding the written exam to be given February 1. GPA must be at least 2.9.

Marquette University
Office of Admissions
1217 W. Wisconsin Ave.
Milwaukee, WI 53233

3911
College of Engineering Scholarships

AMOUNT: Maximum: $7500   DEADLINE: None Specified
FIELDS/MAJORS: Engineering

Open to high school seniors who will be attending school full-time. Contact Admissions after December 1 for information about the written exam. Contact the address below for further information. Written exam will be given February 22. GPA must be at least 2.8.

Marquette University
Office of Admissions
1217 W. Wisconsin Ave.
Milwaukee, WI 53233

3912
College of Nursing Scholarships

AMOUNT: Maximum: $7500   DEADLINE: None Specified
FIELDS/MAJORS: Nursing

Open to high school seniors who will be attending school full-time. Contact Admissions after December 1 for materials. Competition consists of two parts: a) application materials and b) exam and interview held on February 22. Contact the address below for further information. GPA must be at least 2.8.

Marquette University
Office of Admissions
1217 W. Wisconsin Ave.
Milwaukee, WI 53233

3913
Competitive Transfer Scholarships

AMOUNT: Maximum: $2000 DEADLINE: November 15
FIELDS/MAJORS: All Areas of Study

Open to transfer students from two-year schools with at least 24 credits and a minimum GPA of 3.2. November 15 is the deadline for spring 1998, and May 15 is the deadline for fall 1998. Contact the address below for further information.

Marquette University
Office of Admissions
1217 W. Wisconsin Ave.
Milwaukee, WI 53233

3914
Dental Scholarship Program, Continuing Dental Scholarship Program

AMOUNT: $3000-$5000 DEADLINE: March 1
FIELDS/MAJORS: Dentistry

Scholarships are available to incoming as well as continuing students in the School of Dentistry at Marquette. Most based primarily on merit, others consider financial need. Dental scholarship program application/recommendation forms will be required. Contact the School of Dentistry for further information and forms. GPA must be at least 2.9.

Marquette University, School of Dentistry
Office of Admissions
604 N. Sixteenth St.
Milwaukee, WI 53233

3915
Dental Scholarships

AMOUNT: $1000-$4000 DEADLINE: March 1
FIELDS/MAJORS: Dentistry

Open to full-time dental students. These three awards are annual competitions: Dr. John E. and Lucille O. Koss Memorial; Dr. Raymond and Marcella Schweiger Endowed; and the David and Roseann Tolan Family Academic Scholarship. Some criteria varies, but most is standard in looking at academics, extracurricular activities, and financial need. Contact the address below for further information. Must have a GPA of at least 2.8.

Marquette University
Office of Admissions
1217 W. Wisconsin Ave.
Milwaukee, WI 53233

3916
Distinguished Scholars Awards

AMOUNT: None Specified DEADLINE: February 3
FIELDS/MAJORS: All Areas of Study

Open to high school seniors who will be attending school full-time and are in the top 5% of class. Five awards offered annually. Awards are full tuition. Information and applications are available after November 1. Contact the address below for further information. GPA must be at least 3.6.

Marquette University
Office of Admissions
1217 W. Wisconsin Ave.
Milwaukee, WI 53233

3917
Dr. James L. Gutman Family Scholarship

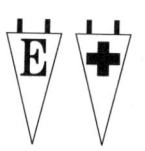

AMOUNT: None Specified DEADLINE: None Specified
FIELDS/MAJORS: Dentistry

Open to full-time dental students of Native American descent. Amounts vary depending upon fund availability. Contact the address below for further information.

Marquette University
Office of Admissions
1217 W. Wisconsin Ave.
Milwaukee, WI 53233

3918
Ignatius Scholar

AMOUNT: Maximum: $7000 DEADLINE: February 3
FIELDS/MAJORS: All Areas of Study

Open to high school seniors who will be attending Marquette full-time. Based on performance, rank, test scores, and extracurricular activities. Transferring students may also apply. Selections will be based on high school and college work completed. Contact the address below for further information. GPA must be at least 3.0.

Marquette University
Office of Admissions
1217 W. Wisconsin
Milwaukee, WI 53233

3919
Indian Fellowship and American Indian Graduate Center Fellowship Program

AMOUNT: None Specified DEADLINE: December 3
FIELDS/MAJORS: All Areas of Study

Open to Native Americans in a postbaccalaureate program. Must be enrolled full-time, demonstrate financial need, and be certified as Indian by tribe. The federal government funds both programs, selects the eligible students, and determines amount of each student's fellowship. Contact the address below for further information about both fellowships.

Marquette University
Office of Admissions
1217 W. Wisconsin Ave.
Milwaukee, WI 53233

3920
Indian Health Service Scholarships

AMOUNT: None Specified DEADLINE: None Specified
FIELDS/MAJORS: Dentistry

Open to full-time students certified as Indian by tribe. These fellowships include tuition, books, instruments, and stipend. For information and application materials, contact the Indian Health Scholarship Programs Office.

Marquette University
Office of Admissions
1217 W. Wisconsin Ave.
Milwaukee, WI 53233

3921
Indian Student Assistance Program Grant

AMOUNT: Maximum: $1100 DEADLINE: None Specified
FIELDS/MAJORS: All Areas of Study

Open to an enrolled member of a federally recognized tribe and/or certified as having one-fourth Indian blood. Must be a resident of Wisconsin and enrolled for at least 6 credits each semester. Must demonstrate financial need. Contact your tribal office for an Indian Certification form and application instructions.

Marquette University
Office of Admissions
1217 W. Wisconsin Ave.
Milwaukee, WI 53233

3922
Marquette Grants

AMOUNT: $500-$7500 DEADLINE: March 1
FIELDS/MAJORS: All Areas of Study

Selected on basis of academic achievement, test scores, and financial need. Must be enrolled full-time. For new freshmen and transfer students entering Marquette for the first-time in the fall. For more information (guide to university-administered scholarships), contact the office of admissions or the financial aid office. GPA must be at least 2.5.

Marquette University
Office of Admissions
1217 W. Wisconsin Ave.
Milwaukee, WI 53233

3923
Metropolitan Milwaukee Association of Commerce Scholarship

AMOUNT: Maximum: $3500 DEADLINE: None Specified
FIELDS/MAJORS: All Areas of Study

Open to high school seniors in the Milwaukee public school system. Must be planning to attend school full-time Contact your high school guidance counselor for information.

Marquette University
Office of Admissions
1217 W. Wisconsin Ave.
Milwaukee, WI 53233

3924
Michael and Maria Laskowski Memorial Awards

AMOUNT: $500 DEADLINE: March 2
FIELDS/MAJORS: All Areas Except Dentistry or Law

Scholarships are available for graduate students at Marquette University in any field of study except dentistry and law. Applicants must be of Polish heritage, reside in Wisconsin, be U.S. citizens, and have a minimum GPA of at least 3.0. Marquette University provides an additional $500 worth of tuition remission. Write to the address listed or call (414) 744-9029 for information.

Polanki, Polish Women's Cultural Club of Milwaukee
Ms Valerie Lukaszewicz, Chairperson
4160 S. First St.
Milwaukee, WI 53207

3925

Minority Engineering Scholarships

AMOUNT: None Specified   DEADLINE: March 1
FIELDS/MAJORS: Engineering

Open to high school seniors who are any of the following: African-American, Native-American, Mexican-American, Puerto Rican, Alaskan Native, or Native Pacific Islander. Grants and research opportunities available. Financial need is considered. Contact the address below for further information.

Marquette University
Office of Admissions
1217 W. Wisconsin Ave.
Milwaukee, WI 53233

3926

National Scholarships and President's Leadership Scholarship

AMOUNT: $3000-$4000   DEADLINE: February 3
FIELDS/MAJORS: All Areas of Study

Both scholarships open to high school seniors who will be attending school full-time. Based on performance, demonstrated leadership ability, and extracurricular activities. Contact the address below for further information. GPA must be at least 2.9.

Marquette University
Office of Admissions
1217 W. Wisconsin Ave.
Milwaukee, WI 53233

3927

Scholarship for Academic Distinction

AMOUNT: Maximum: $6000   DEADLINE: February 3
FIELDS/MAJORS: All Areas of Study

Open to high school seniors who will be attending Marquette full-time. Based on performance, rank, test scores, and extracurricular activities. Transferring students may also apply. Selections will be based on high school and college work. Contact the address below for further information. GPA must be at least 2.9.

Marquette University
Office of Admissions
1217 W. Wisconsin Ave.
Milwaukee, WI 53233

3928

Theater Arts Scholarships

AMOUNT: $500-$2500   DEADLINE: February 15
FIELDS/MAJORS: Theater Arts

Open to high school seniors who will be attending school full-time. Auditions and/or interviews will be held on February 15. Contact the address below for further information.

Marquette University
Office of Admissions
1217 W. Wisconsin Ave.
Milwaukee, WI 53233

MASSACHUSETTS INSTITUTE OF TECHNOLOGY

3929

Undergraduate and Graduate Grants, Loans, and Employment

AMOUNT: None Specified   DEADLINE: None Specified
FIELDS/MAJORS: All Areas of Study

Grants, loans, and employment opportunities are available for MIT students. Awards are based on financial need or academic ability or both. Financial aid forms are available with the admissions applications. Write to the address below for more information. Continuing students may contact the financial aid office for more details.

Massachusetts Institute of Technology
Office of Admissions
77 Massachusetts Ave., Room 3-108
Cambridge, MA 02139

MCHENRY COUNTY COLLEGE

3930

Louise Lundemo Memorial Music Scholarship

AMOUNT: Maximum: $500   DEADLINE: November 25
FIELDS/MAJORS: Music

Open to students who are enrolled in music courses. Auditions will be scheduled for the week following the deadline date. Contact the address below or call (815) 455-8761 for further information.

McHenry County College
Financial Aid Office
8900 Route 14, Room A141
Crystal Lake, IL 60012-2796

MCMURRY UNIVERSITY

3931
Abilene Military Dependent Program

AMOUNT: None Specified   DEADLINE: March 15
FIELDS/MAJORS: All Areas of Study

Awards for students who are dependents of full-time active duty military stationed in Abilene. Awards are for 20% of tuition. Write to the address below for more information. GPA must be at least 2.0.

McMurry University
Box 908 McMurry Station
Abilene, TX 79697

3932
Academic Achievement Scholarship

AMOUNT: $1000-$2150   DEADLINE: March 15
FIELDS/MAJORS: All Areas of Study

Awards for students with a GPA of 3.5 or better. For full-time study. Write to the address below for more information.

McMurry University
Box 908 McMurry Station
Abilene, TX 79697

3933
Activity Scholarship

AMOUNT: $200-$1000   DEADLINE: March 15
FIELDS/MAJORS: Art, Band, Choir, Communications, Theater

Awards for students in art, band, choir, communication, or theater. Must have a GPA of at least 2.0 and be enrolled full-time. Write to the address below for more information.

McMurry University
Box 908 McMurry Station
Abilene, TX 79697

3934
Endowed Scholarship

AMOUNT: None Specified   DEADLINE: March 15
FIELDS/MAJORS: All Areas of Study

Awards for students with a GPA of 2.0 or better and full-time enrollment. Individual award restrictions may apply. Check with the financial aid office for more information.

McMurry University
Box 908 McMurry Station
Abilene, TX 79697

3935
McMurry United Methodist Scholarship

AMOUNT: $1000   DEADLINE: March 15
FIELDS/MAJORS: All Areas of Study

Awards for entering freshmen at McMurry who are recommended by their church in the northwest Texas or New Mexico Conferences and are in the top 50% of their graduating high school class. For full-time study. Write to the address below for more information. GPA must be at least 2.7.

McMurry University
Box 908 McMurry Station
Abilene, TX 79697

3936
Ministerial Scholarship

AMOUNT: $2200   DEADLINE: March 15
FIELDS/MAJORS: All Areas of Study

Awards for ministers, their dependents, and students pursuing a church-related vocation. Must be enrolled full-time with a GPA of 2.0 or better. Write to the address below for more information.

McMurry University
Box 908 McMurry Station
Abilene, TX 79697

3937
Presidential Scholarship

AMOUNT: $600-$3150   DEADLINE: March 15
FIELDS/MAJORS: All Areas of Study

Awards for entering freshmen at McMurry who score a 25 or above on the ACT or 1140 or better on the SAT and are in the top 20% of their graduating high school class. For full-time study. Write to the address below for more information. GPA must be at least 3.2.

McMurry University
Box 908 McMurry Station
Abilene, TX 79697

3938
University Scholars Partnership

GPA 2.5+

AMOUNT: $3000 DEADLINE: March 15
FIELDS/MAJORS: All Areas of Study

Awards for entering freshmen at McMurry who rank in the top 33% of their high school class. For full-time study. Write to the address below for more information. GPA must be at least 2.7.

McMurry University
Box 908 McMurry Station
Abilene, TX 79697

MEMPHIS COLLEGE OF ART

3939
Evelyn Skinker Sculpture Award

AMOUNT: None Specified DEADLINE: June 15
FIELDS/MAJORS: Sculpture

One award is given annually to a student at MCA who shows excellence in sculpting. Contact the Financial Aid Office at the address below for details.

Memphis College of Art
Office of Financial Aid
Overton Park
Memphis, TN 38112

MENLO COLLEGE

3940
Dean's Scholarship

GPA 3.0+

AMOUNT: Maximum: $6500 DEADLINE: March 2
FIELDS/MAJORS: All Areas of Study

Awards are available for freshmen with GPAs ranging from 3.25 to 3.49. Transfer students who have completed fewer than 60 transferable units of college work are also eligible. Write to the address below for additional information.

Menlo College
1000 El Camino Real
Department of Financial Aid
Atherton, CA 94027

3941
Leadership and Service Grant

GPA 2.5+

AMOUNT: Maximum: $5000 DEADLINE: March 2
FIELDS/MAJORS: All Areas of Study

Awards are available for new freshmen with a minimum of 2.8 GPAs who have demonstrated outstanding leadership potential and the ability to make a significant contribution to Menlo College. Write to the address below for additional information.

Menlo College
1000 El Camino Real
Department of Financial Aid
Atherton, CA 94027

3942
President's Scholarship

GPA 3.5+

AMOUNT: Maximum: $10000 DEADLINE: March 2
FIELDS/MAJORS: All Areas of Study

Awards are available to freshmen with GPAs of 3.5 or higher. Transfer students who have completed fewer than 60 transferable units of college work are also eligible. Write to the address below for complete details.

Menlo College
1000 El Camino Real
Department of Financial Aid
Atherton, CA 94027

3943
Transfer Student Awards

GPA 3.0+

AMOUNT: Maximum: $5000 DEADLINE: March 2
FIELDS/MAJORS: All Areas of Study

Awards are available for transfer students with GPAs of 3.0 or higher who have completed 60 transferable units or more college work. Write to the address below for additional information.

Menlo College
1000 El Camino Real
Department of Financial Aid
Atherton, CA 94027

MERCYHURST COLLEGE

3944
Egan Honors Scholarships

AMOUNT: $500-$5505 DEADLINE: May 1
FIELDS/MAJORS: All Areas of Study

Open to admitted incoming freshmen who have demonstrated high academics. Selections based on class rank, GPA, standardized test scores, recommendations, and a writing sample. An essay will also be required. Contact the address below for further information or call (814) 824-2202. GPA must be at least 3.0.

Mercyhurst College
Office of Enrollment
501 E. 38th St.
Erie, PA 16546

3945
Valedictorian/Salutatorian Scholarships

AMOUNT: None Specified DEADLINE: May 1
FIELDS/MAJORS: All Areas of Study

Open to admitted incoming freshmen who are the valedictorian or salutatorian of their class. Selections based on class rank, GPA, standardized test scores, recommendations, and a writing sample. Write to the address below for details or call (814) 824-2202.

Mercyhurst College
Office of Enrollment
501 E. 38th St.
Erie, PA 16546

MEREDITH COLLEGE

3946
A.J. Fletcher/Robert Lewis/Mary Beddingfield and Music Talent Awards

AMOUNT: $350-$7500 DEADLINE: February 15
FIELDS/MAJORS: Music

Different awards for entering freshmen with majors in all areas of music. Preliminary auditions must be arranged prior to February 15 with the Department of Music, Speech, and Theater. These awards stress talent, academic ability, previous music accomplishments, and potential achievements. Six awards are given annually. Request the Special Music Scholarship information and application from the address below.

Meredith College
Office of Admissions
3800 Hillsborough St.
Raleigh, NC 27607

3947
Eleanor Layfield Davis/Ruby C. and Ernest P. McSwain/Lois Outland Awards

AMOUNT: $400-$1500 DEADLINE: February 15
FIELDS/MAJORS: Art

Several awards for entering freshmen majoring in art. A preliminary portfolio review will need to be arranged prior to February 15. Demonstrated ability and potential for success in the field of visual art will be considered. Request the Special Art Scholarship information and application when writing. Contact the address below for further information.

Meredith College
Office of Admissions
3800 Hillsborough St.
Raleigh, NC 27607

3948
Julia Hamlet Harris Scholarships

AMOUNT: $1000-$1500 DEADLINE: February 15
FIELDS/MAJORS: All Areas of Study

Awards for entering freshmen with superior academic credentials. High school records, test scores, and financial need are considered. Awards are renewable if the student remains full-time and maintains a 3.0 GPA. Contact the address below for further information.

Meredith College
Office of Admissions
3800 Hillsborough St.
Raleigh, NC 27607

3949
Meredith Teaching Fellows Awards

AMOUNT: $5000 DEADLINE: February 15
FIELDS/MAJORS: Education

Grants available to education majors at Meredith who have received a North Carolina Teaching Fellows Award. The grant will cover the portions of tuition and room board in excess of the $5000 North Carolina Teaching Fellows Award. Renewable with a minimum 2.5 GPA. Must be a North Carolina resident. Write to the address below for additional information on the Meredith Award or the North Carolina Teaching Fellows Award.

Meredith College
Office of Admissions
3800 Hillsborough St.
Raleigh, NC 27607

3950
Sandra Graham Shelton Scholarship

AMOUNT: $1275 DEADLINE: February 15
FIELDS/MAJORS: Interior Design

Awards for entering freshmen who will interview with the interior design faculty and show examples of their work. Awards are renewable if the student remains full-time and maintains a GPA of 3.0 in the interior design courses. Contact the address below for further information.

Meredith College
Office of Admissions
3800 Hillsborough St.
Raleigh, NC 27607

MESA STATE COLLEGE

3951
Aspinall Foundation Awards

AMOUNT: $1000-$4000 DEADLINE: None Specified
FIELDS/MAJORS: Social Science

Awards for a junior or senior Mesa State students in the field of social science. Applicants must have a GPA of at least 3.0. Contact the Mesa State School of Humanities and Social Science or call 1-800-982-MESA or (970) 248-1396 for more details.

Mesa State College
Office of Financial Aid
PO Box 2647
Grand Junction, CO 81501

3952
Bank One Western Colorado N.A. Scholarship

AMOUNT: Maximum: $1000 DEADLINE: None Specified
FIELDS/MAJORS: Business

Awards for full-time juniors or seniors studying business who participate in the cooperative education program. Applicants must meet qualifications for employment at any of Bank One western Colorado centers. Must have a minimum GPA of 2.5. Contact the School of Professional Studies/Business Administration Department at Mesa State or call 1-800-982-MESA or (970) 248-1396 for more information.

Mesa State College
Financial Aid Office
PO Box 2684
Grand Junction, CO 81501

3953
Boge Chemistry Award

AMOUNT: Maximum: $1000 DEADLINE: None Specified
FIELDS/MAJORS: Chemistry

Awards for outstanding chemistry students at Mesa State College. Write to the address below or call 1-800-982-MESA or (970) 248-1396 for more information.

Mesa State College
Financial Aid Office
PO Box 2684
Grand Junction, CO 81501

3954
Dan A. Brant, Jr. Memorial Scholarship

AMOUNT: Maximum: $1000 DEADLINE: None Specified
FIELDS/MAJORS: All Areas of Study

Awards for students at Mesa State College with GPAs of at least 3.0. Applicants must be walk-on athletes in any varsity sport. For undergraduate study. Contact the Athletic Department or call 1-800-982-MESA or (970) 248-1396 for further details.

Mesa State College
Financial Aid Office
PO Box 2684
Grand Junction, CO 81501

3955
Dr. Henry H. and Margaret Zeigel

AMOUNT: Maximum: $1000
DEADLINE: None Specified
FIELDS/MAJORS: Nursing, Music Theater, Languages/Literature.

Awards for Mesa State sophomores, juniors, or seniors majoring in the four fields listed above. Must have GPAs of 3.0 or higher. Four awards offered annually, one for each field. Contact the School of Professional Studies/Nursing or Humanities and Social Sciences or Fine and Performing Arts or Languages/Literature or call 1-800-982-MESA or (970) 248-1396.

Mesa State College
Financial Aid Office
PO Box 2647
Grand Junction, CO 81501

3956
Eileen Townsend Nagatomo Memorial Scholarship

AMOUNT: Maximum: $1000 DEADLINE: None Specified
FIELDS/MAJORS: Theater

Awards for Mesa State sophomores, juniors, or seniors majoring in theater. Must have GPAs of at least 2.5. Contact the Theater Department or call 1-800-982-MESA or (970) 248-1396 for more information.

Mesa State College
Financial Aid Office
PO Box 2647
Grand Junction, CO 81501

3957
Esther Herr Memorial Scholarship

AMOUNT: Maximum: $1000 DEADLINE: None Specified
FIELDS/MAJORS: Language, Literature, Drama

Awards for Mesa State students enrolled in the School of Humanities and Social Sciences who are studying language, literature, and drama. Must have GPAs of at least 2.75. Three awards offered annually. Contact the School of Humanities and Social Sciences or call 1-800-982-MESA or (970) 248-1396 for more information.

Mesa State College
Office of Financial Aid
PO Box 2647
Grand Junction, CO 81501

3958
Gerlach Music Scholarship

AMOUNT: Maximum: $1000 DEADLINE: None Specified
FIELDS/MAJORS: Music

Award for full-time Mesa State students studying music and enrolled in the School of Humanities and Social Sciences. Must have GPAs of at least 3.0. Preference will be given to keyboard players. Contact the Music Department or call 1-800-982-MESA or (970) 248-1396 for more information.

Mesa State College
Office of Financial Aid
PO Box 2647
Grand Junction, CO 81501

3959
Grand Junction Lion's Club Scholarship

AMOUNT: Maximum: $1000 DEADLINE: None Specified
FIELDS/MAJORS: All Areas of Study

Awards for high school graduates from Mesa County who intend to enter Mesa State. Must have GPAs of at least 3.0 and demonstrate financial need. Recipients must not have additional scholarship money exceeding $1000 per academic year. Renewable. Write to the address below or call 1-800-982-MESA or (970) 248-1396 for more details.

Mesa State College
Office of Financial Aid
PO Box 2647
Grand Junction, CO 81501

3960
Hazel Butler Garms U.S. History Scholarship

AMOUNT: Maximum: $1500 DEADLINE: None Specified
FIELDS/MAJORS: History

Award for Mesa State juniors and seniors studying history. Must have and maintain GPAs of at least 3.0. Contact the Humanities and Social Sciences Department or call 1-800-982-MESA or (970) 248-1396 for more information.

Mesa State College
Office of Financial Aid
PO Box 2647
Grand Junction, CO 81501

3961
Helen Kray Scholarship

AMOUNT: Maximum: $1000 DEADLINE: None Specified
FIELDS/MAJORS: Music

Award for Mesa State sophomores, juniors, or seniors in the music program. Must have GPAs of at least 2.5 and demonstrate financial need. Contact the Music Department or call 1-800-982-MESA or (970) 248-1396 for more information.

Mesa State College
Office of Financial Aid
PO Box 2647
Grand Junction, CO 81501

3962
Madge Huffer Scholarship

AMOUNT: Maximum: $1000 DEADLINE: None Specified
FIELDS/MAJORS: Speech and Theater

Award for full-time Mesa State speech and theater students in the School of Humanities and Social Sciences. Must have GPAs of at least 2.5 and be active participants in speech or theater activities. Contact the School of Humanities and Social Sciences or call 1-800-982-MESA or (970) 248-1396 for more details.

Mesa State College
Office of Financial Aid
PO Box 2647
Grand Junction, CO 81501

3963
Marian Stephens Wethington Memorial Nursing Scholarship

AMOUNT: Maximum: $2000   DEADLINE: None Specified
FIELDS/MAJORS: Nursing

Awards for Mesa State juniors majoring in the field of nursing. Contact the School of Professional Studies/Nursing area or call 1-800-982-MESA or (970) 248-1396 for more details.

Mesa State College
Financial Aid Office
PO Box 2647
Grand Junction, CO 81501

3964
Mary Rait American Association of University Women Grant (AAUW)

AMOUNT: Maximum: $1000   DEADLINE: None Specified
FIELDS/MAJORS: All Areas of Study

Awards for mature women returning to Mesa State for a bachelor's degree after some years of absence from the academic scene. Contact the American Association of University Women or call 1-800-982-MESA or (970) 248-1396 for more details.

Mesa State College
Office of Financial Aid
PO Box 3692
Grand Junction, CO 81501

3965
Mesa County Medical Society Nursing Scholarships

AMOUNT: Maximum: $1000   DEADLINE: None Specified
FIELDS/MAJORS: Nursing

Awards for full-time Mesa State nursing students who agree to work in Mesa County for at least two years following graduation. Must have and maintain a GPA of at least 3.0. Contact the School of Professional Studies/Nursing area or call 1-800-982-MESA or (970) 248-1396 for more details.

Mesa State College
Financial Aid Office
PO Box 2647
Grand Junction, CO 81501

3966
Orchard Mesa Lion's Club Scholarship

AMOUNT: Maximum: $1000   DEADLINE: None Specified
FIELDS/MAJORS: All Areas of Study

Awards for Mesa State junior and senior students who are from Mesa County and have a GPA of at least 3.0. Write to the address below or call 1-800-982-MESA for more details.

Mesa State College
Office of Financial Aid
PO Box 2647
Grand Junction, CO 81501

3967
Red Crawford Tennis Awards

AMOUNT: Maximum: $1000   DEADLINE: None Specified
FIELDS/MAJORS: All Areas of Study

Awards for students at Mesa State College who are active in the tennis program. Must have and maintain a GPA of at least 2.0 and be full-time students. Contact the Physical Education Department/Tennis Coach or call 1-800-982-MESA or (970) 248-1396 for further details.

Mesa State College
Financial Aid Office
PO Box 2684
Grand Junction, CO 81501

3968
Red "Kiwanis" Crawford Scholarship

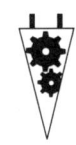

AMOUNT: Maximum: $1250   DEADLINE: None Specified
FIELDS/MAJORS: Electronics Technology

Awards for students at Mesa State College who are Colorado residents and are in the electronics technology program. Contact the United Technical Educational Center (UTEC) on campus or call 1-800-982-MESA or (970) 248-1396 for further details.

Mesa State College
Financial Aid Office
PO Box 2684
Grand Junction, CO 81501

3969
Robert H. and Cynthia B. Cutter Scholarship

AMOUNT: Maximum: $1000   DEADLINE: None Specified
FIELDS/MAJORS: Theater

Awards for students at Mesa State College who are active in the theater program. Must have and maintain a GPA of at least 2.0 and be full-time students. Contact the Theater Department or call 1-800-982-MESA or (970) 248-1396 for further details.

Mesa State College
Financial Aid Office
PO Box 2684
Grand Junction, CO 81501

3970
Rotary Club Scholarship

AMOUNT: Maximum: $1000   DEADLINE: None Specified
FIELDS/MAJORS: All Areas of Study

Awards for Mesa State continuing students with financial need and with special circumstances (major change in life, disadvantaged, etc.). Must have and maintain GPAs of at least 3.0. Write to the address below or call 1-800-982-MESA or (970) 248-1396 for more details.

Mesa State College
Office of Financial Aid
PO Box 2647
Grand Junction, CO 81501

3971
School Academic Scholarship

AMOUNT: Maximum: $1000   DEADLINE: None Specified
FIELDS/MAJORS: All Areas of Study

Awards for Mesa State students from Colorado who have GPAs of at least 3.0. Applicants must be enrolled in at least 12 hours of study. Contact the Chairman of your Academic or Vocational Division at Mesa State or call 1-800-982-MESA or (970) 248-1396.

Mesa State College
Office of Financial Aid
PO Box 2647
Grand Junction, CO 81501

MIAMI-DADE COMMUNITY COLLEGE

3972
Elizabeth Virrick Scholarship

AMOUNT: Maximum: $800   DEADLINE: None Specified
FIELDS/MAJORS: All Areas of Study

Scholarships are awarded to MDCC students who live in the Coconut Grove are of Dade County, who do not qualify to receive funds from government sources. Funds may be applied toward fees and/or books. Two awards are offered annually. Call Collie Coats at (305) 447-3930 for information.

Coconut Grove Cares
Miami-Dade Community College
300 NE Second Ave.
Miami, FL 33132

MIAMI UNIVERSITY

3973
National Merit Scholarships

AMOUNT: $750-$2000   DEADLINE: May 31
FIELDS/MAJORS: All Areas of Study

Scholarships are available at Miami University for full time students who are national merit finalists and name Miami University as their first school of choice. Contact the admissions office or the office of student financial aid for application information. GPA must be at least 3.0.

Miami University
Office of Student Financial Aid
Edwards House
Oxford, OH 45056

MICHIGAN STATE UNIVERSITY

3974
Michigan Dairy Memorial Scholarship

AMOUNT: Maximum: $1000   DEADLINE: April 1
FIELDS/MAJORS: Dairy Science and Related

Open to high school seniors interested in dairy industry studies at Michigan State University. Applications are due April 1 and will be awarded in July. Write to the address below for more information.

Michigan State University, Department of Animal Science
Russel Erickson
1250 Anthony Hall
East Lansing, MI 48824

3975
Michigan Farm Bureau/Marge Karker Scholarship

AMOUNT: Maximum: $1500 DEADLINE: December 1
FIELDS/MAJORS: Agricultural Technology

Open to students enrolled at Michigan State University who are from a Farm Bureau family. If applicant is married or twenty-one years of age, or above, applicant must be a Farm Bureau member. Must have a minimum GPA of 2.6 and be able to demonstrate financial need. Contact the address listed or call 1-800-292-2680 ext. 3202 for further information.

Michigan Farm Bureau
Promotion and Education Department
PO Box 30960-7373 W. Saginaw Hwy.
Lansing, MI 48909

MIDDLE TENNESSEE STATE UNIVERSITY

3976
Academic Service Scholarships

AMOUNT: Maximum: $2000 DEADLINE: March 15
FIELDS/MAJORS: All Areas of Study

Open to incoming freshmen who are in the top 3% of graduating class. A work obligation of five hours per week is required. Renewable if recipient maintains a minimum GPA of 2.5 for the first semester. After that, the student must maintain a 2.5 semester GPA and a 2.9 cumulative GPA each semester. Write to the address below for more details.

Middle Tennessee State University
Office of Student Financial Aid
Murfreesboro, TN 37132

3977
Enrichment Scholarships

AMOUNT: None Specified DEADLINE: March 15
FIELDS/MAJORS: All Areas of Study

Open to students who are qualified for admission to or are currently enrolled in Middle Tennessee State University. Based on potential, area of specialization, and economic status. Write to the address listed for more details. Must have a GPA of at least 3.0.

Middle Tennessee State University
Office of Student Financial Aid
Murfreesboro, TN 37132

3978
Leadership/Performance Scholarship

AMOUNT: Maximum: $2000 DEADLINE: March 15
FIELDS/MAJORS: All Areas of Study

Scholarships for outstanding incoming freshmen based on their achievements in academics, extracurricular activities, and leadership. Renewable if recipients maintain a minimum GPA of 2.8. Write to the address below for more information.

Middle Tennessee State University
Office of Student Financial Aid
Murfreesboro, TN 37132

3979
Matching Scholarship Program

AMOUNT: None Specified DEADLINE: March 15
FIELDS/MAJORS: All Areas of Study

Open to African-American students who are qualified for admission to or are currently enrolled in Middle Tennessee State University. Based on academic potential, area of specialization, and economic status. Applicants must be U.S. citizens. Write to the address below for more details. GPA must be at least 3.0.

Middle Tennessee State University
Office of Student Financial Aid
Murfreesboro, TN 37132

3980
Otis L. Floyd Academic Excellence Scholarship

AMOUNT: None Specified DEADLINE: March 15
FIELDS/MAJORS: All Areas of Study

Open to outstanding African-American incoming freshmen who have a high school GPA of at least 3.2 and an ACT score of at least 25. Renewable if recipients maintain a minimum GPA of 3.0. Write to the address below for more details.

Middle Tennessee State University
Office of Admissions
Murfreesboro, TN 37132

3981
Presidential Scholarship

AMOUNT: Maximum: $3300　DEADLINE: March 15
FIELDS/MAJORS: All Areas of Study

One hundred scholarships guaranteed to incoming freshman who have a GPA of at least 3.5 and an SAT score of 1280 or an ACT score of 29. Renewable with a GPA of 3.0. There are no application forms, but freshmen need to submit a transcript and SAT or ACT score report to the admissions office. Write to the address below for more complete information.

Middle Tennessee State University
Office of Admissions
Cope 208, Att: Linda Puckett
Murfreesboro, TN 37132

3982
Scholastic Achievement Scholarships

AMOUNT: $2000-$2400　DEADLINE: March 15
FIELDS/MAJORS: All Areas of Study

Open to first-time freshmen who are African-American and U.S. citizens. Must have a high school GPA of 3.0 or above. Renewable if recipients maintain a minimum GPA of 2.8 at the end of the second semester. Write to the address below for more details.

Middle Tennessee State University
Office of Admissions
Ron Malone Cope 208
Murfreesboro, TN 37132

MIDLANDS TECHNICAL COLLEGE

3983
Foundation Presidential Scholarships

AMOUNT: $500-$1000　DEADLINE: December 25
FIELDS/MAJORS: All Areas of Study

One scholarship in each of the four academic divisions of Midlands Technical College. For senior year. Contact the Office of Student Aid at the address below for details.

Midlands Technical College
Office of Student Aid
PO Box 2408
Columbia, SC 29202

MIDWAY COLLEGE

3984
Midway Scholarships and Grants

AMOUNT: None Specified　DEADLINE: None Specified
FIELDS/MAJORS: All Areas of Study

Scholarships and grants for women accepted to or enrolled at Midway College. Awards are based on merit, need, or a combination of both. The forty-seven scholarships and grants will also vary in their main concern (i.e., specific majors, specific sports, membership in organizations). Contact the financial aid office at the address below for details.

Midway College
Financial Aid Office
512 E. Stephens St.
Midway, KY 40347-1120

MILLIKIN UNIVERSITY

3985
Long/Vanderburg Scholarship

AMOUNT: Maximum: $10000　DEADLINE: None Specified
FIELDS/MAJORS: All Areas of Study

Open to minority students, admitted to Millikin University, who ranked in the upper third of their high school class. Transfer students must have a minimum GPA of 3.0. Must be U.S citizens or have residential alien status. Renewable if recipients maintain a minimum GPA of 3.0. Contact the address below or call 1-800-373-7733 for further information.

Millikin University
Melissa Watson
1184 West Main St.
Decatur, IL 62522-2084

MILLS COLLEGE

3986
Arthur Vining Davis Science Scholarship

AMOUNT: $2000   DEADLINE: February 15
FIELDS/MAJORS: Science, Mathematics, Computer Science

Scholarship for entering freshman or transfer student who has demonstrated strong ability and interest in science, mathematics, or computer science. Award is based on merit and is renewable as long as the student stays in the same field of study and maintains a 3.0 GPA. Write to the address below for more complete details.

Mills College
Office of Financial Aid
5000 MacArthur Blvd.
Oakland, CA 94613

3987
Carroll Donner Commemorative Scholarship in Music

AMOUNT: $5000   DEADLINE: February 1
FIELDS/MAJORS: Music

Scholarship for first-year female student or undergraduate transfer student who has demonstrated superior music talent. Applicants must audition in person or on tape. Renewable with a 3.2 GPA and full-time enrollment. Write to the address below for more information.

Mills College
Office of Financial Aid
5000 MacArthur Blvd.
Oakland, CA 94613

3988
Regional Scholarships

AMOUNT: $5000   DEADLINE: February 15
FIELDS/MAJORS: All Areas of Study

Awards for entering first-year female students who have demonstrated superior scholastic achievement and distinguished themselves in their extracurricular activities or personal interests. Must have a GPA of 3.2 from high school and an SAT score of at least 1100. Based on both merit and financial need. Ten awards offered annually. Write to the address below for additional information.

Mills College
Office of Financial Aid
5000 MacArthur Blvd.
Oakland, CA 94613

3989
Transfer Scholarships

AMOUNT: Maximum: $5000   DEADLINE: April 1
FIELDS/MAJORS: All Areas of Study

Awards for transfer students who have demonstrated superior scholastic achievement, leadership ability, and/or have contributed significantly to their previous educational institution. Renewable with a 3.2 GPA and full-time enrollment. Based on academics and financial need. Renewable if recipients maintain preset standards. Write to the address below for more details.

Mills College
Office of Financial Aid
5000 MacArthur Blvd.
Oakland, CA 94613

3990
Trustee Scholarships

AMOUNT: Maximum: $10000   DEADLINE: February 15
FIELDS/MAJORS: All Areas of Study

Awards for entering first-year female students who have demonstrated superior scholastic achievement and distinguished themselves in their extracurricular activities or personal interests. Must have a GPA of 3.5 from high school and an SAT score of at least 1200. Based on merit and financial need. Write to the address below for additional information.

Mills College
Office of Financial Aid
5000 MacArthur Blvd.
Oakland, CA 94613

MINNEAPOLIS COLLEGE OF ART AND DESIGN

3991
Shirley and Miles Fiterman, Virginia M. Binger, Wanda Gag Scholarships

AMOUNT: $13934   DEADLINE: March 15
FIELDS/MAJORS: All Areas of Study

Grants and scholarships for seniors at Minneapolis College of Art and Design. Not based on need. Selection is made by faculty. Contact the address below for details. GPA must be at least 3.0.

Minneapolis College of Art and Design
Financial Aid Office
2501 Stevens Ave. S.
Minneapolis, MN 55404

MISSOURI VALLEY COLLEGE

3992

Chamber of Commerce Scholarships

AMOUNT: Maximum: $500 DEADLINE: April 15
FIELDS/MAJORS: All Areas of Study

Three awards open to residents of Saline County, Missouri. Must be first-time students at Missouri Valley College. Contact the address below for further information.

Missouri Valley College
Office of Admissions
500 E. College
Marshall, MO 65340

3993

Missouri Valley College American Humanics Scholarships

AMOUNT: $4000 DEADLINE: April 15
FIELDS/MAJORS: All Areas of Study

Awards open to high school seniors who are/have been members or participants of: Scouts, YMCA/YWCA, Big Brothers/Big Sisters, 4-H, Boys Club of America, Junior Achievement, Campfire, Goodwill Industries, or the American Red Cross. Contact the address below for further information.

Missouri Valley College
Office of Admissions
500 E. College
Marshall, MO 65340

3994

Missouri Valley College Board of Trustees Scholarships

AMOUNT: $5000 DEADLINE: April 15
FIELDS/MAJORS: All Areas of Study

Awards open to high school seniors who have been recommended by a member of the Board of Trustees. Contact the address below for further information.

Missouri Valley College
Office of Admissions
500 E. College
Marshall, MO 65340

3995

Missouri Valley College Boy/Girl State Scholarships

AMOUNT: Maximum: $5000 DEADLINE: April 15
FIELDS/MAJORS: All Areas of Study

Awards open to high school seniors who have been participants of Boys' State or Girls' State. Contact the address below for further information.

Missouri Valley College
Office of Admissions
500 E. College
Marshall, MO 65340

3996

Missouri Valley College Presidential Scholarships

AMOUNT: Maximum: $9700 DEADLINE: April 15
FIELDS/MAJORS: All Areas of Study

Awards open to high school seniors who are residents of Missouri. Must have a minimum SAT of 1240, ACT of 28 and GPA of 3.5. The award is equal to tuition. Contact the address below for further information.

Missouri Valley College
Office of Admissions
500 E. College
Marshall, MO 65340

MOORHEAD STATE UNIVERSITY (MINNESOTA)

3997

Academic Excellence Award

AMOUNT: Maximum: $2000 DEADLINE: June 30
FIELDS/MAJORS: All Areas of Study

Scholarships for incoming freshmen who are National Merit finalists. Award is renewable for three years based on GPA. Write to the address below for more information.

Moorhead State University
Office of Scholarship and Financial Aid
107 Owens Hall
Moorhead, MN 56563

3998
Academic Scholarships

Amount: $500-$750 **Deadline:** March 1
Fields/Majors: All Areas of Study

Scholarships for incoming freshmen who rank in the top 25% of their high school graduating class. Based on high school rank and ACT scores. Write to the address below for more information. GPA must be at least 3.0.

Moorhead State University
Office of Scholarship and Financial Aid
107 Owens Hall
Moorhead, MN 56563

3999
Achievement Scholarships

Amount: Maximum: $500 **Deadline:** March 1
Fields/Majors: All Areas of Study

Open to students who can document achievement in such areas as leadership, contributions to school organizations and activities, and community service. Write to the address below for more information. GPA must be at least 3.0.

Moorhead State University
Office of Scholarship and Financial Aid
107 Owens Hall
Moorhead, MN 56563

4000
Athletic Scholarships

Amount: None Specified **Deadline:** None Specified
Fields/Majors: All Areas of Study

Scholarships for incoming freshmen who demonstrate exceptional athletic talent. Interested applicants should call the men's Athletic Department at (218) 236-2622 or the women's Athletic Department at (218) 299-5824 for more information.

Moorhead State University
Office of Scholarship and Financial Aid
107 Owens Hall
Moorhead, MN 56563

4001
Honors Apprenticeship Scholarships

Amount: Maximum: $2000 **Deadline:** February 1
Fields/Majors: All Areas of Study

Awards for freshmen at Moorhead State University based on academic excellence. Recipients will have the opportunity to work directly with a faculty or staff member.

Renewable for three years. Applicants must rank in the top 5% of their high school graduating class and in the top 5 percentile on the ACT/SAT. Write to the address below for more details. GPA must be at least 3.8.

Moorhead State University
Financial Aid Office
107 Owens
Moorhead, MN 56563

4002
Presidential Scholarships

Amount: Maximum: $500 **Deadline:** March 1
Fields/Majors: All Areas of Study

Open to incoming freshmen who ranked in the top 25% of graduating class. Based on academics and community service. Award is $1000: $500 in the first year and $500 in the second. Recipients must have a minimum GPA of 3.0 to receive the award in the second year. Write to the address below for more information.

Moorhead State University
Office of Scholarship and Financial Aid
107 Owens Hall
Moorhead, MN 56563

4003
Talent Scholarships

Amount: None Specified **Deadline:** None Specified
Fields/Majors: Art, Music, Theater, Speech

Each area has specific eligibility criteria and scholarships are available based on exceptional talent in the areas of art, music, speech, or theater arts. Recipients are selected by department faculty. To apply, contact the following departments directly and ask for either the department chairperson or secretary for scholarship requirements. Art Department: (218) 236-2151; Music Department: (218) 236-2101; Speech-Theater Department: (218) 236-2126. GPA must be at least 3.0.

Moorhead State University
Office of Scholarship and Financial Aid
107 Owens Hall
Moorhead, MN 56563

MOREHEAD STATE UNIVERSITY (KENTUCKY)

4004
Alumni Award

Amount: $500-$750 **Deadline:** March 15
Fields/Majors: All Areas of Study

Open to admitted entering freshmen or transfer students who have at least one parent who is an alumni and an active member of the MSU Alumni Association. Freshmen must have an Admission Index of at least five hundred, and transfer students must have a minimum GPA of 3.0. May be renewed if recipients achieve a minimum GPA of 2.75 during each of the first two semesters and a 3.0 GPA for each semester thereafter. Transfer students must maintain the minimum 3.0 with which they entered MSU. Write to the address below for more information or call 1-800-585-6781.

Morehead State University
Office of Admissions
Morehead, KY 40351

4005
Leadership Award

AMOUNT: Maximum: $650 DEADLINE: March 15
FIELDS/MAJORS: All Areas of Study

Open to incoming freshmen admitted to MSU. Must have exhibited strong leadership and achievement capabilities through school and community activities. Must have a minimum GPA of 2.5. May be renewed if recipients maintain a minimum GPA of 2.5. Contact the address below for further information or call 1-800-585-6781.

Morehead State University
Office of Admissions
306 Howell-McDowell
Morehead, KY 40351

4006
Minority Student Leadership Award

AMOUNT: Maximum: $650 DEADLINE: March 15
FIELDS/MAJORS: All Areas of Study

Open to admitted entering freshmen who are African-American, Native American, Hispanic-American, Asian-American, Alaskan Native, or Pacific Islander. Must be Kentucky residents who have demonstrated achievement in academics and/or extracurricular activities. Renewable if recipients maintain a minimum GPA of 2.5. Contact the address below for further information or call 1-800-585-6781.

Morehead State University
Office of Admissions
306 Howell-McDowell
Morehead, KY 40351

4007
Morehead State University Award

AMOUNT: $1200 DEADLINE: March 15
FIELDS/MAJORS: All Areas of Study

Open to students who have been admitted to MSU as freshmen or transfer students. Must have an Admission Index of at least 550. Transfers must have a minimum GPA of 3.0 for the equivalent of at least one term. Write to the address below for information.

Morehead State University
Office of Admissions
306 Howell-McDowell
Morehead, KY 40351

4008
Presidential Scholarship

AMOUNT: $2000-$6000 DEADLINE: March 15
FIELDS/MAJORS: All Areas of Study

Open to students who have been admitted as freshmen and meet one of the following requirements: be a National Merit Scholar/Finalist; or be your school's valedictorian or salutatorian with a minimum ACT score of 30; or be a National Merit Semi-Finalist or a Kentucky Governor's Scholar with an ACT score of at least 28; or have a minimum GPA of 3.75 and an ACT of at least 28. Contact the address below for further information or call 1-800-585-6781.

Morehead State University
Office of Admissions
306 Howell-McDowell
Morehead, KY 40351

4009
Regents Scholarship

AMOUNT: $750-$2000 DEADLINE: March 15
FIELDS/MAJORS: All Areas of Study

Scholarships are available to entering freshmen admitted to MSU. Must have a minimum ACT score of 20. Renewable if recipients achieve a minimum cumulative GPA of 2.75 during each of the first two semesters and at least a 3.0 GPA for each semester thereafter. Write to the address below for more information or call 1-800-585-6781.

Morehead State University
Office of Admissions
Morehead State University
Morehead, KY 40351

4010
Transfer Student Awards

AMOUNT: $750-$2000 DEADLINE: March 15
FIELDS/MAJORS: All Areas of Study

Open to Kentucky residents transferring from any accredited college or university. Must have completed 12 hours of work with a minimum GPA of 3.0. May be renewed if recipients maintain the 3.0 GPA. Contact the address below for further information or call 1-800-585-6781.

Morehead State University
Office of Admissions
306 Howell-McDowell
Morehead, KY 40351

MOUNT IDA COLLEGE

4011

Mount Ida College-Edith Folsom Hall Scholarship

AMOUNT: $500   DEADLINE: March 1
FIELDS/MAJORS: All Areas of Study

Applicants must be recent female high school graduates who have been accepted by Mount Ida College. Several scholarships available. Write to the address below for details, and be sure to include a SASE.

General Federation of Women's Clubs of Massachusetts
777 Dedham St.
Newton Centre, MA 02159

MOUNT MERCY COLLEGE

4012

Art Scholarships

AMOUNT: $500-$2500   DEADLINE: February 1
FIELDS/MAJORS: Art

Open to high school seniors admitted to Mount Mercy who show talent and potential in visual arts. Recipients must enroll in at least two art courses each year and maintain a minimum GPA of 2.3. A portfolio of ten completed works or slides and a recommendation are required. Write to the address below for details or call (319) 368-6460.

Mount Mercy College
Office of Admission
1330 Elmhurst Dr., NE
Cedar Rapids, IA 52402

4013

Distinguished Honor Scholarships

AMOUNT: Maximum: $5500   DEADLINE: February 1
FIELDS/MAJORS: All Areas of Study

Open to high school seniors admitted to Mount Mercy who have a minimum GPA of 3.2 and have scored at least 23 on the ACT. Participation in school and community activities is also considered. Write to the address below for details or call (319) 368-6460.

Mount Mercy College
Office of Admission
1330 Elmhurst Dr., NE
Cedar Rapids, IA 52402

4014

Holland Presidential Scholar Award

AMOUNT: None Specified   DEADLINE: December 31
FIELDS/MAJORS: All Areas of Study

Open to high school seniors admitted at Mount Mercy with a minimum GPA of 3.5 and an ACT score of at least 26. Awards offer up to full tuition value per year. Participation in school and community activities is also considered. Contact the address below for further information or call (319) 368-6460.

Mount Mercy College
Office of Admissions
1330 Elmhurst Dr., NE
Cedar Rapids, IA 52402

4015

Honor Scholarships

AMOUNT: Maximum: $4000   DEADLINE: February 1
FIELDS/MAJORS: All Areas of Study

Open to high school seniors admitted to Mount Mercy who have a minimum GPA of 3.0 and have scored at least 20 on the ACT. Participation in school and community activities is also considered. Write to the address below for details.

Mount Mercy College
Office of Admission
1330 Elmhurst Dr., NE
Cedar Rapids, IA 52402

4016

Music, Drama Scholarships

AMOUNT: $1000-$2500   DEADLINE: February 1
FIELDS/MAJORS: Music, Drama

Open to high school seniors admitted to Mount Mercy who show talent and potential in music and drama. Applicants need not be majoring in these areas but must participate in ensembles, campus productions, related activities, and be active members of the drama club. All recipients must maintain a minimum GPA of 2.3 for award renewal. Write to the address below for details or call (319) 368-6460.

Mount Mercy College
Office of Admission
1330 Elmhurst Dr., NE
Cedar Rapids, IA 52402

4017
Presidential Scholarships

AMOUNT: Maximum: $7000 DEADLINE: February 1
FIELDS/MAJORS: All Areas of Study

Open to high school seniors admitted at Mount Mercy who have a minimum GPA of 3.5 and have scored at least 26 on the ACT. Participation in school and community activities is also considered. Write to the address below for details or call (319) 368-6460.

Mount Mercy College
Office of Admission
1330 Elmhurst Dr., NE
Cedar Rapids, IA 52402

4018
Social Work Scholarships

AMOUNT: $200-$2500
DEADLINE: February 1
FIELDS/MAJORS: Social Work

Open to full- or part-time students intending to complete a major in social work. Based on academics, demonstrated interest in issues relevant to social work, and involvement in human social services. Must have a minimum GPA of 2.5. Priority given to underrepresented groups in the department: ethnic minorities, students with disabilities, males, and students from regions of the country other than the Midwest. Write to the address below for details or call (319) 368-6460.

Mount Mercy College
Office of Admission
1330 Elmhurst Dr., NE
Cedar Rapids, IA 52402

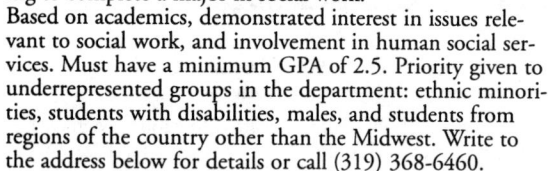

4019
Trustee's Leadership Grants

AMOUNT: Maximum: $1500 DEADLINE: February 1
FIELDS/MAJORS: All Areas of Study

Open to high school seniors and transfer students admitted to Mount Mercy. Recipients are expected to participate in the Emerging Leader's Program and become actively involved in the leadership of the campus. Participation in community service projects, attending seminars, and periodic meetings with the program coordinator are also required. Must maintain a minimum GPA of 2.3. Recipients are reviewed annually for consideration of renewal by the selection committee. Write to the address below for details or call (319) 368-6460.

Mount Mercy College
Office of Admission
1330 Elmhurst Dr., NE
Cedar Rapids, IA 52402

MT. HOLYOKE COLLEGE

4020
Hagop Bogigian Scholarship Fund

AMOUNT: None Specified DEADLINE: March 1
FIELDS/MAJORS: Arts

Scholarships for students of Armenian descent who are enrolled in a four-year bachelor of arts degree program at Mt. Holyoke college. Must have a GPA of at least 3.0. Write to the address below for more information.

Mt. Holyoke College
Financial Aid Office
South Hadley, MA 01075

MURRAY STATE UNIVERSITY

4021
Adults Back To College/Rosa Gasser Scholarship

AMOUNT: None Specified DEADLINE: February 15
FIELDS/MAJORS: All Areas of Study

Scholarships are awarded to a student who is enrolled or planning to enroll either part-time or full-time at MSU, who is twenty-three years of age or older, and who has experienced an interruption in formal education. Write to the address below for more information.

Murray State University
Office of University Scholarships
Ordway Hall, PO Box 9
Murray, KY 42071

4022
Alfred Wolfson Memorial Scholarship

AMOUNT: None Specified DEADLINE: February 15
FIELDS/MAJORS: Biology

Scholarships are awarded to an upperclassman in the field of biology. Write to the address below for more information.

Murray State University
Office of University Scholarships
Ordway Hall, PO Box 9
Murray, KY 42071

4023
Ann Willis Dougherty Memorial Scholarship

AMOUNT: None Specified DEADLINE: February 15
FIELDS/MAJORS: Music, Music Education

Scholarships are awarded to residents of Muhlenberg County, Kentucky, who are enrolled full-time at MSU in the field of music or music education with a GPA of 2.75 or above. Write to the address below for more information.

Murray State University
Office of University Scholarships
Ordway Hall, PO Box 9
Murray, KY 42071

4024
Big Rivers Rural Electric Cooperative Corporation Scholarship

AMOUNT: None Specified DEADLINE: February 15
FIELDS/MAJORS: All Areas of Study

Scholarships are awarded to a resident of one the counties served by Big River Electric Corporation, which includes: Ballard, Breckinridge, Caldwell, Carlisle, Crittenden, Daviess, Graves, Grayson, Hancock, Hardin, Henderson, Hopkins, Livingston, Lyon, McCracken, McLean, Marshall, Meade, Muhlenberg, Ohio, Union, and Webster. Must have a GPA of 3.0 or better. Write to the address below for more information.

Murray State University
Office of University Scholarships
Ordway Hall, PO Box 9
Murray, KY 42071

4025
Celebrate Women Scholarship

AMOUNT: None Specified DEADLINE: February 15
FIELDS/MAJORS: All Areas of Study

Scholarships are awarded to women who are nontraditional, full-time sophomore, junior, senior, or graduate students with a GPA of 3.0 or better. Write to the address below for more information.

Murray State University
Office of University Scholarships
Ordway Hall, PO Box 9
Murray, KY 42071

4026
Dan W. Miller Memorial Scholarship

AMOUNT: None Specified DEADLINE: February 15
FIELDS/MAJORS: All Areas of Study

This scholarship is open to students who have completed their freshman year. Financial need is a major consideration. Write to the address below for more information.

Murray State University
Office of University Scholarships
Ordway Hall, PO Box 9
Murray, KY 42071

4027
Deanna Hughes Parker Memorial Scholarship

AMOUNT: None Specified DEADLINE: February 15
FIELDS/MAJORS: All Areas of Study

Scholarships are awarded to a Murray State University student who is a member of Sigma Sigma Sigma sorority with a GPA of 2.5 or better. Write to the address below for more information.

Murray State University
Office of University Scholarships
Ordway Hall, PO Box 9
Murray, KY 42071

4028
Dianne B. O'Brien Dance Scholarship

AMOUNT: None Specified DEADLINE: February 15
FIELDS/MAJORS: Dance, Physical Education

Scholarships are awarded to applicants with minors or majors in dance or physical education. First consideration will be given to incoming freshmen and returning nontraditional students. Write to the address below for more information.

Murray State University
Office of University Scholarships
Ordway Hall, PO Box 9
Murray, KY 42071

4029
Donna Herndon Student Alumni Association Scholarship

AMOUNT: None Specified DEADLINE: February 15
FIELDS/MAJORS: All Areas of Study

Scholarships are awarded to upperclassmen with no restriction as to area of study or residence. Preference is given to SAA members. Write to the address below for more information.

Murray State University
Office of University Scholarships
Ordway Hall, PO Box 9
Murray, KY 42071

4030
Eleanor McGregor Scholarship

AMOUNT: None Specified DEADLINE: February 15
FIELDS/MAJORS: All Areas of Study

Scholarships are awarded to deserving students who demonstrate financial need and are employed part-time or full-time while attending college. Verification of employment is required. Write to the address below for more information.

Murray State University
Office of University Scholarships
Ordway Hall, PO Box 9
Murray, KY 42071

4031
Elisabeth Maxwell Memorial Scholarship

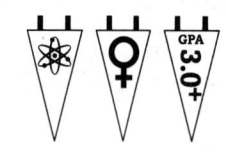

AMOUNT: None Specified DEADLINE: February 15
FIELDS/MAJORS: All Areas of Study

Scholarships are awarded to a female classified as a single parent, head of household, who is entering her junior of senior or who is entering graduate school with a GPA of 3.0 or better. Preference will be given to students pursuing a course of study leading to a career in veterinary science or who have a major in the department of biological sciences. Write to the address below for more information.

Murray State University
Office of University Scholarships
Ordway Hall, PO Box 9
Murray, KY 42071

4032
Elsie P. Alexander Scholarship

AMOUNT: $1000 DEADLINE: February 15
FIELDS/MAJORS: All Areas of Study

Scholarships are awarded to residents of Henry County, Tennessee. Recipient must have graduated in the upper 15% of his or her high school class. Must maintain a GPA of 3.0 or better. Write to the address below for more information.

Murray State University
Office of University Scholarships
Ordway Hall, PO Box 9
Murray, KY 42071

4033
Emma Buckley Scholarship

AMOUNT: None Specified DEADLINE: February 15
FIELDS/MAJORS: All Areas of Study

Scholarships are awarded to needy and deserving students from Woodford and Fayette counties in Kentucky. Write to the address below for more information.

Murray State University
Office of University Scholarships
Ordway Hall, PO Box 9
Murray, KY 42071

4034
Endowed Scholarships in Chemistry

AMOUNT: None Specified DEADLINE: February 15
FIELDS/MAJORS: Chemistry

These scholarships are offered to graduating high school seniors who plan to major in chemistry at Murray State University. Students must demonstrate financial need. Includes the Walter E. Blackburn Scholarship, the Chemistry Alumni Scholarships, and the Pete Panzera Memorial Scholarship. Write to the address below for details.

Murray State University
Office of University Scholarships
Ordway Hall, 1 Murray St.
Murray, KY 42071

4035
Grover Parker/ Murray Lions Club Scholarship

AMOUNT: None Specified DEADLINE: February 15
FIELDS/MAJORS: All Areas of Study

Scholarships are awarded to graduates of Calloway County High School or Murray High School located in Murray, Kentucky, with a GPA of 3.0 or higher. Preferences will be given to current or former members of Future Farmers of America or Future Homemakers of America. Write to the address below for more information.

Murray State University
Office of University Scholarships
Ordway Hall, PO Box 9
Murray, KY 42071

4036
J.B. Wilson Pre-Pharmacy Scholarship

AMOUNT: None Specified   DEADLINE: February 15
FIELDS/MAJORS: Pre-Pharmacy

Scholarships are awarded to a student who has successfully completed the freshman year of study and is enrolled in the pre-pharmacy program. Write to the address below for more information.

Murray State University
Office of University Scholarships
Ordway Hall, PO Box 9
Murray, KY 42071

4037
Joe Dyer Scholarship

AMOUNT: None Specified   DEADLINE: February 15
FIELDS/MAJORS: All Areas of Study

Scholarships are awarded for incoming freshmen or upperclassmen who have a minimum 3.0 GPA. Write to the address below for more information.

Murray State University
Office of University Scholarships
Ordway Hall, PO Box 9
Murray, KY 42071

4038
Kerby and Dorothy Jennings Journalism Scholarship

AMOUNT: None Specified   DEADLINE: February 15
FIELDS/MAJORS: Print Journalism

Scholarships are awarded to a student who is classified as nontraditional and pursuing a degree in print journalism. First priority will be given to Calloway County residents. Write to the address below for more information.

Murray State University
Office of University Scholarships
Ordway Hall, PO Box 9
Murray, KY 42071

4039
Marcus Nickell Education Scholarship

AMOUNT: None Specified   DEADLINE: February 15
FIELDS/MAJORS: Education

Scholarships are awarded to full-time juniors or seniors who are pursuing a degree in the college of education with a GPA of 2.75 or better. Write to the address below for more information.

Murray State University
Office of University Scholarships
Ordway Hall, PO Box 9
Murray, KY 42071

4040
Marian L. Cook Math and Physics Scholarship

AMOUNT: None Specified   DEADLINE: February 15
FIELDS/MAJORS: Mathematics, Physics, Engineering, Physics

Scholarships are awarded to full-time juniors, seniors or graduate students who are pursuing a degree in the field of physics, mathematics, or engineering physics with a GPA of 3.2 or above. Write to the address below for more information.

Murray State University
Office of University Scholarships
Ordway Hall, PO Box 9
Murray, KY 42071

4041
Murray Lions Club-Bryan Tolley Memorial Scholarship

AMOUNT: None Specified   DEADLINE: February 15
FIELDS/MAJORS: All Areas of Study

Scholarships are awarded to a graduate of Murray or Calloway county, Kentucky, high schools who is a sophomore, junior, or senior enrolled full-time at MSU with a GPA of 2.5 or better. Write to the address below for more information.

Murray State University
Office of University Scholarships
Ordway Hall, PO Box 9
Murray, KY 42071

4042
Roy and Dora Griffith Memorial Scholarship

AMOUNT: None Specified   DEADLINE: February 15
FIELDS/MAJORS: All Areas of Study

Scholarships are awarded to a student from Marshall County, Kentucky, who is deserving of financial assistance. Write to the address below for more information.

Murray State University
Office of University Scholarships
Ordway Hall, PO Box 9
Murray, KY 42071

MUSKINGUM COLLEGE

4043
Academic Scholarships

AMOUNT: $2000   DEADLINE: March 15
FIELDS/MAJORS: All Areas of Study

Merit awards based on academic achievement, test scores, and competitive testing. Need is not a factor. Includes the John Glenn Scholarship (full tuition), Presidential Scholarship ($5000-$9000), and the Faculty Scholarship ($2000-$4500). Contact the address below for further information. GPA must be at least 3.0.

Muskingum College
Office of Financial Aid
New Concord, OH 43762

4044
Alumni Grants

AMOUNT: Maximum: $1000   DEADLINE: March 15
FIELDS/MAJORS: All Areas of Study

Open to children and grandchildren of Muskingum College alumni. Eligibility documented by the College. Contact the address below for further information.

Muskingum College
Office of Financial Aid
New Concord, OH 43762

4045
Clergy Grants

AMOUNT: Maximum: $1000   DEADLINE: March 15
FIELDS/MAJORS: All Areas of Study

Open to children of ordained Presbyterian Church U.S.A. ministers engaged in full-time Church work. Contact the address below for further information.

Muskingum College
Office of Financial Aid
New Concord, OH 43762

4046
General Motors/ Equal Employment Opportunity Scholarships

AMOUNT: Maximum: $1000   DEADLINE: March 15
FIELDS/MAJORS: All Areas of Study

Open to minority and female students who have a parent employed by G.M. Contact the address below for further information.

Muskingum College
Office of Financial Aid
New Concord, OH 43762

4047
Muskingum Grants

AMOUNT: $500-$5000   DEADLINE: March 15
FIELDS/MAJORS: All Areas of Study

Need-based grants open to full-time students demonstrating financial need. Academic performance and abilities are also considered. Contact the address below for further information. GPA must be at least 2.7.

Muskingum College
Office of Financial Aid
New Concord, OH 43762

4048
National Presbyterian Scholarships

AMOUNT: $500-$1500   DEADLINE: March 15
FIELDS/MAJORS: All Areas of Study

Open to full-time students who are members of the Presbyterian Church U.S.A. Based on both academics and financial need. This application is available from the Church from December 1 through the deadline.

Muskingum College
Office of Financial Aid
New Concord, OH 43762

4049
Performance Scholarships

AMOUNT: $500-$2000   DEADLINE: March 15
FIELDS/MAJORS: Art, Music, Speech, Theater

Scholarships open to full-time students majoring in the areas listed above. Need is not a factor for these awards. Contact the address below for further information. GPA must be at least 2.7.

Muskingum College
Office of Financial Aid
New Concord, OH 43762

4050
Presbyterian Grants

AMOUNT: Maximum: $1000 DEADLINE: March 15
FIELDS/MAJORS: All Areas of Study

Awards open to full-time students who are communicant members of the Presbyterian Church U.S.A. Contact the address below for further information.

Muskingum College
Office of Financial Aid
New Concord, OH 43762

4051
Science Scholarships

AMOUNT: $1000-$1500 DEADLINE: March 10
FIELDS/MAJORS: Natural, Physical Science

Open to outstanding full-time students pursuing a degree in the above areas. Contact the address below for further information. GPA must be at least 2.9.

Muskingum College
Office of Financial Aid
New Concord, OH 43762

4052
Special Acknowledgment Awards

AMOUNT: $500-$1500 DEADLINE: March 15
FIELDS/MAJORS: All Areas of Study

Awards open to entering freshmen who will be full-time students and were not awarded academic scholarships but can meet the minimum GPA and ACT/SAT standards. Contact the address below for further information. GPA must be at least 2.0.

Muskingum College
Office of Financial Aid
New Concord, OH 43762

NATIONAL UNIVERSITY

4053
Collegiate Honor Award

AMOUNT: $1000 DEADLINE: None Specified
FIELDS/MAJORS: All Areas of Study

Grants for students at National University who have been graduated from an accredited community college or four-year college with a GPA of at least 3.5. Only the GPA from the highest degree earned can be used. Contact the financial aid office at the address below for details.

National University
Financial Aid Office
4025 Camino Del Rio South
San Diego, CA 92108

NAZARETH COLLEGE

4054
Presidential Scholars Program

AMOUNT: $12560 DEADLINE: March 15
FIELDS/MAJORS: All Areas of Study

Scholarships are available to Nazareth College for full-time undergraduate students who demonstrate outstanding academic performance. Must be a U.S. citizen. Write to the address below for details. GPA must be at least 3.1.

Nazareth College
Office of Financial Aid
4245 East Ave.
Rochester, NY 14618

NEW ENGLAND INSTITUTE OF TECHNOLOGY

4055
New England Institute of Technology Americorps Program

AMOUNT: Maximum: $4725 DEADLINE: None Specified
FIELDS/MAJORS: All Areas of Study

Program for full-time undergraduate students with financial need. Must be a U.S. citizen and a resident of Rhode Island. Non-matriculated students are not eligible. Living expenses are also provided for recipients. One to four awards offered annually. Write to the address below for more information.

New England Institute of Technology
Larry Blair, Director of Financial Aid
2500 Post Road
Warwick, RI 02886

NEW MEXICO HIGHLANDS UNIVERSITY

4056
Boatman's Sunwest Academic Scholarships

AMOUNT: Maximum: $1500   DEADLINE: March 1
FIELDS/MAJORS: All Areas of Study

Open to current, accepted, or enrolled students. Must have a minimum GPA of 3.0 to apply and be residents of New Mexico. Contact the address below for further information.

New Mexico Highlands University
Financial Aid Office
201 Felix Martinez Student Svcs. Bldg.
Las Vegas, NM 87791

4057
First State Bank of Taos Academic Scholarship

AMOUNT: None Specified   DEADLINE: March 1
FIELDS/MAJORS: Accounting, Finance, Information Sciences

Open to undergraduates in any of the fields listed above. Must be a resident of Taos County and a full-time student. Award is equal to resident full-time tuition and fees. Contact the address below for further information. Must have a GPA of at least 2.7.

New Mexico Highlands University
Financial Aid Office
201 Felix Martinez Student Svcs. Bldg.
Las Vegas, NM 87791

4058
General Motors Endowed Scholarships

AMOUNT: Maximum: $1000   DEADLINE: March 1
FIELDS/MAJORS: All Areas of Study

Open to undergraduates who are U.S. citizens with a minimum GPA of 3.0. Preference given to women or minorities who are General Motors employees or dependents. Contact the address below for further information.

New Mexico Highlands University
Financial Aid Office
201 Felix Martinez Student Svcs. Bldg.
Las Vegas, NM 87791

4059
GFWC Las Vegas Woman's Club Memorial Scholarship

AMOUNT: Maximum: $1000   DEADLINE: March 1
FIELDS/MAJORS: All Areas of Study

Open to female, nontraditional students from San Miguel or Mora counties. Must have a minimum GPA of 3.0 and be enrolled for 14 or more credit hours. Financial need is a significant factor in selection of recipients. Contact the address below for further information.

New Mexico Highlands University
Financial Aid Office
201 Felix Martinez Student Svcs. Bldg.
Las Vegas, NM 87791

4060
Glenn D. and Billy Parker Daves Endowed Scholarship

AMOUNT: None Specified   DEADLINE: March 1
FIELDS/MAJORS: All Areas of Study

Available to New Mexico residents from any of the following counties: Union, Harding, Roosevelt, Guadalupe, or Otero. Must have a minimum GPA of 3.0 and carry 14 or more credit hours each semester. Contact the address below for further information.

New Mexico Highlands University
Financial Aid Office
201 Felix Martinez Student Svcs. Bldg.
Las Vegas, NM 87791

4061
Legislative Endowment Scholarship

AMOUNT: Maximum: $1000   DEADLINE: March 1
FIELDS/MAJORS: All Areas of Study

Open to returning students or students transferring from a new Mexico two-year institution. Students must be New Mexico residents who can demonstrate financial need. May be renewed. Contact the address below for further information.

New Mexico Highlands University
Financial Aid Office
201 Felix Martinez Student Svcs. Bldg.
Las Vegas, NM 87791

4062
Legislative Gold Scholarships

AMOUNT: None Specified **DEADLINE:** March 1
FIELDS/MAJORS: All Areas of Study

Open to high school seniors who are New Mexico residents with a minimum GPA of 3.75 and an ACT composite score of 25. Renewable for four years by enrolling for 14 credit hours per semester and maintaining a 3.25 the freshman year and 3.5 per semester thereafter. Awards consist of full tuition and fees, $600 towards on-campus housing, and $400 per year book allowance. Contact the address below for further information.

New Mexico Highlands University
Financial Aid Office
201 Felix Martinez Student Svcs. Blvd.
Las Vegas, NM 87791

4063
Legislative Purple and White Scholarships

AMOUNT: None Specified **DEADLINE:** March 1
FIELDS/MAJORS: All Areas of Study

Open to high school seniors who are New Mexico residents with a minimum GPA of 3.25 and an ACT score of at least 22. Renewable by enrolling for 14 or more credit hours per semester and maintaining a 3.0 GPA thereafter. Awards consist of full tuition and fees. Contact the address below for further information.

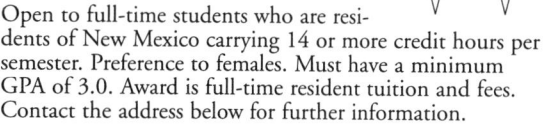

New Mexico Highlands University
Financial Aid Office
201 Felix Martinez Student Svcs. Bldg.
Las Vegas, NM 87791

4064
Legislative Silver Scholarships

AMOUNT: None Specified **DEADLINE:** March 1
FIELDS/MAJORS: All Areas of Study

Open to high school seniors who are New Mexico residents with a minimum GPA of 3.5 and a minimum ACT composite score of 22. Renewable by enrolling for 14 or more credit hours each semester and maintaining a 3.25 GPA for freshman year and 3.5 each semester thereafter. Awards consist of full tuition and fees, $600 towards on-campus housing, and $350 per year book allowance. Contact the address below for further information.

New Mexico Highlands University
Financial Aid Office
201 Felix Martinez Student Svcs. Bldg.
Las Vegas, NM 87791

4065
Leveo V. Sanchez Family Endowed Scholarship

AMOUNT: Maximum: $900 **DEADLINE:** March 1
FIELDS/MAJORS: All Areas of Study

Open to students who are Native American New Mexico residents, preferably from rural communities or pueblos, who enter as freshmen. Must have a minimum high school GPA of 2.5. Renewable if recipient maintains a 2.85 GPA and enrolls for 14 or more credit hours per semester. Contact the address below for further information.

New Mexico Highlands University
Financial Aid Office
201 Felix Martinez Student Svcs. Bldg.
Las Vegas, NM 87791

4066
Luther Sizemore Scholarship

AMOUNT: None Specified **DEADLINE:** March 1
FIELDS/MAJORS: All Areas of Study

Open to undergraduates who are New Mexico residents. Renewable for eight semesters as long as recipient completes 14 or more credit hours and maintains a 2.5 GPA. This award consists of full-time tuition and fees. Contact the address below for further information.

New Mexico Highlands University
Financial Aid Office
201 Felix Martinez Student Svcs. Bldg.
Las Vegas, NM 87791

4067
Marsha Hannah Endowed Scholarship

AMOUNT: None Specified
DEADLINE: March 1
FIELDS/MAJORS: Mathematics, Computer Science

Open to full-time students who are residents of New Mexico carrying 14 or more credit hours per semester. Preference to females. Must have a minimum GPA of 3.0. Award is full-time resident tuition and fees. Contact the address below for further information.

New Mexico Highlands University
Financial Aid Office
201 Felix Martinez Student Svcs. Bldg.
Las Vegas, NM 87791

4068
McDonald's Family Restaurant Scholarship

AMOUNT: None Specified   DEADLINE: March 1
FIELDS/MAJORS: All Areas of Study

Open to undergraduate students who are residents of San Miguel County. Must be enrolled for 14 or more credit hours and maintain a 3.0 GPA per semester. Award is full-time tuition and fees. Contact the address below for further information.

New Mexico Highlands University
Financial Aid Office
201 Felix Martinez Student Svcs. Bldg.
Las Vegas, NM 87791

4069
New Mexico Scholars Scholarships

AMOUNT: None Specified   DEADLINE: March 1
FIELDS/MAJORS: All Areas of Study

Open to high school seniors who are New Mexico residents and have an ACT composite score of at least 25 and be in the top 5% of class. Parents may have no more than a combined family income of $30,000 a year for one student in college or $40,000 a year for more than one student in college. Renewable based on enrolling in 12 or more credit hours per semester with a minimum GPA of 3.0. Contact the address below for further information.

New Mexico Highlands University
Financial Aid Office
201 Felix Martinez Student Svcs. Bldg.
Las Vegas, NM 87791

4070
NMHU Student Senate Scholarship

AMOUNT: None Specified   DEADLINE: March 1
FIELDS/MAJORS: All Areas of Study

Open to full-time undergraduates who are New Mexico residents. Must be enrolled for 14 or more credit hours and maintain a 3.0 GPA. Scholarship is for full-time tuition and fees. Contact the address below for further information.

New Mexico Highlands University
Financial Aid Office
201 Felix Martinez Student Svcs. Bldg.
Las Vegas, NM 87791

4071
Phelps Dodge Mining Company Scholarships

AMOUNT: None Specified   DEADLINE: March 1
FIELDS/MAJORS: Natural Science, Mathematics

Open to full-time students who are New Mexico residents. Must have a minimum GPA of 3.0. Awards equal full-time tuition and fees. Renewable upon reapplication. Contact the address below for further information.

New Mexico Highlands University
Financial Aid Office
201 Felix Martinez Student Svcs. Bldg.
Las Vegas, NM 87791

NEW MEXICO INSTITUTE OF MINING AND TECHNOLOGY

4072
Presidential Scholarships

AMOUNT: $1350   DEADLINE: March 1
FIELDS/MAJORS: All Areas of Study

Awards open to high school seniors with a minimum GPA of 3.0 and an ACT of 27 or better or SAT of 1110 or better. Contact the address below for further information.

New Mexico Institute of Mining and Technology
Financial Aid Office
Campus Station
Socorro, NM 87801

NEW MEXICO STATE UNIVERSITY

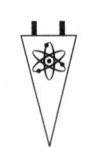

4073
Adrian Berryhill Family Agricultural Scholarship

AMOUNT: Maximum: $1000   DEADLINE: March 1
FIELDS/MAJORS: Animal Science and Range Science

Open to NMSU upperclassmen, one in animal science and one in range science. Must be New Mexico residents (preferably from New Mexico ranching families). Write to the address below for details.

New Mexico State University
College of Agriculture and Home Economics
Box 30001, Box 3AG
Las Cruces, NM 88003

4074
Artesia Data Systems, Inc. Scholarships

AMOUNT: None Specified   DEADLINE: March 1
FIELDS/MAJORS: Business Computer Systems, Accounting

Open to NMSU accounting and business computer systems majors. Based on academics and financial need. Awards are tuition. Information and applications available from January 2 through March 1 in the Advising Center of the College. Must have a GPA of at least 2.7.

New Mexico State University
College of Business Admin. and Economics
Box 30001 Dept. 3AD
Las Cruces, NM 88003-8001

4075
ASWA Scholarship

AMOUNT: None Specified   DEADLINE: March 1
FIELDS/MAJORS: Accounting

Open to NMSU juniors and seniors who have a minimum GPA of 3.0. Preference given to women. Information and applications available January 2 through March 1 in the Advising Center of the College.

New Mexico State University
College of Business Admin. and Economics
Box 30001 Dept. 3AD
Las Cruces, NM 88003-8001

4076
AT&T Computer Science Scholarship

AMOUNT: None Specified   DEADLINE: March 1
FIELDS/MAJORS: Computer Science

Open to sophomores, juniors, seniors, and first-year graduate students who are of Hispanic descent. Must have a minimum GPA of 3.0. Contact the address below for further information.

New Mexico State University
College of Arts and Sciences
Box 30001 Dept. 3335
Las Cruces, NM 88003-8001

4077
AT&T Engineering Scholarship

AMOUNT: Maximum: $500   DEADLINE: March 1
FIELDS/MAJORS: Engineering Technology, Electrical Engineering

Open to minority students who have completed sophomore year with a minimum GPA of 3.0. Contact the address below for further information.

New Mexico State University
College of Engineering
Box 30001 Dept. 3449
Las Cruces, NM 88003-8001

4078
Baxter Black Scholarship

AMOUNT: Maximum: $1000   DEADLINE: March 1
FIELDS/MAJORS: Animal Agriculture

Open to NMSU students interested in animal agriculture, other than pre-vet. Each recipient must be preparing for a career in the livestock industry and must have demonstrated financial need. Write to the address below for more information.

New Mexico State University
College of Agriculture and Home Economics
Box 30001, Box 3AG
Las Cruces, NM 88003-8003

4079
Boeing Scholarship

AMOUNT: None Specified   DEADLINE: March 1
FIELDS/MAJORS: Electrical, Mechanical Engineering

Open to NMSU sophomore, junior, and senior minorities who are U.S. citizens and have a minimum GPA of 3.0. Contact the address listed for further information.

New Mexico State University
College of Engineering
Box 30001, Dept. 3449
Las Cruces, NM 88003-8001

4080
Bonnie Lowenstein Memorial Scholarship

AMOUNT: None Specified   DEADLINE: March 1
FIELDS/MAJORS: Horticulture, Floriculture, Landscape Design, Agronomy, Plant Pathology, Land Management

Open to juniors, seniors, and graduate students majoring in the areas listed above at NMSU. Must have a minimum GPA of 3.0. May be renewable if preset standards are met. Financial need is a consideration but not a deciding factor. Contact the address listed for further information.

New Mexico State University
College of Agriculture and Home Economics
Box 30001 Box 3AG
Las Cruces, NM 88003-8001

4081
C.H. Stith Memorial Scholarship

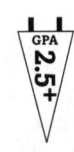

AMOUNT: Maximum: $500 DEADLINE: March 1
FIELDS/MAJORS: All Areas of Study

Open to NMSU undergraduate students with financial need. Recipients must be full-time students with at least a 2.5 GPA to be eligible to receive the full scholarship. Write to the address below for more information.

New Mexico State University
Office of Student Financial Aid
Box 30001 Dept. 5100
Las Cruces, NM 88003

4082
Caroline S. Leland Memorial Piano Scholarship

AMOUNT: $1000 DEADLINE: March 1
FIELDS/MAJORS: Piano

$1000 per year to an incoming freshman who will major in piano or piano pedagogy. Live audition necessary. Apply to Keyboard Coordinator, Department of Music, by March 1. Write to the address below for details.

New Mexico State University
College of Arts and Sciences
Box 30001 Dept. 3335
Las Cruces, NM 88003

4083
Charles E. Stillwell Scholarship

AMOUNT: Maximum: $1000 DEADLINE: March 1
FIELDS/MAJORS: Arts, Sciences

Open to NMSU sophomores with a minimum GPA of 2.75. May reapply as a junior or senior if recipient reaches a minimum GPA of 3.0. Contact the address below for further information.

New Mexico State University
College of Arts and Sciences
Box 30001 Dept. 3335
Las Cruces, NM 88003-8001

4084
Citizens Bank/Robert L. Triviz Memorial Scholarship

AMOUNT: None Specified DEADLINE: March 1
FIELDS/MAJORS: Business Administration

Open to NMSU sophomores, juniors, and seniors who are U.S. citizens and have a minimum GPA of 2.5. Must participate in university or community activities and/or be married holding a part-time job. Contact the address listed for further information.

New Mexico State University
College of Business Admin. and Economics
Box 30001 Dept. 3335
Las Cruces, NM 88003-8001

4085
Claude C. Dove and Essie Dove Scholarship

AMOUNT: Maximum: $500 DEADLINE: March 1
FIELDS/MAJORS: Early Childhood Education

Scholarship shall be granted to a NMSU student with a teaching field emphasis in the area of early childhood education. Based on financial need. Write to the address below for more information.

New Mexico State University
College of Education
PO Box 30001 Dept. 3AC
Las Cruces, NM 88003

4086
Claude Warner Memorial Scholarship

AMOUNT: None Specified DEADLINE: March 1
FIELDS/MAJORS: Agriculture

Open to NSMU juniors and seniors who can demonstrate financial need. Must be residents of New Mexico. Preference given to residents of Otero County. Contact the address listed for further information.

New Mexico State University
College of Agriculture and Home Economics
Box 30001 Box 3AG
Las Cruces, NM 88003-8001

4087
Dona Ana County Medical Society Scholarship

AMOUNT: Maximum: $500 DEADLINE: March 1
FIELDS/MAJORS: Nursing

Open to a NMSU student majoring in nursing who has financial need. Write to the address below for more information.

New Mexico State University
College of Human and Community Services
Suite C, Box 30001 Dept. 3446
Las Cruces, NM 88003

4088
Dona Ana Savings Bank FSB Scholarship

AMOUNT: Maximum: $2500   DEADLINE: March 1
FIELDS/MAJORS: Business

Open to sophomores, juniors, and seniors who are residents of Dona Ana County (for at least one year) and have a declared major in the business college. Renewable if recipients maintain a minimum GPA of 3.0. Financial need will be considered. Contact the address below for further information.

New Mexico State University
College of Business Admin. and Economics
Box 30001 Dept. 3AD
Las Cruces, NM 88003-8001

4089
Edgar M. Kugler/ Phi Delta Kappa Scholarship

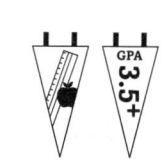

AMOUNT: Maximum: $500   DEADLINE: March 1
FIELDS/MAJORS: Education

Awarded to a NMSU junior or senior in education who has a minimum cumulative GPA of 3.5 and a GPA of 3.75 in professional education. Write to the address below for more information.

New Mexico State University
College of Education
PO Box 30001 Dept. 3AC
Las Cruces, NM 88003

4090
El Paso Natural Gas Company

AMOUNT: $1000   DEADLINE: March 1
FIELDS/MAJORS: Computer Science

$1000 per year awarded to an individual who wishes to study toward a baccalaureate degree in computer science. Award based on scholastic ability and academic potential. Write to the address below for details.

New Mexico State University
College of Arts and Sciences
Box 30001 Dept 3335
Las Cruces, NM 88003

4091
El Paso Natural Gas Co. and IFT Scholarships

AMOUNT: Maximum: $2000   DEADLINE: March 1
FIELDS/MAJORS: Computer Science

Open to NMSU sophomores, juniors, and seniors with a minimum GPA of 3.2. Based on academics, ability, and potential. One sponsor also considers financial need. Contact the address listed for further information about both awards.

New Mexico State University
College of Arts and Sciences
Box 30001 Dept. 3335
Las Cruces, NM 88003-8001

4092
El Paso Natural Gas MBA Fellowship

AMOUNT: None Specified   DEADLINE: March 1
FIELDS/MAJORS: Business

Open to minority students pursuing an MBA. Based on academics and financial need. Contact the address below for further information. Must have a GPA of at least 2.7.

New Mexico State University
College of Business Admin. and Economics
Box 30001 Dept. 3AD
Las Cruces, NM 88003-8001

4093
Elaine Potter Benfer Scholarship

AMOUNT: Maximum: $2400   DEADLINE: March 1
FIELDS/MAJORS: Nursing

Open to a NMSU nursing student or students. Student(s) must be willing to give some time as a Red Cross volunteer. Applications available in the Department of Nursing. Write to the address below for details.

New Mexico State University
College of Human and Community Services
Suite C, Box 30001 Dept. 3446
Las Cruces, NM 88003

4094
Emmett Nations Memorial Scholarship

AMOUNT: Maximum: $600   DEADLINE: March 1
FIELDS/MAJORS: All Areas of Study

Open to freshman or sophomore students enrolled in either the Army or Air Force ROTC at NMSU. Students must be in good academic standing and must be U.S. citizens. Award based on financial need, scholarship, and interest in military career. Write to the address below for more information.

New Mexico State University
Office of Student Financial Aid
Box 30001 Dept. 5100
Las Cruces, NM 88003

4095
Harry and Floyd Lee Memorial Scholarship

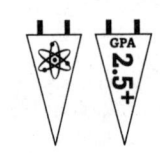

AMOUNT: None Specified DEADLINE: March 1
FIELDS/MAJORS: Animal Science

Open to NMSU juniors and seniors who have minimum GPAs of 2.5 and are U.S. citizens and New Mexico residents. Must have graduated from a New Mexico high school. Contact the address listed for further information.

New Mexico State University
College of Agriculture and Home Economics
Box 30001 Dept. 3AG
Las Cruces, NM 88003-8001

4096
International Telemetering Scholarship

AMOUNT: Maximum: $1700 DEADLINE: March 1
FIELDS/MAJORS: Electrical Engineering, Computer Engineering

Open to a NMSU sophomore, junior, or senior majoring in electrical and computer engineering. Must have no less than a 3.2 GPA. Write to the address below for more information.

New Mexico State University
College of Engineering
Complex I, Box 30001 Dept. 3446
Las Cruces, NM 88003

4097
Johanna Christine Allen Memorial Scholarship

AMOUNT: None Specified DEADLINE: March 1
FIELDS/MAJORS: Accounting

Open to NMSU female students based on academics and activity in university and community affairs. Information and applications available January 2 through March 1 in the Advising Center of the College. Must have a GPA of at least 2.7.

New Mexico State University
College of Business Admin. and Economics
Box 30001 Dept. 3AD
Las Cruces, NM 88003-8001

4098
Joseph J. Bartnik Memorial Scholarship

AMOUNT: None Specified DEADLINE: March 1
FIELDS/MAJORS: Business

Open to NMSU freshmen with a minimum GPA of 3.0. For use during sophomore year. Must not be eligible for other financial aid. Contact the address listed for further information.

New Mexico State University
College of Business Admin. and Economics
Box 30001 Dept. 3335
Las Cruces, NM 88003-8001

4099
Julie S. Papen and Frank Papen, Jr., Memorial Scholarship

AMOUNT: None Specified DEADLINE: March 1
FIELDS/MAJORS: All Areas of Study

Open to NMSU students with a 3.0 GPA or better. Student must have graduated from a high school in New Mexico and be a New Mexico resident. Write to the address listed for details.

New Mexico State University
Student Financial Aid Office
Box 30001 Dept. 5100
Las Cruces, NM 88003

4100
Kringle the Cat Scholarships

AMOUNT: Maximum: $500 DEADLINE: March 1
FIELDS/MAJORS: Animal/Range Science, Agribusiness, Agri-economics, Agricultural Education, Agronomy, Horticulture

Open to one student in each of the four following categories: animal and range science; agricultural economics and agribusiness; agricultural education and agronomy; and horticulture at NMSU. Recipients selected by department heads or committees appointed head. Contact the head of the departments for further information.

New Mexico State University
College of Agriculture and Home Economics
Box 30001 Dept. 3AG
Las Cruces, NM 88003-8001

4101
Linda E. Mitchell and Mr. and Mrs. T.E. Mitchell Memorial Scholarships

AMOUNT: None Specified DEADLINE: March 1
FIELDS/MAJORS: Animal Science

Open to NMSU sophomores, juniors, and seniors majoring in animal science. Preference will be given to New Mexico residents. Contact the address listed for further information about both awards.

New Mexico State University
College of Agriculture and Home Economics
Box 30001 Dept. 3AG
Las Cruces, NM 88003-8001

4102
Lionel D. Haight Scholarship

AMOUNT: None Specified DEADLINE: March 1
FIELDS/MAJORS: Accounting

Open to NMSU accounting majors who can demonstrate scholastic excellence in previous accounting courses and other university work. Award recipients and scholarship amounts are determined by the accounting faculty. Contact the address listed for further information. Must have a GPA of at least 2.7.

New Mexico State University
College of Business Admin. and Economics
Box 30001 Dept. 3AD
Las Cruces, NM 88003-8001

4103
Lloyd W. Lyster Memorial Scholarship

AMOUNT: None Specified DEADLINE: March 1
FIELDS/MAJORS: Civil Engineering

Awarded to an NMSU undergraduate civil engineering major who shows academic promise. Write to the address listed for more information.

New Mexico State University
College of Engineering
Complex I, Box 30001 Dept. 3446
Las Cruces, NM 88003

4104
MCI Scholarship

AMOUNT: Maximum: $5000 DEADLINE: March 1
FIELDS/MAJORS: Electrical Engineering, Computer Engineering

Open to a NMSU freshman or sophomore who is a U.S. citizen, an ethnic minority, or female, majoring in electrical/computer engineering and who is not receiving another corporate scholarship. Write to the address below for more information.

New Mexico State University
College of Engineering
Complex I, Box 30001 Dept. 3446
Las Cruces, NM 88003

4105
Memorial Medical Center Auxiliary Scholarship

AMOUNT: Maximum: $750 DEADLINE: November 15
FIELDS/MAJORS: Medical Fields

Five or six $750 scholarships given in both the fall and spring semesters each year to students in a medically-related curriculum at NMSU. Not open to freshmen. Selection based on GPA of 3.0 or better, with a minimum of 12 credits per semester. Preference given to Dona Ana County residents. Application forms available at the Information Desk, Memorial Medical Center, or write MMC Auxiliary, 2450 Telshor Blvd., Las Cruces, NM 88011.

New Mexico State University
College of Human and Community Services
Suite C, Box 30001 Dept. 3446
Las Cruces, NM 88003

4106
Mobile Oil Foundation and Robert Roberts Scholarships

AMOUNT: None Specified
DEADLINE: March 1
FIELDS/MAJORS: Business Computer Systems

Open to NMSU business computer systems majors. Both awards are based on high academics. Contact the address listed for further information about both awards. Must have a GPA of at least 2.7.

New Mexico State University
College of Business Admin. and Economics
Box 30001 Dept. 3AD
Las Cruces, NM 88003-8001

4107
Molzen and Corbin Associates Scholarship

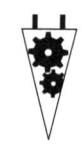

AMOUNT: Maximum: $1000 DEADLINE: March 1
FIELDS/MAJORS: Civil Engineering

Open to a NMSU civil engineering student classified as an upperclassman who is a U.S. citizen with above-average determination and perseverance. Write to the address below for more information.

New Mexico State University
College of Engineering
Complex I, Box 30001 Dept. 3449
Las Cruces, NM 88003

4108
Morgan Nelson Scholarship

AMOUNT: None Specified DEADLINE: March 1
FIELDS/MAJORS: Agronomy, Horticulture, Entomology, Plant Pathology, Human Nutrition, Food Science

Open to NMSU sophomores, juniors, and seniors who have a minimum GPA of 2.5. Contact the address listed for further information.

New Mexico State University
College of Agriculture and Home Economics
Box 30001 Box 3AG
Las Cruces, NM 88003-8001

4109
New Mexico Iris Society Scholarship

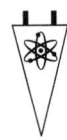

AMOUNT: Maximum: $600 DEADLINE: March 1
FIELDS/MAJORS: Botany, Biology

Open to students majoring in botany or biology. Contact the address below for further information.

New Mexico State University
College of Arts and Sciences
Box 30001 Dept. 3335
Las Cruces, NM 88003-8001

4110
New Mexico Space Grant Graduate Fellowship

AMOUNT: Maximum: $4000
DEADLINE: March 1
FIELDS/MAJORS: Astronomy, Biology, Chemistry, Physics, Computer and Earth Science, Math

Up to $4000 awarded to graduate students in the College of Engineering or in the College of Arts and Sciences majoring in astronomy, biology, chemistry, physics, computer science, earth science, or math at NMSU. Students must have a cumulative GPA of 3.0 and be U.S. citizens. Preference will be given to women and minorities. Applications available from Financial Aid or the Space Grant Office.

New Mexico State University
Student Financial Aid Office
Box 30001 Dept. 5100
Las Cruces, NM 88003

4111
New Mexico Space Grant Undergraduate Scholarship

AMOUNT: $2000
DEADLINE: March 1
FIELDS/MAJORS: Astronomy, Biology, Chemistry, Physics, Computer Science, or Math

Up to $2000 awarded to approximately five undergraduates in the College of Engineering or in the College of Arts and Sciences majoring in astronomy, biology, chemistry, physics, computer science, or math. Students must have a GPA of 3.0 and be U.S. citizens. Women and minority students are greatly preferred. Applications available from Financial Aid or the Space Grant Office or write to the address below for details.

New Mexico State University
Student Financial Aid Office
Box 30001 Dept. 5100
Las Cruces, NM 88003

4112
New Mexico State Police Association Scholarship

AMOUNT: Maximum: $1500 DEADLINE: July 15
FIELDS/MAJORS: All Areas of Study

Open to the dependent son or daughter of a member of the New Mexico State Police Association. Applicants must be between sixteen and twenty-three years old and plan on earning their degree within four years. Preference given to student with financial need, community leadership, 2.5 GPA or student who has received the scholarship in the past and has maintained his or her GPA. Write to the address below for more information.

New Mexico State University
Office of Student Financial Aid
Box 30001 Dept. 5100
Las Cruces, NM 88003

4113
Osuna Nursery Horticulture Scholarship

AMOUNT: None Specified DEADLINE: March 1
FIELDS/MAJORS: Horticulture

Open to NMSU students majoring in horticulture. Must have a minimum GPA of 3.5. Award is annual tuition. Contact the address listed for further information.

New Mexico State University
College of Agriculture and Home Economics
Box 30001 Box 3AG
Las Cruces, NM 88003-8001

4114
Paul W. Price Memorial and A.L. Salsman Memorial Scholarships

AMOUNT: None Specified   DEADLINE: March 1
FIELDS/MAJORS: Agriculture

Open to NMSU agriculture majors with a minimum GPA of 2.25. Contact the address listed for further information.

New Mexico State University
College of Agriculture and Home Economics
Box 30001 Box 3AG
Las Cruces, NM 88003-8001

4115
President's Associates and President's Associates Honors Scholarships

AMOUNT: $2500-$5196   DEADLINE: March 1
FIELDS/MAJORS: All Areas of Study

Scholarships for academically promising entering freshmen at New Mexico State University. Application and five hundred word essay required. Fifteen awards per year. Other, similar programs are available to entering freshmen. Contact the Financial Aid Office at the address below for more information. GPA must be at least 3.0.

New Mexico State University
Office of Student Financial Aid
Box 30001 Dept. 5100
Las Cruces, NM 88003

4116
Robert Lawson Little Memorial Scholarship

AMOUNT: None Specified   DEADLINE: March 1
FIELDS/MAJORS: Range Management

Open to NMSU undergraduates who have a minimum GPA of 2.0 and can demonstrate financial need. Contact the address listed for further information.

New Mexico State University
College of Agriculture and Home Economics
Box 30001 Box 3AG
Las Cruces, NM 88003-8001

4117
Rosina Patterson HTS Scholarship

AMOUNT: None Specified   DEADLINE: March 1
FIELDS/MAJORS: Hospitality, Tourism

Open to NMSU students majoring in either of the fields above. Number of awards and amounts vary from year to year. Contact the address listed for further information.

New Mexico State University
College of Agriculture and Home Economics
Box 30001 Box 3AG
Las Cruces, NM 88003-8001

4118
Sunwest Bank Scholarship

AMOUNT: None Specified   DEADLINE: March 1
FIELDS/MAJORS: Business

Open to NMSU students who are residents of New Mexico transferring from a New Mexico community or junior college with a minimum GPA of 2.5. Based on academics and financial need. Contact the address listed for further information.

New Mexico State University
College of Business Admin. and Economics
Box 30001 Dept. 3AD
Las Cruces, NM 88003-8001

4119
T-4 Cattle Company Scholarship

AMOUNT: Maximum: $500   DEADLINE: March 1
FIELDS/MAJORS: Animal Science

Open to NMSU upperclassmen with preference given to residents of Quay, San Miguel, and Guadalupe counties. Based on financial need, academics, and participation in university activities. Contact the address listed for further information.

New Mexico State University
College of Agriculture and Home Economics
Box 30001 Box 3AG
Las Cruces, NM 88003-8001

4120
Vivien B. Head Music Scholarships

AMOUNT: Maximum: $1300   DEADLINE: March 1
FIELDS/MAJORS: Music

Varying amounts not to exceed $1300 annually to full-time students pursuing degrees in music. The student must be a U.S. citizen, have a 3.0 or better GPA, have a need of financial assistance to obtain an education, and be of good moral character. An essay is required describing the student's career goals and support for the free enterprise system. Personal interview may also be requested. Renewable for a total of eight semesters. Write to the address below for more details.

New Mexico State University
College of Arts and Sciences
Box 30001 Dept. 3335
Las Cruces, NM 88003

NEW MEXICO STATE UNIVERSITY

4121
Wanda H. Bullock Nursing Scholarship

AMOUNT: Maximum: $500 DEADLINE: March 1
FIELDS/MAJORS: Nursing

Open to a NMSU nursing major. Applications are available in the Nursing Department. Write to the address below for more information.

New Mexico State University
College of Human and Community Services
Suite C, Box 30001 Dept. 3446
Las Cruces, NM 88003

4122
William S. May Scholarship

AMOUNT: Maximum: $1000 DEADLINE: March 1
FIELDS/MAJORS: Agricultural Economics, Agribusiness

Open to NMSU juniors and seniors majoring in either of fields above with an interest in agricultural finance. Contact the address listed for further information. Must have a GPA of at least 2.5.

New Mexico State University
College of Agriculture and Home Economics
Box 30001 Box 3AG
Las Cruces, NM 88003-8001

NEW MEXICO TECH

4123
Competitive Scholarship

AMOUNT: Maximum: $700 DEADLINE: March 1
FIELDS/MAJORS: All Areas of Study

Scholarships for NMT entering freshmen who have a high school GPA of at least 3.0, ACT scores of 27 or SAT scores of 1200. Preference to transfer students with a GPA of at least 3.25 and a past high school GPA of at least 3.0. For non-residents of New Mexico. Write to the address below or call 1-800-428-TECH for more information.

New Mexico Tech
Admission Office
801 Leroy Pl.
Socorro, NM 87801

4124
Counselor's Choice Scholarship

AMOUNT: Maximum: $1500 DEADLINE: March 1
FIELDS/MAJORS: All Areas of Study

Scholarships for NMT entering freshmen from New Mexico who are nominated by their high school counselor. Must have a GPA of at least 2.5 and an ACT score of 21 or an SAT score of 860 or better. For U.S. citizens enrolled in full-time study. Renewable. Write to the address below or call 1-800-428-TECH for more information.

New Mexico Tech
Admission Office
801 Leroy Pl.
Socorro, NM 87801

4125
Gold Merit Scholarship

AMOUNT: Maximum: $5000 DEADLINE: March 1
FIELDS/MAJORS: All Areas of Study

Scholarships for NMT entering freshmen who are National Merit finalists and have a high school GPA of 3.0. Must be U.S. citizens or permanent residents and carry at least 12 graded credit hours per semester. Write to the address below or call 1-800-428-TECH for more information.

New Mexico Tech
Admission Office
801 Leroy Pl.
Socorro, NM 87801

4126
Presidential Scholarship

AMOUNT: Maximum: $2700 DEADLINE: March 1
FIELDS/MAJORS: All Areas of Study

Scholarships for NMT entering freshmen who have a high school GPA of at least 3.0 and an ACT scores of 27 or SAT scores of 1200. Must be U.S. citizens and enrolled in full-time study. Renewable. Write to the address below or call 1-800-428-TECH for more information.

New Mexico Tech
Admission Office
801 Larry Pl.
Soccorro, NM 87801

4127
Regents' Scholarship

AMOUNT: $2000 DEADLINE: March 1
FIELDS/MAJORS: All Areas of Study

Scholarships for NMT entering freshmen and transfer students. Freshmen and transfers with less than 30 credits must have a GPA of at least 3.0 and ACT scores of 25 or an SAT score of 1130 or better. Transfers with over 30 credits must have a collegiate GPA of at least 3.0. Must be full-time students and U.S. citizens. Write to the address below or call 1-800-428-TECH for more information.

New Mexico Tech
Admission Office
801 Leroy Pl.
Soccorro, NM 87801

4128
Silver Scholar Scholarship

AMOUNT: Maximum: $4000 DEADLINE: March 1
FIELDS/MAJORS: All Areas of Study

Scholarships for NMT entering freshmen who have a high school GPA of at least 3.5, ACT scores of 30, or SAT scores of 1320. Must be U.S. citizens and enrolled in full-time study. Renewable. Write to the address below or call 1-800-428-TECH for more information.

New Mexico Tech
Admission Office
801 Leroy Pl.
Soccorro, NM 87801

NEW YORK INSTITUTE OF TECHNOLOGY

4129
Martin Luther King Scholarship

AMOUNT: $500 DEADLINE: None Specified
FIELDS/MAJORS: All Areas of Study

Scholarships for minority students at NYIT. Program is designed to increase campus representation of minority students. Based on need and academics. Twenty awards are given annually. Write to the address below for details.

New York Institute of Technology
Old Westbury Campus
Financial Aid Office
Old Westbury, NY 11568

NEW YORK UNIVERSITY

4130
The ASCAP Foundation Frederick Loewe Scholarship

AMOUNT: None Specified DEADLINE: None Specified
FIELDS/MAJORS: Musical Theater Composition

Awards to musical theater composition students at the Tisch School of Arts at New York University. Contact the office of financial aid at New York University for more details.

American Society of Composers, Authors, and Publishers
One Lincoln Plaza
New York, NY 10023

NORTH AMERICAN BAPTIST SEMINARY

4131
Canadian Student Award

AMOUNT: None Specified DEADLINE: July 15
FIELDS/MAJORS: All Areas of Study Offered at NABS

Available to full-time students at NABS. For Canadian students to help offset currency exchange rate losses. Based on September 1 exchange rate. Write to the address below for details.

North American Baptist Seminary
1321 W. 22nd St.
Sioux Falls, SD 57105

NORTH CAROLINA WESLEYAN COLLEGE

4132
Endowed Scholarships, United Methodist Scholarship Loan

AMOUNT: None Specified DEADLINE: June 11
FIELDS/MAJORS: All Areas of Study

Many scholarship programs are administered through the college. Criteria range from GPA to residency, major, or need. Ten to fifteen awards offered annually. Contact the address below for details.

North Carolina Wesleyan College
Director of Financial Aid
3400 N. Wesleyan Blvd.
Rocky Mount, NC 27804

NORTHERN ILLINOIS UNIVERSITY

4133
Academic Finalist Scholarship

[GPA 3.5+]

AMOUNT: $300 DEADLINE: March 1
FIELDS/MAJORS: All Areas of Study

Open to transfer students who have completed a minimum of 45 credit hours with a GPA of at least 3.5. Must be a resident of Illinois. Awards are for a two-year period subject to the recipient maintaining a 3.0 GPA. Awards are $300 per year and tuition waiver. Write to the address below for information.

Northern Illinois University
University Scholarship Committee
Honors House
Dekalb, IL 60115-2854

4134
Academic Finalists Scholarships

[GPA 2.5+]

AMOUNT: None Specified DEADLINE: None Specified
FIELDS/MAJORS: All Areas of Study

Scholarships open to incoming full-time freshmen with demonstrated high academics. These awards pay tuition plus $300 per semester. Renewable if recipients maintain acceptable progress toward their degrees. Contact the address below for further information. GPA must be at least 2.7.

Northern Illinois University
University Scholarship Committee
DeKalb, IL 60115

4135
Faculty Fund Academic Finalists Award

[GPA 2.5+]

AMOUNT: None Specified DEADLINE: None Specified
FIELDS/MAJORS: All Areas of Study

Awards open to incoming full-time freshmen with demonstrated high academics. Renewable if recipients maintain acceptable progress toward their degrees. Awards pay tuition plus $750 per semester. Contact the address below for further information. GPA must be at least 2.9.

Northern Illinois University
University Scholarship Committee
DeKalb, IL 60115

4136
University Scholar Award

[GPA 3.5+]

AMOUNT: None Specified DEADLINE: February 1
FIELDS/MAJORS: All Areas of Study

Open to Illinois residents who are full-time entering freshmen in the top 5% of their high school graduating class. Curricular, cocurricular, and extracurricular activities will be considered. Awards are for a four-year period subject to recipients' maintaining a minimum GPA of 3.3. Awards are for tuition, room, board, activities, and fees. Write to the address listed for further information. Must have a GPA of at least 3.7.

Northern Illinois University
University Scholarship Committee
Dekalb, IL 60115

4137
University Scholar Award for Community College Students

AMOUNT: None Specified DEADLINE: March 1
FIELDS/MAJORS: All Areas of Study

Available to full-time transfer students with at least 45 credit hours and a GPA of 3.5 or above. Award is for two years of paid tuition, books, fees, and room and board if student maintains a 3.3 GPA. Write to the address below for information.

Northern Illinois University
University Scholarship Committee
Honors House
Dekalb, IL 60115

NORTHERN KENTUCKY UNIVERSITY

4138
A. David Nichols Memorial Scholarship

AMOUNT: None Specified DEADLINE: February 1
FIELDS/MAJORS: Law

Open to upper-class law students who are attending Chase College of Law. Must demonstrate financial need and academic merit. Contact the Assistant Dean, Chase College of Law, for further information or call (606) 572-5143.

Northern Kentucky University
Chase College of Law
Office of Admissions
Highland Heights, KY 41099

4139
Albert and Louise Cooper Memorial Scholarship

AMOUNT: Maximum: $650 DEADLINE: February 1
FIELDS/MAJORS: Chemistry

Awards for juniors or seniors with a chemistry major. Must be enrolled for a minimum of 12 credit hours. Contact the Chemistry Department or call (606) 572-5143 for further information.

Northern Kentucky University
Office of Financial Aid-Nunn Dr.
Lucas Administrative Center, #416
Highland Heights, KY 41099

4140
Ambrose H. Lindhorst Scholarship

AMOUNT: Maximum: $2500 DEADLINE: February 1
FIELDS/MAJORS: Law

Open to law students, attending Chase College of Law, who demonstrates a high level of academic promise. Preference will be given to a part-time student who intends to practice in Cincinnati. Renewable for four academic years for part-time students and three academic years for full-time students. Contact the Assistant Dean, Chase College of Law, for further information or call (606) 572-5143.

Northern Kentucky University
Chase College of Law
Office of Admissions
Highland Heights, KY 41099

4141
Arnzen, Parry and Wentz, P.S.C. Scholarship

AMOUNT: Maximum: $1000 DEADLINE: February 1
FIELDS/MAJORS: Law

Open to law students, admitted to Chase College of Law, who are Kentucky residents. Contact the Assistant Dean, Chase College of Law, for further information or call (606) 572-5143.

Northern Kentucky University
Chase College of Law
Office of Admissions
Highland Heights, KY 41099

4142
Bernard J. Gilday, Sr. Scholarship

AMOUNT: Maximum: $1200 DEADLINE: February 1
FIELDS/MAJORS: Law

Open to law students, attending Chase College of Law, who demonstrate financial need and academic merit. Renewable for three academic years for full-time students and four academic years for part-time students. Contact the Assistant Dean, Chase College of Law, for further information or call (606) 572-5143.

Northern Kentucky University
Chase College of Law
Office of Admissions
Highland Heights, KY 41099

4143
Blanch Wiley Shafer Memorial Fund

AMOUNT: None Specified DEADLINE: February 1
FIELDS/MAJORS: Law

Open to law students, attending Chase College of Law, who demonstrate outstanding academic achievement and financial need. Contact the Assistant Dean, Chase College of Law, for further information or call (606) 572-5143.

Northern Kentucky University
Chase College of Law
Office of Admissions
Highland Heights, KY 41099

4144
Ethel Tingley Scholarship

AMOUNT: None Specified DEADLINE: February 1
FIELDS/MAJORS: Law

Open to entering female law students, attending Chase College of Law, who demonstrate financial need. Renewable for three academic years for full-time students and four academic years for part-time students. Contact the Assistant Dean, Chase College of Law, for further information or call (606) 572-5143.

Northern Kentucky University
Chase College of Law
Admissions Office
Highland Heights, KY 41099

4145
Ginny and Theresa Newberry Scholarship

AMOUNT: Maximum: $100 DEADLINE: February 1
FIELDS/MAJORS: All Areas of Study

Award for single mother who is a Kentucky resident. Must have a GPA of 3.0 or higher and demonstrate financial need. Contact the address below or call (606) 572-5143 for further information.

Northern Kentucky University
Office of Financial Aid-Nunn Dr.
Lucas Administrative Center, #416
Highland Heights, KY 41099

4146
Harold J. Siebenthaler Scholarship

AMOUNT: None Specified DEADLINE: February 1
FIELDS/MAJORS: Law

Open to law students, attending Chase College of Law, who demonstrate academic promise and financial need. Must be residents of Hamilton, Butler, Clermont, or Warren counties in Ohio. Contact the Assistant Dean, Chase College of Law, for further information or call (606) 572-5143.

Northern Kentucky University
Chase College of Law
Office of Administration
Highland Heights, KY 41099

4147
John Thomson Memorial Scholarship

AMOUNT: None Specified DEADLINE: February 1
FIELDS/MAJORS: Law

Open to entering law students, attending Chase College of Law, who exhibit high academic promise. Preference will be given to JD/MBA candidates. Contact the Assistant Dean, Chase College of Law, for further information or call (606) 572-5143.

Northern Kentucky University
Chase College of Law
Office of Admissions
Highland Heights, KY 41099

4148
Judge Judy West Scholarship

AMOUNT: None Specified DEADLINE: February 1
FIELDS/MAJORS: Law

Open to Kentucky residents, admitted to Chase College of Law, who are entering law students. Must demonstrate academic promise, commitment to community affairs, and devotion for the study of law. Contact the Assistant Dean, Chase College of Law, for further information or call (606) 572-5143.

Northern Kentucky University
Chase College of Law
Office of Admissions
Highland Heights, KY 41099

4149
Kentucky Bar Association/ Worker's Compensation Section Scholarship

AMOUNT: None Specified DEADLINE: February 1
FIELDS/MAJORS: Law

Open to law students, attending Chase College of Law, who are Kentucky residents. Must demonstrate financial need and academic promise. Contact the Assistant Dean, Chase College of Law, for further information or call (606) 572-5143.

Northern Kentucky University
Chase College of Law
Office of Admissions
Highland Heights, KY 41099

4150
Lange, Quill and Powers P.S.C. Scholarship

AMOUNT: Maximum: $1000 DEADLINE: February 1
FIELDS/MAJORS: Law

Open to second year law students, attending Chase College of Law, who are Kentucky residents. Contact the Assistant Dean, Chase College of Law, for further information or call (606) 572-5143.

Northern Kentucky University
Chase College of Law
Office of Admissions
Highland Heights, KY 41099

4151
Links Scholarship

AMOUNT: Maximum: $750 DEADLINE: February 1
FIELDS/MAJORS: All Areas of Study

Awards for female minorities who are entering freshmen. Must be U.S. citizens or permanent residents. Must be residents of Cincinnati, Ohio. Contact the address below or call (606) 572-5143 for further information.

Northern Kentucky University
Office Financial Aid-Nunn Dr.
Lucas Administrative Center, #416
Highland Heights, KY 41099

4152
LZ Bluegrass of Northern Kentucky Award-Chapter 88 Vietnam Veterans of America

AMOUNT: Maximum: $500 DEADLINE: February 1
FIELDS/MAJORS: All Areas of Study

Award is for student who is either: a Vietnam Era Veteran and served between 1/1/59 and 5/7/75 on active duty, other than: Initial Active Duty, Active Duty Training, Special Active Duty Training for Reserve or National Guard Forces; or student who is a child or spouse of a living or deceased Vietnam Era Veteran. Must demonstrate financial need. Contact the address below or call (606) 572-5143 for further information.

Northern Kentucky University
Office of Financial Aid-Nunn Dr.
Lucas Administrative Center, #416
Highland Heights, KY 41099

4153
Mert Freudenberg Scholarship

AMOUNT: Maximum: $200 DEADLINE: February 1
FIELDS/MAJORS: Applied Sociology, Anthropology

Must be an Applied Sociology/Anthropology major with a cumulative GPA of 3.0 or higher; must have completed more than 30 credit hours but not filed a certificate for graduation. Contact the Social Sciences Department or call (606) 572-5143 for further information.

Northern Kentucky University
Office of Financial Aid-Nunn Dr.
Lucas Administrative Center, #416
Highland Heights, KY 41099

4154
Morris M. Garrett, M.D. Scholarship

AMOUNT: Maximum: $500 DEADLINE: February 1
FIELDS/MAJORS: Radiologic Technologies

Award for student pursuing an associate degree in radiologic technology. Preference will be given to a Campbell County resident. Must demonstrate financial need. Contact the Radiologic Technology Department or call (606) 572-5143 for further information.

Northern Kentucky University
Office of Financial Aid-Nunn Dr.
Lucas Administrative Center, #416
Highland Heights, KY 41099

4155
Robert M. Dennis Scholarship

AMOUNT: Maximum: $1200 DEADLINE: February 1
FIELDS/MAJORS: Law

Open to law students, attending Chase College of Law, who demonstrate financial need. Renewable for three academic years for full-time students; four academic years for part-time students. Contact the Assistant Dean, Chase College of Law, for further information or call (606) 572-5143.

Northern Kentucky University
Chase College of Law
Office of Admissions
Highland Heights, KY 41099

4156
Turfway Park Starting Gate Scholarship

AMOUNT: Maximum: $1500   DEADLINE: February 1
FIELDS/MAJORS: All Areas of Study

Awards for first-time freshmen who had a high school GPA of 3.0 or higher and an ACT composite of 23 or higher. Must enroll for a minimum of 12 credit hours per semester. Contact the address below or call (606) 572-5143 for further information.

Northern Kentucky University
Office of Financial Aid-Nunn Dr.
Lucas Administrative Center, #416
Highland Heights, KY 41099

4157
W. Jeff Ward Scholarship

AMOUNT: Maximum: $2000   DEADLINE: February 1
FIELDS/MAJORS: Law

Open to full-time entering law students, attending Chase College of Law, who demonstrate financial need and academic promise. Priority given to residents of one of the following Kentucky counties: Pike, Floyd, Johnson, Martin, Knott, or Perry. Contact the Assistant Dean, Chase College of Law, for further information or call (606) 572-5143.

Northern Kentucky University
Chase College of Law
Office of Admissions
Highland Heights, KY 41099

4158
Wolnitzek, Bender, Rowekamp & Bonar P.S.C.

AMOUNT: Maximum: $1000   DEADLINE: February 1
FIELDS/MAJORS: Law

Open to Kentucky residents, attending Chase College of Law, who are second-year law students. Must demonstrate financial need and academic merit. Contact the Assistant Dean, Chase College of Law, for further information or call (606) 572-5143.

Northern Kentucky University
Chase College of Law
Office of Admissions
Highland Heights, KY 41099

NORTHWEST MISSOURI STATE UNIVERSITY

4159
Hettie M. Anthony and Patsy Alexander Elmore Fellowships

AMOUNT: Maximum: $2000   DEADLINE: January 15
FIELDS/MAJORS: Home Economics/Related Fields

Applicants must be Kappa Omicron Nu members and doctoral candidates at Northwest Missouri State University. Awards will be announced April 1. Write to the address listed for details.

Kappa Omicron Nu Honor Society
4990 Northwind Dr., Suite 140
East Lansing, MI 48823

NORTHWESTERN COLLEGE

4160
Academic Achievement Scholarship

AMOUNT: Maximum: $1900   DEADLINE: None Specified
FIELDS/MAJORS: All Areas of Study

Awards for freshmen who have an ACT score of at least 23 and are in the top 25% of their graduating class. Renewable with a GPA of 3.0 or better. Write to the address below for more information.

Northwestern College
Financial Aid Office
101 7th St., SW
Orange City, IA 51041

4161
Art Activity Award

AMOUNT: $300   DEADLINE: April 1
FIELDS/MAJORS: Art

Open to students accepted into the college who can demonstrate ability and plan to major in art. Audition deadline is April 1. Contact the Art Department at the address below.

Northwestern College
Financial Aid Office
101 7th St. SW
Orange City, IA 51041

4162
Collegiate Scholarship

AMOUNT: $2000-$3850 DEADLINE: None Specified
FIELDS/MAJORS: All Areas of Study

Awards for freshmen who have an ACT score of at least 26 and are in the top 10% of their graduating class. Renewable with a GPA of 3.0 or better.

Northwestern College
Financial Aid Office
101 7th St. SW
Orange City, IA 51041

4163
Departmental Scholarships

AMOUNT: $500 DEADLINE: None Specified
FIELDS/MAJORS: Most Areas of Study

Awards for Northwestern students based on their academic interests and achievements. Most awards are renewable for sophomore year. Individual criteria may vary. Write to the address below for more information. GPA must be at least 3.0.

Northwestern College
Financial Aid Office
101 7th St. SW
Orange City, IA 51041

4164
Music Activity Award

AMOUNT: $300 DEADLINE: April 1
FIELDS/MAJORS: Music

Open to students who have been accepted into the college and show ability in and plan to participate in music. Audition deadline is April 1. Contact the Music Department at the address below for further information.

Northwestern College
Financial Aid Office
101 7th St. SW
Orange City, IA 51041

4165
National Merit Scholarship

AMOUNT: Maximum: $5750 DEADLINE: None Specified
FIELDS/MAJORS: All Areas of Study

Open to accepted incoming freshmen who have been selected National Merit finalists. Renewable if recipients maintain a minimum GPA of 2.75 through freshman year and at least a 3.0 thereafter. Write to the address below for more information.

Northwestern College
Financial Aid Office
101 7th St. SW
Orange City, IA 51041

4166
National Merit Scholarship

AMOUNT: $5300 DEADLINE: None Specified
FIELDS/MAJORS: All Areas of Study

Awards for freshmen who have been selected as National Merit Finalists. Renewable with a GPA of 3.0 or better. Write to the address below for more information.

Northwestern College
Financial Aid Office
101 7th St. SW
Orange City, IA 51041

4167
Norman V. Pearle Scholarship

AMOUNT: Maximum: $6000 DEADLINE: January 3
FIELDS/MAJORS: All Areas of Study

Awarded to eight freshmen who have an ACT score of at least 25 and a GPA of at least 3.5. Based on a special scholarship competition. Renewable with a GPA 3.0 or better. Write to the address below for more information.

Northwestern College
Financial Aid Office
101 7th St. SW
Orange City, IA 51041

4168
Northwestern Grants

AMOUNT: $200-$2500 DEADLINE: None Specified
FIELDS/MAJORS: All Areas of Study

Awards for Northwestern students who show evidence of good character, leadership abilities, and financial need. Write to the address below for more information.

Northwestern College
Financial Aid Office
101 7th St. SW
Orange City, IA 51041

4169
Presidential Scholarship

AMOUNT: $3900-$4800 DEADLINE: None Specified
FIELDS/MAJORS: All Areas of Study

Awards for freshmen who have an ACT score of at least 28 and are in the top 5% of their graduating class. Renewable with a GPA of 3.0 or better. Write to the address below for more information.

Northwestern College
Financial Aid Office
101 7th St. SW
Orange City, IA 51041

4170
Theater Activity Award

AMOUNT: $300   DEADLINE: April 1
FIELDS/MAJORS: Theater

Open to students who have been accepted into the college. Must demonstrate ability and plan to participate in theater. Audition deadline is April 1. Contact the Theater Department at the address below.

Northwestern College
Financial Aid Office
101 7th St. SW
Orange City, IA 51041

NORTHWESTERN COLLEGE OF IOWA

4171
Academic Achievement Scholarship

AMOUNT: Maximum. $2100   DEADLINE: None Specified
FIELDS/MAJORS: All Areas of Study

Open to accepted incoming freshmen who have a minimum ACT score of 23 and are in the top 25% of graduating class. Renewable if recipients maintain a minimum GPA of 2.75 through freshman year and at least a 3.0 thereafter. Contact the address below for further information or call (712) 737-7130.

Northwestern College of Iowa
Financial Aid Office
Orange City, IA 51041

4172
Art Activity Scholarship

AMOUNT: $100-$500   DEADLINE: None Specified
FIELDS/MAJORS: Art

Open to accepted incoming freshmen who demonstrate ability and plan to major in art. April 1 is the audition deadline. Contact the Art Department for further information or call (712) 737-7130. GPA must be at least 2.6.

Northwestern College of Iowa
Financial Aid Office
Orange City, IA 51041

4173
Collegiate Scholarship

AMOUNT: $2200-$4200   DEADLINE: None Specified
FIELDS/MAJORS: All Areas of Study

Open to accepted incoming freshmen who have a minimum ACT score of 26 and are in the top 10% of graduating class. Renewable if recipients maintain a minimum GPA of 2.75 through freshman year and at least a 3.0 thereafter. Contact the address below for further information or call (712) 737-7130.

Northwestern College of Iowa
Financial Aid Office
Orange City, IA 51041

4174
Music Activity Scholarship

AMOUNT: $300   DEADLINE: None Specified
FIELDS/MAJORS: All Areas of Study

Open to accepted incoming freshmen who demonstrate ability and plan to participate in music. The audition deadline is April 1. Contact the Music Department for further information or call (712) 737-7130. GPA must be at least 2.6.

Northwestern College of Iowa
Financial Aid Office
Orange City, IA 51041

4175
National Merit Scholarship

AMOUNT: Maximum: $5750   DEADLINE: None Specified
FIELDS/MAJORS: All Areas of Study

Open to accepted incoming freshmen who have been selected National Merit finalists. Renewable if recipients maintain a minimum GPA of 2.75 through freshman year and at least a 3.0 thereafter. Contact the address below for further information or call (712) 737-7130.

Northwestern College of Iowa
Financial Aid Office
Orange City, IA 51041

4176
Norman V. Peale Scholarship

AMOUNT: Maximum: $6300   DEADLINE: January 2
FIELDS/MAJORS: All Areas of Study

Open to accepted incoming freshmen who have a minimum ACT score of 25 and at least a 3.5 GPA. Renewable if recipients maintain a minimum GPA of 3.0 Contact the address below for further information or call (712) 737-7130.

Northwestern College of Iowa
Financial Aid Office
Orange City, IA 51041

4177
Northwestern Grants

AMOUNT: $200-$2500   DEADLINE: None Specified
FIELDS/MAJORS: All Areas of Study

Open to accepted incoming freshmen who demonstrate financial need. Must file an FAFSA. Contact the address below for further information or call (712) 737-7130. GPA must be at least 2.6.

Northwestern College of Iowa
Financial Aid Office
Orange City, IA 51041

4178
Presidential Scholarship

AMOUNT: $4300-$5200   DEADLINE: None Specified
FIELDS/MAJORS: All Areas of Study

Open to accepted incoming freshmen who have a minimum ACT score of 28 and are in the top 5% of graduating class. Renewable if recipients maintain a minimum GPA of 2.75 through freshman year and at least a 3.0 thereafter. Contact the address below for further information or call (712) 737-7130.

Northwestern College of Iowa
Financial Aid Office
Orange City, IA 51041

4179
Theater Activity Scholarship

AMOUNT: $300   DEADLINE: None Specified
FIELDS/MAJORS: All Areas of Study

Open to accepted incoming freshmen who demonstrate ability and plan to participate in theater. April 1 is the audition deadline. Contact the Theater Department for further information or call (712) 737-7130. GPA must be at least 2.6.

Northwestern College of Iowa
Financial Aid Office
Orange City, IA 51041

NORTHWESTERN MICHIGAN COLLEGE

4180
Art and Mary Schmuckal Endowed Scholarship

AMOUNT: Maximum: $2400   DEADLINE: April 1
FIELDS/MAJORS: Business

Open to students who are residents of the service area and are enrolled in a business program. Contact the address listed for further information.

Northwestern Michigan College
Financial Aid Office, Admin. Bldg., #142
1701 E. Front St.
Traverse City, MI 49684

4181
Carrie E. Smith Schuyler Scholarships

AMOUNT: Maximum: $400   DEADLINE: April 1
FIELDS/MAJORS: Business, Music

Open to female students who are enrolled in business or music. Contact the address listed for further information.

Northwestern Michigan College
Financial Aid Office, Admin. Bldg., #142
1701 E. Front St.
Traverse City, MI 49684

4182
Chef Pierre, Rotary Charities, and National Cherry Festival Scholarships

AMOUNT: Maximum: $1500   DEADLINE: April 1
FIELDS/MAJORS: Resort Management

Open to students enrolled in the Resort Management Program. Number and amount of awards varies. Contact the address listed for further information.

Northwestern Michigan College
Financial Aid Office, Admin. Bldg., #142
1701 E. Front St.
Traverse City, MI 49684

4183
Corinne J. Naar Mathematics Scholarship

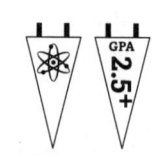

AMOUNT: Maximum: $750 DEADLINE: April 1
FIELDS/MAJORS: Mathematics

Open to mathematics majors. Contact the address listed for further information. Must have a GPA of at least 2.5.

Northwestern Michigan College
Financial Aid Office, Admin. Bldg., #142
1701 E. Front St.
Traverse City, MI 49684

4184
Darrell Keigh Holtsclaw Memorial Scholarship

AMOUNT: Maximum: $1000 DEADLINE: April 1
FIELDS/MAJORS: Aviation

Open to students who have aviation as a career goal. Contact the NMC aviation office for further information. Must have a GPA of at least 2.5.

Northwestern Michigan College
Financial Aid Office, Admin. Bldg., #142
1701 E. Front St.
Traverse City, MI 49684

4185
Dorothy Helms Memorial, John and Nancy Kindra Memorial Scholarships

AMOUNT: $500-$600 DEADLINE: April 1
FIELDS/MAJORS: Health Occupations

Open to students who are enrolled in one of the Health Occupation programs and have a minimum GPA of 2.5. Each scholarship provider offers one award annually. Contact the address listed for further information about both awards.

Northwestern Michigan College
Financial Aid Office, Admin. Bldg., #142
1701 E. Front St.
Traverse City, MI 49684

4186
Earl J. Hathaway Scholarship

AMOUNT: Maximum: $2000 DEADLINE: April 1
FIELDS/MAJORS: Nursing

Open to students who have a minimum GPA of 2.5 and are enrolled at least half-time. Contact the address listed for further information.

Northwestern Michigan College
Financial Aid Office, Admin. Bldg., #142
1701 E. Front St.
Traverse City, MI 49684

4187
Economic Club of Traverse City Scholarship

AMOUNT: Maximum: $1000 DEADLINE: April 1
FIELDS/MAJORS: General Business

Open to students who are residents of the service area, enrolled in the general business program and have a minimum GPA of 3.3. Contact the address listed for further information.

Northwestern Michigan College
Financial Aid Office, Admin. Bldg., #142
1701 E. Front St.
Traverse City, MI 49684

4188
Faye L. Robinett Living Memorial Scholarship

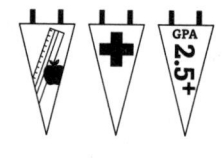

AMOUNT: None Specified DEADLINE: April 1
FIELDS/MAJORS: Nursing, Education

Open to students enrolled in the ADN program or in education. Contact the address listed for further information. Must have a GPA of at least 2.5.

Northwestern Michigan College
Financial Aid Office, Admin. Bldg., #142
1701 E. Front St.
Traverse City, MI 49684

4189
Glen A. Anderson Scholarship

AMOUNT: Maximum: $1000 DEADLINE: April 1
FIELDS/MAJORS: Accounting

Open to students who are majoring in accounting and have a minimum GPA of 3.25. Must be a resident of the service area. Contact the address listed for further information.

Northwestern Michigan College
Financial Aid Office, Admin. Bldg., #142
1701 E. Front St.
Traverse City, MI 49684

4190
Glen Lake Women's Club Scholarship

AMOUNT: Maximum: $2000 DEADLINE: April 1
FIELDS/MAJORS: Health Occupations

Open to students who are Leelanau County residents enrolled in one of the health occupation programs. Contact the address listed for further information.

Northwestern Michigan College
Financial Aid Office, Admin. Bldg., #142
1701 E. Front St.
Traverse City, MI 49684

4191
Gordon and Marlene Rady Scholarship

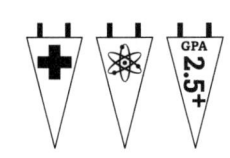

AMOUNT: None Specified DEADLINE: April 1
FIELDS/MAJORS: Nursing, Science, Mathematics

Open to second-year students, from the service area, who are majoring in mathematics, science, or nursing. Number and amounts of awards varies. Contact the address listed for further information. Must have a GPA of at least 2.5.

Northwestern Michigan College
Financial Aid Office, Admin. Bldg., #142
1701 E. Front St.
Traverse City, MI 49684

4192
Grand Traverse Area Rock and Mineral Club Scholarship

AMOUNT: Maximum: $500 DEADLINE: April 1
FIELDS/MAJORS: Earth Science

Open to earth science majors who have a minimum GPA of 2.5. Contact the address listed for further information.

Northwestern Michigan College
Financial Aid Office, Admin. Bldg., #142
1701 E. Front St.
Traverse City, MI 49684

4193
Hettie Molvang and Mabel E. Wayde Memorial Scholarships

AMOUNT: $750-$900 DEADLINE: April 1
FIELDS/MAJORS: Nursing

Open to second-year ADN and LPN students who are residents of Grand Traverse or Wexford counties. Must have a minimum GPA of 2.5. Each scholarship provider offers one award annually. Contact the address listed for further information about both awards.

Northwestern Michigan College
Financial Aid Office, Admin. Bldg., #142
1701 E. Front St.
Traverse City, MI 49684

4194
Jack McChrystal Faculty/Staff Scholarship

AMOUNT: Maximum: $600 DEADLINE: April 1
FIELDS/MAJORS: Liberal Arts

Open to liberal arts majors who have a minimum GPA of 3.25. Contact the address listed for further information.

Northwestern Michigan College
Financial Aid Office, Admin. Bldg., #142
1701 E. Front St.
Traverse City, MI 49684

4195
Jane and John Norton Scholarship

AMOUNT: None Specified DEADLINE: April 1
FIELDS/MAJORS: Liberal Arts

Open to students who are residents of Grand Traverse County and are enrolled in the liberal arts transfer program. Contact the address listed for further information.

Northwestern Michigan College
Financial Aid Office, Admin. Bldg., #142
1701 E. Front St.
Traverse City, MI 49684

4196
Mary Alice Strom-Zonta Club Scholarship

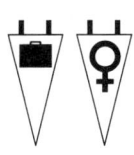

AMOUNT: Maximum: $1200 DEADLINE: April 1
FIELDS/MAJORS: Business

Open to female students who are residents of the Grand Traverse area and are enrolled in a business program. Contact the address listed for further information.

Northwestern Michigan College
Financial Aid Office, Admin. Bldg., #142
1701 E. Front St.
Traverse City, MI 49684

4197
Maude and Olive Marriot Scholarship

AMOUNT: $800-$1000 DEADLINE: April 1
FIELDS/MAJORS: Nursing

Open to students enrolled in the ADN or LPN program. Must be a resident of Antrim County. Contact the address listed for further information. Must have a GPA of at least 2.5.

Northwestern Michigan College
Financial Aid Office, Admin. Bldg., #142
1701 E. Front St.
Traverse City, MI 49684

4198
Preston Tanis Scholarship

AMOUNT: Maximum: $1000 DEADLINE: April 1
FIELDS/MAJORS: All Areas of Study

Open to Grand Traverse area students who graduated from a high school in the same area. Must be able to demonstrate financial need. Contact the address listed for further information.

Northwestern Michigan College
Financial Aid Office, Admin. Bldg., #142
1701 E. Front St.
Traverse City, MI 49684

4199
Ralph E. and Eva B. Wynkoop Scholarships

AMOUNT: Maximum: $1000 DEADLINE: April 1
FIELDS/MAJORS: All Areas of Study

Open to adult students who are enrolled at least half-time and have a minimum GPA of 2.5. Contact the address listed for further information.

Northwestern Michigan College
Financial Aid Office, Admin. Bldg., #142
1701 E. Front St.
Traverse City, MI 49684

4200
Rotary Club of Traverse City Scholarships

AMOUNT: Maximum: $1000 DEADLINE: April 1
FIELDS/MAJORS: All Areas of Study

Open to sophomores who are residents of Grand Traverse or Leelannau counties. Contact the address listed for further information. Must have a GPA of at least 2.0.

Northwestern Michigan College
Financial Aid Office, Admin. Bldg., #142
1701 E. Front St.
Traverse City, MI 49684

4201
Stephen and Peg Siciliano History Scholarship

AMOUNT: Maximum: $200 DEADLINE: April 1
FIELDS/MAJORS: History

Open to students enrolled in the History Program who have a minimum cumulative GPA of 3.25 and a minimum 3.5 in at least 8 semester credit hours of NMC history coursework. Contact the address listed for further information.

Northwestern Michigan College
Financial Aid Office, Admin. Bldg., #142
1701 E. Front St.
Traverse City, MI 49684

4202
Traverse City/Rajkovich Kiwanis Club Scholarship

AMOUNT: Maximum: $500 DEADLINE: April 1
FIELDS/MAJORS: All Areas of Study

Open to Grand Traverse County residents with a minimum GPA of 2.0. Contact the address listed for further information.

Northwestern Michigan College
Financial Aid Office, Admin. Bldg., #142
1701 E. Front St.
Traverse City, MI 49684

4203
W.R. Angell Biology Scholarship

AMOUNT: Maximum: $1500 DEADLINE: April 1
FIELDS/MAJORS: Biology

Open to high school seniors who have demonstrated an interest in the field of biology. Must have a minimum GPA of 3.0 during the last two years of high school and recommendations from your high school biology teaching staff. Renewable for the second year pending completion of at least 36 credits and review of academic standing. Contact the address listed for further information.

Northwestern Michigan College
Financial Aid Office, Admin. Bldg., #142
1701 E. Front St.
Traverse City, MI 49684

NORTHWOOD UNIVERSITY

4204
Northwood University DECA Scholarships

AMOUNT: $1000-$2500   DEADLINE: None Specified
FIELDS/MAJORS: All areas of study

Scholarships for all national and state officers and first-place winners by category. Scholarships are also available for all other active DECA students with a minimum GPA of 2.75. Contact the address below for further information.

Northwood University
Office of Admissions
3225 Cook Rd.
Midland, MI 48640

4205
Northwood University Freedom Scholarships

AMOUNT: $5000   DEADLINE: None Specified
FIELDS/MAJORS: All areas of study

Scholarships available for incoming full-time freshmen. Must have at least a score of 25 on the ACT or 1150 on the SAT and a minimum GPA of 3.0. Renewable if recipients maintain a 3.0 GPA. Contact the address below for further information.

Northwood University
Office of Admissions
3225 Cook Rd.
Midland, MI 48640

4206
Northwood University Free-Enterprise Scholarships

AMOUNT: $4000   DEADLINE: None Specified
FIELDS/MAJORS: All areas of study

Scholarships available to incoming full-time freshmen. Must have at least a 20 score on the ACT or 950 on the SAT and a minimum GPA of 2.7. Renewable if recipients maintain a 2.7 GPA. Contact the address below for further information.

Northwood University
Office of Admissions
3225 Cook Rd.
Midland, MI 48640

4207
Northwood University Transfer Scholarships

AMOUNT: $3000   DEADLINE: May 1
FIELDS/MAJORS: All areas of study

Scholarship available for students transferring to Northwood as full-time juniors who will be enrolled for a minimum of two years. Applicants must have an associate degree and a minimum GPA of 2.7. Contact the address below for further information.

Northwood University
Office of Admissions
3225 Cook Rd.
Midland, MI 48640

OHIO STATE UNIVERSITY

4208
Griffith Foundation Scholarships

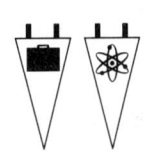

AMOUNT: None Specified   DEADLINE: None Specified
FIELDS/MAJORS: Insurance, Risk Management, Actuarial Science

Scholarships are available for students currently attending Ohio State University and enrolled in one of the programs listed above. Write to the address below for information.

Griffith Foundation for Insurance Education
172 E. State St., #305A
Columbus, OH 43215-4321

OLEAN BUSINESS INSTITUTE

4209
Olean Business Institute Scholarships

AMOUNT: $1000-$2800   DEADLINE: December 1
FIELDS/MAJORS: Business and Related Fields

Scholarships to Olean Business Institute given to freshmen based upon a competitive exam held on the first Saturdays of December and March. Second deadline date is March 7. Write to the address listed for further information.

Olean Business Institute
301 North York Union St.
Olean, NY 14760

OLIVET COLLEGE

4210
Affiliated Churches Grants

AMOUNT: Maximum: $2000   DEADLINE: None Specified
FIELDS/MAJORS: All Areas of Study

Available to entering freshmen who are members of the United Church of Christ or Congregational Christian Churches. Awards are renewable. Contact 1-800-456-7189 or (616) 749-7635.

Olivet College
Office of Admissions
Olivet, MI 49076

4211
Community Responsibility Scholarship

AMOUNT: Maximum: $6000   DEADLINE: None Specified
FIELDS/MAJORS: All Areas of Study

Available to entering freshmen who have demonstrated community involvement. Essay and interview required. This award is not need-based and is renewable. Contact 1-800-456-7189 or (616) 749-7635.

Olivet College
Office of Admissions
Olivet, MI 49076

4212
Heritage Grant

AMOUNT: None Specified   DEADLINE: None Specified
FIELDS/MAJORS: All Areas of Study

Available to entering freshmen. Amounts vary, and the awards are renewable. Contact 1-800-456-7189 or (616) 749-7635.

Olivet College
Office of Admissions
Olivet, MI 49076

4213
International Student Grants

AMOUNT: None Specified   DEADLINE: None Specified
FIELDS/MAJORS: All Areas of Study

Available to entering international students. Awards are for up to one-half of tuition, room, and board. Renewable. Based on both financial need and academics. Call 1-800-456-7189 or (616) 749-7635.

Olivet College
Office of Financial Aid
Olivet, MI 49076

4214
Legacy Fellowship

AMOUNT: None Specified   DEADLINE: None Specified
FIELDS/MAJORS: All Areas of Study

Available to entering freshmen who have participated in the fellowship application process. Essay and interview required. Awards for up to one-half of tuition, room, and board. Renewable. Contact the address below for further information or call 1-800-456-7189 or (616) 749-7635.

Olivet College
Office of Admissions
Olivet, MI 49076

4215
Music Scholarship

AMOUNT: Maximum: $1500   DEADLINE: None Specified
FIELDS/MAJORS: Vocal Music

Awards for entering freshmen based on participation in the choral music program. Audition may be required. Renewable. Contact 1-800-456-7189 or (616) 749-7635.

Olivet College
Office of Admissions
Olivet, MI 49076

4216
Opportunity Grant

AMOUNT: Maximum: $2500   DEADLINE: None Specified
FIELDS/MAJORS: All Areas of Study

Awards for entering freshmen. Based on a minimum high school GPA of 2.25 and an ACT score of at least 17. This award is not need-based. Contact 1-800-456-7189 or (616) 749-7635.

Olivet College
Office of Admissions
Olivet, MI 49076

4217
Presidential Scholarship

AMOUNT: Maximum: $4000   DEADLINE: None Specified
FIELDS/MAJORS: All Areas of Study

Awards for entering freshmen based on a minimum high school GPA of 3.0 and an ACT score of at least 21. This award is not need-based. Contact 1-800-456-7189 or (616) 749-7635.

Olivet College
Office of Admissions
Olivet, MI 49076

4218
Student Employment

AMOUNT: None Specified   DEADLINE: None Specified
FIELDS/MAJORS: All Areas of Study

Available to incoming freshmen. Awards vary and are need-based. Renewable. Call 1-800-456-7189 or (616) 749-7635.

Olivet College
Office of Admissions
Olivet, MI 49076

4219
Transfer Student Grants

AMOUNT: None Specified   DEADLINE: None Specified
FIELDS/MAJORS: All Areas of Study

Available to transfer students. The awards are for up to one-half of tuition and room and board. Based both on financial need and academics. Renewable. Contact 1-800-456-7189 or (616) 749-7635.

Olivet College
Office of Admissions
Olivet, MI 49076

PACIFIC LUTHERAN THEOLOGICAL SEMINARY

4220
Eiichi Matsushita Memorial Scholarship

AMOUNT: None Specified   DEADLINE: October 15
FIELDS/MAJORS: Christian Service, Religion, Theology

Scholarships for students of Asian backgrounds who intend to pursue careers in leadership positions in the Lutheran Church, Asian Ministry. Based on need. Write to the address below for details.

Pacific Lutheran Theological Seminary
Eiichi Matsushita Memorial Scholarship
2770 Marin Ave.
Berkeley, CA 94708

PEACE COLLEGE

4221
Academic Achievement Awards

AMOUNT: $1000   DEADLINE: None Specified
FIELDS/MAJORS: All Areas of Study

Scholarships for students at Peace College with a GPA of at least 3.0. Contact the director of financial aid at the address below for details.

Peace College
Director of Financial Aid
15 East Peace Street
Raleigh, NC 27604

PENNSYLVANIA COLLEGE OF OPTOMETRY

4222
Delaware Optometric Institutional Aid

AMOUNT: Maximum: $4000   DEADLINE: June 1
FIELDS/MAJORS: Optometry

Scholarship for Delaware students who meet academic requirements and enroll at the Pennsylvania College of Optometry. Commission makes final awards July 1. Write to the address listed for more information.

Delaware Higher Education Commission
Carvel State Office Building
820 North French St., #4F
Wilmington, DE 19801

PENNSYLVANIA STATE UNIVERSITY

4223
Elmer R. Deaver Foundation Scholarship

AMOUNT: None Specified   DEADLINE: None Specified
FIELDS/MAJORS: All Areas of Study

Open to enrolled, or planning to enroll, full-time undergraduates. Must have achieved superior academics or manifest promise of outstanding academic success. Must have been an employee of Quaker City Life Insurance Company during the lifetime of Mr. Elmer R. Deaver or the children, spouses, or parents of those employees and applicants who were employed at any time. Contact the address below for further information or call (814) 865-6301. GPA must be at least 3.0.

Pennsylvania State University
Office of Student Aid
314 Shields Building
University Park, PA 16802-1220

4224
Graduate Assistantships and Fellowships

AMOUNT: None Specified DEADLINE: February 1
FIELDS/MAJORS: All Areas of Study

Programs for graduate students at Penn State. Programs are offered through the graduate school, the office of financial aid, and the departments at Penn State. Includes Graham Fellowship and Academic Computer Fellowship for students who use practical and innovative computer applications in their research. Forty awards are given annually. Contact the address below for further information.

Pennsylvania State University
Fellowships and Awards Office
313 Kern Graduate Building
University Park, PA 16802

4225
Minority Scholars Program Fellowship

AMOUNT: Maximum: $13000 DEADLINE: None Specified
FIELDS/MAJORS: All Areas of Study

Programs for African-American, Hispanic, and Native American graduate students at Pennsylvania State. Based upon academic excellence. Twenty fellowships and sixty assistantships are available. Contact the address below for further information.

Pennsylvania State University
Fellowships and Awards Office
313 Kern Graduate Building
University Park, PA 16802

PEPPERDINE UNIVERSITY

4226
Joan Whitney and Charles Shipman Payson

AMOUNT: None Specified DEADLINE: None Specified
FIELDS/MAJORS: Art

Scholarships are available for Maine art students attending Pepperdine University, or visiting artists in residency at Pepperdine who have a connection to the state of Maine. Based on review of portfolio materials. Contact Avery Falkner, Fine Arts Division, Pepperdine University at (213) 456-4155 or write to the address listed for more details.

Maine Community Foundation
245 East Maine St.
PO Box 148
Ellsworth, ME 04605

PFEIFFER COLLEGE

4227
Athletic Grants-in-Aid at Pfeiffer

AMOUNT: None Specified DEADLINE: All Areas of Study
FIELDS/MAJORS: All Areas of Study

Awards for students at Pfeiffer College who will be participating in one of several different sports. Sports for women include basketball, cross country, lacrosse, soccer, softball, swimming, tennis, and volleyball. Sports for men include baseball, basketball, cross country, golf, lacrosse, soccer, and tennis. Contact the Office of Admission and Financial Aid at the address below for complete information.

Pfeiffer College
Office of Admission and Financial Aid
Misenheimer, NC 28109

4228
Children of Ministers Scholarships

AMOUNT: $300-$2000 DEADLINE: None Specified
FIELDS/MAJORS: All Areas of Study

Awards for students at Pfeiffer College who are children of ordained ministers. Contact the Office of Admission and Financial Aid at the address below for complete information.

Pfeiffer College
Office of Admission and Financial Aid
Misenheimer, NC 28109

4229
Freshman Presidential Scholarship and Honor Scholarships

AMOUNT: None Specified DEADLINE: None Specified
FIELDS/MAJORS: All Areas of Study

Scholarships for entering freshmen at Pfeiffer College. Based on a combination of high school grades, test scores, and high school class rank. Contact the Office of Admission and Financial Aid at the address below for details. Also inquire at the advancement office for a complete list of scholarships and the application requirements. GPA must be at least 3.0.

Pfeiffer College
Office of Admission and Financial Aid
Misenheimer, NC 28109

4230
Trustee Incentive Scholarships

AMOUNT: None Specified DEADLINE: None Specified
FIELDS/MAJORS: All Areas of Study

Scholarships for outstanding students at Pfeiffer College. For transfer students or continuing students. Based on GPA. Contact the Office of Admission and Financial Aid at the address below for details. GPA must be at least 3.0.

Pfeiffer College
Office of Admission and Financial Aid
Misenheimer, NC 28109

4231
Undergraduate Programs of Study

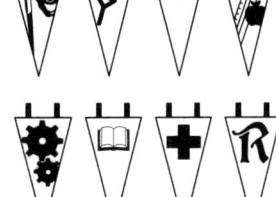

AMOUNT: None Specified
DEADLINE: None Specified
FIELDS/MAJORS: Accounting, Arts Administration, Biology, Business Administration, Chemistry, Christian Education, English, Communication, Computer Information Systems, Criminal Justice, Elementary Education, Engineering, History, Mathematics, Music, Physical Education, Pre-Law, Pre-Med, Psychology, Religion, Secondary Education

Awards for students at Pfeiffer College who excel in one of several different areas of study. Contact the Office of Admission and Financial Aid at the address below for details.

Pfeiffer College
Office of Admission and Financial Aid
Misenheimer, NC 28109

PITTSBURG STATE UNIVERSITY

4232
Honors College Presidential Scholarship

AMOUNT: None Specified DEADLINE: March 1
FIELDS/MAJORS: All Areas of Study

Awards for incoming freshmen at Pittsburg State University who have demonstrated academic ability. Applicants must have an ACT score of at least 28. Renewable for three years. Write to the address listed for more information.

Pittsburg State University
Office of Academic Affairs
203 Russ Hall
Pittsburg, KS 66762

PITTSBURGH INSTITUTE OF MORTUARY SCIENCE

4233
Pittsburgh Institute of Mortuary Science Awards

AMOUNT: None Specified DEADLINE: None Specified
FIELDS/MAJORS: Mortuary Science

Awards for students at the Pittsburgh Institute at any level of study. Write to the address listed for more information.

Pittsburgh Institute of Mortuary Science
Office of Financial Aid
5808 Baum Blvd.
Pittsburgh, PA 15206

PHILLIPS UNIVERSITY

4234
Vocal and Instrumental Music Scholarship

AMOUNT: $500-$1500 DEADLINE: None Specified
FIELDS/MAJORS: Music

Scholarships for music majors at Phillips University. Based on audition or portfolio review. Interview with department head required. Approximately fifteen awards offered annually. Write to address below for additional information.

Phillips University
Financial Aid Office
100 S. University Ave.
Enid, OK 73701

PRINCETON UNIVERSITY

4235
Shelby Cullom Davis Center Postdoctoral Fellowships

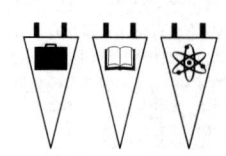

AMOUNT: Maximum: $28000 DEADLINE: December 1
FIELDS/MAJORS: History, Humanities, Business, Economics, Cultural Studies

Seven residential, postdoctoral fellowships at Princeton University's Shelby Cullom Davis Center for Historical Studies. One semester-one-year fellowships. For beginning and established scholars. The topic for the academic years 1996-98 is "animals and human society." Fellows are expected to be in residence at Princeton. Write to the administrator of the Shelby Cullom Davis Center at the address below for further information and application materials.

Princeton University, Department of History
Administrator, Shelby Collom Davis Ctr.
129 Dickinson Hall
Princeton, NJ 08544

PROVIDENCE COLLEGE

4236
Dominic Gencarelli Family Trust

AMOUNT: $1000-$5000 DEADLINE: April 27
FIELDS/MAJORS: All Areas of Study

Scholarships are available for high school seniors of Westerly, Rhode Island, who are planning to attend Providence College, or Westerly residents attending Providence College graduate school. Write to the address below for information.

Westerly High School
James Guarino, Guidance Department
23 Ward Ave.
Westerly, RI 02891

4237
Feinstein Institute Scholarships

AMOUNT: Maximum: $5000 DEADLINE: January 15
FIELDS/MAJORS: Public, Community Service

Open to incoming full-time undergraduates who are interested in pursuing a degree in public and/or community service. Renewable if recipients remain in good standing in the program. Students who are awarded this scholarship may also be eligible for other merit and need-based financial aid. No separate application is necessary. A committee reviews information and materials submitted with the general Providence College application form for evidence of leadership in and commitment to community service in addition to academic achievement. Contact the address below for further information. GPA must be at least 2.9.

Providence College, Feinstein Institute for Public Service
Rick Battistoni, Director
Providence, RI 02918-0001

PURDUE UNIVERSITY

4238
A. Patrick Charnon Memorial Scholarship

AMOUNT: $1500 DEADLINE: April 30
FIELDS/MAJORS: All Areas of Study

Scholarships are for students enrolled in a full-time undergraduate program of study in an accredited four-year college or university. Must maintain good academic standing. Applicants are required to submit a five hundred to one thousand word essay. Contact: A. Patrick Charnon Memorial Scholarship, The Center for Education Solutions, Box 192956, San Francisco, CA 94119-2956 for more information. You will need to included a SASE for a reply.

Purdue University, Indianapolis
Purdue School of Technology
799 West Michigan St.
Indianapolis, IN 46202

4239
Award of Excellence Scholarships

AMOUNT: $1500 DEADLINE: March 1
FIELDS/MAJORS: All Agriculture Programs of Study

Awards open to high school seniors who have a combined SAT score of at least 1100 and are in the top 10% of class. Approximately seventy-five awards offered annually. Contact your Indiana high school guidance office for information and application. GPA must be at least 3.7.

Purdue University-School of Agriculture
Thomas W. Atkinson
1140 Agricultural Administration
West Lafayette, IN 47907

4240
Bill and Mary Earle Scholarship

AMOUNT: $500   DEADLINE: February 1
FIELDS/MAJORS: All Agricultural Programs

Open to students enrolled in the School of Agriculture. Must have a minimum GPA of 2.2 and be essentially a "self-supporting" student. One award offered annually. Write to the address below for more information.

Purdue University-School of Agriculture
Thomas W. Atkinson
1140 Agricultural Administration Bldg.
West Lafayette, IN 47907

4241
Builders Association of Greater Indianapolis Richard Sapp Scholarship

AMOUNT: $500   DEADLINE: February 28
FIELDS/MAJORS: Residential/Light Commercial Industry

Award for a student with an interest in pursuing a career in the residential/light commercial industry. Based on academics, experience, and financial need. Write to the address below for more information.

Purdue University, Indianapolis
Purdue School of Technology
799 West Michigan St.
Indianapolis, IN 46202

4242
C.C. Alexander Memorial Scholarship

AMOUNT: None Specified   DEADLINE: None Specified
FIELDS/MAJORS: Entomology

Open to undergraduates majoring in entomology. Based on academics, character, and financial need. Contact the address below for further information. GPA must be at least 2.7.

Purdue University-Dept. of Entomology
Prof. Gary W. Bennett-Sondra L. Lindsey
Entomology Hall
West Lafayette, IN 47907

4243
Central Soya Freshman and General Mills Freshman Scholarships

AMOUNT: $500-$1000   DEADLINE: February 28
FIELDS/MAJORS: Food Science

Open to high school seniors ranked in the top half of their graduating class and planning to enroll in the Department of Food Science. Must have a minimum SAT score of 1000 or minimum ACT/English/Math scores of 23. Based on academics and extracurricular activities. Four awards offered annually from each of the two companies. Contact the address below for further information about both awards. GPA must be at least 3.0.

Purdue University-Dept. of Food Science
Jennifer Lawrence
Smith Hall, #127C
West Lafayette, IN 47907

4244
Chicago Farmers Scholarship

AMOUNT: $1000   DEADLINE: October 1
FIELDS/MAJORS: Agriculture

Award open to juniors in the School of Agriculture. Based on academics and school and community activities. One award offered annually. Write to the address below for more information. GPA must be at least 2.8.

Purdue University-School of Agriculture
Thomas W. Atkinson
1140 Agricultural Administration Bldg.
West Lafayette, IN 47907

4245
Claude M. Gladdin Minority Scholarships

AMOUNT: Maximum: $1500   DEADLINE: March 1
FIELDS/MAJORS: Forestry, Natural Resources

Open to incoming minority freshmen admitted to forestry and natural resources. Based on academics in high school and professional potential. Two awards offered annually. Contact the address below for further information or call (317) 494-3629. GPA must be at least 2.5.

Purdue University-Dept. of Forestry and Natural Resources
Professor Douglas M. Knudson
West Lafayette, IN 47907

4246
Claude M. Gladdin Scholarships

AMOUNT: Maximum: $500   DEADLINE: March 1
FIELDS/MAJORS: Forestry, Natural Resources

Open to incoming freshmen admitted to forestry and natural resources. Based on academics in high school and professional potential. One to five awards offered annually. Contact the address below for further information. GPA must be at least 2.8.

Purdue University-Dept. of Forestry and Natural Resources
Professor Douglas M. Knudson
West Lafayette, IN 47907

4247
Colonel Fletcher P. Jaquess Scholarship

AMOUNT: $1000   DEADLINE: March 1
FIELDS/MAJORS: Agriculture and Related Areas

Open to high school seniors from Gibson, Posey, Vanderburgh, and Warrick counties in Indiana, planning to enroll in the School of Agriculture. One award offered annually. Information and applications available at your high schools and your county extension offices.

Purdue University-School of Agriculture
Thomas W. Atkinson
1140 Agricultural Administration Bldg.
West Lafayette, IN 47907

4248
Dow Elanco Agricultural Economics Scholarship

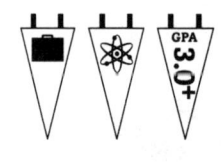

AMOUNT: $1000   DEADLINE: February 1
FIELDS/MAJORS: Agricultural Economics

Open to juniors and seniors majoring in agricultural economics. Must have a minimum GPA of 3.0 and completed AGEC 331. One award offered annually. Write to the address below for more information.

Purdue University-School of Agriculture
Thomas W. Atkinson
1140 Agricultural Administration Bldg.
West Lafayette, IN 47907

4249
Dow Elanco Graduate Scholarship

AMOUNT: $1000   DEADLINE: February 1
FIELDS/MAJORS: Plant Science, Plant Pathology, Forestry, Wildlife, Fisheries

Open to graduate students who have been at Purdue for at least one year. Must be U.S. citizens. Preference for doctoral students. Two awards offered annually. Write to the address below for more information.

Purdue University-School of Agriculture
Thomas W. Atkinson
1140 Agricultural Administration Bldg.
West Lafayette, IN 47907

4250
Dow Elanco Minority Scholarship

AMOUNT: $1000   DEADLINE: February 1
FIELDS/MAJORS: All Agricultural Programs

Open to minority sophomores (who have completed 30 hours at Purdue or Vincennes University) juniors (who have completed 60 hours at Purdue or Vincennes University), or seniors (who have completed 90 hours at Purdue or Vincennes University). One award offered annually. Write to the address below for more information.

Purdue University-School of Agriculture
Thomas W. Atkinson
1140 Agricultural Administration Bldg.
West Lafayette, IN 47907

4251
Dow Elanco Plant Science/Pest Management Scholarship

AMOUNT: $1000   DEADLINE: February 1
FIELDS/MAJORS: Plant Science, Pest Management, Agricultural Communications

Open to juniors and seniors majoring in any of the areas listed above. Must have a minimum GPA of 3.0 and completed 60 hours for juniors and 90 hours for seniors. One award offered annually. Write to the address below for more information.

Purdue University-School of Agriculture
Thomas W. Atkinson
1140 Agricultural Administration Bldg.
West Lafayette, IN 47907

4252
Dow Elanco Purdue Scholar Scholarship

AMOUNT: $3056   DEADLINE: March 1
FIELDS/MAJORS: Agricultural Economics, Biochemistry, Entomology, Horticulture

Open to seniors in Indianapolis public high schools who will be majoring in the fields listed above or any of the following: agronomy, botany, or plant pathology. Based on scholastic record. Award includes tuition, fees, room and board, and a book allowance. One award offered annually. Write to the address below for more information. GPA must be at least 2.8.

Purdue University-School of Agriculture
Karla Hay, School of Agriculture
1140 Agricultural Administration Bldg.
West Lafayette, IN 47907

4253
Farm Bureau Discussion Contest

AMOUNT: None Specified   DEADLINE: None Specified
FIELDS/MAJORS: Agriculture

Discussion contest open to undergraduates in the School of Agriculture. Winning discussions should involve important agricultural issues. Four prizes (awards) offered annually. Sign up for the contest in the Agricultural Economics Department in October and November. GPA must be at least 2.7.

Purdue University-Dept. of Agricultural Economics
Professor Lawrence P. Bohl
Krannert Building, #659
West Lafayette, IN 47907

4254
Farm Credit Services Scholarship

AMOUNT: $1000   DEADLINE: October 1
FIELDS/MAJORS: All Agricultural Programs

Open to sophomores, juniors, and seniors who are Indiana residents and have not won this award previously. Based on academics and evidence of citizenship/leadership. Three awards offered annually. Write to the address below for more information. GPA must be at least 2.7.

Purdue University-School of Agriculture
Thomas W. Atkinson
1140 Agricultural Administration Bldg.
West Lafayette, IN 47907

4255
Gerber Scholarships

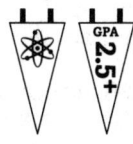

AMOUNT: Maximum: $2500   DEADLINE: February 28
FIELDS/MAJORS: Food Science

Open to high school seniors ranked in the upper half of their graduating class. Must have a minimum SAT score of 1000 or minimum ACT/English/Math scores of 23. Based on academics and extracurricular activities. Two awards offered annually. Contact the address below for further information. GPA must be at least 2.5.

Purdue University-Dept. of Food Science
Jennifer Lawrence
Smith Hall, #127C
West Lafayette, IN 47907

4256
Greiner Scholarships

AMOUNT: $500-$1000   DEADLINE: October 1
FIELDS/MAJORS: Agricultural Engineering

Open to freshmen, sophomores, and juniors in agricultural engineering. Based on academics and financial need. Six or more awards are offered annually. Contact Deb Felix, Room 201, at the address below for further information. GPA must be at least 2.7.

Purdue University-Dept. of Agricultural/Biological Engineering
Professors Gary Krutz, Martin Okos
Agricultural/Biological Engineering, #208
West Lafayette, IN 47907

4257
Hillis D. and M. Wickizer Scholarships

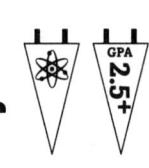

AMOUNT: $2000   DEADLINE: November 1
FIELDS/MAJORS: Agriculture, Related Areas

Open to students enrolled in the School of Agriculture who are residents of Marshall County, Indiana. Preference given to applicants raised on a farm or in a rural atmosphere. Ten awards offered annually. Contact the address below for further information. GPA must be at least 2.5.

Purdue University-School of Agriculture
Thomas W. Atkinson
1140 Agricultural Administration Bldg.
West Lafayette, IN 47907

4258
Indianapolis Landscape Association Scholarship

AMOUNT: Maximum: $1000   DEADLINE: May 15
FIELDS/MAJORS: Horticulture

Open to high school seniors. Based on academics, extracurricular activities, and letters of recommendation. Contact the address below for further information or call (317) 494-1302. GPA must be at least 2.8.

Purdue University-Dept. of Horticulture
Robin Tribbett
Horticulture Bldg., #207-A
West Lafayette, IN 47907

4259
Indiana Society of Farm Managers and Rural Appraisers Scholarship

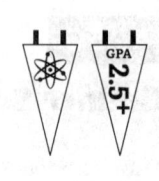

AMOUNT: Maximum: $750   DEADLINE: None Specified
FIELDS/MAJORS: Agricultural Economics

Open to freshmen, sophomores, and juniors. One award based on academics. The other award based on ability to analyze and solve a farm problem. Two awards offered annually. Contact the address below for further information. GPA must be at least 2.7.

Purdue University-Dept. of Agricultural Economics
Professor Lawrence P. Bohl
Krannert Building, #659
West Lafayette, IN 47907

4260
Institute of Food Technologists Freshman Scholarships

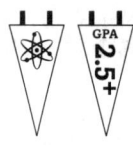

AMOUNT: $750-$1000   DEADLINE: February 15
FIELDS/MAJORS: Food Science

Open to high school seniors enrolling in the Department of Food Science. Previous graduates who are just entering the food science program for a second bachelor's degree are also eligible. Contact the address below for further information. GPA must be at least 2.7.

Purdue University-Dept. of Food Science
Jennifer Lawrence
Smith Hall, #127C
West Lafayette, IN 47907

4261
Jack W. Torr Memorial Scholarship

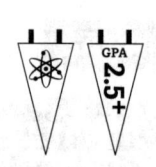

AMOUNT: $500   DEADLINE: August 1
FIELDS/MAJORS: Agriculture, Related Areas

Open to sophomores, juniors, and seniors who are residents of Putnam County, Indiana. Academics, citizenship, and leadership may be considered but are not requirements. One award offered annually. Contact the address below for further information. GPA must be at least 2.7.

Purdue University-School of Agriculture
Thomas W. Atkinson
1140 Agricultural Administration Bldg.
West Lafayette, IN 47907

4262
John F. Benham Citizenship and Leadership Scholarship

AMOUNT: $500   DEADLINE: February 1
FIELDS/MAJORS: Agriculture

Awards open to School of Agriculture seniors who have completed 90 hours of course work (60 taken at a Purdue campus). Must have at least 15 hours remaining and be able to demonstrate financial need. One award offered annually. Write to the address below for more information.

Purdue University-School of Agriculture
Thomas W. Atkinson
1140 Agricultural Administration Bldg.
West Lafayette, IN 47907

4263
John W. Ryan Scholarship

AMOUNT: $800   DEADLINE: December 1
FIELDS/MAJORS: Agriculture, Related Areas

Open to undergraduates who are current members of Purdue Musical Organizations. Based on financial need. One award offered annually. Contact the address below for further information.

Purdue University-School of Agriculture
Thomas W. Atkinson
1140 Agricultural Administration Bldg.
West Lafayette, IN 47907

4264
J.T. Eaton and Company Scholarship

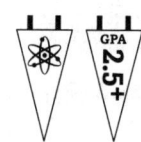

AMOUNT: None Specified DEADLINE: March 31
FIELDS/MAJORS: Entomology

Open to high school seniors who have been admitted to Purdue University. Based on GPA, class rank, SAT scores, and an interest in entomology. One award offered annually. Contact the address below or your Indiana High School counseling office for further information. GPA must be at least 2.7.

Purdue University-Dept. of Entomology
Prof. Gary W. Bennett-Sondra L. Lindsey
Entomology Hall
West Lafayette, IN 47907

4265
Kellogg Food Freshman Engineering Scholarship

AMOUNT: Maximum: $3000 DEADLINE: April 1
FIELDS/MAJORS: Food Science

Open to high school seniors who will be enrolling in the food science program. Based on academics and a well-rounded personality. One award offered annually. Contact Deb Felix, Room 201, Agricultural and Biological Engineering Bldg. GPA must be at least 2.7.

Purdue University-Dept. of Agricultural/Biological
   Engineering
Professors Gary Krutz, Martin Okos
Agricultural/Biological Engineering, #208
West Lafayette, IN 47907

4266
Kraft General Foods Freshman and Kroger Freshman Scholarships

AMOUNT: Maximum: $1000 DEADLINE: February 28
FIELDS/MAJORS: Food Science

Open to high school seniors ranked in the top 10% of their graduating class. Must have a minimum SAT score of 1000 or minimum ACT, English/Math scores of 23. Based on academics and extracurricular activities. One award is offered annually from each of the companies. Contact the address below for further information. GPA must be at least 3.5.

Purdue University-Dept. of Food Science
Jennifer Lawrence
Smith Hall, #127C
West Lafayette, IN 47907

4267
Laurenz Greene Memorial Scholarship

AMOUNT: Maximum: $2500 DEADLINE: April 1
FIELDS/MAJORS: Horticulture

Open to entering freshmen, based on leadership, high school achievements, and SAT scores. Two awards offered annually. Renewable. Contact the address below for further information. GPA must be at least 2.7.

Purdue University-Dept. of Horticulture
Horticulture Student Services Offices
1165 Horticulture Bldg., #207-A
West Lafayette, IN 47907

4268
Mauri Williamson Scholarship for Excellence in Agriculture

AMOUNT: $3000 DEADLINE: March 1
FIELDS/MAJORS: Agriculture, Agricultural/Biological Engineering, Forestry

Open to high school seniors who are U.S. citizens and rank in the top 5% of class. Must have a combined SAT score of at least 1300. One award offered annually. Contact the address below for further information. GPA must be at least 3.6.

Purdue University-School of Agriculture
Thomas W. Atkinson
1140 Agricultural Administration Bldg.
West Lafayette, IN 47907

4269
McCormick Freshman and Universal Flavors Scholarships

AMOUNT: $500-$1000 DEADLINE: February 28
FIELDS/MAJORS: Food Science

Open to high school seniors ranked in the top 10% of their graduating class. Must have a minimum SAT score of 1000 or minimum ACT, English/math scores of 23. Based on academics and extracurricular activities. One award is offered annually from each of the companies. Contact the address below for further information about both awards. GPA must be at least 3.2.

Purdue University-Dept. of Food Science
Jennifer Lawrence
Smith Hall, #127C
West Lafayette, IN 47907

4270
Milk Marketing, Inc. Scholarship

AMOUNT: $1100 DEADLINE: October 1
FIELDS/MAJORS: Animal Science, Agricultural Economics, Food Science, Nutrition

Open to sophomores, juniors, and seniors who have a career interest in the dairy industry. Must have a minimum GPA of 2.5. Two awards offered annually. Contact the address below for further information.

Purdue University-School of Agriculture
Thomas W. Atkinson
1140 Agricultural Administration Bldg.
West Lafayette, IN 47907

4271
Norm Ehmann/Van Waters and Rogers, Pest Control Magazine Scholarships

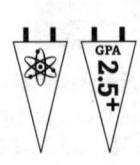

AMOUNT: None Specified DEADLINE: None Specified
FIELDS/MAJORS: Entomology

Open to high school seniors who have been admitted to Purdue University. Based on GPA, class rank, SAT scores, and an interest in entomology. One award from each of the above donors is offered annually. Contact the address below for further information. GPA must be at least 2.7.

Purdue University-Dept. of Entomology
Prof. Gary W. Bennett-Sondra L. Lindsey
Entomology Hall
West Lafayette, IN 47907

4272
North Central Beef Cattle Association Scholarship

AMOUNT: $1000 DEADLINE: November 1
FIELDS/MAJORS: All Agricultural Programs

Open to sophomores, juniors, and seniors with a minimum GPA of 3.0. Must be a resident of any of the following counties in Indiana: Fulton, Laporte, Marshall, Pulaski, St. Joseph, or Starke. Must have a demonstrated interest in the beef industry. One award offered annually. Contact the address below for further information.

Purdue University-School of Agriculture
Thomas W. Atkinson
1140 Agricultural Administration Bldg.
West Lafayette, IN 47907

4273
Pat Baker/Pow Pest Control, Inc. Memorial Scholarship

AMOUNT: None Specified DEADLINE: March 31
FIELDS/MAJORS: Entomology

Open to undergraduates with demonstrated interest in the entomological sciences. Based on positive attitude, academics, interest in entomology, work ethic, and financial need. One award offered annually. Contact the address below for further information. If you are a high school senior in Indiana, get information from your high school counseling office. GPA must be at least 2.7.

Purdue University-Dept. of Entomology
Prof. Gary W. Bennett-Sondra L. Lindsey
Entomology Hall
West Lafayette, IN 47907

4274
Sandage Charitable Trust Scholarship

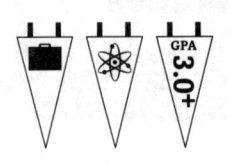

AMOUNT: $500 DEADLINE: June 15
FIELDS/MAJORS: Agricultural Economics, Agronomy, Animal/Food Science, Horticulture

Open to undergraduates with at least 30 credit hours of course work in the School of Agriculture. Must have a minimum GPA of 3.0. Based on activities, experience, creativity, and interest in the business or marketing aspects of agriculture. One award offered annually. Contact the address below for further information.

Purdue University-School of Agriculture
Thomas W. Atkinson
1140 Agricultural Administration Bldg.
West Lafayette, IN 47907

4275
Straszheim Award in Agriculture

AMOUNT: $500 DEADLINE: March 15
FIELDS/MAJORS: Agriculture, Related Areas

Open to high school seniors who rank in the upper 10% of class and are U.S. citizens. Based on academics and participation in school, religious, or community service. One award offered annually. Contact the address below for further information. GPA must be at least 3.5.

Purdue University-School of Agriculture
Thomas W. Atkinson
1140 Agricultural Administration Bldg.
West Lafayette, IN 47907

4276
Eliot Weier Undergraduate Scholarship

AMOUNT: $1000 DEADLINE: None Specified
FIELDS/MAJORS: Botany, Plant Pathology, Plant Science

Open to minority high school seniors. Must have a minimum combined SAT score of 1000 and rank in the top 10% of graduating class. Renewable through school with satisfactory grades. Contact the address below for further information. GPA must be at least 3.5.

Purdue University-Dept. of Botany and Plant Pathology
Professor R.C. Coolbaugh
Lilly Hall of Life Sciences, #I-420
West Lafayette, IN 47907

4277
Terra International, Inc., Scholarships

AMOUNT: $500 DEADLINE: November 1
FIELDS/MAJORS: Agribusiness, Agronomy, Agricultural Systems

Open to juniors and seniors who are U.S. citizens and have a minimum GPA of 3.0. Two awards offered annually. Contact the address below for further information.

Purdue University-School of Agriculture
Thomas W. Atkinson
1140 Agricultural Administration Bldg.
West Lafayette, IN 47907

4278
Willis H. Carrier Graduate Research Fellowship

AMOUNT: Maximum: $20000 DEADLINE: December 1
FIELDS/MAJORS: Research

Open to deserving graduate research students at Purdue University. Contact the address listed for further information. Must have a GPA of at least 3.0.

American Society of Heating, Refrigerating, and
   Air-Conditioning Engineers
Scholarship Program
1791 Tullie Circle NE
Atlanta, GA 30329

4279
Western Termite and Pest Control Scholarship

AMOUNT: None Specified DEADLINE: None Specified
FIELDS/MAJORS: Entomology

Open to Purdue students majoring in entomology. Based on academics, character, financial need, and interest in pursuing a career in the field of entomology. One award is offered annually. Contact the address below for further information. GPA must be at least 2.7.

Purdue University-Dept. of Entomology
Prof. Gary W. Bennett-Sondra L. Lindsey
Entomology Hall
West Lafayette, IN 47907

4280
William and Marilyn McVay Scholarship

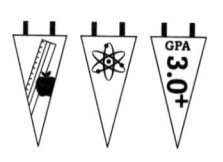

AMOUNT: $750 DEADLINE: March 1
FIELDS/MAJORS: Agriculture and Related Areas

Open to Indiana high school seniors who will be enrolled full-time in the School of Agriculture. Must be in upper third of class and have involvement in agricultural education (FFA). Two awards offered annually. Contact the address below for further information. GPA must be at least 3.0.

Purdue University-School of Agriculture
Thomas W. Atkinson
1140 Agricultural Administration Bldg.
West Lafayette, IN 47907

QUEENS COLLEGE

4281
ASCAP Foundation Louis Armstrong Scholarship

AMOUNT: None Specified DEADLINE: None Specified
FIELDS/MAJORS: Music (composition-jazz)

Annual scholarship for a composition student interested in jazz at Queens College (in the City University of New York). Contact the financial aid office at Queens College. ASCAP does not accept any requests for applications.

RADCLIFFE COLLEGE

4282
Berkshire Summer Fellowship

AMOUNT: Maximum: $3500   DEADLINE: January 15
FIELDS/MAJORS: History

Residential summer fellowships for women historians. Must be in residence for at least one month. For postdoctoral work. Preference given to junior scholars and those who do not normally have access to Boston-area resources. One award is given annually. Write to the address below for details.

Radcliffe College
Mary Ingraham Bunting Institute
34 Concord Ave.
Cambridge, MA 02138

4283
Biomedical Research Fellowship Program

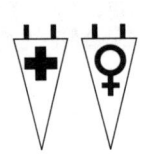

AMOUNT: Maximum: $39700   DEADLINE: October 15
FIELDS/MAJORS: Biomedical Research

Two fellowships are available to women scholars, who have held a Ph.D. for at least two years prior to application, for research in any area of the bio-medical field. Applicant must be a U.S. citizen. Write to the address below for complete details.

Radcliffe College
Mary Ingraham Bunting Institute
34 Concord Ave.
Cambridge, MA 02138

4284
Bunting Fellowship Program

AMOUNT: Maximum: $36500   DEADLINE: October 15
FIELDS/MAJORS: Art, Classics, Drama, Literature

Eight to ten fellowships are available to women scholars and researchers in the fields listed above with a record of significant accomplishments. Applicants must have held a Ph.D. for at least two years prior to application and have had solo exhibits, group shows, published works, etc. Write to the address below for complete details.

Radcliffe College
Mary Ingraham Bunting Institute
34 Concord Ave.
Cambridge, MA 02138

4285
Henry A. Murray Dissertation Award

AMOUNT: Maximum: $2500   DEADLINE: April 1
FIELDS/MAJORS: Social and Behavioral Sciences

Open to doctoral candidates performing dissertation research in the social or behavioral sciences studying individuals in context, in-depth, and across time. Topic should concentrate on issues in human development or personality for populations within the United States. Write to the address below for details.

Radcliffe College
Henry A. Murray Research Center
10 Garden Street
Cambridge, MA 02138

4286
Jeanne Humphrey Block Dissertation Award

AMOUNT: Maximum: $2500   DEADLINE: April 1
FIELDS/MAJORS: Psychology, Sociology, Behavioral Science

Dissertation grant for women doctoral students researching psychological development of women or girls. Proposals should focus on sex and gender differences or some developmental issue of particular concern to women and girls. Must have completed coursework and be current doctoral candidate. Award recipient announced in June. Write to the address below for details.

Radcliffe College
Henry A. Murray Research Center
10 Garden Street
Cambridge, MA 02138

4287
Peace Fellowship

AMOUNT: Maximum: $32000   DEADLINE: January 15
FIELDS/MAJORS: Public Policy, International Peace, Conflict Management

Fellowships are available to women scholars, who have held the Ph.D. prior to application, to support women actively involved in fostering peaceful solutions to conflict among groups or nations. One award is given annually. Write to the address below for complete details.

Radcliffe College
Mary Ingraham Bunting Institute
34 Concord Ave.
Cambridge, MA 02138

4288
Radcliffe Research Grants

AMOUNT: Maximum: $5000   DEADLINE: April 15
FIELDS/MAJORS: History of Women, Human Development

This program offers grants to postdoctoral investigators for research drawing on the center's social science data on human development and social change, particularly the changing life experience of American women. Applicants must already hold a Ph.D. (or other doctoral degree). Applicants will be notified of action on their requests approximately two months after the deadline dates. A second deadline is October 15. Write to the address below for details or call (617) 495-8140.

Radcliffe College
Henry A. Murray Research Center
10 Garden Street
Cambridge, MA 02138

4289
Science Scholars Fellowship Program

AMOUNT: Maximum: $39700
DEADLINE: October 15
FIELDS/MAJORS: See Listing of Fields Below.

Residential fellowship for women who have held a Ph.D. for at least two years. Scholars perform research in a laboratory or with a research group in the Boston area. For study in astronomy, biochemistry, chemistry, computer science, electrical, aerospace, and mechanical engineering, geology, materials science, math, physics, ecology, and evolutionary biology. Must be U.S. citizens. Also for study in molecular and cellular biology, cognitive and neural science, naval architecture, and all fields that relate to the study of oceans. Eight awards are given annually. Write to the address below for complete details.

Radcliffe College
Mary Ingraham Bunting Institute
34 Concord Ave.
Cambridge, MA 02138

RHODE ISLAND COLLEGE

4290
Rhode Island College Americorps Program

AMOUNT: Maximum: $2350   DEADLINE: None Specified
FIELDS/MAJORS: All Areas of Study

Program for undergraduate students at Rhode Island College who are residents of Rhode Island. Non-matriculated students are not eligible to apply. Recipients are provided with living expenses and chosen based on merit. One award is offered annually. Write to the address below for more information.

Rhode Island College
James Hanbury, Director of Financial Aid
600 Mt. Pleasant Ave.
Providence, RI 02908

ROCHESTER INSTITUTE OF TECHNOLOGY

4291
Robert P. Scripps Graphic Arts Grants

AMOUNT: $1000-$3000   DEADLINE: February 25
FIELDS/MAJORS: Graphic Arts (Newspaper Industry)

Awards for full-time undergraduate students majoring in graphic arts as applied to newspaper operations management at Rochester Institute of Technology. Must demonstrate high academic achievement, interest in journalism and graphic arts, and financial need. Renewable. Applicants must be U.S. citizens. Write to the address listed for details. Include a self-addressed mailing label showing the words "Scholarship Application." Also, please state your major and your career goals.

Scripps Howard Foundation
Scholarships Coordinator
PO Box 5380
Cincinnati, OH 45201

ROCKY MOUNTAIN COLLEGE

4292
Academic Scholarships

AMOUNT: $500-$1250   DEADLINE: April 1
FIELDS/MAJORS: All Areas of Study

Awards available to entering or returning students who have demonstrated academic ability. Must have a GPA of at least 3.0. Write to the address below for more information.

Rocky Mountain College
Office of Financial Assistance
1511 Poly Drive
Billings, MT 59102

4293
Art Grants

AMOUNT: None Specified DEADLINE: April 1
FIELDS/MAJORS: Art

Awards available for students at RMC who are studying art. Applicants will be asked to submit a portfolio or slides to the art department. For undergraduate studies. Contact the art department for more information.

Rocky Mountain College
Office of Financial Assistance
1511 Poly Drive
Billings, MT 59102

4294
Equestrian Grants

AMOUNT: None Specified DEADLINE: April 1
FIELDS/MAJORS: Equine Studies

Awards available for students at RMC who are active in equestrian and equine studies. For undergraduate studies. Applicants will need to submit a VHF video of their riding abilities either at home riding or from a horse show. Contact the equestrian department for more information.

Rocky Mountain College
Office of Financial Assistance
1511 Poly Drive
Billings, MT 59102

4295
Girl's State/Boy's State Scholarships

AMOUNT: None Specified DEADLINE: April 1
FIELDS/MAJORS: All Areas of Study

Awards available to entering students at RMC who have a GPA of at least 3.0 and who have been selected as Girl's State or Boy's State delegates. Renewable with satisfactory academic progress. Write to the address below for more information.

Rocky Mountain College
Office of Financial Assistance
1511 Poly Drive
Billings, MT 59102

4296
Matching Fund Scholarship

AMOUNT: Maximum: $500 DEADLINE: June 1
FIELDS/MAJORS: All Areas of Study

RMC will match dollar for dollar the amount that your church commits to fund you (up to $500). A letter from the church stating their commitment to fund you must be submitted to the financial aid office. Write to the address below for more information.

Rocky Mountain College
Office of Financial Assistance
1511 Poly Drive
Billings, MT 59102

4297
RMC Alumni Scholarship

AMOUNT: $500 DEADLINE: April 1
FIELDS/MAJORS: All Areas of Study

Awards available for students at RMC whose parent has also attended RMC for at least one full year. Renewable with satisfactory academic progress. Write to the address below for more information.

Rocky Mountain College
Office of Financial Assistance
1511 Poly Drive
Billings, MT 59102

4298
RMC Athletic Grants

AMOUNT: None Specified DEADLINE: April 1
FIELDS/MAJORS: All Areas of Study

Awards available for students at RMC who are active in athletics. For undergraduate studies. Contact the athletic department or the coach for more information.

Rocky Mountain College
Office of Financial Assistance
1511 Poly Drive
Billings, MT 59102

4299
RMC Forensics Grant

AMOUNT: None Specified DEADLINE: April 1
FIELDS/MAJORS: Forensics

Awards available for undergraduates at RMC who are participating in the forensics program. Contact the office of admissions or the program director to set up an interview or an audition.

Rocky Mountain College
Office of Financial Assistance
1511 Poly Drive
Billings, MT 59102

4300
RMC Honors Scholarships

AMOUNT: $2500 DEADLINE: April 1
FIELDS/MAJORS: All Areas of Study

Awards available to entering freshmen and transfer students at RMC who have a GPA of at least 3.65, an ACT composite of at least 24, or SAT score of at least 1100. Renewable with a GPA of at least 3.5. Write to the address below for more information.

Rocky Mountain College
Office of Financial Assistance
1511 Poly Drive
Billings, MT 59102

4301
RMC Music Grants

AMOUNT: None Specified DEADLINE: April 1
FIELDS/MAJORS: Vocal, Instrumental, Keyboard Music

Awards available for students at RMC who are interested in music. Recipients of vocal grants must enroll in applied music and participate in the choral program at the director's discretion. Contact the office of admissions or the program director to set up an interview or an audition.

Rocky Mountain College
Office of Financial Assistance
1511 Poly Drive
Billings, MT 59102

4302
RMC Theater Arts Grant

AMOUNT: None Specified DEADLINE: April 1
FIELDS/MAJORS: Theater

Awards available for students at RMC who are interested in theater. Recipients must enroll in at least one theater class per year as well as one theater production course per semester. For undergraduate study. Contact the office of admissions or the program director to set up an interview or an audition.

Rocky Mountain College
Office of Financial Assistance
1511 Poly Drive
Billings, MT 59102

4303
Winston Cox Memorial Scholarships

AMOUNT: None Specified DEADLINE: April 1
FIELDS/MAJORS: Business

Awards available to entering or returning students who have a GPA of at least 3.5 and are enrolled in at least one business administration course each semester. Based also on recommendations regarding the applicant's potential in business and on an essay on their career objectives in economics/business administration. Write to the address below for more information.

Rocky Mountain College
Office of Financial Assistance
1511 Poly Drive
Billings, MT 59102

ROSE-HULMAN INSTITUTE OF TECHNOLOGY

4304
Forrest G. Sherer Honorary Scout Scholarship

AMOUNT: $1000 DEADLINE: March 15
FIELDS/MAJORS: Engineering

Scholarships for high school seniors entering Rose-Hulman who have been active in the Wabash Valley Council of the Boy Scouts of America. Four to five awards offered annually. Write to the address below for details.

Rose-Hulman Institute of Technology
5500 Wabash Ave.
Terre Haute, IN 47803

SAN FRANCISCO ART INSTITUTE

4305
San Francisco Art Institute Grants Fund

AMOUNT: None Specified DEADLINE: March 1
FIELDS/MAJORS: All Areas of Study

Scholarships available to students at the Art Institute. Some awards are based on need; some awards on merit. Contact the address below for details.

San Francisco Art Institute
Financial Aid Office
800 Chestnut St.
San Francisco, CA 94133

SAN FRANCISCO CONSERVATORY OF MUSIC

4306
San Francisco Conservatory of Music Scholarship

AMOUNT: $300   DEADLINE: March 1
FIELDS/MAJORS: Music

Scholarships are available to students studying music full-time at San Francisco Conservatory of Music. Write to the address listed for more details.

San Francisco Conservatory of Music
Colin Murdoch, Dean
1201 Ortega St.
San Francisco, CA 94122

SAN FRANCISCO STATE UNIVERSITY

4307
Franam Scholarship for African-American Women

AMOUNT: Maximum: $1500   DEADLINE: May 18
FIELDS/MAJORS: All Areas of Study

Open to entering full-time students and current undergraduate or graduate students who are African-American women attending SFSU at least half-time (full-time preferred). Applicants must have a minimum GPA of 3.5 and demonstrate financial need. Contact the address below for details or call Barbara Hubler at (415) 338-2611.

San Francisco State University
Office of Student Financial Aid
1600 Holloway Ave.
San Francisco, CA 94132

4308
Jacques Johnet Scholarship

AMOUNT: $500-$2000   DEADLINE: September 1
FIELDS/MAJORS: All Areas of Study

Open to full-time undergraduates and graduate students at SFSU who are of Native American heritage. Contact Angela Gonzalez, American Indian Studies Program at (415) 338-2698.

San Francisco State University
Office of Student Financial Aid
1600 Holloway Ave.
San Francisco, CA 94132

4309
Minority Engineering Program Scholarship

AMOUNT: $500-$1000   DEADLINE: April 10
FIELDS/MAJORS: Engineering

Open to entering and current undergraduates at SFSU who are of African-American, Latino, or Native American heritage. Contact the address below for further information or call (415) 338-1328.

San Francisco State University
Richard Gambino, College of Engineering
1600 Holloway Ave.
San Francisco, CA 94132-4011

4310
San Francisco State Future Scholars Scholarship

AMOUNT: Maximum: $1000   DEADLINE: None Specified
FIELDS/MAJORS: All Areas of Study

Open to incoming full-time freshmen, accepted at SFSU, who are California residents and are graduating from California high schools. Applicants must be disadvantaged economically, educationally, and/or environmentally. Call and leave your name and address. Applications will be mailed when available. Rufino de Leon, Jr., Office of Student Financial Aid, (415) 338-2437. GPA must be at least 2.4.

San Francisco State University
Office of Student Financial Aid
1600 Holloway Ave.
San Francisco, CA 94132

4311
San Francisco State Music Scholarship

AMOUNT: $250-$2000   DEADLINE: April 1
FIELDS/MAJORS: Music

Open to entering full-time students and current undergraduates who are music majors at SFSU. Applicants must have a minimum GPA of 3.0. Contact the address below for details or call Mary Grant, Department of Music, at (415) 338-1431.

San Francisco State University
Office of Student Financial Aid
1600 Holloway Ave.
San Francisco, CA 94132

4312
San Francisco State Presidential Scholars Scholarship

AMOUNT: Maximum: $991 DEADLINE: March 14
FIELDS/MAJORS: All Areas of Study

Open to incoming full-time freshmen, accepted at SFSU who have minimum GPA of 3.8. Contact the address below for details or call Gail Whitaker, Presidential Scholars, ADM 447 at (415) 338-2789.

San Francisco State University
Office of Student Financial Aid
1600 Holloway Ave.
San Francisco, CA 94132

4313
San Francisco State University Scholarships

AMOUNT: $300-$2000 DEADLINE: May 10
FIELDS/MAJORS: All Areas of Study

Open to current full-time undergraduates and graduate students at SFSU. Undergraduates must have a minimum GPA of 3.0, and graduates must have at least a 3.5. Applicants must have been enrolled at least half-time in previous semester. Contact the address listed for details or call (415) 337-0200.

San Francisco State University
Office of Student Financial Aid
1600 Holloway Ave.
San Francisco, CA 94132

4314
University Women's Assn. Scholarship for Men and Women

AMOUNT: Maximum: $600 DEADLINE: March 10
FIELDS/MAJORS: All Areas of Study

Open to current undergraduates and graduate students at SFSU who are enrolled at least half-time. Must have been enrolled at least half-time previous semester and have a minimum GPA of 3.0. Contact the address below for details or call (415) 337-0200.

San Francisco State University
Office of Student Financial Aid
1600 Holloway Ave.
San Francisco, CA 94132\

4315
Wallace Diversity Scholarship

AMOUNT: Maximum: $1400 DEADLINE: April 10
FIELDS/MAJORS: Business

Open to incoming and current undergraduates at SFSU who are of African-American, Latino, Native American, or Pacific Islander heritage. Must be enrolled at least half-time and have a minimum GPA of 2.5. Contact the address below for details or call Sharon Collins, College of Business at (415) 338-1276.

San Francisco State University
Office of Student Financial Aid
1600 Holloway Ave.
San Francisco, CA 94132

SAN JOSE STATE UNIVERSITY

4316
Wiggy Sivertsen Scholarship

AMOUNT: Maximum: $750 DEADLINE: None Specified
FIELDS/MAJORS: All Areas of Study

Open to gay and lesbian students or students who have provided service to or worked on behalf of gay and lesbian issues. Must be attending San Jose State at least half-time, be fully matriculated, and be able to demonstrate financial need. May include GPA consideration. Contact the address below for further information.

San Jose State University
Dr. Jill Steinberg, Counseling Center
1 Washington Square
San Jose, CA 95192-0001

SANTA ROSA JUNIOR COLLEGE

4317
Frank P. and Polly O'Meara Doyle Scholarship Program

AMOUNT: $650-$1300 DEADLINE: March 1
FIELDS/MAJORS: All Areas of Study

Applicants must be enrolled at Santa Rosa Junior College. Applications for the Doyle Scholarship Program are made through the registrar of the college. The awards are based on scholastic achievement (GPA), financial need, school activities, and leadership ability. Contact the Scholarship Resource Center at the address below for details. The SRC also has information on other, private scholarships. In all, the University administers more than 2,500 scholarships annually valued between $100 and $2000 (average $600).

Santa Rosa Junior College
Scholarship Resource Center
1501 Mendocino Ave.
Santa Rosa, CA 95401

4318
SRJC Continuing Student Scholarships

AMOUNT: None Specified DEADLINE: March 1
FIELDS/MAJORS: All Areas of Study

More than two hundred scholarships for continuing students at Santa Rosa Junior College. Applicants should have a GPA of at least 2.5 and some amount of financial need. Contact the Scholarship Resource Center for more information on these and other private scholarships administered by SRJC (over 2,500 awards administered each year).

Santa Rosa Junior College
Scholarship Resource Center
1501 Mendocino Ave.
Santa Rosa, CA 95401

4319
Transferring Students Scholarships at SRJC

AMOUNT: None Specified DEADLINE: March 1
FIELDS/MAJORS: All Areas of Study

150 scholarships for students attending Santa Rosa Junior College who will be transferring to four-year institutions. Minimum GPA of at least 3.0. Contact the scholarship resource center for more information on these and other private scholarships administered by SRJC (over 2,500 awards administered each year).

Santa Rosa Junior College
Scholarship Resource Center
1501 Mendocino Ave.
Santa Rosa, CA 95401

SAVANNAH COLLEGE OF ART AND DESIGN

4320
Elizabeth Cooksey Williams Scholarship

AMOUNT: Maximum: $10000 DEADLINE: March 1
FIELDS/MAJORS: All Areas of Study

Scholarships for students at Savannah College of Art and Design who were National Merit Scholarship finalists. Write to the address below for details.

Savannah College of Art and Design
342 Bull St.
PO Box 3146
Savannah, GA 31402

SCHOOLCRAFT COLLEGE

4321
Foundation Scholarships

AMOUNT: $100-$2000 DEADLINE: June 15
FIELDS/MAJORS: All Areas of Study

Scholarships are administered through the financial aid office at Schoolcraft College are available to all students at the College. Contact the financial aid office at the address below for details.

Schoolcraft College
Financial Aid Office
18600 Haggerty Rd.
Livonia, MI 48152

SCHOOL OF VISUAL ARTS

4322
Scholastic Art Awards for Freshmen

AMOUNT: Maximum: $6500 DEADLINE: December 19
FIELDS/MAJORS: Photography

Scholarships available to incoming freshmen. Based on outstanding achievement and financial need. Winners chosen during the second week in May from candidates selected by the Scholastic Art Awards jury. Write to the address below for details. GPA must be at least 3.0.

School of Visual Arts
Office of Admissions
209 East 23rd Street
New York, NY 10010

4323
Silas H. Rhodes Scholarships

AMOUNT: Maximum: $6500 DEADLINE: December 19
FIELDS/MAJORS: All Areas of Study

Scholarships available to incoming freshmen and transfer students with a minimum GPA of 3.0. Recipient freshmen may renew if the GPA of 3.0 is maintained. Recipient transfer students may also renew if they maintain a GPA based on the GPA they had when transferred. Based on portfolio review and short essay (based on essay alone for film applicants). Write to the address below for details.

School of Visual Arts
Office of Admissions
209 East 23rd Street
New York, NY 10010

SCHREINER COLLEGE

4324

Tuition Equalization Grant

AMOUNT: $2800-$2834 DEADLINE: None Specified
FIELDS/MAJORS: All Areas of Study

Grant for students enrolled at least half-time at Schreiner who can demonstrate financial need. Recipients of athletic grants or those pursuing theology or vocational nursing degrees are not eligible. Must be a resident of Texas. 160 awards are given annually. Write to the address below for more information.

Schreiner College
Financial Aid Office
Kerrville, TX 78028

SILVER LAKE COLLEGE

4325

Presidential Honor Scholarship

AMOUNT: Maximum: $2000 DEADLINE: April 15
FIELDS/MAJORS: All Areas of Study

Scholarships available for new full-time undergraduates who live on campus. Must have a minimum GPA of 3.5 and be accepted to Silver Lake College. Must demonstrate involvement in extracurricular and community activities. Write to the address below for further information.

Silver Lake College
Student Financial Aid Office
2406 S. Alverno Rd.
Manitowoc, WI 54220

4326

Presidential Scholarship

AMOUNT: Maximum: $1200 DEADLINE: April 15
FIELDS/MAJORS: All Areas of Study

Scholarships for new full-time students accepted at Silver Lake College. Must have a minimum GPA of 3.0 and live on campus. Must also demonstrate extracurricular and community activities. Write to the address below for further information.

Silver Lake College
Student Financial Aid Office
2406 S. Alverno Rd.
Manitowoc, WI 54220

SMITH CHAPEL BIBLE COLLEGE

4327

Doctoral Teaching Scholarships

AMOUNT: $2538-$32486 DEADLINE: December 16
FIELDS/MAJORS: Ministry, Christian Education, Missionary

Open to doctoral applicants interested in earning a D.Min., Th.D., or Ph.D. Must be Christian leaders residing in the U.S. or Canada, who are being led by the Holy Spirit to enroll in Smith Chapel Bible College for the purpose of earning a doctoral degree (2 Timothy 2:15-16). Also open to senior pastors, ministers of Christian education, or other denominational leaders able to demonstrate exceptional merit, competence, and leadership potential in their church, community, organization, or profession. Additional deadline dates are: May 12 for summer semester and August 11 for fall semester. Contact the address below for further information.

Smith Chapel Bible College
Dr. Abe Johnson, Th.D.
242 Lafayette Circle
Tallahassee, FL 32303

SOUTH DAKOTA STATE UNIVERSITY

4328
Arthur H. Davis Scholarships

AMOUNT: Maximum: $1000 DEADLINE: None Specified
FIELDS/MAJORS: All Areas of Study

Open to incoming freshmen admitted to SDSU who are residents of Butte, Harding, or Lawrence counties. Applicants must demonstrate academic excellence and must have been active in their schools and communities. Students planning to attend SDSU West River Nursing Degree Program are eligible, as well as the Brookings campus attendees. Contact your high school guidance counselor, the address below, or call (605) 688-4121 for further information. GPA must be at least 2.9.

South Dakota State University
Office of Admissions
PO Box 2201
Brookings, SD 57007

SOUTHEASTERN ILLINOIS COLLEGE

4329
Performance and Private Endowed Scholarships

AMOUNT: None Specified
DEADLINE: February 1
FIELDS/MAJORS: All Areas of Study

Scholarships for students at Southeastern Illinois College. Performance scholarships are based on excellence in one of the areas of academics, speech, music, art, and athletics. Private scholarships are based on criteria determined by the sponsors of the awards. A second deadline date is September 1 for the spring term. There are sixty private scholarship sponsors. Contact the financial aid office for details. Must have a GPA of at least 2.5.

Southeastern Illinois College
Financial Aid Office
RR 4, Box 510
Harrisburg, IL 62946

SOUTHERN ILLINOIS UNIVERSITY

4330
Morris Doctoral Fellowship Program

AMOUNT: Maximum: $15000 DEADLINE: January 16
FIELDS/MAJORS: Most Areas of Study

Fellowships are available at SIU for graduate students pursuing a doctorate in one of several areas. Write to the address below for information.

Southern Illinois University, Carbondale
Morris Doctoral Fellowship Program
Dean of the Grad. School, Mailcode 4716
Carbondale, IL 62901

4331
SIUC Valedictorian/ Salutatorian Award

AMOUNT: Maximum: $750 DEADLINE: February 1
FIELDS/MAJORS: All Areas of Study

Open to incoming freshmen who were named valedictorian or salutatorian of an Illinois high school. Must have admission application, academic application, and a letter from high school guidance counselor or principal verifying valedictorian or salutatorian status on file at SIUC. Write to the address below for application.

Southern Illinois University, Carbondale
Terri Williams, New Student Admissions
Mailcode 4710
Carbondale, IL 62901-4710

4332
SIU Academic Scholarship Awards and Grants

AMOUNT: $560-$1125 DEADLINE: February 1
FIELDS/MAJORS: All Areas of Study

Open to incoming freshmen who are in top 10% of high school class. To remain eligible for sophomore through senior years, recipients must maintain full-time enrollment with a minimum GPA of 3.25. Contact the address below for further information.

Southern Illinois University, Carbondale
Terri Williams, New Student Admissions
Mailcode 4710
Carbondale, IL 62901

4333
SIU Foundation Merit Award

AMOUNT: $500-$1000 DEADLINE: February 1
FIELDS/MAJORS: All Areas of Study

High school students who are finalists or semi-finalists in the National Merit Scholarship Program may apply. Admission and academic scholarship application must be on file at the University at Carbondale. To remain eligible for the sophomore through senior years, recipients must remain full-time with a minimum GPA of 3.25. Write to the address below for application.

Southern Illinois University, Carbondale
Terri Williams, New Student Admissions
Mailcode 4710
Carbondale, IL 62901-4710

4334
SIU Multicultural Academic and Grant Awards

AMOUNT: $500-$1000 DEADLINE: February 1
FIELDS/MAJORS: All Areas of Study

Open to African-American and Hispanic-American high school seniors who rank in the top 10% of graduating class. To remain eligible for sophomore through senior years, recipients must maintain full-time enrollment with a minimum GPA of 3.25. Write to the address below for further information.

Southern Illinois University, Carbondale
Terri Williams, New Student Admissions
Mailcode 4710
Carbondale, IL 62901-4710

4335
SIU Multicultural Chancellor's Scholar Award

AMOUNT: $500-$1000 DEADLINE: February 1
FIELDS/MAJORS: All Areas of Study

Open to African-American and Hispanic-American high school seniors who rank in the top 2% of class. To remain eligible for sophomore through senior years, recipients must maintain full-time enrollment and a minimum GPA of 3.5. Write to the address below for further information.

Southern Illinois University, Carbondale
Terri Williams, New Student Admissions
Mailcode 4710
Carbondale, IL 62901-4710

4336
SIU Multicultural Foundation Merit Award

AMOUNT: $500-$1000 DEADLINE: February 1
FIELDS/MAJORS: All Areas of Study

Open to African-American and Hispanic-American high school seniors who have been named semi-finalists or finalists in the National Achievement Scholarship Program for Outstanding Negro Students or in the National Hispanic Scholarship Program. To remain eligible for sophomore through senior years, recipients must maintain full-time enrollment with a minimum GPA of 3.25. Write to the address below for further information.

Southern Illinois University, Carbondale
Terri Williams, New Student Admissions
Mailcode 4710
Carbondale, IL 62901-4710

SOUTHERN OREGON UNIVERSITY

4337
Smullin Scholarships

AMOUNT: Maximum: $1000 DEADLINE: March 1
FIELDS/MAJORS: All Areas of Study

Open to admitted incoming freshmen and current full-time students at SOU. Applicants must be graduating (have graduated) from any high school in the following counties: Lane, Coos, Crook, Curry, Deschutes, Douglas, Jackson, Josephine, Klamath, Lake, and Wallowa. Recipients must maintain a minimum GPA of 2.5. Contact the address below for further information or call (541) 552-6163.

Southern Oregon University, Ashland
Office of Financial Aid
1290 Siskiyou Blvd.
Ashland, OR 97520

SOUTHWEST MISSOURI STATE UNIVERSITY

4338
Anna L. Blair Scholarship

AMOUNT: Maximum: $3200 DEADLINE: March 31
FIELDS/MAJORS: Modern, Classical Languages

Open to full-time students in modern and classical languages who can demonstrate academic excellence. Preference given to a U.S. citizen. Contact the address below for more information. GPA must be at least 3.1.

Southwest Missouri State University
Office of Financial Aid
901 S. National Ave.
Springfield, MO 65804

4339
Army ROTC Scholarship

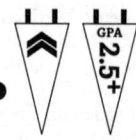

AMOUNT: Maximum: $12000   DEADLINE: None Specified
FIELDS/MAJORS: Military Science

Open to full-time students with a GPA of 2.5 or better. Students must pass a physical fitness test, a written test, and a free physical exam given by a local doctor. Recipients who accept two-, three-, or four-year scholarships will be trained to receive a commission as Second Lieutenants in the regular U.S. Army, Army Reserve, or Army National Guard. Contact the Military Science Department for more information. If you are a high school senior, contact your high school guidance counselor.

Southwest Missouri State University
Office of Financial Aid
901 South National Ave.
Springfield, MO 65804

4340
C. Louis and Thelma Ferrell Van Buren Scholarship

AMOUNT: Maximum: $2050   DEADLINE: None Specified
FIELDS/MAJORS: Science

Student must be a full-time junior or senior enrolled in the College of Natural and Applied Sciences with a GPA of 3.0 or better. Recipient should participate in extracurricular activities. Contact the College of Natural and Applied Sciences for more information.

Southwest Missouri State University
Office of Financial Aid
901 South National Ave.
Springfield, MO 65804

4341
Curl Scholarship

AMOUNT: $2500   DEADLINE: None Specified
FIELDS/MAJORS: Political Science

Student must be a full-time junior or senior political science major enrolled in at least 12 hours of political science. Must have a GPA of 3.0 overall and a GPA of 3.5 in political science. Preference is given to a student from southwest Missouri with a rural background. Contact the Political Science Department for more information.

Southwest Missouri State University
Office of Financial Aid
901 South National Ave.
Springfield, MO 65804

4342
E.R. Smith Scholarships

AMOUNT: Maximum: $2000   DEADLINE: None Specified
FIELDS/MAJORS: All Areas of Study

Open to full-time entering freshmen from Dadeville High School with financial need. Recipient must maintain satisfactory academic progress to renew. Contact the high school counselor for further information.

Southwest Missouri State University
Office of Financial Aid
901 South National Ave.
Springfield, MO 65804

4343
Florence C. Painter Memorial Scholarships

AMOUNT: Maximum: $2500   DEADLINE: March 31
FIELDS/MAJORS: Secondary Education, Spanish

Awards for full-time juniors or seniors with preference given to those planning to teach Spanish. Must have a GPA of 3.0 or better and financial need. Contact the Foreign Languages Department for more information.

Southwest Missouri State University
Office of Financial Aid
901 South National Ave.
Springfield, MO 65804

4344
Forensics Scholarship

AMOUNT: Maximum: $2000   DEADLINE: March 31
FIELDS/MAJORS: Forensics

Awards for students who show promise for achievement in a prominent national debate program. Contact the Communications Department for more information.

Southwest Missouri State University
Office of Financial Aid
901 South National Ave.
Springfield, MO 65804

4345
Future Farmers of America Scholarship

AMOUNT: $2000   DEADLINE: None Specified
FIELDS/MAJORS: Agriculture

Student must be an entering freshman who has placed among the top ten in the southwest Missouri district FFA contest. Contact the Agriculture Department for more information. GPA must be at least 3.6.

Southwest Missouri State University
Office of Financial Aid
901 South National Ave.
Springfield, MO 65804

4346
George H. Klinkerfuss Scholarship

AMOUNT: Maximum: $2500   DEADLINE: March 31
FIELDS/MAJORS: Music, String

Open to full-time entering freshmen music majors. Selected by the string faculty. Contact the Music Department for more information.

Southwest Missouri State University
Office of Financial Aid
901 South National Ave.
Springfield, MO 65804

4347
In-School Players Scholarship

AMOUNT: Maximum: $2000   DEADLINE: March 31
FIELDS/MAJORS: Acting, Music

Open to full-time students having experience in singing and music. Six awards are offered annually. Contact the Theater and Dance Department for more information.

Southwest Missouri State University
Office of Financial Aid
901 South National Ave.
Springfield, MO 65804

4348
Jean Freeman Memorial Scholarship

AMOUNT: $3400   DEADLINE: March 31
FIELDS/MAJORS: All Areas of Study

Student must be a full-time entering freshman from the Ozarks region with a GPA of 2.0 or better. Additional criteria include character, citizenship, potential, and financial need. Preference is given to minority students. Two awards are offered annually. Recipient must complete 24 hours each year with a minimum 2.2 cumulative GPA to renew. Write to the address below for more information.

Southwest Missouri State University
Office of Financial Aid
901 South National Ave.
Springfield, MO 65804

4349
Junior Academy of Science Scholarship

AMOUNT: $2000   DEADLINE: None Specified
FIELDS/MAJORS: Science

Student must receive a number one rating in the district Junior Academy of Science competition. Based on class rank, test scores, and quality of the of the paper presented. Contact the College of Natural and Applied Sciences for more information. GPA must be at least 3.8.

Southwest Missouri State University
Office of Financial Aid
901 South National Ave.
Springfield, MO 65804

4350
Lucy E. Smith Scholarship

AMOUNT: Maximum: $2000   DEADLINE: None Specified
FIELDS/MAJORS: All Areas of Study

Open to full-time entering freshmen from Greenfield High School with financial need. Recipient must maintain satisfactory academic progress to renew. Contact the high school counselor for further information.

Southwest Missouri State University
Office of Financial Aid
901 South National Ave.
Springfield, MO 65804

4351
Madalene Robertson Boritzki Scholarship

AMOUNT: Maximum: $2100   DEADLINE: None Specified
FIELDS/MAJORS: All Areas of Study

Open to seniors planning to attend graduate school with a minimum GPA of 3.5. Must be a member of the Honors College. Contact the Honors College, University Hall, Room 115 or call (417) 836-5872.

Southwest Missouri State University
Office of Financial Aid
901 South National Ave.
Springfield, MO 65804

4352
Marguerite Ross Barnett Memorial Scholarship

AMOUNT: None Specified DEADLINE: None Specified
FIELDS/MAJORS: All Areas of Study

State funded program for undergraduates who are enrolled part-time (6-11 hours) and are employed at least twenty hours per week. Must be able to demonstrate financial need. Contact the address listed for further information.

Southwest Missouri State University
Financial Aid Office
901 South National Ave.
Springfield, MO 65804

4353
Out of State Fee Stipend

AMOUNT: Maximum: $2000 DEADLINE: March 1
FIELDS/MAJORS: All Areas of Study

Open to entering students classified as non-residents. Entering freshmen must have a minimum GPA of 3.25 or rank in the upper one-third of class and score at least a 23 on the ACT. Transfer students must have completed at least 24 hours with a minimum GPA of 3.25. Contact the address below for further information.

Southwest Missouri State University
Financial Aid Office
901 South National Ave.
Springfield, MO 65804

4354
Paul D. and Marian F. Minick Scholarship

AMOUNT: Maximum: $2325 DEADLINE: March 31
FIELDS/MAJORS: All Areas of Study

Student must graduate in the top 15% of their high school class and have a GPA of 3.0 or better. Must be able to demonstrate financial need. Recipient must complete 24 hours each year with a minimum cumulative GPA of 3.0 to renew. Two awards are offered annually. Write to the address below for more information.

Southwest Missouri State University
Office of Financial Aid
901 South National Ave.
Springfield, MO 65804

4355
Phi Theta Kappa Scholarship

AMOUNT: Maximum: $2000 DEADLINE: March 31
FIELDS/MAJORS: All Areas of Study

Open to entering students who are current members of Phi Theta Kappa. Automatically renewed for students who complete 30 hours at SMSU with a minimum GPA of 3.25. Contact the address below for further information.

Southwest Missouri State University
Financial Aid Office
901 South National Ave.
Springfield, MO 65804

4356
Ralph and Elva Harmon Scholarship

AMOUNT: Maximum: $2000
DEADLINE: March 31
FIELDS/MAJORS: Humanities, Arts and Letters, Public Affairs

Student must be a full-time upperclassman majoring in a department within the College of Arts and Letters or the College of Humanities and Public Affairs. Must have a GPA of 3.0 or better and be able to demonstrate financial need. Write to the address below for more information.

Southwest Missouri State University
Office of Financial Aid
901 South National Ave.
Springfield, MO 65804

4357
Ray and Susie Forsythe Scholarship

AMOUNT: $2000 DEADLINE: February 7
FIELDS/MAJORS: Business

Student must be a junior or senior COBA major with leadership characteristics and a GPA of 3.3 or better. Preference is given to SMSU varsity athletes, one being a graduate of Springfield Public Schools. Contact the COBA office for more information.

Southwest Missouri State University
Office of Financial Aid
901 South National Ave.
Springfield, MO 65804

4358
Student Government Association Scholarship

AMOUNT: Maximum: $2000 DEADLINE: March 31
FIELDS/MAJORS: All Areas of Study

Open to full-time students who have completed at lest 12 hours at SMSU with a minimum GPA of 3.0. Must hold an elected or appointed position in SGA, an SGA committee, or other recognized campus organization. Contact the address below for further information.

Southwest Missouri State University
Office of Financial Aid
901 South National Ave.
Springfield, MO 65804

4359
Theater and Dance Activity Scholarship

AMOUNT: Maximum: $2000   DEADLINE: None Specified
FIELDS/MAJORS: Acting, Theater Technician, Dance, Performance Studies

Open to full-time students with outstanding ability to demonstrate acting, performance studies, technical theater, and dance. New students must present a performance audition or technical interview. A videotape may be substituted for the on-site audition. Contact the Theater and Dance Department for more information.

Southwest Missouri State University
Office of Financial Aid
901 South National Ave.
Springfield, MO 65804

SOUTHWEST TEXAS STATE UNIVERSITY

4360
LBJ Achievement Scholarships

AMOUNT: Maximum: $2000   DEADLINE: February 1
FIELDS/MAJORS: All Areas of Study

Open to full-time freshmen (less than 30 credit hours) living on campus. Must have been in the top 25% of senior class. Renewable for second year by maintaining a minimum GPA of 3.0. Also must be a prior Upward Bound, Talent Search, Educational Opportunity Center participant or a past or current migrant/seasonal farm worker. Non-Texas students who receive this award may be eligible to pay resident tuition. Write to the address below for details.

Southwest Texas State University
Scholarship Coordinator
601 University Dr. J.C. Kellam Bldg.
San Marcos, TX 78666-4602

4361
Louise Lindsey Merrick Scholarships

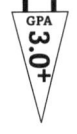

AMOUNT: $1000-$3000   DEADLINE: February 1
FIELDS/MAJORS: All Areas of Study

Open to academically talented high school seniors and junior college transfer students. Traditionally, high school seniors must have a minimum ACT score of 28 or SAT score of 1260. Transfer students must have a minimum GPA of 3.25 to apply. Renewable with a minimum GPA of 3.25. Non-Texas residents who receive this award may be eligible to pay resident tuition. Write to the address below for details.

Southwest Texas State University
Scholarship Coordinator
601 University Dr. J.C. Kellam Bldg.
San Marcos, TX 78666-4602

4362
MLK-Rivera Scholarships

AMOUNT: $1500-$2000   DEADLINE: February 1
FIELDS/MAJORS: All Areas of Study

Open to graduate and transfer students who are Texas residents with financial need. Must be prior Upward Bound, Talent Search, TRIO, free school lunch participant or a migrant/seasonal farm worker. Graduates must have obtained undergraduate degree from SWT with a minimum GPA of 3.0. Undergraduate transfer students must be continuously enrolled in a minimum of 12 semester hours. Write to the address below for details.

Southwest Texas State University
Scholarship Coordinator
601 University Dr. J.C. Kellam Bldg.
San Marcos, TX 78666-4602

4363
New Braunfels Junior Chamber of Commerce Scholarships

AMOUNT: Maximum: $1000   DEADLINE: February 1
FIELDS/MAJORS: All Areas of Study

Open to New Braunfels residents who demonstrate financial need, with preference given to graduates of Comal County high schools. Preference also given to New Braunfels Jaycees or the children of members, past or present. Priority given to non-freshmen. Applicants must be enrolled full-time with a minimum GPA of 3.0. Write to the address below for details.

Southwest Texas State University
Scholarship Coordinator
601 University Dr. J.C. Kellam Bldg.
San Marcos, TX 78666-4602

4364
President's Endowed Scholarships

AMOUNT: $1000   DEADLINE: February 1
FIELDS/MAJORS: All Areas of Study

Open to high school seniors who have been accepted/enrolled at SWT and rank in the upper quarter of class. Renewable with a minimum GPA of 3.25. Non-Texas residents who receive this award may be eligible to pay resident tuition. Write to the address below for details.

Southwest Texas State University
Scholarship Coordinator
601 University Dr. J.C. Kellam Bldg.
San Marcos, TX 78666-4602

4365
Roy F. and Joann C. Mitte Foundation Scholarships

AMOUNT: $5000 DEADLINE: February 1
FIELDS/MAJORS: All Areas of Study

Open to first-time freshmen who are minimally a commended, semi-finalist, or finalist in the National Merit competition, a valedictorian, salutatorian, or in the top 5% of graduating class. All scholarship applicants must provide a resume and essay. Non-Texas residents who receive this scholarship may be eligible to pay resident tuition. Scholarship may be renewable. Write to the address below for details. GPA must be at least 3.7.

Southwest Texas State University
Scholarship Coordinator
601 University Dr. J.C. Kellam Bldg.
San Marcos, TX 78666-4602

4366
University Scholars Scholarships

AMOUNT: $2100 DEADLINE: February 1
FIELDS/MAJORS: All Areas of Study

Open to high school seniors with a minimum ACT score of 27 and SAT of 1230. Selections based on GPA/ACT/SAT scores. A personal interview with school selection committee is required. Scholarships awarded by each of the University's seven undergraduate schools and the College of General Studies. Renewable up to three years. Non-Texas residents who receive this scholarship may be eligible to pay resident tuition. Write to the address below for details. GPA must be at least 3.4.

Southwest Texas State University
Scholarship Coordinator
601 University Dr. J.C. Kellam Bldg.
San Marcos, TX 78666-4602

SOUTHWESTERN OKLAHOMA STATE UNIVERSITY

4367
Distinguished Freshman

AMOUNT: None Specified DEADLINE: March 1
FIELDS/MAJORS: All Areas of Study

Applicants must be first-time entering freshmen who are residents of Oklahoma. Based on high academics. Award is 16 hours paid tuition per semester. Write to the address below for more information. GPA must be at least 3.0.

Southwestern Oklahoma State University
Student Financial Services Office
100 Campus Dr.
Weatherford, OK 73096

4368
Regent's Baccalaureate Scholarship

AMOUNT: None Specified DEADLINE: March 1
FIELDS/MAJORS: All Areas of Study

For incoming freshmen who are residents of Oklahoma. Must have a minimum ACT score of 30, be a National Merit semi-finalist or commended student or a National Achievement semi-finalist or commended student. Awards are tuition, room, and $3000 per year. Renewable if recipients maintain a minimum GPA of 3.25 and complete at least 24 credit hours per year. Write to the address below for more information.

Southwestern Oklahoma State University
Student Financial Services Office
100 Campus Dr.
Weatherford, OK 73096

4369
Salutatorian Scholarship

AMOUNT: Maximum: $300 DEADLINE: March 1
FIELDS/MAJORS: All Areas of Study

Applicant must be a first-time entering freshman residing in Oklahoma. Must be salutatorian of graduating class. Write to the address below for more information.

Southwestern Oklahoma State University
Student Financial Services Office
100 Campus Dr.
Weatherford, OK 73096

4370
Southwestern Scholar

AMOUNT: None Specified DEADLINE: March 1
FIELDS/MAJORS: All Areas of Study

Applicants must be first-time entering freshman residents of Oklahoma. Based on high academics. Award is 12 hours paid tuition per semester. Write to the address below for more information. GPA must be at least 3.0.

Southwestern Oklahoma State University
Student Financial Services Office
100 Campus Dr.
Weatherford, OK 73096

4371
University Scholar

AMOUNT: None Specified DEADLINE: March 1
FIELDS/MAJORS: All Areas of Study

Applicant must be a first-time entering freshman residing in Oklahoma. Must have a GPA of 3.5 or better. Scholarships are renewable. Award is 16 hours paid tuition and fees per semester. Write to the address below for more information.

Southwestern Oklahoma State University
Student Financial Service Office
100 Campus Dr.
Weatherford, OK 73096

4372
Upperclassman Fee Waiver

AMOUNT: None Specified DEADLINE: May 1
FIELDS/MAJORS: All Areas of Study

Applicants can be full-time or part-time undergraduate or graduate students. Must have a GPA of 2.7 or better and be an active member of a university club or organization. Transfer students are welcome to apply. Write to the address below for more information.

Southwestern Oklahoma State University
Student Financial Services Office
100 Campus Dr
Weatherford, OK 73096

4373
Valedictorian Scholarship

AMOUNT: Maximum: $800 DEADLINE: March 1
FIELDS/MAJORS: All Areas of Study

Applicant must be a first-time entering freshman residing in Oklahoma. Must be valedictorian of graduating class. Write to the address below for more information.

Southwestern Oklahoma State University
Student Financial Services Office
100 Campus Dr.
Weatherford, OK 73096

SOUTHWESTERN UNIVERSITY

4374
Beneficiary Grants

AMOUNT: Maximum: $3000 DEADLINE: February 1
FIELDS/MAJORS: All Areas of Study

Open to dependents of United Methodist clergy. Grants are renewable annually if recipients maintain preset standards. Contact the address below for further information.

Southwestern University
Office of Admissions
PO Box 770
Georgetown, TX 78627-0770

4375
Brown Scholar Awards

AMOUNT: $12700 DEADLINE: February 1
FIELDS/MAJORS: All Areas of Study

Awards for high school seniors who rank in the top 5% of their high school class and have at least a 3.7 GPA. Applicants must score at least a 1400 on the SAT and a 32 on the ACT. Finalists will be invited to campus to interview and compete for the award in March. Renewable. Write to the address below for more information.

Southwestern University
Admissions Office
Georgetown, TX 78626

4376
Fine Arts Scholarships and Performance Grants

AMOUNT: $500-$3000 DEADLINE: February 1
FIELDS/MAJORS: Vocal/Instrumental Music, Theater, Art

Open to Southwestern University students majoring in the fields listed above. The awards are renewable. Auditions or portfolio reviews are required. Contact the School of Fine Arts at the address below.

Southwestern University
Office of Admission
PO Box 770
Georgetown, TX 78627-0770

4377
National Achievement Awards

AMOUNT: $7500 DEADLINE: February 1
FIELDS/MAJORS: All Areas of Study

Awards for students who are named semi-finalists in the National Achievement Award Competition. Renewable. Write to the address below for more information.

Southwestern University
Admissions Office
Georgetown, TX 78626

4378
National Hispanic Scholar Awards

AMOUNT: $7500 DEADLINE: February 1
FIELDS/MAJORS: All Areas of Study

Awards for students who are named scholars in the National Hispanic Scholar Recognition Program (NHSRP). Renewable. Write to the address below for more information.

Southwestern University
Admissions Office
Georgetown, TX 78626

4379
National Merit Awards

AMOUNT: Maximum: $7500 DEADLINE: February 1
FIELDS/MAJORS: All Areas of Study

Awards for students who are named finalists in the National Merit Competition and name Southwestern as their first college choice. Renewable. Write to the address below for more information.

Southwestern University
Admissions Office
Georgetown, TX 78626

4380
Presidential Scholar Awards

AMOUNT: Maximum: $10000 DEADLINE: February 1
FIELDS/MAJORS: All Areas of Study

Awards for high school seniors who rank in the top 10% of their class and have at least a 3.7 GPA. Applicants must score at least 1350 on the SAT or a 31 on the ACT. Renewable up to four years. Write to the address below for more information.

Southwestern University
Admissions Office
Georgetown, TX 78626

SPALDING UNIVERSITY

4381
Artistic Grants

AMOUNT: $1000-$2500 DEADLINE: December 1
FIELDS/MAJORS: Art, Creative Writing, Theater

Awarded to students who display outstanding talent in the areas of art, creative writing, or theater. Write to the address below for more information.

Spalding University
Financial Aid Office
851 S. Fourth St.
Louisville, KY 40203

4382
Athletic Grants

AMOUNT: None Specified DEADLINE: December 1
FIELDS/MAJORS: Basketball, Soccer, Volleyball

Awards to men and women in basketball and soccer and to women in volleyball. Contact the Athletic Department or respective coach in the area of interest for more information.

Spalding University
Financial Aid Office
851 S. Fourth St.
Louisville, KY 40203

4383
Gretchen Koo Scholarship

AMOUNT: None Specified DEADLINE: December 1
FIELDS/MAJORS: All Areas of Study

Awarded to a student showing dedication to scholarship and humanitarian and Christian ideals. Write to the address below for more information.

Spalding University
Financial Aid Office
851 S. Fourth St.
Louisville, KY 40203

4384
Honor Scholarship

AMOUNT: Maximum: $4200   DEADLINE: July 1
FIELDS/MAJORS: All Areas of Study

Awards for Spalding undergraduates based on academics and recommendations. Must have a GPA of at least 3.0, average recipient has a GPA of 3.5. Write to the address below for more details.

Spalding University
Financial Aid Office
851 S. Fourth St.
Louisville, KY 40203

4385
J.E. Jinks Scholarship and Anne Gordon Brigham Scholarship

AMOUNT: None Specified   DEADLINE: December 1
FIELDS/MAJORS: Social Work

Scholarship awarded to a social work major selected by departmental faculty. Write to the address below for more information.

Spalding University
Financial Aid Office
851 S. Fourth St.
Louisville, KY 40203

4386
Joseph and Elizabeth Reilly Scholarships and Elizabeth Marcil Scholarships

AMOUNT: None Specified   DEADLINE: December 1
FIELDS/MAJORS: Nursing

Awarded to junior or senior nursing majors. Write to the address below for more information.

Spalding University
Financial Aid Office
851 S. Fourth St.
Louisville, KY 40203

4387
Maddalena and Joseph Perrella Scholarship

AMOUNT: None Specified   DEADLINE: December 1
FIELDS/MAJORS: All Areas of Study

Scholarship awarded to an eligible student of Italian heritage. Write to the address below for more information.

Spalding University
Financial Aid Office
851 S. Fourth St.
Louisville, KY 40203

4388
Medgar Evers/James Chaney Scholarships

AMOUNT: None Specified   DEADLINE: December 1
FIELDS/MAJORS: All Areas of Study

Awarded for two years in alternating years to minority students with high academic achievement from high school. Write to the address below for more information.

Spalding University
Financial Aid Office
851 S. Fourth St.
Louisville, KY 40203

4389
Presidential Scholarship

AMOUNT: $10300   DEADLINE: March 1
FIELDS/MAJORS: All Areas of Study

Approximately five awards for entering freshman based on academics. Must have a GPA of at least 3.25 and maintain a GPA of at least 3.4 for renewal. Campus interview and recommendations are required to apply. Write to the address below for more details.

Spalding University
Financial Aid Office
851 S. Fourth St.
Louisville, KY 40203

4390
ROTC Residence Hall Scholarships

AMOUNT: $2520   DEADLINE: December 1
FIELDS/MAJORS: All Areas of Study

Scholarships are awarded to admitted Spalding students with ROTC scholarships. Write to the address below for more details.

Spalding University
Financial Aid Office
851 S. Fourth St.
Louisville, KY 40203

SPRING ARBOR COLLEGE

4391
Art Scholarship

AMOUNT: None Specified   DEADLINE: February 15
FIELDS/MAJORS: Art

Scholarships are available at Spring Arbor College for undergraduates majoring in art. Applicants will need to submit portfolio. Renewable with annual application. Write to the address below for more details.

Spring Arbor College
Office of Financial Aid
Spring Arbor, MI 49283

4392
Free Methodist Ministerial Discount

AMOUNT: None Specified   DEADLINE: February 15
FIELDS/MAJORS: Christian Ministry

Scholarships are available at Spring Arbor College for undergraduate students who are a) studying to be a full-time minister of the Free Methodist Church, b) dependents of FM ministers (active, retired or deceased), c) ordained FM ministers, and d) FM missionaries or dependents of FM missionaries. Awards range from 25% to 50% of tuition. Write to the address listed for more details. No application required. Minister must submit copy of license.

Spring Arbor College
Office of Financial Aid
Spring Arbor, MI 49283

4393
Marx Grant

AMOUNT: $100-$1500   DEADLINE: February 15
FIELDS/MAJORS: All Areas of Study

Scholarships are available at Spring Arbor College for undergraduates who are residents of Ohio and can demonstrate a significant level of unmet need. Renewable with annual application. Write to the address below for more details.

Spring Arbor College
Office of Financial Aid
Spring Arbor, MI 49283

4394
Music Scholarship

AMOUNT: None Specified   DEADLINE: February 15
FIELDS/MAJORS: Music

Scholarships are available at Spring Arbor College for undergraduates who participate in the Music Department. Will require an audition. Renewable with annual application. Write to the address below for more details.

Spring Arbor College
Office of Financial Aid
Spring Arbor, MI 49283

4395
National Merit or Achievement Finalist or Semi-finalist Scholarship

AMOUNT: None Specified   DEADLINE: February 15
FIELDS/MAJORS: All Areas of Study

Scholarships are available at Spring Arbor College for freshman full-time students who are finalists and semi-finalists in the National Merit or National Achievement Scholarship Competitions. Semi-finalists receive 50% of tuition, and finalists awards are 100% of tuition. Renewable if recipients maintain a minimum GPA of 3.5 Write to the address below for more details.

Spring Arbor College
Office of Financial Aid
Spring Arbor, MI 49283

4396
Racial Minority Group Assistance

AMOUNT: Maximum: $500   DEADLINE: February 15
FIELDS/MAJORS: All Areas of Study

Scholarships are available at Spring Arbor College for financially needy minority undergraduates. Preference given to African-Americans. Write to the address below for more details or call 1-800-968-0011.

Spring Arbor College
Office of Financial Aid
Spring Arbor, MI 49283

4397
Spring Arbor Endowed Scholarships and Grants

AMOUNT: None Specified   DEADLINE: February 15
FIELDS/MAJORS: All Areas of Study

Scholarships are available at Spring Arbor College for undergraduate students. Requirements vary. Includes Stephenson Grant, Fred and Lizzie Sears Grant, Edna C. White Scholarship, Fund for Student Excellence, and the Leadership Scholarship Grant. Write to the address below for more details.

Spring Arbor College
Office of Financial Aid
Spring Arbor, MI 49283

ST. ANDREWS COLLEGE

4398
Warner-Hall, Presbytery Women of the Church, and P.I.E. Scholarships

AMOUNT: $600-$2000   DEADLINE: March 15
FIELDS/MAJORS: All Areas of Study

Scholarships for St. Andrew's students who are members of the Presbyterian Church. Must be nominated by your pastor or youth minister for Warner-Hall Award or by the women of the Church for the Presbytery award. The P.I.E. Award is a matching contribution for students from a local congregation. Write to the address listed or contact your local church for more complete details.

St. Andrews College
Office of Financial Aid
1700 Dogwood Mile
Laurinburg, NC 28352

ST. JOHN'S UNIVERSITY

4399
Saint John's Presidential Scholarship

AMOUNT: Maximum: $11800   DEADLINE: April 1
FIELDS/MAJORS: All Areas of Study

Eighty scholarships for entering students at St. John's University (Queens or Staten Island campus). Must have a high school average of at least 95% (3.6 GPA). Automatically renewable with a 3.0 GPA for four or five years. Obtain a Presidential Scholarship application by writing to "Presidential Scholarship Committee" in care of the address below.

St. John's University
Office of Financial Aid
Grand Central and Utopia Parkways
Jamaica, NY 11439

SAINT LOUIS UNIVERSITY

4400
Athletic Grant-in-Aid Awards

AMOUNT: None Specified   DEADLINE: None Specified
FIELDS/MAJORS: All Areas of Study

A number of awards available to students participating in the NCAA Division I athletic programs. Contact the athletic department or call (314) 977-2500 or 1-800-SLU-FOR-U for more information.

Saint Louis University
Office of Undergraduate Admission
221 N. Grand Blvd.
St. Louis, MO 63103

4401
Dean's Scholarships

AMOUNT: Maximum: $7700   DEADLINE: December 1
FIELDS/MAJORS: All Areas of Study

Awards available for first-time freshmen. Must have a high school minimum GPA of 3.7 and a minimum 28 ACT or 1240 SAT score. This award is a combination of $6200 toward tuition and $1500 toward campus room and board. Community service and extracurricular activities will be considered. One hundred scholarships are awarded annually. Contact the address below or call (314) 977-2500 or 1-800-SLU-FOR-U for further information.

Saint Louis University
Office of Undergraduate Admission
221 N. Grand Blvd.
St. Louis, MO 63103

4402
Ignatian Service Scholarships

AMOUNT: Maximum: $3800   DEADLINE: December 1
FIELDS/MAJORS: All Areas of Study

Awards open to incoming freshmen who have high academic records and can demonstrate strong commitment to the community or religious service. Approximately forty awards offered annually. Contact the address below or call (314) 977-2500 or 1-800-SLU-FOR-U for further information. GPA must be at least 2.8.

Saint Louis University
Office of Undergraduate Admission
221 N. Grand Blvd.
St. Louis, MO 63103

4403
Leadership Scholarships

AMOUNT: Maximum: $3800 DEADLINE: December 1
FIELDS/MAJORS: All Areas of Study

Awards open to incoming freshmen who demonstrate noteworthy leadership qualities and solid academic standing. Approximately forty awards offered annually. Contact the address below or call (314) 977-2500 or 1-800-SLU-FOR-U for further information. GPA must be at least 2.8.

Saint Louis University
Office of Undergraduate Admission
221 N. Grand Blvd.
St. Louis, MO 63103

4404
National Merit Scholarships

AMOUNT: $500-$2000 DEADLINE: December 1
FIELDS/MAJORS: All Areas of Study

Four-year scholarships for incoming freshmen who are National Merit finalists. Must have notified the National Merit Scholarship Corporation that Saint Louis University is their first choice. Financial need is considered. Contact the address below or call (314) 977-2500 or 1-800-SLU-FOR-U for further information. GPA must be at least 3.0.

Saint Louis University
Office of Undergraduate Admission
221 N. Grand Blvd.
St. Louis, MO 63103

4405
Presidential Scholarships

AMOUNT: None Specified DEADLINE: December 1
FIELDS/MAJORS: All Areas of Study

Awards are available for first-time freshmen. Must have a high school minimum GPA of 3.85 and a minimum 30 ACT or 1320 SAT score. Semi-finalists will interview with members of the University Scholarship Committee. Awards also include room and board. Community service and extracurricular activities will be considered. Ten scholarships awarded annually. Contact the address below or call (314) 977-2500 or 1-800-SLU-FOR-U for further information.

Saint Louis University
Office of Undergraduate Admission
221 N. Grand Blvd.
St. Louis, MO 63103

4406
ROTC Scholarship Program

AMOUNT: None Specified DEADLINE: December 1
FIELDS/MAJORS: All Areas of Study

Awards open for both Army and Air Force ROTC members. Program offers scholarships to pay for University costs including a Saint Louis University ROTC matching scholarship. Contact the address below or call (314) 977-2500 or 1-800-SLU-FOR-U for further information.

Saint Louis University
Office of Undergraduate Admission
221 N. Grand Blvd.
St. Louis, MO 63103

4407
University Scholarships

AMOUNT: Maximum: $5600 DEADLINE: December 1
FIELDS/MAJORS: All Areas of Study

Awards available for first-time freshmen. Must have a high school minimum GPA of 3.5 and a minimum 26 ACT or 1170 SAT score. Community service and extracurricular activities are considered. The award is a combination of $4600 toward tuition and $1000 toward campus room and board. Two hundred scholarships are awarded annually. Contact the address below or call (314) 977-2500 or 1-800-SLU-FOR-U for further information.

Saint Louis University
Office of Undergraduate Admission
221 N. Grand Blvd.
St. Louis, MO 63103

ST. MARY OF THE WOODS COLLEGE

4408
Minority Leadership Awards at St. Mary of the Woods

AMOUNT: $500-$2000 DEADLINE: August 1
FIELDS/MAJORS: All Areas of Study

Grants for minority students at St. Mary of the Woods College. Need-based. Minority here is defined as African, Hispanic, Asian, or Native American. Fifty to one hundred awards are offered annually. Write to the address below for details.

St. Mary of the Woods College
Office of Admissions and Financial Aid
Guerin Hall
St. Mary of the Woods, IN 47876

SAINT MARY'S COLLEGE

4409

Saint Mary's College Scholarships and Athletic Grants

AMOUNT: None Specified   DEADLINE: March 2
FIELDS/MAJORS: All Areas of Study

Scholarships for students at St. Mary's based on academics and need. Grants are based on athletic ability. St. Mary's also has a scholarship program for families having more than three children at St. Mary's at one time. Write to the address below for a complete listing of the available programs.

St. Mary's College
Financial Aid Office
PO Box 4530
Moraga, CA 94575

SAINT MARY'S UNIVERSITY

4410

Alumni Scholarships

AMOUNT: $2500   DEADLINE: March 1
FIELDS/MAJORS: All Areas of Study

Open to academically strong freshmen who have at least one parent who graduated from St. Mary's. May be renewed. Contact the address below for further information or call (210) 436-3141. GPA must be at least 2.9.

Saint Mary's University
Office of Financial Assistance
1 Camino Santa Maria
San Antonio, TX 78228-8541

4411

Chaminade Grants/ Employment

AMOUNT: $525   DEADLINE: March 1
FIELDS/MAJORS: All Areas of Study

Open to high achieving non-Texans. These awards are a combination of a grant and employment. May be renewed up to three years. Contact the address below for further information or call (210) 436-3141. GPA must be at least 3.5.

Saint Mary's University
Office of Financial Assistance
1 Camino Santa Maria
San Antonio, TX 78228-8541

4412

Cremer Guarantee Grants

AMOUNT: $3500   DEADLINE: March 1
FIELDS/MAJORS: All Areas of Study

Open to high achieving qualifying freshmen and transfer students who are Texas residents. May be renewed up to three years. Contact the address below for further information or call (210) 436-3141. GPA must be at least 3.5.

Saint Mary's University
Office of Financial Assistance
1 Camino Santa Maria
San Antonio, TX 78228-8541

4413

Presidential Scholarship

AMOUNT: Maximum: $5000   DEADLINE: March 1
FIELDS/MAJORS: All Areas of Study

Open to outstanding incoming freshmen. Renewable based on academic achievement. Contact the address below for further information or call (210) 436-3141. GPA must be at least 3.2.

Saint Mary's University
Office of Financial Assistance
1 Camino Santa Maria
San Antonio, TX 78228-8541

STANFORD UNIVERSITY

4414

Rockefeller Foundation Fellowships in Legal Humanities

AMOUNT: $40000   DEADLINE: November 15
FIELDS/MAJORS: Law, Humanities, Social Science

Postdoctoral fellowships are available at Stanford to support research on theories of interpretation, intention, narrative, and human agency in law and the humanities, especially as these affect subordinated populations. Twelve awards per year. Write to the address below for information.

Stanford University
Stanford Humanities Center
Mariposa House
Stanford, CA 94305

4415

Spencer Postdoctoral Fellowship Program

AMOUNT: $45000
DEADLINE: December 11
FIELDS/MAJORS: Education, Humanities, Social Science, Behavioral Sciences

Postdoctoral fellowships for persons in education, the humanities, or the social and behavioral sciences. They must describe research with relevance to education. Must have Ph.D. or Ed.D. within last five years. Up to thirty fellowships per year. Amount shown may be for one- or two-year awards. This is a non-residential fellowship. Write to the address below for complete details.

National Academy of Education
Stanford University, School of Education
CERAS-108
Stanford, CA 94305

STERLING COLLEGE

4416

National Merit Scholarships

AMOUNT: Maximum: $10076 DEADLINE: March 1
FIELDS/MAJORS: All Areas of Study

Scholarships available at Sterling for undergraduate full-time students who are finalists or semi-finalists in the National Merit Scholarship Competition. Write to the address below for more details.

Sterling College
Financial Aid Office
Sterling, KS 67579

SUL ROSS STATE UNIVERSITY

4417

Alfred W. Negley Memorial Scholarship

AMOUNT: $1000 DEADLINE: April 1
FIELDS/MAJORS: All Areas of Study

Awards for juniors, seniors, and graduate students at Sul Ross who are in any field of study and have a GPA of at least 3.0. Six awards are offered annually. Write to the address below for more information.

Sul Ross State University
Financial Aid Office
Box C-113
Alpine, TX 79832

4418

Baldemar and Araceli B. Garza Scholarship Fund

AMOUNT: $1000 DEADLINE: April 1
FIELDS/MAJORS: English/Spanish

Awards for Sul Ross juniors and seniors studying English or Spanish who have good academic standing. One award is offered annually. Write to the address below for more information. GPA must be at least 3.0.

Sul Ross State University
Financial Aid Office
Box C-113
Alpine, TX 79832

4419

Betty and John Dow Harris Humanitarian Scholarship

AMOUNT: $1000 DEADLINE: April 1
FIELDS/MAJORS: Agriculture or Geology

Awards for undergraduate students at Sul Ross who are U.S. citizens and are majoring in the fields above. One to two awards are offered annually. Write to the address below for more information.

Sul Ross State University
Financial Aid Office
Box C-113
Alpine, TX 79832

4420

Big Bend Telephone Memorial Scholarship

AMOUNT: $1000 DEADLINE: April 1
FIELDS/MAJORS: All Areas of Study

Awards for graduating high school seniors who plan to attend Sul Ross and are from Sanderson, Comstock, or Presidio, Texas. Three to six awards are offered annually. Write to the address below for more information.

Sul Ross State University
Financial Aid Office
Box C-113
Alpine, TX 79832

4421
Budweiser Rodeo Scholarship

AMOUNT: $400-$2000 DEADLINE: August 1
FIELDS/MAJORS: All Areas of Study

Awards for Sul Ross music undergraduates who have a GPA of at least 2.0, participate in rodeo activities, and have NIRA eligibility. Five awards are offered annually. Write to the address below for more information.

Sul Ross State University
Financial Aid Office
Box C-113
Alpine, TX 79832

4422
Clifford B. Casey History Scholarship

AMOUNT: $600-$1000 DEADLINE: April 1
FIELDS/MAJORS: History

Awards for Sul Ross students who are studying history and have good academic standing. Two to four awards are offered annually. Write to the address below for more information. GPA must be at least 3.0.

Sul Ross State University
Financial Aid Office
Box C-113
Alpine, TX 79832

4423
First National Bank in Alpine Scholarship

AMOUNT: $1000 DEADLINE: April 1
FIELDS/MAJORS: Business

Awards for Sul Ross undergraduate students who have a GPA of at least 3.0 prior to each semester. Two awards are offered annually. Write to the address below for more information.

Sul Ross State University
Financial Aid Office
Box C-113
Alpine, TX 79832

4424
Floyd Neill Scholarship

AMOUNT: $1000-$2000 DEADLINE: April 1
FIELDS/MAJORS: All Areas of Study

Awards for all Sul Ross undergraduates who have a GPA of at least 3.5. One award is offered annually. Write to the address below for more information.

Sul Ross State University
Financial Aid Office
Box C-113
Alpine, TX 79832

4425
Houston Livestock Show and Rodeo Academic Scholarship

AMOUNT: $1000 DEADLINE: None Specified
FIELDS/MAJORS: Range Animal Science

Awards for Sul Ross undergraduates who are studying range animal science, are U.S. citizens, and have a GPA of at least 3.0. Eight to twelve awards are offered annually. Write to the address below for more information.

Sul Ross State University
Division of Range Animal Science
Box C-110
Alpine, TX 79832

4426
Houston Livestock Show and Rodeo Scholarship

AMOUNT: $1000 DEADLINE: None Specified
FIELDS/MAJORS: Range Animal Science

Awards for Sul Ross undergraduates who are studying range animal science and are U.S. citizens. Fifteen to twenty awards are offered annually. Write to the address below for more information.

Sul Ross State University
Division of Range Animal Science
Box C-110
Alpine, TX 79832

4427
James B. Gillett Memorial Scholarship

AMOUNT: $1000-$1500 DEADLINE: April 1
FIELDS/MAJORS: Criminal Justice

Awards for Sul Ross juniors and seniors who have good academic standing. Based on three letters of recommendation and a five hundred word essay. Two to four awards are offered annually. Write to the address below for more information. GPA must be at least 3.0.

Sul Ross State University
Financial Aid Office
Box C-113
Alpine, TX 79832

4428

John G. and Evelyn G. Prude Scholarship

AMOUNT: $1500-$2000 DEADLINE: April 1
FIELDS/MAJORS: All Areas of Study

Awards for all Sul Ross students who have financial need and a GPA of at least 3.0. One award is offered annually. Write to the address below for more information.

Sul Ross State University
Financial Aid Office
Box C-113
Alpine, TX 79832

4429

Kathryn Walker-Clayton Williams, Sr. Memorial Scholarship

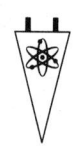

AMOUNT: $1000 DEADLINE: April 1
FIELDS/MAJORS: English

Awards for Sul Ross students who are studying English and have good academic standing. One award is offered annually. Write to the address below for more information. GPA must be at least 3.0.

Sul Ross State University
Financial Aid Office
Box C-113
Alpine, TX 79832

4430

Loyd Oden Memorial Scholarship

AMOUNT: $1000 DEADLINE: None Specified
FIELDS/MAJORS: Industrial Technology

Awards for Sul Ross freshmen who are studying industrial technology and have been recommended by their principal. One to six awards are offered annually. Write to the address below for more information.

Sul Ross State University
Financial Aid Office
Box C-113
Alpine, TX 79832

4431

Mary Moll Jennings Scholarship

AMOUNT: $1200 DEADLINE: April 1
FIELDS/MAJORS: All Areas of Study

Awards for all Sul Ross undergraduates. Freshmen must have a GPA of at least 2.0 to receive the award, and continuing students must have a 3.0 GPA or better. One award is offered annually. Write to the address below for more information.

Sul Ross State University
Financial Aid Office
Box C-113
Alpine, TX 79832

4432

President's Endowed University Scholars Program

AMOUNT: $2000-$2500 DEADLINE: April 1
FIELDS/MAJORS: All Areas of Study

Awards for freshmen at Sul Ross who have obtained an academic seal on their high school diploma and who have an ACT score of at least 25 or an SAT score of at least 1050. Renewable. Four awards are offered annually. Write to the address below for more information. GPA must be at least 3.0.

Sul Ross State University
Financial Aid Office
Box C-113
Alpine, TX 79832

4433

Richard P. "Tiny" Phillips Memorial Scholarship

AMOUNT: $1000 DEADLINE: April 1
FIELDS/MAJORS: Spanish

Awards for Sul Ross undergraduates who have financial need and a GPA of at least 2.5. One award is offered annually. Write to the address below for more information.

Sul Ross State University
Financial Aid Office
Box C-113
Alpine, TX 79832

4434

San Antonio Livestock Scholarship

AMOUNT: $1000 DEADLINE: April 1
FIELDS/MAJORS: Animal Science

Awards for freshmen at Sul Ross who are enrolled in an animal science program. Four awards are offered annually. Write to the address below for more information.

Sul Ross State University
Financial Aid Office
Box C-113
Alpine, TX 79832

4435
Southwest Texas Gas Corporation Scholarship

AMOUNT: $1000   DEADLINE: April 1
FIELDS/MAJORS: All Areas of Study

Awards for all Sul Ross students who are from Alpine, Balmorhea, Ft. Davis, or Marfa, Texas. Must demonstrate financial need. Two awards are offered annually. Write to the address below for more information.

Sul Ross State University
Financial Aid Office
Box C-113
Alpine, TX 79832

4436
Student Deposit Scholarship

AMOUNT: $1000   DEADLINE: April 1
FIELDS/MAJORS: All Areas of Study

Awards for all Sul Ross undergraduates who are from Texas and have a GPA of at least 2.5. Twelve awards are offered annually. Write to the address below for more information.

Sul Ross State University
Financial Aid Office
Box C-113
Alpine, TX 79832

4437
Sul Ross Scholars and Leadership Programs

AMOUNT: $1000   DEADLINE: April 1
FIELDS/MAJORS: All Areas of Study

Awards for freshmen at Sul Ross who have demonstrated academic excellence or leadership. Fifteen awards are offered annually. Write to the address below for more information.

Sul Ross State University
Financial Aid Office
Box C-113
Alpine, TX 79832

SUNY COLLEGE AT OLD WESTBURY

4438
Accounting Scholarships

AMOUNT: Maximum: $500   DEADLINE: None Specified
FIELDS/MAJORS: Accounting

Scholarships are available at SUNY College at Old Westbury for students pursuing a degree in accounting. Includes the Bert N. Mitchell Accounting Scholarship and the Mitchell/Titus & Co. Scholarship Award for Excellence in Accounting. Write to the address listed or call Diane Edey at (212) 709-4500 for more information.

SUNY College at Old Westbury
Office of Financial Aid
Division of Student Affairs
Old Westbury, NY 11568

SUNY, POTSDAM

4439
Bernetta Joy Ortel Memorial Scholarship

AMOUNT: None Specified   DEADLINE: None Specified
FIELDS/MAJORS: All Areas of Study

Awards are available for students transferring to SUNY, Potsdam, from North Country Community College. Write to the address below for more information.

SUNY, Potsdam
Office of Admissions
44 Pierrepont Ave.
Potsdam, NY 13676

4440
Elizabeth and Maurice Baritaud String Scholarship

AMOUNT: None Specified   DEADLINE: None Specified
FIELDS/MAJORS: String Music

Awards are available for freshmen or sophomores at SUNY, Potsdam, who are studying string music at the Crane School of Music. Write to the address below for more information.

SUNY, Potsdam
Office of Admissions
44 Pierrepont Ave.
Potsdam, NY 13676

4441

Frances Aust Silbereisen Scholarship

AMOUNT: None Specified DEADLINE: None Specified
FIELDS/MAJORS: All Areas of Study

Awards are available for students at SUNY, Potsdam, based on financial need. Write to the address below for more information.

SUNY, Potsdam
Office of Admissions
44 Pierrepont Ave.
Potsdam, NY 13676

4442

Mary E. English Scholarship

AMOUNT: None Specified DEADLINE: None Specified
FIELDS/MAJORS: Music Education, Voice, or String Music

Awards are available for freshmen or transfers at SUNY, Potsdam, who are studying in one of the areas listed above. Write to the address below for more information.

SUNY, Potsdam
Office of Admissions
44 Pierrepont Ave.
Potsdam, NY 13676

4443

Mary Lou and Johannes Koulman Scholarship

AMOUNT: None Specified DEADLINE: None Specified
FIELDS/MAJORS: Music

Awards are available for freshmen or transfers at SUNY, Potsdam, who will attend the Crane School of Music. Write to the address below for more information.

SUNY, Potsdam
Office of Admissions
44 Pierrepont Ave.
Potsdam, NY 13676

4444

Minerva Scholarship

AMOUNT: None Specified DEADLINE: None Specified
FIELDS/MAJORS: All Areas of Study

Awards are available for incoming freshmen at SUNY, Potsdam, based on academic achievement, special abilities, and demonstrated talents. Renewable for four years. Write to the address below for more information. Must have a GPA of at least 2.0.

SUNY, Potsdam
Office of Admissions
44 Pierrepont Ave.
Potsdam, NY 13676

4445

Osceola Harvey Hill Memorial Scholarship

AMOUNT: None Specified DEADLINE: None Specified
FIELDS/MAJORS: All Areas of Study

Awards are available for freshmen at SUNY, Potsdam, who were graduates of Alexandria Bay Central High School. Based on academic excellence. Write to the address below for more information.

SUNY, Potsdam
Office of Admissions
44 Pierrepont Ave.
Potsdam, NY 13676

4446

Penny Thompson Barshied Scholarship

AMOUNT: None Specified DEADLINE: None Specified
FIELDS/MAJORS: All Areas of Study

Awards are available for all students at SUNY, Potsdam, based on achievement. Write to the address below for more information. Must have a GPA of at least 2.0.

SUNY, Potsdam
Office of Admissions
44 Pierrepont Ave.
Potsdam, NY 13676

4447

Potsdam Foundation Honors Scholarships

AMOUNT: Maximum: $1000 DEADLINE: None Specified
FIELDS/MAJORS: All Areas of Study

Awards are available for incoming freshmen who have demonstrated excellence in academic performance and/or extracurricular or community activities. Twenty-five of the forty awards are reserved for residents of the following counties: St. Lawrence, Franklin, Jefferson, Clinton, Essex, Lewis, Hamilton, or Warren. Write to the address below for more information.

SUNY, Potsdam
Office of Admissions
44 Pierrepont Ave.
Potsdam, NY 13676

4448
Quentin Reutershan Memorial Scholarship

AMOUNT: None Specified   DEADLINE: None Specified
FIELDS/MAJORS: All Areas of Study

Awards are available for transfer students at SUNY, Potsdam, who have at minimum achieved a second semester sophomore standing and have demonstrated academic excellence and leadership potential through activities at the student's previous institution. Must have a GPA of at least 3.5, financial need, and be considered a non-traditional student. Write to the address below for more information.

SUNY, Potsdam
Office of Admissions
44 Pierrepont Ave.
Potsdam, NY 13676

4449
Rocque F. Dominic Memorial Scholarship

AMOUNT: None Specified   DEADLINE: None Specified
FIELDS/MAJORS: Clarinet Music

Awards are available for freshmen or transfers at SUNY, Potsdam, who are outstanding clarinetists and will attend the Crane School of Music. Write to the address below for more information.

SUNY, Potsdam
Office of Admissions
44 Pierrepont Ave.
Potsdam, NY 13676

4450
Shelly Electric Scholarship

AMOUNT: None Specified   DEADLINE: None Specified
FIELDS/MAJORS: All Areas of Study

Awards are available for students at SUNY, Potsdam, from the North Country, with preference given to those from St. Lawrence County. Based on academic strength and demonstrated need. Write to the address below for more information.

SUNY, Potsdam
Office of Admissions
44 Pierrepont Ave.
Potsdam, NY 13676

4451
Sylvia Levitt Angus Scholarship

AMOUNT: None Specified   DEADLINE: None Specified
FIELDS/MAJORS: All Areas of Study

Awards are available for sophomore transfer students at SUNY, Potsdam. Based on academic achievement. Renewable. Write to the address below for more information.

SUNY, Potsdam
Office of Admissions
44 Pierrepont Ave.
Potsdam, NY 13676

4452
SUNY Empire State Honors Awards for African, Latino, Native Americans

AMOUNT: None Specified   DEADLINE: None Specified
FIELDS/MAJORS: All Areas of Study

Awards are available for freshmen at SUNY, Potsdam, based on academic achievement. Must be an African-American, Latino, or Native American student to apply. Write to the address below for more information.

SUNY, Potsdam
Office of Admissions
44 Pierrepont Ave.
Potsdam, NY 13676

4453
Verna M. Mulvana Scholarship

AMOUNT: None Specified   DEADLINE: None Specified
FIELDS/MAJORS: All Areas of Study

Awards are available for freshmen at SUNY, Potsdam, who were graduates of Salmon River Central High School. Write to the address below for more information.

SUNY, Potsdam
Office of Admissions
44 Pierrepont Ave.
Potsdam, NY 13676

STATE UNIVERSITY OF NEW YORK, SYRACUSE

4454
Syracuse Paper and Pulp Foundation Scholarships

AMOUNT: $1250 DEADLINE: None Specified
FIELDS/MAJORS: Paper Science and Engineering

Awards for undergraduates majoring in the fields above who have a GPA of at least a 3.0 at the State University of New York in Syracuse. The amount of the award is dependent upon the student's GPA. Applicants must be U.S. citizens. Forty-five awards are available annually. Write to the address listed for more information.

State University of New York College of Environmental
    Science and Forest
Director of Financial Aid
115 Bray Hall
Syracuse, NY 13210

SUSQUEHANNA UNIVERSITY

4455
Charles B. Degenstein Scholarship

AMOUNT: Maximum: $7500 DEADLINE: March 1
FIELDS/MAJORS: Business

Available to incoming freshmen who plan to pursue a curriculum in business. Must be ranked in the top 10% of their graduating class and score in the top 15% on national standardized test. Write to the address below for details or call 1-800-326-9672. GPA must be at least 3.5.

Susquehanna University
Office of Financial Aid
512 University Ave.
Selinsgrove, PA 17870

4456
International Student Tuition Scholarships

AMOUNT: None Specified DEADLINE: March 1
FIELDS/MAJORS: All Areas of Study

Available to international students who demonstrate academic ability, potential to contribute to campus life, and financial need. Renewable up to four years. Write to the address below for details or call 1-800-326-9672. GPA must be at least 2.8.

Susquehanna University
Office of Financial Aid
512 University Ave.
Selinsgrove, PA 17870

4457
Lawrence M. and Louise Kresge Isaacs Endowment

AMOUNT: Maximum: $7500 DEADLINE: March 1
FIELDS/MAJORS: Music

Available to freshmen who are majoring in music. Based on audition with the music faculty and high academic achievement. Renewable for a total of four years. Write to the address below for details or call (717) 372-4309. GPA must be at least 3.3.

Susquehanna University
Office of Financial Aid
512 University Ave.
Selinsgrove, PA 17870

4458
Music Scholarships

AMOUNT: $1000-$3000 DEADLINE: March 1
FIELDS/MAJORS: Music-Keyboard, Voice, Band, Orchestra

Available to incoming freshmen who demonstrate a special talent in music. Based on outstanding music auditions in keyboard, voice, or band/orchestral instruments. Renewable for a total of four years. Awards may be given to non-majors if they show exceptional talent in the above fields. Write to the address below for details or contact the music department at (717) 372-4309.

Susquehanna University
Office of Financial Aid
512 University Ave.
Selinsgrove, PA 17870

4459
Presidential Scholarships

AMOUNT: Maximum: $7500 DEADLINE: March 1
FIELDS/MAJORS: All Areas of Study

Available to incoming freshmen who have demonstrated superior academic achievement and personal promise. Renewable for a total of four years. Write to the address below for details or call 1-800-326-9672. GPA must be at least 3.6.

Susquehanna University
Office of Financial Aid
512 University Ave.
Selinsgrove, PA 17870

4460
Scholarships for Distinguished Achievement in Science and Mathematics

AMOUNT: Maximum: $7500 DEADLINE: March 1
FIELDS/MAJORS: Science, Computer Science, Mathematics

Available to incoming freshmen who plan to pursue a curriculum in one of the above fields. Based on high class rank, high national standardized test scores, and overall outstanding academics. Renewable annually for a maximum of four years. Write to the address below for details or call 1-800-326-9672. GPA must be at least 3.5.

Susquehanna University
Office of Financial Aid
512 University Ave.
Selinsgrove, PA 17870

4461
Susquehanna Scholarships

AMOUNT: Maximum: $6000 DEADLINE: March 1
FIELDS/MAJORS: All Areas of Study

Available to incoming freshmen who demonstrate outstanding academic achievement and personal promise. Typically, recipients rank in the top 15% of their graduating class and have scored in the top 20% on national standardized tests. Renewable for a total of four years. Write to the address below for details or call 1-800-326-9672. GPA must be at least 3.5.

Susquehanna University
Office of Financial Aid
512 University Ave.
Selinsgrove, PA 17870

4462
Transfer Student Scholarships

AMOUNT: $4000-$6000 DEADLINE: March 1
FIELDS/MAJORS: All Areas of Study

Available to transfer students with outstanding academic achievement and a GPA of 3.0 or higher. Awards range from $4000 to $6000. Write to the address below for details or call 1-800-326-9672.

Susquehanna University
Office of Financial Aid
512 University Ave.
Selinsgrove, PA 17870

4463
University Assistantship

AMOUNT: Maximum: $9000 DEADLINE: March 1
FIELDS/MAJORS: All Areas of Study

Available to incoming freshmen who demonstrate outstanding academic potential, graduated in the top 5% of their high school class, and scored in the top 10% on national standardized test. These awards include a creative work experience (average of ten hours per week) with a member of the University's faculty or administrative staff. Renewable for a total of four years. Write to the address below for details or call 1-800-326-9672. GPA must be at least 3.5.

Susquehanna University Office of Financial Aid
512 University Ave.
Selinsgrove, PA 17870

4464
Valedictorian/Salutatorian Scholarships

AMOUNT: Maximum: $7500 DEADLINE: March 1
FIELDS/MAJORS: All Areas of Study

Available to incoming students who ranked first or second in their high school graduating class. Renewable for a maximum of four years. Write to the address below for details or call 1-800-326-9672.

Susquehanna University Office of Financial Aid
512 University Ave.
Selinsgrove, PA 17870

SYRACUSE UNIVERSITY

4465
Graduate Newspaper Fellowship/ Internship for Minorities

AMOUNT: $1100 DEADLINE: February 1
FIELDS/MAJORS: Newspaper Journalism

Open to African-American, Asian, Native American, and Hispanic/Latino students who are U.S. citizens at the master's level in newspaper journalism at the Newhouse School of Public Communications. Must have an undergraduate degree in a field other than journalism and have a minimum GPA of 3.0. Award consists of $1100 monthly stipend, moving expenses to Syracuse, travel/academic expenses, and health insurance coverage. For more information, contact the address below or call (315) 443-1124.

Syracuse University
Ms. Jane Lorraine
301 Newhouse I
Syracuse, NY 13244-2100

4466
Syracuse Grants, University Scholarships

AMOUNT: None Specified   DEADLINE: None Specified
FIELDS/MAJORS: All Areas of Study

Merit-based scholarships and need-based grants for undergraduate students at Syracuse University. Renewable based on continued need/GPA. Graduate fellowships and scholarships are based on need and merit. Contact the financial aid office for details.

Syracuse University
Office of Financial Aid
200 Archbold
Syracuse, NY 13244

4467
University African-American Graduate Fellowships

AMOUNT: None Specified   DEADLINE: March 1
FIELDS/MAJORS: All Areas of Study

Six fellowships for African-American graduate students enrolled full-time at Syracuse University. Must enroll in at least one course in African-American studies (3 credit hours). Contact the graduate admissions office for details.

Syracuse University
Office of Financial Aid
200 Archbold
Syracuse, NY 13244

TEXAS A & M UNIVERSITY

4468
Academic Achievement Scholarships

AMOUNT: $2500   DEADLINE: December 9
FIELDS/MAJORS: All Areas of Study

Open to high school seniors in the top 15% of class with a minimum SAT score of 1200 (ACT 27). Must be U.S. citizen or permanent resident. Contact the address below for further information. GPA must be at least 3.5.

Texas A & M University
Office of Academic Scholarships
College Station, TX 77843

4469
Academic Excellence Awards

AMOUNT: $500-$1500   DEADLINE: March 1
FIELDS/MAJORS: All Areas of Study

Scholarships are available to upperclassmen, graduates, and professional students who are enrolled full-time with records of academic excellence, leadership, work experience, and campus activities. Financial need is required in some cases. Approximately six hundred awards per year. Must be a U.S. citizen to apply. Applications available in Room 220 of the Pavilion in January. GPA must be at least 3.1.

Texas A & M University
Student Financial Aid Department
College Station, TX 77843-1252

4470
Academic Incentive Scholarship for Upperclassmen

AMOUNT: Maximum: $1000   DEADLINE: March 1
FIELDS/MAJORS: All Areas of Study

Open to sophomores, juniors, and seniors at Texas A & M with a minimum GPA of 3.4. Applicants may not hold any other multi-year scholarship with an annual value of more than $1000. Applicants must also be U.S. citizens or permanent residents. Write to the address below for details.

Texas A & M University
University Honors Program
101 Academic Bldg.
College Station, TX 77843

4471
Commandant's Leadership Award Scholarships

AMOUNT: $1000-$2500   DEADLINE: None Specified
FIELDS/MAJORS: All Areas of Study

Awards are available to entering freshmen who join the ROTC corps of cadets. Funds are awarded as follows; $2500 each year for first two years, $1500 each year for second two years. Selection based upon academic performance and demonstrated leadership potential. Applicants must be U.S. citizens. Additional awards at lesser values are also available. Write to the office of the Commandant, Division of Student Services, at the address below for details. National ROTC scholarship recipients are given the incentive of residence hall fees waived during the first year ($1354) to come to Texas A & M.

Texas A & M University
Office of the Commandant
College Station, TX 77843

4472
Corps Scholarships

GPA 3.0+

AMOUNT: $500 DEADLINE: None Specified
FIELDS/MAJORS: All Areas of Study

Awards available to incoming freshmen. Selection based upon academic performance and demonstrated leadership potential. Applicants must be U.S. citizens or permanent residents. Some awards give preference to financial need. Write to the office of the Commandant, Division of Student Services, at the address below for details. GPA must be at least 3.0.

Texas A & M University
Office of the Commandant
College Station, TX 77843

4473
Merit Plus Scholarships

AMOUNT: $2000 DEADLINE: None Specified
FIELDS/MAJORS: All Areas of Study

All incoming freshmen who were semi-finalists in the National Merit Scholarship Competition or National Achievement Scholarship Competition who enroll at Texas A & M are eligible for this scholarship. Write to the address below for details.

Texas A & M University
University Honors Program
101 Academic Building
College Station, TX 77843

4474
National Merit and National Achievement Awards for Freshmen

AMOUNT: Maximum: $1500 DEADLINE: January 15
FIELDS/MAJORS: All Areas of Study

All finalists of the National Merit or National Achievement Scholarship Competitions who name Texas A & M as first choice are assured a scholarship in this program. This award can be combined with any other University scholarships earned. Payable in installments of $750 per semester for four years. Write to the address below for details.

Texas A & M University
University Honors Program
101 Academic Building
College Station, TX 77843-4233

4475
Opportunity Award

GPA 2.5+

AMOUNT: $500-$2500 DEADLINE: December 9
FIELDS/MAJORS: All Areas of Study

Open to incoming freshmen with outstanding high school records who have not attended another college or university. Award is based on academic record, activities, leadership skills, test scores, and financial need. Scholarship is for either one or four years. Applicants must be U.S. citizens or permanent residents. Recipients will be notified by mail during the month of April. Apply through Undergraduate Admission Application. GPA must be at least 2.8.

Texas A & M University
Student Financial Aid Department
College Station, TX 77843-1252

4476
President's Achievement Scholarships

GPA 3.0+

AMOUNT: $2500 DEADLINE: December 9
FIELDS/MAJORS: All Areas of Study

Open to high school seniors who are in the top 20% of class with a minimum SAT score of 1050 (ACT 24). Must be U.S. citizen or permanent resident and planning to be a full-time student. Contact the address below for further information. GPA must be at least 3.4.

Texas A & M University
Office of Academic Scholarships
College Station, TX 77843

4477
Tuition Credit Program for Early High School Graduates

AMOUNT: Maximum: $1000 DEADLINE: January 15
FIELDS/MAJORS: All Areas of Study

Open to incoming freshmen who are Texas residents and graduated from a Texas high school in three years instead of four. Applicants must provide proof of early graduation. Must have completed entire high school education in Texas and be a U.S. citizen or permanent resident. Write to address below for details.

Texas A & M University
Student Financial Aid Department
College Station, TX 77843-1252

4478
Two-Year College Scholarship for Transfer Students

AMOUNT: $500-$1000 DEADLINE: June 10
FIELDS/MAJORS: All Areas of Study

Scholarships are available to students transferring from community or junior colleges. Applicants must have an associates degree or have completed a minimum of 60 credit hours. Must be U.S. Citizens or permanent residents. Applications available March 1 through June 1. Write to the address below for details.

Texas A & M University
Student Financial Aid Department
College Station, TX 77843-1252

4479
University Endowed Scholarships/Fellowships

AMOUNT: $2000-$3000 DEADLINE: January 8
FIELDS/MAJORS: All Areas of Study

Open to incoming freshmen ranked in the top 10% of their class by scoring at least 1300 on the SAT (30 ACT). Semi-finalists of the National Merit Scholarship Competition are also eligible. Includes the Lechner, McFadden, and the President's Endowed Scholarships. Non-Texas residents qualify for a tuition waiver. Must be a U.S. citizen or permanent resident. Write to the address below for details. GPA must be at least 3.6.

Texas A & M University
University Honors Program
101 Academic Bldg.
College Station, TX 77843-4233

4480
Valedictorian Scholarship

AMOUNT: $2288 DEADLINE: September 30
FIELDS/MAJORS: All Areas of Study

Open to Texas high school valedictorians only. Certification is required, and Texas A & M must be the first school of enrollment. Award is for the freshman year only. Applicant must be a U.S. citizen or permanent resident. No formal application is required. Write to address below for details.

Texas A & M University
Student Financial Aid Department
College Station, TX 77843-1252

TOWSON UNIVERSITY

4481
Associated Italian American Charities of Maryland, Inc., Scholarship

AMOUNT: Maximum: $1000 DEADLINE: March 15
FIELDS/MAJORS: All Areas of Study

Open to students of Italian heritage who are U.S. citizens. Must have a minimum GPA of 3.0 and be able to demonstrate financial need. Contact Lisa Harrison at (410) 830-2647 for further information.

Towson University
Scholarship Office
8000 York Rd.
Towson, MD 21252-0001

4482
CEEP Scholarships

AMOUNT: $500-$4000 DEADLINE: None Specified
FIELDS/MAJORS: All Areas of Study

Open to minorities who are Maryland residents and U.S. citizens. Must have a minimum GPA of 2.0 and be willing to commit up to ten hours per week involved in activities that benefit the TU community. Applications available March 15. Deadline of April 1 is for continuing students, July 15 deadline is for incoming students. Contact the address below or call Camille Clay (410) 830-2051 for further information.

Towson University
Scholarship Office
8000 York Rd.
Towson, MD 21252-0001

4483
C.T.S.U. Scholarship

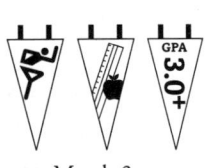

AMOUNT: Maximum: $750 DEADLINE: March 3
FIELDS/MAJORS: Education

Open to full-time junior and senior English majors in high school track. Must have a minimum GPA of 3.0 and be residents of Maryland. Contact the address below or the Dean's office at (410) 830-2570.

Towson University
Scholarship Office
8000 York Rd.
Towson, MD 21252-0001

4484
Cultural Diversity Award

AMOUNT: $1000 DEADLINE: December 1
FIELDS/MAJORS: All Areas of Study

Open to culturally diverse freshmen and transfer students who are U.S. citizens and residents of Maryland. Incoming freshmen must have a minimum GPA of 3.0. Transfer students must have achieved an AA with a minimum GPA of 3.0 and be transferring directly from a Maryland community college. Awards range from $1000 to full tuition and fees. Contact the address below for further information or call (410) 830-2113.

Towson University
Scholarship Office
8000 York Rd.
Towson, MD 21252-0001

4485
Dance Scholarships

AMOUNT: $500-$1500 DEADLINE: March 15
FIELDS/MAJORS: Dance

Open to full-time dance majors accepted in the program by audition. Scholarships renewed each year as long as the criteria are met and recipients remain in good academic standing. Based on talent. Departmental work required of all scholarship recipients. Contact Karen Kohn Bradley at (410) 830-2760 for further information. GPA must be at least 2.8.

Towson University
Scholarship Office
8000 York Rd.
Towson, MD 21252-0001

4486
Diehl Graphsoft Scholarships

AMOUNT: Maximum: $500 DEADLINE: None Specified
FIELDS/MAJORS: Computer Science

Open to outstanding juniors and seniors with a minimum GPA of 3.0 and a course in computer graphics or related area. Contact Kiumi Akingbehin at (410) 830-3701 for further information.

Towson University
Scholarship Office
8000 York Rd.
Towson, MD 21252-0001

4487
George F. Rogers, Jr. Memorial Scholarship

AMOUNT: Maximum: $2000 DEADLINE: None Specified
FIELDS/MAJORS: Mass Communications

Open to enrolled students with a minimum of one and a maximum of two full semesters remaining prior to graduation. Must have a minimum overall GPA of 3.0 and at least a 3.25 in the major. Check with the Department for deadline information. Contact Scholarship Coordinator at (410) 830-3411 for further information.

Towson University
Scholarship Office
8000 York Rd.
Towson, MD 21252-0001

4488
Helen Aletta Linthicum Scholarship

AMOUNT: Maximum: $1000 DEADLINE: December 1
FIELDS/MAJORS: All Areas of Study

Open to Maryland high school valedictorians. Recipients must enroll on a full-time basis once selected for this scholarship. Award is non-renewable and can only be applied to freshman year. Contact the address below for further information or call (410) 830-2113.

Towson University
Scholarship Office
8000 York Rd.
Towson, MD 21252-0001

4489
Henrietta Price Scholarship

AMOUNT: Maximum: $500 DEADLINE: December 15
FIELDS/MAJORS: Occupational Therapy

Open to enrolled full-time students who are Maryland residents. Must be a junior in the bachelor's degree program or a second year student in the master's program. Must also be a member of the American Occupational Therapy Association and the Maryland Occupational Therapy Association. Contact Charlotte E. Exner at (410) 830-2762 for further information. GPA must be at least 2.6.

Towson University
Scholarship Office
8000 York Rd.
Towson, MD 21252-0001

4490
Henry Sanborn Scholarship

AMOUNT: $1000-$1400 DEADLINE: None Specified
FIELDS/MAJORS: Vocal, Piano Music

Open to full-time degree candidates who have completed at least 30 semester hours (15 at TU) with a minimum GPA of 3.0. Contact Carl B. Schmidt at (410) 830-2143 for further information.

Towson University
Scholarship Office
8000 York Rd.
Towson, MD 21252-0001

4491
Jennifer L. Thomas Memorial Scholarship

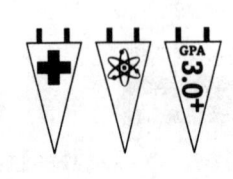

AMOUNT: Maximum: $500 DEADLINE: February 1
FIELDS/MAJORS: Kinesiology

Open to enrolled full-time juniors and seniors who have a minimum GPA of 3.0 and are residents of Maryland. Must have completed at least one semester as a physical education teacher major. Letters of recommendation and an essay will be required. Contact Ray Stinar at (410) 830-2376 for further information.

Towson University
Scholarship Office
8000 York Rd.
Towson, MD 21252-0001

4492
Jeremiah J. German Scholarship

AMOUNT: Maximum: $1000 DEADLINE: April 1
FIELDS/MAJORS: Economics

Open to economics majors completing junior year with a minimum GPA of 3.26. Must have completed Economics 309 and 310. An essay will be required. Topic announced in February, and award announced by June 15. Contact the address below or call (410) 830-2956.

Towson University
Scholarship Office
8000 York Rd.
Towson, MD 21252-0001

4493
Jess Fisher Scholarship

AMOUNT: Maximum: $1000 DEADLINE: None Specified
FIELDS/MAJORS: Pre-Engineering

Open to undergraduates. Based solely on academic merit. Contact the Physics Department at (410) 830-3009 for further information. GPA must be at least 2.8.

Towson University
Scholarship Office
8000 York Rd.
Towson, MD 21252-0001

4494
Loch Raven Kiwanis Foundation Scholarship

AMOUNT: Maximum: $500 DEADLINE: March 15
FIELDS/MAJORS: All Areas of Study

Open to full and part-time female students who are at least twenty-five years of age and have a minimum GPA of 3.0. Contact Lisa Harrison at (410) 830-2647 for further information.

Towson University
Scholarship Office
8000 York Rd.
Towson, MD 21252-0001

4495
Lois D. Odell Outstanding Transfer Student Scholarship

AMOUNT: Maximum: $500 DEADLINE: None Specified
FIELDS/MAJORS: Biology

Open to biology majors transferring with at least 55, but no more than 65 credits. Must have a minimum GPA of 3.2 overall and completed 12 credits in 300 or 400 level biology electives. Application deadline is end of spring semester. Contact Biological Sciences at (410) 830-3042 for further information.

Towson University
Scholarship Office
8000 York Rd.
Towson, MD 21252-0001

4496
Maryland Law Enforcement Officers Scholarship

AMOUNT: Maximum: $1250   DEADLINE: March 1
FIELDS/MAJORS: Law Enforcement

Open to enrolled full-time juniors planning a career in law enforcement but not currently in a law enforcement position. Must have a minimum GPA of 3.0 and be able to demonstrate financial need. Contact John Toland at (410) 830-2933 for further information.

Towson University
Scholarship Office
8000 York Rd.
Towson, MD 21252-0001

4497
Music Department Scholarships

AMOUNT: Maximum: $1000   DEADLINE: June 1
FIELDS/MAJORS: Music

Open to full-time music majors or minors. Based on talent. Contact Carl B. Schmidt at (410) 830-2143 for further information. GPA must be at least 2.5.

Towson University
Scholarship Office
8000 York Rd.
Towson, MD 21252-0001

4498
Outstanding Man and Woman Awards

AMOUNT: Maximum: $1000   DEADLINE: None Specified
FIELDS/MAJORS: All Areas of Study

Open to full-time students who have at least one year of classes left before graduation. Awards based on academics, campus, civic, community involvement, employment, special talents, and an essay. Finalists are interviewed by a selection committee. Contact the address below for further information or call (410) 830-3307. GPA must be at least 3.5.

Towson University
Scholarship Office
8000 York Rd.
Towson, MD 21252-0001

4499
Ronald L. Peterson Scholarship

AMOUNT: Maximum: $1000   DEADLINE: February 1
FIELDS/MAJORS: All Areas of Study

Open to students who have been admitted as entering freshmen and have a minimum GPA of 3.25. Must be children or grandchildren of an alumnus or alumna. Contact the address below for further information or call (410) 830-2234.

Towson University
Scholarship Office
8000 York Rd.
Towson, MD 21252-0001

4500
Teacher Candidates in Urban Schools Scholarship

AMOUNT: $1000-$2000   DEADLINE: March 3
FIELDS/MAJORS: Education

Open to Maryland residents who are full-time incoming freshmen, sophomores, and juniors committed to teaching in urban sites. Preference given to residents of Baltimore. African-American students are encouraged to apply. Contact the address below or Doris Maxwell at (410) 830-4366 for additional information.

Towson University
Scholarship Office
8000 York Rd.
Towson, MD 21252-0001

4501
Warren Internship

AMOUNT: Maximum: $500   DEADLINE: October 25
FIELDS/MAJORS: Occupational Therapy

Open to enrolled students to assist in a third internship or an internship away from home. Must have a minimum GPA of 3.0. An essay and statement of financial need will be required. Eligible students will be scheduled for internships January to August. Contact Nancy Blake at (410) 830-2253 for further information.

Towson University
Scholarship Office
8000 York Rd.
Towson, MD 21252-0001

TRI-STATE UNIVERSITY

4502
Dean's Scholarship

AMOUNT: $4500-$7000 DEADLINE: March 1
FIELDS/MAJORS: All Areas of Study

Awards for students showing high academic achievement. Students must have graduated in the top 33% of their high school class. The school of engineering requires an ACT composite of 24 or SAT of 1110. The schools of art and sciences, business, and the department of technology require an ACT of 23 and SAT of 1070. Contact the address below for further information. GPA must be at least 2.7.

Tri-State University
Office of Financial Aid and Scholarships
300 S. Darling St.
Angola, IN 46703

4503
President's Scholarship

AMOUNT: $8000-$9000 DEADLINE: March 1
FIELDS/MAJORS: All Areas of Study

Awards for students who have superior academic achievement and potential for campus leadership. Applicants must have graduated in the top 10% of their high school class and received a minimum SAT score of 1300 and ACT composite of 29. Renewable if students maintain a 3.2 GPA. Contact the address below for further information. GPA must be at least 3.6.

Tri-State University
Office of Financial Aid and Scholarships
300 S. Darling St.
Angola, IN 46703

4504
Transfer Scholarships

AMOUNT: $4000-$5500 DEADLINE: March 1
FIELDS/MAJORS: All Areas of Study

Awards for students transferring with at least 75 credit hours or an associate's degree. Award of $4000 is available for those with a GPA between 2.5 and 2.9. The $5500 award is for a student with a minimum GPA of 3.0. Contact the address below for further information.

Tri-State University
Office of Financial Aid and Scholarships
300 S. Darling St.
Angola, IN 46703

4505
University Awards

AMOUNT: $1500-$4000 DEADLINE: March 1
FIELDS/MAJORS: All Areas of Study

Awards for high school seniors or transfer college students. Candidates will need to demonstrate success in their high school or college careers. Contact the address below for further information.

Tri-State University
Office of Financial Aid and Scholarships
300 S. Darling St.
Angola, IN 46703

UNITED STATES INTERNATIONAL UNIVERSITY

4506
Athletic Scholarship

AMOUNT: None Specified DEADLINE: March 2
FIELDS/MAJORS: Soccer, Tennis, Cross Country Running

For full-time undergraduates students. Awarded annually to selected team members. For men and women's soccer, tennis, and cross country running teams. Award amount varies. Scholarships are reviewed annually. Contact the athletic department for more information. (619) 635-4630.

United States International University
Financial Aid Office
10455 Pomerado Rd.
San Diego, CA 92131

4507
California Graduate Fellowship

AMOUNT: Maximum: $6490 DEADLINE: March 2
FIELDS/MAJORS: All Areas of Study

For California graduate students who intend to become college or university faculty members. Must be U.S. citizens, U.S. permanent residents, or eligible non-citizens. This award provides tuition and fee assistance. Selections based on parent information, income, educational level, and financial need. Write to the address below for more information.

United States International University
Financial Aid Office
10455 Pomerado Rd.
San Diego, CA 92131

4508
Edward N. Reynolds Graduate Diversity Scholarship

AMOUNT: None Specified DEADLINE: March 2
FIELDS/MAJORS: All Areas of Study

For first-time and continuing full-time domestic traditionally underrepresented ethnic minority graduate students. Must demonstrate academic achievement and/or promise, and financial need. Awarded on a competitive basis. Priority consideration given to those filing their university admissions application by May 1st. Write to the address below for more information. GPA must be at least 2.9.

United States International University
Financial Aid Office
10455 Pomerado Rd.
San Diego, CA 92131

4509
Edward N. Reynolds Undergraduate Diversity Scholarship

AMOUNT: None Specified DEADLINE: March 2
FIELDS/MAJORS: All Areas of Study

For first-time and continuing full-time domestic, traditionally underrepresented, ethnic minority undergraduate students. Must demonstrate academic achievement and/or promise, and financial need. Awarded on a competitive basis. Priority consideration given to those filing their university admissions application by May 1st. Write to the address below for more information.

United States International University
Financial Aid Office
10455 Pomerado Rd.
San Diego, CA 92131

4510
International Presidential Scholarship

AMOUNT: None Specified DEADLINE: March 2
FIELDS/MAJORS: All Areas of Study

For full-time international undergraduates who have demonstrated outstanding scholarly achievement. Must have an incoming GPA of 3.6 or above and be pursuing a degree. Renewable if recipients maintain a minimum GPA of 3.2. This award is for 30% of tuition. Write to the address below for more information.

United States International University
Financial Aid Office
10455 Pomerado Rd.
San Diego, CA 92131

4511
International University Scholarship

AMOUNT: None Specified DEADLINE: March 2
FIELDS/MAJORS: All Areas of Study

For full-time international undergraduates who have demonstrated academic achievement. Must have an incoming GPA of 3.0 or above and be pursuing a degree. Renewable if recipients maintain a minimum GPA of 3.0. This award is for 24% of tuition. Write to the address below for more information.

United States International University
Financial Aid Office
10455 Pomerado Rd.
San Diego, CA 92131

4512
Presidential Scholarship

AMOUNT: None Specified DEADLINE: March 2
FIELDS/MAJORS: All Areas of Study

For full-time domestic undergraduates who have demonstrated outstanding scholarly achievement. Recipients must be U.S. citizens, permanent residents, or eligible non-citizens. Must have an incoming GPA of 3.6 or above and be pursuing a degree. Renewable if recipients maintain a minimum GPA of 3.2. This award is for 30% of tuition. Write to the address below for more information.

United States International University
Financial Aid Office
10455 Pomerado Rd.
San Diego, CA 92131

4513
Ray Marshall Memorial Scholarship

AMOUNT: None Specified DEADLINE: March 2
FIELDS/MAJORS: Hotel/Restaurant Management, Travel, Tourism

Open to full-time, degree-seeking undergraduates of Latino descent. Must be U.S. citizens or permanent residents. The amount of this award varies, up to 60% of tuition. Contact the address below for further information.

United States International University
Financial Aid Office
10455 Pomerado Rd.
San Diego, CA 92131

4514
Ray Marshall Tuition Assistance Scholarships

AMOUNT: None Specified DEADLINE: March 2
FIELDS/MAJORS: Hotel/Restaurant Management, Travel, Tourism

Open to undergraduates who are of Latino descent. Must be employees of hotels or restaurants that have formal programs of monetary support for employee continuing education. This award is for tuition credit only. Amount varies, up to 60% of tuition. Renewable if recipients meet the University's academic standards. Contact the address below for further information.

United States International University
Financial Aid Office
10455 Pomerado Rd.
San Diego, CA 92131

4515
United States International University Grant

AMOUNT: None Specified DEADLINE: March 2
FIELDS/MAJORS: All Areas of Study

For full-time domestic undergraduates with exceptional financial need who are U.S. citizens, permanent residents, or eligible non-citizens. This award is for tuition credit only. Write to the address below for more information.

United States International University
Financial Aid Office
10455 Pomerado Rd.
San Diego, CA 92131

4516
University Scholarship

AMOUNT: $2347 DEADLINE: March 2
FIELDS/MAJORS: All Areas of Study

For full-time domestic undergraduates who have demonstrated academic achievement. Recipients must be U.S. citizens, U.S. permanent residents, or eligible non-citizens. Must have an incoming GPA of 3.0 or above and be pursuing a degree. Renewable if recipients maintain a minimum GPA of 3.0. This award is for 24% of tuition. Write to the address below for more information.

United States International University
Financial Aid Office
10455 Pomerado Rd.
San Diego, CA 92131

UNIVERSITY OF ALABAMA, BIRMINGHAM

4517
David Lloyd Scholarships and Ruby Lloyd Apsey Scholarships

AMOUNT: $2604 DEADLINE: None Specified
FIELDS/MAJORS: Drama and Theater

Applicants must be incoming freshmen who have a minimum ACT score of 25. Write to the address below for more information. GPA must be at least 3.0.

University of Alabama, Birmingham
UAB Department of Theater
Bell Building, UAB Station
Birmingham, AL 35294

4518
Fannie Flagg and Kathy Wates Scholarships

AMOUNT: $250-$1000 DEADLINE: None Specified
FIELDS/MAJORS: Theater, Design

Scholarship is awarded to a promising student for production work in costume shops and/or stage performing. Contact the Office of Student Financial Aid for details. GPA must be at least 2.5.

University of Alabama, Birmingham
UAB Department of Theater
Bell Building, UAB Station
Birmingham, AL 35294

4519
Production Assistantships

AMOUNT: None Specified DEADLINE: None Specified
FIELDS/MAJORS: Design

Assistantships for students in the Department of Theater and Dance at the University of Alabama at Birmingham. For production work on costumes and sets for the department. Write to the address below for information.

University of Alabama, Birmingham
Department of Theater and Dance
Bell Building, UAB Station
Birmingham, AL 35294

4520
UAB Deans Scholarship

AMOUNT: $1000 DEADLINE: None Specified
FIELDS/MAJORS: Theater

Applicants must be incoming freshmen who have a minimum ACT of 22. Renewable. For study at the University of Alabama at Birmingham. Contact the Office of Student Financial Aid for details. GPA must be at least 3.0.

University of Alabama, Birmingham
UAB Department of Theater
Bell Building, UAB Station
Birmingham, AL 35294

4521
UAB Musical Theater Scholarships

AMOUNT: $250-$1000 DEADLINE: None Specified
FIELDS/MAJORS: Musical Theater

Scholarship is awarded to a student majoring in musical theater. A talent audition is required. This would include the following scholarships: Lydia Rogers Scholarship and the William Ozier Memorial Scholarship. Contact the Office of Student Financial Aid for details. GPA must be at least 2.5.

University of Alabama, Birmingham
UAB Department of Theater
Bell Building, UAB Station
Birmingham, AL 35294

UNIVERSITY OF ALASKA SOUTHEAST (JUNEAU CAMPUS)

4522
Alvin G. Ott Fish and Wildlife Scholarship

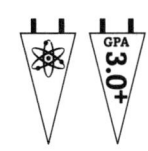

AMOUNT: None Specified DEADLINE: None Specified
FIELDS/MAJORS: Fish and Wildlife

Applicants must have a minimum GPA of 3.0 and be majoring in a field related to fish and wildlife. Write to the address below for more information.

University of Alaska Southeast (Juneau Campus)
Financial Aid Office
11120 Glacier Highway
Juneau, AK 99801

4523
Charles F. Gould Endowment Scholarship

AMOUNT: None Specified DEADLINE: None Specified
FIELDS/MAJORS: All Areas of Study

Applicant must be an Alaska Native, preferably Eskimo, with a minimum GPA of 2.0. Write to the address below for more information.

University of Alaska Southeast (Juneau Campus)
Financial Aid Office
11120 Glacier Highway
Juneau, AK 99801

4524
College of Education Endowments

AMOUNT: None Specified DEADLINE: None Specified
FIELDS/MAJORS: All Areas of Study

Scholarship is to assist in obtaining a college education at the University of Alaska. Recipient must be a full-time student attending any campus of the University of Alaska. Preference will be given to students who show a need for financial assistance. Includes: Richard Mellow Endowment and Andrew Nerland Endowment. Write to the address below for more information.

University of Alaska Southeast (Juneau Campus)
Financial Aid Office
11120 Glacier Highway
Juneau, AK 99801

4525
College of Education Scholarships

AMOUNT: None Specified DEADLINE: None Specified
FIELDS/MAJORS: All Areas of Study

Scholarship is to assist students in obtaining a college education at the University of Alaska. Recipient must be a full-time student attending any campus of the University of Alaska. Includes: Iver and Cora Knapstad Scholarship, Austin E. Lathrop Scholarship, Franklin M. Leach Scholarship. Write to the address below for more information.

University of Alaska Southeast (Juneau Campus)
Financial Aid Office
11120 Glacier Highway
Juneau, AK 99801

4526
Don and Jan O'Dowd/ SWAA Scholarship

AMOUNT: None Specified   DEADLINE: None Specified
FIELDS/MAJORS: All Areas of Study

Applicants must be incoming freshmen with a minimum GPA of 3.0. Applicant must also be an Alaskan resident and a graduate of an Alaska high school. Write to the address below for more information.

University of Alaska Southeast (Juneau Campus)
Financial Aid Office
11120 Glacier Highway
Juneau, AK 99801

4527
Gastineau Rotary Club Scholarship

AMOUNT: $1000   DEADLINE: None Specified
FIELDS/MAJORS: All Areas of Study

This scholarship is open to graduates of Juneau high schools who are entering any degree program offered at the Juneau campus of UAS. Applicants will be judged on the basis of academic achievement, leadership potential, goal-oriented motivation, and financial need. Write to the address below for more information.

University of Alaska Southeast (Juneau Campus)
Financial Aid Office
11120 Glacier Highway
Juneau, AK 99801

4528
Guy A. Woodings Scholarship

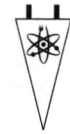

AMOUNT: None Specified   DEADLINE: March 1
FIELDS/MAJORS: Natural Resource Management

Award has preference for Alaska resident majoring in natural resource management with an emphasis in planning and zoning. Write to the address below for more information.

University of Alaska Southeast (Juneau Campus)
Financial Aid Office
11120 Glacier Highway
Juneau, AK 99801

4529
International Sourdough Reunion Memorial Scholarship

AMOUNT: None Specified   DEADLINE: None Specified
FIELDS/MAJORS: All Areas of Study

Applicants must have junior or senior class standing, a minimum GPA of 3.0, and be a resident of either Alaska or the Yukon Territory. Applicants must have graduated from high school in Alaska or in the Yukon Territory. Write to the address below for more information.

University of Alaska Southeast (Juneau Campus)
Financial Aid Office
11120 Glacier Highway
Juneau, AK 99801

4530
John Rutherford Noyes Memorial Scholarship

AMOUNT: None Specified
DEADLINE: None Specified
FIELDS/MAJORS: Education, Science

Applicants must be full-time students attending the University of Alaska Southeast who have a 3.0 or higher GPA. Applicants should demonstrate motivation, as well as academic and leadership potential. Preference will be given to Education and Science majors and to members of the Alaska National Guard. Write to the address below for more information.

University of Alaska Southeast (Juneau Campus)
Financial Aid Office
11120 Glacier Highway
Juneau, AK 99801

4531
Juneau Association of Professional Mortgage Women

AMOUNT: None Specified   DEADLINE: None Specified
FIELDS/MAJORS: Banking, Business Administration

Scholarship is meant to reward academic excellence and to attract students to careers in mortgage banking or related fields. Applicants must have a minimum GPA of 2.5, be a resident of Alaska, be admitted to a Bachelor of Business Administration degree program, have an interest in mortgage banking, and be attending classes as a full-time student. Write to the address below for more information.

University of Alaska Southeast (Juneau Campus)
Financial Aid Office
11120 Glacier Highway
Juneau, AK 99801

4532
Maureen E. Nolan-Cahill Memorial Scholarship

AMOUNT: None Specified   DEADLINE: None Specified
FIELDS/MAJORS: Science, Biological Science, Biology, Health Science, Chemistry, Physics

Applicants must be female students majoring in science (biological science, biology, health science, chemistry, physics), with a GPA of at least 3.0. Applicants must demonstrate financial need. Preference will be given to applicants who are residents of Southeast Alaska and to graduates of Alaskan high schools. Write to the address below for more information.

University of Alaska Southeast (Juneau Campus)
Financial Aid Office
11120 Glacier Highway
Juneau, AK 99801

4533
Mike Miller Scholarship

AMOUNT: None Specified   DEADLINE: None Specified
FIELDS/MAJORS: Liberal Arts, Communications

Applicants must be pursuing a Bachelor of Liberal Arts degree with an emphasis in communications. Applicants must demonstrate academic achievement, leadership potential, and goal-oriented motivation. Write to the address below for more information.

University of Alaska Southeast (Juneau Campus)
Financial Aid Office
11120 Glacier Highway
Juneau, AK 99801

4534
Mil Zahn Memorial/ Alaska Fish and Wildlife Safeguard Scholarship

AMOUNT: None Specified   DEADLINE: None Specified
FIELDS/MAJORS: Natural Resources Management, Justice, Fisheries and Wildlife

Applicants must be majoring in natural resources management, justice, or fisheries and wildlife and have a minimum junior class standing. Write to the address below for more information.

University of Alaska Southeast (Juneau Campus)
Financial Aid Office
11120 Glacier Highway
Juneau, AK 99801

4535
PEO Chapter D Ethel Montgomery Memorial Scholarship

AMOUNT: None Specified   DEADLINE: None Specified
FIELDS/MAJORS: All Areas of Study

Applicants must be full-time female students who are admitted to any degree program on the Juneau campus of UAS and who demonstrate financial need, motivation, and scholastic achievement. Write to the address below for more information.

University of Alaska Southeast (Juneau Campus)
Financial Aid Office
11120 Glacier Highway
Juneau, AK 99801

4536
PEO Chapter G Scholarships

AMOUNT: None Specified   DEADLINE: None Specified
FIELDS/MAJORS: Education

Applicants must be full-time female students who demonstrate motivation, academic achievement, leadership potential, and financial need. One scholarship will be awarded to an education major on the UAS Juneau campus; one scholarship is open to female students who are admitted to any degree program on the UAS Juneau. Write to the address below for more information.

University of Alaska Southeast (Juneau Campus)
Financial Aid Office
11120 Glacier Highway
Juneau, AK 99801

4537
Roger Lang Memorial Scholarship

AMOUNT: None Specified   DEADLINE: None Specified
FIELDS/MAJORS: All Areas of Study

Applicants must be Native Alaskan residents of SE Alaska and must demonstrate motivation, academic achievement, and leadership potential. Undergraduate applicants must have a minimum GPA of 2.5; graduate applicants must have a minimum GPA of 3.0. Write to the address below for more information

University of Alaska Southeast (Juneau Campus)
Financial Aid Office
11120 Glacier Highway
Juneau, AK 99801

4538
Rotary Club of Juneau Scholarships

AMOUNT: None Specified DEADLINE: None Specified
FIELDS/MAJORS: All Areas of Study

Applicants must be Southeast Alaska residents who are entering any degree program offered at the Juneau campus of UAS. Applicants will be judged on the basis of academic achievement, excellence in the arts, leadership potential, goal-oriented motivation, and financial need. Write to the address below for more information.

University of Alaska Southeast (Juneau Campus)
Financial Aid Office
11120 Glacier Highway
Juneau, AK 99801

4539
Southeast Conference Scholarships

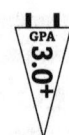

AMOUNT: None Specified DEADLINE: None Specified
FIELDS/MAJORS: All Areas of Study

Applicants must be SE Alaska residents who are full-time students at either the Juneau, Ketchikan, or Sitka campus of UAS. Applicants should demonstrate motivation, academic and leadership potential, and must be in good academic standing with a minimum GPA of 3.0. Write to the address below for more information.

University of Alaska Southeast (Juneau Campus)
Financial Aid Office
11120 Glacier Highway
Juneau, AK 99801

4540
UAS Talent Grants for Resident and Non-Resident Students

AMOUNT: $250-$1000 DEADLINE: None Specified
FIELDS/MAJORS: All Areas of Study

Scholarships are available at the University of Alaska, Juneau, Ketchikan, or Sitka for full-time students. Based on academic achievement, leadership potential, goal-oriented motivation, and financial need. Write to the address below for information. GPA must be at least 3.4.

University of Alaska Southeast (Juneau Campus)
Financial Aid Office
11120 Glacier Highway
Juneau, AK 99801

4541
United Students of UAS-Juneau Full-Time Scholarships

AMOUNT: $1000 DEADLINE: None Specified
FIELDS/MAJORS: All Areas of Study

Scholarships are available at the University of Alaska, Juneau, for full-time students. Based on academic achievement, leadership potential, and goal-oriented motivation. Undergraduate students must have a 3.0 GPA, and graduate students must have a GPA of at least 3.5. Write to the address below for information.

University of Alaska Southeast (Juneau Campus)
Financial Aid Office
11120 Glacier Highway
Juneau, AK 99801

4542
Verna Carrigan Scholarships

AMOUNT: None Specified DEADLINE: None Specified
FIELDS/MAJORS: All Areas of Study

Applicants must be residents of SE Alaska, with preference given to students from the Juneau and Douglas areas, who are entering any degree program at the Juneau campus of UAS. Applicants must demonstrate academic achievement, leadership potential, goal-oriented motivation, and financial need. Write to the address below for more information.

University of Alaska Southeast (Juneau Campus)
Financial Aid Office
11120 Glacier Highway
Juneau, AK 99801

4543
Ward Sims Memorial Scholarship

AMOUNT: None Specified DEADLINE: None Specified
FIELDS/MAJORS: Journalism

Applicants must have junior or senior class standing and be enrolled in the journalism program with a minimum GPA of 2.0. Write to the address below for more information.

University of Alaska Southeast (Juneau Campus)
Financial Aid Office
11120 Glacier Highway
Juneau, AK 99801

4544
William S. Wilson Memorial Scholarship

AMOUNT: None Specified DEADLINE: None Specified
FIELDS/MAJORS: Science

Applicants must be full-time students majoring in science. Preference will be given to undergraduate students, but graduate students will be considered. Write to the address below for more information.

University of Alaska Southeast (Juneau Campus)
Financial Aid Office
11120 Glacier Highway
Juneau, AK 99801

UNIVERSITY OF ALASKA SOUTHEAST (KETCHIKAN CAMPUS)

4545
Al Robertson Memorial Scholarship

AMOUNT: $1000 DEADLINE: None Specified
FIELDS/MAJORS: All Areas of Study

Scholarships are available to members of the graduating class of Ketchikan High School who have a cumulative GPA of at least 2.5. Recipients must be full-time students attending one of the branches of the University of Alaska. Recipients should demonstrate motivation, academic and leadership potential, and must demonstrate financial need. Write to the address below for more information.

University of Alaska Southeast (Ketchikan Campus)
2600 7th Ave.
Ketchikan, AK 99901-5798

4546
Beck Writing Award

AMOUNT: $250 DEADLINE: None Specified
FIELDS/MAJORS: Creative Writing

Scholarships are awarded to full-time or part-time program students at UAS Ketchikan. Preferences are given to students who have completed at least one semester of college-level writing courses with an average grade of B or above and who intend to continue to take English classes. Write to the address below for more information. GPA must be at least 3.0.

University of Alaska Southeast (Ketchikan Campus)
2600 7th Ave.
Ketchikan, AK 99901-5798

4547
Continuing Education Grant

AMOUNT: $500 DEADLINE: None Specified
FIELDS/MAJORS: All Areas of study

Scholarships are awarded to female students attending the UAS Ketchikan campus with plans to enroll in the spring. Applicants must indicate motivation as well as academic and employment potential in selected field. Write to the address below for more information.

University of Alaska Southeast (Ketchikan Campus)
2600 7th Ave.
Ketchikan, AK 99901-5798

4548
Paul Wingren Scholarship

AMOUNT: $1000 DEADLINE: None Specified
FIELDS/MAJORS: All Areas of Study

Scholarships are available to full-time or half-time students at UAS Ketchikan enrolled in a program leading toward a vocational degree/certificate or in coursework leading toward employment or industry certification. Students must have earned at least a 2.0 GPA and be in good academic standing. Preference given to students who are currently employed at least part-time. Write to the address below for more information.

University of Alaska Southeast (Ketchikan Campus)
2600 7th Ave.
Ketchikan, AK 99901-5798

4549
Philis Smith Scholarship

AMOUNT: $1000 DEADLINE: None Specified
FIELDS/MAJORS: All Areas of Study

Scholarships are available to full-time or part-time students at UAS Ketchikan. Must demonstrate motivation and academic leadership potential; must have earned at least a 2.0 GPA; and must be in good academic standing. Write to the address below for more information.

University of Alaska Southeast (Ketchikan Campus)
2600 7th Ave.
Ketchikan, AK 99901-5798

4550
Ralph Yetka Scholarship

AMOUNT: $750 DEADLINE: None Specified
FIELDS/MAJORS: Aviation, Computer Science, Education, Engineering

Scholarships are available to graduates of one of Ketchikan's high schools who will be attending one of the University of Alaska two or four-year campuses. The students must intend to major in aviation, computer science, education, or engineering and must have earned at least a 2.5 GPA over his/her high school or college career. Write to the address below for more information.

University of Alaska Southeast (Ketchikan Campus)
2600 7th Ave.
Ketchikan, AK 99901-5798

4551
Sharon "Christa" McAuliffe Memorial Scholarship

AMOUNT: Maximum: $1000   DEADLINE: None Specified
FIELDS/MAJORS: All Areas of Study

Scholarships are available to full-time students (enrolled or planning to enroll in 12 or more credit hours) at UAS Ketchikan campus. Academic merit, on campus and off-campus involvement, and financial need will be considered. Write to the address below for more information.

University of Alaska Southeast (Ketchikan Campus)
2600 7th Ave.
Ketchikan, AK 99901-5798

UNIVERSITY OF ARKANSAS

4552
Alumni Legacy Scholarships

AMOUNT: None Specified   DEADLINE: None Specified
FIELDS/MAJORS: All Fields of Study

Open to incoming freshman with a minimum of 3.0 GPA and a parent who graduated from UAF who is currently a member of the Arkansas Alumni Association. Award is out-of-state tuition waiver. Renewable if student maintains 24 hours of coursework per year and a GPA of 3.0. Contact the address below for further information or call (501) 575-2801. Students must submit an Arkansas Alumni Legacy Data Form.

University of Arkansas, Fayetteville
Arkansas Alumni Association
PO Box 1070
Fayetteville, AR 72701-1070

4553
Arkansas Alumni Association Scholarships

AMOUNT: None Specified   DEADLINE: March 1
FIELDS/MAJORS: All Fields of Study

Open to incoming students with a minimum of 3.5 GPA who are involved in extracurricular activities and leadership activities. Award is waiver of registration fee. Renewable if students maintain a GPA of 3.2 after 30 hours of coursework per year. Contact the address below for further information or call (501) 575-2801.

University of Arkansas, Fayetteville
Arkansas Alumni Association
PO Box 1070
Fayetteville, AR 72701-1070

4554
Arkansas Alumni Scholarship, Arkansas Scholarship, Chapter Scholarship

AMOUNT: Maximum: $1000   DEADLINE: March 1
FIELDS/MAJORS: All Areas of Study

Scholarships are available for Arkansas residents at the University of Arkansas. Applicants must be graduating high school seniors with a minimum GPA of at least 3.5. Renewable. Write to the address below for information.

Arkansas Alumni Association
PO Box 1070
Fayetteville, AR 72702

4555
Band and Music Scholarships

AMOUNT: None Specified   DEADLINE: None Specified
FIELDS/MAJORS: Music

Available to students majoring in any music field. Student must demonstrate talent by audition. Awards may be renewed. Contact the address below for further information.

University of Arkansas
Chairman, Music Department
201 Music Building
Fayetteville, AR 72701

4556
Chancellor's Scholarships

AMOUNT: $7000-$10000 **DEADLINE:** March 1
FIELDS/MAJORS: All Areas of Study

Open to incoming freshmen with a minimum GPA of 3.5 and ACT score of 33-36 and SAT score of 1470-1600. Applicants may have a 3.5 GPA and be National Merit or Achievement semi-finalists. National Merit or Achievement finalists are also eligible. Renewable if students complete 30 hours with a GPA of 3.2 by the end of spring semester each year. Contact the address below for further information.

University of Arkansas
Office of Admissions
200 Silas H. Hunt Hall
Fayetteville, AR 72701

4557
Freshman Academic Scholarships

AMOUNT: $500-$2000 **DEADLINE:** March 1
FIELDS/MAJORS: All Areas of Study

Available to entering freshmen with minimum GPA of 3.5 who are residents of Arkansas and have not enrolled in any other postsecondary institution. Highly competitive. Renewable for three years if student earns 27 hours with a GPA of 3.0 for freshman year and 30 hours with a GPA of 3.2 for both sophomore and senior years. Awards announced after March 1. Contact the address below for further information.

University of Arkansas
Office of Admissions
200 Silas H. Hunt Hall
Fayetteville, AR 72701

4558
Multicultural Achievement Scholarships

AMOUNT: Maximum: $2000 **DEADLINE:** March 1
FIELDS/MAJORS: All Areas of Study

Offered to students who are members of an ethnic minority with a minimum GPA of 3.0 who have not enrolled in any other postsecondary institution. Renewable if students complete 24 hours with a 2.75 GPA freshman year and complete 27 hours with 3.0 GPA for both sophomore and junior year. Out-of-state fee waiver also available for non-residents. Contact the address below for further information.

University of Arkansas
Office of Admissions
200 Silas H. Hunt Hall
Fayetteville, AR 72701

4559
National Merit Scholarships

AMOUNT: $750-$2000 **DEADLINE:** None Specified
FIELDS/MAJORS: All Areas of Study

Available to entering freshman who are National Merit finalists. Must take PSAT in junior year of high school. Renewable for three years if recipients remain in good academic standing. Contact the address below for further information. GPA must be at least 3.0.

University of Arkansas
Office of Admissions
200 Silas H. Hunt Hall
Fayetteville, AR 72701

4560
Out-of-state Scholarships

AMOUNT: $1000-$6000 **DEADLINE:** March 1
FIELDS/MAJORS: All Fields of Study

Awarded to an out-of-state freshman with minimum GPA of 3.5 who has not enrolled in any other postsecondary institution. Renewable if student earns 27 hours with a 3.0 GPA freshman year and earns 30 hours with GPA of 3.2 for both sophomore and junior years. Awards announced after March 1. Contact the address below for more information.

University of Arkansas, Fayetteville
Office of Admissions
200 Silas H. Hunt Hall
Fayetteville, AR 72701

4561
Sturgis Fellowships

AMOUNT: Maximum: $11000 **DEADLINE:** February 1
FIELDS/MAJORS: Arts, Sciences

Available to students who demonstrate exceptional academic performance as specified by the Fulbright College of Arts and Sciences. Highly competitive. Contact the address below for further information. GPA must be at least 3.2.

University of Arkansas, Fayetteville
Director of Honors Studies
Old Main 517
Fayetteville, AR 72701

4562
Transfer Student Scholarships

AMOUNT: $1000-$2000 **DEADLINE:** March 15
FIELDS/MAJORS: All Areas of Study

Offered to transfer students with a minimum GPA of 3.5 and has earned 45-60 credit hours. Phi Theta Kappa inductees receive priority consideration. Renewable if student earns 30 hours with 3.2 GPA in one year. Contact the address below for further information.

University of Arkansas
Office of Admissions
200 Silas H. Hunt Hall
Fayetteville, AR 72701

4563
University Scholarships

AMOUNT: Maximum: $2500 DEADLINE: March 1
FIELDS/MAJORS: All Areas of Study

Available to entering freshmen with minimum GPA of 3.75 who are residents of Arkansas and have not enrolled in any other postsecondary institution. Highly competitive. Renewable for three years if student earns 27 hours with GPA of 3.0 freshman year and 30 hours with GPA of 3.2 for both sophomore and junior years. Contact the address below for further information.

University of Arkansas
Office of Admissions
200 Silas H. Hunt Hall
Fayetteville, AR 72701

4564
U.S. Army and U.S. Air Force Scholarships

AMOUNT: None Specified DEADLINE: December 1
FIELDS/MAJORS: All Fields of Study

Applicants must have competitive test scores and GPA. Interview is required. Award is full tuition, books, fees, $100 monthly, and room and board. Students must apply between April 1 of junior year and December 1 of senior year of high school. Contact the Professor of Military Science for Army Scholarships at (501) 575-4251 or the Professor for Aerospace Studies for Air Force Scholarships (501) 575-3651. GPA must be at least 3.0.

University of Arkansas, Fayetteville
Office of Admissions
200 Silas H. Hunt Hall
Fayetteville, AR 72701

4565
Wal-Mart Competitive Edge Scholarship

AMOUNT: Maximum: $5000 DEADLINE: March 1
FIELDS/MAJORS: Technology

Scholarships are available to incoming freshmen majoring in technology-related fields. Must have GPAs of 3.5, ACT scores of 27, SAT scores of 1100, and be U.S. citizens. Contact the address below for further information.

University of Arkansas
200 Silas H. Hunt Hall
Fayetteville, AR 72701

UNIVERSITY OF BRIDGEPORT

4566
Academic Excellence and Leadership Scholarship

AMOUNT: Maximum: $19500 DEADLINE: None Specified
FIELDS/MAJORS: All Areas of Study

Open to high school seniors ranked in the top 10% of their graduating classes. Renewable based on satisfactory academics and good standing in the University. Students enrolled in accelerated/professional courses are not eligible for these awards. Contact the address below for further information. GPA must be at least 3.6.

University of Bridgeport
Office of Admissions
126 Park Ave.
Bridgeport, CT 06601

4567
Academic Grant

AMOUNT: Maximum: $6250 DEADLINE: None Specified
FIELDS/MAJORS: All Areas of Study

Open to high school seniors ranked in the top third of their graduating classes. Renewable based on satisfactory academics and good standing in the University. Students enrolled in accelerated/professional courses are not eligible for these awards. Contact the address below for further information. GPA must be at least 3.0.

University of Bridgeport
Office of Admissions
126 Park Ave.
Bridgeport, CT 06601

4568
Academic Scholarship

AMOUNT: Maximum: $12500 DEADLINE: None Specified
FIELDS/MAJORS: All Areas of Study

Open to high school seniors ranked in the top fifth of their graduating classes. Renewable based on satisfactory academics and good standing in the University. Students enrolled in accelerated/professional courses are not eligible for these awards. Contact the address below for further information. GPA must be at least 3.4.

University of Bridgeport
Office of Admissions
126 Park Ave.
Bridgeport, CT 06601

4569
Challenge Grant

GPA 2.5+

AMOUNT: Maximum: $3000 DEADLINE: None Specified
FIELDS/MAJORS: All Areas of Study

Open to high school seniors ranked in the top half of their graduating classes. Renewable based on satisfactory academics and good standing in the University. Students enrolled in accelerated/professional courses are not eligible for these awards. Contact the address below for further information. GPA must be at least 2.5.

University of Bridgeport
Office of Admissions
126 Park Ave.
Bridgeport, CT 06601

4570
Transfer Academic Excellence and Leadership Scholarship

GPA 3.5+

AMOUNT: Maximum: $19500 DEADLINE: None Specified
FIELDS/MAJORS: All Areas of Study

Open to incoming full-time transfer students who have a minimum GPA of 3.75 and at least 24 credits. Renewable based on satisfactory academics, good standing in the University, and remaining full-time. Contact the address below for further information.

University of Bridgeport
Office of Admissions
126 Park Ave.
Bridgeport, CT 06601

4571
Transfer Academic Grant

GPA 3.0+

AMOUNT: Maximum: $6250 DEADLINE: None Specified
FIELDS/MAJORS: All Areas of Study

Open to incoming full-time transfer students who have a minimum GPA of 3.3 and at least 24 credits. Renewable based on satisfactory academics, good standing in the University, and remaining full-time. Contact the address below for further information.

University of Bridgeport
Office of Admissions
126 Park Ave.
Bridgeport, CT 06601

4572
Transfer Academic Scholarship

GPA 3.5+

AMOUNT: Maximum: $12500 DEADLINE: None Specified
FIELDS/MAJORS: All Areas of Study

Open to incoming full-time transfer students who have a minimum GPA of 3.5 and at least 24 credits. Renewable based on satisfactory academics, good standing in the University, and remaining full-time. Contact the address below for further information.

University of Bridgeport
Office of Admissions
126 Park Ave.
Bridgeport, CT 06601

4573
Transfer Incentive Grant

GPA 3.0+

AMOUNT: Maximum: $3000 DEADLINE: None Specified
FIELDS/MAJORS: All Areas of Study

Open to incoming full-time transfer students who have a minimum GPA of 3.0 and at least 24 credits. Renewable based on satisfactory academics, good standing in the University, and remaining full-time. Contact the address below for further information.

University of Bridgeport
Office of Admissions
126 Park Ave.
Bridgeport, CT 06601

UNIVERSITY OF CALIFORNIA, BERKELY

4574
Alumni Club Leadership Scholarship

GPA 3.0+

AMOUNT: Maximum: $1000 DEADLINE: September 30
FIELDS/MAJORS: All Areas of Study

Open to gay, lesbian, and bisexual continuing undergraduates at UC Berkeley, carrying a minimum of 12 units per semester with a minimum cumulative GPA of 3.0. Based on academic achievement and leadership in campus, community, or job activities. Contact the address below for further information.

University of California Gay and Lesbian Assn.
  Alumni House
UC Berkeley-California Alumni Assn.
Scholarship Office
Berkeley, CA 94720-7450

4575
Graduate Opportunity Program

AMOUNT: Maximum: $7000   DEADLINE: January 5
FIELDS/MAJORS: All Areas of Study

Grants for minority graduate students at Berkeley. Based on academic promise and financial need. Must be U.S. citizens or permanent residents. For master's or doctoral degree study. Write to the address below for details.

University of California, Berkeley
Graduate Division
S. Alejandre, Recruitment Coordinator
Berkeley, CA 94720

4576
Mary O'Day Memorial Fellowship

AMOUNT: Maximum: $500   DEADLINE: January 5
FIELDS/MAJORS: Public Health Services

Open to full-time master degree students planning a career in gerontology. Must be U.S. citizens or permanent residents. Contact the address below for further information.

University of California, Berkeley
Office of Financial Aid, Graduate Unit
201 Sproul Hall, #1960
Berkeley, CA 94720

4577
Minna B. Crook, Myrtle C. Lytle and Martha Chickering Fellowships

AMOUNT: $1200-$2700   DEADLINE: January 5
FIELDS/MAJORS: Social Services

Open to full-time master degree students planning a career in public social services. Must be U.S. citizens or permanent residents. Contact the address below for further information.

University of California, Berkeley
Office of Financial Aid Graduate Unit
201 Sproul Hall, #1960
Berkeley, CA 94720

4578
Riva Specht, Wurzel Family and Fred Smith/Don Catalano Fellowships

AMOUNT: $1800-$2700   DEADLINE: January 5
FIELDS/MAJORS: Public Social Services, Public Health Services

Open to full-time master degree students planning a career in public social and/or health services. Must be U.S. citizens or permanent residents. Contact the address below for further information.

University of California, Berkeley
Office of Financial Aid Graduate Unit
201 Sproul Hall, #1960
Berkeley, CA 94720

4579
Solis Family Fellowship

AMOUNT: Maximum: $600   DEADLINE: January 5
FIELDS/MAJORS: Public Services

Open to full-time Latino master degree students planning a career to serve Latino people and communities in the U.S. Must be U.S. citizens or permanent residents. Contact the address below for further information.

University of California, Berkeley
Office of Financial Aid Graduate Unit
201 Sproul Hall, #1960
Berkeley, CA 94720

UNIVERSITY OF CALIFORNIA, IRVINE

4580
Bruce Wade Memorial Scholarship

AMOUNT: Maximum: $1200   DEADLINE: April 4
FIELDS/MAJORS: All Areas of Study

Open to lesbian, gay, or bisexual students who contribute to improving the campus environment for other lesbian, gay, and bisexual students. Must be currently enrolled, have satisfactory academics, and demonstrate service to the LGB campus community. Based on merit, quality of essay submitted, and references. Financial need may be considered as a final selection criterion. Contact the address below for further information. GPA must be at least 2.9.

University of California, Irvine
Lesbian, Gay, Bisexual Resource Center
106 Gateway Commons
Irvine, CA 92697

4581
James J. Harvey Dissertation Fellowship

AMOUNT: $3750 DEADLINE: December 1
FIELDS/MAJORS: Homosexuality

Open to graduate students who have advanced to candidacy for the Ph.D. and are studying male or female homosexuality. Proposals should include a statement by the nominee describing the dissertation project, progress to date, and schedule of completion. Awards include a $3750 stipend and student fees for one quarter. Two to three fellowships are offered annually. Applications for fall quarter are due in early May. Contact the address below for further information.

University of California, Irvine
Research and Graduate Studies
Steve Johnson, Director
120 Administration
Irvine, CA 92697

UNIVERSITY OF CALIFORNIA, LOS ANGELES

4582
Ahmanson and Getty Postdoctoral Fellowships

AMOUNT: $18400 DEADLINE: March 15
FIELDS/MAJORS: Seventeenth and Eighteenth Century Studies

Residential fellowships for scholars who hold a doctorate and would benefit from the interdisciplinary, cross-cultural programs at the Clark Library Center for Seventeenth and Eighteenth Century Studies at UCLA. Topics of study include Western Americana, British Studies, History of Science, Literature, Law, Philosophy, and Musicology. The $18,400 stipend is for two quarters. Write to the fellowship coordinator at the address below for details.

UCLA Center for Seventeenth and Eighteenth Century Studies
395 Dodd Hall, UCLA
405 Hilgard Ave
Los Angeles, CA 90024

4583
Clark Short-Term Fellowships

AMOUNT: $2000-$6000 DEADLINE: March 15
FIELDS/MAJORS: Seventeenth and Eighteenth Century Studies

Residential predoctoral and postdoctoral fellowships at the Center for Seventeenth and Eighteenth Century Studies at UCLA. Supports research, restoration, or dissertation concerns. Terms of fellowships are one to three months. Award amount is $2000 per month. Research topics include History of Printing, Western Americana, British Studies, and Literature. Write to the fellowship coordinator at the address below for details.

UCLA Center for Seventeenth and Eighteenth Century Studies
William Andrews Clark Memorial Library
2520 Cimmarron St.
Los Angeles, CA 90018

UNIVERSITY OF CALIFORNIA, OAKLAND

4584
President's Postdoctoral Fellowship Program

AMOUNT: Maximum: $27000
DEADLINE: December 1
FIELDS/MAJORS: Mathematics, Computer Science, Engineering, Physics

Twenty fellowships are available at Oakland for minority and female postdoctoral scholars committed to careers in university teaching or research. Applicants must be U.S. citizens or permanent residents and hold, or will be holding, the Ph.D. by the year of the award. Write to the address below for information on these and other programs that are available.

University of California, Oakland
Office of the President
300 Lakeside Dr., 18th Floor
Oakland, CA 94612

UNIVERSITY OF CALIFORNIA, SAN DIEGO

4585
Jaye Haddad Memorial Scholarship

AMOUNT: None Specified DEADLINE: None Specified
FIELDS/MAJORS: All Areas of Study

Open to gay, lesbian, bisexual, or transgendered students who have been diagnosed with cancer or AIDS or students with physical disabilities. Must be undergraduates, U.S. citizens, or permanent residents making satisfactory academic progress. Must be able to demonstrate financial need. Contact the address listed for further information. Must have a GPA of at least 2.7.

University of California, San Diego
Scholarship Office 0013
9500 Gilman Dr.
La Jolla, CA 92093

4586
Michael L. Marx and Donald K. Marshall Scholarship

AMOUNT: Maximum: $1000 DEADLINE: February 17
FIELDS/MAJORS: All Areas of Study

Open to gay, lesbian, bisexual, or transgendered sophomores, juniors, and seniors who are striving to reach their full potential while nurturing a positive sense of self-worth. Must be enrolled at the University of California, San Diego, and have a strong academic record and demonstrated financial need. Contact the address below for further information. GPA must be at least 3.0.

University of California, San Diego
Scholarship Office 0013
9500 Gilman Dr.
La Jolla, CA 92093

4587
Regents Scholarships

AMOUNT: $500-$14968 DEADLINE: February 21
FIELDS/MAJORS: All Areas of Study

At least two hundred scholarships are available at UCSD for entering freshmen who have demonstrated high scholastic aptitude and exceptional test scores. Applicants must have a minimum GPA of 3.86. Eligible applicants are automatically considered for this scholarship upon applying to UCSD.

University of California, San Diego
Student Financial Services
9500 Gilman Dr.
La Jolla, CA 92093

UNIVERSITY OF CENTRAL FLORIDA

4588
Abram and Mollie Leftkowitz Scholarship

AMOUNT: None Specified DEADLINE: March 4
FIELDS/MAJORS: All Areas of Study

Open to undergraduates enrolled/admitted to UCF. Applicants must have graduated from a high school in Orange, Seminole, Osceola, or Brevard counties. Religious preference given to Jewish students. Write to the address below for further information.

University of Central Florida
Student Financial Assistance Office
Administration Building, Room 120
Orlando, FL 32816

4589
Achievement, Academic Scholarships

AMOUNT: $1000 DEADLINE: April 1
FIELDS/MAJORS: All Areas of Study

Scholarships are available at the University of Central Florida for full-time incoming freshmen who are National Merit finalists and semi-finalists, valedictorians or salutatorians, or National Achievement Hispanic finalists and semi-finalists. Write to the address below for information.

University of Central Florida
Admission Services
Administration Building, Room 161
Orlando, FL 32816

4590
B. Joseph Teneriello Memorial Scholarship

AMOUNT: None Specified DEADLINE: March 4
FIELDS/MAJORS: Business Management, Computer Science

Open to full-time undergraduates accepted/enrolled at UCF who have a minimum GPA of 2.0. Financial need may be used as a deciding factor. Preference given to applicants who are employees or immediate family members of Mitchell's Formal Wear. Write to the address below for further information.

University of Central Florida
Student Financial Assistance Office
Administration Building, Room 120
Orlando, FL 32816

4591
Council for Continuing Education for Women Scholarship

AMOUNT: Maximum: $1000 DEADLINE: February 15
FIELDS/MAJORS: All Areas of Study

Scholarships are available at CFU for women who are at least twenty-five years of age or above and able to demonstrate financial need. Applicants must have been full-time residents of Central Florida for the previous twelve months. Must also demonstrate a goal for a career, improvement of earning capacity, or employment skills. Write to the address below for further information.

University of Central Florida
Student Disability Services
Administration Building, Room 282
Orlando, FL 32816

4592
Fraternal Order of Police Scholarship

AMOUNT: None Specified DEADLINE: March 4
FIELDS/MAJORS: All Areas of Study

Open to incoming freshmen admitted to UCF who are in the top third of graduating class. Applicants must be graduating from a high school in Orange County and be recommended by a police officer. Financial need may be a deciding factor. Write to the address below for further information. GPA must be at least 2.8.

University of Central Florida
Student Financial Assistance Office
Administration Building, Room 120
Orlando, FL 32816

4593
Harrod Loans

AMOUNT: None Specified DEADLINE: May 29
FIELDS/MAJORS: All Areas of Study

Loans available at UCF for full-time entering freshmen who have a minimum SAT score of 900 and continuing students who have at least a 2.75 GPA. Applicants must be independent students with good moral character. Write to the address below for further information.

University of Central Florida
Student Financial Assistance Office
Administration Building, Room 120
Orlando, FL 32816

4594
Kobrin Family Scholarship

AMOUNT: $500-$1000 DEADLINE: March 4
FIELDS/MAJORS: All Areas of Study

Open to admitted full-time freshmen at UCF who have a minimum GPA of 3.2. Applicants must be residents of Osceola, Seminole, or Orange counties. Preference given to students of the Jewish faith. Write to the address listed for further information.

University of Central Florida
Student Financial Assistance Office
Administration Building, Room 120
Orlando, FL 32816

4595
Milton and Louise Jentes Scholarship

AMOUNT: None Specified DEADLINE: March 4
FIELDS/MAJORS: All Areas of Study

Scholarships are available at UCF for full-time undergraduates who graduated from a high school in Orange or Seminole counties and are of the Jewish faith. Write to the address below for further information.

University of Central Florida
Student Financial Assistance Office
Administration Building, Room 120
Orlando, FL 32816

4596
Project Rebound Scholarship

AMOUNT: Maximum: $5000 DEADLINE: March 4
FIELDS/MAJORS: All Areas of Study

Scholarships are available at UCF for full-time undergraduates who are single heads of households with total responsibility for the care of one or more children. Must demonstrate at least $5000 financial need as determined by the Free Application for Federal Student Aid. Write to the address below for further information.

University of Central Florida
Student Financial Assistance Office
Administration Building, Room 120
Orlando, FL 32816

4597
Robert Morley Scholarship

AMOUNT: None Specified DEADLINE: March 4
FIELDS/MAJORS: All Areas of Study

Open to Christian undergraduates at UCF. Must be able to demonstrate exceptional academic ability and strong faith. Write to the address below for further information. GPA must be at least 3.1.

University of Central Florida
Student Financial Assistance Office
Administration Building, Room 120
Orlando, FL 32816

4598
Sgt. Bobby Conley/John T. Russell Scholarship

AMOUNT: None Specified DEADLINE: May 29
FIELDS/MAJORS: All Areas of Study

Open to full-time students accepted/enrolled at UCF. Applicants must provide an official letter from Christ the King Episcopal Church. Write to the address listed for further information.

University of Central Florida
Student Financial Assistance Office
Administration Building, Room 120
Orlando, FL 32816

4599
Theodore R. and Vivian M. Johnson Disability Scholarship

AMOUNT: None Specified   DEADLINE: April 15
FIELDS/MAJORS: All Areas of Study

Scholarships are available at Florida colleges and universities for full-time students who are handicapped. Applicants must have a GPA of at least 2.0 and be able to demonstrate financial need. Write to the address below for further information.

University of Central Florida
Student Disability Services
Administration Building, Room 282
Orlando, FL 32816

4600
Town and Gown Scholarship

AMOUNT: None Specified   DEADLINE: March 4
FIELDS/MAJORS: All Areas of Study

Open to non-traditional or head of household students at UCF. Applicants must be juniors or seniors and be able to demonstrate financial need. Write to the address below for further information.

University of Central Florida
Student Financial Assistance Office
Administration Building, Room 120
Orlando, FL 32816

4601
UCF Women's Club-Frances H. Millican Endowed Scholarship

AMOUNT: Maximum: $1000   DEADLINE: March 4
FIELDS/MAJORS: All Areas of Study

Scholarships are available at UCF for female full-time undergraduates who are nontraditional students. Must have GPA of at least 3.0 and be able to demonstrate financial need. Nontraditional includes: returning to school after a significant time lapse, beginning studies later in life, or being a single parent or head of household. Write to the address below for further information.

University of Central Florida
Student Financial Assistance Office
Administration Building, Room 120
Orlando, FL 32816

UNIVERSITY OF CINCINNATI

4602
Performing Arts Scholarships

AMOUNT: None Specified   DEADLINE: None Specified
FIELDS/MAJORS: Performing Arts

Scholarships available to undergraduate students who attend or who plan to attend the University of Cincinnati. Awards vary from one-third to full tuition and fees ($12000 in-state, $28000 out-of-state) and can be used for the study of all music, dance, drama, musical theater, theater design, and production programs. Write to the address listed for details.

University of Cincinnati
Paul R. Hilner
College-Conservatory of Music
Cincinnati, OH 45221

UNIVERSITY OF COLORADO, COLORADO SPRINGS

4603
College of Engineering and Applied Science Dean's Scholarship

AMOUNT: None Specified   DEADLINE: March 15
FIELDS/MAJORS: Applied Mathematics, Computer Science, Engineering

Open to incoming high school graduates or college transfer students planning to enroll full-time (minimum 12 credit hours). High school seniors must have a minimum SAT score of 980, ACT of 24 and GPA of 3.2. Transfer students are required to have a minimum GPA of 3.0. Contact the address below for further information.

University of Colorado, Colorado Springs
Office of Financial Aid
1420 Austin Bluffs Pkwy., PO Box 7150
Colorado Springs, CO 80907

4604
Colorado Springs Sky Sox Sport Management Scholarship

AMOUNT: None Specified
DEADLINE: January 15
FIELDS/MAJORS: Sport Management, Sport Medicine

Open to students who have a minimum GPA of 3.0. Must be pursuing sport management or sport medicine as career goals. Contact the address below for further information.

University of Colorado, Colorado Springs
Office of Financial Aid
1420 Austin Bluffs Pkwy., PO Box 7150
Colorado Springs, CO 80907

4605
Karen Possehl Endowment for Women Scholarship

AMOUNT: None Specified DEADLINE: April 15
FIELDS/MAJORS: All Areas of Study

Open to women pursuing degrees, admitted to the University of Colorado at Colorado Springs, who are twenty-five years of age or older. Must have a minimum GPA of 3.0 and be enrolled for at least 12 hours per semester (9 hours if employed full-time). Contact the address below for further information or call (719) 262-3460.

University of Colorado, Colorado Springs
Office of Financial Aid
1420 Austin Bluffs Pkwy., PO Box 7150
Colorado Springs, CO 80907

4606
Marion Sonderman Scholarship

AMOUNT: $2000 DEADLINE: May 24
FIELDS/MAJORS: Political Science, Economics

Open to students who have completed at least 60 semester hours with a minimum GPA of 3.5 in either political science or economics and at least a 3.0 overall. Must be enrolled for a minimum of 9 credit hours during any semester in which the award is received. Contact the address below for further information.

University of Colorado, Colorado Springs
Office of Financial Aid
1420 Austin Bluffs Pkwy., PO Box 7150
Colorado Springs, CO 80907

4607
MCI Scholarship

AMOUNT: $500 DEADLINE: None Specified
FIELDS/MAJORS: Computer Science

Open to minority students who are economically disadvantaged. Must have a minimum GPA of 3.0 overall and a 3.5 in their major courses. Four awards are given annually. Contact the address below for further information.

University of Colorado, Colorado Springs
Office of Financial Aid
1420 Austin Bluffs Pkwy., PO Box 7150
Colorado Springs, CO 80907

4608
Physics Freshman and Undergraduate Scholarships

AMOUNT: Maximum: $1500 DEADLINE: March 31
FIELDS/MAJORS: Physics

Open to high school seniors interested in physics. Must be nominated by a high school science teacher. Based on academics and personal statement. Sophomores, juniors, and seniors based on academics, personal statement, and information from references. Contact Dr. Thomas Christensen, Chair, Department of Physics and Energy Science, Engineering 210, at the address below. GPA must be at least 3.0.

University of Colorado, Colorado Springs
Office of Financial Aid, Dr. Ron Ruminisk
1420 Austin Bluffs Pkwy., PO Box 7150
Colorado Springs, CO 80907

4609
Schantz Scholarship

AMOUNT: $600 DEADLINE: April 4
FIELDS/MAJORS: Arts, Science, Letters

Open to students enrolled in the College of Letters, Arts, and Sciences. Must have a minimum GPA of 3.0 and must have completed at least 30 credit hours at University of Colorado, Colorado Springs. Must be enrolled for a minimum of 9 credit hours each semester. Contact the address below for further information.

University of Colorado, Colorado Springs
Office of Financial Aid
1420 Austin Bluffs Pkwy., PO Box 7150
Colorado Springs, CO 80907

4610
Virginia T. Schuman Scholarship

AMOUNT: None Specified
DEADLINE: March 1
FIELDS/MAJORS: Business, Engineering, Teacher Education

Open to incoming high school graduates or college transfer students. Must have a minimum GPA of 3.0. Contact the address below for further information.

University of Colorado, Colorado Springs
Office of Financial Aid
1420 Austin Bluffs Pkwy., PO Box 7150
Colorado Springs, CO 80907

4611
Zaebst Memorial Scholarship

AMOUNT: $250 DEADLINE: None Specified
FIELDS/MAJORS: Biology

Open to Biology majors. Preference given to juniors and seniors, but graduate students are not excluded. Must have a minimum GPA of 3.5. Contact the address below for further information.

University of Colorado, Colorado Springs
Biology Department
1420 Austin Bluffs Pkwy., PO Box 7150
Colorado Springs, CO 80907

UNIVERSITY OF DELAWARE

4612
B. Bradford Barnes Scholarship

AMOUNT: None Specified DEADLINE: February 7
FIELDS/MAJORS: All Areas of Study

Scholarship for high school seniors who rank in the upper quarter of the class, have a 1200 or better on the SAT or 27 or better on the ACT, and are enrolled full-time at the University of Delaware. Commission makes final awards July 1. Write to the address listed for more information. Must have a GPA of at least 3.0.

Delaware Higher Education Commission
Carvel State Office Building
820 North French St., #4F
Wilmington, DE 19801

UNIVERSITY OF EVANSVILLE

4613
Academic Scholarships

AMOUNT: $2000-$7000 DEADLINE: February 15
FIELDS/MAJORS: All Areas of Study

Awards for students applying for admission to the University of Evansville. Based on strength of academic record, SAT score of at least 1100 or 25 on the ACT, etc. Students who rank first or second in their high school class will be considered for a $5000 academic scholarship. National Merit Finalists will receive an award worth 75% tuition. Write to the address below for more information. GPA must be at least 3.0.

University of Evansville
Office of Financial Aid
1800 Lincoln Ave.
Evansville, IN 47722

4614
Art, Music and Theater Scholarship

AMOUNT: $2000-$7000 DEADLINE: February 15
FIELDS/MAJORS: Art, Music, and Theater

Academic scholarships that takes into account artistic and performing talent as well as academic achievement. Auditions or portfolio presentations are required as part of the application. Write to the address below for more information.

University of Evansville
Office of Financial Aid
1800 Lincoln Ave.
Evansville, IN 47722

4615
Leadership Activity Awards

AMOUNT: $1000-$3000 DEADLINE: February 15
FIELDS/MAJORS: All Areas of Study

Awards for students applying for admission to the University of Evansville. Based on strength of academic record, SAT score of at least 1000 or 21 on the ACT, and activities and involvement in high school. Renewable. Write to the address below for more information. GPA must be at least 2.0.

University of Evansville
Office of Financial Aid
1800 Lincoln Ave.
Evansville, IN 47722

4616
Legacy Scholarships

AMOUNT: Maximum: $4000   DEADLINE: February 15
FIELDS/MAJORS: All Areas of Study

Awards for children and grandchildren of University of Evansville graduates. Must rank in the top half of senior class and score 1000 or better on the SAT or 21 or better on the ACT. Write to the address below for more information. GPA must be at least 2.5.

University of Evansville
Office of Financial Aid
1800 Lincoln Ave.
Evansville, IN 47722

4617
Multicultural Scholars Awards

AMOUNT: $2000-$7000   DEADLINE: February 15
FIELDS/MAJORS: All Areas of Study

Awards for students of color applying for admission to the University of Evansville. Based on strength of academic record and leadership abilities. Renewable. Write to the address below for more information.

University of Evansville
Office of Financial Aid
1800 Lincoln Ave.
Evansville, IN 47722

4618
Sibling Scholarship

AMOUNT: $1000-$1500   DEADLINE: February 15
FIELDS/MAJORS: All Areas of Study

Awards for current students who have a brother or sister who will enroll at University of Evansville. It is $1,500 a year for the first student attending University of Evansville and is given to each for as long as both remain full-time. Entering twins or triplets would each receive $1,000 a year. Write to the address below for more information.

University of Evansville
Office of Financial Aid
1800 Lincoln Ave.
Evansville, IN 47722

4619
University of Evansville United Methodist Scholarships

AMOUNT: Maximum: $2500   DEADLINE: February 15
FIELDS/MAJORS: All Areas of Study

Awards for students who are members of United Methodist Churches and are recommended by their ministers. Renewable. Write to the address below for more information.

University of Evansville
Office of Financial Aid
1800 Lincoln Ave.
Evansville, IN 47722

UNIVERSITY OF FLORIDA

4620
Frederick W. and Grace P. Brecht Scholarship

AMOUNT: None Specified   DEADLINE: April 15
FIELDS/MAJORS: All Areas of Study

Scholarships are available for students that reside in Brevard County, have a GPA of 2.0 or better, are able to demonstrate financial need, and attend the University of Florida full-time. Write to the address below for more information.

University of Florida
PO Box 114025
S-107 Criser Hall
Gainesville, FL 32611

UNIVERSITY OF HAWAII, MANOA

4621
Friends of the Library of Hawaii Scholarships

AMOUNT: $500-$2000   DEADLINE: June 1
FIELDS/MAJORS: Library Science, Information Science

Open to graduate students enrolled in library science at the University of Hawaii. For master's level study. Twelve awards are given annually. Write to the address below for further information.

University of Hawaii
School of Library and Information Studies
2550 the Mall
Manoa, HI 96822

UNIVERSITY OF HAWAII, HILO

4622
American Association of University Women Scholarship

AMOUNT: $150-$500　DEADLINE: February 1
FIELDS/MAJORS: Arts and Sciences

Scholarships are available at the University of Hawaii, Hilo, for full-time female students in the College of Arts and Sciences who are of junior status or higher. Applicants may also be pursuing a postbaccalaureate degree/certificate. Write to the address below for information or call (808) 974-7444. Information also available from Ms. Sherry Amundson, Chair, AAUW Scholarship Committee, 441 Haihai St., Hilo, Hawaii, 96720.

University of Hawaii, Hilo
Financial Aid Office
200 West Kawili Street
Hilo, HI 96720

4623
American Business Women's Association, Nani' O Hilo Scholarship

AMOUNT: None Specified　DEADLINE: February 1
FIELDS/MAJORS: All Areas of Study

Local scholarships are available at the University of Hawaii, Hilo, for full-time female students at any educational level. National scholarships awarded annually to women in their junior, senior, or graduate years of study. Write to the address listed for information and an application.

University of Hawaii, Hilo
Ms. Bernadette V. Baker, ABWA
134 Kimo Place
Hilo, HI 96720

4624
Big Island High School Awards

AMOUNT: $200-$600　DEADLINE: February 1
FIELDS/MAJORS: All Areas of Study

Scholarships are available at the University of Hawaii, Hilo, for full-time students who are graduating from a Big Island high school. Includes the Barney S. Fujimoto Memorial, Hilo High School Class of 1940, Constance E. Masutani Memorial, Dr. Frances F.C. Wong Memorial, James S. Yagi Memorial, and Michio Yoshimura Memorial Art Scholarships. Individual award requirements may vary slightly. Write to the address below for information or call (808) 974-7444.

University of Hawaii, Hilo
Financial Aid Office
200 West Kawili Street
Hilo, HI 96720

4625
Big Island Press Club's Robert Miller Scholarship

AMOUNT: None Specified　DEADLINE: None Specified
FIELDS/MAJORS: Communications, Journalism

Scholarships are available at the University of Hawaii, Hilo, for full-time students who are planning a career in the media. Must be a Big Island resident. Write to the address listed for further information.

University of Hawaii, Hilo
Big Island Press Club
PO Box 1920
Hilo, HI 96720

4626
Daniel G. Fox Prize for Excellence in Computer Science

AMOUNT: Maximum: $500　DEADLINE: February 1
FIELDS/MAJORS: Computer Science

Scholarships are available at the University of Hawaii, Hilo, for full-time senior computer science majors who demonstrate great academic achievement. Write to the address below for information or call (808) 974-7444. GPA must be at least 3.4.

University of Hawaii, Hilo
Financial Aid Office
200 West Kawili Street
Hilo, HI 96720

4627
Hawaii Anthurium Industry Association Scholarship

AMOUNT: Maximum: $1000　DEADLINE: February 1
FIELDS/MAJORS: Agriculture, Floriculture, Horticulture

Scholarships are available at the University of Hawaii, Hilo, for full-time junior agriculture students, majoring in tropical crop production, with a personal and career interest in the horticultural and/or floricultural field. Must have a minimum GPA of 2.5. Write to the address below for information or call (808) 974-7444.

University of Hawaii, Hilo
Financial Aid Office
200 West Kawili Street
Hilo, HI 96720

4628
Hawaii County Farm Bureau Scholarship

AMOUNT: Maximum: $1000   DEADLINE: February 1
FIELDS/MAJORS: Agriculture

Scholarships are available at the University of Hawaii, Hilo, for full-time agriculture students who have accumulated at least 28 credits upon entering sophomore year. Must have graduated from a local high school and have a GPA of at least 3.0. Applicants must also have a sincere interest in promoting the agricultural industry on Hawaii Island. Write to the address below for information or call (808) 974-7444.

University of Hawaii, Hilo
Financial Aid Office
200 West Kawili Street
Hilo, HI 96720

4629
Hawaii Island Chamber of Commerce Scholarship

AMOUNT: Maximum: $700   DEADLINE: February 1
FIELDS/MAJORS: Business, Economics

Scholarships are available at the University of Hawaii, Hilo, for full-time sophomores and juniors with a declared major in either business or economics. The award is to be used in junior or senior year and is payable in two $700 installments. Write to the address below for information or call (808) 974-7444.

University of Hawaii, Hilo
Financial Aid Office
200 West Kawili Street
Hilo, HI 96720

4630
Hilo Medical Center, Kuakini Foundation and Sigma Theta Tau Scholarships

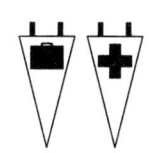

AMOUNT: Maximum: $500   DEADLINE: February 1
FIELDS/MAJORS: Nursing

Scholarships available to students enrolled in the BSN program. Must have a minimum GPA of 2.7 for the Hilo Medial Center Scholarship; a minimum GPA of 3.0 for the Kuakini Foundation Scholarship; and a minimum of 3.3 for the Sigma Theta Tau Scholarship. Must also be active in volunteer, community, or university groups. Write to the address below for information about the award that applies to you or call (808) 974-7444.

University of Hawaii, Hilo
Financial Aid Office
200 West Kawili Street
Hilo, HI 96720

4631
Hilo Women's Club Scholarship

AMOUNT: Maximum: $550   DEADLINE: February 1
FIELDS/MAJORS: All Areas of Study

Scholarships are available at the University of Hawaii, Hilo, for full-time female students who are graduating high school seniors at a Big Island high school. Must have a GPA of at least 3.5. Write to the address below for information or call (808) 974-7444. Information also available from Big Island school counselors.

University of Hawaii, Hilo
Financial Aid Office
200 West Kawili Street
Hilo, HI 96720

4632
J.M. Long Foundation Scholarships

AMOUNT: Maximum: $500   DEADLINE: February 1
FIELDS/MAJORS: Health Related, Business

Scholarships are available at the University of Hawaii, Hilo, for full-time students enrolled in either a health-related or business program. Must be residents of Hawaii. Write to the address below for information or call (808) 974-7444.

University of Hawaii, Hilo
Financial Aid Office
200 West Kawili Street
Hilo, HI 96720

4633
Leon J. Rhodes Student Development Award

AMOUNT: $1200   DEADLINE: February 1
FIELDS/MAJORS: All Areas of Study

Scholarships are available at the University of Hawaii, Hilo, for full-time sophomores who have become good citizens, are self-determined, and have developed successful human relations as a result of their experiences at UHH. The recipient is announced in mid-May. Write to the address below for information or call (808) 974-7444.

University of Hawaii, Hilo
Financial Aid Office
200 West Kawili Street
Hilo, HI 96720

4634
Panaewa Hawaiian Home Lands Community Association Scholarship

AMOUNT: $150-$250   DEADLINE: February 1
FIELDS/MAJORS: All Areas of Study

Scholarships are available at the University of Hawaii, Hilo, for full-time students who are children of members of the Panaewa Hawaiian Home Lands Community Association. Write to the address listed for information, call (808) 974-7444, or contact the Financial Aid Office at the school.

University of Hawaii, Hilo
PHHL Community Association Scholarship
102 Paipai St.
Hilo, HI 96720

4635
Pomare/Hilo Hattie Scholarship

AMOUNT: Maximum: $500   DEADLINE: February 1
FIELDS/MAJORS: All Areas of Study

Scholarships are available at the University of Hawaii, Hilo, for full-time students who are employees or children of employees of Pomare, Ltd. (which does business as Hilo Hattie.) Write to the address below for information or call (808) 974-7444.

University of Hawaii, Hilo
Financial Aid Office
200 West Kawili Street
Hilo, HI 96720

4636
Presidential Achievement Scholarships

AMOUNT: $4000   DEADLINE: February 1
FIELDS/MAJORS: All Areas of Study

Open to juniors who are residents of Hawaii and attending the Hilo, Manoa, or West Oahu campuses. Renewable for qualified seniors. Award consists of $4000, a tuition waiver, and a one-time travel grant. Contact the address below or call (808) 974-7444. GPA must be at least 2.8.

University of Hawaii, Hilo-Manoa-West Oahu
Financial Aid Office
200 West Kawili Street
Hilo, HI 96720

4637
Professional Secretaries Int'l Kohala Coast Chapter Scholarship

AMOUNT: $250   DEADLINE: February 1
FIELDS/MAJORS: Business Administration, Secretarial Science, Office Administration

Scholarships are available at the University of Hawaii, Hilo, for full-time students who are Big Island residents enrolled in one of the areas listed above. Write to the address listed for information, call (808) 880-3303, or see the Financial Aid Office at school.

University of Hawaii, Hilo
Gail Watson, President, PSI
PO Box 383598
Waikoloa, HI 96738

4638
Richard Adap Memorial Scholarship

AMOUNT: Maximum: $500   DEADLINE: February 1
FIELDS/MAJORS: Vocal Music

Open to students in vocal music studies. Must maintain a minimum GPA of 2.5 in music and at least a 2.0 overall and participate in all UHH choral ensembles. An interview and audition are required. Contact the address below, call (808) 974-7444, or contact the Performing Arts Department.

University of Hawaii, Hilo
Financial Aid Office
200 West Kawili Street
Hilo, HI 96720

4639
Rotary Club of South Hilo Scholarship

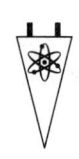

AMOUNT: Maximum: $500   DEADLINE: February 1
FIELDS/MAJORS: Ecology, Environmental Studies

Scholarships are available at the University of Hawaii, Hilo, for full-time students enrolled in ecology or environmental studies programs. Write to the address below for information or call (808) 974-7444.

University of Hawaii, Hilo
Financial Aid Office
200 West Kawili Street
Hilo, HI 96720

4640
Specialist Chad Delos Santos Memorial Scholarship

AMOUNT: Maximum: $1000 DEADLINE: February 1
FIELDS/MAJORS: All Areas of Study

Scholarships are available at the University of Hawaii, Hilo, for full-time students who are members or children of members of the Hawaii Army or Air National Guard. Write to the address below for information or call (808) 974-7444.

University of Hawaii, Hilo
Financial Aid Office
200 West Kawili Street
Hilo, HI 96720

4641
Thomas E. Cook Memorial Scholarship for Humanities

AMOUNT: Maximum: $500 DEADLINE: February 1
FIELDS/MAJORS: Humanities

Scholarships are available at the University of Hawaii, Hilo, from the Church of the Holy Apostles in Hilo. For full-time students enrolled in a humanities program. Applicants must be Big Island residents. Preference given to applicants of Hawaiian ancestry. Write to the address below for information or call (808) 974-7444.

University of Hawaii, Hilo
Financial Aid Office
200 West Kawili Street
Hilo, HI 96720

4642
Travel Women's Hawaii-Hilo Chapter Scholarship

AMOUNT: Maximum: $500 DEADLINE: February 1
FIELDS/MAJORS: Travel and Tourism

Scholarships are available at the University of Hawaii, Hilo, for full-time sophomores planning to pursue a career in the travel industry on the Island of Hawaii. Must be a Hawaiian resident. Write to the address below for information or call (800) 974-7444.

University of Hawaii, Hilo
Financial Aid Office
200 West Kawili Street
Hilo, HI 96720

4643
UHH Scholarships

AMOUNT: $250-$4000 DEADLINE: February 1
FIELDS/MAJORS: All Areas of Study

Scholarships are available at the University of Hawaii, Hilo, for full-time students who are Hawaii residents. Includes the Larry Child Scholarship, the Charles R. Hemenway, the Carol McCall Memorial, the Paul J. Kopecky Memorial, and the Regents Scholarships for academic excellence. Individual requirements may vary slightly. Combined, there are approximately twenty-five awards offered annually. Write to the address below for information or call (808) 974-7444.

University of Hawaii, Hilo
Financial Aid Office
200 West Kawili Street
Hilo, HI 96720

4644
UHHSA Motivated Student Scholarship

AMOUNT: Maximum: $600 DEADLINE: February 1
FIELDS/MAJORS: All Areas of Study

Scholarships are available at the University of Hawaii, Hilo, for full-time students with a GPA of 3.0 or higher who are involved in cocurricular activities. Write to the address below for information or call (808) 974-7444.

University of Hawaii, Hilo
Financial Aid Office
200 West Kawili Street
Hilo, HI 96720

4645
Virginia Pearson Ransburg Delta Kappa Gamma Scholarship

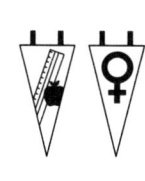

AMOUNT: Maximum: $550 DEADLINE: February 1
FIELDS/MAJORS: Education

Scholarships are available at the University of Hawaii, Hilo, for full-time students enrolled in the teacher education program. Applicants must be from the Federated States of Micronesia, the Republic of Palau, the Marshall Islands, or the Commonwealth of the North Marianas Islands. Preference is given to female applicants. Write to the address below for information.

University of Hawaii, Hilo
Financial Aid Office
200 West Kawili Street
Hilo, HI 96720

4646
Waipunalei Scholarship for the Hawaiian Leadership Program

AMOUNT: $1000   DEADLINE: February 1
FIELDS/MAJORS: All Areas of Study

Scholarships are available at the University of Hawaii, Hilo, for full-time students with a GPA of at least 2.5 who are in the Hawaiian Leadership Development Program. Must be able to demonstrate financial need and be excelling in leadership. Write to the address below for information or call (808) 974-7444.

University of Hawaii, Hilo
Financial Aid Office
200 West Kawili Street
Hilo, HI 96720

4647
Willard D. Keim Memorial Scholarship

AMOUNT: Maximum: $500   DEADLINE: February 1
FIELDS/MAJORS: Political Science

Scholarships are available at the University of Hawaii, Hilo, for full-time political science majors with a 3.0 or better GPA. Must have graduated from a high school in Hawaii. Write to the address below for information of call (808) 974-7444.

University of Hawaii, Hilo
Financial Aid Office
200 West Kawili Street
Hilo, HI 96720

UNIVERSITY OF HOUSTON

4648
Cougar Marching Band Scholarships

AMOUNT: None Specified   DEADLINE: None Specified
FIELDS/MAJORS: All Areas of Study

Open to incoming freshmen enrolled at the University of Houston who intend to participate in the Cougar Marching Band. Contact the marching band office at (713) 743-3175 for details.

University of Houston
School of Music
Scholarship Committee
Houston, TX 77204

4649
School of Music Scholarships

AMOUNT: None Specified   DEADLINE: February 28
FIELDS/MAJORS: Music

Scholarships are available by live or taped audition to students enrolled in Moores School of Music. Based on talent and academics. Music should consist of two contrasting works of substance (no etudes). Contact the scholarship committee at the address below for details.

University of Houston
School of Music
Scholarship Committee
Houston, TX 77204

UNIVERSITY OF ILLINOIS AT CHAMPAIGN URBANA

4650
Avery Brundage Scholarship

AMOUNT: $1000   DEADLINE: January 16
FIELDS/MAJORS: All Areas of Study

Twenty-eight scholarships are available at the University of Illinois for students who participate in amateur athletics programs. For undergraduate study. Write to the address below for information.

University of Illinois at Champaign Urbana
Office of Student Financial Aid
610 E. John Street, 4th Floor
Champaign, IL 61820

4651
Graduate Fellowships, Teaching and Research Assistantships

AMOUNT: None Specified   DEADLINE: February 15
FIELDS/MAJORS: Geography

Privately funded and University funded awards for master's and Ph.D. students in the Department of Geography at the University of Illinois. Most are awarded competitively. Contact the department at the address below for details. Request the brochure "Financial Support for Graduate Study in Geography."

University of Illinois at Champaign Urbana
220 Davenport Hall, Dept. of Geography
607 S. Matthews Ave.
Urbana, IL 61801

4652
Kate Neal Kinley Memorial Fellowship

AMOUNT: $7000 DEADLINE: February 1
FIELDS/MAJORS: Art, Music, Architecture

Fellowships for graduate students in the College of Fine and Applied Arts at the University of Illinois at Champaign Urbana. Three awards per year. Contact the office of the Dean of the College of Fine and Applied Arts at the address below for details.

University of Illinois at Champaign Urbana
College of Fine and Applied Arts
608 E Lorado Taft, 110 Architecture Bldg.
Champaign, IL 61820

4653
Lydia E. Parker Bates Scholarship

AMOUNT: $200-$400 DEADLINE: None Specified
FIELDS/MAJORS: Architecture, Landscape Architecture, Urban Planning, Fine Arts

Scholarships for students in the above areas of study at the University of Illinois at Champaign Urbana. Must maintain a GPA of at least 3.8. Must be able to demonstrate financial need. Approximately two hundred awards per year. Contact your department or the financial aid office for details.

University of Illinois at Champaign Urbana
Lydia E. Parker Bates Scholarship
Financial Aid Office
Urbana, IL 61801

4654
Marvin S. Corwin Scholarship

AMOUNT: None Specified DEADLINE: March 1
FIELDS/MAJORS: Communications

Scholarships for Jewish men and women living in the Chicago metropolitan area, who are identified as having promise for significant contributions in their chosen careers and are in need of financial assistance for full-time academic programs in one of the above fields. Must be above the junior level of study at the University of Illinois at Champaign Urbana. Write to the address below after December 1 for details.

Jewish Vocational Service
Attn: Scholarship Secretary
One South Franklin St.
Chicago, IL 60606

4655
Morgan L. Fitch Scholarship

AMOUNT: Maximum: $2000 DEADLINE: April 1
FIELDS/MAJORS: Real Estate

Scholarships for upperclassmen or graduate students at the University of Illinois at Champaign Urbana. Based on career interests, grades, need, and references. GPAs of at least 3.5 on a 5.0 point scale (2.8 on a 4.0 scale) are required. Must be residents of Illinois and U.S. citizens. Write to the address listed for details.

Illinois Real Estate Educational Foundation
3180 Adloff Ln.
PO Box 19451
Springfield, IL 62794

4656
Fred S. Bailey Scholarships

AMOUNT: $500-$1200 DEADLINE: March 15
FIELDS/MAJORS: All Areas of Study

Scholarships are available at the University of Illinois at Champaign Urbana for students who demonstrate academic ability, financial need, and concern for the needs of others and the betterment of society. More than one hundred awards offered annually. For undergraduates only. For families with income under $50,000 per year. For detailed information please see the Web site: http://www.Mathware.com/Bailey GPA must be at least 2.0.

University of Illinois at Champaign Urbana,
YMCA
Champaign, IL

4657
University of Illinois Scholarship

AMOUNT: None Specified DEADLINE: None Specified
FIELDS/MAJORS: All Areas of Study

Award open to high school seniors in Illinois who have demonstrated outstanding academics. Recipients must maintain a cumulative GPA of 3.4 on a 4.0 scale and progress toward a degree to remain eligible for the scholarship all four years. Contact the address below for further information.

Chicago Illini Club
Financial Aid Office
1200 W. Harrison, Mailcode 334
Chicago, IL 60607

UNIVERSITY OF INDIANAPOLIS

4658
Alumni Scholarship

AMOUNT: None Specified DEADLINE: February 15
FIELDS/MAJORS: All Areas of Study

Scholarships for entering full-time freshmen who rank in the upper 15% of graduating class. Must demonstrate strong college prep curriculum and evidence of leadership potential. Renewable if recipients maintain a minimum GPA of 2.7 and remain full-time. Award is 30% of tuition. Alumni Scholarship Application and recommendation by a University of Indianapolis graduate school is required. Contact the address below for further information.

Financial Aid Office
1400 E. Hanna Ave.
Indianapolis, IN 46227

4659
Dean's Scholarship

AMOUNT: None Specified DEADLINE: February 15
FIELDS/MAJORS: All Areas of Study

Scholarships for entering full-time freshmen who rank in the upper 5-7% of graduating class. Must demonstrate strong college prep curriculum and evidence of leadership potential. Renewable if recipients maintain a minimum GPA of 3.0 and remain full-time. Award is half tuition. Contact the address below for further information.

University of Indianapolis
Financial Aid Office
1400 E. Hanna Ave.
Indianapolis, IN 46227

4660
Presidential Scholarships

AMOUNT: None Specified DEADLINE: December 15
FIELDS/MAJORS: All Areas of Study

Scholarships for entering freshmen at the University of Indianapolis who rank in the top 5% of their high school class. Strong college prep courses, campus interview, and written essays are required. Renewable based on a minimum GPA of 3.3 and full-time attendance. Contact the address below for further information or call (317) 788-3216.

University of Indianapolis
Financial Aid Office
1400 E. Hanna Ave.
Indianapolis, IN 46227

4661
United Methodist Award

AMOUNT: None Specified DEADLINE: February 15
FIELDS/MAJORS: All Areas of Study

Scholarships for entering full-time freshmen or transfer students at the University of Indianapolis who are members of the United Methodist Church. Amount of award may vary according to financial aid packages. Contact the address below for further information.

University of Indianapolis
Financial Aid Office
1400 E. Hanna Ave.
Indianapolis, IN 46227

UNIVERSITY OF IOWA

4662
Biochemistry and Biophysics Freshman Scholarships

AMOUNT: $500-$1000 DEADLINE: February 1
FIELDS/MAJORS: Biochemistry, Biophysics

Open to entering freshmen, admitted to ISU, based on academic excellence, leadership, and participation in high school and community activities. Contact the address below or call (515) 294-2223 for further information.

University of Iowa, Dept. of Biochemistry and Biophysics
Scholarship Unit
1210 Molecular Biology Building
Ames, IA 50011

4663
Freshman Leadership Scholarship

AMOUNT: Maximum: $500 DEADLINE: March 16
FIELDS/MAJORS: Biology, Zoology, Genetics

Open to entering freshmen, admitted to ISU, based on academic excellence and demonstrated leadership. Applicants must have a minimum GPA of 3.0. Contact the address below for further information.

University of Iowa
Biology/Zoology Genetics Club
201 Bessey Hall
Ames, IA 50011

4664
Iowa Federation of Labor, AFL-CIO, Graduate Assistantship

AMOUNT: Maximum: $6500 DEADLINE: March 1
FIELDS/MAJORS: All Areas of Study

Open to University of Iowa graduate students who are members or children of members of any local Iowa unions affiliated with the Iowa Federation of Labor AFL-CIO. One award is offered annually. Write to the address below for complete details.

Iowa Federation of Labor, AFL-CIO
Mark L. Smith, Secretary-Treasurer
2000 Walker St., #A
Des Moines, IA 50317

4665
Medical Technologists Awards

AMOUNT: None Specified DEADLINE: None Specified
FIELDS/MAJORS: Medical Technology

Scholarships are available at the University of Iowa for full-time medical technology majors who are Iowa residents, demonstrate academic excellence, and have financial need. Includes the Iowa Association of Healthcare Recruiters Award, deadline is February 9, and the Iowa Medical Technologists Scholarship Award, deadline is April 1. Individual award requirements will vary. Write to the address listed for information. Must have a GPA of at least 3.0.

University of Iowa Hospitals and Clinics
Clinical Laboratory Science Program
160 Medical Laboratories
Iowa City, IA 52240

UNIVERSITY OF KANSAS

4666
Community College Scholarships

AMOUNT: Maximum: $1000 DEADLINE: January 15
FIELDS/MAJORS: All Areas of Study

Open to community college graduates who have a minimum GPA of 3.0 and will graduate or have already graduated from a Kansas Community College. Awards are made competitively. Contact the address below for further information or call (785) 864-5439.

University of Kansas
University Scholarship Center
135 Strong Hall
Lawrence, KS 66045

4667
Endowment Merit Scholarships

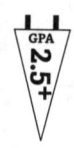

AMOUNT: $500-$1000 DEADLINE: January 15
FIELDS/MAJORS: All Areas of Study

Open to prospective incoming freshmen who are academically competitive and are from economically disadvantaged families. Based on strong high school scores, rank, evaluation of ACT/SAT scores, and involvement in extracurricular and community activities. Must be able to demonstrate financial need. Renewable up to four years based on academics. Contact the address below for further information or call (785) 864-5439. GPA must be at least 2.8.

University of Kansas
University Scholarship Center
135 Strong Hall
Lawrence, KS 66045

4668
Freshmen Honor Scholarships

AMOUNT: Maximum: $500 DEADLINE: January 15
FIELDS/MAJORS: All Areas of Study

Open to prospective incoming freshmen for academic achievement in Kansas high schools. Must have a minimum GPA of 3.0 and be in the top 20% of class. Must also demonstrate participation in extracurricular activities. Contact the address below for further information or call (785) 864-5439.

University of Kansas
University Scholarship Center
135 Strong Hall
Lawrence, KS 66045

4669
Geographic Scholarships

AMOUNT: $500-$2500 DEADLINE: January 15
FIELDS/MAJORS: All Areas of Study

Open to prospective incoming freshmen who are academically strong and participate in extracurricular and community activities. Must be residents of any of the following counties: Barton, Butler, Cherokee, Clark, Clay, Decatur, Douglas, Ford, Greenwood, Harvey, Jackson, Johnson, Kingman, Lincoln, Marshall, Meade, Miami, Mitchell, Morris, Nemaha, Norton, Osage, Pawnee, Pottawatomie, Pratt, Rawlins, Reading, Reno, Rooks, Shawnee, Stanton, Sumner, Thomas, Wabaunsee, Washington, Woodson, and Wyandotte. Contact the address below for further information or call (785) 864-5439. GPA must be at least 2.8.

University of Kansas
University Scholarship Center
135 Strong Hall
Lawrence, KS 66045

4670
Summerfield/Watkins-Berger Scholarships

AMOUNT: Maximum: $1000   DEADLINE: January 15
FIELDS/MAJORS: All Areas of Study

Open to prospective incoming freshmen for outstanding academic and leadership achievement in Kansas high schools. Must have a minimum GPA of 3.5 and be in the top 5% of class. Renewable if recipients maintain a minimum GPA of 3.5. Contact the address below for further information or call (785) 864-5439.

University of Kansas
University Scholarship Center
135 Strong Hall
Lawrence, KS 66045

4671
Whittaker KU Leadership Scholarships

AMOUNT: Maximum: $1000   DEADLINE: January 15
FIELDS/MAJORS: All Areas of Study

Open to prospective incoming freshmen for outstanding academic achievement in Kansas high schools. Must have a minimum GPA of 3.5 and be in the top 20% of class. Must also demonstrate a significant record of leadership activities and community service. Contact the address below for further information or call (785) 864-5439.

University of Kansas
University Scholarship Center
135 Strong Hall
Lawrence, KS 66045

UNIVERSITY OF MAINE

4672
Margaret B. and Mary E. Franklin Scholarship

AMOUNT: None Specified   DEADLINE: March 18
FIELDS/MAJORS: Elementary Education

Awards for graduates of Ellsworth High School who seek a degree in elementary education from the University of Maine at Farmington. Contact the guidance office at Ellsworth High School.

Maine Community Foundation
245 East Maine St.
PO Box 148
Ellsworth, ME 04605

4673
Pulp and Paper Foundation Scholarships

AMOUNT: $1000   DEADLINE: February 1
FIELDS/MAJORS: Pulp and Paper-Related Engineering

Scholarships are available for undergraduate students at the University of Maine who wish to pursue a career in the pulp and paper industry. Freshmen must be in the upper 10% of their high school class and continuing students must have a GPA of 2.8 or better. Twenty-five awards offered annually. Write to the address below for information.

University of Maine Pulp and Paper Foundation
5737 Jenness Hall
Orono, ME 04469

UNIVERSITY OF MASSACHUSETTS

4674
Graduate Student Workshop

AMOUNT: Maximum: $200   DEADLINE: March 1
FIELDS/MAJORS: Law and Legal Education

Awards for students in law who are enrolled in a doctoral program and plan to enter academic careers. Award is to be used to offset the cost of attending the workshop in July. Forty awards are offered annually. Write to the address below for more information.

Law and Society Association
Hampshire House, Box 33615
University of Massachusetts
Amherst, MA 01003

4675
Louis W. and Mary Doherty Scholarship

AMOUNT: $4000-$5000   DEADLINE: March 15
FIELDS/MAJORS: All Areas of Study

Five scholarships are available for residents of Hampden, Hampshire, or Franklin counties in Massachusetts who are attending/plan to attend the University of Massachusetts at Amherst. Write to the address listed for information.

Community Foundation of Western Massachusetts
PO Box 15769
1500 Main St.
Springfield, MA 01115

UNIVERSITY OF MIAMI

4676
Alumni Scholarships

GPA 3.5+

AMOUNT: Maximum: $6073 DEADLINE: February 15
FIELDS/MAJORS: All Areas of Study

Open to high school seniors who are children of University of Miami alumni. Must be Florida residents in the top 20% of class with a minimum GPA of 3.5. Contact the address below for further information.

University of Miami
Office of Admission
PO Box 248025
Coral Gables, FL 33124-4616

4677
Bowman Foster Ashe Scholarship

GPA 3.5+

AMOUNT: $13665 DEADLINE: February 15
FIELDS/MAJORS: All Areas of Study

Open to Isaac Bashevis Singer nominees who were not selected as recipients. Contact the address below for further information. GPA must be at least 3.9.

University of Miami
Office of Admission
PO Box 248025
Coral Gables, FL 33124

4678
George E. Merrick Scholarship and Fay F.W. Pearson Scholarship

GPA 3.5+

AMOUNT: $5200-$6073 DEADLINE: February 15
FIELDS/MAJORS: All Areas of Study

Open to high school seniors in the top 20% of class with a minimum GPA of 3.5. Contact the address.

University of Miami
Office of Admission
PO Box 248025
Coral Gables, FL 33124-4616

4679
Henry King Stanford Scholarships

GPA 3.5+

AMOUNT: $9110 DEADLINE: February 15
FIELDS/MAJORS: All Areas of Study

Scholarships for incoming freshmen who are in the top 10% of class with an ACT of at least 28, a minimum SAT of 1270, and a GPA of 3.75 or better. Renewable. Write to the address below for more information.

University of Miami
Office of Financial Assistance Services
PO Box 248187
Coral Gables, FL 33124

4680
Isaac Bashevis Singer Scholarships

GPA 3.5+

AMOUNT: $18220 DEADLINE: February 15
FIELDS/MAJORS: All Areas of Study

Scholarships for high school seniors in the top 1% of class accepted/enrolled at the University of Miami. Renewable. Write to the address below for more information. GPA must be at least 4.0.

University of Miami
Office of Financial Assistance Services
PO Box 248187
Coral Gables, FL 33124

UNIVERSITY OF MICHIGAN

4681
University of Michigan Club of Washington D.C. Scholarships

GPA 2.5+

AMOUNT: Maximum: $5000 DEADLINE: March 15
FIELDS/MAJORS: All Areas of Study

Open to undergraduates of the University of Michigan who are residents of the Washington D.C. metropolitan area. Incoming freshmen are welcome to apply, but acceptance to the school is a prerequisite to the award. May be renewed up to three years if recipients remain in good academic standing at the University of Michigan. Award is merit and need-based. Contact the address listed for further information or call (202) 554-0585. Must have a GPA of at least 2.9.

University of Michigan Club of Washington D.C.
Scholarship and Recruiting Committee
PO Box 44835
Washington, DC 20026-4835

UNIVERSITY OF MINNESOTA, DULUTH

4682
Academic Scholarships

AMOUNT: None Specified   DEADLINE: February 1
FIELDS/MAJORS: All Areas of Study

Open to entering freshmen based on outstanding scholarship, rank, and ACT test scores. Must be enrolling/accepted into University of Minnesota, Duluth. Contact the address below for further information. GPA must be at least 3.0.

University of Minnesota, Duluth
Admissions Office
20 Campus Center
Duluth, MN 55812

4683
Chemistry-Biochemistry Scholarship

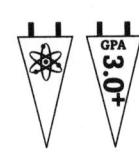

AMOUNT: Maximum: $4200   DEADLINE: None Specified
FIELDS/MAJORS: Chemistry, Biochemistry

Open to entering high ability, full-time freshmen planning to pursue a degree in chemistry or biochemistry. Must be a Minnesota resident, able to demonstrate high academic performance and aptitude, and financial need. Renewable up to five years if recipient maintains a minimum GPA of 3.0. Must be enrolled/accepted into University of Minnesota, Duluth. Contact the address below for further information.

University of Minnesota, Duluth
Admissions Office
20 Campus Center
Duluth, MN 55812

4684
Music Scholarship

AMOUNT: None Specified   DEADLINE: February 1
FIELDS/MAJORS: Music

Scholarships open to music majors. In case of outstanding talent, others will be considered. Must be enrolled/accepted into University of Minnesota, Duluth. Contact the address below for further information.

University of Minnesota, Duluth
Department of Music
10 University Dr.
Duluth, MN 55812

4685
Presidential Scholarship

AMOUNT: $1000   DEADLINE: February 1
FIELDS/MAJORS: All Areas of Study

Awards open to Minnesota high school seniors who rank in the top 5% of their class and demonstrate outstanding scholarship and leadership abilities. Must be enrolled/accepted into University of Minnesota, Duluth. Contact the address below for further information. GPA must be at least 3.5.

University of Minnesota, Duluth
Admissions Office
20 Campus Center
Duluth, MN 55812

4686
President's Outstanding Minority and Morton S. Katz Scholarships

AMOUNT: $1000-$3000   DEADLINE: March 1
FIELDS/MAJORS: All Areas of Study

Awards open to minority high school seniors who have demonstrated high academic potential. Based on rank, ACT scores, and community involvement. Must be enrolled/accepted into University of Minnesota, Duluth. Contact the address below for further information.

University of Minnesota, Duluth
Admissions Office
20 Campus Center
Duluth, MN 55812

UNIVERSITY OF MINNESOTA, MINNEAPOLIS

4687
Adelle and Erwin Tomash Fellowship in History of Information Processing

AMOUNT: Maximum: $12000   DEADLINE: January 15
FIELDS/MAJORS: Computer Science, History of Technology

Fellowships, to be carried out at any appropriate research facility, are available in the history of computers and information processing. Research may be into the technical, social, legal, or business aspects of information processing. Preference is given for dissertation research, but all doctoral students are invited to apply. Write to the Institute at the address below for more details.

Charles Babbage Institute, University of Minnesota
103 Walter Library
117 Pleasant Street, SE
Minneapolis, MN 55455

4688
Minnesota AFL-CIO Scholarships

AMOUNT: $500-$1000 DEADLINE: April 20
FIELDS/MAJORS: All Areas of Study

Awards to members or high school seniors who are children of members of affiliated unions of the Minnesota AFL-CIO or Teamsters. Must be attending/planning to attend schools in Minnesota. Seniors must have a minimum grade of B. One award to a female athlete attending the University of Minnesota. Contact the address below for further information.

Minnesota AFL-CIO
Scholarship Program
175 Aurora Ave.
St. Paul, MN 55103

4689
Minnesota Funeral Directors Association Scholarships

AMOUNT: Maximum: $1000 DEADLINE: March 15
FIELDS/MAJORS: Mortuary Science

Applies to tuition only for the mortuary science program at the University of Minnesota payable in the first quarter of the senior year. Must be a resident of Minnesota and submit high school and/or college transcripts, two essays, and letters of recommendation. Write to the address below for more information.

Minnesota Funeral Directors Association
300 S. Highway 169, Suite 140
Minneapolis, MN 55426

UNIVERSITY OF MINNESOTA, MORRIS

4690
American Indian Tuition Waiver

AMOUNT: Maximum: $4406 DEADLINE: None Specified
FIELDS/MAJORS: All Areas of Study

Open to Native American students admitted to UMM through the regular admissions process. Must provide documentation of tribal affiliation or Indian heritage. Awards are full tuition and are renewable. Contact the address below for further information or call 1-800-992-8863.

University of Minnesota, Morris
Admissions and Financial Aid Office
105 Behmler Hall 600 E. 4th St.
Morris, MN 56267

4691
Freshman Academic Scholarships

AMOUNT: $1100-$2200 DEADLINE: None Specified
FIELDS/MAJORS: All Areas of Study

Open to first-year students based on high school class rank. If you rank in the top 5%, the award is one-half tuition (based on resident tuition). If you rank in the top 10%, the award is one-quarter tuition. These are awarded automatically upon application and admission to UMM. Class ranks must be verified by transcripts or counselors. Non-renewable. Contact the address below for further information or call 1-800-992-8863. GPA must be at least 3.6.

University of Minnesota, Morris
Admissions and Financial Aid Office
105 Behmler Hall 600 E. 4th St.
Morris, MN 56267

4692
Midwest Student Exchange Scholarship

AMOUNT: None Specified DEADLINE: None Specified
FIELDS/MAJORS: All Areas of Study

Allows students from Kansas, Michigan, Missouri, and Nebraska to pay 150% of Minnesota resident tuition. Contact the address below for further information or 1-800-992-8863.

University of Minnesota, Morris
Admissions and Financial Aid Office
105 Behmler Hall 600 E. 4th St.
Morris, MN 56267

4693
Minority Student Tuition Scholarship

AMOUNT: None Specified DEADLINE: None Specified
FIELDS/MAJORS: All Areas of Study

Allows non-resident minority students, who graduate in the top 25% of their class, to qualify for in-state Minnesota tuition. Transferring minority students must have a minimum cumulative GPA of 3.0. Contact the address below for further information or call 1-800-992-8863.

University of Minnesota, Morris
Admissions and Financial Aid Office
105 Behmler Hall 600 E. 4th St.
Morris, MN 56267

4694
President's Outstanding Minority Scholarships

AMOUNT: Maximum: $3000 DEADLINE: April 1
FIELDS/MAJORS: All Areas of Study

Open to ethnic minority students admitted to UMM. This scholarship can be worth up to $3000 depending on financial need and is renewable for up to four years. Applications available in December. Must file the FAFSA. Contact the address below for further information or call 1-800-992-8863.

University of Minnesota, Morris
Admissions and Financial Aid Office
105 Behmler Hall 600 E. 4th St.
Morris, MN 56267

4695
Presidential Scholarships

AMOUNT: Maximum: $8000 DEADLINE: February 15
FIELDS/MAJORS: All Areas of Study

Open to admitted incoming freshmen. There are no minimum criteria to apply for this scholarship, but most recipients are in the upper 10% of senior class and have above average test scores. Awards are $8000 to be distributed over four consecutive years. Applications will be available in December. Contact the address below for further information or call 1-800-992-8863.

University of Minnesota, Morris
Admissions and Financial Aid Office
105 Behmler Hall 600 E. 4th St.
Morris, MN 56267

4696
Transfer Academic Scholarships

AMOUNT: $1100-$2200 DEADLINE: None Specified
FIELDS/MAJORS: All Areas of Study

Open to students transferring to UMM from an accredited institution with at least one year's worth of credits. If students have a minimum cumulative GPA of 3.75, the award is one-half tuition. Students with a GPA between 3.5 and 3.74 qualify for one-quarter tuition scholarships. Can be used during the first year at UMM. Contact the address below for further information or call 1-800-992-8863.

University of Minnesota, Morris
Admissions and Financial Aid Office
105 Behmler Hall 600 E. 4th St.
Morris, MN 56267

4697
Tuition Reciprocity Tuition Scholarship

AMOUNT: None Specified DEADLINE: None Specified
FIELDS/MAJORS: All Areas of Study

Allows students from South Dakota, North Dakota, and Manitoba to pay the Minnesota in-state tuition rate. Students from Wisconsin pay their comparable state rate. Contact the address below for further information or call 1-800-992-8863.

University of Minnesota, Morris
Admissions and Financial Aid Office
105 Behmler Hall 600 E. 4th St.
Morris, MN 56267

UNIVERSITY OF MISSISSIPPI

4698
Albert T. Bledsoe Scholarship

AMOUNT: Maximum: $2500 DEADLINE: March 15
FIELDS/MAJORS: All Areas of Study

Open to entering freshmen at Ole Miss who have a minimum ACT score of 32, at least a 1390 on the SAT, and a GPA of 3.0 or above. Contact the address below for further information or call (601) 232-7226.

University of Mississippi
Office of Financial Aid
University, MS 38677

4699
Brevard Fellowships/Scholarships

AMOUNT: $2000-$12000 DEADLINE: February 15
FIELDS/MAJORS: Engineering, Computer Science

Open to freshmen and transfer students enrolled in engineering and computer science degree programs at Ole Miss. Based on academic performance, leadership, and community activities. Contact the address below for further information or call (601) 232-7407. GPA must be at least 2.7.

University of Mississippi
Office of the Dean
School of Engineering
University, MS 38677

4700
Carrier Scholarships

AMOUNT: Maximum: $6000   DEADLINE: February 1
FIELDS/MAJORS: All Areas of Study

Open to entering Mississippi freshmen, accepted at Ole Miss, who demonstrate exceptional academic ability. Candidate's nominations are forwarded to the Carrier Foundation for consideration. Contact the address below for further information or call (601) 232-7226. GPA must be at least 3.0.

University of Mississippi
Mr. and Mrs. Beckett Howorth
119 Lyceum
University, MS 38677

4701
Christine and Clarence Day Scholarship

AMOUNT: Maximum: $6000   DEADLINE: March 15
FIELDS/MAJORS: Business

Open to outstanding entering freshmen from Mississippi, who plan to pursue careers in business. For additional information and an application form, contact the School of Business Administration at (601) 232-5820.

University of Mississippi
School of Business Administration
University, MS 38677

4702
Fenley Scholarship

AMOUNT: Maximum: $8000   DEADLINE: February 1
FIELDS/MAJORS: All Areas of Study

Open to entering Mississippi freshmen, accepted at Ole Miss, who demonstrate exceptional academic ability. Candidates are nominated and selection is made by special committee. Contact the address below for further information or call (601) 232-7226. GPA must be at least 3.0.

University of Mississippi
Mr. M. Beckett Howorth
119 Lyceum
University, MS 38677

4703
Frederick A.P. Barnard Scholarship

AMOUNT: Maximum: $4460   DEADLINE: March 15
FIELDS/MAJORS: All Areas of Study

Open to entering freshmen at Ole Miss who are National Merit or National Achievement finalists or semi-finalists. Must have a minimum GPA of 3.0. Contact the address below for further information or call (601) 232-7226.

University of Mississippi
Office of Financial Aid
University, MS 38677

4704
George F. Holmes Scholarship

AMOUNT: Maximum: $1000   DEADLINE: March 15
FIELDS/MAJORS: All Areas of Study

Open to entering freshmen at Ole Miss who have a minimum ACT score of 28, at least a 1230 on the SAT, and a GPA of 3.0 or above. Contact the address below for further information or call (601) 232-7226.

University of Mississippi
Office of Financial Aid
University, MS 38677

4705
Hearin-Hess Scholarships

AMOUNT: Maximum: $3000   DEADLINE: February 1
FIELDS/MAJORS: Business

Open to business majors at Ole Miss who have achieved an outstanding record of accomplishments. Contact the address below for further information or call (601) 232-5820. GPA must be at least 3.2.

University of Mississippi
School of Business Administration
University, MS 38677

4706
John G. Adler Scholarships in Engineering

AMOUNT: $2000-$12000   DEADLINE: February 15
FIELDS/MAJORS: Engineering, Computer Science

Open to entering freshmen and transfer students at Ole Miss enrolled in engineering and computer science degree programs. Based on exceptional merit, academic performance, and leadership. Contact the address below for more information or call (601) 232-7407. GPA must be at least 2.8.

University of Mississippi
Office of the Dean
School of Engineering
University, MS 38677

4707
John Millington Scholarship

AMOUNT: Maximum: $1750 DEADLINE: March 15
FIELDS/MAJORS: All Areas of Study

Open to entering freshmen at Ole Miss who have a minimum ACT score of 30, at least a 1310 on the SAT, and a GPA of 3.0 or above. Contact the address below for further information or call (601) 232-7226.

University of Mississippi
Office of Financial Aid
University, MS 38677

4708
John N. Waddell Scholarship

AMOUNT: Maximum: $500 DEADLINE: March 15
FIELDS/MAJORS: All Areas of Study

Open to entering freshmen at Ole Miss who have a minimum ACT score of 26, at least a 1160 on the SAT, and a GPA of 3.0 or above. Contact the address below for further information or call (601) 232-7226.

University of Mississippi
Office of Financial Aid
University, MS 38677

4709
McDonnell-Barksdale Scholarships

AMOUNT: $2000-$6000 DEADLINE: February 1
FIELDS/MAJORS: All Areas of Study

Open to entering Mississippi freshmen who have been accepted at McDonnell-Barksdale Honors College. Contact the address below for further information or call (601) 232-7294. GPA must be at least 3.0.

University of Mississippi
Ms. V. Thurlow
McDonnell-Barksdale Honors College
University, MS 38677

4710
Newman Scholarship

AMOUNT: Maximum: $6500 DEADLINE: February 1
FIELDS/MAJORS: All Areas of Study

Open to entering Mississippi freshmen, accepted at Ole Miss, who demonstrate exceptional academic ability. Candidates are nominated and selection is made by special committee. Contact the address below for further information or call (601) 232-7226. GPA must be at least 3.0.

University of Mississippi
Mr. M. Beckett Howorth
119 Lyceum
University, MS 38677

4711
Pichitino Scholarships

AMOUNT: $2000-$6000 DEADLINE: February 1
FIELDS/MAJORS: All Areas of Study

Open to entering freshmen who have been accepted at McDonnell-Barksdale Honors College. Contact the address below for further information or call (601) 232-7294. GPA must be at least 3.0.

University of Mississippi
Ms. V. Thurlow
McDonnell-Barksdale Honors College
University, MS 38677

UNIVERSITY OF NEBRASKA

4712
Bryan Patterson Prize

AMOUNT: $600 DEADLINE: April 1
FIELDS/MAJORS: Vertebrate Paleontology

Grants to support field work by SVP members. Proposals for the award should be for fieldwork and for fieldwork that is imaginative rather than pedestrian; venturesome rather than safe. Write to the address below for details.

Society of Vertebrate Paleontology
W436 Nebraska Hall
University of Nebraska
Lincoln, NE 68588

UNIVERSITY OF NEW HAMPSHIRE

4713
International Student Scholarships

AMOUNT: None Specified DEADLINE: April 1
FIELDS/MAJORS: All Areas of Study

Scholarship programs are offered to foreign students attending the University of New Hampshire. Inquire directly to the International Student Advisor at the address below.

University of New Hampshire
International Student Adviser
Hood House
Durham, NH 03824

UNIVERSITY OF NEW MEXICO, ALBUQUERQUE

4714
Honeywell Engineering Scholarship

AMOUNT: None Specified   DEADLINE: March 1
FIELDS/MAJORS: Engineering

Awards are available at the University of New Mexico for students admitted to the school of engineering. Must demonstrate financial need, extracurricular activities, and a GPA of at least 3.0. Write to the address below for more information.

University of New Mexico, Albuquerque
Office of Financial Aid
Albuquerque, NM 87131

4715
Ideas in Science Scholarships

AMOUNT: None Specified   DEADLINE: March 1
FIELDS/MAJORS: Engineering

Awards are available at the University of New Mexico for juniors majoring in engineering. Must demonstrate financial need, academic ability (minimum 3.0 GPA), and be a resident of New Mexico. Special consideration is given to students whose program of studies is closely linked to electronic design and applications. Write to the address below for more information. GPA must be at least 3.0.

University of New Mexico, Albuquerque
Office of Financial Aid
Albuquerque, NM 87131

4716
Wal-Mart Competitive Edge Scholarship

AMOUNT: $2500-$5000   DEADLINE: December 1
FIELDS/MAJORS: Mathematics, Engineering, Science

Scholarships are available at the University of New Mexico for entering freshmen enrolled in or planning to enroll in one of the areas listed above. Must be U.S. citizens with a GPA of at least 3.5 and have demonstrated community service and leadership. Write to the address below for information.

University of New Mexico, Albuquerque
Student Financial Aid Office
Mesa Vista Hall North, Room 1044
Albuquerque, NM 87131

4717
Walter Rundell Award

AMOUNT: Maximum: $1000   DEADLINE: July 1
FIELDS/MAJORS: Western History

Open to graduate students pursuing a degree in Western history. Write to the address below for information or call (505) 277-5234.

Western History Association-Award Committee
University of New Mexico
1080 Mesa Vista Hall
Albuquerque, NM 87131

UNIVERSITY OF NORTH CAROLINA, GREENSBORO

4718
C.M. and M.D. Suther Scholarship

AMOUNT: None Specified   DEADLINE: March 1
FIELDS/MAJORS: All Areas of Study

Award open to full-time undergraduates who are residents of North Carolina and can demonstrate financial need. Contact the address below for further information. GPA must be at least 2.7.

University of North Carolina, Greensboro
Financial Aid Office
723 Kenilworth St.
Greensboro, NC 27412

UNIVERSITY OF NORTH CAROLINA, CHAPEL HILL

4719
Gilbert Chinard Scholarships

AMOUNT: Maximum: $1000   DEADLINE: January 15
FIELDS/MAJORS: French History, Literature, Art, and Music

Open to students in the final stage of the Ph.D. dissertation or for those who have received a Ph.D. no longer than six years before time of application. A two-page description of research project and trip as well as a recommendation from the dissertation director will be required. Three awards offered annually. For a research period in France of at least two months. Write to the address below for additional information.

University of North Carolina-Institut Francais
  De Washington
Department of Romance Languages
CB 3170
Chapel Hill, NC 27599

UNIVERSITY OF NORTHERN COLORADO

4720
AAUW Scholarship for Cody Women

AMOUNT: None Specified   DEADLINE: March 1
FIELDS/MAJORS: All Areas of Study

Scholarships are available at UNC for full-time female juniors, seniors, or graduate students from Cody, Wyoming, who demonstrate academic ability and financial need. Write to the address below for information.

University of Northern Colorado, AAUW
American Assoc. of University Women
PO Box 1531
Cody, WY 82414

UNIVERSITY OF NORTHERN IOWA

4721
Art Department Scholarships

AMOUNT: Maximum: $2566   DEADLINE: March 13
FIELDS/MAJORS: Art

Open to incoming freshmen who meet UNI Admissions requirements. Must participate in Art Scholarship Day on UNI campus April 13. Contact the address below for further information. GPA must be at least 2.8.

University of Northern Iowa
William W. Lew, Art Department Head
104 Kamerick Art Building
Cedar Falls, IA 50614

4722
Carver Scholarship

AMOUNT: Maximum: $3600   DEADLINE: March 15
FIELDS/MAJORS: All Areas of Study

Open to Iowa high school graduates who are transfer students of junior standing with a minimum GPA of 2.8. Currently enrolled students (other than freshmen) are also eligible. Financial need is required. Applicants must demonstrate they have overcome obstacles or barriers in life. Essay and two letters of reference are required. Contact the address below for further information or call (319) 273-2700.

University of Northern Iowa
Financial Aid Office
116 Gilchrist Hall
Cedar Falls, IA 50614

4723
Clarence and Carol Letson Scholarship

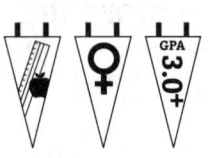

AMOUNT: Maximum: $2566   DEADLINE: March 2
FIELDS/MAJORS: Early Childhood Education

Open to incoming freshmen who can demonstrate financial need. Preference given to females. Renewable if a minimum GPA of 3.0 is maintained. Contact College of Education, 189 Schindler Education Center or call (319) 273-2751. Applications available after December 15.

University of Northern Iowa
Financial Aid Office
116 Gilchrist Hall
Cedar Falls, IA 50614-0024

4724
Excel Scholarship

AMOUNT: $100-$2000   DEADLINE: February 1
FIELDS/MAJORS: Pre-Business, Business Administration

Open to incoming freshmen and transfer minority students enrolled in the College of Business Administration. Must have had four years of high school mathematics. Contact the College of Business Administration for further information or call (319) 273-5894. GPA must be at least 2.8.

University of Northern Iowa
Elizabeth Peterson
204 Business
Cedar Falls, IA 50614

4725
Forensics Scholarship

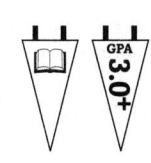

AMOUNT: $100-$2566 DEADLINE: April 1
FIELDS/MAJORS: Forensics Debate

Open to incoming freshmen and transfer students with a minimum high school GPA of 3.0 and experience in forensics. Contact the address below for further information.

University of Northern Iowa
Communications Studies
257 Communications Arts Center
Cedar Falls, IA 50614

4726
Freshman Achievement Scholarship

AMOUNT: Maximum: $1000 DEADLINE: February 1
FIELDS/MAJORS: All Areas of Study

Open to incoming freshmen enrolling directly from high school. Must rank in the top 25% of class. Awards depend on quality of the application, meeting the scholarship deadlines, and availability of funding. $1000 per year for two years. Renewable for the second year by maintaining a minimum GPA of 3.0. 150 to 170 awards offered annually. Contact the address below for further information or call (319) 273-2281.

University of Northern Iowa
Dan Schofield, Office of Admissions
120 Gilchrist Hall
Cedar Falls, IA 50614-0018

4727
Harry and Shirley Hagemann Scholarship

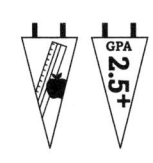

AMOUNT: Maximum: $1000 DEADLINE: March 2
FIELDS/MAJORS: Elementary, Secondary Education

Open to incoming freshmen, current students, and transfer students. Contact College of Education, 189 Schindler Education Center or call (319) 273-2751. Applications available after December 15. GPA must be at least 2.5.

University of Northern Iowa
Financial Aid Office
116 Gilchrist Hall
Cedar Falls, IA 50614-0024

4728
IES Industries Scholarship

AMOUNT: Maximum: $1000 DEADLINE: March 10
FIELDS/MAJORS: Business

Open to an incoming freshmen who has a parent employed by IES. Must be an Iowa resident. Contact Elizabeth Peterson, Management Department (319) 273-6017.

University of Northern Iowa
Elizabeth Peterson
204 Business
Cedar Falls, IA 50614

4729
Mildred Stever Scholarship

AMOUNT: $1000-$2500 DEADLINE: March 2
FIELDS/MAJORS: Physical Education

Open to incoming freshmen in the top 10% of graduating class with a minimum GPA of 3.5. Transfer student must have a minimum GPA of 3.25. May be renewed up to four years if eligible. Contact Rip Marsten at the address below for further information or call (319) 273-6882.

University of Northern Iowa
Health, Physical Ed., and Leisure Services
203 W. Gym
Cedar Falls, IA 50614

4730
Minorities in Teaching Scholarship

AMOUNT: $500-$1500 DEADLINE: March 6
FIELDS/MAJORS: Education

Open to minority incoming freshmen and transfer students who are Iowa residents and participants in the MIT program. Financial need, academics, and leadership will be considered. Preference given to MIT participants from the following Iowa School Districts: Davenport, Des Moines, Cedar Rapids, Muscatine, Sioux City, Waterloo, and South Tama. Contact Evie Waack, Financial Aid Office, (319) 273-2751. Applications available after December 15. GPA must be at least 2.8.

University of Northern Iowa
Financial Aid Office
116 Gilchrist Hall
Cedar Falls, IA 50614-0024

4731
Morris and Lenore Mandelbaum Scholarship

AMOUNT: $1000-$1500 DEADLINE: March 2
FIELDS/MAJORS: Education, Social Science

Open to incoming freshmen graduating from a Des Moines, Iowa, high school majoring in education.

Preference for study in areas of Social Science. Contact College of Education, 189 Schindler Education Center or (319) 273-2751. Applications available after December 15. GPA must be at least 2.5.

University of Northern Iowa
Financial Aid Office
116 Gilchrist Hall
Cedar Falls, IA 50614-0024

4732
Non-Resident Scholarship

AMOUNT: Maximum: $1250 DEADLINE: February 1
FIELDS/MAJORS: All Areas of Study

Open to non-resident incoming freshmen enrolling directly from high school. Must rank in the top 25% of class. Non-resident transfer students must have at least 24 semester hours of coursework and a minimum GPA of 3.5. Renewable for a second year by maintaining a 3.0 GPA. The deadline for transfer students is April 1. Contact the address below for further information or call (319) 273-2281.

University of Northern Iowa
Dan Schofield, Office of Admissions
120 Gilchrist Hall
Cedar Falls, IA 50614-0018

4733
One-year Achievement Award

AMOUNT: Maximum: $1000 DEADLINE: February 1
FIELDS/MAJORS: All Areas of Study

Open to incoming freshmen enrolling directly from high school. Must rank in the top 25% of class. This award is not renewable. Contact the address below for further information or call (319) 273-2281. GPA must be at least 3.0.

University of Northern Iowa
Dan Schofield, Office of Admissions
120 Gilchrist Hall
Cedar Falls, IA 50614-0018

4734
Phi Theta Kappa Scholarship

AMOUNT: $1000-$2000 DEADLINE: April 1
FIELDS/MAJORS: All Areas of Study

Open to transfer students who are members at the community college from which they are transferring. Must demonstrate leadership and campus or community involvement. Must have a minimum GPA of 3.5. Awards are $1000 per year for two years for Iowa residents and $2000 per year for two years for non-residents. Renewable for the second year by maintaining a 3.0 GPA. Five in-state and five out-of-state awards. Contact Jo Loonan or Kelly Christensen at the address below for further information or call (319) 273-2281.

University of Northern Iowa
Dan Schofield, Office of Admissions
120 Gilchrist Hall
Cedar Falls, IA 50614-0018

4735
Scholarship of Distinction

AMOUNT: Maximum: $2000 DEADLINE: February 1
FIELDS/MAJORS: All Areas of Study

Open to incoming freshmen enrolling directly from high school. Must rank in the top 10% of class. Based primarily on high academic achievement. Renewable by maintaining a minimum GPA of 3.0 Contact the address below for further information or call (319) 273-2281.

University of Northern Iowa
Dan Schofield, Office of Admissions
120 Gilchrist Hall
Cedar Falls, IA 50614-0018

4736
Teacher Education Scholarships

AMOUNT: Maximum: $2566 DEADLINE: January 30
FIELDS/MAJORS: Education

Open to incoming freshmen in an Iowa high school. Must have a minimum ACT score of 26 and two recommendations. Fifteen finalists interview on February 20. Contact Dr. Bill Waack, Teacher Education, at the address below or call (319) 273-2265. Applications available after December 15. GPA must be at least 3.0.

University of Northern Iowa
Financial Aid Office
116 Gilchrist Hall
Cedar Falls, IA 50614-0024

4737
Theater Activity Scholarship

AMOUNT: $500-$2000 DEADLINE: March 1
FIELDS/MAJORS: Theater Arts

Open to incoming freshmen in the upper third of graduating class with a minimum GPA of 3.0 and transfer students. Contact Gretta Berghammer, Dept. of Theater (319) 273-6386.

University of Northern Iowa
Financial Aid Office
116 Gilchrist Hall
Cedar Falls, IA 50614

4738
Transfer Achievement Scholarship

AMOUNT: Maximum: $1000 DEADLINE: April 1
FIELDS/MAJORS: All Areas of Study

Open to transfer students, with preference given to students entering from a two-year college who have earned a minimum of 45 semester hours of transferable credit with at least a 3.25 GPA. Award is $1000 per year for two years. Renewable for the second year by maintaining a 3.0 GPA Contact the address below for further information or call (319) 273-2281.

University of Northern Iowa
Dan Schofield, Office of Admissions
120 Gilchrist Hall
Cedar Falls, IA 50614-0018

4739
UNI Music Scholarships

AMOUNT: $150-$2000 DEADLINE: None Specified
FIELDS/MAJORS: Music

Open to incoming freshmen. Based on performance ability, talent, and auditions. Multiple awards with varied criteria. Contact Alan Schmitz at the School of Music for audition dates and deadlines. GPA must be at least 2.5.

University of Northern Iowa
Financial Aid Office
116 Gilchrist Hall
Cedar Falls, IA 50614

4740
Virginia McShane Bettle Scholarship

AMOUNT: Maximum: $1000 DEADLINE: March 2
FIELDS/MAJORS: Elementary Education

Open to incoming freshmen. Preference for full-time students. Contact College of Education, 189 Schindler Education Center or call (319) 273-2751. Applications available after December 15.

University of Northern Iowa
Financial Aid Office
116 Gilchrist Hall
Cedar Falls, IA 50614-0024

4741
Viva Budworth Mondloch Scholarship

AMOUNT: $1000-$1500 DEADLINE: March 2
FIELDS/MAJORS: Education

Open to incoming freshmen and current students. Preference for secondary or K-12 teaching majors. Contact College of Education, 189 Schindler Education Center or call (319) 273-2751. Applications available after December 15. GPA must be at least 2.5.

University of Northern Iowa
Financial Aid Office
116 Gilchrist Hall
Cedar Falls, IA 50614-0024

UNIVERSITY OF OKLAHOMA, NORMAN

4742
A.L. Cosgrove Student Service Award

AMOUNT: $300-$500 DEADLINE: March 15
FIELDS/MAJORS: All Areas of Study

Scholarships are available at OU, Norman, for students who are active members of the Parish, have completed at least 30 credit hours with a minimum GPA of 3.0, and have provided noteworthy service to the Parish and/or the University. Write to the address below for information or call (405) 321-0990.

St. Thomas More University Parish
Scholarship Coordinator
100 East Stinson
Norman, OK 73072

4743
Alice Sowers Physical Therapy Scholarship

AMOUNT: $300-$500 DEADLINE: October 1
FIELDS/MAJORS: Physical Therapy

Scholarships are available at OU, Norman, for full-time senior physical therapy majors with a GPA of at least 3.5. Four awards offered annually. Write to the address below for information or call (405) 271-2131.

University of Oklahoma, Norman-College of Allied Health
Dept. of Physical Therapy
PO Box 26901
Oklahoma City, OK 73190

4744
American Indian Education Grants

AMOUNT: $200-$1500 DEADLINE: None Specified
FIELDS/MAJORS: All Areas of Study

Scholarships are available for OU, Norman, students who are of Native American, Aleut, or Eskimo descent. Must be U.S. citizens and have completed at least one college semester. Preference given to Presbyterians at the undergraduate level. Deadlines are: June 1 and November 15. Write to the address listed for information or call (502) 569-5745.

Presbyterian Church (U.S.A)
Office of Financial Aid for Students
100 Witherspoon St.
Louisville, KY 40202-1396

4745
Arnold and Bess Ungerman Charitable Trust Scholarship

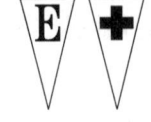

AMOUNT: Maximum: $4000   DEADLINE: May 1
FIELDS/MAJORS: Medicine

Scholarships are available at OU, Norman, for medical students who are of African-American or Native American heritage. Four awards offered annually. Write to the address below for information.

University of Oklahoma, Norman
Director, Office of Financial Aid
OUHSC PO Box 26901
Oklahoma City, OK 73190

4746
Armed Forces Health Professions Scholarship

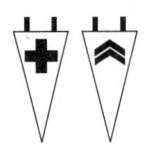

AMOUNT: None Specified   DEADLINE: None Specified
FIELDS/MAJORS: Medicine

Scholarships are available at OU, Norman, for medical students participating in the campus ROTC program. Write to the address listed for information or call: Army (405) 670-5958; Navy (405) 681-2576; Air Force (405) 670-2983.

University of Oklahoma, Norman
Director, Office of Financial Aid
PO Box 26901
Oklahoma City, OK 73190

4747
Barry M. Goldwater Scholarship

AMOUNT: Maximum: $7000   DEADLINE: November 25
FIELDS/MAJORS: Mathematics, Natural Science, Engineering

Scholarships are available at OU, Norman, full-time sophomores and juniors with outstanding academic credentials. Must be intending to pursue a career in mathematics, natural sciences, or engineering. A total of 250 awards are offered nationwide on an annual basis. Write to the address below for information or call (405) 325-5291. GPA must be at least 3.0.

University of Oklahoma, Norman
Honors College
1300 Asp Ave.
Norman, OK 73019

4748
Ben Barnett MBA and Ph.D. Scholars Awards

AMOUNT: $1000-$5000   DEADLINE: February 8
FIELDS/MAJORS: Business Administration

Scholarships are available at OU, Norman, for full-time MBA and Ph.D. student in business administration. Must have high GMAT scores and GPAs. Four awards offered annually. Write to the address below for information or call (405) 325-4107. GPA must be at least 2.7.

University of Oklahoma, Norman
College of Business Administration
307 W. Brooks
Norman, OK 73019

4749
Catholic Foundation of Oklahoma Medical Scholarships

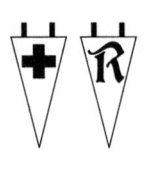

AMOUNT: Maximum: $1000   DEADLINE: March 15
FIELDS/MAJORS: Medicine

Scholarships are available at OU, Norman, for medical students who are Catholics in the Archdiocese of Oklahoma City. Write directly to the Foundation at the address listed for further information or call (405) 721-4115.

University of Oklahoma, Norman
Catholic Foundation, Scholarship Dir.
PO Box 32038
Oklahoma City, OK 73123

4750
Clyde Farrar Fellowship

AMOUNT: Maximum: $5000   DEADLINE: March 1
FIELDS/MAJORS: Electrical Engineering

Scholarships are available at OU, Norman, for full-time graduate students in electrical engineering. One award offered annually. Write to the address below for information or call (405) 325-5911.

University of Oklahoma, Norman
College of Engineering
Room 107, CEC
Norman, OK 73019

4751
College of Medicine Scholarships

AMOUNT: None Specified DEADLINE: None Specified
FIELDS/MAJORS: Medicine

Scholarships are available at OU, Norman, for medical students. Includes the National Health Service Corps, T.A. Ragan, Winstead, and Nina Hinton Memorial, Dr. Pleasant Moseley Haraway, Halverstadt, Southern Medical Association, and William C. Metzgar and Slick Scholarships. Individual award requirements may vary. Write to the address listed for information or call (405) 271-2118.

University of Oklahoma, Norman
Director, Office of Financial Aid
OUHSC, PO Box 73190
Oklahoma City, OK 73190

4752
College of Pharmacy Graduate Awards

AMOUNT: None Specified DEADLINE: February 1
FIELDS/MAJORS: Pharmacy

Scholarships are available at OU, Norman, for graduate pharmacy students. Includes the E. Blanche Sommers, John B. Bruce, Loyd and Maurine Harris, and Roy Sanford Pharmacy Scholarships. Individual award requirements will vary. Write to the address listed for information or call (405) 271-6484.

University of Oklahoma, Norman
Dean, College of Pharmacy
PO Box 26901
Oklahoma City, OK 73190

4753
College of Public Health Graduate Awards

AMOUNT: None Specified DEADLINE: February 1
FIELDS/MAJORS: Public Health

Scholarships are available for graduate public health students at OU, Norman. Includes the OU College of Public Health Alumni Association Scholarship and the Public Health Service Traineeship. Must be a U.S. citizen with a GPA of at least 3.0. Write to the address listed for information or call (405) 271-2232.

University of Oklahoma, Norman
Office of the Dean, OUHSC
PO Box 26901, Chb, Room 139
Oklahoma City, OK 73190

4754
Conoco Fellowship

AMOUNT: Maximum: $8800 DEADLINE: March 1
FIELDS/MAJORS: Chemical Engineering, Materials Science

Scholarship is available at OU, Norman, for full-time graduate students in chemical engineering or materials science. Applicants must be U.S. citizens and not be on leave from a competing company. One award offered annually. Write to the address below for information or call (405) 325-5811.

University of Oklahoma, Norman
Chemical Engineering and Materials Science
100 East Boyd Street, Energy Center
Norman, OK 73019

4755
Construction Science Graduate Student Service Award

AMOUNT: Maximum: $500 DEADLINE: April 15
FIELDS/MAJORS: Construction Science

Scholarships are available at OU, Norman, for graduate students in construction science. Awarded on the basis of service to the department and college. Write to the address below for information or call (405) 325-2444.

University of Oklahoma, Norman, College of Architecture
Division of Construction Science
Gould Hall, #150
Norman, OK 73019

4756
Construction Science Mature Student Award- Flintco Company

AMOUNT: Maximum: $1000 DEADLINE: April 15
FIELDS/MAJORS: Construction Science

Open to admitted OU, Norman, students in construction science. Applicants must be over twenty-eight years of age. Based on academics and financial need. Write to the address below for information or call (405) 325-2444.

University of Oklahoma, Norman, College of Architecture
Division of Construction
Gould Hall, #150
Norman, OK 73019

4757
Cortez A.M. Ewing Public Service Fellowship (Congressional Internship)

AMOUNT: Maximum: $4000 DEADLINE: December 15
FIELDS/MAJORS: Political Science

Available at OU, Norman, for sophomores, juniors, and seniors majoring in political science. Preference is given to students returning to OU in the fall following their summer congressional intern experience. Four to six awards offered annually. Write to the address below for information or call (405) 325-2061. GPA must be at least 2.8.

University of Oklahoma, Norman
Political Science Department
455 West Lindsey
Norman, OK 73019

4758
Elizabeth Ann Burns Memorial

AMOUNT: Maximum: $1000 DEADLINE: August 1
FIELDS/MAJORS: Fine Arts

Scholarships are available at OU, Norman, for full-time students who are members of the Presbyterian Church in Indian Nations Presbytery. Write to the address listed for information or call (405) 321-0933.

First Presbyterian Church
Scholarship Coordinator
PO Box 2066
Norman, OK 73070

4759
FINE Fellowship Program

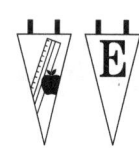

AMOUNT: $7000-$10000 DEADLINE: None Specified
FIELDS/MAJORS: Education

Scholarships are available at OU, Norman, for full-time master's or doctoral level students who are of Native American heritage. Deadlines are: May for summer and August for fall. Write to the address below for information or call (405) 325-1081.

University of Oklahoma, Norman
College of Education
Room 105, ECH
Norman, OK 73019

4760
Frances Weitzenhoffer Memorial Fellowship in Art History

AMOUNT: Maximum: $8000 DEADLINE: March 1
FIELDS/MAJORS: Art History

Fellowships are available at OU, Norman, for full-time graduate art history majors. One award offered annually. Write to the address below for information or call (405) 325-7370.

University of Oklahoma, Norman
Director, School of Art
540 Parrington, Room 122
Norman, OK 73019

4761
Geology Scholarships

AMOUNT: Maximum: $3000 DEADLINE: March 1
FIELDS/MAJORS: Geology, Mineral Science

Scholarships are available at OU, Norman, for full-time geology majors. May be renewed if recipients make satisfactory progress toward graduation. Includes the Harry A. Larsh, Harry J. Brown, and the Heston Geology Fund Scholarships. Write to the address below for information or call (405) 325-3253. GPA must be at least 2.6.

University of Oklahoma, Norman
Director, School of Geology and Geophysics
100 East Boyd Street, Room G-810
Norman, OK 73019

4762
Graduate Assistantships

AMOUNT: Maximum: $14000 DEADLINE: May 1
FIELDS/MAJORS: Anatomy

Graduate assistantships are available at OU, Norman, for students enrolled as graduates in anatomical sciences. Must have earned at least a 3.0 GPA on each anatomy course completed. Advanced graduates are given preference. May be renewed for a total of three to five years. Write to the address below for information or call (405) 271-2085.

University of Oklahoma, Norman
College of Medicine
Department of Anatomical Sciences
OUHSC PO Box 26901
Oklahoma City, OK 73190

4763
Graduate Assistantships

AMOUNT: Maximum: $13000 DEADLINE: January 1
FIELDS/MAJORS: Pharmacology

Open to full-time graduate students in the pharmacology doctoral program. Must have started dissertation research with the faculty mentor. Two awards offered annually. Contact the address below for further information.

University of Oklahoma, Norman
College of Medicine
Department of Pharmacology
OUHSC, PO Box 26901, Library 121
Oklahoma City, OK 73190

4764
Guy Treat Scholarships

AMOUNT: Maximum: $6000 DEADLINE: March 1
FIELDS/MAJORS: Civil Engineering

Scholarships are available at OU, Norman, for full-time juniors majoring in civil engineering. Awards will go to the top students in the program. Six awards offered annually. Write to the address below for information or call (405) 325-5911. GPA must be at least 3.0.

University of Oklahoma, Norman
Director-CEES Room 334 CEC
College of Engineering
Norman, OK 73019

4765
Harry S. Truman Scholarship

AMOUNT: $3000-$27000 DEADLINE: November 25
FIELDS/MAJORS: All Areas of Study

Scholarships are available at OU, Norman, for full-time juniors ranked in the upper 25% of their class. Awards are given for senior year and graduate studies. Maximum of ninety awards offered annually nationwide. Write to the address below for information or call (405) 325-5291. GPA must be at least 3.3.

University of Oklahoma, Norman
Honors College, Dr. Melanie Wright
1300 Asp Ave.
Norman, OK 73019

4766
John S. and Charles F. Barwick Scholarship

AMOUNT: Maximum: $2000 DEADLINE: March 31
FIELDS/MAJORS: All Areas of Study

Scholarships are available at OU, Norman, for entering freshmen who are graduates of Guthrie High School in Oklahoma. Based on academics, character, and financial need. Two awards offered annually. Write to the address listed for information or call (316) 634-2336. Must have a GPA of at least 2.8.

John S. and Charles F. Barwick Scholarship Fund, Inc.
Scholarship Coordinator
2453 Plumthickol Ct.
Wichita, KS 67226

4767
Kerr McGee Corporation Student Scholarships

AMOUNT: Maximum: $4000 DEADLINE: January 30
FIELDS/MAJORS: Accounting

Scholarships are available at OU, Norman, for full-time junior accounting majors. Based on academic ability. Applicants must be residents of Oklahoma. May be renewable for senior year. Write to the address below for information or call (405) 325-4221. GPA must be at least 2.9.

University of Oklahoma, Norman
School of Accounting
200 Adams Hall
Norman, OK 73019

4768
Kerr-McGee Scholarships

AMOUNT: Maximum: $4000 DEADLINE: May 1
FIELDS/MAJORS: All Areas of Study

Scholarships are available at OU, Norman, for students who entered directly from high school and were admitted in '97 and were full-time during fall '97-spring '98. Must be maintaining a minimum GPA of 3.75. Write to the address below for information or call (405) 325-2851.

University of Oklahoma, Norman
OU Scholars Program
1300 Asp Ave.
Norman, OK 73019

4769
McMahon Memorial Scholarships

AMOUNT: Maximum: $5000 DEADLINE: February 15
FIELDS/MAJORS: News Journalism, Broadcasting

Scholarships available at OU, Norman, for admitted entering freshmen. Based on high school GPA, SAT/ACT scores, and personal interviews. Five awards offered annually. Write to the address below for information or call (405) 325-2721. GPA must be at least 3.0.

University of Oklahoma, Norman
School of Journalism and Mass Comm.
860 Van Vleet Oval
Norman, OK 73019

4770
Mercy Hospital Medical Center of Des Moines Scholarship/Loan

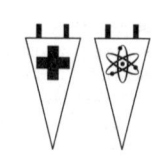

AMOUNT: Maximum: $5000 DEADLINE: December 1
FIELDS/MAJORS: Cytotechnology

Scholarships are available at OU, Norman, for full-time cytotechnology majors who agree to work at Mercy Hospital for at least one year after graduation. Write to the address below for information or call (405) 271-2104.

University of Oklahoma, Norman
Dept. of Clinical Lab Serv., Linda Koch
PO Box 26901
Oklahoma City, OK 73190

4771
National Doctoral Fellowships in Business and Management

AMOUNT: $10000 DEADLINE: February 8
FIELDS/MAJORS: Business Administration

Scholarships are available at OU, Norman, for full-time Ph.D. candidates in business administration and management with high GMAT scores and GPAs. Applicants must be citizens of the U.S. or Canada. Write to the address below for information or call (405) 325-4107. GPA must be at least 2.9.

University of Oklahoma, Norman
College of Business Administration
307 W. Brooks
Norman, OK 73019

4772
National Medical Fellowships

AMOUNT: $500-$4200 DEADLINE: April 1
FIELDS/MAJORS: Medicine

Scholarships are available at OU, Norman, for medical students who are of African-American, Native American, and Hispanic heritage. Based on academic performance and financial need. Information and applications must be requested from the address listed or call (212) 714-1007.

National Medical Fellowships, Inc.
Fellowship Coordinator
110 W. 32nd St., 8th Floor
New York, NY 10001-3205

4773
Native American Seminary Scholarship

AMOUNT: None Specified DEADLINE: None Specified
FIELDS/MAJORS: Theology

Scholarships are available at OU, Norman, for full-time theology students who are of Native American, Aleut, or Eskimo descent. Applicants must be one of the following: a seminary student, a person under the care of presbytery, a member of the Presbyterian Church, or a minister or candidate. Contact the United Ministry Center for deadline information. Write to the address listed for information or call (502) 569-5745.

Presbyterian Church (U.S.A)
Office of Financial Aid for Students
100 Witherspoon St.
Louisville, KY 40202-1396

4774
Noble Foundation Business Administration Scholarships

AMOUNT: $1000-$5000 DEADLINE: February 8
FIELDS/MAJORS: Business Administration, Economics

Scholarships are available at OU, Norman, for full-time MBA and Ph.D. candidates in business administration. Applicants must be U.S. citizens or permanent residents. Must have at least 85% on the GMAT. Write to the address below for information or call (405) 325-4107.

University of Oklahoma, Norman
College of Business Administration
307 W. Brooks
Norman, OK 73019

4775
Nursing Student Assistant Program

AMOUNT: $2000-$4000 DEADLINE: July 10
FIELDS/MAJORS: Nursing

Assistantships are available at OU, Norman, for admitted full-time graduate nursing students. Applicants must be U.S. citizens and Oklahoma residents. Contact the Physician Commission Manpower Training at (405) 271-5848 for more details.

University of Oklahoma, Norman
College of Nursing
PO Box 26901
Oklahoma City, OK 73190

4776
OU Alumni Club of Arizona Scholarships

AMOUNT: Maximum: $1000 DEADLINE: April 1
FIELDS/MAJORS: All Areas of Study

Scholarship available at OU, Norman, for high school seniors who are residents of Maricopa County, Arizona. One award offered annually. Contact the address listed for information.

University of Oklahoma, Norman
Randy Brogdon
127 W. Marlette Ave.
Phoenix, AZ 85013

4777
OU Alumni Club of Dallas Scholarships

AMOUNT: Maximum: $2000 DEADLINE: March 15
FIELDS/MAJORS: All Areas of Study

Scholarships are available at OU, Norman, for high school seniors who are residents of the Dallas area. Up to four awards offered annually. Write to the address listed for information or call (214) 348-8652.

University of Oklahoma, Norman
OU Club of Dallas, Mike Tuttle
PO Box 670753
Dallas, TX 75367-0753

4778
OU Alumni Club of East Texas Scholarships

AMOUNT: None Specified DEADLINE: April 15
FIELDS/MAJORS: All Areas of Study

Scholarships are available at OU, Norman, for entering freshmen who are residents of the East Texas area. Write to the address listed for information or call (903) 534-1977.

University of Oklahoma, Norman
OU Club of East Texas, Mr. Dex Crosby
5935 Old Bullard Rd., #204
Tyler, TX 75703

4779
OU Alumni Club of Fort Worth Scholarships

AMOUNT: Maximum: $1000 DEADLINE: March 1
FIELDS/MAJORS: All Areas of Study

Scholarships are available at OU, Norman, for high school seniors who are residents of the Fort Worth area. Two awards offered annually. Write to the address listed for information.

University of Oklahoma, Norman
OU Club of Fort Worth, Nancy McCann
6504 Tabor
Ft. Worth, TX 76180

4780
OU Alumni Club of Greater New York Scholarships

AMOUNT: Maximum: $1000 DEADLINE: April 1
FIELDS/MAJORS: All Areas of Study

Scholarship available at OU, Norman, for entering freshmen who are residents of the Greater New York area, New Jersey, or Connecticut. One award offered annually. Write to the address listed for information or call (718) 622-0241.

University of Oklahoma, Norman
OU Club of Greater N. Y., Gail Donovan
140 Eighth Ave., #3N
Brooklyn, NY 11215

4781
OU Alumni Club of Houston Scholarships

GPA 3.0+

AMOUNT: Maximum: $2000 DEADLINE: March 15
FIELDS/MAJORS: All Areas of Study

Scholarships are available at OU, Norman, for entering freshmen who are high school seniors and residents of the Houston area. Renewable if students maintain GPAs of at least 3.0 and attend school full-time. Write to the address listed for information or call (713) 951-5600.

University of Oklahoma, Norman
OU Club of Houston, John Teaque
2327 Sheridan
Houston, TX 77030

4782
OU Alumni Club of Love County Scholarships

AMOUNT: None Specified DEADLINE: April 1
FIELDS/MAJORS: All Areas of Study

Scholarships are available at OU, Norman, for undergraduates and graduate students who are residents of Love County, Oklahoma. Contact the address listed for further information or call (405) 276-2323.

University of Oklahoma, Norman
Don and Barbara Sessions
35 Fairway Dr.
Burneyville, OK 73430

4783
OU Alumni Club of McAlester Scholarships

AMOUNT: Maximum: $1000 DEADLINE: April 1
FIELDS/MAJORS: All Areas of Study

Scholarships are available at OU, Norman, for entering freshmen who are residents of Pittsburg County, Oklahoma. Contact your high school guidance counselor for information and an application.

University of Oklahoma, Norman
OU Club of McAlester, Doug Auld
215 N. Sixth
McAlester, OK 74501

4784
OU Alumni Club of Okmulgee County Scholarships

AMOUNT: None Specified DEADLINE: April 1
FIELDS/MAJORS: All Areas of Study

Scholarships are available at OU, Norman, for entering freshmen who are residents of Okmulgee County, Oklahoma. Write to the address listed for information, or contact your high school guidance counselor.

University of Oklahoma, Norman
OU Club of Okmulgee, Shelly O'Mealey
PO Box 68
Okmulgee, OK 74447

4785
OU Alumni Club of San Antonio Scholarships

AMOUNT: Maximum: $1000 DEADLINE: March 31
FIELDS/MAJORS: All Areas of Study

Scholarships are available at OU, Norman, for entering freshmen who are residents of the San Antonio area. Two awards offered annually. Write to the address listed for information or contact your high school guidance counselor.

University of Oklahoma, Norman
OU Club of San Antonio, Michael Bowles
8400 Blanco Rd., #205
San Antonio, TX 78216

4786
OU Alumni Club of Shawnee Scholarships

AMOUNT: None Specified DEADLINE: April 1
FIELDS/MAJORS: All Areas of Study

Scholarships are available at OU, Norman, for entering freshmen who are residents of the Shawnee area. Write to the address listed for information, or contact your high school guidance counselor.

University of Oklahoma, Norman
OU Club of Shawnee, Jeff Diamond
PO Box 336
Shawnee, OK 74802

4787
OU Alumni Club of St. Louis Scholarships

AMOUNT: Maximum: $2000 DEADLINE: April 1
FIELDS/MAJORS: All Areas of Study

Scholarships are available at OU, Norman, for entering freshmen who are residents of the St. Louis area. Three awards offered annually. Contact your high school guidance counselor for further information, write to the address listed, or call (314) 331-0353.

University of Oklahoma, Norman
OU Club of St. Louis, Scholarship Chair
PO Box 1687
St. Louis, MO 63188

4788
OU Medical Scholarships

AMOUNT: $500-$6000 DEADLINE: March 1
FIELDS/MAJORS: Medicine

Open to medical students at OU, Norman. Includes the Blanche Huls, C.E. Williams, Class of 1935 Grace Hassler, Coburn, Dr. Fred S. Clinton, Evelyn A. Maurer, Gale R. Kimball, Larson Memorial, McCabe Memorial, O'Hornett, and Marcella H. Brown Scholarships. Individual award requirements may vary. Write to the address below for information or call (405) 271-2118.

University of Oklahoma, Norman
Director, Office of Financial Aid
OUHSC PO Box 73190
Oklahoma City, OK 73190

4789
OU Sooner Club of Southern California Scholarships

AMOUNT: None Specified DEADLINE: March 15
FIELDS/MAJORS: All Areas of Study

Scholarships are available at OU, Norman, for entering freshmen who are residents of California. Write to the address listed for information or contact your high school guidance counselor.

University of Oklahoma, Norman
OU Club of S. California, Todd Howery
239 Via Ithaca
Newport Beach, CA 90008

4790
Outstanding Transfer Student Award

AMOUNT: $500-$6000 DEADLINE: March 1
FIELDS/MAJORS: Geology, Geophysics

Scholarships are available at OU, Norman, for full-time transfer students with a minimum GPA of 3.0. May be renewed if recipients maintain the minimum GPA of 3.0. Five to ten awards offered annually. Write to the address below for information or call (405) 325-3253.

University of Oklahoma, Norman
Director, School of Geology and Geophysics
100 East Boyd Street, Room 810
Norman, OK 73019

4791
Provost Predoctoral Fellowship

AMOUNT: Maximum: $14000 DEADLINE: March 1
FIELDS/MAJORS: All Areas of Study

Fellowships are available at OU, Norman, for students in good standing in a Ph.D. program. Must be recommended by the graduate program in order to be considered for the fellowship. Write to the address below for information or call (405) 271-2085.

University of Oklahoma, Norman
Dean Graduate College
PO Box 26901 Library 258
Oklahoma City, OK 73190

4792
Roche Biomedical Laboratories, Inc., Scholarship

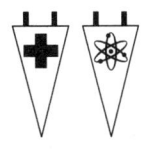

AMOUNT: Maximum: $3000 DEADLINE: None Specified
FIELDS/MAJORS: Cytotechnology

Scholarships are available at OU, Norman, for full-time cytotechnology majors who have been accepted or are enrolled in the program. Write to the address listed for information.

Roche Biomedical Laboratories, Inc.
Financial Assistance Program Admin.
Cytology Dept., 236 Melbane St., #103
Burlington, NC 27215

4793
SDMS Educational Foundation Scholarships

AMOUNT: $500-$1500 DEADLINE: March 31
FIELDS/MAJORS: Sonography

Scholarships are available at OU, Norman, for full-time sonography majors. Ten to fifteen awards (at $500) based on financial need, and two awards (at $1500) are based on academics. Additional deadlines are July 31 and November 30 of each year. Write to the address listed for information or call 1-800-229-9506.

SDMS Educational Foundation
Scholarship Coordinator
12770 Coit Rd., #708
Dallas, TX 75251

4794
Sooner Club of Austin Scholarships

AMOUNT: Maximum: $1000 DEADLINE: March 15
FIELDS/MAJORS: All Areas of Study

Scholarships are available at OU, Norman, for entering freshmen who are residents of the Austin area. Write to the address listed for information or contact your high school guidance counselor.

University of Oklahoma, Norman
Sooner Club of Austin, R. Davis
PO Box 1873
Cedar Park, TX 78613

4795
Tulsa County Medical Society Scholarships

AMOUNT: None Specified DEADLINE: July 1
FIELDS/MAJORS: Medicine

Scholarships available for medical students at OU, Norman, who are residents of the Tulsa metropolitan area (for the past five years). Students are eligible for application after completion of the first year of medical school. Applications available every year beginning April 1, and deadline for submission is July 1. Recipients may make re-application. Write to the address listed for information or call (918) 743-6184.

Tulsa County Medical Society
Scholarship Coordinator
2021 S. Lewis, #560
Tulsa, OK 74014

4796
United Methodist Loan Program

AMOUNT: $900-$1200 DEADLINE: None Specified
FIELDS/MAJORS: All Areas of Study

Low-cost loans are available for members of the United Methodist Church who are enrolled in a degree program at OU, Norman. Applicants must be U.S. citizens or permanent residents and have a minimum GPA of 2.3. Repayment begins six months after borrower discontinues full-time school attendance. Write to the address listed for information or call (405) 321-6266.

Wesley Foundation
Rev. Brad Humphrey
428 W. Lindsey
Norman, OK 73069

4797
Warren R. Lang, M.D. ASCT Scholarship Award

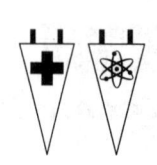

AMOUNT: Maximum: $500 DEADLINE: None Specified
FIELDS/MAJORS: Cytotechnology

Scholarships are available at OU, Norman, for full-time cytotechnology majors who are student members of the ASCT. Recent graduates of an approved school of Cytotechnology are eligible to apply. Write to the address below for information or call (615) 929-6343.

College of Medicine, Dept. of Pathology
Sophie K. Thompson, Chairperson
PO Box 705068
Johnson City, TN 37614

UNIVERSITY OF PENNSYLVANIA

4798
Andrew W. Mellon Fellowships in the Humanities

AMOUNT: $32000 DEADLINE: October 15
FIELDS/MAJORS: Humanities

Fellowship applicants must have held the Ph.D. for a period of no fewer than three and no more than eight years. Applicants must address themselves to an interdisciplinary humanities research project. Duration of award is one year in residence. Three or four awards offered annually. Write for complete details.

University of Pennsylvania
16 College Hall
Chairman, Humanities Coordinating Comm.
Philadelphia, PA 19104

4799
Marcus Foster Fellowship, Fontaine Fellowship

AMOUNT: None Specified DEADLINE: February 5
FIELDS/MAJORS: Education

Fellowships for minority Ph.D./Ed.D. students in the GSE at the University of Pennsylvania. Foster fellowship is renewable. Contact the financial aid office at the address below for details.

University of Pennsylvania, Graduate School of Education
Financial Aid Office
3700 Walnut St.
Philadelphia, PA 19104

4800
NEH Fellowships for Research in Turkey

AMOUNT: $10000-$30000 DEADLINE: November 15
FIELDS/MAJORS: Humanities, Social Sciences

Scholarships are available for graduate students engaged in research in ancient, medieval, or modern times in Turkey, in any field of the humanities and social sciences. Applicants must have fulfilled all preliminary requirements for the doctorate except the dissertation. Award notifications should be sent by January 25. Write to the address below for further information.

University of Pennsylvania Museum
American Research Institute in Turkey
33rd and Spruce Streets
Philadelphia, PA 19104-6324

UNIVERSITY OF PITTSBURGH

4801
Frank B. Sessa Scholarship for Continuing Education

AMOUNT: $750 DEADLINE: March 15
FIELDS/MAJORS: Library and Information Science

Applicants must be members of Beta Phi Mu. An explanation of proposed study or research must accompany application form. For junior, senior, or graduate study. Write to the executive secretary at the address below for details.

Beta Phi Mu International Library Science Honor Society
School of Library and Information Science
University of Pittsburgh
Pittsburgh, PA 15260

UNIVERSITY OF ROCHESTER

4802
African-American Residential Fellowships

AMOUNT: $6000-$30000 DEADLINE: January 30
FIELDS/MAJORS: African Studies

Fellowships are available at the University of Rochester for graduate, dissertation, and postdoctoral research in contemporary topics on the economy, society, politics, and culture of Africa and its Diaspora. Write to the address below for information.

University of Rochester, Frederick Douglas Institute
Assoc. Dir. for Research and Curriculum
302 Morey Hall
Rochester, NY 14627

4803
ASCAP Foundation Max Dreyfus Scholarship

AMOUNT: None Specified DEADLINE: None Specified
FIELDS/MAJORS: Music (Theater-Performance)

Annual scholarship for a student at the Eastman School of Music (University of Rochester). Contact the financial aid office at Eastman. ASCAP does not accept any requests for applications.

American Society of Composers, Authors, and Publishers
One Lincoln Plaza
New York, NY 10023

4804
Link Foundation Energy Fellowship Program

AMOUNT: Maximum: $18000 DEADLINE: December 1
FIELDS/MAJORS: Energy Research

Fellowships are available at the University of Rochester for dissertation research in the development of energy resources and their conservation. To enhance both the theoretical and practical knowledge and application of energy research. Preference given to proposals dealing directly with energy and exploring ideas not yet fully tested, rather than developed programs in progress. Write to the address listed for further information.

Center for Governmental Research, Inc.
Link Foundation Energy Fellowship
37 S. Washington St.
Rochester, NY 14608

4805
Science Scholarship Program

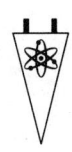

AMOUNT: None Specified DEADLINE: April 15
FIELDS/MAJORS: Science

Scholarship program, awarding high school juniors or seniors (who are outstanding science students) medals and the opportunity to receive scholarships at the University of Rochester. Program participants are nominated by their high schools. Awards are for full tuition. Information should be available from your science teacher or guidance counselor, as students cannot apply directly.

Bausch and Lomb
PO Box 54
Rochester, NY 14601

4806
Urban League Scholarship

AMOUNT: $6000 DEADLINE: January 31
FIELDS/MAJORS: All Areas of Study

Awards open to incoming freshmen. Based solely on financial need. Student must be nominated by a local Urban League office. Students should contact the office nearest them for information and an application. If a student is unable to reach the Urban League office nearest him or her, contact the address below for further information.

University of Rochester
Sharon D. Williams
Office of Admissions
Rochester, NY 14627

UNIVERSITY OF SAN DIEGO

4807
Provost Scholars

AMOUNT: None Specified DEADLINE: February 20
FIELDS/MAJORS: All Areas of Study

A limited number of scholarships are designated in the name of the Provost of the University of San Diego. They are generally reserved for underrepresented students of high achievement who have financial need. Write to the address below for information. GPA must be at least 3.0.

University of San Diego
Office of Financial Aid
5998 Alcala Park
San Diego, CA 92110

UNIVERSITY OF SCRANTON

4808
Claver Award

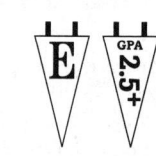

AMOUNT: $1000-$6500   DEADLINE: February 15
FIELDS/MAJORS: All Areas of Study

Open to incoming freshmen who are underrepresented minorities and are able to demonstrate financial need. Contact the address below for further information. GPA must be at least 2.8.

University of Scranton
Office of Financial Aid
Linden and Monroe Ave.
Scranton, PA 18510

4809
Family Tuition Reduction Award

AMOUNT: None Specified   DEADLINE: February 15
FIELDS/MAJORS: All Areas of Study

Open to families that have two or more dependent children in attendance during the same semester as full-time undergraduates. Each student will receive a 10% discount on tuition. Plan also applies when at least one parent is enrolled as a full-time undergraduate student. Contact the address below for further information.

University of Scranton
Office of Financial Aid
Linden and Monroe Ave.
Scranton, PA 18510

4810
Ignatian Scholarship

AMOUNT: None Specified   DEADLINE: February 15
FIELDS/MAJORS: All Areas of Study

Open to incoming freshmen who are typically valedictorians and salutatorians of their high school class with SAT scores ranging from 1400 to 1600 who have shown signs of leadership and caring. Based on exemplary academics. Value of scholarship is full tuition. Contact the address below for further information.

University of Scranton
Office of Financial Aid
Linden and Monroe Ave.
Scranton, PA 18510

4811
Loyola Scholarship

AMOUNT: $2000-$10000   DEADLINE: February 15
FIELDS/MAJORS: All Areas of Study

Open to incoming freshmen who are in the top fifth of their high school class with a minimum SAT score of 1100 who can demonstrate participation in school and community activities. Awards are made in recognition of the student's academic achievement. Value of award is partial tuition. Contact the address below for further information. GPA must be at least 3.4.

University of Scranton
Office of Financial Aid
Linden and Monroe Ave.
Scranton, PA 18510

4812
Transfer Aid Awards

AMOUNT: None Specified   DEADLINE: February 15
FIELDS/MAJORS: All Areas of Study

Xavier Grants are open to transfer students who can demonstrate financial need. Transfers will also be considered for merit based scholarships. Contact the address below for further information.

University of Scranton
Office of Financial Aid
Linden and Monroe Ave.
Scranton, PA 18510

4813
Xavier Grant

AMOUNT: $1000-$8500   DEADLINE: February 15
FIELDS/MAJORS: All Areas of Study

Open to incoming freshmen who are able to demonstrate financial need. Contact the address below for further information. GPA must be at least 2.8.

University of Scranton
Office of Financial Aid
Linden and Monroe Ave.
Scranton, PA 18510

UNIVERSITY OF SOUTH CAROLINA

4814
Mary A. Gardner Scholarship

AMOUNT: Maximum: $300   DEADLINE: April 1
FIELDS/MAJORS: Journalism, Mass Communications

Open to full-time junior and senior journalism majors at USC who have a minimum GPA of 3.0. Must be enrolled in an undergraduate news/editorial program and have a demonstrable interest in pursuing a career in news reporting and/or editing. Write to the address below for further information.

Association for Education in Journalism and
  Mass Communication
University of South Carolina
LeConte College, Rm. 121, Jennifer H. McG
Columbia, SC 29208-0251

UNIVERSITY OF SOUTHERN CALIFORNIA

4815
Asian Pacific American Support Group Scholarships

AMOUNT: $1000-$2500   DEADLINE: March 20
FIELDS/MAJORS: All Areas of Study

Scholarships for Asian-Pacific American students at the University of Southern California. Based on academic achievement, personal merit, and financial need. Must be U.S. citizens or permanent residents enrolled in full-time study and have a GPA of 3.0 or better. For more information, send a SASE to the address below.

Asian Pacific American Support Group Scholarship
  Committee
University of Southern California
Student Union 410, University Park
Los Angeles, CA 90089

UNIVERSITY OF SOUTH FLORIDA

4816
Barbara Schreuder Scholarship

AMOUNT: None Specified   DEADLINE: March 26
FIELDS/MAJORS: All Areas of Study

Scholarships for Eta Chapter members of Pi Gamma Mu (at University of South Florida). Based on scholarship, educational plans, and involvement in campus, community, and PGM activities. Contact Dr. Susan Stoudinger Northcutt at the address listed or Dr. Nancy Hewitt (History, SOC 375) for details.

Pi Gamma Mu, Eta Chapter
University of South Florida
4202 E. Fowler Ave., Soc 375
Tampa, FL 33620

UNIVERSITY OF TENNESSEE, KNOXVILLE

4817
Ronald McNair Program Awards

AMOUNT: $2400   DEADLINE: February 10
FIELDS/MAJORS: Most Areas of Study

Open to highly motivated, disciplined juniors and seniors who are U.S. citizens or permanent residents and can demonstrate financial need. The program also provides for financial assistance to students who are numerically under-represented at the graduate level in the fields listed above. (Includes: African-American, Latino-Americans, and Native Americans). Write to the address below for more information.

University of Tennessee, Knoxville
Ronald McNair Program
900 1/2 Volunteer Blvd.
Knoxville, TN 37996

UNIVERSITY OF TENNESSEE, MARTIN

4818
Alumni Valedictorian Scholarship

AMOUNT: Maximum: $1500 DEADLINE: March 1
FIELDS/MAJORS: All Areas of Study

Scholarships available for all Tennessee valedictorians attending any University of Tennessee campus. Contact the address below for further information.

University of Tennessee, Martin
Office of Financial Assistance
Administration Bldg., Room 210
Martin, TN 38238

4819
Band and Music Scholarships

AMOUNT: $180-$2100 DEADLINE: March 1
FIELDS/MAJORS: All Areas of Study

Scholarships for students who are music majors or who are/will participate in band regardless of major. Based on audition. Contact the address below for further information.

University of Tennessee, Martin
Office of Financial Assistance
Administration Bldg., Room 210
Martin, TN 38238

4820
Cheerleading Training and Scholarship Program

AMOUNT: Maximum: $400 DEADLINE: March 1
FIELDS/MAJORS: All Areas of Study

Scholarships for high school senior cheerleaders. Each participant will be required to take a two-hour course in gymnastics/cheerleading with possible advancement to one of three university squads. Must have a minimum GPA of 2.6. Contact the address below for further information.

University of Tennessee, Martin
Office of Financial Assistance
Administration Bldg., Room 210
Martin, TN 38238

4821
Community College Scholarships

AMOUNT: Maximum: $1500 DEADLINE: March 1
FIELDS/MAJORS: All Areas of Study

Scholarships available to the top student in each of Tennessee's public community colleges who attend any University of Tennessee campus. Contact the address below for further information. GPA must be at least 3.1.

University of Tennessee, Martin
Office of Financial Assistance
Administration Bldg., Room 210
Martin, TN 38238

4822
Harold Conner African-American Scholarships

AMOUNT: None Specified DEADLINE: March 1
FIELDS/MAJORS: All Areas of Study

Scholarships for incoming African-American freshmen who have a minimum GPA of 3.25. Based on high school academics, leadership record, and test scores. Renewable for four years if recipients meet preset standards. Contact the address below for more information.

University of Tennessee, Martin
Office of Financial Assistance
Administration Bldg., Room 210
Martin, TN 38238

4823
Leaders-in-Residence Program

AMOUNT: $1000-$2400 DEADLINE: March 1
FIELDS/MAJORS: All Areas of Study

Scholarships for students who were student council presidents, Beta Club and/or Honor Society presidents, and state officers in high school. Recipients participate in a special leadership program and may compete for residence hall staff positions and $2400 per year awards. Contact the address below for further information.

University of Tennessee, Martin
Office of Financial Assistance
Administration Bldg., Room 210
Martin, TN 38238

4824
National Merit Scholarships

AMOUNT: $800-$2000 DEADLINE: March 1
FIELDS/MAJORS: All Areas of Study

Scholarships for students who were National Merit Scholarship finalists. Contact the address below for further information.

University of Tennessee, Martin
Office of Financial Assistance
Administration Bldg., Room 210
Martin, TN 38238

4825
Salutatorian Freshman Award

AMOUNT: Maximum: $1000 DEADLINE: March 1
FIELDS/MAJORS: All Areas of Study

Scholarships for incoming freshmen who are their high school's salutatorian. Contact the address below for more information.

University of Tennessee, Martin
Office of Financial Assistance
Administration Bldg., Room 210
Martin, TN 38238

4826
University Chancellor's Scholarships

AMOUNT: None Specified DEADLINE: March 1
FIELDS/MAJORS: All Areas of Study

Scholarships for incoming freshmen who have a minimum GPA of 3.5. Renewable for four years if recipients meet preset standards. The scholarships are tuition. Contact the address below for more information.

University of Tennessee, Martin
Office of Financial Assistance
Administration Bldg., Room 210
Martin, TN 38238

4827
University Scholars Scholarships

AMOUNT: Maximum: $3200 DEADLINE: March 1
FIELDS/MAJORS: All Areas of Study

Scholarships for incoming freshmen who have a minimum GPA of 3.5. Renewable for four years if recipients meet preset standards. Contact the address below for more information.

University of Tennessee, Martin
Office of Financial Assistance
Administration Bldg., Room 210
Martin, TN 38238

UNIVERSITY OF TEXAS, AUSTIN

4828
Biology Department Part-Time Employment Opportunities

AMOUNT: None Specified DEADLINE: March 30
FIELDS/MAJORS: Botany, Microbiology, Biology, Zoology

Student or laboratory assistantships for undergraduates at UT, Austin. Assist in laboratories. Both work-study and non-work-study positions available. Write to the department below for details. Application is made through individual faculty members.

University of Texas, Austin
Division of Biological Sciences
Pai 126
Austin, TX 78712

4829
Robert A. Welch Graduate Fellowships in Chemistry and Biochemistry

AMOUNT: None Specified DEADLINE: March 1
FIELDS/MAJORS: Chemistry, Biochemistry

Fellowships for graduate students in the department of chemistry and biochemistry at UT, Austin. Limited teaching duties and enhanced research potentials are afforded to these fellows. Graduate teaching and research assistantships are also available through the department. Contact the department for details.

University of Texas, Austin
Department of Chemistry and Biochemistry
Austin, TX 78712

UNIVERSITY OF TULSA

4830
Mervin Bovaird Foundation Scholarships

AMOUNT: Maximum: $6000 DEADLINE: November 15
FIELDS/MAJORS: All Areas of Study

Scholarships for students enrolled in or applying to the University of Tulsa. High school seniors in Oklahoma are eligible and should contact their high school principals for information. Tulsa Junior College students should contact the President of TJC for information. Seventy-six awards per year. Use the two methods listed to receive further information. Do not contact the organization directly.

Mervin Bovaird Foundation
100 W. 5th St., #800
Tulsa, OK 74103

UNIVERSITY OF VIRGINIA

4831
David Rozkuszka Scholarship

AMOUNT: None Specified DEADLINE: December 1
FIELDS/MAJORS: Library Science

Awards for ALA-accredited master's degree candidate currently working in a library with government documents, with a commitment to government documents librarianship. Write to the address below for additional information.

American Library Association
Susan Tulis, Law Library
University of Virginia, 580 Massie Rd.
Charlottesville, VA 22901

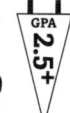

4832
Jefferson Scholars Program

AMOUNT: $10780-$21030 DEADLINE: January 1
FIELDS/MAJORS: All Areas of Study

Full scholarships for entering students at the University of Virginia. Based on leadership, scholarship, and citizenship. Twenty-five awards per year. Renewable for four years. Competition includes regional competition or at-large competition for out-of-state or international students. Write to the address below for details. Must have a GPA of at least 2.8.

University of Virginia Alumni Association
PO Box 3446
University Station
Charlottesville, VA 22903

4833
Woodrow Wilson Memorial Scholarship

AMOUNT: None Specified DEADLINE: None Specified
FIELDS/MAJORS: Law

Scholarships for students in the School of Law at the University of Virginia who are direct descendants of worthy confederates. Must be able to prove lineage. Contact the UDC nearest you for details. If the address is unknown, write to the address below for further information.

United Daughters of the Confederacy
Scholarship Coordinator
328 North Boulevard
Richmond, VA 23220

UNIVERSITY OF WASHINGTON

4834
Uranga Loan

AMOUNT: None Specified DEADLINE: January 12
FIELDS/MAJORS: Foreign Studies

Open to currently enrolled students of Mexican descent who can demonstrate financial need. Contact the address below for further information.

University of Washington
Center for Chicano Studies B 521
Padelford Hall, Box 354380
Seattle, WA 98195

4835
Washington Library Association Scholarships

AMOUNT: None Specified DEADLINE: January 31
FIELDS/MAJORS: Library Science

Scholarships for master's level students who have completed at least 2 quarters of graduate school in library science at the University of Washington. Must be a member of the Washington Library Association. Write to the address below for details or e-mail at wasla@wla.org or wasla@wla.com.

Washington Library Association
Gail Willis
4016-1st Ave., NE
Seattle, WA 98105

UNIVERSITY OF WEST ALABAMA

4836
Annie Pruitt Nursing Award

AMOUNT: $400 DEADLINE: April 15
FIELDS/MAJORS: Nursing

Scholarship for winter quarter of freshman year. Must be a U.S. citizen or permanent resident. Write to the address below for more information.

University of West Alabama
Office of Admissions
Station 4
Livingston, AL 35470

4837
Aver Rumley Memorial Award

AMOUNT: $500   DEADLINE: April 15
FIELDS/MAJORS: Elementary Education

Scholarship for juniors and seniors who are U.S. citizens or permanent residents. Write to the address below for more information.

University of West Alabama
Office of Admissions
Station 4
Livingston, AL 35470

4838
Baldwin County Scholarship

AMOUNT: Maximum: $600   DEADLINE: April 15
FIELDS/MAJORS: All Areas of Study

Renewable scholarship open to all students from Baldwin County, Alabama, who attend Livingston University. Write to the address below for more information.

University of West Alabama
Office of Admissions
Station 4
Livingston, AL 35470

4839
Choctaw County Alumni Chapter Scholarships

AMOUNT: None Specified   DEADLINE: April 15
FIELDS/MAJORS: All Areas of Study

Awards open to incoming freshmen who are residents of Choctaw County, Alabama. Must be U.S. citizens or permanent residents. Contact the address below for further information.

University of West Alabama
Office of Admissions
Station 4
Livingston, AL 35470

4840
Clarke/Washington Alumni Chapter Scholarships

AMOUNT: None Specified   DEADLINE: April 15
FIELDS/MAJORS: All Areas of Study

Awards open to incoming freshmen who are residents of either Clarke or Washington counties in Alabama. Must be U.S. citizens or permanent residents. Contact the address below for further information.

University of West Alabama
Office of Admissions
Station 4
Livingston, AL 35470

4841
Elizabeth Serlina Stallworth Memorial Scholarship

AMOUNT: $600   DEADLINE: April 15
FIELDS/MAJORS: All Areas of Study

Renewable scholarship open to all undergraduates. Write to the address below for more information.

University of West Alabama
Office of Admissions
Station 4
Livingston, AL 35470

4842
Emergency Secondary Education Award

AMOUNT: $3996   DEADLINE: April 15
FIELDS/MAJORS: Math or Science Education

Scholarships for juniors and seniors who are residents of Alabama. Must be U.S. citizens or permanent residents. Write to the address below for more information.

University of West Alabama
Office of Admissions
Station 4
Livingston, AL 35470

4843
First Alabama Bank Scholarship

AMOUNT: $500   DEADLINE: April 15
FIELDS/MAJORS: All Areas of Study

Renewable scholarship for undergraduates who are U.S. citizens and are residents of Sumter County, Alabama. Write to the address below for more information.

University of West Alabama
Office of Admissions
Station 4
Livingston, AL 35470

4844
George W. Skipper Scholarship

AMOUNT: $2229 DEADLINE: April 15
FIELDS/MAJORS: All Areas of Study

Renewable scholarship for all undergraduates from Clarke or Washington counties, Alabama, who work with the local fire department. Must be U.S. citizens or permanent residents. Write to the address below for more information.

University of West Alabama
Office of Admissions
Station 4
Livingston, AL 35470

4845
Gladys K. Ward Memorial Scholarship

AMOUNT: $1245 DEADLINE: April 15
FIELDS/MAJORS: Education

Scholarship for upperclassmen who are majoring in education and are residents of Cuba, Alabama. Must be U.S. citizens or permanent residents. Write to the address below for more information.

University of West Alabama
Office of Admissions
Station 4
Livingston, AL 35470

4846
India Lowry Shields Scholarship

AMOUNT: $2500 DEADLINE: April 15
FIELDS/MAJORS: All Areas of Study

Scholarships for entering freshmen who are residents of Marengo County, Alabama. Must be U.S. citizens or permanent residents. Write to the address below for more information.

University of West Alabama
Office of Admissions
Station 4
Livingston, AL 35470

4847
James P. Homer Scholarship

AMOUNT: $600 DEADLINE: April 15
FIELDS/MAJORS: All Areas of Study

Scholarship open to entering freshmen. Must be a U.S. citizen or permanent resident. Write to the address below for more information.

University of West Alabama
Office of Admissions
Station 4
Livingston, AL 35470

4848
Jefferson/Shelby/St. Clair County Alumni Chapter Scholarships

AMOUNT: None Specified DEADLINE: April 15
FIELDS/MAJORS: All Areas of Study

Awards open to incoming freshmen who are residents of Jefferson, Shelby, or St. Clair counties, Alabama. Must be U.S. citizens or permanent residents. Contact the address below for further information.

University of West Alabama
Office of Admissions
Station 4
Livingston, AL 35470

4849
Julia S. Tutwiler Scholarship

AMOUNT: $750 DEADLINE: April 15
FIELDS/MAJORS: Education

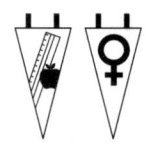

Renewable scholarship open to all freshmen women studying education at UWA. Write to the address below for more information.

University of West Alabama
Office of Admissions
Station 4
Livingston, AL 35470

4850
Languages and Literature Award

AMOUNT: $500 DEADLINE: April 15
FIELDS/MAJORS: English, Literature

Scholarship for juniors and seniors majoring in English or literature. Awards also open to graduate students studying English. Must be U.S. citizens or permanent residents. Write to the address below for more information.

University of West Alabama
Office of Admissions
Station 4
Livingston, AL 35470

4851
Lawrence and Neil Malone Scholarship

AMOUNT: $450 DEADLINE: April 15
FIELDS/MAJORS: Elementary Education

Renewable scholarship for undergraduates who are Baldwin or Mobile counties in Alabama residents and U.S. citizens or permanent residents. Write to the address below for more information.

University of West Alabama
Office of Admissions
Station 4
Livingston, AL 35470

4852
Ralph and Margaret Lyon Graduate Scholarship

AMOUNT: $1200 DEADLINE: April 15
FIELDS/MAJORS: Education

Scholarship for graduate students who are majoring in education. Renewable for LU or UWA graduate students/teachers. Must be U.S. citizens or permanent residents. Write to the address below for more information.

University of West Alabama
Office of Admissions
Station 4
Livingston, AL 35470

4853
Sharon Smith Pafford Memorial Scholarship

AMOUNT: $600 DEADLINE: April 15
FIELDS/MAJORS: English, Band

Renewable scholarship for English or band majors who are U.S. citizens or permanent residents. First preference is for residents of Camden, Tennessee. Write to the address below for more information.

University of West Alabama
Office of Admissions
Station 4
Livingston, AL 35470

4854
Tagged for Success Scholarship

AMOUNT: $2500 DEADLINE: April 15
FIELDS/MAJORS: All Areas of Study

Awards open to upperclassmen who are residents of Alabama. Renewable. Contact the address below for further information.

University of West Alabama
Office of Admissions
Station 4
Livingston, AL 35470

4855
Therman and Martha Sewell Sisk Memorial Award

AMOUNT: $500 DEADLINE: April 15
FIELDS/MAJORS: All Areas of Study

Renewable scholarship for entering freshmen who are U.S. citizens or permanent residents and residents of Sumter County, Alabama. Write to the address below for more information.

University of West Alabama
Office of Admissions
Station 4
Livingston, AL 35470

4856
Trustee Community College Scholarships

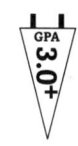

AMOUNT: None Specified DEADLINE: None Specified
FIELDS/MAJORS: All Areas of Study

Awards made in recognition of outstanding academic or leadership achievement while attending a community college. These awards are renewable and reserved for entering transfer students. Must be U.S. citizen or permanent resident. Different awards are granted for specific leadership positions and specific GPAs, and are for full tuition. Write to the address below for more details. GPA must be at least 3.0.

University of West Alabama
Office of Admissions
Station 4
Livingston, AL 35470

UNIVERSITY OF WISCONSIN, MADISON

4857
Advanced Opportunity Fellowships

AMOUNT: Maximum: $17500   DEADLINE: January 15
FIELDS/MAJORS: All Areas of Study

Fellowships available for qualified minority students enrolled at any level in a graduate program. Applicants must be U.S. citizens or permanent residents. See your department and the AOF Fact Sheet at the Office of Fellowships and Minority Programs for specific eligibility requirements and application procedures. Contact your department office for details.

University of Wisconsin, Madison
Graduate School Fellowships Office
217 Bascom Hall, 500 Lincoln Dr.
Madison, WI 53706

4858
E.B. Fred Competition

AMOUNT: Maximum: $17500   DEADLINE: February 1
FIELDS/MAJORS: All Areas of Study

For graduate students who have had an interruption in their formal education for at least five years. Must be in a Ph.D. program. Departments nominate their most academically competitive candidates to a Divisional Fellowship Committee in early February. Write to the address listed for further information.

University of Wisconsin, Madison
Graduate School Fellowships Office
217 Bascom Hall, 500 Lincoln Dr.
Madison, WI 53706-1380

UNIVERSITY OF WISCONSIN, MILWAUKEE

4859
Alumni Association Outstanding Scholar Award

AMOUNT: None Specified   DEADLINE: January 15
FIELDS/MAJORS: All Areas of Study

Available to incoming freshmen who graduated in the top 5% of their senior class and will be enrolled full-time at UWM in the fall. Award covers in-state tuition for eight semesters if student maintains a GPA of 3.25. Contact the address below for further information or call (414) 229-4783.

University of Wisconsin, Milwaukee
Alumni Association
PO Box 413
Milwaukee, WI 53201

4860
UWM Polish American Scholarship Awards

AMOUNT: None Specified   DEADLINE: March 2
FIELDS/MAJORS: Polish Studies

Scholarships are available for Polish-American students majoring in any field and non-Polish students majoring in Polish studies. Applicants must reside in Wisconsin, be U.S. citizens, have a GPA of at least 3.0, and be attending the University of Wisconsin-Milwaukee. Write to the address listed or call (414) 744-9029 for information.

Polanki, Polish Women's Cultural Club of Milwaukee
Ms. Valerie Lukaszewicz, Chairperson
4160 S. First St.
Milwaukee, WI 53207

UNIVERSITY OF WISCONSIN, PLATTEVILLE

4861
AACE International Competition Scholarships

AMOUNT: $500-$2500   DEADLINE: November 1
FIELDS/MAJORS: Cost Management and Related Fields

Awards are available for full-time continuing students at UWP who are enrolled in a degree program related to cost management. Write to the address below for more information or call (608) 342-1125.

University of Wisconsin, Platteville
Professor Stuelke
311 Pioneer Tower
Platteville, WI 53818

4862
A.F. Crow Hybrid Scholarship

AMOUNT: Maximum: $600 DEADLINE: February 1
FIELDS/MAJORS: Agriculture

Awards for incoming freshmen who will be majoring in agriculture. Applicants must be residents of Illinois. Write to the address listed for further information.

University of Wisconsin, Platteville
Office of Admissions and Enrollment Mgt.
Platteville, WI 53818

4863
Agribusiness/Agriculture Economics Alumni Scholarship

AMOUNT: $250-$500 DEADLINE: February 1
FIELDS/MAJORS: Agriculture Economics, Agribusiness

Awards for incoming freshmen who will be majoring in agribusiness or agriculture economics. Based on high school records and activities. Write to the address listed for further information. Must have a GPA of at least 2.9.

University of Wisconsin, Platteville
Office of Admissions and Enrollment Mgt.
Platteville, WI 53818

4864
Agriculture Alumni Association Scholarship

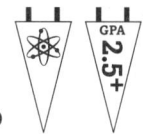

AMOUNT: Maximum: $250 DEADLINE: February 1
FIELDS/MAJORS: Agriculture

Awards for incoming freshmen who will be majoring in agriculture. Based on high school records and activities. Write to the address listed for further information. Must have a GPA of at least 2.9.

University of Wisconsin, Platteville
Office of Admissions and Enrollment Mgt.
Platteville, WI 53818

4865
Agricultural Economics and Agribusiness Alumni Scholarships

AMOUNT: $250-$900 DEADLINE: February 15
FIELDS/MAJORS: Agricultural Economics, Agribusiness

Awards for UWP continuing students majoring in agribusiness or agricultural economics. Based on scholarship and leadership abilities. Write to the address below for more information or call (608) 342-1125. GPA must be at least 2.8.

University of Wisconsin, Platteville
Office of Admissions and Enrollment
Brigham Hall
Platteville, WI 53818

4866
Alpha Gamma Rho Scholarship

AMOUNT: Maximum: $200 DEADLINE: February 1
FIELDS/MAJORS: Agriculture

Awards for incoming freshmen majoring in agriculture. Based on high school academics, activities, and financial need. Must be an FFA member. Write to the address listed for more information. Must have a GPA of at least 2.9.

University of Wisconsin, Platteville
Office of Admissions and Enrollment Mgt.
Platteville, WI 53818

4867
Associated Builders and Contractors of Wisconsin Merit Shop Scholarship

AMOUNT: $500-$2000 DEADLINE: December 15
FIELDS/MAJORS: Building Construction Management

National competition open to full-time UWP continuing students enrolled in building construction management. Number of awards varies from year to year. Write to the address below for more information or call (608) 342-1125.

University of Wisconsin, Platteville
Professor Stuelke
311 Pioneer Tower
Platteville, WI 53818

4868
Associated Builders and Contractors of Wisconsin, Inc. Scholarship

AMOUNT: Maximum: $500 DEADLINE: February 15
FIELDS/MAJORS: Building Construction Management and Related Fields

Open to full-time UWP continuing students majoring in ITM/building construction management. Selection finalized by the faculty of the ITM/BCM program. Write to the address below for more information or call (608) 342-1125.

University of Wisconsin, Platteville
Professor Stuelke
311 Pioneer Tower
Platteville, WI 53818

4869
Building Construction Management Scholarship

AMOUNT: Maximum: $200   DEADLINE: February 1
FIELDS/MAJORS: Building Construction Management

Awards for incoming freshmen who are enrolled or listed as ITM/building construction management major. Write to the address listed for further information.

University of Wisconsin, Platteville
Office of Admissions and Enrollment Mgt.
Platteville, WI 53818

4870
Cenex Scholarships

AMOUNT: Maximum: $750   DEADLINE: February 15
FIELDS/MAJORS: Agricultural Areas, Agronomy, Agribusiness

Available to UWP students who are majoring in the agricultural fields and have completed at least 3 semesters at the time of application. Must be a resident of the Cenex trade area and have a career interest in agribusiness. Based on coursework in cooperative principles, academics, and leadership. Four awards are offered annually. May be renewable for one year. Write to the address below for more information or call (608) 342-1125. GPA must be at least 2.6.

University of Wisconsin, Platteville
Office of Admissions and Enrollment
Brigham Hall
Platteville, WI 53818

4871
Chancellor's Awards

AMOUNT: $500-$1000   DEADLINE: February 1
FIELDS/MAJORS: All Areas of Study

Awards for incoming freshmen who are outstanding applicants as selected by the chancellor. Write to the address below for further information. GPA must be at least 3.6.

University of Wisconsin, Platteville
Office of Admissions and Enrollment Mgt.
Platteville, WI 53818

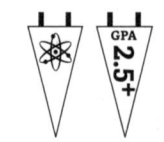

4872
Curt and Linda Hanson Scholarship

AMOUNT: Maximum: $225   DEADLINE: February 1
FIELDS/MAJORS: Agriculture

Awards for incoming freshmen who will be majoring in agriculture. Based on high school academics, financial need, and involvement in agriculture organizations. Write to the address listed for more information. Must have a GPA of at least 2.9.

University of Wisconsin, Platteville
Office of Admissions and Enrollment Mgt.
Platteville, WI 53818

4873
David Laine Memorial Scholarship

AMOUNT: Maximum: $2000   DEADLINE: February 15
FIELDS/MAJORS: Die Casting

Available to full-time UWP students who have a background in die casting. One award offered annually. Write to the address below for more information or call (608) 342-1125.

University or Wisconsin, Platteville
Professor Hauser
316 Pioneer Tower
Platteville, WI 53818

4874
Eastman Cartwright Lumber, Inc. Scholarship

AMOUNT: Maximum: $300   DEADLINE: February 15
FIELDS/MAJORS: Building Construction Management and Related Fields

Available to full-time UWP continuing students who are majoring in a building construction management program. Selection finalized by the BCM faculty. Write to the address below for more information or call (608) 342-1125.

University or Wisconsin, Platteville
Office of Admissions and Enrollment
Brigham Hall
Platteville, WI 53818

4875
Fish Building and Supply Scholarship

AMOUNT: $250-$500   DEADLINE: February 15
FIELDS/MAJORS: Building Construction Management

Available to full-time UWP continuing students who are majoring in a building construction management program. Selection finalized by the BCM faculty. Write to the address below for more information or call (608) 342-1125.

University or Wisconsin, Platteville
Office of Admissions and Enrollment
Brigham Hall
Platteville, WI 53818

4876
Foundry Educational Foundation Scholarships

AMOUNT: $500-$1500 DEADLINE: February 15
FIELDS/MAJORS: Metallurgy, Metal Casting

Available to full-time UWP continuing students who have interest and work experience in metallurgy or metal casting. Based on competitive GPAs. Ten to fifteen awards are offered annually. Write to the address below for more information or call (608) 342-1125. GPA must be at least 2.8.

University or Wisconsin, Platteville
Professor Hauser
316 Pioneer Tower
Platteville, WI 53818

4877
General Engineering Scholarships

AMOUNT: $100-$2000 DEADLINE: February 15
FIELDS/MAJORS: Engineering

Awards are available to UWP engineering majors. Includes the Ward Beetham Memorial, Corporate/Alumni, Engineering Alumni, Paul Faherty, Robert P. Hlavac Memorial, Heinie Miller, Larry Ottensman, and Carl Vietnam Memorial Scholarships. Write to the address below for more information or call (608) 342-1125.

University of Wisconsin, Platteville
Office of Enrollment and Admissions
Brigham Hall
Platteville, WI 53818

4878
General Industrial Engineering Scholarships

AMOUNT: $200-$900 DEADLINE: February 15
FIELDS/MAJORS: Industrial Engineering

Awards open to industrial engineering majors at UWP. Includes the William E. Huff, Industrial Engineering Alumni, Industrial Engineering Alumni at Oscar Meyer, and The Institute of industrial Engineers-Dubuque Chapter Scholarships. Individual award requirements may vary. Write to the address below for more information. GPA must be at least 3.0.

University of Wisconsin, Platteville
Office of Enrollment and Admissions
Brigham Hall
Platteville, WI 53818

4879
George Bullis Scholarship

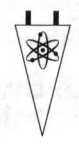

AMOUNT: None Specified DEADLINE: February 1
FIELDS/MAJORS: Mathematics

Awards for incoming freshmen who will be majoring in mathematics or pursuing a career requiring high math aptitude (e.g., mathematics, physics, engineering, etc.). Preference will be given to a National Merit Scholarship finalist. Possibility to extend for entire undergraduate program. Scholarship is for full resident tuition. Write to the address listed for more information.

University of Wisconsin, Platteville
Office of Admissions and Enrollment Mgt.
Platteville, WI 53818

4880
Glen V. Gundy Scholarships

AMOUNT: Maximum: $700 DEADLINE: February 15
FIELDS/MAJORS: Chemistry or Related Area

Available to full-time UWP juniors or seniors majoring in chemistry or a chemistry-related field. Must have completed at least five semesters of course work. One award is offered annually. Write to the address below for more information or call (608) 342-1125.

University of Wisconsin, Platteville
Office of Enrollment and Admissions
Brigham Hall
Platteville, WI 53818

4881
Graphic Arts Technical Foundation Scholarships

AMOUNT: $250-$1000 DEADLINE: February 15
FIELDS/MAJORS: Graphic Communications

Awards available to UWP students who are studying for a career in graphic communications. Must demonstrate potential for success. May be renewable. One to four awards are offered annually. Contact Dr. Virgil Pufahl for more information. GPA must be at least 2.5.

University of Wisconsin, Platteville
Office of Enrollment and Admissions
Brigham Hall
Platteville, WI 53818

4882
Growmark Scholarships

AMOUNT: Maximum: $900   DEADLINE: February 15
FIELDS/MAJORS: Agriculture

Available to UWP upperclassmen who have an interest in the agricultural field. Preference is given to students whose parents hold Farm Bureau or Growmark membership. Must have completed at least 80 credits at the time of application. Two awards are offered annually. Write to the address below for more information or call (608) 342-1125. GPA must be at least 2.5.

University of Wisconsin, Platteville
Office of Admissions and Enrollment
Brigham Hall
Platteville, WI 53818

4883
H.H. Harris Foundation Scholarships

AMOUNT: $400-$1000   DEADLINE: June 1
FIELDS/MAJORS: Metallurgy, Metal Casting

Available to full-time UWP continuing students who have interest and work experience in metallurgy or metal casting. Applications are available in April. Number of awards offered varies. Write to the address below for more information or call (608) 342-1125. GPA must be at least 2.6.

University or Wisconsin, Platteville
Professor Hauser
316 Pioneer Tower
Platteville, WI 53818

4884
Hans F. Seuthe Scholarship

AMOUNT: Maximum: $500   DEADLINE: February 15
FIELDS/MAJORS: Industrial Technology Management, Plastics Processing Technology

Available to full-time UWP upperclassmen with a minimum of 60 credits, who are industrial technology management majors or plastics processing minors. Must have a GPA of 2.75 or above. Write to the address below for more information or call (608) 342-1125.

University or Wisconsin, Platteville
Office of Admissions and Enrollment
Brigham Hall
Platteville, WI 53818

4885
Industrial Technology Alumni Scholarship

AMOUNT: Maximum: $300   DEADLINE: February 15
FIELDS/MAJORS: Industrial Technology Management, Related Areas

Available to full-time UWP seniors who are industrial technology management majors. Academic achievement and extracurricular involvement are equally considered. Write to the address below for more information or call (608) 342-1125. GPA must be at least 2.8.

University or Wisconsin, Platteville
Office of Admissions and Enrollment
Brigham Hall
Platteville, WI 53818

4886
James A. Wilgus Family Scholarship

AMOUNT: Maximum: $900   DEADLINE: February 15
FIELDS/MAJORS: History or Social Science

Open to juniors and seniors at UWP who are majoring in history or the social sciences. Must have a GPA of 3.0 or better. One award is offered annually. Write to the address below for more information or call (608) 342-1125.

University of Wisconsin, Platteville
Office of Enrollment and Admissions
Brigham Hall
Platteville, WI 53818

4887
Jerry Cooper

AMOUNT: Maximum: $500   DEADLINE: February 15
FIELDS/MAJORS: Agriculture

Award for UWP students majoring in any field of agriculture. Write to the address below for more information or call (608) 342-1125.

University of Wisconsin, Platteville
Office of Admissions and Enrollment
Brigham Hall
Platteville, WI 53818

4888
John Deere Dubuque Scholarship

AMOUNT: Maximum: $1250   DEADLINE: February 15
FIELDS/MAJORS: Electrical or Mechanical Engineering

Available to UWP students majoring in electrical or mechanical engineering. One award is offered annually. Write to the address below for more information or call (608) 342-1125.

University of Wisconsin, Platteville
Office of Enrollment and Admissions
Brigham Hall
Platteville, WI 53818

4889
Lands' End Scholarships

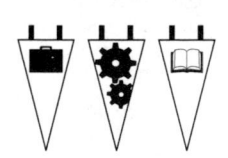

AMOUNT: Maximum: $1250 DEADLINE: February 15
FIELDS/MAJORS: Accounting, Business, Communications, Computer Sciences, Industrial Sciences

Available to UWP full-time students who are majoring in one of the areas above and have at least sophomore standing. Preference is given to graduates of southwestern Wisconsin community high schools. Two awards are offered annually. Write to the address below for more information or call (608) 342-1125.

University of Wisconsin, Platteville
Office of Admissions and Enrollment
Brigham Hall
Platteville, WI 53818

4890
Lula Howery Scholarship

AMOUNT: Maximum: $225 DEADLINE: February 1
FIELDS/MAJORS: Liberal Arts

Awards for incoming freshmen who plan to major in liberal arts. Must demonstrate high academic achievement. Write to the address listed for more information. Must have a GPA of at least 3.1.

University of Wisconsin, Platteville
Office of Admissions and Enrollment Mgt.
Platteville, WI 53818

4891
Matching Monies for Scholarships

AMOUNT: $400-$600 DEADLINE: February 15
FIELDS/MAJORS: Building Construction Management

Open to UWP continuing students who are majoring in a building construction management program. Selection finalized by BCM faculty. Two to four awards offered annually. Write to the address below for more information or call (608) 342-1125. Scholarship co-sponsored by Wausau Homes, Sterling Building Systems, Wisconsin Builders Association, and National Association of Home Builders.

University or Wisconsin, Platteville
Professor Stuelke
311 Pioneer Tower
Platteville, WI 53818

4892
Music Scholarships

AMOUNT: $50-$1000 DEADLINE: February 1
FIELDS/MAJORS: Music

Awards for incoming freshmen who are planning to major in music. Based on musical talent. Write to the address below for more information. You may also call the Music Department for audition dates: (608) 342-1143.

University of Wisconsin, Platteville
Office of Admissions and Enrollment Mgt.
Platteville, WI 53818

4893
National Housing Endowment/Lee S. Evans Scholarship

AMOUNT: Maximum: $1500 DEADLINE: February 15
FIELDS/MAJORS: Building Construction Management and Related Fields

Entry to national competition available to full-time UWP students who are active members of the NAHB. The number of awards varies from year to year. Contact Professor Stuelke for an application and more information or call (608) 342-1125.

University of Wisconsin, Platteville
Professor Stuelke
316 Pioneer Tower
Platteville, WI 53818

4894
Norman R. Powers Scholarship

AMOUNT: Maximum: $150 DEADLINE: February 1
FIELDS/MAJORS: Engineering, Science, Math

Awards for Platteville High School graduates planning to major in engineering. Must have a GPA of 4.0 (or close to it). Write to the address listed for more information.

University of Wisconsin, Platteville
Office of Admissions and Enrollment Mgt.
Platteville, WI 53818

4895
P.E.O. Continuing Education Scholarships

AMOUNT: Maximum: $1000 DEADLINE: February 15
FIELDS/MAJORS: All Areas of Study

Awards for women who are citizens of the U.S. or Canada and are continuing their education after twelve consecutive months as a non-student. Must have at least junior standing with expectations of graduating within 24 months. Write to the address below for more information or call (608) 342-1125.

University of Wisconsin, Platteville
Office of Admissions and Enrollment
Brigham Hall
Platteville, WI 53818

4896
Philip O. Mork Memorial Scholarship

AMOUNT: Maximum: $250 DEADLINE: February 15
FIELDS/MAJORS: Building Construction Management

Available to full-time UWP continuing students who are majoring in a building construction management program. Selection by the BCM faculty. Write to the address below for more information or call (608) 342-1125.

University or Wisconsin, Platteville
Professor Stuelke
316 Pioneer Tower
Platteville, WI 53818

4897
Retirees for Excellence Scholarships

AMOUNT: Maximum: $500 DEADLINE: February 1
FIELDS/MAJORS: All Areas of Study

Awards for incoming freshmen who are in the top 15% of their graduating class. Must demonstrate financial need. Award for first semester is $250. Renewable if recipient maintains a GPA of 2.75. Write to the address listed for further information. Must have a GPA of at least 3.4.

University of Wisconsin, Platteville
Office of Admissions and Enrollment Mgt.
Platteville, WI 53818

4898
Sentry Insurance Youth Leadership Scholarships

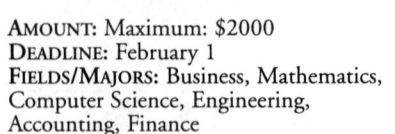

AMOUNT: Maximum: $2000 DEADLINE: February 1
FIELDS/MAJORS: Business, Mathematics, Computer Science, Engineering, Accounting, Finance

Awards for incoming freshmen who are in the top 15% of their graduating class (GPA of 3.3 or better) and are pursuing a degree in one of the fields listed above. Should be able to demonstrate leadership abilities. Write to the address listed for further information.

University of Wisconsin, Platteville
Office of Admissions and Enrollment Mgt.
Platteville, WI 53818

4899
UWP Scholar Award

AMOUNT: Maximum: $2400 DEADLINE: February 1
FIELDS/MAJORS: All Areas of Study

Awards for incoming freshmen who are National Merit finalists. Renewable for up to four years if a 3.5 GPA or better is maintained. Must reapply each year. Write to the address below for further information.

University of Wisconsin, Platteville
Office of Admissions and Enrollment Mgt.
Platteville, WI 53818

4900
Valerie (Beighley) Anderson Scholarships

AMOUNT: $650 DEADLINE: February 15
FIELDS/MAJORS: Liberal Arts, Arts, Humanities

Open to juniors and seniors at UWP majoring in the fields above or the teaching and/or non-teaching majors of English, foreign language, music, or theater. Must have a GPA of at least 3.0. One award is offered annually. Write to the address below for more information.

University of Wisconsin, Platteville
Office of Enrollment and Admissions
Brigham Hall
Platteville, WI 53818

4901
William Eiler Memorial Scholarship

AMOUNT: Maximum: $400 DEADLINE: February 1
FIELDS/MAJORS: Engineering

Awards for incoming freshmen who will be majoring in engineering. Write to the address listed for more information.

University of Wisconsin, Platteville
Office of Admissions and Enrollment Mgt.
Platteville, WI 53818

4902
Wisconsin Academic Excellence Scholar

AMOUNT: Maximum: $2250 DEADLINE: February 1
FIELDS/MAJORS: All Areas of Study

Awards for incoming freshmen who graduated from a Wisconsin high school and has been designated by the high school as first in class. Renewable if a 3.0 or higher GPA is maintained. Write to the address below for further information.

University of Wisconsin, Platteville
Office of Admissions and Enrollment Mgt.
Platteville, WI 53818

4903
Wisconsin Chapter AGC Municipal/Utilities Industry Award

AMOUNT: Maximum: $500 DEADLINE: May 1
FIELDS/MAJORS: Building Construction Management

Awards are available for UWP continuing students who are majoring in a building construction management program. Selection finalized by the Madison AGC Chapter office. Write to the address below for more information or call (608) 342-1125.

University or Wisconsin, Platteville
Professor Stuelke
311 Pioneer Tower
Platteville, WI 53818

4904
Wisconsin Livestock and Meat Council Scholarship

AMOUNT: Maximum: $800 DEADLINE: February 1
FIELDS/MAJORS: Animal Science

Awards for incoming freshmen who will be majoring in animal science. Must be in the upper 50% of graduating class and residents of Wisconsin. Write to the address listed for more information. Must have a GPA of at least 2.5.

University of Wisconsin, Platteville
Office of Admissions and Enrollment Mgt.
Platteville, WI 53818

4905
Wisconsin Pork Producers Scholarships

AMOUNT: $350-$750 DEADLINE: February 15
FIELDS/MAJORS: Animal Science

Available to UWP students who are majoring in animal science with an interest in swine production. Must have 45 credits completed at time of application and demonstrate academic achievement and involvement in student activities. Write to the address below for more information or call (608) 342-1125. GPA must be at least 2.8.

University of Wisconsin, Platteville
Office of Admissions and Enrollment
Brigham Hall
Platteville, WI 53818

4906
Wisconsin Public Service Corporation Scholarship

AMOUNT: Maximum: $2000 DEADLINE: February 15
FIELDS/MAJORS: Electrical, Mechanical Engineering

Available to UWP female and/or minority sophomores majoring in electrical or mechanical engineering. Must have a GPA of 2.0 or better and demonstrate financial need. Renewable. One award is offered annually. Write to the address below for more information or call (608) 342-1125.

University of Wisconsin, Platteville
Office of Enrollment and Admissions
Brigham Hall
Platteville, WI 53818

4907
Wisconsin Rural Rehabilitation Corporation Scholarship

AMOUNT: Maximum: $850 DEADLINE: February 1
FIELDS/MAJORS: Agriculture

Awards for incoming freshmen who will be majoring in agriculture. Must be a Wisconsin farm resident and be able to demonstrate financial need. Write to the address listed for more information.

University of Wisconsin, Platteville
Office of Admissions and Enrollment Mgt.
Platteville, WI 53818

UNIVERSITY OF WYOMING

4908

Student Financial Aid and Scholarships at Wyoming Colleges

AMOUNT: None Specified DEADLINE: None Specified
FIELDS/MAJORS: All Areas of Study

The office of student financial aid at the University of Wyoming can assist students who have been accepted/enrolled at that school in locating scholarships. Write to the address below for details.

University of Wyoming
Office of Student Financial Aid
Box 3335
Laramie, WY 82071

UPPER IOWA UNIVERSITY

4909

Upper Iowa Academic Grants

AMOUNT: None Specified DEADLINE: None Specified
FIELDS/MAJORS: All Areas of Study

Awards are available for new and continuing students. New students will be judged on academic ability (GPA, ACT/SAT scores, etc.). Returning students must have a minimum GPA of 2.0. All recipients must also have applied for financial assistance. Write to the address below for more information.

Upper Iowa University
Financial Aid Office
PO Box 1857
Fayette, IA 52142-1857

4910

Upper Iowa Academic Scholarships

AMOUNT: None Specified DEADLINE: None Specified
FIELDS/MAJORS: All Areas of Study

Awards are available for incoming freshmen who rank in the upper 20% of their high school classes. Transfer and continuing students must have a minimum GPA of 3.2 based on a minimum of 30 semester hours. All recipients must also have applied for financial assistance. Write to the address below for more information.

Upper Iowa University
Financial Aid Office
PO Box 1857
Fayette, IA 52142-1857

4911

Upper Iowa Church Scholarships

AMOUNT: None Specified DEADLINE: None Specified
FIELDS/MAJORS: All Areas of Study

Since Upper Iowa University is a nondenominational private institution and therefore interdenominational in nature, it recognizes the significant contribution religion makes to our society. To qualify for consideration for these scholarships, students must have an application signed by their priest, pastor, rabbi, minister, or other recognized officer within the church community attesting to the student's membership status within that church's organization. Write to the address below for more information. GPA must be at least 2.0.

Upper Iowa University
Financial Aid Office
PO Box 1857
Fayette, IA 52142-1857

4912

Upper Iowa Performance Scholarships

AMOUNT: None Specified DEADLINE: None Specified
FIELDS/MAJORS: Art, Music, Theater

Open to students meeting specific requirements relating to the fields of art, music, and theater. In addition to performance in the activity, applicants may also expect to assist the department in other ways. Based on the recommendations of the specific department. Must be admitted as a regular, full-time student. Must apply for financial assistance. Write to the address below for more information. GPA must be at least 2.0.

Upper Iowa University
Financial Aid Office
PO Box 1857
Fayette, IA 52142-1857

4913

Upper Iowa Presidential Scholarships

AMOUNT: None Specified DEADLINE: None Specified
FIELDS/MAJORS: All Areas of Study

Awards are available for incoming freshmen who rank in the upper 10% of their high school classes, or are valedictorians or salutatorians. Transfer and continuing students must have a minimum GPA of 3.8 based on a minimum of 30 semester hours. All recipients must also have applied for financial assistance. Write to the address below for more information.

Upper Iowa University
Financial Aid Office
PO Box 1857
Fayette, IA 52142-1857

4914
Upper Iowa University Grants

AMOUNT: None Specified   DEADLINE: None Specified
FIELDS/MAJORS: All Areas of Study

Open to students who show strong academic promise, are capable of doing satisfactory college-level work, and can demonstrate financial need. Must be admitted as regular full-time students and apply for financial assistance. Write to the address below for more information. GPA must be at least 3.0.

Upper Iowa University
Financial Aid Office
PO Box 1857
Fayette, IA 52142-1857

VALPARAISO UNIVERSITY

4915
Martin Luther Award

AMOUNT: $3640   DEADLINE: May 1
FIELDS/MAJORS: All Areas of Study

Awards for new students (freshmen or transfers) who are dependents of full-time professional Lutheran church workers. Must have a GPA of at least 2.0. Renewable. Write to the address listed for additional information.

Valparaiso University
Office of Admissions and Financial Aid
Kretzmann Hall
Valparaiso, IN 46383

VANDERBILT UNIVERSITY

4916
Captain Henry Parrish Kernochran Scholarship

AMOUNT: None Specified   DEADLINE: March 1
FIELDS/MAJORS: All Areas of Study

Scholarships for graduate students from Louisiana who are attending Peabody College in Vanderbilt University. Write to the address below for complete details.

Vanderbilt University
Admissions and Financial Assistance
Box 327 Peabody College
Nashville, TN 37203

4917
Eliza M. Claybrooke Memorial Scholarship

AMOUNT: None Specified   DEADLINE: March 1
FIELDS/MAJORS: All Areas of Study

Scholarships for students at Vanderbilt University who are lineal descendants of confederate soldiers or sailors. Write to the address below for details.

Vanderbilt University
Admissions and Financial Assistance
Box 327 Peabody College
Nashville, TN 37203

4918
Fred Russell-Grantland Rice TRA Scholarship

AMOUNT: Maximum: $10000   DEADLINE: January 1
FIELDS/MAJORS: Writing-Sports

Two scholarships for students attending Vanderbilt University with a special interest in the field of sports writing. Applications are made during senior year of high school. Contact the coordinator of special scholarships, undergraduate admissions, Vanderbilt University, 2305 West End Ave., Nashville, TN 37203; (rather than the association) for details and application forms.

Thoroughbred Racing Associations
College Coordinator of Spec. Scholarship
2305 West End Ave.
Nashville, TN 37203

4919
Ida E. Hood and Susan L. Heron Scholarship

AMOUNT: None Specified   DEADLINE: March 1
FIELDS/MAJORS: All Areas of Study

Scholarships for female descendants of Ward Belmont alumnae or a worthy woman in need. For graduate study at Peabody College in Vanderbilt University. Write to the address below for details.

Vanderbilt University
Admissions and Financial Assistance
Box 327 Peabody College
Nashville, TN 37203

4920
John M. Bass Scholarship

AMOUNT: None Specified   DEADLINE: March 1
FIELDS/MAJORS: Elementary Education, Secondary Education

Scholarships for students in the Peabody College at Vanderbilt University who are majoring in elementary or secondary education. Must demonstrate financial need. For graduate study only. Write to the address below for more information.

Vanderbilt University
Admissions and Financial Assistance
Box 327 Peabody College
Nashville, TN 37203

4921
Judge Edward Scott Scholarship

AMOUNT: None Specified   DEADLINE: March 1
FIELDS/MAJORS: All Areas of Study

Scholarships for graduate students in Peabody College at Vanderbilt University from Mississippi. Preference given to students from Bolivar County, Mississippi, or other cities in Mississippi. Write to the address below for more information.

Vanderbilt University
Admissions and Financial Assistance
Box 327 Peabody College
Nashville, TN 37203

4922
Laverne Noyes Scholarship

AMOUNT: None Specified   DEADLINE: March 1
FIELDS/MAJORS: All Areas of Study

Scholarships for graduate students in Peabody College at Vanderbilt University who are descendants of veterans of World War I. Write to the address below for more information.

Vanderbilt University
Admissions and Financial Assistance
Box 327 Peabody College
Nashville, TN 37203

4923
Lizzie Lee Bloomstein Fellowship

AMOUNT: None Specified   DEADLINE: March 1
FIELDS/MAJORS: History and Social Studies

Fellowships for graduate students in the Peabody College at Vanderbilt whose studies include history and social studies. Write to the address below for more information.

Vanderbilt University
Admissions and Financial Assistance
Box 327 Peabody College
Nashville, TN 37203

4924
Louise Burr Jacobs Memorial Scholarship

AMOUNT: None Specified   DEADLINE: March 1
FIELDS/MAJORS: Early Childhood Education

Scholarships for advanced postbaccalaureate students of early childhood education at Peabody College in Vanderbilt University. Write to the address below for more information.

Vanderbilt University
Admissions and Financial Assistance
Box 327 Peabody College
Nashville, TN 37203

4925
Magazine Circle Scholarship

AMOUNT: None Specified   DEADLINE: March 1
FIELDS/MAJORS: All Areas of Study

Scholarships for graduate students in Peabody College at Vanderbilt University who are of the Hebrew faith. Write to the address below for further details.

Vanderbilt University
Admissions and Financial Assistance
Box 327 Peabody College
Nashville, TN 37203

4926
Theda B. Hill Memorial Scholarship

AMOUNT: None Specified   DEADLINE: March 1
FIELDS/MAJORS: All Areas of Study

Scholarships for female graduate students in Peabody College at Vanderbilt University who are from the Commonwealth of Virginia. Write to the address below for complete details.

Vanderbilt University
Admissions and Financial Assistance
Box 327 Peabody College
Nashville, TN 37203

VILLANOVA UNIVERSITY

4927
Elmer Roe Deaver Scholarship

AMOUNT: Maximum: $2000 DEADLINE: None Specified
FIELDS/MAJORS: All Areas of Study

Scholarship available for students who are family members of Quaker City Life Insurance Company employees. Must have a minimum GPA of 3.0. Renewable if recipients maintain conditions of eligibility, including the minimum GPA. Based on academics and financial need. Contact the address below for further information.

Villanova University
Office of Financial Assistance
800 Lancaster Ave.
Villanova, PA 19085

WALKER COLLEGE

4928
Alabama Farmers Federation of Walker County Scholarship

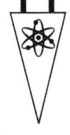

AMOUNT: None Specified DEADLINE: May 1
FIELDS/MAJORS: Agriculture

Open to students planning a career in agriculture or an agriculture-related field. Contact the address listed for further information.

Walker College
Financial Aid Office
1411 Indiana Ave.
Jasper, AL 35501-4967

4929
Artists Guild Scholarship

AMOUNT: None Specified DEADLINE: May 1
FIELDS/MAJORS: Art

Open to outstanding students planning a career in art. Contact the address listed for further information. Must have a GPA of at least 3.0.

Walker College
Financial Aid Office
1411 Indiana Ave.
Jasper, AL 35501-4967

4930
Charlotte B. Flagg Scholarship

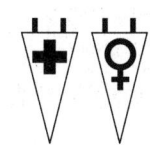

AMOUNT: None Specified DEADLINE: May 1
FIELDS/MAJORS: Nursing

Open to worthy young women in nursing. Contact the address listed for further information.

Walker College
Financial Aid Office
1411 Indiana Ave.
Jasper, AL 35501-4967

4931
D.J. Brasfield, Elza S. Drummond, and Herman E. Drummond Scholarships

AMOUNT: None Specified DEADLINE: May 1
FIELDS/MAJORS: All Areas of Study

Open to outstanding students who are residents of Walker County. Contact the address listed for further information about all three awards. Must have a GPA of at least 3.2.

Walker College
Financial Aid Office
1411 Indiana Ave.
Jasper, AL 35501-4967

4932
Lou Betts Bevill Scholarship, Pauline Lacy Guy Scholarship

AMOUNT: None Specified DEADLINE: May 1
FIELDS/MAJORS: Music

Open to outstanding students in music. Contact the address listed for further information about both awards. Must have a GPA of at least 3.2.

Walker College
Financial Aid Office
1411 Indiana Ave.
Jasper, AL 35501-4967

4933
Nearly New Foundation Scholarship

AMOUNT: None Specified DEADLINE: May 1
FIELDS/MAJORS: All Areas of Study

Open to outstanding female students. Contact the address listed for further information. Must have a GPA of at least 3.2.

Walker College
Financial Aid Office
1411 Indiana Ave.
Jasper, AL 35501-4967

4934
R.D. Dean Collins Scholarship

AMOUNT: None Specified DEADLINE: May 1
FIELDS/MAJORS: Business

Open to students majoring in business. Contact the address listed for further information. Must have a GPA of at least 3.0.

Walker College
Financial Aid Office
1411 Indiana Ave.
Jasper, AL 35501-4967

4935
Sara Ann Guthrie, Son Humphries, and Dr. Francis Nicholson Scholarships

AMOUNT: None Specified DEADLINE: May 1
FIELDS/MAJORS: All Areas of Study

Open to residents of Walker County who graduated from Walker high school or a Walker County high school. The Son Humphries Scholarship is awarded by the Walker County High School Committee. Contact the address listed for further information about all three awards.

Walker College
Financial Aid Office
1411 Indiana Ave.
Jasper, AL 35501-4967

4936
Visual Arts Association Scholarship

AMOUNT: None Specified DEADLINE: May 1
FIELDS/MAJORS: Art

Open to students planning an art career or with an interest in art. Contact the address listed for further information.

Walker College
Financial Aid Office
1411 Indiana Ave.
Jasper, AL 35501-4967

4937
William J. Amundson Scholarship

AMOUNT: None Specified DEADLINE: May 1
FIELDS/MAJORS: Mathematics

Open to outstanding students with an interest in mathematics. Contact the address listed for further information. Must have a GPA of at least 3.0.

Walker College
Financial Aid Office
1411 Indiana Ave.
Jasper, AL 35501-4967

WALTERS STATE COMMUNITY COLLEGE

4938
Douglas Tripp Memorial Scholarship

AMOUNT: None Specified DEADLINE: March 31
FIELDS/MAJORS: Law Enforcement

Available to enrolled WSCC full-time students who are residents of Claiborne County. Based primarily on academic achievement with consideration given to financial need and leadership qualities. Contact the address below for further information or call 1-800-225-4770. GPA must be at least 2.8.

Walters State Community College
Financial Aid Department
500 South Davy Crockett Parkway
Morristown, TN 37813-6899

4939
Dr. J. Eugene and Thelma J. Howard Scholarship

AMOUNT: None Specified DEADLINE: March 31
FIELDS/MAJORS: All Areas of Study

Available to WSCC students who are residents of Jefferson County. Based primarily on academic achievement, with consideration given to financial need and leadership qualities. Contact the address below for further information or call 1-800-225-4770. GPA must be at least 2.8.

Walters State Community College
Financial Aid Department
500 South Davy Crockett Parkway
Morristown, TN 37813-6899

4940
Dr. Luke and Ellen Nabers Memorial Scholarship

AMOUNT: None Specified   DEADLINE: March 31
FIELDS/MAJORS: Pre-Med, Nursing

Available to WSCC full-time students who are enrolled in the fields listed above. Based primarily on academic achievement, with consideration given to financial need and leadership qualities. Contact the address below for further information or call 1-800-225-4770. GPA must be at least 2.8.

Walters State Community College
Financial Aid Department
500 South Davy Crockett Parkway
Morristown, TN 37813-6899

4941
Dr. Truett and Wanda Pierce Scholarship

AMOUNT: None Specified   DEADLINE: March 31
FIELDS/MAJORS: All Areas of Study

Available to WSCC full-time students who are residents of Hancock County. Based primarily on academic achievement, with consideration given to financial need and leadership qualities. Contact the address below for further information or call 1-800-225-4770. GPA must be at least 2.8.

Walters State Community College
Financial Aid Department
500 South Davy Crockett Parkway
Morristown, TN 37813-6899

4942
Edward Franklin Porter Memorial Scholarship

AMOUNT: None Specified   DEADLINE: March 31
FIELDS/MAJORS: All Areas of Study

Available to WSCC full-time students who are first-time students and residents of Cocke County. Based primarily on academic achievement, with consideration given to financial need and leadership qualities. Contact the address below for further information or call 1-800-225-4770. GPA must be at least 2.8.

Walters State Community College
Financial Aid Department
500 South Davy Crockett Parkway
Morristown, TN 37813-6899

4943
E.J. Hardin, Jr. Memorial Scholarship

AMOUNT: None Specified   DEADLINE: March 31
FIELDS/MAJORS: All Areas of Study

Available to WSCC students who are recent graduates from Claiborne County. Based primarily on academic achievement, with consideration given to financial need and leadership qualities. Contact the address below for further information or call 1-800-225-4770. GPA must be at least 2.8.

Walters State Community College
Financial Aid Department
500 South Davy Crockett Parkway
Morristown, TN 37813-6899

4944
George "Eddie" Price Memorial Scholarship

AMOUNT: None Specified   DEADLINE: March 31
FIELDS/MAJORS: All Areas of Study

Available to WSCC full-time students who are graduates of Morristown-Hamblen High School East. Based primarily on academic achievement, with consideration given to financial need and leadership qualities. Contact the address below for further information or call 1-800-225-4770. GPA must be at least 2.8.

Walters State Community College
Financial Aid Department
500 South Davy Crockett Parkway
Morristown, TN 37813-6899

4945
Lon F. Price Endowment Scholarship

AMOUNT: None Specified   DEADLINE: March 31
FIELDS/MAJORS: All Areas of Study

Available to WSCC full-time students able to demonstrate financial need not covered through other sources. Academics and leadership qualities will also be given consideration. Contact the address below for further information or call 1-800-225-4770. GPA must be at least 2.8.

Walters State Community College
Financial Aid Department
500 South Davy Crockett Parkway
Morristown, TN 37813-6899

4946
Marlene and Stephanie Lynn Warren Memorial Scholarship

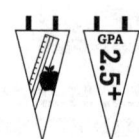

AMOUNT: None Specified DEADLINE: March 31
FIELDS/MAJORS: Elementary Education

Available to enrolled WSCC full-time students who are residents of Hamblen County, preparing for careers in elementary education. Based primarily on academic achievement, with consideration given to financial need and leadership qualities. Contact the address below for further information or call 1-800-225-4770. GPA must be at least 2.8.

Walters State Community College
Financial Aid Department
500 South Davy Crockett Parkway
Morristown, TN 37813-6899

4947
Morristown Lions Club Scholarship

AMOUNT: None Specified DEADLINE: March 31
FIELDS/MAJORS: All Areas of Study

Available to WSCC students who are disabled. Based primarily on academic achievement, with consideration given to financial need and leadership qualities. Contact the address below for further information or call 1-800-225-4770. GPA must be at least 2.5.

Walters State Community College
Financial Aid Department
500 South Davy Crockett Parkway
Morristown, TN 37813-6899

4948
Morristown Optimist Club Scholarship

AMOUNT: None Specified DEADLINE: March 31
FIELDS/MAJORS: All Areas of Study

Available to WSCC full-time students who are first-time students. Award is tuition and books. Based primarily on academic achievement, with consideration given to financial need and leadership qualities. Contact the address below for further information or call 1-800-225-4770. GPA must be at least 2.8.

Walters State Community College
Financial Aid Department
500 South Davy Crockett Parkway
Morristown, TN 37813-6899

4949
Nancy Graham Miller Memorial Scholarship

AMOUNT: None Specified DEADLINE: March 31
FIELDS/MAJORS: Home Economics

Available to WSCC female students seeking a career in the field of home economics. Must be residents of Hawkins, Hancock, or Claiborne counties. Based primarily on academic achievement, with consideration given to financial need and leadership qualities. Contact the address below for further information or call 1-800-225-4770. GPA must be at least 2.8.

Walters State Community College
Financial Aid Department
500 South Davy Crockett Parkway
Morristown, TN 37813-6899

4950
Olen Henderson Marshall Memorial Scholarship

AMOUNT: None Specified DEADLINE: March 31
FIELDS/MAJORS: All Areas of Study

Available to WSCC full-time, degree-seeking students from Grainger County. Must be first-time students. Based primarily on academic achievement, with consideration given to financial need and leadership qualities. Contact the address below for further information or call 1-800-225-4770. GPA must be at least 2.8.

Walters State Community College
Financial Aid Department
500 South Davy Crockett Parkway
Morristown, TN 37813-6899

4951
Rotary Club of Morristown Scholarships

AMOUNT: None Specified DEADLINE: March 31
FIELDS/MAJORS: All Areas of Study

Available to enrolled WSCC full-time students. Based primarily on academic achievement, with consideration given to financial need and leadership qualities. Two awards are offered annually. Contact the address below for further information or call 1-800-225-4770. GPA must be at least 2.8.

Walters State Community College
Financial Aid Department
500 South Davy Crockett Parkway
Morristown, TN 37813-6899

4952
Sevier County Endowment Scholarship

GPA 2.5+

AMOUNT: None Specified DEADLINE: March 31
FIELDS/MAJORS: All Areas of Study

Available to enrolled WSCC full-time students who are residents of Sevier County. Based primarily on academic achievement with consideration given to financial need and leadership qualities. Contact the address below for further information or call 1-800-225-4770. GPA must be at least 2.8.

Walters State Community College
Financial Aid Department
500 South Davy Crockett Parkway
Morristown, TN 37813-6899

4953
William E. Lacy Memorial Endowment Scholarship

GPA 2.5+

AMOUNT: None Specified DEADLINE: March 31
FIELDS/MAJORS: All Areas of Study

Available to WSCC incoming freshmen who will be full-time students. Based primarily on academic achievement, with consideration given to financial need and leadership qualities. Contact the address below for further information or call 1-800-225-4770. GPA must be at least 2.8.

Walters State Community College
Financial Aid Department
500 South Davy Crockett Parkway
Morristown, TN 37813-6899

4954
Winfred E. Moore Memorial Scholarship

GPA 2.5+

AMOUNT: None Specified DEADLINE: March 31
FIELDS/MAJORS: All Areas of Study

Available to WSCC students who are residents of Jefferson County. Based primarily on academic achievement, with consideration given to financial need and leadership qualities. Contact the address below for further information or call 1-800-225-4770. GPA must be at least 2.8.

Walters State Community College
Financial Aid Department
500 South Davy Crockett Parkway
Morristown, TN 37813-6899

4955
WSCC Agriculture and Ornamental Horticulture Alumni Club Scholarship

GPA 2.5+

AMOUNT: None Specified DEADLINE: March 31
FIELDS/MAJORS: Agriculture, Ornamental Horticulture

Available to enrolled WSCC full-time students who are majoring in the fields listed above. Based primarily on academic achievement, with consideration given to financial need and leadership qualities. Contact the address below for further information or call 1-800-225-4770. GPA must be at least 2.8.

Walters State Community College
Financial Aid Department
500 South Davy Crockett Parkway
Morristown, TN 37813-6899

4956
WSCC First Time Student Scholarships

GPA 2.5+

AMOUNT: None Specified DEADLINE: March 31
FIELDS/MAJORS: All Areas of Study

Available to enrolled WSCC full-time students who are first-time students. Includes the Dr. Kenneth V. Pearson Memorial, the Virgil K. Miller, and the Dean Darrell and Mary Simmons Scholarships. Contact the address below for further information or call 1-800-225-4770. GPA must be at least 2.5.

Walters State Community College
Financial Aid Department
500 South Davy Crockett Parkway
Morristown, TN 37813-6899

4957
WSCC Presidential Scholarships

GPA 3.0+

AMOUNT: None Specified DEADLINE: March 31
FIELDS/MAJORS: All Areas of Study

Available to enrolled WSCC full-time students who are valedictorians (or salutatorians as alternates) of high schools within the WSCC service area. Renewable with a minimum GPA of 3.0. Contact the address below for further information or call 1-800-225-4770.

Walters State Community College
Financial Aid Department
500 South Davy Crockett Parkway
Morristown, TN 37813-6899

4958
Xan Leedy Memorial Scholarship

AMOUNT: None Specified   DEADLINE: March 31
FIELDS/MAJORS: Agriculture, Agribusiness

Available to WSCC full-time, degree-seeking students from Grainger County. Must be recent high school graduates. Based primarily on academic achievement, with consideration given to financial need and leadership qualities. Contact the address below for further information or call 1-800-225-4770. GPA must be at least 2.8.

Walters State Community College
Financial Aid Department
500 South Davy Crockett Parkway
Morristown, TN 37813-6899

WARTBURG COLLEGE

4959
Alumni Tuition Grant

AMOUNT: Maximum: $1000   DEADLINE: March 1
FIELDS/MAJORS: All Areas of Study

Available to incoming freshmen who have alumni parents. Must be full-time students. Awards are for $1000 per year. Contact the address below for further information.

Wartburg College
Office of Financial Aid
PO Box 1003
Waverly, IA 50677

4960
Cedar Valley Science Symposium Award

AMOUNT: Maximum: $500   DEADLINE: September 25
FIELDS/MAJORS: Biology, Chemistry, Physics

Available to high school students who have participated in the Cedar Valley Science Symposium. For students to pursue, in-depth, specific areas of biology, chemistry, and physics. Award is $500 per year and is renewable. Symposium is held on a Friday and Saturday in early November. Contact the address below by the end of September for further information.

Wartburg College
Office of Financial Aid
PO Box 1003
Waverly, IA 50677

4961
Exploration in Mathematical Science Award

AMOUNT: Maximum: $500   DEADLINE: March 1
FIELDS/MAJORS: Mathematics, Computer Science, Physics, Engineering

Available to incoming freshmen who participate in the Explorations in the Mathematical Sciences weekend. For students to pursue specific areas of mathematics, computer science, physics, or engineering. Award is $500. Math weekend is held on Friday and Saturday, March 13 and 14. Contact the address below by March 1st for further information.

Wartburg College
Office of Financial Aid
PO Box 1003
Waverly, IA 50677

4962
Meistersinger Music Scholarship

AMOUNT: Maximum: $2500   DEADLINE: December 1
FIELDS/MAJORS: All Areas of Study

Available to incoming freshmen who demonstrate musical talent. Selection based on audition and musical ability. Awarded to vocalists, instrumentalists, and keyboardists. Awards are renewable and range up to $2500 per year. Auditions are held on January 17, 23, and 31. Contact the address below for further information.

Wartburg College
Office of Financial Aid
PO Box 1003
Waverly, IA 50677

4963
Phi Theta Kappa Transfer Students

AMOUNT: Maximum: $5000   DEADLINE: March 1
FIELDS/MAJORS: All Areas of Study

Available to incoming transfer students who are members of Phi Theta Kappa and have completed 30 semester credit hours at a two-year institution. Students must have a GPA of at least 3.3. Four scholarships for up to $5000 per year are awarded for up to two years. Contact the address below for further information.

Wartburg College
Office of Financial Aid
PO Box 1003
Waverly, IA 50677

4964
Presidential Scholarship

AMOUNT: $3000-$6000 DEADLINE: December 1
FIELDS/MAJORS: All Areas of Study

Available to incoming freshmen with a minimum ACT/SAT OR ranked in the top 20% of graduating class OR have a GPA of 3.5 or above. Qualified applicants who participate in an on-campus competition will receive a minimum award of $3000. Awards are based on merit and are renewable for a total of four years if a 2.7 GPA is maintained. Competitions are held on Sunday, February 15. Contact the address below for further information.

Wartburg College
Office of Financial Aid
PO Box 1003
Waverly, IA 50677

4965
Regents Scholarship

AMOUNT: $3500 DEADLINE: December 1
FIELDS/MAJORS: All Areas of Study

Available to incoming freshmen with the minimum ACT/SAT or those who ranked in the top 10% of their graduating class. Qualified applicants who participate in an on-campus competition will receive a minimum award of $3500. Awards are based on merit and are renewable for a total of four years if a 3.0 GPA is maintained. Competitions are held on Sunday, January 18 or February 1. Those who compete for the Regents are not eligible for the Presidential Scholarship. Contact the address below for further information.

Wartburg College
Office of Financial Aid
PO Box 1003
Waverly, IA 50677

4966
Sibling Tuition Grant

AMOUNT: Maximum: $1000 DEADLINE: March 1
FIELDS/MAJORS: All Areas of Study

Available to incoming freshmen who have siblings that are currently attending Wartburg or have graduated from Wartburg. Awards are for $1000 per year. Contact the address below for further information.

Wartburg College
Office of Financial Aid
PO Box 1003
Waverly, IA 50677

4967
Transfer Scholarship

AMOUNT: $1000-$3000 DEADLINE: March 1
FIELDS/MAJORS: All Areas of Study

Available to incoming transfer students who have a GPA of 3.3 or higher. Contact the address below for further information.

Wartburg College
Office of Financial Aid
PO Box 1003
Waverly, IA 50677

WASHINGTON AND LEE UNIVERSITY

4968
Washington and Lee Scholarships

AMOUNT: None Specified DEADLINE: None Specified
FIELDS/MAJORS: All Areas of Study

Scholarships for students at Washington and Lee University who are direct descendants of confederate soldiers. Must be able to prove lineage. Write to the UDC chapter nearest you. If address is not known, write to the address below for further information and address.

United Daughters of the Confederacy
Scholarship Coordinator
328 North Boulevard
Richmond, VA 23220

WASHINGTON COLLEGE

4969
Maryland Council for Dance Scholarships

AMOUNT: None Specified DEADLINE: October 15
FIELDS/MAJORS: Dance

Scholarships are available for dance students, under the age of twenty-three, to assist in the continuation of their dance education and give them an opportunity to experience the audition process. Auditions are held in conjunction with the State Dance Festival, held in mid to late October in locations around the state. Applicants must be residents of Maryland and belong to the Maryland Council for Dance program. Thirty-five awards are offered annually. Write to the address listed for information.

Maryland Council for Dance
Washington College
300 Washington Ave.
Chestertown, MD 21620

WASHINGTON STATE UNIVERSITY

4970
Alberta Hill Academic Excellence Scholarship

AMOUNT: None Specified DEADLINE: February 1
FIELDS/MAJORS: Home Economics

Award open to graduate students at Washington State who have completed one semester of graduate level courses. Contact the address below for further information or call (509) 335-4562. GPA must be at least 3.0.

Washington State University, Scholarship Committee
College of Agriculture and Home Economics
423 Hulbert Hall
Pullman, WA 99164

4971
Alumni/Foundation Leadership Scholarships

AMOUNT: None Specified DEADLINE: None Specified
FIELDS/MAJORS: All Areas of Study

Scholarships are available at Washington State University for full-time entering freshmen with a GPA of at least 3.3 who show participation in community activities. Alumni Leadership Award is open to branch campus students with a minimum GPA of 2.5. Must be a U.S. citizen to apply. Write to the address below for information.

Washington State University
Office of Scholarship Services
Pullman, WA 99164

4972
Arnold and Julia Greenwell Memorial Scholarship

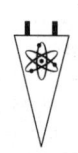

AMOUNT: None Specified DEADLINE: February 1
FIELDS/MAJORS: Agriculture

Award open to junior, senior, and graduate agriculture majors at Washington State with a minimum GPA of 3.0. Contact the address below for further information or call (509) 335-4562.

Washington State University
College of Agriculture and Home Economics
423 Hulbert Hall
Pullman, WA 99164

4973
Benton County Farm Bureau Scholarship

AMOUNT: None Specified DEADLINE: February 1
FIELDS/MAJORS: Agriculture

Award open to agriculture majors from Benton County, Washington, enrolled at Washington State. Contact the address listed for further information or call (509) 786-1000.

Benton County Farm Bureau
Carol Mercer, Executive Secretary
PO Box 665
Prosser, WA 99350

4974
Biological Systems Engineering Scholarships

AMOUNT: None Specified DEADLINE: February 1
FIELDS/MAJORS: Biological Systems Engineering, Agricultural Technology and Management

Award open to sophomores, juniors, and seniors at Washington State majoring in the listed fields. Contact the address below for further information or call (509) 335-4562. GPA must be at least 3.0.

Washington State University, Scholarship Committee
College of Agriculture and Home Economics
423 Hulbert Hall
Pullman, WA 99164

4975
College of Agriculture/ Home Economics Scholarships

AMOUNT: None Specified
DEADLINE: February 1
FIELDS/MAJORS: Agriculture, Home Economics

Awards open to students at Washington State or incoming freshmen who are superior high school seniors. Contact the address below for further information or call (509) 335-4562. GPA must be at least 3.5.

Washington State University, Scholarship Committee
College of Agriculture and Home Economics
423 Hulbert Hall
Pullman, WA 99164

4976
College of Business and Economics Scholarships

AMOUNT: None Specified   DEADLINE: None Specified
FIELDS/MAJORS: Business, Economics

Scholarships are available at Washington State University for full-time students enrolled in a program in one of the areas listed above. Must be a U.S. citizen to apply. Awards based on merit and need. Write to the address below for information.

Washington State University
Office of Scholarship Services
Pullman, WA 99164

4977
College of Engineering and Architecture Scholarships

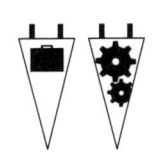

AMOUNT: None Specified   DEADLINE: None Specified
FIELDS/MAJORS: Architecture, Engineering, Computer Science, Construction Management

Scholarships are available at Washington State University for full-time incoming freshmen and transfer students enrolled in a program in one of the areas listed above. Must be a U.S. citizen to apply. Write to the address below for information.

Washington State University
Office of Scholarship Services
Pullman, WA 99164

4978
Dr. Frederick Deforest Heald Memorial and Nellie Townley Heald Awards

AMOUNT: None Specified   DEADLINE: February 1
FIELDS/MAJORS: Plant Pathology

Awards open to students at Washington State with a minimum GPA of 3.0. Must be able to demonstrate financial need. Contact the address below for further information about both awards or call (509) 335-4562.

Washington State University, Scholarship Committee
College of Agriculture and Home Economics
423 Hulbert Hall
Pullman, WA 99164

4979
Ellen Adams Klemgard Scholarship

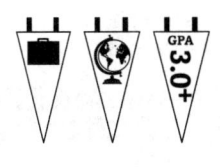

AMOUNT: None Specified   DEADLINE: February 1
FIELDS/MAJORS: Home Economics

Award open to undergraduates at Washington State majoring in home economics. Must have a minimum GPA of 3.0 and be members of Delta Delta Delta. Contact the address below for further information or call (509) 335-4562.

Washington State University, Scholarship Committee
College of Agriculture and Home Economics
423 Hulbert Hall
Pullman, WA 99164

4980
Elmer Kegel Memorial, Norman and Linda Baer Scholarships

AMOUNT: None Specified   DEADLINE: February 1
FIELDS/MAJORS: Forestry Management

Award open to juniors and seniors at Washington State with a minimum GPA of 3.0. Contact the address below for further information about both awards or call (509) 335-4562.

Washington State University, Scholarship Committee
College of Agriculture and Home Economics
423 Hulbert Hall
Pullman, WA 99164

4981
Farmhouse Fraternity Scholarship

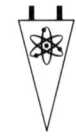

AMOUNT: None Specified   DEADLINE: None Specified
FIELDS/MAJORS: Crop, Soil Sciences

Award open to incoming freshmen who are enrolled/admitted to the Department of Crop and Soil Sciences. Contact the address below for further information or call (509) 335-3471.

Washington State University, Dept. of Crop and Soil Sciences
Dr. Dwane G. Miller
Pullman, WA 99164-6420

4982
Frank and Ethel Lenzie, E.H. Steffen Forestry Scholarships

AMOUNT: None Specified DEADLINE: February 1
FIELDS/MAJORS: Range, Forest Management

Awards open to juniors who have been enrolled at Washington State for at least two semesters and are involved in extracurricular activities. Must have a minimum GPA of 3.0. Contact the address below for further information about both awards or call (509) 335-4562.

Washington State University, Scholarship Committee
College of Agriculture and Home Economics
423 Hulbert Hall
Pullman, WA 99164

4983
Glenn Terrell Presidential and Distinguished Presidential Scholarships

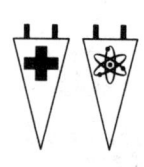

AMOUNT: None Specified DEADLINE: None Specified
FIELDS/MAJORS: All Areas of Study

Scholarships are available at Washington State University for full-time entering freshmen or transfer students who demonstrate outstanding academic ability, leadership skills, and future potential. Must be a U.S. citizen or permanent resident to apply. Write to the address below for information. Must have a GPA of at least 3.7.

Washington State University
Office of Scholarship Services
Pullman, WA 99164

4984
Golf Course Superintendents Association of America Scholarship

AMOUNT: None Specified DEADLINE: None Specified
FIELDS/MAJORS: Crop Science, Turfgrass Management

Award open to undergraduates at Washington State pursuing the turfgrass management option of the crop science major. Contact the address below for further information or call (509) 335-3471.

Department of Crop and Soil Sciences
Washington State University
423 Hulbert Hall
Pullman, WA 99164

4985
Horace W. Bozarth Memorial Scholarship

AMOUNT: None Specified DEADLINE: February 1
FIELDS/MAJORS: Agriculture

Award open to students at Washington State who are residents of Douglas, Okanogan, or Chelan counties. Based on academic achievement. Contact the address below for further information or call (509) 335-4562. GPA must be at least 2.8.

Washington State University, Scholarship Committee
College of Agriculture and Home Economics
423 Hulbert Hall
Pullman, WA 99164

4986
Inland Empire Golf Course Superintendent's Association Scholarship

AMOUNT: None Specified DEADLINE: None Specified
FIELDS/MAJORS: Turfgrass Management

Award open to juniors and seniors at Washington State interested in turfgrass management. Contact the address below for further information.

Washington State University
Department of Crop and Soil Sciences
423 Hulbert Hall
Pullman, WA 99164

4987
Institute of Food Technologists Scholarships and Fellowships

AMOUNT: None Specified DEADLINE: None Specified
FIELDS/MAJORS: Food Science, Human Nutrition

Awards open to undergraduates and graduates at Washington State majoring in food science or human nutrition. Contact the address below for further information.

Washington State University
Dept. of Food Science and Human Nutrition
423 Hulbert Hall
Pullman, WA 99164

4988
John Jacob Harder Memorial Scholarship

AMOUNT: None Specified DEADLINE: February 1
FIELDS/MAJORS: Beef Production, Nutrition

Awards open to juniors and seniors at Washington State who have a minimum GPA of 2.5. Must be residents of Washington and be able to demonstrate financial need. Preference given to students raised on a working cattle ranch. Contact the address below for further information or call (509) 335-4562.

Washington State University, Scholarship Committee
College of Agriculture and Home Economics
423 Hulbert Hall
Pullman, WA 99164

4989
Keith R. Henrickson Memorial Scholarship

AMOUNT: None Specified DEADLINE: February 1
FIELDS/MAJORS: Forestry Management

Award open to undergraduates at Washington State with a minimum GPA of 2.5. Contact the address below for further information or call (509) 335-4562.

Washington State University, Scholarship Committee
College of Agriculture and Home Economics
423 Hulbert Hall
Pullman, WA 99164

4990
Landscape Architecture Foundation Grant Competition

AMOUNT: None Specified DEADLINE: None Specified
FIELDS/MAJORS: Landscape Architecture

Open to juniors, seniors, and graduate students at Washington State majoring in landscape architecture. Contact the address listed for further information or call (202) 223-6229. Must have a GPA of at least 2.8.

Landscape Architecture Foundation
Student Research Grant Competition
1733 Connecticut Ave., NW
Washington, DC 20009

4991
Lewis County 4-H Leaders Council Scholarship

AMOUNT: None Specified DEADLINE: None Specified
FIELDS/MAJORS: Agriculture

Open to incoming freshmen admitted to Washington State who are residents of Lewis County. Must be members (of at least three years) of the 4-H. Contact the address listed for further information or call (206) 748-9121 ext. 218.

Lewis County Cooperative Extension
PO Box 708
345 W. Main Court House Annex
Chehalis, WA 98532-0708

4992
Lindsey C. and Anona F. Staley Scholarship

AMOUNT: None Specified DEADLINE: February 1
FIELDS/MAJORS: Animal Science

Award open to sophomores, juniors, and seniors at Washington State with a minimum GPA of 3.0. Must be able to demonstrate financial need. Contact the address below for further information or call (509) 335-44562.

Washington State University, Scholarship Committee
College of Agriculture and Home Economics
423 Hulbert Hall
Pullman, WA 99164

4993
Mathematics/English/ Honors Scholarship Competition

AMOUNT: $1750-$3500 DEADLINE: None Specified
FIELDS/MAJORS: Mathematics, English

Scholarships are available at Washington State University for full-time students enrolled in a program in one of the areas listed above. Write to the address below for information.

Washington State University
Office of Scholarship Services
Pullman, WA 99164

4994
Mondovi Grange Scholarship

AMOUNT: None Specified DEADLINE: None Specified
FIELDS/MAJORS: Agriculture

Open to students at Washington State who are residents of Lincoln County or the western part of Spokane County. Must be able to demonstrate financial need. Contact the address listed for further information or call (509) 796-2893.

Mondovi Grange
Ms. Earl Williams, Scholarship Committee
Rt. 1 Box 9
Reardan, WA 99209

4995
Multicultural Scholarship Program

AMOUNT: $1750-$3500 DEADLINE: None Specified
FIELDS/MAJORS: All Areas of Study

Scholarships are available at Washington State University for full-time minority entering freshmen or transfer students with a GPA of at least 3.0 who are U.S. citizens. Write to the address below for information.

Washington State University
Office of Scholarship Services
Pullman, WA 99164

4996
National Merit Corporation Scholarships

AMOUNT: $500-$2000 DEADLINE: None Specified
FIELDS/MAJORS: All Areas of Study

Scholarships are available at Washington State University for full-time students who are National Merit Scholarship Finalists who selected WSU as their first college of choice. Must be U.S. citizen to apply. May be renewable up to four years. Write to the address below for information.

Washington State University
Office of Scholarship Services
Pullman, WA 99164

4997
Northwest Turfgrass Association Scholarship

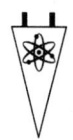

AMOUNT: None Specified DEADLINE: None Specified
FIELDS/MAJORS: Crop, Soil Sciences

Award open to juniors, seniors, and graduate students at Washington State in the Department of Crop and Soil Sciences. Contact the address below for further information or call (509) 335-4562.

Washington State University
Dept. of Crop and Soil Sciences
Pullman, WA 99164

4998
Pacific Seedsman Association Scholarship

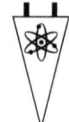

AMOUNT: None Specified DEADLINE: None Specified
FIELDS/MAJORS: Agronomy, Seed Technology

Award open to juniors and seniors at Washington State majoring in agronomy or seed technology. Contact the address below for further information or call (509) 335-4562.

Washington State University
Department of Crop and Soil Sciences
Pullman, WA 99164

4999
Patricia A. Britten Manning Memorial Scholarship

AMOUNT: None Specified DEADLINE: February 1
FIELDS/MAJORS: Animal Science

Award open to female undergraduates at Washington State with a minimum GPA of 2.75. Applicants must be U.S. citizens and be able to demonstrate financial need. Contact the address below for further information or call (509) 335-44562.

Washington State University, Scholarship Committee
College of Agriculture and Home Economics
423 Hulbert Hall
Pullman, WA 99164

5000
Phi Beta Kappa Scholarships

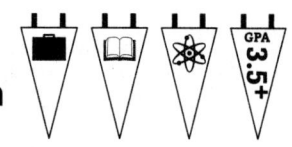

AMOUNT: Maximum: $2500 DEADLINE: None Specified
FIELDS/MAJORS: Liberal Arts, Economics, Science

Scholarships are available at Washington State University for full-time juniors who have exhibited outstanding academic aptitude and have a GPA of at least 3.6 in their junior year. Award given in the senior year. Up to six awards offered annually. Write to the address below for information.

Washington State University
Office of Scholarship Services
Pullman, WA 99164

5001
Phil Jenkins Scholarship

AMOUNT: None Specified DEADLINE: None Specified
FIELDS/MAJORS: Agriculture

Award open to juniors and seniors at Washington State majoring in agricultural fields. Contact the address listed for further information.

Yakima Pom Club
President
PO Box 10812
Yakima, WA 98909

5002
Potash and Phosphate Institute Fellowship

AMOUNT: None Specified DEADLINE: None Specified
FIELDS/MAJORS: Soil, Plant Sciences

Award open to graduate students at Washington State studying soil or plant sciences. Contact the address below for further information or call (509) 335-4562.

Washington State University
Department of Crop and Soil Sciences
Pullman, WA 99164

5003
Pullman Home Economics Association Scholarship

AMOUNT: None Specified DEADLINE: February 1
FIELDS/MAJORS: Home Economics

Award open to undergraduates at Washington State with a minimum GPA of 3.0. Must be able to demonstrate financial need and be a member of one or more student organizations in home economics. Contact the address below for further information or call (509) 335-4562.

Washington State University, Scholarship Committee
College of Agriculture and Home Economics
423 Hulbert Hall
Pullman, WA 99164

5004
Ralph E. Erb Fellowship

AMOUNT: None Specified DEADLINE: February 1
FIELDS/MAJORS: Animal Science, Cattle

Award open to incoming graduate students at Washington State with a minimum GPA of 3.0. Must have an emphasis on dairy cattle endocrinology, reproduction, or nutrition. Contact the address below for further information or call (509) 335-44562.

Washington State University, Scholarship Committee
College of Agriculture and Home Economics
423 Hulbert Hall
Pullman, WA 99164

5005
Roger R. Jones Memorial Scholarship

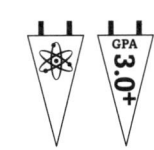

AMOUNT: None Specified DEADLINE: February 1
FIELDS/MAJORS: Forestry

Award open to undergraduates at Washington State majoring in forestry. Contact the address below for further information or call (509) 335-4562. GPA must be at least 3.0.

Washington State University, Scholarship Committee
College of Agriculture and Home Economics
423 Hulbert Hall
Pullman, WA 99164

5006
ROTC Scholarships

AMOUNT: None Specified DEADLINE: None Specified
FIELDS/MAJORS: All Areas of Study

Scholarships are available at Washington State University for full-time students planning to participate in the campus ROTC program. Must be a U.S. citizen to apply. Write to the address below for information.

Washington State University
Office of Scholarship Services
Pullman, WA 99164

5007
Roy Wiggins Memorial, Wildlife Conservation Conclave Scholarships

AMOUNT: None Specified DEADLINE: February 1
FIELDS/MAJORS: Wildlife Conservation, Management, Natural Resources

Awards open to undergraduates at Washington State with a minimum GPA of 3.0. Must be able to demonstrate financial need. Contact the address below for further information about both awards or call (509) 335-4562.

Washington State University, Scholarship Committee
College of Agriculture and Home Economics
423 Hulbert Hall
Pullman, WA 99164

5008
Ruth Lenore Harris Scholarship

AMOUNT: None Specified DEADLINE: None Specified
FIELDS/MAJORS: Dietetics

Award open to students at Washington State planning on a career as a Registered Dietitian or specialist in dietetics. Applications and information are available at the address listed.

Washington State Dietetics Association
Scholarship Coordinator
PO Box 2371
Gig Harbor, WA 98335

5009
Seattle Jaycees Scholarship

AMOUNT: Maximum: $1000 DEADLINE: March 15
FIELDS/MAJORS: All Areas of Study

Available to students enrolled in Washington State University who are active in community service, civic involvement, or volunteerism. Award is renewable. Contact the address listed, enclosing a SASE, for further information, or call (206) 286-2014.

Seattle Jaycees
Scholarship Committee
109 West Mercer
Seattle, WA 98119

5010
Skagit Farmers Supply Scholarship

AMOUNT: None Specified DEADLINE: None Specified
FIELDS/MAJORS: Agriculture

Open to incoming freshmen, admitted to Washington State, majoring in agriculture. Contact the address listed for further information or call (206) 757-6053. Must have a GPA of at least 2.8.

Skagit Farmers Supply
Scholarship Coordinator
PO Box 266, 1276 S. Burlington Blvd.
Burlington, WA 98233

5011
S.O. Graham Research Fellowship

AMOUNT: None Specified DEADLINE: February 1
FIELDS/MAJORS: Plant Pathology

Award open to graduate students at Washington State majoring in plant pathology who can demonstrate financial need. Contact the address below for further information or call (509) 335-4562.

Washington State University, Scholarship Committee
College of Agriculture and Home Economics
423 Hulbert Hall
Pullman, WA 99164

5012
Sports Turf Manager's Association Scholarship

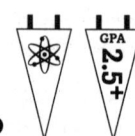

AMOUNT: None Specified DEADLINE: None Specified
FIELDS/MAJORS: Sports Turf Management

Award open to students at Washington State planning careers in sports turf management. Contact the address below for further information or call (509) 335-4562. GPA must be at least 2.8.

Washington State University
Department of Crop and Soil Sciences
Pullman, WA 99164

5013
Stanley P. Swenson Memorial Scholarship

AMOUNT: None Specified DEADLINE: February 1
FIELDS/MAJORS: Human Development, Childhood Education

Award open to juniors and seniors at Washington State with a minimum GPA of 3.0. Contact the address below for further information or call (509) 335-4562.

Washington State University, Scholarship Committee
College of Agriculture and Home Economics
423 Hulbert Hall
Pullman, WA 99164

5014
Visual and Performing Arts Scholarships

AMOUNT: None Specified DEADLINE: None Specified
FIELDS/MAJORS: Art, Fine Arts, Music, Drama

Scholarships are available at Washington State University for full-time students enrolled in a program in one of the areas listed above. Must be a U.S. citizen or permanent resident to apply. Write to the address below for information.

Washington State University
Office of Scholarship Services
Pullman, WA 99164

5015
Washington State Dairy Women's Scholarship

AMOUNT: None Specified DEADLINE: None Specified
FIELDS/MAJORS: Dairy Science, Industry

Open to juniors and seniors at Washington State who have a minimum GPA of 3.0. Contact the address listed for further information.

Washington State Dairy Women
Ann Schakel
6321 Norman Rd.
Stanwood, WA 98292

5016
Washington Home Economics Assn. Scholarship

AMOUNT: None Specified   DEADLINE: None Specified
FIELDS/MAJORS: Home Economics

Open to sophomores and juniors at Washington State who have a minimum GPA of 3.0. Contact the address listed for further information.

Washington Home Economics Association
Mary Wilson, Scholarship Chair
15719 63rd St. Ct.
E. Sumner, WA 98390

5017
Washington Soil Improvement Committee Scholarship

AMOUNT: None Specified   DEADLINE: None Specified
FIELDS/MAJORS: Crop, Soil Sciences

Award open to juniors and seniors at Washington State majoring in either of the listed fields. Contact the address below for further information or call (509) 335-4562.

Washington State University
Department of Crop and Soil Sciences
Pullman, WA 99164

5018
Washington State Federation of Garden Clubs Scholarship

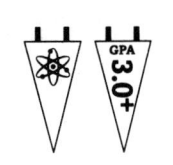

AMOUNT: None Specified   DEADLINE: February 1
FIELDS/MAJORS: Plant Pathology

Award open to juniors and seniors at Washington State with a minimum GPA of 3.0. Must be able to demonstrate financial need. Contact the address below for further information or call (509) 335-4562.

Washington State University, Scholarship Committee
College of Agriculture and Home Economics
423 Hulbert Hall
Pullman, WA 99164

5019
Washington State Nurserymen's Association Scholarship

AMOUNT: None Specified   DEADLINE: February 1
FIELDS/MAJORS: Ornamental Horticulture

Award open to juniors, seniors, and graduate students at Washington State majoring in ornamental horticulture or fruit tree production. Contact the address below for further information or call (509) 335-4562. GPA must be at least 3.0.

Washington State University, Scholarship Committee
College of Agriculture and Home Economics
423 Hulbert Hall
Pullman, WA 99164

5020
Washington/North Idaho Seed Association (Joseph Counsel Memorial) Award

AMOUNT: None Specified   DEADLINE: February 1
FIELDS/MAJORS: Crop, Soil Sciences

Awards open to sophomores and juniors at Washington State majoring in crop and soil science. Contact the address below for further information about both of these awards or call (509) 335-4562. GPA must be at least 3.0.

Washington State University, Scholarship Committee
College of Agriculture and Home Economics
423 Hulbert Hall
Pullman, WA 99164

WASHINGTON UNIVERSITY

5021
Central Institute for the Deaf Scholarships and Awards

AMOUNT: None Specified   DEADLINE: None Specified
FIELDS/MAJORS: Communication Disorders, Speech/Hearing

Scholarships for graduate students at the Central Institute for the Deaf at Washington University of St. Louis. The institute also administers several self-help programs. Write to the address below for details.

Washington University
Central Institute for the Deaf
818 S. Euclid Ave.
St. Louis, MO 63110

5022
Daad Center for Contemporary German Literature Grant

AMOUNT: Maximum: $3000   DEADLINE: January 1
FIELDS/MAJORS: German Literature

Grants for faculty planning to work in the field of German literature at the Center for Contemporary German Literature at Washington University in St. Louis, Missouri. Contact Prof. Paul Michael Luetzeler, Director, at the address listed for more information.

Daad German Academic Exchange Service
Center for Contemp. German Literature
Washington Univ., Campus Box 1104
St. Louis, MO 63130

5023
Financial Awards at Washington University in St. Louis

AMOUNT: None Specified DEADLINE: January 1
FIELDS/MAJORS: All Areas of Study

Several fellowship and scholarship programs are available to graduate students at Washington University in St. Louis. Contact the office of financial aid for details.

Washington University
Office of Financial Aid
Campus Box 1041
St. Louis, MO 63130

5024
Spencer T. Olin Fellowships for Women in Graduate Study

AMOUNT: $20000-$33000
DEADLINE: February 1
FIELDS/MAJORS: See Listing of Fields Below

Fellowships are available at Washington University for female scholars in one of the following fields: Biology, Biomedicine, Humanities, Physics, Math, Social Science, Behavioral Science, Architecture, Business Administration, Engineering, Fine Arts, Law, Medicine, and Social Work. For master's and doctoral level study. Write to the address below for information.

Monticello College Foundation/Washington University
Margaret Watkins, Olin Fellowship Prog.
Campus Box 1187, One Brookings Dr.
St. Louis, MO 63130

WAYNE STATE UNIVERSITY

5025
College of Education Awards

AMOUNT: None Specified DEADLINE: February 20
FIELDS/MAJORS: Education

Open to graduate students enrolled in the College of Education who have a minimum cumulative GPA of 3.0. Information regarding other scholarships and loans from the college will also be provided. Contact the address below for further details or call (313) 577-1623.

Wayne State University
Ms. Barbara Dubrinsky
Room 441, Education Building
Detroit, MI 48202

5026
Departmental Assistantships

AMOUNT: None Specified DEADLINE: None Specified
FIELDS/MAJORS: All Areas of Study

Departments offer teaching and research assistantships to graduate students. The awards provide a stipend, 6-10 credits of graduate tuition per semester, and subsidized health insurance. Fellowships, scholarships, internships, and traineeships may also be available. Contact the department you will be entering approximately twelve months prior to the semester start date. Directly contact the chairperson of your department for further details or call (313) 577-2172.

Wayne State University
Graduate School Scholarship Office
4302 Faculty Administration Bldg.
Detroit, MI 48202

5027
King-Chavez-Parks Future Faculty Fellowships

AMOUNT: $6250 DEADLINE: June 1
FIELDS/MAJORS: All Areas of Study

Open to African-American, Native American, or Hispanic students at the doctoral level at Wayne State. Must be U.S. citizens or permanent residents and plan to pursue a full-time teaching position in a Michigan postsecondary institution within one year of receiving their degree. Students in the College of Education are not eligible at this time. Contact the address below for further information or call (313) 577-2172.

Wayne State University
Graduate Scholarship Office
4302 Faculty Administration Bldg.
Detroit, MI 48202

5028
Munich Fellowships

AMOUNT: None Specified DEADLINE: April 1
FIELDS/MAJORS: All Areas of Study

Available for Wayne State graduate students who have written and oral competence in the German language. Award provides for ten months of study at the University of Munich. It includes tuition and a monthly stipend. Applicants must be U.S. citizens. Write to the address below for further details or call (313) 577-2172.

Wayne State University
Graduate School Scholarship Office
4302 Faculty Administration Bldg.
Detroit, MI 48202

5029
Thesis-Dissertation Research Support

AMOUNT: Maximum: $1000 DEADLINE: None Specified
FIELDS/MAJORS: All Areas of Study

Programs for Wayne State graduate students engaged in approved thesis/dissertation research. Intended to help defray necessary but unusual expenses essential to the performance of thesis or dissertation research. Write to the address below for further details or call (313) 577-2170.

Wayne State University
Graduate School Scholarship Office
4302 Faculty Administration Bldg.
Detroit, MI 48202

5030
Thomas C. Rumble University Graduate Fellowship

AMOUNT: $10250 DEADLINE: February 2
FIELDS/MAJORS: All Areas of Study

Open to full-time students enrolled in the Master of Music or Master of Fine Arts programs. Ph.D. students in all fields, except law and medicine, are also eligible to apply. Recipients may not hold other fellowships, scholarships, assistantships, or internships or hold full-time employment during fellowship period. Law and medical students should consult the Law School and the School of Medicine concerning financial assistance. Contact the address below for further information or call (313) 577-2903.

Wayne State University
Graduate School Scholarship Office
4302 Faculty Administration Bldg.
Detroit, MI 48202

5031
Women of Wayne Alumni Association Scholarships

AMOUNT: None Specified DEADLINE: None Specified
FIELDS/MAJORS: All Areas of Study

Open to women students at Wayne State studying part-time on any level. This award provides tuition assistance for one course per semester. Write to the address below for details or call (313) 577-4103. Information also available at the Alumni House, 441 Ferry Mall, Detroit, MI 48202 or call (313) 577-2300.

Wayne State University
Women's Resource Center
575 Student Center Bldg.
Detroit, MI 48202

WAYNESBURG COLLEGE

5032
Alumni Council Scholarships

AMOUNT: Maximum: $1000 DEADLINE: March 15
FIELDS/MAJORS: All Areas of Study

Available to admitted incoming freshmen who have a minimum GPA of 3.0. Must demonstrate participation in both school activities and community service. A minimum GPA of 3.0 must be maintained to keep this award. Contact the address below for more information or call (412) 852-3208.

Waynesburg College
Financial Aid Office
51 West College St.
Waynesburg, PA 15370

5033
Bonner Scholarships

AMOUNT: $1870-$2870 DEADLINE: March 15
FIELDS/MAJORS: All Areas of Study

Available to admitted incoming freshmen who meet specific academic and financial need criteria and have demonstrated a commitment to community service. Recipients are required to participate in a service program each summer for six to eight weeks. Renewable for four consecutive years contingent upon the fulfillment of program requirements. Students completing the program will be eligible for $1400 in a loan reduction upon graduation. Contact the address below for more information or call (412) 852-3208. GPA must be at least 2.8.

Waynesburg College
Financial Aid Office
51 West College St.
Waynesburg, PA 15370

5034
Presidential Honor Scholarships

AMOUNT: Maximum: $4000 DEADLINE: March 15
FIELDS/MAJORS: All Areas of Study

Available for incoming freshmen, admitted to Waynesburg, who rank in the top 10% of class. Renewable if recipients maintain a minimum GPA of 3.25. Class valedictorians are also eligible to apply for this award. Contact your high school guidance office, the address below, or call (412) 852-3208 for further information.

Waynesburg College
Financial Aid Office
51 West College St.
Waynesburg, PA 15370

5035
Waynesburg Achievement Award

AMOUNT: Maximum: $1000   DEADLINE: March 15
FIELDS/MAJORS: All Areas of Study

Available for incoming freshmen, admitted to Waynesburg, who rank in the top 20% of class. Renewable if recipients maintain a minimum GPA of 3.0. Contact your high school guidance office, the address below, or call (412) 852-3208 for further information.

Waynesburg College
Financial Aid Office
51 West College St.
Waynesburg, PA 15370

5036
Waynesburg Honor Scholarships

AMOUNT: Maximum: $2000   DEADLINE: March 15
FIELDS/MAJORS: All Areas of Study

Available for incoming freshmen, admitted to Waynesburg, who rank in the top third of class. Renewable if recipients maintain a minimum GPA of 3.0. Contact your high school guidance office, the address below, or call (412) 852-3208 for further information.

Waynesburg College
Financial Aid Office
51 West College St.
Waynesburg, PA 15370

5037
Waynesburg Leadership Scholarships

AMOUNT: $1000-$1500   DEADLINE: March 15
FIELDS/MAJORS: All Areas of Study

Available to admitted incoming freshmen who have a minimum GPA of 3.0 and have made significant contributions in cocurricular and service activities. Renewable if recipients maintain a minimum GPA of 3.0. Leadership Scholars will be required to participate in weekly meeting, scheduled service trips, and other program activities. Contact the address below for more information or call (412) 852-3208.

Waynesburg College
Financial Aid Office
51 West College St.
Waynesburg, PA 15370

5038
Waynesburg Outstanding Scholars Scholarships

AMOUNT: None Specified   DEADLINE: March 15
FIELDS/MAJORS: All Areas of Study

Available to admitted incoming freshmen who are graduating in the top 5% of class. Based on class rank, personal recommendations, essays, and an on-campus interview. Renewable if recipients maintain a minimum GPA of 3.3. Recipients are ineligible for any other Waynesburg College scholarships and are required to participate in the Honors Program at the College. Award is full tuition. Contact the address below for more information or call (412) 852-3208.

Waynesburg College
Financial Aid Office
51 West College St.
Waynesburg, PA 15370

WELLESLEY COLLEGE

5039
Alice Freeman Palmer Fellowship

AMOUNT: Maximum: $10000   DEADLINE: January 12
FIELDS/MAJORS: All Areas of Study

Fellowships are available at Wellesley for study or research abroad and in the United States. The holder must be no more than twenty-six years of age at the time of her appointment and unmarried throughout the whole of her tenure. Write to the address below for information.

Wellesley College
Committee on Graduate Fellowships
106 Central Street, Career Center
Wellesley, MA 02181-8200

5040
Anne Louise Barrett Fellowship

AMOUNT: Maximum: $3000   DEADLINE: January 12
FIELDS/MAJORS: Musical, Theory, Composition, History

Open to graduates of Wellesley College studying or performing research in music, especially music theory, composition, or history of music abroad or in the U.S. Awards based on merit and financial need. Contact the address below for further information.

Wellesley College
Sec'y, Committee on Graduate Fellowships
106 Central St., Career Center
Wellesley, MA 02181-8200

5041
Edna V. Moffett Fellowship

AMOUNT: Maximum: $4000   DEADLINE: January 12
FIELDS/MAJORS: History

Fellowships for a young Wellesley alumnae. Preferably for first year of graduate study in history. Contact the address below for further information.

Wellesley College, Fellowships for Wellesley Alumnae
Sec'y, Committee on Graduate Fellowships
106 Central St., Career Center
Wellesley, MA 02181-8200

5042
Fanny Bullock Workman Fellowship

AMOUNT: Maximum: $3000   DEADLINE: January 12
FIELDS/MAJORS: All Areas of Study

Available to Wellesley alumnae. For graduate study in any field. Contact the address below for further information.

Wellesley College, Fellowships for Wellesley Alumnae
Sec'y, Committee on Graduate Fellowships
106 Central St., Career Center
Wellesley, MA 02181-8200

5043
Harriet A. Shaw Fellowship

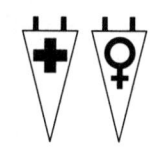

AMOUNT: Maximum: $3000   DEADLINE: January 12
FIELDS/MAJORS: Music, Art

Fellowships are available at Wellesley for study or research in music or art, in the United States or abroad. Preference given to music candidates. Undergraduate work in history of art required of other candidates. Write to the address below for information.

Wellesley College
Committee on Graduate Fellowships
106 Central Street, Career Center
Wellesley, MA 02181-8200

5044
Horton-Hollowell Fellowship

AMOUNT: Maximum: $4000   DEADLINE: January 12
FIELDS/MAJORS: All Areas of Study

Fellowships for Wellesley alumnae for graduate study in any field, preferably in the last two years of candidacy for the Ph.D., or its equivalent, or for private research of equivalent standard. Contact the address below for further information.

Wellesley College, Fellowships for Wellesley Alumnae
Sec'y, Committee on Graduate Fellowships
106 Central St., Career Center
Wellesley, MA 02181-8200

5045
M.A. Cartland Shackford Medical Fellowship

AMOUNT: Maximum: $3500   DEADLINE: January 12
FIELDS/MAJORS: Medicine

Scholarship for women studying medicine. Fellowships are intended to support women with a career objective in general practice, not psychiatry. Write to the address below for information.

Wellesley College
Sec'y, Committee on Graduate Fellowships
106 Central Street, Career Center
Wellesley, MA 02181-8200

5046
Margaret Freeman Bowers Fellowship

AMOUNT: Maximum: $1500   DEADLINE: January 12
FIELDS/MAJORS: Social Work, Law, Public Policy, Public Administration

Fellowships for graduates of Wellesley College studying in any of the above fields or studying for a MBA with career goals in the field of social services. Preference given to candidates with financial need. Contact the address below for further information.

Wellesley College, Fellowships for Wellesley Alumnae
Sec'y, Committee on Graduate Fellowships
106 Central St., Career Center
Wellesley, MA 02181-8200

5047
Mary Elvira Stevens Traveling Fellowship

AMOUNT: Maximum: $20000   DEADLINE: December 15
FIELDS/MAJORS: All Areas of Study

Fellowship is for a full year of travel or study abroad. Candidates must have graduated from Wellesley and be at least twenty-five years of age in the year of application. Any scholarly, artistic, or cultural purpose may be considered. Merit and financial need will also be considered. Contact the address below for further information.

Wellesley College
Alumnae Office
106 Central St.
Wellesley, MA 02181-8201

5048
Mary McEwen Schimke Scholarship

AMOUNT: Maximum: $1000 DEADLINE: January 12
FIELDS/MAJORS: Literature, History

Open for women studying at the graduate level. Purpose of the award is to provide relief from household and child care while studying. Based on scholarly expectation and identified need. Must be over thirty years of age. Preference is given to American studies. Candidates may have graduated from any American institution. Contact the address below for further information.

Wellesley College
Sec'y, Committee on Graduate Fellowships
106 Central St., Career Center
Wellesley, MA 02181-8200

5049
Peggy Howard Fellowship in Economics

AMOUNT: None Specified DEADLINE: April 1
FIELDS/MAJORS: Economics

Open to undergraduates and alumnae of Wellesley College for study and for special projects in economics. Award will be based on merit and financial need. One or two awards offered annually depending on income available. Write to the address below for details.

Wellesley College, Fellowships for Students and Alumnae
Economics Department
106 Central St.
Wellesley, MA 02181-8260

5050
Professor Elizabeth F. Fisher Fellowship

AMOUNT: Maximum: $1000 DEADLINE: January 12
FIELDS/MAJORS: Geology, Geography, Urban, Environmental, Ecological Studies

Open to Wellesley graduates to perform research or undertake further studies in one of the fields listed. Preference is given to geology and geography. Awards will be based on merit and financial need. Contact the address below for further information.

Wellesley College, Fellowships for Wellesley Alumnae
Sec'y, Committee on Graduate Fellowships
106 Central St., Career Center
Wellesley, MA 02181-8200

5051
Ruth Ingersoll Goldmark Fellowship

AMOUNT: Maximum: $1000 DEADLINE: January 12
FIELDS/MAJORS: English Literature, English Composition, Classics

Open to Wellesley alumnae for graduate study in English Literature, English Composition, or the Classics. Awards will be based on merit and financial need. Contact the address below for further information.

Wellesley College, Fellowships for Wellesley Alumnae
Sec'y, Committee on Graduate Fellowships
106 Central St., Career Center
Wellesley, MA 02181-8200

5052
Sarah Perry Wood Medical Fellowship

AMOUNT: Maximum: $24000 DEADLINE: January 15
FIELDS/MAJORS: Medicine

Open to Wellesley alumnae for the study of medicine. Not renewable. Contact the address below for further information.

Wellesley College, Fellowships for Wellesley Alumnae
Sec'y, Committee on Graduate Fellowships
106 Central St., Career Center
Wellesley, MA 02181-8200

5053
Susan Rappaport Knafel and Trustee Scholarships

AMOUNT: $3000-$25000 DEADLINE: January 12
FIELDS/MAJORS: All Areas of Study

Awards for graduating seniors who intend to pursue graduate studies. Two of the three awards include travel and study abroad. Merit and financial need will be considered. Contact the address below for further information about all three awards. GPA must be at least 2.9.

Wellesley College, Secretary, Committee on Graduate Fellowships
Center for Work and Service
106 Central St.
Wellesley, MA 02181-8200

5054
Thomas Jefferson Fellowship

AMOUNT: Maximum: $4000 DEADLINE: January 12
FIELDS/MAJORS: History

For Wellesley alumnae for advanced study in history. Award will be based on merit and financial need. Contact the address below for further information.

Wellesley College, Sec'y, Committee on Graduate Fellowships
Center for Work and Service
106 Central Street
Wellesley, MA 02161-8200

5055
Vida Dutton Scudder Fellowship

AMOUNT: Maximum: $2000   DEADLINE: January 12
FIELDS/MAJORS: Social Sciences, Political Science, Literature

Fellowships for Wellesley alumnae. For study in the field of social science, political science, or literature. Contact the address below for further information.

Wellesley College, Fellowships for Wellesley Alumnae
Sec'y, Committee on Graduate Fellowships
106 Central St., Career Center
Wellesley, MA 02181-8200

WEST CHESTER UNIVERSITY

5056
School of Music Scholarships

AMOUNT: None Specified   DEADLINE: None Specified
FIELDS/MAJORS: Music

Scholarships are available from West Chester University for exceptional students pursuing a degree in music. Write to the address below for further information.

West Chester University
Office of the Dean
Swope Hall
West Chester, PA 19383

WEST VIRGINIA UNIVERSITY

5057
Loyalty Permanent Endowment Fund Valedictorian Scholarships

AMOUNT: $1000   DEADLINE: None Specified
FIELDS/MAJORS: All Areas of Study

Renewable scholarships for every West Virginia High School valedictorian who attends WVU. Only one award per high school. Make certain the financial aid office is aware that you are a valedictorian. Write to the address below for details.

West Virginia University
Financial Aid Office
PO Box 6004
Morgantown, WV 26506

5058
Storer Scholarships

AMOUNT: $2192   DEADLINE: None Specified
FIELDS/MAJORS: All Areas of Study

Scholarships for African-American high school seniors planning to attend WVU. Based on academic achievement. State residency not required. Must have a minimum GPA of at least 3.0. Twenty awards per year. Contact the financial aid office at the address below for details.

West Virginia University
Financial Aid Office
PO Box 6004
Morgantown, WV 26506

5059
WVU National Merit Scholarship

AMOUNT: $500-$2000   DEADLINE: None Specified
FIELDS/MAJORS: All Areas of Study

Scholarships for National Merit Scholarship Finalists who select WVU as their college of choice. Winners of other NMSC scholarships are not eligible. Preference is given to West Virginia residents. Write to the address below for details.

West Virginia University
Financial Aid Office
PO Box 6004
Morgantown, WV 26506

5060
WVU Scholarships

AMOUNT: None Specified   DEADLINE: None Specified
FIELDS/MAJORS: All Areas of Study

Scholarships for students at WVU. Criteria vary for different awards. Programs include WVU foundation, presidential, high school leadership, designated, and departmental scholarships. Contact the financial aid office at the address below for details.

West Virginia University
Financial Aid Office
Mountainlair, 2nd Floor
Morgantown, WV 26506

WESTERN MICHIGAN UNIVERSITY

5061
Academic Scholarship for Michigan Community College Transfers

AMOUNT: Maximum: $500 DEADLINE: March 1
FIELDS/MAJORS: All Areas of Study

Awards for students at Western Michigan who have transferred from Michigan community colleges. Applicants must have a GPA of at least 3.5 and must have completed a minimum of 26 semester hours of transferable course work. No special application is required; students who qualify are automatically considered.

Western Michigan University
Office of Admissions and Orientation
2240 Seibert Administration Bldg.
Kalamazoo, MI 49008

5062
Academic Scholarships

AMOUNT: $250 DEADLINE: March 1
FIELDS/MAJORS: All Areas of Study

Scholarships are available at WMU for full-time undergraduate students who have a minimum GPA of 3.25. Awards will be given to recipients starting with those having a 4.0 GPA and working downward as long as funds are available. Contact the address below for further information.

Western Michigan University
Student Financial Aid
3306 Faunce Student Services Building
Kalamazoo, MI 49008

5063
Achievement Scholarship

AMOUNT: Maximum: $1000 DEADLINE: None Specified
FIELDS/MAJORS: All Areas of Study

Scholarship for admitted freshmen with at least a 3.5 GPA and a minimum ACT score of 20 or SAT of 930. Designed for students planning to enroll at WMU in the same year they graduate from high school. Write to the address below for more information. GPA must be at least 3.5.

Western Michigan University
Office of Admissions and Orientation
Kalamazoo, MI 49008-5120

5064
Army ROTC Scholarships

AMOUNT: Maximum: $12000 DEADLINE: March 1
FIELDS/MAJORS: All Areas of Study

Scholarships are available at WMU for entering freshmen students who will be participating in the ROTC program. Applicants must have a GPA of at least 3.0. Scholarships are also available for current undergraduates who have a minimum GPA of 2.5 and demonstrated leadership abilities. Contact WMU's Army ROTC at (616) 387-8120.

Western Michigan University
Student Financial Aid
3306 Faunce Student Services Building
Kalamazoo, MI 49008

5065
Assistance for Graduate Students

AMOUNT: Maximum: $7350 DEADLINE: February 15
FIELDS/MAJORS: All Areas of Study

Scholarships for graduate students at Western Michigan enrolled in master's or doctoral programs. Programs include graduate college fellows, doctoral associateships, Thurgood Marshall assistantships/grants, and teaching and research assistantships. Contact the address below for further information.

Western Michigan University
Student Financial Aid
3306 Faunce Student Services Building
Kalamazoo, MI 49008

5066
Clifford and Ella Chapman Distinguished Senior Scholarships

AMOUNT: Maximum: $200 DEADLINE: January 31
FIELDS/MAJORS: All Areas of Study

Scholarships are available at WMU for full-time senior students who have a minimum GPA of 3.5 and are U.S. citizens. Work history and extracurricular activities are considered. Contact the address below for further information.

Western Michigan University
Student Financial Aid
3306 Faunce Student Services Building
Kalamazoo, MI 49008

5067
Community College Presidential Scholarship

AMOUNT: Maximum: $1500   DEADLINE: March 1
FIELDS/MAJORS: All Areas of Study

Scholarships are available at WMU for transfer students with a GPA of at least 3.5. Must have a minimum of 26 semester hours of transferable coursework and be selected by your community college president. Contact your college for further information.

Western Michigan University
Student Financial Aid
3306 Faunce Student Services Building
Kalamazoo, MI 49008

5068
Cultural Diversity Scholarship

AMOUNT: None Specified   DEADLINE: February 1
FIELDS/MAJORS: All Areas of Study

Open to students who are U.S. citizens and apply to WMU as freshmen by December 31. Must have a minimum GPA of 3.5 The Office of Admissions must also have applicants' ACT or SAT scores on file for consideration. Committee will consider GPA, test scores, school and community activities, employment experience, and ethnicity. Two types of awards offered: Cultural Diversity Excellence Scholarships, $32,000 in five awards and Cultural Diversity Recognition Scholarships, $8,000 in seventy-five awards. Renewable if student maintains full-time enrollment with at least a 3.25 GPA. Write to the address below for more information.

Western Michigan University
Office of Admissions and Orientation
Kalamazoo, MI 49008-5120

5069
Distinguished Community College Scholars Award

AMOUNT: Maximum: $3000   DEADLINE: March 1
FIELDS/MAJORS: All Areas of Study

Annual scholarships for transfer students entering their first year at Western Michigan University. Must have received an associate's degree with a minimum GPA of 3.75 Contact the office of student financial aid at the address below for details.

Western Michigan University
Student Financial Aid
3306 Faunce Student Services Building
Kalamazoo, MI 49008

5070
Higher Education Incentive Scholarship Competition

AMOUNT: $1200-$4000   DEADLINE: None Specified
FIELDS/MAJORS: All Areas of Study

Scholarships are available at WMU for minority high school seniors who will be entering freshmen with a GPA of at least 3.5. Extracurricular activities will be considered. Contact the address below for further information.

Western Michigan University
Student Financial Aid
3306 Faunce Student Services Building
Kalamazoo, MI 49008

5071
Medallion Scholarships

AMOUNT: None Specified   DEADLINE: December 31
FIELDS/MAJORS: All Areas of Study

Open to seniors who are U.S. citizens and apply to Western Michigan University as freshmen by December 31. Must meet the criteria of at least a 3.8 GPA and a minimum ACT score of 25 or SAT of 1130. Applicants will be invited to one of two on-campus competitions held in February. Designed for students planning to enroll at WMU in the same year they graduate from high school. Primary emphasis on high school academics and the Medallion Competition, without regard to financial need. Committee also considers leadership ability, extracurricular activities, recommendations, and in some cases, personal interviews. Renewable if recipient maintains full-time enrollment with a minimum GPA of 3.25. Medallion participants will receive one of the following three types of scholarships: Medallion Scholarships, $32,000 in fifteen awards, Board of Trustees Scholarships, $24,000 in fifteen awards and WMU Academic Scholarships, $4,800 no quantity of awards specified. Contact the address below for further information.

Western Michigan University
Office of Admissions and Orientation
Kalamazoo, MI 49008-5120

5072
Non-Traditional Student Scholarship

AMOUNT: $200-$400   DEADLINE: None Specified
FIELDS/MAJORS: All Areas of Study

Scholarships for undergraduate or graduate students at Western Michigan University who are considered non-traditional students. A minimum GPA of 2.5 is required of undergraduates; a minimum GPA of 3.2 of graduate students. Contact the address below for further information.

Western Michigan University
Student Financial Aid
3306 Faunce Student Services Building
Kalamazoo, MI 49008

5073
Phi Theta Kappa Alumni Scholarship

AMOUNT: Maximum: $1000 DEADLINE: March 1
FIELDS/MAJORS: All Areas of Study

Scholarships are available at WMU for transfer students with a GPA of at least 3.5, who are members in good standing of Phi Theta Kappa. Associate's degree recommended, but a minimum of 26 semester hours of transferable course work must be completed at time of application. Contact the address below for further information.

Western Michigan University
Student Financial Aid
3306 Faunce Student Services Building
Kalamazoo, MI 49008

5074
Undergraduate Research and Creative Award Program

AMOUNT: Maximum: $1200 DEADLINE: March 1
FIELDS/MAJORS: All Areas of Study

Scholarships are available at WMU for junior or senior students who will be developing a research project with a faculty sponsor. Applicant must be a full-time student with at least a 3.3 GPA after completion of 60 credit hours. March deadline is for fall awards, and November is the deadline for winter awards. Contact Dean, Lee Honors College, (616) 387-3230.

Western Michigan University
Student Financial Aid
3306 Faunce Student Services Building
Kalamazoo, MI 49008

5075
Western Awards for National Merit Scholarship Winner

AMOUNT: Maximum: $3000 DEADLINE: April 1
FIELDS/MAJORS: All Areas of Study

Scholarships are available at WMU for entering freshmen who are National Merit Scholarship winners who choose WMU as their first school of choice. Contact the office of student financial aid at the address below for further information.

Western Michigan University
Student Financial Aid
Faunce Student Services Bldg.
Kalamazoo, MI 49008

WESTERN MONTANA COLLEGE

5076
Alpha Delta Kappa Scholarship

AMOUNT: $500 DEADLINE: February 15
FIELDS/MAJORS: Education

Scholarships for students at Western Montana College majoring in education. Grades are considered. Contact the address below for details.

Western Montana College
Admissions Office
Dillon, MT 59725

5077
Hancock-Emerick Art Award

AMOUNT: Maximum: $200 DEADLINE: March 1
FIELDS/MAJORS: Art

Selection is based on talent and ability in art. Available to undergraduate students at Western Montana College. Grades are also considered for this award. One award is given annually. Write to the address listed for additional information.

Western Montana College
Admissions Office
Dillon, MT 59725

WESTERN NEW MEXICO UNIVERSITY

5078
Board of Regents Scholarship

AMOUNT: $500 DEADLINE: April 1
FIELDS/MAJORS: All Areas of Study

Awards open to undergraduates who are New Mexico residents. Must have a minimum GPA of 3.0. Contact the address below further information.

Western New Mexico University
Financial Aid Office
College Ave., Box 680
Silver City, NM 88061

WESTMINSTER COLLEGE

5079
Alumni Scholarships

AMOUNT: Maximum: $1000 DEADLINE: February 1
FIELDS/MAJORS: All Areas of Study

Available to incoming students who are the sons, grandsons, daughters, or granddaughters of Westminster Alumni. Contact the address below for further information or call 1-800-475-3361.

Westminster College
Enrollment Services
501 Westminster Ave.
Fulton, MO 65251-1299

5080
Churchill Scholarships
GPA 3.5+

AMOUNT: None Specified DEADLINE: February 1
FIELDS/MAJORS: All Areas of Study

Incoming students who have been admitted on or before February 20 will be considered. Select students will be invited to participate in an on-campus competition to determine the winner of the award. Award is for up to full tuition and the opportunity to participate in special honor-related activities. Contact the address below for further information or call 1-800-475-3361. GPA must be at least 3.5.

Westminster College
Enrollment Services
501 Westminster Ave.
Fulton, MO 65251-1299

5081
Dean's Scholarship
GPA 2.5+

AMOUNT: $2500-$4000 DEADLINE: February 1
FIELDS/MAJORS: All Areas of Study

Incoming freshmen who have scored at least a 21 on the ACT or minimum of 970 on the SAT and have a minimum GPA of 2.75 will qualify for this award. Contact the address below for further information or call 1-800-475-3361.

Westminster College
Enrollment Services
501 Westminster Ave.
Fulton, MO 65251-1299

5082
Honor Scholarships
GPA 2.5+

AMOUNT: $2000-$4500 DEADLINE: February 1
FIELDS/MAJORS: All Areas of Study

Incoming freshmen who have demonstrated academic potential but whose GPA does not meet the minimum requirement of 2.75 for other Westminster scholarships may be considered. Contact the address below for further information or call 1-800-475-3361.

Westminster College
Enrollment Services
501 Westminster Ave.
Fulton, MO 65251-1299

5083
Leaderships Awards
GPA 2.5+

AMOUNT: None Specified DEADLINE: February 1
FIELDS/MAJORS: All Areas of Study

Incoming students who have been admitted to Westminster on or before February 20 will be considered. Select students will be invited to participate in an on-campus competition to determine the winner of the award. Students must show potential for leadership in their community or professional activities. Contact the address below for further information or call 1-800-475-3361. GPA must be at least 2.8.

Westminster College
Enrollment Services
501 Westminster Ave.
Fulton, MO 65251-1299

5084
Multi-Cultural Awards
GPA 3.0+

AMOUNT: None Specified DEADLINE: February 1
FIELDS/MAJORS: All Areas of Study

Available to incoming students who have demonstrated high academic achievement and who will contribute to the cultural, ethnic, and geographical diversity of Westminster. Demonstrated financial need is considered. Contact the address below for further information or call 1-800-475-3361. GPA must be at least 3.0.

Westminster College
Enrollment Services
501 Westminster Ave.
Fulton, MO 65251-1299

5085
President's Scholarship

AMOUNT: $3500-$5000 DEADLINE: February 1
FIELDS/MAJORS: All Areas of Study

Incoming freshmen who have scored at least a 24 on the ACT or at least a 1090 on the SAT and have a GPA of at least 2.75 qualify for this scholarship. Contact the address below for further information or call 1-800-475-3361.

Westminster College
Enrollment Services
501 Westminster Ave.
Fulton, MO 65251-1299

5086
Tower Scholarship

AMOUNT: Maximum: $6000 DEADLINE: None Specified
FIELDS/MAJORS: All Areas of Study

Available to incoming freshmen who have scored at least a 25 ACT/1100 SAT and have a GPA of 4.0. The alternative is a minimum ACT of 27/SAT of 1200 and at least a 3.0 GPA. This merit-based award does not consider financial need. Contact the address below for further information or call (412) 946-7100.

Westminster College, Pennsylvania
Scholarship Coordinator
Office of Admissions
New Wilmington, PA 16172-0001

5087
Trustee's Scholarship

AMOUNT: $4500-$7000 DEADLINE: February 1
FIELDS/MAJORS: All Areas of Study

Incoming freshmen who have scored at least a 27 on the ACT or a minimum of 1200 on the SAT and have a GPA of at least 2.75 qualify for this award. Contact the address below for further information or call 1-800-475-3361.

Westminster College
Enrollment Services
501 Westminster Ave.
Fulton, MO 65251-1299

5088
Trustee's Scholarship

AMOUNT: None Specified DEADLINE: None Specified
FIELDS/MAJORS: All Areas of Study

Available to incoming freshmen who have scored at least 27 on the ACT/a 1200 on the SAT and have a GPA of 3.7 or better. The award is for 50% of tuition. Renewable up to four years. This merit-based award does not consider financial need. Contact the address below for further information or call (412) 946-7100.

Westminster College, Pennsylvania
Scholarship Coordinator
Office of Admissions
New Wilmington, PA 16172-0001

5089
Valedictorian-Salutatorian Scholarship

AMOUNT: $500-$1000 DEADLINE: None Specified
FIELDS/MAJORS: All Areas of Study

Available to incoming freshmen who have been designated valedictorian or salutatorian of graduating class. Renewable up to four years. This merit based award does not consider financial need. Contact the address below for further information or call (412) 946-7100.

Westminster College, Pennsylvania
Scholarship Coordinator
Office of Admissions
New Wilmington, PA 16172-0001

5090
Westminster Scholarship

AMOUNT: Maximum: $5000 DEADLINE: None Specified
FIELDS/MAJORS: All Areas of Study

Available to incoming freshmen who have scored at least a 25 ACT/1100 SAT and have a minimum GPA of 3.0. Renewable up to four years. This merit-based award does not consider financial need. Contact the address below for further information or call (412) 946-7100.

Westminster College, Pennsylvania
Scholarship Coordinator
Office of Admissions
New Wilmington, PA 16172-0001

WHARTON SCHOOL OF BUSINESS

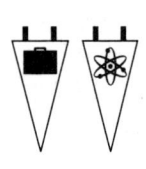

5091
Wharton Doctoral Fellowships in Risk and Insurance

AMOUNT: Maximum: $36000 DEADLINE: February 1
FIELDS/MAJORS: Insurance/Actuarial Science, Risk Management

Doctoral fellowships available at the Wharton School of Business. Must be a U.S. or Canadian citizen. Summer and postdoctoral fellowships are also available. Write to the address below for complete details.

S.S. Huebner Foundation for Insurance Education
Executive Director
3733 Spruce St., 430 Vance Hall
Philadelphia, PA 19104

WHEATON COLLEGE

5092
James E. Burr Scholarship

AMOUNT: Maximum: $2500 DEADLINE: March 1
FIELDS/MAJORS: All Areas of Study

Scholarships are available at Wheaton College for freshmen minority students who have a minimum GPA of at least 3.5, with an ACT composite score of at least 25 or SAT score of 1150 or more. Transfer students are also eligible with a GPA of at least 3.3. Write to the address below or call 1-800-362-2674 or (630) 752-5021 for details.

Wheaton College
Financial Aid Office
Wheaton, IL 60187

5093
National Merit Scholarship

AMOUNT: Maximum: $2000 DEADLINE: March 15
FIELDS/MAJORS: All Areas of Study

Scholarships are available at Wheaton College for undergraduate students who are National Merit scholarship finalists who chose Wheaton College as their first school of choice. Write to the address below or call 1-800-362-2674 or (630) 752-5021 for details.

Wheaton College
Financial Aid Office
Wheaton, IL 60187

5094
President's Achievement Awards

AMOUNT: $750-$2000 DEADLINE: March 15
FIELDS/MAJORS: All Areas of Study

Awards for freshmen named finalists in National Hispanic Scholar Recognition Program or National Achievement Scholarship Program for outstanding Negro students. Write to the address below or call 1-800-362-2674 or (630) 752-5021 for more information.

Wheaton College
Financial Aid Office
Wheaton, IL 60187

5095
President's Award

AMOUNT: Maximum: $4000 DEADLINE: March 15
FIELDS/MAJORS: All Areas of Study

Scholarships are available at Wheaton College for undergraduate students who have a minimum GPA of 3.6, with a composite ACT score of 32 or a SAT score of 1400. Write to the address below or call 1-800-362-2674 or (630) 752-5021 for details.

Wheaton College
Financial Aid Office
Wheaton, IL 60187

5096
ROTC Scholarships

AMOUNT: None Specified DEADLINE: March 15
FIELDS/MAJORS: All Areas of Study

Scholarships are available at Wheaton College for undergraduate students who will be participating in the ROTC program. Write to the address below or call 1-800-362-2674 or (630) 752-5021 for details.

Wheaton College
Financial Aid Office
Wheaton, IL 60187

5097
Special Achievement Award in Music

AMOUNT: $1000-$2500 DEADLINE: March 15
FIELDS/MAJORS: Music

Scholarships are available at Wheaton College for undergraduate students who are enrolled in the music conservatory. Write to the address below or call 1-800-362-2674 or (630) 752-5021 for details.

Wheaton College
Financial Aid Office
Wheaton, IL 60187

5098

Wheaton College Restricted Scholarships, Wheaton Grants

AMOUNT: $5000-$10000 DEADLINE: March 15
FIELDS/MAJORS: All Areas of Study

Scholarships and other awards are available at Wheaton College for undergraduate students who demonstrate academic excellence or financial need or both. Write to the address below or call 1-800-362-2674 or (630) 752-5021 for details.

Wheaton College
Financial Aid Office
Wheaton, IL 60187

5099

Wheaton College Revolving Loan

AMOUNT: None Specified DEADLINE: March 15
FIELDS/MAJORS: All Areas of Study

Low-cost loan available for Wheaton College students. 5% interest rate with repayment beginning after graduation, with ten years to pay back loan. Write to the address below or call 1-800-362-2674 or (630) 752-5021 for details.

Wheaton College
Financial Aid Office
Wheaton, IL 60187

5100

Woten Fund

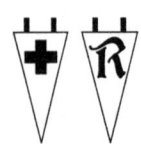

AMOUNT: Maximum: $1100 DEADLINE: March 15
FIELDS/MAJORS: Medicine, Nursing

Awards available to Wheaton College undergraduates planning on becoming missionary nurses or doctors. Write to the address listed or call 1-800-362-2674 or (630) 752-5021 for details.

Wheaton College
Financial Aid Office
Wheaton, IL 60187

WHITWORTH COLLEGE

5101

Alice Woodhead Scholarship

AMOUNT: $400 DEADLINE: April 1
FIELDS/MAJORS: All Areas of Study

Award open to students who are accepted at Whitworth. Must have previously attended for at least one year. Must have a minimum GPA of 2.75 and a high financial need. Contact the address below for further information.

Whitworth College
Office of Financial Aid
300 W. Hawthorne Rd.
Spokane, WA 99251

5102

Eileen "Mom" Hendrick Scholarship

AMOUNT: $200 DEADLINE: March 15
FIELDS/MAJORS: All Areas of Study

Award open to students who are accepted at Whitworth College who demonstrate a strong sense of service to others. Must have at least one year of residency on-campus. Financial need is considered. Contact the address below for further information.

Whitworth College
Office of Financial Aid
300 W. Hawthorne Rd.
Spokane, WA 99251

5103

Estella Baldwin Scholarships for International Students

AMOUNT: $1000 DEADLINE: April 15
FIELDS/MAJORS: All Areas of Study

Awards open to international students accepted at Whitworth College with a minimum GPA of 2.75 and a high financial need. May be renewable. Contact the address below for further information.

Whitworth College
Financial Aid Office
300 W. Hawthorne Rd.
Spokane, WA 99251

5104
James Family Scholarships

AMOUNT: $500-$1000
DEADLINE: April 1
FIELDS/MAJORS: International Business/Relations, Political Science

Award open to students who are accepted at Whitworth College. Must have previously attended for at least one year. Must have a minimum GPA of 3.0 and possess a solid Christian commitment. Contact the address below for further information.

Whitworth College
Office of Financial Aid
300 W. Hawthorne Rd.
Spokane, WA 99251

5105
Lisa M. Plotkin Scholarships

AMOUNT: None Specified   DEADLINE: April 15
FIELDS/MAJORS: All Areas of Study

Award open to sophomores and juniors who are accepted at Whitworth College who are handicapped or majoring in a field to benefit the developmentally disabled. May be renewed. Contact the address below for further information.

Whitworth College
Office of Financial Aid
300 W. Hawthorne Rd.
Spokane, WA 99251

5106
Martha Estelle Frimoth Scholarship

AMOUNT: $500   DEADLINE: March 15
FIELDS/MAJORS: All Areas of Study

Award open to students who are accepted at Whitworth College. Must have previously attended for at least one year. Based on academics, community involvement, and service to others. Must have a minimum GPA of 2.75. Contact the address below for further information.

Whitworth College
Office of Financial Aid
300 W. Hawthorne Rd.
Spokane, WA 99251

5107
Ministerial Dependent Grants

AMOUNT: $1500   DEADLINE: March 1
FIELDS/MAJORS: All Areas of Study

Scholarships for sons and daughters of ordained ministers accepted at Whitworth College. Contact the Financial Aid Office at the address below for details.

Whitworth College
Financial Aid Office
300 W. Hawthorne Rd.
Spokane, WA 99251

5108
Nalos Scholarships

AMOUNT: $700   DEADLINE: March 31
FIELDS/MAJORS: Religion

Award open to juniors and seniors who are accepted at Whitworth College. Must have previously attended for one year. Must have a minimum GPA of 3.0. Contact the address below for further information.

Whitworth College
Office of Financial Aid
300 W. Hawthorne Rd.
Spokane, WA 99251

5109
Sheryl Fardel-Winget Scholarship

AMOUNT: $1000   DEADLINE: March 1
FIELDS/MAJORS: Teacher Education, Special Education

Award open to students who are accepted at Whitworth College. Must have previously attended for at least one year. Must have a minimum GPA of 3.0. Financial need is considered. Contact the address below for further information.

Whitworth College
Office of Financial Aid
300 W. Hawthorne Rd.
Spokane, WA 99251

5110
Sophie Anderson Scholarship

AMOUNT: $350-$500
DEADLINE: October 15
FIELDS/MAJORS: Nursing, Pre-Med, Education, History, Liberal Arts

Awards open to juniors and seniors accepted at Whitworth College who are Washington residents, have a minimum GPA of 3.25, and can demonstrate high financial need. Contact the address below for further information.

Whitworth College
Office of Financial Aid
300 W. Hawthorne Rd.
Spokane, WA 99251

5111
United Parcel Service Scholarship

AMOUNT: $1325 DEADLINE: April 15
FIELDS/MAJORS: All Areas of Study

Awards open to full-time undergraduates accepted at Whitworth College with a minimum GPA of 3.0. Must be able to demonstrate financial need. Contact the address below for further information.

Whitworth College
Financial Aid Office
300 W. Hawthorne Rd.
Spokane, WA 99251

5112
Whitworth Merit and Need Scholarships

AMOUNT: $4000-$7000 DEADLINE: March 1
FIELDS/MAJORS: All Areas of Study

Scholarships based either on merit or on a combination of need and merit for students accepted at Whitworth College. Criteria for each award program differs. Contact the Financial Aid Office at the address below for details. GPA must be at least 3.0.

Whitworth College
Financial Aid Office
300 W. Hawthorne Rd.
Spokane, WA 99251

5113
Whitworth Merit Scholarships

AMOUNT: Maximum: $7000 DEADLINE: March 1
FIELDS/MAJORS: All Areas of Study

Scholarships for incoming freshmen accepted at Whitworth College who are National Merit Scholarship finalists (based on the PSAT/NMSQT test). Contact the Financial Aid Office at the address below for details. GPA must be at least 3.5.

Whitworth College
Financial Aid Office
300 W. Hawthorne Rd.
Spokane, WA 99251

5114
Winner/Christiansen Scholarship

AMOUNT: $700 DEADLINE: April 15
FIELDS/MAJORS: Journalism

Award open to students who are accepted at Whitworth College interested in a career as a professional journalist. Requirements include involvement/commitment to campus media. Must have a minimum GPA of 3.0 and be able to demonstrate financial need. Contact the address below for further information.

Whitworth College
Office of Financial Aid
300 W. Hawthorne Rd.
Spokane, WA 99251

WILLIAMS BAPTIST COLLEGE

5115
Music and Art Awards and Scholarships

AMOUNT: $350 DEADLINE: None Specified
FIELDS/MAJORS: All Areas of Study

Scholarships for students at Williams Baptist College who are artistically or musically talented and wish to participate in groups at WBC. Contact the address below for details.

Williams Baptist College
Financial Aid Office
PO Box 3665
Walnut Ridge, AR 72476

WILSON COLLEGE

5116
The Hagop Bogigian Fund

AMOUNT: Maximum: $1500 DEADLINE: April 30
FIELDS/MAJORS: All Areas of Study

Loans for full-time students at Wilson College who are of Armenian descent. Preference is given to women. Must demonstrate financial need. Write to the address below or call (717) 264-4141 for more information.

Wilson College
Office of Financial Aid
1015 Philadelphia Ave.
Chambersburg, PA 17201

WOFFORD COLLEGE

5117
Anna Todd Wofford Scholarship

AMOUNT: Maximum: $8000   DEADLINE: March 15
FIELDS/MAJORS: All Areas of Study

Four scholarships are awarded to female undergraduate students who rank high in the Wofford scholars competition and demonstrate leadership, academic excellence, and outstanding character. Write to the address below or call (864) 597-4160 for details. GPA must be at least 3.5.

Wofford College
429 North Church Street
Spartanburg, SC 29303

5118
Athletic Grants

AMOUNT: None Specified   DEADLINE: March 15
FIELDS/MAJORS: All Areas of Study

Scholarships are awarded to undergraduate students planning to participate in an intercollegiate sports program. Write to the address below or call (864) 597-4160 for details.

Wofford College
429 North Church Street
Spartanburg, SC 29303

5119
Benjamin Wofford Scholarship

AMOUNT: Maximum: $8000   DEADLINE: March 15
FIELDS/MAJORS: All Areas of Study

Four scholarships are awarded to male undergraduate students who rank high in the Wofford Scholars competition and demonstrate leadership, academic excellence, and outstanding character. Write to the address below or call (864) 597-4160 for details. GPA must be at least 3.5.

Wofford College
429 North Church Street
Spartanburg, SC 29303

5120
Boyd C. Hipp II Scholarship, Marvin L. Holloway Scholarship

AMOUNT: None Specified   DEADLINE: March 15
FIELDS/MAJORS: Business

Scholarships are awarded to juniors and seniors who are business majors and demonstrate academic excellence. Write to the address below or call (864) 597-4160 for details. GPA must be at least 3.3.

Wofford College
429 North Church Street
Spartanburg, SC 29303

5121
Children of Methodist Ministers Grant

AMOUNT: Maximum: $1000   DEADLINE: March 15
FIELDS/MAJORS: All Areas of Study

Scholarships are awarded to children of Methodist ministers. Write to the address below or call (864) 597-4160 for details.

Wofford College
429 North Church Street
Spartanburg, SC 29303

5122
Dewitt L. Harper Scholarship

AMOUNT: $1000-$4000   DEADLINE: March 15
FIELDS/MAJORS: Medicine, Health Services

Scholarships are awarded to undergraduate students who are preparing for a career in the area of medicine or health service and demonstrate leadership, academic excellence, and outstanding character. Write to the address below or call (864) 597-4160 for details.

Wofford College
429 North Church Street
Spartanburg, SC 29303

5123
James C. Loftin Scholarship

AMOUNT: None Specified   DEADLINE: March 15
FIELDS/MAJORS: Chemistry

Scholarships are awarded to juniors and seniors who are chemistry majors and demonstrate academic excellence. Write to the address below or call (864) 597-4160 for details. GPA must be at least 3.3.

Wofford College
429 North Church Street
Spartanburg, SC 29303

5124
John B. Cleveland Endowed Scholarship

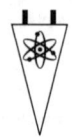

AMOUNT: $1000-$5000 DEADLINE: March 15
FIELDS/MAJORS: Science

Scholarships are awarded to freshmen pursuing a science-related curriculum. Contact your high school guidance counselor, write to the address below, or call (864) 597-4160 for details.

Wofford College
429 North Church Street
Spartanburg, SC 29303

5125
Larry A. McCalla Scholarship

AMOUNT: None Specified DEADLINE: March 15
FIELDS/MAJORS: Pre-Med

Scholarships are awarded to juniors and seniors who are pre-med majors and demonstrate academic excellence. Write to the address below or call (864) 597-4160 for details. GPA must be at least 3.3.

Wofford College
429 North Church Street
Spartanburg, SC 29303

5126
Ministerial Grants and Scholarships

AMOUNT: Maximum: $1000 DEADLINE: March 15
FIELDS/MAJORS: Ministerial Studies

Scholarships are awarded to undergraduate students who plan to study for the ministry. Requirements vary. Write to the address below or call (864) 597-4160 for details.

Wofford College
429 North Church Street
Spartanburg, SC 29303

5127
Neville Holcombe Scholarship

AMOUNT: None Specified DEADLINE: March 15
FIELDS/MAJORS: Pre-Law

Scholarship are awarded to juniors and seniors who are pre-law majors and demonstrate academic excellence. Write to the address below or call (864) 597-4160 for details. GPA must be at least 3.3.

Wofford College
429 North Church Street
Spartanburg, SC 29303

5128
Ruth Winn Wickware Scholarship

AMOUNT: Maximum: $9500 DEADLINE: March 15
FIELDS/MAJORS: Economics, Business Administration

Scholarships are awarded to undergraduate students who are pursuing a degree in economics or business administration. Awards are renewable for a period of up to four years Write to the address below or call (864) 597-4160 for details.

Wofford College
429 North Church Street
Spartanburg, SC 29303

5129
Transfer Student Scholarship

AMOUNT: None Specified DEADLINE: March 15
FIELDS/MAJORS: All Areas of Study

Scholarships are awarded to juniors and seniors who are transferring after graduating from a two-year college. Write to the address below or call (864) 597-4160 for details.

Wofford College
429 North Church Street
Spartanburg, SC 29303

5130
W. Hastings McAlister Scholarship

AMOUNT: Maximum: $14000 DEADLINE: March 15
FIELDS/MAJORS: Medicine, Health Science

Scholarships are awarded to freshmen or transfer students from Spartanburg Methodist College who are preparing for a career in the area of medicine or health science. Preference is given to residents of South Carolina. Contact your high school guidance counselor, write to the address below, or call (864) 597-4160 for details.

Wofford College
429 North Church Street
Spartanburg, SC 29303

5131
W. J. Bryan Crenshaw Endowed Scholarship

AMOUNT: $1000-$5000 DEADLINE: March 15
FIELDS/MAJORS: All Areas of Study

Scholarships are awarded to freshmen who exemplify academic excellence, Christian leadership, and a promise of contribution to society. Renewable. Contact your high school guidance counselor or write to the address below for details. GPA must be at least 3.1.

Wofford College
429 North Church Street
Spartanburg, SC 29303

5132
W. Raymond Leonard Scholarship

AMOUNT: None Specified DEADLINE: March 15
FIELDS/MAJORS: Biology

Scholarships are awarded to juniors and seniors who are biology majors and demonstrate academic excellence. Write to the address below or call (864) 597-4160 for details. GPA must be at least 3.3.

Wofford College
429 North Church Street
Spartanburg, SC 29303

5133
William H. Brabham Scholarship, Lewis P. Jones Scholarship

AMOUNT: None Specified DEADLINE: March 15
FIELDS/MAJORS: History

Scholarships are awarded to juniors and seniors who are history majors and demonstrate academic excellence. Write to the address below or call (864) 597-4160 for details. GPA must be at least 3.3.

Wofford College
429 North Church Street
Spartanburg, SC 29303

5134
Wofford College General Academic Scholarships

AMOUNT: $1000-$2000 DEADLINE: March 15
FIELDS/MAJORS: All Areas of Study

Scholarships are awarded to undergraduate students who demonstrate financial need and have a GPA of at least 2.5. Renewable. Write to the address below or call (864) 597-4160 for details.

Wofford College
429 North Church Street
Spartanburg, SC 29303

5135
Wofford College National Merit Scholarships

AMOUNT: $500-$2000 DEADLINE: March 15
FIELDS/MAJORS: All Areas of Study

Scholarships are awarded to three undergraduate merit scholars who designate Wofford as their first college of choice. Recipients are chosen from among the finalists in the National Merit competition. Write to the address below or call (864) 597-4160 for details. GPA must be at least 3.5.

Wofford College
429 North Church Street
Spartanburg, SC 29303

5136
Wofford College Scholarships

AMOUNT: $1000-$8000 DEADLINE: March 15
FIELDS/MAJORS: All Areas of Study

Scholarships are awarded to undergraduate students who demonstrate leadership, academic excellence, and outstanding character. Write to the address below or call (864) 597-4160 for details. GPA must be at least 3.3.

Wofford College
429 North Church Street
Spartanburg, SC 29303

5137
Wofford Scholars Program

AMOUNT: Maximum: $19000 DEADLINE: March 15
FIELDS/MAJORS: All Areas of Study

Scholarships are awarded annually to incoming freshmen on the basis of exceptional scholarship and leadership. Contact your high school guidance counselor, write to the address below, or call (864) 597-4130 for details. GPA must be at least 3.5.

Wofford College
429 North Church Street
Spartanburg, SC 29303

YORK COLLEGE OF PENNSYLVANIA

5138
Dean's Academic Scholarship

AMOUNT: None Specified DEADLINE: February 1
FIELDS/MAJORS: All Areas of Study

Open to 130 entering full-time freshmen, admitted to York College, with a minimum GPA of 3.25. Must be in the upper two-fifths of their high school class and attain a combined SAT score of 1,150 or better, with a minimum score of 540 on the math and verbal sections. This scholarship pays one-third tuition per year. Renewable if recipients maintain a minimum GPA of 3.25. Write to address below for additional information.

York College of Pennsylvania
Director of Admissions
Country Club Road
York, PA 17405-7199

5139
Hanover Area Scholarship

AMOUNT: None Specified DEADLINE: December 1
FIELDS/MAJORS: All Areas of Study

Open to Hanover High School students who meet current York College registration policy criteria for part-time matriculated or non-matriculated students. Selection will be based on educational goals, financial need, and community involvement. Must be Hanover area residents. Award is tuition for one three-credit course excluding books and fees. Contact the address listed or call (717) 637-6130 for further information.

Hanover Area Chamber of Commerce
Scholarship Coordinator
146 Carlisle St.
Hanover, PA 17331-2500

5140
John Andrews Scholarship

AMOUNT: Maximum: $1200
DEADLINE: February 1
FIELDS/MAJORS: Education, English, History, Humanities, Foreign Languages, Music, Philosophy, Speech

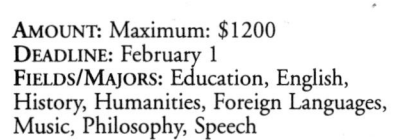

Open to entering full-time freshmen, admitted to York College, majoring in education, English, history, humanities, foreign languages, music, philosophy, or speech. Write to address below for additional information.

York College of Pennsylvania
Director of Admissions
Country Club Road
York, PA 17405-7199

5141
Merit Scholarship

AMOUNT: None Specified DEADLINE: February 1
FIELDS/MAJORS: All Areas of Study

Open to students, attending York College, based on academic achievement at the college level. Students must have completed at least one semester (12 credit hours) and maintained minimum GPA of 3.25. Write to address below for additional information.

York College of Pennsylvania
Director of Admissions
Country Club Road
York, PA 17405-7199

5142
Presidential Scholarship

AMOUNT: None Specified DEADLINE: February 1
FIELDS/MAJORS: All Areas of Study

Open to entering full-time freshmen, admitted to York College, with a minimum GPA of 3.25. Must be in the top one-fifth of their high school class and attained a combined SAT score of 1,200 or better with a minimum score of 540 on the math and verbal sections. This scholarship pays one-half tuition per year. Renewable if recipients maintain a minimum GPA of 3.25. Write to address below for additional information.

York College of Pennsylvania
Director of Admissions
Country Club Road
York, PA 17405-7199

5143
Trustee Honors Scholarship

AMOUNT: None Specified DEADLINE: February 1
FIELDS/MAJORS: All Areas of Study

Open to five entering full-time freshmen, admitted to York College, with a minimum GPA of 3.25. Must be in the top one-fifth of their high school class and attain a combined SAT score of 1,200 or better, with a minimum score of 540 on the math and verbal sections. This scholarship pays full tuition per year. Renewable if recipients maintain a minimum GPA of 3.25. Write to address below for additional information.

York College of Pennsylvania
Director of Admissions
Country Club Road
York, PA 17405-7199

5144
Valedictorian and Salutatorian Scholarships

AMOUNT: None Specified **DEADLINE:** February 1
FIELDS/MAJORS: All Areas of Study

Open to entering full-time freshmen, admitted to York College, with a minimum GPA of 3.25. Must be valedictorians or salutatorians and have a combined SAT score of 1,150 or better, with a minimum score of 540 on the math and verbal sections. This scholarship pays one-half tuition per year. Renewable if recipients maintain a minimum GPA of 3.25. Write to address below for additional information.

York College of Pennsylvania
Director of Admissions
Country Club Road
York, PA 17405-7199

YOUNG HARRIS COLLEGE

5145
Faculty Scholarships

AMOUNT: Maximum: $1200 **DEADLINE:** None Specified
FIELDS/MAJORS: All Areas of Study

Scholarships for incoming freshmen at Young Harris College who have a minimum GPA of 3.2 and who scored at least 1000 on the SAT, with a minimum verbal score of 500. Write to address below for additional information.

Young Harris College
Financial Aid Office
PO Box 247
Young Harris, GA 30582

5146
Fine Arts Scholarships

AMOUNT: $500-$2000 **DEADLINE:** February 1
FIELDS/MAJORS: Art, Music, and Theater

Scholarships for students at Young Harris College who show talent in one of the above areas. Art awards are based on portfolio. Theater and music awards are based on audition. Write to address listed for additional information.

Young Harris College
Financial Aid Office
PO Box 247
Young Harris, GA 30582

INDEXES

Major/Career Objective Index

Special Criteria Index

Geographic Index

Major/Career Objective Index

BUSINESS

Accounting, 51, 52, 53, 110, 151, 227, 458, 459, 711, 712, 722, 802, 899, 978, 1072, 1280, 1440, 1511, 1559, 1618, 1678, 1679, 1680, 1756, 1960, 2068, 2104, 2177, 2198, 2313, 2344, 2350, 2382, 2392, 2393, 2394, 2395, 2552, 2570, 2615, 2706, 2766, 2767, 2773, 2814, 2821, 2853, 2908, 2941, 2950, 2982, 3375, 3385, 3392, 3394, 3456, 4057, 4074, 4075, 4097, 4102, 4438, 4767, 4889

Actuarial Science, 28, 3533, 5091

Administrative Assistant, 2760, 4637

Advertising, 12, 1039, 1126, 1185, 1228, 1389, 1423, 1524, 1670

Agribusiness, 18, 1773, 2140, 2626, 2987, 3572, 3655, 3659, 3675, 3718, 4100, 4277, 4863, 4865, 4870, 4958

Agricultural Economics, 4100, 4252, 4259, 4270, 4274, 4863, 4865

Automotive Aftermarket, 2054

Banking, 487, 1910, 2177, 2515, 3528

Business, 2, 8, 105, 145, 238, 322, 487, 491, 511, 570, 579, 722, 928, 983, 1021, 1028, 1046, 1178, 1198, 1273, 1442, 1455, 1485, 1490, 1559, 1627, 1659, 1685, 1703, 1736, 1757, 1814, 1905, 2068, 2144, 2177, 2313, 2331, 2382, 2434, 2474, 2530, 2536, 2540, 2555, 2616, 2631, 2634, 2697, 2706, 2857, 2867, 2951, 2974, 2981, 3367, 3374, 3383, 3395, 3423, 3444, 3456, 3481, 3864, 3890, 3898, 3952, 4057, 4074, 4075, 4084, 4088, 4092, 4097, 4098, 4100, 4102, 4106, 4118, 4303, 4315, 4357, 4358, 4423, 4455, 4610, 4629, 4632, 4701, 4705, 4728, 4889, 4934, 5120

Business Administration, 308, 729, 828, 1093, 1511, 1891, 1892, 1907, 1996, 2053, 2284, 2518, 2542, 2760, 2766, 2767, 2773, 2775, 2976, 3249, 3292, 3372, 3503, 3531, 3600, 3910, 4084, 4637, 4724, 4748, 4771, 4774, 5128

Business Education, 333, 2767, 2939, 2941

Business Management, 192, 2919, 3503, 4590

Business Technology, 3843

Club Management, 442

Consumer Science, 3675, 3693

Cost Management, 4861

Economic History, 139, 797; of Wisconsin and/or the American Midwest, 1198

Economics, 276, 491, 570, 579, 701, 748, 768, 769, 822, 823, 824, 913, 964, 1007, 1046, 1259, 1442, 1511, 1948, 2068, 2177, 2313, 2515, 2810, 2820, 2839, 2865, 2944, 2952, 3456, 3481, 3503, 3531, 3559, 3638, 3675, 3718, 4492, 4606, 4629, 4774, 5000, 5049, 5128; of Germany, 320

Family and Consumer Sciences, 328

Finance, 487, 517, 620, 621, 722, 983, 1021, 1259, 1511, 1627, 1891, 1892, 2283, 2350, 2382, 2515, 2627, 2630, 3890, 4057

Food Distribution, 2186

Human Resource Management, 1517, 2766, 2767, 2773

Industrial: Relations, 1517; Studies, 2213

Industry, 570, 964, 1007, 5015

Information Networking, 3569

Insurance, 501, 722, 2568, 2951, 3372, 5091

International: Business/Relations, 5104; Economics, 983, 3559; Trade, 1393, 2177, 2313

Management, 282, 579, 722, 977, 2434, 5007; Science, 3503

Market Economics, 3592

Marketing, 12, 171, 282, 620, 722, 977, 1039, 1185, 1252, 2068, 2282, 2289, 2382, 2623, 2624, 2767, 2773; Education, 977; Manufacturing Operations, 621; Travel/Tourism, 1121

Merchandising, 977, 2068

Office Administration, 2760, 2766, 2767, 4637

Personnel, 3372

Pre-Business, 3689, 3722, 4724

Public Administration, 1046, 1511, 1891, 1969, 2323, 3249, 3534, 3581, 5046; Affairs, 2656, 4356; Management, 3600

Purchasing, 579

Quantitative Business, 1295

Real Estate, 22, 179, 487, 658, 860, 862, 2235, 4655

Records Management, 192

Regional Planning, 3681

Resource Management, 262

Retail, 2121

Risk Management, 5091

Sales, 620

Sports Management, 2083, 3567, 4604

Statistics, 722

Turfgrass Management, 173, 847, 895

Water Utility Industry, 533, 1128, 1659, 2202

EDUCATION

Academics, 4329

Aerospace Education, 919

Agricultural Education, 4100

Athletic Training, 2134, 2310, 2945, 3567

Business Education, 333, 2767, 2939, 2941

Child Development, 548

Christian Education, 508, 4327

College Level Teaching, 1946

Deaf Education, 2408

Early Childhood Education, 3672, 3676, 3679, 3696, 3697, 3700, 3703, 3720, 3723, 3726, 3728, 3732, 3734, 3750, 3756, 4085, 4723, 4924, 5013

Earth Science Education, 3565

Education Administration, 1045, 1515, 3378

Education of Visually Impaired or Blind Persons, 547, 1991

Educational Research, 35; Psychology Relating to Gifted/Talented Children, 1030

Elementary Education, 97, 672, 965, 995, 1109, 1144, 1267, 1529, 2711, 2712, 2755, 2757, 2758, 2761, 2774, 2846, 2942, 2954, 3431, 3441, 3570, 3584, 4672, 4740, 4837, 4851, 4920, 4946

English Education, 1640

Environmental Education, 1632

Graphic Arts Education, 2369

Health Education, 791

Hearing Therapy, 106

Human Development, 4288, 5013

Industrial Education, 3739

Intercollegiate Athletics Administration, 713

Interpreting, 676

Jewish Education, 21

Kindergarten Education, 2076

Korean Education, 2210

Legal Education, 4674

Marketing Education, 977

Math Education, 8, 1540, 1846, 2846, 4842

Mentally Handicapped Education, 2293

Middle School Education, 2757, 2758

Music Education, 263, 1566, 2562, 2983, 3253, 3811, 3823, 4023, 4442

Philosophy of Education, 2130

Physical Education, 791, 3487, 3783, 4028, 4729

Physical Science Education, 3580

Preschool Education, 1529, 2076

Reading Research and Disabilities, 1100

School Administration, 3729

Science Education, 8, 1540, 1632, 1846, 4842

Secondary Education, 2, 8, 44, 74, 96, 97, 283, 322, 344, 353, 415, 416, 470, 503, 504, 514, 524, 548, 549, 561, 594, 604, 654, 672, 681, 688, 709, 725, 729, 771, 780, 781, 799, 833, 889, 902, 965, 1046, 1106, 1109, 1144, 1166, 1267, 1436, 1478, 1514, 1515, 1520, 1521, 1529, 1530, 1531, 1539, 1542, 1597, 1673, 1690, 1720, 1738, 1812, 1814, 1818, 1887, 2014, 2062, 2129, 2143, 2206, 2208, 2216, 2223, 2268, 2312, 2314, 2430, 2496, 2498, 2534, 2544, 2563, 2564, 2567, 2607, 2610, 2619, 2693, 2711, 2761, 2798, 2813, 2816, 2828, 2834, 2836, 2856, 2943, 2958, 2979, 2984, 3283, 3310, 3431, 3435, 3444, 3451, 3457, 3484, 3540, 3584, 3638, 3729, 3749, 3757, 3887, 3893, 3949, 4028, 4039, 4085, 4089, 4100, 4343, 4415, 4483, 4500, 4530, 4536, 4550, 4730, 4731, 4741, 4759, 4799, 4845, 4849, 4852, 4920, 5025, 5076, 5110, 5140; History/ American Government/ Social Studies, 1154; Technology, 995

Sign Language, 2408

Spanish Education, 4343

Special Education, 286, 685, 855, 1476, 2126, 2420, 2532, 2719, 2720, 2757, 2758, 2761, 2774, 2807, 2942, 5109

Speech, 94, 106, 465, 791, 917, 922, 1622, 2065, 2127, 2399, 3962, 4003, 4049, 4329, 5021, 5140

Sports Coaching, 1772

Teaching, 480, 836, 904, 981, 983, 1139, 1478, 2214, 2326, 2420, 3567, 4610, 5109

Technology Education, 668, 827, 871, 872, 1350, 1396

Transliterating (Deaf), 676

ENGINEERING

Actuarial/Computer Science, 722

Aeronautics, 60, 235, 953, 2212, 3462

Aerospace Engineering, 107, 1232, 1233, 1234, 1235, 1236, 2109, 2621, 4289

Agricultural Engineering, 207, 923, 1047, 1232, 1285, 2414, 2415, 3719, 3975, 4256, 4268

Aircraft, 31, 1233

Architecture, 65, 80, 95, 185, 186, 199, 221, 381, 426, 476, 479, 804, 1041, 1115, 1137, 1178, 1236, 1243, 1528, 1532, 1636, 1759, 1957, 1965, 1984, 2009, 2025, 2026, 2043, 2053, 2625, 2779, 2890, 3612, 3643, 3645, 3681, 4652, 4653, 4991; History, 186, 1976, 2005, 2427; Writing, 985

Audio Engineering, 230, 1236

Audiology, 94, 465, 2065

Aviation, 31, 36, 60, 75, 235, 298, 1371, 1457, 1637, 1834, 3312, 3319, 3462, 4550; Maintenance, 31; Management, 31; Safety, 1398; Technology, 3340

CAD Technology, 3874

Cereal Chemistry and Technology, 13

Chemical Engineering, 37, 38, 118, 702, 913, 963, 1229, 1230, 1231, 1232, 1235, 1574, 2108, 2290, 2351, 3607, 3613, 3615, 3617, 3618, 3642, 3694, 3715, 3721, 3737, 4754

City Planning, 186, 232, 363, 839, 840, 1263, 1355, 1367, 1534, 1587

Civil Engineering, 150, 181, 204, 223, 242, 702, 820, 861, 1130, 1229, 1230, 1231, 1232, 1233, 1234, 1235, 1236, 1458, 1692, 2008, 2197, 2260, 2637, 2642, 3603, 3610, 3614, 3678, 3737, 4103, 4107, 4764; Construction, 219; Hydraulics, 1125

Computer, 2474, 3511; Engineering, 239, 853, 1232, 1235, 1236, 1310, 1477, 1705, 1943, 3642, 3736, 4096, 4104; Science, 70, 136, 239, 344, 511, 853, 911, 913, 1049, 1272, 1295, 1301, 1477, 1596, 1627, 1659, 1705, 1811, 1943, 1996, 2053, 2200, 2286, 2287, 2382, 2558, 2613, 2894, 2910, 3408, 3460, 3483, 3575, 3642, 3685, 3761, 3890, 3986, 4067, 4076, 4090, 4091, 4110, 4111, 4289, 4460, 4486, 4550, 4584, 4590, 4603, 4607, 4626, 4687, 4699, 4706, 4889, 4961; Systems, 599, 2621, 4074, 4106

Computer/Information Science, 2847, 2864

Consulting Engineering, 495

Data Processing, 599, 1272

Defense Technology, 543

Drafting, 3874

Electrical: Engineering, 383, 647, 853, 854, 913, 1229, 1230, 1231, 1232, 1234, 1235, 1236, 1285, 1310, 1477, 1574, 1705, 1803, 1943, 1957, 2382, 2613, 2621, 3601, 3604, 3607, 3610, 3642, 3714, 3736, 3737, 4079, 4096, 4104, 4289, 4750, 4888, 4906; Related Fields, 1377

Electronics, 385, 608, 723, 815, 1108, 1302, 1538, 1649, 1786; Engineering, 1811, 2247; Technology, 3968

Energy, 880, 1224; Related Studies, 541; Research, 4804;

Engineering Physics, 1233

Engineering Technology, 104, 213, 214, 618, 1086, 1446, 1636, 1937, 2942, 4077

Environmental Engineering, 37, 38, 181, 883, 1816, 1236, 3603

Finishing Technologies, 37

Flight: Operations, 3316, 3318; Training, 3312, 3319

Fluid Power, 2205

Geometric Design, 1130

High-Tech, 472; Research, 983

HVAC Engineering, 933

Hydraulics, 242

Ibero-American Architecture, History of, 643

Imaging Science/Photogrammetry, 1908

Industrial: Education, 3739; Engineering, 6, 8, 24, 25, 30, 64, 107, 136, 183, 247, 270, 307, 344, 366, 401, 446, 476, 477, 479, 488, 494, 543, 579, 596, 615, 620, 621, 622, 699, 700, 704, 774, 775, 786, 787, 804, 848, 854, 882, 910, 959, 974, 1041, 1049, 1093, 1118, 1146, 1178, 1229, 1230, 1231, 1232, 1235, 1236, 1295, 1343, 1359, 1442, 1449, 1573, 1614, 1617, 1641, 1659, 1699, 1703, 1704, 1707, 1781, 1805, 1814, 1905, 1917, 1948, 1959, 1965, 1970, 2000, 2034, 2053, 2082, 2108, 2128, 2190, 2203, 2204, 2206, 2213, 2322, 2372, 2382, 2419, 2432, 2616, 2832, 2894, 2909, 2915, 2935, 3486, 3606, 3611, 3616, 3619, 3620, 3621, 3684, 3690, 3692, 3699, 3709, 3713, 3716, 3725, 3733, 3740, 3741, 3752, 3754, 3761, 3772, 3777, 3875, 3911, 3925, 4040, 4067, 4074, 4076, 4077, 4079, 4080, 4090, 4091, 4096, 4103, 4104, 4106, 4107, 4110, 4111, 4304, 4309, 4454, 4550, 4584, 4603, 4610, 4699, 4706, 4714, 4715, 4716, 4747, 4877, 4878, 4894, 4901, 4961; Technology, 2137, 3739, 4430; Technology Management, 4884, 4885

Information: Science, 41, 70, 924, 975, 1079, 1111, 1272, 1348, 1349, 4057, 4621; Systems, 192, 599; Technology, 3483

Interior Decorating and Design, 216, 221, 1062, 1192, 1380, 1788, 1957, 2513, 3681, 3950

Land Surveying, 25

Magnetic Material Science, 2247

Manufacturing, 488, 1393; Engineering, 178, 360, 440, 1088, 1236, 1250, 1372, 1570, 1765, 2137, 2372, 2374; Engineering Technology, 360, 440, 1250, 1372, 1570, 1765; Operations, 620; Technology, 488, 2374

Manufacturing Engineering, 2409

Marine Engineering, 2106

Material Science Engineering, 2245, 2246, 2249, 2250

Materials Joining, 1589

Mechanical Engineering, 265, 626, 675, 805, 841, 854, 913, 1195, 1229, 1230, 1231, 1232, 1234, 1235, 1236, 1277, 1285, 1415, 1574, 1941, 2108, 2160, 2192, 2382, 2416, 2621, 2622, 3602, 3603, 3607, 3610, 3642, 3737, 4079, 4289, 4888, 4906

Metal Casting, 4876, 4883

Mineral Extractive Disciplines, 446

Minerals Processing/Extracting, 1969, 2245, 2246, 2248

Mining, 1969, 2248, 2436, 3641

Natural Resource Management, 4528, 4534

Naval: Architecture, 2106, 4289; Engineering, 218

Nuclear Engineering, 913, 1785

Ocean Engineering, 1234, 2106

Oilseed Chemistry and Technology, 13

Optics, 2131

Photonic Engineering, 2247

Physics Engineering, 3580

Plastics Engineering, 2108, 4884

Powerplant, 31

Pre-Engineering, 2211, 2419, 2549, 3580, 4493

Pre-Industrial Technology, 2427

Pulp and Paper-Related Engineering, 4673

Radio, 154, 2179

Radiological Technology, 94

Radiology, 793

Radiology Technicians, 184

Remote Sensing, 2196, 2401

Space Related Engineering, 1239

Structural Engineering, 181, 1721

Surveying, 116, 267, 268, 366, 1222, 1325, 1708, 1849, 1850, 1882, 2038

Systems Engineering, 2910, 3619

Technical Fields, 641, 950

Technology, 183, 570, 920, 943, 2213, 2286, 2304, 2409, 2940, 2943, 2974, 3493, 4565; Education, 668, 827, 871, 872, 1350, 1396; Engineering, 2043; Fields, 39, 850

Textile Technology, 323

Traffic Engineering, 1130

Transportation, 150, 623, 624; Planning, 1130; Science, 1130

Water Utility Industry, 533, 1128, 1659, 2202

FINE ARTS

Acting, 4347, 4359

Advertising Art, 1219

Art, 139, 145, 201, 371, 470, 512, 527, 539, 671, 752, 756, 768, 769, 876, 958, 1059, 1134, 1332, 1629, 1879, 1931, 2036, 2301, 2487, 2489, 2504, 2597, 2671, 2683, 2753, 2788, 2819, 2866, 2873, 2913, 2949, 3266, 3320, 3349, 3380, 3414, 3499, 3505, 3506, 3661, 3668, 3792, 3804, 3809, 3853, 3933, 3947, 4003, 4012, 4020, 4049, 4083, 4284, 4293, 4305, 4320, 4323, 4329, 4376, 4381, 4391, 4561, 4609, 4614, 4652, 4719, 4721, 4900, 4912, 4929, 4936, 5014, 5043, 5077, 5146

Art Administration, 466, 496, 1276

Art Conservation, 163, 164, 405, 441, 1159, 1303, 1484, 1978, 2100, 2182, 2230

Art Education, 175, 582

Art History, 1004, 1007, 1115, 1159; Dutch or Flemish, 1958

Art or Music Therapy, 1722

Art Studies, 1519, 2103

Art Theory, 1115

Arts and Literature, 2232, 4356

Arts and Sciences, 2886, 4622

Asian Art Conservation, 2142

Band, 3933, 4458, 4853

Brasses, 3688

Cartooning, 3769

Catholic Liturgical Music, 2498

Ceramic Art, 678

Choir, 3933

Chorale, 2498

Church Music, 745

Cinematography, 194

Clarinet Music, 4449

Classical Music, 886

Commercial Art, 1423, 1884

Costume History, 1843

Creative Art, 1005, 1823

Creative Design, 1219

Culinary Arts, 1384, 2305, 2431

Dance, 347, 371, 2335, 2487, 2504, 2597, 2802, 3552, 4028, 4359, 4485

Decorative Arts, 163, 164, 405, 441, 496, 797, 964, 1159, 1303, 1338, 1484, 1879, 1978, 2009, 2100, 2182, 2230, 2427, 2831, 2887, 4760

Design, 2489, 2504, 2512, 3809, 4518, 4519

Drama, 571, 1174, 2335, 2522, 2550, 2611, 2753, 2913, 3256, 3266, 3268, 3414, 3661, 3853, 3901, 3957, 4016, 4284, 4517, 5014

Drawing, 1206, 1412, 1977, 2301, 3508

Exhibit Interpretation, 1626

Fashion Design, 731, 1788, 2513

Film, 154, 379, 1126, 1346, 1670, 2159, 2301, 3599

Fine Arts, 194, 915, 1119, 1159, 1505, 1843, 1977, 2230, 2301, 2309, 2335, 2545, 2783, 3509, 3765, 3799, 4012, 4016, 4020, 4023, 4028, 4049, 4082, 4083, 4120, 4653, 4758, 5014

Graphic Arts, 220, 909, 1243, 1292, 1524, 1545, 1546, 1613, 1774, 1788, 3681, 3796, 4291, 4881

Graphic Arts Education, 2369

Greek and Roman Art, 430

Guitar, 2576

Instrumental Music, 1565, 1566, 1778, 2504, 2860, 2983, 4301, 4376

Interior Design, 216, 221, 1062, 1192, 1380, 1788, 1957, 2513, 3681, 3950

Jazz Music, 370, 4281

Jewelry-Related Studies, 1180

Keyboard, 3688, 4301, 4458

Leather Art, 1320

Marching Band, 3824

Martial Arts, 641

Movement Studies, 3858

Music, 145, 194, 210, 245, 253, 371, 527, 571, 591, 597, 614, 756, 768, 769, 875, 958, 1492, 1577, 1675, 1740, 1832, 1900, 2006, 2017, 2199, 2335, 2487, 2527, 2554, 2608, 2628, 2639, 2673, 2681, 2709, 2783, 2796, 2806, 2808, 2835, 2843, 2869, 2870, 2903, 2913, 2931, 2934, 2935, 3247, 3253, 3256, 3257, 3266, 3268, 3306, 3349, 3381, 3382, 3391, 3414, 3444, 3453, 3489, 3490, 3505, 3506, 3544, 3628, 3661, 3688, 3774, 3799, 3804, 3810, 3812, 3813, 3814, 3815, 3817, 3818, 3819, 3822, 3826, 3827, 3828, 3829, 3853, 3870, 3899, 3930, 3946, 3955, 3958, 3961, 3987, 4003, 4016, 4023, 4049, 4120, 4263, 4306, 4311, 4329, 4347, 4394, 4443, 4457, 4497, 4555, 4614, 4649, 4652, 4684, 4719, 4739,

4892, 4912, 4932, 5014, 5043, 5056, 5097, 5140, 5146

Music, Theater Performance, 4521, 4802

Music Composition, 208, 209, 2227, 2698

Music Education, 263, 1566, 2562, 2983, 3253, 3811, 3823, 4023, 4442

Music Performance, 263, 2514

Music Research, 2097

Music Theory, 5040

Music Therapy, 106, 1566, 3442

Musical Arts, 46

Orchestra, 2576, 2649, 3396, 3819, 3825, 4458

Organ Music, 2660

Painting, 1206, 1332, 1333, 1412, 1977, 3508

Percussion, 3688, 3820, 3829

Performance Studies, 4359

Performing Arts, 56, 362, 741, 950, 955, 983, 1034, 1059, 1242, 1445, 2561, 2783, 3331, 3764, 4602

Photography, 516, 1412, 1545, 1546, 1610, 1670, 1824, 2036, 2301, 2801, 4322

Piano, 1566, 2514, 2576, 3816, 3822, 4082, 4490

Playwriting, 571, 1145, 1174, 3599

Printmaking, 1977, 3508

Religious Music, 886

Sculpture, 1332, 1333, 1412, 1615, 1977, 2301, 2779, 3939

String Music, 3688, 4346, 4440, 4442

Studio Art, 2831

Theater, 362, 371, 527, 741, 955, 1174, 2199, 2487, 2504, 2597, 2673, 2683, 2783, 2957, 3256, 3453, 3552, 3853, 3928, 3933, 3956, 3962, 3969, 3995, 4003, 4049, 4302, 4376, 4381, 4517, 4518, 4520, 4614, 4737, 4912, 5146

Theater Technician, 4359

Video, 516, 1670, 2301

Violin, 2870

Visual Arts, 46, 369, 404, 496, 530, 741, 983, 1034, 1115, 1430, 2335, 3300, 3331, 3906

Visual Communication, 2513

Vocal, 278, 370, 591, 1578, 1593, 1778, 1975, 2504, 2529, 2562, 2576, 2815, 2978, 3309, 3688, 3817, 3818, 4301, 4376, 4442, 4458, 4490, 4638

Western Art, 404, 530, 1430

Woodwinds, 3688

Worship Arts, 745

HUMANITIES

Arts and Literature, 2232, 4356

Austrian Literature, 808

Bibliography, 636, 2078

Broadcast Journalism, 180, 1227, 1583, 1896, 1985, 1989

Broadcasting, 220, 638, 974, 1268, 1286, 1389, 1524, 1533, 1871, 2614, 2636, 4769

Children's Library Service, 303

Classical Greek Studies, 212, 2937

Classical Languages, 4338

Classical Studies, 139, 744, 797, 1274, 1916, 2009, 2511, 3468

Classics, 1605, 2779, 2874, 2933, 2935, 3285, 4284, 5051

Colonial Literature, 2353

Communication Disorders, 464, 922, 5021

Communications, 12, 296, 319, 372, 385, 608, 723, 724, 815, 1002, 1039, 1108, 1185, 1228, 1302, 1339, 1394, 1423, 1442, 1524, 1538, 1594, 1606, 1649, 1659, 1670, 1871, 2109, 2179, 2224, 2288, 2382, 2391, 2516, 2522, 2571, 2597, 2636, 3482, 3933, 4533, 4625, 4654, 4889; Radio/TV Emphasis, 3384

Comparative Literature, 2800

Composition, 2843, 5040

Creative Writing, 1145, 1223, 1831, 1884, 2036, 2335, 2435, 2838, 3317, 3596, 3853, 4381, 4546

Debate, 897, 2498, 2903, 3866

Editing, 1334

Electronic Media, 1911

English, 187, 524, 1000, 1505, 1996, 2143, 2435, 2593, 2714, 2799, 2823, 3379, 3393, 3500, 3560, 3562, 3566, 3576, 3909, 4418, 4429, 4850, 4853, 4993, 5140; Composition, 5051; Education, 1640; Literature, 5051

Fiction Writing, 3599

Film, 154, 379, 1126, 1346, 1670, 2159, 2301, 3599

Folklore, 2427

Foreign Languages, 1520, 1813, 2553, 2593, 3420, 3909, 5140

Forensics, 2199, 2598, 2783, 3256, 3866, 4299, 4344, 4725

French, 2553, 2881, 3420, 3577; Language, 1433; Literature, 1433

German, 2553, 3577; Language, 937, 941; Literature, 5022

Humanities, 44, 205, 320, 410, 470, 512, 580, 631, 671, 752, 768, 769, 786, 787, 798, 1134, 1314, 1469, 1470, 1519, 1550, 1592, 1598, 1629, 1666, 1786, 1869, 1931, 2079, 2080, 2103, 2120, 2184, 2280, 2411, 2866, 2872, 2878, 2879, 2949, 3287, 3330, 3488, 3499, 3514, 4038, 4049, 4057, 4356, 4414, 4415, 4641, 4798, 4800, 4900, 5140

Interdisciplinary Studies, 2232

Italian Renaissance, 3636

Jewish Language, 1181

Journalism, 187, 194, 296, 319, 324, 642, 724, 983, 1002, 1039, 1061, 1191, 1227, 1228, 1286, 1301, 1328, 1339, 1386, 1389, 1394, 1418, 1437, 1442, 1524, 1545, 1546, 1572,

1580, 1584, 1594, 1670, 1770, 1800, 1811, 1871, 1880, 1905, 2151, 2279, 2382, 2405, 2435, 2498, 2516, 2520, 2528, 2548, 2551, 2571, 2572, 2636, 2749, 3505, 3506, 3517, 3585, 4543, 4625, 4814, 5114; Electronic, 341, 638, 1985, 1988, 1989

Language, 1505, 2827, 3957

Languages, 1705, 3955

Late Medieval Studies, 231

Letters, 4609

Liberal Arts, 12, 373, 781, 1021, 1703, 2280, 2411, 2812, 2862, 4533, 4890, 4900, 5000, 5110

Librarianship, 1243

Library and Information Sciences, 41, 187, 192, 303, 403, 532, 535, 635, 651, 776, 816, 825, 924, 975, 1051, 1079, 1111, 1179, 1336, 1342, 1366, 1427, 1677, 1841, 1914, 2101, 2221, 2222, 4621, 4803, 4831, 4835; Children's or Young Adult, 2039

Library Media, 2757, 2758

Linguistics, 1470, 1592, 2120

Literary Arts, 741

Literature, 194, 205, 371, 1000, 1243, 1550, 1900, 2080, 2120, 2593, 2873, 3514, 3792, 3957, 3995, 4284, 4719, 4850, 5048, 5055

Mass Communications, 1389, 1394, 2749, 4487, 4814

Medieval Studies, 2880

Modern Languages, 4338

Museum: Administration, 2022; Studies, 164, 403, 797, 1004, 1007, 3668

New Media, 983

News: Editing, 1744; Journalism, 4769; Management, 1986, 1987, 1988

Newspaper Journalism, 1672, 4465

Newspaper-Related, 2118

Nineteenth and Twentieth Century Literature, 1591, 2353

Photojournalism, 220, 295, 1220, 1227, 1293, 1583, 1610, 1671, 1702

Poetry, 650, 1145, 1223, 3596

Print Communications, 1874

Print Editorial, 220

Print Journalism, 1468, 1583, 1667, 1668, 2919, 4038

Print/Broadcast, 1572

Proofreading, 1334

Public Relations, 1185, 1228, 1389, 1607, 1670

Public Speaking, 897, 1622

Religious Communications, 1328

Renaissance, 1591; Literature, 2353; Studies, 231

Reporting, 1744

Romance: Language, 2850; Studies, 3285

Russian Literature, 3285

Semantics, 2055, 2120

Seventeenth Century Studies, 4582, 4583

Sports Journalism, 485, 2133

Technical Communication, 2147

Telecommunications, 983, 1896, 3569; Research, 1890

Television, 379, 2159, 2179

Translation, 100

Writing, 319, 362, 1505, 3598; Sports, 4918

MEDICINE

Academic Medicine, 747

Academic Pharmaceutics, 750

Advanced Practice Nursing, 990

Aging Research, 1193

AIDS Research, 55

Allergy/Immunology Medical Research, 653, 1138, 1163, 1870, 1935, 2178

Allied Health, 2071, 2158

Allied Healthcare Providers, 990

Allopathic Medicine, 990, 992

Anatomy, 4762

Anesthetist Nursing, 193

Arthritis Research, 936

Cancer Research, 102, 275, 1160, 1467, 1855, 1857, 1863

Cardiovascular Research, 1856, 1865

Chiropractic Medicine, 414, 736, 1288, 3878

Clinical: Geriatrics, 1193; Healthcare, 492; Pharmacology, 438, 753; Research, 714; Research in Nutrition, 1500

Cystic Fibrosis Research, 436, 980, 1331, 1862, 2172, 2185

Dental: Assisting, 133, 451, 552, 553, 1203, 1249, 1783; Hygiene, 244, 374, 554, 606, 793, 918, 1203, 1525, 1877; Hygiene Education, 88, 1402; Laboratory Technology, 1512; Public Health, 1104; Research, 918, 2169

Dentistry, 193, 411, 510, 555, 602, 611, 721, 791, 959, 961, 990, 994, 1027, 1037, 1168, 1203, 1513, 1523, 1695, 1781, 1798, 2158, 3914, 3915, 3917, 3920

Developmental Neuropsychology, 1949

Dietetics, 3672, 3676, 3679, 3696, 3697, 3700, 3703, 3720, 3723, 3726, 3728, 3732, 3734, 3750, 3756, 5008

Drug Sciences, 1948

Emergency Medical Services, 94

Endoscopic Research, 697, 1741, 2424

Environmental Health, 338, 1646

Epidemiology, 1044, 1920

Epilepsy Research, 254, 1465

Exercise Physiology, 1576

Exercise Science, 2597

Family Medicine, 992

Food and Nutrition, 1076, 1502

Gastroenterology, 225, 1087, 1741, 1769; Research, 682, 1500

Gastrointestinal Disease, 1499

Genetics, 1044, 4663

Geriatrics, 664, 753, 870, 1479, 1928, 2167

Gerontology, 791

Gynecology, 1026

Health, 44, 462, 605, 989, 1798, 1814, 2061, 2232, 2314, 2597, 2868, 3487, 3887; Administration, 322, 492; Education, 791; Policy, 2156; Science, 913, 1027, 1603, 2798, 4532, 5130; Service, 5122; Service Administration, 3534, 3536

Health-Related Fields, 994, 1024, 1561, 1562, 2138, 4632

Healthcare, 2, 234, 284, 350, 460, 661, 683, 904, 991, 1245, 1282, 1403, 1407, 1662, 1971, 2013, 2156, 3431; Administration, 1027; Management, 791

Hearing Therapy, 106

Heart or Stroke Research, 2171

Hemophilia Research, 1238

Hepatomegaly, 1087; Research, 1500;

Home Healthcare, 791

Human Nutrition, 993, 4108

Injury Research, 27

Internal Medicine, 992

Juvenile Diabetes Research, 1247

Kinesiology, 2547, 4491

Lab Technician, 1783

Laboratory Technology, 94, 160

Licensed Practical Nursing, 184, 1783

Liver: Function Disease, 1499; Physiology, 1860; Research, 1352, 1860, 2168

Leukemia Research, 772

Medical Assisting, 1451

Medical Lab, 791; Technicians, 184; Technology, 148

Medical Library Science, 1544

Medical Record: Administration, 905; Technology, 905

Medical Research, 4, 885, 1003, 1921

Medical Secretary, 791

Medical Technology, 133, 791, 1124, 2174, 3246, 3298, 3423, 4665

Medical Therapy, 2174

Medicine, 8, 94, 134, 160, 193, 202, 203, 264, 315, 354, 388, 407, 411, 431, 460, 499, 508, 510, 603, 661, 683, 695, 721, 791, 821, 931, 959, 961, 994, 1003, 1008, 1020, 1041, 1050, 1055, 1082, 1103, 1124, 1162, 1168, 1177, 1307, 1361, 1387, 1463, 1464, 1466, 1494, 1521, 1523, 1606, 1658, 1676, 1694, 1695, 1781, 1830, 1833, 1905, 1930, 1932, 1942, 1950, 1965, 1998, 2041, 2042, 2061, 2063, 2071, 2128, 2156, 2158, 2195, 2390, 2399, 2833, 3431, 3434, 4036, 4087, 4093, 4105, 4108, 4745, 4746, 4749, 4751, 4772, 4788, 4795, 5045, 5052, 5100, 5122, 5130

Mental Health, 206, 649, 714, 917, 1476; Research, 1475; Services, 94

Mental Retardation, 917, 1476

Midwife, 987, 1872

Mortuary Science, 191, 1073, 1085, 1254, 1495, 1548, 1563, 1653, 1655, 2356, 4689

Musculoskeletal Physiology, 1576

Music Therapy, 106, 1566, 3442

Nephrology, 5, 1923

Neural Science, 4289

Neurology, 1964; Research, 1564

Neuromuscular Medicine, 914, 1567

Neurophysiology, 947

Neuroscience, 1044, 1461, 2258

Neurosurgery, 1964

Nurse Practitioner, 1872, 1992

Nursing, 77, 93, 160, 222, 261, 271, 284, 294, 350, 351, 352, 482, 510, 544, 603, 654, 655, 662, 691, 693, 694, 695, 696, 714, 806, 846, 992, 1027, 1070, 1084, 1124, 1307, 1317, 1351, 1382, 1498, 1541, 1631, 1691, 1709, 1710, 1711, 1712, 1713, 1714, 1715, 1727, 1782, 1828, 2087, 2088, 2089, 2090, 2091, 2092, 2093, 2094, 2095, 2163, 2174, 2195, 2319, 2332, 2360, 2429, 2519, 2524, 2525, 2526, 2543, 2556, 2557, 2559, 2687, 2693, 2694, 2708, 2713, 2721, 2935, 2936, 3369, 3423, 3497, 3573, 3578, 3640, 3790, 3793, 3808, 3833, 3834, 3837, 3838, 3907, 3912, 3955, 3963, 3965, 4087, 4093, 4386, 4630, 4775, 4836, 4930, 4940, 5100, 5110; Administration, 345; Assistant, 1783

Nutrition, 94, 169, 791, 865, 1052, 2360, 2852, 4270, 4988

Nutritional Science, 2868, 3672, 3676, 3696, 3697, 3700, 3703, 3720, 3723, 3726, 3728, 3732, 3734, 3750, 3756

Obstetrics, 1026

Occupational Safety, 338

Occupational Therapy, 94, 106, 855, 1315, 1706, 1722, 1826, 1876, 2020, 3340, 3446, 3448, 4489, 4501

Oncology, 1160, 1745; Nursing, 170, 583, 1701, 1746, 1747, 1748, 1749, 1750, 1751, 1810, 2236; Research, 413

Ophthalmology, 1619, 1620, 1621

Optical Engineering, 913, 2131

Optometry, 193, 280, 791, 842, 990, 1240, 1523, 2117, 2407

Osteopathic Medicine, 134, 193, 510, 721, 990, 992, 1464, 1764, 2399

Otolaryngology, 1737, 1839, 1889

Paralysis Research, 140

Pediatric Medicine, 869, 992

Periodontology, 2162

Pharmaceutics, 751, 2303

Pharmacology, 438, 605, 742, 750, 751, 791, 932, 1044, 1608, 1930, 4763

Pharmacy, 94, 510, 659, 750, 932, 1027, 1307, 1866, 2380, 4752

Physical Therapy, 94, 106, 855, 1522, 1706, 1715, 1722, 1825, 1826, 1876, 1982, 2020, 2134, 4743

Physician's Assistant, 990, 992, 1872, 2071, 2174

Physiology, 1044

Plastic Surgery, 1839, 1888, 1889

Podiatric Medicine, 832, 990, 1027

Pre-Med, 1971, 2556, 2557, 2671, 2693, 2710, 3307, 3308, 3645, 4940, 5110, 5125

Pre-Nursing, 2710

Pre-Pharmacy, 2556, 2557, 4036

Pre-Veterinary Medicine, 1758, 3746

Psychiatric Nursing, 1103

Psychiatry, 1966

Psychological Research, 1452

Psychology, 437, 439, 603, 917, 1516, 1526, 1527, 1608, 2593, 2653, 2693, 2859, 2884, 3514, 3557, 3582, 4286

Public Health, 791, 907, 3543, 3551, 4576, 4578, 4753

Radiological Technology, 94

Radiology, 793

Radiology Technicians, 184

Registered Nursing, 2330, 2357

Rehabilitation, 547, 632, 633, 1991

Research Nursing, 1568

Respiratory: Care, 94, 601; Disease, 1921; Therapy, 144, 1188, 1555, 1715, 1962, 2401, 2421

Sports Medicine, 26

Surgical Nursing, 1429

Therapeutic Recreation, 106

Therapy, 1783

Tourette Syndrome-Related, 2254

Toxicology, 703, 751, 907, 1858, 2069

Urology, 4, 5, 1923, 2183

Veterinary: Medicine, 18, 93, 791, 1523, 1626, 1864, 1965, 2140; Science, 1453, 4031

Virology, 1044

Women's Health, 1214

X-Ray Technology, 603

SCIENCE

Agribusiness, 18, 1773, 2140, 2626, 2987, 3572, 3655, 3659, 3675, 3718, 4100, 4277, 4863, 4865, 4870, 4958

Agriculture, 18, 44, 49, 50, 334, 348, 367, 368, 435, 483, 505, 525, 640, 689, 708, 729, 865, 926, 1042, 1148, 1269, 1278, 1301, 1319, 1375, 1453, 1502, 1504, 1629, 1693, 1703, 1704, 1758, 1773, 1799, 1824, 1948, 2001, 2007, 2124, 2175, 2188, 2220, 2315, 2334, 2372, 2533, 2537, 2539, 2565, 2974, 3286, 3650, 3651, 3652, 3654, 3655, 3656, 3657, 3659, 3683, 3693, 3698, 3702, 3704, 3717, 3727, 3738, 3744, 3757, 3761, 3762, 3837, 4086, 4114, 4253, 4254, 4257, 4261, 4262, 4263, 4268, 4272, 4275, 4280, 4345, 4419, 4627, 4628, 4862, 4864, 4866, 4870, 4872, 4882, 4887, 4907, 4928, 4955, 4958, 4994, 5001, 5010; Communications, 865; Systems, 4277

Agronomy, 232, 702, 839, 923, 1263, 1367, 1534, 1587, 3682, 3747, 3760, 4080, 4100, 4108, 4274, 4277, 4870, 4998

Animal: Agriculture, 4078; Behavior, 1626; Ecology, 3747; Husbandry, 1758; Rights, 2072; Science, 18, 865, 1758, 1895, 2140, 3674, 3701, 3746, 3747, 3759, 4073, 4095, 4100, 4101, 4119, 4270, 4274, 4434, 4904, 4905, 4992, 4999, 5004

Applied Mathematics, 4603

Applied Physical Sciences, 728

Applied Science, 644

Aquatic Sciences, 2047

Arboriculture, 1060, 1213, 1261, 2426

Arts and Sciences, 2886, 4622

Astronomy, 749, 911, 953, 1925, 2593, 4110, 4111, 4289

Astrophysics, 749, 953, 1519, 2103

Atmospheric Science, 135, 136, 137, 613, 733, 1043, 1048, 1419, 1585, 1638, 1790

Avian Research, 291, 292, 293, 1266

Baking Industry, 123

Bat Research, 251

Beef Production, 4988

Behavioral: Neurology, 1949; Research, 256; Science, 255, 714, 3479, 4285, 4286, 4415

Biochemistry, 1044, 3613, 3747, 4252, 4289, 4662, 4683, 4829

Biological Engineering, 207, 1232, 2414, 2415, 4268

Biology, 285, 1519, 1641, 1659, 1773, 1855, 1925, 2103, 2290, 2538, 2593, 2601, 2825, 2837, 2848, 2854, 2858, 2876, 2884, 3460, 3556, 3558, 3761, 3789, 3909, 4022, 4031, 4109, 4110, 4111, 4495, 4532, 4611, 4663, 4960, 5132

Biomedical: Engineering, 581, 791, 1236; Life, 2296, 2297; Research, 714, 747, 1603, 4283

Biophysics, 1044, 3747, 4662

Biostatistics, 1044

Bluebird Study, 291, 292, 293

Botany, 259, 361, 839, 1029, 1261, 1263, 1264, 1355, 1367, 1414, 1428, 1534, 1587, 2475, 3284, 4109, 4276, 4828

Cellular Biology, 1044, 4289

Chemistry, 38, 118, 136, 702, 911, 913, 959, 963, 1295, 1574, 1608, 1659, 1965, 2108, 2268, 2290, 2503, 2593, 2659, 2805, 2811, 2849, 2884, 2928, 2935, 2977, 3376, 3450, 3460, 3613, 3695, 3733, 3850, 3953, 4034, 4110, 4111, 4289, 4532, 4683, 4829, 4880, 4960, 5123

Cognitive Science, 4289

Conservation, 232, 262, 363, 387, 489, 490, 708, 839, 1032, 1263, 1264, 1319, 1367, 1414, 1428, 1472, 1547, 1587, 1624, 1799, 1970, 2016; Environmental, 1424; Soil and Water, 2110

Crop and Soil Sciences, 923, 4997, 5017, 5020

Cytotechnology, 148, 1107, 4770, 4792, 4797

Dairy Manufacturing, 2140

Dairy Science, 1502, 1895, 2140, 3653, 3686, 3974, 5015

Defense Technology, 543

Developmental Biology, 1044

Drug Sciences, 1948

Earth Science, 644, 866, 913, 1575, 2436, 4110; Education, 3565

Ecology, 1264, 2202, 4289, 4639, 5050

Electrochemistry, 698, 2180

Energy, 541, 880, 1224; Research, 4804

Enology, 147, 424

Entomology, 285, 923, 4108, 4252, 4264, 4271, 4273, 4279

Environmental, 525; Chemistry, 703, 2069; Control, 232, 363, 1263, 1355, 1367, 1414, 1428, 1534, 1587; Education, 1632; Engineering, 37, 38, 181, 883, 1236, 1816, 3603; Health, 338, 1646; Resource Management, 708; Science, 66, 136, 446, 704, 839, 880, 913, 1224, 1232, 1319, 1659, 1970, 2290, 3449, 3669; Studies, 277, 424, 837, 1453, 1642, 1799, 2242, 4639, 5050

Equine Studies, 1053, 4294

Evolutionary Biology, 4289

Fire Sciences, 1093, 1200

Fish and Wildlife, 10, 1739, 4522, 4535

Floriculture, 232, 363, 795, 839, 840, 940, 1261, 1263, 1264, 1355, 1367, 1547, 1587, 1773, 4080, 4627

Fluid Power, 2205

Food Sciences, 10, 169, 920, 923, 1052, 1285, 1502, 1948, 2304, 3672, 3676, 3679, 3696, 3697, 3700, 3703, 3720, 3723, 3726, 3728, 3732, 3734, 3750, 3756, 4108, 4255, 4260, 4265, 4266, 4269, 4270, 4274

Forensic Science, 149

Forestry, 232, 363, 839, 907, 1152, 1263, 1264, 1355, 1367, 1369, 1414, 1428, 1534, 1587, 1642, 1755, 1968, 2426, 3669, 3705, 3708, 3710, 5005; Management, 4989

Gastric Biology, 1899

Genetics, 1044, 4663

Geodesy, 111, 112

Geodetic Surveying, 111, 112, 1221

Geology, 419, 558, 702, 866, 911, 1029, 1925, 1927, 1969, 2436, 2573, 2593, 2599, 2822, 2845, 2861, 2884, 3565, 3641, 4289, 4761, 4790, 5050

Geophysics, 866, 944, 2050, 3781, 4790

Geoscience Fields, 419

Groundwater Hydrology, 907

Horticulture, 18, 232, 259, 349, 363, 483, 628, 839, 840, 923, 940, 1089, 1151, 1175, 1199, 1258, 1261, 1263, 1264, 1355, 1367, 1428, 1534, 1547, 1587, 1773, 1919, 2016, 2218, 2255, 2347, 2400, 3753, 4080, 4100, 4108, 4113, 4252, 4258, 4267, 4274, 4627

Hydraulics, 242

Hydrologic Science, 136, 137, 223, 613, 866, 1043, 1048, 1419, 2242

Industrial Science, 4889

Irrigation Technology, 173

Kinesiology, 2547, 4491

Land Surveying, 25

Landscape Architecture/Design, 173, 186, 221, 232, 259, 363, 483, 536, 646, 663, 839, 840, 976, 1089, 1261, 1264, 1306, 1311, 1355, 1367, 1428, 1534, 1587, 1636, 1902, 1909, 2417, 2641, 3364, 3365, 3681, 4080, 4653, 4990

Landscape Horticulture, 2244

Large Game Animal Research, 934

Life Sciences, 786, 913, 2298, 3286, 3684

Logistics, 579

Magnetic Material Science, 2247

Marine: Biology, 1739, 2102; Engineering, 2106; Sciences, 336, 866, 921, 1369, 1641, 1968, 2047, 2104

Material Sciences, 37, 38, 476, 911, 913, 1232, 1805, 2306, 2436, 2915, 4289, 4754

Mathematics, 2, 8, 30, 57, 136, 247, 615, 644, 786, 787, 799, 848, 853, 913, 1049, 1505, 1520, 1539, 1614, 1633, 1641, 1705, 1707, 1861, 1917, 1929, 2034, 2053, 2200, 2268, 2593, 2604, 2797, 2877, 2888, 2894, 2949, 3336, 3372, 3408, 3460, 3575, 3667, 3684, 3731, 3761, 3856, 3864, 3888, 3986, 4040, 4067, 4071, 4110, 4111, 4289, 4460, 4584, 4716, 4747, 4879, 4894, 4937, 4961, 4993; Biology, 1044; Education, 1540, 1846, 2846, 4842; Sciences, 911

Meat Science, 564

Metallurgy, 38, 913, 1969, 2245, 2246, 2306, 2436, 4876, 4883

Meteorology, 135, 136, 137, 613, 733, 1043, 1048, 1419, 1790

Microbiological Sciences, 217, 1044, 1955, 2302, 3733, 4828

Microelectronics, 1447

Molecular Biology, 1044, 4289

Morphology, 751

Mortuary Science, 191, 1073, 1085, 1254, 1495, 1548, 1563, 1653, 1655, 2356, 4689

Natural History, 1029, 2229

Natural Resources, 8, 880, 1224, 1632, 1773, 2110, 2261, 2400, 5007; Management, 4528, 4534; Research, 906

Natural Sciences, 57, 246, 247, 1041, 1917, 2531, 2703, 2894, 3499, 3667, 4051, 4071, 4747

Nephrology, 5, 1923
Neural Science, 1964, 4289
Non-Ferrous Metallurgy, 2249
Nuclear Science, 1232, 1785
Ocean Science, 136, 137, 613, 1043, 1048, 1419, 4289
Oilseed Chemistry and Technology, 13
Organic Agriculture, 993
Ornamental Horticulture, 1760, 1961, 2426, 2891, 4955, 5019
Ornithology, 291, 292, 293, 796, 1029; Research, 1686
Outdoor/Environmental Conservation, 2224
Paleontology, 944
Paper Science, 4454
Park/Forestry, 1547
Pathobiology, 1899
Petroleum, 558, 844, 3564; Geology, 944
Photogrammetry, 1956, 2196
Physical Metallurgy, 2250
Physical Science, 40, 511, 644, 2296, 2297, 2298, 2819, 3761, 4051; Education, 3580
Physics, 136, 141, 786, 787, 853, 911, 913, 1574, 1641, 1965, 2107, 2108, 2573, 2593, 2606, 2884, 2888, 2918, 2926, 2935, 3387, 3460, 3580, 4040, 4110, 4111, 4289, 4532, 4584, 4608, 4960, 4961; Engineering, 3580
Plant: Pathology, 232, 363, 839, 923, 1263, 1355, 1367, 1414, 1428, 1534, 1587, 4080, 4108, 4276, 5001, 5018; Sciences, 4276, 5002; Taxonomy, 3284
Pomology, 3744
Pork Production, 1076
Poultry Science, 1895
Preservation, 1243
Range Animal Science, 4425, 4426
Range Management, 2533, 4116
Range Science, 1444, 4100
Regional Planning, 3681
Resource Management, 262
Science, 2, 8, 30, 64, 145, 197, 322, 344, 353, 401, 477, 497, 570, 615, 619, 848, 910, 919, 938, 983, 1029, 1049, 1505, 1520, 1539, 1577, 1614, 1633, 1707, 1781, 1814, 1919, 2034, 2082, 2149, 2200, 2232, 2705, 2829, 2840, 2909, 2949, 2989, 3320, 3336, 3408, 3493, 3505, 3506, 3621, 3845, 3862, 3864, 3875, 3877, 3888, 3986, 4022, 4031, 4034, 4040, 4051, 4067, 4071, 4073, 4078, 4080, 4083, 4095, 4100, 4101, 4108, 4110, 4111, 4113, 4114, 4116, 4119, 4340, 4349, 4460, 4530, 4532, 4544, 4561, 4609, 4716, 4805, 4894, 5000, 5124; Education, 1540, 1632, 1846, 4842; Manufacturing, 2213; Writing, 358
Seed Technology, 4998
Sheep Industry, 1625, 2533
Soil Sciences, 702, 1642, 4997, 5002, 5017, 5020

Sonography, 4793
Space, 866; Research, 953; Sciences, 913; Studies, 2742
Speleology, 251
Statistics, 722
Structural Biology, 1044
Surveying, 116, 267, 268, 366, 1222, 1325, 1708, 1849, 1850, 1882, 2038
Swine Studies, 564
Toxicology, 703, 751, 907, 1858, 2069
Tropical Botany, 838
Turf Management, 173, 847, 895
Vertebrate Paleontology, 318, 4712
Virology, 1044
Viticulture, 147
Water Conservation, 2166
Water Utility Industry, 533, 1128, 1659, 2202
Wildlife, 934, 1369, 1968, 2224, 2398, 2400, 5007
Wind, 3820, 3829
Zoology, 285, 1029, 1626, 3747, 4663, 4828

Social Sciences
Aegean Bronze Age Archaeology, 2778
Aerospace History, 743
African-American Culture, 2022; History, 2427
African: History, 266; Studies, 1243, 4801
Aging Research, 1193
American Popular Culture, 1243
American Studies, 1289, 3379
Anthropology, 946, 1136, 1406, 1519, 1629, 1829, 1925, 2103, 2427, 2593, 2930, 3379, 3514,
Archaeology, 1274, 1629, 1885, 1925, 2009, 2427, 2511, 2779, 2887
Archival Paleography, 636
Armenian Studies, 194
Arms Control, 1013
Asian: History, 266; Studies, 1243, 3285
Austrian Studies, 281
Behavioral Neurology, 1949
Behavioral Science, 255, 714, 3479, 4285, 4286, 4415
Behavioral/Psychosocial Research, 256
Belgian Studies, 912
Biblical Studies, 3480, 3522
Byzantine Studies, 744, 1885, 3363, 3364, 3365
Cartography, 116, 355, 356, 1243, 1324, 1850, 1869
Christian: Ministry, 681, 2717, 3431, 3445, 3802, 4392; Service, 904, 3283; Work, 2661
Church Missionary, 3786
Church-Related Studies, 2031, 2033, 2141
Classical/Near Eastern Archaeology, 2874

Clinical Psychology, 439

Colonial America, 1591

Communal Service, 2341

Community Service, 1181

Conflict Management, 78, 1796, 4287

Costume History, 1843

Counseling, 255, 261, 791, 917

Criminal Justice, 99, 481, 1204, 1337, 1421, 1616, 3428, 3534, 4427

Criminology, 2074, 2593

Cultural: History, 2427; Studies, 246, 1979; Values, 1624

Culture, 2827

Danish Heritage and Culture, 520

Defense Technology, 543

Economic History, 139, 797; of Germany, 320; of Wisconsin and/or the American Midwest, 1198;

Eighteenth Century Studies, 14, 15, 146, 1260, 4582, 4583

Entertainment Law, 1394

Ethnic Studies, 1406

Ethnohistory, 3867

European Studies, 1243

Family and Consumer Sciences, 328

Family Living, 3806

Folklore, 2427

Foreign: Affairs, 513; Languages, 1520, 1813, 2553, 2593, 3420, 3909, 5140; Policy, 1202; Studies, 1952, 2668, 4834

French, 2553, 2881, 3420, 3577; History, 4719

Gay/ Lesbian Studies, 1279, 1308

Gender Studies in Medieval or Early Modern Europe, 1967

Geography, 1243, 1925, 2593, 2952, 3781, 4651, 5050

German: History, 877; Studies, 822, 823, 824, 877, 939, 941, 3285

German-American History, 877

Government, 78, 187, 276, 422, 592, 701, 748, 983, 1140, 1337, 1894, 2256, 2566; American, 3581; Service, 2367, 2368; Studies, 843

Hawaiian Studies, 1406

Helping Professions, 1399, 1426

Hispanic Studies, 1243

Histology, 148

Historical: Preservation, 1127, 1271, 2427; Studies, 3667

History, 34, 187, 205, 403, 515, 524, 570, 600, 610, 701, 822, 823, 824, 1406, 1470, 1519, 1550, 1592, 1629, 1829, 1869, 1996, 2022, 2103, 2143, 2238, 2256, 2569, 2593, 2689, 2709, 2779, 2795, 2830, 2843, 2882, 2952, 3371, 3379, 3514, 3568, 3867, 3960, 4282, 4422, 4886, 4923, 5040, 5041, 5048, 5054, 5110, 5133, 5140; American, 14, 15, 89, 120, 707, 935, 1011, 1023, 1123, 1243, 1260, 1330, 2080, 2120; —, East Texas, 1766; —, Legal History, 1351; —, Military History, 568; —, New England, 1924; Architectural, 186, 1976, 2005, 2427; of Business, 943; of Cartography, 1017; Early American, 3671; European, 266, 2120; of Film, 1243; of Instruction, 2130; of Literacy, 2130; of Map-Making, 356; of Music, 1234; Photography, 1243; Printing and Publishing, 14, 15, 1260, 2078; of Radio, 1243; of Rare Books and Arts, 1243; of Technology, 4687; of Television, 1243; of the Book, 636; of Women, 4288

Home Economics, 18, 90, 101, 169, 328, 435, 595, 669, 1360, 1581, 1654, 1743, 2016, 2360, 2535, 2597, 2658, 3806, 4949, 5003, 5016

Homosexuality, 4581

Human Services, 855, 2193, 2314, 2428, 2658

Ibero-American Architecture, History of, 643

Immigrants, 999

Individual Rights, 3592

Intercultural Studies, 3862

International: Affairs, 748, 1092, 1883, 2883, 3600; Business/Relations, 5104; Development, 3559; Economics, 983, 3559; Peace, 1013, 1796, 4287; Relations, 1092, 1202, 1442, 3542, 3574, 3638; Security, 1202; Studies, 829, 1979, 3862; —, Eastern Europe, 3670; —, Middle East, 3670; Trade, 1393, 2177, 2313

Italian Renaissance, 3636

Japanese Studies, 576, 1164, 1920, 1922, 1934, 2056, 2081

Japanese-American Culture, 1005

Jewish: Culture, 2795; Spiritual, 1624; Studies, 528, 566, 577, 1096, 1098, 1101, 1181, 1818, 2386, 2863, 3860, 3861; Women's Studies, 1718

Justice Studies, 2632, 2636, 4534

Korean: Education, 2210; Research, 1933; Studies, 2947

Land Management, 363, 840, 1263, 1355, 1367, 1414, 1428, 1534, 1587, 4080

Law, 161, 261, 282, 312, 320, 327, 329, 578, 630, 734, 768, 769, 873, 959, 960, 978, 983, 1041, 1064, 1168, 1237, 1246, 1335, 1395, 1523, 1571, 1659, 1762, 1767, 1859, 1905, 1947, 2074, 2077, 2128, 2239, 2817, 3527, 3530, 3554, 3586, 4414, 4674, 4833, 5046; Communications, 3597; Public Policy, 3597

Law Enforcement, 2, 86, 99, 321, 1120, 1762, 2074, 2075, 2296, 4938

Legal: Education, 4674; Field, 2474

Leisure, 2597

Lesbian Studies, 1716, 1717

Material Culture, 2427

Medieval Studies, 2880; Late, 231

Mental Health, 206, 649, 714, 917, 1476; Research, 1475; Services, 94

Mental Retardation, 917, 1476

Middle Eastern Studies, 1243

Military: History, 455; Science, 1013, 2597, 4339

Ministerial Studies, 5126

Ministry, 997, 1867, 2661, 2702, 3436, 4327

Missionary, 997, 2662, 4327

Municipal Government, 900

Museum Studies, 164, 403, 797, 1004, 1007, 3668

Naval History, 567

Norwegian Studies, 1289

Numismatics, 139, 587, 744, 797, 942

Ohio History, 1725

Outdoor Recreation, 1388

Paralegal, 344, 2817

Parapsychology, 670, 929

Philosophy, 748, 2593, 2844, 2851, 3435, 3514, 3579, 3788, 5140; of Education, 2130

Police: Administration, 86; Sciences, 1200

Policy Issues, 3541

Polish Studies, 1161, 2139, 2948, 4860

Political History, 935

Political Science, 187, 276, 317, 422, 701, 729, 761, 762, 763, 822, 823, 824, 843, 945, 1011, 1140, 1176, 1207, 1337, 1511, 1684, 1829, 2128, 2423, 2593, 2656, 2824, 2830, 2839, 2842, 3517, 3563, 3574, 3581, 3638, 4341, 4606, 4647, 4757, 5055, 5104

Population, 44, 1848

Pre-Columbian Studies, 1885, 3364

Pre-Law, 3581, 3645, 5127

Pre-Theology, 3579

Preparation for Ministry, 1868

Psychological Research, 1452

Psychology, 437, 439, 603, 917, 1516, 1526, 1527, 1608, 2593, 2653, 2693, 2859, 2884, 3514, 3557, 3582, 4286

Public: Policy, 78, 945, 983, 1011, 1420, 1553, 1684, 1883, 4287, 5046; Programs, 2420; Recreation, 724; Safety, 337; Sciences, 1892; Service, 91, 1487, 2010, 2323, 4579; Service/Government, 979; Social Service, 4578

Puerto Rican Studies, 3639

Rabbinics, 1818

Recreation, 2636, 3487, 3567

Rehabilitation, 547, 632, 633, 1991

Religion, 176, 258, 357, 364, 378, 639, 927, 931, 1387, 2413, 2501, 3269, 3270, 3273, 3275, 3276, 3277, 3435, 3447, 3514, 3523, 3524, 3531, 3588, 3595, 3788, 4045, 4048, 4050, 5108

Religion (Christian), 3787

Religion/Theology, 1181

Religious, 241, 666, 760, 1590, 2902, 3495, 3587, 3624, 3625, 3626, 3627, 3745, 3773, 3798, 3935, 4296, 4374, 4383, 4742, 5107, 5131; Communications, 1328; Music, 886; Studies, 243, 1101, 2593; Work, 3264

Renaissance, 1591; Studies, 231

Roman Catholic Divinity, 689

Scandinavian Studies, 240

Service to the Disabled, 198

Seventeenth Century Studies, 4582, 4583

Sexuality Studies, 2170

Social and Political Science, 2952

Social Justice/Reform, 205

Social Research, 2886

Social Sciences, 255, 320, 410, 470, 512, 578, 580, 631, 671, 677, 729, 786, 787, 798, 1134, 1314, 1505, 1829, 1859, 1891, 1892, 1931, 2079, 2184, 2232, 2281, 2689, 2709, 2819, 3494, 3531, 3667, 3951, 4285, 4414, 4415, 4731, 4800, 4886, 5055

Social Services, 91, 1818, 4577

Social Studies, 4923

Social Work, 261, 791, 859, 997, 1101, 1945, 1998, 2413, 2593, 2886, 3283, 3534, 3550, 3583, 4018, 4385, 5046

Social/Political Sciences, 768, 769

Society, 943

Sociology, 206, 822, 823, 824, 1608, 1829, 2593, 2839, 2952, 3379, 3583, 3905, 4286

Southern History, 1000

State Government, 1664

Subspecialties Directly Related to Violence, Aggression, and Dominance, 954

Theological Studies, 1431

Theology, 243, 357, 431, 537, 562, 639, 806, 904, 927, 1101, 1124, 1187, 1262, 1387, 1401, 1752, 1981, 2031, 2033, 2141, 2333, 2413, 3269, 3270, 3273, 3275, 3276, 3277, 4773

Theory, 2843

Twentieth Century American History, 945

U.S. Military, 567

U.S. Military History, 1448, 1926

United Methodist Ministry, 3785

United States History, 1353

Urban: Administration, 1093; Government, 2323; Management/Planning, 1969; Planning, 3541, 4653; Studies, 2427, 5050

Welfare, 904

Western Hemisphere History, 79

Western History, 2080, 4717

Women and Public Policy Issues, 2438

Women's: History, 1330, 2427; Issues, 1308; Studies, 572, 1075, 1550, 1635, 1716, 1802

VOCATIONAL

Air Conditioning/Refrigeration, 933

Apparel Merchandising/Design, 3672, 3676, 3679, 3696, 3697, 3700, 3703, 3720, 3723, 3726, 3728, 3732, 3734, 3750, 3756

Arc Welding, 183

Automotive Technology, 740, 1456, 2024

Building Construction, 1759, 4891, 4893; Management, 4868, 4869, 4874, 4875, 4896, 4903

Construction, 479, 1178, 1458, 1636, 1692, 1704, 1805, 2043, 2620, 2638, 2642, 2643; Engineering, 252, 1759; Management, 181, 1458; Science, 4755, 4766

Culinary Arts, 1384, 2305, 2431

Die Casting, 4873

Diesel Mechanics, 740

Drafting, 3874

Fashion Design, 731, 1788, 2513

Food Management, 2305

Food Service, 169, 892, 1052, 1069, 1099, 1299, 1612, 2305, 2431; Communication, 1069; Management, 1881, 2253, 3323

Garden Design, 1961

Grounds Management, 173

Heating/Air-Conditioning, 104, 618, 1937; Engineering, 933; Technology, 214

Heavy Equipment Mechanics, 740

Hospitality, 169, 1099, 1612, 2305, 4117; Management, 2431

Hotel/Motel Management, 69, 335, 433, 434, 484, 616, 706, 778, 1365, 1496, 1508, 1549, 1643, 1656, 1657, 1663, 1689, 1731, 1897, 1901, 2273, 2375

Hotel/Restaurant Management, 442, 892, 1384, 2403, 3323, 3672, 3676, 3679, 3696, 3697, 3700, 3703, 3720, 3723, 3726, 3728, 3732, 3734, 3750, 3756, 4513, 4514

Paralegal, 344, 2817

Printing, 1774

Professional Studies, 2943

Proofreading, 1334

Restoration, 2242

Retail, 2121

Rodeo Activities, 4421

Sports Turf Management, 5012

Surveying, 116, 267, 268, 366, 1222, 1325, 1708, 1849, 1850, 1882, 2038

Travel and Tourism, 69, 71, 189, 224, 237, 282, 335, 433, 434, 484, 616, 706, 755, 778, 1122, 1225, 1365, 1376, 1476, 1496, 1508, 1549, 1623, 1643, 1656, 1657, 1663, 1689, 1731, 1840, 1847, 1897, 2096, 2259, 2273, 2375, 2403, 4117, 4513, 4514, 4642; Management, 2767, 2769, 2771, 2773

Vocational/Technical, 793, 817, 1819, 2346, 4117

Special Criteria Index

2.5 GPA

17, 22, 28, 38, 49, 57, 59, 61, 63, 71, 86, 98, 99, 108, 113, 120, 122, 128, 148, 158, 168, 174, 177, 178, 181, 188, 189, 190, 192, 196, 221, 224, 227, 232, 233, 237, 285, 286, 304, 322, 328, 333, 334, 352, 363, 375, 421, 435, 442, 469, 473, 480, 490, 495, 521, 531, 534, 545, 550, 552, 557, 560, 563, 586, 589, 593, 599, 605, 626, 633, 644, 646, 668, 674, 679, 681, 702, 716, 730, 760, 766, 770, 780, 799, 806, 811, 813, 827, 835, 844, 848, 883, 889, 892, 899, 902, 905, 913, 923, 958, 962, 965, 966, 967, 997, 1033, 1039, 1047, 1056, 1058, 1070, 1072, 1076, 1077, 1078, 1086, 1106, 1107, 1109, 1131, 1140, 1143, 1146, 1158, 1166, 1167, 1178, 1185, 1195, 1215, 1225, 1226, 1263, 1277, 1280, 1284, 1288, 1297, 1306, 1316, 1317, 1321, 1327, 1350, 1355, 1362, 1363, 1367, 1369, 1383, 1384, 1388, 1390, 1397, 1414, 1426, 1428, 1432, 1437, 1456, 1471, 1485, 1498, 1501, 1502, 1503, 1512, 1513, 1530, 1531, 1533, 1534, 1536, 1537, 1547, 1572, 1580, 1583, 1584, 1586, 1595, 1617, 1639, 1667, 1670, 1680, 1681, 1683, 1698, 1706, 1729, 1742, 1774, 1780, 1783, 1789, 1805, 1834, 1847, 1881, 1896, 1904, 1940, 1943, 1968, 1975, 1980, 1983, 1989, 2003, 2012, 2021, 2035, 2037, 2049, 2054, 2070, 2074, 2082, 2083, 2096, 2099, 2117, 2123, 2128, 2133, 2134, 2183, 2189, 2191, 2194, 2207, 2216, 2228, 2235, 2237, 2251, 2253, 2266, 2274, 2291, 2292, 2295, 2304, 2309, 2324, 2335, 2341, 2345, 2350, 2367, 2368, 2369, 2376, 2381, 2396, 2397, 2398, 2414, 2416, 2417, 2418, 2435, 2469, 2473, 2478, 2493, 2494, 2498, 2499, 2502, 2503, 2508, 2526, 2530, 2533, 2535, 2537, 2538, 2539, 2547, 2552, 2554, 2555, 2562, 2568, 2570, 2571, 2578, 2581, 2595, 2617, 2618, 2619, 2626, 2628, 2629, 2632, 2687, 2690, 2691, 2693, 2707, 2708, 2709, 2714, 2719, 2721, 2731, 2737, 2741, 2742, 2746, 2747, 2748, 2766, 2772, 2776, 2801, 2803, 2804, 2808, 2822, 2834, 2837, 2857, 2911, 2914, 2923, 2960, 2961, 2963, 2965, 2966, 2971, 2973, 2978, 2981, 3263, 3268, 3269, 3270, 3272, 3273, 3274, 3275, 3276, 3277, 3278, 3305, 3311, 3313, 3318, 3325, 3326, 3327, 3328, 3333, 3335, 3349, 3353, 3355, 3369, 3370, 3372, 3373, 3386, 3388, 3395, 3399, 3400, 3402, 3409, 3417, 3528, 3561, 3565, 3567, 3568, 3569, 3570, 3574, 3575, 3577, 3578, 3579, 3580, 3581, 3582, 3583, 3584, 3601, 3611, 3612, 3613, 3615, 3616, 3617, 3618, 3646, 3648, 3650, 3651, 3653, 3654, 3656, 3657, 3658, 3659, 3683, 3685, 3686, 3693, 3698, 3699, 3701, 3702, 3708, 3710, 3712, 3713, 3717, 3718, 3719, 3720, 3724, 3727, 3728, 3736, 3738, 3753, 3757, 3759, 3762, 3772, 3795, 3812, 3815, 3830,

3846, 3851, 3852, 3853, 3856, 3862, 3871, 3878, 3882, 3885, 3890, 3901, 3909, 3910, 3911, 3912, 3914, 3915, 3922, 3926, 3927, 3935, 3938, 3941, 3949, 3952, 3956, 3961, 3962, 3975, 3976, 3978, 4005, 4006, 4009, 4018, 4023, 4027, 4039, 4041, 4047, 4049, 4051, 4057, 4065, 4066, 4074, 4081, 4083, 4084, 4092, 4095, 4097, 4102, 4106, 4108, 4112, 4118, 4252, 4254, 4255, 4256, 4257, 4258, 4259, 4260, 4261, 4264, 4265, 4267, 4268, 4270, 4271, 4273, 4279, 4315, 4318, 4328, 4329, 4337, 4339, 4372, 4402, 4403, 4409, 4433, 4436, 4456, 4475, 4485, 4489, 4493, 4497, 4502, 4504, 4508, 4518, 4521, 4531, 4537, 4545, 4550, 4569, 4580, 4585, 4592, 4593, 4616, 4627, 4630, 4638, 4646, 4655, 4667, 4669, 4673, 4681, 4699, 4706, 4718, 4721, 4722, 4727, 4730, 4731, 4739, 4748, 4757, 4761, 4766, 4771, 4808, 4813, 4820, 4832, 4863, 4864, 4865, 4866, 4870, 4876, 4881, 4882, 4883, 4884, 4885, 4904, 4905, 4938, 4939, 4940, 4941, 4942, 4943, 4944, 4945, 4946, 4947, 4948, 4949, 4950, 4951, 4952, 4953, 4954, 4955, 4956, 4958, 4988, 4989, 4990, 4999, 5012, 5033, 5053, 5072, 5081, 5082, 5083, 5085, 5087, 5101, 5103, 5106, 5134

3.0 GPA

2, 6, 11, 12, 13, 19, 25, 31, 51, 53, 59, 69, 70, 88, 96, 104, 106, 107, 135, 144, 147, 149, 187, 194, 203, 207, 213, 214, 215, 223, 239, 244, 247, 252, 271, 294, 296, 317, 335, 341, 349, 353, 360, 366, 372, 374, 379, 381, 386, 433, 434, 447, 453, 458, 470, 478, 479, 481, 482, 484, 485, 486, 487, 497, 504, 505, 511, 514, 515, 554, 555, 558, 559, 575, 594, 613, 616, 618, 620, 622, 624, 648, 654, 655, 671, 676, 700, 706, 711, 712, 715, 719, 720, 731, 735, 737, 761, 762, 763, 769, 773, 774, 778, 789, 815, 828, 831, 833, 836, 839, 841, 845, 850, 853, 854, 857, 860, 862, 867, 882, 887, 890, 896, 898, 904, 911, 918, 921, 949, 950, 956, 959, 963, 978, 979, 981, 982, 993, 999, 1009, 1021, 1028, 1032, 1036, 1043, 1048, 1052, 1063, 1065, 1073, 1104, 1114, 1127, 1133, 1152, 1161, 1170, 1176, 1184, 1188, 1196, 1201, 1207, 1218, 1229, 1230, 1231, 1232, 1233, 1234, 1235, 1236, 1252, 1255, 1261, 1267, 1268, 1270, 1272, 1279, 1285, 1308, 1309, 1329, 1337, 1347, 1357, 1358, 1365, 1368, 1393, 1400, 1402, 1407, 1412, 1434, 1435, 1439, 1440, 1457, 1460, 1469, 1476, 1483, 1494, 1496, 1508, 1509, 1510, 1518, 1522, 1525, 1535, 1540, 1549, 1555, 1563, 1573, 1574, 1577, 1587, 1607, 1613, 1618, 1623, 1627, 1631, 1634, 1637, 1643, 1648, 1649, 1656, 1657, 1659, 1663, 1674, 1689, 1705, 1714, 1723, 1731, 1734, 1757, 1760, 1763, 1765, 1771, 1777, 1779, 1787, 1790,

1792, 1795, 1809, 1812, 1814, 1816, 1822,
1825, 1840, 1850, 1853, 1864, 1874, 1877,
1887, 1897, 1901, 1902, 1915, 1936, 1937,
1962, 1971, 1982, 1988, 1990, 2000, 2004,
2032, 2034, 2047, 2052, 2065, 2066, 2125,
2138, 2139, 2144, 2176, 2184, 2190, 2197,
2198, 2211, 2223, 2241, 2256, 2267, 2268,
2273, 2278, 2279, 2280, 2281, 2282, 2283,
2284, 2285, 2286, 2287, 2288, 2289, 2298,
2303, 2305, 2310, 2316, 2322, 2330, 2331,
2340, 2347, 2351, 2375, 2377, 2378, 2382,
2384, 2388, 2392, 2393, 2401, 2402, 2411,
2419, 2420, 2421, 2429, 2432, 2472, 2479,
2481, 2490, 2496, 2497, 2506, 2513, 2518,
2523, 2531, 2536, 2543, 2551, 2582, 2585,
2588, 2589, 2593, 2597, 2612, 2613, 2615,
2616, 2620, 2621, 2622, 2623, 2625, 2627,
2630, 2631, 2633, 2636, 2637, 2638, 2639,
2640, 2643, 2644, 2653, 2656, 2667, 2674,
2681, 2684, 2694, 2698, 2700, 2701, 2703,
2712, 2715, 2716, 2729, 2732, 2734, 2738,
2739, 2740, 2743, 2744, 2750, 2753, 2754,
2756, 2757, 2759, 2761, 2762, 2765, 2768,
2770, 2771, 2774, 2794, 2797, 2798, 2799,
2800, 2802, 2809, 2810, 2811, 2812, 2813,
2814, 2818, 2824, 2826, 2830, 2831, 2832,
2836, 2840, 2842, 2844, 2845, 2849, 2851,
2852, 2853, 2855, 2856, 2858, 2865, 2867,
2869, 2870, 2893, 2895, 2896, 2897, 2900,
2904, 2906, 2910, 2919, 2920, 2921, 2954,
2972, 2977, 2979, 2980, 2982, 2983, 2984,
2985, 2986, 2987, 2988, 2989, 3250, 3259,
3267, 3271, 3295, 3301, 3307, 3319, 3322,
3330, 3334, 3336, 3337, 3338, 3339, 3342,
3345, 3346, 3347, 3348, 3351, 3352, 3356,
3357, 3359, 3367, 3368, 3371, 3374, 3375,
3376, 3377, 3379, 3381, 3382, 3383, 3384,
3385, 3387, 3389, 3392, 3393, 3403, 3405,
3407, 3410, 3422, 3427, 3429, 3438, 3449,
3450, 3455, 3456, 3458, 3467, 3468, 3470,
3471, 3473, 3479, 3480, 3481, 3482, 3483,
3484, 3486, 3487, 3488, 3489, 3491, 3492,
3493, 3494, 3497, 3520, 3521, 3527, 3530,
3532, 3536, 3537, 3539, 3542, 3545, 3546,
3555, 3566, 3573, 3576, 3591, 3602, 3604,
3605, 3607, 3609, 3614, 3619, 3620, 3630,
3632, 3633, 3634, 3647, 3649, 3652, 3655,
3665, 3678, 3681, 3687, 3689, 3690, 3691,
3696, 3697, 3700, 3703, 3723, 3726, 3729,
3732, 3734, 3737, 3743, 3747, 3749, 3750,
3751, 3756, 3757, 3765, 3768, 3776, 3781,
3800, 3811, 3813, 3814, 3823, 3831, 3832,
3833, 3835, 3836, 3838, 3839, 3841, 3842,
3843, 3845, 3849, 3850, 3854, 3876, 3877,
3879, 3897, 3898, 3903, 3904, 3905, 3908,
3913, 3919, 3924, 3937, 3940, 3943, 3944,
3948, 3950, 3951, 3954, 3955, 3958, 3959,
3960, 3965, 3966, 3970, 3971, 3973, 3977,
3979, 3980, 3982, 3985, 3986, 3987, 3988,
3989, 3991, 3998, 3999, 4002, 4004, 4007,
4010, 4013, 4015, 4020, 4024, 4025, 4031,
4032, 4035, 4037, 4040, 4043, 4054, 4056,
4058, 4059, 4060, 4063, 4067, 4068, 4069,
4070, 4071, 4072, 4075, 4076, 4077, 4079,
4080, 4088, 4091, 4096, 4098, 4099, 4105,
4110, 4111, 4115, 4120, 4269, 4272, 4274,
4276, 4277, 4278, 4280, 4292, 4295, 4311,
4313, 4314, 4319, 4322, 4323, 4326, 4332,
4333, 4334, 4336, 4340, 4341, 4343, 4353,
4354, 4355, 4356, 4357, 4360, 4361, 4362,
4363, 4364, 4366, 4367, 4368, 4370, 4384,
4389, 4404, 4412, 4417, 4422, 4423, 4425,
4427, 4428, 4429, 4432, 4454, 4457, 4462,
4469, 4470, 4472, 4476, 4481, 4483, 4484,
4486, 4487, 4490, 4491, 4492, 4494, 4495,
4496, 4499, 4501, 4511, 4516, 4517, 4520,
4522, 4526, 4529, 4530, 4532, 4539, 4540,
4541, 4546, 4547, 4552, 4558, 4559, 4561,
4564, 4567, 4568, 4571, 4573, 4574, 4586,
4594, 4597, 4601, 4603, 4604, 4605, 4606,
4607, 4608, 4609, 4610, 4612, 4613, 4626,
4628, 4644, 4647, 4657, 4659, 4660, 4663,
4665, 4666, 4668, 4682, 4683, 4693, 4698,
4700, 4702, 4703, 4704, 4705, 4707, 4708,
4709, 4710, 4711, 4714, 4715, 4723, 4724,
4725, 4726, 4729, 4733, 4735, 4736, 4737,
4738, 4742, 4747, 4753, 4762, 4764, 4765,
4767, 4769, 4790, 4807, 4811, 4814, 4815,
4821, 4822, 4856, 4859, 4860, 4878, 4886,
4890, 4897, 4900, 4902, 4914, 4927, 4929,
4931, 4932, 4933, 4934, 4937, 4957, 4963,
4965, 4992, 4995, 5003, 5004, 5005, 5007,
5013, 5015, 5016, 5018, 5019, 5020, 5025,
5032, 5034, 5035, 5036, 5037, 5038, 5058,
5062, 5064, 5074, 5078, 5084, 5086, 5090,
5092, 5108, 5109, 5110, 5111, 5112, 5120,
5123, 5125, 5127, 5131, 5132, 5133, 5136,
5138, 5141, 5142, 5143, 5144, 5145

3.5 GPA

92, 143, 235, 270, 300, 314, 425, 456, 459,
488, 596, 606, 629, 722, 728, 767, 775, 781,
814, 901, 1034, 1112, 1118, 1171, 1172, 1239,
1250, 1343, 1372, 1408, 1442, 1449, 1481,
1542, 1556, 1570, 1602, 1603, 1644, 1660,
1679, 1690, 1699, 1776, 1833, 1893, 1894,
1905, 1938, 1960, 2137, 2298, 2312, 2358,
2370, 2372, 2373, 2374, 2409, 2470, 2471,
2491, 2507, 2509, 2560, 2584, 2586, 2590,
2591, 2600, 2645, 2664, 2682, 2730, 2735,
2736, 2745, 2751, 2782, 2784, 2787, 2788,
2789, 2790, 2792, 2796, 2825, 2828, 2829,
2848, 2861, 2868, 2891, 2905, 2907, 2962,
2967, 3281, 3282, 3291, 3297, 3299, 3315,
3343, 3344, 3354, 3358, 3360, 3398, 3419,
3437, 3454, 3476, 3525, 3529, 3534, 3538,
3610, 3642, 3645, 3660, 3662, 3663, 3692,
3695, 3763, 3766, 3771, 3775, 3791, 3794,
3803, 3840, 3848, 3857, 3894, 3895, 3896,
3900, 3902, 3916, 3932, 3942, 3981, 3990,
3996, 4001, 4008, 4014, 4017, 4053, 4062,
4064, 4089, 4113, 4266, 4268, 4275, 4300,
4303, 4307, 4312, 4325, 4335, 4345, 4349,
4351, 4365, 4371, 4375, 4378, 4380, 4395,
4399, 4401, 4405, 4407, 4410, 4411, 4424,
4448, 4455, 4459, 4460, 4461, 4463, 4468,
4479, 4503, 4510, 4512, 4553, 4554, 4556,
4557, 4560, 4562, 4563, 4565, 4566, 4570,
4572, 4587, 4611, 4631, 4653, 4670, 4671,
4676, 4677, 4678, 4679, 4680, 4685, 4691,
4696, 4716, 4732, 4734, 4743, 4768, 4827,
4862, 4871, 4894, 4899, 4913, 4964, 5000,
5061, 5063, 5066, 5067, 5068, 5069, 5070,
5071, 5073, 5080, 5088, 5095, 5113, 5117,
5135, 5137

ATHLETICS

Athletics, 228, 966, 1241, 1577, 1854, 1875, 2021,
2482, 2652, 2669, 2685, 3268, 3304, 3361,
3397, 3452, 3478, 3589, 3770, 3796, 3954,

4000, 4028, 4298, 4329, 4357, 4400, 4413, 4650, 4688

Basketball, 4382

Cross Country Running, 4506

Soccer, 4382, 4506

Tennis, 3967, 4506

Volleyball, 4382

Disability

Blind, 23, 54

Deaf, 85, 685, 2720

Disability, 197, 250, 289, 290, 417, 463, 500, 543, 546, 612, 625, 644, 677, 754, 783, 784, 793, 804, 817, 871, 928, 966, 969, 1016, 1041, 1066, 1181, 1208, 1257, 1272, 1283, 1300, 1471, 1510, 1557, 1582, 1595, 1596, 1597, 1598, 1599, 1627, 1685, 1778, 1900, 1991, 2030, 2066, 2181, 2209, 2348, 2412, 2706, 2841, 2866, 3430, 3554, 3805, 3880, 3886, 4018, 4585, 4599, 4947, 5021, 5105

Hearing Impaired, 685, 1898

Ethnic

African, 44, 1144, 2173

African-American, 28, 45, 118, 252, 273, 309, 491, 550, 630, 667, 747, 761, 786, 787, 860, 869, 911, 1012, 1021, 1055, 1056, 1349, 1366, 1401, 1425, 1462, 1477, 1511, 1513, 1520, 1522, 1527, 1529, 1530, 1539, 1540, 1565, 1584, 1606, 1710, 1816, 1866, 1867, 1955, 2000, 2003, 2033, 2141, 2165, 2190, 2241, 2296, 2297, 2298, 2324, 2351, 2393, 2419, 2741, 2793, 2809, 3326, 3335, 3417, 3506, 3507, 3532, 3537, 3549, 3644, 3647, 3711, 3715, 3740, 3846, 3869, 3890, 3925, 3979, 3980, 3982, 4006, 4307, 4309, 4315, 4334, 4335, 4336, 4396, 4452, 4465, 4467, 4500, 4617, 4745, 4772, 4822, 5058

African-American Men, 2228

African-Caribbean, 1565

Alaskan Native, 33, 686, 786, 787, 860, 869, 911, 991, 1349, 1511, 1527, 1628, 1867, 1951, 2046, 2064, 2261, 3925, 4006, 4523, 4537, 4744

Aleut, 869, 911, 1511

Armenian, 493, 2300, 2646, 4020, 5116

Asian, 860, 1144

Asian-American, 537, 1021, 1349, 1366, 1437, 1511, 1527, 1529, 1533, 1539, 1540, 1580, 1667, 1867, 2033, 2165, 2393, 2793, 2890, 3333, 3417, 3506, 3507, 4006, 4465

Asian and Pacific Islander, 215, 1522, 4815

Blackfeet Tribe, 288

Caribbean, 2827

Chicano, 860

Cuban-American, 1442

Danish, 1700

Eastern Shawnee, 1733

Greek Cypriots, 1392

Hawaiian, 869, 4641

Hispanic, 491, 786, 787, 860, 1028, 1070, 1081, 1144, 1312, 1366, 1395, 1485, 1513, 1522, 1905, 2012, 2082, 2541, 3333, 3506, 3507, 3559, 4076, 4772, 5026

Hispanic-American, 28, 118, 700, 911, 1021, 1218, 1349, 1477, 1527, 1529, 1539, 1540, 1668, 1867, 1955, 2033, 2165, 2393, 3417, 3547, 3715, 3740, 3869, 3890, 4006, 4334, 4336, 4465

Huguenot, 1057

Hungarian, 1059

Irish-American, 423

Italian-American, 1078, 1112, 1113, 1246, 1604, 4387, 4481

Japanese-American, 20, 56, 91, 611, 897, 1165, 1275, 1301, 1387, 1443, 1558, 1682, 1784, 2002, 2007, 2077, 2239, 2313

Korean, 2946, 2947

Latin-American, 478, 519, 734, 762, 1061, 1191, 1527, 2190, 2339, 2793, 3644, 3647, 4309, 4315, 4425, 4465, 4513, 4514, 4579

Lebanese, 879

Mainland Puerto Rican, 869

Mexican-American, 252, 747, 860, 869, 1606, 1816, 2000, 2351, 2419, 3925

Miami Tribe, 1733

Miccosukee Tribes, 2057

Minorities, 12, 26, 41, 52, 53, 87, 206, 217, 220, 248, 346, 543, 629, 644, 651, 682, 711, 712, 713, 725, 764, 766, 862, 866, 916, 1023, 1066, 1097, 1132, 1188, 1268, 1313, 1455, 1456, 1475, 1512, 1514, 1515, 1516, 1517, 1518, 1524, 1525, 1528, 1532, 1545, 1573, 1607, 1676, 1747, 1748, 1854, 1879, 1883, 1988, 2100, 2114, 2115, 2209, 2223, 2258, 2322, 2331, 2389, 2524, 2568, 2616, 2634, 2641, 2668, 2679, 2712, 2784, 2916, 3278, 3351, 3502, 3551, 3555, 3557, 3608, 3635, 3707, 3778, 3814, 3841, 3877, 3891, 3892, 3985, 4006, 4018, 4020, 4046, 4058, 4065, 4076, 4077, 4079, 4092, 4104, 4110, 4111, 4276, 4388, 4408, 4482, 4484, 4508, 4509, 4558, 4575, 4607, 4686, 4693, 4694, 4730, 4799, 4808, 4817, 4857, 5068, 5092

Modoc Tribe, 1733

Mongolian Heritage, 3666

National Hispanic Scholars, 3546, 3855, 5094

Native Americans, 8, 28, 33, 64, 118, 121, 122, 252, 491, 565, 686, 747, 763, 787, 798, 860, 869, 911, 991, 1021, 1046, 1049, 1144, 1349, 1366, 1483, 1511, 1513, 1522, 1527, 1529, 1539, 1540, 1606, 1628, 1630, 1793, 1806, 1816, 1846, 1867, 1955, 2000, 2033, 2040, 2064, 2165, 2190, 2261, 2351, 2393, 2419, 2632, 2635, 2749, 2759, 2763, 2793, 2892, 2969, 2973, 3320, 3333, 3388, 3417, 3425, 3506, 3507, 3519, 3644, 3647, 3668, 3673, 3715, 3740, 3869, 3890, 3917, 3919, 3920, 3921, 3925, 4006, 4065, 4308, 4309, 4315, 4452, 4465, 4690, 4744, 4745, 4759, 4772, 5026

Native American Sophomores, 1422

Osage Indians, 1385, 1761

Ottawa Tribe, 1733

Pacific Islander, 786, 787, 860, 911, 1349, 1511, 1527, 1955, 3925, 4006, 4315

Polish-American, 1161, 1938, 1940, 2371, 3623, 3924

Polynesian, 2793

Portuguese, 643, 1853

Puerto Rican, 747, 860, 1606, 1816, 3925

Puerto Rican-American, 252, 2000, 2351, 2419

Quapaw Tribe, 1733

Scottish, 2032

Seminole Tribe, 2057

Seneca-Cayuga Tribe, 1733

Serbian, 1294

Spanish, 643, 2553, 3420, 3577, 4418, 4433

Syrian, 879

Welsh, 2376

West Indian Heritage, 1400, 2378

Zuni Tribe, 1025

Military

Air Force, 59, 726, 2517, 4094

Army, 2594, 2595, 4094

Coast Guard, 72

Marines, 72

Military, 32, 40, 58, 125, 126, 127, 128, 130, 132, 158, 193, 195, 196, 274, 342, 409, 445, 457, 523, 556, 557, 637, 718, 759, 765, 834, 852, 867, 957, 1009, 1071, 1074, 1080, 1201, 1253, 1265, 1281, 1304, 1391, 1404, 1408, 1411, 1438, 1454, 1486, 1509, 1588, 1590, 1600, 1633, 1634, 1639, 1683, 1687, 1715, 1723, 1728, 1732, 1782, 1783, 1797, 1804, 1820, 1903, 1936, 1980, 1996, 2027, 2049, 2116, 2187, 2263, 2264, 2270, 2311, 2319, 2336, 2337, 2342, 2343, 2354, 2363, 2364, 2420, 2818, 3251, 3399, 3459, 3492, 3535, 3648, 3881, 3931, 4094, 4390, 4406, 4471, 4530, 4564, 4640, 4746, 4833, 4917, 4922, 5006, 5064, 5096

Navy, 72

ROTC, 4094

Religion

Baha'i Faith, 1287

Brethren Church, 2651, 2662, 2666

Catholic, 2574, 2675, 3893, 4749

Christian Scientist, 76

Christian, 4597

Church of Christ, 2469

Disciples of Christ, 2692

Episcopal Church, 2029

Huguenot, 1057

Jewish, 873, 1182, 1183, 1184, 1340, 1554, 1945, 4588, 4594, 4654

Lutheran, 1714, 4915

Presbyterian, 1609, 1628, 2295, 2299, 3400, 4045, 4048, 4050, 4398, 4744, 4758

Unitarian Universalist, 1412, 1767

United Methodist Church, 2488, 4619, 4661, 4796

Women

2, 16, 17, 26, 50, 89, 96, 107, 113, 125, 134, 151, 154, 221, 238, 270, 276, 306, 307, 346, 354, 419, 457, 492, 511, 515, 520, 523, 540, 548, 549, 550, 569, 592, 593, 594, 596, 672, 680, 682, 699, 710, 713, 718, 746, 798, 871, 890, 896, 911, 1002, 1016, 1097, 1105, 1118, 1169, 1205, 1239, 1259, 1267, 1343, 1372, 1377, 1404, 1405, 1439, 1449, 1473, 1477, 1494, 1514, 1535, 1550, 1571, 1574, 1608, 1662, 1696, 1779, 1802, 1822, 1849, 1850, 1875, 1880, 1900, 1917, 1997, 2053, 2112, 2125, 2146, 2226, 2322, 2360, 2391, 2437, 2540, 2568, 2616, 2650, 2652, 2662, 2663, 2665, 2741, 2753, 2894, 2953, 3316, 3433, 3503, 3515, 3518, 3526, 3550, 3556, 3608, 3635, 3649, 3693, 3715, 3723, 3740, 3761, 3798, 3804, 3833, 3837, 3859, 3887, 3964, 3984, 3987, 3988, 3990, 4011, 4025, 4027, 4031, 4046, 4058, 4059, 4067, 4075, 4097, 4104, 4110, 4111, 4282, 4283, 4284, 4286, 4287, 4289, 4307, 4494, 4532, 4535, 4536, 4584, 4591, 4601, 4605, 4622, 4623, 4631, 4645, 4688, 4720, 4723, 4849, 4895, 4906, 4919, 4926, 4930, 4933, 4949, 4999, 5024, 5031, 5045, 5048, 5116, 5117

Gay, Lesbian, Bisexual, Transgendered

156, 159, 215, 309, 449, 519, 831, 845, 857, 891, 984, 1279, 1308, 1309, 1452, 1506, 1788, 1809, 2045, 2890, 3622, 4316, 4574, 4585, 4586

Men

1533

Geographic Index

ALABAMA
Embry-Riddle University, 3462
Faulkner University, 3521–25
Luleen Wallace College of Nursing, 3907
University of Alabama, Birmingham, 4517–21
University of West Alabama, 4836–56
Walker College, 4928–37

ALASKA
Alaska Pacific University, 2488
University of Alaska Southeast, Juneau Campus, 4522–44
University of Alaska Southeast, Ketchikan Campus, 4545–51

ARIZONA
Academy of Business College, 2474
Arizona State University, 2613–43
Williams Baptist College, 5115

ARKANSAS
Arkansas State University, 2644–45
Harding University, 3634
John Brown University, 3770–75
University of Arkansas, Fayetteville, 4552–65

CALIFORNIA
Armenian Bible College, 2646
California College of Arts and Crafts, 2889–90
California State Polytechnic University, 2891
California State University at Fresno, 2892–93
California State University at Long Beach, 2894
California State University at Northridge, 2895–97
Chapman University, 3045–65
Christian Heritage College, 3088
City College of San Francisco, 3112–14
College of Marin, 3180
College of the Canyons, 3183–85
College of the Siskiyous, 3186–3201
Concordia University, Irvine, 3268–78
Golden Gate University, 3622
Menlo College, 3940–43
Mills College, 3986–90
National University, 4053
Pacific Lutheran Theological Seminary, 4220
San Francisco Art Institute, 4305
San Francisco Conservatory of Music, 4306
San Francisco State University, 4307–15
San Jose State University, 4316
Santa Rosa Junior College, 4317–19
Stanford University, 4414–15
United States International University, 4506–16
University of California, Berkeley, 4574–79
University of California, Irvine, 4580–81
University of California, Los Angeles, 4582–83
University of California, Oakland, 4584
University of California, San Diego, 4585–87
University of San Diego, 4807
University of Southern California, 4815

COLORADO
Adams State College, 2476–80
Colorado College, 3202–5
Colorado Institute of Art, 3206
Colorado State University, 3207–29
Mesa State College, 3951–71
University of Colorado, Colorado Springs, 4604–11
University of Northern Colorado, 4720

CONNECTICUT
Capitol Community College, 2898
Central Connecticut State University, 2938–58
University of Bridgeport, 4566–73

DELAWARE
Delaware State University, 3322
Pennsylvania College of Optometry, 4222
University of Delaware, 4612

FLORIDA
Barry University, 2685–86
Bethune-Cookman College, 2754
Eckerd College, 3400–7
Flagler College, 3527–31
Florida International University, 3532–53
Jacksonville University, 3763–68

Miami-Dade Community College, 3972
Smith Chapel Bible College, 4327
University of Central Florida, 4588–601
University of Florida, 4620
University of Miami, 4676–80
University of Southern Florida, 4816

GEORGIA
American College for the Applied Arts, 2512–13
Columbus State University, 3235–54
Emory University, 3466–76
Georgia Institute of Technology, 3601–21
Savannah College of Art and Design, 4320
Yourn Harris College, 5145–46

HAWAII
East-West Center, 3366
University of Hawaii, Hilo, 4622–47
University of Hawaii, Manoa, 4621

IDAHO
Idaho State University, 3641

ILLINOIS
Bradley University, 2780–87
Devry Institute of Technology, 3338–39
Greenville College, 3630–32
Harold Washington College, 3635
Illinois Institute of Technology, 3642–49
Illinois State University, 3650–59
Knox College, 3849–57
Loyola University, 3894–97
McHenry County College, 3930
Millikin University, 3985
Northern Illinois University, 4133–37
Southeastern Illinois College, 4329
Southern Illinois University, 4330–36
University of Illinois at Champaign Urbana, 4650–57
Wheaton College, 5092–100

INDIANA
Depauw University, 3337
Franklin College, 3585
Hudson Institute, 3638
Indiana State University, 3660–65
Indiana University, 3666
Purdue University, 4238–80
Rose-Hulman Institute of Technology, 4304
St. Mary of the Woods College, 4408

Tri-State University, 4502–5
University of Evansville, 4613–19
University of Indianapolis, 4658–61
Valparaiso University, 4915

IOWA
Iowa State University, 3672–762
Loras College, 3879–93
Mount Mercy College, 4012–19
Northwestern College, 4160–79
University of Iowa, 4662–65
University of Northern Iowa, 4721–41
Upper Iowa University, 4909–14
Wartburg College, 4959–68

KANSAS
Benedictine College, 2753
Fort Hays State University, 3560–84
Kansas State University, 3781
Kansas Wesleyan University, 3782–808
Pittsburg State University, 4232
Sterling College, 4416
University of Kansas, 4666–71

KENTUCKY
Bellarmine College, 2729–31
Centre College Scholarships, 2975
Kentucky Wesleyan College, 3847
Midway College, 3984
Morehead State University, 4004–10
Murray State University, 4021–42
Northern Kentucky University, 4138–58
Spalding University, 4381–90

LOUISIANA
Loyola University, New Orleans, 3898–906

MAINE
Husson College, 3640
Pepperdine University, 4226
University of Maine, 4672–73

MARYLAND
Johns Hopkins University, 3776–79
Towson University, 4481–501
Washington College, 4969

MASSACHUSETTS
American Institute for Economic Research, 2515
Anna Maria College, 2574–87

Archaeological Institute of America Boston University, 2777–79
Brandeis University, 2788–92
Emerson College, 3463–65
Fisher College, 3526
Hampshire College, 3633
Harvard University, 3636
Massachusetts Institute of Technology, 3929
Mount Ida College, 4011
Mt. Holyoke College, 4020
Radcliffe College, 4282–89
University of Massachusetts, 4674–75
Wellesly College, 5039–55

Michigan
Alma College, 2500–509
Grand Rapids Community College, 3623
Great Lakes Christian College, 3624–29
Kendall College or Art and Design, 3809
Michigan State University, 3974–75
Northwest Missouri State University, 4159
Northwestern Michigan College, 4180–203
Northwood University, 4204–7
Olivet College, 4210–19
Schoolcraft College, 4321
Spring Arbor College, 4391–97
University of Michigan, 4681
Wayne State University, 5025–31
Western Michigan University, 5061–75

Minnesota
Bemidji State University, 2732–52
Center for Global Education at Augsburg College, 2668
College of St. Catherine, 3181–82
Concordia College, Moorhead Minnesota, 3255–56
Concordia College, St. Paul, 3257
Minneapolis College of Art and Design, 3991
Moorhead State University, 3997–4003
University of Minnesota, Duluth, 4682–86
University of Minnesota, Minneapolis, 4687–89
University of Minnesota, Morris, 4690–97

Mississippi
University of Mississippi, 4698–711

Missouri
Avila College, 2669–76
Central Methodist College, 2960
Central Missouri State University, 2961–67
Drury College, 3353–59
Evangel College, 3477–97
Logan College of Chiropractic, 3878
Missouri Valley College, 3992–96
Saint Louis University, 4400–407
Southwest Missouri State University, 4338–59
Westminster College, 5079–90

Montana
Rocky Mountain College, 4292–303

Nebraska
Chadron State University, 2976–3044
Concordia College, Seward, 3258–67
Creighton University, 3289–92
University of Nebraska, 4712

New Hampshire
Daniel Webster College, 3311–19
Dartmouth College, 3320–21
Institute of Current World Affairs, 3669–70
University of New Hampshire, 4713

New Jersey
Drew University, 3341–51
Institute for Advanced Study, 3667
Joe Kubert School of Cartoon and Graphic Art, 3769
Lincoln Technical Institute, 3874
Princeton University, 4235

New Mexico
Clovis Rotary Scholarship, 3156
Eastern New Mexico University, 3367–96
Institute of American Indian Arts, 3668
New Mexico Highlands University, 4056–71
New Mexico Institute of Mining and Technology, 4072
New Mexico State University, 4073–122
New Mexico Tech, 4123–28
University of New Mexico, Albuquerque, 4714–17
Western New Mexico University, 5078

New York
Adelphi University, 2481–87
Alfred University, 2489
American Society of Composers, Authors, and Publishers, 3111, 4130
Archaeological Institute of America, 2511
Brooklyn College, 2795–870

City University of New York, 3115
Columbia University, 3230–33
Cornell University, 3284–88
Daemen College, 3294–300
Dowling College, 3340
Fashion Institute of Technology, 3520
Fordham University, 3554–59
Hunter College—University of New York, 3639
Laban/Bartenieff Institute of Movement, 3858
Leo Baeck Institute, 3860–61
Nazareth College, 4054
New York Institute of Technology, 4129
Olean Business Institute Scholarship, 4209
Queens College, 4281
School of Visual Arts, 4322–23
St. John's University, 4399
State University of New York, Syracuse, 4454
SUNY College at Old Westbury, 4438
SUNY, Potsdam, 4439–53
Syracuse University, 4465–67
University of Rochester, 4801–6

NORTH CAROLINA
Appalachian State University, 2592–612
Barton College, 2687–721
Duke University, 3360–62
Elizabeth City State University, 3424–30
Elon College, 3452–61
Meredith College, 3946–50
North Carolina Wesleyan College, 4132
Peace College, 4221
Pfeiffer College, 4227–31
St. Andrews College, 4398
University of North Carolina, Chapel Hill, 4719
University of North Carolina, Greensboro, 4718

OHIO
Antioch University, 2588–91
Ashland University, 2647–67
Baldwin-Wallace College, 2677–84
Bluffton College, 2776
Case Western Reserve University, 2908–22
Cleveland Institute of Art, 3140
Cleveland State University, 3141–55
Columbus College of Art and Design Scholarship, 3234
Denison University, 3324–36
Kent State University, 3810–29
Kent State University, Tuscarawas Campus, 3830–46
Kenyon College, 3848

Lake Erie College, 3859
Miami University, 3973
Muskingum College, 4043–52
Ohio State University, 4208
Rochester Institute of Technology, 4291
University of Cincinnati, 4602

OKLAHOMA
Phillips University, 4234
Southwestern Oklahoma State University, 4367–73
University of Northern Oklahoma, 4742–97
University of Tulsa, 4830

OREGON
Concordia University, Oregon, 3279–83
Lewis and Clark College, 3862–73
Southern Oregon University, 4337

PENNSYLVANIA
Academy of Natural Sciences of Philadelphia, 2475
Allegheny College, 2490–91
Allentown College of Saint Francis De Sales, 2492–99
Beaver College, 2722–28
Bryn Mawr Graduate School of Arts and Sciences, 2873–88
Chatham College, 3087
Clarion University, 3116
Curtis Institute of Music, 3293
Drexel University, 3352
Elizabethtown College, 3431–51
Geneva College, 3586–95
Haverford College, 3637
Juaniata College, 3780
Lincoln University, 3875–77
Mercyhurst College, 3944–45
Pennsylvania State University, 4223–25
Pittsburgh Institute of Mortuary Science, 4233
Susquehanna University, 4455–64
University of Pennsylvania, 4798–800
University of Scranton, 4808–13
Villanova University, 4927
Waynesburg College, 5032–38
West Chester University, 5056
Wilson College, 5116
York College of Pennsylvania, 5138–44

RHODE ISLAND
Brown University, 2871–72
New England Institute of Technology, 4055
Providence College, 4236–37
Rhode Island College, 4290

SOUTH CAROLINA
Charleston Southern University, 3066–86
Clemson University, 3117–39
Coastal Carolina University, 3157–77
Midlands Technical College, 3983
University of South Carolina, 4814
Wofford College, 5117–37

SOUTH DAKOTA
Black Hills State University, 2755–75
North American Baptist Seminary, 4131
South Dakota State University, 4328

TENNESSEE
Carson-Newman College, 2899–907
Memphis College of Art, 3939
Middle Tennessee State University, 3976–82
University of Tennessee, Knoxville, 4817
University of Tennessee, Martin, 4818–27
Vanderbilt University, 4916–26
Walters State Community College, 4938–58

TEXAS
Abilene Christian University, 2469–73
American College of Musicians, 2514
Angelo State University, 2516–73
College Misericordia, 3178–79
Dallas Baptist University, 3301–10
Del Mar College, 3323
McMurry University, 3931–38
Saint Mary's University, 4409–13
Schreiner College, 4324
Southwest Texas State University, 4360–66
Southwestern University, 4374–80
Sul Ross State University, 4417–37
Texas A & M University, 4468–80
University of Houston, 4648–49
University of Texas, Austin, 4828–29

UTAH
Brigham Young University, 2793–94

VIRGINIA
Christopher Newport University, 3089–110
Falmouth University, 3519
George Mason University, 3596
George Washington University, 3598–600
Institute of Early American History and Culture, 3671
University of Virginia, 4831–33
Washington and Lee University, 4968

WASHINGTON
Eastern Washington University, 3397–99
Evergreen State College, 3498–518
University of Washington, 4834–35
Washington State University, 4970–5024
Whitworth College, 5101–114

WASHINGTON, D.C.
Catholic University of America, 2923–36
Center for Hellenic Studies, 2937
Dumbarton Oaks, 3363–65
Georgetown University Law Center, 3597

WEST VIRGINIA
West Virginia University, 5057–60

WISCONSIN
Alverno College, 2510
Edgewood College, 3408–23
Marquette University, 3908–28
Silver Lake College, 4325–26
University of Wisconsin, Madison, 4857–58
University of Wisconsin, Milwaukee, 4859–60
University of Wisconsin, Platteville, 4861–907

WYOMING
Central Wyoming College, 2968–74
University of Wyoming, 4908

REF
LB
2338
C653

The complete
scholarship book.

$22.95

30950

DATE			

SOUTH COLLEGE
709 Mall Blvd.
Savannah, GA 31406

BAKER & TAYLOR

REFERENCE

DO NOT REMOVE FROM LIBRARY